SUNBIRDS

A GUIDE TO THE
SUNBIRDS, FLOWERPECKERS,
SPIDERHUNTERS AND SUGARBIRDS
OF THE WORLD

SUNBIRDS

A GUIDE TO THE
SUNBIRDS, FLOWERPECKERS,
SPIDERHUNTERS AND SUGARBIRDS
OF THE WORLD

ROBERT A. CHEKE

AND

CLIVE F. MANN

ILLUSTRATED BY

RICHARD ALLEN

YALE UNIVERSITY PRESS
NEW HAVEN AND LONDON

Published 2001 in the United Kingdom by Christopher Helm, an imprint of A & C Black Publishers Ltd. and in the United States by Yale University Press.

ISBN 0-300-08940-6
Library of Congress Cataloging in Publication Number 2001090956
Printed in Spain.

A catalogue record for this book is available from the British Library.
The paper in this book meets the guidelines for permanence and durability of the Committee on Production Guidelines for Book Longevity of the Council on Library Resources.

10 9 8 7 6 5 4 3 2 1

CONTENTS

SYSTEMATIC LIST   6

INTRODUCTION   11

ACKNOWLEDGEMENTS   12

STYLE AND LAYOUT OF THE SPECIES ACCOUNTS   13

TOPOGRAPHY   15

MORPHOLOGY   16
    General   16
    Tongues   16
    Plumage, moult and other age-related characters   18
    Karyology   19

RELATIONSHIPS AND TAXONOMY   20
    Possible undescribed species   21

BEHAVIOUR   22
    Food and foraging   22
    Pollination and seed dispersal   22
    Vocalisations   24
    Courtship   24
    Anting   25

BREEDING   26

DISTRIBUTION AND HABITAT   27

PARASITES   28
    Nest parasites   28
    Brood parasites   28
    Endoparasites   28
    Ectoparasites   28

MORTALITY AND PREDATORS   29

PHYSIOLOGY   29

MIGRATION AND OTHER MOVEMENTS   30

ECONOMIC IMPORTANCE   30

CONSERVATION   31

COLOUR PLATES   32

SYSTEMATIC SECTION   129

REFERENCES   361

INDEX   376

SYSTEMATIC LIST

Family Nectariniidae

Subfamily Promeropinae
Sugarbirds
Promerops

1	Gurney's Sugarbird *Promerops gurneyi*	129
2	Cape Sugarbird *Promerops cafer*	131

Subfamily Nectariniinae
Tribe Dicaeini
Flowerpeckers
Prionochilus

3	Olive-backed Flowerpecker *Prionochilus olivaceus*	134
4	Yellow-breasted Flowerpecker *Prionochilus maculatus*	135
5	Crimson-breasted Flowerpecker *Prionochilus percussus*	136
6	Palawan Flowerpecker *Prionochilus plateni*	137
7	Yellow-rumped Flowerpecker *Prionochilus xanthopygius*	137
8	Scarlet-breasted Flowerpecker *Prionochilus thoracicus*	138

Dicaeum

9	Golden-rumped Flowerpecker *Dicaeum annae*	140
10	Thick-billed Flowerpecker *Dicaeum agile*	140
11	Brown-backed Flowerpecker *Dicaeum everetti*	143
12	Whiskered Flowerpecker *Dicaeum proprium*	143
13	Yellow-vented Flowerpecker *Dicaeum chrysorrheum*	144
14	Yellow-bellied Flowerpecker *Dicaeum melanoxanthum*	145
15	White-throated Flowerpecker *Dicaeum vincens*	146
16	Yellow-sided Flowerpecker *Dicaeum aureolimbatum*	147
17	Olive-capped Flowerpecker *Dicaeum nigrilore*	147
18	Flame-crowned Flowerpecker *Dicaeum anthonyi*	148
19	Bicoloured Flowerpecker *Dicaeum bicolor*	149
20	Cebu Flowerpecker *Dicaeum quadricolor*	150
21	Red-striped Flowerpecker *Dicaeum australe*	150
22	Black-belted Flowerpecker *Dicaeum haematostictum*	151
23	Scarlet-collared Flowerpecker *Dicaeum retrocinctum*	152
24	Orange-bellied Flowerpecker *Dicaeum trigonostigma*	153
25	Buzzing Flowerpecker *Dicaeum hypoleucum*	155
26	Pale-billed Flowerpecker *Dicaeum erythrorhynchos*	156
27	Plain Flowerpecker *Dicaeum concolor*	157
28	Pygmy Flowerpecker *Dicaeum pygmaeum*	159
29	Crimson-crowned Flowerpecker *Dicaeum nehrkorni*	160
30	Flame-breasted Flowerpecker *Dicaeum erythrothorax*	160
31	Ashy Flowerpecker *Dicaeum vulneratum*	161
32	Olive-crowned Flowerpecker *Dicaeum pectorale*	162
33	Red-capped Flowerpecker *Dicaeum geelvinkianum*	162

34	Louisiade Flowerpecker *Dicaeum nitidum*	163
35	Red-banded Flowerpecker *Dicaeum eximium*	164
36	Midget Flowerpecker *Dicaeum aeneum*	165
37	Mottled Flowerpecker *Dicaeum tristrami*	166
38	Black-fronted Flowerpecker *Dicaeum igniferum*	166
39	Red-chested Flowerpecker *Dicaeum maugei*	167
40	Fire-breasted Flowerpecker *Dicaeum ignipectum*	168
41	Black-sided Flowerpecker *Dicaeum monticolum*	169
42	Grey-sided Flowerpecker *Dicaeum celebicum*	170
43	Blood-breasted Flowerpecker *Dicaeum sanguinolentum*	171
44	Mistletoebird *Dicaeum hirundinaceum*	172
45	Scarlet-backed Flowerpecker *Dicaeum cruentatum*	174
46	Scarlet-headed Flowerpecker *Dicaeum trochileum*	175

Tribe Nectariniini

Sunbirds and Spiderhunters

Chalcoparia

| 47 | Ruby-cheeked Sunbird *Chalcoparia singalensis* | 177 |

Deleornis

| 48 | Scarlet-tufted Sunbird *Deleornis fraseri* | 179 |
| 49 | Grey-headed Sunbird *Deleornis axillaris* | 180 |

Anthreptes

50	Plain-backed Sunbird *Anthreptes reichenowi*	181
51	Anchieta's Sunbird *Anthreptes anchietae*	182
52	Plain Sunbird *Anthreptes simplex*	183
53	Plain-throated Sunbird *Anthreptes malacensis*	184
54	Red-throated Sunbird *Anthreptes rhodolaema*	186
55	Mouse-brown Sunbird *Anthreptes gabonicus*	187
56	Western Violet-backed Sunbird *Anthreptes longuemarei*	188
57	Kenya Violet-backed Sunbird *Anthreptes orientalis*	190
58	Uluguru Violet-backed Sunbird *Anthreptes neglectus*	191
59	Violet-tailed Sunbird *Anthreptes aurantium*	192
60	Little Green Sunbird *Anthreptes seimundi*	193
61	Green Sunbird *Anthreptes rectirostris*	195
62	Banded Sunbird *Anthreptes rubritorques*	196

Hedydipna

63	Collared Sunbird *Hedydipna collaris*	197
64	Pygmy Sunbird *Hedydipna platura*	201
65	Nile Valley Sunbird *Hedydipna metallica*	203
66	Amani Sunbird *Hedydipna pallidigaster*	205

Hypogramma

| 67 | Purple-naped Sunbird *Hypogramma hypogrammicum* | 206 |

Anabathmis

| 68 | Reichenbach's Sunbird *Anabathmis reichenbachii* | 207 |
| 69 | Príncipe Sunbird *Anabathmis hartlaubii* | 208 |

70   Newton's Sunbird *Anabathmis newtoni*   209

Dreptes

71   São Tomé Sunbird *Dreptes thomensis*   210

Anthobaphes

72   Orange-breasted Sunbird *Anthobaphes violacea*   211

Cyanomitra

73   Green-headed Sunbird *Cyanomitra verticalis*   213

74   Bannerman's Sunbird *Cyanomitra bannermani*   215

75   Blue-throated Brown Sunbird *Cyanomitra cyanolaema*   216

76   Cameroon Sunbird *Cyanomitra oritis*   218

77   Blue-headed Sunbird *Cyanomitra alinae*   219

78   Eastern Olive Sunbird *Cyanomitra olivacea*   221

79   Western Olive Sunbird *Cyanomitra obscura*   222

80   Mouse-coloured Sunbird *Cyanomitra veroxii*   225

Chalcomitra

81   Buff-throated Sunbird *Chalcomitra adelberti*   227

82   Carmelite Sunbird *Chalcomitra fuliginosa*   228

83   Green-throated Sunbird *Chalcomitra rubescens*   229

84   Amethyst Sunbird *Chalcomitra amethystina*   231

85   Scarlet-chested Sunbird *Chalcomitra senegalensis*   233

86   Hunter's Sunbird *Chalcomitra hunteri*   237

87   Socotra Sunbird *Chalcomitra balfouri*   238

Leptocoma

88   Purple-rumped Sunbird *Leptocoma zeylonica*   239

89   Crimson-backed Sunbird *Leptocoma minima*   240

90   Purple-throated Sunbird *Leptocoma sperata*   241

91   Black Sunbird *Leptocoma sericea*   243

92   Copper-throated Sunbird *Leptocoma calcostetha*   246

Nectarinia

93   Bocage's Sunbird *Nectarinia bocagei*   247

94   Purple-breasted Sunbird *Nectarinia purpureiventris*   248

95   Tacazze Sunbird *Nectarinia tacazze*   249

96   Bronze Sunbird *Nectarinia kilimensis*   251

97   Malachite Sunbird *Nectarinia famosa*   253

98   Red-tufted Sunbird *Nectarinia johnstoni*   255

Drepanorhynchus

99   Golden-winged Sunbird *Drepanorhynchus reichenowi*   258

Double-collared group of *Cinnyris*

100   Olive-bellied Sunbird *Cinnyris chloropygius*   259

101   Tiny Sunbird *Cinnyris minullus*   261

102   Miombo Double-collared Sunbird *Cinnyris manoensis*   263

103   Southern Double-collared Sunbird *Cinnyris chalybeus*   264

104   Neergaard's Sunbird *Cinnyris neergaardi*   266

105   Stuhlmann's Double-collared Sunbird *Cinnyris stuhlmanni*   267

106	Prigogine's Double-collared Sunbird *Cinnyris prigoginei*	269
107	Montane Double-collared Sunbird *Cinnyris ludovicensis*	270
108	Northern Double-collared Sunbird *Cinnyris reichenowi*	271
109	Greater Double-collared Sunbird *Cinnyris afer*	272
110	Regal Sunbird *Cinnyris regius*	274
111	Rockefeller's Sunbird *Cinnyris rockefelleri*	275
112	Eastern Double-collared Sunbird *Cinnyris mediocris*	277
113	Moreau's Sunbird *Cinnyris moreaui*	278
114	Loveridge's Sunbird *Cinnyris loveridgei*	280
115	Beautiful Sunbird *Cinnyris pulchellus*	281

Purple-banded Group of *Cinnyris*

116	Mariqua Sunbird *Cinnyris mariquensis*	283
117	Shelley's Sunbird *Cinnyris shelleyi*	285
118	Congo Sunbird *Cinnyris congensis*	286
119	Red-chested Sunbird *Cinnyris erythroceria*	287
120	Black-bellied Sunbird *Cinnyris nectarinoides*	288
121	Purple-banded Sunbird *Cinnyris bifasciatus*	289
122	Tsavo Purple-banded Sunbird *Cinnyris tsavoensis*	291
123	Kenya Violet-breasted Sunbird *Cinnyris chalcomelas*	292
124	Pemba Sunbird *Cinnyris pembae*	293
125	Orange-tufted Sunbird *Cinnyris bouvieri*	293
126	Palestine Sunbird *Cinnyris oseus*	295
127	Shining Sunbird *Cinnyris habessinicus*	297

Maroon Group of *Cinnyris*

128	Splendid Sunbird *Cinnyris coccinigaster*	299
129	Johanna's Sunbird *Cinnyris johannae*	300
130	Superb Sunbird *Cinnyris superbus*	302
131	Rufous-winged Sunbird *Cinnyris rufipennis*	303

White-bellied Group of *Cinnyris*

132	Oustalet's Sunbird *Cinnyris oustaleti*	304
133	White-breasted Sunbird *Cinnyris talatala*	305
134	Variable Sunbird *Cinnyris venustus*	308
135	Dusky Sunbird *Cinnyris fuscus*	310

Olive Group of *Cinnyris*

136	Ursula's Sunbird *Cinnyris ursulae*	311
137	Bates's Sunbird *Cinnyris batesi*	312

Miscellaneous *Cinnyris*

138	Copper Sunbird *Cinnyris cupreus*	313
139	Purple Sunbird *Cinnyris asiaticus*	316
140	Olive-backed Sunbird *Cinnyris jugularis*	318
141	Apricot-breasted Sunbird *Cinnyris buettikoferi*	321
142	Flame-breasted Sunbird *Cinnyris solaris*	321
143	Souimanga Sunbird *Cinnyris sovimanga*	322
144	Madagascar Sunbird *Cinnyris notatus*	324

145	Seychelles Sunbird *Cinnyris dussumieri*	325
146	Humblot's Sunbird *Cinnyris humbloti*	327
147	Anjouan Sunbird *Cinnyris comorensis*	328
148	Mayotte Sunbird *Cinnyris coquerellii*	329
149	Long-billed Sunbird *Cinnyris lotenius*	330

Aethopyga

150	Grey-hooded Sunbird *Aethopyga primigenius*	332
151	Apo Sunbird *Aethopyga boltoni*	332
152	Lina's Sunbird *Aethopyga linaraborae*	334
153	Flaming Sunbird *Aethopyga flagrans*	334
154	Metallic-winged Sunbird *Aethopyga pulcherrima*	335
155	Elegant Sunbird *Aethopyga duyvenbodei*	336
156	Lovely Sunbird *Aethopyga shelleyi*	337
157	Gould's Sunbird *Aethopyga gouldiae*	339
158	Green-tailed Sunbird *Aethopyga nipalensis*	340
159	White-flanked Sunbird *Aethopyga eximia*	341
160	Fork-tailed Sunbird *Aethopyga christinae*	342
161	Black-throated Sunbird *Aethopyga saturata*	343
162	Western Crimson Sunbird *Aethopyga vigorsii*	344
163	Crimson Sunbird *Aethopyga siparaja*	345
164	Javan Sunbird *Aethopyga mystacalis*	348
165	Temminck's Sunbird *Aethopyga temmincki*	348
166	Fire-tailed Sunbird *Aethopyga ignicauda*	349

Arachnothera

167	Little Spiderhunter *Arachnothera longirostra*	350
168	Thick-billed Spiderhunter *Arachnothera crassirostris*	352
169	Long-billed Spiderhunter *Arachnothera robusta*	353
170	Spectacled Spiderhunter *Arachnothera flavigaster*	354
171	Yellow-eared Spiderhunter *Arachnothera chrysogenys*	355
172	Naked-faced Spiderhunter *Arachnothera clarae*	356
173	Grey-breasted Spiderhunter *Arachnothera modesta*	357
174	Streaky-breasted Spiderhunter *Arachnothera affinis*	358
175	Streaked Spiderhunter *Arachnothera magna*	358
176	Whitehead's Spiderhunter *Arachnothera juliae*	360

INTRODUCTION

Sunbirds are typically thought of as being brightly coloured birds with dazzling iridescent plumage and long curved bills, which appear at garden flowers on sunny days chirping agitatedly. Many species have these characteristics, particularly the males, and feed on the nectar of a variety of plants, but others are dull, short-billed, inconspicuous and feed mostly on insects, often high in forest canopies. The true sunbirds, as well as the spiderhunters, also feed extensively on spiders, whose webs are used in their nest fabrics. The sunbirds' other close relatives, the flowerpeckers, have short stubby bills and also feed on insects but take many berries and other fruits, being especially partial to those of mistletoes. The two species of sugarbird are sturdier birds associated with proteas in southern Africa.

Generally, the Nectariniidae lack the very intricate plumage patterns shown by such birds as nightjars (Caprimulgidae), larks (Alaudidae), and cisticolas (genus *Cisticola*). Therefore, taking field descriptions for the purpose of identification does not present the same degree of difficulty as it may in the above groups. Most male sunbirds have striking plumages, and often do not present too many identification problems, except where two or more similar-plumaged species are sympatric. However, most female sunbirds lack striking patterns, tending to be various shades of brown, grey or green, thus creating greater problems in identification. Many flowerpeckers, particularly males, also have striking plumages, but owing to their small size, rapid movements and, often, their fondness for the forest canopy, identification of flowerpeckers is more problematic than for sunbirds.

Two monographs on the sunbirds were published in the nineteenth century. The first was a small illustrated volume which included some original descriptions (Jardine 1843), and the second the lavish and beautifully illustrated book by Shelley (1876-1880). Another monograph, restricted to the sunbirds of southern Africa, was published by Skead (1967) together with a vinyl record of vocalisations. Skead's book has been the source of much useful information repeated here, in what is the first monograph on all the world's sunbirds, together with the spiderhunters, flowerpeckers and sugarbirds. Another major group of nectarivorous passerines, the honeyeaters, are not included. While not claiming to be comprehensive, it is hoped that readers will be able to use this volume to identify any sunbird, spiderhunter, flowerpecker or sugarbird seen, and to gain an insight into its ecology, behaviour and habits, together with pointers to where to seek additional information.

ACKNOWLEDGEMENTS

We are very grateful to the following for help in a variety of ways: M. P. Adams, D. Allan, D. Allen, G. Allport, P. W. Atkinson, A. J. Beakbane, L. Birch, R. Borello, W. D. Borello, N. Burgess, J. A. D. Cape, M. Carswell, M. Catterall, A. S. Cheke, N. G. Cheshire, P. M. Claffey, N. J. Collar, J. A. Coles, T. D. C. Coles, J. T. Couto, A. J. F. K. Craig, J. Dando, L. Daugherty, G. W. H. Davison, J. P. Dean, W. R. J. Dean, J. del Hoyo, C. F. Dewhurst, E. C. Dickinson, J. Elkin, G. R. Graves, D. Harvey, E. P. Figueiredo, B. Finch, C. T. Fisher, L. D. C. Fishpool, J. Fjeldså, C. H. Fry, D. Harvey, A. F. A. Hawkins, C. Helm, M. Herremans, G. Hess, N. D. Hunter, M. P. S. Irwin, S. Jackson, P. J. Jones, H. F. Kaiwala, V. Katenekwa, S. Keith, R. S. Kennedy, S. Kennedy, F. M. Kimmins, D. Kirkup, C. Lotz, M. Louette, E. McIntyre, L. W. Maina, S. Markman, R. Medland, A. M. Moore, D. C. Moyer, P. J. Mundy, H. D. Oschadleus, A. C. Ozóg, D. J. Pearson, M. A. Peirce, P. Poilecot, R. Prys-Jones, E. Pulawska, R. Ranft, N. J. Redman, A. Richford, D. R. Russell, C. Ryall, V. Salewski, H. Sanders, J. Speck, A. J. Stattersfield, F. Steinheimer, Baron R. Stjernstedt, P. Sweet, P. Thomas, B. Treca, J. F. Walsh, M. P. Walters, F. E. Warr, G. Welch, H. Welch, D. R. Wells, M. W. Woodcock.

Specimens from the collections of the following museums have been examined: American Museum of Natural History, New York; Cincinnati Museum Center; Delaware Museum of Natural History; Durban Natural Science Museum; Natural History Museum, Tring; Muséum National d'Histoire Naturelle, Paris; The Merseyside County Museums, Liverpool; Museum of Natural History, Bulawayo; Musée Royale de l'Afrique Centrale, Tervuren; Museum für Naturkunde der Humboldt-Universität, Berlin; National Museum of Zambia, Livingstone; National Museum of Natural History (Smithsonian Institution), Washington; Zoologisk Museum, University of Copenhagen.

Information on recoveries of birds ringed in southern Africa was kindly supplied by SAFRING.

"Anytime the sunbird came from the river side, he would sing *ketekete* (very small). As the saying goes, it is always good to have something small every day rather than something big which will never come again."

Adapted from "The Sunbird and the Lion", pp.32-34 in Kwesi Hutchinson (1994) *Folktales from Ashanti*, Volume 1. Sly Hutchinson, Kumasi, Ghana.

STYLE AND LAYOUT OF THE SPECIES ACCOUNTS

Species accounts in the systematic section are subdivided into headings. The information presented in each heading is outlined below, together with major sources consulted.

Each species is given a sequential number followed by its vernacular and scientific names, and relevant plate number.

The original scientific name and authority are detailed, together with associated reference and type locality, as well as taxonomic comments if appropriate. Alternative vernacular name or names are also listed.

IDENTIFICATION Salient features for identifying the species.
Similar species Details of sympatric or closely allopatric species with which the species in question could be confused, with remarks on how to distinguish the various taxa involved.

VOICE Song A description of the song or songs with onomatopoeic transcriptions in italics. **Call** A description of the call or calls with onomatopoeic transcriptions in italics.

HABITAT The species' usual habitats.

DISTRIBUTION A summary of the species' geographical distribution with, for Afrotropical species, a list of all the countries where the species has been recorded, based mainly on Dowsett (1993). Supplementary information for different countries was obtained according to country, primarily from the following references: Angola (Dean 2000), Australia (Blakers *et al.* 1984), Benin (P. M. Claffey pers. comm.), Bioko, Equatorial Guinea (Pérez del Val 1996), Borneo (Smythies 1960, 1981, MacKinnon & Phillipps 1993, Mann in prep. b), Burkina Faso (Thonnerieux *et al.* 1989), Burma (Smythies 1986), Burundi (Gaugris *et al.* 1981), China including Taiwan (Meyer de Schauensee 1984), Côte d'Ivoire (Thiollay 1985), Democratic Republic of the Congo (Chapin 1954), mainland Equatorial Guinea (Dowsett-Lemaire & Dowsett 1999), Gambia (Gore 1990, Morel & Morel 1990), Ghana (Grimes 1987), the Greater Sunda islands (MacKinnon & Phillipps 1993), the Indian subcontinent (Ali & Ripley 1974, 1983, Grimmett *et al.* 1998), Hong Kong (Viney & Phillipps 1978, 1988), Kenya (Lewis & Pomeroy 1989), Liberia (Colston & Curry-Lindahl 1986, Gatter 1997), Malawi (Benson & Benson 1977, Newman *et al.* 1992), the Malay Peninsula (Medway & Wells 1976), Mali (Lamarche 1981), Mauritania (Lamarche 1988), New Guinea (Rand & Gilliard 1967), Niger (Giraudoux *et al.* 1988), Nigeria (Elgood *et al.* 1994), the Philippines (Dickinson *et al.* 1991), Príncipe (Jones & Tye in press), São Tomé (Jones & Tye in press), Senegal (Morel & Morel 1990), Somalia (Ash & Miskell 1998), southern Africa (Harrison *et al.* 1997), South-East Asia (King *et al.* 1975, Robson 2000), Sudan (Cave & Macdonald 1955), Sumatra (van Marle & Voous 1988), Thailand (Lekagul & Round 1991), Togo (Cheke & Walsh 1996), Wallacea (White & Bruce 1986, Coates & Bishop 1997).

STATUS Comments on the species' status, in different areas if known, ranging from abundant, very common, common, locally common, to scarce or rare, and with remarks on conservation status if appropriate.

MOVEMENTS Comments on any known movements undertaken by the species.

FOOD Types of food eaten.
Known food-plants Scientific names of plants on whose flowers, fruits, seeds or leaves the birds are known to feed. In some cases, authors have not made clear whether the bird has been feeding on a particular plant or using it as a perch, from whence to sally forth after insects or in which to glean leaves for food. Thus the lists may include some plants in these categories. The genera for all vascular plants named are those accepted by Mabberley (1997) and for Afrotropical mistletoes the classification of Polhill & Wiens (1998) has been followed.

HABITS A summary of information on the bird's behaviour, longevity and parasites. Details of blood parasites were derived from Bennett and co-workers (1982, 1985, 1991, 1992).

BREEDING A summary of the species' breeding behaviour. **Nest** A description of the nest. **Eggs** Clutch size (e.g. c/2 indicates a clutch of 2). Measurements of eggs (length from tip to end x maximum breadth in mm). Description of egg. **Laying months** Months when eggs are known to be laid or other evidence of breeding dates, according to region or country.

DESCRIPTION *Scientific name of taxon being described* (if the species is polytypic).

Adult male Description of the adult male.

Adult female Description of the adult female.

Juvenile Description of the juvenile.

Descriptions of non-breeding plumage, nestlings, moult etc. are also included in some accounts, but not invariably in this section.

GEOGRAPHICAL VARIATION A list, in alphabetical order (except where some subspecies form natural groups), of all subspecies of the species in question as recognised in this volume).

Each subspecies is listed, giving the following information:

Scientific name of taxon being described followed by authority and date of type description, and brief summary of the subspecies' range in brackets. If appropriate, comments are also given, e.g. on other subspecies subsumed within it. A brief description of the subspecies is given and how it can be distinguished from others.

MEASUREMENTS All measurements are quoted in mm, except mass in g. After each measurement heading, data are listed alphabetically according to subspecies, with measurements for males listed first, followed by information for females and then juveniles and unsexed birds. For each measurement, data are listed as follows, although full details are not always available: the range (mean, standard deviation [SD] if known, sex and subspecies of the sample). The data used for the range may be additional to those used to estimate means and SDs, but the sample sizes quoted refer to the numbers of birds used to calculate the statistics. Measurements are listed in the following order: **wing**, maximum chord method for folded wing, by which the curvatures of the wing are eliminated; **tail** from the tip of the longest tail feather to the point where the feathers join the body; **bill** from tip of bill to skull unless otherwise stated; **culmen** distance of exposed bill from feathers to tip of bill; **gape** distance from corner of gape to tip of bill; **tarsus** from the depression at the base of its rear joint to the end of the last scale before the toes separate at the front; **mass** of live birds (g). Data were gathered from published figures and unpublished datasets, including those of the authors. In many instances mean and standard deviations were calculated by collating data, but this was not always possible if authors had not quoted standard deviations.

REFERENCES Lists references from which information for the account has been derived, in addition to the authors' unpublished data and those cited above under Distribution.

TOPOGRAPHY

The terminology used to describe the external morphology of a bird, and which is particularly relevant to field identification, varies somewhat from text to text. Figures 1-3 are labelled with the terms as used in this book. Tail feathers are numbered outwards with the central rectrices being T1 and the 10 primaries are also numbered outwards. Many sunbirds, spiderhunters and flowerpeckers have pectoral tufts – groups of elongated feathers emanating from the sides of the chest not from the underwing-coverts. These tufts are usually brightly coloured, often yellow, red or orange in sunbirds and spiderhunters, but white in flowerpeckers, and are prominent in displays. They are often concealed beneath the wings on perched birds.

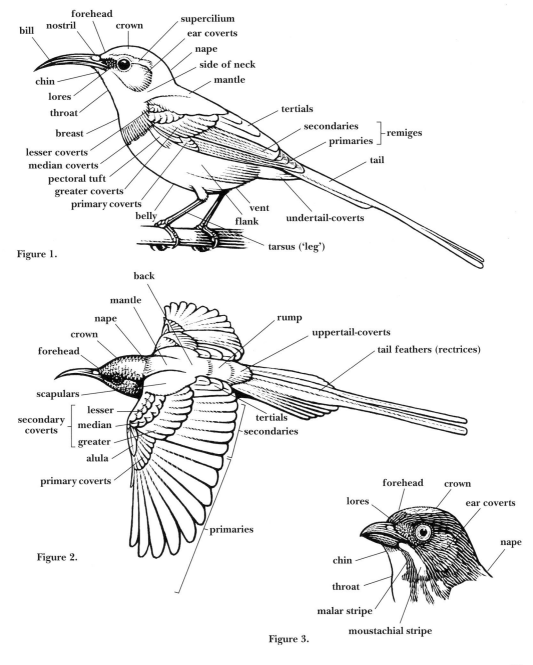

Figure 1.

Figure 2.

Figure 3.

MORPHOLOGY

GENERAL

Summaries of the structure of each genus are provided in the short genus descriptions in the species accounts. Other comments on comparative morphology of different taxa are considered below under "Tongues" and under "Relationships and taxonomy".

The iridescence of sunbirds is produced by internal structural relationships of keratin and melanin granules only, without involvement of air-spaces (Durrer & Villiger 1962, Farquhar *et al.* 1996).

TONGUES

The tongues of nectarivorous birds are adapted to draw nectar from flowers and there are differences between the groups which have taxonomic importance (Delacour 1944). All tongues collect nectar by capillarity, with licking rates of 6-17 per second but speeds of licking respond to changes in sugar concentration and corolla length (Paton & Collins 1989). The range of floral lengths that can be probed without recourse to "nectar-robbing" (see below under food and foraging) is determined by bill length; but the maximum floral lengths which can be probed exceed bill lengths, since sunbirds protrude their tongues beyond the tips of their bills. Rates of nectar extraction, however, decline when the floral length exceeds the bill length. Male sunbirds tend to have longer bills than females, which suggests that males and females may exploit different floral resources or different proportions of the same resources (Paton & Collins 1989).

The tongue of a sugarbird *Promerops* sp. forms an incomplete tube through much of its length. The distal 20% is divided into two lobes, the inner edge of each being bifurcated to form smaller lobes, and the distal 60% of the inner and outer lobes are serrated (Figure 4a).

Tongues of the *Prionochilus* flowerpeckers are triangular, and slightly concave in cross-section. The distal 20% of the tongues are cleft, and each side is bifurcated for the distal 10% of its length, forming a four-pronged tip, with the inner two prongs shorter than the outer two. The outer edges of the tongue are fimbriated (Figure 5a). Tongues of the *Dicaeum* flowerpeckers fall into four groups: (1) broad, flat and non-tubular as found in Bicoloured Flowerpecker *D. bicolor* (Figure 5e), Grey-sided Flowerpecker *D. celebicum*, Yellow-sided Flowerpecker *D. aureolimbatum* and Thick-billed Flowerpecker *D. agile*; (2) narrow to medium broad tongues with their edges curled inwards to form two tubes, one either side of a flat central plate, the tip of which is extended to form two prongs (as in Red-striped Flowerpecker *D. australe* (Figure 5f), Yellow-bellied Flowerpecker *D. melanoxanthum* and Buzzing Flowerpecker *D. hypoleucum*; (3) Narrow tongues with the tips bifid and the centre further divided, the whole tip thus becoming four flat ribbons, much fimbriated at the edges, as found in Olive-capped Flowerpecker *D. nigrilore* (Figure 5g) and (4) long narrow tongues, forming two tubular structures distally (in one specimen of Orange-bellied Flowerpecker *D. trigonostigma* there are two extra lateral extensions, Figure 5b), as found in Flame-breasted Flowerpecker *D. erythrothorax, D. trigonostigma*, Blood-breasted Flowerpecker *D. sanguinolentum*, Pygmy Flowerpecker *D. pygmaeum*, Midget Flowerpecker *D. aeneum* and Scarlet-backed Flowerpecker *D. cruentatum*.

The tongue of the Ruby-cheeked Sunbird *Chalcoparia singalensis* is concave in cross section, the tip is deeply notched and fimbriated, forming two prongs, and the edges of the distal part are fimbriated (Figure 5c).

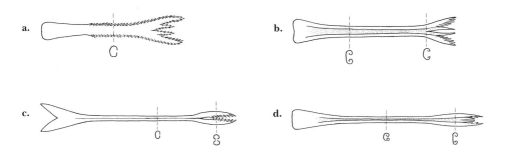

Figure 4. Tongues of **(a) Cape Sugarbird** *Promerops cafer*; **(b) Purple-naped Sunbird** *Hypogramma hypogrammicum*; **(c) Eastern Olive Sunbird** *Cyanomitra olivacea*; and **(d) Crimson Sunbird** *Aethopyga siparaja*.

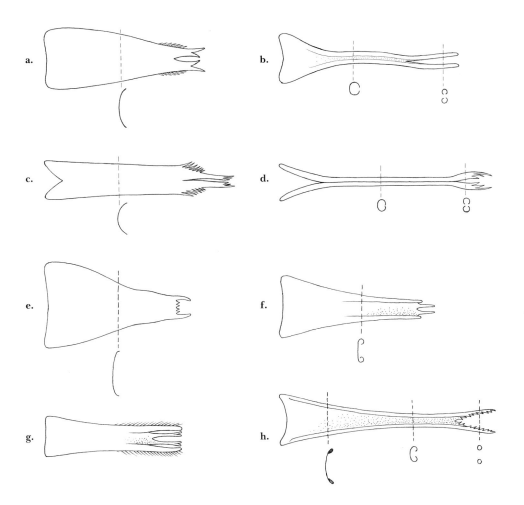

Figure 5. Tongues of **(a) Yellow-breasted Flowerpecker** *Prionochilus maculatus*; **(b) Orange-bellied Flowerpecker** *Dicaeum trigonostigma*; **(c) Ruby-cheeked Sunbird** *Chalcoparia singalensis*; **(d) Plain Sunbird** *Anthreptes simplex*; **(e) Bicolored Flowerpecker** *Dicaeum bicolor*; **(f) Red-striped Flowerpecker** *Dicaeum australe*; **(g) Olive-capped Flowerpecker** *Dicaeum nigrilore*; **and (h) Scarlet-tufted Sunbird** *Deleornis fraseri*.

Tongues of all other sunbirds except those of *Hedydipna* and *Hypogramma* are long and narrow. Those of *Deleornis* taper from a broad base and are concave, with the edges becoming curled over the distal third. The tips are deeply bifurcate, forming two tubes, with serrated inner edges (e.g. Scarlet-tufted Sunbird *D. fraseri*, Figure 5h). Tongues of *Anthreptes* spp. are tubular for much of their length, and bifurcated towards their tips, each side forming partial tubes, deeply notched on the inner edges (Figures 5d, 7b). *Hedydipna* spp. have tongues with edges curled inwards to form two almost complete tubes. The distal 25% is bifurcated forming two complete tubes, the inner edges fimbriated (Figure 7a).

The Purple-naped Sunbird *Hypogramma hypogrammicum* has a tongue with its edges coiled inwards to form two incomplete tubes. The tip is divided into two lobes, serrated on their inner edges, with two prongs in the centre, forming a brush-like structure (Figure 4b). Orange-breasted Sunbird *Anthobaphes violacea* has a tongue with edges curled over much of its length to form two tubes, with the distal 20% bifurcated to form two helical tubes (Figure 6a).

Tongues of *Cyanomitra* spp. are have their edges curled inwards to form a tube. The distal 20% is bifurcated forming two incomplete tubes, serrated on the inner edges (Figure 4c). Those of *Chalcomitra* spp. also have edges curled inwards to form a tube. The tip is bifurcate, forming two tubes, each with jagged inner edges (Figure 6c). Tongues of *Leptocoma* spp. similarly curl inwards to form a tube, becoming two tubes over much of their length. The tip is bifurcate, forming two tubes with serrated inner edges (e.g. Montane Double-collared Sunbird *C. ludovicensis*, Figure 6e). *Cinnyris* spp. have their edges coiled

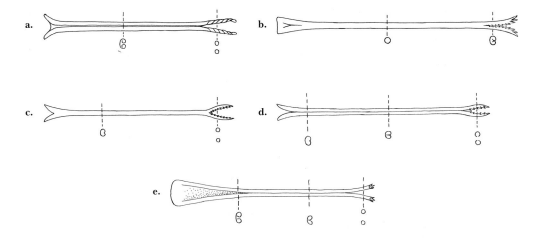

Figure 6. Tongues of **(a) Orange-breasted Sunbird** *Anthobaphes violacea*; **(b) Long-billed Spiderhunter** *Arachnothera robusta*; **(c) Buff-throated Sunbird** *Chalcomitra adelberti*; **(d) Black Sunbird** *Leptocoma sericea*; and **(e) Montane Double-collared Sunbird** *Cinnyris ludovicensis*.

inwards to form two tubes, which separate towards the tip (e.g. Black Sunbird *L. sericea*, Figure 6d). Tongues of *Nectarinia* spp. are extremely long and narrow, coiled into a single tube for most of their length. The bifurcated tip forms two helical tubes, jagged on inner edges (Figure 7c), whereas those of *Aethopyga* spp. have edges curled inwards to form two tubes but the tip is split laterally forming two grooves, or incomplete tubes, with a bifurcate central plate which may help to complete the tubes (Figure 4d). Tongues of *Arachnothera* spp. are also extremely long and narrow with edges curled inwards to form a single tube. The distal 10% is bifurcate, forming two jagged-edged tubes, completed by a central plate (Figure 6b).

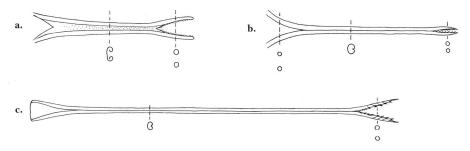

Figure 7. Tongues of **(a) Pygmy Sunbird** *Hedydipna platura*; **(b) Western Violet-backed Sunbird** *Anthreptes longuemarei*; **(c) Tacazze Sunbird** *Nectarinia tacazze*.

PLUMAGE, MOULT AND OTHER AGE-RELATED CHARACTERS

The moulting regimes of sunbirds are complex, being different in different species. The African species can be classified into three main groups (Mackworth-Praed and Grant 1945). (1) Species whose males do not have an intermediate immature plumage, moulting directly from juvenile dress to breeding dress, but do have a non-breeding or eclipse plumage, into which they moult after breeding and moult out of at the start of the following breeding season. Examples include Malachite Sunbird *Nectarinia famosa*, Tacazze Sunbird *N. tacazze*, Purple-breasted Sunbird *N. purpureiventris*, Beautiful Sunbird *Cinnyris pulchellus*, Pygmy Sunbird *Hedydipna platura*, Nile Valley Sunbird *H. metallica*, Copper Sunbird *Cinnyris cupreus*, Purple-banded Sunbird *C. bifasciatus*, Kenya Violet-breasted Sunbird *C. chalcomelas*, Shelley's Sunbird *C. shelleyi*, Oustalet's Sunbird *C. oustaleti*, Variable Sunbird *C. venustus* and Stuhlmann's Double-collared Sunbird *C. stuhlmanni*. (2) Species which have an intermediate immature plumage, into which they moult from their juvenile plumage, but do not have an eclipse plumage and moult from breeding plumage to breeding plumage. Examples include Splendid Sunbird *C. coccinigaster*, Shining Sunbird *C. habessinicus*, Pemba Sunbird *C.*

pembae, Southern Double-collared Sunbird *C. chalybeus*, Regal Sunbird *C. regius*, Amethyst Sunbird *Chalcomitra amethystina* and Scarlet-chested Sunbird *C. senegalensis*. (3) Species which have neither an immature plumage nor an eclipse plumage and moult from juvenile dress into breeding plumage and from one breeding plumage to another. Examples include Bronzy Sunbird *Nectarinia kilimensis*, Golden-winged Sunbird *Drepanorhynchus reichenowi*, Red-chested Sunbird *Cinnyris erythroceria*, Superb Sunbird *C. superbus*, Mariqua Sunbird *C. mariquensis*, Orange-tufted Sunbird *C. bouvieri*, Eastern Double-collared Sunbird *C. mediocris*, Northern Double-collared Sunbird *C. reichenowi*, Olive-bellied Sunbird *C. chloropygius*, Green-headed Sunbird *Cyanomitra verticalis*, Blue-headed Sunbird *C. alinae*, Blue-throated Brown Sunbird *C. cyanolaema*, Western Olive Sunbird *C. obscura*, Socotra Sunbird *Chalcomitra balfouri*, Collared Sunbird *Hedydipna collaris*, Green Sunbird *Anthreptes rectirostris*, Western Violet-backed Sunbird *A. longuemarei*, Kenya Violet-backed Sunbird *A. orientalis*, Uluguru Violet-backed Sunbird *A. neglectus*, Anchieta's Sunbird *A. anchietae* and Grey-headed Sunbird *Deleornis axillaris*.

According to Chapin (1959), sunbirds of the African lowland rain forest have no eclipse plumage, and may nest at any time of the year. However, in the savanna bordering equatorial forest some species do show duller plumage in the off-season. In the dry months of June–August, male Copper Sunbirds *Cinnyris cupreus* and Variable Sunbirds *C. venustus* lose much of their metallic sheen.

The colour of the buccal cavity varies with species and age of sunbirds (Brooke 1970, 1976). In general, breeding males have dark mouths while those of non-breeding males are paler. Males in their post-juvenile moult do not attain adult mouth colours until the moult is nearly complete. The mouths of juvenile sunbirds are usually yellow to orange or pink. The biological significance of these changes is unclear: a relationship to courtship seems unlikely as males tend to display facing away from females (Brooke 1976).

KARYOLOGY

Few studies have been made of the chromosomes of sunbirds but it is known that the Amethyst Sunbird *Chalcomitra amethystina* has a very unusual karyotype made up of a large number of minute chromosomes of average length 1.2μm (Capanna & Geralico 1982), a phenomenon very unusual in birds, especially passerines. The diploid number is 2n = 96-100. Bi-armed chromosomes are heavily outnumbered by acrocentrics. Only the first pair is truly metacentric, while pairs 2 and 3 are sub-telocentric as is the Z heterochromosome. The chromosomes of the Purple-rumped Sunbird *Leptocoma zeylonica* have been described by Bhunya & Das (1991).

RELATIONSHIPS AND TAXONOMY

The classification used in Peters (Paynter 1967) closely followed the Wetmore (1930, 1940, 1951, 1960) system, placing the Nectariniidae (sunbirds and spiderhunters), the Dicaeidae (flowerpeckers, berrypeckers and pardalotes) and Promeropidae (sugarbirds) with other Old World nectarivores, Zosteropidae (white-eyes) and Meliphagidae (honeyeaters). This grouping in turn was placed in an enormous assemblage of Old World insectivores, in the Order Passeriformes.

The Promeropidae has had a chequered taxonomic history, having at times been claimed for, *inter alia*, starlings (Sibley & Ahlquist 1974) and honeyeaters (Salomonsen 1933).

The DNA-DNA hybridisation studies of Sibley & Ahlquist (1974, 1983, 1990) and Sibley & Monroe (1990, 1993) have been accepted in recent years. Although many of their findings lack congruence with other, more traditional, research, and corroboration is frequently lacking, we have accepted their arrangement of the taxa covered in this book as a basis. Thus, we include all species in the single family Nectariniidae. The sugarbirds *Promerops* spp. constitute the subfamily Promeropinae, whereas all other species are included in the subfamily Nectariniinae, subdivided into the tribe Dicaeini (flowerpeckers, but excluding berrypeckers and pardalotes) and the tribe Nectariini (sunbirds and spiderhunters).

The two species of sugarbird are the largest members of the family, and found only in South Africa, Swaziland, Mozambique and Zimbabwe, living in close association with *Protea* vegetation. They have long curved bills, and long tails. The distinctive tongue structure is adapted to nectarivory, although arthropods are also taken, as in other nectar-feeders; it is closer to that of meliphagids than to other members of the Nectariniidae. The skeletal structure of *Promerops* is also closer to those of the meliphagids than to those of the sunbirds, but has been interpreted to suggest that its closest relatives may be neither the sunbirds nor the honeyeaters (Farquhar *et al.* 1996).

The sunbirds and spiderhunters, a morphologically similar group, are distributed over much of Africa, Madagascar and the Indian Ocean islands, the Middle East, the Oriental region, Wallacea, New Guinea and the Solomon Islands, with one species reaching Australia. The baseline for most recent sunbird taxonomy is the revision of Delacour (1944), who reduced the number of genera to five. Amadon (1951) removed the false sunbirds (*Neodrepanis* spp.) of Madagascar, and recognised *Hypogramma* as a separate genus. Various works, culminating in those of Wolters (1977, 1979), brought a number of old genera, most of which had been accepted by Delacour (1944) as subgenera, back into use, and introduced novelties: *Deleornis* for (*Anthreptes*) *fraseri* and (*A.*) *axillaris*, *Paradeleornis* for (*A.*) *seimundi* and (*C.*) *batesi* and *Haplocinnyris* for *C. ursulae* and four new subgenera, *Rhizophorornis* for *A. gabonicus*, *Melanocinnyris* for *C. habessinicus*, *Chrysocinnyris* for *C. loveridgei*, *C. regius* and *C. rockefelleri* and *Cirrothorax* for *C. adelberti*.

Irwin (1993, 1999) is the most recent reviser of sunbirds and with two exceptions his treatment, which accepts 14 genera, is followed here. To his list – *Anthreptes*, *Deleornis*, *Anabathmis*, *Dreptes*, *Anthobaphes*, *Cyanomitra*, *Chalcomitra*, *Leptocoma*, *Nectarinia*, *Hedydipna*, *Cinnyris* (which is further subdivided), *Hypogramma*, *Aethopyga* and *Arachnothera* – we have added two more, *Chalcoparia* for (*Anthreptes*) *singalensis* and *Drepanorhynchus* for (*Nectarinia*) *reichenowi*. Analyses of 195 sonagrams of 65 species of Afrotropical sunbirds did not provide evidence contrary to Irwin's conclusions but general support for them (Maina 1999, L. W. Maina & R. A. Cheke, unpubl.). For instance calls of *Chalcomitra* spp. are generally similar to each other, and most songs of *Cyanomitra* spp. consist of trills with either complex or simple parts at the start or end, and are different from songs of *Cinnyris* spp. Tongue structure lends further support to the acceptance of these genera (Mann in prep. a).

Irwin, whose scheme is also followed by Fry *et al.* (2000), argued that *Anthreptes* is the most primitive, and *Cinnyris* the most derived of the genera. However, it could be argued that *Chalcoparia*, with its non-tubular tongue, recalling that of the flowerpeckers *Prionochilus* spp., is the most primitive, if indeed it is a sunbird at all. *Hypogramma* has a tongue structure which, although partially tubular, is unlike that of any other sunbird, recalling that of *Promerops*, and like *Chalcoparia*, it is perhaps not a sunbird. The tongue and bill structures of the Asian *Aethopyga* and *Arachnothera* not only suggest a close relationship between the two, but could be used as evidence that they are the most highly derived. *Arachnothera* is rather distinct from all other sunbirds in its lack of sexual dimorphism (except for larger size and the presence of pectoral tufts in the males of some species), a different type of nest, and the sharing of incubation by both sexes. White, yellow, orange or red pectoral tufts are present in many sunbirds (and a few flowerpeckers) and are erected during displays.

The genera *Deleornis*, *Anabathmis*, *Dreptes*, *Anthobaphes*, *Cyanomitra*, *Chalcomitra*, *Nectarinia*, *Drepanorhynchus* and *Hedydipna* are confined to Africa and the western Indian Ocean islands, with *H. metallica* reaching Arabia in Yemen. *Chalcoparia*, *Hypogramma*, *Leptocoma*, *Aethopyga* and *Arachnothera* are found only in Asia, with *Aethopyga* occurring also in Wallacea, and *Leptocoma* east to New Guinea. Only *Anthreptes* and *Cinnyris* are found in both Africa and Asia, the latter extending to New Guinea and Australia as well as to the Middle East.

There is much sexual dimorphism amongst sunbirds involving plumage, size and tail length, although in some species the sexes are similar except in size. Most have some iridescent plumage in the males. With two known exceptions (*Chalcoparia* and *Hypogramma*), they have tubular tongues becoming bifid towards the tip. Bills are generally long, and usually curved, although the range and extravagance of the bills of their New World counterparts, the hummingbirds (Trochilidae), is not matched by the sunbirds.

Most of the genera appear to be rather closely related and distinctions between them are not well-marked, except in *Chalcoparia* and *Hypogramma* and, to a lesser extent, *Aethopyga* and *Arachnothera*.

The flowerpeckers (Dicaeini) occur in the Oriental Region, Wallacea, and New Guinea and associated islands, with one species extending into Australia. All are small to very small, with short rounded tails. There is sexual dichromatism in many, but not all, species, with the males having some iridescent, and/or brightly coloured plumage. Compared to sunbirds, their bills are short and blunt. Recent classifications (e.g. Paynter 1967) have placed them in two genera, *Prionochilus* of South-East Asia, the Greater Sundas and the Philippines with rather thick, blunt bills, and the more widespread *Dicaeum*. The latter has more variation in bill structure, being thick and blunt or more slender than *Prionochilus*, and in some are rather pointed and decurved. The division into these genera rests on one character, the length of the outermost primary, long in *Prionochilus*, and vestigial in *Dicaeum*. However, the Yellow-bellied Flowerpecker *D. melanoxanthum* is an exception in having a long outer primary. The tongue structure of *Prionochilus* is non-tubular, recalling that of *Chalcoparia*, whereas that of *Dicaeum* is varied, in some bifid and tubular, recalling that of typical sunbirds. However, some members of this genus, particularly those that are more stout-billed (e.g. *D. agile*), have tongues recalling those of *Prionochilus* (Morioka 1992), whereas others fall into two further groups according to their tongue structure (see generic accounts). This strongly suggests that the genus *Dicaeum* as presently constituted is not a natural grouping, but a lack of spirit specimens of most species prevents a full taxonomic revision at present.

POSSIBLE UNDESCRIBED SPECIES

There are several accounts suggesting the existence of undescribed species, as follows. (A) There have been sightings of an unidentified but distinctive species of sunbird in the Gola Forest, Sierra Leone (Allport 1989, G. Allport pers. comm.). Two mostly black or black-brown *Anthreptes*-like birds were seen feeding together and sallying for insects amongst a mixed-species flock in the middle to lower storey of the forest. The presumed male had a brilliant, almost glossy crimson hood and a breast-band of glossy bluish below it in the pectoral area. A second bird, perhaps a female or immature, was similar but with crimson cap and nape, with red extending from the nape to the front of the carpal joint, possibly attributable to pectoral tufts, and lacking any bluish gloss. The bare parts of both birds were black, the bill being very short and slightly attenuated and down-curved at the tip. (B) Descriptions and illustrations have been provided of yellow-crowned sunbirds seen in the Wadi Tôha (11°48'N 42°45'E), Djibouti, thought by Welch & Welch (1998) to be representatives of an undescribed species, and treated as such by Fry *et al.* (2000) under the name Tôha Sunbird, without the attachment of a formal scientific name. However, birds which had been feeding in pollen-laden flowers, such as those of *Acacia* spp., and had accumulated yellow pollen on their crowns cannot yet be ruled out; females or immature males of Shining Sunbird *C. habessinicus* or of the race *osiris* (or else an unknown form) of Mariqua Sunbird *Cinnyris mariquensis* are possible candidates.

BEHAVIOUR

FOOD AND FORAGING

Co-adaptations between bill morphologies and flower structures have evolved, leading to interspecific ecological differences with short-billed species being unable to probe flowers used as major nectar sources by long-billed species. Indeed some co-adaptations are remarkable, with the "pollen-groove" on the crown of the Golden-winged Sunbird *Drepanorhynchus reichenowi* (Friedmann & Stager 1969 and see Figure 8), being one of the more extreme examples.

When they do feed on the same species of flower(s), a guild of sunbirds with different bill sizes will differ in their foraging efficiencies (Gill & Wolf 1975a, 1978) but interspecific competition is also common (Cheke 1971a). The constraints of territoriality and intraspecific competition also complicate the birds' energetics (Gill & Wolf 1979, Pyke 1979). Effort expended in territory defence is apparently related to the sucrose concentration of ingested food since Bronze Sunbirds *Nectarinia kilimensis* given extra sucrose relaxed their defence of territories (Lott & Lott 1991). The constraints of interspecific competition invoke bizarre behavioural patterns. For instance, female *D. reichenowi* are subordinant to both sexes of *N. kilimensis*, yet they are able to avoid being evicted from the latter's foraging territories by a wing-quivering, tail-spread display evocative of food-begging behaviour, thus exploiting a communication that functions in the reproduction of *N. kilimensis* (Lott 1991).

In addition to foraging for invertebrates by leaf-gleaning, sunbirds also catch insects by sallying like a flycatcher. Flowerheads, seeds and fruits are also sometimes eaten.

POLLINATION AND SEED DISPERSAL

Although arthropods are an important constituent of the diet of many, if not all, members of the Nectariniidae, these birds are intimately associated with flowers. Nectar, fruits, pollen and other parts of flowers are known food sources for all members of the family for which diet items are recorded. Arthropods are also collected at and around flowers. During feeding at flowers pollen is dusted onto the bill, tongue and plumage, and any that is not swallowed will be carried to other flowers, some of which may be receptive members of the same species, and thus pollination is effected. In some cases sunbirds are known to be nectar thieves (or robbers) (Swynnerton 1916), as are some hummingbirds, piercing the bases of corollas thus reducing the chances of pollination.

The means by which sunbirds feed on flowers include direct probing (Figure 8), hovering in front to flowers (Figure 9) and "nectar-robbing" to reach nectar without encountering the pollination apparatus (Figure 10). After feeding, sunbirds often wipe their bills on twigs or branches (Figure 11), presumably to clean off sticky nectar or other debris from plants, or perhaps as a displacement activity.

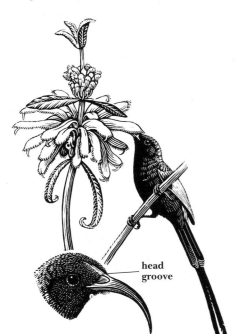

head groove

Figure 8. Male Golden-winged Sunbird *Drepanorhynchus reichenowi* probing floret of *Leonotis* sp., and detail of head to show groove in forehead.

Figure 9. Male Southern Double-collared Sunbird *Cinnyris chalybeus* hovering to feed from floret of *Erica* sp.

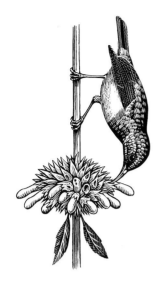

Figure 10 (left). Variable Sunbird *Cinnyris venustus* "nectar-robbing" from base of floret of *Leonotis* sp.

Figure 11 (above). Bill-wiping behaviour by male Seychelles Sunbird *Cinnyris dussumieri*.

Apart from the usual direct pollination from the bill or crown, pollination of *Strelitzia nicolai*, for instance, may be via the feet of *Cyanomitra olivacea*, *C. veroxii*, *Chalcomitra amethystina* and *Hedydipna collaris* (Frost & Frost 1981, see Figure 12). *S. reginae* is probably similarly pollinated by *Cinnyris afer* (Mabberley 1997).

There are no recorded cases of any one species of Nectariniidae being intimately connected with any one particular species of flowering plant leading to the intimate associations recorded for some hummingbirds, but there are some very close associations, e.g. Golden-winged Sunbird *Drepanorhynchus reichenowi* with *Crotalaria* sp. and *Leonotis* spp., and Purple-breasted Sunbird *Nectarinia purpureiventris* with *Symphonia globulifera*. Pollinia (compact packets of pollen), produced only by orchids Orchidaceae and milkweeds Asclepidaceae, become attached to insect pollinators by pollinaria (mechanical clips). In most cases, particularly amongst orchids, there is a very specific relationship between a plant and its pollinator, with often only one species of insect involved, leading to fascinating and bizarre co-adaptations. Recently, two examples of this phenomenon have been found in sunbirds from South Africa. The first involved the Lesser Double-collared Sunbird *Cinnyris chalybeus* and a milkweed *Microloma sagittatum* (Pauw 1998), the second the Orange-breasted Sunbird *Anthobaphes violacea* and pollinia from an as yet unidentified milkweed or orchid (see account for *A. violacea*). In both cases the pairs of pollinia were attached to the tubular tongue tips. In the latter case it appears as if the pollinia were blocking the tongue tubes and preventing them from curling. This could well have a detrimental effect on the species feeding behaviour, and both examples are quite possibly only accidental associations. Another example of a close association between plants and the birds treated here is the Cape sugarbird *Promerops cafer* and the *Protea* species which it pollinates.

Figure 12. Eastern Olive Sunbirds *Cyanomitra olivacea* in different positions for feeding on *Strelitzia* sp. (after Skead 1967).

Figure 13. Mistletoebird *Dicaeum hirundinaceum* depositing mistletoe seeds.

All flowerpeckers for which there is sufficient information spend much time at mistletoes (Loranthaceae and Viscaceae). Larger berries of these plants have the fleshy pericarp removed and eaten by flowerpeckers, and the sticky seeds dropped or wiped onto branches. Smaller fruits are eaten whole and, bypassing the stomach, pass very rapidly through the gut. The fleshy parts are digested in the gut, while the sticky seed passes out of the cloaca and is wiped on a branch (Figure 13). The little information from field studies shows that at least in some species of mistletoe germination can be successful even if the seed has not first been eaten by a flowerpecker, and therefore the relationship is not an obligate one. There is also a close association between many African sunbirds and mistletoes, which have complicated pollination mechanisms (Feehan 1985, Polhill & Wiens 1998).

VOCALISATIONS

Sunbirds call as they flit from food-plant to food-plant, to contact conspecifics, in alarm and in various intraspecific actions such as courtship and feeding young. Males, and in some cases females also, sing, usually from a prominent perch, and some species also utter subsongs. The song is most often in defence or advertisement of a territory, but group displays in leks are also known, particularly in *Cyanomitra* spp. There may be considerable variation intraspecifically, with different dialects known in the Splendid Sunbird *Cinnyris coccinigaster*, for instance (Grimes 1974, Payne 1978). Physiological effects play their part too, as captive male Variable Sunbirds *C. venustus* sing more full song phrases, but less subsong, during the courtship season than otherwise when fed high concentrations of sucrose solutions; and they do not sing at all if no flies are available (Wilhelm *et al.* 1980, 1982).

COURTSHIP

Figure 14. Aerial display of male Cape Sugarbird *Promerops cafer*. Bird rises silently from perch on *Protea* sp., then whips its tail and jerks its wings with an audible *frrt-frrt* and utters a tinny song in descending flight back into proteas (after Skead 1967).

Sunbirds, spiderhunters, flowerpeckers and sugarbirds display to each other when courting and some male displays are elaborate. For instance, male sugarbirds *Promerops* spp. perform spectacular flights (Figure 14), male Copper Sunbirds *Cinnyris cupreus* make bowing motions (Figure 15), male Malachite Sunbirds *Nectarinia famosa* contort themselves into unexpected positions and display their pectoral tufts (Figure 16) and male Greater Double-collared Sunbirds *C. afer* fan their tails and point their heads skywards (Figure 17). Where known, details of such displays are described in the species accounts.

There are numerous recorded instances of cloaca-pecking amongst sunbirds (Figure 18), suggestive of females copulating with more than one male (Birkhead & Møller 1992). Such an extra-pair copulation has been observed in the Purple-rumped Sunbird *Leptocoma zeylonica* (Lamba 1978) and is regular in the Palestine Sunbird *Cinnyris oseus* in which 36% of broods have chicks through extra-pair paternity (Zilberman *et al.* 1999). There is also a bizarre record of a male Long-billed Sunbird *Cinnyris lotenius* repeatedly pecking the cloaca of fledgling Tailorbirds *Orthotomus sutorius* (Neelakantan 1975).

Figure 15 (above). Courtship pose of male Copper Sunbird *Cinnyris cupreus* (after Howells 1971).

Figure 16 (left). Male Malachite Sunbird *Nectarinia famosa* in courtship, displaying pectoral tufts (after Skead 1967).

Figure 17. Courtship display of Greater Double-collared Sunbird *Cinnyris afer*, male with tail fanned momentarily and head pointing skywards (after Skead 1967).

Figure 18. Male Olive-bellied Sunbird *Cinnyris chloropygius* pecking cloaca of female.

ANTING

Sunbirds are known to "ant" (Stewart & Stewart 1964, van Eeden 1981, Alexander 1995b, Cunningham-van Someren 1996). Birds take ants and place them under fluttering, partly extended, wings. During five minutes one Bronze Sunbird *Nectarinia kilimensis* anted once every two seconds

BREEDING

Most sunbirds defend feeding and breeding territories, with males singing from prominent perches and chasing both intra- and inter-specific intruders. In some instances, especially amongst *Cyanomitra* spp., groups of birds sing and display together in leks.

With the exception of the two species of sugarbird *Promerops*, whose nests are cup-shaped (see Plate 1), and those of some spiderhunters (see Figure 19e for Streaked Spiderhunter *Arachnothera magna*) all members of the family Nectariniidae lay eggs in enclosed nests. These are usually purse-shaped bags or pouches, e.g. Midget Flowerpecker *Dicaeum aeneum* (Figure 19g), with or without beards (strands of vegetation hanging loosely below the nest, as in Olive-backed Sunbird *Cinnyris jugularis*: Figure 19f), but some are very long, e.g. that of the Blue-throated Brown Sunbird *Cyanomitra cyanolaema* (Figure 19a), or consist of

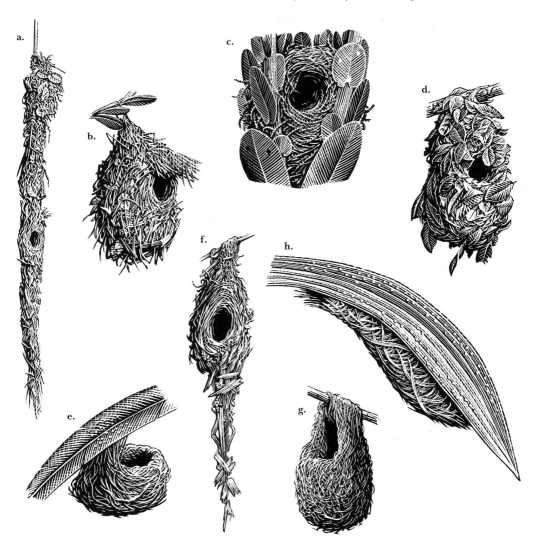

Figure 19. Nests of (a) Blue-throated Brown Sunbird *Cyanomitra cyanolaema*; **(b)** Collared Sunbird *Hedydipna collaris*, showing porch over entrance; **(c)** Orange-breasted Sunbird *Anthobaphes violacea* in bush of *Protea* sp., placed not suspended; **(d)** Western Violet-backed Sunbird *Anthreptes longuemarei*, decorated with dead leaves; **(e)** Streaked Spiderhunter *Arachnothera magna*; **(f)** Olive-backed Sunbird *Cinnyris jugularis*, showing long beard; **(g)** Midget Flowerpecker *Dicaeum aeneum*, purse-like; and **(h)** Yellow-eared Spiderhunter *Arachnothera chrysogenys*, on underside of frond.

structures stuck under palm fronds, e.g. Yellow-eared Spiderhunter *Arachnothera chrysogenys* (Figure 19h). Most sunbird nests are suspended but some are placed in bushes, e.g. that of the Orange-breasted Sunbird *Anthobaphes violacea* (Figure 19c). Many sunbird nests such as those of the Collared Sunbird *Hedydipna collaris* have "porches" projecting above their entrance holes (Figure 19b), while others are decorated with a diversity of objects including caterpillar frass and, as in the case of the Western Violet-backed Sunbird *Anthreptes longuemarei*, dead leaves (Figure 19d).

There is a close association between some species of sunbird and aculeate Hymenoptera, e.g. the Collared Sunbird *H. collaris* often nests close to nests of wasps. There is anecdotal evidence that sunbirds build their nests to face in particular directions, and it has been shown that *A. violacea* does indeed tend to nest in directions away from the prevailing winds (Williams 1993b), perhaps to minimise heat loss by incubating females, eggs or nestlings in the absence of the female or to provide better shelter during storms. The energetics of incubation in this species have also been studied (Williams 1993a).

The nests of *Promerops* are built only by the female, who also undertakes the incubation, which lasts about 17 days, and the majority of the feeding of the chicks, which is carried out for a period of 17-23 days. The young are looked after for a further 3 weeks or more, sometimes for 3 months. *P. cafer* is usually double-brooded, with a normal clutch of 2 eggs.

Sunbirds are frequently double-brooded, and may lay as many as 5 broods in succession. As with sugarbirds, the males of most species take little or no part in either nest-building or incubation, the latter usually taking about 13-15 days. The spiderhunters *Arachnothera* and some flowerpeckers *Dicaeum* are exceptional in that the male is also involved in incubation, and some *Dicaeum* assist with building. Clutches vary from 1 to 4 eggs, 2 being the commonest. There is evidence of polygamy in the Seychelles Sunbird *Cinnyris dussumieri* (Lucking 1996) and it is likely to occur in other species. Extra-pair paternity is common in the Palestine Sunbird *Cinnyris oseus* (Zilberman *et al.* 1999) and is known in the Purple-rumped Sunbird *Leptocoma zeylonica*. The feeding of the chicks is shared between both sexes, and generally lasts 14-19 days. Parental care in *C. oseus* has been studied in detail (Markman *et al.* 1995, 1996, 1999). Co-operative feeding of chicks has been reported in *L. zeylonica* (Ganguly 1986).

DISTRIBUTION AND HABITAT

Members of the family Nectariniidae are found throughout the Afro-tropical region, including the Indian Ocean islands and southern parts of the Arabian Peninsula, extending northwards through north-eastern Africa into the Palaearctic region in the Levant, and then east and south through the Oriental region to Wallacea, New Guinea, the Solomons and Australia. They are often conspicuous, common and numerous members of an avifauna, occurring from sea-level to above the tree-line on high mountains, although each species may have its preferred altitudinal range, which may change seasonally.

Almost all habitats are utilised, although these birds are rarely found far from water in extremely arid areas or deep in large expanses of treeless swamps. Their main food sources, nectar-producing flowers and arthropods, are abundant, albeit seasonally in some cases, more or less throughout their area of distribution, which is principally tropical and subtropical. They can be found on offshore islands of all sizes where suitable food occurs, and there is some evidence of small islands still being colonised.

Some species or groups of species may be particularly associated with certain plants, e.g. sugarbirds with *Protea*, flowerpeckers with mistletoes, some sunbirds with *Leonotis* spp. or *Crotalaria* spp. or mistletoes and spiderhunters with plantains, but the majority are more catholic. All types of forest, mangroves, savanna, bush country, montane vegetation above the tree-line, swamp edge and lakesides, oases and desert fringes, beach vegetation, plantations, areas partly cleared for agriculture, parks, tree-lined roads, gardens and all forms of secondary growth hold varying numbers of this family. Although some species are associated with lower strata within tall forest, and others with the canopy, the majority move freely from one stratum to another depending on the availability of food.

These aspects are discussed further under the generic and specific accounts.

PARASITES

NEST PARASITES

Insects found in sunbird nests, listed by Hicks (1959, 1962, 1971), include Collembola (*Drepanura eburnea* in the nest of an unidentified sunbird), Psocoptera (*Peripsocus pauliani* and *Lepidopsocides* sp. in nests of unidentified sunbirds), Diptera (tropical nest fly *Passeromyia heterochaeta*, Muscidae: Muscinae: Hydrotaeini), and Lepidoptera (*Monopis megalodelta* in nest of unidentified sunbird in Côte d'Ivoire). The larvae of *P. heterochaeta*, which are blood-sucking and attack nestlings, have been found in nests of the Copper Sunbird *Cinnyris cupreus*, Bronze Sunbird *Nectarinia kilimensis* and unidentified *Cinnyris* sp.

BROOD PARASITES

Many sunbird nests of species of *Hedydipna*, *Anabathmis*, *Anthobaphes*, *Cyanomitra*, *Chalcomitra*, *Nectarinia* and *Cinnyris* (but not *Deleornis*, *Anthreptes* or *Drepanorhynchus*, apparently) are parasitised by cuckoos of the genus *Chrysoccoccyx* in Africa, with occasional records of the involvement of Red-chested Cuckoo *Cuculus solitarius*. As many as 11% of the nests of the Dusky Sunbird *Cinnyris fuscus* may be affected in Namibia. In Asia, *Cacomantis* parasitises *Leptocoma* and *Cinnyris*; *Chrysococcyx* parasitises *Aethopyga*, *Cinnyris* and *Arachnothera* (Gould's Bronze-Cuckoo *Chrysococcyx russatus* parasitises Olive-backed Sunbird *Cinnyris jugularis* in Australia); and *Cuculus* and *Hierococcyx* parasitise *Arachnothera*. Flowerpeckers and sugarbirds are, seemingly, not parasitised by cuckoos. In Africa, honeyguides of the genera *Prodotiscus* and *Indicator* are brood parasites of sunbirds.

ENDOPARASITES

Blood parasites of sunbirds, flowerpeckers and sugarbirds include genera such as *Haemoproteus* sp., *Leucocytozoon* sp., *Plasmodium* sp., *Trypanosoma* sp., and microfilariae of nematodes, many unidentified. Those recorded from different birds were listed by Bennett *et al.* (1982), including specific identifications of some *Haemoproteus* sp. and *Leucocytozoon* sp. but all *Haemoproteus* from the Nectariniidae are now considered to be *H. sequeirae* (Bennett *et al.* 1985) and all *Leococytozoon* sp. from sunbirds are now treated as *L. nectariniae* (Bennett *et al.* 1992). Blood parasites of Gurney's Sugarbird *Promerops gurneyi* include *Haemoproteus* sp., microfilariae (Bennett & de Swardt 1989) and *Leucocytozoon deswardti* (Bennett *et al.* 1992). The latter is indistinguishable from, and was previously identified as, *L. annellobiae*, also found in Australia in the blood of the meliphagid *Anthochaera chrysoptera*. *Haemoproteus dicaeus* and *H. nucleophilus* have been described from flowerpeckers (Bennett & Bishop 1991). There are also records of cestodes parasitising the guts of sunbirds e.g. the Olive-backed Sunbird *C. jugularis* (Deardorff *et al.* 1978).

Unless the birds are heavily parasitised it is unlikely that they are pathogenic, but the study of bird parasites is of interest in the light of hypotheses relating sexual selection to them. Females may choose as mates males with brighter plumage, as evidence of their greater fitness regarding resistance to parasites (Hamilton & Zuk 1982) – an advantage, as such resistance is heritable. Given the bright colours of many male members of the Nectariniidae, this group could be ideal for testing such hypotheses.

ECTOPARASITES

No sugarbirds, flowerpeckers, sunbirds or spiderhunters were listed as hosts of feather lice (Mallophaga) by Hopkins & Clay (1952), but *Philopterus turdi* (Denny) is now known from the Cape Sugarbird *Promerops cafer* (Skead 1967), *Philopterus* sp. from the Tacazze Sunbird *Nectarinia tacazze* (Cheke 1972) and *Ricinus timmermanni* from four other species of sunbird (Ledger 1980). Only *Ornithoica exilis* from unidentified sunbirds was amongst the Hippoboscidae listed in the host-parasite check-list of Maa (1969b), but he had earlier listed *Aethopyga shelleyi* as the host of *O. exilis* (Maa 1966) and *Cyanomitra* sp. as a host of *Icosta minor* (Maa 1969a). Feather mites have been recorded from a variety of sunbird hosts (Zumpt 1961).

MORTALITY AND PREDATORS

Infanticide of another pair's offspring has been recorded in the Palestine Sunbird *C. oseus* (Goldstein *et al.* 1986) and adverse weather conditions and predators such as snakes also take their toll of eggs and nestlings. Predator pressure on nests may have accounted for the evolution of the highly camouflaged nature of some sunbird nests. Ejection of nestlings by cuckoos has fatal consequences, but probably the most common cause of the death of nestlings is starvation when the parents die or cannot find enough food or a sufficient variety of it. After fledging, sunbirds are often taken by birds of prey and fall foul of accidents such as deaths caused by entanglement in spiders' webs. Habitat degradation and deforestation will also limit sunbird populations, but despite these many threats some sunbirds live for surprisingly long times, as shown by the results of ringing. The oldest known sunbird was an Amethyst Sunbird *Chalcomitra amethystina* which lived for at least 16 years. Other longevity records include 14 years 5 months (Western Olive Sunbird *Cyanomitra obscura*), at least 13 years (Seychelles Sunbird *Cinnyris dussumieri*), 12 years 6 months (Bronze Sunbird *Nectarinia kilimensis*) and 12 years (Plain-throated Sunbird *Anthreptes malacensis*). A Cape Sugarbird *Promerops cafer* lived at least 7 years 1 month, two species of spiderhunter (Little *Arachnothera longirostra* and Long-billed *A. robusta*) have lived 5 years and a Scarlet-backed Flowerpecker *Dicaeum cruentatum* 4 years.

PHYSIOLOGY

Given their high metabolic rate and small size, sunbirds need to feed during much of the day, e.g. approximately 75% of the time for the Golden-winged Sunbird *Drepanorhynchus reichenowi* (Gill & Wolf 1975b), if they are to balance their energy budgets with inputs from nectar sources and invertebrates. Indeed their name, sunbirds, attributable to their conspicuousness on sunny days, may reflect a physiological need as it is known that the Palestine Sunbird *C. oseus* prefers to feed on aloes in the sun rather than in the shade independent of their nectar concentrations, probably to save energy (Goldstein *et al.* 1987) which might otherwise be spent on keeping warm.

Malachite Sunbirds *Nectarinia famosa* and Tacazze Sunbirds *N. tacazze* take up the three major sugars in nectar – sucrose, glucose and fructose – which are present in two of their main food-plants *Kniphofia snowdenii* and *Lobelia elgonensis* (Cheke 1971a). These sugars and xylose are present in many nectars such as *Protea* sp. and *Faurea* sp. and are also taken up by the Southern Double-collared Sunbird *Cinnyris chalybeus* and the Cape Sugarbird *Promerops cafer*, both of which have extremely high absorption efficiencies (>99%) for sucrose, glucose and fructose, although *P. cafer* is less efficient (47%) at metabolising xylose (Jackson *et al.* 1998) and *C. chalybeus* excretes it (Lotz & Nicolson 1996). Gurney's Sugarbird *P. gurneyi* and Amethyst Sunbird *C. amethystina* also take up sucrose, glucose and fructose, and their preferences for one or the other vary with concentration (Downs & Perrin 1996). Neither the Greater Double-collared Sunbird *C. afer* (Lloyd 1991) nor the Malachite Sunbird *N. famosa* (Downs 1997, 2000) maximise their energy intake when given the opportunity but rather they regulate their overall energy assimilation with regular intake rates throughout the day, with little body weight variation. In experiments, they vary the volume of fluid ingested in relation to the sugar concentrations offered.

When the sugar concentration of nectar is low, *C. chalybeus* may take in excessive quantities of water which need to be disposed of. Under some circumstances, their kidneys may fail to cope with it leading to water retention. The fluid is then probably lost through a mechanism of evaporative water loss (Lotz & Nicolson 1998).

Under normal circumstances, the daily energy intake will be adequate for a sunbird to survive the night but those in high-altitude environments may need to cope with sub-zero nocturnal temperatures. Although unlike hummingbirds sunbirds do not become torpid, experiments on caged birds kept in the open under ambient conditions at 2,690-3,350 m above sea-level in Kenya showed that Eastern Double-collared Sunbirds *C. mediocris*, *N. tacazze*, *N. famosa* and Collared Sunbirds *Hedydipna collaris* were thermolabile to variable extents, dropping their body temperatures by 5-17.5°C below the normal daily level of about 42°C overnight (Cheke 1971b). Such a mechanism would save energy. The suggestion that an adaptive temporary hypothermia was involved was criticised by both Wolf & Gill (1986) and Prinzinger *et al.* (1989) on the mistaken assumption that the experimental birds were in poor health. The latter authors based their argument on the fate of one *C. mediocris* which died in an accidental collision while ignoring data on a second conspecific. Prinzinger *et al.*'s own studies, conducted at unnaturally constant, not fluctuating, temperatures of 5 and 25°C, confirmed that sunbirds are heterothermic (i.e. do not maintain a constant body temperature such as the approximately 42°C usually maintained during the day) and recorded bird temperatures as low as 34.2°C with associated reductions in energy metabolism. They pointed out that such changes are nevertheless within the ranges predicted by general theoretical equations and do not represent an extraordinary phenomenon such as the torpor of hummingbirds and some nightjars. However, Leon & Nicolson (1997) showed that *C. chalybeus* reduces its temperature by 3.6°C on average, with a minimum record of 29.3°C, and wrote that their results are consistent with a hypothermic mechanism and suggest basal metabolic rates 88% less than theoretical predictions.

The first evidence that incubating females in the wild also lower their body temperatures at night was also provided by Cheke (1971b), who found a nearly fledged *N. tacazze* being brooded by an adult female with a body temperature of 34°C whilst still in the nest. Williams (1993a) reported an incubating female *Anthobaphes violacea* as entering temporary hypothermia as it allowed its eggs' temperatures to drop to 29°C at night, but these observations were not, as claimed, "the first data suggesting that sunbirds use hypothermia as an energy conservation mechanism in the field".

MIGRATION AND OTHER MOVEMENTS

Some species of sunbird, e.g. the African race of Palestine Sunbird *C. oseus decorsei*, regularly migrate with the rains in Africa, but most are sedentary or make restricted nomadic movements in response to changes in food abundance. Altitudinal shifts are also common, e.g. *D. reichenowi* moves up and down mountains with the seasons and ringing recoveries have confirmed movements of at least 65 km for this species. Available evidence is summarised for each species in the accounts.

There have been few observations of visible migration by sunbirds, but in Botswana Borello (1992) saw more than 220 sunbirds (Amethyst Sunbirds *Chalcomitra amethystina*, Scarlet-chested Sunbirds *C. senegalensis*, White-bellied Sunbirds *Cinnyris talatala* and Mariqua Sunbirds *C. mariquensis*) moving north-eastward during a spell of 25 minutes and estimated that 1,500 had passed in 3 hours. Herremans (1992) described indirect evidence for movements of the same species, also in Botswana. Tree (1990) summarised data on sunbird movements in relation to nectar sources in Zimbabwe.

Craig & Hulley (1994) discussed movements by sunbirds in South Africa, classifying them into (1) "winter residents" which move annually to a wintering area and remain there; (2) "shoppers", which periodically investigate different areas, feeding opportunistically within their home areas; (3) "tourists", which visit a series of sites on a set itinerary, and (4) "nomads" without home bases, which move unpredictably to new areas whenever food supplies decline.

ECONOMIC IMPORTANCE

The most important, but incalculable, economic contribution which sunbirds, spiderhunters, sugarbirds and flowerpeckers make is to ecosystem health and biodiversity maintenance by their pollination of numerous species of plant, some which are of economic value as crops. To a lesser extent the flowerpeckers, in particular, are responsible for the dispersal of seeds and thus the successful propagation of plants. In some cases such activities may have detrimental effects: *Chalcomitra senegalensis* has been implicated in the pollination of the mistletoe *Tapinanthus bangwensis*, a serious pest of plantation crops including cocoa and in Asia, the Purple Sunbird *Cinnyris asiaticus* spreads mistletoes affecting the gamar tree *Gmelina arborea* and teak *Tectona grandis*. Flowerpeckers also spread mistletoes of economic relevance and the activities of the Scarlet-backed Flowerpecker *Dicaeum cruentatum*, Yellow-vented Flowerpecker *D. chrysorrheum* and sunbirds, probably Purple Sunbird *C. asiaticus*, in this respect, have warranted suggestions for their control by shooting to prevent attacks by Loranthaceae on plantations of Sal trees *Shorea robusta*, an important timber tree (Davidson 1945). A few species of sunbird are also involved as pests of vineyards, for instance *C. asiaticus* and the Purple-rumped Sunbird *Leptocoma zeylonica* attack grapes in India. They puncture the fruits and suck out the juices making them unfit for human consumption, damaging 3.2-45% of a crop (Kumar *et al.* 1984). Also, in the Norton area of Zimbabwe, 100 Scarlet-chested Sunbirds *C. senegalensis* have recently been shot whilst damaging *Protea* flowers being grown for export as cut flowers (J. T. Couto, pers. comm.).

CONSERVATION

The principal means of conserving sunbirds, flowerpeckers, spiderhunters and sugarbirds is by the protection of their habitat. This may involve simply good land husbandry or require concerted efforts to manage protected areas. The latter will be essential for the survival of the Critically Endangered Cebu Flowerpecker *Dicaeum quadricolor*, which is now mostly restricted to a tiny (<15 ha) remnant of forest at Tabunan, within the Central Cebu National Park (Stattersfield *et al.* 1998). This is designated as an Endemic Bird Area (EBA) in the Philippines, two others of which harbour another threatened flowerpecker, the Scarlet-collared Flowerpecker *D. retrocinctum* (Vulnerable). The Black-belted Flowerpecker *D. haematostictum* is also classed as Vulnerable and a fourth Philippine endemic the Whiskered Flowerpecker *D. proprium* is Near-Threatened (Collar *et al.* 1999). Asian sunbirds of conservation concern include the Elegant Sunbird *Aethopyga duyvenbodei* of Indonesia and the recently discovered Lina's Sunbird *A. linaraborae* from the Philippines (Collar *et al.* 1994, 1999).

On the mainland of Africa, the Amani Sunbird *Hedydipna pallidigaster*, Banded Sunbird *Anthreptes rubritorques*, Rockefeller's Sunbird *Cinnyris rockefelleri* and the relatively recently discovered Rufous-winged Sunbird *Cinnyris rufipennis* are classed as vulnerable, as is the island endemic Giant Sunbird *Dreptes thomensis* of São Tomé.

In addition to habitat destruction, its degradation or pollution can also harm sunbirds. For instance, the use of insecticides to control tsetse flies *Glossina* spp. may have been to the detriment of sunbirds in Malawi (de Garine-Witchatitsky *et al.* in press).

PLATE 1: SUGARBIRDS

Sugarbirds are dull brown above with some chestnut on breast and yellow undertail-coverts, and have long, slightly decurved bills and very long tails.

1 **Gurney's Sugarbird** *Promerops gurneyi* **Text and map page 129**

Found only in southern Africa. Two subspecies, the nominate restricted to South Africa, where found in alpine and sour grassland vegetation and grassland bordering Afromontane forests in upland areas; also towns with aloes, *Eucalyptus* plantations. *P. g. ardens* occurs in highlands of eastern Zimbabwe and adjoining Mozambique amongst *Protea–Brachystegia–Erica* scrub.

Sexes differ slightly, females being smaller with shorter tails.

1a **Adult male** (nominate) Dull brown with long slightly decurved bill; brown moustachial stripes, rich chestnut crown and breast-band and streaked belly.

1b **Adult female** (nominate) As male, but tail 34% shorter, head length and wing shorter.

1c **Adult male** (*ardens*) Pectoral band richer and brighter than *gurneyi*; lower back greener, less yellow. Centres of feathers blacker. Cheeks darker.

1d **Adult female** (*ardens*) On nest.

2 **Cape Sugarbird** *Promerops cafer* **Text and map page 131**

Endemic to fynbos of South Africa, preferring stands of mature *Protea* which are in flower on mountain slopes and open ground. Also gardens.

Sexes differ slightly, females being smaller with shorter tails.

2a **Adult male** Stout decurved bill, warm brown chest, very long tail, dull white belly with heavy black streaks and greenish-yellow rump. Forehead and crown greyish-brown.

2b **Adult female** Similar to male but tail shorter.

2c **Adult male** on *Protea* sp.

1a

2a

1c

2b

1b

2c

1d

R.W.A

PLATE 2: *PRIONOCHILUS* FLOWERPECKERS (1)

All species of *Prionochilus* have stout, slightly hook-tipped bills.

3 Olive-backed Flowerpecker *Prionochilus olivaceus* — Text and map page 134

Philippines. Usually below 1,000 m, in forest, secondary growth and at forest edge.
Sexes similar.

3a **Adult** (nominate; Bantan, Dinagat, Mindanao) Mostly olive above, white below with grey sides of throat, breast and flanks.

3b **Adult** (*parsoni*; Luzon) Sides of throat and breast black.

---

4 Yellow-breasted Flowerpecker *Prionochilus maculatus* — Text and map page 135

Malay Peninsula, Sumatra and Borneo. Up to 1,500 m in forest, secondary growth, scrub, cultivation, plantations and at forest edge.
Sexes similar.

4a **Adult** (nominate; Sumatra and Borneo) Mostly olive-green above, with orange patch on crown. Malar stripe and throat white; rest of underparts yellow streaked olive-green.

4b **Adult** (*septentrionalis*; north Malay Peninsula) Greyer ear-coverts and paler lores than nominate, and brighter yellow below.

---

8 Scarlet-breasted Flowerpecker *Prionochilus thoracicus* — Text and map page 138

Southern Vietnam, Malay Peninsula, Sumatra and Borneo. Up to 1,280 m in peatswamp forest, heath forest, beach vegetation, *Casuarina* groves, secondary growth, plantations and forest edge.

8a **Adult male** Black head, with red crown-patch; rest of upperparts yellow, green and black; red patch on breast bordered black; rest of underparts yellow.

8b **Adult female** Head grey; mostly olive-green above, with yellow uppertail-coverts; yellowish and olive below, with orange breast-patch.

8c **Juvenile** Mostly olive and grey, with yellowish central stripe.

PLATE 3: *PRIONOCHILUS* FLOWERPECKERS (2)

All species of *Prionochilus* have stout, slightly hooked bills.

6   **Palawan Flowerpecker** *Prionochilus plateni*   **Text and map page 137**

Philippines. Forest, secondary growth and gardens.

6a   **Adult male** (nominate) Mostly blue-black above, with red on crown, and yellow rump; whitish malar stripe; mostly yellow below, with red patch on breast.

6b   **Adult female** (nominate) Whitish malar stripe and throat; olive-green above, with yellow rump. Sides of breast and flanks grey, rest of underparts yellow.

7   **Yellow-rumped Flowerpecker** *Prionochilus xanthopygius*   **Text and map page 137**

Borneo. Up to 1,760 m in forest, secondary growth, clearings and at forest edge.

7a   **Adult male** Slaty-blue above, orange crown-patch, and yellow rump; below yellow with orange patch on breast; lacks white malar stripe.

7b   **Adult female** Grey and greeny-olive above, with yellow rump; grey throat and flanks; rest of underparts yellow, with some orange on breast; lacks white malar stripe.

5   **Crimson-breasted Flowerpecker** *Prionochilus percussus*   **Text and map page 136**

Malay Peninsula, Sumatra, Borneo and Java. Up to 1,065 m in forest, including mangroves, secondary growth, scrub and old plantations.

5a   **Adult male** (*ignicapillus*; Malay Peninsula, Sumatra and Borneo) Slaty-blue above, with blackish forehead and red crown-patch; white malar stripe; mostly yellow below, with red patch on breast; lacks yellow rump.

5b   **Adult female** (*ignicapillus*) Mostly olive-green, with whitish malar stripe and throat; yellow rump and on breast.

5c   **Juvenile** (*ignicapillus*) Mostly greenish-olive and olive-grey; basal two-thirds of bill pale.

5d   **Adult male** (nominate; Java) With crown feathers raised. Richer yellow below, malar stripe broader and with more extensive red than *ignicapillus*.

PLATE 4: *DICAEUM* FLOWERPECKERS (1)

9   **Golden-rumped Flowerpecker** *Dicaeum annae*   **Text and map page 140**

Sumbawa and Flores, Lesser Sunda Islands.

> **9**   **Adult male** Olive-green above with yellow rump (lacking in female), white throat and malar stripe; rest of underparts yellowish streaked olive-grey.

---

10   **Thick-billed Flowerpecker** *Dicaeum agile*   **Text and map page 140**

India, Sri Lanka, South-East Asia, Greater Sundas, Philippines, Sumba, Flores, Alor and Timor.
Bill stout. Sexes similar.

> **10a**   **Adult** (nominate; peninsular India, northern Burma) Grey-brown above, tinged olive; mostly buffy below with faint darker streaking; white spots on underside of tail.
>
> **10b**   **Adult** (*finschi*; West Java) Bill thinner, more olive above and more heavily streaked below than nominate, and lacks white spots on undertail.
>
> **10c**   **Adult** (*aeruginosum*; Philippines – Cebu, Mindanao, Mindoro, Negros) Olive-green to green above; whitish below, heavily streaked brown.

---

11   **Brown-backed Flowerpecker** *Dicaeum everetti*   **Text and map page 143**

Very restricted distribution in peninsular Malaysia, Sumatra, North Natunas and Borneo.
Bill stout. Sexes similar.

> **11**   **Adult** Browner above than *agile*, lacks streaking below (except *bungurense* on North Natunas) and lacks white spots on undertail.

---

12   **Whiskered Flowerpecker** *Dicaeum proprium*   **Text and map page 143**

Philippines (Mindanao).
Sexes similar.

> **12**   **Adult** Blue-black upperparts and moustachial stripe; chin and malar stripe white; rest of underparts sepia-brown.

---

13   **Yellow-vented Flowerpecker** *Dicaeum chrysorrheum*   **Text and map page 144**

Northern India, Bhutan, Nepal, South-East Asia, south Yunnan, Greater Sundas.
Sexes similar.

> **13**   **Adult** (*chrysochlore*; India, South-East Asia south to Isthmus of Kra) Bright olive-green above; wings and tail black; yellowish-white streaked blackish below; undertail-coverts yellow.

---

14   **Yellow-bellied Flowerpecker** *Dicaeum melanoxanthum*   **Text and map page 145**

Himalayas south and east through Burma to China; south-east Yunnan, northern Thailand and Vietnam in winter.
Thick-billed.

> **14a**   **Adult male** Blackish above; white patches on tail; white and yellow below.
>
> **14b**   **Adult female** Olive-grey above; yellow, white and olive below.

PLATE 5: *DICAEUM* FLOWERPECKERS (2)

15 **White-throated Flowerpecker** *Dicaeum vincens* **Text and map page 146**

South-west Sri Lanka. Up to 1,000 m in rainforest.
Stout bill.

> **15a** **Adult male** Slaty-blue and black above, white throat and undertail-coverts, rest of underparts yellow.

> **15b** **Adult female** Differs from male by grey and olive upperparts.

16 **Yellow-sided Flowerpecker** *Dicaeum aureolimbatum* **Text and map page 147**

Sulawesi area. Up to 2,000 m in forest, woodland, plantations, cultivation and gardens, and at forest edge.
Stout bill. Sexes similar.

> **16a** **Adult** (nominate) Bright olive-green above, with black mask and wings; underparts grey, with bright yellow on sides.

> **16b** **Immature** (nominate) Duller than adult, with paler bill, and less yellow below.

17 **Olive-capped Flowerpecker** *Dicaeum nigrilore* **Text and map page 147**

Philippines. In forest at 900-1,350 m.
Sexes similar.

> **17** **Adult** (nominate) Long, slightly decurved bill. Olive and brown above; blackish mask; throat to belly grey, rest of underparts yellow.

18 **Flame-crowned Flowerpecker** *Dicaeum anthonyi* **Text and map page 148**

Philippines. In forest, particularly mossy forest, from 800 to at least 2,000 m.
Stout bill.

> **18a** **Adult male** (*kampalili*; Mindanao) Glossy blue-black above; crown and undertail-coverts red; rest of underparts grey.

> **18b** **Adult male** (nominate; Luzon) Differs from *kampalili* in having red replaced by orange-buff, and rest of underparts yellowish.

> **18c** **Adult female** (nominate) Olive above, greyish-white below.

19 **Bicoloured Flowerpecker** *Dicaeum bicolor* **Text and map page 149**

Philippines. Below 1,500 m in forest, secondary growth and at forest edge.
Short, stout bill.

> **19a** **Adult male** (*inexpectatum*) Glossy blue-black above, grey below.

> **19b** **Adult female** (*inexpectatum*) Greyish-olive and greenish above, with black tail; grey below.

PLATE 6: *DICAEUM* FLOWERPECKERS (3)

20 **Cebu Flowerpecker** *Dicaeum quadricolor*   **Text and map page 150**

Philippines. Forest.
Very stout bill.

    20a **Adult male** Crown, neck and sides of head black; mantle red; lower back and rump yellowish; greyish below.

    20b **Adult female** Brownish olive-green above, greyish-white below.

    20c **Juvenile** Paler above than female, with pinkish lower mandible.

---

21 **Red-striped Flowerpecker** *Dicaeum australe*   **Text and map page 150**

Philippines. Below 1,000 m in forest, coconut groves, gardens, open country and at forest edge.
Stout bill. Sexes similar.

    21 **Adult** Glossy blue-black above; below white and grey, with red stripe on centre of breast and belly.

---

22 **Black-belted Flowerpecker** *Dicaeum haematostictum*   **Text and map page 151**

Philippines – Panay, Negros, ?Guimaras. Below 1,000 m in forest, at forest edge and in open country.
Stout bill. Sexes similar.

    22 **Adult** Differs from *D. australe* by broader red stripe, bordered black along sides and above.

---

23 **Scarlet-collared Flowerpecker** *Dicaeum retrocinctum*   **Text and map page 152**

Philippines – Mindoro. Forest, forest edge, coconut groves and cultivation below 1,000 m.
Slender, curved bill. Sexes similar.

    23 **Adult** Blue-black above, including wings and tail; rest of head, neck and upper breast blue-black; centre of throat red; rest of underparts grey and white, with red stripe bordered black on centre of breast and belly.

---

24 **Orange-bellied Flowerpecker** *Dicaeum trigonostigma*   **Text and map page 153**

Bangladesh, South-East Asia, Greater Sundas, Philippines. Up to 1,800 m in forest, including mangroves, at forest edge, in scrub, secondary growth, cultivation and gardens.
Bill of medium thickness.

    24a **Adult male** (nominate; Malay Peninsula, Sumatra) Head, upper back, wings and tail dark slaty blue-black; rest of upperparts orange; throat and upper breast grey, rest of underparts orange.

    24b **Adult female** (nominate) Chiefly greyish-brown above, with orange rump; greyish from throat to breast; yellow and orange on belly and undertail-coverts.

    24c **Adult male** (*sibutuense*; Philippines – Sibutu, Omapoy, Sipangkot) Less orange on back and rump, darker on back and bluer on throat than nominate.

    24d **Adult male** (*cinereigulare*; Philippines – Bohol, Leyte, Mindanao, Samar, Biliran) Less orange on back than nominate, no yellow on rump, throat yellow and pale grey.

PLATE 7: *DICAEUM* FLOWERPECKERS (4)

25   **Buzzing Flowerpecker** *Dicaeum hypoleucum*   **Text and map page 155**

Philippines. Up to 1,500 m (but to 1,800 m in Kitanglad range) in forest and at forest edge.
Bill slender.

   25a   **Adult male** (nominate; Basilan, Bongao, Jolo, Siasi, Tawitawi, Malamaui, Sanga Sanga, Manuk
             Manka) Upperparts blackish, underparts pale grey.

   25b   **Adult female** (nominate) Differs from male by olivaceous cast to plumage of upperparts.

   25c   **Adult male** (*pontifex*; Bohol, Dinagat, Leyte, Mindanao, Panaon and Samar) Darker green
             above than *obscurum*, and greyish-white below.

   25d   **Adult male** (*obscurum*; north-west and central Luzon) Mostly olive and olive-green.

---

26   **Pale-billed Flowerpecker** *Dicaeum erythrorhynchos*   **Text and map page 156**

Indian subcontinent and Burma. Up to 2,100 m (Sri Lanka), 150-300 m or lower (Nepal, winter) and to
1,400 m (Nepal, summer) in deciduous forest, mangroves, cultivation, plantations; mango groves,
orchards and open country.
Bill of medium thickness, but markedly down-curved. Sexes similar.

   26   **Adult** Olive-brown above and greyish-white below.

---

28   **Pygmy Flowerpecker** *Dicaeum pygmaeum*   **Text and map page 159**

Philippines. Below 2,000 m in forest, at forest edge and in secondary growth.
Short, quite slender bill.

   28a   **Adult male** Olive-black glossed green above; sides of face and breast grey; yellowish on
             centre of breast and undertail-coverts, rest of underparts grey.

   28b   **Adult female** Duller than male, and lacks gloss.

---

27   **Plain Flowerpecker** *Dicaeum concolor*   **Text and map page 157**

Indian subcontinent, South-East Asia, China, Greater Sundas. Up to 3,660 m, but commoner at lower
altitudes; 300-2,500 m (Nepal); 500-1,500 m (Sumatra); in almost any habitat with trees.
Slender, slightly decurved bill. Sexes similar.

   27a   **Adult** (nominate; south-west India) Olive-brown above, with pale supercilium and lores; below
             yellowish-white.

   27b   **Adult** (*olivaceum*; Indian subcontinent, except south-west India, China, Burma, Thailand south
             to northern peninsular Malaysia) Greener above and greyer below than nominate.

PLATE 8: *DICAEUM* FLOWERPECKERS (5)

29 Crimson-crowned Flowerpecker *Dicaeum nehrkorni*   **Text and map page 160**

Sulawesi. Montane forest, and at edge; 600-2,400 m.
Bill short and slender.

> **29a** **Adult male** Glossy blue-black above, with red crown and rump; mostly grey below with small red spot on breast; whitish abdomen, with blackish stripe down centre.

> **29b** **Adult female** Chiefly dark grey above, with blackish wings and tail; red rump; below grey and white.

---

30 Flame-breasted Flowerpecker *Dicaeum erythrothorax*   **Text and map page 160**

Moluccas. Up to 950 m in scrub, forest and riverine habitats.
Bill short, slender and slightly decurved.

> **30a** **Adult male** (*schistaceiceps*; Morotai, Halmahera, Bacan, Obi and Bisu) Olive-brown above, with golden-green rump; greyish below; large red patch on breast.

> **30b** **Adult male** (nominate; Buru) Differs chiefly from male *schistaceiceps* by white throat.

> **30c** **Adult female** (nominate) Mostly greyish, with white throat to upper breast; rump yellowish-green.

---

31 Ashy Flowerpecker *Dicaeum vulneratum*   **Text and map page 161**

Moluccas. Up to 2,100 m, but usually below 600 m, in coastal and hill forest, gardens, and at forest and plantation edge.
Short bill of medium thickness.

> **31a** **Adult male** Dark brownish-grey above, with red rump; below grey with red patch on breast.

> **31b** **Adult female** Differs from male by whitish throat; lacks red patch on breast.

---

32 Olive-crowned Flowerpecker *Dicaeum pectorale*   **Text and map page 162**

New Guinea – Gebe I, Vogelkop, west Papuan Is. Usually below 1,500 m, but up to 2,350 m rarely, in forest and secondary growth.
Short bill of medium thickness.

> **32a** **Adult male** Olive above with yellowish rump. Grey underparts, with white throat and large red patch on breast.

> **32b** **Adult female** Chiefly olive above and grey below, with white throat, and yellowish centre of abdomen and undertail-coverts.

PLATE 9: *DICAEUM* FLOWERPECKERS (6)

33   Red-capped Flowerpecker *Dicaeum geelvinkianum*   **Text and map page 162**

Mainland New Guinea, except Vogelkop. Sea-level to 1,500 m, rarely to 2,350 m, in forest, at forest edge, in dense savanna, secondary growth, plantations and gardens.
Short bill of medium thickness.

33a   Adult male (nominate) Red cap and rump, and large red patch on breast; dark bluish gloss on shoulder.

33b   Adult female (nominate; Yapen I) Olive-green above; olive-grey below, with white throat, yellowish centre of belly, and whitish-yellow and pink undertail-coverts and vent.

33c   Adult male (*maforense*; Numfor I) Differs from nominate male by darker red on crown and yellowish vent and undertail-coverts.

33d   Adult male (*albopunctatum*; River Kataw, south-central New Guinea) Differs from nominate male by red of breast much more extensive, extending onto throat and chin.

33e   Juvenile Olive-green above, olive-grey below, wings and tail darker; bill mostly pale.

35   Red-banded Flowerpecker *Dicaeum eximium*   **Text and map page 164**

Bismarck Archipelago.
Short stout bill.

35a   Adult male (*layardorum*; New Britain) Head grey, rump red, rest of upperparts blackish-grey. White throat, grey breast with large red patch; belly to undertail-coverts white, with narrow blackish stripe down centre of belly; flanks yellowish-green.

35b   Adult female (*layardorum*) Differs from male in lacking red patch on breast.

34   Louisiade Flowerpecker *Dicaeum nitidum*   **Text and map page 163**

New Guinea – Louisiade Archipelago. Forest and secondary growth.
Short, medium-stout bill.

34a   Adult male Dark brownish-grey glossed blue and green on mantle and wing-coverts; tail glossed blackish; crown dull red. Below mostly grey and green, with white throat and bright red on chest.

34b   Adult female Differs from male by lack of red patch on breast.

36   Midget Flowerpecker *Dicaeum aeneum*   **Text and map page 165**

Solomon Is. At all altitudes in all habitats.
Bill of medium length and thickness.

36a   Adult male Mostly slaty-grey above glossed blue. Centre of throat white, large red patch on breast; sides of neck and breast grey; centre of belly dark grey, flanks yellowish.

36b   Adult female Differs from male by lack of red patch on breast.

37   Mottled Flowerpecker *Dicaeum tristrami*   **Text and map page 166**

Makira I. (Solomon Is.) Mountains.
Short, stout bill.

37   Adult Mostly brown, mottled white on forehead to nape.

38   Black-fronted Flowerpecker *Dicaeum igniferum*   **Text and map page 166**

Lesser Sundas. Up to 1,730 m, but chiefly below 800 m, in degraded forest, woodland, secondary forest, coastal forest, clearings and cultivation.
Longish, slender bill.

38a   Adult male Crown to rump and uppertail-coverts scarlet, glossed violet on back; wings and tail black. Face, sides of neck, pectoral band and stripe on abdomen black; foreneck scarlet; throat and rest of underparts white.

38b   Adult female Crown to upper back, rump and uppertail-coverts scarlet; rest of upperparts brown and blackish. Sides of face and breast brown; throat and rest of underparts whitish.

---

39   Red-chested Flowerpecker *Dicaeum maugei*   **Text and map page 167**

Sulawesi, Lesser Sundas and Nusa Penida. Generally below 1,200 m, but up to 2,000 m on Lombok, in forest, woodland, secondary growth, wooded cultivation and bamboo.
Short bill of medium thickness.

39a   Adult male (nominate; Roti, Sawu, Semau, Timor, Wetar, Romang, Roma and Damar) Head, back, tail, pectoral band and centre of abdomen dark purplish-blue and black; rump, uppertail-coverts, throat and foreneck scarlet; chin and rest of underparts white.

39b   Adult female (nominate) Head, most of upperparts and partial pectoral band grey-brown; rest of underparts white, uppertail-coverts and rump scarlet.

39c   Adult male (*splendidum*; Sulawesi) Differs from male nominate by much narrower pectoral band and abdominal stripe.

---

40   Fire-breasted Flowerpecker *Dicaeum ignipectum*   **Text and map page 168**

Northern and eastern India, Tibet, Burma, South-East Asia, south and central China, Sumatra and Philippines. Hill and montane forest, secondary growth, orchards and cultivation; down to 300 m (winter, Himalayas), 1,440-3,950 m (Himalayas, summer) over 1,000 m (Philippines), above 900 m (Burma) and 900 m (Taiwan, winter), 2,135 m (Taiwan, summer).
Bill of medium length and thickness.

40a   Adult male (nominate; range of species, except Philippines, Thailand, Cambodia, peninsular Malaysia, Sumatra and Taiwan) Glossy greenish-blue above. Black face, sides of breast and centre of abdomen; large scarlet patch on breast; rest of underparts buffy.

40b   Adult female (nominate) Chiefly olive-green above and buffy below.

40c   Adult male (*luzoniense*; Luzon) From nominate by red of breast extending onto throat.

40d   Adult male (*cambodianum*; Thailand and Cambodia) From nominate by scarlet below replaced by buff.

38a

38b

39b

39a

39c

40b

40a

40c

40d

RwA

41 **Black-sided Flowerpecker** *Dicaeum monticolum* Text and map page 169

Mountains of Borneo. Forest, including heath forest, and scrub, at 460-2,540 m.
Bill of medium length and thickness.

41a **Adult male** Glossy blue-black above; face black; chin white; throat and centre of breast scarlet; rest of underparts grey, becoming white on lower belly, and buffy on vent and undertail-coverts.

41b **Adult female** Olive-green above, somewhat buffy on rump; mostly white below, grey on upper flanks and buff on lower flanks; some dark flecking on centre of throat to breast.

42 **Grey-sided Flowerpecker** *Dicaeum celebicum* Text and map page 170

Sulawesi area. In most habitats, from sea-level to 1,000 m.
Bill quite slender, and of medium thickness.

42a **Adult male** (*talautense*; Talaud) Bluish-black above; scarlet throat and upper breast; whitish undertail-coverts; rest of underparts greyish-black.

42b **Adult male** (nominate; Sulawesi, Manadotua, Bangka, Lombok, Togian, Muna and Butung) Differs from male *talautense* by white chin, and paler grey underparts with black stripe on centre of abdomen with creamy-white border.

42c **Adult female** (nominate) Greyish-olive above; flanks grey; throat, breast, centre of belly and undertail-coverts buffy-white.

43 **Blood-breasted Flowerpecker** *Dicaeum sanguinolentum* Text and map page 171

Lesser Sundas, Java and Bali. Lowlands to 1,200 m on Lesser Sundas (but higher on Timor and Flores), but mostly 800-2,400 m on Java and Bali, in forest, woodland, secondary growth, *Casuarina* groves and wooded cultivation.
Slender bill of medium length.

43a **Adult male** (nominate; Java and Bali) Glossy blue-black above with white tips to tail; buffy throat, scarlet breast; sides of breast and flanks grey; belly buff, with black stripe on centre of breast and belly.

43b **Adult female** (nominate) Olive-brown above with scarlet rump and uppertail-coverts; sides of breast grey, rest of underparts buffy.

43c **Adult male** (*wilhelminae*; Sumba) Differs from nominate male by white chin, scarlet throat; buff below replaced by grey and white.

43d **Adult female** (*wilhelminae*) Bill stouter than nominate. Greyer above than nominate female, and buff below replaced by white and grey.

44   Mistletoebird *Dicaeum hirundinaceum*   **Text and map page 172**

Moluccas, Tanimbar, Aru I and Australia. Almost any habitat where mistletoes grow; up to 1,000 m in Snowy Mountains of Australia and up to 250 m on Tanimbar Island.
Rather short bill, of medium thickness.

44a   Adult male (nominate; Australia) Glossy violet blue-black above; throat to breast plus undertail-coverts scarlet; broad black stripe on lower breast and belly; flanks grey; rest of underparts greyish-white.

44b   Adult female (nominate) Greyish-brown above, greyish-white below, with some darker grey on breast; undertail-coverts pink.

44c   Adult male (*fulgidum*; Tanimbar) Differs from nominate male by lack of keel-stripe, paler throat and breast, and orangey instead of greyish-white abdomen.

---

45   Scarlet-backed Flowerpecker *Dicaeum cruentatum*   **Text and map page 174**

Himalayan foothills, China, South-East Asia, Sumatra and Borneo. Generally lowlands up to 1,000 m as in Sumatra and Borneo, but to 1,200 m in China, and to 2,135 m in Nepal, where it probably undergoes vertical seasonal movements. Occurs in forest, at forest edge, in secondary growth, plantations, orchards and gardens.
Bill rather longish and slender.

45a   Adult male (nominate; Himalayas to south China, eastern Thailand, Indochina, Sumatra and Riau Archipelago) Crown to rump scarlet; rest of upperparts, face and sides of breast black; grey flanks, rest of underparts white.

45b   Adult female (nominate) Red lower back, rump and uppertail-coverts; below paler.

45c   Juvenile (nominate) Grey and brown above, with hint of red on uppertail-coverts; buff and grey below.

45d   Adult male (*nigrimentum*/"*pryeri*"; north-east Borneo) Differs from nominate male in having chin to throat black, more black on sides of breast, and flanks greyish-black.

45e   Adult male (*sumatranum*; Sumatra, except Riau) Generally paler and less contrasting than male *nigrimentum*; forehead, face, chin to throat, plus sides of breast and flanks, dark grey.

---

46   Scarlet-headed Flowerpecker *Dicaeum trochileum*   **Text and map page 175**

Southern Borneo, Java, Bali and Lombok. Up to 600 m in woodland, mangroves, cultivation and open areas.
Rather slender bill of medium length.

46a   Adult male (nominate; whole range, except Lombok) Head, back, rump, uppertail-coverts, and chin to upper breast scarlet; rest of upperparts black; rest of underparts grey and white.

46b   Adult female (nominate) Brown above with red wash; scarlet rump and uppertail-coverts; grey and white below.

PLATE 13: AFRICAN *DELEORNIS* AND *ANTHREPTES* SUNBIRDS (1)

48   Scarlet-tufted Sunbird *Deleornis fraseri*   **Text and map page 179**

West and Central Africa from Sierra Leone to Angola. Primary and secondary forests, gallery forest, regenerating forests and forest edges up to 1,550 m.

> **48**   **Adult male** (nominate) Dull green with long straight bill, curved only at tip. Male easily identified if red-orange pectoral tufts seen.

---

49   Grey-headed Sunbird *Deleornis axillaris*   **Text and map page 180**

Central Africa. Dense undergrowth and middle strata of primary forests, forest edges, and secondary forest.

> **49a**   **Adult male** Distinctive dark grey forehead, crown, nape, cheeks and ear-coverts, contrasting with paler grey chin and throat.
>
> **49b**   **Immature** Green head.

---

50   Plain-backed Sunbird *Anthreptes reichenowi*   **Text and map page 181**

East and south-east Africa. Lowland forest or thick bush, gallery forest, forest edges and gardens. Usually near coast.

> **50a**   **Adult male** (nominate; Mozambique to eastern Zimbabwe and north-east South Africa) Small dull sunbird, with distinctive iridescent purplish-blue throat, appearing black in field, bordered with yellow, and short but slightly curved bill.
>
> **50b**   **Adult female** (nominate) Lacks dark forehead and throat.
>
> **50c**   **Adult male** (*yokanae*; coastal forests in south-east Kenya and north-east Tanzania) Throat blackish with bluish feather edges, not purplish-blue.

---

51   Anchieta's Sunbird *Anthreptes anchietae*   **Text and map page 182**

South-central Africa. *Brachystegia* woodland in Angola, Democratic Republic of the Congo, Zambia, Malawi, south-west Tanzania and Mozambique.

> **51a**   **Adult male** Brown upperparts, iridescent dark blue on head and throat, with contrasting bright orangey-red in middle of underparts and yellow sides of breast. Red undertail-coverts.
>
> **51b**   **Adult female** Iridescent blue much less extensive than in male, and brown paler.
>
> **51c**   **Immature** Olive-brown above, mostly yellowish below.

48

49a

49b

50a

50c

50b

51a

51b

51c

52 Plain Sunbird *Anthreptes simplex* **Text and map page 183**

Malay Peninsula, Sumatra and Borneo. Forest, including mangroves, and secondary growth, scrub, cultivation and gardens up to 1,220 m.
Short, slightly curved bill.

52a **Adult male** Olive-green above, with metallic blue or green on forehead; below grey, olive and yellowish-green.

52b **Adult female** Differs from male in lacking metallic feathering on forehead.

53 Plain-throated Sunbird *Anthreptes malacensis* **Text and map page 184**

West Burma, Thailand, Indochina, Malay Peninsula, Greater and Lesser Sundas, Philippines and Sulawesi. In forest, including mangroves, at forest edge, woodland, coastal scrub, plantations, secondary growth, cultivation and gardens, from sea-level to 1,200 m.
Thickish bill, of medium length and slightly decurved.

53a **Adult male** (nominate; South-East Asia, Sumatra, southern Borneo, Java and Bali) Metallic green and purple upperparts with some chestnut on wing-coverts and scapulars; sides of head greenish or brownish; chin and throat pinky-brown bordered metallic purple; lower neck pale pinky-red; rest of underparts greenish-yellow.

53b **Adult female** (nominate) Greyish olive-green above; yellow area around eye and yellowish underparts.

53c **Adult male** (*griseigularis*; Philippines) Differs from nominate male chiefly in having chin and throat grey.

53d **Adult female** (*griseigularis*) Differs from nominate female chiefly in having greyish area around eye, and being grey from chin to upper breast.

54 Red-throated Sunbird *Anthreptes rhodolaema* **Text and map page 186**

Malay Peninsula, Sumatra and Borneo. Forest, at forest edge, in coastal vegetation, secondary growth, clearings and plantations, from sea-level to 800 m.
Bill similar to that of *A. malacensis*.

54a **Adult male** Differs from male nominate *A. malacensis* mainly by pinker, less brownish sides of head and hroat, and maroon band on wing, shoulders and across back.

54b **Adult female** Differs from female nominate *A. malacensis* by much less obvious pale area around eye, and being duller and less yellow below.

47 Ruby-cheeked Sunbird *Chalcoparia singalensis* **Text and map page 177**

North-east Indian subcontinent, South-East Asia, east China, Sumatra, Borneo and Java. In forest, at forest edge, coastal vegetation, secondary growth, clearings, coconut groves and gardens, from sea-level to 1,000 m, but to 1,953 m on Java.
Rather short, almost straight bill.

47a **Adult male** (*assamensis*; north-east Indian subcontinent to northern Burma, northern Thailand, and west and south Yunnan) Upperparts dark glossed green; reddish or copper ear-coverts; chin to breast rufous; rest of underparts yellow.

47b **Adult female** (*assamensis*) Differs from male in being mostly olive-green above and lacks copper on ear-coverts.

PLATE 15: AFRICAN *ANTHREPTES* SUNBIRDS (2)

55   **Mouse-brown Sunbird** *Anthreptes gabonicus*   **Text and map page 187**

West Africa from Gambia to Angola.
Coastal habitats and inland along rivers. Sexes similar.

     55   **Adult** Plain mouse-brown above, greyish-white below; white stripes almost encircling eye
          conspicuous. White tips to all but central tail feathers visible in flight or from underneath.

56   **Western Violet-backed Sunbird** *Anthreptes longuemarei*   **Text and map page 188**

West, central and southern Africa.
Wooded savannas and gallery forests in West Africa, where also occurs in mangroves. Similar main
habitats in East Africa, but also miombo woodland, parks and gardens.
Straight, heavy-looking, bill.

     56a   **Adult male** (nominate; Senegal to Guinea-Bissau) Violet upperparts and throat, contrasting
          with white below and yellow pectoral tufts.

     56b   **Adult female** (nominate) White throat and yellow on underparts; metallic violet uppertail-
          coverts and white eyebrow.

     56c   **Adult male** (*angolensis*; southern Democratic Republic of the Congo, Angola, Zambia, Malawi
          west of the Rift valley, south-west Tanzania) Differs from nominate by metallic green lesser
          wing-coverts; breast washed buff.

57   **Kenya Violet-backed Sunbird** *Anthreptes orientalis*   **Text and map page 190**

South-east Sudan, Ethiopia, Somalia, Rwanda, Uganda, Kenya and north-east Tanzania.
Acacias near water, riverine woodland, dry bushland, open woodland and in junipers in highlands.
Drier habitats than *A. longuemarei*.
Short-billed and stocky.

     57a   **Adult male** Violet above, white below with blue-green rump. More green on lesser wing-
          coverts and rump than nominate *A. longuemarei*.

     57b   **Adult female** White belly and dark blue tail. From female *A. longuemarei* by lack of yellow on
          belly, having only a tinge, and less violet on tail; from female *A. neglectus* by white streak over
          eye.

58   **Uluguru Violet-backed Sunbird** *Anthreptes neglectus*   **Text and map page 191**

Localised sites in Kenya, Tanzania, and northern Mozambique.
Forest and forest edge and thickets at edge of montane forest, from sea-level to 1,250 m in eastern
Tanzania and northern Mozambique and in moist bushed and wooded country in coastal regions in
Kenya and Tanzania.

     58a   **Adult male** Violet upperparts including uppertail-coverts, brown half-collar, bluish-green
          rump, purplish-blue tail and yellowish-green edges to wings and coverts in both sexes. White
          or buffish-brown below (not pure white) with violet chin, yellow pectoral tufts and
          conspicuous cobalt-blue/green flash on shoulder.

     58b   **Adult female** Similar to male but mostly grey below with yellow belly. No white streak over eye.

     58c   **Immature** White streak over eye, bright lemon-yellow on belly and vent. Almost indistinguish-
          able from immature *A. orientalis* and *A. longuemarei*. Immature *A. neglectus* and immature or
          female *A. longuemarei* are bright lemon-yellow on the belly and vent whereas female and
          immature *A. orientalis* have only a faint yellow or buff wash, but edges to wings and coverts
          are brighter yellowish-green in *A. neglectus* than in both of the other species.

56a

55

56b

56c

57a

57b

58a

58c

58b

R·A

PLATE 16: AFRICAN *ANTHREPTES* SUNBIRDS (3) AND AMANI SUNBIRD

59   Violet-tailed Sunbird *Anthreptes aurantium*   **Text and map page 192**

Central Africa from Cameroon to Gabon and the Democratic Republic of the Congo, Central African Republic, Republic of the Congo and Angola. Close to water in forest, gallery forest, seasonally flooded forest, mangroves, swamp forest, edges of salt-pans and wooded savanna.
Longish, slightly decurved bill.

59a   Adult male Brilliant metallic blue, green and violet upperparts contrasting with pale below. Orange pectoral tufts.

59b   Adult female Broad white supercilium.

59c   Immature Greenish-brown above. Conspicuous white or pale yellow supercilium and dark line through eye. Wing edged white. Underparts greyish-white, washed yellow or olivaceous-green. Tail blue with metallic green wash.

66   Amani Sunbird *Hedydipna pallidigaster*   **Text and map page 205**

Coastal *Brachystegia* woodland in south-east Kenya and forest, at forest edges and in open secondary growth in uplands of north-east Tanzania.
Small with short bill and stubby tail.

66a   Adult male Metallic blue-green head and back contrasting with white below.

66b   Adult female Grey above with white supercilium, metallic grey-blue rump, wing-flash and sides of neck.

61   Green Sunbird *Anthreptes rectirostris*   **Text and map page 195**

West, Central and East Africa. Canopy in primary and secondary forests and along tracks and clearings within them, gallery forest, swamp forest, coffee plantations, cultivations and open areas between plantations, including cocoa forest and oil palms, inselbergs and mountains.
Very small with short, straightish bill, giving warbler-like appearance.

61a   Adult male (nominate; Sierra Leone to Ghana) Metallic green above with yellow throat.

61b   Adult female (nominate) Olivaceous above with a scattering of metallic green on shoulders, yellow-olive below, with pale supercilium.

61c   Adult male (*tephrolaema*; Benin to Angola, Sudan, Uganda, Kenya and Tanzania) Metallic green above with grey throat.

62   Banded Sunbird *Anthreptes rubritorques*   **Text and map page 196**

North-east Tanzania. Montane forest.
Very small, short-tailed sunbird.

62a   Adult male Green above, grey below with red breast-band.

62b   Adult female Green above, dull yellowish below without breast-band.

PLATE 17: *HEDYDIPNA* AND *HYPOGRAMMA* SUNBIRDS

63   Collared Sunbird *Hedydipna collaris*   **Text and map page 197**

Senegal to South Africa. Primary, secondary, gallery and coastal forest, coffee groves and swamps, forest
edges, savanna, woodland, thickets, inselbergs, riversides, cultivations and gardens.
Short, stout bill, only slightly decurved.

63a   **Adult male** (nominate; eastern Cape Province from Knysna to southern KwaZulu-Natal, South
Africa) Bright metallic green upperparts, chin and throat, narrow purple breast-band and bright
yellow belly. Green edges to wing-coverts and inner secondaries; dusky olive wash on sides.

63b   **Adult female** (nominate) Dusky olive throat without metallic green and purple band.

63c   **Adult male** (*subcollaris*; Senegal and Guinea-Bissau to coastal Nigeria as far as the Niger delta)
On *Leonotis* sp. From nominate by brown wings, remiges and greater coverts with yellowish-
olive margins.

63d   **Adult female** (*subcollaris*) Differs from nominate by brown wings, remiges and greater coverts
with yellowish-olive margins.

63e   **Juvenile** (*subcollaris*) Warbler-like with pale supercilium and dull green upperparts; paler
below. Older birds with metallic patches.

64   Pygmy Sunbird *Hedydipna platura*   **Text and map page 201**

Sub-Saharan Africa from Senegal to north-west Kenya. Dry savannas, acacia woodland and gardens.
Bill much shorter and straighter than in *Cinnyris pulchellus*.

64a   **Adult male** Long tail, metallic green upperparts and bright yellow below; wings dark brown.
From male *H. metallica* by lack of bluish-purple band between green and yellow of breast.
Male *platura* without streamers also confusable with *H. collaris*, but latter has emerald
upperparts, bluish-green uppertail-coverts, longer bill and violet breast-band.

64b   **Adult male non-breeding** Grey-brown above, yellow and white below with pale supercilium.
Some non-breeding males have green-black bib (not illustrated).

64c   **Adult female** Pale brown above, yellow below and without streamers.

65   Nile Valley Sunbird *Hedydipna metallica*   **Text and map page 203**

Egypt, Sudan, Chad, Ethiopia, Eritrea, Djibouti, Somalia, Saudi Arabia, Yemen and Oman. *Acacia* scrub
and semi-desert. Arid lowlands, river valleys, gardens in irrigated areas. Landscaped areas in towns.

65a   **Adult male** Long tail, metallic green upperparts and upper chest, where green is separated
from yellow belly by purple band (lacking in male *H. platura*).

65b   **Adult male first non-breeding** Similar to adult female with slight gloss to some feather edges.
In subsequent non-breeding plumage, chin and centre of throat matt black (not illustrated).

65c   **Adult female** Dull grey above, whitish supercilium and pale yellow below. From female
H. platura by more prominent supercilium and eye-stripe and paler below.

67   Purple-naped Sunbird *Hypogramma hypogrammicum*   **Text and map page 206**

South-East Asia, Sumatra and Borneo. Occurs in many forest types, and in logged forest and at edge, in
secondary growth and occasionally in gardens, from sea-level to at least 1,160 m.

67a   **Adult male** (*lisettae* ; northern Burma, northern Thailand, northern and central Indochina
and west Yunnan) Male differs from female in being larger, and having metallic purple or
blue on nape, lower back, rump and uppertail-coverts.

67b   **Adult female** (*lisettae*) Olive-green above; below olive-yellow streaked dark olive.

PLATE 18: LITTLE GREEN, BATES'S AND OLIVE SUNBIRDS

60 **Little Green Sunbird** *Anthreptes seimundi*   **Text and map page 193**

West and Central Africa from Sierra Leone to Angola and Uganda. Mature forest, secondary forest, gallery forest, coffee plantations, forest edges and forest-grassland mosaic. Dense undergrowth in forest clearings and abandoned plantations.
Very small. Short, straight, thick bill. Sexes similar.

60a **Adult** (nominate; Bioko) Green, paler below with yellow on belly; pale eye-ring. Brighter yellow below than *kruensis*. From *C. batesi* by straighter bill and more prominent eye-stripe.

60b **Adult** (*kruensis*; Sierra Leone to Togo) On red ironwood *Lophira alata*. Duller and paler below with a greyer tinge, yellow less bright than nominate and *minor*. Chin almost white. Eye-ring less obvious than in nominate and *minor*.

137 **Bates's Sunbird** *Cinnyris batesi*   **Text and map page 312**

West and Central Africa. From Liberia to Angola (Cabinda) and north-west Zambia. Primary forest and edges, forest, secondary growth and cultivated fields with tall trees.
Tiny with short, curved bill and very short tail. Sexes similar.

137 **Adult** Dull green with yellowish belly. Differs from *A. seimundi* by curved bill, darker tail and less obvious or absent supercilium. Perches upright whereas *seimundi* holds itself more horizontal.

78 **Eastern Olive Sunbird** *Cyanomitra olivacea*   **Text and map page 221**

East and south-east Africa. From southern Somalia to South Africa. Lower strata and undergrowth of mature forest, secondary forest, clearings, dense woodland, bushy thickets, coastal scrubland, plantations and gardens.
Long curved bill and yellow or orange pectoral tufts in both sexes.

78a **Adult male** (nominate; South Africa) Dull green upperparts, yellowish below and on wing edges.

78b **Adult female** (nominate) On *Englerina woodfordioides*, showing orange pectoral tufts.

78c **Immature** (nominate) Chin to chest olivaceous-yellow or orangey-yellow. Brighter olive than adult above.

79 **Western Olive Sunbird** *Cyanomitra obscura*   **Text and map page 222**

West and East Africa. From Senegal to Angola; southern Sudan and Ethiopia to Zambia, Zimbabwe and Mozambique.
Bill long and curved. Pectoral tufts only present in males. Separable from *C. batesi*, *A. seimundi* and female *A. rectirostris* by larger size, longer tail and longer bill.

79 **Adult male** (*sclateri*; Melsetter area in eastern Zimbabwe and bordering areas of Mozambique) Drab olive-green, paler below. Paler below than nominate (not illustrated), chest feathers with dusky fringes.

60a

60b

137

78a

78b

79

78c

RwA

PLATE 19: ORANGE-BREASTED, MOUSE-COLOURED, REICHENBACH'S AND CAMEROON SUNBIRDS

72 **Orange-breasted Sunbird** *Anthobaphes violacea* **Text and map page 211**

South Africa. Western Cape Province from Kamiesberg to Cape Town. Endemic to fynbos.

72a **Adult male** On *Erica* sp. Elongated tail, green head, violet breast-band and orange breast.

72b **Adult female** Olive above, olivaceous-yellow below with orange tinge to belly.

---

80 **Mouse-coloured Sunbird** *Cyanomitra veroxii* **Text and map page 225**

East and south-eastern Africa, from Somalia to South Africa. Coastal forests, woodlands, scrubland, mangroves, riverine forest, gardens. Also reaches inland montane forests near coast. *Acacia* scrubland adjoining forest margins.
Dull large sunbird with grey upperparts and dull greyish-white underparts. Sexes similar.

80a **Adult** (nominate; South Africa in eastern Cape Province at Port Elizabeth to east KwaZulu-Natal) Singing male. At very close range a greenish-blue metallic tinge is visible on crown, back and shoulders. Scarlet pectoral tufts.

80b **Adult** (nominate) In flight. Red pectoral tufts with yellow margins.

80c **Immature** (nominate) Pale yellowish below.

80d **Adult** (*fischeri*; South Africa in north-east KwaZulu-Natal and southern Mozambique north to Juba valley in southern Somalia; inland to southern Malawi) Smaller, underparts whiter, upperparts paler and greyer with less gloss than nominate.

80e **Adult** (*fischeri*) In flight. Red pectoral tufts without yellow margins.

---

68 **Reichenbach's Sunbird** *Anabathmis reichenbachii* **Text and map page 207**

West and Central Africa from Liberia to Angola. Coastal areas with sand and palms, swamps, scrub, mangroves, ricefields and forest clearings. Usually near water and occasionally in gardens. Sexes similar.

68a **Adult** Metallic steel-blue head and throat, contrasting with olive back and grey underparts. Yellow vent and pectoral tufts. Dark centres and pale fringes to back and wings give scaly appearance.

68b **Immature** Head dark olive, with black mottling on crown and yellow mottling on face with yellow supercilium. Underparts and cheeks olivaceous-yellow, throat barred dark brown and olive on flanks.

---

76 **Cameroon Sunbird** *Cyanomitra oritis* **Text and map page 218**

Cameroon, Nigeria and Bioko. Montane forest and *Eucalyptus* plantations. Undergrowth within forest, along streams and at forest edges.
Dull olive-green body plumage, contrasting with metallic green or blue and purple head and throat; long curved bill. Sexes similar but female lacks pectoral tufts.

76a **Adult male** (nominate; Mt Cameroon) Metallic feathers of crown and sides of head dull steel-blue, and throat and breast deep purplish-blue.

76b **Adult male** (*bansoensis*; Cameroon at Manenguba, Mt Kupe, Rumpi hills and Bamenda highlands; Obudu plateau and Gashaka-Gumti National Park, Nigeria) Metallic feathers of crown and sides of head bright steel-green, and throat and breast steel-blue. More yellow in mid-belly than in nominate.

76c **Juvenile** (*bansoensis*) Lacks metallic plumage.

72b

72a

80a

80b

80c

68a

68b

80d

80e

76a

76b

76c

RWA

PLATE 20: GULF OF GUINEA SUNBIRDS AND BLUE-HEADED SUNBIRD

69   **Príncipe Sunbird** *Anabathmis hartlaubii*   **Text and map page 208**

Endemic to Príncipe. All habitats, including primary and secondary forest and coconut plantations, except montane forest.
A moderately large sunbird.

> **69a**   **Adult male** Mostly dark olive but with metallic blue throat, which appears black at a distance, and conspicuous yellow flanks. Longish, graduated tail with white tips except in centre.

> **69b**   **Adult female** Mostly dark olive, throat mottled.

70   **Newton's Sunbird** *Anabathmis newtonii*   **Text and map page 209**

Endemic to São Tomé. Steep wooded hillsides, forests, savanna woodland, gardens, edges of shady tracks, plantations and overgrown uncultivated ground.
Small sunbird with olive upperparts.

> **70a**   **Adult male** Dark olive above. Chin and throat metallic green, reflecting violet. Breast bright yellow, belly and undertail-coverts paler yellow. White tips to undertail.

> **70b**   **Adult female** Dark olive above. Pale bars on dark olive throat and upper chest, rest of underparts pale yellowish-white.

71   **São Tomé Sunbird** *Dreptes thomensis*   **Text and map page 210**

Endemic to São Tomé. Usually montane forest, also uncultivated slopes, secondary forest, forest scrub, flowering shrubs along streams, and cultivations.
Sexes similar.

> **71**   **Adult** Unmistakable: huge sunbird appearing mostly black with extensive greenish-yellow patch on vent. Conspicuous long curved bill. Tail graduated, black when closed but white tips to underside of outer feathers visible when spread.

77   **Blue-headed Sunbird** *Cyanomitra alinae*   **Text and map page 219**

Mountains of eastern Democratic Republic of the Congo, south-west Uganda, Burundi and Rwanda. Montane forests up to 3,280 m. Occurs in canopy, but more often at low levels, almost to forest floor. Avoids savanna, preferring primary, secondary and riverine forests.
A long-billed, short-tailed, mid-sized sunbird with blue metallic plumage on hood, saffron tinge to greenish upperparts and blackish underparts. Sexes similar in general.

> **77a**   **Adult male** (nominate; Ruwenzori mountains, Virunga volcanoes, and Bwindi forest, south-west Uganda) Blacker below than female, yellow pectoral tufts.

> **77b**   **Adult female** (nominate). Less black on underparts than male, no pectoral tufts.

> **77c**   **Immature male** (nominate) Spots of metallic plumage on crown, otherwise all upperparts dull olive-green with orangey-yellow tinge on mantle. Chin, throat and upper breast dull blackish-grey with blackish barring; belly, flanks and undertail-coverts greyish-olive.

PLATE 21: GREEN-HEADED, BANNERMAN'S, BLUE-THROATED BROWN AND SOCOTRA SUNBIRDS

73 Green-headed Sunbird *Cyanomitra verticalis* **Text and map page 213**

From Senegal to Zambia. Primary and old secondary forest, clearings, gallery forest, well-wooded savanna, forest-savanna mosaic, thickets, mangroves, plantations, inselbergs and gardens.

73a **Adult male** (nominate; Senegal to Nigeria) Metallic plumage extends onto chin and throat to form hood.

73b **Adult female** (nominate) Differs from male by lack of metallic plumage on chin and throat.

73c **Immature male** (nominate) Slightly mottled grey forehead and crown. Back with olive wash, rest of upperparts as adult male but duller. Forehead, chin, throat, lores and malars blackish-grey. Rest of underparts olive with marked yellow wash.

73d **Adult male** (*viridisplendens*; Sudan, Democratic Republic of the Congo, Uganda, Kenya, Tanzania, Malawi, Zambia) Head and throat brighter brassy green, less dull and bluish than nominate, *bohndorfii* or *cyanocephala*.

73e **Adult male** (*cyanocephala*; coastal areas from mainland Equatorial Guinea and Gabon to Congo estuary, Cabinda, and north-west Democratic Republic of the Congo) Larger; throat and breast with more purple, less steel-blue gloss, and no contrast between the two; abdomen sootier grey, back darker olive than nominate.

74 Bannerman's Sunbird *Cyanomitra bannermani* **Text and map page 215**

Southern Democratic Republic of the Congo, through north-west Zambia to central and north-east Angola. Riverine forest, moist evergreen forest and sometimes adjoining miombo woodland.

74a **Adult male** From male *C. verticalis* by duller, more matt, metallic steel-blue plumage, with greenish reflections on chin and throat, much paler grey chest and belly, smaller, less prominent pectoral tufts and shorter, straighter bill.

74b **Adult female** From female *C. verticalis* by lack of metallic plumage except for faint greenish metallic streaks on crown, and by brighter (more yellowish-) olive upperparts, darker underparts.

75 Blue-throated Brown Sunbird *Cyanomitra cyanolaema* **Text and map page 216**

West, East and Central Africa, from Sierra Leone to Tanzania. Primary forest, forest edges, coastal woodlands, clearings and secondary forest. Gardens, cultivation, riversides, plantations.

75a **Adult male** (nominate; Bioko) Metallic blue throat and forehead.

75b **Adult female** (nominate) Eyebrow and feathers around eye white. Upperparts, and tail brown washed and edged olive-yellow. Uunderparts greyish-white with varying amounts of pale yellowish-green and smoke-grey mottling, brighter on vent.

75c **Immature male** (nominate) Lacks pectoral tufts and metallic feathers on crown and throat, which are brown and grey respectively. Tail and wings edged yellowish olive-green.

75d **Adult female** (*octaviae*; Nigeria to Democratic Republic of the Congo and northern Angola, Uganda and Kenya) Yellower-olive, less greenish on upperparts than nominate.

87 Socotra Sunbird *Chalcomitra balfouri* **Text and map page 238**

Socotra Island. Occurs in all habitats from sea-level to 1,370 m.

87a **Adult male** Dark brown above with pale streaks; white on outer tail feathers. Blackish mask and throat; underparts chiefly whitish and pale brown, with heavy dark barring and mottling on breast and central area of belly; yellow pectoral tufts.

87b **Adult female** Smaller than male, and lacks pectoral tufts.

PLATE 22: SEYCHELLES, CARMELITE, AMETHYST AND GREEN-THROATED SUNBIRDS

145 Seychelles Sunbird *Cinnyris dussumieri*   **Text and map page 325**

Seychelles. Occurs in almost all habitats, including man-made.

145a/b Adult male Sooty greyish-brown above, with white tips to tail. Throat to breast metallic dark blue; rest of underparts greyish-brown and white; pectoral tufts yellow to red.

145c   Adult female Lacks pectoral tufts, and glossy blue below replaced by grey-brown; pale tips to feathers give scaled effect.

82   Carmelite Sunbird *Chalcomitra fuliginosa*   **Text and map page 228**

West Africa, from Sierra Leone to Angola. Coastal plains and lowland woods, coconut palms, mangroves, freshwater swamps, plantations, clearings and gardens. Also in savanna in northern Liberia. Occurs inland along the River Congo.

82a/b Adult male (nominate; north-west Angola to southern Democratic Republic of the Congo, lower Congo inland to Kwanmouth) Metallic purplish-blue forehead. Chin, throat and uppertail-coverts metallic violet; small patch of metallic violet on lesser wing-coverts. Rest dull chocolate-brown, darkest on breast, belly and undertail-coverts. Yellow pectoral tufts. Differs from male *C. rubescens* and *C. amethystina* by metallic forehead reflecting purple not green, generally more chocolate plumage and pale brown hind-neck and mantle.

82c   Adult male in faded plumage (nominate) Bleaching by sunlight leaves head pale brownish or greyish-white, mantle light brown, all metallic feathering duller than when fresh.

82d   Adult female (nominate) Paler than male. Upperparts pale earth-brown with blackish-brown wings and tail, wing-coverts with creamy-white margins and tips. Tail also with white tips. Throat brown, rest of underparts creamy-white with mottled appearance. Differs from female *C. rubescens* and *C. amethystina* by lack of supercilium.

84   Amethyst Sunbird *Chalcomitra amethystina*   **Text and map page 231**

East, Central and south-eastern Africa. From Sudan, Ethiopia, and Somalia to South Africa. Woodlands in savanna, sometimes at edge of evergreen forest or in riverine forest and gardens.

84a   Adult male (nominate; South Africa to Mozambique, south of the Limpopo river, southern Botswana) Iridescent purplish-copper on throat and shoulders, silvery light green on crown visible at close range, contrasting with blackish-brown plumage. Appears all black at a distance.

84b   Immature male (nominate) Similar to adult female but iridescent rosy-purple patch on throat.

84c   Adult female (nominate) Olivaceous grey-brown above, pale grey-brown below with variably heavy mottling, except on belly. Dark throat-patch.

84d   Adult female (*deminuta*; Gabon, Angola, Democratic Republic of the Congo, Republic of the Congo, Namibia, and Botswana [Ngamiland], Zambia) Throat less dusky and much plainer below than nominate, some with hardly any streaking, and moustachial stripe less prominent.

83   Green-throated Sunbird *Chalcomitra rubescens*   **Text and map page 229**

Nigeria to northern Angola and from Sudan to Tanzania and Zambia. Forest, secondary growth and clearings, plantations, farms, edges of villages, well-wooded bush, montane grassland and heaths.

83a   Adult male (nominate; Cameroon to Angola; north-west Zambia; southern borders of Sudan, Uganda, western Kenya, north-west Tanzania) Appears all black at distance but has iridescent green throat-patch and forehead. From male *C. fuliginosa* by much blacker plumage.

83b   Adult female (nominate) Greyish-brown above with contrasting pale belly, heavily streaked and with prominent supercilium. From female *C. cyanolaema* by heavy streaking on breast and white supercilium, without white below eye.

83c   Adult female (*stangerii*; Bioko) Streaking on foreneck and breast heavier and blacker than in nominate and usually white not yellowish below.

145a

145b

145c

82d

82a

82b

82c

84b

84a

84d

84c

83c

83a

83b

RwA

PLATE 23: SCARLET-CHESTED, HUNTER'S AND BUFF-THROATED SUNBIRDS

85   **Scarlet-chested Sunbird** *Chalcomitra senegalensis*   **Text and map page 233**

Sub-Saharan Africa outside forested regions from Mauritania to South Africa. Wooded savannas and semi-arid thorn-scrub; gallery forests, coastal plains, inselbergs, bushy areas, parks, gardens, plantations and farmland. In southern Africa in *Acacia*, miombo, mopane and dry baobab woodland, amongst *Protea* spp. and in coastal scrub.
Large with long curved bill.

     85a   **Adult male** (nominate; Senegal to Nigeria) Vermilion breast contrasting with blackish body and metallic green crown, malar stripe and throat but appears all black at a distance.

     85b   **Adult female** (nominate) Dull brown above, pale brownish-yellow below, boldly mottled with largish black markings and no supercilium. From females of *C. amethystina* and *C. rubescens* by white on alula and associated primary coverts and lack of supercilium (latter present in female *C. hunteri*).

     85c   **Immature male** (nominate) Similar to adult female above but has metallic green on chin and upper neck, dusky black or greyish-black throat and breast, belly yellow with heavy blackish or dark brown mottling and barring with red on chest, metallic colouring on head and blotchy body.

     85d   **Adult male** (*acik*; Cameroon, Sudan, Central African Republic, Democratic Republic of the Congo and north-east Uganda) Red of chest lighter, more matt, lacking gloss and with less pronounced metallic blue barring, and green malar stripe reduced compared with nominate. Differs from male *C. hunteri* by green throat and lack of violet shoulder-patch.

     85e   **Adult male** (*gutturalis*; South Africa to Zambia, Angola, Botswana, Namibia, Democratic Republic of the Congo, Kenya inland to Ukamba, Pemba Island, Zanzibar) Violet metallic shoulder-spot on lesser wing-coverts, which is lacking in nominate, *acik* and *lamperti*.

---

86   **Hunter's Sunbird** *Chalcomitra hunteri*   **Text and map page 237**

North-east Africa: south-east Sudan, Somalia, eastern Ethiopia, northern and eastern Kenya to dry country east of Kilimanjaro in north-east Tanzania, Uganda (single record from Moroto). Bushland, open woodland, and semi-arid grasslands.
Large sunbird with long curved bill.

     86a   **Adult male** Mostly black except for scarlet chest. Differs from mostly allopatric *C. senegalensis* by blacker upperparts and black throat bordered by green moustachials (but this also present in male *C. s. cruentata*), violet uppertail-coverts and shoulder-patch (but this present in male *C. s. cruentata* and *C. s. gutturalis*).

     86b   **Adult female** Mostly greyish-brown above, pale below with heavy mottling on breast and flanks. Paler brown above than female *C. senegalensis*, yellow wash below weaker or lacking and no black throat (present in female *C. s. cruentata*).

     86c   **Immature male** Similar to adult female but black on chin and throat, moustachial stripe green, gorget scarlet with blue bars.

---

81   **Buff-throated Sunbird** *Chalcomitra adelberti*   **Text and map page 227**

West Africa from Sierra Leone to Cameroon. Lowland mature and secondary forests, forest edges and forest clearings near towns and villages, cultivated areas and gardens.
Dumpy, medium-sized sunbird with relatively short bill.

     81a   **Adult male** (nominate; Sierra Leone to Ghana) Pale buff throat contrasts strikingly with overall blackish-brown appearance of rest of plumage. Paler and more rufous below than *eboensis*.

     81b   **Adult female** (nominate) White with yellow wash below, brightest yellow on belly, and brown streaks. Darker below with darker yellowish-grey breast than *eboensis*.

     81c   **Adult male** (*eboensis*; Togo to south-east Nigeria) Throat paler than in nominate and has darker chestnut, less rufous, on underparts below throat.

PLATE 24: ASIAN *LEPTOCOMA* SUNBIRDS (1)

88   Purple-rumped Sunbird *Leptocoma zeylonica*   **Text and map page 239**

Peninsular and eastern India, Sri Lanka and Burma; to 1,400 m in Sri Lanka, occasionally 2,100 m in India; various forest types, jungle, secondary growth, cactus hedges, farmland and gardens. Bill of medium length and slightly curved.

   88a   **Adult male** Deep chestnut back, rest of upperparts metallic green or purple; throat metallic purple; sides of head and lower throat crimson or chestnut; rest of underparts yellow or white.

   88b   **Adult female** Olive-brown above, whitish throat and flanks; rest of underparts yellow.

   88c   **Immature** From female by yellowish throat.

89   Crimson-backed Sunbird *Leptocoma minima*   **Text and map page 240**

South-west India and Sri Lanka. Found chiefly in foothills, but occurs from 300 to 2,100 m; forest, sholas, plantations, gardens. Medium-length bill, slender and decurved.

   89a   **Adult male breeding** Glossy green crown; sides of face blackish; glossy purple rump; blackish wings and tail; rest of upperparts crimson. Glossy purple throat; breast crimson with black lower border; rest of underparts yellowish and whitish.

   89b   **Adult male non-breeding** Crown, neck and mantle olive-green; red band across shoulders and back; rest of back, rump and uppertail-coverts metallic purple; wings and tail black; below dull yellow.

   89c   **Adult female** Olive above; rump and uppertail-coverts red; tail black; wings blackish, with yellow edging; below yellow.

90   Purple-throated Sunbird *Leptocoma sperata*   **Text and map page 241**

North-east India, Bangladesh, South-East Asia, Sumatra, Borneo and Philippines. Occurs in forests, including mangroves, in coastal vegetation, secondary growth, coconut groves, cultivation and gardens. Generally not far from coast, but up to 110 km inland in peninsular Malaysia; normally below 200 m, but up to 1,220 m in peninsular Malaysia. Medium-long, slightly curved bill.

   90a   **Adult male** (nominate; Philippines, except where other forms occur) Metallic green crown, above mostly maroon and metallic green, with red and yellowish on wings; below metallic purple, red, and yellowish.

   90b   **Adult female** (nominate) Olive-green above, browner on wings; mostly yellowish and whitish below.

   90c   **Adult male** (*brasiliana*; range of species, except Philippines) Entirely dark, appearing blackish in poor light. Differs from male nominate by blackish and dark blue replacing crimson, red and yellow of upperparts, and maroon-crimson and sooty-brown replacing red and yellow of underparts.

   90d   **Adult male** (*juliae*; Philippines – Basilan, Jolo, Malampa, Mindanao, Tawitawi, Bongao, Sanga Sanga, Sibutu, Simunul, Malamaui, Siasi and Tonquil) Mauve-red gloss and green on crown; dark crimson above; throat glossed purple, rest of underparts orange-yellow, scarlet and yellow-green.

   90e   **Adult male** (*henkei*; Philippines: mountains of northern Luzon) Differs from nominate in having a black mantle.

88b

88a

88c

89b

89c

89a

90a

90c

90b

90e

90d

RvA

PLATE 25: ASIAN *LEPTOCOMA* SUNBIRDS (2) AND APRICOT-BREASTED SUNBIRD

91 **Black Sunbird** *Leptocoma sericea*   **Text and map page 243**

Wallacea, New Guinea and Bismarck Archipelago. Occurs in most habitats; generally in lowlands, but up to 800 m on Sulawesi, to 1,200 m on Sangihe, and to 1,400 m on Buru and New Ireland.
Longish, curved bill. Male looks blackish in poor light.

91a **Adult male** (*talautensis*; Talaud Island) Crown golden-green; wing-coverts and rump metallic blue and violet; back and chest sooty; throat bronze.

91b **Adult female** (*talautensis*) Brown crown, orange throat to breast; rest of underparts buffy and white.

91c **Adult male** (*auriceps*; Peleng, Banggai, Morotai, Halmahera, Muor, Damar, Ternate, Makian, Mare, Bacan, Obi, Tifore, Sula and Gebe) Crown darker than *talautensis*, throat dark blue.

91d **Adult male** (*aspasioides*; Seram, Ambon, Nusa Laut, Watu Bela and Aru Islands) Wing-coverts and rump greenish-blue.

91e **Adult female** (*aspasioides*) Grey head and throat, olive-grey below.

91f **Adult male** (*chlorolaema*; Kai Islands) Dark green throat; mostly blue-green above.

91g **Adult female** (*christianae*; Louisiade Archipelago, D'Entrecasteaux Archipelago, Trobriands, Marshall Bennett Islands and Woodlark Island) Grey head and throat; rest of upperparts olive-grey; yellowish below.

91h **Adult female** (*sangirensis*; Sangihe, Siau and Ruang) Orange throat; grey-green underparts.

---

92 **Copper-throated Sunbird** *Leptocoma calcostetha*   **Text and map page 246**

Southern Thailand, southern Tenasserim, southern Indochina, Malay Peninsula, Sumatra, Java and Philippines. Chiefly coastal, and below 915 m, occurring in *kerangas*, alluvial, mangrove and secondary forests, coconut and rubber plantations, cultivation and gardens.
Bill of medium length, stout and curved; tail longish, but without elongated central rectrices.

92a **Adult male** Looks blackish in poor light. Upper back, wings and tail black; rest of upperparts metallic green; throat metallic copper-red, breast metallic purple-blue; pectoral tufts yellow; rest of underparts black.

92b **Adult female** Grey-brown crown, rest of upperparts olive-yellow; greyish olive-green below, yellower on belly.

---

141 **Apricot-breasted Sunbird** *Cinnyris buettikoferi*   **Text and map page 321**

Sumba. At forest edge, in secondary growth, cultivation and scrub, in lowlands up to at least 950 m.
Slender, longish, curved bill.

141a **Adult male** Olive-brown above; metallic purplish bluish-green gorget; rest of underparts yellow with orange patch on breast.

141b **Adult female** Differs from male by whitish or yellowish throat, no orange below, and rest of underparts mostly pale yellow.

140 Olive-backed Sunbird *Cinnyris jugularis*   **Text and map page 318**

Nicobars, South-East Asia, south-east China, Hainan Island, Greater Sundas, Philippines, Wallacea, New Guinea, Solomons, Bismarck Archipelago and north-east Australia. Lowlands, and up to 1,700 m, in open country, scrub, mangroves, riverine forest, at forest edge, in secondary growth, agricultural land, plantations and gardens.

Longish, decurved bill.

140a **Adult male** (nominate; Philippines, outside range of *aurora* and *obscurior*) Olive-green above; tail black with white tips; chin to breast plus sides of neck metallic purple-black; occasionally brown band bordering throat; rest of underparts bright yellow.

140b **Adult female** (nominate) Olive-green above, tail black with white tips; supercilium and underparts yellow.

140c **Adult male** (*flammaxillaris*; Burma, Thailand, Cambodia and northern peninsular Malaysia) From nominate male by broad maroon band on breast below metallic purple of chin to upper breast.

140d **Adult male non-breeding** (*flammaxillaris*) Like nominate female, but with metallic black stripe from chin to upper breast.

140e **Adult male** (*aurora*; Philippines – Agutaya, Balabac, Busuanga, Cagayancillo, Culion, Cuyo, Palawan, Dumaran and Calauit) Differs from male nominate by variable amount of orange on breast.

140f **Adult male** (*plateni*; Sulawesi, Talaud, Siau, Sangihe, Manadotua, Manterawu, Bangka, Togian and Salayar) Differs from male nominate by yellow superciliary and malar stripes.

140g **Adult male** (*rhizophorae*; northern Vietnam and Hainan Island) Differs from nominate male by maroon band on upper breast, and rest of breast sooty; remaining underparts greyish-white with a little yellow. Some have bluish gloss on forehead and forecrown.

140h **Adult male** (*teijsmanni*; Tanahjampea, Kalao, Bonerate, Kalaota and Madu) Mostly brownish above; throat glossed purplish-green with a dark chestnut or maroon lower border, with yellow and orange pectoral tufts; below otherwise black glossed purple.

140i **Adult female** (*teijsmanni*) Greyish-olive above, with yellowish supercilium; whitish and pale yellow below.

140j **Adult male** (*clementiae*; Moluccas – Seram, Boano, Ambon, Saparua, Nusa Laut and Watubela) Olive to golden-green above; purple throat; rest of underparts black.

140k **Adult female** (*frenatus*; Wallacea – Morotai, Bacari, Mare, Moti, Ternate, Bisa, Kayoa, Halmahera, Obi, Gomuma, New Guinea, except where *idenburgi* occurs, and northern Queensland) Longer-billed than most subspecies. Differs from female nominate by brighter (more orangey-) yellow supercilium and underparts.

140b

140a

140c

140e

140f

140g

140j

140h

140i

140d

140k

PLATE 27: FLAME-BREASTED, SOUIMANGA AND HUMBLOT'S SUNBIRDS

142 Flame-breasted Sunbird *Cinnyris solaris*   **Text and map page 321**

Lesser Sundas. Scrub, secondary forest, woodland, at forest edge, in cultivation and gardens; chiefly lowlands, but up to 1,000 m on Flores.
Narrow, longish, curved bill.

142a **Adult male** (nominate; range of species, except Wetar) Mostly green above, tail dark brown with large grey tips; forehead, crown, cheeks and throat metallic blue-green and purple; rest of underparts orange and yellow.

142b **Adult female** (nominate) Greenish above, glossy black tail with large white tips; supercilium, lores and underparts yellow.

143 Souimanga Sunbird *Cinnyris sovimanga*   **Text and map page 322**

Madagascar, Glorieuses and Aldabra. Forests, including mangrove, secondary growth and around habitation; *apolis* in subdesert vegetation and adjoining plantations. Lowlands to 2,300 m.
Longish, slender, decurved bill.

143a **Adult male breeding** (nominate; Madagascar, except where *apolis* occurs) Glossy dark green crown, mantle, upper back and wing-coverts; lower back and rump dark olive-grey; tail dark brown, with slight gloss. Throat to breast glossy green, bordered below by glossy blue then brownish-red band; rest of breast sooty-brown; pectoral tufts yellow; rest of underparts yellowish.

143b **Adult male non-breeding** (nominate) Similar to female, but with variable amounts of glossy feathering on shoulder and back, and occasionally some red on breast.

143c **Adult female** (nominate) Dark olive-brown above; greyish supercilium starting in front of eye; chin to upper breast with greyish barring and mottling; rest of breast and flanks yellow with grey streaking, belly yellow; undertail-coverts whitish streaked black; rest of underparts yellowish and grey, with darker streaking on breast, flanks and vent.

143d **Adult male** (*apolis*; south-west Madagascar) Differs from male nominate in having darker and redder breast-band, and yellow of underparts replaced by white and grey.

143e **Adult male** (*abbotti*; Aldabra group – Assumption Island) Differs from male nominate by sooty-brown not yellow on underparts.

146 Humblot's Sunbird *Cinnyris humbloti*   **Text and map page 327**

Grand Comoro and Mohéli. Forest, scrub and gardens; sea-level to 790 m.
Medium-long decurved bill.

146a **Adult male** (nominate; Grand Comoro) Brighter green above than male *mohelicus*, with less gloss on shoulder; throat to upper breast glossy green; rest of breast dull red; belly and vent yellowish-green.

146b **Adult female** (nominate) Olive-green above, unglossed, except for tail; below greyish and yellowish-green with heavy speckling, especially from chin to breast.

146c **Adult male** (*mohelicus*; Mohéli) Dull green above, with large glossy area on shoulder; throat to upper breast glossy bronze-purple bordered below by glossy purple band.

134 Variable Sunbird *Cinnyris venustus*   **Text and map page 308**

West, Central, East and southern Africa. From Senegal to South Africa. Mostly thorn savannas north of the equator, but more wooded areas further south. Varied habitats include forest, forest edge, wooded ravines, savanna, farmland, semi-arid areas, parks, mangroves, plantations, inselbergs, montane savanna, gardens, riverine scrub and herbaceous scrub.

A small sunbird with long curved bill.

134a **Adult male breeding** (nominate; Senegal to northern Cameroon and Ubangi-Shari) Metallic green above, with pale yellow belly beneath broad purple chest-band; chin metallic purple, throat metallic green, upper breast metallic purple, merging with non-glossy black area. Throat and upper breast appear black at a distance.

134b **Adult male non-breeding** (nominate) Similar to adult female but more olive-brown above. Metallic feathers on chin, throat and upper breast; lesser wing-coverts and uppertail-coverts may be retained, sometimes with scattering of metallic feathers on back. Black throat-patch.

134c **Immature male** (nominate) Like adult female but lacks pale tips to outer tail and has throat and breast with dusky markings, those on throat sometimes very conspicuous, appearing as dark streak as birds moult into adult plumage with metallic blotches appearing.

134d **Adult female** (nominate) Lacks metallic plumage and chest-band; yellowish below, greyish-olive above.

134e **Adult male** (*albiventris*; Somalia, eastern and southern Ethiopia, northern and eastern Kenya) White abdomen.

134f **Adult male** (*igneiventris*; eastern Democratic Republic of the Congo, Rwanda, Uganda, Tanzania) Differs from *falkensteini* by middle of chest washed orange-scarlet and pectoral tufts scarlet.

134g **Adult male** (*falkensteini*; Ethiopia and Sudan south to Mozambique and Angola) Deeper yellow underparts than nominate.

134h **Adult male** (*fazoqlensis*; Eritrea, Ethiopia and Sudan) Belly similar to *falkensteini*, but metallic green, not purplish-blue, on throat above purple breast.

PLATE 29: URSULA'S, WHITE-BREASTED AND OUSTALET'S SUNBIRDS

136 Ursula's Sunbird *Cinnyris ursulae*   **Text and map page 311**

Cameroon highlands, Bioko highlands.
Above 950 m in primary and secondary forest and in low shrubs at forest edges. On Bioko, especially in moss forest. Small. Mostly olive-green above and grey below except yellow undertail-coverts, curved bill and short tail. Sexes similar.

136a **Adult** Metallic grey-blue forehead appears shiny in good light.

136b **Adult** Wings outstretched. Reddish-orange pectoral tufts.

133 White-breasted Sunbird *Cinnyris talatala*   **Text and map page 181**

Central and southern Africa from Democratic Republic of the Congo to South Africa. Dry savanna woodland, gardens and parks in towns and occasionally riverine forest.
Small with long curved bill.

133a **Adult male breeding** Metallic green upperparts and throat and broad violet breast-band, contrasting with white belly. Larger-billed than Oustalet's Sunbird *C. oustaleti*, and curvature starts nearer base. Head darker and bluer, middle of throat darker and maroon band thinner than in *C. oustaleti*; pectoral tufts yellow not orange and yellow as in *C. oustaleti*.

133b **Adult male** Wings outstretched. Yellow pectoral tufts.

133c **Adult male non-breeding** Metallic feathers restricted to centre of chin, upper breast, head, back, wing-coverts and uppertail-coverts, with rest of plumage resembling adult female.

133d **Adult female** Dull brown above, white belly and slight streaking on breast. Paler brown above and less heavily streaked below than *C. oustaleti*.

132 Oustalet's Sunbird *Cinnyris oustaleti*   **Text and map page 304**

Central Africa. One population in Angola, another in Malawi, Tanzania and Zambia. *Brachystegia-Isoberlinia* woodland, secondary growth and scrub.
Small with long curved bill.

132a **Adult male breeding** (*rhodesiae*; north-east Zambia to Malawi border and just into south-west Tanzania) Violet-reddish band across chest and lower neck. Chin and throat very dark blue appearing black in field. Above metallic green with bluish tinge. Head greener, middle of throat bluer and maroon band broader than in *C. talatala*; pectoral tufts orange and yellow in nominate, yellow in *C. talatala*.

132b **Adult male** (*rhodesiae*) Wings outstretched. Orange and yellow pectoral tufts.

132c **Adult male non-breeding** (nominate; central Angola) Similar to adult female but greyer on throat and breast and has orange and yellow pectoral tufts and metallic wing- and uppertail-coverts, with some sparse metallic feathering on body.

132d **Adult female** (nominate) Greyish-brown above, paler below. Bill straighter and plumage darker brown above and more heavily streaked below than *C. talatala*.

132b

133b

136a

136b

133a

133d

133c

132a

132d

132c

RW

PLATE 30: ORANGE-TUFTED, PALESTINE, PURPLE, ANJOUAN AND MAYOTTE SUNBIRDS

125 Orange-tufted Sunbird *Cinnyris bouvieri*

Text and map page 293

West and Central Africa. Nigeria to Angola, Zambia, Uganda and Kenya. Mostly grassland, and rocky country at high altitudes; also open woods in savanna, forest patches and edge, and scrub.

125a **Adult male** All metallic except on remiges, belly and upper throat. Lower breast-band broader than in *C. bifasciatus* and chocolate-brown not black underparts. Purple forecrown, orange-yellow pectoral tufts and no blue sheen to metallic head and back.

125b **Adult female** Drab olive above, more yellowish and slightly streaked below, especially on dark throat. Straightish bill, slight malar stripe.

126 Palestine Sunbird *Cinnyris oseus*

Text and map page 295

Cameroon to Sudan and north-west Uganda. Also Arabian Peninsula and south-west Palearctic. Sea-level to highlands in savannas, gardens, orchards, rocky valleys, juniper woods and cypress groves.

126a **Adult male breeding** (nominate; Middle East and Arabia) Multi-coloured iridescent plumage. Orange-red and yellow pectoral tufts distinctive. Shorter bill than *C. bouvieri*.

126b **Adult male non-breeding** (nominate) Upperparts like adult female but wings and tail as in breeding plumage, underparts like adult female or dull black with iridescent patches.

126c **Immature male** (nominate) As adult female but belly brighter yellow, and blackish-blue throat-patch in older birds.

126d **Adult female** (nominate) Dark wings and blackish tail contrasting with dull body. Duller with less yellow below than female *C. bouvieri*, no streaking, bluish-green uppertail-coverts.

139 Purple Sunbird *Cinnyris asiaticus*

Text and map page 316

Oman, southern Iran, Baluchistan, Indian subcontinent to Indochina and south Yunnan. Generally lowlands, but occasionally up to 2,400 m. Light/dry forest, scrub, riverbeds, cultivation, gardens.

139a **Adult male breeding** (*intermedius*; northern Andhra Pradesh, Orissa, Assam and Bangladesh to Indochina and south Yunnan) Dark reddish-brown band on lower breast.

139b **Adult male non-breeding** (nominate; India where other forms do not occur, and Sri Lanka) Olive-brown above, with blackish wings and tail; below yellow, with blue-black stripe from chin to belly.

139c **Adult female** (nominate) Differs from non-breeding male by lack of ventral stripe and glossy areas, and wings olive-brown.

139d **Juvenile** (*intermedius*) Differs from adult female by paler and greyer abdomen.

147 Anjouan Sunbird *Cinnyris comorensis*

Text and map page 328

Anjouan Island. Forest and thickets from 90 to 855 m.

147a **Adult male** Looks black in poor light. Mostly glossy blue-green and black above; throat to upper breast glossy blue-green; narrow dark maroon band across breast.

147b **Adult female** Greenish-olive above; black tail with much white; grey and yellow below, with heavy mottling and streaking.

148 Mayotte Sunbird *Cinnyris coquerellii*

Text and map page 329

Mayotte Island. Occurs in open areas and at forest edge; sea-level to 460 m.

148a **Adult male** Head and upperparts glossy dark green, with some purple; chin to upper breast glossy dark green; narrow purple band on upper breast; centre of breast and belly orange-red.

148b **Adult female** Grey-brown above, with brown wings and black tail; throat to breast grey with darker streaking; rest of underparts yellow.

PLATE 31: SHINING, LONG-BILLED AND AFRICAN DOUBLE-COLLARED SUNBIRDS (1)

127 Shining Sunbird *Cinnyris habessinicus* **Text and map page 297**

North-east Africa and Arabian Peninsula: Sudan, Ethiopia, Eritrea, Djibouti, Somalia, Saudi Arabia, Oman, Yemen, Kenya and Uganda. Rocky or sandy broken country with thorn-bush, especially dry riverbeds, also montane forest, cultivated areas and gardens.
Medium-sized with long, curved bill.

  127a **Adult male** (nominate; Red Sea province of Sudan, Eritrea, Ethiopia) Golden-green metallic head and back, black belly and red breast-band.

  127b **Adult female** (nominate). Uniformly pale underparts, except undertail-coverts.

  127c **Adult female** (*kinneari*; western Saudi Arabia from Asir to Hejaz) Very dark, more blackish-brown than nominate, with scaly appearance to throat and lower underparts.

149 Long-billed Sunbird *Cinnyris lotenius* **Text and map page 330**

South India (to 1,600 m) and Sri Lanka (to 2,100 m). Woodland (occasionally evergreen forest), gardens and farmland.
Rather long, deeply decurved bill.

  149a **Adult male breeding** Looks black in poor light. Head, throat, back, shoulders and rump black glossed green and purple; wings and tail dull blackish. Breast metallic purple bordered below with crimson or maroon band; pectoral tufts yellow; rest of underparts sooty-brown.

  149b **Adult male non-breeding** Dull olive above; tail blue-black. Vent and undertail-coverts white; broad black mesial patch from throat to upper breast; rest of underparts pale yellow.

  149c **Adult female** As non-breeding male, but tail tipped white, and white edges to feathers; lacks black patch on throat and upper breast.

102 Miombo Double-collared Sunbird *Cinnyris manoensis* **Text and map page 263**

Democratic Republic of the Congo, south-east Tanzania, Angola, south-east Zambia, Malawi, northern Mozambique, Botswana and Zimbabwe. Miombo woodland and open savanna, riverine woodland, gardens and parks. Thorn-scrub and highland *Leucospermum* areas in Zimbabwe. *Cryptosepalum* forest in Zambia.
Small; bill appears disproportionately long.

  102a **Adult male** (nominate; Zimbabwe, Malawi north to Nchisi, south-east Zambia, northern Mozambique, south-east Tanzania) On *Tithonia rotundifolia*. Metallic green upperparts and head with greyish back, blue breast-band above red collar, ash-grey belly, often conspicuous yellow pectorals.

  102b **Adult female** (nominate) Dull brown above, pale grey below grading to yellowish on belly and vent.

103 Southern Double-collared Sunbird *Cinnyris chalybeus* **Text and map page 264**

South Africa, Swaziland, Lesotho and extreme south of Namibia. Fynbos, scrub, gardens, *Eucalyptus* plantations, coastal, evergreen montane and inland forests, forest edge, woodland, *Protea* areas of highlands, dune thickets, dry bush.

  103a **Adult male** (nominate; South Africa, Little Namaqualand, Namibia and south-west Cape Province to east of Knysna) Metallic green head and back with very narrow red breast-band below even thinner blue band. Dark grey breast and belly. Narrowness of red breast-band, plus grey not olive belly, separate it from larger male *C. afer*.

  103b **Adult female** (nominate) Greyish-brown above, paler below. Smaller than female *A. violacea* and grey not yellow below.

PLATE 32: AFRICAN DOUBLE-COLLARED SUNBIRDS (2),TSAVO PURPLE-BANDED AND KENYA VIOLET-BREASTED SUNBIRDS

105 Stuhlmann's Double-collared Sunbird *Cinnyris stuhlmanni*   Text and map page 267

Democratic Republic of the Congo, Rwanda, Burundi and Uganda. Highlands in montane forest, forest edges and clearings, bamboo zone, *Hypericum* scrub, amongst *Hagenia* sp. and heathers.

    105a   **Adult male** (nominate; Ruwenzori Mountains) Broad red breast-band with no bronzy tinge to emerald-green iridescence. Bill longer, more curved and heavier and red breast-band much wider than in male *C. prigoginei*.

    105b   **Adult female** (nominate) Dull olivaceous above, yellow wash on belly and vent. More yellow on vent than female *C. prigoginei*.

106 Prigogine's Double-collared Sunbird *Cinnyris prigoginei*   Text and map page 269

A few areas of riparian forest in the Marungu highlands (the only small double-collared sunbird in south-east Democratic Republic of the Congo). Riparian forest along streams in montane areas up to at least 1,900 m, and cornfields and thickets close to streams.

    106a   **Adult male** Narrow red breast-band. Longer wing and tail and heavier than *C. mediocris*, and has smaller red breast-band and narrower strip of blue above it.

    106b   **Adult female** Uniformly olive chin, and throat dark olive with black streaking.

107 Montane Double-collared Sunbird *Cinnyris ludovicensis*   Text and map page 270

Angola highlands, Nyika Plateau of Malawi, and neighbouring eastern Zambia above 1,820 m. Afromontane forest, gallery forest and clearings in highlands, montane grassland and scrub.

    107a   **Adult male** (nominate; highlands of western Angola) Short-billed. Broad red breast-band and greyish-olive underparts. Uppertail-coverts metallic blue with only a hint of violet. From male *C. manoensis* and only sympatric subspecies (*fuelleborni*) of *C. mediocris* by broad breast-band and blue uppertail-coverts. Greyer below, less olive, than *C. mediocris*.

    107b   **Adult female** (nominate) Upperparts dark greyish-brown. Underparts mainly brownish-grey. Greyer than *C. stuhlmanni*. Differs from female *C. manoensis* and *C. mediocris* by non-contrasting greyer upperparts and chin to lower breast, black lores, grey supercilium and only faint yellow wash on belly.

122 Tsavo Purple-banded Sunbird *Cinnyris tsavoensis*   Text and map page 291

Juba area of Somalia, southern Ethiopia and Sudan through dry eastern Kenya to Tsavo National Park and Kibwezi, and north-east Tanzania to Korogwe and Handeni. Dry *Acacia* and *Commiphora* savanna.

    122a   **Adult male** Metallic green upperparts, narrow maroon breast-band and black abdomen. Bill shorter and breast-band narrower, restricted to sides or lacking and more purplish than breast-band of *C. bifasciatus*; lacks eclipse plumage.

    122b   **Adult female** Greyish-green above, tail darker and slightly glossy. Narrow brownish-white supercilium. Sides of face greyish-brown. Underparts pale brownish-white, with yellow tinge below breast streaked greyish-brown. Usually pale-throated unlike most female *C. bifasciatus*.

123 Kenya Violet-breasted Sunbird *Cinnyris chalcomelas*   Text and map page 292

Southern Somalia, E Kenya. Thorn savannas in coastal lowlands from Juba valley to Mombasa and Tsavo.

    123a   **Adult male** Metallic green upperparts, broad purple breast-band above black abdomen. Lacks maroon band of *C. tsavoensis* and *C. bifasciatus*, throat greenish-blue not golden-green.

    123b   **Adult female** Greyish-brown above with light green tinge, uppertail-coverts darker. Tail dark brown, slightly glossy above. Brownish-white supercilium. Paler and less streaked below than *C. tsavoensis* and *C. bifasciatus*. Supercilium more obvious than in female *C. tsavoensis*.

PLATE 33: AFRICAN DOUBLE-COLLARED SUNBIRDS (3)

108 Northern Double-collared Sunbird *Cinnyris reichenowi* Text and map page 271

West, Central and north-east Africa. Nigeria, Cameroon, Central African Republic, Bioko, Democratic Republic of the Congo, Rwanda, Burundi, Uganda, Kenya and Sudan. Montane heathland, montane forest, secondary forest, forest edge, gallery forests, plantations, clearings and gardens. An upland double-collared sunbird, with short bill and tail.

> **108a Adult male** (*preussi*; Bioko, south-east Nigeria, Cameroon) Violet uppertail-coverts and narrow breast-band above broad red lower breast-band and olivaceous-brown belly. Bigger and darker, especially on belly, than *C. chloropygius*, which has green not purple uppertail-coverts. Belly darker, bill and tail shorter than in *C. stuhlmanni*. Has shorter bill and tail than *C. mediocris*, with which it is sympatric in west Kenya, and is bluer, less golden-green above and darker below, with violet not blue uppertail-coverts and broader breast-band.

> **108b Adult female** (*preussi*) Dull olive below with yellow wash. Generally paler above than female *C. chloropygius*, with only slight trace of supercilium. Has browner-olive edges to remiges than those on female *C. chloropygius* and *C. mediocris*, which are greener-olive and less contrasting with the upperparts; female *C. mediocris* lacks even a trace of a supercilium.

109 Greater Double-collared Sunbird *Cinnyris afer* Text and map page 272

South Africa, Lesotho and Swaziland. Open country, valley bushveld, tall scrubland, coastal plains, montane scrub, riverine scrub, *Protea* savanna, fynbos, moist woodland, succulent karoo, parks, gardens and forest edge, especially Afromontane. Avoids forest, unlike *C. chalybeus*. The largest of the double-collared sunbirds.

> **109a Adult male** (nominate; South Africa, Cape Province at Swellendam through southern districts of western Cape Province to Great Fish River) Red breast-band 18-23 mm wide and reaching lower breast. From *C. chalybeus* by larger size, longer and more curved but less robust bill, and (except in young males in first moult) more extensive red on breast. From *C. ludovicensis* and *C. stuhlmanni* by longer bill.

> **109b Adult female** (nominate) On aloe. Smaller and shorter-billed than male. Head dark greyish-olive or bluish-grey. Upperparts greyish-olive or dark brown. Tail brownish-black. Throat and breast grey or greyish-olive with grey-green or light greyish-olive speckling. Usually with pale yellow wash on lower breast and belly.

112 Eastern Double-collared Sunbird *Cinnyris mediocris* Text and map page 277

East Africa. Democratic Republic of the Congo, Kenya, Tanzania, Zambia, Malawi, Mozambique. Montane forests, bamboos, heathland, grassland and gardens. A double-collared sunbird of highland areas with curved bill. *C. m. mediocris* has longer bill and tail than *C. reichenowi*, males with blue not violet narrow breast-band and uppertail-coverts, more golden-green less blue metallic plumage, scarlet breast-band is narrower and not so bright and underparts paler. Female *mediocris* is darker than *C. reichenowi*.

> **112a Adult male** (*fuelleborni*; Tanzania, northern Malawi, Zambia in the Mafinga mountains above 1,800 m) Metallic green body, scarlet breast-band and pale olive belly. Uppertail-coverts grey or metallic green proximally, tipped violet or purplish not blue; broad scarlet to orange-red breast-band broader than in nominate and *usambaricus*.

> **112b Adult female** (*fuelleborni*) Olive above, yellow-green below and brownish on wings. No supercilium.

> **112c Adult male** (*usambaricus*; north-east Tanzania and south-east Kenya) Red breast-band narrower than in nominate or *fuelleborni* and with grey-brown wash below it, uppertail-coverts violet or royal blue, belly more greenish-olive.

PLATE 34: AFRICAN DOUBLE-COLLARED SUNBIRDS (4)

104 Neergaard's Sunbird *Cinnyris neergaardi*   **Text and map page 266**

South-east Africa. Restricted to the coastal belt in Mozambique and South Africa. Coastal sand forests and tall mixed woodlands, coastal scrubland especially where dense, dry sandy thorn-bush and dry woodland. Isolated trees in clearings and villages.
A small short-billed sunbird.

    104a   **Adult male** Iridescent green head, back and throat, red breast-band, black belly and blue rump. From *C. afer* and *C. chalybeus* by black not grey belly and shorter bill.

    104b   **Adult female** Greyish-brown above, paler and unstreaked below. Shorter-billed and greyer than female *C. afer* and *C. chalybeus*.

---

100 Olive-bellied Sunbird *Cinnyris chloropygius*   **Text and map page 259**

West and Central Africa from Senegal to Sudan and to Democratic Republic of the Congo, Rwanda, Burundi, Uganda, Kenya, Tanzania and Angola, with an isolated population in Ethiopia. Clearings and along streams and roads in primary and secondary forest, gallery forest, coffee groves; also farmland, parks, gardens, well-wooded savanna, mangroves, coastal thickets and inselbergs but not to very high altitudes.

    100a   **Adult male** (nominate; south-east Nigeria to Angola; Bioko) On *Hibiscus* sp. Bright metallic green above, throat with red breast-band over olive belly, fewer blue bars in red breast feathers than in male *C. minullus*; bill distinctly curved and longer than *C. minullus*; underwing-coverts usually grey not white as in *C. minullus* (but white in subadult). Smaller, with less extensive scarlet band than *C. reichenowi* and green not violet uppertail-coverts. Bill straighter than *C. mediocris*, uppertail-coverts green not metallic blue.

    100b   **Adult male** (nominate). Hovering in front of *Hibiscus* sp. Yellow pectoral tufts.

    100c   **Adult female** (nominate) Olive upperparts, paler and washed yellow below. From female *C. reichenowi* by supercilium, smaller size and darker, more olive upperparts. Bill longer, more curved; yellower below and less heavily streaked than in *C. minullus*.

---

101 Tiny Sunbird *Cinnyris minullus*   **Text and map page 261**

West and Central Africa. From Sierra Leone to Uganda. More mature forest than *C. chloropygius*, but also occurs at edges, in clearings and forest-savanna mosaic. Less common in man-dominated habitats than *chloropygius*, but enters gardens, cultivated areas, abandoned plots, and around villages.
Very small sunbird with short straightish bill.

    101a   **Adult male** Metallic green upperparts, head and upper throat; blue band on lower throat and scarlet breast-band mottled with metallic blue bars. Belly olive. Like miniature *C. chloropygius* but smaller with shorter tail and shorter, straighter bill, more extensive blue lower throat-band, and more blue bars interspersed within red breast-band. Lower mandible appears almost straight except at tip (curved throughout length in *C. chloropygius*).

    101b   **Adult female** Olive above, yellowish below, with supercilium. Greyer throat than female *C. chloropygius* and paler yellow below than *C. c. kempi*.

---

110 Regal Sunbird *Cinnyris regius*   **Text and map page 274**

East and Central Africa. Democratic Republic of the Congo, Rwanda, Burundi, Uganda and Tanzania. Mixed forest with bamboo, montane evergreen forest, secondary growth, glades, open understorey and scrubland.

    110a   **Adult male** (nominate; highlands in Democratic Republic of the Congo, Uganda and Burundi). Red and bright yellow pattern on underparts and iridescent golden-green above. Unmistakable.

    110b   **Immature male** (nominate) Multi-coloured mixture of adult male and female plumage.

    110c   **Adult female** (nominate) Dull olive above, yellowish and slightly streaked below. From female *C. rockefelleri* by duskier throat, less distinct supercilium. Greener above and yellower below than female *C. stuhlmanni* and *C. reichenowi*. Like female *C. venustus igneiventris* but more olive above and more uniform yellow-olive below including throat.

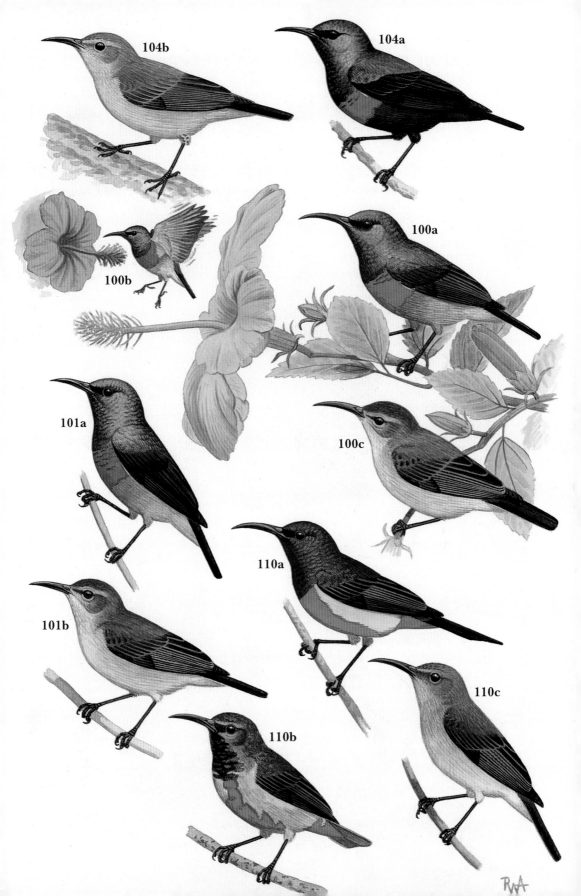

PLATE 35: AFRICAN DOUBLE-COLLARED SUNBIRDS (5) AND COPPER AND DUSKY SUNBIRDS

113 Moreau's Sunbird *Cinnyris moreaui*   **Text and map page 278**

Nguu, Nguru, Ukaguru, Udzungwa and Uvidunda mountains of eastern Tanzania. Moist montane forest and clearings above 1,300 m. Usually in canopy or in bushes at sides of tracks.

113a   **Adult male** Metallic green upperparts, red part of double collar reduced by intrusion of yellow from sides of breast. More yellow on sides of breast and belly brighter than in male *C. mediocris*, but in first adult plumage has abdomen dull like pale male *C. mediocris fuelleborni*.

113b   **Adult female** Greyish throat and olivaceous-yellow underparts.

114 Loveridge's Sunbird *Cinnyris loveridgei*   **Text and map page 280**

The Uluguru mountains in eastern Tanzania. Montane forest and clearings including plantations with a few standing trees and shrubs, and relatively open drier areas with some bamboo.

114a   **Adult male** Blue-green metallic upperparts with gold sheen. Orangey-red band below narrow violet band. Rump non-metallic olive-green.

114b   **Adult female** Greenish-olive above, head and throat greyer, underparts more yellow.

111 Rockefeller's Sunbird *Cinnyris rockefelleri*   **Text and map page 275**

Restricted to montane forest and Afro-alpine moorland in eastern Democratic Republic of the Congo, and, possibly, Burundi and Rwanda. Valleys and streams in tall bamboo and heath zones at 2,050-3,300 m.

111a   **Adult male** All breast and undertail-coverts bright scarlet. From male *C. regius* by lack of yellow on sides of breast (apart from pectoral tufts) and longer bill.

111b   **Adult female** Mostly olive but with yellowish throat, belly and supercilium. Larger and longer-billed with more pronounced supercilium than female *C. regius*.

138 Copper Sunbird *Cinnyris cupreus*   **Text and map page 313**

Senegal to South Africa. Savannas, thorn-scrub, degraded forest, riverine woodland, swamps, mangroves, coastal thickets, cultivated areas, gardens and urban areas.

138a   **Adult male breeding** (nominate; Senegal east to southern Sudan and western Ethiopia, and to south Cameroon, Democratic Republic of the Congo, Uganda, west Kenya, western Tanzania). Appears black at a distance, but has dark metallic plumage appearing coppery or purple.

138b   **Adult male non-breeding** (nominate) Upperparts olive, with a few metallic purple feathers. Lesser coverts and uppertail-coverts tipped metallic purple. Yellowish below with some black feathers. Black remiges and rectrices retained.

138c   **Adult female** (nominate) Dull olive-green above, pale yellowish-buff below. No metallic plumage. From female *C. pulchellus* and *C. venustus* by darker upperparts, brighter supercilium and all pale yellow underparts. Larger than *C. bifasciatus*, more yellowish below.

138d   **Adult male** (*chalceus*; Angola, Zambia, SE Dem. Rep. of the Congo, Malawi, N Mozambique, N Zimbabwe and SW Tanzania) Differs from nominate by greenish sheen to metallic plumage.

135 Dusky Sunbird *Cinnyris fuscus*   **Text and map page 310**

SW Angola, W and S Namibia, SW Botswana, South Africa. Dry country, semi-arid coastal plains with sand-dunes, riverine *Acacia* scrub, inselbergs with scattered bushes, hillside scrub, orchards and gardens.

135a   **Adult male** (nominate; South Africa, Namibia, Botswana) On *Nicotiana glauca*. At close quarters dark brown with metallic bronze-green and purple reflections above and on chest.

135b   **Immature male** (nominate) Black throat.

135c   **Adult female** (nominate) Greyish-brown above, white below.

131 Rufous-winged Sunbird *Cinnyris rufipennis* **Text and map page 303**

At 600-1,700 m on eastern escarpment of the Udzungwa mountains, eastern Tanzania. Moist montane forest with lichens, mosses and epiphytes, also herbaceous glades within 20 m of forest edge.

131a Adult male Bronzy throat-patch and distinctive rufous-red on wings contrasting with violet upperparts, chestnut-red lower breast-band and greyish-green underparts; rufous wings not obvious if views poor.

131b Adult female Rufous on wings and spotted upper- and underparts.

95 Tacazze Sunbird *Nectarinia tacazze* **Text and map page 249**

East Africa. Sudan, Ethiopia, Eritrea, Uganda, Kenya and Tanzania. Forest patches, forest edges, *Eucalyptus* and *Acacia* patches and clearings in grassy areas, bamboo, glades and heathland on mountains. Gardens and cultivated plots.

95a Adult male breeding (nominate; Eritrea, Ethiopia) Appears black with poor views. Purple sheen on mantle and breast distinctive (green on head can cause confusion with *N. kilimensis*).

95b Adult male non-breeding (nominate) Like adult female but wings and tail as in adult male; occasionally metallic tips to body feathers.

95c Adult female (nominate) Dull olive, paler below with distinct white supercilium and malar stripe. Less yellow and less streaked below, face pattern darker and less greyish above than female *N. kilimensis*. Less dusky throat and chest, stronger malar stripe, longer supercilium, bill slightly more curved and longer central rectrices than in female *N. famosa*.

95d Adult male (*jacksoni*; mountains in southern Sudan, Kenya, Uganda and Tanzania) Iridescent purple areas more pinkish than in *N. tacazze*, metallic breast zone broader and extended further posteriorly, central tail feathers 48-62 mm longer than next pair (only 35-46 in *tacazze*).

93 Bocage's Sunbird *Nectarinia bocagei* **Text and map page 247**

West-central Africa. Democratic Republic of the Congo and Angola. Woodlands. Clearings and edges of dambos in miombo woodland, in *Baikiaea plurijuga* woodland, at edges of montane forest at 1,500 m in Angola. Swampy deforested scrubby areas on plateau marshes with flowering shrubs in the Congo.

93a Adult male Appears all black at a distance. Metallic dark violet feathers on head, breast, upperparts and shoulder-patch visible at close range, which may appear as very dark blue.

93b Adult female Pale olive above, black lores and characteristic pattern of pale olive edges to innerwebs of rectrices, T5 with pale outer tip, all outerweb of T6 pale brown. From female *C. cupreus* by less pronounced or no supercilium, darker throat and brighter yellow belly.

93c Immature male Dull olive above as adult female, with a few metallic dark violet feathers interspersed in plumage. Shoulders metallic violet. Underparts with many light yellow-olive feathers contrasting with black remainder. Some violet on throat.

94 Purple-breasted Sunbird *Nectarinia purpureiventris* **Text and map page 248**

Democratic Republic of the Congo, Rwanda, Burundi, Uganda. Glades in montane forest and in gallery forest above 1,900 m. Forest edge, clearings and roadsides, usually in tree-tops.

94a Adult male breeding Iridescent purple, green, copper, pinkish and blue plumage with shortish and straightish bill and elongated tail.

94b Adult male non-breeding On *Symphonia globulifera*. Resembles adult female but with some metallic feathers on mantle, wing-coverts, uppertail-coverts and underparts; black remiges and elongated central tail feathers.

94c Adult female Grey head with black bars; olive upperparts, pale grey below with yellow wash on breast.

96 Bronze Sunbird *Nectarinia kilimensis*   Text and map page 251

Ethiopia, Democratic Republic of the Congo, Rwanda, Burundi, Uganda, Kenya, Tanzania, Angola, Zambia, Malawi, Mozambique and Zimbabwe. Secondary growth, woodland and scrub at forest edges, cultivations, gardens, bushes at edge of dambos and montane grassland.

96a   **Adult male** (nominate; highlands of eastern Democratic Republic of the Congo, Kenya, Uganda, northern Tanzania) Greener than *arturi*, lacking as much metallic copper wash on head; neck and mantle less purplish-bronze, more golden-green. At a distance confusable with male *N. tacazze*, *N. famosa* and *N. johnstoni* but bill shorter and more decurved.

96b   **Adult female** (nominate) More olive above than *gadowi*; brighter, more extensive, yellow wash below. Like female *N. tacazze*, *N. famosa* and *N. johnstoni* but bill shorter and more decurved. Throat whitish so malar stripe does not show as in *N. tacazze* and *N. famosa*, breast yellow with dark streaks (blotches or speckles on female *N. famosa*).

96c   **Immature male** (nominate) On *Kniphofia* sp. White-tipped throat feathers. Upperparts and chest tinged olive, abdomen pale yellow. Scattering of metallic feathers.

96d   **Adult male** (*arturi*; south-eastern Tanzania, Malawi west of the Rift, Zambia, eastern highlands of Zimbabwe) Iridescent green plumage with reflections of brighter green, gold, bronze or red.

96e   **Adult male** (*gadowi*; highlands of central Angola) Deeper and purer green on head and throat, less golden on breast and upperparts than nominate and *arturi*.

96f   **Adult female** (*gadowi*) Greyer above than nominate and *arturi*, and less yellow below.

98 Red-tufted Sunbird *Nectarinia johnstoni*   Text and map page 255

Democratic Republic of the Congo, Rwanda, Uganda, Kenya, Tanzania, Zambia and Malawi. Afro-alpine moorland with giant lobelias, proteas and giant groundsels, open *Hagenia–Hypericum* forest, *Hypericum* and *Kotschya–Erica* scrub, bamboo.

98a   **Adult male breeding** (nominate; Kenya, northern Tanzania) Duller bluer-green than male *N. famosa* with scarlet, not yellow, pectoral tufts.

98b   **Adult male** (nominate) On *Lobelia* sp. Very long tail; metallic green, appearing all dark at distance.

98c   **Adult male non-breeding** (nominate) In flight. Head and body brownish, otherwise as breeding birds. Scarlet pectoral tufts.

98d   **Adult female** (nominate) Greyish-brown above, no prominent supercilium or malar stripe (present on female *N. famosa*, *N. tacazze* and *N. kilimensis*). Scarlet pectoral tufts.

97 Malachite Sunbird *Nectarinia famosa*   Text and map page 253

Sudan, Ethiopia and Eritrea to South Africa. In South Africa from sea-level to 2,800 m, but prefers upland fynbos, karoo vegetation types, alpine grassland, riverside scrubland, thorn-bush and gardens but avoids forests. Elsewhere sage-bush and heath-zone up to 3,000 m.

97a   **Adult male breeding** (nominate; Namibia, South Africa, Lesotho, western Swaziland, Zimbabwe) Bright green metallic plumage and elongated tail. Similar to male *N. johnstoni* but has yellow not red pectoral tufts and brighter, greener, less bluish plumage.

97b   **Adult male non-breeding** (*cupreonitens*) On *Protea* sp. Like adult female but retains black flight feathers, metallic gloss on wings and uppertail-coverts, and sometimes sparse metallic tips to body feathers. Male nominate undergoes similar eclipse but long central tail feathers are not lost.

97c   **Adult male non-breeding** (nominate) In flight. Yellow pectoral tufts.

97d   **Adult female** (nominate) Olivaceous-grey above, yellowish mottled blackish below, with prominent pale supercilium and malar stripe, lacking in female *N. johnstoni*, and more olive, less grey above. Like female *N. tacazze* but yellower below, shorter tail and no elongated central tail feathers. From female *N. kilimensis* by longer, straighter bill, darker upperparts, mottled not streaked underparts and more marked malar stripe.

PLATE 38: GOLDEN-WINGED, SHELLEY'S, RED-CHESTED AND CONGO SUNBIRDS

99 Golden-winged Sunbird *Drepanorhynchus reichenowi* **Text and map page 258**

Democratic Republic of the Congo, Uganda, Kenya and Tanzania. Bushy grassland, montane forest edges, bamboo clearings above 1,170 m and up to 3,300 m; cultivated plots.

99a **Adult male** (nominate; southern and western Uganda to western and central Kenya, south to Crater highlands, Kilimanjaro and Usambaras in Tanzania) Brilliant gold on wings and elongated tail and markedly decurved bill. Coppery-green and reddish iridescence on head, mantle and chin to upper breast.

99b **Adult male** (nominate) In flight.

99c **Adult female** (nominate) Gold wings and tail, markedly decurved bill. Olivaceous upperparts, pale below with dark mottling on breast and belly.

99d **Immature male** (nominate) Similar to adult female but sides of face, chin and throat black, rest of underparts olive heavily barred black. Wings and tail edged less bright yellow.

117 Shelley's Sunbird *Cinnyris shelleyi* **Text and map page 285**

Democratic Republic of the Congo, Tanzania, Zambia, Malawi, Mozambique, Zimbabwe, Namibia and Angola. *C. s. shelleyi* almost restricted to *Brachystegia* woodland, but occurs in *Baikiaea* woodland in Zambia and sometimes in *Acacia* woodland and gardens. *C. s. hofmanni* in woodland, scrubland, gardens and thick riparian scrub.

117a **Adult male** (nominate; Zambia east of 26°E to south-east Democratic Republic of the Congo, Katanga, Malawi, northern Mozambique and south-west Tanzania) Scarlet breast-band and sooty-black belly, wings and tail. Differs from male *C. manoensis* by black belly, black wings and tail and violet not blue-green uppertail-coverts.

117b **Adult female** (nominate) Grey greenish-brown above. Tail dark brown. Thin brownish-white supercilium. Pale brownish below, with lower parts tinged greenish-yellow; extensive mottling on chin and throat, dark streaks on breast, flanks and undertail-coverts. Smaller, shorter-billed and duskier below than very similar female *C. mariquensis*.

119 Red-chested Sunbird *Cinnyris erythroceria* **Text and map page 287**

Sudan, Ethiopia, Democratic Republic of the Congo, Rwanda, Burundi, Uganda, Kenya and NW Tanzania. Close to rivers, marshes and lakes, mostly in savanna areas but also swamp grass, forest, cultivation.

119a **Adult male** Iridescent green upperparts and throat, red and black on breast and belly, and slightly elongated tail. From male *C. pulchellus melanogaster* by lack of yellow patches on sides of breast. *C. nectarinoides* is allopatric.

119b **Adult female** Dark but pale-tipped graduated tail, dark throat with yellow malar stripe. Female *C. p. melanogaster* has square-ended tail and less heavily streaked underparts.

119c **Immature male** Like adult female but greener. Chin and throat blacker.

118 Congo Sunbird *Cinnyris congensis* **Text and map page 286**

Republic of the Congo and Democratic Republic of the Congo. Forested banks of rivers, trees on river islands and clearings near villages.

118a **Adult male** Metallic green upperparts, bluer on uppertail-coverts, metallic green chin and throat separated from scarlet breast-band by narrow blue band. Belly black. From male *C. chloropygius* by long tail, black belly and no pectoral tufts. *C. pulchellus* is allopatric.

118b **Adult female** Upperparts dull, dark brownish-olive. Tail graduated. Lores blackish; short pale line above eye, pale line from lower mandible down neck. Chin grey, lower throat mottled blackish-brown, rest of underparts pale yellow, brightest in mid-belly, mottled and streaked on breast and flanks. Darker above with darker throat than female *C. chloropygius*.

106

PLATE 39: MARIQUA, PURPLE-BANDED, PEMBA AND MADAGASCAR SUNBIRDS

116 Mariqua Sunbird *Cinnyris mariquensis*   **Text and map page 283**

Sudan, Ethiopia and Eritrea to South Africa. Dry *Acacia* savanna, riverine forest and bushland, swamp-fringing forest. Gardens in towns and cities.

116a Adult male (nominate; South Africa in KwaZulu-Natal; southern Mozambique to Matabeleland in Zimbabwe, south-west Zambia, northern and eastern Botswana; northern Namibia and southern Angola) Iridescent areas show as golden-green; dark red breast.

116b Adult female (nominate) Crown to rump and face brown. Uppertail-coverts and tail very dark brown. Thin brownish-white supercilium above and behind eye. Larger and more heavily streaked below than female *C. bifasciatus*.

116c Adult male (*suahelicus*; Rwanda; Burundi; central Uganda; interior of Kenya from the equator through Tanzania to Mwenzo in north-east Zambia; eastern Democratic Republic of the Congo, Kwanza valley, Angola) On *Erythrina* sp. Greyer abdomen and shorter-billed than nominate. Larger with longer, more decurved bill than *C. bifasciatus*.

116d Adult male (*osiris*; Eritrea, Ethiopia, Somalia to northern Kenya, northern Uganda and south-east Sudan) Posterior margin of metallic throat more violet blue than nominate. Upper violet breast-band broader. Lower maroon breast-band darker and narrower.

121 Purple-banded Sunbird *Cinnyris bifasciatus*   **Text and map page 289**

From Gabon to Kenya, and south to South Africa. Coastal bush, mangrove swamps, riverine forest, open savanna woodland with thickets, mixed broad-leaved and miombo woodland, dry and moist evergreen forest, semi-open areas including cultivation and gardens.

121a Adult male breeding (nominate; Gabon to Namibia) Dark; shows blue breast-band at close quarters. Smaller with shorter, less decurved bill and bluer uppertail-coverts than *C. mariquensis*. Smaller than *C. bouvieri* but with two breast-bands. Bill longer, breast-band less purplish than in *C. tsavoensis*.

121b Adult female (nominate) Above brown, except narrow white stripe over eye. Primaries narrowly edged yellowish-white. Chin and throat whitish with olive tinge on throat. Less streaked on chest and belly than female *C. mariquensis* and less yellow below.

121c Adult male non-breeding (*microrhynchus*) (Eastern and southern Africa) Retains glossy wing-coverts and uppertail-coverts, dark wings, blackish throat and some dark on underparts.

124 Pemba Sunbird *Cinnyris pembae*   **Text and map page 293**

Pemba Island, off south-east Tanzania. Many habitats including towns and villages.

124a Adult male Upperparts, chin and throat and median wing-coverts iridescent green with blue reflections. Glossy violet band on breast above black abdomen. Differs from *C. chalcomelas* by smaller size, sheen on upperparts distinct from *C. chalcomelas* in Kenya (violet not green).

124b Adult female Greenish grey-brown above. Tail greyish-brown with dark blue gloss above, edged dark olive. White supercilium. Below plain unstreaked pale creamy or pale yellow.

144 Madagascar Sunbird *Cinnyris notatus*   **Text and map page 324**

Madagascar and Comoro Islands. Various forest types, including mangrove, secondary forest, plantations, parks and gardens; at all altitudes on Mohéli, but most frequent 400-500 m.

144a Adult male (nominate; Madagascar) Mainly glossy blue and purple above; chin to breast glossy green bordered with a narrow violet band below; rest of underparts blackish.

144b Adult female (nominate) Above brown tinged olive with slight scaling; narrow pale supercilium; most of underside heavily mottled and streaked darkish.

144c Adult male (*moebii*; Grand Comoro) Purple and violet gloss on chin to breast.

PLATE 40: SPLENDID, SUPERB AND JOHANNA'S SUNBIRDS

128 Splendid Sunbird *Cinnyris coccinigaster*   **Text and map page 299**

West and Central Africa. From Senegal to Sudan, Cameroon, Central African Republic, Gabon, Democratic Republic of the Congo and Uganda. Savannas, secondary forest, forest edge, riversides, farmland, coastal thickets, inselbergs, scrubland, plantations, residential areas with adequate vegetation.
A large, long-billed sunbird.

>   **128a**   **Adult male** Appears black at a distance but has purple head, green back and wing-coverts, steel-blue reflections on mantle and rump, blue and scarlet breast, black belly and blue undertail, giving multi-coloured appearance. From male *C. superbus* and *C. johannae* by violet-purple head, throat and breast, red and blue on lower breast, black belly and blue undertail.
>
>   **128b**   **Adult male** Hawking for termites. Yellow pectoral tufts.
>
>   **128c**   **Adult female** Dark brownish-grey above, yellow with grey and brown streaks below. Dark bars on white throat, light streaking on underparts and belly plain yellow (belly of *C. johannae* heavily streaked and chin white); female *C. superbus* has orange undertail-coverts and distinct supercilium. Paler yellow below and less curved bill than female *Chalcomitra senegalensis*. Larger and longer-billed than female *Cinnyris erythroceria*.
>
>   **128d**   **Immature male** Similar to adult female but lacks grey forehead, upperparts browner and ashier. Chin and throat greyish-black, becoming glossy-purple on subadult; other underparts pale yellow with some dark mottling on breast.

129 Johanna's Sunbird *Cinnyris johannae*   **Text and map page 300**

West and Central Africa. From Sierra Leone to Angola (Cabinda). Upper and middle strata of mature forest, old secondary forest, along tracks and in clearings, also, rarely, in gardens or cocoa plantations. Mostly in lowland humid southern forests in West Africa, but some records as far north as 8°19'N.
A large forest species with very long bill and short tail.

>   **129a**   **Adult male** (nominate; southern Nigeria and southern Cameroon to Democratic Republic of the Congo east to Kasai, upper Congo and Kivu) Purple and bright red below; crown, head, throat and back metallic green. Differs from male *C. superbus* by yellow (as against no) pectoral tufts, crown metallic green (steel blue-green in *C. superbus*), brighter red below, throat green above and purple at base (mostly blue with some purple in *C. superbus*).
>
>   **129b**   **Adult female** (nominate) Heavily streaked underparts. From female *C. superbus* by white chin and throat, very heavily streaked underparts.

130 Superb Sunbird *Cinnyris superbus*   **Text and map page 302**

West and Central Africa. From Sierra Leone to Uganda, Kenya, Tanzania and Angola. Canopy and fairly dense undergrowth along streams in primary and secondary forest and coffee groves, forest edges and clearings in wooded lowlands.
A large, long-billed and short-tailed sunbird.

>   **130a**   **Adult male** (nominate; Cameroon and Gabon to northern Angola) Appears all black in poor light. Larger than *C. coccinigaster* with longer bill and dark red underparts below breast, metallic green or blue crown. Male *C. johannae* similar but brighter red below and crown metallic green.
>
>   **130b**   **Adult female** (nominate) Olive above and yellow below, unstreaked breast and orange-red wash on undertail-coverts. Long pale supercilium and more yellow below than either *C. coccinigaster* or *C. johannae* and latter has heavily streaked, not plain, underparts. Orange undertail-coverts distinguish female *C. superbus* from both other species and longer bill also separates *C. superbus* from *C. coccinigaster*.

128d

128c

128a

128b

129a

130a

129b

130b

RwA

PLATE 41: BEAUTIFUL AND BLACK-BELLIED SUNBIRDS

115 Beautiful Sunbird *Cinnyris pulchellus*   **Text and map page 281**

West and East Africa. From Senegal to Eritrea, and to Democratic Republic of the Congo, Uganda, Kenya and dry interior Tanzania. Thorn savannas, mainly in dry sahel and savanna belt of West Africa and edges of rivers, but recorded in mangrove scrub, beaches and gardens.
Slim with shortish curved bill and (in male) elongated tail.

115a   **Adult male breeding** (nominate; Senegal to Nigeria, Sudan, Eritrea, western Ethiopia, north-east borders of Democratic Republic of the Congo to north of Lake Albert, Uganda east to Akole, north-west Kenya to Baringo) On *Bombax* sp. Long central tail feathers, mostly bright metallic green plumage and red breast-band, bordered yellow. Differs from smaller *Hedydipna platura* and *H. metallica*, which are entirely yellow below, by scarlet breast-band bordered yellow; longer bill and lacks *H. platura*'s purple uppertail-coverts.

115b   **Adult male non-breeding** (nominate) Resembles adult female, but with black remiges and rectrices. Grey-brown above, dusky yellow below, but retains green metallic chin, throat, wing-coverts and a few such feathers on rump and uppertail-coverts, although metallic on chin and throat may be replaced by whitish patch. Some lose the long tail, others do not.

115c   **Adult female** (nominate) On *Bombax* sp. Upperparts dull brown with faint yellow wash from crown to rump and darker brown on wing- and tail-coverts. Narrow pale supercilium behind eye. Tail blackish-brown with slight bronze-green or bluish gloss, narrowly tipped white, outer pair with white along outerwebs. Chin and throat whitish, rest of underparts suffused yellow and slightly mottled dark blackish-brown on breast and flanks. Remiges dark brown, edged pale olive as are greater wing-coverts. Differs from female *H. platura* by dull yellow underparts and longer bill. More obvious supercilium than in female *C. venustus*; smaller and paler than female and immature *C. cupreus*.

115d   **Immature male** (nominate) Similar to adult female but with a vertical black streak on throat and upper chest, bordered with creamy-white moustachial stripe.

115e   **Adult male** (*melanogaster*; west and central Kenya south to Tanzania) Differs from nominate by longer bill, black abdomen, undertail-coverts with metallic green-blue tips, red patch larger and central tail feathers less projecting. From *C. nectarinoides* by yellow borders to red breast-patch.

120 Black-bellied Sunbird *Cinnyris nectarinoides*   **Text and map page 288**

North-east Africa. Southern Ethiopia, Somalia, Kenya and Tanzania. Open dry thorn savannas with *Acacia* spp., and riverine vegetation in dry country.
A smallish sunbird of arid parts of the Horn of Africa and East Africa.

120a   **Adult male** (nominate; northern Kenya from Guaso Nyiro east of highlands to Tsavo and Taita and north-east Tanzania) Metallic golden-green upperparts, black belly, yellow pectoral tufts and elongated central tail feathers. Tail less elongated than in male *C. pulchellus melanogaster* and lacks yellow patches on sides of red breast-patch.

120b   **Adult female** (nominate) Upperparts dull yellowish-olive, with dark brown streaks on crown and mantle. Pale yellow streak above eye. Chin to throat, sides of breast and flanks pale yellow with greyish-black streaks; malar streak, centre of belly and undertail-coverts pale yellow without blackish streaks. From female *C. pulchellus melanogaster* by dark streaking on breast and flanks. Female *C. tsavoensis* white below and much more heavily streaked.

120c   **Immature male** (nominate) Similar to adult female but remiges edged more yellowish, chin and throat all brownish-grey with pale yellow malar stripe. Breast mottled not streaked.

120d   **Adult male** (*erlangeri*; Juba River area in south-east Ethiopia, southern Somalia and north-east corner of Kenya) Breast-band of males redder, less orange and less deep than in nominate; no yellow pectoral tufts. Metallic plumage much bluer.

115a

115b

115c

115d

115e

120d

120b

120a

120c

RW

PLATE 42: *AETHOPYGA* SUNBIRDS (1)

150 Grey-hooded Sunbird *Aethopyga primigenius*   **Text and map page 332**

Philippines – Mindanao. Forest and forest edge above 1,000 m. Sexes similar.

    150a **Adult male** (nominate; range of species except Mt Hilong-Hilong) Head, neck and throat grey; back olive-green; tail brown tipped white; breast and mid-belly white, rest of underparts yellow.

    150b **Adult male** (*diuatae*; Mt Hilong-Hilong) From nominate by darker throat, with greyish mesial stripe of varying intensity ending in yellow spot; darker grey below.

151 Apo Sunbird *Aethopyga boltoni*   **Text and map page 332**

Philippines – Mindanao. At 820-2,300 m, usually above 1,500 m, in montane mossy forest.

    151a **Adult male** (nominate; Mt McKinley, Mt Apo and Mt Kitanglad) Metallic green forehead; pale yellow rump. Below mostly yellow, with much orange on breast; pectoral tufts orange.

    151b **Adult female** (nominate) Olive-grey above, greener on back with little yellow on rump; throat to upper breast olive-grey with indistinct pale streaking; pectoral tufts pale yellow.

152 Lina's Sunbird *Aethopyga linaraborae*   **Text and map page 334**

Philippines – eastern Mindanao. In montane mossy forest from 975-1,980 m, and probably higher.

    152a **Adult male** Metallic green and blue forehead, cheek-patch, wing-coverts and uppertail-coverts; blackish-grey head and tail, latter edged violet and tipped white; underparts yellow, with orange on breast and scarlet pectoral tufts. Bill longer than *A. boltoni*.

    152b **Adult female** Differs from female *A. boltoni* by orangey edging to wing feathers, lack of yellow on rump, greater contrast between throat and sides of neck, less orange but more streaking below.

153 Flaming Sunbird *Aethopyga flagrans*   **Text and map page 334**

Philippines. Up to 1,350 m in forest, secondary growth and at forest edge.

    153a **Adult male** (nominate) Crown and uppertail-coverts metallic blue-green; chin metallic purple, throat to breast dull black, with bright reddish-orange mesial stripe.

    153b **Adult female** (nominate; Catanduanes and Luzon, except north-east) Olive-green above, grey below, pale yellow patch on breast.

    153c **Adult male** (*guimarasensis*; Guimaras and Panay) Differs from nominate by blood-red hindcrown to mantle, much brighter yellow below, and less orange on belly.

154 Metallic-winged Sunbird *Aethopyga pulcherrima*   **Text and map page 335**

Philippines. Mostly submontane, from lowlands to 1,500 m, in forest and edge, and secondary growth.

    154a **Adult male** (nominate; Basilan, Dinagat, Leyte, Mindanao, Samar and Biliran) Forehead, spot behind eye, wing-coverts, uppertail-coverts and tail metallic green; rump bright yellow.

    154b **Adult female** (nominate) Olive-green above, with yellow rump; underparts dull olive-grey.

    154c **Adult male** (*jefferyi*; Luzon) Differs from male nominate by dark metallic blue forehead, yellow lower back as rump; metallic green of wing-coverts extends onto remiges; paler below.

155 Elegant Sunbird *Aethopyga duyvenbodei*   **Text and map page 336**

Sulawesi – Sangihe and Siau. Up to 900 m in bamboo, secondary growth, plantations and forest edge.

    155a **Adult male** Metallic green crown; sides of head and neck maroon-red; dark green back and mantle; rump yellow; uppertail-coverts metallic purple; blackish tail tipped and edged white.

    155b **Adult female** Golden-olive above; yellow below with olive band on breast.

PLATE 43: *AETHOPYGA* SUNBIRDS (2)

156 Lovely Sunbird *Aethopyga shelleyi*   **Text and map page 337**

Philippines. Below 2,000 m in forest, at forest edge, in secondary growth and scrub.
Bill medium-long, fine and decurved.

  156a Adult male (nominate; Balabac, Busuanga, Culion and Palawan) Differs from male *rubrinota*
  by whole crown glossy purple and green, no cheek spot; more red on breast; grey of
  underparts paler.

  156b Adult female (nominate) Olive-green above; below greyish, tinged yellow. Tail not elongated,
  and rounded.

  156c Adult male (*rubrinota*; Lubang) Forecrown glossy green; rest of crown and nape dark green;
  wings yellowish-green; sides of head, neck, and upper back dark red; lower back and rump
  bright yellow; uppertail-coverts, tail, malar stripe and spot behind eye glossed blue-green;
  chin to breast yellow, with traces of red in centre; rest of underparts grey. Tail graduated, with
  elongated central feathers.

157 Gould's Sunbird *Aethopyga gouldiae*   **Text and map page 339**

Himalayas, from Sutlej valley to eastern India, Tibet south to Chittagongs, north-west Burma; west,
central and south China; southern Laos and southern Vietnam. In various forest types, and evergreen
scrub-jungle. Altitude varies with range; generally breeding at 1,200-4,270 m, but 330-2,700 m in winter.
Medium to shortish decurved bill.

  157a Adult male (nominate; Himalayas and Tibet) Differs from male *dabryii* by more purple throat,
  crimson supercilium, and breast mostly yellow with variable amount of scarlet streaking.

  157b Adult female (nominate) Tail square. Head and nape grey; rest of upperparts olive, with
  yellow rump; throat grey, rest of underparts yellowish-grey.

  157c Adult male (*dabryii*; east Nagaland, China and Pome, east Tibet; in winter to Manipur and
  north Cachar, Burma) Long graduated tail with very elongated central feathers, outer ones
  tipped buffish. Glossy purple-blue crown, malar, auricular area and throat; sides of head, nape
  and back crimson; rump bright yellow; uppertail-coverts and uppertail metallic blue; scarlet
  breast; rest of underparts yellow.

  157d Adult male (*annamensis*; southern Laos and southern Vietnam) Differs from male nominate
  by lack of yellow on rump and more scarlet on sides of breast.

  157e Adult female (*annamensis*) Differs from female nominate by yellow lower breast and belly,
  yellow of rump extending onto lower back and uppertail-coverts.

158 Green-tailed Sunbird *Aethopyga nipalensis*   **Text and map page 340**

Himalayas from Mussoorie to eastern India, south to Chittagongs, Burma, Thailand, Laos, Vietnam,
north-west Yunnan; central and south-west China. Forest, orchards and gardens. Altitude varies
geographically; generally 300-3,665 m, lower in winter.
Medium to longish bill, markedly decurved; long white-tipped tail with elongated central feathers in
both sexes.

  158a Adult male (*karenensis*; south-east Burma) Central rectrices much more elongated than
  female. Crown, nape and throat, uppertail-coverts and tail metallic blue-green; crimson-brown
  patch on sides of neck; back and wings bright olive-green; yellow rump; rest of underparts yellow.

  158b Adult female (*karenensis*) Grey head and throat to upper belly; rest of upperparts olive-green;
  rest of underparts yellow.

  158c Adult male (*koelzi*; Bhutan, Tibet and eastern India, south to Chittagongs, north-west Yunnan,
  northern Vietnam, central and south-west China) Differs from male *karenensis* by crimson-
  brown extending onto back, breast streaked scarlet.

  158d Adult female (*koelzi*) Differs from female *karenensis* by olive crown and nape, hint of yellow on
  rump.

159 White-flanked Sunbird *Aethopyga eximia*   **Text and map page 341**

Mountains of Java. In forest, at forest edge, in clearings and alpine scrub above tree-line; 1,200-3,000 m, especially common above 2,400 m.
Medium-long, slender, decurved bill.

159a **Adult male** Longish, graduated tail; crown, and narrow band on throat metallic purple-blue; yellow rump; uppertail-coverts and tail metallic blue-green; chin to upper breast red; pectoral tufts, underwing-coverts and long fluffy flank feathers white; rest of plumage chiefly olive.

159b **Adult female** Square or rounded tail; dull olive above, greyer on head, paler grey on throat; olive-green below, white underwing-coverts, pectoral tufts and flanks.

160 Fork-tailed Sunbird *Aethopyga christinae*   **Text and map page 342**

Central Laos, Vietnam and south-east China. Forest, and at forest edge, chiefly on lower hills.
Bill shortish, slender and decurved.

160a **Adult male** (*latouchii*; south-east China, northern Vietnam and central Laos) Central tail feathers elongated into short black spikes. Crown, nape, uppertail-coverts, and central rectrices metallic green; outer rectrices tipped white. Rump yellow, rest of back and wings yellowish-olive; throat dark red, rest of underparts olive-yellow.

160b **Adult female** (*latouchii*) Rounded tail; chiefly olive-green above, with darker crown; chin to breast yellowish-grey, rest of underparts buffish-yellow.

160c **Adult male** (nominate; Hainan Island) Differs from *latouchii* in having black back rather than yellowish-olive, and breast dark red, concolorous with throat, not yellow.

161 Black-throated Sunbird *Aethopyga saturata*   **Text and map page 343**

Himalayas, from Garhwal to eastern India, Nepal, Bhutan, south-east Tibet; Bangladesh, west and south-east Yunnan, west Kwangsi and South-East Asia. Forest and forest edge, jungle, scrub, secondary growth and along streams; usually 1,000-2,200 m, but down to 305 m in winter.
Shortish, slender, decurved bill.

161a **Adult male** (*anomala*; southern Thailand to Trang) Graduated tail with elongated central feathers. Crown, nape, uppertail-coverts and tail metallic purple; back and sides of neck crimson-brown; wings blackish-brown; throat to upper breast dull smoky-black, bordered purple; yellowish band on breast; rest of underparts greyish.

161b **Adult male** (*petersi*; eastern Burma, northern Thailand, Laos, northern Vietnam, south-east Yunnan and west Kwangsi) Differs from male *anomala* by glossy blue crown and malar area, yellow rump; chin to breast unglossed black; rest of underparts chiefly yellow, with scarlet streaking on breast.

161c **Adult male** (*assamensis*) Differs from male *anomala* by yellow rump, blackish extending onto upper belly, and rest of underparts olive-green and grey.

161d **Adult male** (*assamensis*) In flight.

161e **Adult female** (*assamensis*; north-east India, northern Burma to west Yunnan) Tail rounded. Chiefly olive-green above with yellow rump, and olive and yellowish below.

161f **Adult male** (*johnsi*; southern Vietnam) Differs from male *petersi* by generally brighter plumage, breast scarlet with yellow streaking.

163 Crimson Sunbird *Aethopyga siparaja*   **Text and map page 345**

Himalayan foothills from Kangra east to north-east India, south through South-East Asia; Yunnan; Nicobars, Greater Sundas, Philippines and Sulawesi. In various forest types, including mangroves, and at forest edge, in scrub, secondary growth and gardens; usually below 915 m, but to 1,500 m in Sulawesi, 1,800 m in Nepal (summer) and 1,190 m in Borneo.
Bill shortish to medium-long, slender and decurved.

163a   Adult male (nominate; Malay Peninsula, Sumatra, except Aceh, Borneo and probably this form on Java). Tail graduated, with central feathers elongated. Forehead to centre of crown, malar stripe and tail glossed purple or purple-green; rest of crown, sides of neck, shoulder and mantle crimson; rest of wings olive-grey; rump yellow. Chin to upper breast scarlet, with fine yellow streaks; rest of underparts yellowish-grey.

163b   Adult male (*seheriae*; Himalayan foothills east to Sikkim, eastern India and western Bangladesh) Larger than male nominate, with much longer central rectrices, bronzy-green forehead, forecrown and tail, olive hindcrown and rump (latter with concealed yellow patch), paler lower breast and belly.

163c   Adult female (*seheriae*) Tail rounded. Olive and greyish-olive above, becoming brighter and yellower on rump and uppertail-coverts; tail dark with pale tips; below grey and olive, with yellow streaking and undertail-coverts.

163d   Adult male (*flavostriata*; northern Sulawesi) Differs from nominate male by much red on wings, broad yellow rump, more extensive scarlet below with strong yellow streaks, and much darker belly.

163e   Adult male (*magnifica*; Philippines) Larger and longer-billed than male *flavostriata*; graduated tail. Also differs from male *flavostriata* by blackish wings, with red shoulder, bright orange-yellow rump, and blackish belly and vent.

163f   Adult female (*magnifica*) Mainly olive and grey-green, with red edging to black tail, and varying amounts of red on scapulars, wing-coverts, rectrices and back.

162 Western Crimson Sunbird *Aethopyga vigorsii*   **Text and map page 344**

India – Western Ghats. Occurs up to 900 m in wooded country, preferably in foothills.
Larger and more robust, and with a longer, thicker bill, than allopatric *A. siparaja*.

162a   Adult male Tail graduated, with central rectrices slightly elongated. Crown, uppertail-coverts and tail metallic green; sides of head, nape, mantle, back and shoulder dull crimson; rump pale yellow; malar stripe and cheek-spot metallic purple; chin to upper breast scarlet streaked yellow, and bordered below with narrow dark brownish-grey band; rest of underparts grey.

162b   Adult female Rounded tail. Chiefly olive above, becoming more yellowish on rump and uppertail-coverts; tail blackish with pale tips; underparts grey.

PLATE 46: *AETHOPYGA* SUNBIRDS (5)

164 Javan Sunbird *Aethopyga mystacalis*   **Text and map page 348**

Java. Forest, secondary forest, edge; generally 800-1,985 m, occasionally down to sea-level and up to 2,300 m.
Shortish, decurved bill.

164a   Adult male Graduated tail, with elongated central feathers. Head, breast, back and shoulders bright crimson, rest of wings blackish; breast streaked yellow; crown (except forehead), malar stripe, uppertail-coverts and tail iridescent purple; lower breast to vent grey, whitish on flanks.

164b   Adult female Tail rounded; grey head, paler on throat, flanks whitish; rest of plumage olive.

165 Temminck's Sunbird *Aethopyga temmincki*   **Text and map page 348**

South-west Thailand, peninsular Malaysia, Sumatra and Borneo. Occurs in various forest types; generally submontane, but recorded from close to sea-level to 1,985 m.
Shortish, decurved bill.

165a   Adult male Graduated tail, with elongated central rectrices. Head, back, shoulders, tail and chin to breast scarlet; upper rump yellow, lower rump and uppertail-coverts brownish, glossed purple; sides of crown, nape and moustachial stripe glossed purple; remiges blackish edged golden; rest of underparts grey.

165b   Adult female Tail rounded. Head grey; rest of plumage olive, more yellow below, with reddish wash on wings and tail.

166 Fire-tailed Sunbird *Aethopyga ignicauda*   **Text and map page 349**

Himalayas east to Bangladesh, Tibet and China; Burma. Found chiefly in coniferous forest with dense undergrowth, and above tree-line; 3,000-4,880 m in summer, 610-2,900 m in winter.
Medium-long, slightly decurved bill.

166a   Adult male breeding (nominate; range of species except Chin Hills, Burma) Crown and throat metallic purple; sides of face black; wings olive, rump yellow; rest of upperparts scarlet. Breast bright yellow washed orange; rest of underparts pale yellow and grey.

166b   Adult male (nominate) In flight. Tail graduated, with very elongated central rectrices. Shows much red above.

166c   Adult male non-breeding (nominate) Similar to female, but uppertail-coverts and graduated tail scarlet, latter with slightly elongated central feathers; rump yellow, lower breast to vent more yellow.

166d   Adult female (nominate) Tail rounded; head to upper breast grey; rest of underparts yellowish; above olive, yellowish on rump.

PLATE 47: SPIDERHUNTERS (1)

All spiderhunters have long to very long, robust, decurved bills and rounded tails. The sexes are similar, except that in species where there are pectoral tufts they are lacking in the female, which is also smaller.

167 Little Spiderhunter *Arachnothera longirostra*   Text and map page 350

India, South-East Asia, west Yunnan, Greater Sundas and the Philippines. Forests, secondary growth, plantations and gardens. Generally below 1,000 m, but up to 1,500 m in southern India, 2,000 m, possibly 2,200 m, in Sumatra and 2,100 m in China.

  167a **Adult** Mainly olive above and yellow below; throat and area around eye whitish; dark grey stripe through eye and blackish moustachial stripe.

  167b **Adult male** In flight. Orange pectoral tufts; tail dark with white tips and edges.

168 Thick-billed Spiderhunter *Arachnothera crassirostris*   Text and map page 352

Malay Peninsula, Sumatra and Borneo. Forests and secondary growth, around bananas and gingers. Found from lowlands up to 1,350 m.

  168 **Adult** Shorter and much stouter bill than similar-sized *A. longirostra*. Mainly dark olive above, tail tipped and edged yellow; yellow around eye, with dark stripe through eye; chin to breast greyish-yellow, rest of underparts yellow. Orange-yellow pectoral tufts in male.

169 Long-billed Spiderhunter *Arachnothera robusta*   Text and map page 353

Malay Peninsula, Sumatra, Borneo and Java. Canopy of forests, sometimes secondary growth. Found from lowlands locally up to 1,700 m.

  169 **Adult** Larger and much longer-billed than previous two species. Mainly dark olive above, with blackish tail tipped white. Mostly yellow below, with green streaking from throat to breast. Male has orange-yellow pectoral tufts.

170 Spectacled Spiderhunter *Arachnothera flavigaster*   Text and map page 354

Malay Peninsula, Sumatra and Borneo. Occurs in low and middle storey of various forest types, at edges and in secondary growth, cultivation, clearings; chiefly lowlands, but up to 1,500 m on Sumatra, and possibly to 1,800 m on Borneo.

  170 **Adult** Similar size to *A. robusta*, but with much shorter, thicker bill. Olive above; broad yellow orbital ring and triangular ear-patch; throat to breast greenish-olive, rest of underparts yellow.

171 Yellow-eared Spiderhunter *Arachnothera chrysogenys*   Text and map page 355

Malay Peninsula, Sumatra and islands, Borneo and West Java. Forest, secondary vegetation, plantations and gardens. Mainly lowlands up to 1,400 m, but up to 1,835 m in peninsular Malaysia.

  171 **Adult** (nominate; range of species, except eastern Borneo) Smaller, with a longer, finer bill, narrower orbital ring and smaller ear-patch than *A. flavigaster*.

All spiderhunters have long, robust bills and rounded tails. The sexes are similar, except in those species that have pectoral tufts, which are lacking in the female, and which is also smaller.

172 Naked-faced Spiderhunter *Arachnothera clarae* — Text and map page 356

Philippines. Occurs in forest, at forest edge, in scrub and around bananas; lowlands, and up to 1,400 m. Long, stout bill only slightly decurved.

172a Adult (*philippinensis*; Leyte, Samar and Biliran) Olive-green above with brown edges to remiges; green below. Naked forehead, lower face pinkish; black naked skin in front of eye.

172b Adult (*luzonensis*; Luzon) Differs from *philippinensis* in being less green, more olive-grey below, and having forehead feathered.

173 Grey-breasted Spiderhunter *Arachnothera modesta* — Text and map page 357

Southern Burma, Thailand, Cochinchina, peninsular Malaysia, Sumatra and Borneo. Occurs in forest, including secondary forest, and at forest edge, in plantations, orchards and around bananas; lowlands up to 1,200 m.
Longish, stout, slightly decurved bill.

173 Adult (nominate; Malay Peninsula and Borneo) Golden olive-green above, olive-grey below, with dark streaking, particularly on throat and breast, with little on flanks and belly; dark terminal band on tail.

174 Streaky-breasted Spiderhunter *Arachnothera affinis* — Text and map page 358

Borneo, Java and Bali. Forest, at forest edge and around plantains; usually 900-1,600 m, but as low as 305 m.

174 Adult (*everetti*; Borneo) Larger than *A. modesta*, greener above and more extensively streaked below.

175 Streaked Spiderhunter *Arachnothera magna* — Text and map page 358

Nepal, Bhutan, northern and north-east India south through Chittagongs, Burma, north-west and south-west Thailand, Indochina, Yunnan and Malay Peninsula. Forests, thickets, old cultivation and gardens; chiefly submontane and montane, occurring up to 2,200 m, but lower in winter in north of range.

175 Adult (nominate; north and north-east India, Nepal, Bhutan and Bangladesh, to northern Burma and peninsular Malaysia) Bill long, stout and decurved. Golden-olive above, yellowish-white below; heavily streaked above and below with black; black subterminal bar on tail.

176 Whitehead's Spiderhunter *Arachnothera juliae* — Text and map page 360

Mountains of Borneo. Forests, and at forest edge; 930-2,100 m.

176 Adult Long, stout, decurved bill. Mainly blackish and blackish-brown; heavily streaked with white on head and body; yellow rump and undertail-coverts.

172a

172b

173

174

175

176

RWₜ

Family Nectariniidae
Subfamily Promeropinae

SUGARBIRDS
PROMEROPS

Promerops Brisson, 1760, *Ornithologia*, 1, p.34; 2, p.460. Type, by tautonymy, "Le Promérops" *Promerops promerops* Brisson = *Merops cafer* Linnaeus.

Two species restricted to southern Africa, formerly overlapping with some evidence of hybridisation in a narrow zone of sympatry at the edges of their ranges. However, atlas data from the 1990s failed to detect any sites where both species occurred. The monotypic *Promerops cafer* is restricted to the south and south-east of South Africa. *P. gurneyi* occurs in the east and north of South Africa, Swaziland and eastern Zimbabwe along the border with Mozambique. *P. gurneyi* has two subspecies: the nominate in South Africa and *ardens* comprising the Zimbabwe and Mozambique populations. The two species are the only representatives of the Promeropidae, a family which has been subsumed within the honeyeaters Meliphagidae of Australia by some authors (e.g. Mayr & Amadon 1951, White 1963), with the starlings by others (Sibley & Ahlquist 1974) and as the Promeropinae within the Nectariniidae on the basis of DNA-DNA hybridisation studies (Sibley & Monroe 1990).

Long, slender, down-curved bill with subapical hair-thick groove on maxilla, smooth cutting edge, no internal serrations. Culmen slightly raised. No feathers on longitudinal nostrils with operculae. Twelve tail feathers. Stiff feathers on forehead and crown. Hind toe and claw not longer than tarsus. Cup-shaped nest.

1 GURNEY'S SUGARBIRD
Promerops gurneyi   Plate 1

Promerops gurneyi Verreaux, 1871, *Proc. Zool. Soc. London*, p.135, Natal, South Africa.

Alternative names: Gurney's Long-tailed Sugarbird, Natal Sugarbird, Natal Long-tailed Sugarbird, Chestnut-headed Sugarbird

IDENTIFICATION Dull brown with long, slightly de-curved bill, brown moustachial stripes, rich chestnut crown and breast-band, streaked belly, bright yellow undertail-coverts and long tail.
Similar species General shape as female Cape Sugarbird *Promerops cafer* (2), from which it differs in having russet-red or chestnut chest and crown, and bill lighter; also, tails not markedly different in length between the sexes, and tail of male shorter (137-170 mm) than tail (222-320) of male *P. cafer*. *P. cafer* is bolder and noisier.

VOICE Call A loud *clack* or a *chit*, sometimes oft-repeated and may be preceded by *tirry-tirry-tirry-tirry*..., increasing in speed until switching to the *chit-chit*. The latter variable and described as *shirruk, shirruk, shirruk*; *swirratik-swirratik*, a quiet *tsik-tsik-tsik-tsik*; *tseek-tseek-tseek*, and a soft *tsip-tswit-tswit-tswit-tswittit, tswittit*..., recalling Greater Honeyguide *Indicator indicator*. Alarm call is either *chit* or a *skirrrt*, like sound of cloth being ripped. Scolding call when intruders near nest is a rapid *tree, tree, tree*..., and *chiddly, chiddly, chick, chick, chick* accompanies birds chasing predators or reacting to other threats. **Song** Similar to song of *P. cafer*, being a series of repetitive, jangling *wheezy, wheezy whisk, whisk, wheezy, wheezy, wheezy, whisk, wheezy* with variations such as *surdle-swiddly, ee, awk*; *speedle, sponky, ta-link*; *sirky, sinkle, sernkle*; *zink, zonky, zinkzank*, etc., with pauses between each repetition. Bouts may last 5 minutes and singing sessions continue for 20 minutes, with bill usually brought forward and down at start of each bout. Respond to songs of other males and to those of *P. cafer*. Some songs recall Fork-tailed Drongo *Dicrurus adsimilis* or Willow Warbler *Phylloscopus trochilus*. Occasionally sing at night.

DISTRIBUTION Eastern Cape to the Drakensberg mountains and escarpments in the north of South Africa. Golden Gate National Park, Bethlehem, Orange Free State. Soutpansberg, Waterberg and Blouberg of northern Transvaal. KwaZulu-Natal and Transkei but not Lesotho. Hhouho valley in Swaziland and nearby at 1,460 m, 13 km south-east of Amsterdam, Transvaal. Known range, historically, only overlaps with *cafer* in eastern Amatole and Pirie mountains above Alice and King William's Town, respectively, but 1990s data suggest complete allopatry. It strays into lower and mid-Natal, Qudeni in western Zululand. Isolated population in eastern Zimbabwe and adjacent Mozambique.

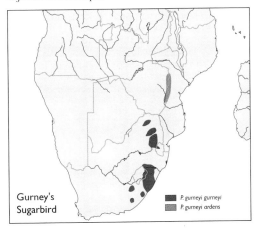

Gurney's Sugarbird

■ *P. gurneyi gurneyi*
▨ *P. gurneyi ardens*

HABITAT Alpine and sour grassland vegetation types and grassland bordering Afromontane forests in upland areas. *Protea roupelliae* or *Protea multibracteata* heath at 1,500-

1,800 m in the Natal Drakensberg, straying into forest patches and marginal scrub of *Leucosidea sericea, Buddleja salviifolia* and *Myrsine africana. Protea caffra* heath in Witwatersrand, *P. lacticolor* heath on Amatole mountains. Towns with aloes, *Eucalyptus* plantations. *Protea–Brachystegia–Erica* scrub in Zimbabwe, near Melsetter, *Protea* scrub in the Chimanimani mountains.

STATUS Common in both South Africa and Zimbabwe in suitable *Protea* habitat but threatened where this is replaced by bananas, sugarcane and other commercial crops or damaged by burning. Large stands of *Protea subvestita* habitat have been destroyed as this species is not fire-resistant.

MOVEMENTS Local movements and wanderings occur, when recorded in habitats lacking proteas, including coastal thorn scrub. For instance, when *Protea roupelliae* cease to flower in the Lydenburg area in March, birds wander 5.7-10.5 km (mean 7 km) to lower altitudes, including suburban areas, to seek nectar, but return to original sites to breed when flowering re-starts in August–September. There is also site-fidelity to the wintering sites. Seasonal movements between neighbouring mountains. One ringing recovery involved movement of 37 km.

FOOD Nectar, spiders and insects including small flies. Hawk for insects, flying up and down or horizontally from perches.
Known food-plants *Aloe arborescens, Buddleja salviifolia, Callistemon* sp., *Erythrina lysistemon, Erythrina* sp., *Eucalyptus* sp., *Faurea speciosa, Grevillea* sp., *Greyia* sp., *Greyia radlokoferi, G. sutherlandii, Halleria* sp., *Halleria lucida, Kniphofia* sp., *Leonotis leonotis, Leucosidea sericea, Leucospermum* sp., *Myrsine africana, Protea caffra, P. gaguedi (= P. abyssinica), P. lacticolor, P. nerifolia, P. repens, P. roupelliae, P. subvestita.*

HABITS Usually singly or in pairs, occasionally in groups of 6-10 birds. Flight slightly undulating with rapid wing-beats, occasionally bobbing and jerky. When leaving perch on a *Protea*, jump up, over and down, recalling diving cormorant *Phalacrocorax* sp. Aerial displays much less dramatic than those of *P. cafer*, lacking exaggerated flappings, but nevertheless spectacular, consisting of vertical flights up to 10 m and descents with choppy wing-beats, sometimes accompanied by soft, husky *zikky, zikky...* calls. *Frrt-frrt* noise made by modified P6 of some birds during display-flight (or when released after handling). Tend to hide amongst *Protea* for up to 15 minutes and then re-appear on top of *Protea* bush to sing or chase conspecifics. Flick wings excitedly when feeding or in sight of danger. Strongly territorial, exchanging songs with neighbours, and will fly directly at intruders, including both conspecifics and other species such as Cape Weavers *Ploceus capensis* and Red-winged Starlings *Onychognathus morio*. Will tolerate competing Malachite Sunbirds *Nectarinia famosa* (97) on same bush but not on same flower.

Moult September–March, primaries renewed descendantly from P1 to P10, secondaries moulted ascendantly and tail feathers moulted centrifugally from T1 outwards to T6. Body moults occur throughout the year.

Longevity of a male at least 5 years 11 months. Host to the blood parasite *Leucocytozoon deswardti*, previously identified as, and indistinguishable from, *L. annellobiae*, also found in Australia in the blood of the meliphagid Brush Wattlebird *Anthochaera (Anellobia) chrysoptera*. This suggests that these birds may have shared a common ancestor before becoming separated by continental drift some 40 million years ago. Also host to *Haemoproteus* sp., *Plasmodium cathemerium, P. vaughani, Trypanosoma avium* and microfilariae.

BREEDING Coincides with peak flowering by *Protea roupelliae* in habitat dominated by that plant. Nests in solitary *Protea* trees (3-4 m above ground), in or on edges of clusters of *Protea* bushes or on south-western edges or centres of bushes. Construction by female only, completed in 5 days. Incubation, also by female only, 16-17 days, nestling period 21-23 days. Both sexes feed nestlings on small winged insects including mantids and beetles; also, probably, nectar. When parent alights on nest, young respond by craning necks, begging with open bills. Faeces taken and deposited 5 m away from nest. Fledglings remain dependent on parents for 2-3 months. **Nest** Similar to that of *Promerops cafer*, placed 0.8-6 m up, but perimeter much neater. Bulky exterior made of dry heath stalks, twigs of *Stoebe vulgaris, Pteridium* spp., *Helichrysum* spp., *Cliffortia linearifolia* and sticks of *Widdringtonia nodiflora* and other species. Nest with external width 100-125 mm, external depth 45-60 mm, cup 50-60 mm wide, 35-44 mm deep, neat, made of fine stalks neatly lined with brown fluff from *Protea* at its base. Sometimes lined with leaves of *Buddleja salviifolia*. **Eggs** c/1-2. Ground colour pale salmon to pale coffee-brown with purple darkening at obtuse end and some flecks and scrolls of dark brown; 20.9-25 (mean 22.9, SD 1.67, n=6) x 16.2-17 (mean 16.7, SD 0.28), mass 2.5g. **Laying months** South Africa: September–February, mostly October–December in Natal Drakensberg, November–January at Lydenburg, April and June in King William's Town mountains; Zimbabwe: October.

DESCRIPTION *P. g. gurneyi*
Adult male Forehead, crown and nape reddish-chestnut brown, crown feathers lanceolate and sharp. Ear-coverts fuscous. Neck dull brown, with dark streaks, mantle similar but streaks bolder. Back fuscous, also streaked and with olive-green wash. Rump and uppertail-coverts greenish-yellow. Upperwing all fuscous, primaries without bulges or emarginations on webs of P4-6 in most birds, but 43.5-65.9% of males do have them (maximum width of bulge 10.6-16.1, mean 13.7, SD 1.03, 64 males), and their widths are correlated with wing length. Occasionally bulge also present on P7. Underwing-coverts and axillaries silvery-grey. Tail blackish-brown. Throat and cheeks light buff, usually with faint brown malar stripe. Breast tawny to chestnut, slightly blotched with light buff. Chest and upper belly light buff, streaked tawny-brown. Lower belly and flanks light buff, with heavy brown streaking. Undertail-coverts bright yellow. Iris hazel. Bill, legs and feet black.
Adult female As male, but tail 34% shorter, head length shorter (mean 54, 32 males, mean 52.2, 34 females), wing shorter and lower mass. Only 8.7% of females with wing bulge on 6th primary (maximum width of bulge 9.9-12.0 in 80 females, mean 11.1, SD 0.67, 13 females).
Juvenile Newly hatched nestlings naked with blackish-grey down on head, back and wings only. Gape yellow, base of bill pale orange. Eyes open and feathers begin sprouting after 5 days, when legs black and claws already sharp. Fully feathered by 12-14 days. Breast and crown dark brownish, rump and undertail-coverts greenish-yellow. Juveniles have greenish-russet downy feathers on breast and secondaries edged brownish, not whitish as in adults, and the nestling gape colour is retained for about 6 months.

GEOGRAPHICAL VARIATION

P. g. ardens Friedmann, 1952 (North of the Limpopo river. Eastern districts of Zimbabwe above 1,000 m – mostly 1,100-2,300 m – where *Protea* spp. present and adjoining mountains of Mozambique near Manica e Sofala and probably to headwaters of the R. Pungwe. Absent from South Africa) Pectoral band richer and brighter than *gurneyi*; lower back greener, less yellow. Centres of feathers blacker. Cheeks darker.

P. g. gurneyi (Verreaux, 1871) (South Africa, south of the Limpopo river. East Cape Province at Elliotdale to interior Natal, Orange Free State and east and north Transvaal, Swaziland) Described above.

MEASUREMENTS Males significantly larger and heavier than females but no evidence of seasonal variation in mass. **Wing** 87-95 (male *ardens*), 86-101 (mean 94.4, SD 3.2, 159 male *gurneyi*), 82-84 (female *ardens*), 77-96 (mean 87.0, SD 3.57, 195 female *gurneyi*), 71-99 (mean 86.4, SD 3.7, 93 unsexed *gurneyi*); **tail** 120-174 (male *ardens*), 94-187 (mean 150.1, SD 17.36, 159 male *gurneyi*), 117-118 (female *ardens*), 88-155 (mean 111.1, SD 10.3, 195 female *gurneyi*), 60-166 (mean 105.5, SD 12.7, 92 unsexed *gurneyi*); **bill** 31.8-36 (male *ardens*), 30.0-38.1 (mean 34.1, SD 1.8, 97 male *gurneyi*), 31-32 (female *ardens*), 28.9-36 (mean 32.5, SD 1.5, 115 female *gurneyi*), 25-37.2 (mean 33.0, SD 1.9, 94 unsexed *gurneyi*); **culmen to feather line** 25.8-31.9 (mean 28.9, SD 1.14, 62 male *gurneyi*), 25.2-30.6 (mean 27.7, SD 1.29, 80 female *gurneyi*); **tarsus** 19.6-26 (male *ardens*), 19.4-29.6 (mean 21.8, SD 1.13, 159 male *gurneyi*), 24 (female *ardens*), 17-31.7 (mean 20.9, SD 1.29, 195 female *gurneyi*), 17.4-23.1 (mean 20.9, SD 1.0, 94 unsexed *gurneyi*); **mass** 30-45 (mean 37.4, SD 2.63, 158 male *gurneyi*), 23-43 (mean 32.6, SD 3.8, 195 female *gurneyi*); 24.0-40.0 (mean 32.5, SD 4.0, 90 unsexed *gurneyi*).

REFERENCES Bennett *et al.* (1992), Bennett & de Swardt (1989), Craib (1981), Skead (1963, 1967), Steyn (1973), de Swardt (1989, 1990, 1991a, 1992a, 1997), de Swardt & Bothma (1992), de Swardt & Schoeman (1997), Tarboton *et al.* (1987), Wooler (1982).

---

2   CAPE SUGARBIRD
Promerops cafer   Plate 1

Merops cafer Linnaeus, 1758, *Syst. Nat.* ed.10, 1, p.117, Ethiopia; restricted to Cap de Bonne Espérance [= Cape of Good Hope] by Brisson, 1760, *Ornithologia*, 2, p.462.

Alternative names: Sugarbird, Long-tailed Sugarbird, Cape Long-tailed Sugarbird

IDENTIFICATION Dull brown with stout, decurved bill, warm brown chest, very long tail in male, yellow undertail-coverts, dull white belly with heavy black streaks and greenish-yellow rump. Crown may appear pale with dusting of pollen.

Similar species Gurney's Sugarbird *Promerops gurneyi* (1), from which *P. cafer* differs by lack of chestnut on crown, paler breast, heavier bill, longer tail and, especially, elongated tail of male. *P. cafer* is bolder and noisier. In poor light, a silhouette view of Malachite Sunbird *Nectarinia famosa* (97) could be mistaken for a sugarbird.

VOICE Call A loud *tcheenk, tcheenk*, soft, much-repeated

skidge, skidge, skwidge, skwidge or *skeedge, skeedge*, interspersed with *sit, wotty-geenkle* or *tcheekarik, rikkarik* and ending with drongo-like wheeze. Rhythmical repetitious *clack-clack-clack...* or *tsit-tsit-tsit...*, preceded by *tirry, tirry, tirry...* Various hissing sounds. Alarm call an excited *chick*, repeated irregularly and explosively a number of times, with an occasional *chiddy* interjected or a high-pitched *tweet-tweet-tweet*. Also a ratchet-like alarm call, especially during nesting, reminiscent of a rusty gate. Serious danger alerted by *sssssrrrr* or *sssrrr, sssrrr, sssrrr*. Subsong of male a creaking and clanging call, interjected by an occasional *chick* preceded and followed by *tip-tid-y-y-tid-y-y* or *tiddy-tiddy* with some notes recalling Fork-tailed Drongo *Dicrurus adsimilis*.
Song Characteristic and prolonged series of jumbled, jangling and churring notes, variously described as *tseedle wankle, tsee-weedle, eedle, eenkle; surdly, eedle-ee, yank; tseedle, eedle-ankle ankle, ee, sa, seedle-a, styonk; zeedle, tazinkel-zeenkel, zeenkle, zeenkle; zeenkle, eenkle-zeenkle; weenkle, eenkle*. May sing at night, especially when moonlit. Females also utter similar but quieter song. Breeding males use specialised wing feathers to produce a clacking sound during undulating display-flight.

DISTRIBUTION Endemic to the fynbos biome in the Cape Province of South Africa from the Cedarburg mountains to the Cape peninsula and east to Port Elizabeth and Grahamstown, straying as vagrant to Jagersfontein, southern Orange Free State, perhaps in response to drought. Range only overlaps with *gurneyi* in mountains above King William's Town, but recent data suggest complete allopatry.

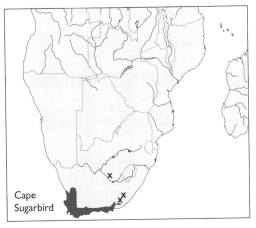

Cape
Sugarbird

HABITAT A bird of the fynbos, preferring stands of mature *Protea* which are in flower on mountain slopes and open ground. *Protea lacticolor* heath on Amatole mountains. Close to towns it moves into gardens by day, returning to *Protea* heaths to roost, and frequents botanical gardens. In Tsitsikamma area of the southern Cape, it occurs in dense mixed *Berzelia* and *Protea*. It also occurs in *Eucalyptus* and sisal plantations, and restionaceous tussock marsh with *Eucalyptus lehmanni*.

STATUS Common in suitable habitat (up to 4.1 birds per ha in tall sparse scrubland dominated by *Protea nitida*) but vulnerable to encroaching agriculture, water impoundment, urbanisation, invasions by alien plants such as *Hakea* sp. and *Pinus* sp. into preferred areas, and uncontrolled burning of *Protea* habitat.

131

MOVEMENTS Nomadic, moving from place to place with changing climate and in search of flowering *Protea* on upland heaths and *Leucospermum conocarpodendron* on coastal plains. Also move in response to burning, waiting for burnt areas to re-grow mature plants. Occupy breeding territories for only part of the year, returning to same sites to breed, except where rich food sources allow residence, e.g. in botanical gardens. One ringed bird travelled 160 km; other recoveries include movements of 10, 17 and 33 km. One bird seen at sea 45 kilometres SSW of Cape Point, South Africa, in May (J. Graham, pers. comm.).

FOOD Nectar, spiders and insects including small beetles and moths. Newly hatched chicks are fed regurgitated nectar, with insects added when a few days old. Different probing strategies used on different species of *Protea*, a genus for which they are important pollinators. May make up to 42 probes in a single flower of *Protea neriifolia* in anti-clockwise or clockwise rotations of it, whilst perched on top. Up to 3 birds may feed simultaneously on one *Protea neriifolia* flower. Hovers above Sisal flowers *Agave sisalana* and feeds whilst airborne. *P. cafer* is an efficient pollinator for *Mimetes hirtus*, brushing its head and throat against pollen-bearing parts and stigmata as it forages for nectar. The birds are particularly attracted to partially-opened inflorescences. Males probe from top into floral bracts of *Protea lepidocarpodendron* more often than females.
Known food-plants *Agave sisalana*, *Aloe* spp., *Erica* spp., *Eucalyptus* sp., *Eucalyptus lehmanni*, *Halleria lucida*, *Kniphofia* spp., *Kniphofia uvaria*, *Leonotis oxymifolia*, *Leucospermum* sp., *Leucospermum conocarpum*, *L. conocarpodendron*, *L. cordifolium*, *Mimetes fimbriifolius*, *M. hartogii*, *M. hirtus*, *Oldenburgia grandis*, *Protea aristata*, *P. aurea*, *P. barbigera*, *P. cynaroides*, *P. incompta*, *P. lacticolor*, *P. lepidocarpodendron*, *P. longifolia*, *P. multibracteata*, *P. neriifolia*, *P. repens* (= *P. mellifera*), *P. subvestita*, *Tecoma* sp., *Watsonia tubularis*.

HABITS Specialised brush-tipped tongue used for extracting nectar from flowers. Pollen becomes encrusted on crown and so sugarbirds act as important pollinators of *Protea* spp. May compete with Orange-breasted Sunbirds *Anthobaphes violacea* (72) for nectar. Probe into leaf-ends of *Protea* bushes, apparently to wipe bill clean of excess liquid. Also hawk up to 10 m above the ground for insects, in manner of flycatcher, from vantage point such as a silvertree *Leucadendron argenteum*, when insects caught in flight with audible snap. Larger prey taken back to perch and killed by being dashed against a branch with a quick sideways movement of the head in a bee-eater-like manner. Require food intake of 10-13 kJ per hour of daylight.

Both sexes roost together in lower branches of a *Protea* bush and have central meeting places and "play centres". Bathe in tops of *Protea* bushes after heavy rain.

Tend to hide amongst *Protea* for up to 15 minutes and then re-appear on top of *Protea* bush to sing or chase conspecifics. Flight strong and direct without the diversions so common in sunbirds; but, like sunbirds, faeces are ejected in a strong liquid jet. Longevity of a female up to 7 years 1 month. Host to feather lice *Philopterus turdi*.

BREEDING Form long-term monogamous pairs. Strongly territorial in breeding season and both sexes also occupy feeding territories in non-breeding season, when birds most aggressive early in the day. Males with longest tails most successful in attracting mates and females mated to longer-tailed males lay more eggs. However, such females do not provision young more than those mated with shorter-tailed males. Indeed provisioning rates of sexes within pairs positively correlated. Territory advertised with calls from prominent perch. Display-flight reaching up to 10 m above perch, with whipping of tail up and down over back, followed by undulating movements, when clacking noise (*frrrt-frrt-frrrt*) made by primary feathers or tail. Males repel intruders by flying straight towards site where intruder perched or feeding, perching in front of the site, singing excitedly and repeatedly flicking wings. Females occasionally join males in such defences. Frequency of male displays positively correlated with frequency of intrusions by strange males and increase during females' fertile periods. Females with nests "wing-quiver" by holding wings slightly above their backs and flapping or quivering them, an action sometimes also performed by males, perhaps as a displacement activity. Female disturbed from nest will adopt a drooping wing posture, and a pseudo-brooding posture occurs, with breast feathers expanded, when observer near nest. Hovers and chatters 2 m above potential mammal predators such as Small Grey Mongoose *Herpestes pulverulenta*.

Copulation resulting in fertile eggs may occur hidden amongst bushes as only copulations observed have been after egg-laying. These couplings were very conspicuous, occurring on tops of bushes or a *Leucadendron argenteum* tree within territories; they may have a social function such as pair-maintenance rather than a reproductive role. Nest built exclusively by female. Building may be very rapid: one completed in 3 days with complete clutch of 2 eggs 5 days later (Martin 1953). First egg laid in early morning 1-6 days after nest completion, second egg laid in afternoon. Incubation, by female, 17-18 days. Most feeds (76%) by female. Male also removes faeces, which are taken to a *Protea* bush latrine near edge of territory. Young probably fed nectar when very young; thereafter given insects (Coleoptera, Diptera, Hymenoptera, Lepidoptera, Neuroptera, Orthoptera) and spiders. Nestling period 17-21 days. Night brooding ceases after 11-16 days. Post-nestling period three weeks; then adults may chase young away. 56.5% of 46 nests unsuccessful. Nestling mortality 67%, attributable to rain, low temperatures, and attacks by Argentine ants *Iridomyrmex humilis*, snakes including Olive House Snake *Lamprophis ornatus* in stomach of which 2 young found, rodents, cats, Small Grey Mongoose, Fiscal Shrikes *Lanius collaris* and Southern Boubous *Laniarius ferrugineus*. After clutch failure, females alter behaviour from direct trajectories 1-2 m above ground, to undulating, conspicuous, flights for longer distances invariably followed by "mate-guarding" male. Once incubation re-starts such behaviour ceases but appears again 10 days after hatching. **Nest** An untidy cup 60-190 mm (mean 110) high, internal diameter 550-800 mm (mean 700), external diameter 100-180 mm (mean 135), internal depth 40-70 mm (mean 60). Made of dry heather twigs, sometimes including pliable springy grasses or bracken. Lining of brown *Protea* fluff and fibre-like plant stems including those of *Leptocarpus paniculatus*, *Thamnochortus fructicosus*, *Serruria* sp., *Helichrysum* sp. and unidentified Restionaceae. Placed in *Protea*, *Erica*, bracken, bramble, *Rhus* spp. and at least 12 other species including the silvertree *Leucadendron argenteum*, in which may be 30-240 cm or more up but mostly 90-160 cm high. Usually placed low (mean height of 90 nests 1.2 m above ground) in centre of bush for optimal shelter. Some nests very loosely constructed and fragile, others compact and sturdy.
Eggs c/1-2, rarely 3. Oval. Colour variable, sometimes in same clutch, ranging from a pale buff or coffee colour to

dull salmon-pink with overlay of dark brown and purple spots and scrawls. Occasionally with dense ring composed of fine lines, coarse lines and zig-zag markings of purplish-brown. 21.4-25.0 (mean 23.4, SD 1) x 16.5-20.7 (mean 17.5, SD 0.5). **Laying months** January to August and November, but mainly during April–May, sometimes linked to flowering of *Protea*. Double broods not infrequent and triple broods occasional.

DESCRIPTION

Adult male Forehead feathers stiff and bristly, light brown (fuscous) with feather edges pale warm buff, giving streaked appearance. Crown and cheeks dark brown, crown darker as feathers have black centres. Crown feathers lanceolate and sharp. Lores dark brown. Neck, mantle and back dark brown, streaked with black, occasionally brightish olive-green. Feathers have dark centres with light brown edges, becoming paler near rump. Rump yellowish-olive. Lesser and median wing-coverts as back. Primary and greater wing-coverts fuscous finely edged light buff. Primaries 4-6 with rounded bulges on innerwebs and heavy emarginations on narrow outerwebs. Tail blackish-brown, occasionally with greenish-olive edging to outerwebs, with elongated central feathers projecting 175-191 mm beyond rest of tail. Elongated feathers dark brown above and below. Remaining rectrices paler brown above and markedly so below, giving contrast with underside of elongated feathers. Moustachial stripes very dark brown, almost black. Malar streak pale buff, almost white. Chin and upper throat whitish-buff. Chest and breast light brown, sometimes mottled whitish and with darker, tawny, patches on sides of breast decreasing towards belly. Belly pale buff. Flanks light buff heavily streaked fuscous. Undertail-coverts bright yellow. Iris reddish-brown. Bill black. Legs dark brown. Feet black.
Adult female Smaller than male. Forehead and crown unicolorous dark brown; otherwise as male but lacks elongated tail.
Nestling Hatch with eyes closed. Body and head pale pink, legs and feet even paler. Gape pale yellow, bill paler yellow with black tip under egg-tooth. Culmen only slightly curved. Mouth pale pink, becoming brighter later. Claws yellow, becoming grey later. Body covered with long light-brown or grey down which remains on head for a few days after fledging. Feathers break through 11 days after hatching. Fledgling has dark grey back and down remaining on head. Breast-band indistinct and crown dark. Throat greyish with buff tinge at sides. Gape light yellow and obvious. Tail short and stubby.
Juvenile Greyer than adults, without brown wash on upper breast-band. Upperparts as adult female but tertials and wing-coverts edged with rich reddish-brown. Streaking less distinct. Primaries 4-6 lack bulges of adult. Tail short (56 mm). Upper chest darkish without clear demarcation of adult's chocolate chest. Lower chest pale pinkish-buff without dark centres to feathers. Flanks also lack dark-centred feathers. Base of lower mandible pale. Lacks yellow on vent.

Broekhuysen (1971) described an albino bird which was very light smoky-grey. Sides of head and neck darker. Bill and legs normal darkish colour, rump yellow.

GEOGRAPHICAL VARIATION None.

MEASUREMENTS Wing 88-98 (mean 91.4, SD 2.99, 30 males), 76-84 (mean 82.3, SD 3.10, 28 females); **tail** 109-380 (mean 195.3, SD 76.3, 9 males), 82-160 (mean 104.3,

SD 20.25, 6 females); **bill** 37-44 (mean, 39.3, SD 2.6, 7 males), 31-39 (mean 34.7, SD 2.87, 7 females), 30-36 (unsexed); **culmen** (tip to feathers) mean 31.0, SD 1.0 (27 males), mean 29.9, SD 1.0 (18 females); **tarsus** 22.3-26 (mean 24.5, SD 1.3, 9 males), 24-28 (mean 25.4, SD 1.6, 7 females), 21-24 (unsexed); **mass** mean 36.8, SD 2.2 (25 males), mean 37.5 (57 males), mean 31.8, SD 1.9 (21 females), mean 31.5 (40 females), 36.5 (unsexed), 2.9-4.8 (mean 3.6, hatchlings), 28.3-30.3 (fledglings).

REFERENCES Broekhuysen (1959, 1971), Burger *et al.* (1976), Collins (1983a,b,c), Fraser (1997d), Fraser *et al.* (1989), Fraser & McMahon (1992), Henderson & Cherry (1998), Martin (1953), Martin & Mortimer (1991), Mostert *et al.* (1980), Rebelo (1987b), Seiler & Fraser (1985), Seiler & Prys-Jones (1989), Seiler & Rebelo (1987), Skead (1967), Steyn (1997), de Swardt & Buys (1992), Winterbottom, (1962, 1964).

Subfamily Nectariniinae
Tribe Dicaeini

FLOWERPECKERS
PRIONOCHILUS

Prionochilus Strickland, 1841, *Proc. Zool. Soc. London* 9, p.29, type, by subsequent designation, *Pardalotus percussus* Temminck and Laugier (G. R. Gray, 1841, *List Gen. Birds*, ed.2, p.46).
Chalritociris Oberholser 1923 *Ohio Journ. Sci.*, 23: 239. Type by original designation *Pardalotus percussus* Temminck and Laugier.
Not preoccupied by *Prionocheilus* Chevrolat, 1837, Coleoptera.

Six species, three occurring in the Philippines only, one endemic to Borneo, and two in South-East Asia and the Greater Sundas. All small with short, rounded tails and ten long primaries. Bill short, broad and deep, edges finely serrated. Tongue triangular, and slightly concave in cross-section; distal 20% of tongue cleft, and each side cleft again for distal 10%. Slight fimbriations on outer edges of tongue. Berries, particularly those of Loranthaceae, play an important part in diet. These have a laxative effect, and as they by-pass the blind-ending stomach which is closed by sphincter, pass rapidly through the digestive tract. Nests pendant and domed, like those of sunbirds and *Dicaeum*.

3   OLIVE-BACKED FLOWERPECKER
Prionochilus olivaceus   Plate 2

Prionochilus olivaceus Tweeddale, 1877, *Ann. Mag. Nat. Hist.* (4) 20, p.536, Dinagat, Philippine Islands.

IDENTIFICATION Sexes similar. Golden-olive above, with blackish-brown primaries and tail. Juvenile more olive and yellow below.
Similar species None.

VOICE High *tsoo-eet*, second note rising, and a high rattling trill.

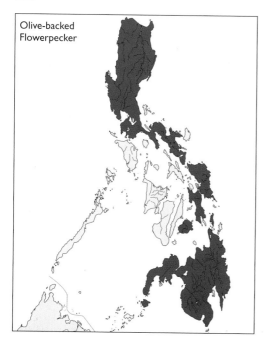

Olive-backed Flowerpecker

DISTRIBUTION Endemic to Philippines (Luzon, Basilan, Dinagat, Mindanao, Leyte, Samar and Bohol).

HABITAT Uncommon in flowering and fruiting trees, in forests, at forest edge and in secondary growth, usually below 1,000 m.

STATUS Uncommon.

MOVEMENTS Unknown.

FOOD Nothing recorded, but presumably includes fruit, and possibly also nectar and/or pollen, of mistletoes.
Known food-plants None.

HABITS Occurs singly or in mixed flocks; other habits unknown.

BREEDING Nest Unknown. **Eggs** Unknown. **Laying months** August in Basilan, probably earlier in Samar.

DESCRIPTION *P. o. parsoni*
Adult Upperparts golden-olive; tail and primaries blackish-brown edged olive; lores and sides of throat and breast black streaked white on lower flanks; loral spot white; vent, undertail-coverts and centre of chin to belly white. Iris brick-red; bill and feet black.
Juvenile Chest grey tinged olive; loral spot greyish; central white streak below has olive-grey tinge, yellowish on belly; bill pale brown.

GEOGRAPHICAL VARIATION
P. o. olivaceus Tweeddale, 1877 (Basilan, Dinagat and Mindanao) Differs from *parsoni* by having sides of face, throat and breast pale olive-grey.
P. o. parsoni McGregor, 1927 (Luzon in the Sierra Madre Mts., Isabela, Mt Sicapo-o, Sablan, Pangil, Matnog and Mt Isarog; Catanduanes) Described above.
P. o. samarensis Steere, 1890 (Leyte, Samar and Bulusan Lake, Sorsogon Province, Luzon; possibly Bohol) Differs from *olivaceus* by having sides of breast browner, tending to streak at posterior end; probably not valid and should perhaps be included in *olivaceus*.

MEASUREMENTS Wing 51-58 (male *parsoni*), 51-60

(female *parsoni*); **tail** 28 (unsexed *parsoni*); **bill** 9.6-11.3 (mean 10.6, SD 0.64, 5 male *parsoni*), 10.0, 10.7, 10.9 (3 female *parsoni*); **gape** 9.6-10.7 (male *parsoni*), 10.4-11.5 (female *parsoni*); **tarsus** 14 (unsexed *parsoni*); **mass** no data.

REFERENCES Bourns & Worcester (1909-1910), Dickinson *et al.* (1991), duPont (1971), McGregor (1927), Salomonsen (1960a).

---

4 YELLOW-BREASTED FLOWERPECKER
Prionochilus maculatus   Plate 2

Pardalotus maculatus Temminck & Laugier, 1836, *Pl. Col., Livr.* 101, pl.600, fig.3, Borneo.

Alternative name: Yellow-throated Flowerpecker

IDENTIFICATION Olive-green above with orange crown-patch and black tip to tail; underparts yellow streaked olive-green; whitish moustachial stripe; greenish-olive malar stripe. Juvenile duller, with no streaking or orange on crown.
Similar species Brown-backed Flowerpecker *Dicaeum everetti* (11) and Thick-billed Flowerpecker *D. agile* (10) are brown above with much less obvious brown streaking below; Yellow-vented Flowerpecker *D. chrysorrheum* (13) has bright yellow undertail-coverts, and all three lack orange crown-patch.

VOICE Harsh, metallic chittering calls and a high-pitched *tswik*.

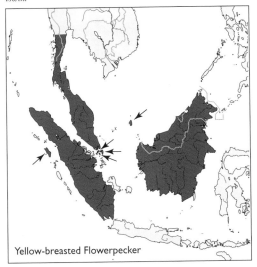

Yellow-breasted Flowerpecker

DISTRIBUTION The Malay Peninsula, Thailand, Sumatra (including Nias and Riau), North Natunas and Borneo.

HABITAT Lowlands and hills up to 1,500 m in the middle and lower storeys of lowland and hill dipterocarp, alluvial, peatswamp and secondary forests, forest edge, scrub, old rubber, *Albizia* plantations and cultivation.

STATUS Not uncommon in Borneo and Sumatra; uncommon Thailand.

MOVEMENTS Unknown.

FOOD Berries, nectar and/or pollen of mistletoes.
Known food-plants None.

HABITS Forages at all levels in forest, and frequently found close to ground. Usually in pairs, or solitary. Host to *Haemoproteus dicaeus*, *Leucocytozoon* sp. and microfilariae.

BREEDING Nest Undescribed. **Eggs** c/2. Undescribed. **Laying months** Sumatra: Belitung, March; Borneo: Kalimantan Tengah, Tanjung Puting National Park, juveniles May and August, Sabah, enlarged gonads February, April, May–July.

DESCRIPTION *P. m. maculatus*
Adult Sexes similar. Head dark olive-green with orange patch on crown; tail dark with black tip; rest of upperparts olive-green; malar stripe greenish-olive; moustachial stripe and throat white, lores paler, rest of underparts yellow broadly streaked olive-green, with less streaking on brighter yellow centre of abdomen. Iris red; bill black, lower mandible black or bluish-grey, paler at base of lower mandible, legs and feet grey.
Juvenile Upperparts dull greenish-olive; underparts dull greyish-olive with yellowish centre to belly; no orange on centre of crown; bill pale.

GEOGRAPHICAL VARIATION
P. m. maculatus (Temminck & Laugier, 1836) (includes *opistatus*) (throughout mainland Sumatra, except Riau; Borneo) Described above.
P. m. natunensis (Chasen, 1935) (North Natunas) From *maculatus* by brighter and yellower underparts, with dark markings more olive and less grey; throat more washed with yellow.
P. m. oblitus (Mayr, 1938) (rest of Malay Peninsula, including Penang and Singapore) From *maculatus* by larger size, longer tail; upper throat white or whitish, not yellow; forehead grey; upperparts darker and less citrine, particularly crown and uppertail-coverts; ear-coverts, malar stripe and streaks on sides of breast and flanks greenish or greyish-green, not olive; smaller orange crown-patch.
P. m. septentrionalis Robinson & Kloss, 1921 (north Malay Peninsula south to Trang, Pattani and Narathiwat) Both sexes differ from *oblitus* in having much greyer ear-coverts, with little or no green wash; white throat-stripe narrower; underparts much brighter yellow, almost orange-chrome in middle of breast; from *maculatus* by smaller orange crown-patch.

MEASUREMENTS Wing 51-53 (mean 52, 4 male *maculatus*, Brunei), 51-52 (male *natunensis*), 51-56 (mean 53.7, 3 male *oblitus*), 50-55 (mean 53, SD 1.63, 7 male *septentrionalis*), 50-54 (female *maculatus*), 51 (female *natunensis*), 52, 54 (2 female *oblitus*), 51-52 (mean 51.7, SD 0.5, 4 female *septentrionalis*), 49-57 (mean 53.1, 14 unsexed *maculatus*, Brunei); **bill** 11.2-12.5 (mean 11.8, SD 0.47, 6 male *septentrionalis*), 10.5-12.3 (mean 11.8, SD 0.87, 4 female *septentrionalis*), 11.6-12.1 (unsexed *maculatus*); **gape** 11.6-12.4 (male *maculatus*), 10.5-12.6 (female *maculatus*), 12 (male *natunensis*), 11-15 mm (mean 13.5, 14 unsexed *maculatus*); **mass** 7.5-7.9 (mean 7.6, 4 male *maculatus*, Brunei), 6.6-8.9 (mean 7.7, 14 unsexed *maculatus*, Brunei), 7.7-11.8 (mean 9.1, 3 male *oblitus*), 7.8, 7.9 (2 female *oblitus*).

REFERENCES Chasen (1934), Danielsen & Heegaard (1995), King *et al.* (1975), MacKinnon & Phillipps (1993),

Mann (1996, in prep. a,b), van Marle & Voous (1988), Medway (1972), Medway & Wells (1976), Nash & Nash (1988), Sheldon *et al.* (in press), Smythies (1957, 1981), Verheugt *et al.* (1993).

5 CRIMSON-BREASTED FLOWERPECKER
Prionochilus percussus   Plate 3

Pardalotus percussus Temminck & Laugier, 1826, *Pl. Col., Livr.* 66, pl. 394, fig.2, Java

IDENTIFICATION Male slaty-blue above with scarlet crown-patch; below bright yellow with red patch on breast, and white moustachial stripe bordered black. Female is olive-green above with orange crown-patch; below mostly greyish-olive.

Similar species Yellow-rumped Flowerpecker *Prionochilus xanthopygius* (7) (on Borneo only) has a yellow rump; Palawan Flowerpecker *P. plateni* (6) is allopatric, occurring on the Philippines only; Scarlet-breasted Flowerpecker *P. thoracicus* (8) has yellowish uppertail-coverts, black tail and white undertail-coverts; male Fire-breasted Flowerpecker *Dicaeum ignipectum* (40) has underparts rich buff, not yellow, and black below red patch on breast, whereas female has yellowish rump, lacks white malar stripe and has buff rather than greyish-olive and yellow underparts. Female from female Black-sided Flowerpecker *D. monticolum* (41) by whitish malar stripe and yellow centre of belly, not cream. Male differs from male Blood-breasted Flowerpecker *D. sanguinolentum* (43) by lack of black patch along centre of belly, whereas female differs from female of that species by lacking red rump.

VOICE Female call *see-sik*, fast at times.

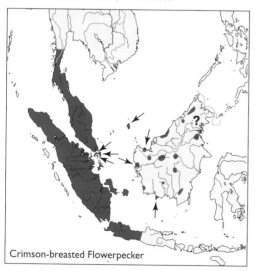

Crimson-breasted Flowerpecker

DISTRIBUTION The Malay Peninsula (including peninsular Burma, and from 10°30'N in peninsular Thailand), mainland Sumatra (rare, but present in Bukit Barisan Selatan National Park; recorded Riau and Lingga Archipelagos) and east coast islands, Borneo (rare), North Natunas and West Java.

HABITAT The lower and middle storeys (upper of secondary forest) and occasionally canopy of lowland dipterocarp forest, alluvial forest, peatswamp forest, lower montane forest and secondary forest; mangroves, scrub and old plantations; up to 1,065 m.

STATUS Rare on mainland Sumatra and Borneo, uncommon Thailand. Barito Ulu, Kalimantan Tengah: commoner at higher altitudes; in Borneo not usually found with *P. xanthopygius*, which is by far the commoner. Probably rare on Java.

MOVEMENTS Unknown.

FOOD Presumably includes fruit, and possibly also nectar and/or pollen, of mistletoes.
Known food-plants None.

HABITS Occurs in all storeys of primary forests, but in upper storey of secondary forest. Host to *Haemoproteus dicaeus, Leucocytozoon* sp., *Trypanosoma* sp. and microfilariae.

BREEDING Nest Unknown. **Eggs** c/1; *ignicapillus*: white 12.5-13.1 x 9.7-10.0; *percussus*: elongate-oval, white with purplish-brown spots forming cap 14.8-16.4 x 11.2-11.6 (mean 15.9 x 11.2). **Laying months** Borneo, Sarawak, Kuching, April, dependent young, Burito Ulu, July, Kalimantan Tengah, Tanjung Puting National Park, July. Juveniles Pasoh, Malay Peninsula, early May; Ketambe, Aceh, late August; Bukit Lawang, Sumatra Utara, late April; Krui, Lampung, Sumatra, May–June.

DESCRIPTION *P. p. ignicapillus*
Adult male Upperparts are slaty-blue with black forehead; scarlet patch on crown; white moustachial stripe with blackish border below; underparts bright yellow with red patch in centre of breast. Flanks dark grey; underwing-coverts and pectoral tufts white; remiges edged pale blue. Iris brown or orange-brown; bill black, basal half of lower mandible pale; legs and feet black or bluish.
Adult female Upperparts are olive-green; dull orange crown-patch; whitish malar stripe; pale greyish throat, sometimes with yellowish tinge; underparts greyish-olive, yellow on centre, and whitish undertail-coverts.
Juvenile Upperparts dull greenish-olive; underparts dull olive-grey, whitish in centre of belly.

GEOGRAPHICAL VARIATION
> *P. p. ignicapillus* (Eyton, 1839) (Malay Peninsula, Sumatra except Batu Island, and Borneo) Described above.
> *P. p. percussus* (Temminck & Laugier, 1826) (Java) Male has more extensive red on chest, and is deeper yellow than *ignicapillus*.
> *P. p. regulus* (Meyer de Schauensee, 1940) (Batu Island, Sumatra) Male from *ignicapillus* by entire dorsal surface being paler, red crown-spot much smaller, entire lower surface more greenish-yellow and chest-streak deep orange and not scarlet; female differs in having lower surface much duller, yellow spot on centre of breast not brighter than yellow on centre of abdomen.

MEASUREMENTS Wing 51-58 (male *ignicapillus*), 56 (male *regulus*), 47-54 (female *ignicapillus*), 51.5, 52 (2 female *regulus*); **bill** 10.0-12.5 (male *ignicapillus*), 10.2-10.9 (female *ignicapillus*); **culmen** 9 (male *regulus*), 8-8.5 (2 female *regulus*); **gape** 10.7-12.0 (male *ignicapillus*), 10.5-11.1 (female *ignicapillus*).

136

REFERENCES Baker (1934), Bennett & Bishop (1991), Hellebrekers & Hoogerwerf (1967), Holmes (1996), King *et al.* (1975), MacKinnon & Phillips (1993), Mann (in prep. b), van Marle & Voous (1988), Medway & Wells (1976), Meyer de Schauensee (1940), Nash & Nash (1988), Smythies (1957, 1960, 1981), Verheugt *et al.* (1993), Wilkinson *et al.* (1991).

6   PALAWAN FLOWERPECKER
Prionochilus plateni   Plate 3

Prionochilus Plateni Blasius, 1888, *Braunschweigische Anzeigen* 37, p.336, Puerto Princesa, Palawan.

IDENTIFICATION Adult male blue-black above with red crown-patch and yellow rump; white malar stripe and chin; below yellow with red patch on breast. Adult female olive-green above with yellowish crown and rump; yellowish below with white malar stripe, chin and throat; sides of chest and flanks grey. Juvenile as female but lacks malar stripe, greyer below, bill pale at base.
Similar species Female Bicoloured Flowerpecker *Dicaeum bicolor* (19) from female of this species by grey underparts washed olive, not yellowish, and greenish rump, not yellowish; male from both sexes of Red-striped Flowerpecker *D. australe* (21) by yellow rump, not black glossed blue, and yellow on underparts, not grey; male from both sexes of Pygmy Flowerpecker *D. pygmaeum* (28) by red below. The very similar Crimson-breasted Flowerpecker *Prionochilus percussus* (5) and Yellow-rumped Flowerpecker *P. xanthopygius* (7) are allopatric.

VOICE Unknown.

DISTRIBUTION Endemic to south-west Philippines,

Palawan
Flowerpecker

occurring on Balabac, Palawan, Culion, Busuanga and Calauit.

HABITAT Flowering and fruiting trees in forest, secondary growth and gardens.

STATUS Common.

MOVEMENTS Unknown.

FOOD Presumably includes fruit, and possibly also nectar, and/or pollen, of mistletoes.
Known food-plants None.

HABITS Occurs singly or in mixed flocks; other habits unknown. Host to *Haemoproteus dicaeus.*

BREEDING Nest Unknown. **Eggs** Unknown. **Laying months** Male in breeding condition August.

DESCRIPTION *P. p. plateni*
Adult male Upperparts dark greyish-blue, centre of crown red, rump yellow; chin and malar stripe white separated by greyish-blue line; throat, breast and belly yellow; red patch in middle of breast. Iris dark brown; bill black, base of lower mandible grey; feet black.
Adult female Upperparts olive-green; centre of crown and rump yellowish; malar stripe whitish separated from whitish chin and throat by grey; sides of neck and flanks grey; rest of underparts yellowish.
Juvenile As adult female but without white malar stripe; much greyer below with almost no yellow; pale base to bill.

GEOGRAPHICAL VARIATION
  P. p. culionensis (Rand, 1948) (Busuanga, Culion, Calauit and Calamianes) Male differs from *plateni* in having underparts and rump more orange-yellow, less clear yellow; red pectoral spot larger; white malar stripe smaller. Female is deeper yellow below with greater tendency towards an orange pectoral spot. Slightly smaller on average.
  P. p. plateni Blasius, 1888 (Balabac and Palawan) Described above.

MEASUREMENTS Wing 52-56 (mean 54, SD 1.41, 6 male *plateni*), 50-53 (mean 51, SD 1.05, 10 female *plateni*), 50-58 (unsexed); **tail** 23-29 (unsexed); **bill** 11.4-12.5 (males), 11.3-12.7 (females), 10-12 (unsexed); **gape** 11.2-12.4 (males), 11.6-12.5 (females); tarsus 13-16 (unsexed); **mass** 8-9 (8 unsexed).

REFERENCES Blasius (1888), Dickinson *et al.* (1991), duPont (1971), Hartley & McGowan (1991).

7   YELLOW-RUMPED FLOWERPECKER
Prionochilus xanthopygius   Plate 3

Prionochilus xanthopygius Salvadori, 1868, *Atti R. Accad. Sci. Torino*, 3, p.416, Sarawak, Borneo.

IDENTIFICATION Adult male slaty-blue above with red crown-patch and yellow rump; underparts yellow with orange breast-patch. Adult female olive-grey above with dull orange crown-patch and yellow rump; chin and throat whitish; sides of face grey; flanks olive-grey; rest of underparts yellow, more orange on upper breast. Juvenile is greyer than female with pale bill.

Similar species Male differs from male Crimson-breasted Flowerpecker *Prionochilus percussus* (5) in lacking black on head and a malar stripe but having a yellow rump and a smaller red patch on breast; female differs from female of that species by lacking malar stripe, being olive-grey, not greenish, above, and having a yellowish rump; from female Scarlet-breasted Flowerpecker *P. thoracicus* (8) by being smaller and duller, and has white not yellowish undertail-coverts; female from female Black-sided Flowerpecker *Dicaeum monticolum* (41) by yellowish centre of belly, not creamy. Allopatric to Palawan Flowerpecker *P. plateni* (6).

VOICE High-pitched chittering calls in flight, similar to many other flowerpeckers. *Tsee-oo*, with first note rising, second on level tone. *Ship-ship* or *ship-ship-ship. Tsik-tsik*, which may become fast. Fast descending series of 7-9 staccato notes on same pitch.

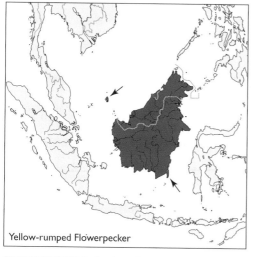

Yellow-rumped Flowerpecker

DISTRIBUTION Endemic to Borneo, where it is widespread and common; once recorded on Bungarun Island, North Natunas.

HABITAT Lowland and hill dipterocarp forests, peat-swamp forest, heath forest and secondary forest, at forest edge and in clearings, *Albizia*, cocoa plantations, overgrown rubber; lowlands to 1,760 m.

STATUS Common and widespread in Borneo.

MOVEMENTS Unknown.

FOOD Flowers, pollen, stamens, nectar, ripe fruit pulp, buds, tiny beetles and spiders; possibly mistletoes.
Known food-plants *Eugenia* sp., *Lantana* sp., *Psidium* spp., *Trema orientalis.*

HABITS Found at all heights in vegetation, frequently close to ground. Restless and active, as other flowerpeckers.

BREEDING Nest Unknown. **Eggs** Reddish-white background flecked with red and grey to purple marks; 14.6-16.7 (mean 15.9) x 11.3-12.3 (mean 11.8). **Laying months** Sabah: enlarged gonads February–April, June, July, September; Penampang River, juveniles August; Barito Ulu, Kalimantan Tengah, July and August; adult collecting nest material Sungai Kinabatangan, February; Sarawak: male fledgling October 1893, 1,300 m up Mt Mulu.

DESCRIPTION
Adult male Slaty-blue head, back, wings and tail; red patch on crown; orange patch on upper breast; rump and rest of underparts yellow. Flanks olive and grey; white underwing-coverts and pectoral tufts; undertail-coverts yellowish-white. Iris brown; bill black, feet black.
Adult female Blue-grey crown, with very small dull orange-red patch; back greeny-olive with yellow rump; throat whitish; sides of face grey; flanks olive-grey; rest of underparts yellow, some orange on upper breast, and undertail-coverts whitish.
Juvenile As adult female, but more bluish-grey above and bill pale; much greyer below with almost no yellow; uppertail-coverts olive, and yellow of rump less distinct; wings and tail blackish-brown, former edged blue-grey. Bill pale.

GEOGRAPHICAL VARIATION None.

MEASUREMENTS Wing 48-58 (mean 54.1, 24 males), 49-53 (mean 50.8, 7 females), 48-54 (mean 51.4, 8 unsexed juveniles); **bill** 9.5-10.9 (mean 10.1, SD 0.61, 6 males), 9.7-11.6 (mean 10.4, SD 0.75, 6 females); **gape** 9.5-14.1 (mean 11.5, 15 males), 10.5-12.5 (mean 11.3, 9 females), 11.2-12.4 (mean 11.7, 6 unsexed juveniles); **mass** 6.5-8.6 (mean 7.7, 24 males), 6.9-8.6 (mean 7.5, 8 females), 6.5-8.2 (mean 7.6, 8 unsexed juveniles).

REFERENCES MacKinnon & Phillipps (1993), Mann (1996, in prep.), Nash & Nash (1988), C. R. Robson (*in litt.*), Salomonsen (1960a), Sheldon *et al.* (in press), Schönwetter (1980-1984), Smythies (1957, 1960, 1981).

8 SCARLET-BREASTED FLOWERPECKER
Prionochilus thoracicus   Plate 2

Pardalotus thoracicus Temminck & Laugier, 1836, *Pl. Col., Livr.* 101, Pl. 600, figs. 1-2, Borneo.

IDENTIFICATION Adult male has black head with red crown-patch; tail and wings mostly black; back and mantle green, rump and uppertail-coverts yellow; below red and yellow; yellow on upperparts conspicuous in flight. Adult female is olive-green above, with greyish head, yellowish uppertail-coverts and black tail; below greyish, olive and yellow, with orange-yellow on breast. Juvenile is greyer than female with pale base to bill.
Similar species Female from female Crimson-breasted Flowerpecker *Prionochilus percussus* (5) by white throat, yellowish rump, black tail, and yellow undertail-coverts; female is larger and brighter than female Yellow-rumped Flowerpecker *P. xanthopygius* (7) and has yellow undertail-coverts; female from female Fire-breasted Flowerpecker *Dicaeum ignipectum* (40) and Black-sided Flowerpecker *D. monticolum* (41) by orange and yellow on underparts; female from Orange-bellied Flowerpecker *D. trigonostigma* (24) by black tail and yellowish (not orange-yellow or orange) uppertail-coverts and rump.

VOICE Metallic, clicking twitter. Very high-pitched insect-like series of about 6 *seek* notes. Harsh *chink*.

DISTRIBUTION Southern Vietnam, the Malay Peninsula, Sumatra (rare – Aceh, Lampung, Utara, Riau, Lingga Archipelago and Belitung) and Borneo.

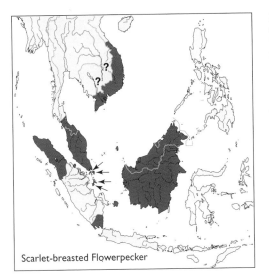
Scarlet-breasted Flowerpecker

BREEDING Nest In low bush. **Eggs** Unknown. **Laying months** Malay Peninsula: juveniles, January and August to October; Borneo: Sabah, enlarged testes March; Kalimantan Tengah, Tanjung Puting National Park, July. Recently fledged young, Barito Ulu, July, August and September. Sumatra: Belitung, young in nest January.

DESCRIPTION
Adult male Head black, with small red patch on crown; back and mantle green; lesser wing-coverts, rump and uppertail-coverts yellow, rest of wings and tail black; throat and breast red, belly and undertail-coverts yellow. Iris brown. Bill dark brown to black; legs dark slate.
Adult female Head greyish, with or without dull olive-yellow patch on crown; rest of upperparts olive-green; yellowish uppertail-coverts, tail black; sides of face grey, throat pale grey; orange-yellow breast-patch; rest of underparts greyish-olive, with extensive area of yellow on belly and undertail-coverts.
Juvenile As female, but greyer below; base of bill pale. Young males show some yellow and red on breast, and occasionally tiny amount of red on crown.

GEOGRAPHICAL VARIATION None known, but there is the possibility of an undescribed subspecies on Riau Archipelago, Sumatra.

MEASUREMENTS Wing 58-66 (mean 61.1, SD 2.51, 10 males), 47-57 (mean 52.1, SD 4.14, 7 females), 49-61 (unsexed); **tail** 24-32; **bill** 10.3-11.9 (mean 10.9, SD 0.68, 10 males), 9.2-10.9 (mean 9.8, SD 0.63, 7 females); **gape** 10.1-12.0 (males), 9.7-11.3 (females), 11-13 (unsexed); **tarsus** 12.5-16 (unsexed); **mass** 8.9 (male).

REFERENCES Holmes (1996), King *et al.* (1975), MacKinnon & Phillipps (1983), Mann (1996, in prep. b), van Marle & Voous (1988), Medway & Wells (1976), Nash & Nash (1988), Parrott & Andrew (1996), Rajathurai (1996), Sheldon *et al.* (in press), Smythies (1957, 1960, 1981), Wilkinson *et al.* (1991).

HABITAT Lowlands up to 1,280 m, in peatswamp forest, heath forest and secondary forest, at forest edge, in *Casuarina* groves, beach vegetation and rubber plantations. Upland forest on ultrabasic soil, fire-padang *kerangas*.

STATUS Uncommon in lowlands of Borneo; rare resident in Sumatra and uncommon in Thailand.

MOVEMENTS Possibly nomadic in some areas.

FOOD Insects, spiders, berries and possibly pollen. **Known food-plants** *Eugenia* sp., unidentified mistletoes Loranthaceae.

HABITS Sometimes behaves like nuthatch *Sitta* sp., climbing on tree-trunks. Forages at all heights. Takes insects from spiders' webs and tree-trunks.

DICAEUM

Dicaeum Cuvier 1817, *Règne Animale* 1: 410.
Type by subsequent designation (G. R. Gray, 1840, *List Gen. Birds* ed.1, p.13), *Certhia erythronotum* Gmelin – *Certhia erythronotus* Latham – *Certhia cruentata* Linnaeus.
Pachyglossa 'Hodgson' = Blyth 1843, *Jour. Asiat. Soc. Bengal* 12: 1009. Type by monotypy, *P. melanozantha* Blyth.
Piprisoma Blyth, 1844 *Jour. Asiat. Soc. Bengal* 13: 394. Type by monotypy *Fringilla agilis* Tickell.
Acmonorhynchus Oates, 1890, *Fauna Brit. Ind., Bds.* 2: 381. Type by monotypy, *Prionochilus vincens* Sclater.
Salomonsen (1960b,c, 1961) placed all species of flowerpecker, with the exception of the 6 species assigned to *Prionochilus*, in the genus *Dicaeum*. The present work accepts 38 species, occurring in tropical Asia, Wallacea, the New Guinea region and Australia.

This genus is not well defined, as there is no single character, or combination of characters, that can be used to separate all members of this genus from *Prionochilus*. Similar in nesting, digestive tract structure and overall morphology to *Prionochilus*, but the outermost primary is short, except in *D. melanoxanthum*. Bill is short and triangular, of variable thickness and curvature, with finely serrated edges; nostrils exposed, but partly covered by a membrane; rictal bristles short.
Tongue structure is highly variable, and since spirit specimens are required, only those species where these exist have been examined. On tongue structure, *Dicaeum* can be divided into four groups. Species in Group 1 (*agile, bicolor, celebicum, aureolimbatum*) (Figure 5e), have broad, flat, non-tubular tongues similar to *Prionochilus* (Figure 5a). Species in Group 2 (*melanoxanthum, australe, hypoleucum*) have narrow to medium broad flat tongues with the sides towards the distal end rolled inwards to form tubes, some with a small amount of fimbriations (Figure 5f). Group 3 contains only one species, *nigrilore*, which has a long, narrow tongue, with tip bifid and the centre further divided, resulting in the tip

becoming four flat ribbons, much fimbriated at their edges (Figure 5g). Those in Group 4 (*trigonostigma, erythrothorax, sanguinolentum, pygmaeum, aeneum, cruentatum*) have long narrow tongues, forming two tubes distally, with few or no fimbriations (Figure 5b); one specimen of *trigonostigma* has 2 extra lateral ribbon-like extensions. Tongue and bill forms are obviously adaptive, and presumably polygenic. Tongue shape would also be under the 'environmental' influence of the bill shape, hence a narrow bill would result in a narrow tongue. It is probable that *Dicaeum*, as presently constituted, does not form a monophyletic group (Mann in prep. a), and a comprehensive revision is required.

9 GOLDEN-RUMPED FLOWERPECKER
Dicaeum annae   Plate 4

Acmonorhynchus annae Büttikofer, 1894, in Weber, *Reise Niederl. Ost-Ind.*, 3, p.301, Pl.18, fig. 4, Flores, Lesser Sunda Islands.

IDENTIFICATION Adult is olive-green above with yellow rump (latter lacking in female); white throat and malar stripe; rest of underparts pale yellowish streaked olive-grey. Juvenile like female but greyer, with less distinct malar stripe; bill pale.
Similar species None.

VOICE Series of thin *see* notes on same pitch with last three notes longer and more widely spaced.

DISTRIBUTION Endemic to Sumbawa and Flores, Lesser Sundas Islands.

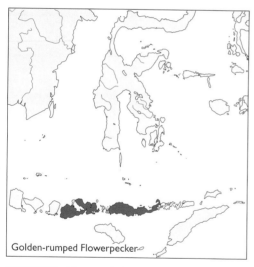
Golden-rumped Flowerpecker

HABITAT Deciduous and degraded forest, woodland and cultivation. Occurs from sea-level to 1,530 m on Sumbawa, and to 1,800 m on Flores.

STATUS Locally common, but also locally uncommon or rare; most frequent in closed canopy semi-evergreen forest.

MOVEMENTS Unknown.

FOOD Presumably includes fruit, and possibly also nectar and/or pollen, of mistletoes.
Known food-plants None.

HABITS Occur singly, in pairs or in groups.

BREEDING No information.

DESCRIPTION *D. a. annae*
Adult male Upperparts are olive-green, rump yellow; throat and malar stripe white; rest of underparts pale yellowish streaked olive-grey; white pectoral tufts. Bill and feet blackish; iris unrecorded, probably brown.
Adult female Similar to male but lacks yellow rump.
Juvenile As female, but throat and belly greyer, malar stripe less distinct; bill paler, especially lower mandible.

GEOGRAPHICAL VARIATION
D. a. annae (Büttikofer, 1894) (Flores) Described above.
D. a. sumbavense Rensch, 1931 (Sumbawa) Slightly smaller than nominate and slightly more olive above, tips of flight feathers duller and less green. This form is doubtfully separable.

MEASUREMENTS Wing 56-63 (male *annae*), 55-57 (male *sumbavense*), 55-57 (female *annae*), 54-56 (female *sumbavense*); **bill** 10.5, 11.2 (2 female *annae*); **gape** 10.4-12.6 (male *annae*), 11.5-12.5 (female *annae*), 10.4-11.6 (3 male *annae*); **mass** 10.3 (female *annae*), 9.7 (unsexed *sumbavense*).

REFERENCES Butchart *et al.* (1993), Büttikofer (1894), Coates & Bishop (1997), Salomonsen (1960b), White & Bruce (1986).

10 THICK-BILLED FLOWERPECKER
Dicaeum agile   Plate 4

Fringilla Agilis Tickell, 1833, *Journ. Asiat. Soc. Bengal*, 2, p.578, Borabhúm and Dolbhúm, Bengal.

Alternative name: Striped Flowerpecker (Philippine forms)

IDENTIFICATION Rather nondescript, with a thick bill. Adult is mostly grey-brown above with olive tinge, or greenish-brown above; underparts mostly buffy with indistinct to distinct dark streaking; variable amounts of white on tips of underside of outer tail feathers. Juvenile differs in being washed yellow below and has less streaking. Wags tail from side to side.
Similar species From Yellow-breasted Flowerpecker *Prionochilus maculatus* (4) by lack of heavy olive-green streaking below; Brown-backed Flowerpecker *Dicaeum everetti* (11) is browner, lacks streaking below and white tips to tail, and has a thicker bill; Buzzing Flowerpecker *D. hypoleucum* (25) and Plain Flowerpecker *D. concolor* (27) have much finer bills, and lack streaking below. From female Yellow-bellied Flowerpecker *D. melanoxanthum* (14) by lack of yellow on belly and undertail-coverts; from female White-throated Flowerpecker *D. vincens* (15) by lack of pale yellow on belly. Pale-billed Flowerpecker *D. erythrorhynchos* (26) has a pale bill and no streaking below; female Fire-breasted Flowerpecker *D. ignipectum* (40) is green above with a yellowish rump.

140

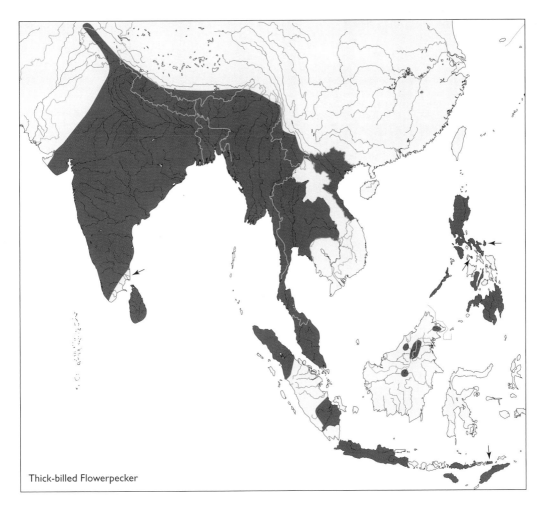

Thick-billed Flowerpecker

VOICE Call Loud, sharp *chik-chik-chik-chik*. **Song** A short series of 6-8 notes on different pitches. Very high-pitched *chit-chit* notes, and series of rattling notes *tititiititi* unlike other flowerpeckers. Twitters during display.

DISTRIBUTION The Indian Peninsula from outer Himalayas (from about 1,500 m) between a line from Kangra to Deesa in the west and Darjeeling to Midnapore in the east, southwards; Sri Lanka, Burma, Thailand, north Vietnam, Laos, Malay Peninsula, Borneo, Sumatra (rare), Java, Bali (one record), Philippines, Sumba, Flores, Alor and Timor.

HABITAT Lowlands up to 3,000 m, in a variety of forest types, including peatswamp forest, woodland, *Albizia falcataria* plantations, coconut palms, orchards, secondary growth, at forest edge and in gardens. In tree-tops and shrubs, amongst flowers and fruit, including exotics in gardens, but especially associated with *Loranthus* and *Viscum* mistletoes. In Nepal 150 m to perhaps 3,000 m, but below 915 m in winter.

STATUS Not uncommon and widespread in India and Thailand. Rare and local in Pakistan. Probably local in Bangladesh. Widespread and frequent in Nepal. Infre–quent or scarce in Sri Lanka, where it occurs in northern forests, Uva and parts of the Central Province. Rare in

Burma, where found up to 1,200 m. Uncommon in the Philippines. Very scarce, Sabah. Rare on Sumatra, Java and Alor, uncommon to rare on Flores, moderately common on Sumbawa and Besar, uncommon on Sumba and sparse on Timor. Common in parts of southern Laos.

MOVEMENTS Seasonal altitudinal movements in Himalayas; in Nepal up to 1,980 m (possibly to 2,135 m or even 3,000 m) in summer, but below 915 m in winter.

FOOD Wild fruits, berries and flowers; spiders, and insects including tiny caterpillars, e.g. *Eurema blanda*.
Known food-plants Pipal and other wild figs *Ficus* sp., *Lantana* sp., unidentified mistletoes Loranthaceae, *Madhuca indica*, *Viscum* spp. Soft juicy parts of flowers of flamboyant (mohur) *Delonix regia* tree.

HABITS Occurs singly, in pairs, small groups or loose parties, and with other species; acrobatic. Wags tail from side to side when perched, a diagnostic feature. Forages in low bushes up to 30 m, but chiefly in canopy of fruiting trees; gleans from slender branches and twigs. Berries of Loranthaceae are revolved in bill to strip off edible peri-carp, and viscous seed is wiped onto an adjoining branch with a sweeping side-to-side movement of the head. Presumed male fluttered over another, presumed female, in leafless tree at 5 m, showing white median stripe and white flecking on centre of crown, whilst twittering excitedly.

BREEDING Often nest in mango trees *Mangifera indica*, also recorded on *Lantana* sp. bush. **Nest** An inconspicuous pear-shaped pouch of soft felted fibres, flower buds, spiders' webs and vegetable down including that of Loranthaceae, with entrance on side, suspended from twig 2-9 m from ground, looking like dry leaf. Said to be springy and to recover its shape after crushing. **Eggs** c/2-4. Pale pinkish-white blotched and speckled pale or deep brick-red. Races *agile* and *zeylonicum*: 14.8-17.1 (mean 15.8, n=85) x 10.5-12.1 (mean 11.4); *modestum*: 15.0-16.1 (mean 15.3, n=13) x 10.8-12.0 (mean 11.5). **Laying months** Indian subcontinent: January–August. India: January to June. Male with enlarged testes at Djiring, South Annam, March 1927. Sri Lanka: April, May.

DESCRIPTION *D. a. agile* Sexes similar.
Adult Above grey-brown with faint olive tinge to back, and more olive tinge to rump; tail and remiges brown, former edged olive-green; throat buffy-white with faint brown streaking at sides; rest of underparts buffy with obscure brown streaking, browner on flanks; pectoral tufts, present in both sexes, whitish; large white tips to underside of outer tail feathers, narrow white tips to next pair. Bill thick. Presumed male in display shows distinct white median stripe and white flecking on centre of crown and nape. Iris brown, dull orange or light brick-red; bill bluish in nominate, black in others, or more frequently brownish with yellowish area on lower mandible; feet slaty-brown (nominate), black or grey.
Juvenile Washed yellow below and with less streaking than adult.

GEOGRAPHICAL VARIATION Forms on the Philippines constitute a distinct group and were previously separated as Striped Flowerpecker *D. aeruginosum*. There is a cline from north to south in the Philippines, showing a decrease in ventral streaking and an increase in greenish on the back. Those on Luzon are sufficiently differentiated to be separated as *D. a. striatissimum*, whereas those on Mindanao are somewhat intermediate between the nominate and *striatissimum*.

Agile group
　　D. a. agile (Tickell, 1833) (Indian Peninsula, from outer Himalayas of West Punjab to Nepal, Bhutan, Assam, Meghalaya and Nagaland south through Gujarat and Bengal to entire peninsula except extreme south-east of Tamil Nadu; north Burma) Described above.
　　D. a. finschi Bartels, 1914 (West Java) Much more olive above than nominate; underparts greyish-white, breast moderately streaked grey, more so than nominate; no spots on undertail; bill thin.
　　D. a. modestum (Hume, 1875) (includes *remotum* [Robinson & Kloss, 1915]) (Malay Peninsula, including southern Tenasserim and peninsular Thailand; Borneo) Above olive, moderately streaked below; tail spots faint; bill thin. Juvenile less streaked than adult, belly and undertail-coverts with yellow wash.
　　D. a. obsoletum (Müller, 1843) (Timor; rare) Greyish-olive above, less olive than nominate, and browner on rump; darker than *D. annae*. Almost pure white

below, with no streaking on breast; tail spots faint; bill thick.
　　D. a. pallescens (Riley, 1935) (Bangladesh, Burma, Thailand except peninsula, and north Vietnam) Much greyer above and more heavily streaked below than nominate, and bill less deep (mean of 9, 3.7 mm compared to 4.3 mm).
　　D. a. sumatranum (Chasen, 1939) (includes *atjehense* Delacour, 1946 and may be synonymous with *modestum*) (Sumatra; known only by the type from Aceh, and three records from Aceh, Utara and Selatan) Whitish tips to tail like *modestum*, but general coloration more like *finschi*.
　　D. a. tinctum (Mayr, 1944) (Sumba, Flores and Alor; rare) Brownish-olive above, greener than nominate and darker than *D. annae*. Creamy underparts, with fine greyish streaking on breast less obvious than in nominate; faint spots on undertail; bill thick.
　　D. a. zeylonicum (Whistler, 1944) (Sri Lanka, up to 1,200 m) Differs from *agile* in being darker, more olive-grey and less yellow, more heavily streaked below, and slightly smaller; rump more olive, less yellow.

Aeruginosum group
　　D. a. aeruginosum (Bourns & Worcester, 1894) (Philippines – Cebu [not since 1950s], Mindanao, Mindoro and Negros) Olive-green above, more green on lower back, rump and uppertail-coverts; underparts whitish heavily streaked medium brown, heaviest on breast; faint whitish patches on underside of outer tail feathers. Juvenile grey rather than brown, lacking greenish wash of adult; almost no streaking below; bill paler on lower mandible.
　　D. a. affine (Zimmer, 1918) (Philippines – Palawan) Upperparts more greyish-olive than *aeruginosum* and *striatissimum*, with broader bright olivaceous edging and underparts paler, more narrowly and obscurely streaked below. Terminal white spots on rectrices brighter, smaller and more sharply defined. Smaller, with a shorter, broader and more obtuse bill.
　　D. a. striatissimum Parkes, 1962 (Philippines – Lubang, Luzon, Romblon, Sibuyan and Catanduanes) Upperparts darker, browner or sootier, and less greenish, and underparts more heavily and extensively streaked on flanks and abdomen than *aeruginosum*. White spot on innerweb of outer rectrix is fainter, larger and less sharply defined.

MEASUREMENTS Wing 62-68 (male *aeruginosum*), 63-68 (male *affine*), 57-65 (male *agile*), 57-60 (male *?deignani*), 61 (male *finschi*), 53-62 (male *obsoletum*), 56-62 (male *pallescens*), 54-57 (male *zeylonicum*), 60 (female *affine*), 55-64 (female *agile*), 57-60 (female *?deignani*), 50-61 (female *pallescens*), 53-58 (female *zeylonicum*), 64-65 (unsexed *striatissimum*); **tail** 35 (male *affine*), 32 (female *affine*), 29 (female *pallescens*); **bill** 9.4 (male *aeruginosum*), 8.0-9.5 (mean 8.7, SD 0.53, 6 male *agile*), 8.3-9.3 (mean 8.8, SD 0.41, 6 female *agile*), 10 (unsexed *agile*); **culmen from base** 8 (female *affine*); **gape** 10.3, 10.5 (2 male *aeruginosum*), 9.6-10.5 (male *agile*), 10.4-12.5 (male *?deignani*), 10.3 (male *finschi*), 9.5-10.3 (male *obsoletum*), 10.4-12.4 (male *pallescens*), 8.8-10.8 (male *zeylonicum*), 9.1-11.1 (female *agile*), 9.6-11.9 (female *?deignani*), 9.3-11.6 (female *pallescens*), 9.9-10.05 (female *zeylonicum*); **mass** no data.

REFERENCES Ali (1969), Ali & Ripley (1974), Bourns & Worcester (1894), Coates & Bishop (1997), Corlett (1998),

Deignan (1960), Dickinson *et al.* (1991), duPont (1971), Evans *et al.* (2000), Fleming *et al.* (1976), Grimmett *et al.* (1998), Hale (1996), Hellebrekers & Hoogerwerf (1967), Inskipp & Inskipp (1985), King *et al.* (1975), MacKinnon & Phillipps (1993), Madge (1986), Mann (in prep. a,b), van Marle & Voous (1988), Medway (1972), Medway & Wells (1976), Riley (1935), Salomonsen (1960b), Sheldon (1985), Wait (1931), Whistler (1949), White & Bruce (1986).

---

11 BROWN-BACKED FLOWERPECKER
Dicaeum everetti   **Plate 4**

Prionochilus everetti Sharpe, 1877, *Ibis*, p.16, Bintulu, western Borneo.

IDENTIFICATION Adult is olive-brown above; underparts grey-brown, whitish on throat, centre of breast and belly (streaked below in *D. e. bungurense*).
Similar species Thick-billed Flowerpecker *Dicaeum agile* (10) is less brown, has streaks below, white spots on tail and a finer bill. Plain Flowerpecker *D. concolor* (27) has a finer bill. Yellow-breasted Flowerpecker *Prionochilus maculatus* (4) is olive-green above, with orange crown-patch, and heavily streaked below.

VOICE Sharp, metallic *chip-chip*.

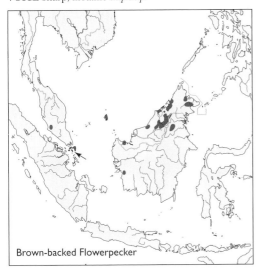

Brown-backed Flowerpecker

DISTRIBUTION Selangor (Malay Peninsula), Riau Archipelago (Sumatra; 2 collected), Sarawak, Brunei, Labuan (Sabah), "central" Borneo, and North Natunas.

HABITAT *Kerangas* (heath forest), mangroves, forest edge, secondary forest and plantations around villages; up to 975 m.

STATUS Uncommon or rare throughout its range. Listed as near-threatened by Collar *et al.* (1994).

MOVEMENTS Unknown.

FOOD Spiders, tiny insects and flowers. Probably also fruit, and possibly also nectar and/or pollen, of mistletoes Loranthaceae.
Known food-plants None.

HABITS Little recorded; often forages low.

BREEDING Nest Small whitish felt-like pouch probably of *lalang* (a long grass) or kapok, or other vegetable down, 5-6 m high in jungle tree, suspended from end of branch.
Eggs Unknown. **Laying months** Sabah, Lumahat, February; active testes March.

DESCRIPTION *D. e. everetti*
Adult Sexes similar; upperparts olive-brown, darker on tail; edges of secondaries greenish. Underparts grey-brown; throat, centre of breast and belly white. Iris whitish to pale yellow or orange; bill grey or dark brown, or grey upper mandible and brown lower mandible with yellowish patch; feet grey or dark brown.
Juvenile Unknown.

GEOGRAPHICAL VARIATION Two subspecies, but race *bungurense* may prove to belong to *D. agile*.
  D. e. bungurense (Chasen, 1934) (Bunguran Is., North Natunas) Larger than nominate (wing 63.5); darker above and greyer below, with marked streaking on throat, breast and centre of belly. White spots on tail lacking.
  D. e. everetti (Sharpe, 1877) (includes *D. e. sordidum* [Robinson & Kloss, 1918]) (range of species except where *bungurense* occurs) Described above.

MEASUREMENTS Wing 63.5 (male *bungurense*), 54-60 (unsexed *everetti*); **tail** 32.5 (male *bungurense*), 32 (unsexed *everetti*), 9.9-10.2; **bill** 11.5 (male *bungurense*); **gape** 9.5-11.4 (unsexed *everetti*); **depth of bill at front of nostril** 4.1, 4.2 (unsexed *everetti*); **tarsus** 9.9-10.2 (male *bungurense*); **mass** no data.

REFERENCES Chasen (1931), Collar *et al.* (1994), MacKinnon & Phillipps (1993), Mann (in prep. a), van Marle & Voous (1988), Sharpe (1877), Sheldon (1985), Sheldon *et al.* (in press), Smythies (1957, 1960, 1981).

---

12 WHISKERED FLOWERPECKER
Dicaeum proprium ▼   **Plate 4**

Dicaeum proprium Ripley & Rabor, 1966, *Proc. Biol. Soc. Wash.* 79, pp.305-306, Mt Mayo, Limot, Mati, Davo Province, Mindanao, Philippines.

IDENTIFICATION Adult male is mostly blue-black above with bluish gloss; underparts mostly pale brownish, whitish on throat and moustachial stripe, with blue-black malar stripe. Female is less glossed above, and slightly browner below. Juvenile is less glossed, and lacks malar stripe.
Similar species Male Flame-crowned Flowerpecker *Dicaeum anthonyi* (18) has orange crown, and some yellow below; Pygmy Flowerpecker *D. pygmaeum* (28) and male Bicoloured Flowerpecker *D. bicolor* (19) lack blue-black malar stripe and sepia wash below, and former also has an olive-yellow rump.

VOICE Four or five high-pitched notes, first two higher than others. High insect-like trills, with lower *tsenk* notes possibly made by a second bird. High *swink* and *chenk* notes with buzzing quality. These are run into a song, with rising and falling notes.

DISTRIBUTION Endemic to Mindanao, Philippines. Recorded on Mt Mayo, Mt Kitanglad, Mt Matutum, Mt

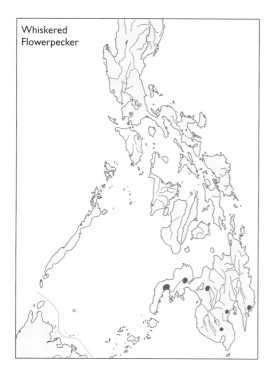

Whiskered
Flowerpecker

MEASUREMENTS Wing 62, 62, 62 (3 males), 56 (female);
tail 22-29 (males), 20 (female); bill 9.5, 11, 11.1 (3 males),
9.7 (female); tarsus 12-14 (male), 13 (female); mass 10.2,
10.2 (2 males).

REFERENCES Collar *et al.* (1994, 1999), Dickinson *et al.*
(1991), duPont (1971), Ripley & Rabor (1966).

13   YELLOW-VENTED FLOWERPECKER
Dicaeum chrysorrheum   Plate 4

Dicaeum chrysorrheum Temminck & Laugier, 1829, *Pl. Col.*,
Livr. 80, pl. 478, fig. 1, Java.

IDENTIFICATION Adult is bright olive-green above with
black wings and tail; mostly yellowish-white below heavily
streaked greyish-black, with yellow undertail-coverts.
Juvenile is generally duller and paler.
Similar species Yellow-breasted Flowerpecker *Prionochilus
maculatus* (4) has olive-green streaking and lacks yellow
undertail-coverts. Speckled Piculet *Picumnus innominatus*
has conspicuous white supercilia and moustachial stripes,
and lacks yellow on undertail-coverts.

VOICE *Zeet*; repeated *zit-zit-zit* in flight; repeated *chip-a-
chip-treee*; soft squeak; loud, deep, hoarse contact calls.

Piapayungan, Mt Sugarloaf and Mt Apo and at Lake Sebu
and Mainit, Manticao.

HABITAT Uncommon above 900 m amongst flowering
and fruiting trees in forest, forest edge and secondary
growth.

STATUS A rare and little known species once considered
to be globally threatened by habitat destruction and
classified as Vulnerable (Collar *et al.* 1994), now downlisted
to near-threatened (Collar *et al.* 1999). Restricted to forest,
forest edge and secondary growth above 900 m on
Mindanao, where it is uncommon to locally common. No
recent records except Mt Kitanglad, Mt Apo and Sitio Siete
near Lake Sebu in South Cotabato province.

MOVEMENTS Unknown.

FOOD Presumably includes fruit, and possibly also nectar
and/or pollen, of mistletoes Loranthaceae.
Known food-plants None.

HABITS Nothing recorded.

BREEDING Nothing recorded.

DESCRIPTION
Adult male Upperparts blue-black with bluish gloss,
primaries dark brown; chin, upper throat and moustachial
stripe greyish-white, separated by blue-black malar stripe;
lower throat and rest of underparts pale sepia-brown,
darker and greyer on flanks; pectoral tufts white; undertail-
coverts greyish-white. Bill blackish, paler at base of lower
mandible; feet dark brownish.
Adult female Differs from male only in being slightly less
glossy above and slightly darker brown below.
Juvenile Little or no gloss above, and lacks malar stripe.

GEOGRAPHICAL VARIATION None recorded.

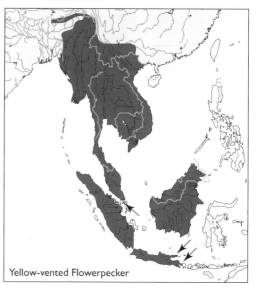

Yellow-vented Flowerpecker

DISTRIBUTION The Himalayan foothills from Nepal
(east of Dhankuta, Tamur river) eastward through north-
eastern India, including Sikkim, Bhutan, Arunachal
Pradesh, Patkai range, Meghalaya, Nagaland, Manipur,
Tripura, Mizo Hills and Chittagong Hills, to Burma,
Thailand, Indo-China and south Yunnan; southwards
through Malay Peninsula (recently found again in Singapore) to Sumatra, Borneo and Java (one record for Bali
at Bali Barat National Park).

HABITAT Hills up to at least 1,200 m, but to over 2,000 m
in Sikkim (*chrysochlore*); 245 m in Nepal; lowlands and hills
to 700 m (Sumatra); lowlands to 1,700 m (Borneo); lowlands to 1,500 m (Burma); up to 880 m (Malay Peninsula).

Lowland and hill dipterocarp forests, lower montane forest, lower montane secondary forest, alluvial forest and peatswamp forest; in open jungle, at forest edge and in woodlands, particularly where mistletoes Loranthaceae occur, highland *kerangas*, *Albizia*, old rubber, gardens and orchards.

STATUS Common in India south of Brahmaputra. Rare in Nepal, Bhutan and Bangladesh. Uncommon throughout plains and foothills of Burma, up to 1,500 m. Uncommon, Borneo. Few records from Sumatra in Aceh, Utara, Riau, Barat, Jambi and Selatan. Rare in Bali and apparently also Java.

MOVEMENTS Unknown.

FOOD Berries, particularly Loranthaceae, and presumably Viscaceae, small figs, nectar, small beetles and other insects.
Known food-plants Mistletoes, figs.

HABITS Aggressive. Feeds at all levels; occasionally perches on wires.

BREEDING Building and incubation by both sexes. **Nest** Takes only 4-5 days to build and is well concealed, below 8 m. Similar to other flowerpeckers, but uses more moss on exterior, and more grass and fibre. One made of soft cotton down, very fine grass seed ends, bound with cobwebs, scraps of moss and shreds of grass. Another all of *Bombax* sp. cotton with a few shreds of grass and fibre to hold it together. **Eggs** c/2-3; white. Race *chrysochlore*: 14.5-16.0 (mean 15.3, n=22) x 10.4-11.4 (mean 11.0). **Laying months** India: April–August.

DESCRIPTION *D. c. chrysochlore* Sexes similar.
Adult Upperparts bright olive-green; wings and tail black; throat white with greyish-black moustachial streak; breast and belly yellowish-white heavily streaked greyish-black; undertail-coverts bright golden-yellow. Bill dark grey or blackish; iris orange or orange-red; feet dark grey.
Juvenile Underparts more greyish, with finer, less defined, streaks; upperparts duller.

GEOGRAPHICAL VARIATION
D. c. chrysochlore Blyth, 1843 (Himalayan foothills from Nepal east through Darjeeling, Sikkim, Bhutan, ?Arunachal Pradesh, Patkai Range, Meghalaya, Nagaland and Manipur south to Tripura, Mizo Hills and Chittagong Hills east to Burma, Indochina and Thailand south to Isthmus of Kra) Described above.
D. c. chrysorrheum Temminck & Laugier, 1829 (south from Isthmus of Kra to Sumatra – Aceh, Utara, Riau, Barat, Jambi and Selatan; Borneo, Java and Bali) Differs from *D. c. chrysochlore* in having breast and belly creamy-white streaked blackish, and undertail-coverts yellow or orange. Juvenile *chrysorrheum* differs from adult in having undertail-coverts pale yellow and rest of underparts greyish with dull greyish-brown streaks.

MEASUREMENTS Wing 57-61 (male *chrysochlore*), 52-61 (mean 58.4, SD 2.59, 10 male *chrysorrheum*), 55-58 (female *chrysochlore*), 53-60 (mean 57.2, SD 2.25, 8 female *chrysorrheum*), 55-62 (unsexed *chrysochlore*); **bill** 11.7-14.3 (mean 12.5, SD 0.98, 6 male *chrysochlore*), 10.3-11.9 (mean 11.5, SD 0.85, 10 male *chrysorrheum*), 11.3-12.6 (mean 11.9, SD 0.56, 6 female *chrysochlore*), 10.0-12.2 (mean 11.6, SD 0.84, 8 female *chrysorrheum*), 13-14 (unsexed *chrysochlore*); **gape** 11.6-14.2 (male *chrysochlore*), 11.8-13.3 (male *chry-*

sorrheum), 11.0-13.4 (female *chrysochlore*), 11.1-14.4 (female *chrysorrheum*); **mass** 9 (female *chrysochlore*).

REFERENCES Ali & Ripley (1974), Fleming *et al.* (1976), Green (1991), Gretton (1990), Grimmett *et al.* (1998), Hellebrekers & Hoogerwerf (1967), Inskipp & Inskipp (1985), King *et al.* (1975), MacKinnon & Phillipps (1993), Mann (1996, in prep. b), van Marle & Voous (1988), Medway & Wells (1976), Sheldon *et al.* (in press), Smythies (1957, 1981, 1986).

---

14 YELLOW-BELLIED FLOWERPECKER
Dicaeum melanoxanthum   Plate 4

Pachyglossa melanoxanthum Blyth (ex Hodgson ms), 1843, *Journ. Asiat. Soc. Bengal*, 12, p.1010, Nepal.

IDENTIFICATION Thick-billed. Adult male is slaty-black above with white patches on tail; mostly yellow below, with blackish sides to neck and breast, white centre of throat and upper breast. Adult female is olive-grey above, and on sides of neck and head; centre of throat and breast white; rest of underparts yellow, flanks more olive.
Similar species Thick-billed Flowerpecker *Dicaeum agile* (10) and Plain Flowerpecker *D. concolor* (27) lack yellow on belly and undertail-coverts; female from female Orange-bellied Flowerpecker *D. trigonostigma* (24) by lack of yellow-orange or orange on rump; female from Pale-billed Flowerpecker *D. erythrorhynchos* (26) by yellow on underparts.

VOICE Unknown.

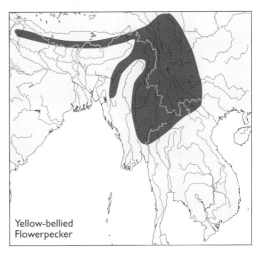

Yellow-bellied Flowerpecker

DISTRIBUTION The Himalayas from Almora eastwards (including Nanda Devi National Park) through Nepal (west and central), Sikkim, Bhutan and Arunachal Pradesh, south through Nagaland and Manipur; east to Burma (Shan States), north Yunnan, south-central and south-west China. North Thailand, south-east Yunnan and extreme north Vietnam in winter only.

HABITAT Found amongst tall trees in open forest, bushy areas at edge of forest, clearings in rain forest, and pine forest; between 1,400 and 3,915 m in summer, down to

775 m in winter. In Nepal 1,050-1,550+ m in winter, 2,440-3,000 m in summer; 2,350 m at Shipuri Lekh in December.

STATUS Not uncommon 1,600-2,400 m in Southern Shan States of Burma. Rare winter visitor to north Thailand. Local and frequent in Nepal. Scarce and local in India. Rare in Bhutan. Vagrant to Bangladesh.

MOVEMENTS Vertical seasonal movements. Winter visitor only to north Thailand, south-east Yunnan and north Tonkin.

FOOD Insects. Diet presumably also includes fruit, and possibly also nectar and/or pollen of mistletoes. Possibly eats mistletoe leaves in winter in Nepal.
Known food-plants None.

HABITS Little known, solitary and elusive. Occurs in foliage of tall trees and creepers, moving incessantly. Sometimes sallies from dead branches for insects like a flycatcher.

BREEDING Nest Unknown. **Eggs** c/3; white, 14.9-15.7 (mean 15.0) x 11.4-12.0. **Laying months** India: Juvenile Dibhrughar, June 1880; Burma: breeding on Loi Mai, April.

DESCRIPTION
Adult male Upperparts slaty-black with slight gloss; wings and tail black, two outer pairs of tail feathers with large white patch on innerweb, sometimes reduced or absent on penultimate feather; 10th primary reduced; sides of neck and breast dull greyish-black; centre of throat and upper breast white, rest of underparts bright yellow. Upper mandible black, lower grey; iris chestnut; feet black.
Adult female Upperparts, sides of head and neck olive-grey; centre of throat and breast white; centre of belly and undertail-coverts yellow, flanks olive-yellow.
Juvenile Unknown.

GEOGRAPHICAL VARIATION None recorded.

MEASUREMENTS Wing 68-76 (mean 73.1, SD 2.02, 10 males), 63-69 (mean 66.2, SD 0.5, 4 females); **bill** 9.5-11.5 (mean 10.3, SD 0.52, 10 males), 9.3-11.2 (mean 10.1, SD 0.73, 5 females); **gape** 10.5-11.8 (male), 9.7-10.2 (female); **mass** no data.

REFERENCES Ali & Ripley (1974), Fleming (1968), Fleming *et al.* (1976), Grimmett *et al.* (1998), Mann (in prep. a), Smythies (1986).

---

15   WHITE-THROATED FLOWERPECKER
Dicaeum vincens   Plate 5

Prionochilus vincens P. L. Sclater, 1872, *Proc. Zool. Soc. London*, p.730, Ceylon.

Alternative name: Legge's Flowerpecker

IDENTIFICATION Adult is slaty-blue above with black wings and tail; large white terminal spots on tail; below bright yellow with white throat. Adult female has grey head, with dull olive back; wings and tail dark brown; below pale yellow with whitish throat and olive flanks.
Similar species Female from Thick-billed Flowerpecker *Dicaeum agile* (10) by pale yellow belly.

VOICE Call *Tchip, tchip-twee-see-see, tzee tzee tzee.* Repeated high-pitched *tee-too.* **Song** Reported to have two songs, apparently undescribed.

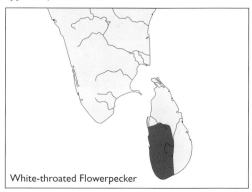
White-throated Flowerpecker

DISTRIBUTION Endemic to Sri Lanka, where it is confined to the south-western quarter (including Sinharaja Forest) in the wet zone up to 1,000 m.

HABITAT Tall trees and creepers in rainforest up to 1,000 m.

STATUS Confined to dense forests of the wet lowland zones of Sri Lanka, reaching 1,000 m in the Central Province. Common below 900 m. Listed as near-threatened by Collar *et al.* (1994).

MOVEMENTS Unknown.

FOOD Nectar, berries, spiders and small insects.
Known food-plants None.

HABITS Solitary, in pairs or family parties. Mainly at tops of tall trees, but sometimes forages low; acrobatic.

BREEDING Nest Typical of flowerpeckers, 18-38 m up in dipterocarp tree. **Eggs** c/2; pinky-white speckled pinky-brown, much heavier at broad end; 14.8-15.4 x 11.1-11.2. **Laying months** January–August.

DESCRIPTION
Adult male Slaty-blue upperparts and sides of face, paler on rump, wings and tail black, latter with large white terminal spots; throat to upper breast white, lower breast and belly bright yellow, undertail-coverts white. Iris brown or reddish-brown, upper mandible black, lower blue-grey basally, feet black.
Adult female Head grey, back dull olive; wings and tail brownish-black, outer feathers with large white spots; throat whitish, belly pale yellow and flanks olive. Underwing-coverts white, undertail-coverts whitish.
Juvenile Resembles female but with yellow wash on throat.

GEOGRAPHICAL VARIATION None recorded.

MEASUREMENTS Wing 58-60 (mean 58.8, SD 0.75, 6 males), 55-59 (mean 56.8, SD 1.33, 6 females); **bill** 10.8-12.5 (mean 11.6, SD 0.78, 5 males), 10.5-11.9 (mean 11.1, SD 0.55, 6 females).

REFERENCES Ali & Ripley (1974), Banks & Banks (1986), Collar *et al.* (1994), Grimmett *et al.* (1998).

---

16   YELLOW-SIDED FLOWERPECKER
Dicaeum aureolimbatum   Plate 5

Prionochilus aureolimbatus Wallace, 1865, *Proc. Zool. Soc. London* p.477, pl.29, fig.1, mountains of Minahassa, northern Celebes.

IDENTIFICATION Adult is olive-green above; cheeks and underside greyish-white; sides of breast and flanks bright yellow.
Similar species None.

VOICE High-pitched *s-uit*, less high-pitched and strident than Grey-sided Flowerpecker *D. celebicum* (42), and at less frequent intervals; series of 5-6 rapidly repeated short, dry, staccato *tuk* notes. Sharp, clear *zit-zit-zit*, sometimes run together 4-5 times.

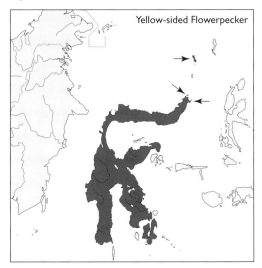
Yellow-sided Flowerpecker

DISTRIBUTION Endemic to Sulawesi and certain adjacent islands, including Banka, Kabaena, Lembeh and Sangihe in the north and Muna and Butung in the south.

HABITAT Common up to 2,000 m in forest, woodland, plantations and cultivation. Found in primary forest, tall secondary forest, at forest edge, in mixed plantations and suburban gardens.

STATUS Widespread and common on Sulawesi and Sangihe.

Locally common in parts of Sulawesi, where occurs in low bushes in scrubland and at forest edges between 50 and 1,100 m. Rare on Siumpu island in *Lantana camara* thicket; common on Kabaena island.

MOVEMENTS Unknown.

FOOD Fruits of mistletoes and small figs, and possibly also nectar and/or pollen; insects and spiders.
Known food-plants Mistletoes, figs, wild cherries.

HABITS In singles, pairs and small groups and with *D. celebicum*, which displaces it from feeding bushes; mostly middle storey or medium-sized trees. An occasional member of bird parties. Restless; less upright than *celebicum*, posture being more similar to a white-eye *Zosterops*. Larger

fruits squeezed before being swallowed, and beak wiped on branch afterwards.

BREEDING Nest Unknown. **Eggs** Race *aureolimbatum*: white, with violet or red spots, or grey, with dense purple-brown flecking; 15.1-16.4 (mean 15.3, n=3) x 11.0-11.1 (mean 11.1). **Laying months** Immatures regularly Sangihe late August–early September; fledglings November.

DESCRIPTION *D. a. aureolimbatum* Sexes similar.
Adult Bright olive-green above, duller on crown, brighter green on rump; auriculars blackish-grey; cheeks dark grey, underside greyish-white tinged ashy on foreneck; sides of breast, flanks and undertail-coverts bright yellow. Wings and tail blackish-brown, moustachial stripe greyish-white. Underwing-coverts white. Bill and feet blackish.
Juvenile Sides of chest yellow, less bright than adult; flanks grey, undertail-coverts whitish. Bare parts pinky-brown.

GEOGRAPHICAL VARIATION

> *D. a. aureolimbatum* (Wallace, 1865) (Sulawesi, Bangka, Lembeh, Muna and Butung; ?Kabaena) Described above.
> *D. a. laterale* Salomonsen, 1960 (replaces name *sanghirensis*; Sangihe) Differs from *aureolimbatum* in being duller above and having paler sides to breast and greyish-olive flanks; yellow confined to sides of breast forming an incomplete band, and on undertail-coverts.

MEASUREMENTS Wing 44-54 (mean 51.6, 21 unsexed *aureolimbatum*), mean 50.6 (SD 1.21, 6 unsexed *?aureolimbatum*); **tail** 24-29 (mean 26.7, 21 unsexed *aureolimbatum*); **bill** 9.0-11.1 (mean 10.2, 21 unsexed *aureolimbatum*), mean 10.4 (SD 0.53, 6 unsexed *?aureolimbatum*); **tarsus** 11.5-13.0 (mean 12.3, 21 unsexed *aureolimbatum*); **mass** no data.

REFERENCES Coates & Bishop (1997), M. Catterall (pers. comm.), Coomans de Ruiter (1951), Holmes & Wood (1979), Riley (1997), Schönwetter (1980-1984), Wallace (1865), Watling (1983), White & Bruce (1986).

---

17   OLIVE-CAPPED FLOWERPECKER
Dicaeum nigrilore   Plate 5

Dicaeum nigrilore Hartert, 1904, *Bull. Brit. Orn. Cl.* 15 p.8, Mt Apo, 3,000 ft., Mindanao.

IDENTIFICATION Adult is brown and olive above; black on lores and below eye; below mostly yellow with white chin and yellow undertail-coverts; long curved bill.
Similar species Buzzing Flowerpecker *Dicaeum hypoleucum* (25) and female Bicoloured Flowerpecker *D. bicolor* (19) differ in lacking black lores and patch under eye, and former is yellow below.

VOICE High *tseep-tseep*... Rapid trill of about 30 high notes, rising and falling, some quite sweet and unflowerpecker-like.

DISTRIBUTION Endemic to Mindanao, Philippines.

HABITAT Forests at 900-1,350 m.

STATUS Not uncommon.

MOVEMENTS Unknown.

FOOD Presumably includes fruits, and possibly also nectar and/or pollen, of mistletoes Loranthaceae.

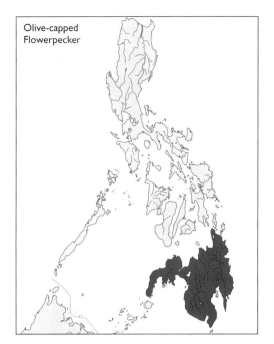

Olive-capped
Flowerpecker

Known food-plants None.

HABITS Frequents flowering and fruiting trees in forests.

BREEDING Nest Unknown. **Eggs** Unknown. **Laying months** Birds of both sexes with enlarged gonads on Mt Malindang in April and May.

DESCRIPTION *D. n. nigrilore*
Adult Sexes similar; top of head light olive; back brownish; rump olive; tail and wings dark brown; lores and patch under eye black; chin white; throat, breast and belly grey; flanks and undertail-coverts dull yellow. Iris brown; bill black; feet greyish-black.
Juvenile Unknown.

GEOGRAPHICAL VARIATION
   D. n. diuatae Salomonsen, 1953 (Mt Hilong-Hilong in the Diuata Mts) Much duller, more olive-green than nominate. Flanks and undertail-coverts olive-greenish, not yellow; abdomen suffused yellow not white; top of head darker and duller green; mantle darker blackish-brown; back green like rump, not brown; wing-coverts and secondaries have much broader green edge on outerwebs of feathers; measurements similar to nominate.
   D. n. nigrilore Hartert, 1904 (Mt Apo, Mt Malindang, Mt McKinley, Mt Kitanglad, Mt Matutum, Mt Mayo and Daggayan) Described above.

MEASUREMENTS Wing 54-55 (55 male *nigrilore*); **tail** 29; **bill** 16-16.4 (male, *nigrilore*); **gape** 14.7-15 (male *nigrilore*); **tarsus** 15; **mass** no data.

REFERENCES Dickinson *et al.* (1991), duPont (1971), Rand & Rabor (1960), Salomonsen (1960b).

---

18   FLAME-CROWNED FLOWERPECKER
Dicaeum anthonyi   Plate 5

Prionochilus anthonyi McGregor, 1914, *Phil. J. Sci.* 9 p.531, Mt Polis, Ifugoa Subprovince, Luzon, 2,000 m.

IDENTIFICATION Adult male is mostly glossy blue-black above with orange-yellow or red crown; below yellowish with white or grey chin and throat, and orange-yellow or red undertail-coverts. Adult female olive above and greyish-white below, becoming browner on flanks; buff undertail-coverts.
Similar species Palawan Flowerpecker *Prionochilus plateni* (6) has a yellow rump. Male Whiskered Flowerpecker *Dicaeum proprium* (12) lacks orange and orange-yellow; female from Buzzing Flowerpecker *D. hypoleucum* (25) by olive rather than olive-brown upperparts, and greyish-white rather than greyish-olive underparts.

VOICE Nothing recorded.

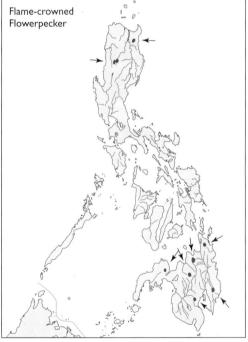

Flame-crowned
Flowerpecker

DISTRIBUTION Endemic to Luzon and Mindanao, Philippines.

HABITAT Forest, particularly mossy forest, above 800 m to at least 2,000 m.

STATUS Uncommon. Listed as near-threatened by Collar *et al.* (1994, 1999).

MOVEMENTS Unknown.

FOOD Presumably includes fruit, and possibly also nectar and/or pollen, of mistletoes.
Known food-plants None.

HABITS Forages, singly, in pairs or in mixed flocks, in fruiting and flowering trees in forests.

BREEDING Nothing recorded.

DESCRIPTION *D. a. anthonyi*
Adult male Forehead and lores black; crown orange-yellow; rest of upperparts black glossed blue; chin and throat white; breast and belly yellowish; undertail-coverts orange-yellow. Iris brown; bill black; feet black or blackish-slate, soles pale yellow. Yellowish on undertail-coverts.
Adult female Upperparts, cheeks and sides of neck olive, underparts greyish-white.
Juvenile Unknown.

GEOGRAPHICAL VARIATION
D. a. anthonyi (McGregor, 1914) (Luzon – Mt Polis, Mt Tabuan, Mt Puguis and Dipalayag) Described above.
D. a. kampalili Manuel & Gilliard, 1953 (Mindanao – Mt Pasian, Mt Kampalili, Mt McKinley, Mt Kitanglad, Mt Apo and Daggayan) Male differs from *anthonyi* in having a glossy red crown, grey underparts with red undertail-coverts, and in being smaller. Female much browner below with buff undertail-coverts.
D. a. masawan Rand & Rabor, 1957 (Mindanao – Mt Malindang) Male differs from *kampalili* by having breast and flanks washed yellow, and much yellower belly.

MEASUREMENTS Wing 56-57 (male *anthonyi*), 54-55 (male *kampalili*), 54 (female *kampalili*); **tail** 31 (male *anthonyi*), 25 (male *kampalili*); **bill** 12 (male *anthonyi*), 11.8 (male *kampalili*), 12.4 (female *kampalili*); **tarsus** 16 (male *anthonyi*); **mass** 9.6 (male *kampalili*), 11.7 (female *kampalili*).

REFERENCES Collar *et al.* (1994, 1999), Dickinson *et al.* (1991), duPont (1971), McGregor (1914), Salomonsen (1960b).

---

19   BICOLOURED FLOWERPECKER
Dicaeum bicolor   Plate 5

Prionochilus bicolor Bourns & Worcester, 1894, *Occas. Pap. Minnesota Acad. Nat. Sci.* 1 p.20, Hills at back of Ayala, Zamboanga, Mindanao.

IDENTIFICATION Bill thick and curved. Adult male black, glossed blue above; underparts grey with whitish median line. Adult female mostly greyish-olive, brown and greenish above, with black tail; below olive-grey with paler median stripe.
Similar species Female distinguished from female Palawan Flowerpecker *Prionochilus plateni* (6) by lack of yellowish on rump and underparts, and from Thick-billed Flowerpecker *Dicaeum agile* (10) by lack of streaking below. Male Whiskered Flowerpecker *D. proprium* (12) has blue-black jugular stripe and sepia wash on underparts; Olive-capped Flowerpecker *D. nigrilore* (17) has long curved bill, black lores and patch under eye; female from Buzzing Flowerpecker *D. hypoleucum* (25) by being greener, less brown, above; Pygmy Flowerpecker *D. pygmaeum* (28) has an olive-yellow rump.

VOICE *Swip-swip...*, becoming a rapid trill, slower and lower-pitched towards end.

DISTRIBUTION Endemic to the Philippines (Luzon, Mindoro, Catanduanes, Negros, Guimaras, Bohol, Leyte, Mindanao, Samar and Dinagat).

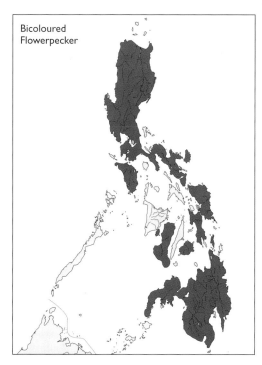

Bicoloured Flowerpecker

HABITAT Forest below 1,500 m, at forest edge and in secondary growth.

STATUS Fairly common.

FOOD Presumably includes fruit and possibly also nectar and/or pollen of mistletoes.
Known food-plants None.

HABITS Forages singly, in groups or mixed flocks, in fruiting and flowering trees in forests.

BREEDING Nest Unknown. **Eggs** Undescribed. **Laying months** South Luzon: female with ripe egg April, fledglings March.

DESCRIPTION *D. b. inexpectatum*
Adult male Upperparts black, glossed blue to below eye; underparts grey with whitish streak down middle; throat, moustachial stripe, belly and undertail-coverts whitish. Iris red; bill black, feet black.
Adult female Upperparts greyish-olive, browner on crown, greener on lower back, rump and uppertail-coverts; tail black; underparts grey with olive wash, and lighter streak down middle; underwing-coverts white; undertail-coverts whitish. Iris red; bill brown on upper mandible, with pale yellowish-brown lower mandible; feet black.
Juvenile Unknown.

GEOGRAPHICAL VARIATION
D. b. bicolor (Bourns & Worcester, 1894) (Bohol, Leyte, Mindanao, Samar and Dinagat) Male from *inexpectatum* by purple iridescence on upperparts; below with almost no grey on flanks; female is darker glossy green above, with underparts like *viridissimum*.
D. b. inexpectatum (Hartert, 1895) (Luzon, Mindoro and Catanduanes) Described above.
D. b. viridissimum Parkes, 1971 (Negros and Guimaras) Male differs from *inexpectatum* by green iridescence

on upperparts, and female by underparts washed olive-green.

MEASUREMENTS Wing 48-52 (mean 51.2, SD 1.64, 5 male *inexpectatum*), 47-51 (mean 49.0, SD 0.02, 4 female *inexpectatum*); **tail** 24 (male *inexpectatum*); **bill** 9-10 (mean 9.5, SD 0.33, 5 male *inexpectatum*), 9.4-9.7 (mean 9.5, SD 0.15, 4 female *inexpectatum*); **gape** 9.8-11 (male *inexpectatum*), 9.4-10.8 (female *inexpectatum*); **tarsus** 12 (male *inexpectatum*); **mass** no data.

REFERENCES Bourns & Worcester (1894), Dickinson *et al.* (1991), duPont (1971), duPont & Rabor (1973), Goodman & Gonzales (1990).

20 CEBU FLOWERPECKER
Dicaeum quadricolor Plate 6

Prionochilus quadricolor Tweeddale, 1877, *Proc. Zool. Soc. Lond.* p.762, pl. 77, fig. 2, Cebu.

IDENTIFICATION Adult male black, greenish-yellow and orange-red above; greyish-white below. Adult female brownish olive-green above, greyish-white below.
Similar species Pygmy Flowerpecker *Dicaeum pygmaeum* (28) lacks orange-red tips to back. Female Buzzing Flowerpecker *D. hypoleucum* (25) is dark brown with olive tinge above, greyish-white below with buffy centre of belly and vent.

VOICE Series of *tsip-tsip* notes, which may develop into a trill. *Trik-trik* developing into trill. Very hard *tit-tit*. Very high *see-ip*, rather insect-like, which may be repeated. High-pitched *sit-sit-sit*.

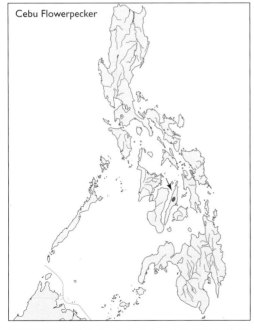
Cebu Flowerpecker

DISTRIBUTION Endemic to Cebu, Philippines, where confined to c.30 ha area of forest at Tabunan. Now also known to occur at Nug-as and Mt Lantoy.

HABITAT Rare forest denizen of which little is known, except that it occurs in closed-canopy forest and utilises open-canopy forest.

STATUS Re-discovered in 1992 after it was considered extinct, having not been seen previously since 1906. Globally threatened species classified as Critically Endangered, dependent upon survival of its remnant habitat. It was re-discovered in a 3 km² patch of forest within which only 30 ha of closed-canopy forest, upon which the species seems to be dependent, remains. However, it is known to utilise open-canopy forest also and adaptation to this habitat may offer hope, given that the remnant forest, although within Central Cebu National Park, is under threat. Competition with the more aggressive *D. australe* is an additional threat.

FOOD Small fruit of forest tree, and possibly also nectar and/or pollen, of mistletoes.
Known food-plants None.

HABITS Never seen in groups larger than four.

BREEDING Birds seen chasing each other, March. **Nest** Undescribed. **Eggs** Undescribed. **Laying months** June, also juvenile seen December and singing male March.

DESCRIPTION
Adult male Top of head and hindneck black; back black but feathers have bright orange-red tips; lower back and rump greenish-yellow; tail and wings black; whitish throat, malar stripe, and centre of breast, rest of underparts grey. Iris dark brown; bill and feet glossy black. Legs bright pink, apparently only in breeding season.
Adult female Upperparts brownish olive-green, underparts greyish-white.
Juvenile Similar to female, but paler above, and has pinkish lower mandible.

GEOGRAPHICAL VARIATION None recorded.

MEASUREMENTS Wing 53 (male), 54 (unsexed); **tail** 28.8 (male), 30 (unsexed); **bill** 9.4 (male), 10 (unsexed); **tarsus** 14 (male), 13 (unsexed); **mass** no data.

REFERENCES D. Allen (pers. comm.), BirdLife International (2000), Bourns & Worcester (1909-1910), Collar *et al.* (1994, 1999), Dickinson *et al.* (1991), duPont (1971), Dutson *et al.* (1993), Magsalay *et al.* (1995), Tweeddale (1877a).

21 RED-STRIPED FLOWERPECKER
Dicaeum australe Plate 6

Pipra australis Hermann, 1783, *Tab. Aff. Anim.*, p.223. "New Guinea", corrected to the Philippines and restricted to Luzon by Salomonsen (1960b).

Alternative name: Red-keeled Flowerpecker

IDENTIFICATION Adult glossy blue-black above, white and grey below with scarlet stripe on centre of breast and belly. Juvenile is blackish-brown above, grey below, buffy on centre of abdomen.
Similar species From Scarlet-collared Flowerpecker *Dicaeum retrocinctum* (23) by white, not black, throat with red spot; from Pygmy Flowerpecker *D. pygmaeum* (28) by red on breast and belly.

VOICE High insect-like *suit-suit...*, becoming a trill. Series of high-pitched up and down notes, *tik-tik*, becoming a trill.

DISTRIBUTION Endemic to the Philippines, occurring on Basiao, Basilan, Biliran, Bohol, Burias, Cabo, Calicoan, Camiguin North, Camotes, Catanduanes, Cebu, Dinagat, Leyte, Lubang, Luzon, Marinduque, Maripipi, Masbate, Mindanao, Naranjos, Samar, Sarangani, Siargao, Ticao and Verde.

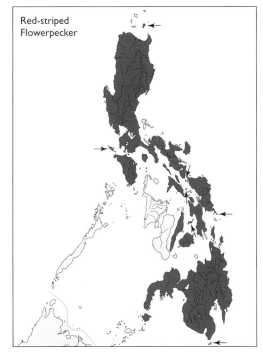

Red-striped Flowerpecker

HABITAT Below 1,000 m in forest, at forest edge, in gardens, coconut groves and in open country.

STATUS Common.

MOVEMENTS Unknown.

FOOD Presumably includes fruit, and possibly also nectar and/or pollen, of mistletoes.
Known food-plants None.

HABITS Forages singly, in groups and in mixed flocks, in fruiting and flowering trees. Host to *Haemoproteus dicaeus* and *H. nucleophilus*.

BREEDING Nest Unknown. **Eggs** Unknown. **Laying months** Cebu: June; Luzon: juveniles August, adults with enlarged gonads August; Mindanao: August; Samar: August.

DESCRIPTION Sexes similar.
Adult Upperparts black glossed blue; chin and throat white; breast and belly grey with scarlet stripe down middle. Iris dark brown. Bill dark brown to black. Feet greyish-brown or black.
Juvenile Blackish-brown above, unglossed, to below cheeks, and malar region. Axillaries whitish; underparts grey, slightly buffy on centre of abdomen; orange-red base to bill.

GEOGRAPHICAL VARIATION None. However, the species previously included *D. haematostictum*, which has now been separated.

MEASUREMENTS Wing 51-60 (mean 54.5, SD 2.41, 10 males), 49-57 (mean 52.2, SD 2.2, 10 females); **tail** 28 (unsexed); **bill** 11-14.5 (mean 12.1, SD 1.01, 9 males), 10.6-12.6 (mean 11.8, SD 0.64, 10 females); **tarsus** 9 (unsexed); **mass** 11 (male).

REFERENCES duPont (1971), Dickinson *et al.* (1991), Salomonsen (1960b).

---

22   BLACK-BELTED FLOWERPECKER
Dicaeum haematostictum   Plate 6

Dicaeum haematostictum Sharpe, 1876, *Nature* 14, p.298, Guimaras, Philippines.

Alternative name: Visayan Flowerpecker, Guimaras Flowerpecker, Red-keeled Flowerpecker

IDENTIFICATION Adult glossy blue-black above, white and grey below with scarlet stripe on centre of breast and belly, bordered black above at sides. Juvenile blackish-brown above, grey below, buffy on centre of abdomen.
Similar species From Scarlet-collared Flowerpecker *Dicaeum retrocinctum* (23) by white, not black, throat with red spot; from Pygmy Flowerpecker *D. pygmaeum* (28) by red on breast and belly. The allopatric Red-striped Flowerpecker *D. australe* lacks the black border to the scarlet breast- and belly-stripe.

VOICE *Seet seet*, which may become a trill; *chip*; rapid ticking notes. *Chip-seet-seet*, followed by short trill.

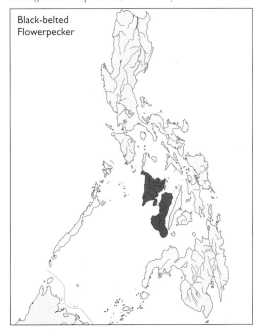

Black-belted Flowerpecker

DISTRIBUTION Endemic to the Philippines, where occurs on Guimaras, Negros and Panay.

HABITAT Forest, forest edge and open country, below 1,250 m. Also agricultural land, coconut groves, gardens.

STATUS A globally threatened species considered to be

151

Endangered by Collar *et al.* (1994), but now Vulnerable (Collar *et al.* 1999). In 1992 it was recorded on a few low-land sites on Panay and it may now be extinct on Guimaras given the extent of deforestation there. It was common on Negros in the 1950s, but it is now uncommon or rare there except on Mount Talinis.

MOVEMENTS Unknown.

FOOD Fruit, berries, flowers, insects, spiders and possibly nectar and/or pollen from mistletoes.
Known food-plants None.

HABITS Forages singly, in groups and in mixed flocks, in fruiting and flowering trees.

BREEDING Nest Suspended from end of branch some distance from ground. Another 7-11 m high in tree-fern.
Eggs c/1; very pale greenish-white, profusely spotted towards larger end, heavily clouded lilac undermarkings, and olive-brown specks over rest of shell. 16.5-17 x 12-12.4.
Laying months Negros: March, enlarged testes January–March, nests August–September, juveniles August.

DESCRIPTION Sexes similar.
Adult Upperparts black glossed blue; chin and throat white; black collar on upper breast; rest of breast and belly grey with broad scarlet stripe down middle. Iris dark brown or black. Bill dark brown to black. Feet greyish-brown or black.
Juvenile male Dark greyish-brown above, and on sides of neck and cheeks; underparts grey. Iris hazel. Proximal half of lower mandible and base of upper mandible cream.
Male in transition Blackish-brown above and on cheeks and malar region, unglossed except for shoulder; much less red and black on underparts than in adult, which are chiefly grey, becoming slightly buffy on centre of abdomen; yellow base to lower mandible.

GEOGRAPHICAL VARIATION None. Previously included in *D. australe*, but accorded species status by Collar *et al.* (1999) following Brooks *et al.* (1992).

MEASUREMENTS Wing 51-59 (mean 55.4, SD 2.61, 12 males), 50-57 (females); **bill** 10.8-14 (mean 12.1, SD 1.09, 11 males), 11.2-12.7 (females); **mass** no data.

REFERENCES Brooks *et al.* (1992), Collar *et al.* (1994, 1999), duPont (1971), Dickinson *et al.* (1991), Mann (in prep. a), Meyer (1933), Schönwetter (1980-1984), Ogilvie-Grant & Whitehead (1898), Salomonsen (1960b).

---

23   SCARLET-COLLARED FLOWERPECKER
Dicaeum retrocinctum   Plate 6

Dicaeum retrocinctum Gould, 1872, *Ann. Mag. Nat. Hist.* ser.4, 10 p.114, Manila (male), Mindanao (female); [error = Mindoro; inferentially corrected to Mindoro by Whitehead (1899)].

IDENTIFICATION Adult blue-black above with scarlet collar; red patch on black chin and throat; black-bordered scarlet stripe on centre of breast and belly; rest of underparts greyish-white.
Similar species From Red-striped Flowerpecker *Dicaeum*

australe (21) and Pygmy Flowerpecker *D. pygmaeum* (28) by black throat with red spot, and slender, decurved bill.

VOICE High *chip chip....*

DISTRIBUTION Endemic to Mindoro, Philippines, although also reported from Panay and Negros.

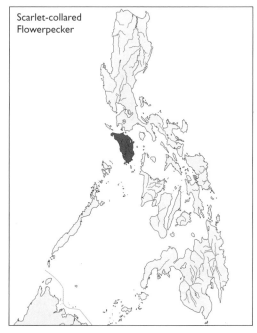

Scarlet-collared Flowerpecker

HABITAT Forest, forest edge, cultivation and coconut groves, below 1,200 m. Poorly tolerant of degraded land.

STATUS Although described as fairly common on Mindoro (Dickinson *et al.* 1991), listed as globally threatened, status Vulnerable, by Collar *et al.* (1999) owing to its dependence on lower-altitude closed-canopy forest and the almost complete disappearance of this habitat.

MOVEMENTS Unknown.

FOOD Fruit, and possibly also nectar and/or pollen of mistletoes.
Known food-plants *Ficus* spp., *Muntingia* sp., epiphytes, ?Loranthaceae, vines.

HABITS Forages singly, in groups and mixed flocks amongst flowering or fruiting trees. Often high in canopy, but occasionally low down in bushes.

BREEDING Nest Unknown. **Eggs** Unknown. **Laying months** April, enlarged gonads April–June.

DESCRIPTION Sexes similar.
Adult Bill slender and decurved. Upperparts including tail blue-black, with a scarlet collar on hindneck, sometimes incomplete; chin and throat to upper breast black with red patch; sides of throat, lower breast, belly and undertail-coverts grey-white; scarlet stripe bordered black on centre of breast and belly. Remiges blackish-brown. Underwing-coverts white. Iris dark red-brown. Bill and feet black.
Juvenile Unknown.

GEOGRAPHICAL VARIATION None.

MEASUREMENTS Wing 51, 52, 53 (3 males); **tail** 25 (unsexed); **bill** 12.1, 12.5, 14.6 (3 males), 12.7, 13 (unsexed); **gape** 11.1-12.3 (males), **tarsus** 15 (unsexed); **mass** no data.

REFERENCES Collar *et al.* (1994, 1999), Curio (1994a,b), Curio *et al.* (1996), Dickinson *et al.* (1991), duPont (1971), Dutson *et al.* (1992), Whitehead (1899).

24 ORANGE-BELLIED FLOWERPECKER
Dicaeum trigonostigma   Plate 6

Certhia trigonostigma Scopoli, 1786, *Del. Flor. Fauna. Insubr.*, fasc. 2, p.91, Malacca, Malaysia.

IDENTIFICATION Adult male slaty-blue or grey, and orange above, grey and orange below. Adult female greyish olive-brown with yellow or orange rump; grey-brown below with yellow belly, becoming orange on lower belly and undertail-coverts. Juvenile lacks yellow and orange, and is more greyish-olive.
Similar species Male unlike any other flowerpecker. Female from female Scarlet-breasted Flowerpecker *Prionochilus thoracicus* (8) by orange or orange-yellow rump, and lack of black tail; females of Yellow-bellied Flowerpecker *Dicaeum melanoxanthum* (14) and Fire-breasted Flowerpecker *D. ignipectum* (40) lack orange or orange-yellow rump; female Blood-breasted Flowerpecker *D. sanguinolentum*

(43), Scarlet-backed Flowerpecker *D. cruentatum* (45) and Scarlet-headed Flowerpecker *D. trochileum* (46) have red rumps, and latter has red on back.

VOICE Call Continually utters a low shrill chirp. A long drawn-out *zeeee*. A repeated *sit* from male birds only. Prolonged buzzing *brrr-brrr*; a repeated *zit-zit-zit* by male birds even during flight. Rapid and repeated *chit-it-chit-it-chit*. **Song** High-pitched rapid sissiping.

DISTRIBUTION Bangladesh, eastern Assam, Sundarbans, Burma, Thailand, Malay Peninsula, Sumatra and islands, Borneo, Natunas, Java, Bali and Philippines. One record, Arunachal Pradesh, India.

HABITAT Various types of forest and at forest edge, including dipterocarp forest, lower montane forest, peat-swamp forest, alluvial forest, *Melaleuca* forest, heath forest and mangroves, scrub, cultivation, highland *kerangas*, *Albizia* plantations, *Eucalyptus* plantations, overgrown rubber, gardens and secondary growth; up to 1,800 m.

STATUS Common in the Philippines. Recently rediscovered at Nug-as, Cebu, but not common. Common and widespread in peninsular Malaysia, entering gardens in towns and reaching foothills. Rare outside southern Tenasserim in Burma. Locally common, Bangladesh.

MOVEMENTS Unknown.

FOOD Fruits, berries, seeds, minute insects, nectar and pollen.
Known food-plants *Eugenia* sp., unidentified mistletoes

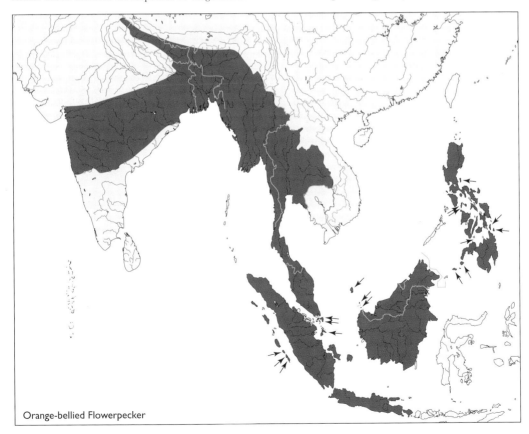

Orange-bellied Flowerpecker

Loranthaceae, banana *Musa* sp., mangrove fruits, flowers and fruits of rubber *Hevea brasiliensis* and coffee *Coffea* sp., sedge seeds, figs *Ficus* sp.

HABITS Feeds on flowering and fruiting trees at all heights. Wipes cloaca on perch after defecating, thus presumably aiding dispersal of Loranthaceae seeds; in captivity has trouble passing ordinary fruit. Host to *Haemoproteus dicaeus*, *Trypanosoma* sp. and microfilariae.

BREEDING Nest Has form and size of a goose egg of fine green moss, clubmoss or fern, lined with white fibres and small feathers, suspended 2-13 m above ground by small end from slender twig of tall tree or in bush; *Imperata* sp. pappus and fibre may be used, with caterpillar frass as decoration; cobweb may be used for binding. Nests on Samar pocket-shaped with side entrance, suspended from slender boughs or stems of large leaf. Outside of green moss bound together with spiders' webs, and lined with dark brown down from young fern fronds, in neglected clearings some distance from forest; a nest from Taiping, peninsular Malaysia, mostly of plant down with rootlets used to surround the opening and the attachment and to form very sparse covering on rest of outside. One from Nias Island, Sumatra, was a very compact pocket, mostly of moss and rootlets, lichen giving felt-like appearance, with decorations of plant material. **Eggs** c/2-3; bluish-white, with tiny brown specks and, at larger end, longer dark brown spots. On Samar: pure white, 15 x 12. *cinereigulare*: 14.0-15.7 (mean 14.8, n=10) x 10.7-11.4 (mean 10.8); *dayakanum*: 15.7-16.4 (mean 15.9, n=5) x 10.7-13.0 (mean 11.4); *flaviclunis*: 13.8-16.1 (mean 15.4, n=22) x 10.7-11.4 (mean 11.0); *rubropygium*: 14.3-17.6 (mean 15.5, n=10) x 10.8-11.9 (mean 11.2); *trigonostigma*: 14.6 x 10.3; *xanthopygium*: 17.0 x 12.0. **Laying months** Bangladesh: April–May; Borneo: Kuching, Sarawak, March; Sabah: fledgling September, nests July, September–December, enlarged sex organs February–April, June, August. India: May, September; Malaya: January–May, July, nestlings March, juveniles January and May to September; Java: West Java, February–May, October, December; Philippines: Samar, July and August, and Siquijor, February; Sumatra: eggs July, Juvenile P. Rupat, Riau Archipelago, August.

DESCRIPTION *D. t. trigonostigma*
Adult male Head to below eye, neck, upper back, wings and tail dark slaty-blue; triangular orange patch on upper back; lower back and rump orange. Throat to upper breast pale grey; rest of underparts bright orange, becoming more yellow on belly. Iris brown or pale brown; bill blackish, paler on lower mandible; feet dark grey, indigo or blackish.
Adult female Olive-brown upperparts, with olive-yellow, sometimes tinged orange, rump; throat, breast and flanks grey-brown, belly yellow, becoming orange on lower belly and undertail-coverts.
Juvenile Similar to female, but throat, breast and flanks greyish-olive, lacking all yellow or orange. Bill bright yellow tipped light brown; iris dark brown; legs pale slate-blue. See also under *sibuyanicum* (below).

GEOGRAPHICAL VARIATION Species breaks down into two groups, one Sundaic west to Assam (nominate *trigonostigma* group; the first six forms below), and one in the Philippines (*dorsale* group, in which males have the orange of the back separate from that of the rump, or rump may lack orange or yellow).

Trigonostigma group
D. t. antioproctis Oberholser, 1912 (Simeulue Island off Sumatra) Female greenish, with a less olive rump, and less olive below than nominate. Probably invalid, and should be merged with other west Sumatran island forms in nominate.
D. t. dayakanum Chasen & Kloss, 1929 (Borneo) Male differs from *trigonostigma* by being blacker above, having more extensive orange on back, darker grey throat to upper breast, whereas female has rump more greenish-orange, throat yellowish-white, breast grey with some orange, and abdomen yellow.
D. t. flaviclunis Hartert, 1918 (Java and Bali) Rump of male is purer yellow. Female has brighter yellow rump, and is more yellow below, tending to orange on centre of breast. Juvenile is browner and lacks all yellow and orange.
D. t. megastoma Hartert, 1918 (Natunas) As nominate but with much longer bill.
D. t. rubropygium Baker, 1921 (Arunachal Pradesh, eastern Assam and Sundarbans; Burma, from Tenasserim through the Karen hills and Karenni to the plains of southern Burma and Arakan; and Thailand south to Krabi) The male is more orange below, the female more orange on uppertail-coverts, than nominate, with which it intergrades in south peninsular Thailand.
D. t. trigonostigma (Scopoli, 1786) (Surat Thani south through Malay Peninsula to Singapore; Sumatra and satellites [Banyak islands, Nias, Batu Islands, Mentawai Islands]; Riau Archipelago; Lingga Archipelago; Karimata Island) Described above.

Dorsale group
D. t. assimile Bourns & Worcester, 1894 (Philippines – Jolo, Tawitawi [previously, probably no longer] and Siasi) Male differs from *cinereigulare* in having yellow rump, dark grey chin and throat, and paler orange breast and belly.
D. t. besti Steere, 1890 (Philippines – Siquijor) Male differs from *cinereigulare* by having less yellow on throat, and being larger (wing 52 versus 49; bill 11 versus 9).
D. t. cinereigulare Tweeddale, 1878 (Philippines – Bohol, Leyte, Mindanao, Samar, Calicoan and Biliran) Male differs from nominate *trigonostigma* by having a small orange triangle on back, no yellow on rump, a greyish band across centre of yellow throat, and breast and belly darker orange. The female has a yellow throat, and more orange in centre of breast. Male differs from *besti* in having lower throat and neck grey washed yellow.
D. t. cnecolaemum Parkes, 1989 (Philippines – Tablas) Male differs from *intermedium* by throat washed yellow rather than pale, neutral grey, breast slightly deeper orange-yellow, and blue dorsum slightly less blackish, especially forehead. Immature males yellow on chin, rather than grey as in *intermedium*, and green of dorsum less greyish. No females of *intermedium* examined, but are possibly greyer on throat than in this form, as in immature males.
D. t. dorsale Sharpe, 1876 (Philippines – Masbate, Negros and Panay) Male differs from *trigonostigma* in having dark blue rump and less orange above, and more orange breast and belly. Female differs in being yellow below, orangey on centre of breast.
D. t. intermedium Bourns & Worcester, 1894 (Philip-

pines – Romblon) Male differs from *sibuyanicum* by having chin and throat much paler grey, washed pale yellow; olive-green patch on rump very small or absent. The female is duller below.

D. t. isidroi Rand & Rabor, 1969 (Philippines – Camiguin Sur) Male larger (wing 56 versus 51) than *cinereigulare* and *besti* with chin and throat much paler yellow, sides of throat greyish-white without yellow wash.

D. t. pallidius Bourns & Worcester, 1894 (Philippines – Cebu; believed extinct since 1920, but recently rediscovered at Nug-as) Male differs from *dorsale* by having upperparts lighter blue, and underparts uniform yellow with trace of orange on breast.

D. t. sibutuense Sharpe, 1893 (Philippines – Sibutu, Omapoy and Sipangkot) Male has less orange on back than nominate, very little yellow on rump, above more bluish, and throat very dark grey. It differs from *assimile* in dark olive-green rump. The female is much greener above than *trigonostigma*, particularly on the back which tends to greenish-yellow on rump; throat to breast is greyer with some orange on upper breast (one specimen out of two examined had an orange feather on back).

D. t. sibuyanicum Bourns & Worcester, 1894 (Philippines – Sibuyan) Male differs from *trigonostigma* in rump being very dark olive-green with no yellow; chin and throat grey; rest of underparts less orange, more greeny-yellow. Female lacks yellow on rump. Juvenile male has upperparts olive-green; wings and tail black; remiges edged blue; tertials edged green; below light olive washed greenish-yellow on chin, centre of breast and abdomen; bill bright yellow tipped light brown.

D. t. xanthopygium Tweeddale, 1877 (Philippines – Luzon, Marinduque, Mindoro and Polillo) Male has top of head and upperparts dark slaty-blue, with a bright orange-red patch on middle of back, yellow uppertail-coverts and rump, and blue-black tail; lores and sides of head black; chin, throat and upper breast yellow, centre of breast and belly orange; vent and undertail-coverts yellow tinged green. Female from *trigonostigma* by being olive rather than grey below.

MEASUREMENTS Wing 50-53 (mean 51.8, 10 male *besti*), 47.5-51 (mean 49.4, 7 male *dayakanum*, Brunei), 50-52 (mean 51, 10 male *cinereigulare*, Samar), 49-52 (mean 50, 4 male *cinereigulare*, Bohol), 49-52 (mean 51.2, 10 male *cinereigulare*, Mindanao), 55-57 (mean 55.6, 10 male *isidroi*), 54-57 (male *sibuyanicum*), 53 (male *xanthopygium*), 46, 47 (female *dayakanum*, Brunei), 49-52 (unsexed *cinereigulare*), 45 (unsexed juvenile *dayakanum*, Brunei); **tail** 25 (male *xanthopygium*); **bill** 11 (male *besti*), 12 (male *xanthopygium*), 9 (unsexed *cinereigulare*); **culmen** 13-14 (mean 13.3, 10 male *besti*), 11.0-13.5 (mean 12.4, 10 male *cinereigulare*, Samar), 12-13 (mean 12.5, 4 male *cinereigulare*, Bohol), 12-13.5 (mean 12.7, 10 male *cinereigulare*, Mindanao), mean 14.0 (10 male *isidroi*), 12-12.5 (unsexed *trigonostigma*), 13.5-14.1 (unsexed *sibuyanicum*); **gape** 12.1-13.8 (mean 12.8, 8 male *dayakanum*, Brunei), 11.5, 12.8 (female *dayakanum*, Brunei), 12.7 (unsexed juvenile *dayakanum*, Brunei); **tarsus** 12 (male *xanthopygium*); **mass** 5.8-7.0 (mean 6.6, 8 male *dayakanum*, Brunei), 6.6, 7.3 (female *dayakanum*, Brunei), 6.2 (unsexed juvenile *dayakanum*, Brunei).

REFERENCES D. Allen (pers. comm.), Booth (1969), Brooks *et al.* (1992), Dickinson *et al.* (1991), duPont (1971), Dutson *et al.* (1996), Grimmett *et al.* (1998), Hellebrekers & Hoogerwerf (1967), Holmes (1996), MacKinnon & Phillipps (1993), Mann (in prep. a,b), Medway & Wells (1976), Nash & Nash (1985), Ogilvie-Grant & Whitehead (1898), Parkes (1989), Rand & Rabor (1967), Richardson & Baker (1981), Scopoli (1786), Sheldon *et al.* (in press), Singh (1995), Smythies (1957, 1960, 1981, 1986).

25 BUZZING FLOWERPECKER
Dicaeum hypoleucum   Plate 7

Dicaeum hypoleucum Sharpe, 1876, *Nature* 14, p.298, Basilan, Philippines.

IDENTIFICATION Adult olive-brown or blackish above with dark brown primaries and tail; underparts greyish-olive. Juvenile is dark olive-grey above, below grey tinged greenish-yellow; bill pale.

Similar species Plain Flowerpecker *Dicaeum concolor* (27) and Brown-backed Flowerpecker *D. everetti* (11) are all allopatric to *D. hypoleucum*. From Thick-billed Flowerpecker *D. agile* (10) by lack of streaking below; from Olive-capped Flowerpecker *D. nigrilore* (17) by lack of black lores and patch under eye; from Flame-crowned Flowerpecker *D. anthonyi* (18) by olive-brown, not olive, upperparts, and greyish-olive, not greyish-white, underparts; Bicoloured Flowerpecker *D. bicolor* (19) female is greener, less brown, above.

VOICE High buzzing notes *see-see-see*, followed by rapid trilled *cheenjet*. Very metallic *chimp chimp*, equally spaced at first, but later running into a trill.

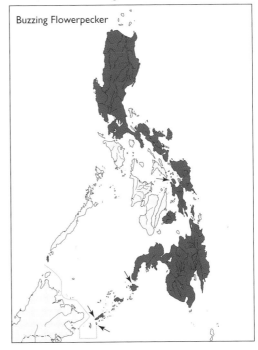

Buzzing Flowerpecker

DISTRIBUTION Endemic to the Philippines, occurring on Basilan, Bicol, Bohol, Bongao, Catanduanes, Dinagat, Jolo, Leyte, Luzon, Malamaui, Manuk Manka, Mindanao, Panaon, Samar, Sanga Sanga, Siasi and Tawitawi.

HABITAT Forests and at forest edge below 1,500 m, but to 1,800 m in Kitanglad range.

STATUS Common.

MOVEMENTS Unknown.

FOOD Fruit of figs is the only definitely known item, but perhaps also nectar and/or pollen of figs and mistletoes. **Known food-plants** *Ficus* spp.

HABITS Forages singly, in groups or mixed flocks on fruiting and flowering trees (particularly *Ficus*).

BREEDING Nest Unknown. **Eggs** Undescribed. **Laying months** Basilan, September.

DESCRIPTION *D. h. obscurum* Sexes similar.
Adult Upperparts olive-brown; tail and primaries dark brown; underparts greyish-olive. Iris brown, bill black, feet brownish or black.
Juvenile Dark olive-grey above; underparts grey with greenish-yellow tinge; bill paler.

GEOGRAPHICAL VARIATION
  D. h. cagayanensis Rand & Rabor, 1967 (north-eastern Luzon – Sierra Madre Mts including Mt Cagua) Below paler and yellower, less olive, than *obscurum*.
  D. h. hypoleucum Sharpe, 1876 (Basilan, Bongao, Jolo, Siasi, Tawitawi, Malamaui, Sanga Sanga and Manuk Manka) Male differs from *pontifex* by having upperparts blackish and underparts paler; female more olivaceous. This distinctive form may warrant specific status.
  D. h. mindanense Tweeddale, 1877 (Zamboanga Peninsula, Mindanao) Smaller than nominate. Upperparts, cheeks and ear-coverts dusky olive-green; below greyish-white, particularly on breast; flight feathers dark brown edged olive-green on outerwebs; tail feathers dark brown faintly edged olive; axillaries and underwing-coverts white; bill longer than head.
  D. h. obscurum Ogilvie-Grant, 1894 (includes *lagunae* Parkes, 1962) (north-western and central Luzon – north-central mountains, Laguna province, and probably southern Sierra Madre Mts., Bicol and Catanduanes) Described above.
  D. h. pontifex Mayr, 1946 (Bohol, Dinagat, Leyte, Mindanao, Panaon and Samar) Differs from *obscurum* in having greyish-white underparts, darker green above.

MEASUREMENTS Wing 53-56 (mean 55.1, 10 male *cagayensis*), 50-54 (mean 52.3, SD 1.50, 6 male *hypoleucum*), 48-53 (mean 51.0, SD 1.87, 5 female *hypoleucum*), 55, 55 (2 unsexed juvenile *hypoleucum*); **tail** 27; **bill** 13.2-14.8 (mean 13.8, SD 0.57, 6 male *hypoleucum*), 13.1-15 (mean 14.2, SD 0.79, 5 female *hypoleucum*), 11.8, 12.2 (2 unsexed juvenile *hypoleucum*); **tarsus** 14; **mass** no data.

REFERENCES Dickinson *et al.* (1991), duPont (1971), Rand & Rabor (1967), Tweeddale (1877).

---

26   PALE-BILLED FLOWERPECKER
Dicaeum erythrorhynchos   Plate 7

Certhia erythrorhynchos Latham, 1790, *Lath. Index Orn.* I. p.299, India; restricted to Bombay by Baker, 1926, *Fauna Brit. India, Birds*, ed.2, 3, p.432.

Alternative name: Tickell's Flowerpecker

IDENTIFICATION Adult olive-brown above and greyish-white below; juvenile greyer; short, slender, pale bill.
Similar species From Plain Flowerpecker *Dicaeum concolor* (27) by pale bill and lack of supercilium; from female Yellow-bellied Flowerpecker *D. melanoxanthum* (14) by lack of yellow below; from Thick-billed Flowerpecker *D. agile* (10) by pale bill and lack of streaking below.

VOICE Call High-pitched repeated *pit*; almost incessant sharp *chik-chik-chik*. **Song** A series of twittering notes and a cricket-like reel.

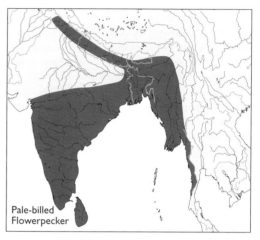
Pale-billed
Flowerpecker

DISTRIBUTION The Himalayan foothills and plains of Uttar Pradesh (including Rajaji National Park) to Nepal, Bengal, Arunachal Pradesh, Bhutan, Bangladesh, Bihar, and Deccan from Baroda and Jabalpur southwards; Burma, south to Tenasserim; Sri Lanka.

HABITAT Canopy of deciduous forest with mistletoes (Loranthaceae and *Viscum* spp.), mangroves, at edges villages and towns in cultivated grounds, plantations, mango groves, orchards and figs in open country; to 2,100 m in Sri Lanka, 152-305 m in Nepal in terai and lower foothills, but up to 1,400 m in summer.

STATUS Widespread in India, where locally abundant, e.g. southern Gujarat, Bombay and Pune, but absent from dry north-western areas. Common at all altitudes in Sri Lanka. Common in Bangladesh. Widespread and frequent in Nepal. Not uncommon in Burma.

MOVEMENTS Seasonal vertical movements in Himalayan foothills.

FOOD Chiefly berries, but also fruit, nectar, spiders and small insects. Tests ripeness of berries with mandibles before feeding. Swallows berries of *Loranthus* sp. and *Viscum* sp. whole, broad end first. After 3-4 berries have been eaten, birds retire to rest on branch for a few minutes with feathers puffed out; then sticky, slimy, seeds passed out, broad end first, onto branches after speedy digestion – a final, jerky and dipping movement of the posterior of the body, and pivoting of body to position it almost along rather than astride the branch, leaves the seeds stuck, after which the bird flies off to seek more.
Known food-plants *Dendrophthoe falcata* (mainly eats ripe fruits), guava *Psidium* sp., *Loranthus* (? = *Taxillus*) *longiflorus*, mango *Mangifera indica*, unidentified Loranthaceae, fruits of *Scurrula parasitica*, and *Viscum* spp.

HABITS Occurs in parties of up to 10+ in winter; singles or pairs at other times. Usually in canopy; restless, continually flitting from branch to branch; flies high and rapidly; defends feeding territory. Host to *Haemoproteus dicaeus*.

BREEDING Both sexes build nest, care for young and probably incubate. Nestlings fed on peeled *Loranthus* berries. **Nest** A small oval purse of fine grass, vegetable down, bark, moss, cocoons and caterpillar frass, felted and pinkish-brown, suspended from twig amongst leaves 1.5-12 m above ground, sometimes also secured to supporting branch at back and often well concealed by surrounding foliage. One nest of *ceylonense* hammock-like, suspended from twigs at each end. Lined with soft silky down and fibres. Another suspended 11 m up from *Grevillea robusta* tree in a tea field and profusely decorated with berries, lichen and flat white material resembling shed reptile skin. **Eggs** c/1-3. Unmarked white. Some eggs of *ceylonense* spotted. Race *ceylonense:* 14.4-15.4 (mean 14.6, n=4) x 10.3-11.0 (mean 10.5); *erythrorhynchos:* 13.1-15.5 (mean 14.5, n=36) x 10.1-11.1 (mean 10.4). **Laying months** India: February–June in north, February–May and August–September in south; Nepal: January–June; Sri Lanka: January–July, peak March, but also September and November.

DESCRIPTION *D. e. erythrorhynchos* Sexes similar.
Adult Plain olive-brown above; remiges dark brown with pale edging; rectrices dark brown with pale tips; greyish-white underparts, buffier on belly; underwing-coverts whitish. Iris hazel-brown; bill pale horny-brown, pinkish-flesh at gape and on lower mandible except tip, and pale pink in mouth; feet dark slate.
Juvenile Greyer above and below than adult. Orange-yellow at gape and on lower mandible except tip.

GEOGRAPHICAL VARIATION
    D. e. ceylonense Babault, 1920 (Sri Lanka) Differs from *erythrorhynchos* in being darker, more olive above and below, and lower mandible dark brown instead of pinkish. Iris yellowish-brown, bill plumbeous-brown, feet greyish.
    D. e. erythrorhynchos (Latham, 1790) (India, Nepal, Bhutan, Bangladesh and Burma) Described above.

MEASUREMENTS Wing 46-50 (male *ceylonense*), 46-52 (male *erythrorhynchos*), 43-50 (female *ceylonense*), 46-52 (female *erythrorhynchos*); **tail** 22-27 (male *erythrorhynchos*), 22-25 (female *erythrorhynchos*); **bill** 12-13 (male *ceylonense*), 11-13 (male *erythrorhynchos*), 12-13 (female *ceylonense*), 11-13 (female *erythrorhynchos*); **gape** 9.8-11.9 (male *ceylonense*), 10.7-12.8 (male *erythrorhynchos*), 9.7-12.8 (female *ceylonense*), 10.4-12.5 (female *erythrorhynchos*); **tarsus** 12-13 (male *ceylonense*), 11-13 (male *erythrorhynchos*), 12-13 (female *ceylonense*); **mass** 4-8 (mean 6.5, 17 unsexed *erythrorhynchos*).

REFERENCES Ali (1969), Ali & Ripley (1974), Fleming *et al.* (1976), Grimmett *et al.* (1998), Inskipp & Inskipp (1985), Latham (1790), Smythies (1986), Wait (1931), Whistler (1949).

---

27   PLAIN FLOWERPECKER
Dicaeum concolor   **Plate 7**

Dicaeum concolor Jerdon, 1840, *Madras Journ. Lit. Sci.* 11, p. 227, Malabar coast, India.

IDENTIFICATION Adult olive-brown above, with pale lores and supercilium; yellowish-white below. Juvenile duller; browner above, ashier below. Short, slender, slightly curved blackish bill.
Similar species From Pale-billed Flowerpecker *Dicaeum erythrorhynchos* (26) by supercilium and blackish bill, and is also dumpier. From Thick-billed Flowerpecker *D. agile* (10) and Brown-backed Flowerpecker *D. everetti* (11) by much finer bill. From Fire-breasted Flowerpecker *D. ignipectum* (40) female by being smaller, with a longer, more curved bill, no metallic lustre above except on tail, and more olivaceous below; female Yellow-bellied Flowerpecker *D. melanoxanthum* (14) has yellow below; female Black-sided Flowerpecker *D. monticolum* (41) is olive-green rather than olive-brown above.

VOICE Call *Tik-tik-tik*; sharp *chek*; *chirp-chirp-chirp*; also twitters. **Song** A high-pitched trilling.

DISTRIBUTION The Himalayan foothills of the eastern half of Nepal eastwards through Sikkim, north Bengal and Bhutan to Arunachal Pradesh, south through Assam, Nagaland and Manipur to Chittagong Hills, Thailand, Indochina, south through Malay Peninsula; south-west India north to Khandala and Mahableshwar (including Wynaad); South and Middle Andamans; central and south China (Hunan, east Szechuan south to Yunnan, Kwangsi and Kwangtung), Hainan Island and Taiwan; Hong Kong (vagrant); Sumatra, Borneo (particularly Sabah, and Kelabit uplands, Sarawak), Java and Bali.

HABITAT Dependent on Loranthaceae, and found in various forest types, evergreen and moist deciduous, including hill and montane forests, chiefly at the edge, and groves of trees in open country, secondary growth, plantations, other cultivation and trees around villages. Often around vines with fruit or flowers. Occurs from sea-level to 3,660 m, but probably commonest in foothills and submontane localities; in Nepal usually 305-1,525 m, but up to 2,500 m; in Sumatra, 500-1,500 m.

STATUS Local to common in Indian subcontinent. Common in Thailand in the northern and eastern plateaus and south-western provinces. Widely but sparsely distributed in Burma, where common on coastal islands of Arakan from Myebon to Ruywa. Very uncommon in Borneo. Not rare in Java. Vagrant to Hong Kong.

MOVEMENTS None recorded, but probably moves vertically in higher parts of range.

FOOD Insects, spiders, berries and nectar.
Known food-plants Mistletoes Loranthaceae: *Dendrophthoe falcata*, *D. pentandra* (*Dicaeum* spp. probe with their bill sideways into the top of the flowerbud of *D. pentandra*, the corolla jerks open, and the liquid nectar, which completely fills it, shoots out), *Helixanthera intermedia*, fruits of *Scurrula parasitica*, *Taxillus cuneatus*, *T. recurvus*.

HABITS Usually single, but sometimes in pairs or small parties; often in tree-tops, but also very low. Restless. Host to *Leucocytozoon* sp. and feather mites *Monojoubertia marquardti*.

BREEDING Both sexes involved in all activities. **Nest** A very small hanging purse (c.70 x 50 mm) made chiefly of floss of *Bombax malabarica* and other fibres and vegetable down, on trees or high bushes 6-12 m above ground, although sometimes much lower amongst nettles and

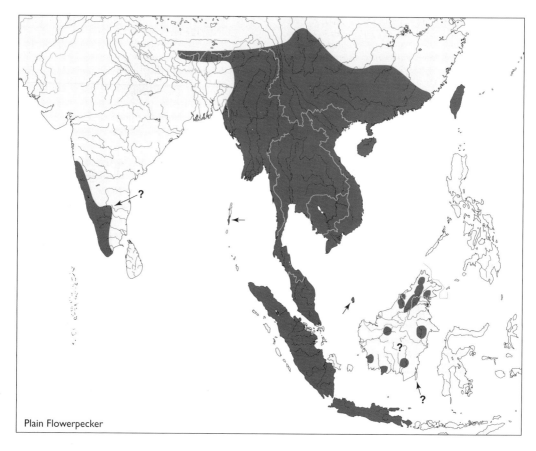

Plain Flowerpecker

briars. **Eggs** c/2-3. Race *borneanum*: 13.8 x 11.0; *concolor*: 13.9-16.4 (mean 14.7, n=25) x 10.1-11.2 (mean 10.6); *olivaceum*: 13.0-15.9 (mean 14.6, n=45) x 9.9-11.7 (mean 10.3). Unmarked white, but eggs from Sabah pale orange-pink thickly flecked burnt-sienna towards broad end and few fine spots of chestnut. **Laying months** Nepal and north India: March–September; South India: January–May; Andamans: chiefly May and June; Sabah: March, enlarged testes, June and July.

DESCRIPTION *D. c. concolor*

Adult Sexes similar. Olive-brown above, with dark centres to crown feathers; pale lores and supercilium; yellowish-white below; white shoulder on closed wing. Iris brown to dark brown; bill bluish-grey, dark horny-brown on culmen, feet brownish-black.

Juvenile Browner, duller and less olive than adult and underparts ashier; also lacks dark centres to feathers of crown.

GEOGRAPHICAL VARIATION

D. c. borneanum Lönnberg, 1925 (Malay Peninsula from Perak and Penang south to Singapore; Sumatra and Borneo) Quite green above, brighter on rump; throat to breast grey; flanks yellowish-green; centre of belly buffish-white. Feet plumbeous.

D. c. concolor Jerdon, 1840 (south-west India; includes *subflavum* Baker, 1921) Described above.

D. c. minullum Swinhoe, 1870 (Hainan Island) Slightly greener above than nominate. Olive-green above, brownish on head, back and scapulars; yellowish on rump. Dark centres of coronal feathers give spotted appearance. Tail tipped white. Throat and belly dusky-yellowish; clearer, nearly primrose on vent. Flanks greyish-olive; axillaries and carpal edged white.

D. c. olivaceum Walden, 1875 (Indian subcontinent except south-west, China, Burma and Thailand south to north peninsular Malaysia) Slightly more olive-green above than nominate; underparts duller and ashier with slight buffy-yellow tinge. Differences less obvious in worn plumage. Iris brown, bill plumbeous-grey or black.

D. c. sollicitans Hartert, 1901 (Java and Bali) Greener above than nominate, and has smaller bill. From *olivaceum* by larger, more distinct, buff patch on lores filling space between bill and eye; bill slightly broader at base, and possibly has a shorter wing. Feet plumbeous.

D. c. uchidai Kuroda, 1920 (Taiwan) Similar to *olivaceum* but tail shorter and generally darker. Above deep olive, paler on rump and uppertail-coverts; sides of breast and flanks tinged olive, tail blackish-brown faintly tinged green. Juvenile has basal half of lower mandible and basal edge of upper mandible yellowish. Margins of terminal third of both mandibles finely serrated.

D. c. virescens Hume, 1873 (South and Middle Andamans) Much greener above than nominate or *olivaceum*, and yellow on vent and belly; lores whitish but no white on forehead, and supercilium almost absent.

MEASUREMENTS Wing 45-52 (male *concolor*), 46 (male *minullum*), 43-48 (male *olivaceum*), 46-48.5 (male *uchidae*), 44-52 (female *concolor*), 44 (female *minullum*), 41-45 (female *olivaceum*), 45 (female *uchidae*), 44.5 (unsexed *sollicitans*), 43.5-45 (unsexed juvenile *uchidae*); **tail** 22-23 (male *uchidae*), 21 (female *uchidae*), 10.5-11 (unsexed juvenile *uchidae*); **bill** 12-13 (male *concolor*), 11-12 (male *olivaceum*), 12-13.5 (female *concolor*), 11-12 (female *olivaceum*); **culmen** 9-9.4 (male *uchidae*), 10 (female *uchidae*), 8.6-9 (unsexed juvenile *uchidae*); **gape** 10.3-10.4 (male *borneanum*), 11.3-13.2 (male *concolor*), 10.6 (male *minullum*), 8.6-10.7 (male *olivaceum*), 11.2 (male *sollicitans*), 11.2 (male ?*subflavum*), 11.0-11.6 (male *virescens*), 11.2-11.6 (female *borneanum*), 10.7-12.7 (female *concolor*), 8.9-10.3 (female *olivaceum*), 10.7-12.3 (female *virescens*); **mass** 5-8 (mean 6.2, 15 unsexed *concolor*), 4-6 (unsexed *olivaceum*).

REFERENCES Ali (1969), Ali & Ripley (1974), Atyeo (1971), Cooper (1991), Davidar (1985); Grimmett *et al.* (1998), Hartert (1901), Hellebrekers & Hoogerwerf (1967), Inskipp & Inskipp (1985), King *et al.* (1975), Kuroda (1920), MacKinnon & Phillipps (1993), Mann (in prep. a,b), van Marle & Voous (1988), Medway & Wells (1976), Salomonsen (1960c), Sheldon *et al.* (in press), Smythies (1957, 1960, 1981), Swinhoe (1870).

---

28   PYGMY FLOWERPECKER
Dicaeum pygmaeum   Plate 7

Pygmy Flowerpecker

Nectarinia pygmea (*pygmea* in text, *pygmaea* on plate) Kittlitz, 1833, *Mém. Pres. Acad. Imp. Sci. St. Pétersbourg* 2, p.2, pl.2, Luzon; restricted to "vicinity of Manila" by Parkes, 1962, *Postilla*, no.67, p.6.

IDENTIFICATION Adult male mostly olive-black glossed green above, with yellowish rump; below grey, white and buffy. Female similar but duller.
Similar species From Cebu Flowerpecker *Dicaeum quadricolor* (20) by lack of orange-red tips to back feathers; from Palawan Flowerpecker *Prionochilus plateni* (6), Red-striped Flowerpecker *D. australe* (21) and Scarlet-collared Flowerpecker *D. retrocinctum* (23) by lack of red below; Whiskered Flowerpecker *D. proprium* (12) has blue-black jugular stripe; male Bicoloured Flowerpecker *D. bicolor* (19) has black rump glossed blue.

VOICE High *schenk-schenk....*

DISTRIBUTION Endemic to the Philippines. Occurs on Balabac, Bohol, Boracay, Calagna-an, Calauit, Calayan, Camiguin Sur, Cebu, Corregidor, Culion, Fuga, Gigante Islands, Guimaras, Leyte, Lubang, Luzon, Maestre de Campo, Marinduque, Masbate, Mindanao, Mindoro, Negros, Palawan, Polillo, Romblon, Samar, Semirara, Sibay, Sibuyan, Sicogon, Siquijor and Ticao. Possibly also Tawi Tawi – this could be previously unrecorded subspecies (Allen 2001).

HABITAT Forest, forest edge and in secondary growth below 2,000 m. Up to limits of dipterocarp forest (1,200 m) on Mindanao.

STATUS Common.

MOVEMENTS Unknown.

FOOD Presumably includes fruit, and possibly also nectar and/or pollen, of mistletoes.

Known food-plants None.

HABITS Forages singly, in groups and mixed flocks at fruiting and flowering trees, often near water.

BREEDING Nest Unknown. **Eggs** Unknown. **Laying months** North Luzon: February; Palawan, December; Samar: July.

DESCRIPTION *D. p. pygmaeum*
Adult male Top of head, back, wings and tail olive-black glossed green; rump dull olive-yellow; face, sides of throat and flanks grey; chin and centre of throat white; rest of underparts buffy. Iris dark brown, bill black, feet brownish-black.
Adult female As male but duller and lacks gloss.
Juvenile Unknown.

GEOGRAPHICAL VARIATION
   D. p. davao Mearns, 1905 (Mindanao and Camiguin Sur) Differs from *pygmaeum* in having face, sides of throat and flanks darker; belly and undertail-coverts more yellowish; back glossed greeny-blue.
   D. p. fugaensis Parkes, 1988 (Fuga, Babuyanes group, and perhaps Calayan) Male closest to *salomonseni* and *pygmaeum* but flanks grey rather than greenish; entire dorsum much blacker than in these forms and slightly iridescent, especially crown, approaching blue-black of *davao*. Greenish rump more restricted and contrasts with adjacent area of back as in the last form, where green rump is absent. Female and immature male greyer and less green on flanks than *salomonseni* and *pygmaeum*, with greenish rump-patch much smaller.
   D. p. palawanorum Hachisuka, 1926 (Balabac, Palawan, Culion and Calauit) Differs from *pygmaeum* in being larger and slightly lighter above with gloss confined to shoulders (little on crown and back); duller olive-yellow rump; underparts paler. Female similar to nominate.

D. p. pygmaeum (Kittlitz, 1833) (Philippines outside ranges of other subspecies) Described above.
D. p. salomonseni Parkes, 1962 (north and north-west Luzon) Larger and slightly lighter than nominate, with a duller olive-yellow rump.

MEASUREMENTS Wing 45-48 (male *pygmaeum*), 50 (unsexed *palawanorum*), 43-45 (female *pygmaeum*), 50 (male *salomonseni*); **tail** 25 (male *pygmaeum*); **bill** 9.5-10.4 (mean 9.9, SD 0.3, 6 male *pygmaeum*), 8.6-11.2 (mean 10.1, SD 0.96, 6 female *pygmaeum*); **gape** 9.5-10.4 (male *pygmaeum*), 10.1-12.8 (female *pygmaeum*); **tarsus** 11 (male *pygmaeum*); **mass** no data.

REFERENCES Allen (pers. comm. 2001), Dickinson *et al.* (1991), duPont (1971), Parkes (1988).

---

29 CRIMSON-CROWNED FLOWERPECKER
Dicaeum nehrkorni   Plate 8

Dicaeum Nehrkorni Blasius, 1886, *Braunschweigische Anzeigen*, Rurukan, northern Celebes

Part of the *D. nehrkorni-erythrothorax-vulneratum-pectorale-geelvinkianum-nitidum-eximium-aeneum* superspecies.

IDENTIFICATION Adult male glossy blue-black above, with crimson crown and rump; below grey and white, with crimson breast-spot, and blackish median line on abdomen. Adult female is duller with little or no red on crown; below grey and white.
Similar species Male from male Red-chested Flowerpecker *Dicaeum maugei* (39) by crimson crown; female from female *D. maugei* by thinner bill and much less red on uppertail-coverts; both sexes from Grey-sided Flowerpecker *D. celebicum* (42) by crimson rump.

VOICE Call Short, sharp *zit-zit*. Very hard repeated *tit* notes. High-pitched insect-like trill.

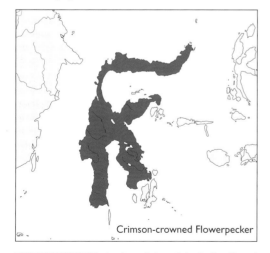
Crimson-crowned Flowerpecker

DISTRIBUTION Endemic to Sulawesi, including Dongi Dongi and Dumoga-Bone National Park, Butung island and possibly Kabaena island.

HABITAT Hill and montane forest, and at forest edge; 200-2,400 m. (A report of one in mangroves at sea-level on Butung is probably erroneous.)

STATUS Widespread and apparently uncommon, but may be overlooked as behaviour inconspicuous.

MOVEMENTS Unknown.

FOOD Includes fruit, and possibly also nectar and/or pollen, of mistletoes and wild cherries.
Known food-plants Loranthaceae and wild cherries.

HABITS Singly or in pairs, or in mixed-species flocks, mostly in canopy. Sings from leafless branch in canopy.

BREEDING Nothing recorded.

DESCRIPTION
Adult male Upperparts glossy blue-black; crown and rump bright crimson; throat, breast and sides grey, with small crimson spot on breast; white pectoral tufts; abdomen white with blackish-brown median line. Bill dark brown to black; feet blackish.
Adult female Duller than male, with little or no red on crown and lacking breast-spot and keel-stripe; little white on head. One specimen has a slight amount of red on hindcrown.
Juvenile Similar to adult female, but initially has no red on rump.

GEOGRAPHICAL VARIATION None.

MEASUREMENTS Wing 48, 49, 51 (3 males), 43, 47 (2 females); **bill** 10.4, 11.9, 13.9 (3 males), 9.6, 11.0 (2 females); **mass** no data.

REFERENCES Blasius (1886), Bostock & Sujatnika (1993), M. Catterall (pers. comm.), Coates & Bishop (1997), Rozendaal & Dekker (1989), Watling (1983), White & Bruce (1986).

---

30 FLAME-BREASTED FLOWERPECKER
Dicaeum erythrothorax   Plate 8

Dicaeum erythrothorax Lesson, 1828, *Voy. Cocquille, Zool.*, 1 (1826) p.672; atlas, pl.30, figs. 1 and 2, Buru, southern Moluccas

Part of the *D. nehrkorni-erythrothorax-vulneratum-pectorale-geelvinkianum-nitidum-eximium-aeneum* superspecies.

IDENTIFICATION Adult male mostly olive and brown above with yellowish-green rump; head and face glossed green; underparts whitish, grey and yellow with orange-red patch on upper breast. Adult female lacks red; juvenile as female but less green on rump, and greyer below.
Similar species None.

VOICE Nothing recorded.

DISTRIBUTION Endemic to Moluccas occurring on Morotai, Halmahera, Bacan, Obi, Bisa and Buru.

HABITAT Up to 800 m in scrub, forest and riverine habitats. Up to 950 m on Bacan.

STATUS Common to uncommon on Halmahera; common on Buru.

MOVEMENTS Unknown.

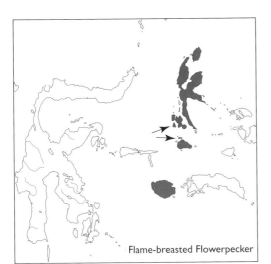

Flame-breasted Flowerpecker

31 ASHY FLOWERPECKER
Dicaeum vulneratum   Plate 8

Dicaeum vulneratum Wallace, 1863, *Proc. Zool. Soc. London*, p.32, Ceram, Moluccas.

Part of the *D. nehrkorni-erythrothorax-vulneratum-pectorale-geelvinkianum-nitidum-eximium-aeneum* superspecies.

IDENTIFICATION Adult male dark brownish-grey above with red rump; mostly ashy-grey below with scarlet patch on upper breast. Adult female lacks red below. **Similar species** None.

VOICE Call Hard, staccato *tst*, often in flight. **Song** On Seram three high-pitched, metallic, disyllabic notes lasting 1.5 sec. On Ambon song thin, very high-pitched trisyllabic note.

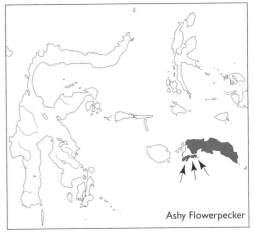

Ashy Flowerpecker

FOOD Presumably includes fruit, and possibly nectar and/or pollen, of mistletoes.
Known food-plants None.

HABITS Found in pairs, groups and mixed-species flocks in canopy; very active.

BREEDING Nest in Natural History Museum, Tring, with 1 chick, collected by Doherty, Buru, November 1897. **Nest** Suspended from twig by broad attachment and partly concealed by large leaves. Oval pouch with entrance just above centre. Made of plant fibre, some dried grass, giving felted appearance. Unlined. 9 x 5.5 cm. **Eggs** Undescribed, but measured (Schönwetter 1980-1984); *erythrothorax*: 14.2-15.2 (mean 14.7, n=2) x 10.5-10.6 (mean 10.6). **Laying months** October or November.

DESCRIPTION *D. e. erythrothorax*
Adult male Upperparts olive, with rump yellowish-green; wing-coverts and remiges dark brown with broad olive edging; head and face grey glossed green; throat white, breast grey, with orange-red patch on foreneck; flanks olive-yellow; middle of abdomen whitish-yellow. Bill black; feet black; iris brown.
Adult female As male but lacks red.
Juvenile As female, but less green on rump, greyer below, less olive on flanks.

GEOGRAPHICAL VARIATION
D. e. erythrothorax Lesson, 1828 (Buru) Described above.
D. e. schistaceiceps G. R. Gray, 1860 (Morotai, Halmahera, Bacan, Obi and Bisu) From *erythrothorax* by more golden rump and grey throat concolorous with breast; wing-coverts dark brown without broad olive edging; flanks olive-green, not olive-yellow.

MEASUREMENTS Wing 49-54 (mean 51.8, 8 male *erythrothorax*), 51, 53 (2 female *erythrothorax*), 50, 50.5 (2 unsexed *schistaceiceps*); **bill** 9.3-10.8 (mean 10.3, 8 male *erythrothorax*), 10.2, 10.9 (2 female *erythrothorax*); **mass** no data.

REFERENCES Bishop (1992), Coates & Bishop (1997), Jepson (1993), Schönwetter (1980-1984), White & Bruce (1986).

DISTRIBUTION Endemic to Moluccas, occurring on Seram, Ambon, Saparua and Seram Laut.

HABITAT Primary forest and disturbed gardens in hills. Coastal forest and plantation edge, forest-edge shrubs. Found from sea-level to 2,100 m; up to 1,375 m on Seram but mainly below 1,000 m.

STATUS Common in coastal forest and at plantation edge and in forest-edge shrubs, but more abundant in primary forest and disturbed gardens in hills. Common on Seram, moderately so on Ambon.

MOVEMENTS Unknown.

FOOD Nectar from unidentified plants. Presumably also berries, and/or pollen, of mistletoes.
Known food-plants None.

HABITS Occurs singly, in pairs or in mixed-species flocks. In crowns of trees, as well as shrubs.

BREEDING No information.

DESCRIPTION
Adult male Dark brownish-grey above with scarlet rump; face ashy-brown; underparts are ashy-grey with large scarlet patch on foreneck; vent and undertail-coverts white. Bill and feet black; iris brown.
Adult female As male but lacks red on chest, and has white throat and centre to breast and abdomen.
Juvenile As female, but rump yellowy-green, not red.

GEOGRAPHICAL VARIATION None.

MEASUREMENTS Wing 49-51 (mean 49.9, SD 0.69, 7 males), 45, 46, 46 (3 females); **bill** 10.4-11.5 (mean 10.8, SD 0.38, 7 males), 9.5, 9.7, 10.6 (3 females); **mass** no data.

REFERENCES Bowler & Taylor (1989), Coates & Bishop (1997), Wallace (1863), White & Bruce (1986).

---

32 OLIVE-CROWNED FLOWERPECKER
Dicaeum pectorale   Plate 8

Dicaeum pectorale S. Müller, 1843, *Land. Volk.*, in Temminck, *Verh. Nat. Gesch. Nederland. Overz. Bezit.*, 1 (1839-1844), p.162, Lobo, Triton Bay, New Guinea.

Part of the *D. nehrkorni-erythrothorax-vulneratum-pectorale-geelvinkianum-nitidum-eximium-aeneum* superspecies. Could perhaps be considered conspecific with *geelvinkianum* and/or *nitidum*.

IDENTIFICATION Adult male is olive above with yellow rump; below white and grey with large scarlet breast-patch. Adult female has no scarlet, and has darker grey streaking on chin to breast. Juvenile is more olive, less grey below.
Similar species None; Red-capped Flowerpecker *Dicaeum geelvinkianum* (33) and Louisiade Flowerpecker *D. nitidum* (34) are allopatric.

VOICE Short, dry, buzzy, insect-like note; a high upslur. Latter like similar call of Black Sunbird *Leptocoma sericea* (91), but is uttered as a single note, not repeated.

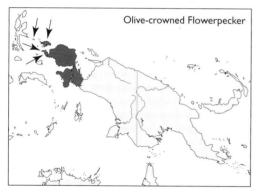

Olive-crowned Flowerpecker

DISTRIBUTION Endemic to New Guinea occurring on Gebe Island, Vogelkop and West Papuan Islands.

HABITAT Canopy of forest and secondary growth in lowlands and lower mountains; sea-level to 1,500 m, rarely to 2,350 m.

STATUS Not uncommon.

MOVEMENTS Unknown.

FOOD Spiders; fruits, presumably including those of mistletoes.
Known food-plants None.

HABITS Solitary or in pairs.

BREEDING No information except on nestling (see below).

DESCRIPTION *D. p. pectorale*
Adult male has olive upperparts, yellowish on rump; throat, undertail-coverts and centre of abdomen whitish; large scarlet patch on breast; sides of head, flanks and rest of underparts grey. Iris brown; bill and feet dark brown.
Adult female Differs from male in having no scarlet on breast, and chin to breast streaked darker grey, centre of abdomen and undertail-coverts yellowish.
Juvenile As female, but more olive, less grey below. Nestling has brownish down above, greyish below.

GEOGRAPHICAL VARIATION
  D. p. ignotum Mees, 1964 (Gebe Island) Darker, less greenish, more olive, above than *pectorale*, and slightly paler, less yellowish on centre of belly and undertail-coverts; wing and bill slightly larger. This form does not bridge nominate and *erythrothorax*, although geographically between them, indicating that they are distinct species.
  D. p. pectorale S. Müller, 1843 (Misol, Waigeu Islands and Vogelkop) Described above.

MEASUREMENTS Wing 53.5, 54 (2 male *ignotum*), 48-53 (mean 50.8, SD 1.92, 6 male *pectorale*), 48, 50 (female *pectorale*); **tail** 26 (male *pectorale*); **bill** 10.4-10.9 (mean 10.6, SD 0.21, of 4 male *pectorale*), 9.2 (female *pectorale*); **gape** 11 (female *pectorale*); **tarsus** 12 (male *pectorale*); **mass** no data.

REFERENCES Beehler *et al.* (1986), Mees (1964), Meyer (1874), Rand & Gilliard (1967), Salomonsen (1960c).

---

33 RED-CAPPED FLOWERPECKER
Dicaeum geelvinkianum   Plate 9

Dicaeum geelvinkianum Meyer, 1874, *Sitzungsz. K. Akad. Wiss., Math. Naturwiss. Wien*, Cl., 70, Abt. 1, p.120, Jobi, Mysore and Mafoor [= Japen, Biak and Numfor]; restricted to Japen by Sharpe, 1885, *Cat. Birds Brit. Mus.*, 10, p.34.

Alternative name: Red-crowned Flowerpecker

Part of the *D. nehrkorni-erythrothorax-vulneratum-pectorale-geelvinkianum-nitidum-eximium-aeneum* superspecies. Could perhaps be considered conspecific with *pectorale* and/or *nitidum*.

IDENTIFICATION Adult male varies from dark olive-brown to slightly glossy black above; red cap and rump; below grey and white with red chest-patch. Adult female lacks red below. Juvenile lacks red.
Similar species None; Olive-crowned Flowerpecker *Dicaeum pectorale* (32) and Louisiade Flowerpecker *D. nitidum* (34) are allopatric. *Myzomela* spp. are similar-sized but have longer, decurved, bills, and lack red cap.

VOICE A buzzy single note, a down-slurred *bszzrt*.

DISTRIBUTION Endemic to New Guinea, including islands in Geelvink Bay and D'Entrecasteaux Archipelago but absent from Vogelkop.

HABITAT Canopy of forest, forest edge, secondary growth, dense savanna, plantations and gardens in lowlands and

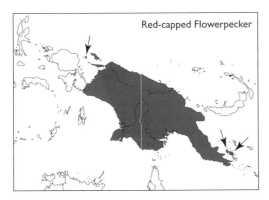

Red-capped Flowerpecker

lower mountains from sea-level to 1,500 m, rarely up to 2,350 m.

STATUS Common at lower altitudes throughout its range.

MOVEMENTS Unknown.

FOOD Spiders and fruit, swallowed whole, and possibly also nectar and/or pollen, of mistletoes.
Known food plants None.

HABITS Active, nervous birds, preferring tree-tops where they feed on fruiting and flowering trees and forage for spiders.

BREEDING Nest Pear-shaped with a side entrance near the top, made of grey animal silk and reddish-brown strips from ferns, suspended from a short slender *Croton* sp. tree.
Eggs c/2-3. Race *rubrocoronatum*: white. 13.3-15.2 (mean 14.2, n=3) x 10.9-11.0 (mean 11.0). **Laying months** New Guinea: Fergusson Island, November–December.

DESCRIPTION *D. g. setekwa*
Adult male Bright red cap and rump; wings and tail dark brown; rest of upperparts very dark olive-green; wings and tail dark brown, shoulder darker with slight bluish gloss; white throat; red patch on chest; rest of underparts olive-grey, centre of belly yellowish-buff, vent and undertail-coverts white or pink. Pectoral tufts white. Iris brown. Bill and feet blackish.
Adult female As male but lacks red below and is paler on belly.
Juvenile Similar to female but little or no red above, and much of bill pale.

GEOGRAPHICAL VARIATION
D. g. albopunctatum D'Albertis & Salvadori, 1879 (Kataw river, south-central New Guinea) From *rubrigulare* by white areas between red tip and dusky base of feathers of head, rump and uppertail-coverts. Red pectoral patch extending onto entire throat and chin and sides of breast.
D. g. centrale Rand, 1941 (Balim river, 1,600 m, central New Guinea; replaces *setekwa* at higher altitudes) Larger than *diversum* with more greyish breast, lighter flanks and slightly darker upperparts.
D. g. diversum Rothschild & Hartert, 1903 (north coast of Irian Jaya) Like *rubrocoronatum* but has somewhat lighter and more scarlet crown and uppertail-coverts, and more steel-blue, not purple, upper surface, which is also more tinged olive. Male blacker than *setekwa*, less olive above, red slightly darker, breast-patch smaller.

D. g. geelvinkianum Meyer, 1874 (Japen Island) Differs from *maforense* by bright red crown and uppertail-coverts, and more greenish upperparts.
D. g. maforense Salvadori, 1875 (Numfor Island) Male differs from *setekwa* in having dull dark red crown, rump and uppertail-coverts, and yellowish vent and undertail-coverts.
D. g. misoriense Salvadori, 1875 (Biak Island) Male like *maforense* but with much less red on breast; duller above with bright carmine rump.
D. g. obscurifrons Junge, 1952 (west New Guinea) Similar in size to *centrale*, but more greenish, less violet on upperparts; underparts darker; red on head and uppertail-coverts less bright, more brownish-red, nearest to *maforense*, which is smaller and has breast-patch less vivid.
D. g. rubrigulare D'Albertis & Salvadori, 1879 (Fly River, south New Guinea) From *rubrocoronatum* by neck in front being entirely red.
D. g. rubrocoronatum Sharpe, 1876 (south-east New Guinea) Male has a vermilion crown and rump, and rest of upperparts blackish glossed purple and blue, except lower back which is dark olive; yellower below than nominate; red pectoral patch very small. Female lacks red below; above slightly glossed blue on dark greeny-brown.
D. g. setekwa Rand, 1941 (up to 915 m along Snow Mts, south-west New Guinea) Described above.
D. g. violaceum Mayr, 1936 (D'Entrecasteaux Archipelago) Male similar in size to *rubrocoronatum* but duller and lighter above, and gloss purplish-violet, not steel-blue; red of crown, rump and breast-spot average darker; underparts more washed grey; abdomen not yellowish-green but greyish-olive.

MEASUREMENTS Wing 58 (male *centrale*), 52 (male *diversum*), 52 (male *maforense*), 58 (male *obscurifrons*), 53 (male *rubrocoronatum*), 50-52 (mean 51, 10 male *setekwa*), 53 (male *violaceum*), 42-48 (mean 46.4, 10 female *setekwa*); **tail** 25 (unsexed of unknown subsp.); **bill** 9.5-11.1 (mean 10.3, 10 male *setekwa*), 9.3-10.7 (mean 9.9, 10 female *setekwa*); **gape** 9.1-11.7 (mean 10.5, 10 male *setekwa*); **tarsus** 12 (unsexed of unknown subsp.); **mass** no data.

REFERENCES Beehler (1978), Beehler *et al.* (1986), D'Albertis & Salvadori (1879), Mayr (1936), Meyer (1874), Rand (1941), Rand & Gilliard (1967), Rothschild & Hartert (1896), Schönwetter (1980-1984).

34   LOUISIADE FLOWERPECKER
Dicaeum nitidum   Plate 9

Dicaeum nitidum Tristram, 1889, *Ibis* p.555, Sudest [= Tagula] Island, Louisiade Archipelago, New Guinea

Part of the *D. nehrkorni-erythrothorax-vulneratum-pectorale-geelvinkianum-nitidum-eximium-aeneum* superspecies. Could perhaps be considered conspecific with *pectorale* and/or *geelvinkianum*.

IDENTIFICATION Adult male has dark brownish-grey upperparts glossed dark blue and green; cap dull red, rump and breast-patch brighter red; throat yellowish-white, greyish sides to throat and breast; rest of underparts

163

yellowish-green, paler, more yellowish near vent; pectoral tufts and undertail-coverts white. Adult female is duller and lacks red below. Juvenile lacks red completely.

Similar species None; Olive-crowned Flowerpecker *Dicaeum pectorale* (32), Red-capped Flowerpecker *D. geelvinkianum* (33) and Mistletoebird *D. hirundinaceum* (44) are allopatric.

VOICE Short, dry, buzzy, insect-like note. A high upslur given singly, unlike similar but repeated call of Black Sunbird *Leptocoma sericea* (91).

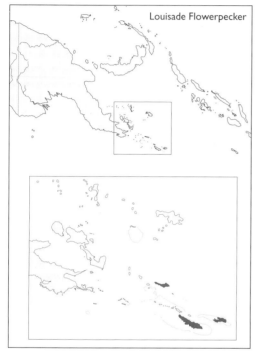
Louisade Flowerpecker

DISTRIBUTION Endemic to Louisiade Archipelago in New Guinea.

HABITAT Canopy of forest and secondary growth.

STATUS Unknown.

MOVEMENTS Unknown.

FOOD Fruits, presumably including those of mistletoes, and spiders.
Known food-plants None.

HABITS Solitary, or in pairs, in canopy.

BREEDING No information.

DESCRIPTION *D. n. nitidum*
Adult male Dull red cap, brighter red rump; rest of upperparts dark brownish-grey glossed blue and green, particularly on mantle and wing-coverts; remiges dark blackish-brown, edged greenish; tail glossy blackish; bright red patch on breast; chin, throat, abdomen and undertail-coverts whitish; rest of underparts and sides of head greyish to yellowish-green. Pectoral tufts white. Iris brown; bill black, base of lower mandible whitish; feet black.
Adult female Differs from male in lacking red breast-patch.
Juvenile Differs from female in lacking red on upperparts.

GEOGRAPHICAL VARIATION
D. n. nitidum Tristram, 1889 (Tagula and Misima Islands) Described above.
D. n. rosseli Rothschild & Hartert, 1914 (Rossel Island) Male differs from nominate in having shoulders glossed blue-green; and in being less blackish, more a dark olive-green above.

MEASUREMENTS Wing 55.5, 56, 57 (3 male *nitidum*), 58, 58, 59 (3 male *rosseli*); **tail** 26 (unsexed, unknown subsp.); **bill** 10.5, 11.1 (2 male *nitidum*), 10.6, 11.2, 11.9 (3 male *rosseli*); **tarsus** 14 (unsexed, unknown subsp.); **mass** no data.

REFERENCES Beehler *et al.* (1986), Rand & Gilliard (1967), Rothschild & Hartert (1914), Tristram (1889).

---

35   RED-BANDED FLOWERPECKER
Dicaeum eximium   Plate 9

Dicaeum eximium Sclater, 1877, *Proc. Zool. Soc. London* p.102, Pl. 14, fig. 2, New Ireland, Bismarck Archipelago.

Part of the *D. nehrkorni-erythrothorax-vulneratum-pectorale-geelvinkianum-nitidum-eximium-aeneum* superspecies.

IDENTIFICATION Adult male dark grey, blackish or bronze-green above with crimson rump; below white, grey and yellowy-green; red spot on breast. Adult female lacks red below, and underparts are more isabelline-white and yellowish-olive. Juvenile is greyer than female below.
Similar species None.

VOICE Very high single squeaky notes. *Tzick* call.

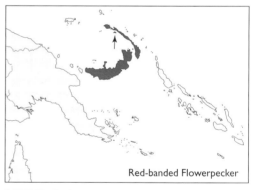
Red-banded Flowerpecker

DISTRIBUTION Endemic to Bismarck Archipelago, occurring on New Britain, New Ireland, New Hanover and Dyaul Island.

HABITAT Nothing recorded.

STATUS Unknown.

MOVEMENTS Unknown.

FOOD Presumably includes fruit, and possibly also nectar and/or pollen, of mistletoes.
Known food-plants None.

HABITS Nothing recorded.

BREEDING May be double-brooded. **Nest** Below 2 m, often low in ferns, without an obvious porch, although roof may overhang rest of nest. **Eggs** Race *layardorum*: white, elongated, comparatively large; 15.5-19.0 (mean 16.9, n=12) x 9.5-13.0 (mean 10.9). **Laying months** Unknown.

DESCRIPTION *D. e. layardorum*
Adult male Blackish above with grey head. Red rump; white throat and red spot on breast; underparts immediately below this grey, then yellowy-green. Thin blackish stripe down centre of belly. Iris brownish-red or reddish-brown. Bill black; feet blackish-slate.
Adult female Above dark grey, rump crimson; throat, chest, centre of belly and vent isabelline white; flanks yellowish-olive. Less white on throat than male and lacks red below.
Juvenile As female, but greyer below; throat-streak narrower.

GEOGRAPHICAL VARIATION
  D. e. eximium Sclater, 1877 (New Ireland and New Hanover) Above olive-brown or bronze-green; crown and sides of head brownish contrasting with back; rump scarlet; below white with narrow scarlet breast-band; grey of sides of breast darker, flanks olive greenish-brown and abdomen darkish slate; iris dark brown.
  D. e. layardorum Salvadori, 1880 (New Britain) Described above.
  D. e. phaeopygium Salomonsen, 1964 (Dyaul Island) Head, back and rump dark brown, whereas rump in nominate and *layardorum* is red.

MEASUREMENTS Wing 51, 52, 54 (3 male *layardorum*), 50-56 (males, unknown subsp.), 49 (female *eximium*), 47, 49 (2 female *layardorum*), 48.5-50.5 (females, unknown subsp.), 51 (unsexed *eximium*); **bill** 9.3, 9.6, 10.4 (3 male *layardorum*), 9.8-12 (males, unknown subsp.), 9.7 (female *eximium*), 9,7, 10.7 (2 female *layardorum*), 10-11.2. (females, unknown subsp.); **mass** no data.

REFERENCES Meyer (1933), Salomonsen (1960c), Salvadori (1880), Schönwetter (1980-1984), Sclater (1877).

---

36 MIDGET FLOWERPECKER
Dicaeum aeneum   Plate 9

Dicaeum aeneum Pucheran, in Jacquinot and Pucheran, 1853, *Voy. Pôle Sud, Zool.*, 3, p.97; atlas pl. 22, fig.4, San Jorge (near Santa Isabel), Solomon Islands.

Alternative name: Solomons Flowerpecker

Part of the *D. nehrkorni-erythrothorax-vulneratum-pectorale-geelvinkianum-nitidum-eximium-aeneum* superspecies.

IDENTIFICATION Adult male is slaty-grey glossed metallic-blue above, with black tail; below white, grey and olive with scarlet breast-patch. Adult female lacks red below, has olive flanks, and is generally buffier below. **Similar species** None.

VOICE A distinctive rapid *tik-tik-tik-tik* and high-pitched short squeaky calls delivered with open bill. Very high *sweet sweet*; very high chipping becoming a short trill. Brief trisyllabic call.

DISTRIBUTION Endemic to Solomon Islands, occurring on North Solomons, Guadalcanal, Florida and Malaita Islands.

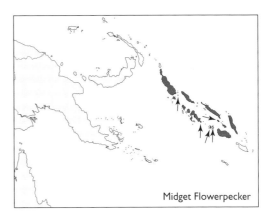
Midget Flowerpecker

HABITAT All habitats at all altitudes (recorded at 520 m).

STATUS Common from coast to high mountains.

MOVEMENTS Unknown.

FOOD Insects and fruits, sometimes hovering to feed, and possibly also nectar and/or pollen, of mistletoes. **Known food-plants** *Trema* sp., *Ziziphus* sp.

HABITS Usually single or in pairs. Rapid flight through undergrowth. Bobs head on alighting. Host to *Haemoproteus nucleophilus*.

BREEDING Both sexes feed young and remove excreta. **Nest** Pear-shaped with side entrance and rounded bottom, unlike untidy base of sunbird nests; made of grasses and fine vegetable material, poorly concealed on low horizontal branch or suspended 1-2 m above ground in ornamental shrub or *Hibiscus* bush. **Eggs** Unknown. **Laying months** Northern Solomons: November; Guadalcanal: female with enlarged ovaries July.

DESCRIPTION *D. a. aeneum*
Adult male Upperparts and wings slaty-grey with metallic blue gloss; sides of head grey; tail black; bright scarlet patch on breast; middle of upper throat whitish; sides of throat and breast grey; flanks citrine-olive; middle of upper abdomen dark grey, middle of lower abdomen and undertail-coverts buffy-white. Iris brown or dark brown; bill and feet black.
Adult female Differs from male in lacking red below and having olive flanks; middle of throat, breast and abdomen buffy-white.
Juvenile Perhaps whiter on throat and yellower on belly than female.

GEOGRAPHICAL VARIATION
  D. a. aeneum Pucheran, 1853 (northern Solomons – Bougainville, Choiseul and Ysabel) Described above.
  D. a. becki Hartert, 1929 (Florida and Guadalcanal) Male differs from nominate in having greenish gloss above instead of blue.
  D. a. malaitae Salomonsen, 1964 (Malaita Island) From other two by gloss on upperparts reduced to a faint bluish tinge, and has a much thinner, longer bill. Slate on underparts is slightly paler. Flank colour intermediate between the other two forms.

MEASUREMENTS Wing 47-53 (male *aeneum*), 51-54 (male *becki*), 50-54 (male *malaitae*), 45-51 (female *aeneum*), 47-50 (female *becki*), 47-49 (female *malaitae*); **bill** 11-13 (male *aeneum*), 11-13 (male *becki*), 13.5-15.5 (male *malaitae*), 10.5-13 (female *aeneum*), 11-13 (female *becki*), 13-15 (female *malaitae*); **mass** 7.1-8.8 (mean 8.0, S.D. 0.71, 5 male *aeneum*), 8.5 (female *aeneum*).

REFERENCES Hadden (1981), Kratter *et al.* (2001), Mayr (1945), Pucheran (1853), Salomonsen (1960c), Schodde (1977).

37   MOTTLED FLOWERPECKER
Dicaeum tristrami   Plate 9

Dicaeum tristrami Sharpe, 1884, *Proc. Zool. Soc. London* (1883) p.579, San Christobal island [=Makira], Solomon islands.

Alternative name: San Cristobel Midget Flowerpecker

IDENTIFICATION Adult mostly brown above, mottled white on forehead and back; whitish supercilium and ear-coverts; brownish-white mottling on chin to breast. Juvenile has pale bill and less marked mottling below. **Similar species** None.

VOICE Hard, high, metallic and emphatic *tschip-tschip*.

DISTRIBUTION Endemic to Makira Island, Solomons.

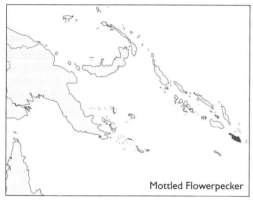

Mottled Flowerpecker

HABITAT Mountainous areas, primary forest, forest edge and secondary growth.

STATUS Particularly abundant in mountains; uncommon in lowlands.

MOVEMENTS Unknown.

FOOD Presumably includes fruit, and possibly also nectar and/or pollen, of mistletoes. **Known food-plants** None.

HABITS Nothing recorded.

BREEDING Nest Unknown. **Eggs** Unknown. **Laying months** Female with enlarged ovaries October–December.

DESCRIPTION Sexes similar.
Adult Upperparts brown, paler on mantle, mottled white on forehead, crown and nape; wings brown; tail blackish; eyebrow and ear region whitish; cheeks dark brown; throat to upper breast brown with pale edges to feathers giving mottled or scaled effect; rest of underparts pale brownish-white. Iris dark brown; bill black, paler at base of lower mandible; feet dark slate or black.

Juvenile From adult by pale bill and less well marked scaling below.

GEOGRAPHICAL VARIATION None.

MEASUREMENTS Wing 55-61 (mean 58.4, SD 1.90, 10 males), 50-57 (mean 58.9, SD 2.29, 8 females); **bill** 10.4-12.4 (mean 11.6, SD 0.66, 10 males), 10.9-12.8 (mean 11.6, SD 0.66, 8 females); **gape** 11.1 (female); **mass** 11-13 (mean 11.8, SD 0.62, 13 males), 10-12.5 (mean 11.2, SD 0.70, 8 females).

REFERENCE Doughty *et al.* (2000), Mayr (1945).

38   BLACK-FRONTED FLOWERPECKER
Dicaeum igniferum   Plate 10

Dicaeum igniferum Wallace, 1863, *Proc. Zool. Soc. London*, p.494, Flores, Lesser Sunda islands.

Forms superspecies with *D. maugei*.

IDENTIFICATION Adult male dark scarlet on crown, neck, mantle, uppertail-coverts and rump; back glossed violet; forehead, scapulars and tail black; face, sides of neck and pectoral band black; foreneck and throat scarlet; rest of underparts white with black median band. Adult female duller than male, mainly greyish and whitish below, lacking black pectoral band and red on throat and foreneck; brownish-grey pectoral band, forehead and sides of face; lower back brown; rump red. Juvenile as female but red above confined to rump.
Similar species Male from male Blood-breasted Flowerpecker *Dicaeum sanguinolentum* (43) by violet-glossed scarlet upperparts, not dark glossy blue; juvenile from female of that species by white underparts rather than ochre or ochre-buff.

VOICE Call Thin, high-pitched *see-saw* notes rapidly repeated 4-5 times. **Song** Very rapid, descending series of short, thin, dry notes lasting 6 seconds.

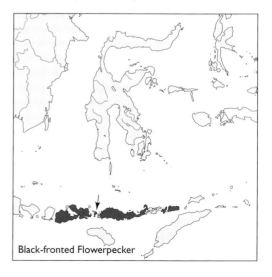

Black-fronted Flowerpecker

DISTRIBUTION Endemic to Lesser Sunda Islands, occurring on Sumbawa, Komodo, Flores, Pantar and Alor.

HABITAT Degraded forest and woodland, tall secondary forest, scrubby monsoon coastal forest, clearings, lightly wooded cultivation, semi-deciduous forest; up to 1,730 m, but chiefly below 800 m.

STATUS Widespread and common. Less common in semi-deciduous forest.

MOVEMENTS Unknown.

FOOD Presumably includes fruit, and possibly also nectar and/or pollen of mistletoes.
Known food-plants None.

HABITS Occurs singly, in pairs, groups and mixed parties; male sings from exposed branch in lower canopy.

BREEDING No information.

DESCRIPTION *D. i. igniferum*
Adult male Whole upperside from crown to rump dull scarlet, glossed violet on back; forehead, face, sides of neck, pectoral band, scapulars and wings black, somewhat purplish on scapulars and wings; throat white, foreneck scarlet; rest of underparts white with black median band down abdomen. Bill blackish. Feet black.
Adult female Duller above than male, with less gloss. Greyish-brown forehead, sides of face, lower throat and pectoral band; rest of underparts whitish; crown to upper back, and rump scarlet; rest of upperparts brown.
Juvenile Like female, but red above confined to rump; bill entirely pale, darkening towards tip.

GEOGRAPHICAL VARIATION
  D. i. cretum Rensch, 1929 (Alor and Pantar) Slightly larger than nominate with broader black line below; possibly not valid.
  D. i. igniferum (Blyth, 1843) (Sumbawa, Komodo and Flores) Described above.

MEASUREMENTS Wing 50-53 (mean 50.2, SD 0.5, 4 male *igniferum*), 48-49 (mean 48.5, SD 0.58, 4 female *igniferum*); **bill** 11.0-11.8 (mean 11.3, SD 0.38, 4 male *igniferum*), 11.2-12.2 (mean 11.5, SD 0.49, 4 female *igniferum*); **mass** no data.

REFERENCES Coates & Bishop (1997), Salomonsen (1961), Wallace (1863), White & Bruce (1986).

---

39   RED-CHESTED FLOWERPECKER
Dicaeum maugei   Plate 10

Dicaeum maugei Lesson, 1830, *Traité Orn.*, p.303, Timor.

Forms a superspecies with *D. igniferum*.

IDENTIFICATION Adult male dark glossy purplish-blue above with scarlet rump; face blackish, with scarlet on foreneck and throat; black from face and sides of neck to median abdominal stripe; chin and rest of underparts white. Adult female brownish-grey above, with scarlet rump and uppertail-coverts, and black tail; sides of face, neck and partial pectoral band brownish-grey. Juvenile as female, but has paler bill.
Similar species From Blood-breasted Flowerpecker

Dicaeum sanguinolentum (43) by red rump and throat and whiter underparts. Male from male Crimson-crowned Flowerpecker *D. nehrkorni* (29) by lack of crimson on crown, and female from female of this species by thicker bill and more extensive red on uppertail-coverts; male from Grey-sided Flowerpecker *D. celebicum* (42) and Blood-breasted Flowerpecker *D. sanguinolentum* (43) by scarlet rump; female from female Scarlet-headed Flowerpecker *D. trochileum* (46) by dark purplish-blue above, not brown.

VOICE Call High-pitched *tsit*. High-pitched 2-3 note whistle like Sangihe Hanging-parrot *Loriculus catamene*.

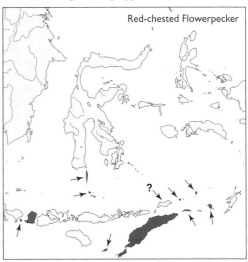

Red-chested Flowerpecker

DISTRIBUTION Endemic to Wallacea. Occurs on Salayar, Tanahjampea (Sulawesi), Roti, Sawu, Timor, Wetar (possibly), Romang, Damar, Moa, Babar, Lombok (Lesser Sundas) and Nusa Penida (Bali).

HABITAT Woodland generally not above 1,200 m on Timor, but up to 2,000 m on Lombok; around mistletoes Loranthaceae. In primary and secondary forest and woodland, degraded forest, wooded cultivation and bamboo.

STATUS Generally moderately common to common.

MOVEMENTS Unknown.

FOOD Presumably includes fruits, and possibly nectar and/or pollen, of mistletoes.
Known food-plants None.

HABITS Singly or in pairs.

BREEDING Nest One of race *neglectum* in Natural History Museum, Tring, collected by A. Everett, 27 May 1896 at 500 m, Lombok, Indonesia. Compact oval purse attached to palm frond, made of thick layerings of pappus, loosely covered with fine vegetable fibre and a few dead leaves and fragments of lichen. Large entrance hole (30 x 25 mm) near apex. Short beard (55 mm) from base of entrance hole. 110 x 65 mm. **Eggs** c/2; white; 16.0 x 10.8. **Laying months** Indonesia: Lombok at 500 m, May.

DESCRIPTION *D. m. maugei*
Adult male Glossy dark purplish-blue above; face blackish; rump scarlet; underparts creamy; scarlet patch on foreneck bordered blackish below extending from the face down sides of neck; blackish median stripe on abdomen.

167

Iris dark; bill and feet black.

Adult female Scarlet rump and uppertail-coverts; tail black; rest of upperparts grey-brown. Sides of neck, face and partial pectoral band greyish-brown; rest of underparts white.

Juvenile As female but with paler bill.

GEOGRAPHICAL VARIATION

D. m. maugei Wallace, 1863 (includes *romae*) (Lesser Sundas – Roti, Sawu, Semau, Timor, Wetar, Romang, Roma and Damar) Described above.

D. m. neglectum Hartert, 1897 (Nusa Penida and Lesser Sundas – Lombok) Male is similar to nominate but red below slightly darker, black band slightly broader and bill slightly longer and slenderer.

D. m. salvadorii Meyer, 1884 (Lesser Sundas – Moa and Babar) In male scarlet is more extensive below, and black border of scarlet area is much narrower than in nominate.

D. m. splendidum Büttikofer, 1893 (Sulawesi group – Salayar and Tanahjampea) Male similar to *salvadorii* but red below lighter, black breast-band all but absent, and bill slightly smaller. Female has some reddish on upper back.

MEASUREMENTS (nominate) **Wing** 53-59 (mean 54.2, SD 3.10, 8 males), 53-54 (mean 53.2, SD 0.5, 4 females); **bill** 8.7-11.8 (mean 10.6, SD 0.94, 8 males), 10.0-11.3 (mean 10.6, SD 0.56, 4 females); **mass** no data.

REFERENCES Bruce (1987), Coates & Bishop (1997), Hartert (1904), MacKinnon & Phillips (1993), Salomonsen (1961), White & Bruce (1986).

---

40 FIRE-BREASTED FLOWERPECKER
Dicaeum ignipectum   Plate 10

Myzante ignipectus Blyth (ex Hodgson ms), 1843, *Journ. Asiat. Soc. Bengal*, 12, p.983, Nepal and Bhutan.

Alternative name: Buff-bellied Flowerpecker

Forms a superspecies with *D. monticolum, D. celebicum, D. sanguinolentum* and *D. hirundinaceum*.

IDENTIFICATION Adult male metallic greenish-blue above; buff, yellow and olive below, with scarlet on breast, and black on belly. Adult female is mostly olive-green above, greyer on crown, yellower on rump and uppertail-coverts; below buffy, more olive on flanks. Juvenile is paler below than female, with white on chin and throat.

Similar species Female and immature larger than Plain Flowerpecker *Dicaeum concolor* (27) with a shorter, less curved bill, metallic lustre above, and less olivaceous below. Male Crimson-breasted Flowerpecker *Prionochilus percussus* (5) has yellow below, not rich buff, and lacks black below red; female Scarlet-breasted Flowerpecker *P. thoracicus* (8) is orange and yellow below; Thick-billed Flowerpecker *D. agile* (10) lacks green above and yellowish on rump; female Orange-bellied Flowerpecker *D. trigonostigma* (24) has yellow-orange or orange rump.

VOICE Call Sharp metallic *chip*; high-pitched *tsik* repeated about twice per second. Also high-pitched repeated *see*; twittering trill; metallic *chip...chip...chip* with greater spacing between notes than in Scarlet-backed Flower-

pecker *D. cruentatum* (45). **Song** A high-pitched, strident *see-bit, see-bit, see-bit, see-bit* and a long series of clicks uttered from a perch and on the wing, or a shrill *titty-titty-titty...*, recalling the rapid snipping sound of a pair of scissors.

DISTRIBUTION Northern and eastern India, Nepal, Bhutan, Tibet, Burma, Thailand, Indochina, south and central China, Hainan, Taiwan, Malay Peninsula, Philippines and Sumatra.

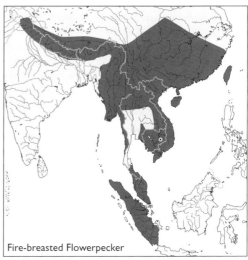
Fire-breasted Flowerpecker

HABITAT Flowering and fruiting trees, and particularly amongst mistletoes Loranthaceae in upper and middle storeys of hill and montane forests, subtropical evergreen and deciduous oak forests, rhododendrons, secondary growth, orchards and other cultivation; 600-3,950 m (915-2,700 m in Nepal; Philippines above 1,000 m; 800-2,200 m in Sumatra and Malay Peninsula).

STATUS Common and widespread throughout most of its range. Locally common in higher hills of Burma, rare below 900 m. Not uncommon in montane forests of Sumatra. Uncommon in forests and forest edge, usually above 1,000 m in Philippines.

MOVEMENTS Vertical movements in areas with well-marked seasons; down to 300 m in winter, 1,440-3,950 m in summer, in Himalayas, northern India and China; 900 m in Taiwan in winter, 2,135 m in summer; in Nepal 1,830-2,700 m in summer, 915-2,285 m in winter.

FOOD Insects, spiders, nectar, fruit and berries, particularly mistletoes Loranthaceae.
Known food-plants Unidentified Loranthaceae.

HABITS Singly or in pairs in breeding season; may be in groups or mixed parties in non-breeding season. Keep to tops of trees, hopping ceaselessly from branch to branch.

BREEDING In Burma, race *ignipectum* nests in trees in rocky ravines running through dense forest. **Nest** An oval purse, about 90 x 60 mm, of soft vegetable down held together by grass, rootlets and cobwebs and sometimes decorated with green moss; entrance hole on side near top, with or without a porch; in trees 3-9 m above ground. **Eggs** c/2-3; white. Race *ignipectum*: 13.0-16.0 (mean 14.5, n=22) x 10.0-11.0 (mean 10.3). **Laying months** Hong Kong: mostly October–March; Indian subcontinent: March–

June; Malaya: young, Fraser's Hill, August; Burma: Kalaw, February, Upper Chindwin, April, Taunggyi crags, May, Sinlum Bhamo, June; Nepal: March–April in Chitlang and Kathmandu valleys, and possibly Jiri in May. Sumatra: nest March, Batak Highlands.

DESCRIPTION *D. i. ignipectum*
Adult male Upperparts metallic greenish-blue; face and sides of breast black, throat buffy-white; underparts rich buff with scarlet patch on breast, black stripe in centre of belly below this; flanks olive; undertail-coverts and lower belly yellow. Iris brown or black. Bill black with whitish patch at base of lower mandible. Feet dark horny or black.
Adult female Crown greyish-olive, rest of upperparts olive-green, yellower on rump and uppertail-coverts; lores buffy-white; underparts pale buff or cinnamon-buff washed olive on flanks. Bill black with yellow to orange patch at base of lower mandible.
Juvenile As female but chin and throat white, with buff on underparts paler and duller than adult.

Male hybrid with *D. cruentatum* from Fokien, South China, has scarlet crown, back and rump mixed with some glossy blue-black; rest of upperparts glossy blue-black; sides of face and neck sooty-black; underparts buff, with broad red band on chest.

GEOGRAPHICAL VARIATION
D. i. apo Hartert, 1904 (Mindanao and Negros) Differs from *luzoniense* by glossy-green sides of head, not slaty, darker olive-green flanks, and lighter and brighter yellow undertail-coverts.
D. i. beccarii Robinson & Kloss, 1916 (Sumatra) Male is glossy blue-green above, darker buff (rustier) below with a cinnamon breast-band and narrow black stripe in centre of belly; no red below.
D. i. bonga Hartert, 1904 (Philippines – Samar) As *luzoniense* and *apo* but smaller (wing 47 vs 53-55 mm). Sides of head as dark as or darker than latter, and upperparts more steel-blue.
D. i. cambodianum Delacour & Jabouille, 1928 (Cambodia, and north-east and south-east Thailand) Male is metallic blue-green or green above and lacks scarlet below; throat, breast and centre of belly rich buff.
D. i. dolichorhynchum Deignan, 1963 (peninsular Malaysia) Male has black stripe down centre of lower breast and belly; band of red on chest narrower than nominate. Female is greyer above and browner below than nominate.
D. i. formosum Ogilvie-Grant, 1912 (Taiwan) Male differs from nominate in being glossy steel-blue above; red below extends onto chin.
D. i. ignipectum (Blyth, 1843) (Himalayas from Kashmir east through Arunachal Pradesh, including Nepal, Sikkim and Bhutan, to northern Burma, north-ern Indochina and China in Fukien, Hopeh, south Shensi, south Szechwan, south-east Tibet from Yigrong valley to north Yunnan, and south to Tali and Mengtsz; Kwangsi, Kwangtung and Hainan; and India south through Meghalaya, Nagaland and Manipur to Mizo Hills) Described above.
D. i. luzoniense Ogilvie-Grant, 1894 (Philippines – Luzon) Male from *ignipectum* by being dark glossy-green above, with dull blackish sides of head and neck, and more extensive red on breast extending to throat but not chin; flanks olivaceous-grey. Female from nominate by darker upperparts with a slight greenish

gloss, greyish-white underparts washed olive on flanks, and undertail-coverts orange-yellow.

MEASUREMENTS Wing 48.5-50.5 (male *formosum*), 46-53 (mean 47.7, 10 male *ignipectum*), 54 (male *luzoniense*), 47 (female *formosum*), 43-49 (mean 46.1, 10 female *ignipectum*), 48-48.5 (juvenile female *formosum*), 47 (unsexed *bonga*); **tail** 24-26 (male *formosum*), 25-30 (male *ignipectum*), 32 (male *luzoniense*), 23.5 (female *formosum*), 23-26 (female *ignipectum*), 23.5-24.5 (juvenile female *formosum*); **bill** 8.9-12 (mean 10.8, 9 male *ignipectum*), 9 (male *luzoniense*), 9-12 (mean 10.2, 10 female *ignipectum*); **tarsus** 12-14 (male *ignipectum*), 12 (male *luzoniense*), 12-14 (female *ignipectum*); **culmen** 8-9 (male *formosum*), 7.9 (female *formosum*), 7.9 (juvenile female *formosum*); **mass** 4-8 (male *ignipectum*), 5.5-6.1 (female *ignipectum*).

REFERENCES Ali & Ripley (1974), Corlett (1998), Dickinson *et al.* (1991), duPont (1971), Fleming *et al.* (1976), Hartert (1904a), Inskipp & Inskipp (1985), King *et al.* (1975), Kuroda (1920), MacKinnon & Phillipps (1993), van Marle & Voous (1988), Medway & Wells (1976), Meyer de Schauensee (1984), Salomonsen (1961), Smythies (1986), Viney & Phillipps (1988).

---

41   BLACK-SIDED FLOWERPECKER
Dicaeum monticolum   Plate 11

Dicaeum monticolum Sharpe, 1887, *Ibis*, p. 452, Mt Kinabalu, northern Borneo.

Forms superspecies with *D. ignipectum*, *D. celebicum*, *D. sanguinolentum* and *D. hirundinaceum*. Some authors would include it in one of the first two species, while others would lump all in the latter species. It is particularly close to some forms of *D. celebicum*.

IDENTIFICATION Adult male glossy bluish-black above; breast scarlet bordered black; rest of underparts white, dark grey and creamy. Female is olive-green above, greyish below, with white pectoral tufts. Juvenile darker than female.
Similar species Grey-sided Flowerpecker *Dicaeum celebicum* (42), Fire-breasted Flowerpecker *D. ignipectum* (40), Mistletoebird *D. hirundinaceum* (44) and Blood-breasted Flowerpecker *D. sanguinolentum* (43) are all allopatric. Female Crimson-breasted Flowerpecker *Prionochilus percussus* (5) has whitish malar stripe and, like Yellow-rumped Flowerpecker *P. xanthopygius* (7), has yellow on belly, not cream; female from Plain Flowerpecker *D. concolor* (27) by olive-green upperparts, not olive-brown.

VOICE A sharp, piercing, metallic *zit*. Rapid ticking; repeated *tit-tit*. *Tsweet-tsweet*, second note slurred down and up.

DISTRIBUTION Endemic to Borneo; known from a few localities in Sarawak (Gunung Penrissen, Gunung Dulit, Bario, Gunung Mulu), Sabah (Crocker Range, Gunung Kinabalu, Gunung Trus Madi), and Kalimantan Barat (Gunung Liang Kubung).

HABITAT Hill dipterocarp and montane forest at 460-2,540 m, scrub and *kerangas*.

STATUS Uncommon to common.

MOVEMENTS Unknown.

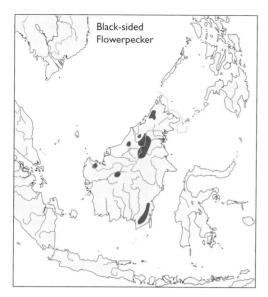

Black-sided
Flowerpecker

FOOD Fruits, berries, seeds, aphids, flies, leafhoppers etc.
Known food-plants Mistletoes Loranthaceae.

HABITS Usually forages low, but occasionally in canopy.

BREEDING Nest Made of moss lined with tree-fern pith,
decorated on outside with lichen. **Eggs** Unknown. **Laying
months** Sarawak: Bario, young November–February;
Sabah: enlarged testes December.

DESCRIPTION
Adult male Upperparts glossy bluish-black; face black; chin
white, throat and breast scarlet bordered black; malar region
and sides of neck sooty-black; upper flanks and upper belly
dark grey, lower belly white, lower flanks and sides of belly
olive; breast scarlet, bordered greyish-black; vent and
undertail-coverts buffy-yellow. Underwing-coverts and pectoral tufts white. Iris brown or black; bill black; feet brown.
Adult female Upperparts olive-green, with buffy wash on
rump; underparts pale greyish; whitish on throat and some
whitish mottling on breast; creamy on centre of belly, and
buffy on lower flanks; white pectoral tufts.
Juvenile As female but darker below. Some fine dark
streaking on chin to breast.

GEOGRAPHICAL VARIATION None.

MEASUREMENTS Wing 47-54 (mean 49.7, SD 1.85, 11
males), 42-48 (mean 46.2, SD 1.58, 14 females); **bill** 10-14
(mean 11.2, SD 0.51, 15 males), 9.9-12.8 (mean 11.2, SD
0.86, 15 females); **mass** no data.

REFERENCES MacKinnon & Phillipps (1993), Mann (in
prep. b), Salomonsen (1961), Sheldon *et al.* (in pressw),
Smythies (1957, 1960, 1981).

---

42   GREY-SIDED FLOWERPECKER
Dicaeum celebicum   Plate 11

Dicaeum celebicum S. Müller, 1843, *Land. Volk.*, in Temminck,
Verh. Nat. Gesch. Nederland. Overz. Bezit., 1 (1839-1844),
p.162, Celebes.

Forms superspecies with *D. ignipectum, D. monticolum, D.
sanguinolentum* and *D. hirundinaceum.* It is particularly close
to *D. monticolum* and possibly conspecific with it; some
consider it conspecific with *D. hirundinaceum*, while others
lump all four.

IDENTIFICATION Adult male black, slightly glossed
purple above with sooty face; scarlet on throat and black
median band on abdomen; rest of underparts white,
creamy-yellow and sooty-olive. Adult female is greyish-olive
above; underparts as male but lacks red and black. Juvenile
is darker than female.
Similar species Male differs from male Red-chested Flowerpecker *Dicaeum maugei* (39) by lack of scarlet rump; both
sexes differ from Crimson-crowned Flowerpecker *D.
nehrkorni* (29) by lack of crimson rump.

VOICE Thin, high-pitched upslurred *seeei* lasting 0.75
seconds at 0.5-5.0 second intervals; short *tjjt* repeated;
short, rather dry, slightly muted, unmusical *trri-tri*; single
high-pitched *tsip*; in flight a sharp *chip, chip, chip...*

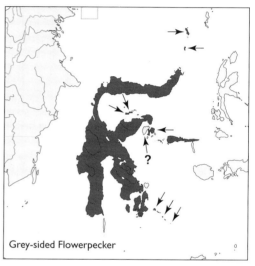

Grey-sided Flowerpecker

DISTRIBUTION Endemic to Sulawesi and neighbouring
islands (Tukangbesi archipelago, Siumpu, Kabaena, Banggai, Manadotua, Bangka, Lembeh, Togian, Muna, Butung,
Sangihe, Siau and Talaud) and Moluccas (Sula).

HABITAT Sea-level to 1,000 m; in most habitats, including
montane forest, primary and tall secondary forest, and at
forest edge, in plantations, lightly wooded cultivation, gardens, secondary scrub and around habitation; sometimes
in towns. Particularly found in *Lantana camara* patches on
Siumpu island.

STATUS Widespread and generally common. Common
throughout Sulawesi up to 1,000 m. Commoner than
Yellow-sided Flowerpecker *Dicaeum aureolimbatum* (16) in
degraded habitats.

MOVEMENTS Unknown.

FOOD Fruits of mistletoes, wild cherries and *Lantana
camara*, nectar and pollen; tiny spiders and insects.
Known food-plants Flowering coconuts, wild cherries, *Lantana camara*, Loranthaceae and Viscaceae.

HABITS Singly or in pairs; usually in outer canopy and

foliage, gleaning from bare outer twigs. Sits quivering wings for 30 or more seconds before swallowing fruit, then wipes bill on branch. Larger fruits of wild cherries are pierced and pulp squeezed out, whereas smaller fruits are swallowed whole. Restless and aggressive, particularly to *D. aureolimbatum*; maintains upright posture. Host to feather mite *Monojoubertia cristata*.

BREEDING Nest Pear-shaped purse with slit-like upper side entrance; constructed of fine grasses and down, and covered with bits of dry leaves, small twigs and spiders' web. Another nest about 1.5-2.0 above ground in *Casuarina equisitifolia* tree was attached to an outer branch; pendant-shaped ball, woven of fine grasses, with twigs and dried leaves attached to outside with slit-like entrance near top, below a small overhanging porch. A third, empty nest was similar, but covered with spiders' webs and leaf debris on one side. **Eggs** c/3; race *celebicum*: white, daubed with pale grey, which may be an artefact; 13.2 x 9.8. **Laying months** Unknown.

DESCRIPTION *D. c. celebicum*
Adult male Black glossed dull purplish (amethyst) upperparts; face sooty; throat white, with scarlet patch on lower throat and breast; abdomen creamy-white with black median band; flanks sooty-olive; undertail-coverts whitish. Bill dark brown, feet blackish.
Adult female Greyish-brown above; whitish-grey throat and breast; flanks dark olive-grey; centre of belly and vent buffy-white.
Juvenile As female but darker below, more greenish on upper breast, and darker, greyer on throat; bill paler.

GEOGRAPHICAL VARIATION
    D. c. celebicum S. Müller, 1843 (Sulawesi, Manadotua, Bangka, Lembeh, Togian, Muna and Butung) Described above.
    D. c. kuehni Hartert, 1903 (Tukangbesi archipelago) Male differs from nominate in being more bluish-purple above, paler abdomen is greyish-white with lighter and greyer olive sides.
    D. c. sanghirense Salvadori, 1876 (Sangihe, and perhaps Siau) Male has dark inky-blue glossed upperparts, abdomen less yellow, more greyish-white, flanks purer dark grey, less olivaceous.
    D. c. sulaense Sharpe, 1884 (Banggai and Sula) Male is lighter and more purplish-blue above than *kuehni*, flanks dark greyish-olive, and median stripe on abdomen greyish, not black.
    D. c. talautense Meyer & Wiglesworth, 1895 (Talaud) Male lighter, less glossy and more blue, or purplish-blue, above than nominate; flanks and abdomen uniform greyish-black. Female is generally darker below. So distinctive it may warrant specific separation.

MEASUREMENTS Wing 45.5-54 (all subspp.), 45.5-51 (mean 48, 9 male *celebicum*), 44-48 (mean 46.2, 4 female *celebicum*); **tail** 27-28.5 (mean 27.7, 5 male *celebicum*), 22.2-25 (mean 24.1, 4 female *celebicum*); **bill** 9.4-11.6 (mean 10.1, 9 male *celebicum*), 9.75-11.0 (mean 10.3, 5 female *celebicum*); **tarsus** 11-12 (mean 11.4, 5 male *celebicum*); **mass** no data.

REFERENCES Atyeo (1971), M. Catterall (pers. comm.), Coates & Bishop (1997), Holmes & Wood (1979), Riley (1997), Salomonsen (1961), Schönwetter (1980-1984), Stones *et al.* (1997), White & Bruce (1986).

43 BLOOD-BREASTED FLOWERPECKER
Dicaeum sanguinolentum   Plate 11

Dicaeum sanguinolentum Temminck & Laugier, 1829, *Pl. Col., livr.* 80, pl.478, fig.2, Java; restricted to West Java by Robinson & Kloss, 1923, *Journ. Fed. Malay States Mus.,* 11, p.57.

Forms superspecies with *D. ignipectum, D. monticolum, D. celebicum* and *D. hirundinaceum*.

IDENTIFICATION Adult male is dark glossy blue above with white-tipped tail; breast scarlet; black stripe on centre of lower breast and belly; rest of underparts pinky or orange-buff; white pectoral tufts. Adult female is olive-brown above with scarlet rump; underparts olive or orange-buff streaked olive-grey; white pectoral tufts. Juvenile more olive or grey than female.
Similar species Male Red-chested Flowerpecker *Dicaeum maugei* (39) has scarlet rump; male Crimson-breasted Flowerpecker *Prionochilus percussus* (5) lacks black patch on centre of belly and female lacks both red rump and olive-grey streaking below; Orange-bellied Flowerpecker *D. trigonostigma* (24) has yellow-orange or orange rump, not red; male Black-fronted Flowerpecker *D. igniferum* (38) has upperside dull scarlet mottled purple, whereas juvenile of that species from female by white underparts, not ochre or orange-buff; female from female Scarlet-headed Flowerpecker *D. trochileum* (46) by ochre or orange-buff underparts rather than dull white, and from juvenile of that species by scarlet rump, not orange.

VOICE Call A variety of sharp high-pitched clicks and buzzing and a harder, sharper, two-note call. **Song** Jerky series of 4-5 thin very high-pitched sweet notes of 1-2 seconds' duration.

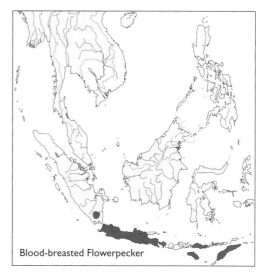
Blood-breasted Flowerpecker

DISTRIBUTION The Lesser Sundas (Flores, Sumba and Timor), Java (including Gunung Gede-Pangrango National Park), Bali and once Lampung, Sumatra.

HABITAT Lowlands up to 1,200 m on Lesser Sundas, but higher on Timor and Flores; presumably not where *D.*

igniferum and *D. maugei* occur in lowlands; mostly 800-2,400 m on Java & Bali. Hill and mountain forest, and at forest edge; in primary and secondary forest, and amongst *Casuarina*; in open and degraded woodland, and lightly wooded cultivation; found particularly amongst Loranthaceae and *Viscum*.

STATUS Common and widespread on Sumba, common on Flores but confined to high elevations and uncommon on Timor. Widespread at 800-2,400 m on Bali and Java. Presumed vagrant to Sumatra.

MOVEMENTS Unknown. If truly vagrant to Sumatra, it seems likely some movements, perhaps chiefly vertical, occur.

FOOD Presumably includes fruit, and possibly also nectar and/or pollen of mistletoes. Chironomid larvae and spiders.
Known food-plants *Viscum* sp. and unidentified mistletoes Loranthaceae in Java.

HABITS Singly or in pairs in tree-tops.

BREEDING Nest Unknown. **Eggs** Race *sanguinolentum*: lustreless white 11.5-15.5 (mean 14.2, n=10) x 7.8-10.8 (mean 10.0). **Laying months** Java: West Java, January, August, October.

DESCRIPTION *D. s. sanguinolentum*
Adult male Upperparts dark glossy blue with white tips to tail; throat and belly pinky-buff; breast scarlet with broad black stripe along centre of lower breast and belly; flanks orange-buff; white pectoral tufts. Iris blue or brown; bill black; feet dark grey.
Adult female Dull olive-brown above; scarlet rump and uppertail-coverts; underparts ochre or orange-buff streaked olive-grey, sides of breast greyish; white pectoral tufts.
Juvenile Greyer than female.

GEOGRAPHICAL VARIATION
D. s. hanieli Hellmayr, 1912 (Timor) Male has only a small red patch on foreneck, creamy-white throat and chin, white abdomen with yellowish tinge, and yellowish flanks. Female unknown.
D. s. rhodopygiale Rensch, 1928 (Flores) Male differs from nominate in having orange-pink, not buff, undertail-coverts, and from other forms in buff not whitish abdomen, blackish flanks and much thinner bill.
D. s. sanguinolentum Temminck & Laugier, 1829 (Java, Bali and Sumatra – presumably vagrant) Described above.
D. s. wilhelminae Büttikofer, 1892 (Sumba) Male similar to *D. maugei* but with no red on rump, dark grey flanks and brighter violet dorsal gloss, abdomen whitish; bill shorter and thicker. From nominate male in having white chin, with scarlet throat to breast, and grey belly and flanks. Female differs from nominate by olive-grey rather than olive-brown upperparts, and pale buffy-white and grey underparts. Juvenile as female but white and grey below suffused olive; bill paler.

MEASUREMENTS (nominate) **Wing** 46-51 (mean 48.4, SD 1.67, 9 males), 46-48 (mean 46.7, SD 0.96, 4 females); **bill** 10.7-12.0 (mean 11.4, SD 0.52, 9 males), 11.1-12.2 0 (mean 11.7, SD 0.51, 4 females); **mass** no data.

REFERENCES Coates & Bishop (1997), Hellebrekers & Hoogerwerf (1967), MacKinnon & Phillipps (1993), Salomonsen (1961), Schönwetter (1980-84), White & Bruce (1986).

44   MISTLETOEBIRD
Dicaeum hirundinaceum   Plate 12

Motacilla hirundinaceum Shaw & Nodder, 1792, *Nat. Misc.*, 4, pl. 114, New Holland, Australia

Alternative names: Australian Flowerpecker, Australian Flower Swallow, Mistletoe Flowerpecker, Moo-ne-je-tang.

Forms superspecies with *D. ignipectum*, *D. monticolum*, *D. celebicum* and *D. sanguinolentum*.

IDENTIFICATION Adult male is glossy blue-black above; scarlet throat, breast and undertail-coverts; black streak on centre of lower breast and belly; rest of underparts grey. Adult female is greyish-brown above; below grey mottled dark on throat and breast; scarlet undertail-coverts with white tips. Juvenile differs from female in having a pink, not blackish, bill.
Similar species None; all other flowerpeckers are allopatric.

VOICE High-pitched double or treble note and a warble. **Call** Sibilant calls and dry *tick* note. Flight call is a sharp *dzee!*; *pretty-sweet* or *tsew!* Alarm call is a sharp *trrit-trrit* or a throaty *krik-krik*. Contact call a *see* or *seep*. **Song** *Wissweet... wissweet...* or *wit-wissweet... wit-wissweet...*, usually oft-repeated, and given by both sexes. Also a clear, penetrating *kinsey kinsey kinsey* or *wichy wichy wichy* or *swizit swizit, weet weet swizit* or *witsoo witsoo witsoo...*, *wiss wiss wiss...*, sung by territorial males, usually from high perches in tall trees. Also a soft warbling song that includes mimicry of Mulga Parrot *Psephotus varius*, Variegated Fairy-wren *Malurus lamberti*, Rufous Whistler *Pachycephala rufiventris*, Grey Fantail *Rhipidura fuliginosa*, Weebill *Smicrornis brevirostris*, Striated Pardalote *Pardalotus striatus*, Chestnut-rumped Thornbill *Acanthiza uropygialis*, Inland Thornbill *A. apicalis*, Yellow-rumped Thornbill *A. chrysorrhoa*, Southern White-face *Aphelocephala leucopsis*, Silvereye *Zosterops lateralis*, White-fronted Honeyeater *Phylidonyris albifrons*, New Holland Honeyeater *P. novaehollandiae*, Jacky Winter *Microeca fascinans*, White-browed Babbler *Pomatostomus superciliosus*, Grey Shrike-thrush *Colluricincla harmonica*, Black-faced Woodswallow *Artamus cinereus*, Dusky Woodswallow *A. cyanopterus* and Willie Wagtail *Rhipidura leucophrys*.

DISTRIBUTION The Moluccas (Watubela, Tayandu and Kai) and Tanimbar (Lesser Sundas), Aru Islands and Australia (except Tasmania, and driest, treeless, deserts). Thought to have entered Australia late, perhaps at most 2 million years after New Guinea separated, and pre-adapted to feed on Loranthaceae and Viscaceae.

HABITAT Forests and edge, woodland, secondary growth and scrub wherever mistletoes grow; all wooded habitats including sclerophyll woodland and open savanna woodland, savanna grassland, semi-arid scrub, low mallee (eucalypts), mulga (dominated by *Acacia aneura*), mangroves, village trees. More frequent in riparian zones in arid areas; prefers mature eucalypt stands and larger

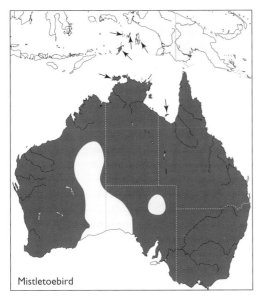

Mistletoebird

woodland trees in open country. Rare above 1,000 m in Snowy Mountains of Australia. Sea-level to 250 m on Tanimbar Islands.

STATUS Moderately common Yamdena and Kai islands. Common throughout mainland Australia in suitable habitat. Density in eucalypt woodland forest 0.08-0.52 birds per ha.

MOVEMENTS Non-breeders are highly nomadic in some areas, linked to fruiting by mistletoes.

FOOD Insects (including moths, aphids and syrphid flies) and spiders, especially when feeding young for first few days after hatching; mistletoe berries and other berries and fruits; nectar; pollen. In South Australia, *Amyema quandang* produces ripe fruit continuously, and the fruits are mainly only eaten by two dispersers: this species, and the Spiny-cheeked Honeyeater *Acanthagenys rufogularis*, which also pollinates the plants when taking nectar from the flowers. The mistletoe fruits are adeptly squeezed from their cases by *D. hirundinaceum*, swallowed, by-passing the blind sac of a stomach (used to digest insects and spiders - the proventriculus, gizzard and duodenum of dicaeids are all in the same plane) to enter the intestine directly. The still-sticky stones are excreted rapidly (820±29 seconds, much faster than the 2,434±36 taken by *A. rufogularis*). At first they adhere to the bird's cloaca but by aligning its body along a branch and, with a deft wiping motion followed by three sideways jumps to detach the clinging thread, the Mistletoebird fastens the seed to its perch. Many such seeds are often linked together by gelatinous threads along branches. 85% germinate and 43% produce seedlings, more than the 31% passed through the guts of honeyeaters.

Known food-plants Loranthaceae including *Amyema congener*, *A. miquelii*, *A. quandang*, *A. preissi*, 2 other *Amyema* spp., *Dendrophthoe* sp., *Elytranthe* sp., *Lepeostegeres* sp., *Lysiana* sp., *Lysiana exocarpi*, *Macrosolen* sp., *Muellerina celastroides*, *Scurrula* sp. and 2 other unidentified genera; *Atriplex* sp., *Chrysanthemoides monolifera*, *Coprosma lucida*, *Crataegus* sp., *Fuchsia* spp., *Ligustrum* sp., *Lycium ferocissimum*, *Malus pumila*, *Schinus areira*.

HABITS Non-breeders highly nomadic (see above); usually in pairs when breeding, but solitary males common, and both sexes solitary outside breeding season. Maintains upright posture. Moves rapidly, often high; flies swiftly; restless; deposits defecated mistletoe seeds on branches. Flicks wings when foraging for insects at rate of 18 flicks per minute. Catches insects by snatching and hawking. Can become torpid in cold weather. Singly or in pairs in mid-storey to canopy.

Host to *Haemoproteus* sp. and feather mites *Monojoubertia securigera* and *M. parvisecurigera*.

BREEDING Territorial, with male defending territory of 13-25 ha, chasing intruding males in high-speed weaving flights over boundaries throughout year but especially August–January, and singing from exposed perches. Courtship involves male flitting around female making excited calls, perching nearby and partially fanning tail; also chasing flights through and above trees. Female usually builds and incubates alone, but both parents feed young. Incubation c.12 days; young stay in nest c.15 days. **Nest** Neat pear-shaped purse with felt-like or silken consistency made of matted plant down, debris, lichen, feathers, dried blossom and cobwebs with slit entrance on side, suspended 1-15 m high from thin leafy twigs. 155 x 105 mm. May be decorated with brown or grey matter including excreta of insect larvae, or faded wattle-blossom. Nest placed 1.7-2.6 m up in bullock bush *Alectryon oleifrons* and western myall *Acacia papyrocarpa*, but up to 18 m inside forest. **Eggs** c/3-4; white. Race *hirundinaceum*: 16.3-17.8 (mean 17.0, n=26) x 10.7-12.7 (mean 11.5); *ignicolle*: 13.5 x 11.0. **Laying months** Season variable, but mostly September–April (October–March in Australia, timed to coincide with fruiting of mistletoes).

DESCRIPTION *D. h. hirundinaceum*
Adult male Head and upperparts glossy violet blue-black; scarlet orbital ring; throat, breast and undertail-coverts scarlet; broad blackish streak on centre of lower breast and belly; flanks grey and rest of abdomen greyish-white. Iris grey, light brown, red or deep brown. Bill blackish or dark grey on upper mandible, lower mandible dark grey to brown. Legs dark grey, dark brown or black, feet dark brown, blackish or grey. Mouth salmon-pink, flesh-colour in centre.
Adult female Greyish-brown above; greyish-white below with some darker mottling on throat and breast; undertail-coverts pale scarlet, with whitish tips giving a scaled effect.
Juvenile Differs from female in having a pink, not blackish, bill; and indistinct, slightly rufous scaling on throat.

Clinal variation in size and colour, northern birds smaller, females in north paler and whiter below, compared to greyer and browner in south; western birds more variable.

GEOGRAPHICAL VARIATION
D. h. fulgidum P. L. Sclater, 1883 (Tanimbar Islands) Male differs from *keiense* in being paler pink below, with only a little grey-green on sides of abdomen. Female differs in having a deep crimson rump.
D. h. hirundinaceum (Shaw & Nodder, 1792) (Australia except Tasmania) Described above.
D. h. ignicolle Gray, 1858 (Aru Island) Male differs from nominate in having white of underparts replaced by dull yellowish, and grey replaced by olive-green.
D. h. keiense Salvadori, 1875 (Watubele, Tayundu and Kai) Male differs from nominate in having purplish-

173

blue upperparts; narrow red band across breast, pale grey-green flanks, whitish lower abdomen and rest of underparts pale pink-orange without keel-stripe. Female differs by being olive-brown above with a reddish rump.

MEASUREMENTS Some clinal variation in the nominate, with birds in northern Australia smaller than those in the south. **Wing** 57-66 (mean 61.9, SD 2.68, 10 male *hirundinaceum*), 51 (male *ignicolle*), 55-60 (mean 57.7, SD 1.67, 8 female *hirundinaceum*); **tail** 23 (male *ignicolle*); **bill** 9.0-12.7 (mean 10.7, SD 0.98, 10 male *hirundinaceum*), 9.9-11.5 (mean 10.9, SD 0.53, 8 female *hirundinaceum*); **culmen** 10 (male *ignicolle*); **tarsus** 12 (male *ignicolle*); **mass** 8-10 (unsexed).

REFERENCES Attenborough (1995), Atyeo (1971), Ballingall (1990), Beehler *et al.* (1986), Blakers *et al.* (1984), Coates & Bishop (1997), Close (1991), Hall (1974), Longmore (1991), Murphy *et al.* (1993), Pizzey & Knight (1997), Reid (1983, 1987, 1989, 1990, 1997), Richardson & Wooler (1988), Salomonsen (1961), Serventy (1970), Simpson (1997), Simpson & Day (1984), White & Bruce (1986).

---

45   SCARLET-BACKED FLOWERPECKER
Dicaeum cruentatum   Plate 12

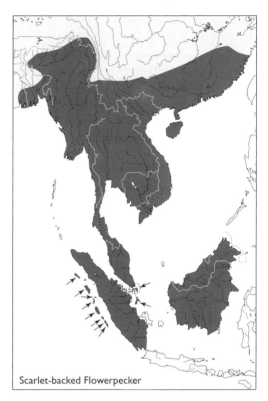

Scarlet-backed Flowerpecker

Certhia cruentata Linnaeus, 1758, *Syst. Nat.*, ed. 10, 1, p.119; based on "The Little Black, White and Red Indian Creeper" of Edwards, 1748 *Nat. Hist. Birds* 2 (1747), pl.81, Bengal.

Alternative name: Pryer's Flowerpecker

IDENTIFICATION Adult male red and glossy blue-black above; below black, grey and white. Adult female brown and olive above; crimson lower back, rump, uppertail-coverts and black tail; buff and grey below. Juvenile buffier below than female, and has pale base to bill.
Similar species Female from female Orange-bellied Flowerpecker *Dicaeum trigonostigma* (24) by red rump; female Scarlet-headed Flowerpecker *D. trochileum* (46) has whitish (not buff or grey) underparts.

VOICE Noisy. **Call** *Chip-chip* and *chip-chip.....chip-chip*; loud stream of clicking staccato notes *tchik-tchik-tchik*; high-pitched *chizee*; constant twittering; sharp squeaks; shrill call. **Song** Up and down *see-sip-see-sip-see-sip*; also continually repeated *see-bit see-bit see-bit.*

DISTRIBUTION The Himalayan foothills eastwards from extreme eastern Nepal to Bhutan, Assam and Arunachal Pradesh, south through Bengal, Nagaland, Manipur, Chittagongs and Burma, to Thailand, Indochina and Malay Peninsula; Fukien, Kwangtung, Kwangsi, southern Yunnan and Hainan Island in China; Sumatra and Borneo.

HABITAT Lowlands generally up to 1,000 m, but as high as 1,200 m in China and 2,135 m in Nepal; highland *kerangas*; associates with Loranthaceae in various forest types, including alluvial forest, and at edge, in orchards, plantations, groves of trees in cultivation, secondary growth and gardens.

STATUS Very common in Thailand. Common in the Calcutta area of India. Common resident in Borneo and Sumatra in secondary forest, gardens and plantations up to 1,000 m. Common in lowlands of Peninsular Malaysia in open scrub, especially near the coast. Common throughout Burma in plains and hills. Rare in Nepal and Bhutan; locally common Bangladesh. Status uncertain in India.

MOVEMENTS Probably undergoes vertical seasonal movements in higher parts of range.

FOOD Insects, spiders, small figs, green seeds, berries and nectar. Fruits of mistletoes.
Known food-plants Limes, *Ficus* spp., unidentified Loranthaceae, fruits of *Loranthus scurrula*, *Macrosolen cochinchinensis* (= *Loranthus ampullaceus*), *Scurrula parasitica*, and perhaps Viscaceae.

HABITS Active and aggressive. Usually in pairs or family parties in tree-tops, but also forages on bushes. Hawks flying insects from perch, and catches them by hovering. Strong swift flight with erratic dipping paths. Greatest longevity recorded 4 years. Host to *Haemoproteus dicaeus*, *Plasmodium vaughani* and *Trypanosoma* sp., and feather mites *Monojoubertia marquardti*.

BREEDING Building and incubation by both sexes, the latter taking 10-11 days. **Nest** Tiny oval or pear-shaped purse, 90 x 60 mm, of vegetable down bound together by grass, rootlets and cobwebs. Entrance near top; sometimes has a porch. Suspended from terminal twig, hidden by leaves, 2-15 m but usually 6-9 m above ground, often in mango tree *Mangifera indica*. **Eggs** c/2-4. Race *cruentatum*: 13.1-15.3 (mean 14, n=62) x 9.4-11.1 (mean 10.2); *nigrimentum*: 13.5-14.7 (mean 14.0, n=4) x 9.9-10.2 (mean

10.0). Greyish-white, unmarked, or with a few faint brownish flecks. **Laying months** India and Nepal: March–August, chiefly May and June; Peninsular Malaysia: January–June; Burma: February–April; Sumatra: building, Deli, November and December; Hong Kong: June–August; Sabah: November–January, April, May; enlarged testes January–March, June; Thailand: January–April, July.

DESCRIPTION *D. c. cruentatum*

Adult male Crown, back and rump deep red; sides of head black; wings and tail glossy blue-black; sides of throat and breast black; flanks grey; centre of throat, breast and belly pale buff; white pectoral tufts. Iris brown; bill black or blackish-green, feet black or blackish-green.

Adult female Uppertail-coverts scarlet; tail black; wings dark brown; rest of upperparts olive with orange tinge on back; throat greyish-white; buff underparts with grey flanks.

Juvenile As female, but buffier below, no red on rump and paler base to orange bill.

Hybrid with *D. trochileum* recorded from Samarinda, Kalimantan Timur, Borneo.

GEOGRAPHICAL VARIATION

D. c. batuense Richmond, 1912 (Mentawai Islands) Male from *sumatranum* by smaller bill, centre of chin, throat and chest buffy-white as *cruentatum* but light area not as broad; sides of head, neck and body slightly darker than *sumatranum*; from *cruentatum* by lighter red upperparts; sides of neck, body and flanks smoky-grey and not blackish; scapulars greenish, not bluish gloss, and forehead black. Female from *cruentatum* by narrower white median line on underparts.

D. c. cruentatum (Linnaeus, 1758) (includes *siamense*; Nepal and north-east India to south China, east Thailand and Indochina; Riau Archipelago, Sumatra) Described above.

D. c. ignitum (Begbie, 1834) (peninsular Malaysia) Male is slightly darker on flanks than nominate; less than 25% are of the "*pryeri*" form also found on Borneo (see under *nigrimentum*).

D. c. niasense Meyer de Schauensee & Ripley, 1939 (Nias Island – doubtfully separable, and should probably be included in *sumatranum*) Male similar to *batuense* but wing-coverts purplish-blue and not greenish-blue, buff centre of underside only reaching to upper chest; throat darker grey; from *sumatranum* by more purplish-blue wing-coverts, grey of underparts darker and bill stouter.

D. c. nigrimentum Salvadori, 1874 (Borneo, probably throughout; in north-east Sabah "*pryeri*" occurs) Variable, and probably includes other quite distinct forms such as "*pryeri*" from Sandakan and "*hosei*" from "Borneo". Black on throat and upper breast, and more black on flanks (Tawau and Lamag); creamy line through throat and breast ("Borneo", Labuan and Gunung Dulit); as previous but a little scarlet on breast (Gunung Kalulong); as previous but black on chin (Gunung Kinabalu); very narrow buffy line through throat ("Sarawak"); those from Labuan mostly have a black (but some a buffy) throat. Female from Banjarmasin has some red on crown and back (could be immature male or intersex). Those with black throat ("*pryeri*", less than 25% of population) represent a non-geographical colour morph; "*hosei*" is somewhat intermediate (Moulton 1914, Chasen & Kloss 1930, Salomonsen 1961).

D. c. simalurense Salomonsen, 1961 (Simeulue Island) Male from *batuense* by larger size, with upperparts darker red, more scarlet, and gloss of wing-coverts stronger and bluer, which also distinguishes it from *niasense* and *sumatranum*, but it is similar to *cruentatum* in colour.

D. c. sumatranum Cabanis, 1878 (Sumatra and satellite islands, except where other forms occur) Males are smaller, and have lighter red upperparts than nominate; forehead black; wings duller; smoky-grey throat, sides of neck, sides of breast and flanks rather than black; median parts of throat and chin whitish; scapulars with greenish, not bluish, gloss.

"***D. c. pryeri***" Sharpe, 1881 (Sabah – Sandakan, Lamag, Tawau; Malay Peninsula) A non-geographical morph. Black of throat in male extends to breast.

"***D. c. hosei***" Sharpe, 1897 (Sulawesi, Gunung Masarang – locality erroneous, presumed Borneo) Black on chin and upper throat of male, but buffy-white centre of lower throat to breast. A morph, intermediate between *nigrimentum* and "*pryeri*".

Possibly an undescribed form in Sabah.

MEASUREMENTS Wing 43-49 (mean 45.3, male *batuense*), 46 (male *niasense*), 47, 48 (male *nigrimentum*, Brunei), 50, 51 (male *simalurense*), 43 (female *batuense*), 47 (female *simalurense*), 46-51 (unsexed *cruentatum*); **tail** 25-28 (unsexed *cruentatum*); **bill** 10.3-12.4 (mean 11.4, SD 0.71, 10 male *cruentatum*), 10.6-12.1 (mean 11.2, SD 0.57, 7 female *cruentatum*), 12 (unsexed *cruentatum*); **gape** 10.5, 11.1 (male *nigrimentum*, Brunei); **culmen** 9 (male *niasense*), 12 (female *batuense*); **tarsus** 13 (unsexed *cruentatum*); **mass** 7-8 (male *cruentatum*), 5.5, 5.7 (male *nigrimentum*, Brunei).

REFERENCES Ali & Ripley (1974), Atyeo (1971), Chasen & Kloss (1930), Corlett (1998), Davidson (1945), Fleming *et al.* (1976), Gretton (1990), Grimmett *et al.* (1998), Inskipp & Inskipp (1985), King *et al.* (1975), MacKinnon & Phillipps (1993), Mann (in prep. b), van Marle & Voous (1988), McClure (1974), Medway & Wells (1976), Meyer de Schauensee (1984), Moulton (1914), Redman *et al.* (1984), Salomonsen (1961), Sharpe (1881, 1897), Sheldon *et al.* (in prep.), Smythies (1957, 1960, 1981, 1986), Stresemann (1940).

46 SCARLET-HEADED FLOWERPECKER
Dicaeum trochileum   Plate 12

Certhia trochilea Sparrman, 1789, *Mus. Carlsonianum*, fasc. 4 no. 80, "America?" [error = Java *fide* Stresemann 1923, *Orn. Monatsb.*, 31, p.41].

IDENTIFICATION Adult male scarlet and black above; scarlet chin to breast, otherwise greyish-white below. Adult female brown above with red wash; scarlet rump and uppertail-coverts; dull white and grey below. Juvenile is greenish-brown above with orange on rump.

Similar species Female from that of Scarlet-backed Flowerpecker *Dicaeum cruentatum* (45) by reddish wash on crown and mantle.

VOICE Call High-pitched *zit-zit-zit*, much shorter than *buzz-chip* of other flowerpeckers. **Song** A sweet series of very high-pitched double notes that see-saw abruptly up and down for 2.0-3.5 seconds. A buzzing *seeeeep...seeeeep*.

DISTRIBUTION South-east Borneo, Java (including Baluran National Park, Pulau Dua, Gede-Pangrango National Park, Bogor), Madura, Bali, Bangka, Karimunjawa, Bawean, Kangean, Lombok and a few records from Lampung, Sumatra.

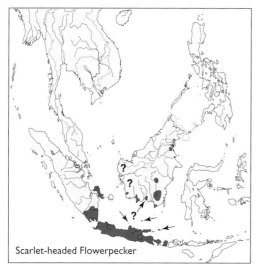

Scarlet-headed Flowerpecker

HABITAT Up to 600 m in woods, lightly wooded cultivation, cultivation, open areas and mangroves; towns. Associated with mistletoes.

STATUS Common in gardens and open areas of lowlands of Java, its outlying islands, and Bali. Uncommon in Sumatra. Apparently uncommon on Lombok.

MOVEMENTS Unknown.

FOOD Nectar and/or pollen and berries of mistletoes. Insects and small spiders.
Known food-plants *Dendrophthoe pentandra* (*Dicaeum* spp. probe with their bill sideways into the top of the flower bud of *D. pentandra*, the corolla jerks open, and the liquid nectar, which completely fills it, shoots out) and unidentified Loranthaceae in Java.

HABITS Recorded at 5 m above ground in crown of *Rhizophora* tree. Singly or in pairs in upper tree levels amongst fruits and mistletoes; also seen foraging low.

BREEDING Nest Unknown. **Eggs** Race *trochileum*: variable shape of oval-elongate to oval with distinctly different ends; generally white unglossed or faintly glossed; some have a few markings, one with sharply defined red-brown point. 13.5-16.7 (mean 15.8, n=50) x 10.2-11.5 (mean 10.8). **Laying months** Java: West Java, February–July.

DESCRIPTION *D. t. trochileum*
Adult male Head, upper back, rump, uppertail-coverts and chin to upper breast scarlet (scarlet fades to orange-yellow in older skins); flanks and lower breast grey; wings and tail black; belly greyish-white; white underwing-coverts and pectoral tufts. Iris brown; bill black; feet black.
Adult female Upperparts brown, washed red on head and mantle; rump scarlet; underparts dull white.
Juvenile Greenish-brown above; orange patch on rump;

greyish below, paler on throat and centre of belly.

Hybrid with *D. cruentatum* recorded from Samarinda, Kalimantan Timur, Borneo.

GEOGRAPHICAL VARIATION
   D. t. stresemanni Rensch, 1928 (Lombok) Shorter bill than nominate; female paler above and below than nominate, particularly on head and flanks. Doubtfully valid.
   D. t. trochileum (Sparrmann, 1789) (range of species except Lombok) Described above.

MEASUREMENTS Wing 52-56 (mean 52.9, SD 1.45, 10 male *trochileum*), 50-54 (mean 51.1, SD 1.54, 9 female *trochileum*); **bill** 10-13.1 (mean 12 .3, SD 0.55, 10 male *trochileum*), 10.9-12.6 (mean 11.9, SD 0.54, 9 female *trochileum*), 9 (unsexed *stresemanni*); **mass** no data.

REFERENCES Bishop (1985), Coates & Bishop (1997), Hellebrekers & Hoogerwerf (1967), MacKinnon & Phillipps (1993), Mann (in prep. b), Smythies (1957, 1960, 1981), White & Bruce (1986).

Tribe Nectariniini

SUNBIRDS AND SPIDERHUNTERS
Chalcoparia

Chalcoparia Cabanis 1851, *Mus. Hein.*, 1, p.103. Type by monotypy *Motacilla singalensis* Gmelin.

One species in tropical Asia. Small; tail rounded; sexes differ, only male having metallic plumage. Bill shorter than head, culmen very slightly curved, lower mandible straight, lacking the serrations found in all other sunbirds. Nostrils exposed and operculated. Tongue covered with a horny plate, concave in cross-section, with the tip deeply notched and fimbriated; the edges of the distal part also fimbriated. This is unlike the tongue of any other sunbird, and comes closest to some flowerpeckers, particularly *Prionochilus*. Habits reminiscent of white-eyes *Zosterops* spp., small babblers.

47 RUBY-CHEEKED SUNBIRD
Chalcoparia singalensis   Plate 14

Motacilla singalensis Gmelin, 1788, *Syst. Nat.*, 1 (2), p.964, Ceylon [error]; Malacca designated by Oberholser, 1912, *Smiths. Misc. Coll.*, 60 (7), p.21.

Alternative name: Rubycheek

IDENTIFICATION Adult male dark above, with metallic green gloss; copper ear-coverts and cheeks; breast and throat rufous, rest of underparts yellow. Adult female is mostly olive-green above, more yellowish on wings; underparts as male. Juvenile like female but with a yellow throat. **Similar species** Both sexes distinguished from males of Plain-throated Sunbird *Anthreptes malacensis* (53), Red-throated Sunbird *A. rhodolaema* (54) and Fork-tailed Sunbird *Aethopyga christinae* (160) by rufous throat and breast.

VOICE Song A shrill, rising trill ending in brief double note, followed immediately by a descending trill, ending in two distinctly separated notes, *tirrr-titi, trirrr, tir, tir.* **Call** A shrill chirp *seet-seet* or *tear-tear*, often uttered in flight from bush to bush.

HABITAT The upper storey of a variety of forest types and forest edge, including lowland and hill dipterocarp, *Melaleuca*, peatswamp, heath and secondary forests, clearings, scrub jungle, mangroves, coastal vegetation, luxuriant vegetation by riverbanks, *Albizia, Gmelina*, cocoa, coconut groves and village gardens; lowlands generally up to 1,000 m, but to 1,950 m on Java. In Nepal favours low branches and bushes around villages as well as in forest.

DISTRIBUTION Eastern Nepal, Arunachal Pradesh and north-eastern India to Bangladesh, Burma, Thailand, Indochina, west and south Yunnan, Malay Peninsula, Natunas, Sumatra, Borneo and Java.

STATUS Common in Thailand and Indian subcontinent; locally frequent in India. Locally common in Bangladesh. Very local and rare in Nepal. Rare in Bhutan. Widespread but uncommon on Sumatra and Java. Common Sabah, but less so in most other parts of Borneo.

MOVEMENTS Unknown.

FOOD Feeds at spiders' webs. Caterpillars, ants, sandflies and other winged insects, fruits, pollen and nectar.
Known food-plants *Casuarina* sp.

HABITS Occurs singly or in small groups of up to 10 birds,

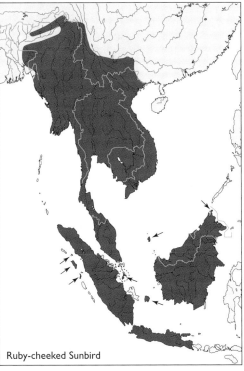

Ruby-cheeked Sunbird

when it behaves as a small flock. Rather tit-like behaviour. Very active. A deep and vigorous jerking of tail during male's song. May be high in trees on exposed perches or around low bushes. Probes flowers for nectar, and gleans insects from leaves. Host to *Haemoproteus sequeirae.*

BREEDING Male feeds female in courtship. Nests under lips of steep banks, never in open. Also often nests in rubber plantations. **Nest** Pear-shaped, shaggy, of very fine vegetable fibres, mixed with fern stalks, black roots, cobwebs, moss and dry grass; large entrance with porch, suspended from drooping twigs of bushes about 2 m (about 5 m in peninsular Malaysia) above ground. 160 x 60 mm. **Eggs** c/2. Purplish-grey, marked with purplish-black, or purplish-brown, clouds and hair lines, occasionally entirely dark grey, underlying shell marks. Race *assamensis*: pale pink, mauve or white, with fine lines and speckles of brown-grey or purplish-grey or dark reddish-brown, 16.0-18.3 (mean 16.9, n=8) x 11.7-12.3 (mean

12.1); *internotus*: 16.0-17.7 (mean 16.8, n=7) x 11.3-12.0 (mean 11.8); *phoenicotis*: 15.1-17.8 (mean 16.8, n=28) x 10.8-12.4 (mean 11.8); *sumatrana*: 15.0-17.1 (mean 16.1, n=2) x 11.4-11.5 (mean 11.5). **Laying months** Borneo: Sabah, January–May, August, enlarged gonads March, June, July; Sarawak, juveniles August–September; southern Borneo, nest-building June, juveniles June–July; India: end March to June; Java: West Java, February–July; peninsular Malaysia: July; Burma: March, May–August.

DESCRIPTION *C. s. assamensis*

Adult male Above brilliant metallic green; ear-coverts and cheeks copper, bordered below by purple line; throat and breast rufous, rest of underparts lemon-yellow. Wings blackish; tail black with some greeny-blue. Iris red, bill blackish, feet greenish-grey.

Adult female Olive-green above, yellowish wings, throat and breast rufous, rest of underparts lemon-yellow.

Juvenile As female, but throat yellow, concolorous with breast.

GEOGRAPHICAL VARIATION

C. s. assamensis (Kloss, 1930) (includes *rubigentis* [Baker, 1930]) (Chitwan eastwards in Nepal, east to Sikkim, Bhutan, Darjeeling, Assam, Nagaland, Manipur, Bangladesh to north Burma and north Thailand, west and south Yunnan) Described above.

C. s. bantenensis (Hoogerwerf, 1967) (West Java) Size as *sumatranus*, *borneanus* and *phoenicotis*, but tail shorter than latter; wing longer than *koratensis*. Differs from first three forms by small area of brown on chin, throat and foreneck, and much clearer greenish-yellow on underparts. Browner on throat and foreneck than *koratensis*. Juvenile is yellower below and brighter olive-green above than *phoenicotis* or *sumatrana*.

C. s. borneana (Kloss, 1921) (Borneo) Male has similar amount of chestnut-red on underparts to nominate. From *C. s. interposita* by rufous of foreneck and upper breast rather deeper in both sexes. Those in southern Borneo slightly larger than those in north.

C. s. internota (Deignan, 1955) (south Burma, south Thailand) Reddish-brown of throat and breast not clearly defined, unlike *interposita* and *assamensis*, forming a link between these two. Throat and upper breast in either sex darker than in *assamensis*, paler than *interposita*; yellow of underparts more greenish than in *assamensis*, more golden than in *interposita*.

C. s. interposita (Robinson & Kloss, 1921) (southern Thailand) Male has less chestnut-red on throat and upper breast than nominate, but more than *koratensis*. Less green than nominate, with less brown on chin, throat, foreneck and breast, but less brightly yellow than *koratensis*. More extensive rufous below than *assamensis*, but throat paler, and bluish, not greenish, on shoulder.

C. s. koratensis (Kloss, 1918) (includes *stellae* [Deignan 1950]) (eastern Thailand, Laos, Vietnam) Male has less extensive rufous, which is paler, on throat than *assamensis* and well separated from yellow of rest of underparts.

C. s. pallida (Chasen, 1934) (North Natuna Islands) Male distinguished from nominate by less intense, less sharply defined, and less extensive rufous on underparts, and from *bantenensis* and *borneana* by less yellow below.

C. s. panopsia (Oberholser, 1912) (west coast islands of Sumatra) Male as nominate, but female has upperparts lighter, more greenish, and posterior parts of underparts more brightly yellowish.

C. s. phoenicotis (Temminck, 1822) (East and Central Java) Not well marked. Rufous of throat merges imperceptibly into yellow of rest of underparts; green gloss on back is darker than in *assamensis*.

C. s. singalensis (Gmelin, 1788) (Malay Peninsula from Perak southwards) Male has more chestnut-red on throat, foreneck and upper breast than *interposita* and generally less yellow below.

C. s. sumatrana (Kloss, 1921) (mainland Sumatra and Belitung) Male is more bluish above, and darker and more extensive rufous below, than *assamensis*.

MEASUREMENTS Wing 54-57 (male *bantenensis*), 53-56 (male *borneana*), 52-54 (male *koratensis*), 53-55 (3 male *pallida*), 54-58 (male *phoenicotis*), 53-56 (male *sumatrana*), 54 (female *borneana*; Brunei), 53 (female *pallida*), 52-54 (female *phoenicotis*), 52-53 (female *sumatrana*), 52-55 (unsexed *assamensis*); **tail** 41-43 (male *bantenensis*), 38-43 (male *borneana*), 40-44 (male *koratensis*), 40 (male *pallida*), 43-48 (male *phoenicotis*), 39-45 (male *sumatrana*), 38-41 (female *phoenicotis*), 36-42 (female *sumatrana*), 54 (juvenile female *bantenensis*), 41-43 (unsexed *assamensis*); **bill** 15-17 (male *assamensis*), 14-16 (female *assamensis*); **culmen** 12-13.2 (male *bantenensis*), 11.1-13.8 (male *borneana*), 12-12.9 (male *koratensis*), 12-13.2 (male *phoenicotis*), 11.9-12.9 (male *sumatrana*), 11.9-13.2 (female *phoenicotis*), 12-13.2 (female *sumatrana*), 11.5 (juvenile female *bantenensis*); **gape** 13.5-14.3 (male *assamensis*), 13.5-15.9 (3 male *borneana*, Brunei), 15 (male *pallida*), 12.8-13.5 (female *assamensis*), 13.5 (female *borneana*, Brunei); **tarsus** 15-17 (unsexed *assamensis*), 17 (male *pallida*); **mass** 8.2-9.1 (3 male *borneana*, Brunei), 8.6 (female *borneana*, Brunei).

REFERENCES Ali & Ripley (1974), Deignan (1955), Fleming *et al.* (1976), Hellebrekers & Hoogerwerf (1967), Hoogerwerf (1967), Inskipp & Inskipp (1985), MacKinnon & Phillipps (1993), Mann (1996), van Marle & Voous (1988), Medway & Wells (1976), Nash & Nash (1988), Oberholser (1912), Sheldon *et al.* (in press), Smythies (1960, 1981, 1986, 1999).

DELEORNIS

Deleornis Wolters 1977 *Bonn. Zool. Beitr.* 28 (1977) p. 82-101.

Two species formerly included within *Anthreptes*. Stout birds with outer tail feathers 4-7 mm shorter than rest, in nearly square tails. Bill short, nearly straight and stouter than in *Anthreptes*, from which further distinguished by completely straight, not slightly curved, lower mandible. Tongue tapers from base to tip, and is shallow dish-shape in cross-section for much of length, with edges curled inwards to form two incomplete tubes. Distal 25% cleft, with the curled edges forming two much fimbriated tubes (Figure 5h). No metallic plumage. Sexes similar apart from red-orange or orange-yellow pectoral tufts of males. Probably entirely insectivorous. Warbler-like behaviour.

48 SCARLET-TUFTED SUNBIRD
Deleornis fraseri **Plate 13**

Anthreptes fraseri Jardine and Selby, 1843, *Illustr. Orn.*, (new series) pl.52 and text, Fernando Po.

Alternative name: Fraser's Sunbird

The distinct Grey-headed Sunbird, often considered a race of *D. fraseri*, is here separated as *D. axillaris* (49). The two forms are largely allopatric and do not intergrade where they meet in the Democratic Republic of the Congo.

IDENTIFICATION A large dull green sunbird with a long straight bill, curved only at the tip. Females appear smaller. Males easily identified if red-orange pectoral tuft seen, which is often conspicuous.
Similar species The only lowland sunbird with orange pectoral tufts, distinguishing males from superficially similar Bates's Sunbird *Cinnyris batesi* (137) and Little Green Sunbird *Anthreptes seimundi* (60) and females of Green Sunbird *A. rectirostris* (61). Western Olive Sunbird *Cyanomitra obscura* (79) has curved bill. Separable from pale-legged and straight-billed Grey Longbill *Macrosphenus concolor* by bill characters (slightly curved dark upper mandible and pale horn lower mandible), pale eye-ring and dark legs.

VOICE Call Repeated squeaking calls including *psi*. **Song** Race *cameroonensis*: series of high-pitched *tsserr-tseep* notes, repeated at one-second intervals; sometimes only *tseep* notes uttered. Alternatively, *tsserr* immediately followed by 4-5 *tseep* notes, a pause of 4-6 seconds, followed by repetition of the sequence. The first *tsserr* is sometimes omitted, giving *tseep-tseep-tseep-tseep*. Race *idius*: similar to *cameroonensis*, but two or more *tsserr* may follow each other and these are commoner, with fewer *tseep* notes. Also a rapid *tzuc-zui-zui-zui-zui*.

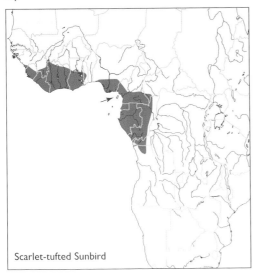
Scarlet-tufted Sunbird

DISTRIBUTION West and Central Africa. Forested habitats from Sierra Leone to Angola, including Bioko. Recorded Guinea, Sierra Leone, Liberia, Côte d'Ivoire, Ghana, Togo, Nigeria, Mali, Cameroon, Equatorial Guinea including Bioko, Gabon, Angola, Republic of the Congo and Democratic Republic of the Congo.

HABITAT Primary and secondary forests, gallery forest, regenerating forests and forest edges up to 1,550 m. Inhabits cocoa plantations in lowlands of Bioko.

STATUS Locally common. Common Liberia, reaching 1,100 m. Locally not uncommon resident in Ghana, where common in Bia National Park. Uncommon in Togo. Common resident in south-east Nigeria, less so in south-west. Widespread and common in Equatorial Guinea; 18-22 pairs per km² in Gabon. Uncommon resident in Angola.

MOVEMENTS Unrecorded, but probably sedentary, as a bird re-trapped in same territory three times over 10 years 11 months.

FOOD May be entirely insectivorous, feeding on small insects (beetles, grasshoppers, butterflies, moths, caterpillars, termites, winged ants) and spiders.
Known food-plants None.

HABITS Active. Feeds on insects, alone or in small groups, by foraging along branches at all levels but usually c.20 m high, in well-wooded and forest habitats, lower in plantations. Forages warbler-like amongst live and dead leaves and very occasionally in flowers. Seldom perches on branches >2.0 cm in diameter. Bioko subspecies does not associate with other sunbird species, but mainland races join bird parties involving other sunbirds, e.g. Collared Sunbird *Hedydipna collaris* (63), *Anthreptes seimundi*, *A. rectirostris*, Blue-throated Brown Sunbird *Cyanomitra cyanolaema* (75), Buff-throated Sunbird *Chalcomitra adelberti* (81) and Johanna's Sunbird *Cinnyris johannae* (129). Forages 3-50 m up, but usually in tops of forest trees, keeping in touch with noisy cries. Associates with Chestnut-capped Flycatcher *Erythrocercus mccalli* in forests of Gabon. Males are aggressive towards each other and defend territories. Aggressive displays by males accompanied by shrill cries and involve head and tail projected forwards, wings drooping, tail spread, bill wide open showing red-orange gape and pectoral tufts much in evidence. Longevity: at least 10 years 11 months. Another bird re-trapped after 8 years 5 months. Host to feather mites *Anisodiscus megadiscus*, *Favetta heteroclyta*, *Heteralges ostracopus*, *Monojoubertia grandiloba*, *Pterodectes mesocaulus*, *Pteronyssus garioui* and *Xolalges glossopus*.

BREEDING Young fed by both parents. **Nest** Unknown, but nest-building, Liberia, 9-15 m on outer twigs of understorey trees. **Eggs** Unknown. **Laying months** Angola: breeding condition February, August, September; Cameroon: juvenile March, breeding condition March, October; Democratic Republic of the Congo: July, October; Equatorial Guinea (Bioko): fledgling March; Gabon: breeding condition June, October, dependent young March, November; Ghana: October, breeding condition June; Liberia: dependent young November, January, nest-building September, November, December, enlarged gonads October, November, wing-moult October, January–April; Nigeria: breeding condition April, November; juveniles with unossified skulls January, April, June–August, October; Republic of the Congo: January, October, November.

DESCRIPTION *D. f. fraseri*
Adult male Crown to uppertail-coverts bright olive-green. Wings and tail brown with outerwebs edged yellow-olive. Axillaries pale yellow. Underwing-coverts grey-white. Underparts yellow-olive, contrasting with upperparts.

Pectoral tufts orange-red, yellow at base. Pale yellow or white eye-ring. Eye hazel. Bill dull brown, base of lower mandible olive-yellow. Legs and feet olive, claws yellow-horn.
Adult female Similar to male but lacks pectoral tufts and is smaller.
Juvenile Entirely pale olive above, duller than adult and paler below with yellow wash on belly. Bill darker than in adult.

GEOGRAPHICAL VARIATION
D. f. cameroonensis (Bannerman, 1921) (southern Nigeria and Cameroon to Republic of the Congo, western Democratic Republic of the Congo, Gabon to north-west Angola) Distinguished from *fraseri* by duller olive-green underparts with less yellow. Lighter below than *idius*.
D. f. fraseri (Jardine & Selby, 1843) (Bioko) Described above.
D. f. idius (Oberholser, 1899) (Sierra Leone east to Togo) Smaller and darker than the other two races. Tail darker brown, less green. Eye reddish-brown. Upper mandible horn, lower mandible yellowish-horn. Legs and feet greenish-slate, claws flesh-coloured.

MEASUREMENTS Wing 64-75 (mean 69.4, 20 male *cameroonensis*), 71-80 (mean 74.6, 5 male *fraseri*), 59-66 (mean 62.7, 9 male *idius*), 58-63 (mean 59.9, 20 female *cameroonensis*), 63-72 (mean 68.2, 5 female *fraseri*), 55-60 (mean 57.2, 11 female *idius*); **tail** 42-56 (mean 49.6, 20 male *cameroonensis*), 47-55 (male *fraseri*), 39-45 (mean 43.1, 9 male *idius*), 37-42 (mean 39.6, 20 female *cameroonensis*), 42-44 (female *fraseri*), 37-41 (mean 39, 11 female *idius*), 33-36 (unsexed *cameroonensis*); **bill** 19-21.5 (mean 19.8, 20 male *cameroonensis*), 17-18 (male *fraseri*), 15.5-18 (mean 16.8, 9 male *idius*), 16.5-18.5 (mean 17.5, 20 female *cameroonensis*), 16-17 (female *fraseri*), 15-17.5 (mean 16.3, 11 female *idius*); **tarsus** 15.5-17.4 (mean 16.2, 20 male *cameroonensis*), 15-16.5 (mean 15.9, 20 female *cameroonensis*), 15-17 (unsexed *fraseri*); **mass** 10-11.3 (mean 10.4, SD 1.02, 10 male *idius*), 9.0-12.3 (mean 9.8, SD 0.95, 15 female *idius*), 13 (male *cameroonensis*), 11.5-15.3 (mean 12.9, 3 unsexed *cameroonensis*).

REFERENCES Bannerman (1948), Brosset & Erard (1986), Christy & Clarke (1994), Fry *et al.* (2000), Gatter (1997), Pérez del Val (1996), C. Ryall (*in litt.*), Zumpt (1961).

49   GREY-HEADED SUNBIRD
Deleornis axillaris   **Plate 13**

Camaroptera axillaris Reichenow, 1893, *Orn. Monatsb.* 1, p.32, Uvamba, Semliki valley, Toro, western Uganda.

This species, often considered a race of *D. fraseri*, is here treated as distinct following Sclater (1930) and Mackworth-Praed and Grant (1973). The two forms are largely allopatric and do not intergrade where they meet in the Democratic Republic of the Congo.

IDENTIFICATION Mostly warbler-like green sunbird originally described as a *Camaroptera*, but adult with distinctive dark grey forehead, crown, nape, cheeks and ear-coverts, contrasting with paler grey chin and throat. Juvenile has green head.
Similar species Juveniles may be mistaken for white-eyes *Zosterops* spp.

VOICE Song A prolonged and undulating reel of rising and falling notes. Recalls song of Grey Longbill *Macrosphenus concolor* but consists of regular wave-like up-and-down sounds whereas *M. concolor* rolls its notes.

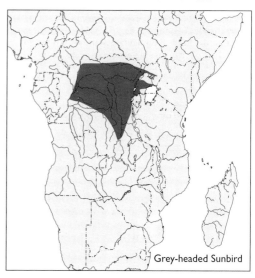
Grey-headed Sunbird

DISTRIBUTION Central Africa. Middle Congo and Ubangi rivers from about 16°E to Kasai, upper Congo, Manyema, north to Api. Democratic Republic of the Congo including Ituri forest and south and west Uganda, including Semliki valley, Ruwenzoris and Bwamba, Budongo, Kalinzu and Mabira forests. One record, Bukoba, north-west Tanzania.

HABITAT Dense undergrowth and middle strata of primary forests, often at tops of trees at forest edges, amongst creeper-covered trees, in secondary forest and clearings.

STATUS Common in Democratic Republic of the Congo in forests from Lukolela to the Ituri and Semliki valley. Common in Budongo forest, Kifu and Kasyoha-Kitomi forests, Uganda, 700-1,550 m.

MOVEMENTS Unrecorded; probably resident.

FOOD Insects, including Orthoptera, Coleoptera, lepidopteran larvae and ant pupae; spiders; small fruits.
Known food-plants None. Possibly does not visit flowers.

HABITS Actions recall white-eyes. Occurs in groups of 4-6 at mid-height of trees and joins bird flocks in canopy but also forages amongst vines and creepers around tree-trunks, often low.

BREEDING Nest Unknown. **Eggs** Unknown. **Laying months** Democratic Republic of the Congo: probably during rains, birds in breeding condition July, October; Uganda: April–August.

DESCRIPTION
Adult male Forehead, crown, cheeks and nape dark grey; chin and throat pale grey, contrasting with head; back and rump rich green. Flight feathers dark brown, edged bright yellowish-green, but edges of P1-2 very narrow and barely

discernible as yellowish-green. Rectrices yellowish-green above and below. Chest, centre of belly and undertail-coverts pale greenish-yellow. Flanks dark olive. Axillaries white or washed yellow especially at wing edge. Bright orange pectoral tufts, yellowish at base. Legs brown, greenish-grey or olive. Bill stout, upper mandible black, dark brown or greyish-horn, lower mandible pale brown, pale horn or pinkish-grey; finely serrated. Feet olive-brown, greenish or bluish-grey. Claws yellow. Iris brown, reddish-brown, dull red, orange, hazel or sepia.

Adult female As male, but no pectoral tufts. The implication that the head of the female is green (White 1963) is erroneous, but it is true of juvenile *D. axillaris* (see below); M. P. S. Irwin in Fry *et al.* (2000) followed White and wrote that female *D. axillaris* is green-headed, as in *D. f. cameroonensis*. Legs greenish-grey, feet similar or slate. Upper mandible black or brownish-horn, lower grey, sometimes tinged olive; tip, cutting edges and lower mandible sometimes pinky-yellowish. Legs dark grey. Feet grey,

tinged olive, claws and soles greyish. Iris hazel, light brown or pale sepia.

Juvenile Crown, neck, forehead and nape concolorous dark olive-green like back. Supercilium pale yellowish-green. Chin, throat and rest of underparts including belly concolorous pale olive-green. Iris light brown. Feet greenish-olive, claws yellow.

GEOGRAPHICAL VARIATION None.

MEASUREMENTS Wing 65-74 (mean 66.8, SD 2.4, 6 males), 57-66 (mean 60.1, SD 2.88, 5 females); **tail** 45-52 (mean 48.7, SD 2.66, 6 males), 41-43 (mean 42, SD 1, 5 females); **bill** 18-19.5 (mean 18.7, SD 0.61, 6 males), 16.5-19 (mean 17.1, SD 0.89, 5 females); **tarsus** 17-20.5 (mean 18.1, SD 1.43, 5 males), 17-19 (mean 17.4, SD 0.89, 5 females); **mass** 11-15 (mean 12.3, 32 males), 8.3-13 (mean 10.3, 18 females).

REFERENCES Bannerman (1948), Chapin (1954), B. Finch (pers. comm.), Fry *et al.* (2000).

ANTHREPTES

Anthreptes Swainson 1832 in Swainson and Richardson *Fauna Bor. Amer.*, 2 (1831) p.495. Type, by original designation and monotypy, *Cinnyris javanica* Swainson = *Certhia malacensis* Scopoli.

Small, short-billed sunbirds with warbler-like habits and, except those species with slight bill curvature, appearance. Tongue long and narrow, forming a tube for 80% of length; distal 20% bifid, becoming broader and forming two semitubes; tips on each side forming three points (Figure 5d). Sexes often similar, but some species with marked dichromatism. Plumage sometimes completely dull, sometimes with extensive iridescence. Basal third of bill always uncurved. Fine serrations on mandibles. Outer primary less than half the length of its neighbour. Tail feathers never elongated and tail square at end.

50 PLAIN-BACKED SUNBIRD
Anthreptes reichenowi   Plate 13

Anthreptes reichenowi Gunning, 1909, *Ann. Transvaal. Mus.*, 1, p.173. Mzimbiti, near Beira, Portuguese East Africa (Mozambique).

Alternative names: Blue-throated Sunbird, Blue-throated Little Sunbird, Plain-backed Little Sunbird, Gunning's Sunbird, Zambesi Blue-headed Sunbird

IDENTIFICATION Small dull sunbird, male with distinctive iridescent purplish-blue throat, appearing black in field, bordered with yellow, and short but slightly curved bill.

Similar species Male Amani Sunbird *Hedydipna pallidigaster* (66) has bluish-green head and back and white belly, female is also white below but grey above. Male Collared Sunbird *H. collaris* (63) distinguished by iridescent green, not blue, throat, which is uniform without yellow at sides. Male Variable Sunbird *Cinnyris venustus* (134) has longer, decurved bill, throat is darker blue and lacks yellow at sides. Female *A. reichenowi* is dull above without iridescent green, as on back of female Collared, and bill much shorter than in female Variable. Immature males of White-breasted Sunbird *Cinnyris talatala* (133) and *C. venustus* also have dark throats but differ by presence of small green shoulder-flashes and no blue on foreheads.

VOICE Call *Tik tik; zlui.* Alarm call: *wee-wee-wee* or *tew-tew-*

tew or *eea-eeea-eeea.* **Song** Race *reichenowi*: Simple. A pleasing warble of 4-5 seconds' duration consisting of 3-5 different notes each repeated 4-6 times in sequence, descending from start to finish: *tseep-tseep-tseep-tseep tswee-tswee-tswee-tswee cher-cher-cher-cher chooo-chooo-chooo-chooo zip-zip-zip-zip.* Different parts of the song, especially the final flourish, may be omitted. Recalls Willow Warbler *Phylloscopus trochilus.*

DISTRIBUTION Eastern and south-east Africa. Coastal forests of Kenya (Sokoke-Arabuko forest, Home, Diani and Jadini forests, lower Tana river, Mrima, Shimba Hills), Tanzania and Mozambique south to Praia da Zavora. Also recorded Nuanetsi and Hunyani rivers, Mutare, Gona-re-Zhou National Park, and Haroni-Rusitu in Zimbabwe. In South Africa there is a specimen from Letaba district, a sight record from Punda Maria and reports from Tzaneen and north-eastern KwaZulu-Natal.

HABITAT Lowland forest or thick bush, gallery forest, forest edges and gardens. Usually near coast but occasionally in inland riverine forest running through savanna.

STATUS Listed as near-threatened by Collar *et al.* (1994). Restricted to a few sites but not uncommon within them, but these are threatened by deforestation.

MOVEMENTS Unknown but seems to wander inland.

FOOD Mostly insectivorous, taking lepidopteran larvae, termites and many spiders. Possibly also feeds on nectar.
Known food-plants *Albizia* sp., *Diospyros* sp., *Kigelia* sp., unidentified mistletoes Loranthaceae, *Mimusops* sp.

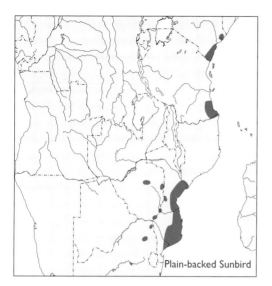

Plain-backed Sunbird

HABITS Unobtrusive birds which behave much like white-eyes *Zosterops* spp. or warblers, leaf-gleaning and searching for insects in flowers at all levels. Single or in pairs but join mixed-species flocks. Mobs African Barred Owlet *Glaucidium capense*.

BREEDING Territorial. Males sing from canopy. Courtship involves male chasing female until she settles; male then perches above female, flicks wings, displays pectoral tufts and sings; female quivers wings. **Nest** Pouch made of grass, twigs, bark, and leaves bound with cobwebs and sometimes with spider or insect cocoons as decoration or with black threads of fungal mycelia ?*Marismius* sp. Oval, entrance with hood of grass stems near top. No beard. Attached 5 m up by 5 cm wrap, rather than point or loop, along side-branch of liana across void in degraded forest. Height 115 mm, width 65 mm, diameter of entrance hole 35 mm. **Eggs** c/2-3. Race *reichenowi*: 15.1-15.5 (mean 15.3, n=5) x 10.4-11.1 (mean 10.9). White, spotted or flecked with dull reddish or brown, sometimes including mauve, with most near the blunt end. **Laying months** East Africa: March–May, July–November; Mozambique: June, October–November; Tanzania: November; Zimbabwe: September–November.

DESCRIPTION *A. r. reichenowi*
Adult male Crown, nape and ear-coverts dull greenish-yellow, feathers on crown edged deep blue. Neck, mantle, rump and uppertail-coverts bright olive-green. Tail light brownish-green, edged bright olive-yellow. Remiges and wing-coverts bright olive-yellow, edged brighter yellow, bend of wing yellow. Cheeks and sides of neck lime-green. Throat and upper breast deep purplish-blue with brighter iridescent reflections in good light, bordered with yellow on sides of throat. Lower breast, belly, flanks and undertail-coverts lemon-yellow with brighter yellow wash. Pectoral tufts lemon-yellow. Iris brown. Bill brown, bluish-grey at base. Legs and feet brown or bluish-grey.
Adult female As male but lacks blue on head, throat is dull green mottled grey, and paler yellow below.
Juvenile Immature male has throat-streak mottled with dark blue iridescent patches and pale yellow, rest of plumage as female, lacking iridescence on forehead, but more olive above. Older birds have metallic plumage on front of crown. Juvenile female similar to adult but more olive.

GEOGRAPHICAL VARIATION
A. r. reichenowi Gunning, 1909 (lowland forest from Beira, Mozambique, to Nuanetsi and Hunyani rivers in eastern Zimbabwe and north-east South Africa) Described above.
A. r. yokanae Hartert, 1921 (coastal forests from Sokoke in south-east Kenya to Amani in north-east Tanzania) Smaller (wing 51-56) than *reichenowi* (53-57); abdomen greener-yellow; pectoral tufts paler; throat of male blackish with bluish feather-edges, not purplish-blue. Iris of male dark red-brown, female's dark brown. Feet blue-grey. Bill of female dark slate.

MEASUREMENTS Wing 53-57 (mean 55.1, 27 male *reichenowi*), 49-54 (mean 51.3, 21 female *reichenowi*); **tail** 36-44.5 (mean 38.4, 26 male *reichenowi*), 31-38 (mean 35.0, 21 female *reichenowi*); **bill** 16-19 (mean 16.8, 27 male *reichenowi*), 14-18 (mean 16.0, 20 female *reichenowi*); **tarsus** 13.5-20 (mean 15.7, 27 male *reichenowi*), 14.5-19 (mean 16.6, 21 female *reichenowi*); **mass** 6.7-8.8 (mean 7.7, 14 male *reichenowi*), 5-10 (mean 7.2, 5 male *yokanae*), 6.5-7.8 (mean 7.06, 13 female *reichenowi*), 6-10 (mean 7.2, 8 female *yokanae*).

REFERENCES Allan & Tree (1997), Evans (1997), Hipkiss *et al.* (1994), Hustler (1985), Irwin (1995a,b), Skead (1967), Williams (1951c, 1953d).

51   ANCHIETA'S SUNBIRD
Anthreptes anchietae   Plate 13

Nectarinia anchietae Barbosa du Bocage, 1878, *J. sci. Math. Phys. Nat. Lisboa* 6, p.208, Caconda, "in the interior of Benguella" [=Huíla], Angola.

Alternative name: Red-and-blue Sunbird

IDENTIFICATION Both sexes unmistakable. Brown upperparts, iridescent dark blue on head with contrasting bright orangey-red in middle of underparts and yellow sides of breast. Appear plump when perched; yellow conspicuous in flight.
Similar species None.

VOICE Call A loud and distinctive monosyllabic *cheou* by male and *choo-wee* by female, followed by bill-wiping. **Song** Subsong of male *twi-tsui-tsi-twi* from perch at top of tree (e.g. *Terminalia sericea*) or a similar simple sequence of ascending *tzer-chip-chip-chip*, lasting a second but repeated up to 20 times. Full song a more complex sequence involving variations on *tseu-werr, tsoo-wit, tser-wit-tsui-tsi, chip-choo-chip, witchoo-witchoo, chip-chip, chip-up-chip-up, chipyoo-chipyoo* repeated up to 40 times, with some scolding bursts recalling parts of songs of *Acrocephalus* spp.

DISTRIBUTION South-central Africa. Angola from north-western Huíla and Huambo to northern Bié, and north to Lunda Sul and Lunda Norte to Katanga, Democratic Republic of the Congo; Zambia in Eastern Province plateau south to Chipata and Chadiza and west of the Luangwa valley; also in Northern Province where widespread, and a scattering of other sites. Malawi west of the Rift Valley. Also recorded from south-west Tanzania and Mozambique.

HABITAT *Brachystegia* woodland, to which the species is endemic. Strays into degraded woodland, especially in rocky areas.

Anchieta's Sunbird

STATUS Uncommon resident in miombo woodland in Angola. Locally common in Zambia. Uncommon in Malawi. Locally not uncommon in south-west Tanzania.

MOVEMENTS May wander, as present at some sites in Zambia during rains, but absent in dry season.

FOOD Insects, nectar.
Known food-plants *Faurea saligna*, *Protea* sp., *Tecoma* sp. Fruits of *Macaranga asas* and *Ochthocosmus africanus*.

HABITS Active, usually singly or in pairs; joins mixed-species parties. Sits on branches looking from left to right agitatedly. Tends to feed in the canopy. Behaves more like *Cinnyris* sunbird than warbler fashion of other *Anthreptes*.

BREEDING Territorial. **Nest** Domed with side entrance; made of seeds, twigs and flower parts of *Protea* sp., held together with leaves of *Indigofera* sp. and awns and glumes of *Loudetia superba*, decorated with *Protea* seeds. Positioned 1-6.5 m above ground, in *Protea* bush, *Monotes* or suspended from outer branch of *Pterocarpus angolensis*. Females carry fluff for nest building. Lined with pappus from *Faurea saligna*. **Eggs** c/1-2. 17.5-18.0 (mean 17.8, n=2) x 11.5 (mean 11.5). Smooth but not glossy. Bluish-white or grey with black spots and sepia and grey scrawls, mostly at larger pole. **Laying months** Malawi: September–December, nest-building end August; Zambia: April–May.

DESCRIPTION
Adult male Forehead and crown dark iridescent blue, rest of upperparts including tail, which is slightly glossy above, brown. Face brown. Lores metallic blue. Chin to upper breast iridescent blue, sides of breast bright yellow, middle of breast to upper belly very bright orangey-red, rest of underparts greyish-brown except undertail-coverts bright orange-red and pectoral tufts yellow. Remiges, scapulars, shoulder and wing-coverts brown. Outer edges of primaries buff. Yellow patch on bend of wing. Axillaries and underwing-coverts buffish-brown. Iris dark brown. Bill, legs and feet black.
Adult female Resembles male but blue only on forehead, and lores brown. Chin and throat also brown with dark iridescent blue tips. Sides of breast duller yellow, washed olive. Less extensive area of orangey-red in middle of belly.
Juvenile Immature resembles adult female but paler above with short buffy-white supercilium to just behind eye and

whitish feathers below eye; chin to upper breast brownish-olive and lower breast and middle of belly and rest of underparts pale olive-yellow.

GEOGRAPHICAL VARIATION None described.

MEASUREMENTS Wing 61-67 (mean 64.3, 69 males), 59-64 (mean 61.3, 17 females); **tail** 35-46 (mean 42.4, 48 males), 35-43 (mean 39.2, 21 females); **bill** 15.5-18 (mean 16.5, 48 males), 15-17 (mean 15.9, 21 females); **tarsus** 15.5-19 (mean 16.6, 43 males), 15.5-16 (mean 15.8, 16 females); **mass** 8 (1 male).

REFERENCE Benson *et al.* (1971), Chapin (1954), Fry *et al.* (2000).

---

52   PLAIN SUNBIRD
Anthreptes simplex   Plate 14

Nectarinia simplex Müller, 1843, *Land. Volk.*, in Temminck, *Verh. Nat. Gesch. Nederland. Overz. Bezit.*, 1 (1839-1844), p.173, Sumatra and Borneo.

IDENTIFICATION Adult male dull olive-green above with metallic blue or green forehead; sides of head and throat grey; otherwise greyish-olive below, yellowish-green on centre of belly and undertail-coverts. Adult female lacks metallic coloration. Juvenile is browner above and generally paler than female, and has a paler bill.
Similar species Female from female Plain-throated Sunbird *A. malacensis* (53), Red-throated Sunbird *A. rhodolaema* (54) and Olive-backed Sunbird *Cinnyris jugularis* (140) by lack of bright yellow in plumage; female from female Purple-throated Sunbird *Leptocoma sperata* (90) by lack of pale markings on face; female from female Copper-throated Sunbird *L. calcostetha* (92) by olive-green, not grey-brown, crown; female from female Black-throated Sunbird *Aethopyga saturata* (161) by lack of yellow rump; female from female Crimson Sunbird *A. siparaja* (163) by lack of olive-yellowish on rump; female Temminck's Sunbird *A. temmincki* (165) is olive-brown above and has red tinge to wings and tail.

Plain Sunbird

183

VOICE Metallic chirps, trills and high-pitched *seep*.

DISTRIBUTION Burma (southern Tenasserim), south-west and peninsular Thailand and Malaysia, Sumatra (including Nias, but not Riau or Jambi), North Natunas and Borneo.

HABITAT A variety of forest types, including lowland dipterocarp forest, coastal scrub forest including mangroves and betel palms, and secondary forest, scrub, *Albizia*, old rubber plantations, *Trema orientalis*, cocoa, cultivation and gardens up to 1,220 m.

STATUS Locally common on Borneo and Sumatra; uncommon in Thailand; very rare in Burma.

MOVEMENTS No records.

FOOD Caterpillars and other insects, nectar, fruits and seeds.
Known food-plants Seeds of *Acacia mangium*; *Bauhinia* sp., *Ficus* sp., *Manihot esculenta*; fruits of *Poikilospermum suaveolans*.

HABITS An active bird, frequenting exposed as well as concealed branches when feeding. Leaf-gleans like a warbler. Host to *Haemoproteus sequeirae* and microfilariae.

BREEDING Nest Untidy, made of grass and fibres with ends sticking out in all directions, lined with thickly felted down, and without porch. Eggs c/2; 18.6-20.1 (mean 19.3, n=2) x 12.9-13.0 (mean 12.9); white, suffused with mauve-grey over most of egg; dark purple-grey blotches, spots and streaks sparsely distributed over whole egg. Laying months Borneo: Sabah, fledged young early April, enlarged gonads February–June, August; peninsular Malaysia: April and earlier, fledgling May and juvenile May; Burma: March; Sumatra: May–June (Krui), pair with juvenile May, Nias.

DESCRIPTION
Adult male Dark metallic blue or green forehead; dull olive-green above, with greyish sides of head; throat grey, rest of underparts greyish-olive with centre of belly and undertail-coverts yellowish-green. Iris reddish-brown, bill black, feet brown or greenish.
Adult female As male, but forehead olive-green as rest of upperparts.
Juvenile As female, but bill pale yellowish-brown or orange-yellow and feet orange-yellow; browner above, paler below.

GEOGRAPHICAL VARIATION Forehead of male metallic green in Malay Peninsula and Sumatra, metallic purple on Borneo, but no subspecies recognised; the Bornean birds should perhaps be separated subspecifically.

MEASUREMENTS Wing 61-68 (mean 63.7, 12 males, Brunei), 56-62 (mean 59.7, 7 males, Sabah), 63 (male, peninsular Malaysia), 56-63 (mean 58.2, 10 females, Brunei), 52-57 (mean 55.4, 8 females, Sabah); gape 16.6-18.9 (mean 17.7, 12 males, Brunei), 15-18.5 (mean 16.7, 7 males, Sabah), 11.2-16.9 (mean 15.2, 7 females, Brunei), 16-16.5 (mean 16.1, 7 females, Sabah); mass 8.3-10.7 (mean 9.4, 12 males, Brunei), 9.2 (male, peninsular Malaysia), 7.1-11.8 (mean 8.5, 11 females, Brunei).

REFERENCES Dymond (1994), Ford (1995), Holmes (1996), Lambert (1991), MacKinnon & Phillipps (1991), Mann (1996), van Marle & Voous (1988), Medway & Wells (1976), Müller (1843), Sheldon *et al.* (in press), Smythies (1986), Thompson (1966).

53   PLAIN-THROATED SUNBIRD
Anthreptes malacensis   Plate 14

Certhia malacensis Scopoli, 1786, *Del. Flor. Fauna. Insubr.*, fasc. 2, p.91, Malacca (ex Sonnerat 1782 *Voy. Indes Orient. Chine* 2, p.209).

Alternative names: Brown-throated Sunbird, Grey-throated Sunbird

FIELD IDENTIFICATION Large; heavy, thick bill. Adult male has dark glossed upperparts, with some chestnut; brownish or grey throat; reddish collar on lower neck, rest of underparts yellowish. Adult female mostly greyish olive-green above, and greenish-yellow below, with a yellow eye-ring. Juvenile differs from female in having a paler bill.
Similar species Female from female Plain Sunbird *Anthreptes simplex* (52) by bright yellow on underparts; male from male Red-throated Sunbird *A. rhodolaema* (54) by more brownish, less pinkish-red on throat and sides of head, and female has a more obvious yellow eye-ring and brighter yellow underparts; both sexes of Ruby-cheeked Sunbird *Chalcoparia singalensis* (47) have rufous throat and breast; female Purple-throated Sunbird *Leptocoma sperata* (90) lacks eye-ring, and has yellow below confined to vent; the smaller female *L. sperata* has much less obvious eye-ring, and brown edges to flight feathers; female Purple Sunbird *Cinnyris asiaticus* (139) lacks yellow eye-ring and is brighter; female Copper-throated Sunbird *L. calcostetha* (92) has greyish-white throat; female Olive-backed Sunbird *C. jugularis* (140) is bright yellow below, and has yellow supercilium, not eye-ring; Flame-breasted Sunbird *Cinnyris solaris* (142) has blackish tail with white tips; all female *Aethopyga* lack yellow eye-ring; Temminck's Sunbird *A. temmincki* (165) and Javan Sunbird *A. mystacalis* (164) have a red wash on tail and wings; Fire-tailed Sunbird *A. ignicauda* (166) is olive below; Gould's Sunbird *A. gouldiae* (157) is yellowish on rump; Green-tailed Sunbird *A. nipalensis* (158) is olive-green below with white tips to outer tail feathers; White-flanked Sunbird *A. eximia* (159) is dark olive-green below and has white flanks; Crimson Sunbird *A. siparaja* (163) is grey and olive below.

VOICE Call High-pitched chirps *kelichap*, *tweet-tweet-tweet*, or simple melodious *wee-chuuw*, *wee-chuuw*. On Lombok a hard *swit*; drawn-out, thin, high-pitched *siiewei*, rapid nasal chatter *tititi* at medium pitch. *A. m. extremus* has a short two-note, slightly piercing call, first note rising, second falling, repeated rapidly 7-10 times over 5-6 seconds. *A. m. rubrigena* has a loud incessant *chip* or *cheep*. Song From prominent perch gives a *swit-swit-sweet* or *sweet-sweet*. *A. m. rubrigena* song is a *wee-chew-chew-wee*.

DISTRIBUTION Western Burma, Tenasserim, south-east, central and peninsular Thailand, Indochina, peninsular Malaysia, Borneo, Greater and Lesser Sundas, North Natunas, Philippines and Sulawesi.

HABITAT Peatswamp forest, heath forest, *Melaleuca* forest, riverine forest, selectively logged forest, degraded forest, at forest edge, in woodland, mangroves, coastal scrub, bamboos, open swamp, *Casuarina*, *Albizia* plantations, coconut groves and other cultivation, gardens and secondary growth, from sea-level up to 1,200 m. In Sabah, less common in plantations than *A. rhodolaema*.

STATUS Common in scrubland, Sulawesi, Greater Sundas and Thailand.

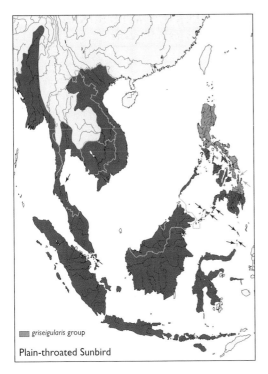

griseigularis group

Plain-throated Sunbird

MOVEMENTS Unrecorded.

FOOD Insects, spiders, fruits, especially if over-ripe, and nectar. More insects (caterpillars, small black beetles, butterflies) taken than nectar, but known pollinator of the ornamental *Nicolaia elatior*, buds of which are used as spices; nectar thief of mistletoes.
Known food-plants *Allamanda* sp., *Canna* sp., *Citrus* sp., *Cocos nucifera*, *Erythrina* sp., *Eugenia grandis*, *Hibiscus* spp. including *rosa-sinensis*, unidentified mistletoes Loranthaceae, *Morinda citrifolia*, *Nicolaia* (= *Etlingera*) *elatior*, *Spathodea* sp.

HABITS Occurs singly, in pairs and occasionally in larger groups. Frequently found low in vegetation, but feeds at all heights, and sings from prominent perch. Leaf-gleans. Joins mixed-species parties, e.g. with Black Sunbird *Leptocoma sericea* (91), Yellow-sided Flowerpecker *Dicaeum aureolimbatum* (16) and Pale-bellied White-eye *Zosterops consobrinorum* on Sulawesi. Pugnacious, often chasing other small birds away from flowers. 10% of 190 ringed at Rantan Panjang, peninsular Malaysia, were still alive after 6 years, and 2 individuals after 12 years. During breeding season chase individuals of same sex. Host to *Haemoproteus sequeirae*, *Akiba* sp., *Leucocytozoon nectariniae*, *Plasmodium polare* and microfilariae.

BREEDING Fledging period 15 days. **Nest** 1-13 m above ground, suspended from near ends of leafy twigs; pear-shaped, made of grass, plant fibres or casuarina twigs, with cobwebs and slivers of bark on outside; short tail, and entrance one-third from top with eave; lined with tree-cotton, *Imperata* pappus or moss. **Eggs** c/2. Race *malacensis*: 16.2-19.5 (mean 17.6, n=90) x 11.8-14 (mean 12.7); usually oval, slightly pointed at one end, but considerably elongated or slightly pyriform varieties occur. Ground colour white or creamy-stone, often considerably clouded with

grey, pale purplish-brown or purplish-black. Speckled and blotched dark purplish-brown with much black scribbling, most prominent at large end where a well-defined zone may be formed. Usually dull without gloss, occasionally faintly glossed. Others dull pink with thick grey scribblings, spotted black and russet. Race *celebensis*: 17.0 x 12.5 (n=2).
Laying months Borneo: may breed all year; southern Borneo, May, July, juveniles July–August; Sabah: nests January–March, May, July, family parties April–July, November, active gonads January–March, June–August; Indonesia: Java, February–August, Sumatra, June; peninsular Malaysia: December–August, may be at least double-brooded; Philippines: recently fledged young, Talicod, July; Sangihe: males in moult late August–early September; Sulawesi: Peleng Island, Banggai group, nest November, Butung, March–November; Thailand: February–July, September.

DESCRIPTION *A. m. malacensis*
Adult male Metallic green upperparts, with metallic purple back, rump, uppertail-coverts and shoulder; tail blackish-brown edged glossy blue-green; remiges brown edged greeny-yellow, some rufescent-olive or chestnut on wing-coverts and some chestnut on scapulars; sides of head olive-green, or greeny-brown; chin and throat pale pinky-brown, with metallic purple lateral borders; collar on lower neck pale pinky-red and rest of underparts greenish-yellow, brighter on breast and upper belly; bright yellow pectoral tufts. Iris red, bill black, feet grey or olive-brown.
Adult female Greyish olive-green above; wings and tail brown with yellowish edging, yellowish eye-ring and bright greenish-yellow underparts.
Juvenile As female, but bill paler.

GEOGRAPHICAL VARIATION This highly polytypic species is best divided into at least two groups.

Malacensis group
　A. m. anambae Oberholser, 1917 (Anambas) Male has paler throat, and is richer yellow below than nominate. Poorly marked.
　A. m. borneensis Riley, 1920 (Sabah and islands, Brunei, Borneo) Male similar to *mjobergi*, but smaller, and female duller below. Not well differentiated.
　A. m. cagayanensis Mearns, 1905 (Philippines – Cagayan Sulu) Male is much brighter below than *wiglesworthi* and has olive rather than red edges to remiges.
　A. m. celebensis Shelley, 1877 (Sulawesi, Manterawu, Manadotua, Bangka, Talisei, Togian, Labuan Blanda, Butung, Muna and Kabaena) (includes *citrinus* [Stresemann 1932] and *nesophilus* [Eck 1976]) Male is like *rubrigena* but duller and greener below, with pinkish-brown or dull chestnut on wing-coverts. Female is pale greyish-yellow below.
　A. m. chlorigaster Sharpe, 1877 (Philippines – Cebu [where now extinct], Lubang, Masbate, Negros, Panay, Sibuyan, Tablas and Marinduque; ?Romblon, ?Ticao) Male differs from *paraguae* in having chin and throat more reddish-brown, breast and belly more yellowish, and red of wing-edgings very dark.
　A. m. convergens Rensch, 1929 (Sumbawa, Komodo, Padar, Flores, Adonara, Satonda, Lomblen, Pantar and Alor; ?Lombok) Male differs from *malacensis* in being more greenish-yellow below, and flight feather margins have greenish-brown rather than olive-green margins.
　A. m. extremus Mees, 1966 (Banggai Islands and Sula) Male is larger, greener and less yellow below, with a

185

more greyish gular patch, and generally duller than *celebensis* and *citrinus* with a larger, broader and stronger bill. It is smaller than *heliocalus*, and greener below than that and *convergens*.

A. m. heliocalus Oberholser, 1923 (includes *sanghirara* [Hachisuka 1926]) (Sangihe and Siau) Male is brighter and yellower below than *celebensis*, with a longer wing.

A. m. heliolusius Oberholser, 1923 (Philippines – Basilan, west and central Mindanao, and Talicod) Male differs from *chlorigaster* in olive-brown, not reddish, cheeks, paler red wing-coverts and edgings, and generally brighter.

A. m. iris Parkes, 1971 (Philippines, Sibutu; ?Sitanki; intergrades with *wiglesworthi* on Bongao) Male differs from *wiglesworthi* in having steel-blue crown and back, brighter yellow underparts, and greyer flanks and undertail-coverts, and female lacks the reddish wash on wing-coverts and edgings.

A. m. malacensis (Scopoli 1786) (southern Burma, Indochina, Thailand, Malay Peninsula, Sumatra including islands; Anamba Islands and Karimata Island; Kalimantan; Java; Bali and possibly Lombok; those in Sarawak are either this or intergrades with *borneensis*) Described above.

A. m. mjobergi Bangs & Peters, 1927 (Maratuas) Male has cheeks concolorous with throat, and not olive-green as in nominate. Not well marked.

A. m. paraguae Riley, 1920 (Philippines – Balabac, Culion, Palawan and Calauit) Male differs from *malacensis* in having purple-green on head and back, edges of wings greenish or faintly orange, lores and patch behind eye greenish-brown, sometimes with an orange tint, chin and throat dull reddish, and belly duller yellow.

A. m. rubrigena Rensch, 1931 (Sumba) Male differs from *convergens* in lacking chestnut on scapulars and greater wing-coverts, with only edges of wing-coverts vivid matt red-brown. It differs similarly from *celebensis* and *chlorigaster*, and to a lesser extent from nominate. It is less olive below than former, and less pure yellow than nominate. Female is greyer on head and nape than female *convergens*, *celebensis*, *chlorigaster* and nominate.

A. m. wiglesworthi Hartert, 1902 (Philippines – Bongao, Tawitawi and probably Pangamian, all in Sulu Archipelago) Male differs from *heliolusius* by even brighter yellow underparts, with redder cheeks, and paler and brighter edging of remiges.

Griseigularis group

A. m. birgitae Salomonsen, 1953 (Philippines – Luzon; ?Mindoro) Male is similar to *griseigularis* but has a much longer bill (19 mm), and the underparts are duller and darker.

A. m. griseigularis Tweeddale, 1878 (Philippines – north-east Mindanao, Samar, Sakuyok, Leyte, Bucas Grande, Dinagat, Siargao and Camiguin Sur) Male differs from *paraguae* in having top of head and upper back metallic green, sides of face redder, chin and throat grey, rest of underparts dull olive-green. Female from nominate female in having greyish-white nares, eye-ring and moustachial stripe, and grey from chin to upper breast.

MEASUREMENTS Wing 66-69 (mean 67.3, 12 male *borneensis*, Brunei), 64-70 (mean 66.6, 10 male *borneensis*, Sabah, mainland), 67-72 (mean 69.1, 8 male *borneensis*,

Sabah, islands), 67-70 (mean 68.3, 7 male *celebensis*), 64-69 (male *citrinus*), 65-69 (male *convergens*), 67-71 (13 male *extremus*), 73-77 (male *heliocalus*), 65 (male *paraguae*), 64-69 (mean 67, male *rubrigena*), 59-65 (mean 62.1, 8 female *borneensis*, Brunei), 61-65.5 (mean 62.8, 12 female *borneensis*, Sabah, mainland), 62-66 (mean 64.2, 5 female *borneensis*, Sabah, islands), 64 (female *celebensis*), 60.5-64.5 (female *citrinus*), 64-66.5 (7 female *extremus*), 61-63 mm (mean 63, female *rubrigena*); **tail** 40-46 (mean 45.0, 7 male *celebensis*), 35-39.5 (male *citrinus*), 46 (male *convergens*), 37-42 (13 male *extremus*), 49 (male *paraguae*), 41-45 (mean 43.5, male *rubrigena*), 32.5 (female *celebensis*), 33-36 (female *citrinus*), 36-37 (7 female *extremus*), 37.5-40 (mean 39, female *rubrigena*); **bill** 16.5 male (*borneensis*, Brunei), 18.5-21.5 (mean 20.3, 7 male *celebensis*), 18-20 (male *citrinus*), 20-21.8 (13 male *extremus*), 15-18 (male *malacensis*, Indonesia), 15.2 (female *borneensis*, Brunei), 18.3 (female *celebensis*), 17-19.5 (female *citrinus*), 19.5-20.5 (7 female *extremus*), 13.5-16.9 (female *malacensis*, Indonesia), 19 (unsexed *griseigularis*); **culmen** 18.5-19 (mean 18.5, male *rubrigena*), 17-18.5 (mean 18.0, female *rubrigena*); **gape** 18.2-20.9 (mean 19.5, 12 male *borneensis*, Brunei), 18-20 (mean 19.8, 11 male *borneensis*, Sabah, mainland), 20.5-22 (mean 21.1, 8 male *borneensis*, Sabah, islands), 17.1-19.5 (male *celebensis*), 17.1-19.5 (male *malacensis*, Tenasserim), 18 (male *paraguae*), 16.0-20.1 (mean 18.6, 8 female *borneensis*, Brunei), 17-21 (mean 18.9, 12 female *borneensis*, Sabah, mainland), 19-20 (mean 19.6, 5 female *borneensis*, Sabah, islands), 17.4-19.6 (female *celebensis*), 17.2-19.0 (female *malacensis*, Tenasserim); **tarsus** 14.7-16.2 (mean 15.7, 7 male *celebensis*), 16 (male *paraguae*); **mass** 11.1-13.5 (mean 12.0, 12 male *borneensis*, Brunei), 7.4-13.1 (mean 10.7, 8 female *borneensis*, Brunei).

REFERENCES Bishop (1992), Brooks *et al.* (1995), Bruce (1987), M. Catterall (pers. comm.), Classen (1987), Coates & Bishop (1997), Dickinson *et al.* (1991), Dutson *et al.* (1996), Hellebrekers & Hoogerwerf (1967), Holmes & Wood (1979), Hoogerwerf (1966), Jones *et al.* (1994), MacKinnon & Phillipps (1993), Mann (1996), Medway & Wells (1976), Nash & Nash (1988), Riley (1997), Sheldon *et al.* (in prep.), Smythies (1986), Watling (1983), White & Bruce (1986), Zimmer (1918).

54   RED-THROATED SUNBIRD
Anthreptes rhodolaema   Plate 14

Anthreptes rhodolaema Shelley, 1878, *Monog. Nectariniidae*, p.313, pl. 101, Malacca and Sumatra; restricted to Malacca by Riley, 1934, *Proc. Biol. Soc. Washington*, 47, p.116.

Alternative name: Rufous-throated Sunbird

IDENTIFICATION Adult male dark above, with metallic green crown and mantle, and violet back and rump; below yellowish-olive. Adult female dull olive above, olive-yellow below, and has a narrow yellowish eye-ring.
Similar species Female from female Plain Sunbird *Anthreptes simplex* (52) by brighter yellow underparts; female from female Plain-throated Sunbird *A. malacensis* (53) by much less obvious eye-ring, and less yellow below, and male from male of this species by pinker, less brownish throat and sides of head; both sexes of Ruby-cheeked Sunbird *Chalcoparia singalensis* (47) have rufous of throat extending

to breast; female Purple-throated Sunbird *Leptocoma sperata* (90) has brownish edges to wing feathers; female Copper-throated Sunbird *L. calcostetha* (92) has white undertail-coverts; female Olive-backed Sunbird *Cinnyris jugularis* (140) has black tail with white tips; female Crimson Sunbird *Aethopyga siparaja* (163) has yellow below confined to undertail-coverts, and the tail is black; female Temminck's Sunbird *A. temmincki* (165) is olive-brown above with reddish tinge to wings and tail.

VOICE Call Typical chirps and metallic trill; high-pitched trills. **Song** High *sit sit sit see* and slurred *sit sit sit swèèr*.

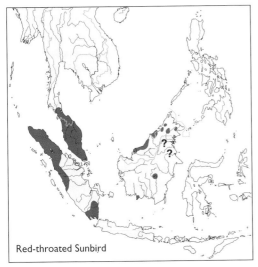

Red-throated Sunbird

DISTRIBUTION Burma (South Tenasserim), south peninsular Thailand, peninsular Malaysia, Sumatra (Aceh, Barat, Utara, Lampung, Riau, Jambi) and Borneo; possibly Palawan.

HABITAT Various forest types, including lowland and hill dipterocarp forests, heath forest, peatswamp forest and secondary forest, *Albizia* plantations, cocoa, tall tree plantations, clearings and coastal vegetation. Generally lowland, but up to 800 m.

STATUS Uncommon in southern Thailand. Scarce in southern Tenasserim. Very uncommon, Borneo, but in Sabah commoner in plantations than *A. malacensis*. Rare on Sumatra.

MOVEMENTS No records.

FOOD Insects (caterpillars, Orthoptera), spiders, pollen, nectar and small fruits.
Known food-plants *Casuarina* sp., *Manihot esculenta*, Orchidaceae, Zingiberaceae.

HABITS In courtship male points head up, tail down, lowers wings and utters high-pitched trills.

BREEDING Nest built only by female. **Nest** Matted plant fibres on suspensor cord, with pad at base, lined with dead leaves, and decorated with lichen-covered bark forming a tail; entrance hole in upper half, with eave, which may cover most of front of nest; total length of nest 310 mm; in trees at edge of clearings 9-20 m above ground. **Eggs** c/ 1; 14.6-14.7 (mean 14.7, n=2) x 10.6-10.9 (mean 10.8). Pale lavender-purple, spotted, blotched and lined with

dark brown. **Laying months** Southern Borneo: nest-building June; Sabah: active gonads June–September.

DESCRIPTION
Adult male Dark metallic green crown and mantle; sides of face dull maroon, ear-coverts brown; violet-glossed stripe from bill along side of neck; violet-glossed shoulder; band across upper back maroon; rest of back, rump and uppertail-coverts violet; wings brown, greater coverts edged rufous, remiges edged bright olive; tail blackish-brown with bluish-green gloss. Throat pale pink with dull red sides and narrow band bordering upper breast; rest of underparts yellowish-olive. Iris red, bill black, feet olive.
Adult female Dull olive upperparts, olive-yellow underparts, brighter on lower breast and belly; narrow eye-ring.
Juvenile As female, but greyer below, yellow confined to centre of throat to belly.

GEOGRAPHICAL VARIATION None.

MEASUREMENTS Wing 68 (male, Brunei), 66-71 (mean 68.7, 7 males, Sabah), 62 (female, Brunei), 63-66 (female, Sabah); **gape** 19.9 (male, Brunei), 18-20 (mean 19.4, 7 males, Sabah), 17-19 (female, Sabah); **mass** 11.2 (male, Brunei), 11.6 (female, Brunei).

REFERENCES Dickinson *et al.* (1991), duPont (1971b), Holmes (1996), MacKinnon & Phillipps (1993), Mann (in prep. b), Medway & Wells (1974), Nash & Nash (1988), Sheldon *et al.* (in prep.), Shelley (1878), Smythies (1986).

55   MOUSE-BROWN SUNBIRD
Anthreptes gabonicus Plate 15

Nectarinia gabonica Hartlaub, 1861, *J. Orn.* 9, p.13 (descr.), p.109 (type locality), Gabon.

Alternative names: Brown Sunbird, Mouse-coloured Sunbird

IDENTIFICATION Appears neat and compact, recalling warbler. Mouse-brown above, greyish-white below with no metallic feathers. White stripes almost encircling the eye are conspicuous and characteristic. White tips to all but central tail feathers visible in flight or from underneath. Black bill, only slightly decurved, appears large.
Similar species Female Blue-throated Brown Sunbird *Cyanomitra cyanolaema* (75) also has white around eye but has longer, decurved bill. Immature Collared Sunbird *Hedydipna collaris* (63) has yellowish not white around eye and is yellowish below. Greyish underparts distinguish *A. gabonicus* from female Western Violet-backed Sunbird *A. longuemarei* (56), which is mostly white below with yellow vent, violet tail and uppertail-coverts and lacks white below eye.

VOICE Call A soft *tsurp-tseep-tseep* sometimes uttered in flight, a single plaintive *tseep* or *sqee* or a harsh *tserr* repeated every 1-2 seconds. *Sip-sip-sip-sip* in flight. **Song** A typical sunbird twittering chatter, *tser-tser-tsew-tsi-tsi-tsi-tsi-tsi-tseuuur*, delivered from top of tall tree. Occasionally only the first *tser-tser-tsew* part is uttered or call is elaborated to *wit-wit-sqee-witter-witter*.

DISTRIBUTION West Africa. Gambia to Angola (Cabinda only). Known from Senegal, Gambia, Guinea, Sierra

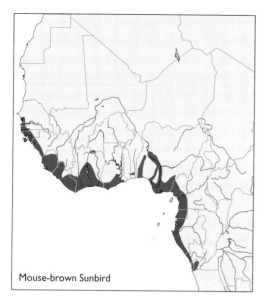

Mouse-brown Sunbird

Made of dry grass and dead leaves and decorated with cobwebs. Side entrance with short porch. No beard. Lined with pappus, grass and feathers. **Eggs** c/1-2. 16.8-18.0 (mean 17.3, n=3) x 12.2-12.7 (mean 12.4). Ovate, smooth, unglossed. Ashy-grey, with slight violet wash and irregular dark lines and spots or greenish-grey with dense cloudy marks and grey and brown streaks. **Laying months** Cameroon: January–April; Democratic Republic of the Congo: September; Gabon: April, June; Gambia: December, February, March, nest-building August; Liberia: October–March; Nigeria: January; Sierra Leone: February–March, July–September.

DESCRIPTION

Adult male Band on forehead, lores, patch below eye and stripe from before, behind and below eye white. Rest of upperparts and wings mouse-brown with slight olive-green tinge to outerwebs of remiges and terminal half of uppertail-coverts. Distinct white border to wing below carpal joint, about 8 mm long. Tail dark brown, all except central pair of rectrices with broad white tips and olive-green fringe to outerwebs. Distal edge of tips of outer tail feathers white on both surfaces. Axillaries and underwing-coverts white. Iris red or brown. Bill black, broad at base, almost straight. Legs and feet black, latter sometimes paler, more greyish.

Adult female Olive-green tinge to outerwebs of flight and tail feathers less noticeable than in males. Iris hazel.

Juvenile Similar to adult but more olivaceous above and on wings; lemon-yellow wash on underparts, especially belly and vent. Nestling black and naked.

GEOGRAPHICAL VARIATION None described.

MEASUREMENTS Wing 56-60 (mean 57.4, SD 1.01, 9 males), 53-59 (mean 55.2, SD 2.13, 6 females); **tail** 35-50 (mean 39.2, SD 4.38, 9 males), 33-47 (mean 36.2, SD 3.27, 5 females); **bill** 12-17 (mean 15.9, SD 0.60, 9 males), 14.5-16.5 (mean 15.5, SD 0.77, 6 females); **tarsus** 15-18.5 (mean 16.4, SD 1.01, 9 males), 13.5-17 (mean 16.2, SD 0.75, 6 females); **mass** no data.

REFERENCES Bannerman (1948), Cheke (1999), Christy & Clarke (1994), Gatter (1997), Serle (1949), Walsh (1967).

Leone, Liberia, Côte d'Ivoire, Ghana, Benin, Nigeria, Burkina Faso, Cameroon, mainland Equatorial Guinea, Gabon, Republic of the Congo, Democratic Republic of the Congo and Cabinda (Angola).

HABITAT Coastal swamps, especially mangroves (*Avicennia* sp. and *Rhizophora* sp.) and coconut groves along coast. Also occurs inland in gallery forest beside the larger perennial rivers in Sierra Leone and Liberia (e.g. 86 birds along 100 km of rivers Cestos, Dube and Cavalla and along St Paul River at least as far as near Bong Mine), Ghana (Opintin gallery forest), Gabon (M'Passa on Ivindo river) and reaches as far as the Northern Guinea savanna in the interior of south-western Burkina Faso and Nigeria, where found 339 km inland. Sometimes in farmland, gardens and amongst coconuts on Liberian coast.

STATUS Not uncommon within its specialised mangrove habitat, rare elsewhere. Abundant along coast of Liberia, where occurs at 6-15 birds per km, and also common along rivers. Not uncommon, Ghana. Common resident in mangroves in Nigeria, rarer inland. Common in Cameroon and Sierra Leone. Uncommon resident in mangrove forest along the coast of Cabinda. Threatened wherever mangroves are being destroyed.

MOVEMENTS Probably moves up rivers from the coast during wet seasons, to return in dry periods.

FOOD Insects.
Known food-plants None.

HABITS Energetic birds which forage singly, in pairs or small groups, for insects at all heights, but usually below 3 m. Hunt in tree foliage like warblers, with quick acrobatic movements, often close to, or only 1 m above, water in overhanging vegetation. Feed in mangrove trees and on lianas. Associates rarely with other sunbird species, e.g. Scarlet-chested Sunbird *Chalcomitra senegalensis* (85).

BREEDING Territorial. Female incubates. **Nest** Suspended overhanging water from tip of branch in mangroves or beside rivers, precariously close (30-150 cm) to high tide or flood-level. Often in open, occasionally in gardens.

56　WESTERN VIOLET-BACKED SUNBIRD
Anthreptes longuemarei　　　Plate 15

Cinnyris longuemarei Lesson, 1831, *Illustr. Zool.* pl. 23., "Senegambia superior" [= Senegal]

Alternative names: Violet-backed Sunbird, Uganda Violet-backed Sunbird, Plum-coloured Sunbird, Blue Sunbird, Longuemare's Sunbird

IDENTIFICATION Male easily identified by distinctive violet above and on throat, contrasting with white below and yellow pectoral tufts. Dull brown female told by contrasting white throat and yellow underparts, metallic violet uppertail-coverts and white eye-brow. Straight heavy-looking bill.

Similar species Female from female Mouse-brown Sunbird *A. gabonicus* (55) by yellow below and metallic violet uppertail-coverts. Sympatric with Kenya Violet-backed Sunbird *A. orientalis* (57) in Uganda at Fatiko, Masindi and Soroti and on eastern part of Uganda/Sudan border and western Kenya, but *A. longuemarei* prefers moister habitats and male told by violet back and rump (blue-green in *A. orientalis*); female *longuemarei* has yellow on belly and violet tail, female *orientalis* has white belly and dark blue tail; immature *longuemarei* has yellow to immature *orientalis*'s white underparts. Uluguru Violet-backed Sunbird *A. neglectus* (58) distinguished by greyish-brown not white underparts and female lacks white streak over eye. Immature Variable Sunbird *Cinnyris venustus* (134) is also yellow below but smaller with a decurved bill and blue not violet tail. Yellow-bellied Hyliota *Hyliota f. flavigaster* is superficially similar but has wing-bar.

VOICE Call Four note *t-claa-tee-tee* and alarm call of *skee*. Race *angolensis*: a quiet *chip-chip* with shorter notes than Amethyst Sunbird *Chalcomitra amethystina* (84) uttered from top of tree. An oft-repeated sharp *tit* when feeding or alarmed. Race *longuemarei*: harsh *cha-cha-cha*. **Song** Race *angolensis*: a fast sequence of ascending and descending chattering notes *wit-to-do-dis*, repeated 5-6 times, followed by final flourish of *zit-zit-zit-chit-chit*.

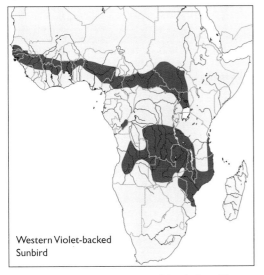

Western Violet-backed Sunbird

DISTRIBUTION Senegal, Gambia, Guinea-Bissau, Guinea, Sierra Leone, Côte d'Ivoire, Ghana, Togo, Benin, Nigeria, Mali, Burkina Faso, Chad, Sudan, Cameroon, Central African Republic, Gabon, Republic of the Congo, Democratic Republic of the Congo, Burundi, Uganda (north-west and central areas below 1,500 m, occasional near Lake Victoria), Kenya, Tanzania, Angola, Zambia (widespread), Malawi, Mozambique and Zimbabwe.

HABITAT Wooded savannas, including *Acacia* woodland, and gallery forests running through savanna, in West Africa, where also occurs in mangrove e.g. especially amongst *Avicennia* sp. in Gambia. Similar main habitats in East Africa, where also sometimes in gardens or lakeside scrubland. Prefers miombo woodland in Angola, Malawi and Zimbabwe, where also frequents *Uapaca* woodland, but only occurs in miombo in Zambia. Found from sea-level but usually above 1,000 m in southern Africa.

STATUS Uncommon in most West African savannas.

Scarce but sometimes locally common in Gambia. Locally common Senegal. Rare in Ghana. Uncommon in Togo and Nigeria. Common in southern Sudan. Common in savannas of Democratic Republic of the Congo. Not uncommon in wooded savanna west of the Budongo forest, Uganda. Scarce in southern Africa: local and uncommon in Malawi and Zambia. Not uncommon resident in miombo woodland in Angola.

MOVEMENTS Moves north into northern Nigeria, May, and travels north, January–April, to breed in Northern Guinea savanna woodland in dry season in Togo, where some also probably resident in Southern Guinea savanna. Probably migrant in Mali. Apparently sedentary in Zimbabwe apart from local wanderings in the dry season and juvenile dispersals. Probably sedentary, Uganda. Migrant to Kenya.

HABITS Usually in pairs or groups of 3-12 birds. Restless. Forages like warbler, sometimes hanging upside-down, probing into bark and hawking for insects. Buoyant flight with fast wing-beats. A female seen feeding in miombo woodland was attacked by Souza's Shrike *Lanius souzae*. Pre-roost family party of four, perched in a line on a branch, played at dislodging end bird, which would return and hang upside-down before regaining position. Joins mixed-species parties: *A. l. nyassae* associates with Scarlet-chested Sunbird *Chalcomitra senegalensis* (85), *Eremomela* spp., *Hyliota* spp. and *Parus* spp. Male preens female.

FOOD Mainly insects including beetles, caterpillars, small Diptera and Hymenoptera. Also spiders, nectar, small fruits and seeds up to the size of a pea. Nectar-robs.
Known food-plants *Adansonia digitata*, *Aloe cameronii*, *Bauhinia* sp., *Bombax* sp., *Brachystegia* sp., *Callistemon* sp., *Erythrina* spp. including *E. abyssinica*, *Faurea speciosa*, *Leonotis leonurus*, unidentified mistletoes Loranthaceae, *Parinari macrophylla*, *Spathodea* sp., *Tacazzea* sp., *Tecoma capense*, *Vitex* sp.

BREEDING Territorial. Male courtship involves drooping wings and fanning out tail. Female only builds, but male is in attendance, watchful, and chases away intruders such as male *Chalcomitra senegalensis* and Brubru *Nilaus afer*. Building may take a month with visits by female, calling *quip quip quip* or *cheep* or *churr* on arrival and departure, every 15-20 minutes in morning and late afternoon. Building involves anchoring material to roof with web, by clinging upside down in entrance hole and reaching to back of nest. Incubation is only by female but both sexes feed young in and out of the nest. Adults with young roost side by side 4 m up in tree. **Nest** Race *haussarum*: bag-like, flimsy, pouch, resembling bundle of dead leaves, with side entrance near top, attached 4-6.5 m up to thin upright branch of almost leafless thorn tree or *Mitragyna inermis*, made of fine vegetable fibres and silky material but extensively decorated outside with dry brown dead leaves including those of *Mitragyna* and leaf fragments, papery bark, leaf petioles, insect frass and grass stems held together with cobwebs; lined with papery bark, pappus of *Bombax* sp. and cobweb; entrance extensively reinforced with cobweb, one entrance concealed by leaves on each side; no porch, no beard; sometimes in association with tailor ants *Oecophylla* sp., the nests of which are similar to those of the bird, invoking possibility of protective nest mimicry; length 135 mm, external diameter 60 mm, maximum internal diameter of chamber 40 mm;

189

longuemarei: an untidy structure of dead leaves, grass and cobwebs, suspended in open view but resembling bunch of dead leaves, about 5 m up in tree; *nyassae*: typical sunbird-type, untidy loose oval bag with entrance near top suspended 7.5 m in tree amongst bunch of dry seed pods; made of fine yellowish-white grass stems held together with cobwebs, lined with fine material; outside covered with dry circular leaves of wild rubber tree, giving it neat and pretty appearance. Depth 150 mm, width 100 mm, entrance hole 40 mm in diameter, base of nest inside 50 mm below entrance. Another made of fine fibres, grass stems, twiglets, and insect silk held together by cobwebs, decorated with dead leaves e.g. of *Brachystegia* sp. Lined with vegetable down. Height 154 mm, width across front 102 mm, internal depth below lip of entrance hole 39 mm. **Eggs** c/1-2; *angolensis*: greenish-white or pale buff with deep brown or black scribblings; 18.1-20.2 (mean 19.6, n=7) x 12.0-13.0 (mean 12.9); *nyassae*: pale buff, smoky-buff, white or pale blue with mostly lengthwise scribblings and hair-lines of blackish-brown and slate-grey, denser at blunt end; 17.0-20.2 (mean 19.5, n=5) x 12.0-13.5 (mean 12.7). **Laying months** East Africa: March. Democratic Republic of the Congo: February, September, enlarged gonads March; Gambia: May; Ghana: February; Kenya: January; Malawi: September, nest-building April, November; Nigeria: February, November; Sudan: February; Togo: February, March; Zambia: February, July, September, December; Zimbabwe: August–December.

DESCRIPTION *A. l. longuemarei*

Adult male Upperparts metallic violet, rump bluer. Wings dark brown, lesser wing-coverts metallic violet. Tail blackish with metallic violet wash. Underparts white. Yellow pectoral tufts. Iris dark brown. Bill almost straight, heavy-looking. Upper mandible greenish-black, lower mandible greenish-brown. Buccal cavity dark pink. Iris dark brown. Legs and feet dark olive-greenish.

Adult female Forehead and upperparts brown (greyish-brown with faint olive wash when fresh, becoming darker) except metallic violet uppertail-coverts. Conspicuous white eyebrow. Ear-coverts brown. Chin to breast white, belly yellow. Axillaries and underwing-coverts white with yellow tinge. Tail brown with strong metallic violet wash. No pectoral tufts.

Juvenile Juvenile male olive-green above, with metallic violet uppertail-coverts. Other metallic violet plumage appears first on crown and lesser wing-coverts. Slight white eyebrow, breast and belly yellow, becoming white. Tail with dark blue wash. No pectoral tufts.

GEOGRAPHICAL VARIATION

A. l. angolensis Neumann, 1906 (southern Democratic Republic of the Congo and Angola to Kasai, Katanga, Manyema, Zambia, Malawi west of the Rift Valley, Zobue northwards to Lake Malawi at Nkhotakota and north of Karonga; south-west Tanzania) Males with whole of lesser wing-coverts metallic green; breast washed buff; females pale below but brighter yellow on belly and vent than *nyassae*. Flight feathers of juvenile edged with yellow-green.

A. l. haussarum Neumann, 1906 (synonymised with *longuemarei* by White 1963 and by Fry *et al.* 2000) (Liberia east to Nigeria, north Cameroon, south Sudan, upper Uelle of Democratic Republic of the Congo, north Uganda to Kavirondo; vagrant to west Kenya) Tips of lesser wing-coverts at wing-bend and feathers on wing-border metallic green.

A. l. longuemarei (Lesson, 1831) (Senegal to Guinea-Bissau) Males have lesser wing-coverts with only a trace of green edges, sometimes none. Described above.

A. l. nyassae Neumann, 1906 (East Zimbabwe, north Mozambique, Malawi east of the Rift Valley, Mulanje and Thyolo further north, also Phirilongwe area; south-east Tanzania north to Dar-es-Salaam) Males purer violet above than *angolensis* without any greenish; underparts white; females darker brown above and less yellow on abdomen than *angolensis* and crown with more violet gloss.

MEASUREMENTS Wing 74-82 (mean 78.7, 46 male *angolensis*), 73-77 (16 male *haussarum*), 72-76 (3 male *longuemarei*), 76-82 (mean 78.3, SD 2.06, 7 male *nyassae*), 66-72 (mean 69.3, 25 female *angolensis*), 62-71 (7 female *haussarum*), 65-68 (5 female *longuemarei*), 65-70 (mean 68, SD 1.63, 7 female *nyassae*); **tail** 49-60 (mean 54.0, 46 male *angolensis*), 49-55 (16 male *haussarum*), 46-50 (3 male *longuemarei*), 52-57 (mean 54.6, SD 1.62, 7 male *nyassae*), 43-49 (mean 46.1, 25 female *angolensis*), 45-49 (7 female *haussarum*), 40-44 (5 female *longuemarei*), 43-48 (mean 44.9, SD 1.68, 7 female *nyassae*); **bill** 16-19 (mean 17.1, 46 male *angolensis*), 15-17.5 (16 male *haussarum*), 15-17 (3 male *longuemarei*), 17-20 (mean 18.8, SD 1.07, 7 male *nyassae*), 15.5-18.0 (mean 16.7, 25 female *angolensis*), 15-16 (7 female *haussarum*), 14-15 (5 female *longuemarei*), 17-19 (mean 18.1, SD 0.67, 7 female *nyassae*); **tarsus** 16.5-19 (mean 17.1, 46 male *angolensis*), 16-18 (16 male *haussarum*), 16-18 (3 male *longuemarei*), 19-22 (mean 20.6, SD 0.98, 7 male *nyassae*), 16.5-20 (mean 17.0, 25 female *angolensis*), 16-18 (7 female *haussarum*), 16-18 (5 female *longuemarei*), 17-20 (mean 18.7, SD 1.07, 7 female *nyassae*); **mass** 11.5-13.0 (2 male *angolensis*), 12.0-13.0 (mean 12.6, 5 male *haussarum*), 10.7-13.0 (mean 11.8, 25 male *nyassae*), 12.0-13.0 (mean 11.3, 10 female *haussarum*), 9.8-13.4 (mean 11.13, 20 female *nyassae*).

REFERENCES Bannerman (1948), Barlow *et al.* (1997), Krienke (1941), Medland (1991), Newby-Varty (1945), Pettet (1977), Priest (1938), Skead (1967), Tree (1997k), Walsh (1966), Walsh *et al.* (1990), Wells (1966), White (1963).

57 KENYA VIOLET-BACKED SUNBIRD
Anthreptes orientalis   Plate 15

Anthreptes orientalis Hartlaub, 1880, *J. Orn.* 28 p.213, Lado, on Bahr-el-Jebel (White Nile), Sudan.

Alternative name: Eastern Violet-backed Sunbird

IDENTIFICATION Short-billed and stocky. Male violet above, white below with blue-green rump. Female with white belly and dark blue tail.

Similar species Western Violet-backed Sunbird *Anthreptes longuemarei* (56) is sympatric in Uganda at Fatiko, Masindi and Soroti and on eastern part of Uganda/Sudan border, but *orientalis* prefers drier areas. Male *orientalis* has more green on lesser wing-coverts and rump; females lack yellow on belly, having only a tinge, and less violet on tail. Immature *orientalis* dull white not yellow below. Uluguru Violet-backed Sunbird *A. neglectus* (58) distinguished by greyish-brown not white underparts and female *neglectus* lacks white streak over eye.

VOICE Call *Chwee* and *tswee-tswee*. **Song** A short twittering of rapid ascending and descending and somewhat harsh notes, *too-wit-woo-tweu, zeet-zeet*, from top of tree.

DISTRIBUTION South-east Sudan, Ethiopia, Somalia, Rwanda, Uganda (mostly north and east, below 1,300 m), Kenya and north-east Tanzania.

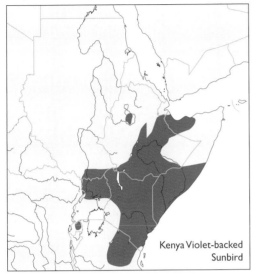
Kenya Violet-backed Sunbird

HABITAT Table-topped acacias near water, riverine woodland, dry bushland and open woodland. Also in *Juniperus* sp. at forest edge in highlands. Drier habitats than *A. longuemarei*.

STATUS Common in Sudan and Ethiopia. Fairly common, presumed resident, in Somalia south of 7°N and locally common in north-west Somalia west of 46°E. Uncommon resident in Kenya, e.g. in Tsavo East National Park. Fairly common in Uganda.

MOVEMENTS Unknown.

FOOD Insects and nectar.
Known food-plants *Leonotis* sp., unidentified mistletoes Loranthaceae.

HABITS Found in pairs or small groups and in mixed-species parties. Forages in warbler-like manner, sometimes creeping about foliage, and searches small branches and bark. Also hawks for insects. When feeding may simultaneously fan tail and flick wings in rapid succession. Dominant over Black-bellied Sunbird *C. nectarinoides* (120) when defending mistletoe flowers. Reduces metabolism at night by 44% at constant ambient temperature of 5°C and by 51-57% at 25°C. Host to *Haemoproteus* sp.

BREEDING Territorial. **Nest** Suspended from end of branch low in small bush, sometimes associated with wasps' nests. Neat oval with side-top entrance and short porch. Loosely woven of grass, vegetable down, hair and wool, with characteristic external ornamentation of plant material with old egg capsules of praying mantises. **Eggs** 17.0-19.0 (mean 17.9, n=5) x 12.0-12.5 (mean 12.3). Greenish-grey with dark grey, black or brown speckles. **Laying months** East Africa: January–February, April–August, October–December; Ethiopia: April–June; Kenya: October; Somalia: April–June; Sudan: November–March; Uganda: enlarged testes May.

DESCRIPTION
Adult male Upperparts, except iridescent violet uppertail-coverts and violet-blue tail, iridescent bluish-green. Chin and lores iridescent violet. Throat to undertail-coverts white. Flanks greyish, thighs whitish mixed with brown. Remiges and wing-coverts, except iridescent violet median wing-coverts and scapulars, brown. Outer primaries with yellowish outer margins. White tips to innerwebs of T5-6. Axillaries and underwing-coverts white. Iris dark brown. Bill, legs and feet black.
Adult female Upperparts, apart from violet-blue uppertail-coverts and tail, brown. Outerweb of T6 brown. Eye-stripe, lores and ear-coverts brown. Whitish supercilium. Underparts all whitish except for yellow-tinged belly and flanks.
Juvenile Similar to female but underparts, especially middle of belly, whitish tinged yellow or buff. Crown, mantle and wing-coverts usually light grey-brown, sometimes dark brown.

GEOGRAPHICAL VARIATION Populations from Somalia to north-east Kenya used to be separated as *A. o. neumanni* Zedlitz, 1916 on the basis of smaller size (wing 61-64). Birds from Dodoma, Tanzania, were described as *A. o. barbouri* by Friedmann (1931), who considered them similar to *orientalis* but with much larger females (although little bigger – wing 65 – than the biggest females of the latter), and with both sexes having stouter bills (culmen 21 in *barbouri* female, 17 in *orientalis*), but without more information to justify subspecific status, the differences are here attributed to clinal variation.

MEASUREMENTS Wing 61-72 (mean 67.2, 41 males), 58-64 (mean 61.2, 31 females); **tail** 44-52 (mean 48.9, 41 males), 40-46 (mean 43.2, 31 females); **bill** 15-18 (mean 16.7, 41 males), 15-18 (mean 16.0, 31 females); **tarsus** 16-21 (mean 17.2, 41 males), 16-21 (mean 16.8, 31 females); **mass** 8-12.0 (mean 10.4, 15 males), 8-12.0 (mean 10.2, 9 females).

REFERENCES Ash & Miskell (1983), Friedmann (1931), Fry *et al.* (2000), Kahindi & Kageci (1995), Prinzinger *et al.* (1989), Prinzinger & Jackel (1986).

---

58 ULUGURU VIOLET-BACKED SUNBIRD
Anthreptes neglectus   Plate 15

Anthreptes longuemarei neglectus Neumann, 1922, *Orn. Monatsb.* 30 p.13, Uluguru Mountains, Tanganyika Territory [= Tanzania].

IDENTIFICATION Violet upperparts including uppertail-coverts, brown half-collar, bluish-green rump and purplish-blue tail, in both sexes. Male is white or buffish-brown below with violet chin, yellow pectoral tufts and conspicuous cobalt blue-green flash on wing-shoulder. Green edgings to primaries of male not discernible in field. Female is mostly grey below but with yellow belly. Juvenile has white supercilium.
Similar species Kenya Violet-backed Sunbird *A. orientalis* (57) is sympatric along River Tana in Kenya and Western Violet-backed Sunbird *A. longuemarei* (56) is sympatric on coast of Tanzania but *neglectus* is a true forest bird, unlike *orientalis* or *longuemarei*. Males distinguished by greyish-brown not white underparts, females by greyish-brown, not pure white, underparts and lack of white streak over eye. Unless shoulder-flash already visible, immature almost

191

indistinguishable from those of *orientalis* and *longuemarei* but immature *neglectus* and immature or female *longuemarei* are bright lemon-yellow on belly and vent whereas female and immature *orientalis* have only a faint yellow or buff wash.

VOICE Call *Tsssp* repeated up to four times in succession, sometimes followed by a second-long melodious warbling trill, also described as a thin sibilant warble. Also a repetitive *sweep-sweep-sweep* or *seep-sureep, sureep...*

Uluguru Violet-backed Sunbird

DISTRIBUTION East Africa. Kenya: Shimba Hills (wildlife sanctuary and Mkongani forest), Tana River forest (including Kitere forest in Tana River primate reserve, only site north of Mombasa), Buda forest reserve and Jadini forest. Also many sites in Tanzania including the Uluguru, Ukaguru and Udzungwa mountains (Mwanihana forest and 1,400 m in Ndundulus), north Nguu mountains, Ngurus, West Usambaras and Mt Nilo in East Usambaras in Tanzania, and north Mozambique at River Lurio and Netia.

HABITAT Forest and forest edge and thickets at edge of montane forest, from sea-level to 1,250 m in eastern Tanzania (e.g. Uluguru mountains, East Usambaras mountains) and northern Mozambique, up to 1,800 m, and in moist bushed and wooded country in coastal regions in Kenya and Tanzania. Prefers submontane forest but also found in damaged forests, riverine forests and agricultural zones including tea plantations with shade trees.

STATUS Vulnerable and classed as near-threatened. Locally common in East Usambaras and in the Kimboza forest reserve in the Ulugurus but scarce in the Ngurus and uncommon in the Nguu mountains at 1,300-1,500 m.

MOVEMENTS Unknown.

FOOD Insects and probably nectar. Fine sand in one stomach. **Known food-plants** *Grevillea* sp., unidentified mistletoes Loranthaceae.

HABITS Found in pairs or groups of up to 10 birds, often in mixed parties (with up to 18 other species) in dense forest foliage, in canopy, or foraging for insects 5-10 m above ground, occasionally as low as 1 m. Male preens female. Nest-building female seen pulling strips of thin fibrous material, possibly cobweb, from a *Podocarpus usambarensis* tree, 3-4 m up at forest edge along roadside. Bird then dropped 10-20 cm with folded wings before flapping vigorously, breaking free and flying off trailing the fibre.

BREEDING Territorial. Fledglings fed by male and almost certainly by female too. **Nest** Hung from twig 8 m up overhanging a road, at edge of forest. Untidy oval with side-top entrance, made of grass, moss and lichens; with beard. Lined with white pappus. **Eggs** Unknown. **Laying months** East Africa: December, January and March. Mate-guarding and nest-building September.

DESCRIPTION
Adult male Reddish-violet forehead and crown leading onto dull black nape. Reddish-violet mantle, back and uppertail-coverts, latter metallic. Metallic blue-green rump. Tail metallic violet above, black below. Outer tail feathers tipped white. Faces dark brown. Upper throat metallic reddish-violet. Sides of neck, throat and underparts white but belly, flanks and undertail-coverts washed buff. Remiges dark brown with greenish outer edges. Scapulars reddish-violet. Greater wing-coverts with green edges. Shoulder and median coverts iridescent green. Axillaries and underwing-coverts white. Pectoral tufts yellow or orange. Iris dark brown. Bill black. Feet grey-black.
Adult female Similar to male. Iridescent blue-violet above, no obvious supercilium, but blackish-brown on central forehead and extensive yellow on belly, undertail-coverts and thighs; rest of underparts buffish-grey with olive streaks at sides of belly.
Juvenile Crown, mantle and wing-coverts dusky brown, occasionally with violet metallic wash; iridescence on upperparts may be limited to uppertail-coverts, tail and bend of wing; flight feathers edged yellow-green; carpal patch usually iridescent; belly and vent washed lemon-yellow; bold white supercilium from lores to at least 5 mm behind eye in both sexes.

GEOGRAPHICAL VARIATION None described but a female collected from the River Tana, Kenya, was smaller (wing 61.5 mm, tail 43.5) than usual, with yellow on belly paler and less extensive, and may represent an undescribed subspecies (Keith 1968).

MEASUREMENTS Wing 68-75 (mean 71.1, 11 males), 63-68 (mean 64.8, 6 females); **tail** 50-56 (mean 52.9, 11 males), 47-49 (mean 48.3, 6 females); **bill** 15.5-18.0 (mean 17.3, 11 males), 16-18 (mean 16.5, 6 females); **tarsus** 16.5-18.5 (mean 17.4, 11 males), 16-17.5 (mean 16.6, 6 females); **mass** 12.8-15.5 (mean 14.2, SD 1.19, 4 males), 12.3-15 (mean 13.6, 2 females).

REFERENCES Alexander (1995a), Butynski (1994), Evans (1996), Fjeldså *et al.* (1997), Fry *et al.* (2000), Hipkiss *et al.* (1994), P. J. Jones (pers. comm.), Keith (1968), Sclater & Moreau (1933), Seddon *et al.* (1999), Stuart & Jensen (1985).

59 VIOLET-TAILED SUNBIRD
Anthreptes aurantium   Plate 16

Anthreptes aurantium J. & E. Verreaux, 1851, *Rev. Mag. Zool.* (Paris), ser.2, 3, p.417, Gabon.

IDENTIFICATION Easily told by combination of longish, slightly decurved bill, brilliant metallic blue, green and

violet upperparts and contrasting pale underparts. Orange pectoral tufts in male. Female with broad white supercilium.
Similar species Male Western Violet-backed Sunbird *A. longuemarei* (56) has all head and back violet not metallic green or blue, yellow not orange pectoral tufts, and is usually allopatric.

VOICE High-pitched calls in flight, otherwise unknown.

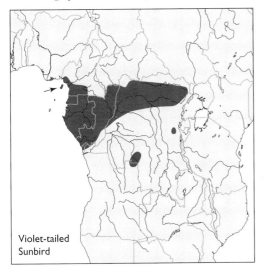

Violet-tailed Sunbird

DISTRIBUTION Central Africa from Cameroon to Gabon and the Democratic Republic of the Congo, where it reaches the Ituri forest. Also recorded from Central African Republic, Republic of the Congo and north-east Angola.

HABITAT Forest, usually secondary forest, gallery forest particularly along rivers, seasonally flooded forest, mangroves, swamp forest, edges of saltpans and wooded savanna. Always close to water.

STATUS Rare in most localities but common in Gabon where 1 pair or party every 500-800 m of river. Uncommon resident in gallery forest in northern Lunda Norte, Angola.

MOVEMENTS Unknown, probably sedentary.

FOOD Spiders and insects, including caterpillars, unidentified pupae and winged ants but also small berries and fruits; possibly nectar.
Known food-plants *Globimetula* sp., *Macaranga assas* (fruits), *Mussaenda erythrophylla.*

HABITS Active and agile, foraging silently from water's edge to canopy, but principally low down, in pairs or groups of up to four. Tame.

BREEDING Territorial. Only female seen to feed nestlings, which are sometimes fed with small fruits. **Nest** Suspended from ends of branches, 1-3 m above water, from trees e.g. *Cynometra alexandri* or shrubs beside or growing in rivers. Oval or pear-shaped with side entrance with short porch, and beard of dead leaves. Made of dry leaves, brown fibres, black fungal threads, and filaments from spiders' webs, particularly those of the social spider *Agelena republicana.* The latter are so numerous that nest may appear as part of a web complex. Lined with white plant down. **Eggs** c/1-2. 18.0-19.2 (mean 18.6, n=3) x 12.0-13.1 (mean 12.6).

Elongated. Clear bluish-grey with brown or purplish-black lines, thicker and darker at larger pole forming ring.
Laying months Cameroon: March; Democratic Republic of the Congo: April, June; Gabon: April, November, December, dependent young March, nest-building January, September; Republic of the Congo, building nest November.

DESCRIPTION
Adult male Upperparts brilliant metallic blue or green of various hues and varying with different reflections; crown bluish-green, mantle violet or purplish-blue, back greenish, rump and uppertail-coverts blue. Wings brown, coverts and secondaries with broad metallic green edges. Tail violet or blue, with green edges. Chin and throat metallic green; lores, ear-coverts and sides of head blackish with little gloss. Bright orange pectoral tufts. Rest of underparts including underwing-coverts and axillaries pale buff, more greyish-white on belly. Iris dark brown. Bill slightly decurved, black, grey at base of lower mandible. Legs and feet greyish-black or bluish-grey.
Adult female Similar to male above but bluer, less purple, before assuming metallic plumage. Chin to chest and sides of neck greyish-white, rest of underparts pale yellow, with olive tinge on flanks. Underwing-coverts white, axillaries white with yellow wash. Iris dark brown. Bill and feet dark grey.
Juvenile Greenish-brown above. Conspicuous white or pale yellow supercilium and dark line through eye. Wing edged white. Underparts greyish-white, washed with yellow or olivaceous-green except throat. Tail blue with metallic green wash.

GEOGRAPHICAL VARIATION None described as subspecies but Chapin (1954) noted that males from Gabon and the lower River Congo have more buff on the breast and more violet on the throat than birds from the Ituri forest. A few adult females have white not yellow bellies.

MEASUREMENTS Wing 63-68 (mean 65.9, 13 males), 59-62 (mean 60.5, 8 females); **tail** 41-49 (mean 46.3, 13 males), 38-43 (mean 40.2, 8 females); **bill** 15-17 (mean 16.5, 12 males), 16-17 (mean 16.3, 6 females); **tarsus** 15.5-18 (mean 16.3, 12 males), 15.5-18 (mean 16.2, 8 females); **mass** no data.

REFERENCES Bannerman (1948), Brosset & Erard (1986), Chapin (1954).

---

60   LITTLE GREEN SUNBIRD
Anthreptes seimundi   Plate 18

Cinnyris seimundi Ogilvie-Grant, 1908, *Bull. Br. Orn. Club* 23, p.19, "Fernando Po and West Africa..."; type from Banterbari, Fernando Po *fide* Sclater 1930, *Syst. Av. Aethiop.,* p.711.

Alternative name: Seimund's Little Green Sunbird

Taxonomic note When *A. seimundi* was included in *Nectarinia, N. s. minor* (see below) was preoccupied by *N. (Cinnyris) angolensis minor* Oustalet (= *N. [Chalcomitra] rubescens*) and became *N. s. traylori* Wolters, 1965; with reclassification back to *Anthreptes,* the subspecific name reverts to *A. s. minor*).

IDENTIFICATION A very small green sunbird, paler below with yellow on belly, a short, straight, thick bill, disproportionately long for the bird's size, and pale, narrow, eye-ring.

Similar species Bates's Sunbird *Cinnyris batesi* (137) is very similar but darker, has a more curved bill, greyish-olive not yellowish underparts, brown not green tail, and no yellow eye-ring; *A. seimundi* holds itself more horizontally and appears more uniform below. Scarlet-tufted Sunbird *Deleornis fraseri* (48) is also similar but slightly larger, lacks yellow on belly and males have orangey-red pectoral tufts. Also similar to females and young of Grey-headed Sunbird *D. axillaris* (49). Western Olive Sunbird *Cyanomitra obscura* (79) and Eastern Olive Sunbird *C. olivacea* (78) also similar but about twice as big and with longer, much more decurved bill and yellow pectoral tufts except in females of *C. obscura*. Can also be confused with female Olive-bellied Sunbird *Cinnyris chloropygius* (100), which has dark blue, not green, tail and longer, finer, all-black, more curved bill.

VOICE Call An oft-repeated high-pitched and squeaky *twip twip twip*. **Song** Race *kruensis*: *twip* or *psee* repeated 7-8 times per second in rapid burst; *minor*: a disyllabic *pse-ee* or *pss-upp* repeated every second.

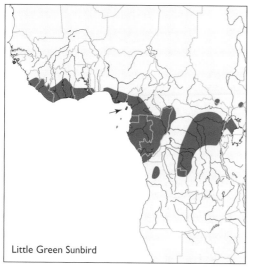

Little Green Sunbird

DISTRIBUTION West and Central Africa. Guinea, Sierra Leone, Liberia, Côte d'Ivoire, Ghana, Togo, Nigeria, Cameroon, Central African Republic, Equatorial Guinea (Bioko and mainland Rio Muni), Gabon, Republic of the Congo, Democratic Republic of the Congo, Angola, Rwanda, Uganda (south-west and as far north and east as Budongo and Kifu forests) and Sudan (Bengengai and Talanga forests).

HABITAT All levels from understorey to canopy of mature forest, secondary forest, gallery forest, coffee plantations, forest edges and forest-grassland mosaic. Dense undergrowth in forest clearings and abandoned plantations.

STATUS Rare in Guinea. Uncommon in Liberia, Ghana, Togo and Nigeria. Not uncommon in forests of Cameroon; uncommon in Equatorial Guinea; *minor* rare in Itombwe Mountains, Democratic Republic of the Congo, but abundant at Talanga forest in Sudan and sometimes fairly common in Uganda up to 1,500 m. Not uncommon resident in northern Angola.

MOVEMENTS Sedentary. Resident in Uganda and, probably, elsewhere.

FOOD Insects including small beetles and caterpillars; small spiders; small fruits, seeds and fruit of *Ficus* spp.; nectar. **Known food-plants** *Erythrina* sp., *Lophira alata*, unidentified mistletoes Loranthaceae, *Macaranga assas*, fruits of *Ochthocosmus africanus* and *Urera hypsilodendron*.

HABITS Feeds fast and methodically e.g. in vines on *Musanga* sp. tree, usually in small monospecific parties of up to 8 birds or in association with *D. axillaris*, constantly calling. Probes small figs in flight while hovering above them. Prefers middle (3-25 m) to tops of forest trees. Occasionally a member of bird armies e.g. with Green Sunbird *A. rectirostris* (61), Blue-throated Brown Sunbird *Cyanomitra cyanolaema* (75), Buff-throated Sunbird *Chalcomitra adelberti* (81) and Johanna's Sunbird *Cinnyris johannae* (129). Perches horizontally. Host to *Trypanosoma avium*.

BREEDING Territorial. Incubation only by female. **Nest** Small compact oval with side-top entrance, about 100 mm long, made of fibre and cobwebs with some hanging loosely but otherwise no beard, suspended near end of leafy twig covered above by foliage, 10 m from ground in a tall tree. Another suspended from a yam vine. Lining of thistledown. A third was made of bark fibres and dry leaves, a fourth attached to petiole of a yam *Dioscorea* sp. **Eggs** c/2. Race *minor*: 14.0-15.0 (mean 14.5, n=4) x 11-11.5 (mean 11.3). Cream, unglossed, covered with fine brown freckles. **Laying months** Cameroon: April–May, July, November–December; Democratic Republic of the Congo: February, September; Gabon: November; Ghana: breeding condition February; Liberia: July, dependent young February, April; Nigeria: breeding condition July, November; Republic of the Congo: October; Sierra Leone: February; Uganda: November–February, August.

DESCRIPTION *A. s. seimundi*
Adult male Upperparts bright olive-green. Eye almost completely encircled by pale yellow. Wings dark brown with yellowish margins. Tail dark brown with olive wash on outerwebs. Throat dull greenish-yellow, more yellow on belly and all yellow along mid-rib. No pectoral tufts. Undertail-coverts yellow. Axillaries and underwing-coverts white with yellow edging. Iris dark brown. Bill fine and short, dark brown, paler at base of lower mandible (slightly yellowish in *kruensis*). Legs and feet greenish-black.
Adult female Similar to male but smaller.
Juvenile Both sexes have dark crowns and sides of underparts greyer than adults.

GEOGRAPHICAL VARIATION
A. s. kruensis (Bannerman, 1911) (Sierra Leone to Togo) Duller and paler below with a greyer tinge, yellow less bright than *minor*. Chin almost white. Eye-ring less obvious than in *minor* and *seimundi*.
A. s. minor Bates, 1926 (south-east Nigeria, south-east Central African Republic to Democratic Republic of the Congo [Bas Vele district], including Itombwe Mountains, Talanga [Imatong Mountains] and Bangangai forests in Sudan and north-west Angola west to Lusambo, and Uganda [Budongo forest]) Greener on belly and flanks, less yellow and more olive below and smaller than nominate, but retains yellow mid-rib and has faint yellow supercilium. Iris dark brown. Adult male has upper mandible greenish-black, lower brownish-yellow with greenish-brown tip.

Legs and feet greenish-black. Adult female has bill black, base of lower mandible yellow, feet black, iris dark brown.

A. s. seimundi (Ogilvie-Grant, 1908) (Bioko) Described above.

MEASUREMENTS Wing 49-53 (mean 51.5, 7 male *kruensis*), 48-57 (mean 53.3, 23 male *minor*), 54-57 (4 male *seimundi*), 45-50 (mean 48.8, SD 1.6, 10 female *kruensis*), 44-55 (mean 49.2, 20 female *minor*), 49, 52 (2 female *seimundi*); **tail** 20-29 (mean 22, 4 male *kruensis*), 26-32 (mean 28.3, 23 male *minor*), 30-32 (4 male *seimundi*), 22-25 (mean 22.4, SD 1.7, 10 female *kruensis*), 23-29 (mean 25.8, 20 female *minor*), 26, 26 (2 female *seimundi*); **bill** 13-16 (8 male *kruensis*), 14-17 (mean 15.8, 23 male *minor*), 15 (male *seimundi*), 13-16 (mean 15.5, SD 0.5, 10 female *kruensis*), 13-15.5 (mean 14.9, 20 female *minor*), 13, 13 (2 female *seimundi*); **tarsus** 14-15 (4 male *kruensis*), 14-16 (mean 15.4, 23 male *minor*), 16-16.5 (4 male *seimundi*), 13-16.5 (mean 15.0, 20 female *minor*), 15, 15 (2 female *seimundi*); **mass** 6.3-6.8 (mean 6.5, SD 0.21, 4 male *kruensis*), 6.5-11 (mean 7.6, 17 male *minor*), mean 5.9 (SD 0.7, 10 female *kruensis*), 5.0-6.5 (mean 5.7, 6 female *minor*).

REFERENCES Bannerman (1948), Bates (1927), Benson & Irwin (1966), Brosset & Erard (1986), Fry *et al.* (2000), Traylor & Archer (1982), Wolters (1965).

61 GREEN SUNBIRD
Anthreptes rectirostris   Plate 16

Certhia rectirostris Shaw, 1811-12, *General Zool.* 8 p.246, no locality; Gambia designated by Sclater 1930 *Syst. Av. Aethiop.* p.709; amended to Ashanti, Gold Coast, by Bannerman 1948 *Birds Trop. West Africa*, 6, p.242.

Alternative names: Yellow-chinned Sunbird (*A. r. rectirostris*), Yellow-chin Sunbird (*A. r. rectirostris*), Grey-chinned Sunbird (*A. r. tephrolaema*)

A. r. rectirostris and *A. r. tephrolaema* sometimes treated as separate species (e.g. by Chapin 1954). *Anthreptes pujoli* is this species, its description having been based on a fledgling (Erard 1979).

IDENTIFICATION A very small sunbird, males with metallic green above and distinctive yellow (*A. r. rectirostris*) or grey (*A. r. tephrolaema*) throat, bordered with metallic green and orange but latter difficult to see in the field. Short straightish bill gives warbler-like appearance. Females difficult to tell in the field, being olivaceous above with a scattering of metallic green on shoulders, yellow-olive below, with pale supercilium.
Similar species Male separated from Collared Sunbird *Hedydipna collaris* (63) by smaller size, non-metallic throat-patch, dull brown and olive tail and shorter straightish bill. Females resemble miniature Western Olive Sunbird *Cyanomitra obscura* (79) and Eastern Olive Sunbird *C. olivacea* (78).

VOICE Call *Pweet-pweet-pweet-* etc., also *pseek-pseek-pseek-* etc. delivered more rapidly than *pweet* call, and *de-de-de-de* repeated when flitting from leaf to leaf. Race *tephrolaema*: high-pitched *pseep-pseep* or *psee-psee* or *pweet-pweet* or *pseek-pseek* repeated at 1.5-2.5 second intervals; an ascending

peep or descending *tsi*; *huit-huit-huit-huit*. **Song** Race *tephrolaema*: a complex high-pitched twittering of rapid notes such as *tser-tsit-tseee-too, tepu-ti-du-tepu-di-do, chup-chup-chup, churr*, rising and falling and ending in *tser-tser-tser*; or a less complicated chattering *tser-tser-tsip-tsip-tsip-tsip-tse-tswoo-tsi-tsi*, lasting 1.5-2 seconds, oft-repeated. Another rendering is *tieû-tieû! tiu-tiu-tiu-tiup, tiu-tiu-tiup, tiu-tiu-tiup.*

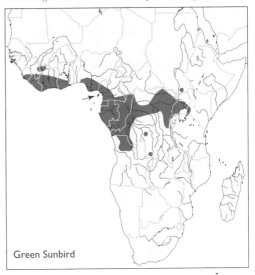

Green Sunbird

DISTRIBUTION West and Central Africa. *A. r. rectirostris* known from Guinea, Sierra Leone, Liberia, Côte d'Ivoire, Mali, Ghana; *A. r. tephrolaema* recorded from Benin (Pobé forest), Nigeria, Cameroon, Equatorial Guinea (including Bioko), Central African Republic, Gabon, Angola, Republic of the Congo, Democratic Republic of the Congo, Sudan (foothills of Imatong mountains), Uganda (forests of south and west, up to 1,500 m), Kenya above 1,000 m and north-west Tanzania (Minziro forest).

HABITAT Canopy in primary and secondary forests and along tracks and clearings within them, gallery forest, swamp forest, coffee plantations, cultivations and open areas between plantations, including cocoa forest and oil palms, inselbergs and mountains. More usually found in clearings or secondary forest than in primary forest, e.g. on Bioko usually avoids primary forest, occurring from the coast up to Moka (1,300 m).

STATUS Uncommon throughout most of its range, but possibly overlooked. Commoner in Liberia than elsewhere. Not uncommon in Ghana and on Bioko. Uncommon resident in Nigeria. Widespread at forest edges, Equatorial Guinea. Occurs at densities of 3-5 pairs per km² in Gabon. Not uncommon resident in Angola. Rare in extreme south of Sudan. Uncommon in Democratic Republic of the Congo. Common and widespread in south and west Uganda and west Kenya, 700-2,150 m.

MOVEMENTS Some seasonal movements may occur.

FOOD Insects including termites and moth larvae, spiders, small berries, fruits and seeds. Possibly nectar.
Known food-plants Arils of *Alchornea cordifolia* (intact seeds of which are defecated), fruits of *Ochthocosmus africanus*, arils of *Xylopia aethiopica*, small fruits of *Macaranga* sp.

HABITS Occurs in pairs or family parties of up to seven

birds at mid-height of trees in primary and secondary forest and at forest edges in clearings with large trees remaining. Seldom below 20 m, usually 25-50 m up. Forages on twigs <3 cm in diameter. Joins mixed-species flocks, e.g. with *H. collaris*, Little Green Sunbird *Anthreptes seimundi* (60), Blue-throated Brown Sunbird *Cyanomitra cyanolaema* (75), Buff-throated Sunbird *Chalcomitra adelberti* (81) and Johanna's Sunbird *Cinnyris johannae* (129), paradise-flycatchers *Terpsiphone* spp. and/or Speckled Tinkerbird *Pogoniulus scolopaceus*. Searches for food, mostly insects, on and below leaves, along branches and tree-trunks, in warbler-like manner. Occasionally sallies off branches to make flycatcher-like captures. Host to *Haemoproteus sequeirae* and microfilariae.

BREEDING Territorial; males sing 10-20 m up in trees, but probably co-operative breeder. Only female incubates. Young fed by both parents and sometimes by other adult helpers within a group. **Nest** Race *rectirostris*: suspended high from tangled vine in tree or 2 m from ground in kola tree, beside river, or 40 m up in mature forest. Globular, made of stems bound with spiders' webs, decorated with kola tree flowers and lined with white vegetable silk. Race *tephrolaema*: globular, built of fibres and lichens or green moss, sometimes amongst dead vegetation, lined with cottony vegetable down or brown material possibly from ferns and rootlets, and suspended 1.5-10 m above ground from a branch, liana or thorny vine attached to tree. Short beard of loose moss. 130 mm high, 100 mm deep, side entrance 40 mm in diameter. **Eggs** c/2. Ovate. Grey with violet tone and irregular dark grey-green spots and lines. **Laying months** Cameroon: April–February, June, July, November; Democratic Republic of the Congo: January–April, July, September; Gabon: dependent young March; Ghana: December; Kenya: August; Liberia: September–December, groups with many immatures January–April; Nigeria: June; Republic of the Congo: February, September–October; Uganda: August and birds in breeding condition June and November, also juveniles April.

DESCRIPTION *A. r. rectirostris*
Adult male Head, neck, mantle and scapulars metallic green with golden tinge, especially on ear-coverts. Metallic plumage sometimes reaches rump and uppertail-coverts but these usually olive. Tail blackish-brown, edged olive. Remiges dark brown with olive edges. Wing-coverts brown, lesser coverts with metallic green or blue edges, greater coverts edged olive. Chin and throat lemon-yellow, bordered by metallic green chest-band with lower border of orange. Ashy-grey below band, merging into pale yellow of belly and uppertail-coverts. Lemon-yellow pectoral tufts. Underwing-coverts and axillaries white, latter with yellow tips. Iris dark brown or reddish-brown. Bill, legs and feet black. Mouth dull yellow.
Adult female All upperparts olive-green, more yellowish on rump and uppertail-coverts and slight metallic green reflections on head and back. Lesser wing-coverts with metallic green edges. Chin white, rest of underparts pale yellowish, more olive on breast and brightest on belly. Wings and tail dark brown with olive edges. Bill black. Feet black.
Juvenile Shortly after fledging, lacks any metallic feathers, being similar to adult female, with olive-brown upperparts, yellow wash below, more olivaceous on chest, slight yellowish supercilium, small pale spots on tips of wing-coverts especially on median coverts, bill mostly black but extreme base of lower mandible orange-horn, and gape-

flanges orange-red. Later, male gains some metallic feathers on crown and mantle, chin and throat greyish-white, breast pale ash, belly and undertail-coverts bright yellow. Iris dark. Upper mandible dark brown, lower yellow. Feet slate-black. Males develop yellow throat before metallic or orange plumages.

GEOGRAPHICAL VARIATION
A. r. rectirostris (Shaw, 1811) (Sierra Leone to Ghana) All of throat lemon-yellow. Described above.
A. r. tephrolaema (Jardine & Fraser, 1851) (includes *elgonense* van Someren, 1921) (southern Nigeria to mouth of Congo river and north-west Angola; in Democratic Republic of the Congo as far east as west Katanga, Kasai, upper Congo; south Sudan at Imatong mountains; Uganda; western Kenya; Bioko). Male with chin and upper throat grey; lower throat metallic green in broader band than *rectirostris* and reaching further up throat; abdomen greyer, less yellow than *rectirostris*. Undertail-coverts dull yellow. Male with iris red, red-brown or brown, female iris chestnut, brown or dark brown. Female darker and browner above than *rectirostris*. Throat of juveniles greyer than in *rectirostris* and tinged yellow.

MEASUREMENTS Wing 55-60 (mean 59, S. D. 1.1, 6 male *rectirostris*), 53-65 (25 male *tephrolaema*), 53-58 (24 female *rectirostris*), 52-58 (19 female *tephrolaema*); **tail** 29-33.5 (mean 28.8, SD 0.9, 6 male *rectirostris*), 31-37 (22 male *tephrolaema*), 25-32.5 (24 female *rectirostris*), 28-37 (16 female *tephrolaema*); **bill** 12-16 (mean 15.2, SD 0.4, 6 male *rectirostris*), 12-15 (22 male *tephrolaema*), 11.5-15 (4 female *rectirostris*), 12-15 (16 female *tephrolaema*); **tarsus** 13.5-16 (11 male *rectirostris*), 13-15 (22 male *tephrolaema*), 13.5-16 (4 female *rectirostris*), 13-16 (16 female *tephrolaema*); **mass** 10-12 (mean 11, SD 1, 6 male *rectirostris*), 10.0 (male *tephrolaema*), 7-12 (mean 9.9, 17 female *rectirostris*), 10.0 (female *tephrolaema*).

REFERENCES Bannerman (1948), Brosset & Erard (1986), Button (1967), Chapin (1954), Christy & Clarke (1994), Dowsett-Lemaire (1996), Erard (1979), Fry *et al.* (2000), Pérez del Val (1996), Quantrill & Quantrill (1998).

---

62   BANDED SUNBIRD
Anthreptes rubritorques   Plate 16

Anthreptes rubritorques Reichenow, 1905, *Orn. Monatsb.* 13 p.181, Mlalo, Usambara Mountains, German East Africa [= Tanzania].

Alternative names: Banded Green Sunbird, Usambara Grey-chin Sunbird

IDENTIFICATION Very small, short-tailed sunbird. Male green above, grey below with red breast-band. Female green above, dull yellowish below with no breast-band.
Similar species Male resembles allopatric Green Sunbird *A. rectirostris* (61), but bluer on back, grey on throat more extensive and green breast-band less greenish, not metallic, and edged red not orange. Females differ from those of *rectirostris* by metallic feathers on head and back. Male Amani Sunbird *Hedydipna pallidigaster* (66) has bluish-green upperparts and breast, no red breast-band, red pectoral tufts and white belly; female grey above, white below.

VOICE Call A plaintive *chip* or *teuu* uttered every second for 30-60 seconds by male when following nest-building female. Also a disyllabic *thk-eeer*. **Song** The far-carrying *chip* call may be repeated at an accelerated pace to create song.

DISTRIBUTION North-east Tanzania. Restricted to montane forested areas in the East Usambaras (1,000-1,350 m on Mt Nilo), West Usambaras, Nguus, Ngurus, Ulugurus (where rare and known from only five specimens), and Udzungwa mountains in Eastern Tanzania, 900-1,600 m, where threatened by deforestation.

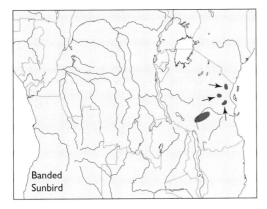

Banded Sunbird

HABITAT Mid-altitude submontane forest down to 750 m, and forest edges. Also in scrub near maize plantations and on boundaries of submontane forest with miombo woodland.

STATUS Vulnerable and classed as threatened, status Vulnerable. Locally common in Usambaras, local but uncommon in Udzungwas, uncommon or rare elsewhere.

MOVEMENTS Probably sedentary.

FOOD Nectar, insects including larvae of *Dysdercus* sp., berries and fruits.
Known food-plants *Erythrina abyssinica*, *Grevillea* sp., berries of *Macaranga kilimandscharica*, fruits of *Rubus* sp.

HABITS Forages in pairs or small parties high in trees, usually in the canopy or subcanopy of mature trees, occasionally in mixed-species flocks. Flocks of 60 reported as regular in the East Usambaras and occasional in the West Usambaras. Nest-building female seen collecting fibre from central rachis of *Albizia* sp.

BREEDING Male sings from canopy for extended periods, June–January. Female active in nest-building with attendant male. Male perches near nest as sentry, calling often. Only female incubates and feeds young. **Nest** A neat oval, with high side-top entrance but no beard. Built with lichens *Usnea* sp., cobwebs and feathery bracts of a flowering climber, decorated with needles of *Casuarina* sp., suspended 15 m or more up in canopy of mature *Newtonia* sp. trees, or at forest edge in *Widdringtonia* sp., 300-1,500 m a.s.l. Lined with pappus, including on roof. Another consisted of a ball of unidentified brown fibres, without covering of lichen, fixed on top of a palm frond and anchored by three palm leaflets penetrating nest structure. This nest was 2 m out on the frond 1.5 m from its tip, overhanging a bank, 6 m from the ground. **Eggs** c/2? Unknown. **Laying months** Tanzania: January, July, September, building August, ovaries enlarged November.

DESCRIPTION
Adult male Upperparts and face metallic green. Tail green with purplish reflections. Underparts grey, except narrow red breast-band and yellowish middle of belly and undertail-coverts. Pectoral tufts orangey-yellow. Remiges brown with olive-green edges to outerwebs. Secondary coverts dull iridescent green, scapulars and median and lesser coverts brighter metallic green. Axillaries and underwing-coverts white. Iris black or brown. Bill, legs and feet black.
Adult female Similar to male but duller above with green metallic feathering on upperparts and ear-coverts less dense, whitish not grey throat, lacks breast-band, rest of underparts olive, brightest in mid-belly, and tail brownish with olive edges.
Juvenile Blackish above with olive wash, yellow-olive below. Gape yellow, mouth orangey-red. Iris reddish-brown; bill, legs and feet black.

GEOGRAPHICAL VARIATION None described.

MEASUREMENTS Wing 56-62 (mean 60, SD 2.28, 6 males), 56 (1 female); tail 33-38 (mean 36.3, SD 1.97, 6 males), 33 (1 female); bill 13-17 (mean 15.7, SD 0.81, 6 males), 15 (1 female); **tarsus** 15-17 (mean 16, SD 0.63, 6 males), 16 (1 female); **mass** 10.5-11.9 (mean 10.7, SD 0.41, 11 males).

REFERENCES Collar & Stuart (1985), Collar *et al.* (1994), Evans (1997), Hipkiss *et al.* (1994), P. J. Jones (pers. comm.), Moreau (1944), Moreau & Moreau (1937), Seddon *et al.* (1999), Stuart & Hutton (1977).

HEDYDIPNA

Hedydipna Cabanis 1851 *Mus. Hein.*, 1, p. 101. Type by original designation *Cinnyris platurus* Vieillot.

Four species of small sunbirds with short, nearly straight, stubby bills, broad at base. Curvature of bill starts at base. Tongue narrow and flat for about 75% of length, with edges rolled inwards to form two tubes. Distal 25% bifid, forming two complete tubes, with inner edges fimbriated (Figure 7a). Males of two species short-tailed, others with elongated central rectrices.

63   COLLARED SUNBIRD
Hedydipna collaris   Plate 17

Cinnyris collaris Vieillot, 1819, *Nouv. Dict. Hist. Nat.*, nouv. éd., 31, p.502, Gamtoos River, Cape Province, South Africa.

IDENTIFICATION Small sunbird with bright metallic green upperparts, male with similarly coloured chin and throat, purple breast-band and bright yellow or orange-yellow belly. Underparts of female all yellow. Bill short, stout and only slightly decurved.
Similar species Male Pygmy Sunbird *Hedydipna platura* (64)

similar to male *H. collaris* but has elongated tail, coppery-green upperparts, shorter, finer bill, violet uppertail-coverts and no breast-band. Female *H. collaris* separable from male *H. platura* by short tail and yellow not metallic green throat. Variable Sunbird *Cinnyris venustus* (134) also has yellow belly and metallic green upperparts but with longer, finer, more decurved bill, much more extensive purple area on breast, and orange and red pectoral tufts; female brown not grey above. Male Northern Double-collared Sunbird *Anthreptes reichenowi* (108) is superficially similar but has dark blue, not green, throat bordered on either side by yellow, the green being less intense and yellow underparts duller. Green Sunbird *A. rectirostris* (61) has grey not yellow belly. Juvenile Collared (race *sub-collaris*) is mostly plain olive-green above, not metallic apart from shoulder-patch, and before it gains yellow underparts it can be confused with the larger Green Hylia *Hylia prasina* and with both the Little Green Sunbird *A. seimundi* (60) and Bates's Sunbird *Cinnyris batesi* (137); both separable by lack of metallic shoulder-patch and *C. batesi* has longer, more curved bill.

VOICE Call Varied. Male's usual call is a loud *tsweet-tsweet*, or *tseet-tseet*, or *tserp-tserp*, or *cherreee* or *tsewrew*; also has a high-pitched *chi-chi* in courtship and a repeated *tsk-tsk* in flight between food-plants. An incessant twittering chirp and squeaks similar to calls of cordonbleus *Uraeginthus* spp. Race *subcollaris*: *see-suuu*. Alarm call: *seep seep seep*. Race *elachior*: alarm call a high-pitched trisyllabic *pur-su-ee*, contact call a rising *dreee*. **Song** Race *elachior*: a short sequence of clear whistling *tsee-ou* notes, sometimes following an introductory tw-note *dzer-dzer*, recalls incantation of "busy-busy-busy...busy"; *collaris* or ?*zuluensis* in South Africa: also introduced by *dzer* but sequence deeper and more like *chip-chip-chip...chip*. Repetitions of *chirreee*; *tseep, t,t,t,t,t; twirree, twirree, ee, ee*, a drawn-out *chwrr,r,r,r,r,r,ee*. Female also sings, even from nest; *subcollaris*: high-pitched *tsi-tsu-tsu-tsu-tsi-tsu-tsu-tsu-tsu-tsi* interspersed between single notes.

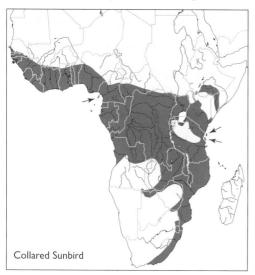

Collared Sunbird

DISTRIBUTION Sub-Saharan Africa. Recorded from Senegal, Gambia, Guinea-Bissau, Guinea, Sierra Leone, Liberia, Côte d'Ivoire, Ghana, Togo, Benin, Nigeria, Mali, Burkina Faso, Sudan, Ethiopia, Somalia, Equatorial Guinea including Bioko, Cameroon, Central African Republic, Gabon, Republic of the Congo, Democratic Republic of the Congo, Rwanda, Burundi, Uganda, Kenya, Tanzania including Zanzibar, Mafia island and Pemba, Angola, Zambia, Malawi, Mozambique, Namibia, Botswana, Zimbabwe, Swaziland and South Africa.

HABITAT Occurs in many habitats including primary forest, secondary forest, gallery forest, coastal forest, coffee plantations and swamps, but prefers open areas such as forest edges, clearings, roadsides in forests, savanna, woodland including *Brachystegia* and *Uapaca zanzibarica* formations, thickets from coast to mountains, inselbergs, riversides, open bush, cultivations, gardens, cocoa and *Eucalyptus* plantations. Occurs up to 2,600 m in Burundi, 2,400 m in Uganda, 1,600 m in Liberia and 1,200 m on Bioko.

STATUS Common and widespread resident throughout most of its range but mostly at coast in Senegal and Gambia, where it has become commoner since 1980s. Common widespread resident in Ghana, Togo and Nigeria. Widespread and common in Equatorial Guinea. Common in Gabon, where 1 pair per hectare. Common in extreme south of Sudan. Common in Democratic Republic of the Congo. Locally very common, Somalia. Common in moister regions of Uganda. Common in Malawi but absent from Nkata Bay District. Common and widespread in Zambia. Common in most of Burundi. Abundant Zanzibar.

MOVEMENTS Mainly sedentary, with ringing recoveries up to 7 km from marking location. However, some local wandering in search of nectar sources, and may undergo some altitudinal movements, e.g. in Drakensberg Mountains of South Africa.

FOOD Searches actively for insects by leaf-gleaning in trees, e.g. in *Acacia* sp. in the manner of a warbler or tit, but occasionally makes sallying flights to catch insects in the air or hover in front of flowers. Food mostly insects (adults and larvae, including ones 2 cm long, which may be struck against a perch before being swallowed, ant pupae, termites), small spiders, small snails, small seeds, small fruits e.g. of *Macaranga* sp., *Rauwolfia* sp., *Tetrorchidium didymostemon* and berries including those of *Alchornea cordifolia* (Euphorbiaceae). Attracted to sweet liquid exudate from exit-holes of fig-wasp *Elisabethiella baijnathi* in figs of *Ficus burtt-daveyi*.

Known food-plants *Acacia abyssinica, Achyrospermum carvalhi, Acrocarpus fraxinifolius, Albizia* sp., *Alchornea cordifolia* (seeds up to 8.5 mm long), *Aloe* sp., *Anthocleista* sp, *Berlinia grandiflora, Burchellia bubalina, Caesalpinia pulcherrima, Catunaregam* sp., *Chrysanthemoides* sp. (berries), *Clematis simensis, Clerodendrum johnstonii, Combretum paniculatum, Dombeya goetzenii, Englerina woodfordiodes, Erythrina* sp., *Eucalyptus* sp., *Faurea saligna, Ficus burtt-daveyi, Fuchsia* sp., *Gouania* sp., *Grevillea banksii, Grewia similis, Halleria lucida, Helinus mystacinus, Hibiscus* sp., *Kalanchoe* sp., *Lantana* sp., *Leonotis mollissima, L. nepetifolia, Leucas densiflora*, fruits of *Macaranga* sp., *Macrorungia pubinervis, Mimusops caffra*, fruits of *Ochthocosmus africanus, Petrea nobilis*, fruits of *Rauwolfia* sp., *Ruspolia hypocrateriformis, Salvia* sp., *Schotia speciosa, Stereospermum* sp., *Strelitzia nicolai, Symphonia globulifera, Tecoma capensis, Tetrorchidium didymostemon, Trema orientalis* (berries), *Triumfetta macrophylla*, arils of *Xylopia aethiopica* and various unidentified mistletoes Loranthaceae.

HABITS Occurs in pairs or small family groups (4-6 birds) and often a member of mixed-species groups. In West Africa, sometimes associates with Scarlet-chested Sunbird *Chalcomitra senegalensis* (85), Buff-throated Sunbird *C. adelberti* (81), *Anthreptes seimundi*, *A. rectirostris*, Blue-throated Brown Sunbird *Cyanomitra cyanolaema* (75) and Johanna's Sunbird *Cinnyris johannae* (129). In southern Africa, associates with *C. venustus*, Amethyst Sunbird *Chalcomitra amethystina* (84, *C. senegalensis*, Mouse-coloured Sunbird *Cyanomitra veroxii* (80), Western Violet-backed Sunbird *A. longuemarei* (56), Greater Double-collared Sunbird *Cinnyris afer* (109), Malachite Sunbird *Nectarinia famosa* (97), Cape Batis *Batis capensis*, white-eyes *Zosterops* sp., Yellow-throated Seicercus *Seicercus atricapillus* and Bleating Bush-warbler *Camaroptera brachyura*. Often forages in low bushes and overgrown areas at edges of clearings or plantations, but also feeds on creepers on forest trees and high up in canopy. Vertical foraging range in Liberia 1-25 m. Sometimes hangs upside-down to feed. Territorial, sings from vantage points, e.g. top of *Thevetia* sp. bush. Will attack its reflection in windows and known to enter houses to feed on cut flowers. Sometimes aggressive: male pecked female Eastern Double-collared Sunbird *Cinnyris mediocris* (112) in same feeding tree (*Dombeya goetzenii*). Known to indulge in active anting, picking up black ants from twigs and placing them under their wings whilst perched in a *Herria reticulata* shrub. Such behaviour may involve up to 3 birds at a time, last 10 minutes, and include shivering with wings out in apparent ecstasy, followed by "shower-baths" as the birds knock dew-drops off leaves onto their wings and mantle whilst poking at the ants with their bills, ruffling their plumage and shaking the moisture onto it. Reduces metabolism at night by 39% at constant ambient temperature of 5°C and by 61-65% at 25°C. Maximum longevity 11 years. Host to *Haemoproteus sequeirae*, *Leucocytozoon nectariniae*, *Nuttalia* sp., *Plasmodium vaughani* and *Trypanosoma avium*.

BREEDING Territorial. Males chase each other flicking wings audibly. Male courtship display involves bending slightly forwards, jumping alternately 40 degrees to the bird's left and then 40 degrees to the right of its starting point, whilst continuously flapping its wings up and down and calling *chi-chi*. May display to more than one female, which respond with *chi-chi* calls. There are other records of a male with at least three females, but may also be polyandrous, as group of three (two males and a female) seen associating together before one male chased the female and pecked vigorously at its cloaca. The behaviour was repeated several times with the female behaving as if soliciting by raising its vent and fluttering its wings (P. J. Jones, Kibale, Uganda). Males also chase females in weaving flights. Incubation period 17-19 days. Only female builds, but often accompanied by male. Building may take only 1.5 days, but a week more usual. Usually only female incubates but male sometimes does so (van Someren 1956). Only female broods, but may be fed at nest by male. Nestling period 14-16 days. Both parents feed nestlings but female does most. Young recorded taken from nest by monkeys. Family groups still together 2 weeks after fledging. Occasionally double-brooded. Begging young make repetitive *dree-didlee-dree-didlee* calls. Parasitised by Klaas's Cuckoo *Chrysococcyx klaas* and seen feeding young Red-chested Cuckoo *Cuculus solitarius* but this bird was also fed by Fischer's Slaty Flycatcher *Dioptrornis fischeri*. **Nest** A neat ovoid pear-shaped structure of grass e.g. *Panicum*

maximum and fibres including *Marismius*, dead leaves, leaf mould, spiders' nests or webs, twigs, rootlets, asparagus tendrils, held together with cobwebs, sometimes decorated with lichen, bark, seeds or flowers. Lined with vegetable down, mostly kapok or fibres of *Galopina* sp., or horsehair, feathers or rootlets. Entrance hole at the side with pronounced porch projecting 30 mm above and also slightly down edges of entrance, made as a continuation of nest itself rather than just tufts of grass seed-heads tucked in. Beard of dead leaves and cobwebs. Suspended from branch 2-8 m above ground, or on cactus *Cereus* sp. or from rope in disused room, sometimes close to nest of pugnacious social wasp. 90-165 mm high; 55-76 mm wide; 65-88 mm deep; diameter of entrance 25-45 mm, situated 40 mm below apex. Race *elachior*: 1 m up in small mangrove tree at shore edge; 2 m up from drooping branch in tree, 5-6 m up in small tree in thick undergrowth among coconut palms; 7-8 m up on bough of forest tree. Two within 10 cm of hornet's or wasp's nests, the latter built before the sunbird's nest. Sometimes in houses, e.g. in rafter in bedroom. Ellipsoid. Entrance 30 mm in diameter, no porch, no beard. Made of fibre, grass-heads, tiny flower-heads, leaves, plant stems held together with gossamer. Lined with thick felt of cotton-grass down. 82 mm long, 52 mm wide, greatest antero-posterior measurement 64 mm. Race *garguensis*: 90 mm long with 75 mm long beard, made of dry grass, fibres, bark, silk and lined with pappus; one, 2,000 m up in Ruwenzoris, amongst leaves of *Lobelia gibberoa*. Race *somereni*: 90 x 90 mm, suspended under a branch 1.5-8 m high, once under web of spider *Agelena consociata*. **Eggs** c/1-4. Race *collaris*: 15-16.9 (mean 15.7, n=11) x 10.7-11.3 (mean 11), white to cream, variably marked with dark olive and grey, generally denser at broad end; *elachior*: blunt ovate, smooth and slightly glossy. White ground colour, tinged pinkish-brown with handsome markings of blotches, suffusions, irregular lines and speckles in various shades of brown. Pale ashy-grey secondary blotches concentrated at larger pole. 15.0-15.3 (mean 15.1, n=3) x 11.4-11.5 (mean 11.4); *garguensis*: 14.0-16.0 (mean 15, n=4) x 10.9-11.1 (mean 11) bluish-white spotted with brown and grey; *somereni* c/1-2. 14.4-14.6 (n=2) x 10.5-11.0; whitish background, liberally marked with fine brown lines and spots or clear green with little brown mottles at larger end or pale reddish with denser red marks at wider end; *subcollaris*: 15.4-17.5 (mean 16.4) x 11.5-12.1 (mean 11.8); ovate with background of white, greyish-green, light brown, light green or pale blue, with slight gloss, marked with black specks and thin lines and scrawls, forming a ring at larger pole. *zambesiana*: 15 x 11 (n=2); *zuluensis*: colour as *collaris*, 15.6-16.7 (mean 16.0, n=3) x 11-11.2 (mean 11.1). **Laying months** Angola: May and October; Benin: December; Botswana: June, October. Cameroon: January–June, October–December; Republic of the Congo: September–November; Côte d'Ivoire: building July, December, dependent young March, May–September and December; Democratic Republic of the Congo: January, September (*somereni*), August (*garguensis*); East Africa: January–December; Gambia: October; Ghana: July, November, dependent young February, April, July, August, November, December, nest-building March, April, June, October; Gabon: November–April, July, dependent young January, September; Kenya: January, May (*garguensis*), July, August (*elachior*), November; Liberia: all months, peak October–April; Malawi: September–May, September, October; Mozambique: March–May; Nigeria:

January, April, July, September, October, December; Senegal: December; Somalia: December; South Africa: September–February (*collaris*); November (*zuluensis*); Togo: March, September; Uganda: March, May, June, September (*garguensis*); Zambia: January, March–April, August–September, December; Zanzibar: April–November; Zimbabwe: September–January, April–May. Adults in middle stages of wing moult (primaries 5-7 growing), Liberia, March, May and November.

DESCRIPTION *H. c. subcollaris*
Adult male Head, neck, chin, throat, back and rump metallic golden-green, uppertail-coverts more bluish. Wings brown, remiges and greater coverts with yellowish-olive margins. Lesser wing-coverts metallic green. Tail glossy purplish-blue, outer pair of rectrices browner and all with metallic green edges to outerwebs. Breast-band of purple between metallic green throat and bright yellow breast and belly. Yellow pectoral tufts. Flanks and thighs greenish-olive. Undertail-coverts yellow. Underwing-coverts white with yellow streaks. Axillaries yellow. Iris dark brown. Bill and feet black or greenish-black.
Adult female Distinguished from male by white chin, throat pale yellow not metallic green, and rest of underparts also pale yellow without purple breast-band. Bill and feet black.
Juvenile Nestlings have black down, with iridescent green on head and mantle. Newly fledged young have feathers of head grey, tipped olive; forehead usually bright olive, later with faint metallic green sheen, crown and nape greyer, lores grey, cheeks and sides of throat yellow-olive; prominent yellow streak above eye and less prominent one below, the two almost meeting behind. Back, wings and uppertail-coverts bright olive, tail brown edged olive. Metallic patch on shoulders (c.0.5 cm in diameter on example from Abidjan, October). Chin, throat and upper breast pale grey-white merging into clear pale yellow on belly. Undertail yellow-olive. Lower mandible horn or pinkish-horn, upper mandible dark grey. Iris dark, legs black. Belly becomes yellow before chin.

GEOGRAPHICAL VARIATION The greatly reduced amount of metallic plumage on juvenile *H. c. subcollaris*, and the presence of metallic plumage on even the nestlings of *H. c. somereni* (Chapin 1954), led Field (1971) to suggest that *subcollaris* should be given specific rank. Bannerman (1921b) had previously split *H. collaris* into two species (*Anthreptes hypodila* and *A. collaris*) on the same basis, supported by the presence of the metallic green edging on the remiges and wing-coverts of *A. collaris*. *A. hypodila subcollaris*, *A. h. hypodila* and *A. h. zambesiana* were quoted as having young birds without metallic plumage until after the first moult. Further research is required to establish the amount of metallic feathering on nestlings and juveniles of the other races to see if they indeed split into natural groups.
　　H. c. collaris (Vieillot, 1819) (eastern Cape Province from Knysa to south KwaZulu-Natal, South Africa) Males with green edges to wing-coverts and inner secondaries; purple breast-band narrow; dusky olive wash on sides; females with dusky olive throat.
　　H. c. djamdjamensis (Benson, 1942) (restricted to the Alghe and Sagan river area of south-west Ethiopia) Similar to *zambesiana* but males brighter yellow below; females much yellower below than *elachior* and richer yellow than *zambesiana* with deep yellow extending to lower throat.

H. c. elachior (Mearns, 1910) (includes *jubaensis* [van Someren, 1932]) (Zanzibar; coastal East Africa including Lamu island from Dar-es-Salaam to Juba area in Sudan, south of 4°N in Somalia, inland as far as Kilosa, Moshi and the Kenya highlands) Underside, particularly of females, paler than *zambesiana*.
H. c. garguensis (Mearns, 1915) (includes *ugandae* [van Someren, 1921] and *philipsi* [White, 1950]) (western Kenya, Uganda, southern Sudan east of the Nile, Rwanda, Burundi, Kivu, western Tanzania from Mondoli to Rukwa, Katanga, Zambia except in range of *zambesiana* and south as far as Ngoma, Angola from Alto Zambesi to Vila Luso and Malange) Male has underside deep yellow with flanks tinged greener than in *zambesiana*; female has throat to chest olive-grey with dusky green flanks.
H. c. hypodila (Jardine, 1851) (Bioko) Differs from *subcollaris* by less brilliant metallic parts and duller yellow below.
H. c. somereni (Chapin, 1949) (south-east Nigeria at coast near Calabar, Cameroon to Cabinda, north-west Angola south to Cuanza Norte and along the escarpment to Cuanza Sul; northern Democratic Republic of the Congo except Katanga, south-west Sudan west of the Nile) Underparts palest and dullest yellow of all races, flanks dusky olive; female with dusky yellow throat. Nestlings and juveniles with metallic plumage.
H. c. subcollaris (Hartlaub, 1857) (includes *nigeriae* to which less richly coloured inland birds were formerly assigned [White, 1950]) (Senegal and Guinea-Bissau to Benin and coastal Nigeria as far as Niger delta). Described above.
H. c. zambesiana (Shelley, 1880) (includes *chobiensis* [Roberts, 1932]) (Angola from northern Malanje east to Moxico, Lunda Norte and possibly north-western Lunda Sul; southern Democratic Republic of the Congo, Zambia [Eastern Province, Luangwa and Middle Zambezi valleys and upstream to Barotse Province and along the River Kafue], Zimbabwe [Zambezi valley to Victoria Falls, Ngamiland and south Barotseland], south-western Tanzania, Zanzibar, Mafia island, Malawi, Mozambique and Botswana) Males with secondaries edged yellowish, wing-coverts with little or no green on margins; underparts deep yellow with little or no olive on flanks. Females purer yellow than *zuluensis*. Gape yellow for first three months, becoming black later.
H. c. zuluensis (Roberts, 1931) (includes *patersonae* [Irwin, 1960] and *beverlyae* [Irwin, 1961]) (north-eastern KwaZulu-Natal, eastern Swaziland, eastern Transvaal lowveld, southern Mozambique north to Gorongoza, Limpopo valley and eastern highlands of Zimbabwe) Secondaries edged yellow and, compared to nominate, wing-coverts with narrower green edges in males which are purer yellow below with greenish suffusion on flanks. Flight feathers as in *zambesiana*.

MEASUREMENTS Wing 50-55 (mean 52.9, 10 male *collaris*), 49-55 (mean 51.3, 11 male *elachior*), 54-57 (mean 54.9, 17 male *garguensis*), 51-55 (27 male *hypodila*), 52-55 (mean 53.7, 10 male *somereni*), 47-53 (mean 50.8, SD 1.4, 10 male *subcollaris*), 46.0-57.0 (mean 51.4, SD 1.1, 26 male *zambesiana*), 48-52 (mean 49.4, 10 female *collaris*), 50 (female *elachior*), 49-53 (mean 50.9, 10 female *garguensis*), 48-52 (13 female *hypodila*), 46-51 (mean 48.8, SD 1.5, 10 female *subcollaris*), 46-53.0 (mean 48.5, SD 1.2, 16 female *zambesiana*, significantly shorter than males, P<0.001); **tail** 33-41 (mean 36.2, 10 male *collaris*), 40 (male *garguensis*), 28-33 (27 male *hypodila*), 30-34 (mean 30.3, SD 2.4, 10 male *subcollaris*), 30.5-43.0 (male *zambesiana*), 32-36 (mean 33.9, 10 female *collaris*), 27-32 (13 female *hypodila*), 25-29 (mean 27, SD 1.1, 10 female *subcollaris*), 31.0-37.0 (female *zambesiana*); **culmen** 13.0-17.0 (unsexed *zambesiana*); **bill** 14-16 (mean 14.9, 10 male *collaris*), 16-17 (2 male *garguensis*), 13-14.5 (27 male *hypodila*), 15-16 (mean 15.6, 10 male *somereni*), 13-15 (mean 16, 10 male *subcollaris*), 13-15 (mean 14.7, 10 female *collaris*), 12-14 (13 female *hypodila*), 13-16 (mean 15.9, SD 0.3, 10 female *subcollaris*); **tarsus** 16-17 (mean 16.3, 10 male *collaris*), 16 (male *garguensis*), 15-16 (27 male *hypodila*), 15-16 (31 male *subcollaris*), 16-17 (mean 16, 10 female *collaris*), 15-16 (13 female *hypodila*), 15-16 (13 female *subcollaris*), 14.0-18.0 (unsexed *zambesiana*); **mass** 6.3-11.0 (mean 7.8, 28 male *collaris*), 5.3-8.0 (mean 6.7, 25 male *elachior*), 6.2-9.3 (mean 7.9, 18 male *garguensis*), 7.0 (male *somereni*), 7.0-8.5 (mean 7.4, SD 0.8, 10 male *subcollaris*), 6.3-9.4 (mean 7.4, SD 0.5, 28 male *zambesiana*), 7.5-9.4 (mean 8.3, 24 male *zuluensis*), 5.8-9.7 (mean 7.4, SD 0.67, 15 female *collaris*), 5.4-8.5 (mean 6.4, 17 female *elachior*), 7.3-9.1 (mean 8.1, 15 female *garguensis*, one bird 7.9 on first capture, 9.1 36 months later), 7.0 (female *somereni*), 6.5-7.5 (mean 7.0, SD 0.7, 10 female *subcollaris*), 5.8-9.7 (mean 6.9, SD 0.5, 20 female *zambesiana*, significantly lighter than males, P<0.01), 6.5-8.3 (mean 7.4, 14 female *zuluensis*).

REFERENCES Alexander (1995b), Bannerman (1921b, 1948), Barlow *et al.* (1997), Blackwell & Wells (1965), Britton & Britton (1977), Brosset & Erard (1986), Cheke (1971a), Colston & Curry-Lindahl (1986), Field (1971), Fry *et al.* 2000), Hanmer (1981, 1997), Irwin (1961), Pérez del Val (1996), Prinzinger *et al.* (1989), Prinzinger & Jackel (1986), Serle (1943), Sevastopulo (1980a,b), Skead (1962, 1967), Sykes (1984), Tree (1997l).

---

64 PYGMY SUNBIRD
Hedydipna platura   **Plate 17**

Cinnyris platurus Vieillot, 1819, *Nouv. Dict. Hist. Nat.*, nouv. éd., 31, p.501, Senegal.

Alternative name: Pygmy Long-tailed Sunbird

IDENTIFICATION Adult males in breeding plumage easily distinguished by small size, short bill, long tail, metallic green upperparts and bright yellow below; wings dark brown. Female pale brown above, yellow below and without streamers. Non-breeding birds of both sexes and immatures grey-brown above, yellow and white below with pale supercilium. Some non-breeding males have green-black bib.
Similar species Confusion with male Beautiful Sunbird *Cinnyris pulchellus* (115) possible if underparts or bill not seen: bill is much shorter (9-11 vs 15 mm) and straighter than in *pulchellus*, which has yellow only on pectoral tufts. Nile Valley Sunbird *Hedydipna metallica* (65) is mostly or entirely allopatric (some overlap reported but not confirmed at Ennedi, north-east Chad, where *metallica* breeds, and overlaps also in Sungikai and Rashad areas of Kordofan, Sudan) but males separable principally by bluish-purple band between green and yellow of breast on

metallica, the metallic plumage of which has only slight violet tinge, less coppery. Females very similar but *platura* tends to have less pronounced supercilium. Male *platura* without streamers also confusable with Collared Sunbird *H. collaris* (63), but latter has emerald not coppery-green upperparts, bluish-green uppertail-coverts, longer bill and violet breast-band.

VOICE Call *Twee* or *twee-weet* or *tsuup-tsuup-tsuup* or *tsei*. Female utters *cheek* when nest-building and male makes shrill chirps from nearby perch on approach to and departure from nest. Contact call by male *cheek-cheek*. **Song** Recalls feeble Skylark *Alauda arvensis*: complex sequence lasting 3-4 seconds repeated after short (10-second) intervals involving phrases such *pseu-pseu-pseu-der-dzer-dzer, tsi-tsi-tsi, pser-eee* and some trilling. Variations include sequences such as *pserr-pserr-pserr, tseu-i, ti-ti-ti-ti-ti-ti, pserr-pserr, pser-eu*; songs with a trill followed by *pserr* repeated as many as 8 times or the *tseep* call repeated 10 times in succession.

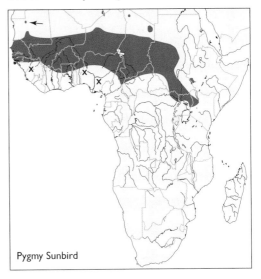

Pygmy Sunbird

DISTRIBUTION Sub-Saharan Africa from Senegal to north-west Kenya, generally as far north as 17°N, but isolated populations north of 20°N in Chad and Mauritania. Recorded from Senegal, Gambia, Guinea-Bissau, Guinea, Sierra Leone, Côte d'Ivoire, Ghana, Togo, Benin, Nigeria, Mauritania, Mali, Burkina Faso, Niger, Chad, Sudan, Ethiopia, Cameroon, Central African Republic, Democratic Republic of the Congo, Uganda and Kenya.

HABITAT Dry savannas from Sahel zone to Northern Guinea savanna. Found in acacia woodland, thorn scrub, savanna woodland and gardens.

STATUS Widespread and common in suitable habitat. Common in Senegal, except in north. Uncommon Mauritania, where reaches beyond 17°N up to the Adrar region. Not uncommon in Togo, November–April. Common in Nigeria. Locally common in north of Uganda, mainly below 1,500 m. Fairly common in south and south-western Sudan.

MOVEMENTS Resident in north of range, e.g. Aïr in Niger, but partial migrant from there also. Birds move south during dry season to breed, e.g. some birds migrate from the Sahel south to breed in savanna areas of Ghana,

Togo and Nigeria (October–April, some occurring in northern Ghana as early as mid-August). In most of southern range, only a dry-season visitor, returning north with onset of rains, March–May. However, population in north-west Nigeria only present during rains, April–August, perhaps coming from south-west Niger where only present October–April. Birds breeding in Uelle, Democratic Republic of the Congo, late December–March, may be migrants from Sudan. Breeding visitor to north-west Uganda, October–March.

Before moving, may gather in loose pre-migratory flocks of 20-30 birds. In Mauritania moves in relation to flowering by unidentified Loranthaceae that parasitise *Acacia* spp.

FOOD Nectar, insects including larvae, ants and termites, e.g. *Pseudacanthotermes* cf. *militaris*, spiders, and flower parts including pollen and *Acacia* petals.
Known food-plants *Aloe* spp., *Acacia albida*, *Azadirachta indica*, *Balanites aegyptiaca*, *Bombax ceiba*, *B. costatum*, *Cassia sieberiana*, *Calotropis procera*, *Delonix regia*, *Dichrostachys glomerata*, *Erythrina senegalensis*, *Euphorbia pulcherrima*, *Ficus* sp., *Hibiscus* sp. including *H. sino-ornata*, unidentified mistletoes Loranthaceae parasitic on *Acacia* spp., *Jacaranda mimosifolia*, *Parkia clappertoniana*, fruiting *Salvadora* sp., *Pterocarpus erinaceus*, *Tapinanthus globiferus*, *Vitellaria paradoxum*, *Vitex doniana*.

HABITS Occurs singly, in pairs or family parties and amongst loose flocks of other sunbirds, warblers and white-eyes. Active and restless. Flicks wings. Flight rapid with whirring wing-beats, and frequent darting movements. May hang upside-down or hover in front of flowers to obtain nectar. Aggressive to other birds in breeding season. Host to *Haemoproteus* sp., *Trypanosoma* sp. and microfilariae.

BREEDING Territorial. Males sing from perch. Male display involves cocking tail and drooping wings and bowing to female. Nest construction and incubation by female, who seldom leaves the nest. Male may sing beside nest. May be 2 or more days between nest completion and laying. Incubation lasts about 14 days. Both parents feed the young in the nest, at intervals of 13 minutes (female) and 23 minutes (male), and after fledging. Male chirps several times from perch on way to and from feeding chicks in nest. Female cleans nest by removing pellets. Time between hatching and fledging 12-15 days. Occasionally double-brooded in same nest; second brood may fledge only 34 days after first. Nest sometimes in association with wasps. **Nest** Oval domed purse, attached firmly to branches, 1.5-4 m above ground, in body of *Acacia*, *Bougainvillea* or other thornbushes such as *Balanites aegyptiaca* or *Dichrostachys cinerea*, or in *Citrus* bush. Constructed of fine grass, cotton lint and small leaves bound together with cobwebs and cotton strands, occasionally with feathers as well. Decorated with dead leaves, seeds, caterpillar frass and cocoons. May be lined with fine vegetable down from seed-pods of *Calotropis procera*. Height of nest 85-100 mm, width 45-53 mm, maximum depth 62 mm. Entrance hole 30 mm in diameter, about 50 mm from base, with small porch 25 mm long. No hanging beard. **Eggs** c/1-2. White, glossy with fragile shell. 14.2-16.1 (mean 15.1, n=6) x 10.3-11.6 (mean 10.7). **Laying months** A dry-season breeder. East Africa: October, December. In much of West Africa at height of dry season; Burkina Faso: February–March; Cameroon: February; Democratic Republic of the Congo: February; Gambia: February–March, September; Mali: male displaying to female November; Mauritania: January–March and August–September; Niger: December; Nigeria: December–April; Senegal: February, March; Togo: February–March.

DESCRIPTION

Adult male All upperparts, including head, metallic green with bronze or coppery-red sheen, except rump and uppertail-coverts metallic purplish-blue. Lesser wing-coverts and outer margins of inner median and greater coverts also metallic green. Innerwebs of inner median and greater coverts black. Flight feathers dark brown with narrow grey-white fringes along parts, inner secondaries with blue sheen, tertials black edged glossy blue-green on outer edges and tips. Tail feathers black with steel-blue gloss, especially marked on central pair (elongated 55-80 mm beyond others with racquet-shaped broadening at tips. Chin, throat and upper breast metallic green with bronze sheen, rest of underparts, including thighs and undertail-coverts, bright yellow but flanks and undertail-coverts paler. Yellow sometimes demarcated from metallic green by thin violet line, but this never as extensive as in *H. metallica*. Yellow of lower breast and belly sometimes tinged orange. Axillaries black or greyish-black, intermixed with yellow, especially on shafts. Underwing-coverts and axillaries black or greyish-black. Iris black or dark brown. Short decurved black bill, legs and feet black. **Non-breeding plumage** Male moults long tail feathers immediately after breeding, occasionally while still feeding young. In West Africa, male in breeding plumage October–March and begins to lose it and enter eclipse plumage, April. In western Sudan and northern Kenya males in eclipse June and July. The eclipse plumage resembles that of adult female including rectrices and remiges, but metallic green on wing-coverts and black underwing-coverts and axillaries are retained, with some green sometimes also remaining on body and uppertail-coverts, and on throat to form bib. In worn plumage, reddish tinge of head and body is lost, green is duller, yellow paler and remiges browner. After breeding, adults have partial moult of head, body and upperwing-coverts, some or all of tertials and central tail feathers, sometimes all of tail. Pre-breeding moult involves primaries descendantly. This is unusual in that remiges and rectrices are moulted twice per annum, i.e. once into female-like non-breeding plumage and once into breeding plumage.

Adult female Lacks metallic plumage. Upperparts ash-brown with olive tinge on rump. Wings and back brown with wings and wing-coverts darker than back. Wing-coverts have paler brown margins. Rump pale greenish-yellow. Tertials with pale edges. Tail very dark brown, with dark blue gloss, outer margins of outermost pair edged pale. Broad pale buff stripe above eye. Ear-coverts darker than rest of head and tinged olive. Underparts and axillaries pale yellow, throat paler and flanks greener. Underwing-coverts white, inner ones pale yellow. Lores pale grey. Faint pale eye-ring. Iris brownish-black; bill, legs and feet black.

Juvenile Very young male indistinguishable from female until underparts become bright yellow, with deeper yellow feathers emerging on lower breast and abdomen and metallic green on lesser wing-coverts. After first moult, wings and tail are darker, shortly followed by appearance of metallic green feathers on throat and parts of crown, and metallic violet on rump. Immature female has grey-brown upperparts, off-white or greyish-white underparts washed greenish-yellow, occasionally with buff tinge. Eye-stripe yellowish, throat grey. Mouth flesh-coloured and inside of mandibles yellow. Iris blackish, bill dusky brown, feet dark greenish-grey. Post-juvenile moult partial, involving head, body, and lesser and median wing-coverts; sometimes may be complete.

GEOGRAPHICAL VARIATION None recognised but *H. p. adiabonensis* described from northern Ethiopia as being shorter-winged (Zedlitz 1910).

MEASUREMENTS Wing 52-60 (mean 58.5, 10 males); 53-57 (mean 54.5, 11 females); **tail** with elongations 91-113 (mean 99.7, 10 males); tail without elongations 32-37 (22 males), 31-35 (mean 33.2, 10 females); **bill** 9-13 (mean 12.2, 10 males), 10.8-12.5 (mean 11.8, 10 females); **tarsus** 13-17 (mean 13.7, 10 males); 12.8-14.6 (mean 13.5, 10 females); **mass** 6.0-7.5 (mean 6.8, 16 males), 6-7 (mean 6.4, 8 females), 5.7-7.0 (mean 6.7, 19 unsexed, Zaria, Nigeria).

REFERENCES Ash & Miskell (1983), Bannerman (1948), Bates (1927, 1934), Chapin (1954), Cramp & Perrins (1993), Fry *et al.* (2000), Korb & Salewski (2000), Mackworth-Praed & Grant (1945), Pettet (1977), Serle (1940), Skinner (1969), Thonnerieux *et al.* (1989), Walsh *et al.* (1990), Zedlitz (1910).

---

65 NILE VALLEY SUNBIRD
Hedydipna metallica Plate 17

Nectarinia metallica Lichtenstein, 1823, *Verz. Doubl. zool. Mus. Berlin* p.15, Dongola, Sudan.

Alternative name: Pygmy Sunbird

IDENTIFICATION Male in breeding plumage easily identified by long tail, metallic green upperparts and upper chest, where green is separated from yellow belly by purple band. Female dull grey above with whitish supercilium, pale yellow below.
Similar species Pygmy Sunbird *Hedydipna platura* (64) is mostly or entirely allopatric (some overlap reported but not confirmed at Ennedi, north-east Chad, where *H. metallica* reported to breed, and in Kordofan, Sudan) and slightly smaller, except wing. Male *platura* lacks violet breast-band; green of *metallica* much more emerald and greeny than *H. platura* without coppery tinge; female *platura* has less prominent supercilium and eye-stripe. Confusion of males without tail elongations with Collared Sunbird *H. collaris* (63) possible but *metallica* has violet on lower back and rump, unlike back of *collaris* which is uniform green.

VOICE Call *Tschi, peee, pee-ee* or *pee-e-ee, cheeit cheeit, tee-weee* with second note rising; contact call *pee*. **Song** High-pitched warble of trills, hisses and gurgles including *pruiit-prruiit-ptuiit-tiriririri-tiriniri*. A twittering subsong with chatters, trills and squeaks recalling cork rubbed jerkily on glass.

DISTRIBUTION North-east Africa and Arabia. Recorded from Egypt, Sudan, Chad, Ethiopia, Eritrea (migrant visitor), Djibouti, Somalia (migrant visitor), Saudi Arabia, Yemen and Oman.

HABITAT *Acacia* scrub and semi-desert. Arid lowlands, river valleys, gardens in irrigated areas. In Ethiopia, usually

below 1,200 m. Usually from sea-level to 1,600 m in Yemen but also up to 2,200 m. Landscaped areas of industrial city in Yanbu area, Saudi Arabia.

STATUS Common; locally abundant non-breeding visitor across all northern Somalia to east coast south to 9°N. In Egypt common in Nile Valley from Qena to Aswan. Fairly common in central and north-eastern Sudan except in extreme north-east. Abundant in Tihamah coastal plains of Saudi Arabia.

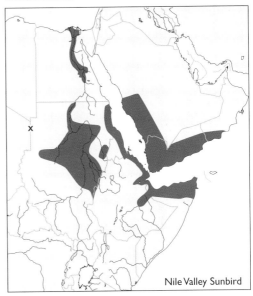

Nile Valley Sunbird

MOVEMENTS In Egypt, influx of winter visitors since 1980s, October–March, to Cairo area, where known to breed, and one record at Hungeda on Red Sea Coast, April 1990. Regular migrant in east Eritrea to coastal plains January–February when *Acacia* spp. bloom, until June. Non-breeding migrant to Somalia and east Ethiopia, September–May, perhaps involving birds from Arabia. Winter movements involve influxes north of Tropic of Cancer in Saudi Arabia, with birds arriving from mid-October; a group of 70 seen together in Saudi Arabia may have been migrating. Visits Oman, November–February.

FOOD Insects including aphids (Aphididae) taken from Cruciferae and *Duranta* sp., parts of flowers and nectar. Feeds by perching on plants and by hovering in front of flowers, as well as sallying for flying insects. Head often becomes covered in pollen. Nectar-robs flowers with long florets.
Known food-plants *Acacia* sp. (including parts of flowers of *A. nilotica*), *Althaea* sp., *Antirrhinum* sp., *Bauhinia* sp., *Bignonia* sp., *Bombax* sp., *Calotropis procera*, *Capparis* sp., *Carica papaya*, *Citrus* spp., *Clarkia* sp., *Euphorbia* sp., *Faidherbia* sp., *Hibiscus* sp., *Jacaranda* sp., *Justicia* sp., *Lantana camara*, unidentified mistletoes Loranthaceae, *Petunia* sp., *Rhazya stricta*, *Rorippa* sp., *Salvia* sp., *Tecoma* sp., *Trapeolum majus*, *Ziziphus* sp.

HABITS Restless but tame. Flicks wings and spreads tail or flicks it whilst making contact calls. Usually in pairs, but gregarious in non-breeding season, sometimes in parties of up to 30 at flowering *Bombax* sp. trees, and group of 70 recorded. Also associates with other species e.g.

203

Shining Sunbird *Cinnyris habessinicus* (127), Chiffchaff *Phylloscopus collybita* and Graceful Warbler *Prinia gracilis*. Gleans shoots, stems and leaves for insects. Wipes bill after feeding on insects but not after nectar-feeds. Seen bathing in early morning dew, Cairo. Subservient to Little Green Bee-eaters *Merops orientalis* hawking for insects at edge of tree.

BREEDING Territorial. Male sings from perch while flicking wings, spreading tail and shivering body to enhance plumage characters. Courtship display by male involves rocking body to and fro and turning head from side to side; initially passive female then joins in these dancing movements before copulation. Dancing hovering display-flight, with wings whirring and pair chasing each other, also reported. Both sexes assist with nest-building, taking about 12 days. Female only incubates. May be double-brooded. **Nest** Elongated, flask-shaped pouch with whole of back attached to branch, 2 m up in middle of tree or outer branches of *Acacia* sp. Made of plant down, wool and fibre, spider egg cases, small leaves, grass stems, rootlets, feathers, held together with cobwebs and lined with white down and feathers. Entrance hole one-third way down from top with porch. 120 x 50 mm. Another, Arabia, pendent from branch of *Salvadora persica*, 1.5 m above ground. One, Egypt, 2.2 m up in flowering shrub, included many nylon strings within its structure in addition to animal hair, wool, string of natural fibres, leaves, twigs and seed-pod. Others up to 5 m from ground, in forks or suspended from twig made of plant fibres, rootlets, dead leaves, flowers, feathers, plant down and seeds, bound with spiders' web, lined with down and feathers. Height 90-120 mm, width 50 mm, outer circumference 140-170 mm, entrance hole without porch 25 mm in diameter with base 54 mm above base of cup. **Eggs** c/1-3, perhaps 4 occasionally; subelliptical, smooth and glossy; white with pink flush when fresh, larger pole finely speckled rufous on larger grey marks; 15.0-19.0 (mean 16.9, n=12) x 11.0-12.0 (mean 11.5); weight 1.13g. **Laying months** Arabia: February–May; December, Diutu River. Egypt: in Cairo area, forms pairs October–March, starts singing December, and males in full breeding dress by February, territorial squabbles March and nest built by May with fledglings later in same month; also fledglings September; Eritrea: possibly January–July; Oman: May; Saudi Arabia: January–April; Sudan: January–November; Yemen: March–April, fledged young November.

DESCRIPTION

Adult male Bill short, decurved. Head, neck, mantle, scapulars, lesser and median wing-coverts and back dark metallic emerald with slight tinge of dark purplish-blue. Rump and uppertail-coverts dark glossy bluish-purple varying in colour with angle of light. Upper chest dark metallic emerald with dark purplish-blue band (sometimes very narrow or partly interrupted) across lower margin above bright yellow of rest of underparts, with paler flanks and white intermixed in undertail-coverts. Tail, with central pair of feathers elongated 49-72 mm beyond end of T2, black with dark metallic blue sheen, edges brighter, sometimes greenish. Remiges, tertials, primary coverts, greater upperwing-coverts and bastard wing black. Remiges with brown tinge especially on outer edges. Tertials with bluish gloss, greater coverts with metallic bluish-green edges. Axillaries and underwing-coverts matt black. Iris dark brown or black-brown. Bill, legs and feet black. **Non-breeding plumage** Male similar to adult female

but chin and centre of throat matt black, with slight gloss to some feather edges. Remiges, tertials and rectrices brownish-black with faint blue-green sheen, not brown as in adult female. Male first adult non-breeding plumage apparently lacks black on throat and so indistinguishable from female. Male in worn plumage has duller green, more bluish metallic feathering, more of black in centre of feathers showing, yellow underparts paler with undertail-coverts whitish; tail, tertials and greater upperwing-coverts matt black and remiges dark greyish-brown. Females in worn plumage lose yellowish-green sheen on upperparts, becoming uniform brownish-grey with supercilium and eye-stripe less obvious; underparts duller yellow, throat whitish, remiges and rectrices dark greyish-brown lacking white on edges; white spot on tip of innerweb of T6 mostly wears off. Adult post-breeding moult partial, involving head, body, T1 and some tertials and wing-coverts. Adult pre-breeding moult is complete with primaries lost descendantly. Unusual in that remiges and rectrices are moulted twice per annum, i.e. once into female-like non-breeding plumage and once into breeding plumage. Birds along Red Sea to Ethiopia, eastern Sudan and Somalia are in breeding plumage February–June, moult into eclipse plumage May–August and moult back into breeding dress, December–March.

Adult female Sides of neck and upperparts light brownish-grey with faint yellowish-green sheen to forehead and neck; rump and uppertail-coverts with broad yellowish-green edges. Supercilium yellow with light brown stripe from above lores through eye to ear-coverts. Underparts dull yellow, brighter on chest and centre of belly. Remiges dark brownish-grey with narrow whitish edges to tips and outerwebs except on outer primaries. Median and lesser coverts light brownish-grey, edged paler grey, other coverts and tertials darker grey, edged pale greyish-white. Central rectrices dark brownish-grey with thin white edges; T2-T5 black, also with thin white edges, T6 brownish-grey, innerweb with basal half black with white spot on tip, outerweb edged white. Axillaries dark grey-brown, underwing-coverts yellowish-white with greyish-brown bases.

Juvenile Upperparts pale greenish-grey, with faint yellowish-green on rump and forehead, ear-coverts darker. Lores pale grey; supercilium dull yellow. Underparts yellow, paler on chin, throat and cheeks. T2-T5 darker grey than in adult female and spot on tip of T6 less obvious. Remiges brownish-grey; outerwebs edged dull greenish, tips edged whitish; median and lesser coverts edged pale green.

GEOGRAPHICAL VARIATION None described.

MEASUREMENTS Wing 54-60 (mean 56.8, SD 1.32, 30 males), 51-56 (mean 53.8, SD 1.26, 13 females); tail with elongations 87-108 (mean 97.6, SD 5.26, 13 males), 30-37 (mean 33.5, SD 1.85, 13 females); **tail without elongations:** 36-41 (mean 38.1, SD 1.63, 14 males); **bill** 12.6-14.8 (mean 13.6, SD 0.60, 29 males), 12.1-14.0 (mean 13.2, SD 0.76, 13 females); **tarsus** 14.8-15.8 (mean 15.3, SD 0.30, 12 males), 14.3-15.3 (mean 14.6, SD 0.34, 11 females); **mass** 7.0-7.5 (mean 7.2, 3 males), 7 (female).

REFERENCES Baha el Din (1992), Cramp & Perrins (1993), Evans (1992), Evans & Dijkstra (1993), Jennings (1995), Mackworth-Praed & Grant (1945), Rahmani *et al.* (1994), Simmons & Hurrell (1951).

66   AMANI SUNBIRD
Hedydipna pallidigaster   Plate 16

Anthreptes pallidigaster Sclater and Moreau, 1935, *Bull. Br. Orn. Club* 56 p.17, Sigi valley, 4 miles east of Amani, north-eastern Tanganyika Territory [= Tanzania].

IDENTIFICATION A very small sunbird, frequenting tree-tops. Male has distinctive metallic blue-green head and back contrasting with white below. Female grey above with white supercilium, metallic grey-blue rump, wing-flash and sides of neck.
Similar species Male unmistakable but female could be confused with female Plain-backed Sunbird *Anthreptes reichenowi* (50), which is olive not grey above with yellowish not white underparts.

VOICE Call A loud *chip*, a soft *zee-eeeee*, and a loud *seer-seer*, followed by twittering flight note, easily recognisable. Also *seeeet-seeeet*. **Song** A very complex, barely audible, jingling, bubbly and bustling song, typical of sunbirds, consisting of a series of rising and falling high-pitched, very short, chirps, in an apparently chaotic delivery with few repetitions.

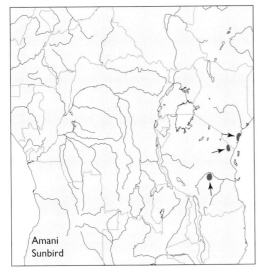

Amani
Sunbird

DISTRIBUTION Coastal south-east Kenya (Arabuko-Sokoke forest) and north-east Tanzania (in and near East Usambaras mountains and Ndundulu mountains, Udzungwas).

HABITAT Limited to coastal *Brachystegia* woodland in the Arabuko-Sokoke forest in Kenya and to the Udzungwa and East Usambaras mountains (up to 1,000 m on Mt Nilo) in Tanzania, where found in forest, at forest edges and in open secondary growth.

STATUS Vulnerable. 2,900-4,700 pairs (1 pair per 1.5-2.4 ha) estimated present in Sokoke forest in late 1970s. Only 320 km² of suitable habitat left in Usambaras.

MOVEMENTS Nomadic in response to flowering of preferred trees, wandering from miombo woodland into adjacent forest.

FOOD Spiders, lepidopteran larvae, and probably nectar.
Known food-plants *Erythrina* sp., *Grevillea* sp., unidentified mistletoes Loranthaceae.

HABITS Forages alone, in pairs, in groups of up to 60 at flowering trees or in mixed-species flocks, e.g. with fly-catchers, Black-headed Apalis *Apalis melanocephala* and *Anthreptes reichenowi yokanae*. Also with woodpeckers, drongos *Dicrurus* sp., weavers and *Cyanomitra olivacea* (78). Interacts aggressively with Collared Sunbird *H. collaris* (63). Gleans in canopy foliage 5-15 m above ground, often hanging upside-down like a tit *Parus* sp., and forages for insects in the air.

BREEDING Incubation by female only. Both sexes feed fledglings. **Nest** Like nest of *H. collaris* but 400 mm long including beard, with shroud of *Usnea* and distinct porch also of *Usnea*, suspended 7-14 m up in *Brachystegia spiciformis* tree. Made of fine grass-like fibres and small quantities of plant down. Well camouflaged, resembling bunch of lichen. **Eggs** c/3 (16.1 x 11.0; 15.7 x 11.0; 15.4 x 10.9 mm, all weighing 1 g each). Beige, heavily marked with brown, especially at rounded end. Numerous loosely scattered very dark brown, almost black spots, and some chocolate-brown markings up to 2 mm long, no streaks. **Laying months** March, May–June, September–October, December.

DESCRIPTION
Adult male Head to mantle dark iridescent purplish blue-green. Back and rump blackish. Uppertail-coverts and tail metallic purplish-blue. Centre of throat down to upper chest, within metallic part, dark purplish inky-blue border-ed with dark green; rest of underparts greyish-white. Pectoral tufts orange, yellow basally. Iris dark brown. Wings blackish-brown, lesser and median coverts and scapulars iridescent purplish blue-green. Underwing-coverts and axillaries white. Iris dark brown. Bill, legs and feet black.
Adult female Upperparts dark grey with slight metallic sheen. Metallic plumage on lesser and median coverts, sides of hind-neck and uppertail-coverts dull silvery green. Lores and cheeks blackish. White supercilium. Ear-coverts greyish-white. Underparts all white. Wing dark brown. Underwing-coverts white. Tail with white tips (1 mm broad) above and below. Bill black. Feet black. Juvenile like adult female but pale yellow wash on lower breast, belly and vent. White patch from above centre of eye to base of bill. Uppertail dark blue without white tips. Juvenile male with white throat tinged purplish.

GEOGRAPHICAL VARIATION Males in Ndundulu mountains brighter metallic blue, less greenish; may represent an undescribed subspecies (Dinesen *et al.* 1993).

MEASUREMENTS Wing 52-54 (mean 52.4, 11 males), 48-52 (mean 50.5, 6 females); **tail** 31-39.5 (mean 32.5, 11 males), 29.6-33 (mean 30.4, 6 females); **bill** 12-14 (mean 13.2, 11 males), 11.4-15 (mean 13.1, 6 females); **tarsus** 17.5-18.5 (mean 18.1, SD 0.58, 3 males), 16-18.5 (mean 16.9, 3 females); **mass** 6-7.2 (mean 6.4, 5 males), 6.6-8.0 (mean 7.4, 4 females).

REFERENCES Britton & Britton (1978), Collar & Stuart (1985), Collar *et al.* (1994), Dinesen *et al.* (1993), Hipkiss *et al.* (1994), Seddon *et al.* (1999), Stuart & Hutton (1977).

HYPOGRAMMA

Hypogramma Reichenbach 1853, *Handb. spec. Orn., Icon. Synops. Avium, Scansoriae, Tenuirostres,* continuatio no. XI, p. 314. Type by monotypy *Anthreptes nuchalis* Blyth = *Nectarinia hypogrammica* Müller.

One species, in tropical Asia. Medium-sized sunbird, somewhat babbler-like in behaviour. Longish bill, with curved culmen, but straight lower mandible. Sexes differ; male has tufts of elongated feathers at base of lower back and metallic nuchal patch, characters found in no other sunbird. Tongue quite unlike that of any other sunbird: rolled at edges to form two semi-tubes for much of its length. Distal 20% split centrally and inner edges deeply fimbriated, and each half split again for half that length, to form a quadrifid brush tip.

67   PURPLE-NAPED SUNBIRD
Hypogramma hypogrammicum Plate 17

Hypogramma hypogrammicum S. Müller, 1843, *Land. Volk.,* in Temminck, *Verh. Nat. Gesch. Nederland. Overz. Bezit.,* 1 (1839-1844), p.173, Sumatra and Borneo.

Alternative names: Blue-naped Sunbird, Banded Sunbird

IDENTIFICATION Adult male dark olive-green above with metallic purple or blue on nape, lower back, rump and uppertail-coverts; outer tail feathers tipped white; below white to olive-yellow boldly streaked dark olive. Adult female is smaller than male and lacks metallic coloration.
Similar species None.

VOICE Call Single, strident *schewp, tsit-tsit.* **Song** A high, strong *sweet sweet sweet, sweet, sweet.*

DISTRIBUTION Burma, Thailand, Laos, Vietnam, Cambodia, west Yunnan, peninsular Malaysia, Sumatra and Borneo, including North Natuna Islands.

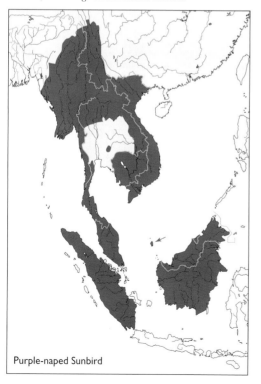

Purple-naped Sunbird

HABITAT All storeys, but most frequently in understorey, of primary and secondary forests, including freshwater swamp forest and heath forest, up to at least 1,160 m. Tall riverine swamps; tall secondary growth, older *Albizia* sp. plantations, overgrown rubber, open swamp, riparian forest. Often more numerous in recently logged forest, where the densities of small flowering plants are greater. Occasional in gardens.

STATUS Locally common on Borneo and Sumatra; uncommon in Thailand. Common in parts of southern Laos.

MOVEMENTS None known.

FOOD Nectar, fruits, seeds, insects including mosquitoes, spiders.
Known food-plants *Plagiostachys* spp. and other unidentified Zingiberaceae, wild plantains; fruits of *Callicarpa longifolia* and *Poikilospermum suaveolens*; *Dillenia excelsa* seeds.

HABITS Fans and flicks tail; usually forages low, from ground-level to 5 m. Often keeps in cover, but not particularly shy. Behaviour more reminiscent of a small babbler than a sunbird. Host to *Leucocytozoon* sp. and microfilariae.

BREEDING Nest One was pear-shaped, made of grass, rootlets, hair and bark, suspended from underside of plantain leaf. Another was a pendant ball, untidy, a little prolonged and very narrow at the top end, composed of scraps of bark, lichen, dry moss, leaves, bound with cobwebs and adorned with oddments hanging fluttering some 150 mm below bottom of nest. Lining of cotton down. No porch. Attached to betel palm over 6 m from ground. **Eggs** c/2-3; 18.0 x 13.0-13.2, n=2); whitish, with a lilac-grey suffusion over most of egg, heavier in places; dark grey and black scribblings, and irregular blotching, more prominent at broad end. **Laying months** Peninsular Malaysia: building March; juveniles January–October; Sabah: nest-building January, active gonads January–March, May–August, November, December; South Borneo: Sarawak, Kuching, August, juvenile August.

DESCRIPTION *H. h. hypogrammicum*
Adult male Upperparts dark olive-green; metallic purple-blue band on nape, lower back, rump and uppertail-coverts; underparts greyish-white on throat becoming olive-yellow on belly, dark olive-green on vent and either olive-yellow or yellow on undertail-coverts; throat, breast and upper belly streaked dark olive; tail dark olive, outer feathers tipped white. Iris red or brown, bill black or brownish-black, feet brown, brownish-green or olive.
Adult female As male, but smaller and lacks metallic colouring.
Juvenile Unrecorded.

H. h. hypogrammicum S. Müller, 1843 (Sumatra, Borneo) Described above.

H. h. lisettae (Delacour & Jabouille, 1926) (northern Burma, northern Thailand, north and central Indochina, west Yunnan) Gloss of male is distinctly purple, and collar narrower than in most nominate. Undertail-coverts brighter yellow than nominate; ground colour of breast and abdomen paler yellow, and no white shows through metallic blue of rump.

H. h. mariae (Ripley, 1959) (Cambodia, south Indochina) Bill longer than in nominate or *nuchale*, and equal to that of *lisettae*. Differs from *lisettae* and *nuchale* in having upper surface of central rectrices black narrowly edged olive-green; all except central rectrices broadly tipped beneath with white as in *nuchale* and *natunensis*, thus differing from nominate (narrowly tipped white) and *lisettae* (tipped yellowish-white). Underparts less yellow than any other form.

H. h. natunense (Chasen, 1935) (North Natuna Islands) Similar to *nuchale* but bill larger and throat more finely marked.

H. h. nuchale (Blyth, 1843) (southern Burma, southern Thailand, peninsular Malaysia) Gloss of male more purple and less blue than in nominate.

MEASUREMENTS Wing 66-71 (mean 68.4, 16 male *hypogrammicum*, Borneo), 63-67 (male *lisettae*), 61-70 (mean 65.5 9 male *nuchale*), 61-67 (mean 63.5, 13 female *hypogrammicum*, Borneo), 61 (female *lisettae*), 60-64 (mean 62.7, 3 female *nuchale*), 66.7-68 (unsexed *natunensis*); **tail** 50-53 (male *lisettae*), 47 (female *lisettae*), 50 (unsexed *natunensis*); **bill** 25 (male *hypogrammicum*, Borneo); **culmen** 21-22 (male *lisettae*), 21 female *lisettae*), 18.1 (unsexed *natunensis*); **gape** 20.0-26.2 (mean 23.1, 14 male *hypogrammicum*, Borneo), 19.0-23.9 (mean 22.6, 11 female *hypogrammicum*, Borneo), 23 (unsexed *natunensis*); **mass** 9.8-15.2 (mean 12.6, 16 male *hypogrammicum*, Borneo), 7.8-12.3 (mean 10.4, 9 male *nuchale*), 10.0-13.5 (mean 11.7, 21 female *hypogrammicum*, Borneo), 9.7-12.8 (mean 11.1, 3 female *nuchale*).

REFERENCES Duckworth & Kelsh (1988), Evans *et al.* (2000), Ford (1995), Gaither (1994), Lambert (1991), MacKinnon & Phillipps (1993), Mann (1996), Medway (1972), Medway & Wells (1976), Mitra & Sheldon (1993), Muller (1843), Nash & Nash (1988), Sheldon *et al.* (in press), Smythies (1999).

ANABATHMIS

Anabathmis Reichenow 1905 *Vog. Afr.*, 3, p. 467. Type by subsequent designation Sclater 1930 *Syst. Av. Aethiop.* p. 707 *Nectarinia reichenbachii* Hartlaub.

Two medium-sized and one small West African sunbirds, all with some iridescent bluish-violet plumage on chin and throat in males and on head in *A. reichenbachii*. Tails graduated with all except central pair tipped pale. Bill strong with curvature beginning at base, relatively shorter and finer than those of *Cyanomitra*. Island species sexually dimorphic, mainland species with sexes similar.

68   REICHENBACH'S SUNBIRD
Anabathmis reichenbachii   Plate 19

Nectarinia reichenbachii Hartlaub, 1857, *Syst. Orn. Westafr.*, p.50, Gabon

IDENTIFICATION Metallic steel-blue head and throat, contrasting with olive back and grey underparts in combination with yellow vent and pectoral tufts are distinctive. Dark centres and pale fringes to back and wings give scaly appearance. Immature has yellow below, brown on head and heavily marked underparts.
Similar species Blue-throated Brown Sunbird *Cyanomitra cyanolaema* (75) is similar but male has brown below the blue and is otherwise dull brown, lacking yellow; female has brown crown, white around eye, mottled throat and breast and is off-white below. Green-headed Sunbird *C. verticalis* (73) is larger, has a dark iridescent green hood, longer tail with white tips, lacks yellow below and is longer-billed, but call is similar. Cameroon Sunbird *Cyanomitra oritis* (76) is superficially similar but allopatric.

VOICE A very noisy bird. **Call** A disyllabic *chirr-up*, a plaintive *psi-ou* or *tewy-tewy* and *tchui tchui tchu-ih, tchu-ih, tiyi, tiyi*. **Song** Complex high-pitched jangling, continuing for a minute or more, including sequence *tser-pit-too-tu-wee* repeated amongst variations of *witssooo* and *weee*, trills, slurs and whistles. A variation includes *tser-pert-ta-tee* repeated

3-4 times in quick succession at intervals of 3-4 seconds, sometimes with a chirping *tsee-tsoo* end sequence.

DISTRIBUTION West and Central Africa. Liberia, Côte d'Ivoire, Ghana, Togo, Nigeria, Cameroon, Equatorial Guinea (Rio Muni only, absent from Bioko), Gabon, Republic of the Congo, Democratic Republic of the Congo (east to middle and upper Congo and Kivu), Angola.

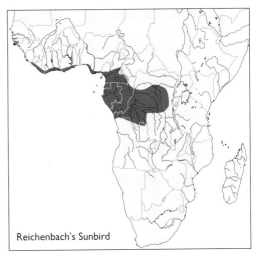

Reichenbach's Sunbird

HABITAT Coastal areas with sand and palms, coastal swamps, coastal scrub bordering lagoons, mangroves, ricefields and forest clearings. Usually near water, at edges of forest in low thickets and other shady areas along streams and rivers. Occasionally in gardens.

STATUS Common in Cameroon and locally not uncommon in Nigeria and parts of Côte d'Ivoire. Locally very common in Republic of the Congo, in low bushy vegetation over water all along the coast and inland to Lake Nanga. Uncommon resident in Angola. Elsewhere scarce or rare, e.g. rare in Liberia, Ghana, Togo and Itombwe Mountains, Democratic Republic of the Congo.

MOVEMENTS Probably sedentary.

FOOD Insects and nectar.
Known food-plants *Cocos nucifera*, *Englerina gabonensis*, *Globimetula braunii* (has specialised edges to corolla segments which respond to probes by sunbird bill to cause reflex action, and further sunbird probes split corolla tube causing stamens to coil inwards explosively), *Psychotria djumaensis*, *Sabicea africana*.

HABITS Forages in pairs or family groups 5-30 m up amongst flowers and leaves of trees overhanging water, in the forest canopy, emergent forest trees and forest edges but never more than 500 m from water. Hawks for insects. Sits on same perch for long periods, returning to same perch after flights. Some habits unusual as recorded moving with tail spread, wings drooping and performing series of turns and pirouettes recalling behaviour of Blue Fairy Flycatcher *Elminia longicauda*. Occasionally joins mixed-species parties and associates with Collared Sunbird *Hedydipna collaris* (63), *C. verticalis*, Western Olive Sunbird *C. obscura* (79) and Olive-bellied Sunbird *Cinnyris chloropygius* (100). Roosts in tall weeds. Host to the filaria *Pelecitus spiralis*.

BREEDING Territorial. Sings vigorous song all year from prominent place, e.g. top of coconut palm *Cocos nucifera*, with upright stance, wings drooping and tail fanned. Nest takes 5 days to build. Female incubates. One nest destroyed by chimpanzees *Pan troglodytes*. **Nest** Typical sunbird bag or pouch, but small, made of fine strips of grass, dry leaves, plantain leaves and fibres, held together by cobwebs. Inside of plant fibres unlined. Suspended from horizontal branch 3-5 m above water. **Eggs** c/1. 16.8-17.7 (mean 17.4, n=4) x 12.0-13.0 (mean 12.5). Unglossed. Light chocolate or greyish-buff with fine darker speckles concentrated at larger end. **Laying months** Cameroon: May, June, September–December; Republic of the Congo: September, October, December; Gabon: February, October, November; Liberia: immature bird September.

DESCRIPTION
Adult male Head, except black lores, metallic dark steel-blue with violet and green reflections. Rest of upperparts olive-green, but with mottled appearance on mantle as centres of feathers brown and rump and uppertail-coverts similarly admixed with olive-yellow. Wings dark brown, with olive edges. Graduated tail blackish-brown with broad buffish-white tips to all rectrices except central pair. Chin and throat metallic dark steel-blue with violet and green reflections. Breast pale grey. Pectoral tufts yellow or orange-yellow. Belly, undertail-coverts and ends of elongated flank feathers yellow. Axillaries and underwing-coverts white. Iris dark brown. Bill, legs and feet black.

Adult female As male, but slightly smaller and pectoral tufts paler yellow.
Nestling Olive above, throat grey with olive wash, breast and belly yellowish.
Juvenile Changes from nestling plumage as follows: head and throat become brown, upperparts brown with olive wash, underparts yellow with brownish mottling; brown cheeks and ear-coverts become yellow, as does streaking on throat, which then becomes all yellow; dark, but dull metallic feathers appear on throat and sides of head; full metallic colour appears on head and throat but some yellow remains, breast becomes buff; belly, undertail-coverts and newly emerged pectoral tufts turn yellow. After post-juvenile moult, upperparts, remiges and rectrices as adult but head dark olive, with black mottling on crown and yellow mottling on face with yellow supercilium. Underparts and cheeks olivaceous-yellow, throat barred dark brown and olive on flanks.

GEOGRAPHICAL VARIATION None described.

MEASUREMENTS Wing 58-63 (mean 59.1, 10 males), 54-57 (mean 55.9, 10 females); tail 44-50 (mean 48.8, 10 males), 40-46 (mean 42.2, 10 females); bill 17-19.0 (mean 18.2, 10 males), 17-19 (mean 18, 10 females); tarsus 16-18 (mean 17.5, 10 males), 15-17 (mean 16.4, 10 females); mass 9.8-13 (3 males).

REFERENCES Bannerman (1948), Bartlett & Anderson (1987), Brosset & Erard (1986), Cane & Carter (1988), Demey (1986), Dowsett *et al.* (1993), Eccles (1985), Kirkup (1998), Mabberley (1997).

69 PRINCIPE SUNBIRD
Anabathmis hartlaubii   Plate 20

Nectarinia hartlaubii Hartlaub (ex Verreaux ms), 1857, *Syst. Orn. Westafr.*, p. 50 "Angola" [= Príncipe, see Dohrn 1866, *Proc. Zool. Soc. London* p.326].

Alternative names: Hartlaub's Sunbird, Prince's Island Sunbird

IDENTIFICATION Unmistakable. A moderately large sunbird, mostly dark olive but with metallic blue throat in male, which appears black at a distance, and conspicuous yellow flanks. Longish, graduated tail with white tips except in centre. Throat of female mottled.
Similar species None.

VOICE Call A grasshopper-like 2-3 note *dreee* or *too-wee*, repeated incessantly, and a thin *wee wee*, uttered when foraging. Also high-pitched *psit-sit*, *tissss* or *tssit*. Female produces ventriloquial piping note in subdued tone at one-second intervals. Song An oft-repeated *peek-oo-wee*, *peek-oo-wee* or *pstes-to-tchou*, *pstes-to-tchou* (recalling "it gets to you", lasting 0.5 seconds), with occasional whistling *twee* interspersed. Also *tik-e-tik*, *tik-e-tik*, *tik-e-tik*, *ee-tik* and a rapid *tiu-tiu-huit-tiu-tiu-huit*.

DISTRIBUTION Príncipe, where it is the only endemic sunbird, but *Cyanomitra obscura* also occurs there.

HABITAT All habitats on Príncipe including primary and secondary forest and coconut plantations, except montane forest.

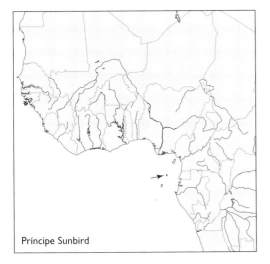

Príncipe Sunbird

STATUS Endemic to Príncipe, where quite common to abundant in plantations including coconut and forest re-growth, but not common in dense woodland.

MOVEMENTS Restricted to within Príncipe.

FOOD Insects, particularly ants and aphids, and nectar. **Known food-plants** *Cocos nucifera*, *Erythrina* sp., *Musa* sp.

HABITS Usually in pairs or parties of 3-10 birds. Feeds at flowers and forages on twigs and leaves, usually at lower levels in trees, and occasionally on ground. Most vocal in late afternoon.

BREEDING Nest Oval, 170-200 mm long, suspended from twigs 1-7 m above the ground, with a small lateral entrance 40 mm in diameter. Composed of loosely woven hairy strips from palm bark and dead leaves. Small porch above entrance, rudimentary beard. Lined with flowers and vegetable down. **Eggs** c/2. White background mostly obscured by dense reddish spots. **Laying months** February, but apparently breeds throughout the year.

DESCRIPTION
Adult male Upperparts olive, ear-coverts brownish-olive. Wings brown with olive margins. Graduated tail dark blue with slight metallic gloss. All rectrices except central pair tipped buffish-white. Uppertail-coverts black, with metallic greenish edges. Chin, throat and upper breast metallic dark blue with violet reflections. Breast greenish-olive, belly brighter with yellow wash. Undertail-coverts and flanks white basally, tipped yellowish-olive. Axillaries and underwing-coverts white. Iris chestnut-brown. Bill, legs and feet black.
Adult female Similar to male except throat lacks metallic plumage, being olive with darker barring, paler near chin. **Juvenile** Similar to adult female but dark greyish-brown on throat and chest. Male similar to adult but lacks metallic plumage, chin and throat being sooty-grey.

GEOGRAPHICAL VARIATION None described.

MEASUREMENTS Wing 60-66 (mean 62.5, 10 males), 55-60 (mean 58.3, 9 females); **tail** 49-56 (mean 54.2, 10 males), 42-48 (mean 45.3, 9 females); **bill** 19-24 (mean 23.5, 10 males), 19-21 (mean 20, 9 females); **tarsus** 19-22 (mean 20, 10 males), 17.5-19.5 (mean 18.5, 9 females); **mass** 10.4 (unsexed).

REFERENCES Bannerman (1948, 1951), Christy & Clarke (1998), Jones & Tye (in press), de Naurois (1994).

70   NEWTON'S SUNBIRD
Anabathmis newtonii   Plate 20

Cinnyris newtonii Barbosa du Bocage, 1889, *Journ. Sci. Mat. Phys. Nat. Lisboa* series 1, 11 (1886), p.250, São Tomé.

Alternative names: Newton's Yellow-breasted Sunbird, Yellow-breasted São Tomé Sunbird, São Tomé Sunbird, Newton's Sunbird

IDENTIFICATION Olive upperparts, yellow belly; throat and breast dark iridescent greenish-blue on male, dark olive with pale bars on female.
Similar species None. The only small sunbird occurring on São Tomé.

VOICE *Call* A high-pitched disyllabic *tsee-ee*, repeated every second, a loud *bzueeh*, a repetitive *jit-jit-jit...* and a variety of calls made by foraging parties. *Bink*, recalling Chaffinch *Fringilla coelebs*, a rising *zee-eep* and a grating *zhreeeuw*. Young beg with incessant *bjuit, bjuit, bjui*. **Song** A high-pitched chattering jangle of rapid, rising and falling, very short notes, *tsee, ti, to, wee, tzeee, tsuwee*, with many variations, in sequences lasting more than 2 minutes.

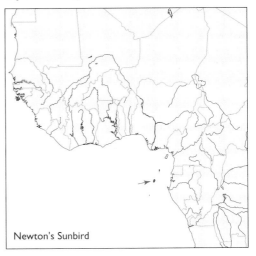

Newton's Sunbird

DISTRIBUTION São Tomé.

HABITAT Steep wooded hillsides up to 1,800 m, forests up to top of Pico de São Tomé, savanna woodland, gardens, edges of shady tracks, plantations including those of coffee, cocoa, coconuts and bananas and overgrown un-cultivated ground.

STATUS Endemic to São Tomé, where widespread and common in all habitats with tall trees.

MOVEMENTS Differing views on the bird's abundance have led to suggestions that it may undergo seasonal altitudinal shifts, e.g. Eccles (1988) noted none in gardens at low elevations during April despite abundance of flowers.

FOOD Nectar, insects including small beetles, spiders.

Known food-plants *Canna* sp., *Cestrum levigatum*, *Erythrina* sp., *Leea tinctoria*, *Musa* sp., *Rubus* sp.

HABITS Occurs in pairs, small parties of up to 10 birds and loose associations of 30. Joins São Tomé Speirops *Speirops lugubris*, São Tomé White-eye *Zosterops ficedulinus* and other species in foraging parties. Acrobatic feeder, often at flowers high up at tops of trees, and searches undersides of leaves. Active with fast flight through forest understorey. Four or five males may sing loudly whilst perched together and bowing in all directions, displaying white underwing-coverts with open bills and turning from side to side.

BREEDING Display involves males staying on a perch, beating their wings and singing. May be cooperative breeder. Parasitised by Emerald Cuckoo *Chrysococcyx cupreus insularum*. **Nest** Bag with side entrance near top, made of leaves, moss and plant filaments and suspended from low branches of shrub, e.g. cocoa. Lined with wool, vegetable down and feathers. Porch above side-top entrance and beard below it. **Eggs** c/2; 15 x 11. Oval, greyish-white with dense covering of small violet spots. **Laying months** August–February, juveniles April, June and family parties July–August.

DESCRIPTION
Adult male Forecrown pale olive, hindcrown and rest of upperparts and ear-coverts darker olive, becoming grey when worn. Lores black. Uppertail-coverts black with hint of metallic green at tips. Tail black, central pair of rectrices with glossy sheen, others broadly tipped white with outer pair as much white as black. Wings dark brown, broadly edged dark olive. Sides of neck dark olive. Chin and throat metallic green, reflecting violet, more purplish on upper breast. Breast bright yellow, belly and undertail-coverts paler. Axillaries and underwing-coverts white, except those at wing-border black tipped white. Iris dark chestnut. Bill, legs and feet black.
Adult female Similar to male but throat and sides of neck dark olive not metallic, appearing scaly as bases of feathers darker, and breast is pale yellow concolorous with belly, not bright yellow.
Juvenile As adult female but without yellow below. Gape yellow. Immature male dark olive above, chin and throat dark grey with yellow mottling. Breast and belly pale yellow.

GEOGRAPHICAL VARIATION None described.

MEASUREMENTS Wing 51-57 (mean 54.0, 10 males), 47-52 (mean 49, 8 females); **tail** 31-42 (mean 38.6, 10 males), 28-35.5 (mean 33.2, 8 females); **bill** 16-18 (mean 17.5, 10 males), 14.5-18 (mean 16.7, 8 females); **tarsus** 15-19 (mean 18.1, 10 males), 15.0-17.5 (mean 16.6, 8 females); **mass** 7 (male), 6.1 (female).

REFERENCES Atkinson *et al.* (1991), P. W. Atkinson (*in litt.*), Bannerman (1948, 1951), Christy & Clarke (1998), Eccles (1988), Jones & Tye (in press), de Naurois (1979, 1994), Snow (1950).

DREPTES

Dreptes Reichenow 1914, *J. f. Orn.* 62, p. 488. Type by original designation *Nectarinia thomensis* Bocage.

A monotypic genus restricted to São Tomé. The largest sunbird, substantially bigger than all other species, with long curved bill and dark brown plumage, except slight iridescence on head and chest and greenish-yellow on vent. Long graduated tail, with all but central pair of rectrices tipped white. No pectoral tufts. Sexes similar.

71   SÃO TOMÉ SUNBIRD
Dreptes thomensis   Plate 20

Nectarinia thomensis Barbosa du Bocage, 1889, *Journ. Sci. Mat. Phys. Nat. Lisboa* series 2, 1, p.143, St Miguel, São Tomé.

Alternative names: São Tomé Giant Sunbird, Giant Sunbird, Dusky São Tomé Sunbird

IDENTIFICATION An unmistakable huge sunbird appearing mostly black with extensive greenish-yellow patch on vent. Conspicuous long curved bill. Tail black when closed but white tips to underside of outer tail feathers visible when graduated tail spread.
Similar species None.

VOICE A noisy bird, but silent near nest. **Call** Powerful calls of *cheep*, usually given in flight. Birds in lek utter harsh, emphatic, *tic-tic-tic-tic-tic-tic*, followed by series of *tsi-tsu-huee*, *tsi-tsiu-tsiu* or *huit-huit-rruit-rruit*. **Song** Unusual sequence of three strident notes of one-second duration, *chee-cheep-eeep* or *tsweet-chut-uu* or *huèt-tsip-tsuit*, sometimes followed by chuckling *chut, chut, chit chit*; the first part of the song, *tsweet*, sometimes repeated without final flourish.

São Tomé Sunbird

DISTRIBUTION Endemic to São Tomé.

HABITAT Usually montane forest, but has occurred on uncultivated slopes, in secondary forest, forest scrub, flowering shrubs along streams, and cultivations up to 1 km away from forest.

STATUS Endemic to the island of São Tomé, where mostly restricted to primary forests and threatened by clearances. Occurs commonly in mid- and high-altitude forest at Lagoa Amélia and along Rio Xufexufe in south-west of the island and the Rio Ana Chaves in central region. Recorded from the coast in south-west, but distribution in lowland forest patchy.

MOVEMENTS Strays from forest as far as 1 km to reach cultivations.

FOOD Nectar, insects, pulp of fruits.
Known food-plants Epiphytes, *Musa* sp.

HABITS Generally occurs at low densities, but concentrates at flowering shrubs (when, e.g., seven birds foraging in 0.25 ha), feeding in canopy of forest and at flowers near ground. Active, constantly moving from tree to tree. Probes flowers, leaf-gleans and feeds from underside of leaves in hovering flight. Also remarkable feeding method involving searching bark, into which it probes like tree-creeper *Certhia* spp. or Spotted Creeper *Salpornis spilonotus*.

BREEDING May be polygynous, as twice as many females as males seen at sites. Seemingly territorial around nest-site. **Nest** Pouch, suspended 4-10 m up from end of long hanging branches, including those of bamboo. Composed of plant fibres and moss. Small porch above side entrance. Long beard of plant fibres. **Eggs** c/2. 21.5 x 15.0. Long, white with small red spots. **Laying months** São Tomé: September–January.

DESCRIPTION
Adult male A huge sunbird. Crown, mantle, back, cheeks and throat sooty-black with steel-blue edges to all feathers. Feathers on rump long and greyer. Metallic blue tips to uppertail-coverts. Wings dark brown. Lesser and median coverts with metallic steel-blue tips. Tail long, graduated, black with dark blue gloss. Rectrices, except three central pairs, tipped white, outer rectrices with broadest such tips. T6 28-48 mm shorter than T1. Breast dark brown with narrow metallic tips, belly feathers lack these but have yellow tinge. Flank feathers long, olive-yellow but grey basally. Undertail-coverts buff. Axillaries and underwing-coverts pale greyish-buff with broad white tips. Iris dark brown or red. Bill, legs and feet black.
Adult female Similar to male but smaller.
Juvenile Young male resembles adult but is smaller.

GEOGRAPHICAL VARIATION None described.

MEASUREMENTS Wing 88-94 (mean 91.6, 11 males), 79-84 (mean 82.0, 10 females); **tail** 84-98 (mean 89.0, 11 males), 69-76 (mean 74.5, 9 females); **bill** 36-43 (mean 40.5, 10 males), 30-36 (mean 32.9, 10 females); **tarsus** 27-31 (mean 29.5, 11 males), 22-28 (mean 26.3, 10 females); **mass** 26.2 (1 male), 18.0-18.9 (mean 18.5, SD 0.40, 4 females).

REFERENCES Atkinson *et al.* (1994), P. W. Atkinson (*in litt.*), Bannerman (1948, 1951), Christy & Clarke (1998), Jones & Tye (1988, in press), de Naurois (1993, 1994), Sargeant (1994), Snow (1950).

ANTHOBAPHES

Anthobaphes Cabanis 1851 *Mus. Hein.* 1, p.103. Type by monotypy *Certhia violacea* Linnaeus.

A monotypic genus. *Anthobaphes violacea* is an endemic of the South African fynbos. A smallish sunbird with thin bill and long graduated tail. Tongue long and narrow, with edges curled inwards to form two tubes. Distal 23% bifid forming two separate tubes with the walls helical; no fimbriations (Figure 6a). Male outer tail feathers 14 mm shorter than T5 and central tail feathers elongated 28 mm beyond T2. Green iridescence on head of male. No pectoral tufts. Female olive with orange wash on belly.

72   ORANGE-BREASTED SUNBIRD
Anthobaphes violacea   Plate 19

Certhia violacea Linnaeus, 1766, *Syst. Nat.* ed. 12, 1, p.188, Cape of Good Hope, South Africa.

Alternative names: Wedge-tailed Sunbird, Violet-headed Sunbird

IDENTIFICATION Elongated tail, green head, violet breast-band and orange breast of male distinctive. Female olive above, olivaceous-yellow below with orange tinge to belly. **Similar species** Female is superficially similar to females of Southern Double-collared Sunbird *Cinnyris chalybeus* (103) and Greater Double-collared Sunbird *C. afer* (109) but has brighter yellow wash on breast and belly. Female Malachite Sunbird *Nectarinia famosa* (97) told by shape, malar stripe and dark patches below. Female Amethyst Sunbird *Chalcomitra amethystina* (84) much browner and heavily marked below.

VOICE Call *Seep-seep, seep-seep, seep-seep,* or *tsearp* with a twangy quality making it sound as *sshraynk* or *sshraynk-sshraynk*. Anxiety call: *eet-eet* or *dzeeu-dzeeu*. *Ke-ke-ke* uttered when two males chasing each other and excited males utter a bell-like tinkle. Males maintain regular bursts of *sskraying-sskraying-sskraying*. Female utters a tinny *sshraynk*. **Song** A complex high-pitched warble of a mixture of chattering whistles, *piou*, melodious sequences and a characteristic descending snarling *tzzurr* or *jeeeu*, interspersed at intervals of 1.5-11 seconds. Also a subsong, interspersed with *sshraynk*. Females sing occasionally.

DISTRIBUTION South Africa. West Cape Province from Kamiesberg to Cape Town and vagrant east to King William's Town.

HABITAT Endemic to fynbos of South Africa. Mountain slopes with heaths and *Protea* spp. Stands of *Protea lepidocarpodendron* with a long flowering season in the Cape Peninsula and of *P. nereiflora* with a short concentrated flowering season. Habitat preferences overlap with those

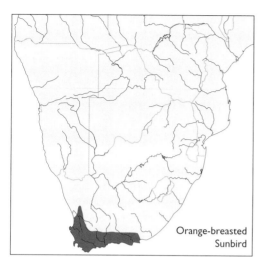

Orange-breasted
Sunbird

of Cape Sugarbird *Promerops cafer*. Wanders to karoo vegetation. Occurs in gardens and parks.

STATUS Common in suitable habitat with densities of 7.1 birds per ha in tall open shrubland dominated by *Protea nitida* and *P. neriifolia*. Threatened wherever urban and agricultural development or fires destroy habitat or where invasive plants are ousting native vegetation.

MOVEMENTS Moves in the southern summer from lower to higher altitudes (moving up at least 320 m and for up to 8 km distances laterally), when flowering plants scarce at lower altitudes.

FOOD Insects and nectar. Coleoptera, Diptera including Chironomidae, Muscidae and Syrphidae, Hymenoptera including ants, Lepidoptera, Orthoptera including Acrididae, Blattidae; also spiders. When feeding on *Protea lepidocarpodendron*, it clings to side of flower like a woodpecker and thrusts bill at rightangles into the bracts to reach the nectar. Feed from 66 different species of *Erica* by clinging to stems and probing up into florets. May have co-evolved with the *Erica* spp. as ornithophilous ones have thicker stems than would be needed solely for flower support and nutrient supply, and are thicker-stemmed than both entomophilous and anemophilous species. Catch insects in air, as a flycatcher, but also hawk for insects in spectacular flights beginning with vertical climb and ending with tumbling return to perch with prey. Sometimes feed on ground, probing into grass in wader-like manner, presumably for insects but observer only noted spider taken; both dry and wet grass probed, so drinking unlikely. Unidentified pollinia – similar to but shorter and more kidney-shaped than those from milk-weeds found on tongues of *C. chalybeus* (Pauw 1998; see Introduction and account 103) – noted fixed to tongue of a spirit specimen at Natural History Museum, Tring (*A. violacea* and *C. chalybeus* are the only ones on which pollinia have been recorded so far).

Known food-plants *Agapanthus* sp., *Erica* spp. including *E. coccinea*, *E. gilva*, *E. mammosa*, *E. perspicua*, *E. phylicaefolia*, *E. plunkenetii* and *E. speciosa*, *Eucalyptus* sp., *Hedera helix*, *Leonotis leonurus*, *L. oxymifolia*, *Leucospermum conocarpodendron*, *Liparia spherica*, *Lobelia pinifolia*, *Lobostemon fructicosum*, *Mimetes fimbriifolius*, *M. hartogi*, *M. hirtus*, *Protea lepidocarpodendron*, *P. mellifera*, *Tecoma* sp., *Watsonia tabularis*.

HABITS Tame. Occurs singly, in pairs, small groups and family parties. Gregarious during non-breeding season, when forms loose groups of 50-100 birds, known as "parliaments", which roam over feeding zones. Also associates with *C. chalybeus*. Birds often scratch each others' heads and rub their bills. Respond inquisitively to wheezing alarm calls of *Promerops cafer*. Bathe in dew and rain-drops on ends of *Leucospermum* sp. or *Protea* spp. bushes, followed by preening. May compete for nectar from proteas with *P. cafer* in fynbos. Adult seen taken by swooping Red-breasted Hawk *Accipiter rufiventris*. Longevity up to 5 years.

BREEDING Linked to timing of flowering *Erica* spp. Defends breeding territory, using same site in successive years, and same mate if birds re-join. Aggressive territorial defence involves physical contact with intruder followed by chase. Prominent *Protea* or *Erica* bush or small tree used by male as perch to survey territory. Level of aggression reflected in postures of male, ranging from feathers on head erect (changing visual effect from green to black) with neck stretched, to bent-forward stoop with drooping, quivering, wings and tail held down, stiff and bent forwards. Pectoral tufts may or may not be displayed. Male displays also include stretching wing out, singing, spreading both wings to expose pectoral tufts and jerking tail up and down. Female has a pseudo-begging posture when crouches with tail vertical, wings drooping, and moves back and forth. Also performs "chat-crouches" when bill held downward, tail up and wings drooping held away from body. Nest built only by female, but male joins forays for material, singing on return. Building takes 5-18 days, and 1-8 days after completion (mean 3 days) first egg laid. Eggs usually laid in early morning, occasionally in evening. Incubation 14-15 days, coverage by female 65%. When incubating, female's tail becomes twisted to one side, so bird with crooked tail likely to be nesting. Hatching rate 65%. Nestling period 15-22 days, coverage by female 53% for days 2-4 and 23% for next 17 days until fledging. Male assists with feeding young, providing 34% of feeds. 56% of diet of young insects (Acrididae, Blattidae, Chironomidae, Coleoptera, Hemiptera, Lepidoptera, Muscidae including *Dipteron* sp., Orthoptera, Syrphidae), 42% spiders, remainder vegetable matter. Adults swallow faeces for first 5 days, then carry them away. Fledging rate 68%. Young return to nest to roost for up to 15 days after fledging and may be accompanied by female who actively guides young to nest for first week. Young dependent on adults for nearly 3 weeks after fledging. May form permanent pair-bonds, as same pair found to nest together in three successive years. Nest predators include mice, cats, mongooses, birds of prey and Southern Boubou *Laniarius ferrugineus*. Parasitised by Klaas's Cuckoo *Chrysococcyx klaas*. **Nest** Oval, domed, with side-top entrance lacking porch, and placed, usually low (76% <1 m above ground, but sometimes up to 10 m high), in the lee of a bush such as a *Protea* sp. or *Elytropappus rhinocerotis* or *E. scaber*, to provide shelter during cold months when the *Erica* are flowering. Also nests in *Acacia cyclops*, *Anthospermum* sp., *Brunia* sp., *Eucalyptus* sp., *Hakea* sp., *Helichrysum* sp., *Indigofera* sp., *Maytenus* sp., *Metalasia* sp., bracken and small pines. Made of rootlets, twigs, leaves from heaths and sometimes grass, bound with cobwebs. Thickly lined with downy plant material from *Protea* sp. or *Eriocephalus* sp. Feathers, green vegetation or spiders' cocoons may be used as external decoration. Height 85-120 mm, 64-90 mm wide, 75-100 mm deep with entrance hole of 20-40 mm diameter. May re-use same nest. Nests tend to be facing south-east to east or north-west. **Eggs** c/ 1-2 (31% c/1, 69% c/2). 14.9-18.2 (mean 16.8, n=28) x 10.8-13.5 (mean 12.3). Variable. Mostly white or whitish, occasionally greenish-grey, heavily dotted with small greyish-brown or chocolate-brown spots and streaks all over but more so at blunt end. **Laying months** All months, with peak during May–August. Double- or triple-brooded.

DESCRIPTION

Adult male Head, chin, throat, sides of breast, neck and mantle iridescent green, basal two-thirds of feathers brown. Median and lesser wing-coverts and back pale yellowish-green, becoming darker on uppertail-coverts. Remiges, primary and greater coverts brown with pale yellowish-green outer margins. Tail brownish-black, edged brownish-olive, more so on outerwebs. Central rectrices elongated and blacker, without contrasting edges, outer rectrices paler, also lacking contrasting edges. Middle of breast violet, merging into rusty-orange of belly. Lower belly chrome-yellow. Flanks yellow and orange with olive wash. Pectoral tufts bright yellow. Axillaries and underwing-coverts greyish-brown. Iris dark brown. Bill and feet black.

Adult female Head greyish-olive. Neck, mantle and back dark yellowish-green, paler on rump and uppertail-coverts. Tail brown with yellow outer edges. Wings as male. Throat

and breast dark yellowish-green, with grey intermixed. Belly and undertail-coverts yellow. Iris dark brown. Bill and feet black.

Juvenile Young hatch naked, weighing 1.2 g, with yellow bill becoming grey-tipped and then pink on day 6, before greyish-horn by day 12. Juvenile similar to adult female but browner upperparts and darker below. Young male first develops orange patches on breast and lower neck, which extend onto collar; vent then becomes yellow-orange and metallic blue-green spots appear on scapulars. Tail develops full length last; birds with undeveloped tail have been seen singing. One male was paired when aged 11 months.

GEOGRAPHICAL VARIATION None described.

MEASUREMENTS Wing 53-57 (mean 55.6, 10 males), 51-53 (mean 52.2, 5 females); **tail** 71-80 (mean 76, 10 males), 45-52 (mean 46.4, 5 females); **bill** 24-25 (mean 24.5, 10 males), 21-23 (mean 22.4, 5 females); **tarsus** 16-18 (mean 16.9, 10 males), 16 (female); **mass** 9-11.3 (mean 10.0, 30 males), 8.6-9.7 (mean 9.1, 3 females).

REFERENCES Broekhuysen (1963), Collins (1983b,c), Fraser (1989, 1997b), Fraser *et al.* (1989), Fraser & McMahon (1991, 1992), Oatley (1997), Siegfried *et al.* (1985), Skead (1967), Spottiswood (1993), Williams (1993a,b), Winterbottom (1962), Wooler (1982).

CYANOMITRA

Cyanomitra Reichenbach 1854, *Handb. Spec. Orn. Synops. Avium Scansoriae* p.291. Type by subsequent designation (G. R. Gray 1855 *Cat. Gen. Subgen. Birds*, p. 137) *Certhia cyanocephala* Shaw.

Eight species of medium-sized sleek sunbirds with long heavy bills, slightly but distinctly curved. Tongue long and narrow with rolled edges forming a single complete tube. Distal 25% broadens out and is bifid, forming two almost complete tubes, the inner edges of which are jagged. Varying amounts of iridescent plumage, usually blue or green, in 5 species, others with none. Males and some females with pectoral tufts. Males larger than females, three species with sexes otherwise alike. Found in moist habitats.

73   GREEN-HEADED SUNBIRD
Cyanomitra verticalis   Plate 21

Certhia verticalis Latham, 1790, *Ind. Orn.* 1, p.298, Africa; restricted to Senegal by Sclater and Mackworth-Praed, 1918, *Ibis* p.622.

Alternative names: Olive-backed Sunbird, Green-headed Olive Sunbird

IDENTIFICATION Large, long-billed sunbird. Males easily identified by metallic green or blue hood (appearing black at a distance), contrasting with yellowish-green back, wings and tail; apart from hood area, rest of underparts whitish or grey. Females similarly identifiable but with metallic feathering restricted to crown and sides of face. Young birds with crown and throat black, latter leading via yellow band to dull olive underparts.

Similar species Bannerman's Sunbird *Cyanomitra bannermani* (74) has duller steel-blue, not green, metallic parts but with green reflections. The Blue-headed Sunbird *C. alinae* (77) has violet-blue metallic parts and brownish-orange tinge to green above, underparts blackish with yellow tinge on belly. The Western and Eastern Olive

Sunbirds *C. obscura* (79) and *C. olivacea* (78) are similar in size, shape and body colours but lack metallic feathers. Blue-throated Brown Sunbird *C. cyanolaema* (75) has brown on face between blue crown and throat and is brown above.

VOICE May mimic other species. **Call** A quiet *tsk*, and a loud *cheerick*, *pzurrp* or *tweezee* repeated at 0.3-2 second intervals; a plaintive *chi-u-wee*, *chee*, (*viridisplendens*); also *tchouee*, like call of Reichenbach's Sunbird *Anabathmis reichenbachii* (68). Alarm call: *chaa* or *pss-chaa*. **Song** Race *boehndorffi*: a quiet *tsk*, repeated at intervals of 0.5-4.5 seconds in a series lasting 10-17 seconds, followed by a rapid burst of *tse* 9-11 times; *viridisplendens*: similar, but *tsk* may be followed by a wheeze and series of 5-8 *tse* preceded by brief melodious warble.

DISTRIBUTION West, East and Central Africa. Senegal, Gambia, Guinea, Guinea-Bissau, Sierra Leone, Liberia, Côte d'Ivoire, Ghana, Togo, Benin, Nigeria, Mali (Kangaba and Siby), Burkina Faso, Sudan, Cameroon, Equatorial Guinea, Central African Republic, Gabon, Republic of the Congo, Democratic Republic of the Congo, Angola, Rwanda, Burundi, Kenya, Uganda (up to 2,230 m), Tanzania, Malawi, Zambia.

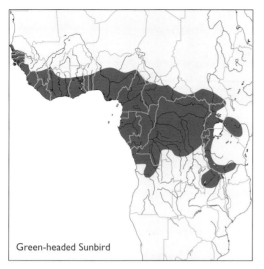

Green-headed Sunbird

HABITAT Primary forest, old secondary forest, forest clearings, gallery forest, well-wooded savanna, forest-savanna mosaic, coastal plains, coastal thickets, mangroves, banana plantations, coffee plantations, broad-leafed bush, flowering trees, shrubs, fields, inselbergs and gardens. Also occurs at high altitudes, especially so in East Africa e.g. up to 2,400 m, but typically above 1,700 m in Kenya and at 2,000-2,150 m on Nyika Plateau of Zambia.

STATUS Common but not abundant throughout most of its range. Scarce in Gambia and Senegal. Not uncommon, Liberia and Togo. Common in Nigeria. Very common in Cameroon. Common Gabon, where occurs at densities of 12-20 pairs per km². Not uncommon resident in Angola. Common in southern Sudan. Locally common in Kenya. Common widespread resident, Uganda.

MOVEMENTS Unknown, probably resident.

FOOD Nectar and insects including beetles, caterpillars, dipterans, homopterans including cicadas, hymenopterans and small orthopterans; spiders (8 in one beakful noted by J. Chapin); also takes small fruits, seeds and sap from oil palms *Elaeis guineensis*. Feeds on trunks and branches of trees.
Known food-plants *Adansonia digitata, Agelanthus brunneus, A. sansibarensis, A. subulatus, Alangium* sp., *Albizia zygia, Baikiaea* sp., *Berlinia grandiflora, Bersama abyssinica englerana, Bridelia brideliifolia, Caesalpinia* sp., *Canthium gueinzii, Carica papaya, Clematis brachiata, Clerodendrum johnstonii, Dendrophthoe pendens, Englerina woodfordiodes, Erythrina* sp. including *E. tomentosa, Halleria lucida, Hypericum revolutum, Ixora* sp., *Leonotis decadonta, L. mollissima* (= *L. raineriana*), *Musa* sp., *Phragmanthera usuiensis, Symphonia globulifera, Syzygium cordatum, Tapinanthus constrictiflorus, Tecoma capensis, Xylopia aethiopica* (fruits), unidentified Zingiberaceae.

HABITS Forages singly or in pairs, sometimes in family parties, usually very active high in the canopy, but also joins other sunbirds such as Variable Sunbird *Cinnyris venustus* (134) or mixed-species flocks. Occasionally found in lower strata, in shrubs and near forest floor, preferring shady areas. Gleans leaves, hover-gleans and chases insects in flight. A female catching insects over the ground near a tangle of vines flew backwards for 0.5 m without gaining

or losing height. Males seen to gather in groups of up to 30 in fruiting *Xylopia aethiopica* trees, Gabon, February, each defending an area of diameter 2-4 m by singing and jumping up and down in one place adopting aggressive postures with pectoral tufts sticking out from the body, tails raised and bill pointing at adversary. Female greeted by head straight out, lowering of tail and rapid wing-beats. Sometimes become heavily dusted with pollen. Maximum longevity: 3 years 8 months. Host to *Haemoproteus sequeirae* and to the feather mites *Anisodiscus dolichogaster, Boydaia nectarinia* and *Xolalges glossopus*.

BREEDING Territorial; territory sometimes consists of whole of a small forest patch of 0.5-10 ha. Pair defended same territory for at least three seasons. Both parents feed young. Parasitised by Klaas' Cuckoo *Chrysococcyx klaas*. **Nest** Race *boehndorfii*: 12 m high on prickly liana, above a stream. Like large nest of *Cyanomitra obscura*, globular, pocket-shaped and covered with strips of bark and dead leaves with beard, of streamers or loose end, hanging 0.5 m down from base of side entrance. Race *cyanocephala*: coarsely woven domed entrance half-way up side; *verticalis*: untidy globular nest suspended from branch of shrub overhanging a stream, others suspended from telephone wire or from beam of deserted hut; *viridisplendens*: suspended, 1.5-7 m above ground, from small tree or bush, composed of dried grass, dried banana bark and fibres woven with cobwebs, cocoon silk or vegetable lint and lined with banana bark and fibres. Nest sometimes has streamers 300 mm long below nest stemming from just beneath entrance hole. **Eggs** c/2. Race *boehndorfii*: 18-18.5 (mean 18.3, n=2) x 13.5 (mean 13.5), oval, slightly pointed at smaller end, lacking gloss with pale pink background marked with small dots and short lines of deep chocolate-brown and markings of lilac-grey all over or at larger pole only; *viridisplendens*: 19-19.5 (mean 19.3, n=4) x 14 mm, variable in colour. White to pinkish-brown background with dense dark mottling. **Laying months** East Africa: March–October and building November. Cameroon: March, April, June, July, September, October, dependent young September; Republic of the Congo: September; Democratic Republic of the Congo: February, may breed all year; Gabon: November–December, nest-building March, December; Ghana: copulation October, juveniles November; Liberia: family parties January, April–June; Malawi: December–February, April; Nigeria: July, nest-building March, moults January; Sierra Leone: August–September; Uganda: March, April, May, July–September, November; Zambia: December–May.

DESCRIPTION *C. v. verticalis*
Adult male Head, nape, throat and upper breast metallic green, appearing dark blue in some lights. Lores black. Rest of upperparts golden-olive. Wings brown. Lesser wing-coverts golden-olive, as are margins of greater coverts and remiges. Tail brown with golden-olive on outerwebs. Underparts beneath metallic throat dark grey, flank feathers with greenish-yellow tips. Large cream-coloured pectoral tufts with yellow wash. Axillaries and underwing-coverts grey. Iris dark brown. Bill, legs and feet greenish-black. Moults primaries, November–January, Kakamega Forest, Kenya.
Adult female Very distinct from adult male as only forehead, crown, nape, ear-coverts and line below eye metallic green or metallic blue in some lights. Lores black. Rest of upperparts as male. All underparts pale grey, but chin and malars paler, almost white. No pectoral tufts. Axillaries and underwing-coverts white.

Juvenile Immature male has grey, slightly mottled, fore-head and crown and back with olive wash. Rest of upper-parts as adult male but duller. Forehead, chin, throat, lores and malars blackish-grey. Rest of underparts olive with marked yellow wash. Immature female as young male but throat paler grey.

GEOGRAPHICAL VARIATION

C. v. boehndorffi (Reichenow, 1887) (South Cameroon and interior of Gabon, middle Congo, south from southern Democratic Republic of the Congo south to northern Angola through Uíge to Cuanza Norte and Cuanza Sul, and east through Malanje to northern Lunda Norte and east to Ubangi-Chari and Kasai) Upperparts of adult male greener, less olive-yellow, and underparts darker grey than *verticalis*. Larger (wing 64-70) than *verticalis* (60-65). Female has bright-er green (less golden-green) crown and cheeks, darker olive (less yellow) back and greyer (less white) under-parts than *verticalis*. Male has greener metallic throat than *cyanocephala*, and this contrasts with the breast. Immatures have whole crown dull black contrasting with olive back.

C. v. cyanocephala (Shaw, 1811) (Coastal areas from mainland Equatorial Guinea and Gabon to the mouth of the Congo, Cabinda, and north-western Democratic Republic of the Congo) Similar to *boehndorffii* but throat and breast with more purple, less steel-blue, gloss, and no contrast between the two, and abdomen sootier-grey. Larger and with darker olive back than *verticalis*.

C. v. verticalis (Latham, 1790) (Senegal to Nigeria) Described above.

C. v. viridisplendens (Reichenow, 1892) (includes *niassae* [Reichenow, 1910]) (Bahr-el-Ghazal, south Sudan, and north-east Democratic Republic of the Congo east to Uganda and Kenya highlands as far as Mt Kenya; Tanzania, west of a line from the Crater highlands through Iringa to Ufipa and Rungwe; north Malawi; east Democratic Republic of the Congo to Manyema; north-east Zambia from Fort Rosebery to Serenje and north to Isoka) Head and throat brighter brassy-green, less dull and bluish than *boehndorfii*, *cyanocephala* or *verticalis*. Populations in Bwindi (Impenetrable) forest, west Uganda, much smaller and may represent undescribed subspecies.

MEASUREMENTS Wing 63-70 (mean 66.8, 10 male *boehndorfii*), 65-68 (7 male *cyanocephala*), 60-69 (mean 65.9, 15 male *verticalis*), 65-72 (mean 69.1, 47 male *viridisplendens* western Kenya and East Usambaras, Tanzania), 59-60 (2 male *viridisplendens*, Bwindi [Impenetrable] forest, western Uganda), 60-65 (6 female *boehndorfii*), 59-61 (2 female *cyanocephala*), 58-65 (mean 61.9, 10 female *verticalis*), 63-68 (mean 64.5, 20 female *viridisplendens* western Kenya and East Usambaras, Tanzania); **tail** 44-50 (16 male *boehndorfii*), 45-48 (7 male *cyanocephala*), 41-47 (mean 46.1, 10 male *verticalis*), 54-58 (2 male *viridisplendens*), 40-45 (6 female *boehndorfii*), 41 (2 female *cyanocephala*), 35-43 (mean 41.6, 10 female *verticalis*); **bill** 23-28.5 (mean 27.4, 16 male *boehndorfii*), 21-23 (7 male *cyanocephala*), 21-30 (mean 27.5, 15 male *verticalis*), 21-29 (mean 27.0, 12 male *viridisplendens*), 20-27.5 (mean 25.9, 4 female *boehndorfii*), 22 (2 female *cyanocephala*), 21-28 (mean 26.5, 10 female *verticalis*), 24.0-27.5 (mean 25.6, SD 1.03, 7 female *viridisplendens*); **tarsus** 17-20 (16 male *boehndorfii*), 18-19 (7 male *cyanocephala*), 17-19 (mean 17.9, 10 male *verticalis*),

18-19 (2 male *viridisplendens*), 17-18 (6 female *boehndorfii*), 16 (2 female *cyanocephala*), 16-18 (mean 17.3, 10 female *verticalis*); **mass** 14.5 (male *boehndorfii*), 13.8, 15 (2 male *cyanocephala*) 10.4-13.7 (mean 12.5, 10 male *verticalis*), 13.4-16.6 (mean 15.2, 45 male *viridisplendens*, western Kenya and East Usambaras, Tanzania), mean 14.7, (SD 1.79, male *viridisplendens*, Kivu, Democratic Republic of the Congo), 12.9-15.5 (mean 15.0, 11 male *viridisplendens*, Malawi), 9.7-11.0 (2 male *viridisplendens*, Bwindi [Impenetrable] forest, western Uganda), 10.7-13.5 (3 female *verticalis*), 11.2-15.5 (mean 13.7, 20 female *viridisplendens*, western Kenya and East Usambaras, Tanzania), mean 13.1 (SD 1.71, female *viridisplendens*, Kivu, Democratic Republic of the Congo), 11.8-13.8 (mean 12.7, 5 female *viridisplendens*, Malawi).

REFERENCES Bannerman (1948), Blancou (1939), Brosset & Erard (1986), Cheke (1978), Dowsett-Lemaire (1989), Fry *et al.* (2000), Kramer (1975), Kunkel (1964), Ng'weno (1990), Zumpt (1961).

74   BANNERMAN'S SUNBIRD
Cyanomitra bannermani   Plate 21

Cyanomitra verticalis bannermani Grant & Mackworth-Praed 1943, *Bull. Br. Orn. Club* 63 p.63, Kayoyo, Katanga, southern Belgian Congo [southern Democratic Republic of the Congo].

Alternative names: Bannerman's Blue-headed Sunbird, Blue-headed Sunbird

Nectarinia sororia Ripley, 1960, *Postilla*, no. 43, p.2, Duque de Bragança, Melange District, Angola, is based on the female of this species.

IDENTIFICATION Medium-sized olive-green sunbird with blue metallic hood in males, female with greyish-brown crown and metallic plumage only on some feather tips.
Similar species Similar to Green-headed Sunbird *C. verticalis* (73) (allopatric in Zambia, sympatric in north-east Angola) but male differs in having duller, less metallic steel-blue plumage, with greenish reflections, on the chin and throat, a much paler grey chest and belly, smaller and less prominent pectoral tufts and a shorter, straighter bill. Female told by lack of metallic plumage, except for faint greenish metallic streaks on crown, and by brighter olive, more yellowish, upperparts and darker underparts. Where sympatric with *verticalis*, *bannermani* is larger.

VOICE Call A brief *chuk*. **Song** A series of 4-5 *chuk*, followed by a rising wheeze *purz-urr-wee*.

DISTRIBUTION Katanga, southern Democratic Republic of the Congo, through north-west Zambia (Mwinilunga south to the Mundwiji Plain, Matonchi and forests in western Zambezi District) to central (Cacola) and north-east Angola (on the central plateau from southern Cuanza Sul east through northern Bié, Duque de Bragança, Malan-je District, Lunda Norte, southern Lunda Sul and northern Moxico).

HABITAT Riverine forest and thick woodland along streams. Also mid-strata of moist evergreen forest and its edges, from which sometimes wanders into adjoining miombo woodland.

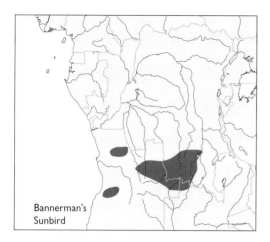

Bannerman's
Sunbird

STATUS Not uncommon in Katanga, Democratic Republic of the Congo. Uncommon resident in Angola. Not uncommon in Zambia.

MOVEMENTS Unknown.

FOOD Nectar, termites (*?Pseudacanthoptermes* sp.) and spiders.
Known food-plants None.

HABITS Undescribed but probably similar to *C. verticalis*.

BREEDING Only one nest described (Colebrook-Robjent 1990), which was near ground in gallery forest. Female incubates. **Nest** Bulky and broad (main nest 100 mm wide, 90 mm deep but extraneous material made nest up to 190 mm broad) with porch of fine twisted stems, suspended from vine 1.2 m above water, well hidden by overhanging vegetation. Base of nest chamber 180 mm below attachment to vine. Nest made of long coarse grass stems, much of which hung down to 340 mm below base of chamber, with roof of black fibrous stems. No cobwebs utilised. Decorated outside with curling strips of banana bark and adorned with large leaves, especially at rear. Diameter of entrance 42 mm, lower lip 84 mm above base of chamber (90 mm high and 40 mm wide), lined with soft fine stems. **Eggs** c/2. Regular ovals without gloss. Warm, pinky-brown background, densely marked all over with irregular streaks of dark purplish-brown, giving dull claret or smudged puce appearance. 19.6 x 13.9 and 18.3 x 13.6. **Laying months** Zambia: September; active gonads March and September.

DESCRIPTION
Adult male Top and sides of head and neck metallic greenish-blue. Remainder of upperparts olive-green. Uppertail dark greyish-brown, tips of T3-T6 and outerweb of T6 paler; outerwebs of T1-T5 edged yellowish olive-green. Lores black. Chin, throat and upper breast metallic greenish-blue as head, with which they merge. Some individuals more steely-blue on throat, others dull bluish. Pectoral tufts pale yellow. Remainder of underparts grey, becoming darker on belly and flanks. Upperwing dark grey-brown. Primaries edged dull yellow; alula and primary coverts with olive-green fringes. Axillaries, underwing-coverts and inner borders of undersides of flight feathers pale grey. Throat and upper breast tinged violet. Bill black. Iris dark reddish-brown. Legs and feet black.
Adult female Crown feathers dark brown bordered dark grey, but some, especially on sides of crown, with dull

metallic light green edges, giving mottled appearance. Neck grey. Mantle, back and rump bright yellowish olive-green, with concentration of feathers with bright yellow intermixed on mantle and upper back. Flight feathers edged olive-green. Uppertail black with bright yellowish olive-green edges. Chin, throat, breast and chest smoke-grey. Belly paler with some feathers almost white. Undertail-coverts dull grey. Bill, legs and feet black.
Juvenile Immature male like female, but throat darker grey and only traces of metallic green on forehead. Crown and remainder of upperparts bright olive-green.

GEOGRAPHICAL VARIATION None described.

MEASUREMENTS Wing 68-71 (mean 69.0, SD 1.33, 10 males), 64-66 (mean 64.7, SD 0.76, 3 females); **tail** 40-53, (mean 48, SD 3.74, 10 males), 42-46 (mean 44.3, SD 2.08, 3 females); **bill** 21-25 (mean 24.1, SD 0.94, 8 males), 21-23 (mean 21.8, SD 1.04, 3 females); **tarsus** 18-20.5 (mean 19.4, SD 0.76, 10 males), 19 (1 female); **mass** 14.1 (1 female).

REFERENCES Benson *et al.* (1971), C. Carter (unpublished recording at Library of Wildlife Sounds, London), Colebrook-Robjent (1990), Grant & Mackworth-Praed (1943), Ripley (1960).

---

75 BLUE-THROATED BROWN SUNBIRD
Cyanomitra cyanolaema   Plate 21

N.[*ectarinia*] *cyanolaemus* Jardine and Fraser, 1851, *Contrib. Orn.*, p.154, Clarence, Fernando Po [= Malabo, Bioko].

Alternative name: Blue-throated Sunbird

IDENTIFICATION A drab brown sunbird, but easily told if well seen by steely metallic blue-violet forehead and throat of male and by white feathers around eye of female. If these not seen, male identifiable by dark head contrasting with paler upperparts and female by pale underparts and white or pale throat.
Similar species Green-headed Sunbird *Cyanomitra verticalis* (73) has more extensive green, not blue, iridescence, lacks brown face and is olive above not brown. Blue-headed Sunbird *C. alinae* (77) has longer bill and shorter tail, all head metallic violet-blue and orange tinge to upperparts. Female similar to Mouse-brown Sunbird *Anthreptes gabonicus* (55) as both have white around eye, but *C. cyanolaema* has longer bill and is white with mottling below and yellowish-olive or olivaceous-grey vent.

VOICE Call A harsh *tschuk*, a *tsit* or *chip* and sharp rising and falling *tssew*. **Song** A long series of twitterings, including *psit* but consisting mostly of short staccato descending trills of *ptssew*.

DISTRIBUTION West, East and Central Africa. Guinea, Sierra Leone, Liberia, Côte d'Ivoire, Ghana, Togo, Nigeria, Cameroon, Central African Republic, Equatorial Guinea (Bioko and Rio Muni), Gabon, Republic of the Congo, Democratic Republic of the Congo, northern Angola, Rwanda, Uganda (up to 1,500 m in south and west), Kenya (Kakamega forest) and Tanzania (Gombe Stream Game Reserve).

HABITAT Primary forest, forest edges and clearings and secondary forest. Forest patches, gardens, cultivations, river-

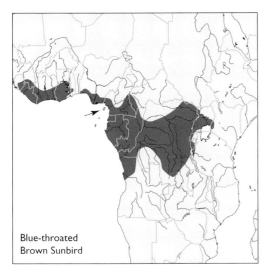

Blue-throated
Brown Sunbird

sides, coastal woodlands, coconut and cocoa plantations. Occasionally strays into gallery forest in savanna, e.g. to Tamale and Mole Game Reserve in Ghana. Reaches 1,500 m in Liberia and Kenya, and 1,350 m in Democratic Republic of the Congo.

STATUS Uncommon throughout much of its range, less so in Liberia, Côte d'Ivoire, Cameroon and Gabon. Not uncommon in Ghana and Nigeria. Rare in Togo. Widespread and common in Equatorial Guinea. Locally common resident in Angola, Democratic Republic of the Congo, Uganda and Tanzania.

MOVEMENTS Mostly sedentary but some local movements, e.g. birds reaching Tamale and Mole Game Reserve in northern Ghana during wet season.

FOOD Insects including small caterpillars, spiders (sometimes taken from their webs), seeds, small fruits, flowers, fruit pulp.
Known food-plants *Albizia gummifera*, *Anthocleista* sp., *Caesalpinia* sp., *Combretum platypterum*, *Erythrina* sp., fruits of *Macaranga assas*, *M. barteri* and *Musanga cecropioides*, *Maranthes* sp., *Musa* sp., *Pentadesma* sp., *Spathodea campanulata*, seeds of *Tetrorchidium didymostemon*, fruits of *Xylopia aethiopica*, epiphytes, mistletoes, vines.

HABITS Usually seen as singletons or in pairs at midheight or tops of trees, occasionally low down when crossing clearings or feeding on low bushes or banana plants. Perch on branches up to 50 cm in diameter. Forage at heights of 0-45 m by gleaning amongst dry leaves and by hovering, and takes invertebrates from sides of houses. Joins mixed-species flocks, e.g. with Little Green Sunbird *Anthreptes seimundi* (60), Green Sunbird *A. rectirostris* (61), Buff-throated Sunbird *Chalcomitra adelberti* (81) and Johanna's Sunbird *Cinnyris johannae* (129). Occurs in groups of 4-7 but once up to 45 singing males observed, Gabon, at apparently traditional sites, at start of rains on dead branches or fruiting or flowering *Xylopia* trees, jumping from branch to branch, facing each other, singing, pectoral tufts exposed, chest inflated, head thrown back, bill wide open, wings drooping, tail spread out in a fan and lowered. Behaviour recalled quarrelling House Sparrows *Passer domesticus*. Females came to observe but did not participate and no copulations seen. Foreheads

sometimes covered in pollen and sometimes mites. Host to the cestode *Staphylepis ambilateralis*.

BREEDING Territorial. For lekking display see above. Incubation by female only lasts 14 days. **Nest** *cyanolaema*: bulky nest of pale fibres with very prominent porch of fine dried grass decorated with dead leaves above and below large entrance hole. Suspended on thick wire from eaves on outside of two-storey house. Long beard entwined in thinner wire below nest. Whole strusture 1 m long. Race *octaviae*: on shrub or bush, 1.8-12 m high, in open part of forest, site of fallen trees, or track through primary forest or clearing in secondary forest. One hanging from thorny vine over river, 5 m above water. Others in swampy woodland attached to drooping end of frond of rattan palm, anchored by hooklets. Remarkable structures resembling bundle of dead vegetation, with extensive beard, whole nest complex may be almost 1 m from top to bottom. One rope-like with bulge for nest proper in middle. Composed of twigs, stems, dried leaves, *Marasmius* (which may continue to grow on the nest), cobwebs, vegetable fibres and moss, lined with bark fibres. Short porch of bark shreds above entrance, of which one had diameter of 35 mm, situated 260 mm below top of nest which itself was 200 mm high, with upward prolongation of 200 mm, and 95 mm deep. Cup deep, often padded with mammal hairs including those of gorilla *Gorilla gorilla*. **Eggs** c/2. Long oval-shaped, lacking gloss. Pinkish-brown to brown, cream-coloured or buff, greyish around larger end, with dense coating of very small brown or dark purplish-grey markings. Others greyish-violet with dark brown markings. Race *octaviae*: 15.8-20.0 (mean 17.6, n=29) x 11.9-14.0 (mean 12.9). **Laying months** Cameroon: June, July, dependent young February; Democratic Republic of the Congo: March, but may breed all year; Equatorial Guinea (Bioko): January; Gabon: December–April; in breeding condition Cabinda, August–September; Liberia: dependent young February, March, December; Nigeria: August, November; Republic of the Congo: October; Uganda: April–September.

DESCRIPTION *C. c. cyanolaema*
Adult male Forehead, chin and throat dark metallic steel blue-green with violet tinge. Crown behind forehead and upperparts brown. Remiges and rectrices brown, some of latter with pale tips. Breast brown, becoming paler greybrown on belly and undertail-coverts. Flanks greyer brown with cinnamon tinge. Pectoral tufts lemon-yellow or cream. Underwing-coverts and axillaries greyish-white. Inside of mouth black. Iris dark brown. Bill black. Legs and feet black. Soles of feet yellowish.
Adult female Crown, malars and ear-coverts dark brown. Eyebrow and feathers around eye white; lores brown, whitish below. Upperparts, wing and tail brown with olive-yellow wash, and all these feathers edged olive-yellow, especially when fresh, with broadest edging on wing-coverts, secondaries, rump and uppertail-coverts. Some rectrices with pale tips. Chin and throat white or buff. Rest of underparts greyish-white with varying amounts of mottling with pale yellowish-green and smoke-grey, brighter on vent. Axillaries and underwing-coverts white. Iris dark brown. Bill black. Legs and feet black. Soles of feet yellowish.
Juvenile male Similar to adult male but lacks pectoral tufts and metallic feathers on crown and throat, which are brown and grey respectively. Olive-yellow feather fringes less marked than in adult but underparts washed olive.

Tail edged yellowish olive-green. Upper mandible greenish-black, lower mandible yellow with greenish-black tip.
Juvenile female Brown above with hint of olive and olive-green edges to feathers, especially on tail, visible in field. Underparts grey-brown with dull yellow wash. Bill brown, gape flanges orange. Legs and feet black.

GEOGRAPHICAL VARIATION
C. c. cyanolaema (Jardine, 1851) (Bioko) Described above.
C. c. magnirostrata (Bates, 1930) (Sierra Leone and Liberia, possibly Côte d'Ivoire, Ghana and Togo) Darker than *cyanolaema* and males usually darker and browner (less grey) below than *octaviae*. Bill heavier and longer (24-28, males) than *octaviae* (22-26), otherwise similar to it but slightly larger on average. Five males from Ghana have bills 25.5-28 and wings 70-71, confirming presence of *magnirostrata* there and probably Togo, not *octaviae* as stated by Grimes (1987) and Cheke & Walsh (1996) respectively. Nigerian birds examined were *octaviae*.
C. c. octaviae Amadon, 1953 (Nigeria and Cameroon to Democratic Republic of the Congo (except southeast Katanga) south to Cuanza Norte and Lunda Norte in north Angola; east to Uganda in Budongo Forest, and Kenya in Kakamega Forest) Females yellower olive, less greenish on upperparts than nominate.

MEASUREMENTS Wing 64-74 (29 male *cyanolaema*), 68-71 (mean 70.1, SD 1.4, 13 male *magnirostrata*), 65-73 (mean 68.4, 10 male *octaviae*), 62-70 (16 female *cyanolaema*), 63-68 (mean 65.8, SD 2.5, 5 female *magnirostrata*), 63-67 (mean 65, 10 female *octaviae*); **tail** 50-55 (28 male *cyanolaema*), 47-57 (mean 49.7, SD 1.4, 13 male *magnirostrata*), 50-61 (mean 54.9, 10 male *octaviae*), 42-50 (16 female *cyanolaema*), 44-50 (4 female *magnirostrata*), 44-50 (mean 46.7, 10 female *octaviae*); **bill** 20-23 (28 male *cyanolaema*), 24-28 (mean 25.7, 10 male *magnirostrata*), 22-26 (mean 24, 10 male *octaviae*), 20-22 (16 female *cyanolaema*), 23-26 (mean 25.4, 5 female *magnirostrata*), 22-24 (mean 23.2, 10 female *octaviae*); **tarsus** 16-17 (28 male *cyanolaema*), 16-17 (2 male *magnirostrata*), 16-17 (mean 16.6, 10 male *octaviae*), 15-17 (16 female *cyanolaema*), 16 (female *magnirostrata*), 16-17 (mean 16.5, 10 female *octaviae*); **mass** 11.0 (male *cyanolaema*), 13.9-18.8 (mean 15.3, 12 male *magnirostrata*), 14.5-20 (mean 16.9, 16 male *octaviae*), 14.0-16.6 (mean 15, 7 female *magnirostrata*), 13.5-20 (mean 17, 12 female *octaviae*).

REFERENCES Bates (1911, 1927), Brosset (1974), Brosset & Erard (1986), Burger (1987), Mariaux & Vaucher (1991), Prigogine (1971).

---

76 CAMEROON SUNBIRD
Cyanomitra oritis   Plate 19

Cinnyris oritis Reichenow, 1892, *J. Orn.*, 40, p.191. Buea, 950 m, Mt Cameroon.

Alternative names: Blue-headed Sunbird, Cameroon Blue-headed Sunbird

IDENTIFICATION A medium-sized sunbird with dull olive-green plumage, contrasting with metallic green or blue and purple head and throat, and long curved bill which gives bird top-heavy appearance. Sexes similar but

female lacks pectoral tufts. Forehead sometimes dusted with silvery pollen.
Similar species Purple throat and olivaceous-yellow, not grey, underparts distinguish *C. oritis* from the Green-headed Sunbird *Cyanomitra verticalis* (73) and the Blue-throated Brown Sunbird *C. cyanolaema* (75). Reichenbach's Sunbird *Anabathmis reichenbachii* (68) is superficially similar but nowhere sympatric with *oritis*.

VOICE Call An oft-repeated ticking, *tick tick tick tick*; *pseep* at 0.5-2 second intervals, but usually at 0.5 second gaps; and a trisyllabic *tch-tch-tchwee* repeated at 2 second intervals. *C. o. poensis*: quiet *chip* or *chip-chip*, sounding deeper than the calls of most sunbirds. Alarm call: *jeep*. **Song** A jingling song of metallic notes, recalling start of song of Wren *Troglodytes troglodytes*, and a quiet warble with middle part 3-4 repeats of *tsi*. Both songs are uttered in 2-3 second bursts.

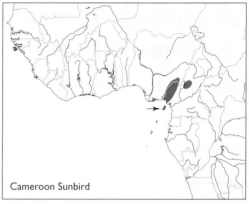

Cameroon Sunbird

DISTRIBUTION Cameroon, Nigeria and Bioko.

HABITAT Montane forest (1,200-2,100 m) on Mt Cameroon. Also found in *Eucalyptus* plantations. Occurs at 800-2,800 m in primary and secondary forest and forest edges and clearings on Bioko. Occurs in undergrowth within forest, along streams and at forest edges.

STATUS Not uncommon resident on Obudu Plateau, and common widespread resident Gotel mountains, Nigeria. Common on Mt Cameroon from 570 m up and in highlands of north and north-east of Cameroon. Common in primary and secondary forest and forest clearings at 800-2,000 m on slopes of Pico Basille, Pico Biao and the Caldera da Luba on Bioko.

MOVEMENTS Some altitudinal movements may occur seasonally on Mt Cameroon where reaches down to 570-670 m only in June–September.

FOOD Insects, nectar and plant material.
Known food-plants *Leea guineensis*, *Lobelia columnaris*, *Psychotria manni*, unidentified Rubiaceae.

HABITS Feeds singly or in small groups in shrubs and flowering trees within forest and at forest edge in remnant strips. Associates with Northern Double-collared Sunbird *Cinnyris reichenowi*. Perches on low branches to feed on flowers opposite. May congregate at flowering trees. Moult February–March. Tame.

BREEDING Nest Race *bansoensis*: concealed by screen of ferns and suspended 1 m above ground from a fern above a rocky bank by stream. Pear-shaped, loosely built with blades of grass, rootlets and moss, lined with fibres and silk-cotton. Side entrance with porch extending 50 mm, with beard of dry grass. Much moss at attachment point. **Eggs** c/2; *bansoensis*: 18 x 12.5, ovate, smooth, unglossy; covered all over with dark brown speckling, darker at wider pole; *oritis*: 18.0 x 12.0; *poensis*: 17 x 13. **Laying months** Bioko: egg in oviduct April, young January and June, males in breeding condition January–April. Cameroon: March, April, July, November, December; Nigeria: dependent young April.

DESCRIPTION *C. o. oritis*
Adult male Head, throat and upper breast metallic steel-blue, reflecting violet in some lights especially on throat and breast. Eye-ring bright pale blue. Remainder of body olive-green with underparts brighter and washed yellow, becoming brighter yellow on flanks. Pale yellow pectoral tufts. Remiges and rectrices dark brown, bordered with olive-green and with broadest margins on secondaries but those on primaries brighter. Iris dark brown. Bill, legs and feet black.
Adult female As male but lacks pectoral tufts. Iris dark brown. Bill black. Feet blackish.
Juvenile Dull greenish-olive upperparts and dusky crown, no metallic plumage. Chin, throat and upper neck brown to grey, rest of underparts olive with yellow wash.

GEOGRAPHICAL VARIATION
C. o. bansoensis Bannerman, 1922 (Cameroon at Manenguba, Mt Kupe, Rumpi hills and Bamenda highlands; Obudu Plateau and Gashaka-Gumti National Park, Nigeria) Differs from *oritis* in having metallic feathers of crown and sides of head bright steel-green rather than dull steel-blue, and throat and breast steel-blue instead of deep purplish-blue. More yellow in middle of belly. Head brighter and glossier green than *poensis*, abdomen yellower. Smaller than both *oritis* and *poensis* (bill <29 mm).
C. o. oritis (Reichenow, 1892) (Mt Cameroon, Cameroon) Described above.
C. o. poensis Alexander, 1903 (Bioko, Equatorial Guinea) Darker olive than *oritis*; metallic head more greenish and extending onto hindneck, sides of neck and further down breast.

MEASUREMENTS Wing 58-63 (mean 61.5, 10 male *bansoensis*), 62-65 (mean 63.3, 3 male *oritis*), 59-63 (4 male *poensis*), 51-62 (mean 56.2, 12 female *bansoensis*), 57 (1 female *oritis*); **tail** 39-48 (mean 42.7, 10 male *bansoensis*), 38-40 (mean 39.0, 3 male *oritis*), 35-38 (mean 36.5, 12 female *bansoensis*), 36-41 (4 male *poensis*), 34 (1 female *oritis*); **bill** 25-29 (mean 27.9, 10 male *bansoensis*), 28-33 (mean 31.8, 10 male *oritis*), 25-27 (4 male *poensis*), 25-29 (mean 27.7, 12 female *bansoensis*), 28 (1 female *oritis*); **tarsus** 18-21 (mean 19.5, 10 male *bansoensis*), 18-19 (3 male *oritis*), 20 (4 male *poensis*), 17-22 (mean 19, 12 female *bansoensis*); **mass** 9.8-13.8 (mean 12, 73 male *bansoensis*), 10.8-13.8 (male *oritis*), 8.7-11.9 (mean 10.4, 41 female *bansoensis*), 9.2-10.7 (female *oritis*).

REFERENCES Bannerman (1948), Fry *et al.* (2000), Pérez del Val (1996), Serle (1965), Stuart & Jensen (1986).

---

77   BLUE-HEADED SUNBIRD
Cyanomitra alinae   Plate 20

Cyanomitra alinae Jackson, 1904, *Bull. Br. Orn. Club* 14 p.94, Ruwenzori.

Alternative name: Ruwenzori Blue-headed Sunbird

IDENTIFICATION A long-billed, short-tailed, medium-sized sunbird with blue metallic plumage on hood, saffron tinge to brown upperparts and blackish underparts. Sexes similar in general.
Similar species Similar to Green-headed Sunbird *C. verticalis* (73) but metallic feathers violet-blue rather than green, and mantle saffron; breast to belly sooty-black in some races. Juvenile *alinae* has the saffron mantle and more uniform dusky colours below than *verticalis*. Confusion with Blue-throated Brown Sunbird *C. cyanolaema* (75) also possible, but again separable by distribution of metallic plumage and colours above and below.

VOICE Call Final two notes of a *tcii tcii tcii yehu* call distinctive. The call is produced in a continuous burst, slightly rising and falling in pitch, and may be a song. Other calls *ssee* or *tsee* and *chip*. **Song** A soft twittering, ending with loud *chip* calls every 3-4 seconds.

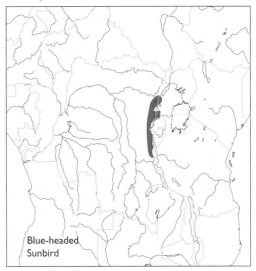

Blue-headed Sunbird

DISTRIBUTION Mountains of eastern Democratic Republic of the Congo, south-west Uganda, Burundi and Rwanda.

HABITAT Montane forests at 1,400-2,700 m (1,850-2,350 m on southern Itombwe massif) and up to 3,280 m in Ruwenzoris. Occurs in canopy, but more often at low levels, almost to forest floor. Avoids savanna, preferring primary, secondary and riverine forests.

STATUS Fairly common in montane forest at 1,400-2,700 m in the Ruwenzoris, Ankole and abundant in the Bwindi (Impenetrable) forest in south-west Uganda. Common in Rwanda. Very common above 1,850 m in the Itombwe mountains. Abundant in Burundi above 1,750 m in forested mountains of the Zaire-Nil crater from the Rwanda border south to Teza and Bugarama. Elsewhere status unclear, but apparently scarce in the Kivu area.

MOVEMENTS Unknown, probably resident.

FOOD Insects, small spiders and nectar. Probes flowers with long bill from perches and when hovering.
Known food-plants *Agelanthus brunneus*, *Balthasaria schliebenii*, *Brillantaisia* sp., *Canarina eminii*, *Erythrina* sp., *Impatiens niamniamensis*, *Ixora burundensis*, unidentified

Loranthaceae, *Lobelia gibberoa*, *Phragmanthera usuiensis*, *Pseudosabicea* sp., *Symphonia gabonensis*, *S. globulifera*, *Tapinanthus constrictiflorus*.

HABITS Usually seen singly or in pairs at mid-height or low down in trees. Joins mixed-species flocks and associates with white-eyes *Zosterops* spp. Territorial regarding nest site and main food-plant *Balthasaria schliebenii*. Disputing males face each other on tree-tops, calling excitedly, until one flies at the other followed by much fluttering, with birds sometimes falling together gripping each other's feet, before the procedure is repeated. Prefers the forest canopy.

Occurs sympatrically with *C. verticalis* over much of its range, and at similar altitudes on the Lendu Plateau, but tends to range up to higher altitudes elsewhere. No altitudinal overlaps between the ranges of the two species in the Virungas and the Rugege forest, and overlaps from 50 m (Itombwe Mountains) to 700 m (mountains west of Lake Kivu) elsewhere, except Mt Kabobo and Mt Marungu where *verticalis* is absent.

BREEDING Territorial. **Nest** *tanganijicae*: 165 mm high, 85 mm wide, 75 mm deep with 30 mm wide entrance 60 mm from the top, suspended 2 m above ground from a bush or shrub and constructed with moss, lichens (*Usnea* sp.), grass, roots and dry leaves (bamboo leaves at high altitudes), lined with fine grass or seeding flowerheads e.g. *Panicum* sp. or *Thalictrum rhychocarpum*, pappus of *Gynura vitellina* and small feathers. Side entrance with pronounced porch. **Eggs** c/1-2; reddish-brown or reddish-grey with irregular dark blotches, darker at larger pole; *alinae*: 17.3-17.8 x 13.0-13.1 (n=2); *tanganijicae*: 20.2 x 13.2-14.6 (n=2). **Laying months** Democratic Republic of the Congo: January to May and breeding condition October and November. Juvenile birds north of Lale Tanganyika, June.

DESCRIPTION *C. a. alinae*

Adult male Top and sides of head to hindneck and sides of neck metallic bluish-green with violet reflections; mantle and back bright saffron; scapulars, rump and uppertail-coverts olive-green. Tail slightly graduated, blackish-brown, tips of T5-T6 paler, more olive; outerwebs of tail feathers edged olive-green. Lores sooty-black. Chin to upper breast metallic violet-blue, merging with greener sides of head; pectoral tufts yellow; lower breast, upper flanks and belly dark sooty-brown, merging with dull olive-green lower flanks, tibiae and undertail-coverts. Median and lesser wing-coverts bright metallic green, rest of upperwing blackish-brown, primaries edged olive-yellow, secondaries and tertials edged olive-green. Axillaries, underwing-coverts and inner borders of undersides of remiges greyish-white. Iris brown, reddish-brown, dark hazel or dark chestnut. Bill black. Legs black or olive-black. Feet black or olive-black.

Adult female As male but lacks pectoral tufts, and metallic plumage on crown duller green, lacking blue sheen. Iris crimson or hazel. Bill black. Feet black.

Juvenile male Spots of metallic plumage on crown, otherwise all upperparts dull olive-green with orangey-yellow tinge on mantle. Chin, throat and upper breast dull blackish-grey with blackish barring, belly, flanks and undertail-coverts greyish-olive.

GEOGRAPHICAL VARIATION

C. a. alinae Jackson, 1904 (Ruwenzori Mountains, Virunga volcanoes, and Bwindi [Impenetrable] forest, south-west Uganda) Described above.

C. a. derooi (Prigogine, 1975) (Two main populations, one west of Lake Albert, the other west of Lake Edward) Differs from *alinae* by deep green (much less blue) crown and by bluer, less purple on metallic underparts; from *tanganijicae* by shorter bill. Back darker, with redder tinge, than other races and breast darker, blackish grey.

C. a. kaboboensis (Prigogine, 1975) (restricted to 1,980-2,480 m on Mt Kabobo) Differs from *alinae*, *tanganijicae* and *derooi* by deep grey belly, slightly washed with black, appearing paler, resembling females of other races, lower belly and undertail-coverts with less olive wash and lack of metallic green shoulder-patches. Neck and throat steel-blue, with greener reflections than in other races. Female also lacks shoulder-patches; crown and metallic feathers of underparts greener and less blue, belly pale grey, vent and undertail-coverts less olive. Mantle golden-olive, closer to colour of *tanganijicae* than *alinae*.

C. a. marungensis (Prigogine, 1975) (restricted to 1,660-1,710 m on Marunga) Differs from *alinae*, *tanganijicae* and *derooi* by light grey, much brighter belly and lack of metallic patch on lesser wing-coverts, and from *kaboboensis* by paler belly and less robust, shorter bill.

C. a. tanganjicae (Reichenow, 1915) (includes *vulcanorum* [Hartert, 1920]) (mountains west of Lake Kivu including Mt Kahuzi, Itombwe mountains, north-west of Lake Tanganyika and Rugege [Nyungwe] forest in Rwanda, south-east of Lake Kivu and mountains of Burundi) Head greener and less blue than *alinae*.

MEASUREMENTS Wing 59-68 (mean 64.2, 46 male *alinae*), 58.5-64 (mean 61.7, 28 male *derooi*), 65-69 (mean 67.4, 9 male *kaboboensis*), 65.5 (1 male *marungensis*), 60-71 (mean 64.8, 44 male *tanganjicae*), 57-62 (mean 59.2, 28 female *alinae*), 55.5-59 (mean 57.4, 8 female *derooi*), 58-62 (mean 60.8, 4 female *kaboboensis*), 60, 60.5 (2 female *marungensis*), 58-63 (mean 60.7, 19 female *tanganjicae*); **tail** 37-46 (mean 44.2, 42 male *alinae*), 38-46 (mean 41.5, 29 male *derooi*), 46-49.5 (mean 47.5, 9 male *kaboboensis*), 41 (1 male *marungensis*), 39-48 (mean 43.5, 44 male *tanganjicae*), 35.5-40 (mean 38.5, 27 female *alinae*), 35-37 (mean 36, SD 0.95, 9 female *derooi*), 36-40 (mean 38.5, 4 female *kaboboensis*), 38-39 (2 female *marungensis*), 35-41.5 (mean 37.6, 17 female *tanganjicae*); **bill** 27.5-32 (mean 29.6, 44 male *alinae*), 27-30 (mean 28.7, 29 male *derooi*), 31-33 (mean 32.2, 9 male *kaboboensis*), 29 (1 male *marungensis*), 27.5-34 (mean 31.5, 39 male *tanganjicae*), 26-30 (mean 28.9, 10 female *alinae*), 26-29 (mean 27.5, 9 female *derooi*), 31.5-32 (mean 31.6, 4 female *kaboboensis*), 27.5, 28 (2 female *marungensis*), 29-33 (mean 31.1, 17 female *tanganjicae*); **tarsus** 16-20 (mean 18, 6 male *alinae*), 18-21 (mean 19.4, 10 male *derooi*), 20-23 (mean 21.5, 9 male *kaboboensis*), 20-23 (mean 21.0, 10 male *tanganjicae*), 18-19 (mean 18.5, 4 female *alinae*), 18-21 (mean 19, SD 0.94, 10 female *derooi*), 20-22 (mean 20.7, 4 female *kaboboensis*), 18 (1 female *marungensis*), 19-22 (mean 20.8, 10 female *tanganjicae*); **mass** 12-14.5 (mean 13.5, 5 male *alinae*), 11-16 (mean 13.5, 23 male *tanganjicae*), 10-13 (mean 11.3, 8 female *alinae*), 10-15 (mean 11.7, 23 female *tanganjicae*).

REFERENCES Bennun (1986), Dowsett & Prigogine (1974), Dowsett-Lemaire (1990), Prigogine (1971, 1972, 1975, 1984).

78 EASTERN OLIVE SUNBIRD
Cyanomitra olivacea Plate 18

Cinnyris olivaceus A. Smith, 1840, *Ill. Zool. S. Afr.*, text to pl. 57, footnote, Durban, South Africa.

Alternative name: Olive Sunbird, Olive-coloured Sunbird

IDENTIFICATION A large, mostly dull green sunbird, paler below with long curved bill and yellow or orange pectoral tufts in both sexes. Some subspecies have a yellow or orange wash on the throat and upper breast. Young are lighter grey below with light greenish-grey throats. Presence often detected by distinctive voice.

Similar species Western Olive Sunbird *Cyanomitra obscura* (79) is indistinguishable in the field but its female lacks pectoral tufts. Bates's Sunbird *Cinnyris batesi* (137), Little Green Sunbird *Anthreptes seimundi* (60) and females of Green Sunbird *A. rectirostris* (61) are all smaller with shorter tails, the latter two with shorter, straighter bills. Mouse-coloured Sunbird *Cyanomitra veroxii* (80) is superficially similar but grey above, greyish-white below, with red pectoral tufts and different voice.

VOICE Call *Tsk-tsk-tsk* and *tsick* or *tut-tut-tut* or *slik-slik-slik...* A piping *tseeng-tseeng-tseeng-tseeng-...*; a stuttering *ch, ch, ch*; *choyt*; *chwip, chwip, chwip...*, *chip,p,p,p,p*. An insect-like *phit zeet* or *woot zeet*, or *wip-wip-wip-wip...* repeated again and again, sometimes as "midday" call. A guttural *phweep-phweep* used to defend feeding territories. Alarm note: *tsink-tsink-tsink* or *jet-jet-jet* or harsh *tk*. **Song** Race *alfredi*: a descending series of notes *dee-dee-dee-di-doo*. Also a simple sweet long-drawn song of *tschi* notes, repeated every 0.5 seconds all at much the same pitch, interspersed with short melodic phrases and ending in a series of 4 *tsk* per second; *olivacea*: a monotonous warble, lasting a minute or more, of repeated whistling notes, rising and falling in pitch with occasional melodic phrases, described as *tsee-tsee-tsee-*, *tseedlee, eedlee-id-id-id-seedle, eedle-ee-ee-ee*. Also a slowish warble, including a reedy *see-weetee-wee-tee-to-tip* and *tsee-tsee-tsee...* Rival males may sing concurrently in a "choir", assembled in a tree, producing a delightful chorus with rising and falling notes including *sweety weety...*

DISTRIBUTION East and south-east Africa. Southern Somalia, eastern Kenya, eastern mainland Tanzania to Malawi, Zanzibar, Zambia east of the Luangwa valley, Mozambique and South Africa (eastern Mpumalanga, Swaziland, KwaZulu-Natal and Eastern Cape).

HABITAT Lower strata and undergrowth of mature forest, secondary forest and clearings. Also dense woodland, bushy thickets, coastal scrubland, dune forests, banana and eucalyptus plantations, occasionally in gardens. Up to at least 1,800 m, straying to 2,150 m.

STATUS Common at Mt Nilo, East Usambaras, Tanzania, where occurs at density of 13.1 per 500 metre-net hours. Uncommon presumed resident in riverine vegetation along lower Juba river in Somalia. Locally common in Malawi. Common (5-7 pairs per ha) in coastal areas of KwaZulu-Natal, South Africa; scarcer inland.

MOVEMENTS Mainly sedentary but may make local movements in response to changes in distribution of nectar sources. Some post-breeding altitudinal movements may occur, accounting for presence of race *alfredi* within range of race *olivacina*, e.g. at Massinga. Longest ringing recovery distance 4 km.

FOOD Insects, spiders, nectar, small berries and fruits.
Known food-plants *Achyrospermum carvalhi, Agelanthus kraussianus, Antidesma venosum, Burchellia* sp., *Dracaena flagrans* (nectar-robbed), *Englerina woodfordiodes, Erythrina* sp., *Eugenia malacensis, Fuchsia* sp., *Gardenia tigrina* (nectar-robbed), *Grevillea banksii, Halleria lucida, Hibiscus tiliaceus, Ipomoea* sp., *Jacaranda* sp., *Kigelia africana, Leonotis leonurus, L. mollissima,* unidentified Loranthaceae, *Macrorungia pubinervia, Mimusops caffra, Schotia brachypetala, Strelitzia nicolai, Tecoma* sp., *Tetrorchidium didymostemon* (fruits), *Trema guineensis* (berries).

HABITS Usually single and unobtrusive but sings loudly and often in mixed-species flocks. Occasionally in groups of up to 100 in flowering trees. Flicks wings incessantly. Hovers in front of flowers, leaf-gleans and hawks for insects from a perch and searches spiders' webs. Hovers along eaves and gutters. Searches up tree-trunks like a treecreeper *Certhia* sp. Comes to bird-baths. Responds to its reflection in windows. Aggressive towards Southern Double-collared Sunbirds *Cinnyris chalybeus* (103) and Greater Double-collared Sunbirds *C. afer* (109). Maximum longevity from ringing data 4 years. Assembles in groups for singing displays in breeding season. Defends feeding territory using guttural *phweep-phweep* call and prevents females taking food until after copulation. Defends clumps of *Leonotis leonurus* intra-specifically and interspecifically, gaining 57 kJ of energy per day from the flowers and using 5.4 of these on defence per day. Primary moult lasts 107-130 days, during November–March in Kakamega forest, Kenya.

Bird from Amani, Tanzania, was the neotype host of the blood parasite *Haemoproteus sequeirae*. Also host to *Leucocytozoon nectariniae, Plasmodium relictum, P. rouxi, P. vaughani, Nuttalia* sp., *Trypanosoma avium* and microfilariae including those of *Chandlerella inversa*, for which it is the type host.

BREEDING Territorial and probably polygynous, as male seen to copulate with several females which nest in its territory. Males gather in assemblies of 10-20 birds singing and vying amongst each other for tallest perches in lekking displays. Male performs fluttering display flight. Incubation 12-15 days, fledging period 13-17 days. Both sexes

Eastern Olive Sunbird

feed young in nest. Young are prone to jump out of nest if approached when only 11-12 days old. Parasitised by Emerald Cuckoo *Chrysococcyx cupreus*. **Nest** Can be built in 2 days. Race *changamwensis*: placed 0.3-6 m up. One suspended from creeper over stagnant pool and others in or on houses, e.g. inside or under eaves of thatched houses, from a wire suspended from the roof in a disused grass hut, on wire supporting mosquito net which was lowered each afternoon and night, and on a ceiling mobile. Untidy, resembling bundle of rubbish, with beard of 700 mm. Race *olivacea*: suspended 0.5-2 m up from branch in forest or over stream or amongst exposed roots in eroded banks; also uses houses, electric flex, etc. Elongated pear-shape of dry grass, fibres, twigs, rootlets, lichen, moss and leaves bound together by cobwebs; with untidy long porch and straggling beard up to 260 mm long. Lined with seed-down, feathers and fine grass. Height 90-130 mm; width 80 mm; depth 70 mm; entrance hole 40 mm in diameter. **Eggs** c/1-2, rarely 3. Race *changamwensis*: 16.9 (mean 17.3, n=2) x 12.0; *olivacea*: 18-19.4 (mean 18.5, n=3) x 12.7-13 (mean 12.9), greyish-white, spotted and streaked with greyish-brown. **Laying months** East Africa: January–December; Kenya: June; Malawi: September, November–January; Mozambique: November; South Africa: August–April; Tanzania: January, December.

DESCRIPTION *C. o. olivacea*
Adult male Forehead to nape and sides of face brownish-black, forehead and crown with very slight metallic blue tinge. Neck, mantle, back, chin and throat olivaceous-green, sometimes with orangey-yellow wash on chin, throat and upper breast, brighter green on rump and uppertail-coverts. Remiges dark brown, outerwebs, except on outer two primaries, edged yellowish-green. Wing-coverts edged olive-green, those on alula and outer 4 primaries darker. Tail dark brown edged yellowish-green, except outer rectrices. Breast and belly yellowish-green, becoming darker yellowish-olive on lower belly, flanks and undertail-coverts. Pectoral tufts bright yellow, sometimes with pale orange admixed. Axillaries and underwing-coverts whitish-grey tipped yellowish-green. Iris dark brown. Bill and legs black.
Adult female As male.
Juvenile Nestlings have bright orange gapes and mouths and are greyer than adults. Background colour of throats of juvenile *olivacea* and *olivacina* are rust-coloured but pale yellow in *alfredi*, *changamwensis* and *neglecta*. Chin to chest olivaceous-yellow. Brighter olive than adult above. Feet pale pinkish-grey. Bill grey.

GEOGRAPHICAL VARIATION Females of all subspecies have pectoral tufts.
  C. o. alfredi Vincent, 1934 (includes *intercalans* [Clancey, 1978]) (southern Tanzania from Rungwe to Songea; Zambia [east of Luangwa with isolated population at Marble Hill south-east of Lusaka], Malawi [except far north], northern Mozambique north of the Zambesi) Slightly greener and smaller (wing 55-67, bill 24-27), crown less grey, paler below and bill less stout than *olivacea*.
  C. o. changamwensis (Mearns, 1910) (includes *puguensis* van Someren, 1939) (coastal Somalia, Kenya and Tanzania inland to Taita, Usambaras, Pugu hills and South Pare mountains; Mafia island; also Zanzibar, based on a bird collected by R. H. W. Pakenham, Izani forest, Zanzibar, 12 September 1937, ascribed by him to *C. obscura granti*, unsexed but with fully ossified skull, with bright yellow pectoral tufts and

yellow on the throat and thus appearing to be *changamwensis*, a conclusion supported by bill width in front of nostrils of 3.4 [3.0-3.6 in *changamwensis*; 3.6-4.2 in *granti*] and by the existence of a similar specimen discussed below under *C. obscura granti*; these specimens represent the only records of the species in Zanzibar and provide a case of sympatry between *C. olivacea* and *C. obscura*) Upperside brighter and greener, underside slightly paler than *neglecta* and smaller (male wing 56-69, bill 22-24). Similar to *alfredi* but greener above, yellower below.
  C. o. neglecta Neumann, 1900 (includes *chyulu* van Someren, 1939) (central and north-eastern Kenya, Chyulu Hills and eastern edge of highlands, to north-eastern Tanzania including Usambaras) Slightly duller above, darker on crown and greyer below than *alfredi*.
  C. o. olivacea (Smith, 1840) (includes *daviesi* [Haagner, 1907], South Africa; Pondoland to Natal and south Zululand) General colour dark and greenish, including underparts; large (male wing 61-70; bill 27-29). Described above.
  C. o. olivacina (Peters, 1881) (coastal parts of southern Tanzania and Mozambique and north-east KwaZulu-Natal). Slightly paler above and below and smaller than *alfredi* with smaller and finer bill (male wing 57-63; bill 21-23); pectoral tufts lack orange.

MEASUREMENTS Wing 62-64 (mean 63, 5 male *alfredi*), 56-69 (mean 61.2, 25 male *changamwensis*), 61-70 (mean 65.1, 10 male *olivacea*), 57-63 (mean 59.9, 6 male *olivacina*), 51-61 (mean 55.9, 18 female *changamwensis*), 59-64 (mean 61.2, 10 female *olivacea*), 55-66 (mean 60.4, 30 unsexed *alfredi*); **tail** 49-62 (mean 53.9, 10 male *olivacea*), 47-53 (mean 50.1, 10 female *olivacea*); **bill** 27-29 (mean 28.1, 10 male *olivacea*), 21-24 (mean 22.7, 6 male *olivacina*), 27-28 (mean 27.7, 10 female *olivacea*); **tarsus** 16-18 (mean 17.1, 10 male *olivacea*), 16-17 (mean 16.3, 10 female *olivacea*); **mass** 6.8-10.9 (mean 8.2, 95 male *changamwensis*), 9.2-15.0 (mean 12.6, 126 male *olivacea*), 6.2-9.5 (mean 7.6, 88 female *changamwensis*), 7.3-8.0 (female *olivacea*), 7.3-8.0 (mean 7.6, 3 female *olivacina*), 8.3-10.7 (mean 9.5, 159 unsexed *alfredi*), 9-14.7 (mean 11.8, 490 unsexed *olivacea*).

REFERENCES Aspinwall (1971), Bannerman (1948), Britton & Britton (1977), Clancey (1978a,b, 1992-1993), Frost & Frost (1980), Fry *et al.* (2000), Mann (1985), Moreau & Moreau (1940), Sclater & Moreau (1933), de Swardt (1992b), Swynnerton (1908), Tree (1997h).

---

79   WESTERN OLIVE SUNBIRD
Cyanomitra obscura   Plate 18

N.[ectarinia] obscurus Jardine, 1843, Nectariniadae, in *Nat. Library*, 13, p.253, Fernando Po [= Bioko].

Alternative name: Guinean Olive Sunbird, Guinea Olive Sunbird, Olive Sunbird

IDENTIFICATION Large, drab, olive-green sunbird, paler below, the pectoral tufts of the male being the only bright plumage but often obscured; bill long and curved.
Similar species Female told from that of Eastern Olive Sunbird *Cyanomitra olivacea* (78) by lack of pectoral tufts. Immature Green-headed Sunbird *C. verticalis* (73) has blackish-grey on head and chest. Separable from Bates's

Sunbird *Cinnyris batesi* (137), Little Green Sunbird *Anthreptes seimundi* (60) and female Green Sunbird *A. rectirostris* (61) by larger size and longer tail and bill.

VOICE Call A harsh *tschaa-tschaa-tschaa* every 5 seconds; *tsk* or *tic*, *der-der-der* and *cooee*. *C. o. guineensis* utters a call in the middle of the day, consisting of a continuous series of *chip* notes every 0.5 seconds or alternating high and low notes every second: *weep... wup... weep... wup.* **Song** A slow build-up to a descending series of sweet clear notes *dee-dee-dee-di-doo*, uttered by both sexes, and a similar series but with ascending and descending notes ending in a flurry of *chip-chop-chip-chip*. Rival males may sing concurrently. Song of *C. o. obscura* a rapid, oft-repeated, guttural *hoo-hoo-hoo*. Song of *C. o. cephaelis* rises and falls, speeds and slows "like a squeaky wheel cranked at different speeds": *pi, pi, pi, pi, pi-pi-pi-pi, pi.*

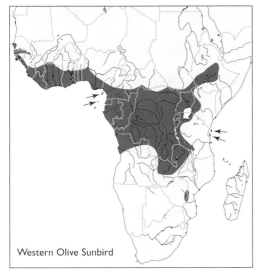

Western Olive Sunbird

DISTRIBUTION West and East Africa. Senegal, Guinea, Guinea-Bissau, Sierra Leone, Liberia, Côte d'Ivoire, Mali (south of Kangaba), Ghana, Togo, Benin, Nigeria, Cameroon, Central African Republic, Equatorial Guinea (Rio Muni and Bioko), Príncipe, Gabon, Republic of the Congo, Democratic Republic of the Congo, southern Sudan, Ethiopia as far north as central area, Rwanda, Burundi, Uganda, western Kenya, western Tanzania (and Zanzibar and Pemba), Angola, central and western Zambia, northern Malawi, highlands of eastern Zimbabwe along Mozambique border, southern Mozambique.

HABITAT Prefers lower strata (0-6 m) of mature forest, secondary forest, gallery forest, forest patches, riverine forest, coffee plantations, abandoned plantations (e.g. cloves on Zanzibar), cultivated zones and clearings but found low down in bushes or on ground if flowers present, providing shade available. Also occurs in mangroves, coastal thickets, gardens and montane scrub, in moist wooded areas, bushes around villages and occasionally in urban areas. Still common up to 1,500 m in Liberia. Rarely above 1,800 m in Ethiopia.

STATUS Common throughout most of its range. Up to 5 per 100 m of net per day in primary forest on Bioko, increasing to 12 in secondary forest and abandoned plantations. Uncommon Senegal, unrecorded so far in Gambia. Abundant from coast to mountains, Liberia. Common resident in Togo. Common and locally abundant in Nigeria. Widespread and common in Equatorial Guinea. Abundant (four birds per hectare) in primary forest in Gabon. Common in extreme south of Sudan. Common in Democratic Republic of the Congo. Common resident in Angola. Abundant in Burundi from level of Lake Tanganyika to 1,800 m. Common and widespread in evergreen or riparian forest west of the Luangwa valley in Zambia. Locally common in Kenya. Very common in Budongo forest, Uganda. Locally common in Rwanda. Common but elusive on Pemba and Zanzibar. Common in plantations and forest regrowth on Príncipe.

MOVEMENTS Mainly sedentary (one bird re-trapped six times in 3 years 8 months) but may make local movements in response to changes in distribution of nectar sources. Apparently non-breeding visitor to Senegal, December–March. One controlled 3 km away after 2 months.

FOOD Insects including larvae, termites, small black beetles, small Hemiptera and flies, spiders, nectar, pollen, small berries, flower stamens, seeds and fruits including those up to 5 mm in diameter and banana pulp. Competes at flowers of *Tecoma stans* with honeybee *Apis mellifera* which deters sunbirds by flying at their faces.
Known food-plants Fruits of *Afromomum* sp., *Carica papaya*, *Ceiba pentandra*, *Cephaelis mannii*, *Englerina woodfordiodes*, unidentified mistletoes Loranthaceae, *Macaranga assas* (fruits), *M. barteri* (fruits), *Musa* sp., *Musanga cecropioides* (fruits), *Oxyanthus troupini*, *Passiflora* sp., *Symphonia globulifera*, *Syzygium congolense*, *Tecoma* sp. including *T. stans*, *Tetrorchidium didymostemon* (fruits), *Xylopia aethiopica* (seeds).

HABITS Usually single or in pairs but also occurs in mixed-species flocks. Shy, quick-moving and inquisitive. Frequents tops of forest trees up to at least 30 m but more often forages close to ground (0-10 m). Active and restless, difficult to observe but presence often betrayed by scolding calls, sometimes by 1-4 birds simultaneously and lasting 2-3 minutes. Searches leaves and twigs in warbler-like manner. Often joins mixed-species groups. Probably not territorial as many birds caught at same site, and probably changes mate often as birds often re-trapped with different partners. Group display of 7-8 males seen, in absence of females, at start of rains in Gabon, involved singing and jumping up and down, puffing up breast, displaying pectoral tufts, head held high and projecting backwards, wings drooping and tail at 45°. Aggressive if nest approached and defends feeding territories, e.g. *Symphonia globulifera* and *Syzygium congolense* trees. Comes to bird-baths. Annual survival rate (both sexes) 51%, with 23% of population surviving for 5 years, and four birds estimated to have been at least 7 years old. A male of at least 14 years 5 months and a female at least 7 years 9 months in Kakamega forest, W. Kenya, and birds more than 7 years old also reported from Zimbabwe, but oldest West African record 5 years one month. At least two records of birds being killed following entanglement in spider's web.

Parasitised by *Leucocytozoon* sp. Race *guineensis* is host of feather mites *Pellonyssus zosteropus* and *Lasioseius cinnyris* and the cestode *Staphylepis ambilateralis.* Race *ragazzi* is host to the feather mites *Monojoubertia grandiloba* and *Anisodiscus* nr. *megadiscus.* Race *cephaelis* is host to the filaria *Chandlerella inversa.*

BREEDING For lekking behaviour see above. Only female builds nest and incubates. Eggs laid at 24-hour intervals. Female certainly but probably also male feeds young. Sixteen of 23 nests in Gabon destroyed by predators. Parasitised by Emerald and Klaas's Cuckoo *Chrysococcyx cupreus* and *C. klaasi*. One nest with unidentified young honeyguide *Indicator* sp. in Gabon. **Nest** Suspended from branches or shrubs, one from creeper over stagnant pool. Race *cephaelis*: suspended 0.3-5 m above ground from end of branch, liana or other creeper, sometimes over water, made of green mosses, *Marasmius* and spiders' webs, fine grasses or dry leaves, stems and black fibres; with porch. Lined with seed-down and soft fibres. 190-220 mm high, 75-90 mm wide, 75-90 mm deep with entrance 30 mm in diameter or 40 x 50 mm, 80 mm from top of nest. Extensive beard from base of nest entrance. Race *obscura*: made of vegetable material with lateral entrance, suspended from tangled shrub, nail on wall of house, occasionally inside house; *zanzibarica*: usually >1 m above ground, but one only 0.3 m up. **Eggs** c/1-3. Colour variable but usually clear grey or brown-grey, strongly and irregularly marked with olive-grey, grey-green, violet-grey or brown mottling, especially at larger end; *cephaelis*: c/1-2. 15.8-18.0 (mean 17.4, n= 45) x 11.9-13.2 (mean 12.5), some with green or brown background, mottled with yellowish-brown, dark brown and grey; *obscura*: 13 x 18. **Laying months** Angola: October–March with August–September in Cabinda; Cameroon: February–August, birds in breeding condition in all months except March; Democratic Republic of the Congo: February, June–October; Côte d'Ivoire: building March; East Africa: January–December; Equatorial Guinea (Bioko): 2 young in mid-January, birds in active moult February; Gabon: all months but principally in dry season June–September; Ghana: fledglings May–July; Nigeria: January, November; Príncipe: November–January; Sudan: June–August; Uganda: February, April–June, August, September; Zanzibar: September–April; Zimbabwe: September–March, peak November–December.

DESCRIPTION *C. o. guineensis*
Adult male All upperparts olive-green but crown darker than mantle and back. Inconspicuous pale stripe above eye and buff patch in front of it. Ear-coverts and cheeks with faint white speckling. Wings dark brown with olive-yellow margins to remiges and coverts. Tail dark brown with outerwebs edged olive-yellow. Chin to undertail-coverts greyish with olive wash. Pectoral tufts lemon-yellow. Underwing-coverts white. Axillaries yellowish-white. Iris dark brown. Bill greenish-black but lower edge of upper mandible pale at base. Legs brown, feet greenish-black.
Adult female Similar to male but no pectoral tufts and shorter tail. Iris brown. Bill black except orange or light orange-brown basal half of lower mandible. Legs olive, feet yellowish posteriorly.
Juvenile Nestlings have orange gapes. Tibio-tarsal skin pinkish-orange for first six months, changing to pinkish-yellow for a year, then yellowish-brown for another year. Juveniles similar to adults above but generally darker olive with brownish crown. Chin and sides of throat white. Rest of underparts with brighter yellow suffusion and grey feather-bases giving more speckled appearance.

GEOGRAPHICAL VARIATION
  C. o. cephaelis Bates, 1930 (Ghana to Gabon, Democratic Republic of the Congo, Angola from Golungo Alto in Cuanza Norte east to northern Lunda Norte,

and from southern Malanje south along the escarpment to Gabela in Cuanza Sul; an isolated record from Namibe; Burundi; Príncipe) Similar to *ragazzii*, sharing pale base to lower mandible, yellow in life, but with shorter bill and paler underparts, tinged yellow-green. From *guineensis* by light buffish-flesh tone to pale part of lower mandible, as opposed to pale blackish of *guineensis*.
  C. o. granti Vincent, 1934 (Zanzibar and Pemba islands; includes *pembae* Granvik, 1934) Colour similar to *obscura* but bill straighter and shorter. As pointed out by Pakenham (1979), some doubt remains about the absence of pectoral tufts in female *granti*. If this is disproved, then *granti* would revert to *C. olivacea* and no longer be an isolated population closer to populations of *olivacea* on the mainland than to those of *obscura*. Fry & Keith (2000) place it in *C. olivacea* on geographical grounds anyway. However, Pakenham cited a tufted female "*granti*" collected in Zanzibar on 16 October 1927 by J. H. Vaughan as the main source of the doubt: it was noted as non-breeding and could have been wrongly sexed, but it has a bill-width of 3.3 in front of the nostrils and, like Pakenham's specimen reported under *C. olivacea changamwensis* above, appears also to be that subspecies, as originally suggested by Vaughan. If so, the case for *granti* being within *obscura* and not *olivacea* is supported. Pakenham may not have considered the possibility of representatives of what are now considered to be two species being co-present on Zanzibar.
  C. o. guineensis Bannerman, 1921 (Guinea-Bissau to Togo, where overlaps with *cephaelis*) Described above. Similar to *cephaelis* but generally darker, bill with black base to lower mandible and shorter wings.
  C. o. obscura (Jardine, 1843) (Bioko) Paler, greyer (less greenish) below than *cephaelis*, but still with yellowish tinge, and larger (significantly so in both sexes, P<0.001) with heavier bill. Differs from *guineensis* by larger size, paler underparts, and pale basal half of lower mandible.
  C. o. ragazzii (Salvadori, 1888) (includes *vincenti* Grant & Mackworth-Praed, 1943 and *lowei* Vincent, 1934) (Sudan [Boma hills and Imatong mountains], central to south-west Ethiopia, Uganda, western Kenya, Tanzania; north-eastern and southern [Katanga] Democratic Republic of the Congo; northern Zambia from Mwinilunga and Kasempa to Copperbelt and Abercorn; extreme north of Malawi) Colour similar to *obscura* but deeper green above and duller below. Pale base to lower mandible, yellow in life.
  C. o. sclateri Vincent, 1934 (Melsetter area in eastern Zimbabwe and bordering areas of Mozambique) Similar to *obscura* but paler below, chest feathers with dusky fringes. T5-6 often with pale brownish-olive tips. Juvenile has olivaceous throat and breast.

MEASUREMENTS Wing 59-68 (mean 63.3, SD 0.27, 56 male *cephaelis*), 55-62 (mean 59.7, 7 male *granti*), 54-62 (mean 58.4, 12 male *guineensis*), 60-70 (mean 65.9, SD 0.3, 37 male *obscura*), 57.0-73 (mean 66.8, 47 male *ragazzii*), 62-67 (male *sclateri*), 50-60 (mean 56.8, SD 0.38, 37 female *cephaelis*), 52-56 (female *granti*), 51-55 (mean 54.7, SD 1.9, 12 female *guineensis*), 55-64 (mean 60.7, SD 0.6, 12 female *obscura*), 51.5-65.0 (mean 57.9, 41 female *ragazzii*), 55-60 (female *sclateri*); **tail** 45-56.5 (male *cephaelis*), 42-53 (male *granti*), 35-52 (mean 40.3, SD 2.5, 13 male *guineensis*),

46.0-66.0 (mean 58, 5 male *ragazzii*), 36-43 (female *cephaelis*), 39-43 (female *granti*), 37-39 (mean 38.4, SD 0.9, female *guineensis*), 38.0-56.0 (mean 47.8, 5 female *ragazzii*); **culmen** 20.0-27.5 (*ragazzii*); **bill** 21-28 (male *cephaelis*), 21-26 (mean 25.4, SD 0.8, 13 male *guineensis*), 23-28 (male *obscura*), 22-28 (mean 26.2, 5 male *ragazzii*), 20-26 (female *cephaelis*), 20.5-25 (mean 24.2, SD 0.9, 12 female *guineensis*), 25-27 (mean 26, 6 female *ragazzii*), 20-23 (mean 20.6, 7 unsexed *granti*), 23-28 (unsexed *ragazzii*); **tarsus** 15-18 (male *cephaelis*), 14-18 (male *guineensis*), 15-22 (mean 17.8, 5 male *ragazzii*), 14-17 (female *cephaelis*), 16-17 (female *guineensis*), 17-18 (mean 17.6, 5 female *ragazii*), 15.0-19.0 (unsexed *ragazzii*); **mass** 10.0-12.8 (mean 11.1, 24 male *cephaelis*), 8.0-11.0 (mean 9.7, 18 male *guineensis*), 9.0-13.8 (mean 11.5, 65 male *ragazzii*, one bird varied by 1.4 g on recapture), 9.2-12.4 (mean 10.5, 20 male *sclateri*), 7.8-11.5 (mean 9.5, 14 female *cephaelis*), 7.7-9.8 (mean 8.6, 14 female *guineensis*), 7.9-12.2 (mean 10.0, 67 female *ragazzii*), 9.2-13.5 (mean 11.2, 77 male *sclateri*), 8.0-11.8 (mean 9.8, 67 female *sclateri*).

REFERENCES Akinpelu (1989), Bannerman (1948, 1951), Brosset & Erard (1986), Chabaud (1979), Cheke (1978), Clancey (1978a,b, 1992-1993), Dranzoa (1997), Fain & Mariaux (1991), Hanmer (1997), Jones & Tye (2000), Kirkpatrick & Smith (1988), Mann (1985), Mariaux & Vaucher (1991), Pérez del Val (1996), Prigogine (1971), Tree (1997h), Tye & MacAulay (1993).

80   MOUSE-COLOURED SUNBIRD
Cyanomitra veroxii   Plate 19

Cinnyris veroxii A. Smith, 1831, *S. Afr. Quart. J.*, 1st. ser., no. 5, p.13, eastern Cape Province *fide* Sclater, 1930, *Syst. Av. Aethiop.* p.702, South Africa.

This taxon is sometimes referred to as *C. verroxii* or *C. verreauxi* (e.g. Delacour 1944), the latter to reflect the name of the collector of the type, but *veroxii* was used in the original description, and could mean ferocious if derived from the Latin *ferox*, so according to article 32 (a) of the International Code of Zoological Nomenclature should stand (Clancey 1968, 1969).

Alternative name: Grey Sunbird, Verreaux's Sunbird

IDENTIFICATION Dull, large sunbird with grey upperparts and dull greyish-white underparts. At very close range a greenish-blue metallic tinge is visible on crown, back and shoulders. Scarlet pectoral tufts. Sexes similar. Young pale yellowish below. Song is characteristic.
Similar species Eastern Olive Sunbird *C. olivacea* (78) and Western Olive Sunbird *C. obscura* (79) are similar in shape and size and one or other may co-occur with *C. veroxii*. As its English name implies, *veroxii* is grey where the others are olive and has red, not yellow or orange, pectoral tufts. Confusion may arise with immature males of the double-banded sunbirds *Cinnyris* spp. when their bands begin to show, creating the impression of red pectoral tufts.

VOICE Call *Chip*, and *chip-chop*; *chip-choy-choy*; *zzip*; *tzeep-tjip-cha*; *sit*, *tsway-sit so*; alarm call an agitated twittering, including *skirree*, *rirree*, *rirree...* and *tsink*, *tsink*, *tsink* and *cheetee*, *teree-ree-tee-tee-ree...* **Song** Characteristic and sung all year: *cherr-chip-chee-churruoo* or *cherr-chip-cher-yooo* or *jip, jip,*

jip, joy-ee, falling slightly in pitch and lasting about a second and repeated every 2-5 seconds, occasionally initiated with a quieter *tsa-tsu*. Subsong a trilling series of rapid *tserr-tserr*, interspersed with short melodic phrases. Two males may sing to each other for 30 minutes or more, beginning with *zzik* repeated every 0.5 seconds interspersed by *chip-chop-chop* or variants every 30 seconds.

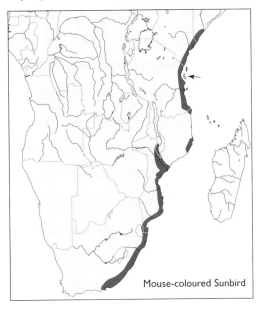

Mouse-coloured Sunbird

DISTRIBUTION East and south-east Africa. Somalia, Kenya, Tanzania, Malawi (Nchalo, Lengwe National Park), Mozambique, Swaziland, South Africa.

HABITAT Coastal forests, woodlands, scrubland including scrub with baobabs *Adansonia digitata*, *Euphorbia* thickets, mangroves, riverine forest, gardens. Also penetrates inland montane forests near coast, acacia scrubland adjoining forest margins.

STATUS Rare in Somalia where occurs along coast south of 2°15'N and up to 240 km up the Juba River. Scarce in Kenya, where localised along coast but also found 50 km up the Tana River and a vagrant further inland at 1,200 m. Scarce along coast in Tanzania, where also vagrant inland, but *zanzibarica* common in coral-rag bush in Zanzibar. Scarce on Mozambique coast but reaches 250 km up the Zambesi River. Not uncommon in South Africa along KwaZulu-Natal and Eastern Cape coasts, also extending 80 km inland in thickly wooded valleys. Rare in Malawi where only known from extreme south.

MOVEMENTS Local movements may occur, with seasonal movements from forest to acacia woodland reported. May irrupt westwards in wet summers, e.g. in 1987-1988 one bird reached as far west as Cape Town. Roams widely during a day in search of food-plants.

FOOD Insects including larvae of Lepidoptera, spiders, spiders' eggs, and nectar.
Known food-plants *Aloe* spp., *Erythrina* sp., *Halleria lucida*, *Kigelia africana*, *Leonotis leonurus*, unidentified mistletoes Loranthaceae, *Mimusops caffra*, *Scadoxus puniceus*, *Schotia* sp., *Strelitzia nicolai*, *Viscum* sp.

HABITS Shy and restless. Flight fast and erratic. Feeds in tops of trees and in denser open areas, where also feeds low down. Flycatches for airborne insects and hovers to take spiders from webs. Occasionally congregates at aloes. Flicks wings to show pectoral tufts. Chases congeners. Reduces metabolism at night by 47% at constant ambient temperature of 5°C and by 50-55% at 25°C.

BREEDING Bird displaying to another in song bouts for 30 minutes thrusts head and neck up and forward with primaries fanned and half-lowered to sides of body when making *chip-chop-chop* notes (see above), but relaxes wings when trilling with lower mandible moving up and down rapidly. May keep up such displays on and off all morning or more. Predators at nest include boubous *Laniarius* sp., monkeys and snakes. **Nest** Suspended 1-6 m above ground from forest tree or shrub or amongst exposed roots in eroded bank or rocky crevice. Sometimes nests in or on houses or huts such as cow-stalls, e.g. on wire attached to mosquito net in house, from creeper on porch or verandah and in garage. Nests repeatedly in same site, but makes fresh nest each year. Elongated pouch, often with long neck and wispy beard, with extensive porch overhanging entrance. Often but not invariably made of black rhizomorphs of horse-hair blight *Marasmius*; other material includes fine rootlets, twiglets, dead leaves, bark fibres, vegetable down, moss, lichen and dried grass. When no *Marasmius* used, cobwebs predominate as binding material. Decorated outside with bits of bark, web, leaves etc. Lined with fine dry grass, no pappus, above lining of dead leaves; grass lining may be 1 cm thick and carpeting all interior, but thinner (3 mm) on roof. Porch 85 mm long, 60 mm wide and 10 mm thick. Nest height 120-170 mm, excluding neck of 110 mm; width 50-75 mm, depth 80 mm, entrance hole 30-40 mm in diameter. One nest of race *zanzibarica* placed close to many hanging wasp nests at seashore. **Eggs** Race *fischeri*: c/2; *veroxii*: c/1-3 (mean of 45 clutches 2.2), 16.5-19.9 (mean 18.1, n=49) x 11.9-13.2 (mean 12.5), greyish-white, buffish or dark brown, darker at wider pole, usually plain but sometimes spotted and streaked greyish-brown or reddish-brown; *zanzibarica*: c/2, dark brown, almost oval. **Laying months** East Africa: February, April–July, September–December; Kenya: May–July, September, November, December; South Africa: September–February, peak November–December; Zanzibar: breeding condition November–April.

DESCRIPTION *C. v. veroxii*
Adult male Crown and nape dark brown with feathers tipped metallic bluish-green. Lores dark olive-grey. Sides of face grey, olive-grey or brownish-grey. Mantle grey. Neck,

rump and uppertail-coverts brownish-grey with feathers tipped metallic bluish-green, greener than crown, less so from lower back to tail. Remiges and greater wing-coverts dark brown, edged pale brown, secondaries edged pale greenish. Rectrices dark grey-brown with green gloss above, edged pale greyish-green, outer feather and tip of T5 paler. Median and lesser wing-coverts similar in centres, but broadly tipped metallic bluish-green. Chin, throat and breast pale greyish-buff or pale grey. Rest of underparts light greyish-olive or pale pinkish-grey. Axillaries, underwing-coverts and inner borders of undersides of remiges greyish-white. Pectoral tufts scarlet. Iris dark brown. Bill and feet black.
Adult female As male, rarely with yellow in pectoral tuft.
Juvenile Mantle olive-green not grey; throat whitish, belly yellowish-olive, brighter on breast; lacks pectoral tufts. Gape of birds 1-2 months old bright orange and still orange after 1 year.

GEOGRAPHICAL VARIATION
  C. v. fischeri (Reichenow, 1880) (coastal lowlands of north-east KwaZulu-Natal and southern Mozambique north to Juba valley in southern Somalia; inland to southern Malawi) Underparts whiter, upperparts paler and greyer with less gloss than *veroxii*, and smaller (wing 60-63) than *veroxii* (wing 62-68).
  C. v. veroxii (Smith, 1831) (lowland forest from eastern Cape Province at Port Elizabeth to east KwaZulu-Natal) Described above.
  C. v. zanzibarica Grote, 1932 (Zanzibar) Paler below than other races, upperside greyer, less glossy, lacking green metallic tinge of *fischeri*, and smaller (wing 59-61) but heavier than both *veroxii* and *fischeri*.

MEASUREMENTS Wing 60-63 (mean 61.0, 6 male *fischeri*), 62-68 (mean 65.5, 6 male *veroxii*), 59-61 (mean 59.8, 6 male *zanzibarica*), 54-55 (4 female *fischeri*), 57-62 (mean 59, 8 female *veroxii*); **tail** 50-56 (mean 52.3, 6 male *veroxii*), 50-54 (mean 51.9, 8 female *veroxii*); **bill** 26-28 (mean 26.5, 6 male *veroxii*), 23-26 (mean 25.1, 8 female *veroxii*); **tarsus** 16-18 (mean 16.8, 6 male *veroxii*), 15-17 (mean 16, 8 female *veroxii*); **mass** 8.5-11.2 (mean 10.4, 10 male *fischeri*), 9.4-11.5 (mean 10.4, 8 male *veroxii*), 13.9-18.8 (mean 15.3, 12 male *zanzibarica*), 7.0-9.8 (mean 8.5, 9 female *fischeri*), 8.6-11.7 (mean 9.7, 10 female *veroxii*), 14-16.6 (mean 15, 7 female *zanzibarica*), 9.2-13.1 (mean 11.3, 31 unsexed *veroxii*).

REFERENCES Britton & Britton (1977), Fuggles-Couchman (1984), Hanmer (1979, 1981), Pakenham (1979), Prinzinger *et al.* (1989), Prinzinger & Jackel (1986), Skead (1967), Tree (1997g).

CHALCOMITRA

Chalcomitra Reichenbach 1854, *Handb. spec. Orn., Icon. Synops. Avium, Scansoriae*, p.277. Type by subsequent designation (G. R. Gray 1855, *Cat. Gen. Subgen. Birds* p. 137) *Certhia amethystina* Shaw.

Seven species of medium to large, stocky sunbirds with square-ended tails and heavy, markedly decurved bills. Tongue similar to *Cyanomitra* but broadens at tip, and bifurcation less deep (Figure 6c). Most sexually dimorphic, some markedly so, others only slightly. Two species with pectoral tufts, rest without. Mostly brown-bodied with some metallic feathering on males, on head at least, except in *C. balfouri*.

81   BUFF-THROATED SUNBIRD
Chalcomitra adelberti   **Plate 23**

Cinnyris adelberti Gervais, 1834 (July), *Mag. Zool.* [Paris] 3 (1833), cl.2, pl.19, Senegal[?] (but possibly Sierra Leone).

IDENTIFICATION Somewhat dumpy, medium-sized sunbird with relatively short bill. Adult male unmistakable if pale buff throat seen, contrasting strikingly with overall blackish-brown appearance of rest of plumage. Female brown above, streaked brown below on greyish-white chin and yellowish-olive breast and belly, brightest yellowish on belly.
Similar species None. Females separable from those of allopatric Green-headed Sunbird *Cyanomitra verticalis* (73) by streaking below and absence of supercilium.

VOICE Call *Tseep*, *chip* and *pitchew* (*adelberti*); *pitchew-tlweet* (*eboensis*). **Song** A complicated rapid introductory twittering for about 15 seconds, followed by a long series of *pttioooou* calls repeated every 1-3 seconds for more than a minute (*adelberti*), also a relaxed *tserr-pit-cherr-choou* lasting 1.5-2 seconds, repeated every 4-6 seconds (*adelberti*); loud *tseep...tseep...tseep* (*eboensis*).

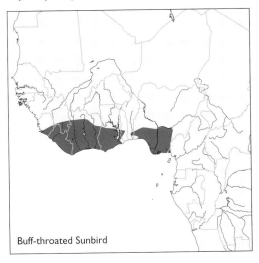

Buff-throated Sunbird

DISTRIBUTION West Africa. Guinea, Sierra Leone, Liberia, Côte d'Ivoire, Ghana, Togo, Benin, Nigeria, Cameroon.

HABITAT Lowland mature and secondary forests, forest edge and clearings near towns and villages, where also visits cassava fields, other cultivated areas and gardens. Attracted to trees with ants' nests. Occurs up to 1,000 m in Liberia.

STATUS Uncommon or locally common in forest habitats in West Africa from Sierra Leone to south-east Nigeria, where locally common, and Cameroon. Not uncommon in Liberia and Ghana. Common in Togo. Rare in Cameroon except in Ekok area near border with Nigeria.

MOVEMENTS Local dispersals occur in relation to flowering of trees, with southward movements in dry season in Liberia and Nigeria.

FOOD Insects, including ants and small caterpillars; spiders; nectar. Nectar-robs larger flowers.

Known food-plants *Bombax* spp., *Carica papaya*, *Convolvulus* sp., *Daniella* sp., *Ficus* sp., *Hibiscus* sp., *Pouteria alnifolia*, *Rhipsalis* sp., *Spathodea campanulata*.

HABITS Tame. Forage on branches <10 cm in diameter, >20 m up in the mid-stratum or tops of trees, singly, but usually in pairs, occasionally in groups of up to 10 birds or as part of mixed flocks e.g. with Little Green Sunbird *Anthreptes seimundi* (60), Green Sunbird *A. rectirostris* (61), Blue-throated Brown Sunbird *Cyanomitra cyanolaema* (75) and Johanna's Sunbird *Cinnyris johannae* (129). Associates at flowering trees with other sunbirds such as Superb Sunbird *C. superbus* (130). Hover in front of ants' nests suspended from trees, apparently taking ants from them; obtains insects by leaf-gleaning, hovering below leaves and branches and sometimes by aerial sallies from a perch. Sometimes sits in tops of tall trees, either silently for long periods or calling occasionally. Reduces metabolism at night by 52% at constant ambient temperature of 5°C and by 49-53% at 25°C.

BREEDING Butterfly-like display-flight by singing male. Males chase each other. Both parents feed young and remove faecal pellets. **Nest** 2-5 m above ground, in shade of canopy of creepers around dying tree or in mango *Mangifera indica* or *Raphia* palm. Untidy dome structure 250 mm x 250 mm, similar to nest of Scarlet-chested Sunbird *Chalcomitra senegalensis* (85), of fibrous plant material such as grass stems suspended amongst dry leaves at end of twig. Bottom a straggly beard of wispy fibres and/or spiders' webs. Entrance at side, hole 50-70 mm in width with slight overhanging porch. Lining white, fibrous, probably kapok (*Bombax* sp. or *Ceiba pentandra*). **Eggs** c/4; undescribed. **Laying months** Côte d'Ivoire: juveniles September–October; Ghana: nest-building December; Liberia: nest-building July and juveniles June–July; Nigeria: October–March, a dry-season nester.

DESCRIPTION *C. a. adelberti*
Adult male Crown to back of eye bright metallic green, merging into blackish-brown on back of head and neck. Mantle and back paler brown, uppertail-coverts blackish-brown. Eye-ring and lores black. Lesser wing-coverts light chestnut with rufous hue. Rest of wing-coverts and remiges dark brown with narrow chestnut edges. Tail blackish-brown. Chin and upper throat black. Malar stripe metallic green, becoming wider posteriorly. Lower throat pale buff, becoming cream-coloured through bleaching in birds with old feathers, forming conspicuous wide bib. Bib has black border separating it from bright chestnut underparts. Axillaries and underwing-coverts chestnut. Iris brown. Bill, legs and feet black.
Adult female Upperparts earth-brown, wings and tail darker. Throat greyish-white with olive-brown streaks. Rest of underparts cream with olive wash and light streaking of olive-brown. Axillaries and underwing-coverts with yellow tinge.
Juvenile Immature male similar to female but underparts more olive-brown. Adult plumage is gradually assumed during moult at end of dry season (February–March) with black chin, buff throat and black bar below throat appearing before metallic feathers on crown and throat. Before adult body feathers appear, brown back becomes bleached.

GEOGRAPHICAL VARIATION
   C. a. adelberti (Gervais, 1834) (Sierra Leone to Ghana) Described above.

C. a. eboensis (Jardine, 1843) (Togo to south-east Nigeria) Males with darker chestnut, less rufous, on underparts below throat which is paler than in *adelberti*. Females paler below with paler yellowish-grey breast with pale brown marks.

MEASUREMENTS Wing 60-67 (mean 63.2, 10 male *adelberti*), 62-64 (5 male *eboensis*), 55-63 (mean 58.8, 6 female *adelberti*), 56-57 (2 female *eboensis*); **tail** 31-39 (mean 37, 10 male *adelberti*), 38-40 (5 male *eboensis*), 29-36 (mean 34, 6 female *adelberti*), 30-32 (2 female *eboensis*); **bill** 17-21 (mean 18.9, 10 male *adelberti*), 18-20 (5 male *eboensis*), 16-20 (mean 19.3, 6 female *adelberti*), 18-19 (2 female *eboensis*); **tarsus** 14-16 (mean 15, 10 male *adelberti*), 16-17 (5 male *eboensis*), 14-15 (mean 14.8, 6 female *adelberti*), 16-17 (2 female *eboensis*); **mass** 8.9-11.0 (mean 10.1, 7 male *adelberti*), 9.9 (male *eboensis*), 8.3-10.1 (mean 9.4, 4 female *adelberti*).

REFERENCES Bannerman (1948), Button (1967), Fry (1965), Gatter (1997), Gray (1972), Prinzinger *et al.* (1989), Prinzinger & Jackel (1986), Serle (1957), Turner & Forbes-Watson (1979).

82   CARMELITE SUNBIRD
Chalcomitra fuliginosa   Plate 22

Certhia fuliginosa Shaw, 1811-12, *Gen. Zool.* 8, p.222, Malimba, Portuguese Congo.

IDENTIFICATION A very distinctive large sunbird but variable in colour. Appears dark with buff nape and mantle tinged with reddish, becoming even paler above in worn, bleached plumage.

Similar species Male told from Green-throated Sunbird *Chalcomitra rubescens* (83) and Amethyst Sunbird *C. amethystina* (84) by metallic forehead reflecting purple not green, generally more chocolate plumage, and pale brown hindneck and mantle. Female separable by lack of supercilium.

VOICE Call *Tsit.* **Song** A descending trill of *pttrreeeee* of about 0.5 seconds duration, repeated every 2-3 seconds, and a trilling *dree-dree* all at the same pitch (*aurea*).

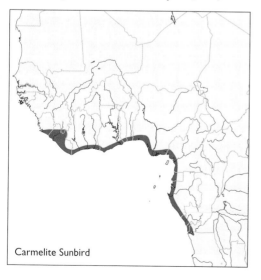

Carmelite Sunbird

DISTRIBUTION West Africa. Sierra Leone, Liberia, Côte d'Ivoire, Ghana, Togo, Benin, Nigeria, Cameroon, Equatorial Guinea, Gabon, Republic of the Congo, Cabinda, Democratic Republic of the Congo and Angola.

HABITAT Coastal lowland woods, coastal plains, coconut palms, mangroves, freshwater swamps, plantations, at edges of clearings and roads through secondary and coffee plantations and gardens. Also in savanna in northern Liberia. Occurs inland along the River Congo. Avoids primary forest.

STATUS Rare to locally common, Liberia. Locally common Côte d'Ivoire. No recent records in Ghana or Togo. Common in Nigeria. Not uncommon in Cameroon. Common on coasts of Republic of the Congo and Democratic Republic of the Congo. Uncommon to locally common resident in Angola. Threatened by destruction of mangroves.

MOVEMENTS Common in Lagos area, July–October, but not at other times so may disperse along coast. Also noted 50 km inland at Abeokuta, Nigeria.

FOOD Insects, with larger ones sucked dry and discarded. Nectar.

Known food-plants *Canna* sp., *Ceiba pentandra*, ?*Cocos nucifera*, *Coffea* spp., *Delonix regia*, *Hibiscus* sp., *Moringa pterygosperma*, *Musa* sp., *Russelia* sp.

HABITS Often in small parties of 8 or more birds. Feeds by perching on and hovering in front of flowers and reaching up to them from the ground. Host to feather mites *Anisodiscus dolichogaster*, *Pterodectes hologaster* and *Proctophyllodes legaci*.

BREEDING Female builds with male in attendance. **Nest** In rubber plantation, 3 m from ground, suspended by gossamer strands and fibres from end of rubber tree branch. A small domed pouch, circular entrance on side with porch, and short beard. Made of fibres, skeletons of rubber leaves, and some moss, finely woven with gossamer and black fibres, decorated with bits of bark. Thickly lined with plant down. Others hung from avocado trees, shrubs, wire on telegraph pole and low bush over water. **Eggs** c/2. Race *aurea*: 19-21.7 (mean 20.1, n=4) x 13.1-14.6 (mean 13.7); long ovate, smooth and glossy. Brownish-white largely covered with streaks, spots and blotches of brown or lilac-grey, concentrated at larger pole. **Laying months** Cabinda: breeding condition August–September; Cameroon: September–November; Gabon, January–February, July, December; Liberia: juveniles and immature in wing-moult October; Nigeria: September, November, dependent young October and November, nest-building January; Republic of the Congo, September–December.

DESCRIPTION *C. f. aurea*
Adult male Metallic purplish-blue forehead. Chin, throat and uppertail-coverts metallic violet. Large pectoral tufts lemon-yellow. Remainder of body plumage dull chocolate-brown, darkest on breast, belly and undertail-coverts. Wings and tail very dark chocolate-brown, wings with small patch of metallic violet on lesser wing-coverts below carpal joint. Axillaries and underwing-coverts dark brown. Iris brown. Bill, legs and feet black. Very prone to bleaching of feathers by sunlight and thus males in old plumage may appear with head pale brownish or as pale as greyish-white, mantle light brown, all metallic feathering duller than when fresh including undertail-coverts which become tinged with metallic green instead of the usual violet.

Adult female Paler than male. Upperparts earth-brown with dark brown wings and tail, wing-coverts with creamy-white margins and tips. Tail-feathers also with white tips. Throat brown, rest of underparts creamy-white with dark centres to feathers giving mottled appearance.

Juvenile Male similar to adult female but cheeks to chin and throat sooty-brown, lacking moustachial stripe, and heavy dark brown mottling on breast.

GEOGRAPHICAL VARIATION Chapin (1954) reported a probable hybrid between *C. f. fuliginosa* and *C. amethystina deminuta*; see also Hall & Moreau (1970) and Louette (1989). The latter described another hybrid, pointed out that coastal birds were smaller than those from inland at Kinshasa, and advocated the validity of *C. f. nigrescens*, which has a darker mantle than the nominate, concolorous with the rest of the plumage, for the populations in the Democratic Republic of the Congo and Angola. He also argued that there is apparent introgression between the population of *fuliginosa* inland and *amethystina*.

C. f. aurea (Lesson, 1847) (coasts from Sierra Leone to Gabon) Described above. Male paler brownish above with less glossy forehead and throat than *fuliginosa*.

C. f. fuliginosa (Shaw, 1811) (includes *nigrescens* Oustalet, 1893, but see Louette 1989) (north-west Angola [Gabela] to southern Democratic Republic of the Congo, lower Congo inland to Kwanmouth) Male darker above, with very slightly more metallic plumage, female darker on hind-neck than in *aurea* and with brownish area on throat and foreneck.

MEASUREMENTS Wing 67-72 (mean 70.2, 10 male *aurea*), 66.0-70.5 (mean 68.6, 15 male *fuliginosa/nigrescens*, coastal Democratic Republic of the Congo), 68.5-73.5 (mean 70.5, 15 male *fuliginosa/nigrescens*, Kinshasa, Democratic Republic of the Congo), 62-67 (mean 64.3, 8 female *aurea*); **tail** 42-46 (mean 43.5, 10 male *aurea*), 40.5-46.5 (mean 43.6, 15 male *fuliginosa/nigrescens*, coastal Democratic Republic of the Congo), 40.5-46.0 (mean 43.0, 15 male *fuliginosa/nigrescens*, Kinshasa, Democratic Republic of the Congo), 35-41 (mean 39, 8 female *aurea*); **bill** 21-26 (mean 24.6, 10 male *aurea*), 20-25 (mean 23.3, 8 female *aurea*); **culmen** 23.0-25.5 (mean 24.2, 15 male *fuliginosa/nigrescens*, coastal Democratic Republic of the Congo), 25.0-26.5 (mean 25.7, 15 male *fuliginosa/nigrescens*, Kinshasa, Democratic Republic of the Congo), **tarsus** 16-18 (mean 17, 10 male *aurea*), 17 (3 female *aurea*); **mass** 11.6 (male *fuliginosa*), 12.2 (female *aurea*).

REFERENCES Bannerman (1948, 1951), Fry *et al.* (2000), Hall & Moreau (1970), Louette (1989), Zumpt (1961).

---

83 GREEN-THROATED SUNBIRD
Chalcomitra rubescens   Plate 22

Cinnyris rubescens Vieillot, 1819, *Nouv. Dict. Hist. Nat.*, nouv. éd. 31, p.506, Kingdom of Congo and Cacongo.

Taxonomic note *Chalcomitra angolensis* is this species.

IDENTIFICATION Male appears all black at a distance but iridescent green throat-patch visible at close quarters. Female greyish-brown above with contrasting pale belly, heavily streaked and with prominent supercilium.

Similar species In West Africa, almost black appearance and green throat of male unlikely to lead to confusion with other species, except the much lighter-coloured and browner Carmelite Sunbird *Chalcomitra fuliginosa* (82). Female told by heavy streaking on breast and white supercilium, without white below eye possessed by female Blue-throated Brown Sunbird *Cyanomitra cyanolaema* (75). In East Africa, male separable from male Amethyst Sunbird *Chalcomitra amethystina* (84) by green throat-patch extending to upper breast, bordered by violet band, and absence of metallic feathers on shoulders or uppertail-coverts; female almost indistinguishable from female Amethyst but darker above and more boldly streaked below.

VOICE Call *Chip* (*rubescens*). **Song** A complex sequence of twittering notes in a rapid delivery, including phrases of *weet-to-weeto-ro* (*rubescens*, East Africa). A long song sequence lasting nearly 4 minutes, starting with a rapid series of *chip* (6-7 per second), followed by musical twittering, a 4-second burst of very rapid *chi* notes (11-12 per second), more musical twittering, bursts of *chip, chip, chip*, a trill tailing off in volume, more musical twittering, the repeated sequences of 20 or more further bursts of *chip* sometimes accelerating, the later ones preceded by 1-9 *choueee* calls (*rubescens*, West Africa). Some individual variation in proportions of musical passages and *chip-chip* in the songs. *Chir-chip* repeated 5 times followed by 4 repetitions of *chip*, the whole sequence repeated continuously for 3 minutes or more (*strangerii*, Bioko).

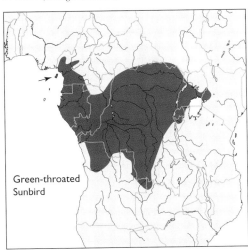

Green-throated Sunbird

DISTRIBUTION West, Central and East Africa. Nigeria, Cameroon, Equatorial Guinea (Bioko and Rio Muni), Central African Republic, Gabon, northern Angola, Republic of the Congo, Democratic Republic of the Congo, Sudan, Rwanda, Burundi, Uganda (up to 1,500 m), western Kenya, north-west Tanzania, Zambia (northern Mwinilunga province at confluence of Rivers Mbulungu and Zambezi, Lisomo stream and the District HQ).

HABITAT Forest, forest edges, secondary growth and clearings up to 1,500 m. Gallery forests in wooded savanna. Cocoa and rubber plantations, farms, edges of villages, well-wooded bush, gardens with tall trees. Montane grassland and heaths.

STATUS Common in suitable habitat. Rare in Nigeria, where known from Gashaka-Gumti Game Reserve, subspecies not identified. Not uncommon in Cameroon.

Common in Bioko up to 1,200 m and locally common in mainland Equatorial Guinea at forest edges. Common and widespread in Gabon with 5-6 pairs per km² in proximity of habitations. Common in Democratic Republic of the Congo. Uncommon in Sudan. Not uncommon resident in Angola. Common and widespread in forests and woodlands of Uganda, but avoids dry areas especially in the north. Locally common in Nandi and Kakamega forests, Kenya. Rare and localised in Tanzania and Zambia.

MOVEMENTS Probably sedentary but may wander, as records in Zambia all from September–October.

FOOD Insects, including ants and caterpillars, small spiders, pollen, small fruits and nectar. Stomach of one bird contained orange ball of rubber 4.5 x 2.5 mm, latex presumably ingested with other plant juices.
Known food-plants *Albizia zygia, Carica papya, Dalbergia* sp., *Erythrina abyssinica, Fiscus* sp., *Leonotis nepetifolia,* unidentified mistletoes Loranthaceae, *Musa* spp., *Spathodea campanulata.* Forages for insects in *Musanga* tree.

HABITS Singly or in groups of up to 5 at flowering trees, when likely to chase each other. Dominates Olive-bellied Sunbird *Cinnyris chloropygius.* Prefers to forage high in trees, usually 15-30 m up but sometimes as low as 5 m. May hang upside-down when foraging and feeding, like tit *Parus* sp. Sometimes hovers in front of flowers or small figs while feeding and at edges of trees whilst hawking for insects, which it also does in short flycatcher-like sallies for 2-3 m away from its perch. When not feeding, perches looking from side to side with jerky head movements. Males sing from vantage points on dead trees or wires to defend territories. Sometimes aggressive: males chase each other, their females and other species of sunbird. Roosts in mango trees.

BREEDING Male sings and chases females during breeding season. Only female feeds newly hatched young, but male present. **Nest** Race *rubescens*: 200 mm high with a 50 mm beard, 70 mm wide and 70 mm deep. Diameter of entrance 25 mm, located 110 mm from the apex, with overhanging porch. Made of *Usnea* and other lichens, cobwebs, moss roots, hairs from tree-ferns *Cyathea* sp., and mats of silk vegetation from Asclepiadaceae and attached to a *Macaranga* bush. Thickly lined with soft silky pappus. Another suspended 7 m up in large tree beside road, made of fine dry vegetable material and dried leaves, lined with plant down, and decorated outside with bark, lichens and caterpillar frass. **Eggs** c/2; *rubescens*: 17.0-19.0 (mean 18.2, n=5) x 11.2-12.5 (mean 12.0); distinctive with unusual pattern. Glossy, brownish or creamy-white with many lavender-grey, dark brown or grey-brown stripes, parallel to the length of the egg but closer together at the bigger end, which appears darker. **Laying months** Angola: breeding condition October; Cameroon: April, July, August, October; Democratic Republic of the Congo: March, November; East Africa: May–July, October–December; Gabon: nest-building September, males singing and chasing females September–February; Uganda: eggs June, August, breeding condition July, September–November; Zambia; active gonads October.

DESCRIPTION *C. r. rubescens*
Adult male Band on forehead and lores black. Anterior part of crown metallic green with blue fringe posteriorly merging into 3 mm deep iridescent fringe of metallic violet at rear of crown. Nape, ear-coverts and rest of upperparts

very dark brown burnished with golden-bronze. Remiges and tail yet darker brown than back, except outerwebs of rectrices concolorous with back. Chin black, throat iridescent green with bright purple fringe below. Malar streak of iridescent bluish-green separated from throat-patch by 1 mm wide streak of brown. Rest of underparts dark brown with golden-bronze tinge. No pectoral tufts. Iris dark brown. Bill, legs and feet black. Non-breeding plumage suggested to occur in *stangerii*, the Bioko race, as Alexander recorded a male with female plumage, except for presence of metallic green on forehead and throat, with enlarged gonads, and such a male with moulting shoulder patches seen singing, Bioko, February 2001. Bird was accompanied by a juvenile. Bannerman (1948) doubted the existence of such an eclipse dress and thought precocity more likely. Birds in worn plumage may appear paler through bleaching and thus, when moulting, new feathers appear much darker than old.
Adult female Ear-coverts and lores brown. Prominent white supercilium. All upperparts earth-brown, darkest on forehead. Remiges and rectrices darker brown than back, remiges edged pale. Rectrices with narrow white tips. Throat variable, greyish-white or streaked brown ranging to entirely black. Breast yellowish-white with prominent olive-brown streaks. Belly yellow with less marked streaking. Undertail-coverts pale yellow with dark centres. Underwing-coverts mottled greyish-brown with white tips. Axillaries very pale yellow. Iris dark brown. Bill, legs and feet black.
Juvenile Immature male similar to adult female but throat, destined to become metallic green, grey with white tips to feathers. Future metallic malar stripe region demarcated with barred feathers. Metallic plumage appears first on throat, then on crown. Immature female similar to adult female but streaks on underparts tend to be darker and less olive. Juvenile has pinkish-yellow gape.

GEOGRAPHICAL VARIATION
C. r. crossensis (Serle, 1963) (Cameroon, Mamfe and to west of Bamenda; Nigeria, Cross River and Taraba States, as far west as Buanchor) Resembles *rubescens* but male lacks any metallic on throat and breast except on malars. Only known female, collected at the type (male) at Mamfe on 10 March 1953, with heavy streaking below and without any yellowish wash although a few greenish-olive feathers present, but indistinguishable from *stangerii* or *rubescens*.
C. r. rubescens (Vieillot, 1819) (?Nigeria; Cameroon to Cabinda south through Democratic Republic of the Congo except south-east Katanga, and Uíge to Cuanza Norte, Cuanza Sul and Malanje, and east to northern Lunda Norte in Angola; north-west Zambia [Mwinilunga], southern borders of Sudan, Uganda, west Kenya, north-west Tanzania) Described above.
C. r. stangerii (Jardine, 1842) (Bioko) Male with metallic plumage on chin to upper breast all emerald-green, as head, not as golden-green as in *rubescens*. Iridescent purple band on hindcrown usually narrower and stretching less far behind eyes than in *rubescens*. Female with foreneck and breast-streaking heavier and blacker than in *rubescens* and usually white not yellowish below. Immature male differs from adult female by being darker below with blacker centre to chest and belly feathers, giving barred rather than streaked appearance, and more uniform dark, rather than mottled grey, chins. For possible eclipse plumage see under non-breeding plumage in description of nominate.

MEASUREMENTS Wing 63, 66 (2 male *crossensis*), 63-71 (mean 68.2, 12 male *rubescens*), 59 (female *crossensis*), 58-67 (6 male *stangerii*), 58-63 (mean 60.4, 11 female *rubescens*); tail 38, 43 (2 male *crossensis*), 39-48 (mean 44.9, 12 male *rubescens*), 37 (female *crossensis*), 34-42 (mean 36.9, 11 female *rubescens*); bill 19, 20 (2 male *crossensis*), 18-23 (mean 24.6, 12 male *rubescens*), 20 (female *crossensis*), 18-22 (mean 21, 11 female *rubescens*); tarsus 16, 17 (2 male *crossensis*), 15-19 (mean 16, 12 male *rubescens*), 15 (female *crossensis*), 15-16 (mean 15.5, 10 female *rubescens*); mass 8-14 (mean 11.3, 19 male *rubescens*), 6.5-11.0 (mean 9.4, SD 1.78, 5 female *rubescens*).

REFERENCES Bannerman (1948), Benson *et al.* (1971), Brosset & Erard (1986), Chapin (1954), Cheke (2001), Demey & Njabo (2001), Green (1990), Hopkins *et al.* (1999), Moore (1995), Prigogine (1971), Serle (1957, 1963).

84   AMETHYST SUNBIRD
Chalcomitra amethystina   Plate 22

Certhia amethystina Shaw, 1811-12, *Gen. Zool.* 8, p.195, Cape of Good Hope, South Africa.

Alternative name: Black Sunbird, Amethyst-throated Sunbird

IDENTIFICATION Large sunbird. Male appears all black at a distance but iridescent plumage (purplish-copper on throat and shoulders, silvery light green on crown) clearly visible at close range. Iridescence on throat may sometimes appear red. Iridescent green patch on forehead clearly visible at close range and in good light appears as a silvery light green sheen.
Similar species Male separable from those of Green-throated *Chalcomitra rubescens* (83) and Carmelite Sunbird *C. fuliginosa* (82) by iridescent green on forehead and crown without any violet, violet and blue shoulder-flash and lack of pectoral tufts. Female has paler upperparts and usually less heavily marked below than female *rubescens*. However, females very variable, some with no streaking and reminiscent of female Miombo Double-collared Sunbird *Cinnyris manoensis* (102). Female and juvenile resemble those of Scarlet-chested Sunbird *Chalcomitra senegalensis* (85), but latter always have some white on alula and associated primary coverts. Amethyst is more yellowish below, generally much paler with greater contrast between the greyish upperparts and greenish abdomen, with only slight streaking visible on upper chest. Both Amethyst and Scarlet-chested Sunbirds utter *chip* calls but *choop* of Scarlet-chested distinctive and different from equivalent *chup* variation of Amethyst. Young and females confusable with those of Mariqua Sunbird *Cinnyris mariquensis*, but breast of Amethyst usually more heavily marked and bill more curved.

VOICE Call Common note, including when in flight, a single *chip* or *tschiek*, with some calls sounding more like *chup* (but not the *choop* of *C. senegalensis*), plus *zit-zit* and *zeebe-zeebu*, *tzwit-tzuit-zit* and *williet, williet, williet...* and *tsick-tipperit*. A quiet *chip* or *chip-chip*, a *tser-zip* and *zit-zit* (*amethystina*); both *chip* and *chop, chip-chop, cher-chip, cher-chop, chip-chip* or *ptcher-chiiizzz*, with a wheezing finish or *cherr-chip cherr-chou* (*kirkii*). A stuttering *chee, chee, chee, chee* or *ssweek-ssweeek-ssweeek*, between birds chasing each other at flowers. Alarm call: *t,t,t,t,t,t...* or *jit-jit-jit-jit...* and a more

urgent *choy, tit-choy, tit-chree*. Song A very complex sequence of rising and falling twitters uttered very rapidly (*amethystina*); complex, involving *chip-chip-chip-chee* uttered from top of tree or *der-chip-cher-chu* (*kirkii*). May sing from exposed position or hidden in tree for a whole morning, with short breaks between sessions, some of which last an hour. Young male still in juvenile plumage noted singing and females also produce a soft warble.

DISTRIBUTION East, Central and south-east Africa. Sudan, Ethiopia, Somalia, Gabon, Republic of the Congo, Democratic Republic of the Congo, Burundi, north-east Uganda, Kenya, Tanzania, Angola, Zambia, Malawi, Mozambique, Namibia, Botswana, Zimbabwe, Swaziland, Lesotho and South Africa.

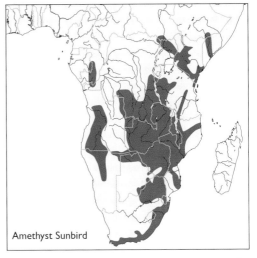

Amethyst Sunbird

HABITAT Woodlands in savanna, including miombo woodland and *Baikiaea* woodland, sometimes at edge of evergreen forest or in riverine forest. Slopes with *Aloe* spp. and *Protea* spp. and gardens.

STATUS In Somalia uncommon presumed resident restricted to Juba valley. In Sudan only known from Didinga and Imatong mountains, 1,500-2,100 m, where common. Fairly common in wooded savannas of Republic of the Congo and Democratic Republic of the Congo. Common in Kenya. Uncommon in Uganda, where only known from north-east (Mt Moroto and Mt Lonyili). Not uncommon in Tanzania. Common and widespread in Malawi, Zambia and Zimbabwe. Common in Mozambique, South Africa and Swaziland but absent from Lesotho.

MOVEMENTS A wanderer and partial migrant. Moves east-west in Zimbabwe with birds coming from the west mostly present, May–August. Active eastward movements noted in Botswana, where scarcer June–September. An adult male ringed Lusaka, February, recovered 116 km north, May of same year. An immature ringed North West Province of South Africa recovered Pretoria North, 75 km away 35 months later, and another 120 km distant after 30 months. Move at least 26 km during seasonal shifts from suburban areas of Lydenburg to and from mountains. Common in Tanzania at Iringa and Songea only April–October.

FOOD Insects including termites, aphids and hoverflies (Syrphidae), many spiders, nectar. Gleans rose-bushes for aphids and may take termites as they emerge from ground.

Often hawks for insects like a flycatcher from tops of trees. Sometimes rubs termites on branch before eating them and takes spiders back to perch before swallowing them. Male seen to kill spider, the owner of a large globular nest in a *Mimosa* tree into which the bird then made a 25 mm opening to feed, together with a female, on the spiderlings. The pair then took over the nest for their own use, which they began to use even when it was still crawling with spiderlings which they continued to eat. Hovers in front of flowers to take nectar or grab spiders and seen to probe into fallen oranges. Oozing coconut sap also taken.

Known food-plants *Acacia sieberiana, Aloe* spp., *Abutilon* sp., *Acrocarpus fraxinifolius, Baikiaea* spp. including *B. plurijuga, Bauhinia* sp., *Bombax* sp., *Brunsfelsia* sp., *Canna* sp., *Cassia* sp., *Cestrum* sp., *Combretum flagrans, C. mozambicensis, Crotalaria australis, Dalbergia nitidula, Diospyros* sp., *Erythrina* spp. including *E. caffra, E. humeana* and *E. tomentosa, Eucalyptus* sp., *Euphorbia* sp., *Grevillea banksii, Halleria lucida, Hibiscus* sp. (nectar-robbed), *Ipomoea lobata, Kigelia africana, Kniphofia* sp., *Leonotis* sp. including *L. mollissima,* unidentified mistletoes Loranthaceae, *Melia azedarach, Petrea* sp., *Phragmanthera dschallensis* (parasite of *Acacia* spp., especially *A. drepanolobium*), *Protea angolensis, P. gaguedi, P. welwitschia, Prunus* sp., *Salvia* sp., *Schotia brachypetala, Strelitzia* sp. including *S. augusta, S. nicolai* and *S. reginae, Syzygium* spp. including *S. cordatum, Tecoma capense, Tithonia tagetiflora, Watsonia* sp.

HABITS Active, restless and conspicuous singly, in pairs or small groups. Flies erratically and seldom in a straight line. Mixes with other sunbird species such as *Chalcomitra senegalensis,* White-breasted *Cinnyris talatala* (133), Western Violet-backed *A. longuemarei* (56), Greater Double-Collared *C. afer* (109), Collared *Hedydipna collaris* (63) and Malachite *Nectarinia famosa* (97) at flowering trees, but also can be aggressive towards conspecifics, to other sunbirds such as Southern Double-Collared *C. chalybeus* (103) and also to Klaas's Cuckoo *Chrysococcyx klaas.* Aggressive display, e.g. towards Ruddy Waxbill *Lagonosticta rubricata,* involves throwing up head and pointing gaping bill skywards. Antagonistic behaviour of adult male to juvenile involves bizarre slow butterfly-like flight with wings flapping slowly and body moving at an angle down towards the younger bird. Males also fly at each other, interlock their feet and "fence" with their bills as they fall to the ground.

Bobs head up and down gently and rhythmically when perched. Final part of flight to perch may involve jerky motion with body held vertically. Respond to its reflection in window. Reduces metabolism at night by 51% at constant ambient temperature of 5°C and by 55-70% at 25°C. Maximum longevity 7 years 4 months.

Host to feather lice *Ricinus timmermanni,* ticks *Hyalomma aegyptium* and blood parasites *Haemoproteus sequeirae, Leucocytozoon nectariniae, Plasmodium circumflexum, P. vaughani, Trypanosoma everetti* and microfilariae.

BREEDING Courtship behaviour of *C. a. amethystina* involves male hopping about drooping first one wing then the other, then both at once, then fluttering each one. Female hangs head down in rigid motionless posture. Male chases female incessantly, to the detriment of nest-building activities and before building begins. Male stays very close behind during chases which are acrobatic with many changes in direction and accompanied by sharp clicks, probably wing-claps. Cloaca-pecking occurs, sometimes involving several stabbing actions in succession. After cloaca-pecking, one male seen with small black object,

possibly faecal, in tip of beak (Skead 1967). Observations suggest that function of cloaca-pecking in this and, perhaps, other sunbirds may be sperm-competition as occurs in Dunnocks *Prunella modularis* (Davies 1983, 1987) and other species (Birkhead & Møller 1992), in which faecal material and packets of sperm, presumably from other males in earlier matings, are released by female after pecks by male before he copulates with her. Soliciting female stretched head and neck horizontally, extended left wing and uttered quiet warble while swaying body slowly from side to side and fanning tail off-centre. One female attended during two successive broods by male in immature plumage. May nest in trees or shrubs alongside buildings, and in same place repeatedly. Only female builds nest and incubates (for 13-18 days). Both parents feed pulli, which hatch naked and blind, with egg tooth and with pale orange skin, during nestling period of 14-19 days. Chicks out of nest beg with *tseeep-tseeep...* call and are fed by both parents. Nests susceptible to being blown down in exposed areas. Often double-brooded. Parasitised by *Chrysococcyx klaas* and by Emerald Cuckoo *C. cupreus.* Host of Green-backed Honeybird *Prodotiscus zambesiae.*

Nest Race *amethystina*: pear-shaped, side-entrance, pendent 2-6 m above ground from branches or twigs of trees, e.g. *Acacia* sp., *Brachystegia* sp., *Eucalyptus* sp., conifers, mangroves, or from man-made structures such as clothes line, electric flex or bare wire, made of fine grass or fibres, wool, hair, bark and held together with cobwebs, decorated with leaves and lichen, lined with white woolly plant seed material, e.g. kapok or asclepiad pappus or from seeds of *Tarchonanthus* sp., feathers or even with red petals of *Lagerstroemia* sp. A prominent porch, often of *Eragrostis* sp. grass above entrance, which is 35-55 mm in diameter. Sometimes with beard. 128-171 mm high, 64-89 mm wide, 64-72 mm deep. Race *deminuta*: suspended from tree, 2-6 m up, oval or pear-shaped with porch. Made of fine grass and fibres held together with cobwebs; decorated with lichen, dead leaves, bark and wood splinters; lined thickly with plant down. Race *kirkii*: 127 x 89 x 76 mm, neatly made of plant down with a few fine dried grass strips, dead leaves, wood shavings, plant stems, bound with insect-web, thickly lined, decorated with a few small heaps of red-brown excreta of wood-boring insect larvae or with scale-like patches of lichen providing good camouflage. Lined with white pappus. No beard. No porch. Others in tamarind tree or suspended from string on verandah. Length 120 mm, greatest breadth 53, greatest antero-posterior measurement 45 mm, length of cavity 78 mm, entrance hole 28 mm with lower lip 43 mm above base of nest. **Eggs** c/1-4, usually 2 laid on successive days. Race *amethystina*: 17.0-23.2 (mean 19.5, n=34) x 12.0-14.0 (mean 13.1), white, cream, greenish-grey, pale green or light grey, marked with dense cover of spots, streaks, mottles, lines and smudges. Race *deminuta*: 16.8-19 x 12.3-13.5; cream or fawn-coloured, spotted or mottled with dark brown and grey. Race *kirkii*: 15.5-20.4 (mean 18.8, n=61) x 10.5-13.9 (mean 12.8), smooth, ovate, dirty white marked with elongated streaks, blotches and spots of olive-brown, chocolate-brown and slate-grey, usually denser at blunt end. **Laying months** Angola: May, October, and in breeding condition October, December; Botswana: October, November, January, March; Democratic Republic of the Congo: September–November; East Africa: January, March–December; Malawi: September–February, April; Mozambique: January; Somalia: August; South Africa: January–December; Zambia: August–March; Zimbabwe: July–April.

DESCRIPTION *C. a. amethystina*

Adult male Crown blackish-brown with iridescent green patch on forehead, appearing in good light as a silvery light green sheen or even as gold. Cheeks and lores dark blackish-brown. Nape, neck, mantle, back and rump blackish-brown. Uppertail-coverts purplish-violet. Remiges, tail, primary and greater coverts dull black. Lesser and median wing-coverts dark blackish-brown but carpals iridescent coppery-violet, as are chin and throat. Rest of underside dark blackish-brown. Some birds with indications of yellow pectoral tufts. Buccal cavity very dark brown to black. Iris dark brown. Legs and bill black. Probably no non-breeding plumage although eclipse seen in captive male. Wing moult of *amethystina* recorded April–June, with interrupted moult noted May (Grahamstown, South Africa).

Adult female Olivaceous grey-brown above, pale grey-brown below but with variable extent of heavy mottling, except on belly. Uppertail-coverts dark brown. Tail blackish-brown with greyish-white tips. Slight white supercilium. Sides of face greyish-brown, lores darker blackish-brown. Throat, breast and flanks with greyish-brown or dark brown streaks, sometimes very dense such that throat is almost black. Prominent white moustachial stripe, especially obvious in dark-throated individuals. Lesser and median coverts olive-grey. Remiges, primary and greater coverts dark greyish-brown. Remiges edged buff, paler on primaries. Underwing-coverts and axillaries brownish. Iris dark brown. Legs and bill black. Buccal cavity yellow-grey. Almost completely albinistic female recorded.

Juvenile Nestling pale orange. Juvenile has gape yellow. Throat blacker than adult female's, lacking radiating dotted lines but with pale moustachials, and more heavily spotted and yellowish below, giving barred rather than streaked look. Buccal cavity yellow-grey, becoming dull vermilion in males during post-juvenile moult. Immature male has an iridescent rosy-purple patch on throat.

GEOGRAPHICAL VARIATION

C. a. amethystina (Shaw, 1811) (includes *adjuncta* Clancey, 1975) (South Africa, Cape Province at Swellendam to KwaZulu-Natal, east Transvaal; Mozambique, south of the Limpopo River, south Botswana). Described above.

C. a. deminuta Cabanis, 1880 (Gabon, Angola from Huíla, northern Benguela, Huambo and Bié north to Cuanza Sul and Malanje, and east to Moxico, Lunda Norte and Lunda Sul, middle of Democratic Republic of the Congo to Kasai and Katanga and west to Gungu and north-west to Djambala in the Republic of the Congo, Namibia [Ovamboland] and Botswana [Ngamiland], Zambia [in north and west, mainly west of a line along Muchinga escarpment to Lusaka and Livingstone, outside range of *kirkii* except in Kasama and Mpika in west of Western Province and Kalabo where ranges overlap with some intergradation], ?Zimbabwe) Males with bills shorter (24-28) than *amethystina* (25-32) but uppertail-coverts also purplish-violet. Females with variable amounts of yellow on underparts and without blackish bases to throat feathers and therefore throats do not appear dusky as in *amethystina*. Much plainer below than *amethystina*, some with hardly any streaking and moustachial less prominent.

C. a. kirkii (Shelley, 1876) (includes *doggetti* [Sharpe, 1902] and *kalckreuthi* [Cabanis, 1878]) (Tanzania,

Mafia Island, Kenya north to Juba valley in Somalia, north-east Uganda [Mt Moroto and Kidepo National Park], south-east Ethiopia and south-east Sudan, ?Democratic Republic of the Congo, Malawi, Mozambique from Coguna northwards, Zambia [east of Muchinga escarpment in Eastern Province and throughout Western, Central, and Southern Provinces plus Barotse Province except its far north], Zimbabwe) Similar to *deminuta* (i.e. smaller than nominate) but males lack metallic purplish-violet on uppertail-coverts, which are blackish-brown or dull black.

MEASUREMENTS Wing 71-75 (mean 73.5, 10 male *amethystina*), 67-71 (mean 69.3, 10 male *deminuta*), 62-72 (mean 65, 20 male *kirkii*), 65-70 (juv/imm male *kirkii*), 60.0-67.5 (mean 61.8, 10 female *kirkii*), 61-67 (juv/imm female *kirkii*); **tail** 38.0-43.5 (mean 40.8, 15 male *deminuta*), 42.0-49.5 (mean 43.8, 10 male *kirkii*), 36-43.5 (juv/imm male *kirkii*), 34.0-46.5 (mean 38.3, 10 female *kirkii*), 34-43 (juv/imm female *kirkii*); **bill** 25-32 mean 29.7, 10 male *amethystina*), 24-28 (mean 26.3, 10 male *deminuta*), 24-27 (mean 25.5, 10 male *kirkii*), 24-27 (juv/imm male *kirkii*), 22.5-25.5 (mean 23.5, 10 female *kirkii*), 22.5-25.5 (juv/imm female *kirkii*); **culmen** 25.0-28.0 (mean 26.6, 15 male *deminuta*), 22.0-27.0 (*kirkii*); **tarsus** 15.0-18.5 (mean 16.3, 10 male *kirkii*), 15.5-18.5 (juv/imm male *kirkii*), 15.0-18.5 (mean 15.7, 10 female *kirkii*); **mass** 9.5-18.5 (mean 14.7, SD 1.21, 178 male *amethystina*), 12 (male *deminuta*), 9.2-14.7 (mean 11.0, 27 male *kirkii*), 10.6-12.6 70 (juv/imm male *kirkii*), 8.3-16.9 (mean 12.7, SD 1.25, 76 female *kirkii*), 9.9-12.2 (mean 10.2, 22 female *kirkii*).

REFERENCES Barnicoat (1984), Borello (1992), Capanna & Geralico (1982), Clancey (1975), Cowles (1936), Craig & Simon (1991), Fry *et al.* (2000), Hall & Moreau (1970), Hanmer (1997), Herremans (1992), Ledger (1980), Louette (1989), Oatley (1997), Oatley & Best (1997), Oxlee (1988), Prinzinger *et al.* (1989), Prinzinger & Jackel (1986), Sclater & Moreau (1933), Serle (1943), Skead (1953, 1967), de Swardt & Schoeman (1997), Tree (1991, 1997j).

---

85   SCARLET-CHESTED SUNBIRD
Chalcomitra senegalensis   Plate 23

Certhia senegalensis Linnaeus, 1766, *Syst. Nat.*, ed. 12, 1, p.186, Senegal.

Alternative names: Scarlet-breasted Sunbird, Scarlet-throated Sunbird

IDENTIFICATION Large with long curved bill. Adult males easily identified, except where sympatric with Hunter's Sunbird *Chalcomitra hunteri* (86), by vermilion breast contrasting with blackish body and metallic green crown, but appears all black at a distance. Purple shoulder of male *gutturalis* and *cruentata* almost never visible in the field. Female dull brown above, pale brownish-yellow below, boldly mottled with largish black markings and no supercilium.

Similar species Male *C. hunteri* separable by its violet uppertail-coverts and prominent violet shoulder-patch. *C. hunteri* has black chin and upper throat and so its green moustachials are also distinctive except where the similar-throated *C. senegalensis cruentata* is present. Poor views of males, or views from behind only, can lead to confusion with Amethyst Sunbird *C. amethystina* (84) especially if purplish-red throat of latter produces bright red reflections which can happen in some lights; Amethyst male has violet not black uppertail-coverts. Females and juveniles of *C. senegalensis* resemble those of *C. amethystina* and of Green-throated Sunbird *C. rubescens* (83) but differ by presence of white on the alula and associated primary coverts and lack of supercilium; female *senegalensis* also usually has heavier mottling on throat and breast and is less yellowish below. Both *C. amethystina* and *C. senegalensis* utter *chip* calls, but *choop* of *senegalensis* diagnostic. Female and immature *C. senegalensis* browner and underparts less yellow than those of Splendid Sunbird *Cinnyris coccinigaster* (128).

VOICE Call *Choop* or *tjoyp* and *chip-chip tsee-tsee* and *chip-chip-chip* or *a-zee-zee, a-zee-zee, a zeee-ee* uttered both from perches and in flight, often at one-second intervals, but sometimes with the rate of delivery of the *chip* calls accelerating. Also *sshup* and *tsk*, and single *chip* or *chip-chip-chip* when feeding (*gutturalis*). A loud, frequently repeated *cheep, chew, cheep, chew...* (*acik*). Quarrelling *senegalensis* utter *eu-eu-eu-eu... i-i-eu-eu-eu* alarm notes. **Song** A five-syllable *chip-choop-chip-choo-choo*, or *chip-choop-choo-chip-chip* lasting 1.5-2 seconds or four-syllable *chip-choop-choo-chip*, followed by *chip* repeated 5 times per second and an even faster series of *chi* or by musical twittering, including a very fast whistling *weetodu-weetodu*, which may occur at any time amongst a series of the *chip* calls etc. (*gutturalis*). Other renderings of the *gutturalis* song include *tip, teeu, tip, tip..., cheep, chew, cheep, chew..., chip, chip, chap, chip..., tsiyi, tsiyi, tsiyi, tsé* and *tyo, tyo, tyo*. An agitated series of rising and falling notes in a jumbled twittering series of variations on *weet* or *weetu* (*senegalensis*). Singing sessions may last an hour or more. Immature males also sing.

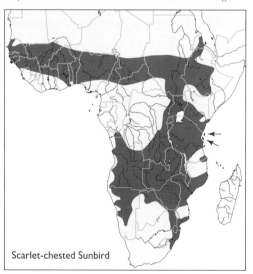

Scarlet-chested Sunbird

DISTRIBUTION Sub-Saharan Africa outside forested regions. Mauritania (migrant visitor), Senegal, Gambia, Guinea-Bissau, Guinea, ?Sierra Leone, ?Liberia, Côte d'Ivoire, Ghana, Togo, Benin, Nigeria, Mali, Burkina Faso, Niger, Chad, Sudan, Ethiopia, Eritrea, Cameroon, Central African Republic, Democratic Republic of the Congo, Rwanda, Burundi, Uganda, Kenya, Tanzania including Zanzibar and vagrant to Pemba, Angola, Zambia, Malawi,

Mozambique, Namibia, Botswana, Zimbabwe, Swaziland and South Africa.

HABITAT Wooded savannas and semi-arid thorn-scrub as far north as 15°N in West Africa. Also frequents gallery forests in dry savannas, coastal plains, inselbergs, bushy areas, parks, gardens, plantations and farmland. Usually between 1,200 and 2,400 m in Ethiopia, mostly below 1,500 m in Uganda. In southern Africa occurs in acacia, miombo, mopane and dry baobab woodland, amongst *Protea* spp. and in coastal scrub.

STATUS Abundant and widespread in savanna woodland. Rare visitor to Mauritania. Common and widespread in Senegal and Gambia. Abundant Ghana and Togo. Common in Nigeria. Common in Sudan south of 13°N. Locally common to abundant in Ethiopia. Abundant on Zanzibar, but rare on Pemba where only seen in extreme south. Common in northern Democratic Republic of the Congo. Locally common resident in Angola. Common and widespread in Kenya and Uganda. Common to abundant in Malawi, Zimbabwe and South Africa but absent from central Kalahari.

MOVEMENTS Complex. Some sedentary but nomadism and migration common. Birds move into plateau of Zimbabwe during dry season, March–July, probably from northern Botswana. Irruptions may also occur into Zimbabwe during drought years, and from the west e.g. during June–September of 1987. Influxes to Kenya in dry seasons, February–April and September–November. In Tanzania, moves to uplands to breed. Visitor to Namibia, November–April. In West Africa, probably moves north with the rains but evidence for migrations equivocal, as present along north-south transects throughout the year in Nigeria casting doubt on movements (P. J. Jones pers. comm.), but in Mauritania mostly recorded only in wet season, June to October, rarely November: probably some resident and some migrant birds.

Ringing recoveries of *gutturalis* in southern Africa include distances of up to 153 km by males, but one female travelled 360 km within Zimbabwe over 24 months.

FOOD Nectar and insects, including ants, beetles, crickets, flies, leafhoppers, moths, termites (e.g. *Pseudacanthotermes* cf. *militaris*) and caterpillars; spiders. Usually searches by moving from twig to twig but may hover in front of flowers and also makes sallies from habitual perches to take insects on the wing. Hovers in front of leaves e.g. of *Acacia tortilis*, presumably in search of insects, and take caterpillars in similar manner from *Terminalia sericea*; both sexes hover in front of grass-heads 0.3-1 m above ground, from which female seen taking insect. Inspect ants' nests in trees. Hover in front of spiders' webs and vigorously pluck the spiders' prey from webs e.g. in *Brachystegia spiciformis* or *Acacia tortilis* trees. Sometimes feed by searching the bark of a tree like a Spotted Creeper *Salpornis spilonota*, involving upside-down movements, or peck into crevices of dead trees. Also leaf-glean upside-down in *Brachystegia* trees and sometimes perch upside-down whilst feeding from *Kigelia africana* flowers (from which it also robs nectar), and *Hibiscus* flowers. Round pea-sized balls of white or greenish-white rubber, probably from *Manihot glaziovii* have been found in stomachs.

Known food-plants *Acacia sieberiana, Acrocarpus fraxinifolius, Albizia coriaria, A. lebbek, A. zygia, Aloe arborescens, A. tauri, Baikiaea* spp. including *B. plurijuga, Bauhinia* sp., *Bombax costatum, Caesalpinia pulcherrima, Callistemon* sp., *Canna* sp.,

Carica papaya, Carissa edulis, Cassia singueana, C. sieberiana, Ceiba pentandra, Citrus limon, Combretum flagrans, C. mozambicensis, C. paniculatum, Cordyla africana, Crossopteryx febrifuga, Crotalaria sp., *Dalbergia nitidula, Daniellia oliveri, Delonix regia, Erythrina abyssinica, E. humeana, E. senegalensis, Euphorbia pulcherrima, Gmelina arborea, Grevillea banksii, Halleria lucida, Hevea brasiliensis, Hibiscus* sp., *Hippeastrum equestre, Kigelia africana* (both directly into flowers and nectar-robbing from base), *Kniphofia* sp., *Leonotis* spp. including *L. leonurus* and *L. nepetifolia*, unidentified mistletoes Loranthaceae, *Macrosphyra longistyla, Manihot glaziovii, Musa* sp., *Parkia clappertoniana, Phragmanthera dschallensis* (parasite of *Acacia* spp., especially *A. drepanolobium*), *Protea angolensis, P. gaguedi, P. welwitchia, Prunus* sp., *Schotia brachypetala, Spathodea campanulata, Symphonia globulifera, Syzygium codatum, Tacazzea apiculata, Tapinanthus bangwensis, T. globiferus, Tecoma capense, Thevetia peruviana, Tithonia* sp., *Vernonia* sp., *Vitellaria paradoxum, Vitex doniana*.

HABITS Noisy, encountered singly or in pairs but often gregarious, e.g. in groups of 20 in dry season, sometimes associating with other sunbird species such as Beautiful Sunbird *Cinnyris pulchellus* (115) and Pygmy Sunbird *Hedydipna platura* (64) in West Africa, and *Chalcomitra amethystina*, White-bellied Sunbird *Cinnyris talatala* (133) and Western Violet-backed Sunbird *Anthreptes longuemarei* (56) in Central or southern Africa. As many as 20 may congregate in a flowering shrub or tree (e.g. *Kigelia africana*) in the dry season. Perches on edges of trees looking from side to side occasionally bill-wiping. Aggressive; males chase each other and drive females off flowers, seemingly defending these as part of feeding territory. They also attack *A. longuemarei* and females also known to attack birds, including Miombo Double-collared Sunbird *Cinnyris manoensis* (102), which approach their nests too closely. Female recorded damaging nest of Purple-banded Sunbird *C. bifasciatus* (121) and robbing it of its lining, but also as victim, as one seen being attacked by Glossy-backed Drongo *Dicrurus adsimilis*. Responds to reflections in windows. One bird, a female, seen on at least 12 occasions to immerse its head in a bird-bath and then rub its forehead, lores and bill on the rough bark of a nearby perch, perhaps to remove clinging pollen. Reduces metabolism at night by 42% at constant ambient temperature of 5°C and by 58-64% at 25°C. Maximum longevity at least 11 years. Host to feather mites *Anisodiscus dolichogaster, Boydaia nectarinia, Pterodectes hologaster, Ptilonyssus cinnyris, Proctophyllodes legaci* and *Sternostoma nectarinia* and to blood parasites *Haemoproteus sequeirae, Leucocytozoon nectariniae, Plasmodium* sp., *Trypanosoma everetti* and microfilariae.

BREEDING Territorial with male advertising territory from song-perch, usually very conspicuous on top of tree or tall bush. Courtship involves male swaying from side to side in front of female and pivoting body. Nest built quickly (3-6 days) by female, but male seen with cobweb, and accompanies female on forays for material. Nests in open woodland, large gardens, over water, and in villages, occasionally on or in buildings, often in same tree or same general area year after year; in one case built nest on base of previous one to create double-storied structure hanging from iron bar. Nest may face any direction in relation to tree from which it is suspended, often near or over water. Sites 1.5-10 m above ground include in *Cassia* tree, in creeper and on light flex on house verandah (many others also close to houses), in branches of tree including one overhanging a drive, in *Acacia* sp. tree, in tree growing

from *Macrotermes* sp. termite mound, and in *Araucaria* sp., *Bougainvillea* sp., *Brachystegia* sp., *Colophospermum mopane, Delonix regia, Eucalyptus* sp., *Grevillea* sp., *Jacaranda* sp. and *Opuntia* sp. Sometimes nests in association with other animals, e.g. within 5 m of nest of Wahlberg's Eagle *Aquila wahlbergi* and surrounded by colony of sociable spiders *Eresus purcelli* or near wasps' or hornets' nest. Known to rob feathers for own nest from nests of Variable Sunbird *Cinnyris venustus* (134) and Penduline Tit *Anthoscopus* sp. Incubation period 13-15 days. Both parents feed chicks with small white moths, small black beetles and other winged insects; nestling period 17-20 days. Young return to nest to roost for at least 4 nights after fledging. One seen taking nectar on its own only 9 days after leaving nest. Sometimes double- or triple-brooded; sometimes but not always builds new nest each time, once starting anew only 11 days after young fledged from previous one. Young occasionally taken from nest by snakes, e.g. boomslang *Dispholidus typus* in both Nigeria and South Africa, and fledglings by Fiscal Shrike *Lanius collaris*. Often double-and sometimes triple-brooded. Parasitised by Klaas's Cuckoo *Chrysococcyx klaas* and Emerald Cuckoo *C. cupreus*. Host of Greater Honeyguide *Indicator indicator* and probably also of Wahlberg's Honeybird *Prodotiscus regulus*, as latter seen chased by pair of Scarlet-chested Sunbirds. **Nest** Domed bulky ellipsoidal or fig-shaped nest, with porch of dead grass-heads overhanging for 40 mm. Suspended with gossamer and bark-fibre. Made of cobweb with interwoven pieces of bark, bark-fibre, dried leaves, gossamer and grass. Decorated with brown leaf skeletons, grass seeds, wool, string, feathers, scraps of paper including newspaper and caterpillar frass. Lined with white vegetable down, hair and feathers to depth of 10 mm. Short beard of grass, leaves, and bark stretches up to 50 mm below base. Single attachment, from tips of branches often above termite hill or near water, roof spars and electric light-bulbs, allows nest to sway in wind. Sometimes high up, e.g. 15 m up in *Eucalyptus* sp.; 130-230 mm tall, 75-80 mm wide, 80 mm deep and with entrance hole 35 mm in diameter. Nests of *gutturalis* on Zanzibar 1-9 m up in bushes or trees; one within 0.5 m of a wasp's nest. In Nigeria, *senegalensis* is triple-brooded, sometimes with 2-3 broods in same nest. **Eggs** c/1-3. Race *acik*: 17.8-19.0 x 12.3-13.0 mm (n=3), dirty white or fawn or light green with brown or grey streaks and blotches, denser at broad end; *gutturalis*: 17.1-20.5 (mean 18.9, n=83) x 12.0-14.0 (mean 13.0), colour mostly as *acik* but some less marked and some bluish-white, greenish or pinkish. Markings of brown, grey or chocolate streaks, mottles, lines, spots and blotches varying from few to very dense, sometimes forming ring. Race *senegalensis*: 18.1-21.0 (mean 19.5, n=12) x 11.7-13.0 mm (mean 12.4), cylindrical or elongated ovate lacking gloss with four types recognised: (i) dull grey background with many darker longitudinal streaks; (ii) purplish background with darker streaks and spots mainly at larger end; (iii) bluish-green background with small darker green spots and a dark green band; (iv) light pinkish-cream background with pale grey spots and crooked lines and spots of chocolate-brown. Race *lamperti*: 16.8-20.1 (mean 18.4, n=10) x 12.3-14.0 (mean 12.7). **Laying months** Angola: dependent young May and in breeding condition August–September; Botswana: August–December; Cameroon: May, July; Democratic Republic of the Congo: March, August–October; East Africa: January–December; Eritrea: August; Ethiopia: July, August; Gambia: June, December, nest-building July; Ghana: May, July–September, nest-building March; Kenya:

January, February, August; Malawi: February–May, July–December; Mozambique: September–March; Namibia: November–April; Niger: July; Nigeria: February–October, double-brooded and where 8 sets of eggs taken from same nest in orange tree; South Africa: August–January; Sudan: July–September; Tanzania: March, May; Togo: dependent young September, nest-building August; Uganda: March–June, August, October; Zambia: July–March; Zanzibar: January–March and June–October; Zimbabwe: July–April, June; may nest twice a year, at six monthly intervals, in same nest.

DESCRIPTION C. s. senegalensis

Adult male Lores black. Crown metallic emerald with golden sheen. Rest of upperparts very dark brown, often appearing black. Wings and tail brown when fresh, fading to cinnamon-brown. Lesser wing-coverts and scapulars blackish-brown. Uppertail-coverts brown with darker brown fringes. Chin and upper throat metallic green with bronze sheen, bordered by contrasting bright metallic green malar stripe widening posteriorly. Lower throat and entire breast bright vermilion, each feather with narrow metallic purplish-blue or bluish-green subterminal bar. Flanks, belly, undertail-coverts, axillaries and underwing-coverts very dark brown. Iris dark brown. Bill, legs and feet greenish-black. For non-breeding plumage see under *gutturalis* below.

Adult female Upperparts earth-brown. Wings and wing-coverts brown, outer greater coverts with narrow white edges. Tail brown, becoming darker towards tip, with narrow white edges. Chin and throat dark brown with narrow bars of lighter brown giving mottled appearance. Breast and belly pale yellow, heavily marked with dark brown, especially on belly. Undertail-coverts dark brown with yellowish-white tips. Axillaries light brown. Underwing-coverts mottled brown and white. Buccal cavity yellowish-pink to yellow-grey.

Juvenile Nestling has cream gape, olive back, greenish-yellow underparts and dark, mottled throat. Immature male similar to adult female above but has metallic green on chin and upper neck, dusky or greyish-black throat and breast, belly yellow with heavy blackish or dark brown mottling and barring with red on chest, metallic colouring on head, and blotchy body. Buccal cavity brownish-grey to black or dusky red. Adult plumage assumed gradually with metallic feathers appearing here and there, a red gorget and, later, red chest and blotchy body. Sometimes white patches on wings. Metallic feathers on crown appear last.

GEOGRAPHICAL VARIATION

C. s. acik (Hartman, 1866) (includes *adamauae* Reichenow, 1915) (northern Cameroon, to west and south Sudan, Central African Republic, Ubangi-Shari, and north-eastern Democratic Republic of the Congo, savannas of the Uelle to north end of Lake Albert and north-east Uganda in arid areas e.g. Teso and Karamoja) Male has red of chest lighter, more matt, and with less pronounced metallic blue barring, and green malar stripe reduced compared with *senegalensis*.

C. s. cruentata (Rüppell, 1845) (south-eastern Sudan at Boma hills, Eritrea, Ethiopia, northern Kenya) Male as *gutturalis* but chin and upper throat black without green gloss but bordered with green moustachial stripe; violet shoulder-spot smaller, wings lighter brown than in *acik* and noticeably contrasting with back; female without white edges to primary coverts and alula, paler yellow on belly than *acik*.

C. s. gutturalis (Linnaeus, 1766) (includes *saturatior* [Reichenow, 1891] and *inaestimata* [Hartert, 1899]) (South Africa [eastern Cape Province, KwaZulu-Natal and Transvaal] to Mozambique; Malawi; Zambia; north-western Zimbabwe; Angola from Cuando Cubango west through Cunene and Huíla, north across Huambo and Bié to Luanda, Bengo, southern Cuanza Norte and Malanje, and east to Lunda Norte, Lunda Sul and Moxico; northern Botswana; northern Namibia; north to lower Democratic Republic of the Congo, Kasai, west of Lake Tanganyika; south-east Kenya inland to Ukamba; Pemba Island; Zanzibar) Male has violet metallic shoulder-spot on lesser wing-coverts (lacking in *senegalensis*, *acik* and *lamperti*) and female generally yellower below. Clinal, decreasing in size towards coast. Gape white for first 3 months, pale yellow thereafter until 7-8 months, remaining dull yellow up to at least 12 months and becoming black after 20 months. Full breeding plumage not attained until 2 years old. Some males enter an eclipse plumage (October–November in Malawi) of a mixture of new female-like plumage and old breeding dress, and also adopt partial eclipse plumage (noted April, August and December in Malawi).

C. s. lamperti (Reichenow, 1897) (includes *aequatorialis* [Reichenow, 1899] and *erythrinae* [Stoneham, 1933]) (eastern Democratic Republic of the Congo from Lake Albert to north end of Lake Tanganyika, Rwanda, Burundi, Uganda, Kenya from a little north of the equator to Chyulu hills in south-east, south Sudan in the Imatong mountains and Leboni forest, western Tanzania and south and east of Lake Victoria to Moshi) Male similar to *acik* but with heavier, longer (28-31) bill (22-26, *acik*); female with paler, less heavily marked underparts.

C. s. senegalensis (Linnaeus, 1766) (Senegal to Nigeria) Described above.

MEASUREMENTS Wing 65-70 (25 male *acik*), 72-78 (mean 74.6, 10 male *cruentata*), 69-81 (mean 72.8, SD 1.6, 47 male *gutturalis*), 69-77 (juv/imm male *gutturalis*), 69-76 (mean 72.2, 10 male *lamperti*), 63-69 (mean 67.2, 10 male *senegalensis*), 59-61 (7 female *acik*), 63-72 (mean 66.1, SD 1.5, 49 female *gutturalis*, significantly shorter than males), 64-71 (juv/imm female *gutturalis*), 59-63 (mean 61.7, 10 female *senegalensis*); **tail** 42-47 (25 male *acik*), 48.5-56.5 (male *gutturalis*), 42-52 (juv/imm male *gutturalis*), 42-52 (mean 45.7, 10 male *senegalensis*), 34-41 (7 female *acik*), 39.5-49 (female *gutturalis*), 38-48.5 (juv/imm female *gutturalis*), 37-44 (mean 40.2, 9 female *senegalensis*); **bill** 21-24 (25 male *acik*), 27-32 (male *gutturalis*), 26-32 (juv/imm male *gutturalis*), 26-29 (mean 27.5, 10 male *lamperti*), 20-26 (mean 22.3, 10 male *senegalensis*), 18-20 (7 female *acik*), 24.5-29 (female *gutturalis*), 24-29 (juv/imm female *gutturalis*), 19-24 (mean 21.6, 9 female *senegalensis*); **tarsus** 15-17 (25 male *acik*), 17-19.5 (male *gutturalis*), 17-19.5 (juv/imm male *gutturalis*), 15-19 (mean 16.3, 10 male *senegalensis*), (7 female *acik*), 16-19.5 (female *gutturalis*), 16-19.5 (juv/imm female *gutturalis*), 15-17 (mean 15.5, 9 female *senegalensis*); **mass** 11.1-17.2 (mean 13.3, SD1.0, 54 male *gutturalis*), 11.7-16.5 (juv/imm male *gutturalis*), 11.4-16.0 (mean 13.9, 39 male *lamperti*), 7.5-12.7 (mean 10.5, 55 male *senegalensis*), 9.6-15.3 (mean 11.9, SD 1.0, 60 female *gutturalis*, significantly lighter than males, P<0.001), 10.4-15.1 (juv/imm female *gutturalis*), 12.1-14 (mean 13.3, 12 female *lamperti*), 6.8-11.0 (mean 8.9, 28 female *senegalensis*, significantly lighter than males P<0.01), 7.5-14 (unsexed *senegalensis*).

REFERENCES Bannerman (1948), Edwards (1988), Elgood *et al.* (1994), Fry *et al.* (2000), Hanmer (1981, 1989), Korb & Salewski (2000), Lees (1999), Murray (1968), Oatley (1995, 1996a, 1997), Pettet (1977), Prinzinger *et al.* (1989), Prinzinger & Jackel (1986), V. Salewski (*in litt.*), Skead (1967), Thonnerieux *et al.* (1989), Tree (1991, 1997i), Zumpt (1961).

86   HUNTER'S SUNBIRD
Chalcomitra hunteri   Plate 23

Cinnyris hunteri Shelley, 1889, *Proc. Zool. Soc. London*, p.365, pl.41, fig.2, Useri river, east of Mt Kilimanjaro, Kenya-Tanganyika boundary.

IDENTIFICATION Large sunbird with long curved bill. Males mostly black except for scarlet chest. Female mostly greyish-brown above, pale below with heavy mottling on breast and flanks.
Similar species Very similar to Scarlet-chested Sunbird *Chalcomitra senegalensis* (85), but nearly always allopatric with *hunteri* preferring drier country. Male *hunteri* is blacker above with black throat bordered by green moustachials, and violet uppertail-coverts and shoulder-patch. Female *hunteri* paler brown above, less evident or absent yellow wash below, and without black throat (present in female *C. senegalensis cruentata*).

VOICE Call A *chip* or *tew* repeated 2-4 times in rapid succession with these phrases recurring every 1-3 seconds, and a descending *choo*. Also *choo-choo-choo* or *tchi-tchi-tchi-tch...* **Song** A complicated twittering of rising and falling notes, including a whistle and trill, followed by *chip*, *chip-choo* and *chip* repeated every 1-2 seconds.

DISTRIBUTION North-east Africa. South-east Sudan, Somalia, eastern Ethiopia, north and east Kenya to dry country east of Kilimanjaro in north-east Tanzania, Uganda (single record from Moroto).

Hunter's Sunbird

HABITAT Bushland and open woodland with *Acacia* spp. and *Commiphora* spp. or *Dobera* sp. and *Albizia* sp., and semi-arid grasslands. Not above 1,500 m in Ethiopia.

STATUS Fairly common and widespread resident throughout Somalia, except in north-east and extreme west. Uncommon in Ethiopia. Common resident in dry habitats in Kenya, but avoids open grassland. Very rare in Uganda.

MOVEMENTS Unrecorded, but may move north from Kenya to Somalia, January–February.

FOOD Nectar, insects and fruit pulp.
Known food-plants *Acacia* sp., *Acrocarpus fraxinifolius*, *Aloe* sp., *Commiphora* sp. (fruit pulp probed), *Delonix elata*, *Erythrina* sp., *Kigelia africana*.

HABITS Difficult to approach. Takes nectar from flowers when perched and by hovering in front of them. Searches for insects amongst leaves and branches and catches them in mid-air like a flycatcher.

BREEDING Only female builds nest, although male may accompany female on journeys for building materials. Female continues to add to lining of nest after starting incubation. Second egg laid the day after the first. **Nest** Typical sunbird type, ellipsoid, made of fine grass, rootlets, dead leaves, bark, feathers, paper and bound with spiders' webs; decorated with lichen; profusely lined throughout chamber with feathers including those of Vulturine Guineafowl *Acryllium vulturinum*. Domed nest proper 120 mm high with distinct porch of 24 mm. Suspended by 125 mm of grass and with 200 mm beard. One nest attached to electric flex holding light bulb 1 m from side wall, reaching to within 1.5 m of bar inside house, attachments stretching 200 mm above and below nest, latter forming beard. Others in trees 1.3-2 m up, one 2 m from ground in *Platycelyphium voense*, another suspended 1.5 m up in thorn-tree. Length 126 mm, greatest breadth 64 mm, greatest antero-posterior measurement 78 mm, length of cavity 105 mm. Entrance 34 mm in diameter, near upper pole with lower lip 47 mm above base. **Eggs** c/1-2. Long, ovate with smooth lustreless surface. White, pale greenish-grey or olive-grey with many brown streaks and markings in pastel shades of brown and grey, or finely speckled with dark grey especially at larger pole. 19-19.5 x 11.6-13 (n=2) mm. **Laying months** Kenya: February, June, October and December; Somalia: May, July.

DESCRIPTION *C. h. hunteri*
Adult male Iridescent green forehead and crown. Uppertail-coverts and base of rump iridescent violet. Rest of upperparts, face and neck black. Tail blackish-brown. Green moustachial stripes border black chin and upper throat above scarlet gorget. Scarlet breast feathers have indistinct iridescent blue and green bands with blue bars, reflecting violet or yellow, more conspicuous on lower throat and sides of breast. Metallic violet patch on lesser wing-coverts. Remiges blackish-brown. Underwing-coverts and axillaries black. Iris brown. Bill, legs and feet black.
Adult female Greyish-brown above. Uppertail-coverts dark brown. Tail dark greyish-brown, central rectrices paler than others; T5-T6 tipped white. Ear-coverts and cheeks greyish-brown, darker on lores. Chin and throat dark greyish-brown with pale brown bars. Moustachial stripes very pale brown and narrow. Pale brownish-white below with heavy greyish-brown mottling on breast and flanks. Remiges dark brown, primaries with whitish edges, tertials

and greater wing-coverts edged buff, median and lesser wing-coverts with greyish-brown tips. Axillaries buff, underwing-coverts greyish-brown with paler tips. Iris brown. Bill, legs and feet black.

Juvenile As adult female but no moustachial stripe and underparts more heavily barred and mottled. Immature male similar but black on chin and throat, moustachial stripe green, and scarlet gorget with blue bars.

GEOGRAPHICAL VARIATION An aberrant subadult male from Eil Dab, Somalia, has the breast-patch buff instead of red, recalling Buff-throated Sunbird *Chalcomitra adelberti* (81). Witherby (1905) thought that this was a colour change caused by contact with carbolic powder sprinkled in the packing box, an explanation doubted by Clancey (1986).

   C. h. hunteri (Shelley, 1889) (extreme north-eastern Tanzania and adjacent Kenya, north to southern Ethiopia and west to Uganda) Described above.
   C. h. siccata (Clancey, 1986) (north-east Kenya including north-west shore of Lake Turkana, south Ethiopia [near Mega], plateau regions of Somalia) Black of adult male more brownish rather than jet; breast more orange-red than scarlet; buffish subterminal barring to lower part of red breast area more prominent.

MEASUREMENTS Wing 66.5-72.5 (mean 70.8, SD 1.98, 10 male *hunteri*), 67-73 (mean 70.1, SD 1.93, 16 male *siccata*), 59-64 (mean 62.4, 5 female *hunteri*), 63.5 (female *siccata*); **tail** 42-51 (mean 46.7, SD 2.86, 10 male *hunteri*), 40-48 (mean 44.9, SD 2.02, 16 male *siccata*), 28-42 (mean 39.9, 5 female *hunteri*), 40 (female *siccata*); **bill** 23-28 (mean 25.8, 10 male *hunteri*), 25-27 (mean 26.2, 5 female *hunteri*); **tarsus** 16-18 (mean 17.2, 10 male *hunteri*), 16-18 (mean 16.6, 5 female *hunteri*); **mass** 10-14 (mean 11.9, 12 male *hunteri*), 10 (female *hunteri*).

REFERENCES Archer & Godman (1961), Clancey (1986), Lack (1976, 1985), Serle (1943).

---

87   SOCOTRA SUNBIRD
Chalcomitra balfouri   Plate 21

Cinnyris balfouri Sclater and Hartlaub, 1881, *Proc. Zool. Soc. London*, p.169, pl.15, fig.2, Socotra.

Alternative name: Socotra Island Sunbird

IDENTIFICATION Large, deep-chested, robust; stout bill and legs. Adult male mostly brown above streaked pale; white on outer tail feathers; whitish supercilium, black around eye and lores, black and white pattern in moustachial area; below mostly grey and brown with pale scaling, and yellow pectoral tufts. Adult female is smaller and lacks pectoral tufts. Juvenile differs from female in having paler feet and a brown rather than red iris.
Similar species None.

VOICE Call Squeaky, strident *zii* or *zee*; apparent alarm or territorial dispute call is a repeated harsh, grating *tcheep-up* or *tchee*. Shrill, hoarse alarm notes uttered by male from top of bushes. **Song** Loud and varied, sung from top of bush. A series of quick jangling notes in short bursts or longer. Also mimics other species including Socotra Warbler *Incana incana*.

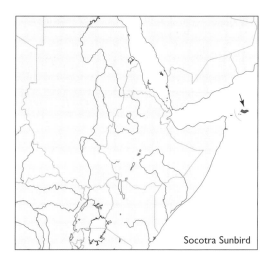

Socotra Sunbird

DISTRIBUTION Endemic to Socotra and Abd el Kuri.

HABITAT Occurs in all habitats from sea-level to 1,370 m, amongst scattered trees and bushes, but commoner where vegetation is more substantial; found amongst dragon's blood trees *Dracaena* sp., *Rhus thyrsiflora*, *Buxus hildebrandtii*, *Carphalea obovata*, *Sterculia* spp., *Adenium obesum socotranum* and *Euphorbia arbuscula*. Avoids bare limestone plateaus.

STATUS Common; 50 may be seen in a day. Populations may be reduced where overgrazing occurring.

MOVEMENTS Sedentary.

FOOD Insects, including small cicadas, spiders; small fruits (including *Euphorbia*) and seeds; possibly nectar, e.g. of *Calotropis procera*.
Known food-plants *Aloe* spp., *Calotropis procera*, *Euphorbia* sp.

HABITS Conspicuous, vivacious and noisy. Usually in pairs or singly; active forager; occasionally catches insects in mid-air or on ground; chases other conspecifics noisily from territory. Sings from prominent perch, with pectoral tufts widely spread. Makes loud sound with wings in flight: *thrip, thrip*.

BREEDING Five visits to nest in 1.25 hours; parents frequent area of radius 80 m from nest and remove faecal sacs. Fledglings solicit with calls and wing-quivering. **Nest** Dome-shaped 80 mm high x 60 mm wide; large oval entrance; made of fine, loosely woven grasses and cobwebs lined with white woolly plant material and possibly goat hair; one concealed amongst branches at 2.5 m in *Euphorbia arbuscula* tree on rocky hillslope at 100 m altitude, another suspended among thick bush and creepers. **Eggs** c/3. Undescribed. **Laying months** Probably January to May; 3 four-day pulli 30 March; juveniles March; 2-3 fledged young February, being cared for by parents at 1,200 m; recently empty nest February; young in nest May.

DESCRIPTION
Adult male Above dull brown streaked pale on crown with some streaking on nape and mantle; lores and around eye sooty-black; narrow greyish-white supercilium extending to rear of ear-coverts. Primaries dark brown; secondaries dull brown edged greyish-white and olive, forming pale panel; dull brown coverts with greyish fringes. Slight blue gloss on blackish tail; white on outerwebs and tips of outer

tail feathers, white tips on next, and small amounts of white on tips of others. Narrow dull black moustachial stripe, white submoustachial stripe, becoming broader towards cheeks; sooty-black malar stripe; clear-cut chin and throat dark grey-brown with darker mottling; breast feathers dark brown with broad grey tips giving a marked scaled effect; belly pale grey, with slight scaling on upper belly and sides; rear flanks pale greyish-brown; large bright yellow pectoral tufts; underwing-coverts pale greyish-white. Vent and undertail-coverts white. Bill blackish, moderately decurved and thick-based around nostril. Feet blackish. Iris red or reddish-brown.

Adult female As male but smaller, lacks pectoral tufts, has barred submoustachial stripe and less clean-looking chin and lower breast.

Juvenile As adult but iris brown, feet dark grey with yellowish soles, lower mandible pale yellowish. Thought to moult into adult plumage at first moult.

GEOGRAPHICAL VARIATION None described.

MEASUREMENTS Wing 60-67 (mean 65.6, 12 males), 57-60 (mean 58.6, 10 females); **tail** 47-53 (mean 49.6, 12 males), 42-46 (mean 44.1, 6 females); **bill** 22-24.5 (mean 23.1, 12 males), 20-22 (mean 20.7, 6 females); **gape** 19.2-22.6 (mean 21.3, 7 males), 19.2-20.4 (mean 19.7, SD 0.58, 4 females); **tarsus** 20-21 (mean 20.9, 12 males), 17-20 (mean 18.3, 6 females); **mass** 8-15 (33 unsexed).

REFERENCES Forbes (1903), Martins *et al.* (1993), Ogilvie-Grant & Forbes (1903), Porter & Martins (1993), Ripley & Bond (1966), Sclater & Hartlaub (1881), Showler & Davidson (1996).

LEPTOCOMA

Leptocoma Cabanis, 1851, *Mus. Hein*, 1, p. 104. Type by original designation *Nectarinia hasseltii* Temminck = *Certhia brasiliana* Gmelin.

Five species in tropical Asia. Small sunbirds with curved weak bills. Tail short and square to rounded or graduated and fairly long. Nasal operculum feathered. Much velvety feathering, but metallic plumage restricted. Tongue rolled to form a single tube proximally, becoming a double tube with a common medial wall and then two separate tubes over distal 10% (Figure 6d).

88   PURPLE-RUMPED SUNBIRD
Leptocoma zeylonica   Plate 24

Certhia zeylonica Linnaeus, 1766, *Syst. Nat.* ed.12, 1, p.188, Ceylon.

Alternative name: Indian Purple-rumped Sunbird

IDENTIFICATION Adult male mostly metallic green or purple above except for deep chestnut back and nape; throat metallic purple; sides of head and lower throat-band crimson or chestnut; rest of underparts yellow or whitish. Adult female brown above with olive tinge, rufous edging on wings; whitish throat and flanks; rest of underparts yellow. Juvenile from female by completely pale yellow underparts.

Similar species Young and female from young of Purple Sunbird *Cinnyris asiaticus* (139) by rufous tinge to edges of secondaries and tertials on latter, and also greyish-white throat and flanks; female from female Long-billed Sunbird *C. lotenius* (149) by lack of grey throat; both sexes from corresponding sexes of Gould's Sunbird *Aethopyga gouldiae* (157) by lack of yellowish rump, and male of latter also has an elongated tail.

VOICE Call *L. z. zeylonica* has a constant chirp, like opening and closing of a large pair of scissors, *sweety-swee, sweety sweety-swee*. **Song** Song of *L. z. flaviventris* is a sharp, twittering *tityou, tityou, tityou, trr-r-r-tit, tityou*, etc. Feeble, mousy *sisiswee, sisiswee...* almost identical to that of Crimson-backed Sunbird *Leptocoma minima* (89), but lower-toned and quieter than that of *C. asiaticus*.

DISTRIBUTION Peninsular India south from Nasik, Jabalpur and Lohardaga; Assam and south Bengal; Bangladesh and Arakan (Burma); Sri Lanka.

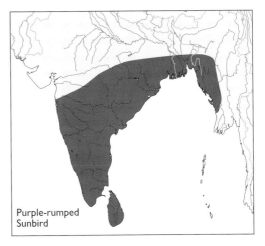

Purple-rumped Sunbird

HABITAT Forest, deciduous jungle, secondary jungle, dry cultivated land, cactus hedges, tamarind and babool trees, farmlands and gardens in plains and lower hills, but up to 1,050 m in Kerala and 1,400 m in Sri Lanka, occasionally to 2,100 m in India. Prefers deciduous biotope in India and wet zone in Sri Lanka.

STATUS Common in India and Bangladesh, including in towns. Common throughout Sri Lanka.

MOVEMENTS Ascends to highest altitudes in Sri Lanka during the north-east monsoon.

FOOD Nectar, small insects, *Trigona* bees, soft caterpillars, spiders; grapes, causing birds to be considered a pest around Hyderabad, India.

Known food-plants *Acanthus ilicifolius, Anisomeles indica,*

239

A. malabarica, Bombax malabarica, Butea monosperma, Dendrophthoe falcata (= Loranthus longiflorus, having deep corolla with slits; when sunbirds insert bills into slits they trigger separation of the fused elements and release the top of the corolla, exposing pollen), Hamelia patens, Erythrina indica, Gliricidia sp., unopened Hibiscus rosa-sinensis, Leonotis nepetifolia, Moringa oleifera and Vitis sp. grapes, which are pierced and juice sucked out, those on periphery of vineyards suffering most, with damage ranging from 3.2 to 45%. Believed to pollinate both Dendrophthoe falcata and the narrow-tubed Hamelia patens.

HABITS Usually single or in pairs; very active, flitting amongst foliage; aggressive and territorial; acrobatic and often hovers. Robs nectar from flowers with large corollas; important in propagating mistletoes Loranthaceae. Singing male pivots from side to side opening and closing wings and tail. Host to Haemoproteus sequeirae and Plasmodium sp.

BREEDING Territorial and pugnacious. Defends territory of radius 150-250 m around the nest by singing from high perch, making warning calls at, pursuits of and attacks on conspecific male intruders. Display involves male flying towards female, perching near her, singing, occasionally spreading and closing wings, flicking tail from side to side and pivoting on perch. Copulation in trees, bushes or creepers most frequent; once observed by one pair 3 times in 4 hours, during nest-building especially near the time of its completion, but also occurs after female has begun laying and ceases after hatching of eggs. Extra-pair copulations occur but are rare (seen once in 3 years' study of 9 pairs, when was also observed by male's mate whilst incubating in their nest!). Female responds to warning calls of her mate but not to those of other males. Nest constructed mostly by female (66% of construction activity), but male brings materials and incorporates them if she is absent. 10-17 collecting trips made per hour at height of building period, which takes 9-18 days altogether. First egg laid 24-48 hours after nest-lining completed, subsequent eggs laid at intervals of 22-26 hours, usually in mornings between 06h60 and 10h00. In Pune, India, eggs incubated by female for 11-14 days, whilst male guarded. Second egg hatches 11-14 hours after first; 95% hatching success. Both parents feed young on nectar and soft-bodied insects with 15 feeding trips per hour; both parents remove faecal sacs to 20-30 m away from nest, but this task is usually done by the female who, after feeding the young, waits for them to defecate; young fledge after 11-14 days; second brood sometimes started 15-18 days after departure of first brood; fledging rate 83% of hatchlings, and overall success rate 79%. One record of cooperative feeding of chicks. Female death by egg-binding with second egg of clutch recorded Baj Baj, West Bengal. Visits by children, cats and dogs may cause desertion. Parasitised by Plaintive Cuckoo Cacomantis merulinus. **Nest** Pendant pear-shaped or oval purse of grass, fibres, and other oddments, held together with cobweb, lined with soft vegetable down, and decorated with lichen, bark, moss, caterpillar frass, broken leaves and a variety of other rubbish; a side-top entrance, most with a porch similar to those of Cinnyris asiaticus; from 1-15 m in trees e.g. jambul tree and shrubs, Citrus aurantiifolia, attached to branch tips and occasionally attached at bottom to thicker twig, but sometimes outside or inside dwellings, attached to creepers, trellises or wires, even pendant electric light bulbs; old nests may be re-used. Nests often near spider's web. 200-300 mm high, 7-9 mm wide at thickest part. **Eggs** c/2-3. 14.4-18.2 (mean 16.4, n=100) x 11.0-12.7 (mean 11.8); mass 0.875-0.950 g (mean 0.920, n=18). Ovoid, slightly glossy, plain greyish-white, or grey with greenish or buff tinge, flecked and speckled greyish-brown, particularly around broad end. **Laying months** India: nests in every month, but peaks March–May in Bengal, December–April in south India, and again July–September, after monsoon; in Pune most nest in rains June–September; Sri Lanka: every month, but chiefly February–June, often with second brood August–November.

DESCRIPTION L. z. flaviventris
Adult male Crown metallic green, nape and back deep chestnut, rump and uppertail-coverts metallic purple, metallic green patch on shoulder; throat metallic purple, sides of head and band across lower throat deep chestnut; breast and centre of belly lemon-yellow; flanks greyish-white; vent and undertail-coverts yellowish-white. Iris orange-brown or reddish-brown; bill brownish-black; mouth dull orange-pink or pinkish-brown; feet and claws horny-brown or black; soles yellowish-flesh.
Adult female Brown above with olive tinge, rufous edges to remiges; throat and flanks greyish-white; throat grey, some with buffy wash or slightly yellowish wash; breast and centre of belly lemon-yellow; vent and undertail-coverts yellowish-white.
Juvenile Nestling light fleshy-pink, eyes open after 36-72 hours. Juvenile as female but whole underparts very pale lemon-yellow.

GEOGRAPHICAL VARIATION
L. z. flaviventris (Hermann, 1804) (includes sola [Vieillot, 1819]) (India, Bangladesh and Burma) Described above. Male sometimes has more extensive postocular iridescence, which may be tinted bronze and not green.
L. z. zeylonica (Linnaeus, 1766) (Sri Lanka) Smaller than flaviventris.

MEASUREMENTS Wing 51-58 (male flaviventris), 50-57 (male zeylonica), 51-56 (female flaviventris), 50-54 (female zeylonica); **tail** 30-38 (male flaviventris), 30-35 (male zeylonica), 30-35 (female flaviventris), 29-32 (female zeylonica); **bill** 17-19 (male flaviventris), 17-18 (male zeylonica), 16-18 (female flaviventris), 16-18 (female zeylonica); **gape** 14.5-16.2 (male zeylonica), 16.5-19.0 (male flaviventris), 13.5-15.5 (female zeylonica); **tarsus** 15-17 (male flaviventris), 14-16 (male zeylonica), 14-15 (female flaviventris), 15-16 (female zeylonica); **mass** 7-11 (male flaviventris), 7-9 (female flaviventris).

REFERENCES Ali (1969), Ali & Ripley (1974), Bharucha (1982), Chattopadhyay (1980), Choudhury (1991), Ganguly (1986), Kumar et al. (1984), Lamba (1978), Leandri (1950), Raju (1998), Raju & Reddi (1989), Sengupta (1974), Wait (1931).

89   CRIMSON-BACKED SUNBIRD
Leptocoma minima   Plate 24

Cinnyris minima Sykes, 1832, Proc. Zool. Soc. London, p.99, Ghauts, Dukhun [India].

Alternative name: Small Sunbird

IDENTIFICATION Adult male is mostly crimson above,

with green crown, metallic lilac-purple rump and blackish wings and tail; throat purple; breast crimson bordered black; rest of underparts yellowish and whitish. Non-breeding male has crown, neck and mantle olive-green, and lilac-purple extends up back; crimson band across shoulders and upper back; dull yellowish below. Adult female is olive above, with crimson rump, uppertail-coverts and blackish tail; underparts yellow. Juvenile is yellower below than female.

Similar species Male from Purple-rumped Sunbird *Leptocoma zeylonica* (88) by deep crimson back, not chestnut, and lack of metallic shoulder-patch; broader crimson collar below bordered black; male Western Crimson Sunbird *Aethopyga vigorsii* (162) is olive and grey below rather than dull yellow. Female Purple Sunbird *Cinnyris asiaticus* (139) and Long-billed Sunbird *C. lotenius* (149) from female of this species by red rump, and former is also olive, not brown, above.

VOICE Call A constant metallic *chik* when feeding. **Song** Squeaky *see-see-whi-see-see-siwee* etc., for 5-10 seconds at a stretch and frequently repeated after short pauses.

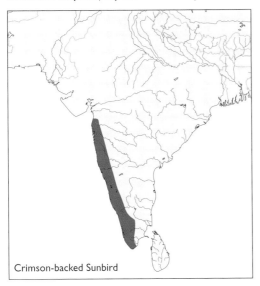
Crimson-backed Sunbird

DISTRIBUTION India in the Western Ghats from north of Bombay south to the hills of southern Kerala.

Wait (1934) listed four records including two nests from Sri Lanka. Both clutches from these were collected by W. W. A. Philips for the Stuart Baker collection and were in the Natural History Museum (NHM), Tring, but are now lost, presumed stolen. Measurements quoted in Baker's unpublished manuscript catalogue in the NHM are within the range for *L. minima* and smaller than those of *L. zeylonica* (see below). Moreover, Ripley (1961) referred to a record from Point Pedro, Sri Lanka. However, all records from that country have been considered dubious (Henry 1971, Ali & Ripley 1974); the species is not listed for Sri Lanka by Grimmett *et al.* (1998).

HABITAT Forest, sholas, shade trees in plantations including those of tea and coffee, gardens, chiefly in foothills, but occurs 300-2,100 m.

STATUS Locally common.

MOVEMENTS Undergoes local movements, and absent from Nilgiris October–March.

FOOD Insects, spiders and nectar.
Known food-plants *Dendrophthoe memecylifolia*, *D. falcata*, *Elytranthe parasitica**, *Erythrina* sp., *Helixanthera intermedia*, *Macrosolen parasiticus*, *Scurrula obovata**, *S. parasitica**, *S. rhopalocarpa**, *Taxillus cuneatus*, *Tolypanthus lagenifera** (the plants marked * are dependent for pollination on the birds that open their buds).

HABITS Solitary, in pairs of groups of 3-4 birds. Male pivots from side to side when singing. Acrobatic, flitting and hovering in front of flowers, and clinging upside-down, when feeding. Male defends territory around flowering trees against others of same species and against flower-peckers. Host to *Haemoproteus sequeirae*.

BREEDING Nest A neat round hanging pouch of fibres, moss and cobwebs; suspended from tip of twig under 2 m from ground in bush or sapling on edge of path or clearing, commonly on *Strobilanthes* plants. **Eggs** c/2, 13.2-15.2 (mean 14.1, n=22) x 9.5-10.9 (mean 10.3). White, densely ringed with dark reddish spots, and speckled reddish. **Laying months** India: Bombay, February, March, May, December; Kerala, September–April, Nilgiris, May–October. [Sri Lanka: c/2, Anarigala(?), Matugama, Kulutwa(?), 22 March 1921, 2 April 1921 (c/2, one egg 14.1 x 10.2, other 13.9 x 10.3, noticeably smaller than those of *L. zeylonica*); see above under Distribution].

DESCRIPTION
Adult male Crown iridescent green; sides of face blackish; wings and tail blackish-brown with lilac gloss; back and shoulder deep metallic red; metallic purple-lilac rump; purple throat; crimson upper breast bordered with broad blackish collar; belly dull yellow; bright lemon pectoral tufts; flanks greyish-white. Iris dark brown, bill and feet blackish. **Non-breeding plumage** (from April/May to August) As female, but upper back and shoulders metallic-red, rump and uppertail-coverts metallic purple-lilac; lesser wing-coverts metallic-red, forming a broad band with adjacent part of back.
Adult female Above olive, lower rump and uppertail-coverts deep maroon-crimson; remiges and wing-coverts dark brown edged olive-yellow; below dull yellow. Iris dark brown, bill and feet blackish but paler than in male.
Juvenile As adult female, but yellower below.

GEOGRAPHICAL VARIATION None.

MEASUREMENTS Wing 44-50 (male), 42-46 (female); **tail** 27-31 (male), 26-27 (female); **bill** 14-17 (male), 14.5 (female); **gape** 12.6-15.7 (male), 12.3-13.8 (female); **tarsus** 12-13 (male), c.13 (female); **mass** 4-6 (male), 4-5 (female).

REFERENCES Ali & Ripley (1974), Davidar (1985), Grewal (1993), Grimmett *et al.* (1998), Henry (1971), Khan (1977), Sykes (1832), Wait (1931).

90 PURPLE-THROATED SUNBIRD
Leptocoma sperata   Plate 24

Certhia sperata Linnaeus, 1766, *Syst. Nat.* ed. 12, p.186, Philippine islands; restricted to Manila by Salomonsen, 1953, *Vidensk. Medd. Dansk naturhist. Foren.* 115, p.255.

Possibly forms a superspecies with *L. sericea*, which is much larger and longer-billed. *L. sperata* is a very markedly polytypic species, but as some of the forms are linked by variable, hybrid populations, it was thought better not to split it into a number of species.

IDENTIFICATION Adult male is very varied; crown iridescent green; sides of face blackish; throat iridescent purple; rest of upperparts mostly deep red or black; wings may have yellowish edges; rump and tail iridescent blue or green; rest of underparts various shades of yellow, or red and yellow, or red and black. Adult female mostly olive-green, brighter below. Juvenile is similar to female.

Similar species Female from female Plain Sunbird *Anthreptes simplex* (52) by pale markings on face, and latter has grey throat and sides of head; from Plain-throated Sunbird *A. malacensis* (53) and Red-throated Sunbird *A. rhodolaema* (54) by lack of bright yellow below; female Copper-throated Sunbird *Leptocoma calcostetha* (92) has greyish-white throat, and male of that species from male *L. s. brasiliana* group by green on lower back, rump and wing-coverts, larger size, and lack of red below; female Olive-backed Sunbird *Cinnyris jugularis* (140) has black tail with white tips; male Purple Sunbird *C. asiaticus* (139) from male *L. s. brasiliana* by sooty-brown belly and vent of latter, and from female by olive upperparts and brighter yellow underparts; male Flaming Sunbird *Aethopyga flagrans* (153) has back and wing-coverts bright olive-yellow washed orange, whereas female is greyer below; female Metallic-winged Sunbird *A. pulcherrima* (154) is olive-grey below, and has yellow rump; female Lovely Sunbird *A. shelleyi* (156) is more greyish-olive below, less yellowish-green than female of this species; both sexes of Gould's Sunbird *A. gouldiae* (157) and Black-throated Sunbird *A. saturata* (161) have yellow rumps, and male also has a long tails, and female of former has grey throat; female Green-tailed Sunbird *A. nipalensis* (158) has white tips to tail; female from female Fork-tailed Sunbird *A. christinae* (160) by yellow underparts, brighter on belly; female from female Crimson Sunbird *A. siparaja* (163) by less grey, more yellow, underparts and shorter tail (28 as opposed to 35); female Temminck's Sunbird *A. temmincki* (165) is browner above, with greyer head and red wash on wings and tail; female from female Fire-tailed Sunbird *A. ignicauda* (166) by much yellower underparts, and lack of orange tinge on uppertail-coverts and tail.

VOICE Call A feeble *chip chip*; sharp metallic chirp *si-si-si*; occasional *wheep* or double-noted whistle with first note rising and second falling; also high *tiswit..titwitwit*; *chit chit chit chit* in flight. **Song** Thin high-pitched *psweet, psweet, psweet, psweet, psweet, psweet..psit-it, psit-it, psweet, psweet...*

DISTRIBUTION Assam, Tripura, Manipur, Bangladesh, west and central Burma, Thailand, Cambodia, southern Laos, southern Vietnam, peninsular Malaysia, Sumatra (including Riau), West Java, Borneo, Maratua Island, Anamba Islands, Natuna Islands and the Philippines.

HABITAT Forests including riverine, *Melaleuca* and peat-swamp forest, mangroves, coastal vegetation, secondary growth, *Albizia* plantations, overgrown rubber, cultivation, coconut groves, gardens; generally not far from coast, but up to 110 km inland in peninsular Malaysia, and normally in lowlands, rarely over 200 m, but up to 1,220 m in peninsular Malaysia and 1,000 m in Sabah.

STATUS Local in India; plentiful Sylhet, Bangladesh, October–mid January. Locally common in Thailand; generally uncommon on Greater Sundas; widespread on coast of peninsular Malaysia, but local inland.

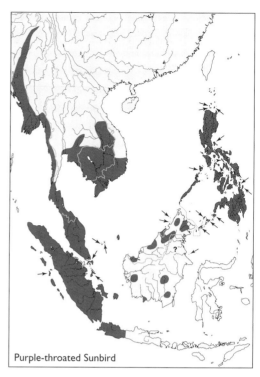

Purple-throated Sunbird

MOVEMENTS Some seasonal movements in India and Bangladesh.

FOOD Nectar, fruit, seeds, insects (including caterpillars and green aphids). Takes insects from spiders' webs. **Known food-plants** *Justicia brandegeeana, Hibiscus* sp.

HABITS Singly, in pairs, small groups or flocks of up to 30; also in mixed flocks with other sunbirds, flowerpeckers and white-eyes; often forages high and in exposed positions. Hovers to take insects or water from leaves, and nectar from flowers; also hangs over flowers to take nectar. Host to *Haemoproteus sequeirae* and *Plasmodium* sp.

BREEDING Nest Lacks beard and attached to branches or tips of palm fronds 1.5-6.5 m above ground. **Eggs** c/2; Highly glossed brown, with fine spots of darker brown coalescing to form ring or cap at broad end. Eggs in captivity brownish-fawn, greyish-brown at larger end separated from other colour by darkish-brown band, slight flecking of brown and grey; or pinkish-fawn, darkish brown fleckings at larger end which merge together, small grey and brown flecks over rest of egg; 13 x 9. Eggs, Sabah, creamy-white streaked with reddish-brown or purplish-brown; *brasiliana*: 13.1-14.7 (mean 13.7, n=11) x 9.6-11.0 (mean 10.3). **Laying months** Bangladesh: February, May; Java: January, May–June; peninsular Malaysia: February–July; Philippines: Negros, January, Palawan, December, Siquijor, February, Samar, April, active ovary Marinduque, April; Borneo: Sabah, September, enlarged testes January, February, April, June; southern Borneo, juvenile August; Thailand: April, May, July.

DESCRIPTION *L. s. sperata*
Adult male Top of head metallic coppery-green or golden-green; sides of neck, scapulars and mantle maroon; lower back, rump and uppertail-coverts metallic green; tail black;

wing black with remiges edged orange-red; lores, sides of face to ear-coverts, and malar area blackish; chin and throat metallic purple or violet-purple, breast and upper belly scarlet, more orange in some; belly and undertail-coverts yellowish-olive or -green, yellower in some. Iris brown or dark brown, bill and feet black.

Adult female Olive-green, much brighter below, becoming yellow and whitish from lower breast to vent; edges of wings brownish.

Juvenile Similar to female.

GEOGRAPHICAL VARIATION A highly polytypic species which falls into several groups.

Philippine group

L. s. henkei (A. B. Meyer, 1884) (Philippines: mountains of north Luzon; linked to nominate through hybrid, previously *L. s. theresae* [Gilliard, 1950], in central Luzon) Male differs from *sperata* in having a black mantle. Broad hybrid zone with nominate.

L. s. juliae (Tweeddale, 1877) (Philippines: Basilan, Jolo, Malanipa, central and west Mindanao, Tawitawi, Bongao, Sanga Sanga, Sibutu, Simunul, Malamaui, Siasi, Tonquil; linked to nominate through hybrid *L. s. juliae* x *L. s. sperata* [*trochilus* (Salomonsen, 1952)] known previously as *L. s. davaoensis* [see below], from Davao to Gingoog City, Mindanao). Male differs from *sperata* in having variable amounts of mauve-red gloss mixed with green on crown; dark crimson instead of reddish-brown above; remiges edged red or brownish-red; tail more purple-blue; breast bright orange-yellow, with varying amounts of scarlet, and belly to vent yellow-green. Male "*L. s. davaoensis*" (Delacour, 1945) is variable with orange-maroon breast.

L. s. sperata (Linnaeus, 1766) (includes *marinduquensis* duPont, 1971, which was described [duPont 1971a] as having female differing from nominate by lower back, rump and uppertail-coverts being dark red, outer margins of remiges burnt-orange. No such features are present on the one female specimen examined, and photographs of the type show a bird indistinguishable from *Aethopyga siparaja magnifica*, so we suspect a misidentification. Also includes *trochilus* [Salomonsen, 1953], *manueli* [Salomonsen, 1952] and *theresae* [Gilliard, 1950], the last being a hybrd *henkei* x *sperata*, with intergradation of maroon and black on mantle) (Philippines outside range of other forms; Maratuas) Described above. Those of central Luzon have greyer bellies. Hybridisation with *L. s. juliae* occurs in eastern Mindanao.

Sundaic and South-East Asian group

L. s. axantha (Oberholser, 1932) (Natuna Islands) Similar to *eumecis* but larger; female darker, more olivaceous, less purely yellow below; brighter, more yellowish, less greyish above.

L. s. brasiliana (Gmelin, 1788) (includes *hasseltii* [Temminck, 1825] and *phayrei* [Blyth, 1843], Burma) (Assam, Tripura, Manipur, Bangladesh hills east through Burma to southern Thailand south through peninsular Malaysia to Sumatra and Borneo) Male differs from *sperata* in having upper back black, rump and shoulder-patch metallic purple-blue, breast and upper belly deep maroon-crimson, rest of underparts sooty-brown; female is olive above, with a black tail, yellow below, brighter on belly.

L. s. emmae (Delacour & Jabouille, 1928) (Cambodia,

southern Laos, southern Vietnam) Male differs from *brasiliana* in gloss of back more bluish and less green.

L. s. eumecis (Oberholser, 1917) (Anamba Islands) Larger than *brasiliana*, particularly bill; female lighter above, paler, more greenish and less golden below.

L. s. mecynorhyncha (Oberholser, 1912) (Sumatra: Simeulue, Banyak, Nias and Mentawai) From *oenopa* by much longer bill. Possibly invalid and could be merged with *brasiliana*.

L. s. oenopa (Oberholser, 1912) (Sumatra: Nias) From *brasiliana* by somewhat larger bill; male usually darker on lower underparts; female more greenish above, darker and duller below. Possibly invalid and could be merged with *brasiliana*.

MEASUREMENTS Wing 49.5-55 (mean 51, male *axantha*), 46-50 (male *brasiliana*), 49 (male *eumecis*), 50 (male *henkei*), 49-51 (male *juliae*), 50-55 (male *sperata*), 40 (female *sperata*), 44-48 (female *brasiliana*), 46-46.5 (female *eumecis*), 46-49 (female *juliae*); **tail** 28-29 (unsexed *brasiliana*), 32 (unsexed *sperata*), 27 (female *sperata*); **bill** 16-17 (unsexed *brasiliana*), 17.9 (female *sperata*), 18 (unsexed *sperata*); **exposed culmen** 13.5-14 (mean 13.7, male *axantha*), 14.8-16 (male *eumecis*); **gape** 14.0-16.3 (male *brasiliana*), 16.2 (male *henkei*), 16.6-17.6 (male *juliae*), 15.8-19.0 (male *sperata*), 13.3-16.3 (female *brasiliana*), 14.8-17.5 (female *juliae*); **tarsus** 12-13 (unsexed *brasiliana*), 14 (female *sperata*), 13 (unsexed *sperata*); **mass** no data.

REFERENCES Ali & Ripley (1974), Bourns & Worcester in MacGregor (1909-1910), Dickinson *et al*. (1991), duPont (1971a,b), Gill (1969), Grimmett *et al*. (1998), Helle-brekers & Hoogerwerf (1967), Hill (2000), MacKinnon & Phillipps (1993), Mann (in prep. a), Medway & Wells (1976), Nash & Nash (1988), Oberholser (1912), Reed (1971), Rabor (1977), Rajathurai (1996), J. Riley (pers. comm.), Sheldon *et al*. (in press), Smythies (1999).

---

91 BLACK SUNBIRD
Leptocoma sericea   Plate 25

Cinnyris sericeus Lesson, 1827, *Dict. Sci. Nat.* (éd. Levault), 50, p.21, near Dorey, New Guinea.

Possibly forms superspecies with *L. sperata*.

IDENTIFICATION Adult male chiefly black, with glossy greenish or golden crown, variously coloured iridescent throat; wing-coverts and rump glossy green or blue. *L. s. grayi* has dark red above. Adult female much smaller than male with no metallic colour; crown and nape grey (brown in *L. s. talautensis*), mantle olive-grey or olive-green; white tips to tail feathers; throat whitish-grey (orange in *L. s. talautensis* and possibly *sangirensis*); rest of underparts pale yellowish or yellowish grey-green. Juvenile greener on crown, yellower on throat and greyer below than female; young male *L. s. talautensis* has orange throat. Immature male at later stages shows some adult plumage.

Similar species Papuan Black Myzomela *Myzomela nigrita* has white underwing, and sometimes red on crown in male, whereas female is olive and brown, with dull red on forehead, face and chin; Dwarf Honeyeater *Oedistoma iliolophus* is greyer than female, lacks white tips to tail feathers, and has narrow but conspicuous white eye-ring; Pygmy Honeyeater *O. pygmaeum* is very much smaller, with

243

shorter bill; Black Berrypecker *Melanocharis nigra* has a much shorter, straight bill; female from Slaty-chinned Longbill *Toxorhamphus poliopterus* by latter's much longer bill and grey head and chin conspicuously separated from bright yellow breast; female from female Yellow-bellied Longbill *T. novaeguineae* by shorter bill, lack of yellow eye-ring, and underparts only partially yellow, not entirely so. Male Olive-backed Sunbird *Cinnyris jugularis idenburgi* (140) told from male of this species by dark olive-green underparts, whereas *C. j. buruensis* and *C. j. keiensis* are bright or golden-green above; male *C. j. teijsmanni* has chestnut band on upper breast and is brownish above. These forms of *jugularis* have non-iridescent olive or brown crowns. Females possibly confusable with *C. jugularis* and Plain-throated Sunbird *Anthreptes malacensis* (53) in poor light in areas of overlap. Female *A. malacensis* has a yellow eye-ring and underparts; female Crimson Sunbird *Aethopyga siparaja* (163) has yellow below confined to undertail-coverts, and a black tail. Female from *C. jugularis* by lack of supercilium and grey or orange throat, not yellow or whitish.

VOICE Call High-pitched, thin, sibilant notes, singly or in series; also a rapid series of identical upslurs followed by a slow trill at lower pitch; a rapid series of notes alternating between two pitches. Clear, hollow *peep*; occasionally rapid, shrill, slurred *zi-zi-zi-zi-zi*; single weak upslurs, one per second, and variations on this; occasional single harsh note. Short *pit-pit-pit* in flight; clear high-pitched downslurred *swee* whilst foraging. **Song** Rapid sweet tinkling cadence lasting 1.5-4.0 seconds.

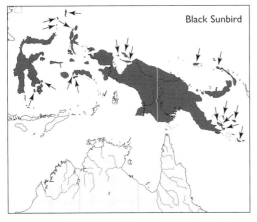

Black Sunbird

DISTRIBUTION Taliabu (Sula group), Sulawesi and nearby islands, Talaud Islands; Banggai Islands; Dagasuli, Bisa, Kayoa, Buru, Seram, Ambon, Nusa Laut, Seram Laut, Watubela, Kai, Loleba Besar and Loleba Kecil (Moluccas); Gebe, New Guinea region and Bismarck Archipelago.

HABITAT Lowland woods and forest canopy and at edge, in riverine habitats, mangroves, scrub, disturbed habitats, coconut plantations and other cultivation, secondary scrub and gardens; lowlands, but up to 1,200 m on Sangihe and 1,400 m on Buru, where it occurs in all habitats except forest interior. Competes pugnaciously with *C. jugularis*; on Siau it is replaced at lower altitudes by that species, and similarly on Batjan (Moluccas) it is always above 100 m, whereas *jugularis* is always below this altitude, the two occurring in the same habitats. Occurs up to 1,400 m on New Ireland (Bismarcks) and throughout Sulawesi from sea-level to 800 m.

STATUS Common in most areas where it occurs.

MOVEMENTS None known.

FOOD Arthropods, fruit and nectar.
Known food-plants Coconut palms *Cocos nucifera* for the attracted insects, as well as the plant products; flowering shrubs.

HABITS Forages in open; active and pugnacious. Singly, in pairs, or in small family parties, although up to c.35 on Talaud, or in mixed feeding flocks with flowerpeckers, white-eyes and monarchs. Hover-gleans and gleans; hovers in front of flowers; acrobatic. Usually in outer foliage of crowns and secondary growth, in lower levels at edge; in understorey on Bismarcks. Chases other males out of territories with threat display involving wing-flapping and singing; also chases away Dusky Myzomela *Myzomela obscura*. Host to *Haemoproteus* sp.

BREEDING Nest Made of fibres, bark and bast, lined with bark; 160-220 x 50 mm, drop-shaped, fastened 3-9 m above ground to end of bough, vine, bamboo or palm frond; perpendicular longitudinal entrance hole, 40 x 20 mm, on side of upper half, with pronounced protecting porch. Much neater than nest of *C. jugularis* and without beard. **Eggs** c/2-3, White tinged cream, with small brown spots all over, concentrated as brown ring around broad end, or pale brownish speckled brown. Race *aspasioides*: 16.0-17.3 (mean 16.6, n=6) x 11.5-12.5 (mean 12.0); *christianae*: 16.8-19.5 (mean 17.8, n=11) x 12.1-13.0 (mean 12.0); *caeruleogula*: 15.0-17.8 (mean 16.4, n=20) x 11.0-12.4 (mean 11.7); *sangirensis*: 16.0 x 11.5 (n=2); *grayi*: 15.5 x 12.0 (n=2); *auriceps*: 15.2-17.1 (mean 16.0, n=6) x 11.5-12.3 (mean 11.8); *sericea*: 16.8-18.7 (mean 17.7, n=4) x 11.9-13.7 (mean 12.7). **Laying months** Indonesia: Moluccas, occupied nests at Manusela National Park, Seram, late August–September, Seram, November, and Butung, Sulawesi, August and September; Papua New Guinea, mainland, breeding condition Fly River, November, Lake Daviumbu, late September, Brown River, late August and October; Madang, building September; Papua New Guinea, various islands, May–January, March. Presence of juveniles and moulting males August–early September on Sangihe, Talaud and Siau suggests breeding June–July. Eggs, Feni Island, New Ireland, May.

DESCRIPTION *L. s. sericea*
Adult male Chiefly blackish, with head and mantle iridescent bluish-green, green iridescence on wing-coverts, uppertail-coverts and rump, latter sometimes edged purple; reddish-purple or purple iridescence, with some blue, or purplish-blue, on throat. Iris brown; bill and feet blackish.
Adult female Grey head, throat paler grey, back and wings olive-grey, belly pale yellow.
Juvenile As female, but has dirtier grey underparts; young male *talautensis* has an orange throat with dark blue glossy streaks.

GEOGRAPHICAL VARIATION There is an east-west cline in some characters in the subspecies *aspasioides*, *cochrani*, *mariae* and *auriceps*.

    L. s. aspasioides (G. R. Gray, 1860) (includes *L. s. chlorocephala* [Salvadori, 1874]) (Seram, Ambon, Nusa Laut, Watubela and Aru Islands) Male differs from nominate by greener crown; wing-coverts and rump less pure (more bluish-) green; dark blue or purple-blue throat, not purple, and with longer bill on average than all forms except *christiana*. Adult female from nominate by olive-grey, not yellow, underparts.

L. s. auricapilla (Mees, 1965) (Kayoa Islands, known from two specimens) Male as *auriceps* except crown is extremely golden-green (as in *maforensis*), wing-coverts and rump violet or purplish-blue.

L. s. auriceps (Mees, 1965) (includes *L. s. morotensis* [Shelley, 1877]) (Peleng and Banggai Islands, Morotai, Halmhera, Muor, Damar, Ternate, Makian, Mare, Bacan, Obi, Tifore, Sula, Gebe) Male has crown more green to golden-green than nominate, but darker than *talautensis*, and wing-coverts, rump and throat glossed blue. Some clinal variation.

L. s. caeruleogula (G. R. Gray, 1860) (New Britain, Rook Island, Umboi Island) Similar to *corinna* but smaller; male wing 59-61, compared with 65-66 of *corinna*.

L. s. chlorolaema (Salvadori, 1874) (Kai Islands) Male similar to nominate, but the only form to have a rather dark green or grass-green throat; green crown, blue-green shoulder to lower back, uppertail-coverts, rump and sides of tail.

L. s. christianae (Tristram, 1899) (Louisiade Archipelago, D'Entrecasteaux Archipelago, Trobriands and Marshall Bennett group, and Woodlark Island) A large, long-billed form. Male has a dark green crown, with throat glossed blue with almost no purple, the brightest of any form. Those from last three groups of localities tend somewhat towards *vicina*. Female yellower below than nominate.

L. s. cochrani (Stresemann & Paludan, 1932) (Misol and Waigeu) Similar to nominate, but perhaps slightly smaller. Male has throat bright blue as in *caeruleogula*, not violet, but differs from latter by wing-coverts and rump being bright green, or blue-green with yellow suffusion, and has a finer bill.

L. s. corinna (Salvadori, 1878) (Bismarck Archipelago, except Feni Island) Large. Male has crown glossed green or blue-green; throat glossed purple-blue or purple; wing-coverts and rump more bluish-green than nominate.

L. s. cornelia (Salvadori, 1878) (Tarawai Island) Similar to nominate and *mysorensis* but has much larger wing, male 70-72, compared to 58-63 for nominate and 62.5-66 for *mysorensis*. Male has crown, back and rump glossed blue-green; throat glossed purple-violet.

L. s. eichhorni (Rothschild & Hartert, 1926) (Feni Island) Male has throat glossed bluish-purple, unlike steel-blue of *corinna*; crown more greyish- or graphite-green than moss-green of *corinna* and wing-coverts and rump bluer. Female as *corinna*.

L. s. grayi (Wallace, 1865) (north Sulawesi, Lembeh, Manadotua, Bangka) Male is like *porphyrolaema* but upper back and lower breast dull brownish-red instead of sooty; purple and blue throat; small blue shoulder-patch; blue rump.

L. s. maforensis (Meyer, 1874) (Mafor or Numfor Island) Male is only form to have green back and golden crown; green of wing-coverts and rump slightly duller and more bluish than nominate.

L. s. mariae (Ripley, 1959) (Kofiau Island) Male similar to *cochrani* but throat-gloss pansy-violet rather than steel-blue; cap greener than this form or nominate, less yellow-green than *auriceps*; wing-coverts and rump yellowish blue-green. Female brighter yellow below than *cochrani* or *auriceps*, nearer nominate.

L. s. mysorensis (Meyer, 1874) (Schouten Islands, ?Biak Island) Male differs from *cornelia* by blackish, usually unglossed, underparts, although occasionally some violet gloss of throat, and has a longer bill; from nominate by larger size and more bluish-green above.

L. s. nigriscapularis (Salvadori, 1875) (Meos Num, Rani Island) Male differs from nominate by second and third rows of scapulars black like *porphyrolaema* and *sanghirense*, and third row green, but unlike other forms with bright green backs and blue-tinted upper-wings it has velvety-black primaries.

L. s. porphyrolaema (Wallace, 1865) (Sulawesi [except north], Muna, Labuan Blanda, Butung, Togian, Siumpu and Kabaena) Male has greenish-blue only on lesser wing-coverts and rump, crown green or golden, or slightly bronze-green, throat rich purple bordered laterally with greenish-blue; back and chest sooty.

L. s. proserpina (Wallace, 1863) (Buru Island) Male has black wing-coverts, with only scapulars greenish metallic blue, rump greenish-blue, crown green or bluish-green, as *eichhorni*; throat purple or purplish-blue.

L. s. salvadorii (Shelley, 1877) (Yapen Island) Male similar to *nigriscapularis* but much larger; rump and edges of rectrices bluish, less greenish; crown more greenish than nominate.

L. s. sangirensis (Meyer, 1874) (Sangihe, Siau and Ruang) Male is like *porphyrolaema* but throat bronzy bordered purple, and blue laterally only on chin; crown green tinged golden; wing-coverts and rump bluish. The female probably has throat orange like immature male, and pale grey-green underparts. Juvenile has underparts bright yellow.

L. s. sericea (Lesson, 1827) (New Guinea, except southeast) Described above.

L. s. talautensis (Meyer & Wiglesworth, 1894) (Talaud Island) Male like *sangirensis* but crown glossed golden-green; wing-coverts and rump glossed blue and tinged violet, bronze throat bordered blue and violet; bill slightly longer than previous form. Female and immature male have brown crown, nape, back and shoulders and orange throat and upper breast, more pronounced than in *sangirensis*; rest of underparts buffy and white.

L. s. veronica (Mees, 1965) (Liki Island) Larger, but with same-sized bill as nominate. Male has crown slightly more bluish-green than nominate or *corinna*; wing-coverts and rump more bluish-green than nominate; entire underparts from breast downwards steel-blue.

L. s. vicina (Mayr, 1936) (south-east New Guinea) Male similar to *cornelia* but throat blue; female similar to *christinae*, but immature male and female have back dull greyish-green, not bright citrine; abdomen pale greyish-yellow not bright sulphur-yellow.

MEASUREMENTS Wing 59-61 (male *caeruleogula*), 62-65.5 (male *christianae*), 70-72 (male *cornelia*), 65-66 (male *corinna*), 60-61.5 (male *eichhorni*), 62.5-66 (male *mysorensis*), 62-63 (male *nigriscapularis*), 59-61.5 (mean 60.1, 9 male *porphyrolaema*), 61-65 (male *proserpina*), 71 (male *salvadorii*), 59-61 (male *sangirensis*), 58-63 (male *sericea*), 66.5 (male *veronica*), 58.5-59.5 (female *christianae*), 54-54.5 (female *eichhorni*), 63 (female *nigriscapularis*), 50.5-55 (female *proserpina*), 51-52 (female *sangirensis*); **tail** 39-41 (mean 40.2, 9 male *porphyrolaema*); **bill** overall species range of bill to skull, 18.9-24.3 (males), 17.9-23 (females), 20 (male *corinna*), 23 (male *eichhorni*), 17-18 (male *nigriscapularis*), 19-20.5 (mean 19.7, 9 male *porphyrolaema*), 19.5-21.4 (male *sericea*), 19.5 (female *corinna*), 23 (female *eichhorni*), 17 (female *nigriscapularis*), 18 (female *sericea*); **culmen** mean 22.8 (male *christianae*), 22 (female *christianae*); **gape** 19.1-20.9 (mean 20.4, 6 male *cornelia*), 23.9 (male *mysorensis*), 22.0-24.8 (male *proserpina*), 17.5-18.8 (male *sangirensis*), 20.0-22.0 (female *proserpina*), 16.9-18.7 (female *sangirensis*); **tarsus** 12-13.5 (mean 13.1, 9 male *porphyrolaema*); **mass** no data.

REFERENCES R. Allen (pers. comm.), Beehler *et al.* (1986), Bishop (1992), M. Catterall (pers. comm.), Coates (1990), Coates & Bishop (1997), Bowler & Taylor (1989), Holmes & Wood (1979), Jepson (1993), Mayr (1936), Mees (1965), Meyer (1874), Rand (1942a), Riley (1997), Ripley (1959), Robson (1992), Watling (1983), White & Bruce (1986).

92 COPPER-THROATED SUNBIRD
Leptocoma calcostetha   Plate 25

Nectarinia calcostetha Jardine, 1843, *Nat. Libr. ornith.* 13, p.263, "E. Ind. Islands ?"; restricted to Java by Oberholser, 1923, *Journ. Washington Acad. Sci.* 13, p.229.

Alternative name: Macklot's Sunbird

IDENTIFICATION Longish tail. Adult male appears blackish, with various colours of iridescence; pectoral tufts yellow. Adult female has olive-yellow upperparts, except for grey-brown crown; underparts greyish olive-green, yellower on belly; whitish throat and white undertail-coverts. Juvenile differs from female by yellowish throat and small amount of scaling on throat and breast.
Similar species Female Plain Sunbird *Anthreptes simplex* (52) from female by greenish crown; female Plain-throated Sunbird *A. malacensis* (53) from female by yellow eye-ring and throat; female Red-throated Sunbird *A. rhodolaema* (54) from female by yellow throat and brighter yellow underparts; male from male Purple Sunbird *Cinnyris asiaticus* (139) by belly and undertail-coverts black, and without reddish-brown band separating breast from belly; female from female *C. asiaticus* by greyish-white throat and white undertail-coverts; female from female Purple-throated Sunbird *Leptocoma sperata* (90) by lack of greenish-yellow throat; male from *L. s. brasiliana* group by green on lower back, rump and wing-coverts and lack of red below; female from female Lovely Sunbird *Aethopyga shelleyi* (156) by greyish-white throat and grey underparts; female Gould's Sunbird *A. gouldiae* (157) from female by yellowish rump, and lacks white below; female Green-tailed Sunbird *A. nipalensis* (158) from female by white tips to tail, and darker olive-green without white below; female White-flanked Sunbird *A. eximia* (159) from female by olive-green underparts and white flanks; female Fork-tailed Sunbird *A. christinae* (160) from female by lack of greyish-white throat; female Black-throated Sunbird *A. saturata* (161) from female by yellow on rump; female Crimson Sunbird *A. siparaja* (163) and female Temminck's Sunbird *A. temminckii* (165) from female by lack of white on undertail-coverts and greyish-white throat, latter also with red wash on wings and tail.

VOICE A deep trill, more melodious and less descending than Yellow-bellied Prinia *Prinia flaviventris*.

DISTRIBUTION Southern Tenasserim, southern Thailand, Cambodia, Cochinchina, peninsular Malaysia, Sumatra (islands and coast, including Riau), Borneo, Java; Balabac and Palawan (Philippines).

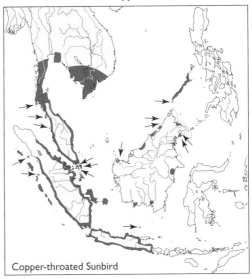

Copper-throated Sunbird

HABITAT *Kerangas* (heath forest), alluvial and secondary forests, mangroves, beach vegetation, coconut groves, rubber plantations, cultivation and gardens; chiefly coastal below 915 m.

STATUS A not uncommon resident on Sumatra and Borneo. Uncommon on Java. Scarce in southern Tenasserim, Burma.

MOVEMENTS Unknown.

FOOD Nectar, and presumably also arthropods.
Known food-plants *Acacia* sp., mangrove trees.

HABITS Very active, flitting from flower to flower; frequently in amongst foliage. Usually at low to mid-storey, and at crowns of low trees. Characteristic dipping flight. Maximum longevity record 4.5 years. Host to *Haemoproteus sequeirae*.

BREEDING Cooperative nest-building observed; some nests may be decoys. **Nest** Pear-shaped bag with oval entrance in top half with eave; made of fine grass, fibre, kapok and hairs, loosely woven, but solid at base, decorated with plant fragments, occasionally felted with spiders' webs or lined with egrets' feathers; total length 125 cm; on branches of mangroves, bushes, casuarinas and nipah fronds, occasionally suspended over water, from less than 1 to about 2.5 m above ground. **Eggs** c/2; 15.0-18.3 (mean 16.7, n=11) x 11.2-12.8 (mean 11.9); glossy; greyish-clay to warm brown, evenly marked with very small dark brown spots, forming a cap or pale green, heavily suffused with olive-brown; variable number of dark brown round spots. **Laying months** Borneo: March–May, Sabah, nest-building and completion May, enlarged testes June; Java: April–June, August, September; peninsular Malaysia: January–June; Sarawak: chicks July; Sumatra: Nias, female at nest in mangroves May.

DESCRIPTION

Adult male Top of head metallic green; hindneck, upper back, wings and tail black; lower back, rump and wing-coverts metallic green; chin and throat metallic coppery-red bordered metallic purplish-blue; breast metallic purplish-blue; pectoral tufts yellow; belly and undertail-coverts black. Iris brown; bill and feet black.
Adult female Top of head grey-brown; rest of upperparts olive-yellow; greyish-white throat, undertail-coverts white; rest of underparts greyish olive-green, yellower on belly.
Juvenile As female, but throat yellow, not greyish-white, with some dark scaling on throat and upper breast.

GEOGRAPHICAL VARIATION None.

MEASUREMENTS Wing 58-61 (males), 53-56 (females); **tail** 42 (unsexed); **bill** 20 (male); **gape** 18.6-21.8 (males), 18.3-19.8 (females); **tarsus** 14 (male); **mass** no data.

REFERENCES DuPont (1971b), Dymond (1994), Helle-brekers & Hoogerwerf (1967), Holmes (1996), Jardine (1843), King *et al.* (1975), MacKenzie (1981), MacKinnon & Phillipps (1993), McClure (1974), Medway & Wells (1976), Rajathurai (1996), Sheldon *et al.* (in press), Smythies (1960, 1981, 1986, 1999).

NECTARINIA

Nectarinia Illiger 1811, *Prodr. Syst. Mamm. Avium,* p.210. Type by subsequent designation (G. R. Gray 1840, *List Gen. Birds,* ed. 1, p.12) *Certhia famosa* Linnaeus.

Six species of sleek medium-sized sunbirds with straightish or curved medium to long bills. Tongue very long and narrow with edges rolled inwards to form a tube. Distal 10% bifid, opening out to form two tubes of helical structure with somewhat jagged edges (Figure 7c). Males with iridescent plumage all over and square-ended or graduated tails with elongated central rectrices, protruding 45-130 mm beyond T2. Pectoral tufts present in only two species. Females dull, mostly olive above and paler below, tails dark with iridescent sheen.

93   BOCAGE'S SUNBIRD
Nectarinia bocagei   Plate 36

Nectarinia bocagei Shelley, 1879, *Monog. Nectariniidae,* p.21, pl.6, fig.2, Angola; type from Caconda cf. Sclater, 1930, *Syst. Av. Aethiop.* p.683.

IDENTIFICATION Male appears all black at a distance but metallic dark violet feathers on head, breast, upperparts and shoulder-patch visible at close range, and these may appear as very dark blue in some lights. Female pale olive above and black lores and blackish undertail with pale tips and edges.
Similar species Male separable from Copper Sunbird *Cinnyris cupreus* (138), the only sympatric dark sunbird, by larger size and longer bill. Female lacks supercilium, and has darker throat and brighter yellow belly.

VOICE Call A loud *wiep-wiep; tsiek-tsiek* by quarrelling males. **Song** Undescribed.

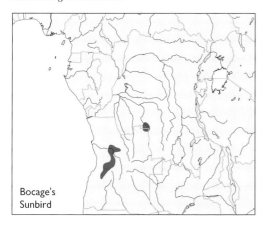

Bocage's Sunbird

DISTRIBUTION West-central Africa. Democratic Republic of the Congo (southern Kwango); Angola in central highlands, northern Huíla, Benguela to Huambo and northern Bié, northern Malanje and western Lunda Sul, with an apparently isolated population at Ninda in Moxico.

HABITAT Woodlands. Angola: clearings and at edges of dambos in miombo woodland. *Baikiaea plurijuga* woodland at Ninda in Moxico, eastern Angola. Edges of montane forest at 1,500 m. Democratic Republic of the Congo: swampy deforested scrubby areas on plateaus. Occurs in south-west in marshes with flowering shrubs.

STATUS Uncommon to locally common resident in Angola. Uncommon in Democratic Republic of the Congo.

MOVEMENTS Unknown.

FOOD Nectar and probably insects.
Known food-plants *Erythrina* sp., unidentified mistletoes Loranthaceae, *Sabicea africana.*

HABITS Occurs in small flocks in dry season.

BREEDING Courtship display involves aerial pursuits with fast zig-zagging flights. **Nest** Large and thick, made of fibres and/or whitish-yellow soft woolly material from trunks of raffia palms, and placed in small raffia palms in drier areas of marshland. Thickly lined with soft woolly material from raffia. **Eggs** c/2. 18.0-19.7 (mean 18.9, SD 0.73, n=6) x 13.2-14.5 (mean 13.9, SD 0.47). Thickly stippled with small brownish-grey spots, obscuring whitish ground colour. One of two eggs in Natural History Museum, Tring, more or less uniform but stipples less dense at narrow end; other egg with very dense stippling only at larger pole, rest showing more white. **Laying months** Angola: Huambo, 26 February; Democratic Republic of the Congo: January, October.

DESCRIPTION
Adult male Upperparts dark iridescent violet with blue-green reflections. Tail black with violet fringes, graduated,

with elongated central feathers protruding 32-35 mm beyond rest of tail. Chin to upper breast dark iridescent violet with blue-green reflections, rest of underparts black. All wing feathers black with dark violet edges except lesser wing-coverts violet. Underwing-coverts and axillaries black. Iris dark brown. Bill, legs and feet black. **Non-breeding plumage** Unrecorded in Angola but shown by birds in Democratic Republic of the Congo, which moult into greyish eclipse, resembling adult female but still with elongated central rectrices. Birds in both nuptial and eclipse plumages in October.

Adult female Upperparts pale olive, greenish-olive on rump. Tail blackish-brown with bluish tinge, graduated, central rectrices protruding up to 6 mm beyond rest of tail. Characteristic undertail pattern of pale olive edges to innerwebs, T5 with pale outer tip, all outerweb of T6 pale brown. Ear-coverts and cheeks very dark brown, lores blackish. Chin and throat olivaceous-yellow, rest of underparts olivaceous-yellow with dark brown streaks. Remiges dark greyish-brown with pale olive edges, tertials, greater wing-coverts, primary wing-coverts and alula with pale greenish-brown fringes. Remiges greyish-brown underneath. Axillaries greenish-yellow, underwing-coverts grey with yellow tips. Iris black or very dark brown. Feet black. Bill black. Mouth dull yellow-ochre anterior to palate, shading to grey and pale sepia.

Juvenile Juvenile like adult female but chin grey with pale tips, breast grey. Belly pale yellow mottled grey. Primaries with broader pale edges. Axillaries and underwing-coverts grey. Immature male dull olive above as adult female, with a few metallic dark violet feathers interspersed. Shoulders metallic violet. Underparts with many light yellow-olive feathers contrasting with black remainder. Some violet on throat.

GEOGRAPHICAL VARIATION None described, but different habitat preferences and apparent lack of eclipse plumage in Angolan birds suggest possible subspeciation.

MEASUREMENTS Wing 70-75 (mean 72.9, SD 1.91, 10 males), 63-69 (mean 68.7, 8 females); **tail** 66-97 (mean 87.1, SD 10.23, 10 males), 49-55 (mean 53.3, 8 females); **bill** 25-28 (mean 26.3, SD 1.11, 7 males), 24-27 (mean 24.8, 8 females); **tarsus** 17-21 (mean 19.1, SD 1.59, 10 males), 17-20 (mean 17.8, 8 females); **mass** 14.5, 15 (2 males).

REFERENCES Dean (2000), Lippens & Wille (1976), Schouteden (1959), Wille (1964).

94   PURPLE-BREASTED SUNBIRD
Nectarinia purpureiventris   Plate 36

Cinnyris purpureiventris Reichenow, 1893, *Orn. Monatsb.* 1, p.61, Migere, western Mpororo [= south-western Uganda] cf. Chapin, 1954, *Bull. Amer. Mus. Nat. Hist.*, 75B, p.273.

Alternative name: Rainbow Bird

IDENTIFICATION Male a beautiful kaleidoscopic pattern of iridescent purple, green, copper, pinkish and blue with shortish and straightish bill and elongated tail. Female duller with distinctive black-barred grey head; olive upperparts, pale grey below with yellow wash on breast.
Similar species None. Only sympatric sunbird with similar shape is Bronze Sunbird *Nectarinia kilimensis* (96) whose

male is green above, blackish below, without purple or pinkish colours, female bronze above with a pale supercilium, streaked yellow below.

VOICE Call *Tsi-tsi-tsi-tsi.* Also *zay-zay-zit* or *zay-zay-zit-zit-zit-zit.* When feeding utters sharp conversational *ts-wick, ts-tswick, nts-tswick.* **Song** Rapid wheezy splutterings, twitters and squeaks, produced explosively for several seconds.

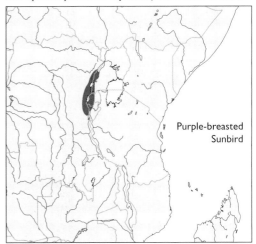

Purple-breasted Sunbird

DISTRIBUTION Democratic Republic of the Congo, Rwanda, Burundi, Uganda. Within 4° of the equator, in highlands over 1,500 m, from south-west Uganda, including Bwamba forest, Bwindi (Impenetrable) forest, Kalinzu forest and Ruwenzori, west of Lake Edward south to mountains around Lake Kivu and Plateau of Itombwe mountains north-west of Lake Tanganyika.

HABITAT Glades in montane forest and in gallery forest above 1,500 m. Forest edge, clearings and roadsides, usually in tree-tops.

STATUS Common. In Uganda, locally common resident in valleys of Ruwenzori forests, 1,500-2,700 m.

MOVEMENTS Local movements in relation to flowering by trees likely, as birds in Mubuku valley varied from very common in August–November to almost absent at other times. Similar altitudinal shifts in December–January from 2,350-2,500 m down to 1,750-2,000 m in Rwanda.

FOOD Insects (Diptera including *Bradysia* sp., Homoptera and Hymenoptera), small spiders and nectar. **Known food-plants** *Albizia gummifera, Erythrina* sp., *Lobelia gibberoa, Symphonia gabonensis, S. globulifera,* flowers of vines.

HABITS Very active, constantly moving at flowers and occasionally taking insects on the wing. Seldom seen more than a few hundred metres away from a *Symphonia globulifera* in bloom. One or other individuals of these trees bear masses of flowers in any month, and flowering portions defended as feeding territories by both sexes against other sunbirds, but groups of up to 12 *purpureiventris* will feed together peacefully. Also feed lower down at forest edges. Males chase females, other males and other species. Host of feather mites *Sternostoma nectarinia.*

BREEDING Territorial. Displaying male sings from perch with head up, wings drooping, tail often fanned and raised almost vertically. Courting males chase females. Nest built initially only by female; male may help at later stages. **Nest** Compact oval i 16-125 mm high (sometimes with elongated beard up to 170 mm below with straggling lichens), 65-75 mm wide, 65-70 mm deep, entrance hole 30-35 mm in diameter; usually attached 2-3 m above the ground, suspended from branch of a *Maesa rufescens* or *Macaranga* sp., but occasionally 8-24 m up in large trees, e.g. *Alangium* sp., sometimes concealed amongst *Usnea* sp. Composed of mosses, lichens (*Usnea* sp. and *Peltigera* sp.), grass-heads, flower stalks of *Thalictrum rhynchocarpum*, and *Panicum* sp., decorated with lichens and grass-heads, and lined with pappus of *Gynura vitellina* and a few feathers. Indistinct porch. **Eggs** c/1-2; 19.4-20.5 (mean 20.0, n=2) x 13.1-14.2 (mean 13.7); clear grey with little grey-olive speckles, most numerous near blunt end where they form a circlet. **Laying months** Democratic Republic of the Congo: April–August, November; Rwanda: January, February; Uganda: October and November.

DESCRIPTION

Adult male Crown and sides of head iridescent black with purplish reflections. Forehead and lores unglossed black. Back of neck and mantle iridescent green, rest of upperparts a mixture of iridescent black, purple, copper and green. Long uppertail-coverts copper-green. Tail graduated, central rectrices elongated 70-115 mm beyond others, black with green fringes. Chin and throat black with blue-green sheen. Upper breast purplish- or coppery-green above iridescent blue band. Belly, flanks and lesser wing-coverts iridescent purple, reflecting blue. Vent black. Undertail-coverts purple. Wings black with broad coppery-green fringes to tertials and greater coverts. Underwing-coverts and axillaries black. Iris dark brown. Bill, legs and feet black. **Non-breeding plumage** Shown periodically, but at no particular time of year, with records in January, March, August and October to December; some adult males lose a large proportion of their metallic plumage on head and body and resemble young males, but told in the hand by speckled, opaque bone of skull. New olive or grey feathers then sprout on head, upper back and sides of breast and a regular moult of remiges and rectrices takes place and testes are reduced. At this time, they resemble adult females but with metallic feathers on mantle. **Adult female** Top of head and neck light brownish-grey with black barring from dark centres of feathers. Rest of upperparts light olivaceous-green, uppertail-coverts yellowish. Tail dark greyish-brown, graduated with central tail feathers edged olive and elongated about 5 mm beyond rest. Outerwebs of T2-T5 edged olivaceous-green. T3-T6 tipped pale grey, T6 with outerweb grey also. Sides of head greyish-brown, lores darker. Underparts pale grey with varying amounts of dark barring, yellow wash on breast. Wing greyish-brown edged olivaceous-green but with median and lesser wing-coverts all olivaceous-green. Underwing-coverts grey edged olivaceous-green, axillaries more greenish. Iris dark brown. Bill, legs and feet black. **Juvenile** Young male resembles female but has broad blackish stripe of dark spots on foreneck in which metallic feathers soon appear. Metallic plumage then appears on lesser wing-coverts, body, greater wing-coverts, scapulars and belly as new remiges and rectrices develop. Long tail acquired before any metallic on head. Thus, young male can become partially metallic within 4 months of birth, whilst retaining one or two areas of thin cartilage on the skull until 6 or 7 months old. Such parti-coloured birds may be seen at any time of year, and some with incom-

pletely ossified skulls attain breeding plumage and have swollen gonads, and so can breed before they are a year old.

GEOGRAPHICAL VARIATION None described.

MEASUREMENTS Wing 63-72 (mean 66.7, 9 males), 56-62 (mean 59.4, 8 females); **tail** 115-167 (mean 139, 9 males), 48-63 (mean 59.4, 8 females); **bill** 20-23 (mean 22, 9 males), 19-22 (mean 20, 8 females); **tarsus** 15-17 (mean 16.2, 9 males), 15-16 (mean 15.6, 8 females); **mass** 10.0-13.5 (mean 11.7, 32 males), 10-12.5 (mean 10.9, 12 females).

REFERENCES Chapin (1954, 1959), Dowsett-Lemaire (1990), Fry *et al.* (2000), Prigogine (1971), Zumpt (1961).

95　TACAZZE SUNBIRD
Nectarinia tacazze　　　　　　　　Plate 36

Certhia tacazze Stanley, 1814, in Salt, *Voyage Abyssinia, App.*, 4, p.58, Abyssinia; probably from Tacazze River northern Abyssinia *fide* Sclater, 1930, *Syst. Av. Aethiop.* p.683.

IDENTIFICATION A large, long-tailed, long-billed sunbird. Male appears black at distance or in poor light, but has distinctive purple sheen. Female dull olive, paler below with distinct white supercilium and malar stripe.
Similar species Green on head of male can cause confusion with Bronze Sunbird *Nectarinia kilimensis* (96), but purple on mantle and breast distinctive; female *kilimensis* greyer above, yellower and more streaked below, face pattern lighter. Female Malachite Sunbird *N. famosa* (97) similar but has duskier throat and chest, less pronounced malar stripe, shorter supercilium, slightly straighter bill and less protruding central rectrices.

VOICE Call *Chup, chup, chup, seee chup chup, seee chup...*, followed by a harsh metallic chattering. **Song** A long series of twitters *sweet-siuswitterr tseu seet-swirursittii, tsit-tsit-tsit-chitichitichiti...* or *tew tew tew tew tew.*

DISTRIBUTION East Africa. Sudan, Ethiopia, Eritrea, Uganda, Kenya and Tanzania.

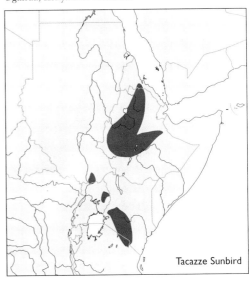

Tacazze Sunbird

249

HABITAT Forest patches, forest edges, *Eucalyptus* and *Acacia* patches and clearings in grassy areas, bamboo, glades and heathland on mountains. Gardens and cultivated plots. Rarely below 1,800 m in Ethiopia. Reaches 4,000 m on Mt Kenya: 1,800-4,200 m on Mt Elgon, Uganda.

STATUS Common to abundant in montane areas.

MOVEMENTS Altitudinal migrant on Kenyan side of Mt Elgon, where non-breeding visitor to lower slopes during cool wet seasons, June–August, but resident at high altitudes. Very common 2,800 m, December, but absent at this height, July. Has occurred down to 1,650 m in Nairobi. Leaves mountains in south Sudan when *Lobelia* spp. cease to flower.

FOOD Nectar with sucrose and glucose demonstrated in stomach contents in similar proportions to those of main food-plants *Lobelia elgonensis* and *Kniphofia snowdenii*. Insects include the bibionid fly *Dilophus erythraea* taken from *Lobelia elgonensis*, other Diptera, Hymenoptera, Psocoptera, Neuroptera, Hemiptera, small Coleoptera; spiders and mites. Sometimes hovers in front of flowers while feeding but may also perch on neighbouring plant to lean across to food flower. Catches flying ants in flight. Comes to sugared water in gardens.
Known food-plants *Acrocarpus fraxinifolius*, *Aloe* sp., *Antirrhinum majus*, *Callistemon* sp., *Canna* sp., *Dombeya goetzenii*, *Echinops amplexicaulis*, *Ekebergia* sp., *Englerina woodfordiodes*, *Erica arborea*, *Eucalyptus* sp., *Faurea saligna*, *Fuchsia* sp., *Hagenia abyssinica*, *Hypericum keniense*, *Impatiens elegantissima*, *Kigelia africana*, *Kniphofia ?rogersi*, *K. snowdenii*, *Leonotis mollissima*, *Lobelia aberdarica*, *L. elgonensis*, *L. gibberoa*, *L. keniensis*, *L. telekii*, unidentifed mistletoes Loranthaceae, *Musa* sp., *Protea gaguedi*, *P. kilimandscharica*, *Usnea* sp.

HABITS Usually singly or in pairs but large congregations may occur around nectar sources in non-breeding season. Noisy and aggressive; males chase each other and defend territories against each other and Malachite Sunbirds *N. famosa* where these species overlap. Hawks for insects. Mob predators, e.g. Mountain Buzzard *Buteo oreophilus*. One male stayed in same territory continuously for 6 years and another lived at least 8 years. Can survive cold nights by temporary hypothermia, dropping body temperature to as low as 27°C under natural conditions in Kenyan highlands. In laboratory, reduces metabolism at night by 43% at constant ambient temperature of 5°C and by 51-74% at 25°C. Host to *Leucocytozoon* sp., the feather lice *Philopterus* sp. and feather mites *Proctophyllodes legaci*.

BREEDING Territorial, males defending nesting areas aggressively against all sunbirds but especially conspecifics. Nest built by female in 3-8 days with male in attendance. Incubation by female only, for 14-17 days, and female removes faecal sacs. Young fed by both parents. Nestling period c.19 days. Fledglings return to roost in nest for at least 6 nights. Parasitised by Klaas's Cuckoo *Chrysococcyx klaas* and attacked by Fiscal Shrike *Lanius collaris*. **Nest** Race *jacksoni*: on a low branch in a fir, made of dead leaves, strips of bark and cobwebs lined with fluff from door-mat, chicken feathers and horse hairs. Another 200 mm in length, 100 mm wide and 80 mm deep, suspended in giant heather *Erica* sp. and composed of dead *Erica* strands wrapped in thick felt of pale *Usnea*, decorated with light brown flaky bark, seed down, feathers, plant fibres, rootlets and grass stems. Lined with feathers and woolly material.

Narrow side-top entrance, 25 mm across, chamber small in relation to nest size owing to thickness (10 mm) of walls providing good insulation for sub-zero temperatures at high altitudes (>3,000 m) in Cherangani Mountains, Kenya. Occasionally have short beard of lichen. Usually 1.5-10 m up, suspended from thin branch of *Acacia mearnsii*, *Cedrus* sp., *Erica* sp., *Eucalyptus* sp., *Podocarpus* sp., rose bush or creepers on walls. Occasionally double-brooded. **Eggs** c/1-2. Greenish-blue with dark brown marks and faint pink spots. Race *jacksoni*: 20.3-21.6 (mean 20.9, n=2) x 14.0-14.5 (mean 14.2); *tacazze*: 19.5-20.0 (mean 19.7, n=2) x 13.5-14.0 (mean 13.8). **Laying months** East Africa: January–December. Ethiopia: May, July, August–November; Kenya: April, July, September; Tanzania: breeds December–February at 2,100-3,000 m in Arusha National Park.

DESCRIPTION *N. t. tacazze*
Adult male Head to mantle iridescent green tinged purple and bronze, more purplish on rest of upperparts. Tail black, fringed with iridescent purplish-black, long and graduated with central rectrices extending up to 50 mm beyond others. Chin to breast bronze-green, more purplish lower down and black on rest of underparts. Wing black with purple iridescence on median and lesser wing-coverts. Underwing-coverts and axillaries black. Iris brown. Bill, legs and feet black. **Non-breeding plumage** Like adult female but wings and tail as in adult male (see below under *jacksoni*). In Ethiopia, starts to moult into non-breeding dress December, and back into breeding plumage from March.
Adult female Greyish-olivaceous brown above. Tail dark brown, graduated, with central pair of rectrices elongated about 5 mm beyond others giving pointed appearance. Outerwebs of outer tail feathers brownish-white, extending onto end of innerweb. Other rectrices with broad (T5) or narrow (T3-T4) white tips. Ear-coverts darker than upperparts which, together with prominent brownish-white supercilium and off-white malar stripe, gives distinct face pattern. Throat greyish-brown, leading to olivaceous grey breast and flanks, lightly mottled blackish; belly and undertail-coverts olivaceous-yellow. Wings dark brown, edged olivaceous. Underwing-coverts dark grey with yellowish tips, axillaries olivaceous-yellow. Iris brown. Bill, legs and feet black. A female with albinistic primaries and tail feathers and generally much paler grey plumage, except on the back, seen at Asmara, Eritrea.
Juvenile As adult female but middle of throat black, underparts yellower and upperparts greyer.

GEOGRAPHICAL VARIATION
N. t. jacksoni Neumann, 1899 (mountains in southern Sudan, Kenya highlands on both sides of the Rift Valley to Meru, Uganda [Morong'ole and Kidepo National Park], Kilimanjaro and Mt Hanang in Tanzania) Iridescent purple areas more pinkish than in *tacazze*, metallic zone on breast broader and extended further posteriorly, central tail feathers 48-62 mm longer than next pair (only 35-46 in *tacazze*). Male *jacksoni* has a non-breeding dress similar to adult female, but black flight feathers and tail with elongated central feathers are retained, as are metallic wing- and uppertail-coverts and, occasionally, metallic tips to body feathers. Some individuals which probably breed twice a year (e.g. in Kenya) may not enter non-breeding dress.
N. t. tacazze (Stanley, 1814) (Eritrea, Ethiopia) Described above.

MEASUREMENTS (All values for *jacksoni* from western Kenya) **Wing** 71-84 (mean 79.7, SD 2.67, 20 male *jacksoni*), 77-83 (mean 79.8, 10 male *tacazze*), 64-75 (mean 70.3, SD 2.42, 21 female *jacksoni*), 67-73 (mean 70.5, 10 female *tacazze*); **tail** 65-142 (mean 118.7, SD 18.63, 17 male *jacksoni*), 98-106 (mean 103, 10 male *tacazze*), 58-66 (mean 63.0, SD 2.24, 14 female *jacksoni*), 48-56 (mean 54, 10 female *tacazze*); **bill** 28-34 (mean 30.4, SD 1.79, 18 male *jacksoni*), 30-34 (mean 32.5, 10 male *tacazze*), 27-32 (mean 29.4, SD 1.63, 15 female *jacksoni*), 28-31 (mean 29.7, 10 female *tacazze*); **tarsus** 18-24 (mean 20.3, SD 1.55, 18 male *jacksoni*), 18-20 (mean 19.3, 10 male *tacazze*), 18-22 (mean 19.4, SD 1.19, 14 female *jacksoni*), 17-19 (mean 18, 10 female *tacazze*); **mass** 12-17.9 (mean 15.7, SD 0.85, 19 male *jacksoni*), 12.3-18.3 (mean 15.5, 10 male *tacazze*), 12.0-15.5 (mean 13.6, SD 0.88, 20 female *jacksoni*, one bird 1.2 g heavier on recapture and can lose 2g overnight at high altitudes), 13.5-16.2 (mean 14.3, 10 female *tacazze*). *jacksoni*: may lose as much as 2 g overnight.

REFERENCES Cheke (1971a,b, 1972, 1978), Fry *et al.* (2000), S. Kennedy *per* D. Harvey (*in litt.*), Mackworth-Praed & Grant (1945), Prinzinger *et al.* (1989), Prinzinger & Jackel (1986), Sheppard (1958).

---

96 BRONZE SUNBIRD
Nectarinia kilimensis **Plate 37**

Nectarinia kilimensis Shelley, 1884, *Proc. Zool. Soc. London*, p.655, 5,000ft. Kilimanjaro.

Alternative name: Bronzy Sunbird

IDENTIFICATION Large sunbird, male with elongated central tail feathers, appearing black at a distance with bronze reflections on head, back and breast, coppery on rump, shoulder-flash and lower breast; female greyish-olive above, with white supercilium, yellowish and heavily streaked below.
Similar species At a distance when colours not discernible male may be confused with male Tacazze Sunbird *Nectarinia tacazze* (95), Malachite Sunbird *N. famosa* (97) and Red-tufted Sunbird *N. johnstoni* (98), but bill shorter and more decurved. Female similar to same species but bill as male, throat whitish so malar stripe less obvious than in female *tacazze* and *famosa* and breast yellow with dark streaks, not blotches or speckles of female *famosa*.

VOICE Call A loud shrill oft-repeated *pea-view* and *choo-ee, choo-choo* or *jer-jooey* or *dzu-wee*. *Chee-wit* when near nest to signal to young; if uttered at fast rate, every 0.5 seconds, indicates alarm, as does a continuous *peep*. Agitation indicated by high-pitched chittering. A high-pitched musical squeak used as greeting call and when approaching nest. Female calls *psew-psew-seep* or *tsew-eep*. Female on nest occasionally makes a high-pitched *ooee ooee chee chee chee* (the *chee* notes slightly lower). Nestling utters weak *seep*. **Song** *Chee-wit* repeated at one-second intervals in territorial song, with female sometimes duetting. Also *jer-jooey, jer-jooey-jooey, tik-tik, jer-jooey*, followed by *tyup, tyup-tyup-tyeek-tyeek* or shorter version of *jer, ju-jer, wip-wip*.

DISTRIBUTION East Africa. Ethiopia (two records, from Jimma and Dilla area), Democratic Republic of the Congo, Rwanda, Burundi, Uganda, Kenya, Tanzania, Angola, Zambia, Malawi, Mozambique and Zimbabwe.

Bronze Sunbird

HABITAT Secondary growth, woodland and scrub at forest edges, cultivations, gardens. At edges of Afromontane forest. Prefers areas with trees. Occurs 1,000-2,200 m in eastern highlands of Zimbabwe. Bushes at edge of dambos and montane grassland above 1,370 m in Zambia.

STATUS Locally common resident in Angola. Common in highlands of Democratic Republic of the Congo, 1,200-2,300 m, where reaches 2,700 m. Common and widespread in south and west of Uganda, up to 2,300 m and even as low as 1,000 m and common at 1,300 m on north shore of Lake Victoria. Common below 2,100 m in Kenya and Tanzania.

MOVEMENTS Nomadic in Zimbabwe. Local wanderings in relation to food supply likely in Uganda as most records at Kampala in December–April. Disperses after breeding, Malawi.

FOOD Nectar taken from flowers by hovering and from perches. Insects including ants, beetles, homopterans, hymenopterans, dipterans, termites and tipulids; spiders. Catches insects by hawking and gleaning.
Known food-plants *Acrocarpus fraxinifolius*, *Agelanthus sansibarensis*, *A. subulatus*, *Aloe* spp., *Astralagus crassicarpus*, *Balthasaria* sp., *Bridelia brideliifolia*, *Canna* spp., *Crotalaria* sp., *Erythrina* spp. including *E. abyssinica*, *E. humeana* and *E. tomentosa*, *Faurea speciosa*, *Fuchsia* sp., *Grevillea banksi*, *Halleria lucida*, *Impatiens gomphophylla*, *Kigelia africana*, *Kniphofia* sp., *Leonotis decadonta*, *L. mollissima*, *L. nepetifolia*, *L.* aff. *pole-evansii*, *Lobelia giberroa*, *L. mildbraedii*, unidentified mistletoes Loranthaceae, *Musa* sp., *Pentas schimperana*, *Phragmanthera dschallensis* (parasite of *Acacia* spp., especially *A. drepanolobium*), *P. usuiensis*, *Protea angolensis*, *P. gaguedi*, *P. madiensis*, *P. petiolaris*, *P. repens*, *P. welwitschii*, *Prunus* sp., *Spathodea* sp., *Symphonia globulifera*, *Syzygium cordatum*, *S. guineense*, *Tecoma* spp. including *T. capensis*, *Tephrosia* sp., *Triumfetta* sp.

HABITS Occurs in pairs throughout year, and may mate for life, as ringed pair nested together 15 times during four years. Foraging behaviour includes leaf-gleaning in trees. Associates with *N. famosa*, Variable Sunbirds *Cinnyris venustus* (134) and Southern Double-collared Sunbirds *C. chalybeus* (103). Closely associated in equatorial areas with

251

Erythrina abyssinnica, some of which may be flowering at any time of year. Race *arturi* has increased in the highlands of Zimbabwe following the introduction of the commercial growing of *Protea* spp. Males in moult there February–July, females May–June. Sometimes fearless of man, as recorded feeding on insects and spiders from cobwebs in an occupied classroom. Attacks reflection in windows and a breeding male sang at its image in a mirror. Known to "ant", with males anting whilst perched in a *Hamelia patens* shrub. Reduces metabolism at night by 41% at constant ambient temperature of 5°C and by 51-72% at 25°C. Longevity up to 12 years 6 months. Host of *Leucocytozoon nectariniae*, feather mites *Ptilonyssus cinnyris* and microfilariae.

BREEDING Defends territories, often with clumps of *Leonotis* sp. within them, against all species of intruding sunbirds, Black-headed Weavers *Ploceus cucullatus* and African Paradise-flycatchers *Terpsiphone viridis*. Female attacked Lesser Honeyguide *Indicator exilis*. Nest built by female in 5-21 days. Incubation and brooding by female only, with incubation in bouts of 20 minutes with 10-minute absences in between, taking 14-16 days all told. Male may accompany female on forays for material. Nests sometimes re-used. May be multiple-brooded. In some cases male never feeds chicks but in others both parents do so, at rate of 7.5-12 times per hour, in between broodings of 26.5-28 minutes per hour. Brooding female may remain in nest but move to side when male comes to feed chick. After ceasing to brood, female feeds on *Leonotis*, catches insects for a few minutes and then returns to chick. Older nestling may make hole at back of nest to protrude bill while simultaneously presenting cloaca to nest hole for parents to remove faecal sac. Nestling period usually 14-16 days, once extended for 22 days. Fledglings continue to be fed by female after she has begun new nest, but independent after 3-4 weeks. Young return to roost in nest for 5-6 days after fledging. Parasitised by Klaas's Cuckoo *Chrysococcyx klaas* and by Didric Cuckoo *C. caprius*. Female seen taking egg (probably of *C. klaas*) out of her nest and dropping it, before she had laid any of her own eggs. The tropical nest-fly *Passeromyia heterochaeta*, whose larvae are blood-sucking and attack nestlings, has been found in a nest, July, Nairobi, Kenya. **Nest** Attached to stem of bush 0.8-13 m up, suspended from tree, or hung amongst reeds with sites overhanging empty space or water. Examples of nests include: 5 m above a river in an overhanging tree, 1.7 m up in a *Hypericum revolutum* bush, 2 m up in outer branches of *Maytenus heterophylla*, 4 m above a marsh suspended from *Buddleja salviifolia*, 5 m up in *Erythrina*, 3 m up in *Maesa lanceolata*, and 0.8 m up on stems of *Cirsium* sp. Large sturdy structure of dried grass, leaves, bark, fibres, thistledown and lichen woven with spiders' webs. Nest hole 40 mm in diameter, about two-thirds from top, with base reinforced with much cobweb, usually with prominent porch of fibres and seedless grass-heads; slight beard below. Lined with grass inflorescences or down from e.g. *Clematis* sp. 120-200 mm long, width 80-90 mm. Internal measurements 100 x 60 mm. One nest of *arturi* suspended 2.5 m up from horizontal branch of pine, made of dry pine needles lined with plant down. **Eggs** c/1-2. Race *arturi*: white, whitish or pale bluish-cream, with spots of varying size and blotches of greyish-brown, sepia or dark grey. 20.0 x 13.0-13.5; *kilimensis*: 19.9-21.0 (mean 20.5, n=3) x 13.3-13.5 (mean 13.4); pale creamy- or bluish-white, with varying densities of lilac or ash-brown spotting. **Laying months** Angola: February–March; East Africa: all months.

May nest 4-5 times in equatorial regions e.g. in Democratic Republic of the Congo, taking 40-50 days for each cycle. Democratic Republic of the Congo: nests all year; Kenya: November–August; Malawi: February, March, June, July, December; Uganda: February, April–August, October–November; Zambia: December; Zimbabwe: September–May.

DESCRIPTION *N. k. arturi*
Adult male Head, throat, breast, neck, mantle, back, median and lesser wing-coverts and uppertail-coverts iridescent green with reflections of varying intensities of brighter green, gold, bronze or red. Tail blackish-brown. Central rectrices elongated with narrow edges of dark red on proximal portion of both webs. Remiges, primary and greater wing-coverts brown. Belly and flanks very dark brown or black. Undertail-coverts very dark brown. Gape dull black, matching bill. Legs dark horn. Feet grey, some with yellow soles. Iris dark brown.
Adult female Crown, nape, ear-coverts, lores, neck, mantle, back and rump greyish-olive. Yellow supercilium and malar stripe. Uppertail-coverts dark brown. Tail blackish-brown with white edges to outer 2-3 pairs of rectrices. Underparts dark yellowish with brown streaks. Undertail-coverts yellow.
Juvenile As female. Throat mottled grey and whitish with yellow tinge at sides. Young male has white-tipped throat feathers. Upperparts and chest tinged olive, abdomen pale yellow. Bill dull black, light horn in unfledged chick. Subadults show range of gape colours including chrome-yellow.

GEOGRAPHICAL VARIATION
N. k. arturi Sclater, 1906 (south-eastern Tanzania from Rungwe to Njombe and Kilosa, Malawi west of the Rift, Zambia, eastern highlands of Zimbabwe) Described above.
N. k. gadowi Bocage, 1893 (highlands of central Angola from the Serra da Chela and Tundavala in south-central Huíla north along the escarpment through western Huíla and Huambo to southern Cuanza Sul; northern Bié; sight record from Calandula in Malanje) Male deeper and purer green on head and throat, less golden on breast and upperparts than *arturi* and *kilimensis*. Female greyer above.
N. k. kilimensis Shelley, 1884 (highlands along eastern Democratic Republic of the Congo from west of Lake Albert to Mt Kabobo and Marungu, Kenya, Uganda, northern Tanzania to Ufipa) Male greener than *arturi*, being more golden-green, less purplish-bronze on head, neck and mantle.

MEASUREMENTS Wing 69-75 (mean 72.6, 15 male *arturi*), 71-79.0 (mean 75.5, 88 male *kilimensis*), mean 72.1 (SD 1.07, male *kilimensis*, Kivu, Democratic Republic of the Congo), 63-69 (mean 66.3, female *arturi*), 64-71 (mean 68.0, 40 female *kilimensis*), mean 68.1 (SD 1.18, female *kilimensis*, Kivu, Democratic Republic of Congo); **tail** 105-122 (adult male *arturi*, including central rectrices), 54.5-67.0 (adult male *arturi*, excluding central rectrices), 115-135 (mean 124.8, 10 male *kilimensis*, including central rectrices), 55-63 (adult female *arturi* including central rectrices), 48-58 (adult female *arturi* excluding central rectrices), 54-59 (mean 55.5, 10 female *kilimensis*); **bill** 26.5-31.0 (mean 28.2, SD 1.3, 13 male *arturi*), 27-31 (mean 29, 10 male *kilimensis*), 25.0-29.0 (mean 27.1, 7 female *arturi*), 27-29 (mean 28.1, 10 female *kilimensis*); **culmen** 27.8-31.5 (mean 27.9, male *arturi*), 26.5-31.0 (mean 27.5, female *arturi*); **tarsus** 15.5-20.0 (mean 17.4, male *arturi*), 18-20 (mean 19.2, 10 male *kilimensis*), 15.0-20.5 (mean 16.8, female *arturi*), 18-19 (mean 18.4, 10 female *kilimensis*); **mass** 13.5-18.6 (mean 16.3, 17 male *arturi*), 14.0-19.9 (mean 16.7, 271 male *kilimensis*), 11.7-16.1 (mean 14.0, SD 0.74, 13 female *arturi*), 13.3-16.7 (mean 14.7, 96 female *kilimensis*).

REFERENCES Antikainen (1990), Beesley (1972), Chapin (1978b), Cunningham-van Someren (1996), C. F. Dewhurst (pers. comm.), Dowsett-Lemaire (1989), Fry *et al.* (2000), Gardiner & Meikle (1985), Hanmer (1997), Jackson (1970), Kramer (1975), Löhrl (1979), Lott (1991), Lott & Lott (1991), Manson & Lane (1989), Prinzinger & Jackel (1986), Skead (1967), Swynnerton (1908), Tree (1997a), Zumpt (1961).

---

97 MALACHITE SUNBIRD
Nectarinia famosa   Plate 37

Certhia famosa Linnaeus, 1766, *Syst. Nat.*, ed. 12, 1, p.187, Cape of Good Hope, South Africa.

Alternative names: Yellow-tufted Malachite Sunbird, Long-tailed Emerald Sunbird, Green Sugarbird

IDENTIFICATION Males distinctive with bright green metallic plumage and elongated tail. Female olivaceous-grey above, yellowish mottled blackish below, with prominent pale supercilium and malar stripe.
Similar species Both sexes like equivalents of Red-tufted Sunbird *Nectarinia johnstoni* (98) but male has yellow not red pectoral tufts, female has pale supercilium and malar stripe (lacking in female *N. johnstoni*) and is more olive, less grey, above. Female like female Tacazze Sunbird *N. tacazze* (95), but yellower below with shorter tail and unelongated central tail feathers, and told from female Bronze Sunbird *N. kilimensis* (96) by longer, straighter bill, more marked malar stripe, darker upperparts and mottled not streaked underparts.

VOICE Call Contact call is a fluid *tseuu, tseuu* or *tsi-tseer.* Other variants are *ssseeep, sseeem, sweeenk* and an emphatic *chip.* Alarm call: repetitive trill *treeeee* or slower *tjoep, tjoep, tjoep...* Aggressive attacks accompanied by screeching whinny. **Song** A series of whistles for 1.5-2.5 seconds, sometimes with high and low notes alternating: *tseuu, tseuu* notes followed by *pesui pesui pesui*, or a stutter followed by a repeated wheeze: *tik, tik, tik, tik, tik, tik, tik-heezy, heezy, heezy, heezy.* Males in breeding and eclipse plumage may sing a rapid warble, sometimes interspersed with *chip* calls.

DISTRIBUTION East and southern Africa. Sudan, west and south-eastern highlands of Ethiopia and Eritrea, Democratic Republic of the Congo, Rwanda, Burundi, Uganda, Kenya, Tanzania, Zambia, Malawi, Mozambique, Namibia, Zimbabwe, Lesotho, western Swaziland and South Africa.

HABITAT In South Africa from sea-level to 2,800 m, but prefers upland fynbos. Common there in Cape of Good Hope Nature Reserve but less commonly in restionaceous plateau fynbos; also frequents karoo vegetation types, alpine grassland, riverside scrub, thorn-bush and gardens but avoid forests. Sage-bush and heath zone up to 3,000 m in Arusha National Park, Tanzania. In Ethiopia rarely

below 2,400 m. Open habitats, scrubby moorland, forest edge, *Protea* moorland and bamboo in Kenya highlands. Protea moorland above 1,800 m on Nyika plateau, Malawi and Zambia.

STATUS Locally common in suitable upland habitat. About 2.3 birds per ha in upland mixed fynbos, with 1,000 birds present in the Cape of Good Hope Nature Reserve (7,750 ha), 0.5 birds per ha in *Protea nitida* scrubland and 3.5 birds per ha in *Protea roupelliae.* Uncommon in Ethiopia. Only known from above 1,800 m in Imatong Mountains, Sudan. Common 1,600-2,900 m in south-west highlands of Uganda, where also recorded Mts Morongole and Lonyili in Karamoja. Locally common in highlands of Kenya, Tanzania and Democratic Republic of the Congo, 1,200-2,800 m.

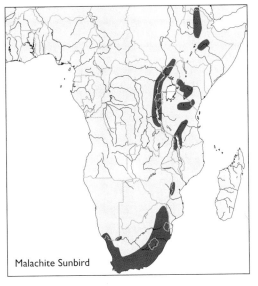

Malachite Sunbird

MOVEMENTS Disperse in response to shortages of flowering plants. Nomadic in Zimbabwe and South Africa, where one recovered 161 km away from ringing location at Cape, another at Ficksburg 149 km away from ringing site at Bloemfontein and another found 41 km over stretch of sea, but probably travelled as much as 150 km taking an overland route. A third bird recaptured 99 km away and a fourth 54 km east of ringing site. Bird ringed at Bloemfontein recovered near Gumtree, Eastern Free State, may have moved 500 km. Thought to undertake local movements in Ethiopia. Wanders altitudinally, Kenya, reaching as low as 1,400 m and probably also wanders in Uganda.

FOOD Nectar with sucrose and glucose demonstrated in stomach contents in similar proportions to those of main food-plants *Lobelia elgonensis* and *Kniphofia snowdenii.* Insects include the bibionid fly *Dilophus erythraea* taken from *Lobelia elgonensis*, other Diptera (including Tabanidae), Hymenoptera, Psocoptera, Neuroptera, Hemiptera, small Coleoptera, Lepidoptera; spiders and mites. One record of two small lizards being taken as prey. Some plant species heavily used in one year may be almost ignored in subsequent seasons. Chins may become dusted red and yellow by pollen.
Known food-plants *Acacia sieberiana, Acrocarpus fraxinifolius, Agave* sp., *Aloe arborescens, A. broomii, A. claviflora, A. ferox,*

253

A. graminicola, A. granidentata, A. mzimbana, A. nuttii, A. saponaria, A. spectabilis, A. striata, Astracantha gummifera, Buddleja salviifolia, Chasmanthe sp., *Cotyledon macrantha, C. orbiculata, Crocosmia* sp., *Digitalis* sp., *Erica arborea, E. gilva, E. mammosa, Erythrina* spp. including *E. abyssinica* and *E. lysistemon, Gladiolus natalensis, Grevillea banksii, Greyia sutherlandi, Hagenia abyssinica, Halleria lucida, Hyobanche* sp., *Hypericum revolutum, Impatiens gomphophylla, Jacaranda* sp., *Kigelia africana, Kniphofia* spp. including *K. grantii, K. linearifolia, K. ?rogersi, K. snowdenii, Leonotis decadonta, L. leonurus, L. mollissima* (= *L. raineriana*), *L. nepetifolia, L. oxymifolia, L.* aff. *pole-evansii, Lobelia aberdarica, L. elgonensis, L. gibberoa, Leucospermum conocarpum, Lycium* sp., *Melianthus villosus, Mimetes hartogii, Nicotiana* sp., *Phragmanthera dschallensis* (parasite of *Acacia* spp., especially *A. drepanolobium*), *Opuntia* sp., *Phygelius capensis, Protea angolensis, P. caffra, P. cynaroides, P. gaguedi, P. kilimandscharica, P. lacticolor, P. madiensis, P. multibracteata, P. neriifolia, P. petiolaris, P. roupelliae, P. welwitschii, Strelitzia* sp., *Sutherlandia frutescens, Tecoma capensis, Usnea* sp., *Vinca* sp., *Watsonia* spp. including *W. tabularis.*

HABITS Sometimes seen singly, but also in pairs and loose groups of 30-40 birds, with assemblies at feeding areas. As many as 1,350 birds ha recorded feeding in patch of *Leonotis leonurus*. Timid with man but highly aggressive towards conspecifics, other species of sunbirds including *N. tacazze* and Eastern Double-collared Sunbird *Cinnyris mediocris* (112), and other birds including Egyptian Goose *Alopochen aegyptiacus*, Laughing Dove *Streptopelia senegalensis*, White-rumped Swift *Apus caffer*, Rock Martin *Psalidoprocne fuliginosa*, Pearl-breasted Swallow *Hirundo dimidiata*, Hoopoe *Upupa epops*, Cape Robin-chat *Cossypha caffra*, Karoo Prinia *Prinia maculosa*, Fiscal Shrike *Lanius collaris*, Starling *Sturnus vulgaris*, Cape Sparrow *Passer melanurus* and Cape Canary *Serinus canicollis*. Victims may be gripped on back from behind and even forced to ground. Will fly long distances to attack intruders on feeding territories; one bird timed flying next to vehicle at 56 kph! Rival males grapple with feet in mid-air, clutching one another's breasts, and tumble to ground. However, may be dominated by Orange-breasted Sunbird *Anthobaphes violacea* (72) or sugarbirds *Promerops* spp (1,2). Responds to reflections in windows. Display-flights include high flight followed by vertical descent towards other bird, zig-zagging flight with wings held out straight at body-level, head and tail raised, and moth-like flapping flight. Singing may be accompanied by head pointing skywards and wings held back half-spread, vibrating and showing pectoral tufts.

Sometimes hawks for insects, flying up from prominent perch and tumbling back; spectacular when many birds feeding this way together. Occasionally perch on ground to feed from low flowers e.g. *A. claviflora* and *Hyobanche* sp. Bathes in dew and rain-drops in plants and also in bird-baths and garden sprays. Longevity up to 7 years 2 months. Thermolabile during cold nights at high altitude when bird's core temperature can drop to 32°C.

Bird from Paardeplaats, South Africa, was the type host of the blood parasite *Leucocytozoon nectariniae*. Also host to *Haemoproteus sequeirae, Plasmodium polare, Trypanosoma avium* and microfilariae. Host to feather lice *Ricinus timmermanni* and feather mites *Proctophyllodes legaci*.

BREEDING Territorial. Male *famosa* courtship display involves whistling calls from perch, flicks of down-drooping wings, then an accelerated warbling and wing-flapping, sometimes with tail cocked at sharp angle and waved up and down or from side to side. Pectoral tufts sometimes shown at same time. Male then flies vertically before hovering above female and lowering himself down to copulate with wings quivering rapidly. Alternatively, before flight and copulation, male may crouch with head in shoulders, ruffled feathers and fanned tail. Receptive female utters *pseeep-pseeep* calls. If unsuccessful, male will pursue female relentlessly for up to 15 minutes. Extra-pair copulations occur, as one male displaying to female turned attentions to newly arrived female, copulated with her and then returned to copulate with first female. Also much cloaca-pecking takes place especially during court-ship periods and once seen immediately prior to copulation. Male *cupreonitens* display involves perching below female, crouching forwards with tail held erect and body feathers fluffed out, making yellow pectoral tufts very conspicuous, whilst uttering incessant high-pitched squeaking calls. Male then pursued the seemingly uninterested female wherever she went until copulation. Only females build nest, during which they may steal down from nests of Southern Penduline Tits *Anthoscopus minutus*. Male accompanies building female on forays for material. Nest may be completed in as little as 3 days, but usually 7-30 days. Only female incubates, for 13 days. Males of some pairs feed nestlings, others do not. Nestling period 14-18 days. Both parents feed fledglings, which roost in nest for up to 14 nights. Both sexes remove faecal sacs. Double- and triple-brooded, sometimes re-using nest. Parasitised by Red-chested Cuckoo *Cuculus solitarius* and Klaas's Cuckoo *Chrysococcyx klaas*. **Nest** From near ground to 20 m up in a tree or bush, often overhanging water, gully or quarry or within road culvert. In *Protea* sp., asclepiad shrubs, *Acacia saligna, Eucalyptus* sp., pines, *Hakea* sp., *Bougainvillea* sp., weeds, reeds, ferns or driftwood on riverbanks. Also 3 m up on wire. Another unusual nest, lined with sheep's wool, was attached to vertical sides of a hessian sack, hanging from a beam in a barn, secured by cobwebs. Another in coarse baling twine suspended from roof, with adults entering barn through broken window pane. Nest is oval or pear-shaped, with a side-top entrance usually with porch of grass-heads which may almost encircle the hole (*famosa*) but also often lack porch (*cupreonitens*), and often placed within bush (not suspended) with entrance facing inwards. Made of grass, fibres, leaves, twigs, rootlets and held together with cobwebs. Externally decorated with lichen or white cocoons and sometimes with beard. Lined with grass, hair, feathers (up to 385), plant-down, pappus, asclepiad down, wool and cotton. Height 14.0 cm, width 4.5 cm, depth 9.0 cm., diameter of entrance hole 4.9 cm. **Eggs** Race *cupreonitens*: c/1; 16.6-21.0 (mean 18.6, n=4) x 12.0-13.5 (mean 12.9); greyish- or greenish-white with freckles of grey and brown, darker at larger pole; *famosa*: c/1-3; 17.5-22.0 (mean 19.2, n=51) x 12.4-16.0 (mean 13.3), slightly elongated, dull, smooth or glossy; cream, light brown, greenish-brown, olive-white or white, densely freckled, spotted, streaked and mottled, more heavily at larger pole, with brown, grey, olive, often so dense that little ground colour visible. **Laying months** East Africa: May–December but may moult and breed at any time of year with individuals following their own cycles. Ethiopia: July–September; Kenya: August, December (at 3,400 m); Lesotho, November–January; Malawi: June; Namibia: April; South Africa: Cape Peninsula area, May–November, Eastern Cape, August–January, highlands of KwaZulu-Natal November–February, Transvaal, August–February; Zambia: June; Zimbabwe: August–March.

DESCRIPTION *N. f. famosa*

Adult male Head, mantle, neck, back and underparts except lower belly and undertail-coverts, brilliant metallic malachite-green. Rump and uppertail-coverts darker green. Tail dark brownish-black, edged dark green on outerwebs except on outer feathers. Central pair of rectrices elongated to protrude up to 80 mm beyond others, edged green on both vanes, more so proximally. Remiges and alula dark brownish-black, secondaries edged green. Primary, greater, median and lesser wing-coverts dark brownish-black, edged green. Lower belly and undertail-coverts green in white base wash. Pectoral tufts bright yellow.

Non-breeding plumage Male of *cupreonitens* similar to adult female but with black flight feathers and tail with elongated central feathers retained, as is metallic gloss on wing and uppertail-coverts; occasionally sparse metallic tips remain on body feathers. Male of *famosa* has a similar eclipse with metallic green noticeable on wing-coverts, rump and uppertail-coverts but, in contrast, the long central tail feathers are lost. Moulting *famosa*, Grahamstown, South Africa, January–May; some May birds show interrupted moult with two distinct feather generations. In Malawi eclipse September–March, after breeding.

Adult female Crown, nape, ear-coverts, lores and cheeks brown. Neck, mantle, back, rump and uppertail-coverts brown with greyish-olive suffusion. Tail olive-black. Outertail feathers with white edges and tips; second to outermost pair with white edges to outerwebs. Remiges and wing-coverts brown with yellowish-olive margins to outerwebs. Throat and breast dull yellow with brown blotches and yellowish-olive wash, belly similar but less blotched and sometimes quite bright yellow or greenish-yellow. Flanks olive. Pale yellow malar stripe.

Juvenile As adult female, but upperparts greener and underparts and malar stripe yellower, some males with blackish centres to throat. Young male develops first metallic feathers on head or wing-coverts.

GEOGRAPHICAL VARIATION

N. f. cupreonitens Shelley, 1876 (includes *aeneigularis* Sharpe, 1891, *centralis* van Someren, 1916, and *subfamosa* Salvadori, 1884) (above 1,200 m in Eritrea, Ethiopia, southern Sudan, eastern highlands of Democratic Republic of the Congo south to Mt Kabobo and Marungu, Tanzania, Uganda, Zambia south to the Zambesi River, Kenya, Zimbabwe, northern Malawi, northern Mozambique) Male more golden-green above with blue from chest to undertail-coverts darker and less green than in *famosa*. Bill shorter (26-31) than *famosa* (30-36) and central tail feathers shorter (94-120) than *famosa* (110-151). For eclipse plumage see description of nominate.

N. f. famosa (Linnaeus, 1766) (includes *major* Roberts, 1936) (Namibia, South Africa, Lesotho, western Swaziland, Zimbabwe). Described above.

MEASUREMENTS Wing 70.0-80.5 (mean 73.5, 23 male *cupreonitens*), 76-86 (mean 78.4, 10 male *famosa*), 61.5-76.0 (mean 67, SD 1.58, 5 female *cupreonitens*), 68-73 (mean 70.2, 10 female *famosa*); **tail including central rectrices** 102.0-158.0 (mean 115.8, SD 12.42, 13 male *cupreonitens*), 118-147 (mean 126.1, 10 male *famosa*), 44-64 (mean 51.6, SD 7.44, 5 female *cupreonitens*), 45-53 (mean 48, 10 female *famosa*); **tail excluding central rectrices** 49.0-60.0 (male *cupreonitens*), 38.5-55.0 (female *cupreonitens*); **bill** 29-33.5 (mean 31.3, 33 male *cupreonitens*), 33-36 (mean 35, 10 male *famosa*), 26-32 (mean 29.7, SD 1.97, 7 female *cupreonitens*),

30-34 (mean 32.3, 10 female *famosa*); **culmen** 29.5-34.5 (*cupreonitens*); **tarsus** 15.5-20.0 (mean 17.2, 12 male *cupreonitens*), 16-18 (mean 17.4, 10 male *famosa*), 16-20 (mean 17.2, SD 1.68, 5 female *cupreonitens*), 16-18 (mean 16.5, 10 female *famosa*); **mass** 12.0-18.7 (mean 13.8, 91 male *cupreonitens*), 15.5-22.5 (mean 17.6, 90 male *famosa*), 9.1-17.5 (mean 12.1, 76 female *cupreonitens*), 11.5-17.5 (mean 14.5, 93 female *famosa*). Race *cupreonitens* may lose 1 g overnight.

REFERENCES Cheke (1971a,b, 1978), Craig & Simon (1991), Dean & Milton (1998), Dowsett-Lemaire (1988, 1989), Fraser (1989, 1997a), Fraser *et al.* (1989), Fry *et al.* (2000), Ledger (1980), Lloyd (1989), Mackworth-Praed & Grant (1945), Moffet (1990), Oatley (1995), Porter (1956), Scammell (1963), Siegfried (1985), Skead (1967), de Swardt (1995), Taylor (1946), Underhill & Fraser (1989), Uys (1981b), Wolf (1975), Wolf & Wolf (1976), van Wyk (1984).

98 RED-TUFTED SUNBIRD
Nectarinia johnstoni   Plate 37

Nectarinia johnstoni Shelley, 1885, *Proc. Zool. Soc. London*, p.227, pl.14, 11,000ft. Kilimanjaro.

Alternative names: Scarlet-tufted Malachite Sunbird, Red-tufted Malachite Sunbird

IDENTIFICATION Large sunbird, denizen of very high altitudes. Male with very long tail and metallic green plumage, appearing all dark at a distance. Female greyish-brown above, with pectoral tufts but without prominent supercilium or malar stripe.
Similar species Malachite Sunbird *Nectarinia famosa* (97) is very similar but male has yellow, not scarlet, pectoral tufts and is brighter, less bluish, green; and female lacks pectoral tufts and, along with female Tacazze *N. tacazze* (95) and Bronze Sunbirds *N. kilimensis* (96), shows prominent supercilium and malar stripe.

VOICE Harsher than that of *N. famosa*. **Call** A sharp metallic *tspk*, often uttered in flight, or a rapid *tsp-tk tsp-tk* or ticking *tiki-tiki-tiki* (by male). Also *chk-k* or *cha-cha*. Birds call frequently, so presence easily detected. **Song** Nominate sings from a perch on a rock or more often from a *Lobelia*, *Protea* or *Senecio*; song usually commences as a soft, almost inaudible warble, rising in pitch to a sharp *tsk tee, tsk tee, tk tk tk*, followed by a high long trill rising towards a peak of *s-s-s-s-s-s-s-s-s-s-*. Singing males may flick their wings, fan their pectoral tufts and occasionally sometimes fly straight up as much as 10 m before diving back to original perch. Song of *salvadorii* simpler: an accelerated repetition of dry *tserrep tserrep tserrep* notes following some *tsec* notes, lasting 1.3-2 seconds, uttered during breeding season.

DISTRIBUTION East Africa. Democratic Republic of the Congo, Rwanda, Uganda (south-west highlands, on Ruwenzoris and Virunga volcanoes), Kenya, Tanzania, Zambia and Malawi.

HABITAT Afro-alpine moorland with giant lobelias, proteas and giant groundsels *Senecio* sp. Open *Hagenia–Hypericum* forest, *Hypericum* scrub and bamboo. *Protea* grassland and *Kotschya–Erica* scrub above 1,980 m on Nyika plateau, Malawi and Zambia, which is not high enough for afro-alpines such as giant lobelias and groundsels. In

Uganda, occurs in hollows and valleys at 3,300-4,400 m in afro-alpine moorland with giant lobelias, tree heathers *Erica* spp., and giant groundsels.

STATUS Abundant in afro-alpine moorland, 3,000-4,500 m.

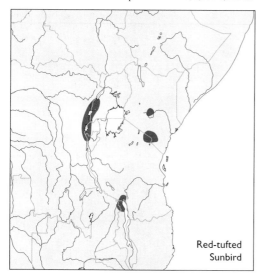
Red-tufted Sunbird

MOVEMENTS Altitudinal wanderer in Kenya. Vagrant to North Pare mountains, 60 km from Mt Kilimanjaro. Migrant to Nyika plateau in Malawi, where absent May–June.

FOOD Insects including Chironomidae and other Diptera, Coleoptera and Lepidoptera; spiders, small snails, nectar and pollen. Often feeds hovering in front of inflorescences of *Lobelia*, catching insects, mainly bibionids and chironomids, and occasionally sweeping through swarms and capturing them like a flycatcher with snap of bill audible at close quarters. Whilst foraging in giant lobelias *Lobelia telekii* or *L. keniensis*, birds run up the inflorescences like a Eurasian Treecreeper *Certhia familiaris*. Prefers to visit younger male flowers at the apex of the inflorescences of *L. telekii*, which contain twice as much sugar as the older female flowers lower down. *Lobelia keniensis* is home to bibionid flies which form the most important item of food (90% of stomach contents of nominate *johnstoni*). Also, rosettes of *L. keniensis* hold pools of water holding chironomid larvae which form an important part of the diet of the nominate race. Feeds small lycaenid butterfies *Harpendireus aequatorialis* and Diptera to young in nests, which they catch on the wing.
Known food-plants *Aloe* sp., *Erica* sp., *Hypericum* sp. including *H. keniense*, *Kniphofia* sp., *Lobelia deckenii*, *L. keniensis* (= *L. gregoriana*), *L. telekii*, *Leonotis decadonta*, *L. mollissima*, *L.* aff. *pole-evansii*, *Protea angolensis*, *P. kilimandscharica*, *P. madiensis*, *P. petiolaris*, *P. welwitschii*, *Senecio brassica*, *S. keniodendron*, *Tecoma capensis*.

HABITS Territorial in the alpine zone, with size of territory varying with altitude and consequent availability of food from 1,700 to 3,300 m². Thus, populations denser in the lower alpine zone than in the peak region. Also annual variations in territory size in relation to numbers of *Lobelia telekii* inflorescences. Territories contain about four times the number of flowers visited by their owners during a day, but those with more flowers have more intruders. After intrusions, defending males tend to feed near site of the incursion. Both non-breeding birds without territories and territorial birds may intrude, hence territory-holders always kept busy. Territories of males which pair and attempt to breed are about twice as big and with twice as many flowers as those of unpaired males. Males feeding nestlings tend to lose territorial bouts at *Lobelia telekii* inflorescences. Non-breeding parties of 10 or more males, sometimes with females and Mountain Chats *Pinarochroa sordida*, aggregate on moorland especially where there are good stands of *Protea*. Ornaments (long tails of males and pectoral tufts) are condition-dependent sexual signals and long-tailed males tend to be bigger birds overall, but ornaments vary in size with environmental variables (tails 172.3 ± 15.2 mm long, pectoral tufts 9.1 ± 1.3 in bad year, 188.8 ± 15.3, 9.7 ± 1.7 in good year). Males with wider pectoral tufts and longer tails able to defend more *Lobelia* inflorescences and larger territories, and changes in aggressive interactions and mean lengths of encounter followed experimental manipulation of ornaments.

Tame, allowing observers to approach to within a few metres. Often bathes, splashing in recently melted water in leaves of groundsel or giant lobelia. Adults seen to roost communally (at least three birds) in holes in matted dead-leaf clusters of tree groundsel *Senecio keniodendron*, originally excavated by Mountain Chats *Pinarochroa sordida*. Immature birds roost in disused nests.

BREEDING Territorial, with *Lobelia* and *Senecio* used as song-posts. Not all territorial males attract mates. Only 57-87% do so in a year. Nests between 3,300 and 4,200 m on Mt Kenya. Male *johnstoni* display involves approaching female, perching close but usually below her, raising bill at slight angle, puffing out feathers, holding tail curved up over back, raising wings half-open, uttering high-pitched *psurr-psurr-psurr* and turning body clockwise, thus displaying metallic feathers to full advantage. Only female incubates but both sexes feed nestling, with male only involved during last week of nestling's stay in nest except when there are two young. Female takes faecal sacs and drop them 30 m or more away from nest. On Nyika plateau territories of race *salvadorii* established in *Protea* grassland and *Kotschya–Philippia* scrub on rocky outcrops. Males sing and display from prominent perches, chasing away conspecifics and Montane Double-collared Sunbird *Cinnyris ludovicensis* (107). Display involves male approaching female, stretching neck out and depressing head until bills almost touch, whilst uttering a soft churring call. Female may also flutter wings before copulation, and may sometimes initiate proceedings by advancing on a male with wings drooped and fluttering. Uncooperative females chased by males in zig-zag jerky flight. Display-flight involves fast vertical flight, with males chasing each other or pursuing a female, but occasionally occurs along a path following contours.

Occasionally dives at and then feeds female, which assumes chick's begging posture with vibrating wings, one of the few examples of courtship feeding in sunbirds. Females do all incubation and brooding. After feeding chicks, female feeds on *Protea welwitschii*, then hunts insects and spiders. Chicks are brooded for 10 minutes per hour in day. They are fed at rate of 5-12 visits per hour and leave nest 22 days after hatching. Female alone cares for fledglings for up to two weeks. Involvement of one male in fledgling care consisted of occasional aggressive forays at young which elicited vigorous begging, accompanied by *seep, seep* calls, but they were not fed; another male was attentive and fed young regularly. Adults leave territory once young independent. **Nest** Race *dartmouthi*: woven into small heathland bush, <1 m up or 15 m up in *Hagenia* tree; oval, made of white wool from unidentified flowers or of *Usnea* sp. and pappus with brown fibres especially around the lateral entrance, lined with pappus; 140 mm high and 120 mm wide; *johnstoni*: in *Erica* bushes in the moorland zone and lined with woolly tomentum stripped from the backs of *Senecio keniensis brassica* leaves, or hair of rodents or hyrax; also in *Lobelia telekii* inflorescences; in tops of grass tussocks or amongst dead leaves below the terminal rosettes of *Senecio keniodendron* at higher elevations. Above 4,100 m, most in tussocks of *Festuca pilgeri*, but *S. keniodendron* inflorescence and *Erica arborea* also used. Race *salvadorii*: 1.8-2 m up, deep in *Erica* bush. **Eggs** c/1-2. 19-20.5 x 12-13.5; white, streaked pinkish-brown, especially at larger pole. Usually only one egg, but two may be laid if nest in high-quality territory; 4% of nests have c/2. **Laying months** Race *dartmouthi*: Democratic Republic of the Congo: December, nest-building June; Uganda: Ruwenzoris above 3,600 m, November–January; *johnstoni*: East Africa: January, February, May, July–October, December, perhaps all year in the alpine zone; *salvadorii*: Malawi: January, October, December; Zambia: active gonads January.

DESCRIPTION *N. j. dartmouthi*

Adult male Head black with green iridescence on crown, sides of head and neck. Rest of upperparts metallic green, bluish on rump and violet-blue on uppertail-coverts. Tail black, central pair of rectrices thin and very long, protruding up to 115 mm beyond rest and with both webs at base edged bluish-green. Outer webs of T2-T6 with fringes bluish-green. Underparts iridescent green, becoming bluer below from chest, violet-blue on upper belly and flanks and black on lower belly, thighs and undertail-coverts. Pectoral tufts bright scarlet. Wing black, with iridescent green median and lesser wing-coverts, iridescent blue edges to greater wing-coverts and alula edged bluish-green. Underwing-coverts and axillaries black. Iris brown or hazel. Bill, legs and feet black. **Non-breeding plumage** Male eclipse plumage recorded in *johnstoni* on Mt Kenya but not in *dartmouthi* in Ruwenzoris or Kivu volcano populations. Non-breeding male has head and body brownish, otherwise as breeding birds.
Adult female Upperparts brownish-grey, face darker. Tail very dark brown with blue sheen. Outer rectrices with outerwebs and tips edged buff. Underparts off-white, mottled dark brownish-black, with yellow wash on breast and flanks, latter dark brown. Undertail-coverts brown. Pectoral tufts 22-25% smaller than those of males but also scarlet, sometimes more orangey than male. Wing blackish-brown, edged paler. Underwing-coverts and axillaries blackish-brown. Iris brown or hazel. Bill, legs and feet black.
Juvenile Similar to adult female but lacks pectoral tufts.

GEOGRAPHICAL VARIATION

N. j. dartmouthi Ogilvie-Grant, 1906 (eastern Democratic Republic of the Congo and western Uganda, above 2,700 m in Ruwenzori mountains, and Kivu volcanoes) Described above. Male bluer than either *johnstoni* or *salvadorii* with short bill of latter but long wing of former. Male metallic plumage bluish-green. Female darker below, centre of abdomen dusky yellow; throat, breast and flanks dark sepia-brown.
N. j. itombwensis Prigogine, 1977 (Itombwe mountains, 2,350-3,100 m) Male differs from *johnstoni* and *salvadorii* by deeper blue, purplish and green metallic colour on back, throat, chest, belly and proximal fringes to

edges of elongated tail feathers, and resembles *dartmouthi* which, however, is even more bluish especially on rump and uppertail-coverts. Female resembles *salvadorii* but underparts slightly tinged brown (lighter grey in *salvadorii*); generally lighter, much paler below, especially on lower belly, than *johnstoni*, undertail-coverts off-white not dull brown. Also paler below than *dartmouthi*: chest and belly greyish-brown (*dartmouthi* has dark sepia-brown underparts); centre of abdomen dusky white, tinged light brown (*dartmouthi* has a much darker belly with centre of abdomen dusky yellow generally restricted to small patch); undertail-coverts greyish-white intermixed with brownish-grey (dark brown in *dartmouthi*).
N. j. johnstoni Shelley, 1885 (includes *idius*) (Kenya, where common from the edge of the forest [at 3,000 m] to the foot of the main peak at 4,500 m on Mt Kenya, Aberdares, Mt Meru and Olosirwa; Kilimanjaro in north Tanzania) Male metallic plumage green. Female has breast and flanks olive-tinged sepia-brown; throat greyish; centre of abdomen dusky white, sometimes tinged yellow.
N. j. salvadorii Shelley, 1903 (name replaces *nyikensis*: when *Leptocoma sericea salvadorii* was included in *Nectarinia*, *salvadorii* was preoccupied and replaced by *nyikensis*) (northern Malawi on Nyika Plateau at 2,000-2,450 m, and Livingstone mountains, Zambia, southern Tanzania above 2,100 m) Male smaller-winged (72-78) than *johnstoni* (80-86) and bill shorter (24-27; 29-32 in *johnstoni*). Male metallic plumage green. Female paler below; resembles *johnstoni* but a little paler and greyer on malar region, throat and centre of abdomen.

MEASUREMENTS Wing 81-88 (mean 84.4, 8 male *dartmouthi*), 80-86 (25 male *johnstoni*), 75-80 (mean 78.4, SD 1.14, 5 male *itombwensis*), 72.5-80 (mean 78.8, 5 male *salvadorii*), 74-77 (mean 75.3, 4 female *dartmouthi*), 67.5-73.5 (mean 69.6, SD 1.52, 5 female *itombwensis*) 69-75 (13 female *johnstoni*), 66-70 (10 female *salvadorii*); **tail including elongated central rectrices** 130-210 (mean 144, 8 male *dartmouthi*), 119-153 (mean 135, SD 14.98, 5 male *itombwensis*), 156-204 (25 male *johnstoni*), 110-195 (10 male *salvadorii*); **tail** 46-53 (mean 48.4, 4 female *dartmouthi*), 43.5-49 (mean 47.6, SD 1.14, 5 female *itombwensis*), 45-53 (13 female *johnstoni*), 43.5-48 (9 female *salvadorii*); **bill** 24.5-30 (mean 28.1, 8 male *dartmouthi*), 27.5-31 (mean 30.6, SD 0.55, 5 male *itombwensis*), 33-36 (mean 34.5, 8 male *johnstoni*), 26-29 (mean 27.6, 9 male *salvadorii*), 24-27 (mean 26.3, 4 female *dartmouthi*), 26-29 (mean 28, SD 1.41, 4 female *itombwensis*), 31-32 (2 female *johnstoni*), 25.0-28.0 (mean 26.1, 6 female *salvadorii*); **exposed culmen** 29-32.5 (25 male *johnstoni*), 24-26.5 (10 male *salvadorii*), 28.5-30.5 (11 female *johnstoni*), 21-26 (9 female *salvadorii*); **tarsus** 19-21 (mean 19, 8 male *dartmouthi*), 18-20 (mean 19, SD 0.71, 5 male *itombwensis*), 17.5-21 (25 male *johnstoni*), 16-19 (10 male *salvadorii*), 19-21 (mean 20, 4 female *dartmouthi*), 18-19 (mean 18.6, SD 0.55, 5 female *itombwensis*), 17.5-19 (13 female *johnstoni*), 15-16.5 (9 female *salvadorii*); **mass** 14-17 (mean 15.7, 3 male *dartmouthi*), 14, 16 (2 male *johnstoni*).

REFERENCES Burd (1995), Chapin (1954), Coe (1961, 1967), Dowsett-Lemaire (1988, 1989), Evans (1991, 1996), Evans & Barnard (1995), Evans & Hatchwell (1992a,b), Evans & Thomas (1992), Prigogine (1977), Williams (1951), Young (1982), Young & Evans (1993).

DREPANORHYNCHUS

Drepanorhynchus reichenowi Fischer & Reichenow 1884, *J. Orn.* 32, p.56, 1,500-2,000 m, Lake Naivasha, Kenya. Type by original designation *Drepanorhynchus reichenowi* Fischer.

Monotypic genus of a montane species of large sunbird with characteristic markedly decurved bill. Male has long tail with elongated central rectrices. Both sexes with golden wings and tails. Groove in head from bill through forehead to forecrown becomes worn, losing feathers and accumulating pollen (Figure 8).

99 GOLDEN-WINGED SUNBIRD
Drepanorhynchus reichenowi Plate 38

Drepanorhynchus reichenowi Fischer, 1884, *J. Orn.* 32, p.56, 1,500-2,000 m, Lake Naivasha, Kenya.

Alternative name: Golden-wing Sunbird

IDENTIFICATION Unmistakable with brilliant golden on wings and tail and markedly decurved bill. Male with iridescence of coppery-green and reddish on head, mantle and chin to upper breast. Female has olivaceous upperparts, pale below with dark mottling on breast and belly. Gold on wings and tail.
Similar species None.

VOICE Call A weak rasping note *jwee* and *tweep*. A rapid *cha-cha-cha-cha-cha* and a fast *chuk-chi-chi-chek*, *cher-cher-cher*.
Song Short bursts of twitters interspersed with high *chi-chi-chi* and a chatter.

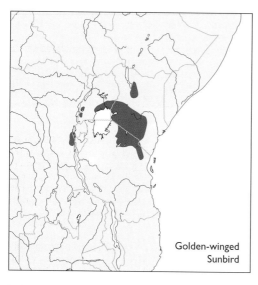

Golden-winged
Sunbird

DISTRIBUTION East Africa. Democratic Republic of the Congo, Uganda, Kenya and Tanzania.

HABITAT Bushy grasslands, montane forest edges, forest clearings and bamboo clearings above 1,170 m and up to 3,300 m. Also cultivated plots and gardens.

STATUS Common above 2,400 m in the Itombwe mountains, Democratic Republic of the Congo. Common in Kenya at 1,200-3,400 m. Common, Mt Elgon, Uganda, where also occurs on north shore of Lake Victoria and north-west Ankole. Widespread and locally common in Tanzania.

MOVEMENTS Moves up and down mountains with the seasons, in relation to flowering patterns. Ringing recoveries have confirmed movements of at least 101 km by a female and 65 km for a male. The latter was ringed at Kariobangi, 1,600 m, and recovered at South Kinangop, 2,530 m, confirming altitudinal shift.

FOOD Insects (Coleoptera, Diptera, Hymenoptera and unidentified larvae) and nectar. Catches flying ants in flight. Forms feeding territories in extensive patches of *Leonotis nepetifolia*.
Known food-plants Unidentified Acanthaceae, *Acrocarpus fraxinifolius*, *Aloe graminicola*, *Crotalaria* spp. including lion's-claw flower *C. agatiflora*, *Erythrina abyssinica*, *Fuchsia* sp., *Ipomoea batatas*, *Jacaranda mimosifolia*, unidentified Leguminosae, *Leonotis mollissima* (= *L. raineriana*), *L. nepetifolia*, *Phragmanthera dschallensis* (parasite of *Acacia* spp., especially *A. drepanolobium*).

HABITS Singly or in pairs and occasionally in large feeding assemblies. Does not join mixed-species flocks in Democratic Republic of the Congo but feeds with other montane sunbirds in Kenya. Develops yellow coating of pollen on crown when feeding on *Crotalaria agatiflora*, with which it may have co-evolved. Aggression of territorial defence increases late in the day. Can obtain 76% of energy requirements from territory. Longevity at least 9 years 6 months. Type host of feather louse *Ricinus timmermanni*.

BREEDING Territorial. **Nest** Race *lathburyi*: globular, made of fine grasses, lined with plant down, 1.5 m up in *Leonotis elliottii*; *reichenowi*: on top of thistle, 1 m up; *shellyae*: 190 mm high, 70 mm wide, entrance hole 30 mm in diameter (40 mm below the top), made of dry grass, clothed in pappus, with a porch; placed 1.5 m above ground in an isolated bush, or made of dry flower stalks, *Usnea* sp. and gossamer, lined with pappus. No porch. **Eggs** Race *reichenowi*: c/1; 19.8-21.0 (mean 20.6, n=3) x 13.0-14.6 (mean 13.8); whitish with heavy grey-brown mottling forming patch at larger pole; *shellyae*: 20.5 x 14.2. **Laying months** Democratic Republic of the Congo: May; East Africa: January–April, June–December. Kenya: January, October; Tanzania: February.

DESCRIPTION *N. r. reichenowi*
Feathers on forecrowns of both sexes do not form conjoined edge where they meet base of upper mandible, but form a V of bare unfeathered skin, pointing backwards across crown. This may be only small but can be up to 9.5 mm in length and 3.2 mm wide at its widest near bill, and size may increase with wear when birds probe and pollinate flowers. This crown groove accumulates pollen.
Adult male Upperparts black with bronzy-gold reflections on crown, mantle and back, less golden on rump and uppertail-coverts. Tail black and very long, graduated, with central rectrices protruding up to 70 mm beyond rest and with golden-yellow edges. T2-T6 with golden only on

outerwebs. Underparts black with copper and golden reflections on chin and breast. Wing black but appearing gold as feathers broadly edged golden-yellow; median and lesser wing-coverts more coppery. Primary and secondary wing-coverts and alula edged green. Underwing-coverts and axillaries black. Iris dark brown. Bill, legs and feet black. **Non-breeding plumage** Male has glossy bronze of head, foreneck and back replaced by dull black, with a few metallic feathers left on lower foreneck and back. Males in eclipse in Kenya, February–June, but June–October in the Democratic Republic of the Congo. Male in Tanzania in eclipse, November.

Adult female Top of head, lores and ear-coverts dark brown with olivaceous tinge on crown. Rest of upperparts olivaceous-green, faintly mottled brown. Graduated dark brown tail with golden-yellow edges has central rectrices protruding up to 10 mm beyond rest. Chin and throat pale yellow, rest of underparts darker olive-yellow heavily mottled dark brown on middle of breast and belly. Wing brown edged yellow, appearing all yellow when folded, as male. Underwing-coverts blackish-brown, tipped olivaceous-yellow, axillaries olivaceous-yellow. Iris dark brown. Bill, legs and feet black. **Juvenile** Similar to adult female but sides of face, chin and throat black and rest of underparts olive heavily barred black. Wings and tail edged less bright yellow.

GEOGRAPHICAL VARIATION

D. r. lathburyi (Williams, 1956) (northern Kenya on isolated peaks 1,700-2,300 m up in the Matthews range, Mt Nyiru, Mt Uraguess and Mt Kulal) Smaller (wing 75-80) than *reichenowi* (79-86), bill more strongly decurved; male metallic plumage said to have stronger red reflections but much individual variation and some nominate

even redder than two specimens of *lathburyi* examined. *D. r. reichenowi* Fischer, 1884 (includes *alinderi* Laubmann, 1928]) (south and west Uganda to west and central Kenya, south to Crater highlands, Kilimanjaro and Usambara in Tanzania) Described above. *D. r. shellyae* (Prigogine, 1952) (mountains of Democratic Republic of the Congo north-west of Lake Tanganyika, above 2,100 m) Bill less curved than *reichenowi*; length of culmen from tip to base in straight line 27.5-29 (30-32 mm in *lathburyi*). Crown of female grey (not green like mantle).

MEASUREMENTS Wing 75-80 (male *lathburyi*), 78-86 (mean 81.6, 14 male *reichenowi*), 78-83.5 (mean 80.5, 8 male *shellyae*), 67-74 (mean 69.5, 30 female *reichenowi*), 70 (female *shelleyae*); **tail** 115-140 (including elongated central rectrices, mean 131.5, 14 male *reichenowi*), 117-131 (including elongated central rectrices, mean 125, 8 male *shellyae*), 67-74 (excluding elongated central rectrices, mean 70.4, 8 male *shellyae*), 52-67 (mean 54.8, 10 female *reichenowi*), 68-71 (mean 69.8, 6 female *shellyae*), 56-61 (mean 57.8, 6 female *shellyae*); **bill** 28-31 (mean 29.2, 14 male *reichenowi*), 25-29 (mean 26.8, 10 female *reichenowi*); **culmen** 28-32 (mean 29.7, 8 male *shellyae*), 26-29 (mean 28.2, 6 female *shellyae*); **tarsus** 16-19 (mean 17.8, 14 male *reichenowi*), 16-18 (mean 17.5, 10 female *reichenowi*), **mass** 12.8-17.5 (mean 15.7, 65 male *reichenowi*), 11-15.9 (mean 13.7, 32 female *reichenowi*).

REFERENCES Backhurst (1973, 1977), Chapin (1954), Friedmann & Stager (1969), Gill & Wolf (1975a,b, 1977, 1978, 1979), Ledger (1980), Lott (1991), Prigogine (1952, 1971), Pyke (1979), Sheppard (1958), Travis (1982), Williams (1956), Wolf (1975).

CINNYRIS

Cinnyris Cuvier 1817, *Règne Animale*, 1, p.411. Type by subsequent designation (G. R. Gray 1855 *Cat. Gen. Subgen. Birds* p.19), *Certhia splendida* Shaw 1811 = *Certhia coccinigaster* Latham 1801.

Fifty species of mostly medium-sized sunbirds with fine, slightly or strongly curved, short or medium-length bills. Tongue long and narrow, sides curved inwards to form two tubes, distal 15% bifid with no obvious fimbriations except at very tip. Males with iridescent plumage especially on upperparts, and usually with pectoral tufts; females plain and lack pectoral tufts. Can be subdivided into six groups (Irwin 1999): 16 species of double-collared sunbirds; 12 species of purple-banded sunbirds; 4 species in the maroon group, based on the colour of the underparts of *C. superbus* and its two close relatives, with the somewhat arbitrary inclusion of *C. rufipennis*; 4 species of white-bellied sunbirds; 2 olive species, and 12 species in a miscellaneous group comprising *C. cupreus* and those which do not occur in Africa.

100 OLIVE-BELLIED SUNBIRD
Cinnyris chloropygius   Plate 34

Nectarinia chloropygia Jardine, 1842, *Ann. Mag. Nat. Hist.* 10, p.188, Aboh, Niger river, Nigeria.

IDENTIFICATION Small sunbird, male with bright metallic green upperparts and throat with red chest-band above olive belly. Female with olive upperparts, paler and washed with yellow below.
Similar species Like large version of the Tiny Sunbird *Cinnyris minullus* (101) but male fewer or no blue bars amongst red breast feathers; bill distinctly curved and longer than in *minullus*; underwing-coverts usually grey not white like

those of *minullus*, except in subadult plumage when also white. Female yellower below and less heavily streaked than *minullus*. Similar also to Northern Double-collared Sunbird *C. reichenowi* (108) but smaller, male with less extensive scarlet band and green not violet uppertail-coverts. In eastern Africa, confusion with Eastern Double-collared Sunbird *C. mediocris* (112) possible but bill is straighter and uppertail-coverts are green not metallic blue. Female *chloropygius* has paler throat and underparts and is yellower below than female (unstreaked) *reichenowi* and (lightly mottled) *mediocris*. Pale belly and short tail distinguish male from male Beautiful Sunbird *C. pulchellus* (115). Confusion with Miombo Double-collared Sunbird *C. manoensis* (102) possible in Angola, but male *manoensis* has purple band between throat and breast and female is grey.

VOICE Call *zeet-zeet* or *psee* and an incessant series of *chip* notes, repeated 3-4 times per second. **Song** Race *chloropygius*: a short burst lasting 3-4 seconds, beginning with *pisr-pisr* notes followed by a very rapid series of rising and falling *sisisisisi-sisisisi-si* and other notes in a hurried jumble delivered from conspicuous perch; *kempi*: similar but shorter, about 2 seconds, rising for the first half during the *sisisi* phase and falling for the second which is less complex, consisting of high-pitched chirps.

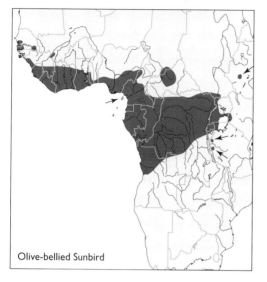

Olive-bellied Sunbird

DISTRIBUTION West and Central Africa with an isolated population in Ethiopia. Senegal, Guinea-Bissau, Guinea, Sierra Leone, Liberia, Côte d'Ivoire, Ghana, Togo, Benin, Nigeria, Mali, Chad, Sudan, Ethiopia, Cameroon, Central African Republic, Equatorial Guinea (Bioko and Rio Muni), Gabon, Republic of the Congo, Democratic Republic of the Congo, Rwanda, Burundi, Uganda, Kenya, Tanzania and Angola.

HABITAT In the lower strata of trees and thickets at the edges of clearings and along streams and roads in primary and secondary forest, gallery forest and coffee plantations; also farmland, parks, gardens, well-wooded savanna, mangroves, coastal thickets and inselbergs but not to very high altitudes. Race *orphogaster* prefers scrubland to montane forest at 1,500 m in the Itombwe mountains of the Democratic Republic of the Congo and only occurs between 1,000 and 1,750 m in Kenya.

STATUS Common, sometimes abundant, throughout the forest zones in West Africa. Uncommon in Senegal and no records from Gambia. Not uncommon in Togo. Common in Nigeria. Locally common in mainland Equatorial Guinea at forest edges. Occurs at densities of 5-7 per 10 ha, in vicinity of habitations, Gabon. Rare in extreme south of Sudan. Abundant in Democratic Republic of the Congo. Common in western Kenya and north-west Tanzania. Common and widespread up to 2,300 m in Uganda, mostly in south. Abundant in Burundi. Locally common resident in Angola. Rare and isolated in Ethiopia.

MOVEMENTS Partially migratory, some birds moving north with the rains in West Africa, March–June.

FOOD Insects including small caterpillars and beetles; spiders, nectar, seeds and flower parts. Small shells, quartz, sand grains and grit have been found in stomachs.

Known food-plants *Allamanda cathartica* (nectar-robbed), *Bougainvillea* sp., *Canna* sp., *Clerodendrum* sp., *Coffea* sp., *Cogniauxia podolaena*, unidentified Convolvulaceae, *Erythrina* sp., *Heliconia* sp., *Hibiscus* sp. (nectar-robbed) including *H. rosa-sinensis* (nectar-robbed, with pink flowers preferred to red ones), *Ipomoea* sp., *Maerua* sp., *Manihot esculenta*, *M. utilissima*, *Musa* sp., *Ochthocosmus africanus* (fruits), *Psidium guajava*, unidentified Rubiaceae, *Solanum* sp., *Spathodea nilotica*, *Thevetia peruviana* (nectar-robbed), *Yucca* sp.

HABITS Active birds which feed at any time of day including the hottest periods, usually low down, 0.5-3 m up but sometimes up to 10 m. Tame, allowing close approaches when feeding and known to enter houses to feed on cut flowers. Occasionally hover in front of flowers. Advertises its presence with *zit-zit* calls when moving from place to place or flower to flower. Solitary, in pairs or in small groups of six or more birds. Fast flight. Males sometimes defend feeding territories. Aggressive towards *C. minullus*, other sunbirds and even sphingid moths feeding on preferred flowers. Prefer pink to red *H. rosa-sinensis* flowers, perhaps as consequence of nectar-depletion in red ones exploited by butterflies (*Nepheronia thalassina*, *N. pharis*, *Borbo* sp., *Papilio dardanus*, *P. fourcas*), which prefer the red flowers. Host to *Haemoproteus sequeirae*, *Plasmodium elongatum* and *Trypanosoma* sp., the cestode *Staphylepis ambilateralis* and feather mites *Anisodiscus dolichogaster*, *Monojoubertia grandiloba*, *Paralgoides anoplopus*, *Pterodectes hologaster* and *Xolalges glossobus*.

BREEDING Territorial. Incubation by female only; young fed by both parents. Parasitised by Emerald Cuckoo *Chrysococcyx cupreus* and Cassin's Honeybird *Prodotiscus regulus*. **Nest** Untidy structure of coarse grass, strips of bark and leaves loosely entwined in the fabric, suspended 1-10 m high from branch of bush or palm. Has short straggly beard and is lined with fine grass, seed-down, feathers or wool. Ovoid, 120-150 mm tall, 70 mm wide and 70 mm deep, with pronounced porch at entrance hole (20-25 mm across) slightly above the mid-point on the side and about 65 mm below the top. **Eggs** c/1-3; *chloropygius*: 14.0-15.5 (mean 14.5, n=11) x 10.5-11.5 (mean 10.7); *kempi*: 13.5-15.5 (mean 14.4, n=5) x 9.9-11.5 (mean 10.5); white; *orphogaster*: 14.8-18.6 (mean 15.3, n=12) x 10.7-11.9 (mean 11.1); long pointed ovals, plain white to clear grey with big patches or stripes and grey or brown spots often concentrated at larger end. **Laying months** Angola: March, December, in breeding condition February, April, December; Cameroon: February–June, August–December; Democratic Republic of the Congo: January–April, June, August–December; East Africa: February, April, May–November; Equatorial Guinea (Bioko): September; Ethiopia: July; Gabon: August, December–March; Ghana: dependent young February, April, September, October, nest-building March, June, August, October; Liberia: February, November, dependent young September, October, December, March, April; Nigeria: May–October; Republic of the Congo: January, September, October; Sierra Leone: October–November; Uganda: February, March, July–September, November.

DESCRIPTION *C. c. chloropygius*
Adult male Upperparts from crown to uppertail-coverts, head and throat metallic green. Lores black. Throat feathers merge into blue at base above 10 mm-wide scarlet breast-band. Rest of underparts olive except for bright

yellow pectoral tufts. Wings brown, secondaries with narrow olive edges. Greater wing-coverts also edged olive when fresh. Tail black glossed dark blue. Underwing-coverts and axillaries dull white with yellow or grey tinge. Iris brown or dark brown. Bill, legs and feet black.

Adult female Olive above. Pale stripe before and behind eye. Wings brown, remiges and coverts with greenish-olive margins. Tail blackish with dark blue gloss. Chin off-white, throat pale olive. Rest of underparts olive with distinct yellow wash. Iris brown. Bill and legs black. Mouth flesh-coloured.

Juvenile Nestlings have belly with yellow wash and grey throats. Immature male as adult female but browner on upperparts. Subadult male has metallic feathers on crown and back, throat and chest with upperparts becoming metallic first; belly red with a few yellow feathers and grey throat. Some subadult males may retain white underwing-coverts of immature plumage, even when metallic feathers attained, causing confusion with *C. minullus*. Moult in December in Côte d'Ivoire.

GEOGRAPHICAL VARIATION

C. c. bineschensis Neumann, 1903 (only known from type-locality Detschabassa near Tepi in Kaffa, Binescho region, south-west Ethiopia [Neumann 1905] and nearby sites at Tepi, c.1,250 m at 7°12'N 35°25'E, and Gezmaret, c.1,200 m at 7°7'N 35°26'E [Atkins 1994]; these birds are 650 and 700 km from their nearest conspecifics in Kenya and Sudan, respectively) Abdomen of male sooty, even more so than in *orphogaster*.

C. c. chloropygius (Jardine, 1842) (includes *luehderi* Reichenow, 1899 and *insularis* Reichenow, 1920) (south-east Nigeria to Cameroon, lower Congo, Cabinda and north-west Angola south through Uíge to Cuanza Norte and Malanje, and south along the escarpment to Quitondo and Gabela in Cuanza Sul, east to Ubangi and middle Congo River; Bioko). Described above.

C. c. kempi Ogilvie-Grant, 1910 (Senegal to south-west Nigeria) Male has lighter, more olive abdomen than *chloropygius* and narrower, more orangey breast-band. A pale-bellied *kempi*-like specimen recorded from Mt Cameroon, so range may be wider or subspecies in need of revision.

C. c. orphogaster Reichenow, 1899 (includes *uellensis* Reichenow, 1912) (Congo Basin, Lisala and Kasai, and north-east Angola in northern Lunda Norte to Democratic Republic of the Congo, upper Congo, Kivu and Manyema, Burundi; southern edge of Sudan, Uganda, Kenya [Kakamega forest, central and south Nyanza] and north-west Tanzania) Male has darker abdomen than *chloropygius*. Nestling has brownish-grey iris, pinkish-grey bill and feet, corners of mouth yellow.

Note *Cinnyris ogilvie-granti*, described as *Anthreptes ogilvie-granti* by Bannerman (1921a), is not a separate species but represents a well-marked aberrant dress of female *C. chloropygius*, known from Cameroon and the Democratic Republic of the Congo (Bates 1927, Bannerman 1948, de Roo-de Ridder & de Roo-de Ridder 1969, Prigogine 1978), characterised by the possession of male features. Some *"ogilvie-granti"* have light yellow pectoral tufts and maximal development of red on the breast, but all have at least some red on the breast and are without any metallic plumage. Underparts are richer-coloured than normal female *C. c. orphogaster* and there is a slight metallic lustre to the upperparts. Chin and throat is dull olive-yellow, instead

of pale greyish-white with a faint olive wash, breast bright orange-red instead of pale yellow with indistinct streaks; belly bright sulphur-yellow instead of pale whitish-yellow; a slight purple and greenish sheen distributed over the whole of the underparts, but more pronounced on the head, the lesser wing-coverts and uppertail-coverts. Those with long bright yellow pectoral tufts are adult female *"ogilvie-granti"*, as immatures lack the tufts even if possessing red breasts as bright as males.

MEASUREMENTS Wing 45-54 (mean 48.2, 10 male *chloropygius*), 45-49 (mean 47.3, 14 male *kempi*), 52-56 (mean 53.3, 10 male *orphogaster*), 43-48 (mean 44.6, 10 female *chloropygius*), 43-46 (mean 45.7, 3 female *kempi*), 45-49 (mean 47.2, 12 female *orphogaster*); **tail** 27-38 (mean 33.3, 10 male *chloropygius*), 25-33 (mean 28.5, SD, 2.65, 4 male *kempi*), 22-32 (mean 26.1, 10 female *chloropygius*), 25-30 (mean 26.0, 3 female *kempi*); **bill** 15-21 (mean 19.5, 10 male *chloropygius*), 17-19 (mean 18.0, 14 male *kempi*), 20-22 (mean 21, 10 male *orphogaster*), 15-20 (mean 18.5, 10 female *chloropygius*), 16-18 (mean 17, 3 female *kempi*); **tarsus** 14-16 (mean 15.5, 10 male *chloropygius*), 14-16 (mean 15, SD 0.82, 4 male *kempi*), 13-15 (mean 13.9, 10 female *chloropygius*), 13-14 (4 female *kempi*); **mass** 7.1 (male *chloropygius*), 4.7-6.5 (mean 5.4, 9 male *kempi*), 5.5-8.0 (mean 6.3, 37 male *orphogaster*), 5.0 (female *kempi*), 5-7.5 (mean 6.1, 14 female *orphogaster*).

REFERENCES Ash (1994), Atkins (1994), Bannerman (1921a), Bates (1927), Brosset & Erard (1986), Button (1967), Chapin (1954), Fry *et al.* (2000), Mariaux & Vaucher (1991), Prendergast (1983), Prigogine (1971, 1978), de Roo-de Ridder & de Roo-de Ridder (1969), Traylor & Parelius (1967), Waltert & Faber (2000), Zumpt (1961).

---

101   TINY SUNBIRD
Cinnyris minullus   Plate 34

Cinnyris minullus Reichenow, 1899, *Orn. Monatsb.*, p.170, Jaounde [= Yaoundé], Cameroon.

IDENTIFICATION A very small sunbird with short straightish bill. Male has metallic green upperparts, head and upper throat, blue band on lower throat, and scarlet breast-band mottled with metallic blue bars. Belly olive. Female olive above, yellowish below and with supercilium. **Similar species** Resembles miniature Olive-bellied Sunbird *Cinnyris chloropygius* (100) but male has more extensive blue lower throat-band, and more blue bars interspersed within red breast-band. These are difficult to see in the field, so *minullus* is more easily told by its smaller size, shorter tail and shorter and straighter bill. Lower mandible appears almost straight except at tip, whereas it is curved throughout its length in *chloropygius*. Female has greyer throat than female *chloropygius* and is paler yellow below than *C. c. kempi*; *minullus* tends to have purer white underwing-coverts than greyer-tinged *chloropygius*. Both species respond to playback of recordings of each other's songs as well as their own.

VOICE Call A *chip* or *chip-chip*. **Song** A monotonous series of high-pitched mouse-like squeaky *tsi-tsi-tsi* or *suisui-sui-sui* notes, lasting about 15 seconds, or a shorter series of *tsi* or 2 *tweee*, followed by a melodic warble including *chip* notes, for 2-3 seconds.

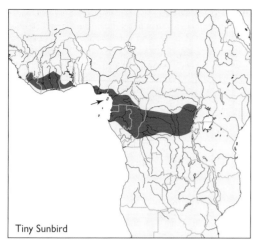

Tiny Sunbird

DISTRIBUTION West and Central Africa. Sierra Leone, Liberia, Côte d'Ivoire, Ghana, Nigeria, south Cameroon, Equatorial Guinea [Bioko and Rio Muni], Gabon, Republic of the Congo, Democratic Republic of the Congo [middle Congo south to Kwango and Kasai, east to upper Congo], Uganda as far west as Bwamba, 700 m, and Kibale forest, 1,700 m).

HABITAT Prefers more mature forest than *chloropygius*, being more often found in forest or secondary forest, but also occurs in forest edge, clearings and forest-savanna mosaic. Less common in man-dominated habitats than *chloropygius*, but occurs in gardens even in urban areas such as Abidjan and Malabo, and in cultivated areas such as cocoa plantations, abandoned plots and around villages.

STATUS Widespread and not uncommon, but rarer than *C. chloropygius*. Rare in Nigeria and mainland Equatorial Guinea. Occurs at densities of 2-3 per 10 ha, Gabon. Common Democratic Republic of the Congo. In Uganda scarce, occurring as far east as Kibale.

MOVEMENTS Probably sedentary.

FOOD Nectar, pollen, small insects.
Known food-plants *Anthocleista* sp., *Delonix regia*, *Leea* sp., unidentified Leguminosae, *Mussaenda* sp., creepers on forest margins.

HABITS Similar to those of *C. chloropygius*, with which it is interspecifically territorial. Defends feeding territories erratically, depending on availability of flowers. Attends flowers but also forages for insects, gleaning leaves. Forages 5-50 m up, most often above 20 m, perching on branches <5 cm in diameter. Forages singly or in pairs but, unlike *chloropygius*, joins mixed bird armies in upper strata of forest.

BREEDING Male sings from tops of tall trees. Pairs may have site fidelity for nest locations, as breeding observed in same place in successive years. Eggs laid at 24-hour intervals. Female only incubates; both sexes feed nestlings. **Nest** Placed 1.5-3 m up on leafy branch or in lime tree or thin trunk at forest edge, with opening towards clearing. Distinguishable from those of *C. chloropygius* by different materials used in the construction and lack of a beard. Small, ovoid, beautifully made, and always with some bark in structure, entwined with rootlets e.g. of epiphytic plant, grass stems and dead leaves held together with cobwebs and filaments of *Marasmius*, lined with kapok, fine grass

or pappus, and decorated with lichen, bark, dry leaves or dry palm flowers. 130 mm high, 75 mm wide with pronounced porch of *Marasmius* above 25 mm-wide side entrance 90 mm below top. **Eggs** c/1-2; 13.8-15.5 (mean 14.4, n=10) x 10.0-10.9 (mean 10.4); distinct from those of *C. chloropygius*. Long ovals, plain white tinged green or bluish, unglossy, very strongly marked with grey brown or dark brown spots around the larger end or with irregular grey or dark lilac-grey blotches with larger ones around the biggest end; easily told from those of *C. chloropygius* by smaller size and lack of stripes. **Laying months** Cameroon: April–June, October; Côte d'Ivoire: recently fledged juvenile July; Democratic Republic of the Congo: March, June, December; East Africa: July–August; Gabon: occupied nests September, November, dependent young September; Liberia: courtship display and nest-building October.

DESCRIPTION
Adult male Upperparts, head, chin and upper throat metallic green, bluer on uppertail-coverts. Metallic green merges on lower throat into thin metallic blue band above scarlet breast-band. Numerous patches of metallic blue within scarlet breast-band, 10-15 mm wide. Lemon-yellow pectoral tufts. Wings very dark brown, greater wing-coverts narrowly edged metallic green. Lesser and median wing-coverts metallic green. Tail black washed metallic bluish-purple. Belly and undertail-coverts dark olive. Inner borders of undersides of remiges greyish-white. Axillaries yellowish-white. Underwing-coverts white, often pure snow-white. Iris dark brown. Bill, legs and feet black.
Adult female Upperparts dark olive-green. Wings dark brown, remiges with dark yellowish margins and coverts edged olive-yellow. Tail very dark brown with blue gloss, outer feather and distal half of T5 paler brown. Narrow olivaceous-yellow supercilium. Throat grey, rest of underparts olive with yellow wash especially on belly. Axillaries yellowish-white. Underwing-coverts white, often pure snow-white. Iris very dark brown. Bill black but horn colour basally, yellowish at base of lower mandible. Legs and feet black.
Juvenile Buccal cavity of nestling orange, gape white. Juvenile as adult female, but throat darker grey, forming distinct bib, bordered whitish-grey laterally concolorous with chin. Supercilium much shorter and less noticeable, although feathers immediately above and just behind eye pale yellowish-olive. Underparts brightly washed with yellow. Gape pinkish orange-yellow. Iris very dark brown. Bill, legs and feet black.

GEOGRAPHICAL VARIATION *C. m. amadoni* (Eisentraut, 1965) (Bioko) and *C. m. marginatus* Ogilvie-Grant, 1907 (Semliki valley and Ituri forest in Democratic Republic of the Congo) have been described but are no longer considered valid. The Bioko race was named on the basis of slightly larger size (6 males with wings 49-51, mean 50.3; three females with wings 46.5-48.5, mean 47.7).

MEASUREMENTS Wing 45-51 (mean 48.1, 11 males), 43-48 (mean 45, 7 females); **tail** 25-29 (mean 28.4, 10 males), 23-26 (mean 25, 7 females); **bill** 14-18 (mean 16.5, 10 males), 13-16 (mean 16.5, 7 females); **tarsus** 13-14 (mean 14.1, 10 males), 13-15 (mean 13.9, 7 females); **mass** 5.0-6.5 (mean 5.8, 7 males), 4.5-6.5 (mean 5.7, 8 females).

REFERENCES Bannerman (1948, 1951), Bates (1911), Brosset & Erard (1986), Chapin (1954), Christy & Clarke (1994), Eisentraut (1965), Fry *et al.* (2000), Pérez del Val (1996), Prigogine (1971).

102 MIOMBO DOUBLE-COLLARED SUNBIRD
Cinnyris manoensis   **Plate 31**

Cinnyris manoensis Reichenow, 1907, *Orn. Monatsb.* 15, p.200, Langenburg [= Missale], Mano area, west of Lake Nyassa, Malawi.

Alternative name: Miombo Sunbird

Taxonomic note Includes *C. chalybeus gertrudis, C. c. bractiatus, C. c. zonarius* and *C. c. namwera.* Placed by some authors with *C. chalybeus.*

IDENTIFICATION Adult male has green head and mantle, greyish back, blue breast-band (reflects up throat when seen from below) above red breast-band (appears very thin when seen directly from the front), yellow pectoral tufts (easily seen and often conspicuous), ash-grey belly; bill appears long for such a small species. Adult female pale grey below becoming yellowish on belly and vent, dull brown above.
Similar species Female resembles variants of White-breasted Sunbird *Cinnyris talatala* (133) which have pale grey bellies, but are larger. Young juveniles up to six weeks old confusable with those of Variable Sunbird *C. venustus* (134) and Shelley's Sunbird *C. shelleyi* (117). Females also confusable with female *C. venustus.* Montane Double-collared Sunbird *C. ludovicensis* (107) sympatric with *C. m. pintoi*, male of which is separable by its lack of violet on uppertail-coverts, olive back without iridescence except on tips of uppertail-coverts, and narrower, duller red breast-band. Southern Double-collared Sunbird *C. chalybeus* (103) is similar but allopatric. In Malawi occasionally sympatric with Eastern Double-collared Sunbird *C. mediocris* (112), which differs by green not grey rump, violet not blue uppertail-coverts and olive belly of male, and much greener, less grey female.

VOICE Call A *zit* or *chip-chip* or *zip-chip-chip-chip* or *zip-chip* or *chip-chip-chip* or *zip-zip-zip*, usually from perch in a tree (e.g. from top of *Cassia abreviata* or *Pericopsis angolensis*) but also in flight. **Song** A descending trill of one second's duration, sometimes preceded by 5-7 *zit* call, and a complicated warble, uttered in bursts of 7-8 seconds, of rising and falling chirps of *tsee-see-tseu-twee-tzeee* or *tsee-tseeo-tzee-tse*, often following a *chip-chip* call.

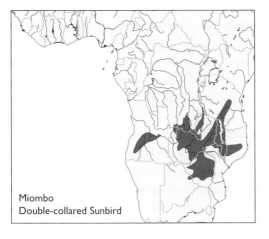
Miombo
Double-collared Sunbird

DISTRIBUTION Democratic Republic of the Congo, south-east Tanzania to Songea, Angola, south-east Zambia, Malawi, northern Mozambique, Botswana and Zimbabwe.

HABITAT Miombo woodland and open savanna. Up to 1,830 m, Ngwazi, Mufindi district, Tanzania. Miombo woodland, thorn-scrub and highland *Leucospermum* areas in Zimbabwe. *Cryptosepalum* forest in Zambia. In eastern highlands of Zimbabwe from 750 m up to 2,200 m. Riverine woodland, gardens and parks.

STATUS Local and uncommon in Tanzania. Locally common resident in Angola. Common in Zimbabwe. Uncommon in Zambia.

MOVEMENTS Moves locally in relation to flowering sources. Nomadic in Zimbabwe. One bird recovered 29 km away from ringing site.

FOOD Nectar, insects and spiders. Probes directly into flowers but also nectar-robs, e.g. from *Hibiscus*, gleans for insects amongst mopane trees *Colophospermum mopane*, hovers to feed from flowers, e.g. *Combretum zeyheri*, hawks for insects and takes spiders.
Known food-plants *Acrocarpus* sp., *Aloe* spp., *Bauhinia* sp., *Brachystegia speciformis, Callistemon citrinus, Cassia abreviata, C. singuena, Combretum flagrans, C. zeyheri, Faurea saligna, Leonotis* sp., *Erythrina abyssinica, Eucalyptus* sp., *Hibiscus* sp., *Holmskioldia* sp., *Jacaranda mimulopsis, Kniphofia* sp., *Leonotis* sp., unidentified mistletoes Loranthaceae, including a species parasitising *Brachystegia stipulata, Maranthes floribunda, Pyrostegia venusta, Salvia* sp., *Spathodea* sp., *Strelitzia* sp., *Tecoma capense, Tithonia rotundifolia, Gladiolus* sp.

HABITS Males defend feeding areas against each other. Interspecific reactions include holding the body stiff and elongated whilst rocking to and fro as if the legs were a pivot. Dominant over *C. talatala* and Purple-banded Sunbird *C. bifasciatus* (121) at *Cassia singuena* trees, where feeds on nectar exuding from beans opened at ends by Common Bulbuls *Pycnonotus barbatus* and Black-collared Barbets *Lybius torquatus.* Observed chasing a Laughing Dove *Streptopelia senegalensis* and pulling feathers from it, presumably for nesting material. Longevity more than 8 years.

BREEDING Bizarre displays include male swinging upside-down on perch when singing to female with nest material, and pair pivoting together very fast in half or full circles on perch for 5 minutes. Pre-copulatory display involves male in full song joined on perch by female, birds face each other, bow to each other, throw back their heads, bow again and repeat head movements and bowing in sequence for 10 seconds before male jumps on female's back to effect copulation. Parent may thrust bill deep into chick's throat and make pulsating actions suggestive of pumping liquids. May nest on verandahs of houses. **Nest** Pear-shaped or round nest made of grass bound with cobweb or white plant down with few grass stems. Fixed by twigs through top of dome, 2-6 m up, often to mass of cobwebs, out in open on bush. **Eggs** c/1-3. 16.1-17.9 (mean 16.7, n=16) x 11.2-12.0 (mean 11.8). **Laying months** Malawi: May–October, fledglings, March (*pintoi*); Mozambique: May; Zambia: August, October, November; Zimbabwe: all year, peak September–November.

DESCRIPTION *C. m. manoensis*
Adult male Head to back and scapulars metallic green, reflecting bronze. Rump pale olivaceous-brown. Iridescent bluish or purplish on tips of uppertail-coverts. Tail dark

brown with slight gloss, outer feather paler edged greyish-white on outer margin. Chin to upper breast metallic green, reflecting bronze, leading to narrow (2 mm deep) violet-blue band above larger (10 mm deep) scarlet band on lower breast. Belly and vent pale olivaceous or greyish-brown. Yellow pectoral tufts. Wing greyish-brown, edged lighter brown; lesser wing-coverts metallic green, reflecting bronze. Underwing-coverts off-white, axillaries with yellow wash. Iris dark brown. Bill, legs and feet black.

Adult female Upperparts dark greyish-brown, rump washed olive. Tail dark brown with slight gloss, outer feather paler with outer margin edged brownish-white. Sides of face dark brown. Underparts brownish-grey, slightly speckled, becoming paler on belly with slight yellow tinge. Wing greyish-brown, edged pale brown. Underwing-coverts white, axillaries with yellow wash.

Juvenile similar to adult female, but see below under *pintoi*.

GEOGRAPHICAL VARIATION

C. m. amicorum (Clancey, 1970) (Mt Gorongoza, Mozambique) Slightly larger than *manoensis*. Male greener above than *manoensis* and upper breast-band more violet, less blue. Belly darker. Female darker above and browner below than *manoensis*.

C. m. manoensis Reichenow, 1907 (includes *gertrudis* Grote, 1926 and *bractiatus* Vincent, 1933) (Zimbabwe, Malawi north to Nchisi, south-east Zambia, northern Mozambique, south-east Tanzania to Songea, intergrading with *pintoi* towards Iringa and Rungwe and in Zambia east of the Luangwa rift). Male with uppertail-coverts metallic blue or violet.

C. m. pintoi (Wolters, 1965) (replaces *intermedius* preoccupied by *C. asiaticus intermedius*) (central Angola on the central plateau from central and northern Huíla north to Huambo, east through Bié and south-eastern Malanje to northern Moxico to Katanga, Democratic Republic of the Congo, and Zambia west of the Luangwa rift; Malawi north of Nchisi and south-west Tanzania north-east to Iringa and Mlalo) Male lacks blue or violet on uppertail-coverts, which are greyish or narrowly tipped glossy green; underparts paler grey and bill shorter than *manoensis*. Juvenile *pintoi* resembles adult female but is more olive with a perceptibly swollen gape, white at first, darkening to yellow and olive-green (persisting well into second year). Outerwebs of primaries of immature females are olive contrasting with grey-olive of innerwebs. Underparts strongly washed yellow. Juvenile males do not attain full adult dress until end of third year, before which they have many dull olive feathers on head, back and breast, and red and blue chest-bands are irregular. No white on tail. Adults moult in November–December in Malawi; subadults start earlier and moult for longer; a partial post-juvenile moult of remiges occasional.

MEASUREMENTS Wing 63-67 (mean 64.3, 3 male *amicorum*), 59-67 (mean 63.3, 10 male *manoensis*), 57-64.5 (male *pintoi*), 56-64 (juv/imm male *pintoi*), 57-61 (mean 58.8, 10 female *manoensis*), 52-60 (female *pintoi*), 46-59 (juv/imm female *pintoi*); **tail** 45-47 (mean 45.8, 3 male *amicorum*), 42-47 (mean 45.2, 10 male *manoensis*), 37-45 (male *pintoi*), 40-44 (juv/imm male *pintoi*), 38-42 (mean 40, 10 female *manoensis*), 35-42 (female *pintoi*); **bill** 23-27 (mean 24.3, 10 male *manoensis*), 19-27 (male *pintoi*), 21-25 (juv/imm male *pintoi*), 20-24 (mean 22.1, 10 female *manoensis*), 19-23 (female *pintoi*), 17-22 (juv/imm female

pintoi); **tarsus** 16-18 (mean 16.9, 10 male *manoensis*), 14-19 (male *pintoi*), 14-19 (juv/imm male *pintoi*), 16-17 (mean 16.5, 10 female *manoensis*), 14-20 (female *pintoi*), 15-19.5 (juv/imm female *pintoi*); **mass** 8.1-12.8 (mean 10.0, SD 0.86, 50 male *manoensis*), 8.5-11.0 (male *pintoi*), 6-11.2 (mean 9.0, SD 0.91, 49 female *manoensis*), 6.5-10.9 (female *pintoi*), 8.4-10.6 (juv/imm male *pintoi*), 6.8-10.0 (juv/imm female *pintoi*).

REFERENCES Ade (1984), Fry *et al.* (2000), Hanmer (1997), Haugaard (1995), Lane (1992), Macdonald (1958), Manson (1986), V. Salewski (*in litt.*), Tree (1990, 1997d), Vincent (1949).

103 SOUTHERN DOUBLE-COLLARED SUNBIRD
Cinnyris chalybeus   Plate 31

Certhia chalybea Linnaeus, 1766, *Syst. Nat.*, ed. 12, 1, p.186, Cape of Good Hope, South Africa.

Alternative names: Lesser Double-collared Sunbird, Smaller Double-collared Sunbird, Grey-bellied Double-collared Sunbird, Red-collared Sunbird

IDENTIFICATION Small sunbird with narrow red breast-band on males, but this often indistinct in the field. Female nondescript greyish-brown above, paler below.

Similar species Narrowness (8-10 mm) of breast-band of male *chalybeus* distinguishes it from the larger Greater Double-collared Sunbird *Cinnyris afer* (109), which has much broader (18-23 mm) band and longer, less curved, stouter bill. Male Shelley's Sunbird *C. shelleyi* (117) has black not grey belly and green rump. Male Neergaard's Sunbird *C. neergaardi* (104) has black belly and blue rump. Female *chalybeus* is smaller than female Orange-breasted Sunbird *Anthobaphes violacea* (72) and is grey not yellow underneath.

VOICE Call *Cher-cher. Swik-swik. Chee-chee. Zzik, zzik* or *zz zz zz zhik.* A plaintive *tseet* or *tseet-tseet.* **Song** Begins and ends with a series of 6-12 nasal harsh hissing *ptzzer* or *sswit-sswit* or *sssweee* notes or series of *siz, siz, siz* and consists of a melodic warble of rising and falling notes varying on *tsee,* with a sequence of characteristic rising *weeto-weeto-weet* interspersed, which may be fuller, e.g. *weeta witta witta-weeta, witta witta, witta witta wit,* or consist of other variants, but also rises and falls. Males may sing to each other from prominent perches such as dead twigs for 15 minutes or more, sometimes flashing their pectoral tufts. May sing in flight when also performs wing-clapping display. Both sexes have a subsong.

DISTRIBUTION South Africa, Swaziland, Lesotho and extreme south of Namibia.

HABITAT Fynbos, scrub, gardens, *Eucalyptus* plantations, coastal evergreen montane forests and inland forests, forest edge, woodland, riverine woodland, *Protea* areas of highlands, dune thickets, dry bush.

STATUS Common. Occurs at densities of one bird per ha in closed woodland dominated by *Brabejum stellatifolium* and *Cunonia capensis.*

MOVEMENTS Local dispersals in search of food occur,

with ringing recoveries up to 34 km from site of marking. Post-breeding dispersals may be regular with birds arriving in areas such as near Rondevlei, December, and dispersing from there presumably to breed elsewhere, April. Birds leave arid western regions in July–December, and move into south-eastern Cape Province, May–November. Bird suddenly appear, Knysna, when aloes begin to bloom, June.

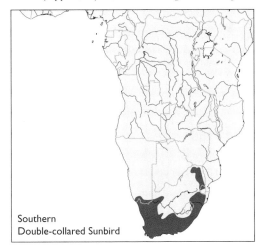

Southern
Double-collared Sunbird

FOOD Nectar, insects including ants, larvae, small beetles, Diptera including Culicidae; spiders. Also takes grass seeds and probes fruits of *Ficus* sp. Prefers sucrose, glucose and fructose, which it digests with 100% efficiency, to xylose, which it excretes. After feeding on flowers of *Satyrium odorum*, wipes clinging pollinia off bill. Robs nectar from *Strelitzia* sp. by piercing base of flowers and probing with its long tongue. Attracted to sweet liquid exudate from exit-holes of fig-wasp *Elisabethiella baijnathi* in figs of *Ficus burtt-daveyi*. Feeds directly from *Canna indica* flowers using the spathe as a perch, but also nectar-robs them by piercing holes just above the outer whorl of the perianth and through the base of an inner segment, and may re-use old holes. Has remarkable association with the milkweed *Microloma sagittatum*, collecting pollinia on tongue which attach to it by tongue slotting into specialised groove, and passing them on to pollinate other flowers (Pauw 1998), but whether this is a chance association or of regular occurrence is unknown. Ball of rubber latex in a bird's stomach presumably represented a mis-feed from probing petals during feeds for nectar on *Manihot glaziovii*. Drinks from bird baths.

Known food-plants *Albuca canadensis*, *Aloe* spp. including *A. humilis* and *A. swynnertonii*, *Babiana* sp., *Bauhinia* sp., *Cadaba* sp., *Canna indica*, *Carissa* sp., *Cissus juttae*, *Cotyledon orbiculata*, *Cunonia capensis*, *Erica* spp. including *E. gilva*, *Erythrina tomentosa*, *Eucalyptus* spp., *Ficus* spp. including *F. burtt-daveyi* (fruits probed for exudates), *Gardenia tigrina* (nectar-robbed), *Gladiolus* sp., *Grevillea banksii*, *Halleria lucida*, *Justicia guttata*, *Kniphofia rhodesiana*, *Lachenalia pendula*, *Lantana* sp., *Leonotis leonurus*, *L. oxymifolia*, *Leucospermum* sp. including *L. conocarpum*, *Lobostemon fructicosum*, unidentified mistletoes Loranthaceae, *Lycium* sp., *Manihot glaziovii*, *Melia azedarach*, *Microloma sagittatum*, *Musa* sp., *Nicotiniana* sp., *Pelargonium inquinans*, *Phygelius capensis*, *Protea caffra*, *P. lacticolor*, *Prunus* sp., *Salvia africana-lutea*, *S. aurea*, *Satyrium odorum*, *Schotia brachypetala*, *Strelitzia* sp., *Tecoma capensis*, *Virgilia* sp.

HABITS Very energetic, active, restless and noisy bird. Tame but aggressive towards conspecifics; males attack and cling to each other by their feet in mid-air, tumbling to the ground as they do so. Subservient to *Cinnyris afer*, Dusky Sunbird *C. fuscus* (135) and Amethyst Sunbird *Chalcomitra amethystina* (84). Joins mixed-species feeding groups e.g. with Collared Sunbird *Hedydipna collaris* (63) or Mouse-coloured Sunbirds *Cyanomitra veroxii* (80). In the Cape of Good Hope Peninsula forms large parties with *Anthobaphes violacea* during non-breeding season. Flight rapid and erratic, sometimes accompanied by wing sounds, *frrrt-frrrt*. Hovers in front of flowers to feed. Sometimes hawks for insects. Will bathe by flying through sprays of garden hoses. Adult taken by Brown-hooded Kingfisher *Halcyon albiventris*. Longevity up to 8 years 2 months.

BREEDING Territorial, with nest-site fidelity. Male often pecks cloaca of female, actions sometimes but not invariably followed by copulation, suggesting likelihood of extra-pair copulatory activity. One peck may be made, two quick pecks or a series of excited ones. Male will peck female flushed from eggs. One male pecked vent of juvenile he was feeding. Only female builds nest, but is often accompanied on forays by male, taking 7-30 days for completion. May be double-brooded and use same nest more than once. Several females may roost in nest when it is completed. Eggs laid on successive days, earliest-laid hatching first. Only female incubates for 13-16 days. Nestlings fed by both parents during 15-19 days in nest. Both parents remove faecal sacs. Ten-day-old young seen to pass faecal sacs to parents for removal. Fledglings return to nest to roost for at least first 3 nights, once for 9 nights. Parents feed fledglings for up to 27 days after leaving nest. Predators of eggs include Striped Mouse *Rhabdomys pumilio*. Nests destroyed by Grey-headed Bush-shrike *Malaconotus poliocephalus* and Pied Starlings *Spreo bicolor*. Parasitised by Klaas's Cuckoo *Chrysococcyx klaas*. **Nest** May be very low, <0.2 m above ground, but usually c.1.5 m high in Ericaceae. Also known to nest in *Acacia cyclops*, *Elytropappus* sp., *Helichrysum* sp., *Melianthus* sp., *Metalasia* sp., *Olea* sp., *Sideroxylon* sp. Also nest in gardens, 6 m up at top of willow tree and 8 m in *Podocarpus falcatus*. A nest, probably of this species, made of discarded tissues and silvery chocolate wrapping in a lay-by, another included bits of plastic and hen's egg shell. Other unusual nests include from electric flex and modifications of nests of tent caterpillar *Eurodope* sp. and Karoo Prinia *Prinia maculosa*. Nest is pear-shaped or oval, compact with entrance at side near top, sometimes with porch of grass-stems. Made of dry grass, fibres, lichen, kapok, wool, feathers, *Usnea barbata* (in highland forest areas), twigs and rootlets held together with cobwebs. Outside also covered with cobwebs, sometimes giving grey appearance. One nest made of winged seeds of *Galium tomentosum*, also used for decorating outside of nest. Decorations may also include spider cocoons, string, plastic strips and bits of newspaper. Lined with feathers including those of poultry, hairs, woolly plant-down and kapok or, in highland areas, bark and seed-heads in *Usnea*-based nest; latter also had short beard of *Usnea*, but beards usually lacking in nests of this species. Height 100-130 mm, width 60-90 mm, depth including porch 90-120 mm, diameter of entrance 25-30 mm. **Eggs** c/1-3, *chalybeus*: 15.6-18 (mean 16.6, n=6) x 11-12.3 (mean 11.6), cream, grey, greyish-white or greenish-white almost obscured by mottling, lines and spots of brown, grey, sepia or black; *subalaris*: 14.6-18.5 (mean 16.6, n=36) x 10.9-13.2 (mean 11.7). **Laying months** South Africa: April–December. Sometimes lay two consecutive broods in same nest. *C. c. subalaris:* c/3, November.

DESCRIPTION *C. c. chalybeus*
Adult male Head, throat, upper breast, neck, mantle, back and rump metallic green, bases of feathers brown. Uppertail-coverts iridescent bright blue. Rectrices black with slight blue sheen. T5-T6 paler, T6 with narrow brownish-white outer margin. Remiges, primary and greater wing-coverts dark brown, lesser wing-coverts metallic green. A narrow band (2 mm deep) of iridescent bluish-violet below edge of green on upper breast. Below this a scarlet breast-band about 8-10 mm deep. Pectoral tufts yellow. Belly smoky-grey, merging into olive-grey on lower belly, flanks and undertail-coverts. Underwing-coverts pale brown. Buccal cavity yellow, black, mauve or brownish-black with a white centre patch. Iris dark brown. Bill and feet black. **Non-breeding plumage** Eclipse plumage resembling adult female dress assumed after breeding but wings and tail as breeding plumage, metallic feathers usually retained on mantle, back and uppertail-coverts, with a few left on chin throat and head, and a scattering of red feathers on lower breast. **Adult female** Crown and nape greyish-olive. Mantle, back, rump, median and lesser wing-coverts and uppertail-coverts yellowish-olive or distinctly greenish, with some grey feathering. Tail black. Remiges, primary and greater wing-coverts dark brown. Pale yellow patch on bend of wing. Throat and breast olive-grey, merging to more greyish-olive on belly. Axillaries and underwing-coverts pale greyish-yellow. Buccal cavity orange, becoming pink when about to lay. Iris dark brown. Bill and feet black. **Juvenile** Nestling dark pink. Bill dark horn with dark tip. Gape white. Juvenile as adult female, buccal cavity orange, becoming yellow with pink centre patch in male during post-juvenile moult. Immature male similar to adult male but olivaceous feathers admixed with metallic plumage on head, mantle, sides of face, chin, throat and sides of chest.

GEOGRAPHICAL VARIATION
  C. c. chalybeus (Linnaeus, 1766) (includes *albilateralis*) (South Africa: Little Namaqualand, Namibia and south-west Cape Province to east of Knysna) Described above.
  C. c. subalaris Reichenow, 1899 (includes *capricornensis*) (South Africa: Pondoland to KwaZulu-Natal and Transvaal) Males with darker grey abdomen, more olive tinged grey, than *chalybeus*. Bill slightly longer (24-26) than *chalybeus* (21-23). Female darker and greener above, greener below.

MEASUREMENTS Wing 55-59 (mean 56.6, 10 male *chalybeus*), 57.5 (male *subalaris*), 49-54 (mean 51.7, 12 female *chalybeus*); tail 43-47 (mean 45, 10 male *chalybeus*), 43 (male *subalaris*), 35-39 (mean 37.1, 10 female *chalybeus*); bill 21-23 (mean 21.9, 10 male *chalybeus*), 24-26 (mean 24.8, 8 male *subalaris*), 18-20 (mean 19.3, 10 female *chalybeus*); tarsus 16-18 (mean 16.8, 10 male *chalybeus*), 16-18 (mean 16.8, 10 female *chalybeus*); mass 6.0-9.5 (mean 8.5, 51 male *chalybeus*), 6.0-9.5 (mean 7.2, 37 female *chalybeus*), 6.0-10.0 (mean 8.0, SD 0.69, 72 male *subalaris*), 6.0-9.5 (mean 7.32, SD 0.68, 55 female *subalaris*).

REFERENCES Berrington (1997), Chenaux-Repond (1975), Clancey & Irwin (1978), Compton *et al.* (1996), Follet (1990), Fraser (1989, 1997c), Fraser *et al.* (1989), Fry *et al.* (2000), Leon & Nicolson (1997), Lotz & Nicolson (1996), Martin (1983), Martin *et al.* (1991), McCardle

(1989), Oatley (1995b, 1997), Pauw (1998), Rebelo (1987a), Schmidt (1964, 1991), Skead (1967), Swynnerton (1916), Uys (1981a), Vincent (1949), von Korff (1997).

---

104 NEERGAARD'S SUNBIRD
Cinnyris neergaardi   Plate 34

Cinnyris neergaardi Ogilvie-Grant, 1908, *Bull. Br. Orn. Club* 21, p.93, Coguno, Inhambane District, Portuguese East Africa [= Mozambique].

Alternative names: Coguno Double-collared Sunbird, Neergard's (*sic*) Sunbird

IDENTIFICATION A small, short-billed sunbird. Male has iridescent green head, back and throat, red breast-band, black belly and blue rump. Female greyish-brown above, paler and unstreaked below.
Similar species Male Greater Double-collared Sunbird *C. afer* (109) and Southern Double-collared Sunbird *C. chalybeus* (103) are similarly coloured, but bellies are grey not black and bills are longer. Shelley's Sunbird *C. shelleyi* (117) is very similar but allopatric, with a green, not blue rump. Can be confused with Purple-banded Sunbird *C. bifasciatus* (121) but male has yellow pectoral tufts and red breast-band and female has paler unstreaked underparts.

VOICE Noisy. Male sings from tops of woodland canopy. **Call** A thin *weesi-weesi-weesi*. **Song** A *tswui-tsu* followed by rapid burst of *ti-ti-ti-ti...*, for 1-3 seconds, the whole sequence repeated over and over again in succession of vocalisations, sometimes omitting the initial flourish.

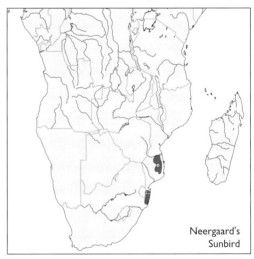

Neergaard's
Sunbird

DISTRIBUTION South-east Africa. Mozambique, South Africa. Restricted to the coastal belt from just south of Richard's Bay, KwaZulu-Natal, in South Africa, north to Panda and Inhambane in Mozambique. In Mozambique occurs in two widely separated populations, one restricted to coastal sand forests south of Maputo and the other in tall mixed woodland north of the Limpopo River.

HABITAT Coastal scrubland, especially with dense dry sandy thorn-bush and dry woodland. Isolated trees in clearings and villages.

STATUS Listed as near-threatened by Collar *et al.* (1994). Not uncommon at Makane's Point, River Pongola, bordering Mosi swamp near the South Africa/Mozambique border (Clancey 1952), Mkuzi, False Bay, Ndumu and Tembe. May be threatened by deforestation in Mozambique.

MOVEMENTS Apparently wanders in non-breeding season, perhaps along north–south route, as may be only present in southern Mozambique in southern summer.

FOOD Nectar, small insects and spiders.
Known food-plants *Aloe* spp., *Schotia capitata*, *Syzygium cordatum*.

HABITS Forages in canopy of trees, sometimes with Amethyst Sunbird *C. amethystina*.

BREEDING Female, accompanied by male, collects nest-lining material. **Nest** Well concealed but chunky, hidden in thick clump of *Usnea*, suspended 5-6 m up in thorn-tree e.g. *Acacia burkeii* and made of cream-coloured fibrous material, feathers and down, and camouflaged with insect larvae and other debris. Lined with white fibres from seed-pods of the creeper *Strophanthus luteolus*. **Eggs** c/2; reported by Priest (1948) as 16.1-16.8 (mean 16.6, n=4) x 11.0-11.6 (mean 11.2) and coloured slaty-blue, spotted with dark grey, but there is doubt about the accuracy of these records (Chittenden 1995). **Laying months** Mozambique: Floresta Licuati, September–January; South Africa: recently finished nest but without eggs, Mkuzi, November; eggs October and November, Kosi Bay, KwaZulu-Natal, but records doubtful (see above), July.

DESCRIPTION
Adult male Head, neck, mantle, back, median and lesser wing-coverts and throat iridescent bright green, basal two-thirds of feathers brown. Uppertail-coverts bright blue. Tail very dark brownish-black. Remiges, primary and greater wing-coverts and alula black. Thin band below green gorget of iridescent blue. Breast scarlet with some blue speckling. Belly and undertail-coverts matt black. Pectoral tufts yellow. Axillaries black. Underwing-coverts brown. Iris dark brown. Bill and feet black.
Adult female Greyish-brown above, more olive on rump. Tail very dark brown, outer rectrices paler, especially on outerweb. Narrow buffish-white supercilium. Sides of head dark grey-brown. Underparts pale greyish-brown with faint yellow wash on lower breast and belly. Wing dark greyish-brown, primaries edged greyish-white, broader pale grey-brown margins to secondaries, tertials and greater wing-coverts. Lesser and median wing-coverts greyish-brown. Underwing-coverts and axillaries off-white. Iris dark brown. Bill and feet black.
Juvenile resembles adult female.

GEOGRAPHICAL VARIATION None described.

MEASUREMENTS **Wing** 52-57 (mean 54.2, 11 males), 49-51 (mean 49.6, 4 females); tail 35-38 (mean 36.6, 11 males), 30-33 (mean 31, 4 females); **bill** 17-17.5 (mean 17.4, 11 males), 15-16 (mean 15.6, 4 females); **tarsus** 15-17 (mean 16.4, 11 males), 14-15 (mean 14.7, 4 females); **mass** 6.2-7.1 (mean 6.5, 7 males), 5.6-5.9 (mean 5.7, 3 females).

REFERENCES Anon. (1980), Chittenden (1995), Clancey (1952, 1971), Fry *et al.* (2000), Johnson (1997).

105 STUHLMANN'S DOUBLE-COLLARED SUNBIRD
Cinnyris stuhlmanni   Plate 32

Cinnyris stuhlmanni Reichenow, 1893, *Orn. Monatsb.* 1, p.61, Central Africa: type from upper western slope of Ruwenzori and not Nsangani in Ukondju, Semliki valley (Chapin, 1954, *Bull. Amer. Mus. Nat. Hist.* 75B, p.252).

Alternative names: Ruwenzori (or Rwenzori) Double-collared Sunbird, Rwanda (or Ruanda) Double-collared Sunbird (*C. s. graueri* only)

Taxonomic note Treated by some authors as subspecies of *Cinnyris afer*.

IDENTIFICATION A large upland sunbird. Male with very conspicuous broad red breast-band and no bronzy tinge to emerald-green iridescence. Abdomen olivaceous. Female dull olivaceous above with yellow wash on belly and vent.
Similar species Male Prigogine's Double-collared Sunbird *Cinnyris prigoginei* (106) has much narrower breast-band, shorter, less decurved, bill and is more violet on upper breast-band and uppertail-coverts. Female *prigoginei* has less yellow on vent. Greater Double-collared Sunbird *C. afer* (109) has longer, more decurved bill and is bronzier-green above, paler below. Male Montane Double-collared Sunbird *C. ludovicensis* (107) is shorter-billed, female greyer. Northern Double-collared Sunbird *C. reichenowi* (108) is smaller, shorter-billed and paler below.

VOICE **Call** A harsh *tsp* note similar to that of Red-tufted Sunbird *Nectarinia johnstoni* (98), and *chee-chee*. A long *tseeeep*. **Song** Race *graueri*: a pleasant warble, rising in pitch towards end, then dropping, *chee-oo, che che, chee-oo, che che, se, se, se, se, se, se, se, che chit, che chit, che chit*; race *schubotzi*: a short (2.5-3 seconds) jumble of notes interspersed with *jit* or *jeep*; race *stuhlmanni*: a short bright song.

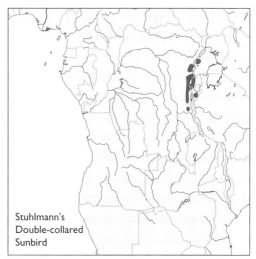

Stuhlmann's
Double-collared
Sunbird

DISTRIBUTION Democratic Republic of the Congo, Rwanda, Burundi and Uganda (Ruwenzori mountains at 2,000-4,000 m and Virunga volcanoes).

HABITAT Occurs in montane areas of the Virunga

volcanoes in Uganda, 2,270-3,600 m, in montane forest and the bamboo zone, but principally in *Hypericum* scrub at 2,700 m and higher, above the bamboo zone. In the Kivu highlands occurs amongst *Hagenia* sp., *Hypericum* spp. and *Erica* spp. In the Ruwenzoris confined to the upper bamboo zone at 2,100-3,700 m, and above the bamboo amongst giant heathers *Erica* spp., *Hagenia* trees and shrubs. In mountains west of Lake Kivu and the Nyungwe forest, Rwanda, frequents forest edges and clearings above 2,000 m.

STATUS Abundant in Burundi near the Rwanda border in the Ruhwa, Lua and Kabulantwa valleys. Common in the Kivu mountains between 2,750 and 3,500 m, where recorded as high as 3,780 m although rare below 2,400 m; uncommon in Ruwenzoris in Democratic Republic of the Congo. Abundant on Mount Muhavira in Virunga mountains, Uganda, above 2,750 m.

MOVEMENTS Unknown.

FOOD Nectar and insects including small beetles and small caterpillars; spiders.
Known food-plants *Balthasaria schliebenii*, *Crotalaria agatiflora*, *Hypericum revolutum*, *Kniphofia princiae*, *Lobelia gibberoa*, *L. mildbraedii*, *Symphonia globulifera*, unidentified tall shrubs with spikes of whitish flowers and unidentified creepers.

HABITS Shy. Occurs singly or in pairs, probing flowers and nectar-robbing them, but may occur in abundance with 30 seen in a single *Hypericum* tree. Subservient to Blue-headed Sunbird *Cyanomitra alinae* (77) and Purple-breasted Sunbird *Nectarinia purpureiventris* (94), but feeds amicably with *N. johnstoni*. Occasionally feeds on flowers near ground. Forages tit-like amongst leafy branches of trees.

BREEDING Territorial. Male displays in front of female, hopping around with quivering wings drooped like begging juvenile and simultaneously warbling, with the pectoral tufts raised and spread out, fan-like, at right angles to the body. When ignored by female, male flies straight up as if flycatching and returns to perch. Only female builds nest and incubates. **Nest** *graueri*: oval and small, usually well concealed, 2-5 m up in *Hypericum* sp. tree, on ends of thickly leaved drooping branches or bamboos near ravines or open patches of forest; one made mostly of *Usnea* sp. with some moss, entrance-surround and lining of fine brown fibres; lined also with white pappus and feathers; others made of flower stalks of *Thalictrum* sp., *Usnea* sp., strips of bamboo leaves, moss and pappus held together with cobwebs, lined with pappus and doves' feathers; side-top entrance with small projecting porch of *Thalictrum* sp. and moss sometimes projecting up and out in tatty spire, also beard 150-200 mm long. 133 x 89 x 127 mm. Attachment twig entwined with lichen and cobweb for 50 mm. Race *stuhlmanni*: an oval ball of moss with entrance hole in side, unlined. Well concealed in thick moss, pendant 1-6 m up from the ends of branches of tree-heaths. **Eggs** c/1; *graueri*: white, unglossed, mostly obscured by ash-grey freckles and clouds, with dark ring at larger pole, sometimes with pale brown streaks; 20.0-20.5 x 12.0-12.9; *stuhlmanni*: dark olive, freckled with a darker shade of olive, giving uniform appearance; 19.0 x 13.0. **Laying months** Democratic Republic of the Congo: June, September, December, nest-building March (*graueri*); East Africa: January, September, December; Uganda: September (*graueri*), December (*stuhlmanni*).

DESCRIPTION *C. s. stuhlmanni*
Adult male Uppertail-coverts metallic violet-blue. Rest of upperparts, scapulars, lesser and median wing-coverts and head to upper breast metallic emerald-green. Narrow (3 mm) metallic violet band on upper breast above broad (16-22 mm) scarlet band, mottled brown. Rest of underparts dark olive. Pectoral tufts yellow. Tail very dark brown and slightly glossed, graduated, with central rectrices up to 13 mm beyond outer feather. Remiges dark brown, edged olivaceous-brown. Underwing-coverts and axillaries grey. Iris dark brown. Bill and feet black. **Non-breeding plumage** Like adult female but wings darker and metallic wing-coverts retained.
Adult female Upperparts dark olive-green, lores and ear-coverts darker and greyer. Tail dark brown. Underparts greyish-olive, faintly barred darker. Pale in mid-belly with slight yellow tinge. Wing dark brown, edged paler with brighter yellow tinge on margins of primaries. Lesser and median coverts dark olive-green. Underwing-coverts and axillaries white with yellow wash.
Juvenile Undescribed.

GEOGRAPHICAL VARIATION
   C. s. chapini Prigogine, 1952 (mountains from west of Lake Edward to north-west of Lake Tanganyika and Mt Kabobo, 2,200-3,200 m) As nominate but smaller, bill shorter (22-25), breast-band darker, belly dark grey. Resembles *graueri* but bill longer.
   C. s. graueri Neumann, 1908 (Kivu volcanoes and Rwanda above 1,800 m; Virunga volcanoes, 2,270-3,600 m, where collected on Mts Muhavura, Mgahinga and Sabinio, south-western Kigezi, Uganda) Like *stuhlmanni* but smaller and shorter-billed (17.5-21.5), male with breast-band brick-red, uppertail-coverts more violet-blue. Abdomen buff-grey, less olivaceous. Juvenile undescribed, but immature male retains juvenile feathers on upperparts and breast, suggesting moult from juvenile to first adult breeding plumage. Latter resembles full adult but breast-band less extensive and duller, with metallic green margins on upperparts narrower and lack of red on undertail-coverts. Evidence suggests moult from breeding dress to breeding dress with no eclipse plumage in this subspecies.
   C. s. schubotzi Reichenow, 1908 (Burundi and Nyungwe forest, Rwanda, and mountains north-east of Bujumbura, Burundi) Close to *chapini* but female with throat and upper breast much the darkest grey of all subspecies.
   C. s. stuhlmanni Reichenow, 1893 (Ruwenzori mountains) Described above.

MEASUREMENTS Wing 65.5-70 (8 male *chapini*), 63.5-67.5 (mean 65.5, 12 male *graueri*), 64-69 (mean 67.2, 10 male *stuhlmanni*), 60-61 (2 female *chapini*), 58-61 (5 female *graueri*), 58-61 (mean 59.7, 3 female *stuhlmanni*); **tail** 56-63 (8 male *chapini*), 55-59 (15 male *graueri*), 53.5-58.5 (mean 55.7, 10 male *stuhlmanni*), 45-50.5 (2 female *chapini*), 45-47 (5 female *graueri*), 43-47 (mean 45, 3 female *stuhlmanni*); **bill** 20.5-24.5 (mean 23.6, 22 male *chapini*), 16.5-21.5 (mean 20.3, 12 male *graueri*), 23-28 (mean 26.9, 10 male *stuhlmanni*), 20-23.5 (mean 22.8, 3 female *chapini*), 16.0-20.5 (mean 19.1, 10 female *graueri*), 22.5-23.5 (mean 23, 3 female *stuhlmanni*); **tarsus** 19-20 (mean 19.3, 6 male *stuhlmanni*), 19 (female *stuhlmanni*); **mass** 6-8 (mean 7, 6 male *graueri*), 10-11.5 (mean 10.9, 7 male *stuhlmanni*), 5-7 (mean 6, 7 female *graueri*), 9-10.5 (mean 10.0, 3 female *stuhlmanni*).

REFERENCES Chapin (1954), Clancey & Irwin (1978), Dowsett-Lemaire (1990), Gyldenstolpe (1924), Fry *et al.* (2000), Mackworth-Praed & Grant (1945), Prigogine (1952, 1979), Williams (1952).

---

106 PRIGOGINE'S DOUBLE-COLLARED SUNBIRD
Cinnyris prigoginei **Plate 32**

Cinnyris afer prigoginei Macdonald, 1958, *Bull. Br. Orn. Club* 78, p.9, Sambwe, 6,100 ft., Marungu Highlands, Congo.

Alternative name: Marungu Sunbird

Taxonomic note This sunbird has been treated (1) as a subspecies of *Cinnyris afer*, (2) as a subspecies of *C. ludovicensis*, and (3) as a hybrid swarm from crosses between *C. mediocris* and *C. stuhlmanni*. Specimens pre-dating Macdonald's description were ascribed to *C. chalybeus manoensis*.

IDENTIFICATION The only small double-collared sunbird inhabiting the Marungu Highlands in the Democratic Republic of the Congo. Male has narrow red breast-band. **Similar species** Greater Double-collared Sunbird *Cinnyris afer* (109), Montane Double-collared Sunbird *C. ludovicensis* (107), Eastern Double-collared Sunbird *C. mediocris* (112), and Stuhlmann's Double-collared Sunbird *C. stuhlmanni* (105). Male shares characters with *C. mediocris* (short tail, low tail/wing ratio [75.6], small chest-band [10 mm]) and *C. stuhlmanni chapini* (wing length 62.5, colour of breast-band purplish, colour of chest-band dark red, colour of uppertail-coverts blue purplish). Also similar to *C. s. graueri* but male has more olive belly, narrower red breast-band; bill 19-22.5; uppertail-coverts violet with green not bluish edges. *C. prigoginei* is larger (longer wing and tail) and heavier than *C. mediocris*, and has smaller red breast-band and narrower strip of blue above it.

VOICE Similar to those of *C. afer* and *C. ludovicensis*.

DISTRIBUTION East-central Africa. Restricted to a few areas of riparian forest in the Marungu highlands in the south-east of the Democratic Republic of the Congo. Only recorded from Kasiki, the Lufoko River, Matafali, Pande and Sambwe.

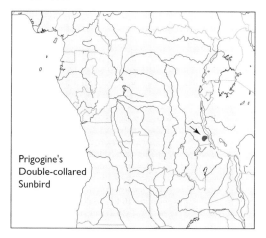

Prigogine's
Double-collared
Sunbird

HABITAT Riparian forest, with *Syzygium cordatum*, *Ficalhoa laurifolia* and *Ilex mitis*, along streams in montane areas up to at least 1,900 m, and cornfields and thickets close to streams.

STATUS Said to be common along the edge of the Lufoko River, but threatened by deforestation and streambank erosion by cattle in its restricted habitat (Collar & Stuart 1985).

MOVEMENTS Unknown.

FOOD Nectar (presumably).
Known food-plants None.

HABITS Unknown.

BREEDING Enlarged testes, February, and enlarged ovaries, April.

DESCRIPTION
Adult male Iridescent colours of head and mantle bluish-green (as in *C. stuhlmanni graueri*, not yellowish-green as in *C. l. whytei* and races of *C. chalybeus*) with a very slight golden sheen. Rump blue. Flight feathers and wing-coverts black (or palish dark brown when worn), outer edges of primaries paler. Uppertail black with bluish sheen and white tips. Iridescent colours of uppertail-coverts purplish-blue, almost violet basally (not bluish or green-bluish as in *mediocris*), with green edges. Iridescent colours of narrow breast-band purplish-blue (as in *C. stuhlmanni graueri*, not bluish as in races of *chalybeus* and *C. mediocris*, and not broad as in *afer*) and bluer than uppertail-coverts. Red chest-band dark red (not light red as in *mediocris*), and very narrow, 10 mm deep, even narrower at centre. Pectoral tufts bright yellow. Underwing-coverts pale. Outer fringes of innerwebs of underside of primaries white. Belly yellowish-olive, washed brownish-grey proximally, but not as rich or olive as *C. mediocris fuelleborni* or *C. m. bensoni*, giving light greyish-brown tone to lower belly. Undertail-coverts also light greyish-brown. Undersides of tail feathers dark brown centrally with off-white edges. Bill black, stouter and more curved than in *C. stuhlmanni*. Iris dark brown. Feet black. **Non-breeding plumage** Birds in worn plumage have non-metallic olive mixed with metallic green on crown, sides of head and back and lack olive on lower abdomen, which is thus greyish resembling *C. stuhlmanni*. Primaries and wing-coverts brown not black.
Adult female General colour of all upperparts from forehead to rump uniformly olive not grey. Uppertail black, outer tail feathers edged white. Flight feathers dark brown or black. Outer edges of primaries edged olive-green, secondaries with more yellow-green edges. Chin and throat dark olive with black streaking. Upper breast dark olive. Lower breast and belly pale olive with flanks and vent yellowish-olive. Undertail black with broad white outer edges. Bill black, pale at base. Legs and feet black.
Juvenile Unknown.

GEOGRAPHICAL VARIATION None described.

MEASUREMENTS Wing 60-65 (mean 62.8, SD 1.63, 16 males), 60-61 (mean 60.3, SD 0.5, 4 females); **tail** 44-54 (mean 47.8, SD 1.33, 16 males), 39-43.5 (mean 42.8, SD 2.01, 4 females); **bill** 19.5-23 (mean 22.05, SD 0.48, 16 males), 19-22 (mean 20.3, SD 1.53, 3 females); **tarsus** 15-20 (mean 17.8, SD 2.04, 6 males), 16, 18 (females); **mass** 9.7-10.9 (mean 10.3, SD 0.59, 4 males), 8.0 (female).

REFERENCES Benson & Prigogine (1981), Chapin

(1954), Clancey & Irwin (1978), Collar & Stuart (1985), Dowsett & Dowsett-Lemaire (1993), Dowsett & Prigogine (1974), Macdonald (1958), Prigogine (1979), Schouteden (1949).

107 MONTANE DOUBLE-COLLARED SUNBIRD
Cinnyris ludovicensis   Plate 32

Nectarinea [*sic*] *ludovicensis* Barbosa du Bocage, 1870, *Journ. Sci. Math. Phys. Nat. Lisboa* 2 (1868), p.41, Biballa, Mossamedes, Angola (see Bocage, 1881, *Orn. D'Angola*, p.169).

Alternative names: Ludwig's Double-collared Sunbird, Bocage's Montane Double-collared Sunbird

Taxonomic note Treated by some authors as subspecies of *Cinnyris afer*.

IDENTIFICATION A short-billed double-collared sunbird, with broad red breast-band and greyish-olive underparts in males.
Similar species Like nominate Greater Double-collared Sunbird *Cinnyris afer* (109) but bill shorter (19-22, instead of 30-32), uppertail-coverts metallic blue with only a hint of violet (those of *afer* are distinctly violet), underparts deep olive not light olive as in *afer*, median coverts metallic green not dark brown, and remiges narrowly edged olive-brown not pale buff. Belly more olive. Broad breast-band and blue uppertail-coverts separate male from male Miombo Double-collared Sunbird *C. manoensis* (102) and only sympatric subspecies of Eastern Double-collared Sunbird *C. mediocris fuelleborni* (112). Females separable from female *manoensis* and *mediocris* by non-contrasting, greyer upperparts and chin to lower breast, black lores, grey supercilium and only faint wash of yellow on belly. Females greyer on throat and chest than *C. afer*.

VOICE Call A sharp *tsic*; alarm call a fast series of *tchep tschep tchep tchep*, with gaps between notes shorter than in *C. mediocris*. **Song** Race *whytei*: a bustling jumble of high notes, consisting of *ti, ti, titi pitsy-pitsy, chu-chu-chu pitsy-pitsy, titititipitsy, pichew, chichichichi*... Also a shorter version, lasting 2-2.5 seconds, uttered during breeding season (January–August on Nyika Plateau): a sharp dry nervous strophe often preceded by one or two sharp *tsic* sounds.

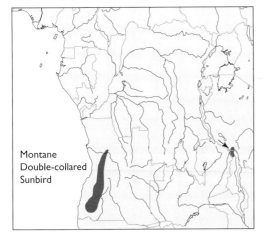

Montane
Double-collared
Sunbird

DISTRIBUTION Angola highlands from Huila to Mt Moco and Gabela. Nyika plateau of Malawi and neighbouring east Zambia above 1,820 m.

HABITAT Edges of hillside forest, Afromontane forest, gallery forest and in clearings in highlands, montane grassland and bracken-briar. Scrub and secondary growth 1.5-4 m high, forest edges and open grassland.

STATUS *C. l. ludovicensis* is a locally common resident in highlands of Angola. *C. l. whytei* is common in scrub and secondary growth 1.5-4 m tall, above 1,900 m on the Nyika plateau, but avoids forest.

MOVEMENTS Unknown. Birds on Nyika plateau remain in same area all year.

FOOD Nectar and insects.
Known food-plants *Agelanthus sansibarensis, A. subulatus, Aloe mzimbana, Bersama abyssinica englerana, Borreria dibrachiata, Canthium gueinzii, Chlorphytum engleri, Clerodendrum quadrangulatum, Crotalaria goetzei, Dendrophthoe pendens, Englerina inaequilatera, Geniosporum rotundifolium, Gladiolus natalensis, Halleria lucida, Hypericum revolutum, Impatiens gomphophylla, Kniphofia grantii, K. linearifolia, Leonotis decadonta, L. mollissima, L. aff. pole-evansii, Lobelia giberroa, Pentas schimperana, Phragmanthera usuiensis, Protea madiensis, P. petiolaris, P. welwitschii, Syzygium cordatum, Tecoma capensis*.

HABITS Solitary or in pairs. Probes and nectar-robs flowers. Subservient to *C. mediocris*, Green-headed Sunbird *Cyanomitra verticalis* (73), Bronze Sunbird *Nectarinia kilimensis* (96), Red-tufted Sunbird *N. johnstoni* (98) and Malachite Sunbird *N. famosa* (97) but dominant over Variable Sunbird *C. venustus* (134).

BREEDING *C. l. whytei* hold small territories, 0.1-0.5 ha, in *Tecoma capensis* bushes at forest edge or in *Kotschya-Erica* scrub in rocky outcrops, with males singing from prominent perches and chasing away conspecific intruders. 2-3 broods per season; nest re-used; sometimes builds in same tree in successive years; in one case, egg of second brood laid only 1-2 days after fledgling of previous brood left nest. Nest-building, incubating and brooding by female only. Incubation 14-15 days. Male occasionally feeds chicks and becomes responsible for fledglings, with one in sole charge for 19 days. *Nest* Suspended from leaf rachis, e.g. 1.8-5 m up on outside of *Hagenia abyssinica* tree, 2 m up in *Buddleja salviifolia*, suspended 1.5-2.5 m up in *Erica benguelensis*, 2.5 m up in *Rhus longipes*, 1.5 m up in thick foliage of *Anthospermum* sp. **Eggs** c/1. Race *whytei*: 16.5-18.3 x 11.5-13.2.
Laying months Angola: breeding condition October–December; Malawi: February–August; Zambia: copulation May.

DESCRIPTION *C. l. ludovicensis*
Adult male Head to scapulars and rump plus chin to upper breast metallic green with golden sheen; uppertail-coverts metallic blue tinged violet. Tail black with blue gloss above. Lores black; very thin (c.2 mm wide) violet-blue band separating green of breast from broad (17-23 mm) scarlet or orangey-red lower breast-band. Pectoral tufts yellow. Underparts deep olive. Lesser and median coverts metallic green, remainder of upperwing dark brown; remiges narrowly edged olive-brown. Underwing with coverts and axillaries pale grey, inner borders of flight feathers grey-buff. Bill black. Eyes dark brown. Legs black. No data on non-breeding plumage, but no evidence of one in the relatively well studied *whytei*.

Adult female Upperparts dark greyish-brown, darker on uppertail-coverts. Tail blackish-brown. T6 and distal T5 paler brown with greyish-white edges at tips of innerwebs. Ear-coverts and cheeks greyish-brown, thin supercilium pale buff. Lores blackish-brown; chin grey-buff; throat and upper breast brownish-grey with buff mottling. Rest of underparts brownish-grey, but centre of lower breast and belly paler and slightly olive-yellow. Upperwing dark grey-brown with olive-brown edges. Primaries narrowly edged goldish olive-brown. Underwing has coverts and axillaries greyish-white and inner borders of flight feathers greyish-white. Bill black. Eyes dark brown. Legs black.
Juvenile Unknown.

GEOGRAPHICAL VARIATION

C. l. ludovicensis (Bocage, 1870) (highlands of western Angola from eastern Namibe and western Huíla north through Huambo to Cuanza Sul and western Malanje) Described above.

C. l. whytei Benson, 1948 (montane grassland above 1,800 m in Malawi, Nyika plateau, and adjacent parts of Zambia) Male upper breast-band steelier-blue and wider (3 mm) than nominate and red breast-band darker, more scarlet, less yellowish-red, and narrower (12-16), and has some dusky bars within it. Females darker on chin and throat than nominate. Underparts duller than nominate, less yellow and more greenish. Slightly smaller than nominate but tail relatively longer.

MEASUREMENTS Wing 64-67 (mean 65.2, 9 male *ludovicensis*), 58-67 (mean 61.9, 19 male *whytei*), 56-59 (mean 57.8, 8 female *ludovicensis*), 60 (female *whytei*); **tail** 45-54 (mean 50.1, 9 male *ludovicensis*), 50-53 (mean 51.1, 10 male *whytei*), 35-43 (mean 39.8, 8 female *ludovicensis*), 50 (female *whytei*); **bill** 19-22 (mean 20.6, 9 male *ludovicensis*), 18-21.1 (mean 19.1, 19 male *whytei*), 17-20 (mean 18.3, 8 female *ludovicensis*), 17.5-19.5 (mean 18.8, SD 1.15, 3 female *whytei*); **tarsus** 17-20 (mean 18.1, 9 male *ludovicensis*), 15-19 (mean 16.4, 9 male *whytei*), 16-20 (mean 17.5, 8 female *ludovicensis*), 15.3 (female *whytei*); **mass** 9, 10 (2 male *ludovicensis*), 7 (female *ludovicensis*), 7.1-10.8 (mean 9.3, 38 male *whytei*, with up to 0.5 g variation within 3-day period: Dowsett 1983), 7.4-9.0 (mean 8.1, 14 female *whytei*).

REFERENCES Bennun (1986), Benson (1949), Dowsett (1983), Dowsett-Lemaire (1988, 1989a), Fry *et al.* (2000).

---

108 NORTHERN DOUBLE-COLLARED SUNBIRD
Cinnyris reichenowi   Plate 33

Cinnyris reichenowi Sharpe, 1891, *Ibis*, p.444, Sotik, East Africa.

Alternative names: Preuss's Double-collared Sunbird, Nandi Double-collared Sunbird

IDENTIFICATION An upland double-collared sunbird of medium size, with short bill and tail. Male has violet uppertail-coverts and narrow breast-band above broad (up to 19 mm) red lower breast-band and olivaceous-brown belly. Female has only slight trace of supercilium above eye and is dull olive below, apart from yellow wash in middle of belly.

Similar species Bigger and darker than Olive-bellied Sunbird *Cinnyris chloropygius* (100) with a more complicated call. Belly appears much darker than that of Olive-bellied. Crown appears blue in some lights. Males of *chloropygius* have a much paler belly, olive rather than brown, and green not purple uppertail-coverts. Scarlet breast-band is broader in male *reichenowi* (up to 19 mm, only 12.5 mm in *chloropygius*), which also has purple breast-band between the scarlet band and the green throat (lacking or vestigial in *chloropygius*). Stuhlmann's Double-collared Sunbird *C. stuhlmanni* (105) has paler belly in males, longer bill and longer tail. *C. reichenowi* has shorter bill and tail than Eastern Double-collared Sunbird *C. mediocris* (112), with which it is sympatric in western Kenya, and male is bluer, less golden-green above, with violet not blue uppertail-coverts and broader breast-band and darker below. Only slight trace of supercilium above eye distinguishes female from female *C. chloropygius*, which is generally darker above. Female *reichenowi* has browner-olive edges to remiges than those of female *C. chloropygius* and *C. mediocris*, which are greener-olive and contrast less with the upperparts; female *mediocris* lacks even a trace of a supercilium.

VOICE Call Race *preussi*: *Psee, pzeet; zeet-zeet. Zeee-zeee-e-zit* from perch. Race *reichenowi*: a harsh *jijijijiji*, a *chick* or *chip-chip*; alarm note: *seeeeep*. **Song** Race *preussi*: a series of *chup-chup-ch-ch-ch-ch*, for up to 20 seconds, or a 2-note *tsup-tsup* followed by series of melodic or harsh warbles, then gaps with 6-10 *psee* before the warble is repeated. Also a jumble of wheezy rapidly repeated notes. Race *reichenowi*: 2 well-spaced notes, followed by short, rapid twitter – *tsip... tsweet..susususrisrisri- tsew-tsutsu-tsu*.

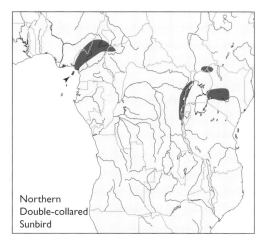

Northern
Double-collared
Sunbird

DISTRIBUTION West-central and north-eastern Africa. Nigeria (Obudu and Mambilla plateaus and Gashaka-Gumti Game Reserve), Cameroon, Central African Republic (Sarki), Equatorial Guinea (Bioko), Democratic Republic of the Congo, Rwanda, Burundi, Uganda, Kenya and Sudan.

HABITAT Montane heathland, e.g. Mt Cameroon (up to 2,780 m) and highlands of Bioko, where breeds. Usually at 1,200-2,400 m in Bwindi forest, Uganda, where some overlap in range with *C. stuhlmanni*. In East African mountains occurs in montane forest, secondary forest, forest edge, gallery forests, plantations of *Eucalyptus* sp. and *Acacia mearnsii*, clearings and gardens.

STATUS Common. Abundant in Nigeria on the Obudu and Mambilla plateaus. Common in mountains of southern Sudan above 1,800 m and in mountains of Democratic Republic of the Congo at 1,500-2,000 m. Abundant in Burundi along the mountains of the Zaire-Nil crater from the Rwanda border, south to the Tanzanian border between 1,300 and 2,400 m.

MOVEMENTS Altitudinal migrant. Moves up and down mountains in Cameroon, appearing lower than the breeding range in the wet season, July–September, when becomes the commonest sunbird at Kumba (300 m). Moves up and down mountains in East Africa, where present Mt Elgon, Kenya, December, but absent July. One of the few forest species to migrate.

FOOD Insects including larvae, spiders, nectar.
Known food-plants *Alangium* sp., *Albizia* sp., *Aloe* sp., *Brillantaisia* sp., *Convolvulus*, *Englerina woodfordiodes*, *Erythrina* sp., *Impatiens niamniamensis*, *Lobelia columnaris*, *Mitragyna* sp., *Oxyanthus troupinii*, *Pavetta* sp., *Physalis peruviana*, *Pseudosabicea* sp., *Psychotria* sp., *Salvia* sp., *Symphonia globulifera*, *Syzygium* sp., *Toxocarpus* sp., *Triumfetta cordifolia*, *Virectaria* sp., thistles, creepers.

HABITS Active. At mid-height to tops of trees, sometimes in mixed-species flocks. Looks from side to side from perches. Within his territory, male sings prodigiously from buildings and low shrubs including banana plants and in flight. During these displays, pectoral tufts may be invisible, visible but flat, or erect and fully displayed. Male aggressive throughout the year, especially towards other males, and mid-air fights may lead to grounding and battles with bills and claws. Also attacks *C. chloropygius* and Cameroon Sunbird *Cyanomitra oritis* (76). Associates with Black-capped Speirops *Speirops lugubris* and Oriole-finch *Linurgus olivaceus*. Maximum recorded longevity 2 years 11 months. Host to feather mite *Ptilonyssus cinnyris*.

BREEDING Territorial. Males chase each other and regularly burst into song at start of breeding season. In Cameroon, pair off in September and October when gonads enlarge. Only female builds, but male sometimes accompanies her in search of material. **Nest** Ellipsoidal domed structure overhanging path in forest. Made of dried grass overlaying dry moss, lichens and plant fibres, bound with cobwebs, lined with feathers of other birds, e.g. Olive Pigeon *Columba arquatrix sjostedi* and Yellow-breasted Boubou *Laniarius atroflavus*, also vegetable down, and attached by creeper string to mass of dry rotten wood and moss in such a way as to appear part of the moss. Small side entrance near top, with short porch. No beard. 95 mm high, 70 mm wide. Usually low, 2-5 m above ground but some 6-15 m high in moss-covered branches of forest trees or in cypress tree. One 3 m high, suspended from *Convolvulus* sp., hanging from roof of shed. **Eggs** c/1-2. 14.5-18.3 x 9.8-12. Ovate, smooth, unglossed, mauvish with dark pinkish-grey shades and profuse blackish-brown speckles or brown with darker stains or grey with grey blotches and blackish stripes. **Laying months** Cameroon: August–February; Democratic Republic of the Congo: May, November; East Africa: August, November–December; Kenya: July; Nigeria: November, nest-building December; Uganda: January, August.

DESCRIPTION *C. r. preussi*
Adult male Head, mantle, back, cheeks and throat metallic green, reflecting steel-blue in some lights, with pale shafts to feathers and black bases. Grey-brown rump with olive

or occasionally metallic green tips. Uppertail-coverts metallic purple. Tail black with blue gloss. Remiges and greater coverts dark-brown with olive-yellow margins. Lesser wing-coverts metallic green. Throat metallic green. Narrow purple band below throat above scarlet breast. Belly pale brown, thighs and vent with olive tinge. Undertail-coverts pale brown. Bright lemon-yellow pectoral tufts. Axillaries and underwing-coverts brown. Iris black or dark brown. Bill, legs and feet black.
Adult female Crown to uppertail-coverts and cheeks dark olive-green. Underparts paler, chin grey, throat grey with olive wash, rest of underparts greyish-olive, belly washed yellow. Tail very dark brown. Wings with olive-yellow margins. Axillaries pale yellow. Underwing-coverts white. Iris dark brown. Bill, legs and feet black.
Juvenile Immature male as adult female. In West Africa, begins to assume adult plumage from start of rains, end March, with metallic plumage appearing on rump and uppertail-coverts and scarlet on breast.

GEOGRAPHICAL VARIATION
C. r. preussi Reichenow, 1892 (includes *parvirostris* [Eisentraut, 1965] of Bioko and *genderuensis* [Reichenow, 1910]) (Bioko; south-east Nigeria on the Obudu and Mambilla plateaus and Gashaka-Gumti Game Reserve; Cameroon from Mt Cameroon and Kumba to Bamenda, Tibati and Genderu mountains) Described above.
C. r. reichenowi Sharpe, 1891 (= *kikuyuensis* [Mearns 1915]) (includes *ericksoni* [Hartlaub 1891]) (mountains of east Democratic Republic of the Congo from west of Lake Albert to north-west of Lake Tanganyika and Mt Kabobo; Burundi; southern Sudan in the Imatong mountains; Ruwenzori; south-west Uganda in the Bwindi [Impenetrable] forest; Kenya from Elgon and Uraguess to highlands on either side of Rift) Bill shorter (14-15) than *preussi* (16-19) and abdomen more olive.

MEASUREMENTS Wing 55-60 (mean 58.3, 10 male *preussi*), 48-55 (mean 52.8, 28 male, *reichenowi*), 50-55 (mean 53.4, 10 female *preussi*), 48-52.5 (mean 49.9, 14 female *reichenowi*); **tail** 35-46 (mean 42.6, 10 male *preussi*), 38-39 (mean 38.3, 3 male *reichenowi*), 30-37 (mean 35.8, 10 female *preussi*), 33-35 (mean 34.5, 4 female *reichenowi*); **bill** 16-22 (mean 19.4, 10 male *preussi*), 14-17 (mean 16.2, 13 male *reichenowi*), 15-20 (mean 19, 10 female *preussi*), 14-16 (mean 15, 3 female *reichenowi*); **tarsus** 16-18 (mean 17, 10 male *preussi*), 18-19 (mean 18.3, 3 male *reichenowi*), 15-16 (19 female *preussi*), 14-17 (mean 16.5, 13 female *reichenowi*); **mass** 5.2-8.0 (mean 6.8, 43 male *reichenowi*); 5.3-8.5 (mean 6.9, 20 female *reichenowi*).

REFERENCES Bannerman (1948, 1951), Bates (1927), Bennun (1986), Dowsett-Lemaire (1990), Eisentraut (1965), Fry *et al.* (2000), Grimes (1971), Louette (1976), Serle (1951), Zumpt (1961).

109 GREATER DOUBLE-COLLARED SUNBIRD
Cinnyris afer   Plate 33

Certhia afra Linnaeus, 1766, *Syst. Nat.*, ed. 12, 1, p.186, Cape of Good Hope, South Africa.

Alternative names: Larger Double-collared Sunbird, Red-breasted Sunbird

IDENTIFICATION The largest of the double-collared sunbirds. Adult male distinguished by depth of red breast-band, being 18-23 mm and reaching lower breast. Female usually with pale yellow wash on lower breast and belly.

Similar species Told from Southern Double-collared Sunbird *Cinnyris chalybeus* (103) by larger size, longer, more curved but less robust bill, much more extensive red on breast in male (except young male in first moult when band is narrower), and clearer, louder voice. Male differs from both Montane *C. ludovicensis* (107) and Stuhlmann's Double-collared Sunbird *C. stuhlmanni* (105) by longer bill (30-32), from latter by slight bronzy tinge to metallic green upperparts and from former by violet (not metallic blue) uppertail-coverts, light olive (not deep olive) underparts, dark brown median coverts with only a few green subterminal fringes, and pale buff (not olive-brown) edges to primaries. Neergaard's Sunbird *C. neergaardi* (104) has shorter bill and male has black belly; Shelley's *C. shelleyi* (117) is allopatric.

VOICE Call A harsh *sskert. Tsig-tsig; chay,ing-chay,ing; ch,ch,ch, cher-rrreee* during chases. A drawn-out whistled *tssweeee; thoyee-thoyee-thoyee; pheet* uttered by newly-fledged birds. Alarm call a stuttering *ss,ss,ss,ss...* **Song** Loud. A musical twittering of whistling variations on *weetu*, rising and falling, increasing and decreasing in volume, interspersed with bursts of 20 or more *tsi* notes, followed by 3-4 *tsk* notes or by a rapid burst of *weet* changing to *tscheep* repeated 5 times per second for half a minute (*afer*). Female has song indistinguishable from that of male.

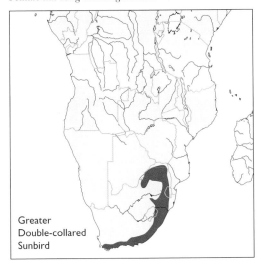

Greater Double-collared Sunbird

DISTRIBUTION South Africa, Lesotho and Swaziland.

HABITAT Open country, valley bushveld, tall scrubland, coastal plains, montane scrub, riverine scrub, *Protea* savanna, fynbos, moist woodland, succulent karoo, parks, gardens and forest edge, especially Afromontane. Avoids forest, unlike *C. chalybeus*.

STATUS Common in south-west and southern Cape. Locally common in upland KwaZulu-Natal.

MOVEMENTS A wanderer in relation to flowering patterns. Moves during seasonal shifts from suburban areas of Lydenburg, South Africa, to and from mountains.

FOOD Nectar; juices of fruits such as figs *Ficus* sp. and grapes *Vitis* sp.; insects including ants, small beetles (Coleoptera), Diptera, scale insects (Homoptera), larvae of Lepidoptera, moths on the wing and other insects during aerial sallies from perches; spiders, often taken from webs during hovering flight. Gleans insects and spiders by probing in flowers and dead and living leaves, and hunts amongst them by hovering. Attracted to sweet liquid exudate from exit-holes of fig-wasp *Elisabethiella baijnathi* in figs of *Ficus burtt-davyi*. When feeding on *Strelitzia reginae*, alights on spathe, presses against swollen stigma, depositing pollen from another flower on it, while pollen lying in the "arrow" of flower is deposited on the bird's feathers; and pollination also possible via bird's feet (Mabberley 1997).

Known food-plants *Acacia sieberiana, Aloe* spp., *Ananas comosus, Canna* sp., *Cotyledon* sp., *Erica* spp., *Erythrina* sp., *Ficus* spp. including *F. burtt-davyi, Gasteria* sp., *Hibiscus* sp., *Plumbago auriculata, Protea caffra, P. roupelliae, Pyrostegia venusta, Schotia* sp., *Spermacoce dibrachiata, Strelitzia reginae, Symphonia globulifera, Tecoma* sp., *Vitis* sp.

HABITS Active, occurring singly, in pairs, in small groups and in mixed-species parties, e.g. with white-eyes *Zosterops* spp. Aggressive, males chasing each other, as do females. Males may sing to each other when perched only 0.3 m apart, swaying their bodies from side to side as they sing. Sing with head held up, pointing to sky. Non-singer may bob head up and down. Displaying male and submissive female may swing upside-down from perches. Male sometimes displays aggressively by fanning tail and showing pectoral tufts. Bathes in dew, rainwater and bird-baths. Responds to image in reflections. Sometimes hawks for insects. Moults primaries November–March, with primaries moulted descendantly from P1 to P10. Secondaries and tail moult recorded December–March. Longevity up to 6 years 3 months. Host to blood parasites *Haemoproteus sequeirae, Leucocytozoon nectariniae* and *Plasmodium relictum* and feather mites *Anisodiscus megacaulus* and *Ptilonyssus cinnyris*.

BREEDING Male display involves chasing towards female along branch and singing, whilst either swaying from side to side or bobbing head up and down, sometimes showing pectoral tufts. A responsive female elicits full display by male of more vigorous singing with head held up and tail fanned. May also stretch body vertically, ruffle feathers, quiver body, half-open wings, fan tail to one side and bob up and down to female, who may follow suit. Sequence may be oft-repeated with variation of female swinging upside-down on perch. Display-flights involve jerky flight with body held nearly vertical just before landing on perch. Cloaca-pecking common, especially during nest-building, suggesting high frequency of extra-pair copulations). Only female builds nest, taking 10-24 days; uses silk from spiders' webs in aloes, cacti, window panes, walls, around houses and electric light flexes to do so. Male accompanies search flights and harries and chases female during building. Females may steal material from nests of other birds, e.g. African Paradise-flycatcher *Terpsiphone viridis*. Only female incubates, for 15 days. Nestlings fed by both parents, male starting to feed immediately after eggs hatch. Down feathers present on chicks and wing and tail in pin by 4th. day. Body feathers and wing and tail feathers complete by day 9. Nestling period 13-15 days. Fledglings return to roost in nest for 3 or more days after first flight and are fed for at least 10 days after first flights. Both parents feed fledglings. Triple-brooded in some seasons, breeding attempts immediately following on from each other. Parasitised by Klaas's Cuckoo *Chrysococcyx klaas*. **Nest** 1.5-7 m up in trees or shrubs, e.g. *Acacia, Euclea, Euphorbia, Opuntia* and *Schotia*, usually near top and often in same site year after year. Usually fixed within tree or bush, but occasionally hanging. Some compact, others untidy. Oval with side-top entrance and pronounced porch, projecting 35-60 mm, of 60-80 grass stems of *Eragrostis* sp. or *Panicum* sp., 80-90 mm in length. Made variously of grasses (up to 538 stems), bits of bark, twigs (up to 42), rootlets, leaves (up to 136), lichen, string, rags, bunches of small fruits e.g. *Scutia myrtina*, leaf mould, feathers, sheep's wool and hare's fur, bound together and secured to site with cobwebs. Outside decorated with large leaves, discarded snake skin, lichen and coloured cloth. Lined with feathers (up to 539 in one nest) and wool fibres. Nest 127-150 mm high, entrance diameter 30-39 mm, height below entrance 50-52 mm, width 60-85 mm, depth 60-83 mm. **Eggs** c/2. Race *afer*: 17.0-19.5 (mean 18.4, n=10) x 11.8-13.1 (mean 12.4), white, grey or greenish-white, heavily marked with indistinct clouding of slate-grey or olive and a few chocolate-brown or reddish-brown speckles, streaks, lines and spots. **Laying months** South Africa: all year.

DESCRIPTION *C. a. afer*
Adult male Head, neck, mantle and rump metallic green with blue reflections, bases of feathers brown. Uppertail-coverts iridescent violet. Tail brownish-black. Remiges, primary and greater wing-coverts brown. Median and lesser wing-coverts metallic green. Throat metallic green, separated from scarlet breast and upper belly by narrow band of bluish-violet. Lower belly and undertail-coverts dark olive-buff. Iris dark hazel. Bill and feet black.
Adult female Smaller and shorter-billed than male. Head dark greyish-olive or bluish-grey. Upperparts and median and lesser wing-coverts greyish-olive or dark brown. Tail brownish-black. Remiges, primary and greater wing-coverts brown. Throat and breast grey or greyish-olive with grey-green or light greyish-olive speckling. Undertail-coverts greyish-olive or grey. Axillaries and underwing-coverts pale green. Bill and feet black.
Juvenile Similar to adult female.

GEOGRAPHICAL VARIATION
C. a. afer (Linnaeus, 1766) (South Africa, Cape Province at Swellendam through southern districts of western Cape Province to Great Fish River) (Intergrades between *afer* and *saliens* occur between Great Fish River and Great Kei River) Described above.
C. a. saliens (Clancey, 1962) (South Africa from east of the Great Kei River, eastern Cape Province, to upper districts of KwaZulu-Natal, Free State, Lesotho, western Swaziland and highveld of Northern Province) Male differs from *afer* in larger size and lighter, non-metallic ventral parts: red breast-band is lighter, rest more yellowish, less dark brownish-olive. Female paler and greyish, more reticulated on throat and breast and greener or yellowish (less grey) on lower mesial ventral surface. Apart from (possibly clinal) size differences, these characters are not convincing; their arbitrariness and a lack of differences in moult regimes between *afer* and *saliens* led Lloyd & Craig (1989) to doubt the validity of *saliens* and to recommend further fieldwork on the two taxa.

MEASUREMENTS Wing 62-68 (mean 65.1, 10 male *afer*),

67-74 (mean 69.1, SD 2.26, 23 male *saliens*), 52-64 (mean 60.6, SD 3.60, 10 female *afer*), 60-64 (mean 61.4, 10 female *saliens*); **tail** 51-56 (male *afer*), 54-64 (mean 54.7, SD 2.80, 23 male *saliens*), 42-54 (mean 46.3, SD 6.07, 10 female *afer*), 54-56 (mean 54.4, 10 female *saliens*); **bill** 26-28 (mean 27.6, 5 female *afer*), 30-32 (mean 31, 10 male *saliens*), 30-32 (mean 31, 10 female *saliens*); **tarsus** 16.6-19 (male *afer*), 18-19 (mean 18.6, 10 male *saliens*), 15.9-18.1 (mean 16.6, SD 0.98, 10 female *afer*), 17-19 (mean 17.8, 10 female *saliens*); **mass** 9.0-18.0 (mean 12.0, SD 0.9, 123 male *afer*), 11-13 (mean 12.1, 9 male *saliens*), 9-14 (mean 10.2, SD 0.90, 66 female *afer*), 8.1-11.2 (mean 9.7, 6 female *saliens*); birds tend to be heavier in moulting season, November–January.

REFERENCES Benson & Prigogine (1981), Clancey (1962), Clancey & Irwin (1978), Dowsett (1983), Harebottle (1999), Harrison (1997a), Hutton (1985), Lloyd (1989), Lloyd & Craig (1989), MacDonald (1985), Oatley & Best (1997), Schoeman (1990), Skead (1954, 1967), de Swardt (1991b), de Swardt & Schoeman (1997), Zumpt (1961).

110 REGAL SUNBIRD
Cinnyris regius Plate 34

Cinnyris regia Reichenow, 1893, *Orn. Monatsb.* 1, p.32, central Africa; restricted to western Rwanda by Gyldenstolpe, 1924, *Kongl. Svensk. Vet.-Akad. Handl.*, 1, p.94; amended to Ruwenzori by Schouteden, 1937, *Rev. Zool. Bot. Africa* 30, p.166.

IDENTIFICATION Male unmistakable with contrasting red and bright yellow pattern on underparts and iridescent golden-green above. Female dull olive above, yellowish and slightly streaked below.
Similar species Female told from female Rockefeller's Sunbird *Cinnyris rockefelleri* (111) by duskier throat and less distinct supercilium, from female Stuhlmann's *C. stuhlmanni* (105) and Northern Double-collared Sunbird *C. reichenowi* (108) by greener upperparts and yellower underparts, and from female Variable Sunbird *C. venustus igneiventris* (134) by being more olive above and more uniform yellow-olive below including throat.

VOICE Call *Djer, dzit, dit* or *didit*. *Tchic-tchic* or *thickathic* on take-off. **Song** Race *regius*: 1-2 second bursts of a warbling twitter of rapid rising and falling notes; usually followed by single *tsi*, repeated every 1-3 seconds depending on length of gaps between warbles, which may last up to 10 seconds.

DISTRIBUTION East and Central Africa. Democratic Republic of the Congo, Rwanda, Burundi, Uganda and Tanzania.

HABITAT Mixed forest with bamboo in places, montane evergreen forest. Variety of habitats from 1,500 to 3,100 m (1,900-2,350 m on southern Itombwe massif). Forests, secondary growth, glades, open understorey, bamboo and scrubland.

STATUS Common in mountains of Democratic Republic of the Congo at 1,500-3,100 m. Common above 2,400 m in Uganda. Known in Burundi from Ijenda, Mt Heha, Rwegura and Teza and in Tanzania from Mt Kungwe and

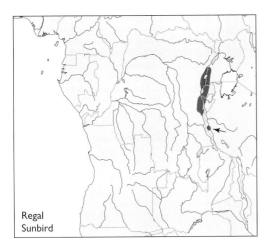

Regal
Sunbird

Mahale highlands, where locally common. Common above 2,200 m in Nyungwe forest, Rwanda, but less numerous down to 1,700 m.

MOVEMENTS Unknown.

FOOD Nectar and insects.
Known food-plants *Albizia* sp., *Canthium* sp., *Englerina woodfordiodes*, *Impatiens* spp. including *I. gesneroides*, *I. niamniamensis* and *I. stuhlmanni*, *Ipomoea* sp., *Lobelia gibberoa*, *Oxyanthus troupinii*, *Pavetta* sp., *Sericostachys* sp., *Symphonia gabonensis*, *S. globulifera*, *Syzygium* sp., *Triumfetta cordifolia*, *Virectaria* sp., vines. Pollen of unidentified Anthemideae found on skin of *C. regius* but may be from contamination (Iwarson 1979).

HABITS Usually seen singly or in pairs. Host of feather mites *Ptilonyssus cinnyris* and *Sternostoma nectarinia*.

BREEDING Nest Typical *Cinnyris* shape, often attached to end of fern frond or 4 m up in bamboo, or 5 m up in *Polyscias fulva* tree, or in *Mimulopsis* sp. Small, oval, made of fibres, moss and tendrils, with a thick lining of *Clematis* and asclepiad down and feathers including those of turaco *Tauraco* sp., green pigeon *Treron* sp. and weaver *Ploceus* sp. A nest of *regius* was 160 mm high, 90 mm wide, 85 mm deep with a 35 mm wide entrance hole 70 mm below the top, attached to a *Syzygium* sp. tree and composed of mosses, remains of *Panicum* sp. flowers, partially decomposed flowers of ?*Dracaena* sp. and roots of polypodiaceous ferns and lined with tufts from *Gynura vitellina*, hairs from treeferns *Cyathea* sp. and a few feathers of *Tauraco* spp. or plant down of *Sericostachys* sp. **Eggs** c/1; 17.1 x 12.2; clear grey with deeper grey speckles, more numerous near the deep grey-brown larger pole. **Laying months** Democratic Republic of the Congo: April–May; East Africa: July–August. Rwanda: nest-building December; Uganda: April–June, October, copulation, nest-building and young birds May–June.

DESCRIPTION *C. r. regius*
Adult male Head to scapulars and rump plus chin to upper breast, median and lesser wing-coverts iridescent emerald-green. Uppertail-coverts violet. Graduated tail very dark brown, violet-tinged, with central rectrices protruding 3 mm beyond rest, outer feather paler. Lores black. Narrow violet upper breast-band, scarlet lower mid-breast and belly. Sides of breast and flanks bright yellow. Thighs and vent olivaceous-green. Undertail-coverts red. Wing dark brown, edged olivaceous-green. Underwing has coverts off-white with yellow wash, axillaries dull olive, remiges grey. Iris dark brown or hazel. Bill black, legs black.

Adult female Upperparts dark olivaceous-green. Tail dark brown, outer feather paler. Chin and throat darkish olive with some yellowish streaks, breast darker olive. Rest of underparts yellowish-green. Wing dark brown. Outerwebs of secondaries elongated and brownish-olive contrasting with dark olive upperparts and pale yellowish below. Lesser and median wing-coverts olive. Underwing has coverts white with yellow wash, axillaries pale greenish, innerwebs of remiges fringed pale grey. Iris dark brown. Bill black, feet black.

Juvenile Male as adult female but has throat-patch iridescent green, iridescent shoulder-patches, red patches on chest, belly and base of undertail-coverts; belly pale not bright yellow. Immature male is a multi-coloured mixture of adult male and female plumage: as in adult male on wings, lesser wing-coverts, tail, upper- and undertail-coverts and breast; as in female on upperparts, sides of face and neck to chest but with a few metallic feathers.

GEOGRAPHICAL VARIATION
C. r. anderseni Williams, 1950 (western Tanzania at Mt Kungwe, in Kungwe-Mahale mountains) Male with scarlet breast changing posteriorly to orange and leaving abdomen olive-yellow and duller (instead of extending over mid-abdomen); flanks more olive; undertail-coverts yellowish-orange not red; bill broader at base. Upperparts of female not pure olive but washed grey.
C. r. regius Reichenow, 1893 (includes *kivuensis*) (Ruwenzori mountains in eastern Democratic Republic of the Congo and western Uganda at 1,800-3,000 m, Bwindi [Impenetrable] forest, south-west Uganda; highlands of south-east Democratic Republic of the Congo, Kigezi and mountains from west of Lake Albert and north-west of Lake Tanganyika to Mt Kabobo; Burundi, Rwanda) Described above.

MEASUREMENTS Wing 54-55 (male *anderseni*), 52-57 (mean 54.6, 11 male *regius*), 48.5-50 (female *anderseni*), 45-53 (mean 49.6, 7 female *regius*); **tail** 40-44 (male *anderseni*), 36-51 (mean 48.8, 11 male *regius*), 33-35 (female *anderseni*), 30-40 (mean 35.6, 7 female *regius*); **bill** 17-18 (male *anderseni*), 15-21 (mean 18.7, 15 male *regius*), 16.5-19 (mean 18.1, 7 female *regius*); **exposed culmen** 16.5-17 (male *anderseni*), 14-17 (male *regius*), 15-15.5 (female *anderseni*), 13.5-16 (female *regius*); **tarsus** 17.5-18 (male *anderseni*), 16.5-20 (mean 17, 11 male *regius*), 17 (female *anderseni*), 15-19.5 (mean 16.8, 7 female *regius*); **mass** 5-8 (mean 7.1, 37 male *regius*), 5.5-7.0 (mean 6.1, 14 female *regius*).

REFERENCES Dowsett-Lemaire (1990), Prigogine (1971), Williams (1950a), Zumpt (1961).

111 ROCKEFELLER'S SUNBIRD
Cinnyris rockefelleri   Plate 35

Cinnyris rockefelleri Chapin, 1932, *Amer. Mus. Novit.*, no.570, p.16, Mt Kandashomwa at 2,750 m, west of Ruzizi valley, eastern Belgian Congo.

IDENTIFICATION Small sunbird. Male unmistakable, as all breast bright scarlet, as are undertail-coverts. Female mostly olive but with yellowish throat, belly and supercilium.

Similar species Male similar to the partly sympatric Regal Sunbird *C. regius* (110), but lacks yellow on sides of breast (apart from pectoral tufts) and has longer bill. Female has more pronounced supercilium and is longer-billed than female *C. regius*.

VOICE Call A harsh *shick shick* contact call. **Song** Undescribed.

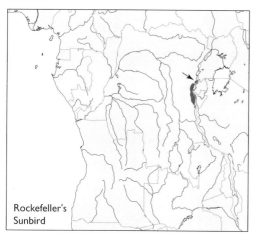

Rockefeller's
Sunbird

DISTRIBUTION Democratic Republic of the Congo and, possibly, Burundi and Rwanda. Restricted to about 250 km² in high montane forest and afro-alpine moorland in mountain ranges in eastern Democratic Republic of the Congo, north-west of Lake Tanganyika. Known from the type locality, Mt Kandashomwa, west of the Ruzizi valley in the Itombwe mountains; elsewhere in the Mt Kandashomwa area in the northern end of the Itombwes 80 km north of Itombwe at Mt Kahusi, Mt Muhi, Muusi and Lake Lungwe; at Mt Kabushwa, west of Lake Kivu; at Mt Karisimbi in the Virunga mountains north of Lake Kivu, and at lower elevations about 35 km south-west of Kandashomwa at Ngusa (2,240 m) and Nzombe (2,050 m); Sight records from Rwegura in the Nyungwe forest, Burundi, are in need of confirmation and a bird in the Rwanda part of this forest (J. P. Vande weghe in Dowsett-Lemaire 1990) may have been a vagrant.

HABITAT Along valleys and streams in tall bamboo and heath zones at 2,050-3,300 m, preferring thickets near streams to bamboo groves. Also found in arborescent heather.

STATUS Unknown, but probably threatened, and treated as such by Collar & Stuart (1985) and Collar *et al.* (1994). Deforestation is a likely threat is in its restricted habitat, but it was locally common on Mt Kandashomwa in 1929. Occurs within the Kahuzi-Biega National Park which may afford it adequate protection.

MOVEMENTS Unknown.

FOOD Nectar, presumably, and also insects which were recorded from stomach of one specimen.
Known food-plants None.

HABITS Noisy and active, usually encountered alone or in pairs at mid-height in trees, occasionally joining mixed-species parties.

BREEDING No information except that some birds do not breed in July, when they were moulting outer primaries. **Nest** Unknown. **Eggs** Unknown. **Laying months** Unknown. Enlarged gonads May.

DESCRIPTION
Adult male Head, neck, mantle to rump and scapulars bright metallic green with golden sheen, latter more marked at distal ends of feathers in some lights; basal two-thirds of metallic feathers (invisible on unruffled bird) very dark brown to black; uppertail-coverts glossy bright violet-blue for distal 12 mm or so, blackish-brown basally with metallic green bands (narrowing at middle) across centres and on tips. Lores black. Tail blackish above with faint bluish gloss. Chin to upper breast metallic green like head, bordered by narrow (4 mm) glossy violet band; lower breast below breast-band and upper belly bright scarlet, with invisible basal half of feathers black, bordered by yellow band which merges into scarlet portion; some birds have belly brighter scarlet than lower breast as some yellow feathers intermixed; small pectoral tufts bright yellow; lower belly, flanks and thighs deep olive-green, some feathers with bright olive-green streaks; undertail-coverts scarlet, in patch up to 17 mm long. Lesser and median coverts edged olive-green; rest of upperwing blackish-brown, remiges with outer halves of outerwebs edged brightish olive-green, especially so on secondaries which have markedly long, protruding outerwebs (conspicuous on folded wing). Underwing has outer edges of innerwebs of flight feathers bordered white, coverts whitish, some with olive tips. Bill black. Iris brown. Legs and feet black.
Adult female Forehead and crown dark olive and black, giving mottled appearance; feathers dark blackish-brown edged olive-green all round. Distinct pale olive supercilium runs 1 cm from bill to 3 mm behind eye. Lores black. Neck, mantle, back, scapulars, rump and uppertail-coverts uniform dark olive-green. Ear-coverts paler yellowish-olive. Lesser upperwing-coverts broadly edged olive-green. Tail slightly rounded, central rectrices 3 mm longer than outermost, dark brown with faint dark blue gloss on both webs. Chin and throat bright yellowish olive-green. Chest and breast duller, darker olive-green. Lower belly and undertail-coverts bright olive-green with yellowish tinge but not as bright as chin and throat. Flight feathers dark brown with extensive edging of yellowish olive-green; outerwebs of secondaries with pronounced elongations, as in male. No pectoral tufts. Underwing has coverts white with yellowish edges, visible as patch at top of folded wing, flight feathers grey-brown with innerwebs edged white. Bill black. Legs and feet black.
Note: Female *rockefelleri* was reported by Hendrickx & Massart-Lis (1952) as having a faint green metallic gloss on forehead, crown and nape and a green metallic gloss on back, scapulars and upperwing-coverts; and their description of metallic fringes to the mantle was used as a feature distinguishing female *rockefelleri* from female *C. regius kivuensis*. However, no metallic plumage at all was visible on the two specimens examined. According to its label, one of these was the specimen used in the description of the female.
Juvenile Unknown.

GEOGRAPHICAL VARIATION None described.

MEASUREMENTS Wing 55.5-58 (mean 57.2, SD 0.79, 10

males), 51-52 (mean 51.3, SD 0.58, 3 females); **tail** 36-45 (mean 39.5, SD 3.1, 10 males), 30-34 (mean 32 ,SD 2.83, 2 females); **bill** 20-23.5 (mean 22.4, SD 1.05, 9 males), 22, 22 (2 females); **tarsus** 18-20 (mean 18.8, SD 0.67, 9 males), 17, 17 (2 females); **mass** "*poids* 52, 52.2 and 55 g", presumably meaning 5.2, 5.22 and 5.5 g, on labels of three males collected by Prigogine.

REFERENCES BirdLife International (2000), Collar *et al.* (1994), Collar & Stuart (1985), Dowsett-Lemaire (1990), Gaugris (1976), Gaugris *et al.* (1981), Hendrickx & Massart-Lis (1952), Prigogine (1971).

---

112 EASTERN DOUBLE-COLLARED SUNBIRD
Cinnyris mediocris   Plate 33

Cinnyris mediocris Shelley, 1885, *Proc. Zool. Soc. London*, p.228, Kilimanjaro 12,000 ft.

IDENTIFICATION A conspicuous small sunbird of highland areas. Male with curved bill, metallic green body, scarlet breast-band and pale olive belly. Female olive above, yellow-green below and brownish on wings.

Similar species Slight overlap in range of nominate *mediocris* with that of Northern Double-collared Sunbird *Cinnyris reichenowi* (108), above 1,800 m in Kenyan highlands. Nominate *mediocris* has longer bill and tail, male with blue not violet narrow breast-band and uppertail-coverts, more golden-green less blue metallic plumage, narrower and duller scarlet breast-band, and paler underparts. Female *mediocris* is darker than *reichenowi*. Confusion also possible with similar but altitudinally allopatric Olive-bellied Sunbird *C. chloropygius* (100), males of which have uppertail-coverts metallic green concolorous with rest of upperparts, and darker olive underparts; female has brighter yellow underparts. Montane Double-collared Sunbird *C. ludovicensis* (107) is larger but with a shorter, straighter bill, blue uppertail-coverts and narrow breast-band, unlike the races of *mediocris* which it meets, which have violet uppertail-coverts. Female *ludovicensis* has greyish-brown belly. Male Miombo Double-collared Sunbird *C. manoensis* (102) has green-tipped olive uppertail-coverts, and female is greyish-brown not olive. Similar Loveridge's Sunbird *C. loveridgei* (114) and Moreau's Sunbird *C. moreaui* (113) are allopatric.

VOICE Call A harsh nasal *chek chek*; *tse*; *tseep, tseep* and a falling *tse-ee*; alarm call a fast series of *tchep tschep tchep tchep*. **Song** Two *tseep* notes 0.5 seconds apart, followed by a downslurred *ts-szurr* and a rapid rattle-like warble for 2-7 seconds, with much frequency modulation. Also described as *peety-ja-teece-ja-teece-ja-teece-ja tsrrt-tsrrt-ja-peety-peety-peety-ja* and variants thereof, likened to the jingling of a light chain. Similar to song of *C. loveridgei* but slower and notes more discernible in the rattle.

DISTRIBUTION East Africa. Kenya, Tanzania, Zambia, Malawi, Mozambique.

HABITAT Montane forests, bamboos, heathland, grassland and gardens.

STATUS Common. Occurs at density of 6 per 500 net metre hours, 600-1,500 m, on Mt Nilo, East Usambaras, Tanzania.

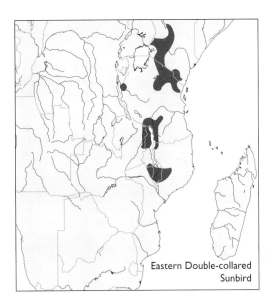
Eastern Double-collared Sunbird

MOVEMENTS Retreats to lower altitudes in non-breeding season.

FOOD Nectar, insects including the bibionid fly *Dilophus erythraea* and other Diptera, Hymenoptera, Neuroptera, unidentified larvae; spiders and small gastropod molluscs. Agile while feeding; for instance feeds from end of spur of *Impatiens papilionacea*, then turns to grip spur itself while hanging upside-down to feed from mouth of flower. Also nectar-robs from *Kniphofia* sp. and *Leonotis* sp. Forages for insects on undersides of maize leaves and catches flying ants in flight.

Known food-plants *Abutilon* sp., *Acacia abyssinica*, *Achyrospermum* sp., *Acrocarpus fraxinifolius*, *Aeollanthus repens*, *Agelanthus sansibarensis*, *A. subulatus*, *Bersama abyssinica englerana*, *Bridelia brideliifolia*, *Brillantaisia ulugurica*, *Canthium gueinzii*, *Carduus kinensis*, *Clematis brachiata*, *C. simensis*, *Clerodendrum johnstonii*, *C. quadrangulatum*, *Crotalaria goetzei*, *Dendrophthoe pendens*, *Dombeya goetzenii*, *Echinops amplexicaulis*, *Ekebergia* sp., *Englerina inaequilatera*, *E. woodfordiodes*, *Erica arborea*, *Erythrina* spp. including *E. abyssinica*, *Faurea saligna*, *Geniosporum paludosum*, *Hagenia abyssinica*, *Halleria lucida*, *Hoslundia opposita*, *Hypericum keniense*, *H. revolutum*, *Hypoestes aristata*, *Impatiens elegantissima*, *I. gomphophylla*, *I. papilionacea*, *Ipomoea involucrata*, *Kniphofia ?rogersi*, *K. snowdenii*, *Laggera* sp., *Leonotis decadonta*, *L. mollissima*, *Leucas densiflora*, *Lobelia aberdarica*, *L. elgonensis*, *L. giberroa*, unidentified mistletoes Loranthaceae, *Momordica* sp., *Pavetta subumbellata*, *Pentas decora*, *P. schimperana*, *Phragmanthera usuiensis*, *Plectranthus sylvestris*, *Protea kilimandscharica*, *Prunus* sp., *Rubus steudneri*, *Rytignia neglecta*, *Salvia* sp., *Syzygium cordatum*, *Tecoma capensis*, *Triumfetta macrophylla*, *Usnea* sp.

HABITS Feeds singly, in pairs and in mixed-species groups in forest, encompassing up to 14 species often led by White-headed Woodhoopoes *Phoeniculus bollei*. Aggressive, dominant over *C. ludovicensis* but subservient to Tacazze Sunbird *Nectarinia tacazze* (95), Malachite Sunbird *N. famosa* (97) and Green-headed Sunbird *Cyanomitra verticalis* (73). Pair maintains same territory, a forest patch of about 0.2 ha, year after year for at least six years. Can use temporary hypothermia to survive cold night-time temperatures at high altitudes, one female dropping body temperature 17.5°C down to 23.5°C. Longevity at least 6 years 1 month. Host to *Leucocytozoon nectariniae*.

BREEDING Territorial. Male assists nest-building by breaking off bits of lichen and bringing them to nest for female to weave in; when enthusiastic male tried to weave material in himself female flew at him chattering, leaving him to drop the lichen and flee. Nest-building female visits nest every minute at mid-day peak of activity. Males display pectoral tufts to other males while courting female. Male sings from nearby perch as female incubates. Male repeatedly defended nest against approaches by female Variable Sunbird *C. venustus falkensteini* (134) but failed to prevent latter from laying in the nest (presumably the female *venustus* had suffered loss of her own nest). **Nest** Domed pouch with side entrance. Kenya (Aberdares): made of *Usnea*, some long grass strands, with crescent-shaped seeds still attached. Heavy lining of vegetable down and a few feathers. Suspended from drooping dead *Hypericum* sp. bough 2.5 m above ground. Another lined with soft white seed down, 2 m above ground at end of hanging conifer branch. Another in *Acacia* sp. bush. **Eggs** c/1-2; *mediocris*: 16.0-17.5 (mean 16.5) x 10.8-12.0. Pale greenish-white with finely suffused greyish-brown marks nearly obscured by background. **Laying months** East Africa: January–June, August–December. Kenya: July, December; Malawi: April–October; Zambia; active gonads May.

DESCRIPTION *C. m. mediocris*
Adult male Uppertail-coverts blue. Rest of upperparts, lesser and median wing-coverts and chin to breast iridescent golden-green. Tail very dark brown and glossy, slightly graduated, outer feather and distal half of T5 paler and tipped white on innerwebs and on outerweb of T6. Lores black. Thin (depth 2-6 mm) band of violet-blue on breast between end of green and scarlet breast-band. Yellow pectoral tufts, 11-21 mm long. Belly and vent dull olive. Wing dark greyish-brown, remiges and greater wing-coverts with buff edges. Underwing-coverts off-white, axillaries pale greenish. Iris dark brown or black. Bill, legs and feet black. Post-breeding moult lasts 96 days, on average, July–November, Malawi.
Adult female Upperparts dark olive-green, lores darker. Tail greyish-brown and glossy, slightly graduated, outer two feathers tipped brownish-white on innerwebs and on outerweb of T6. Iris dark brown or black. Chin and throat olivaceous-green with yellow speckling. Rest of underside olivaceous-yellow, darker on breast and flanks. Remiges dark brown, edged olivaceous-green. Median and lesser wing-coverts dark olive. Underwing-coverts white with yellow wash, axillaries olivaceous-yellow. Bill, legs and feet black.
Juvenile As adult female but underparts darker. Gape yellow, bill dull brown with pale tip.

GEOGRAPHICAL VARIATION
C. m. bensoni Williams, 1953 (mountains of Malawi, except extreme north in the Karonga district, and Nyika plateau in Zambia above 1,800 m and northern Mozambique; birds from Nyika plateau in Malawi intermediate with *fuelleborni*: see Benson & Benson 1977) Similar to *fuelleborni* with uppertail-coverts violet instead of blue, but breast-band darker red, more brownish-olive above and sooty-green below.
C. m. fuelleborni Reichenow, 1899 (Tanzania from Iringa to Songea and Rungwe and Njombe district,

northern Malawi in the Karonga district, Zambia in the Mafinga mountains above 1,800 m; birds from Nyika plateau in Malawi intermediate with *bensoni*: see Benson & Benson 1977) Male with uppertail-coverts grey or metallic green proximally, tipped violet or purplish instead of blue; broad scarlet to orange-red breast-band (11-20 mm deep) broader than *mediocris* and *usambaricus*, often with yellow laterally but distinct from pectoral tufts, and paler than in *bensoni*; abdomen greener golden-olive. Undertail-coverts sometimes scarlet-tipped, scarlet-washed or all scarlet. Female darker than *usambaricus*. Young male in first metallic dress appears more mottled than adult and pectoral tufts are shorter.
C. m. mediocris Shelley, 1885 (Kenya highlands on both sides of the Rift north-west to Kulal, northern Tanzania from Crater highlands to Kilimanjaro, North Pare Mtns and Mt Hanang) Described above.
C. m. usambaricus Grote, 1922 (north-east Tanzania at Usambara and South Pare Mountains and Taita Hills, south-east Kenya) Male with red breast narrower (6-8) than *mediocris* (10-13) and with grey-brown wash below it, uppertail-coverts violet or royal blue instead of blue, belly more greenish-olive. Female greener.

MEASUREMENTS Wing 54-60 (mean 57.5, SD 1.51, 16 male *bensoni/fuelleborni*), 52-62 (mean, 56.3, SD 2.16, 22 male *mediocris*), 52-59 (mean 54.8, SD 2.10, 10 female *bensoni/fuelleborni*), 48-54 (mean 51.6, SD 1.29, 11 female *mediocris*); **tail** 44.5-49.5 (mean 46.4, SD 1.68, 8 male *bensoni/fuelleborni*), 38-53 (mean 46.2, SD 4.13, 17 male *mediocris*), 40 (female *bensoni*), 33-44 (mean 41.0, SD 4.11, 10 female *mediocris*); **bill** 16.4-24.6 (mean 22.3, SD 1.73, 27 male *bensoni/fuelleborni*), 15-22 (mean 19.0, SD 2.0, 21 male *mediocris*), 15.7-22.5 (mean 20.1, SD 1.17, 18 female *bensoni/fuelleborni*), 14-20.5 (mean 17.9, SD 1.75, 10 female *mediocris*); **tarsus** 15.3-19.5 (mean 17.5, SD 1.20, 16 male *bensoni/fuelleborni*), 16-20 (mean 18.3, SD 1.38, 18 male *mediocris*), 14.0-17.7 (mean 16.0, SD 1.15, 9 female *bensoni/fuelleborni*), 14-19.0 (mean 16.9, SD 1.73, 10 female *mediocris*); **mass** 7.0-9.8 (mean 8.6, SD 0.60, 55 male *bensoni/fuelleborni*), 6.4-9.6 (mean 7.5, SD 0.56, 20 male *mediocris*), 6.8-9.2 (mean 7.8, SD 0.48, 56 female *bensoni/fuelleborni*), 5.2-9.0 (mean 7.0, SD 0.74, 10 female *mediocris*), unsexed *bensoni/fuelleborni*: up to 0.5 g variation in a 3-day period (Dowsett 1983); in *mediocris*, birds may lose 1.4 g overnight, and those at 3,350 m are significantly heavier (range 7.6-9.4, mean 8.0, 8 males) than birds caught at 2,690 m (range 6.4-8.5, mean 7.3, 12 males) (Cheke 1971b).

REFERENCES A. J. Beakbane (*in litt.*), Benson & Benson (1977), Cheke (1971a,b, 1972), Dowsett (1983), Dowsett & Dowsett-Lemaire (1984), Dowsett-Lemaire (1988, 1989), Sclater & Moreau (1933), Stuart & van der Willigen (1980), Williams (1950, 1978).

---

113 MOREAU'S SUNBIRD
Cinnyris moreaui   Plate 35

Cinnyris mediocris moreaui W. L. Sclater, 1933, *Ibis*, p.214, Maskati, Nguru Range, 6,000 ft., east central Tanganyika.

IDENTIFICATION A highland sunbird, male with metallic green upperparts, red part of double collar reduced by intrusion of yellow from sides of breast. Underparts yellowish-olive. Female has greyish throat and olivaceous-yellow underparts.

Similar species Male *moreaui* in first adult plumage has abdomen dark and dull similar to pale examples of the Eastern Double-collared Sunbird *Cinnyris mediocris fuelleborni* (112). Intermediates between *moreaui* and *mediocris* occur on Mt Bismarck and elsewhere. Male with abdomen yellower, less olive, than the allopatric Loveridge's Sunbird *C. loveridgei* (114), with bill shorter (22.5-23 vs 24-25). Female slightly smaller than *loveridgei* with crown green, not grey, and more olive below.

VOICE Call Chirps every second or two from exposed branch. **Song** A rapid, almost musical cascade of high-pitched notes similar to song of *C. mediocris*.

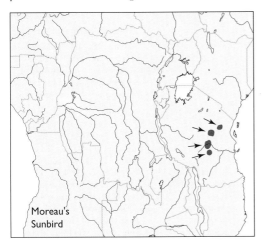

Moreau's Sunbird

DISTRIBUTION Nguu, Nguru, Ukaguru, Udzungwa and Uvidunda mountains of eastern Tanzania, including sites at Mt Kiboriani, west of the Ukagurus, and Mwanihana Forest.

HABITAT Moist montane forest and clearings above 1,300 m in Nguru, Nguu, Udzungwa, Uvidunda and Ukaguru mountains of Tanzania. Usually in canopy or in bushes at sides of tracks. Joins mixed-species groups.

STATUS Listed as near-threatened by Collar *et al.* (1994), as forest strongholds affected by agricultural clearance and firewood-gathering, but very common in suitable localised habitat: 27.6 caught per 10,000 net-metre hours in Ukagurus. Common in Mwanihana Forest, 1,500-1,850 m, and abundant above 1,300 m in the Mamiwa Kisara Forest Reserve in the Ukagurus.

MOVEMENTS Unknown.

FOOD Presumably nectar and insects.
Known food-plants *Achyrospermum carvalhi*.

HABITS Found in forest canopy or in bushes along roads through forest but avoids pine and scrub. Often in mixed-species flocks. Forages 1-3 m up in mid-storey. Collects water from surface of lichen in canopy of leafless *Albizia* sp.

BREEDING Nest Built by female. Small domed purse, made of leaves or dry grasses and silk from insect's nest, entrance hole near top, placed in low vegetation, beside road through forest or higher, e.g. 3 m up, suspended

from bracken or 2 m up in upright stem of small shrub, or 10 m high in tall tree. **Eggs** Pale whitish with grey-brown marks, similar to eggs of *C. mediocris*. **Laying months** 2 young in nest, edge of rainforest, 1,800 m, Masenge, Ukaguru Mountains, Kilosa district, 26 December. Five females had brood-patches in August–September, Mamiwa Kisara forest, Ukagurus, but another had new feathers on the patch indicative of recently completed breeding. 2 occupied nests, another being built and 2 fledglings caught, same site, August–September.

DESCRIPTION
Adult male Upperparts to rump, scapulars, lesser and median wing-coverts, and chin to breast iridescent bronzy-green. Feathers of rump non-metallic olive-green. Uppertail-coverts metallic green, merging to glossy purplish-violet at tip. Tail very dark brown, faintly glossed and slightly graduated, outer feather paler. Narrow band (2 mm deep) below green on chest glossy blue reflecting violet. Underneath this band, a band or patch 10-15 mm deep on middle of lower breast ranges from red to orange, bordered by yellow on sides of breast. Abdomen bright olive to yellowish-olive. Pectoral tufts not sharply defined, yellow feathering continued on either side of red breast-patch. Wing very dark brown, edged olivaceous-yellow. Underwing-coverts and axillaries pale greenish-yellow. Iris dark brown or black. Bill black. Legs black.
Adult female Upperparts olive-green with metallic greenish-grey fringes to feathers of mantle and crown. Tail very dark brown, outer feather paler. Breast and abdomen bright olive-yellow, chin and throat greyer. Remiges and greater wing-coverts very dark brown, edged yellowish-olive. Underwing-coverts and axillaries pale greenish-yellow. Iris dark brown. Bill black. Legs black.
Juvenile male Head, nape, mantle, rump and uppertail-coverts dusky greyish-olive; chin, throat, upper breast, flanks and undertail-coverts dusky yellowish-olive, becoming slightly brighter and more yellowish on lower breast and centre of abdomen; wings dusky brown, with warm olive-brown margins; rectrices blackish, with narrow olive margins. From this plumage moults into one closely resembling adult male but with some olive-green feathers amongst first metallic feathers on crown, red breast-patch duller and less extensive, metallic fringes to upperparts narrower with many non-metallic feather bases exposed, interrupting continuous metallic appearance of adult. Abdomen duskier, less yellowish than adult. First adult male dress differs from older males, as red patch duller and less extensive, metallic fringes on upperparts narrower giving scaly appearance, and belly duskier.
Immature female resembles adult but metallic greyish-green fringes to upperparts less pronounced; duller (less yellowish-) green below.

GEOGRAPHICAL VARIATION None described, but males in Rubeho mountains, Tanzania, are darker with scarlet, not orange, breast-bar completely separating the yellow lateral tufts, indicative of intergradation with *C. mediocris fuelleborni*. Indeed *C. moreaui* is intermediate between *C. mediocris* and *C. loveridgei* and Stuart & van der Willigen (1980) suggested that *moreaui* has resulted from hybrids of these two species. A further complication is a report that male *C. mediocris* at Mufindi in the Udzungwas are *moreaui*-like (Jensen & Brøgger-Jensen 1992).

MEASUREMENTS Wing 53-59 (mean 56, 24 males), 50-54 (mean 51.5, 20 females); **tail** 29-43 (mean 39.1, 24 males), 32-36 (mean 34.1, 20 females); **bill** 19.7-26.4 (mean 23.7, 24 males), 19.2-24.8 (mean 22.8, 20 females); **tarsus** 17.0-20.0 (mean 18, 24 males), 16.9-19 (mean 17.7, 20 females); **mass** 6.8-9.6 (mean 8.5, 56 males), 5.1-10.4 (mean 8.0, 43 females).

REFERENCES Evans & Anderson (1993a,b), Fjeldså *et al.* (1997), Fry *et al.* (2000), Fuggles-Couchman (1986), Jensen & Brøgger-Jensen (1992), Sclater & Moreau (1933), Seddon *et al.* (1999), Stuart & van der Willigen (1980), Williams (1950 b,c).

114 LOVERIDGE'S SUNBIRD
Cinnyris loveridgei   Plate 35

Cinnyris loveridgei Hartert, 1922, *Bull. Br. Orn. Club* 42, p.49, Uluguru Mountains, eastern Tanganyika [= Tanzania].

IDENTIFICATION Small montane short-tailed sunbird with long curved bill. Male double-collared with blue-green metallic upperparts with gold sheen. Orangey-red band below narrow violet one. Breast often appears more orangey than some illustrations suggest. Feathers of the rump non-metallic olive-green. Basal uppertail-coverts metallic green, terminal ones purplish blue-violet. Female greenish-olive above, head and throat greyer, underparts yellower.
Similar species Female very similar to female Moreau's Sunbird *Cinnyris moreaui* (113) but slightly larger. Very similar to Eastern Double-collared Sunbird *C. mediocris* (112), but is allopatric with it and with *C. moreaui*.

VOICE Call A harsh metallic *tsk* or *pzit*, uttered by both sexes. **Song** A short (3-4 seconds) warble of very high-pitched *tsi* notes delivered so fast that they recall an insect such as a grasshopper; sometimes preceded by a few double notes of *tsp-tee, tsp-tee, tsp-tee.*

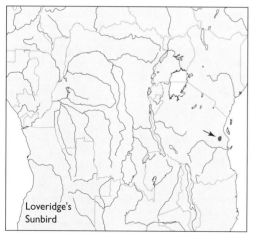

DISTRIBUTION Restricted to the Uluguru mountains in east Tanzania. Prefers high ground; found at 1,520-2,580 m at Kimhandu, 1,685-2,475 m at Lanzi, 1,200-1,960 m at Tegetero, 2,000-2,500 m at Tchenzema and up to 2,400 m on the Lukwangule plateau.

HABITAT Montane forest preferred, but also inhabits

clearings including plantations with a few standing trees and shrubs, and relatively open drier areas with some bamboo.

STATUS Near-threatened (Collar *et al.* 1994) restricted-range species, but locally abundant in suitable habitat in montane forests. Apparently adaptable and tolerant of habitat changes, remaining common in face of cultivation.

MOVEMENTS No evidence of vertical migration.

FOOD Spiders, larval Lepidoptera, Diptera, small beetles, mayflies (Ephemeroptera) and nectar.
Known food-plants Flowers of indigenous pea crop and an *Albizia*-like tree.

HABITS Highly mobile, rapid fliers, appearing vigorous and "temperamental". Feeds in forest canopy and down at undergrowth level, usually gleaning on twigs and leaves, but sometimes hawks from a perch like a flycatcher.

BREEDING Nest Bulky, oval structure (150 mm long, 90 mm wide) with large side-top entrance 50 mm in diameter and no porch. Made of dry grass, dead leaves and hair-like seed stems of *Thalictrum* sp., bound together with cobwebs. Dead leaves and loose ends of dry grass in untidy bundle hanging from base but well concealed by foliage and suspended, about 2 m above ground, from below horizontal branch of coniferous tree. Inner lining of fine shredded grass and some plant-down. **Eggs** Unknown. **Laying months** August, October–March.

DESCRIPTION
Adult male Upperparts to rump, scapulars, lesser and median wing-coverts, and chin to breast iridescent green. Feathers of rump non-metallic olive-green. Basal uppertail-coverts metallic green, terminal ones purplish blue-violet. Tail very dark brown, slightly glossy above, graduated. Lores black. Narrow (3 mm) band of metallic violet on upper breast, above orangey-red breast-patch, fusing with warm cadmium-yellow on sides of breast and abdomen, latter tinged olive with faint orange wash in centre. Pectoral tufts not sharply defined; yellow feathering continues onto sides of breast. Wing very dark brown edged golden-olive. Underwing-coverts pale greyish-olive, axillaries yellow. Iris brown. Bill and feet black.
Adult female Crown and sides of face greyish. Rest of upperparts olive-green, feathers of mantle with greenish-grey or bluish-grey metallic fringes. Tail very dark brown, outer feather paler. Chin greyish-olive, throat dark olivaceous-green. Breast and abdomen bright olive-tinged cadmium-yellow. Wing dark greyish-brown, primaries fringed pale brown, secondaries and tertials widely edged yellowish. Primary and greater wing-coverts dark greyish-brown edged olivaceous-green. Median and lesser wing-coverts dark olive-green. Underwing-coverts and axillaries white with yellow wash. Iris brown. Bill and feet black.
Juvenile Male differs from adult female by presence of distinct pale grey throat and upper breast; rest of underparts pale greyish-green. Crown grey, merging to greenish-grey on nape and upperparts, feathers of mantle fringed with bluish metallic as in adult female. Rest of plumage resembles adult female. Male moults directly into adult dress.

GEOGRAPHICAL VARIATION None described, but *C. moreaui* sometimes included within *loveridgei*.

MEASUREMENTS Wing 52-62 (mean 57.6, 20 males), 51-59 (mean 54.3, 15 females); **tail** 38-43 (mean 40.1, 9 males), 35-37 (mean 36, 3 females); **bill** 25-27 (mean 25.9, 7 males), 23-24 (mean 23.7, 3 females); **tarsus** 19-21 (mean 19.6, 7 males), 18-19 (mean 18.3, 3 females); **mass** 9.0-12.0 (mean 10.6, 25 males), 8.0-10.0 (mean 9.0, 24 females).

REFERENCES Stuart & van der Willigen (1980), Svendsen *et al.* (1995), Williams (1950, 1951a).

115 BEAUTIFUL SUNBIRD
Cinnyris pulchellus   Plate 41

Certhia pulchella Linnaeus, 1766, *Syst. Nat.* ed. 12, 1, p.187, Senegal.

Alternative name: Beautiful Long-tailed Sunbird

IDENTIFICATION Male distinctive with long central tail feathers, mostly bright metallic green plumage and red breast-band, bordered with yellow. Male of race *melanogaster* has all-black belly, male nominate *pulchellus* has iridescent green belly and black only on thighs and vent. Non-breeding male resembles adult female but retains long tail and some metallic feathering. Juvenile male has dark throat-streak before metallic feathers obtained. Female dull brown above, pale supercilium, and pale yellow underparts.
Similar species Yellow-bordered scarlet breast-band distinguishes male from superficially similar but smaller Pygmy Sunbird *Hedydipna platura* (64) and Nile Valley Sunbird *H. metallica* (65), which are entirely yellow below and have elongated feathers which broaden out at ends (unlike evenly wide feathers of *pulchellus*); *pulchellus* has longer bill than *platura* and no purple uppertail-coverts. Adult female *pulchellus* told from female *platura* by dull not bright yellow underparts and longer bill (14-16 mm vs 9-10 mm). Female and immature *pulchellus* daintier with more obvious supercilium than those of Variable Sunbird *Cinnyris venustus* (134) and are smaller and paler than female and immature Copper Sunbird *C. cupreus* (138). Male *C. p. melanogaster* differs from Black-bellied Sunbird *C. nectarinoides* (120) by yellow borders to red breast-patch, latter only having yellow pectoral tufts in nominate *nectarinoides* or no yellow in race *erlangeri*. Female *pulchellus* has more prominent supercilium and brighter yellow underparts with less streaking.

VOICE Call Repeated *zit-zit*, *chip-chip*, *tsi-chip* or *tsick-tsick* when feeding; *je-je-je-je*. Female call a single or disyllabic note distinct from male call. **Song** A subdued warble. Race *melanogaster*: a jumbled twittering of incoherent notes uttered rapidly and strung together for 30 seconds or more, creating impression of nervous agitation. Nominate *pulchellus*: an almost melodic warble of rising and falling high-pitched notes, involving *ti-tsu-tswee* and similar variants, lasting for nearly one minute, sometimes including rising series of 3-4 *tsi*. Warble may be interspersed with long sequence of rapid scolding *che*, at rate of 5-8 per second and continued for more than a minute with a few bursts of *chip-chip*.

DISTRIBUTION West and East Africa. Senegal, Gambia, Guinea-Bissau, Guinea, Sierra Leone, Côte d'Ivoire, Ghana, Togo (as far south as 9°17'N), Benin, Nigeria, Mauritania (resident and migrant visitor as far south as

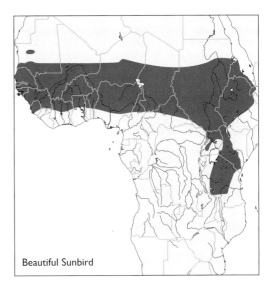

Beautiful Sunbird

8°N), Mali, Burkina Faso, Niger (migrant visitor), Chad, Sudan, west Ethiopia, Eritrea, Cameroon, Central African Republic, Democratic Republic of the Congo (north-east borders to north of Lake Albert), Rwanda (vagrant), Uganda, Kenya and dry interior of Tanzania.

HABITAT Thorn savannas, mainly in dry sahel and savanna belt of West Africa and edges of rivers, but recorded on the coast of Sierra Leone in mangrove scrub, beaches and gardens. Also occurs in gardens in Senegal, Gambia and Nigeria. Usually below 1,800 m in Ethiopia. Usually below 1,300 m in Uganda in semi-arid areas such as *Acacia* bush and usually near water.

STATUS Common in suitable habitat, including gardens, throughout West Africa. Common and widely distributed in Mauritania up to 20°N. Common and widespread in Senegal and Gambia. Common resident and wet-season visitor to northern Ghana with similar status in Togo and Nigeria. Frequent to locally abundant in Ethiopia. Very common in Sudan, south of Atbara. Common resident in north Uganda.

MOVEMENTS Movements in West Africa complex, with apparently resident birds in all but far northern part of range, with migrants shifting with rains, to breed in wet season (February–October in south, May–September in north or only June–August in far north). Thus, southern populations move north, February–April, breed, and return September–October. In sahelian northern part of range some subpopulations present in dry season and migrate south to Northern Guinea savanna at onset of rains to breed. In Nigeria reaches furthest south September–March, and furthest north April–October. Movements may be related to flowering regimes of mistletoes Loranthaceae (e.g. *Tapinanthus globiferus*) parasitic on *Acacia* spp.; Arabic name *tuyr al-annaba* means *Tapinanthus* bird.

FOOD Insects (including those attracted to flowers of *Ziziphus mauritiana*, small spiders, nectar and small flowers (*Acacia* sp.).
Known food-plants *Acacia* sp., *Albizia coriara*, *Aloe* sp., *Bombax* sp., *Calotropis procera*, *Combretum paniculatum*, *Commiphora* sp., *Delonix elata*, *Gmelina arborea*, *Hibiscus sino-ornata*,

Jacaranda mimosifolia, unidentified Loranthaceae parasitic on *Acacia* spp. and on *Vitellaria parkii, Manihot glaziovii, Moringa pterygosperma, Tapinanthus globiferus* (mistletoe parasite of jujube tree *Ziziphus mauritiana* and *Acacia* spp.).

HABITS Flight direct. Often seen singly but occasionally gregarious with several feeding in the same tree, when may be very active and chase each other. Frequents villages and gardens and may feed as low as 1 m from ground. Host to feather lice *Ricinus timmermanni* and blood parasite *Haemoproteus sequeirae*.

BREEDING Breeds during rainy seasons. Territorial. Males aggressive to other males in breeding season and display from tops of trees, showing colours of underparts with upright pose, and flick wings and twitch fanned tail from side to side. Courtship behaviour of males to females involves wings and tail spread out. May be polygamous as males occasionally court two females at once. Female only incubates and broods but male also attends nest. **Nest** 120 mm high, sometimes with 35 mm long attachment, 50 mm wide, internal depth 35 mm. Entrance hole in centre, 25 mm in diameter. Longitudinal purse-shape, composed of dry fibres, bark, twigs, dried grass, leaves, cobweb (especially at entrance and attachment), vegetable down, plant stems, feathers, snake skin and cobwebs, lined with white and grey feathers or vegetable down, sometimes decorated with lichen, and suspended 1-6 m above ground from branches of trees e.g. *Acacia* sp., *Bauhinia reticulata, Citrus sp.* (lime or orange), *Tamarindus indica, Ziziphus mauritiana.* Usually no porch or beard but some with substantial porch and occasionally with beard. Race *melanogaster*: hanging from tip of branch, 0.3 m long, with beard, lined with feathers, made of dry leaves and vegetable matter, woven with cobwebs, 1 m up in *Acacia mellifera*. **Eggs** Race *melanogaster*: c/1-2; soft-toned bright green with violet-grey spots and clouds, and purple-black S-shaped flourishes and spots, the former more towards the pointed end, the latter towards the blunt end; 16.0-17.0 (mean 16.5, n=4) x 11.0-12.0 (mean 11.5); *pulchellus*: c/1-2; 15.1-18.0 (mean 16.6, n=34) x 9.9-12.4 (mean 10.9). Elongated ovate, sometimes slightly glossy and variable in colour. Usually pale bluish-grey, green, brown or greyish-white with dark grey, brown or ashy longitudinal streaks, blotches and spots especially at larger pole. Sometimes tinged olive and marked with dark sepia or so heavily marked with pale brown or grey as to appear uniform greyish. **Laying months** East Africa: January–December; Burkina Faso: June; Chad: July–August; Eritrea: July; Gambia: June–March; Ghana: July–September, where assumes breeding plumage between March and May, loses it by October; Kenya: May, June (*melanogaster*), July (*pulchellus*); Mali: July; Mauritania: June–October; Niger: June–July; Nigeria: February, June–October, mostly in wet season June–August; Senegal: June–October; Sudan: July, September, October; Tanzania: March (*melanogaster*); Togo: nest-building October, singing July; Uganda: February–March, May–June, August–October.

DESCRIPTION *C. p. pulchellus*
Adult male Crown and all upperparts including rump bright metallic green; lesser and wing-coverts metallic green, median and greater wing-coverts, flight feathers dark brown. Uppertail-coverts tipped bright metallic green shading into blue towards dark brown base. Tail bluish-black, inner rectrices narrowly edged metallic green; central pair of rectrices very narrow, fringed metallic green broadly at base but narrowly along elongated part and

remain same width along all exposed length. Elongations protrude 55-65 mm beyond end of adjacent pair. Chin, throat and upper breast same metallic green as upperparts, with golden reflections and narrow band of metallic blue below green. Scarlet patch in centre of breast below which feathers tipped yellow. Abdomen and sides of body bright metallic green, undertail-coverts more metallic blue. Thighs and vent black. Axillaries and underwing-coverts black. Coverts along border of wing metallic green. Eye black or very dark brown. Bill, legs and feet black. **Non-breeding plumage** Resembles adult female, but with black remiges and rectrices. Grey-brown above, dusky yellow below, but green metallic chin, throat, wing-coverts and a few such feathers on rump and uppertail-coverts retained. Metallic on chin and throat may also be lost, giving whitish throat-patch. Some lose the long tail, perhaps first-year birds, others do not. Hence birds which do not lose tail seem to moult wings and tail only once a year, at start of breeding season, but moult body feathers twice per annum. Thus, after breeding, males moult metallic feathers (except tail and lesser wing-coverts) and may have fresh non-breeding plumage but well-worn elongated tail and tatty wings until start of following breeding period. Birds in equatorial regions may omit eclipse plumage but in West Africa, Eritrea and Sudan eclipse extends from October and November until start of rains in following March–June. In Tanzania moult out of breeding dress in July.

Adult female All plumage dull with no metallic feathers. Upperparts dull brown with faint yellow wash from crown to rump and darker brown on wing- and tail-coverts. Narrow white or pale yellow supercilium behind eye. Ear-coverts darker brown. Tail blackish-brown with slight bronze-green or bluish gloss. Tail feathers narrowly tipped white, outer pair more broadly with white along margin of outerweb. Chin and throat whitish, rest of underparts suffused yellow and slightly mottled dark blackish-brown on breast and flanks. Remiges dark brown, edged pale olive as are greater wing-coverts. Other wing-coverts, alula and tertials edged pale brown. Undertail-coverts, axillaries and underwing-coverts white with yellow tinge. Eye black or very dark brown. Bill, legs and feet black.

Juvenile Male similar to adult female but with a vertical black streak on throat and upper chest, bordered with creamy-white moustachial stripe, a plumage seen July to October, and underparts duller. Immature male acquires metallic green on throat and lesser wing-coverts before rest of body. Female resembles adult female but sometimes brighter yellow below and lacks black throat of immature male.

GEOGRAPHICAL VARIATION The two subspecies may warrant specific rank (Chapin 1954). Overlaps in range only involve migrants and post-breeding dispersers.

   C. p. melanogastra (Fischer & Reichenow, 1884) (west and central Kenya south through dry interior of Tanzania to Rukwa and 160 km north-west of Arusha; one record from Democratic Republic of the Congo at south-east base of Ruwenzoris) Bill longer. Male has abdomen black instead of metallic green, undertail-coverts with metallic green-blue tips, red patch larger and central tail feathers projecting less far (28-45) beyond rest. Female with less blackish throat and more dusky streaking below.

   C. p. pulchellus (Linnaeus, 1766) (includes *aegra* [Hartert, 1921] and *lucidipectus* [Hartert, 1921]) (Senegal and Guinea-Bissau to Nigeria, Sudan, Eritrea, west Ethiopia, north-east borders of Democratic

Republic of the Congo to north of Lake Albert, Uganda east to Akole, north-west Kenya to Baringo) Described above.

MEASUREMENTS Wing 55-65 (mean 61.7, 14 male *melanogaster*), 56-61 (mean 58.4, 18 male *pulchellus*), 52 (female *melanogaster*), 47-56 (mean 52.6, 12 female *pulchellus*); **tail with elongations** 74-131 (mean 93.2, 10 male *pulchellus*), 41 (female *melanogaster*), 33-41 (mean 36, 10 female *pulchellus*); **tail without elongations** 39-44 (30 male *pulchellus*), 34-37 (12 female *pulchellus*); **bill** 21, 22 (2 male *melanogaster*), 15-19 (mean 18.2, 10 male *pulchellus*), 20 (female *melanogaster*), 14-18 (mean 14.6, 10 female *pulchellus*); **tarsus** 17 (2 male *melanogaster*), 14-16 (mean 14.9, 10 male *pulchellus*), 18 (female *melanogaster*), 14-16 (mean 14.6, 10 female *pulchellus*); **mass** 7.0-9.5 (mean 8.4, 37 male *melanogaster*), 5.6-10.2 (mean 7.5, 37 male *pulchellus*), 7.1-9.7 (mean 8.1, 3 female *melanogaster*), 5.6-8.0 (mean 6.6, 27 female *pulchellus*), 5.3-6.7 (mean 6.1, 16 unsexed *pulchellus*). Male *pulchellus* significantly heavier than females (Fry 1970).

REFERENCES Bannerman (1948), Chapin (1954), Fry (1970), Fry *et al.* (2000), Koenig (1956), Ledger (1980), Mundy & Cook (1972), Newby (1980), Pettet (1977), Serle (1943), Thonnerieux *et al.* (1989).

116 MARIQUA SUNBIRD
Cinnyris mariquensis   Plate 39

Cinnyris mariquensis A. Smith, 1836, *Rep. exped. C. Afr.*, p.53, north of Kurrichane, western Transvaal, South Africa.

Alternative names: Marico Sunbird, Southern Bifasciated Sunbird, Western Bifasciated Sunbird

IDENTIFICATION A medium-sized long-legged species with upright stance on perches. Iridescent areas of male show as golden-green; dark red (maroon) breast of male conspicuous at close quarters and contrasts with black belly. Green upperparts contrast with dark primaries and tail when male seen from above.
Similar species Similar to Purple-banded Sunbird *Cinnyris bifasciatus* (121) but is larger and has longer, more decurved bill and male with broader (12-13 vs 7-10 mm) maroon breast-band and narrower violet band. Female and juvenile resemble those of *bifasciatus* but are larger and more heavily streaked on the chest and belly and tend to have a yellowish patch in the middle of their chests (the inconsistency further compounded by orange or yellow deposits of pollen on chests). Juvenile also resembles juvenile Shining Sunbird *C. habessinicus* (127) but the black throat-patch continues onto the breast and flanks as a series of large, blackish, drop-like spots; the underparts, strongly washed yellow, are also distinctive. Juvenile, especially immature male with dark throat-patch, also confusable with that of the smaller, straighter-billed White-breasted Sunbird *C. talatala* (133), which are much less heavily streaked on breast (markings do not stretch so far down the abdomen) and their bellies are usually whitish without yellow wash (if present it does not extend onto belly or flanks), although very young birds do have yellow below with few or no spots. Female also confusable with some female Amethyst Sunbird *Chalcomitra amethystina* (84), but have throat mottled grey, radiating out to breast,

flanks and belly. Colour of lower breast-band of male *mariquensis* distinguishes it from Shelley's Sunbird *Cinnyris shelleyi* (117).

VOICE Call A *chip-chip*, with up to 10 *chips* per second. *Schitz-schitz* sometimes uttered. Also a *cherrr-ip-yoo* similar to song of *C. bifasciatus* but slower. Juvenile begging call a continuous *dearr*. **Song** Race *mariquensis*: a very complex sequence of alternating but discrete bursts of *chur-chur*, *tser-tser*, *chip-chip-chip*, *tsi-tsi*, and other notes intermingled in a continuous vocalisation including *b-r-r-zi*, whistles, some typical sunbird-type melodic warbles and trills; may last a few minutes; *suahelicus*: a long sequence of jumbled twitters, high-pitched, and varying with some whistles, short trills and melodic phrases.

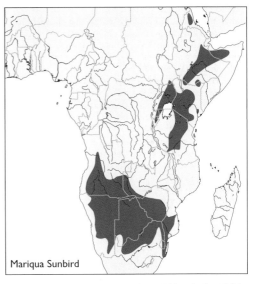

Mariqua Sunbird

DISTRIBUTION East and southern Africa. Sudan, Ethiopia, Eritrea, Somalia, Rwanda, Burundi, Uganda, Kenya, Tanzania, Angola, Zambia, Mozambique, Namibia, Botswana, Zimbabwe, Swaziland and South Africa.

HABITAT Dry *Acacia* savanna or at *Acacia* savanna/riverine forest edges. 1,200-1,500 m in Uganda in various bush habitats, including gardens, from moist woodland near Lake Victoria to dry *Acacia* scrub and woodland in north-east and south-west. Riverine bushland and swamp-fringing forest in Okavango delta. *Acacia robusta* woodland and grassy areas with *Acacia* sp., *Combretum* sp. and *Aloe* spp. Occasional in gardens in towns and cities.

STATUS Common in Didinga mountains, Sudan. Common presumed resident in Somalia. Frequent to locally abundant in Ethiopia, where usually below 2,100 m. Locally common resident in Angola. Common and widespread in Kenya, Uganda and Tanzania (scarce in southern Tanzania), north-eastern South Africa, Botswana, southwestern Zimbabwe and Namibia.

MOVEMENTS Nomadic in Zimbabwe. A recovery 51 km away from ringing site in South Africa. Leaves arid Kalahari areas during droughts. Probably wanders in Mozambique and Uganda, as presence at Kampala erratic.

FOOD Nectar; insects including Diptera, Lepidoptera (larvae and moths), Hymenoptera, termites; spiders.

283

Known food-plants *Acacia erubescens, Aloe* sp., *Bauhinia* sp., *Cadaba termitaria, Callistemon* sp., *Crotalaria* sp., *Erythrina* sp., *Geranium* spp., *Grevillea* sp., *Jacaranda* sp., *Kigelia* sp., *Kniphofia* sp., *Leonotis leonurus*, unidentified mistletoes Loranthaceae including those on *Acacia nigrescens, Peltophorum africanum, Phragmanthera dschallensis* (parasite of *Acacia* spp., especially *A. drepanolobium*), *Plicosephalus kalachariensis* (parasitising *Acacia tortilis*), *Schotia* sp., *Tecoma* sp., *Thevetia* sp.

HABITS Territorial; defends feeding territories throughout year and nest area in breeding season; males chase each other. Sings from tops of trees e.g. *Eucalyptus*. Males may conduct singing duels near to each other, in upright pose. Usually single or in pairs, not in groups, but associates with White-breasted Sunbird *Cinnyris talatala* (133) and Scarlet-chested Sunbird *Chalcomitra senegalensis* (85). Gleans insects from leaves, sometimes hanging upside-down. Hawks for insects like a flycatcher *Muscicapa* sp. Hovers in front of grass-heads to take insects and in front of flowers for nectar. Drinks from bird-baths throughout the year in Botswana, even when plenty of food available. Aggressive; chases away Cape White-eyes *Zosterops pallidus* and pugnacious at bird-baths, where juvenile male seen to attack adult male *C. talatala*. Host of feather mite *Ptilonyssus cinnyris*.

BREEDING Male courts female by flying around her, hovering in front of her for 5 seconds and then alighting beside her. Only female builds but male accompanies her on forays for material, occasionally carrying it. First egg laid in early morning on successive days, first laid 12 days after start of nest-building. Incubation for 13.5-14.5 days by female only, starting after second egg laid. One female brought food to nestlings every two minutes. Fledglings return to nest to roost. Parasitised by Didric Cuckoo *Chrysococcyx caprius* and Klaas's Cuckoo *C. klaas*. One nest ripped apart by Red-faced Mousebirds *Colius indicus*. **Nest** Fixed 1-8 m up in tree or shrub e.g. 2 m above ground in canopy of peach tree, 4.5 m up in a leafless sapling of *Acacia bussei*, and in pines, *Eucalyptus* sp. and *Jacaranda* sp. trees; also over pool, and one <1 m from wasp's nest. Same site used in successive years and even same nest has been used twice in a season. First material is a long piece of white down attached to a branch, camouflaged with *Eucalyptus* resin, before construction begins on nest, porch and entrance. A thick-walled, whitish oval with rudimentary porch, made of white down or woolly material and fine grass. Lined with goose-down or other feathers and decorated with dark material such as *Eucalyptus* resin and bark, seeds of *Ziziphus mucronata*, small flowers, feathers and seed capsules, attached with spiders' webs. Height 128 cm, width 64 mm, diameter of entrance hole (20-30 mm below apex) 39 mm. **Eggs** c/1-3, usually 2. Race *mariquensis*: cream, white, greyish- or greenish-white, with dense covering of streaks, dots, lines and blotches of pale brown, black, grey, dark grey or olive, occasionally forming ring at larger pole but usually covering whole egg. 15.2-20.5 (mean 17.4, n=10) x 11.0-13.4 (mean 11.6); *osiris*: 15.0-19.3 (mean 17.3, n=3) x 11.0-12.8 (mean 11.7); *suahelicus*: 17-18 x 12-14. **Laying months** Botswana: November. East Africa: January–December. Ethiopia: May; Mozambique: July; Somalia: March; South Africa: August–April; Uganda: February, June, August, September, November; Zambia: February, September, October; Zimbabwe: January–July and September–October.

DESCRIPTION *C. m. mariquensis*
Adult male Head, neck, mantle, throat, upper breast, median and lesser wing-coverts, back and rump metallic green, with golden reflections, basal two-thirds of feathers dark blackish-brown. Uppertail-coverts metallic dark bluish-green. Tail very dark brown, all except outer two pairs of rectrices edged metallic green. Narrow band of iridescent, bright, dark violet-blue below gorget and above purple-maroon breast-band (8-10 mm deep), which is intermixed with violet. Rest of underparts black. Remiges very dark brown but slightly paler than rectrices. Underwing-coverts and axillaries black. Iris dark brown. Bill and feet black.
Adult female Crown, nape, ear-coverts, cheeks, neck, mantle, back and rump brown. Uppertail-coverts and tail very dark brown. Outer tail feather with broad white patch at tip of innerweb and white fringe to outer edge. Thin brownish-white supercilium above and behind eye. Throat and breast off-white or pale pinkish-white with heavy black markings, density of which varies. Belly also with brown blotches but washed with varying shades of pale yellow. Undertail-coverts streaked blackish-brown and white with yellow wash. Axillaries and underwing-coverts whitish.
Juvenile Juvenile male resembles adult female but has black or smoky-grey throat, bordered white. Malar streak and underparts washed yellow. Breast heavily streaked black. Short yellowish-white supercilium and shoulder-patch noticeable, latter sometimes appearing as two spots. Remiges and tertiaries with light brown tips, broader on secondaries and tertials, contrasting with rest of brown plumage. Central tail feathers glossy dark blue with green tinge, outer pair brown with white edges above and below. Adjacent pair tipped white. Bill flanges orange-yellow. In older juvenile, throat is metallic green as are shoulders and uppertail-coverts; purple and maroon breast-bands then appear, belly loses mottling and yellow, assuming black of adult.

GEOGRAPHICAL VARIATION
C. m. mariquensis Smith, 1836 (includes *lucens* [Clancey, 1973] and *ovamboensis* Reichenow, 1904, which are recognised by Fry *et al.* 2000) (South Africa in KwaZulu-Natal; southern Mozambique to Matabeleland in Zimbabwe, south-west Zambia, northern and eastern Botswana; northern Namibia and south Angola from Cuando Cubango and Cunene to southern Huíla) Described above.
C. m. osiris (Finsch, 1872) (includes *hawkeri* Neumann, 1899) (Eritrea, Ethiopia, Somalia [west of 47°E and north of 8°N] to northern Kenya, northern Uganda and south-east Sudan) Male with black abdomen and posterior margin of metallic throat more violet-blue. Upper violet breast-band broader. Lower maroon breast-band darker and narrower. Female more heavily marked on throat and breast. White on tail of juvenile male and female less extensive.
C. m. suahelicus Reichenow, 1891 (Rwanda; Burundi; central Uganda; interior of Kenya from the equator through Tanzania to Mwenzo in north-east Zambia, east Democratic Republic of the Congo, Kwanza valley, Angola) Male with greyer, less deep black abdomen and shorter-billed than *mariquensis*.

MEASUREMENTS Wing 58.5-73.5 (mean 69.0, SD 2.95, 38 male *mariquensis*), (mean 67.2, 15 male *suahelicus*), 58-68 (mean 64.5, SD 1.26, 12 female *mariquensis*); **tail** 44.5-52 (mean 47.5, 10 male *mariquensis*), 38-43 (mean 42.1, 7 female *mariquensis*); **bill** 23-25.5 (mean 23.7, 10 male *mariquensis*), 20-22 (mean 21.3, 10 male *suahelicus*), 21.5-24.5 (mean 22.8, 7 female *mariquensis*); **tarsus** 17-19.5 (mean 18.1, 10 male *mariquensis*), 16-19 (mean 18.1, 7 female *mariquensis*); **mass** 10.0-14.2 (mean 11.7, SD 0.97, 41 male *mariquensis*), 9.1-13.3 (mean 11.7, 64 male *suahelicus*), 7.0-12.3 (mean 10.2, SD 0.94, 25 female *mariquensis*), 8.3-11.3 (mean 10.1, 7 female *suahelicus*).

REFERENCES W. D. Borello (pers. comm.), Clarke (1985), Fry *et al.* (2000), Herremans (1997a), Milstein (1963), Oatley (1995), Tree (1991), Vincent (1949), Zumpt (1961).

---

117 SHELLEY'S SUNBIRD
Cinnyris shelleyi   Plate 38

Cinnyris shelleyi Alexander, 1899, *Bull. Br. Orn. Club* 8, p.54, Zambezi river, 60 miles below junction of Kafue-Zambezi rivers (*Ibis* 1899, pp.556, 642).

Alternative names: Shelley's Double-collared Sunbird, Zambesi Valley Double-collared Sunbird, Zambesi Valley Sunbird

IDENTIFICATION Male easily identified by its scarlet breast-band and sooty-black belly, wings and tail.
Similar species Male Miombo Double-collared Sunbird *Cinnyris manoensis* (102) lacks black belly and has brown wings and tail and blue-green not violet uppertail-coverts; female is unstreaked below. Female *shelleyi* is very similar to female Mariqua Sunbird *C. mariquensis* (116) but is smaller, shorter-billed and duskier below. Allopatric Southern Double-collared Sunbird *C. chalybeus* (103) is similar but male has grey not black belly and female is paler below with speckling on breast. Male Neergaard's Sunbird *C. neergaardi* (104), also allopatric, has black belly but blue, not green, rump.

VOICE Call A *chip, tsk* or rapid, declining, chattering *didi* or *chitter*. A high *seep-seep*. **Song** A rapid burst of warbling, 1-8 seconds long, including *chibbee-cheeu-cheeu*.

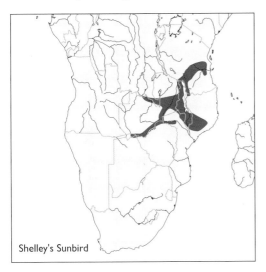

Shelley's Sunbird

DISTRIBUTION South-eastern Africa. Democratic Republic of the Congo, Tanzania, Zambia, Malawi (Blantyre north to Edingeni and at edge of Lake Malawi), Mozambique (north only, records from south now rejected), Namibia, Zimbabwe. Reaches 100 km west into Namibia along the Caprivi strip. May occur in Angola as seen at the edge of the River Mashi (= River Cuando) floodplain, nearby in Zambia.

HABITAT *C. s. shelleyi* almost restricted to *Brachystegia* woodland, but also occurs in *Baikiaea* woodland at Livingstone in Zambia and occasionally in *Acacia* woodland and gardens. Found at 425-1,200 m in Malawi. *C. s. hofmanni* found in woodland, scrubland, gardens and thick riparian scrub.

STATUS Uncommon. Locally common in eastern Tanzania, 500-1,200 m. Sparsely distributed in Malawi. Uncommon and sparsely distributed, mostly on plateaus, in Zambia.

MOVEMENTS Probably sedentary, but the type specimen was obtained away from usual plateau habitat.

FOOD Nectar, insects including Diptera and small Lepidoptera, spiders.
Known food-plants *Holmskioldia* sp., *Lagerstroemia* sp., unidentified mistletoes Loranthaceae parasitising *Acacia albida*, *Tecoma* sp. Avoids aloes.

HABITS Males perch on tree-tops to sing. Forages in upper reaches of trees.

BREEDING A nest, which had contained 2 young, had its lining pulled out by the female after the young had fledged; she then re-lined it before re-laying. Double-brooded. **Nest** 102-120 mm high, entrance hole with diameter of 30 mm and depth of nest inside 30 mm. Placed 2-3 m up in *Lagerstroemia* sp. or *Tecoma* bush. Made of old leaves, leaf ribs, bark and grass or greenish and grey lichen, lightly held together with cobwebs. Thickly lined with chicken feathers or feathers of doves or francolins, which protrude from and conceal the entrance. **Eggs** c/1-2; *shelleyi*: 15.0-17.5 (mean 16.1, n=6) x 11.0-12.0 (mean 11.4). Pale olive ground colour with a few fine specks of dull purple or black smudges all over or restricted to zone, 3.5 mm broad, surrounding the larger pole. **Laying months** East Africa: October. Malawi: August; Zambia: August–November. Zimbabwe records from November (Newby-Varty 1945, 1948) considered by Brooke (1964) to be based on a misidentification.

DESCRIPTION *C. s. shelleyi*
Adult male Head, throat and neck metallic emerald with bright yellowish-green, gold and copper reflections. Mantle, back, median and lesser wing-coverts similar to head but with less varied reflections. Uppertail-coverts dark emerald. Remiges, primary and greater wing-coverts and alula dark brownish-black. Tail dark brownish-black, central pair finely edged metallic green. Lores black. Thin bluish-violet band below green gorget above broad (10-15 mm wide) scarlet breast-band. Belly, flanks and undertail-coverts very dark brown. Wing very dark brown, remiges fringed olivaceous-yellow. Axillaries and underwing-coverts brown. Iris brown. Bill and feet black.
Non-breeding plumage Wings and tail as in breeding dress, but metallic feathering restricted to chin and throat and uppertail-coverts; chin to throat as adult male, red band present, but rest of underparts similar to adult female although some black may remain on belly; upperparts as

adult female apart from some metallic on head and mantle.

Adult female Grey greenish-brown upperparts, sides of face darker. Tail very dark brown, outer feather paler, broadly tipped white. Thin brownish-white supercilium. Underparts pale brownish, with lower parts tinged greenish-yellow and extensive mottling on chin and throat and dark streaks on breast, flanks and undertail-coverts. Wing dark brown, primaries with off-white margins, secondaries edged pale green. Underwing-coverts and axillaries brownish-white and dark at base. Iris brown. Bill and feet black.

Juvenile Young of both sexes have black chins and throats, bordered by pale moustachial stripes, dark upper breast and dark marks on breast and flanks; otherwise similar to adult female but yellower on underparts. Immature male has scarlet breast-band.

GEOGRAPHICAL VARIATION

C. s. hofmanni Reichenow, 1915 (east Tanzania from Ruvu and Pangani rivers to Morogoro region) Bill shorter (18-20) and more curved than *shelleyi* (20-23) and female greener above and with orange-red on breast. Male with blacker flanks, belly and undertail-coverts.

C. s. shelleyi Alexander, 1899 (Zambia east of 26°E to south-east Democratic Republic of the Congo, Katanga, Malawi, northern Mozambique and south-west Tanzania) Described above.

MEASUREMENTS Wing 58-62 (mean 59.4, 5 male *hofmanni*), 62-66 (mean 64.0, 11 male *shelleyi*), 56-57 (female *hofmanni*), 58-60 (mean 58.7, 4 female *shelleyi*); tail 35-43 (male *hofmanni*), 40-45 (mean 43.1, 11 male *shelleyi*), 31-34 (female *hofmanni*), 38-42 (mean 39.5, 4 female *shelleyi*); bill 18-19 (mean 18.7, 6 male *hofmanni*), 21-23 (mean 21.8, 11 male *shelleyi*), 20-23 (mean 21.4, 4 female *shelleyi*), 19 (female *hofmanni*); tarsus 15, 16 (2 male *hofmanni*), 15-17 (mean 16.0, 11 male *shelleyi*), 15-18 (mean 16.3, 4 female *shelleyi*); **mass** 8.0 (2 male *hofmanni*).

REFERENCES Brooke (1964), Fry *et al.* (2000), J. del Hoyo (pers. comm.), Newby-Varty (1945, 1948), Skead (1967), Tree *et al.* (1991).

---

118 CONGO SUNBIRD
Cinnyris congensis   Plate 38

Nectarinia congensis van Oort, 1910, *Orn. Monatsb.* 18, p.54, Boma, lower Congo; error, corrected to Irebu by Chapin, 1954, *Bull. Amer. Mus. Nat. Hist.* 75B, p.268.

Alternative names: Congo Black-bellied Sunbird, Long-tailed Congo Sunbird

IDENTIFICATION Adult male has metallic green upperparts, bluer on uppertail-coverts, metallic green chin and throat separated from scarlet breast-band by narrow blue band. Belly black. **Similar species** Male Olive-bellied Sunbird *Cinnyris chloropygius* (100) lacks long tail and has olive not black belly and yellow pectoral tufts. Female *congensis* is darker above and has darker throat than *chloropygius*, and is streaked on lower abdomen not on breast. Beautiful Sunbird *Cinnyris pulchellus* (115) is similar but allopatric.

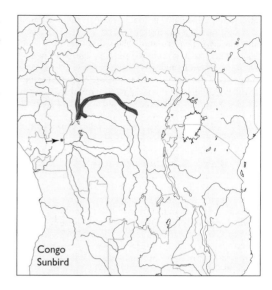

Congo
Sunbird

VOICE Unknown.

DISTRIBUTION Republic of the Congo and Democratic Republic of the Congo. Occurs along the northern arc of the Congo River from Lukolela in the west to mouth of the Lomami River at Isangi, west of Kisangani. Also up the Ubangi River as far as Impfondo, the lower Momboyo River and between R. Léfini and town of N'go in Congo west of Congo River, the most southerly record apart from the supposedly erroneous type-locality of Boma.

HABITAT Forested banks of rivers, trees on river islands and clearings near villages.

STATUS Common along forested banks of the Congo River.

MOVEMENTS Sedentary, staying along river margins but strays to islands in mid-river.

FOOD Small spiders, and probably insects and nectar. **Known food-plants** *Caesalpinia regia*.

HABITS Unknown.

BREEDING Nest Information based solely on sighting by Chapin of male beside a nest suspended from a bush, hanging 2 m above river. **Eggs** Unknown. **Laying months** Breeding condition July–December, but may breed all year round.

DESCRIPTION

Adult male Head, throat, neck and rest of upperparts metallic green, but much bluer on uppertail-coverts. Median and greater wing-coverts black with faint purplish-blue tinge, inner greater coverts narrowly edged metallic green. Flight feathers black. Tail sooty-black, narrowly edged metallic blue-green; graduated, central feathers narrow and elongated, projecting 46-75 mm beyond rest of tail; other feathers with wider metallic edges. Lores black. Chin to upper breast metallic green like head, bordered by line of metallic blue; below this, a broad scarlet band (24 mm deep, 15 mm wide) across lower breast, some feathers with narrow subterminal blue band and some near throat with blue tips; rest of underparts sooty-black, except some long flank feathers and undertail-coverts tipped metallic green. Lesser and median coverts metallic green; upperwing otherwise sooty-black. Axillaries and underwing-coverts sooty-black. Iris dark brown. Bill black. Legs black. Non-breeding plumage unknown but see under juvenile male.

Adult female Upperparts dull, dark brownish-olive. Tail graduated, central feathers 3-4 mm longer than T2, about 10 mm longer than outermost; feathers blackish-brown with dull greenish sheen, especially on edges; T1 with or without narrow pale tips, rest with pale brownish-white tips to innerwebs increasing in extent outwardly; T6 also has distal half of outerweb pale brown. Lores blackish; short narrow pale line from above to behind eye. Chin grey, upper throat with variable amount of dark mottling, lower throat heavily mottled blackish-brown, forming patch; pale line from base of lower mandible down side of neck, separating dark throat from olive face; rest of underparts pale yellow, brightest in centre of belly, mottled and streaked on breast and flanks; undertail-coverts yellowish-white. Upperwing olive-brown; underwing-coverts greyish-brown with whitish tips. Bill brownish-black; legs blackish.

Juvenile Undescribed, but a November male, probably juvenile moulting into adult dress but possibly a bird in non-breeding dress, has crown and rest of head dark brown with mottling of sparse iridescent green feathers, becoming denser on back. Wings and tail as adult but with less iridescence. Chin and throat black with iridescent green at edges, appearing bright blue in some lights. Scarlet breast-band diffuse, interspersed with black and a few yellow feathers. Centre of belly black but rest of belly and flanks with streaks of dull yellowish-ochre.

GEOGRAPHICAL VARIATION None described.

MEASUREMENTS Wing 62-66 (mean 64.7, SD 0.88, 15 males), 56-59 (4 females); **tail, middle rectrices (T1)** 75-151 (mean 108.4, SD 18.74, 14 males), **next pair (T2)** 49-52 (9 males), 41-45 (4 females); **bill** 18-22 (mean 20.1, SD 1.50, 12 males), 16-20 (4 females); **tarsus** 15.5-19 (mean 17.2, SD 0.86, 15 males), 15.5-16.5 (4 females); **mass** no data.

REFERENCES Bannerman (1948), Chapin (1954), Fry *et al.* (2000).

---

119 RED-CHESTED SUNBIRD
Cinnyris erythroceria   Plate 38

Nectarinia erythrocerca (*sic*) Hartlaub, 1857, *Syst. Orn. Westafr.*, p.270, no locality; White Nile, south of lat. 8°N, designated by Sclater, 1930, *Syst. Av. Aethiop.* p.684.

Taxonomic note It is commonly accepted (e.g. by Sclater 1930, Chapin 1954, Hall & Moreau 1970) that the original name was misspelt, since *erythrocerca* means red-tailed although the bird's tail is black, whereas *erythroceria* means red-hearted (from *ceros*, heart) and is highly appropriate (the original description included the phrase *pectore intense rubro*). *Nectarinia nectarinoides beveni* is this species.

IDENTIFICATION Adult male has mostly iridescent green upperparts and throat, contrasting with red and black on breast and belly, and slightly elongated tail. Female has dark but pale-tipped tail and dark throat with yellow malar stripe. **Similar species** Male Beautiful Sunbird *Cinnyris pulchellus melanogaster* (115) also has black belly, green metallic

plumage and elongated tail but has yellow patches on sides of breast. Female *C. p. melanogaster* has square-ended tail and less heavily streaked underparts. Black-bellied Sunbird *C. nectarinoides* (120) is allopatric.

VOICE Call A *jik* or *trink*, uttered in series. **Song** Brief but pleasant twitter: *tsi-si-sip-see-see-swee* or *tsi-tsi-tsi-tsi-tsi-tsi-tsi-tsip.*

DISTRIBUTION East Africa. Sudan (lower Bahr-el-Ghazal and southwards from Lake No), Ethiopia (vagrant to Lake Abaya), Democratic Republic of the Congo south to Kivu, Rwanda, Burundi, Uganda, Kenya and north-west Tanzania from Bukoba to southern side of Lake Victoria.

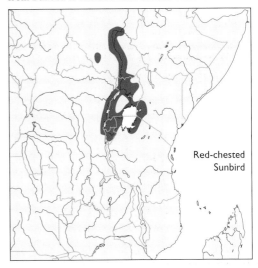

Red-chested Sunbird

HABITAT Close to rivers, marshes and lakes mostly in savanna areas but also swamp grass, forest, bushland, cultivated zones and even gardens with swimming pools. Occurs up to 1,800 m in Uganda.

STATUS Common in Uganda, especially around Lake Victoria and on its islands, and around shores of Lakes Albert, Edward and Kivu. Not uncommon in southern Sudan.

MOVEMENTS Probably sedentary.

FOOD Nectar, insects including small Coleoptera and Diptera; spiders.
Known food-plants *Erythrina* sp., *Hibiscus* sp. (nectar-robbed), *Spathodea* sp., *Tamarindus* sp.

HABITS Usually in pairs, feeding low in bushes but sometimes up in trees. Active, conspicuous and aggressive.

BREEDING Territorial. **Nest** Small, inconspicuous, elongated and egg-shaped, sometimes with entrance hole at side near top protected by porch, others with no porch; daintily woven of dry grass, down, dry leaves, bark strips, cobwebs, etc. Thickly lined throughout, almost felted, with plant down, feathers and wool. Egg-cup lined with feathers. Outside decorated with leaf skeletons, dead *Bougainvillea* flowers, *Tecoma* flowers, and other materials. Suspended 2-5 m above ground from *Bougainvillea* sp. (3 records) and *Tecoma* sp. (2), conifer branch (1). 135 x 60 mm. **Eggs** c/1-3 (?4), usually c/1. 16.5-17.8 (mean 16.9, n=4) x 10.2-12.2 (mean 11.4). White or bluish-white or dull grey with longitudinal streaks and small blotches of grey or ash-brown. **Laying months** East Africa: all months. Uganda: February–November.

DESCRIPTION

Adult male Forehead, crown and sides of head and chin to throat metallic green. Metallic bluish-green from nape to rump and on scapulars. Uppertail-coverts violet. Tail very dark brown, glossy bluish above and fringed bluish-green. Central tail feathers narrow and elongated 18-25 mm beyond rest of tail. Lores black. Narrow violet-blue band across upper breast above broader red band. Rest of underparts black. Wing very dark brown edged bluish; median and lesser wing-coverts iridescent green-blue. Underwing-coverts and axillaries black. Iris dark brown or hazel. Bill black, feet black.

Adult female Greenish-brown above, mottled dark on forehead and crown, sides of face darker. Graduated tail very dark brown, glossed bluish; outer feather with buff edge proximal to tip and on outer edge, T4 and T5 also with buff near tips of innerwebs. Thin pale yellowish-brown supercilium and broad greenish-yellow malar stripe. Abdomen pale greenish-yellow with heavy streaking on breast and upper belly. Undertail-coverts brownish-white with dark centres. Thighs dark greenish-brown. Wing very dark brown, remiges fringed greenish-yellow. Axillaries and underwing-coverts pale greenish-yellow, latter with dark centres. Iris dark brown or hazel. Bill black, feet black.

Juvenile Similar to adult female but greener. Chin and throat blacker.

GEOGRAPHICAL VARIATION None described.

MEASUREMENTS Wing 61-67 (mean 63.3, 12 males), 54-61 (mean 56.8, 11 females); **tail** 61-77 (mean 69.4, 12 males), 41-46 (mean 43.8, 11 females); **bill** 18-21 (mean 19.7, 12 males), 17-20 (mean 18.4, 11 females); **tarsus** 15-20 (mean 16.8, 12 males), 15-19 (mean 15.8, 11 females); **mass** 8.2-10.0 (mean 9.2, 57 males), 7.4-9.5 (mean 8.4, 52 females).

REFERENCES Chapin (1954), Fry *et al.* (2000).

---

120 BLACK-BELLIED SUNBIRD
Cinnyris nectarinoides　　　　Plate 41

Cinnyris nectarinoides Richmond, 1897, *Auk*, p.158, Plains east of Kilimanjaro.

Alternative name: Smaller Black-bellied Sunbird

IDENTIFICATION A smallish sunbird of arid parts of the Horn of Africa and East Africa. Male with metallic golden-green upperparts, black belly, yellow pectoral tufts and elongated central tail feathers.

Similar species Male Beautiful Sunbird *C. pulchellus melanogaster* (115) also has black belly but has more elongated tail and yellow patches on sides of red breast-patch; female has dark streaking on breast and flanks. Female Tsavo Purple-banded Sunbird *C. tsavoensis* (122) rather similar but is white below and much more heavily streaked.

VOICE Call A *tsk*, *chip* or *che*. **Song** Race *nectarinoides*: a series of 6-20 staccato *tsk*, *chip* or *che*, at a rate of 6-7 per second, leading into a short warble of rising and falling *tsi* notes finishing in an accelerating flourish. The whole sequence lasts 2-8 seconds, but usually only 2-3, and is repeated again and again with gaps of up to 12 seconds during songs of 3.5 minutes or more.

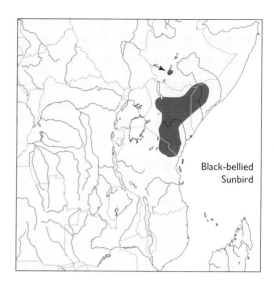

Black-bellied
Sunbird

DISTRIBUTION North-east Africa. Southern Ethiopia, Somalia, Kenya and Tanzania.

HABITAT Open, dry, thorn savannas with *Acacia* spp., and riverine vegetation in dry country.

STATUS Rare in Ethiopia, seen Lake Abaya. Uncommon in Somalia, known from upper River Juba. Locally common in Kenya, 50-1,300 m, where known from River Daua in north-east, Wajir, North Uaso Nyiro Reserve, River Tana, Kitui, Kibobo, Tsavo West National Park and, commonly, along Athi-Galana, Tivo and Tsavo rivers in Tsavo East National Park.

MOVEMENTS No information.

FOOD Insects including small Diptera and lepidopteran larvae; spiders and nectar.

Known food-plants *Acacia* sp., *Adansonia digitata*, unidentified mistletoes Loranthaceae.

HABITS Subservient to Kenya Violet-backed Sunbird *Anthreptes orientalis* (57) when feeding at Loranthaceae. Feeds high up in riverside trees.

BREEDING Nest Domed purse-shaped nest with tapering support above, side entrance usually with porch and beard, placed in low tree or shrub. Made of fine grass- and seed-heads, held together with cobweb, decorated with bark and dead leaves and lined with feathers of vegetable down. **Eggs** c/1-2; *nectarinoides*: pale olive-grey or olive-brown almost completely covered with light chocolate and with darker streaks and brighter flecks; 16-17.9 x 11.5-11.6; *erlangeri*: pale brownish-olive with medium dark olive-brown stripes and speckles, especially at the larger pole; also pale yellowish-green with swirling olive-brown striations. Resemble larks' eggs; 16.5 x 12.5. **Laying months** East Africa: April–August, November and female with egg in oviduct January.

DESCRIPTION *C. n. nectarinoides*

Adult male Head to rump and lesser wing-coverts metallic golden-green with blue reflections, bases of feathers black. Uppertail-coverts dark metallic blue, sometimes with purple fringes. Wings brownish-black, primaries browner, secondaries with faint purplish-blue gloss. Chin and throat

288

metallic golden-green, bases of feathers black. Metallic dark blue to purple band across chest above broad (13-19 mm deep) orangey-red breast-band. Yellow pectoral tufts. Rest of underparts black with some whitish streaks on flanks. Tail black above with faint glossy greenish-blue margins and indistinct glossy blue bands across feathers; central rectrices elongated 16-22 mm beyond remainder. Iris brown or black. Bill black. Feet black. **Non-breeding plumage** A male collected, Taita, August, has fresh tail feathers, rump and uppertail-coverts but rest of upperparts dull brown, with blotches of green metallic feathers. Some metallic on centre and lower throat, breast-band and rest of underparts admixed with whitish-yellow.

Adult female Upperparts dull yellowish-olive, with dark brown streaks on crown and mantle. Pale yellow streak above eye. Wings dark brown with pale yellowish outer margins to flight feathers. Tail black above with faint glossy greenish-blue margins and indistinct glossy blue bands across feathers; outer feathers broadly tipped white on inner margin and thin white strip along outer margin; innerweb of end of next pair also tipped white. Chin to throat, sides of breast and flanks pale yellow with greyish-black streaks; malar streak, centre of belly and undertail-coverts pale yellow without blackish streaks. Iris brown. Bill black. Feet black.

Juvenile Similar to adult female but remiges edged more yellowish, chin and throat all brownish-grey with pale yellow malar stripe. Breast mottled not streaked.

GEOGRAPHICAL VARIATION

C. n. erlangeri (Reichenow, 1905) (Juba River area in south-east Ethiopia, south Somalia and north-east corner of Kenya) Breast-band of males redder, less orange and less deep (12 mm); no yellow pectoral tufts. Metallic plumage much bluer (less golden-) green.

C. n. nectarinoides Richmond, 1897 (north Kenya from Guaso Nyiro east of highlands to Tsavo and Taita and north-east Tanzania) Described above.

MEASUREMENTS Wing 51-55 (mean 53.5, 13 male *nectarinoides*), 53 (male *erlangeri*), 47-49 (mean 47.8, 5 female *nectarinoides*); **tail** 54-64 (mean 54.3, 13 male *nectarinoides*), 55 (male *erlangeri*), 31-33 (mean 32.4, 5 female *nectarinoides*); **bill** 17-19 (mean 17.8, 13 male *nectarinoides*), 19 (male *erlangeri*), 17-18 (mean 17.2, 5 female *nectarinoides*); **tarsus** 14-15 (mean 14.6, 13 male *nectarinoides*), 16 (male *erlangeri*), 13-15 (mean 14.2, 5 female *nectarinoides*); **mass** 4-6 (mean 5.1, 6 male *nectarinoides*), 4 (female *nectarinoides*).

REFERENCES Fry *et al.* (2000), Mackworth-Praed & Grant (1955), Zimmerman *et al.* (1996).

---

121 PURPLE-BANDED SUNBIRD
Cinnyris bifasciatus   Plate 39

Certhia bifasciata Shaw, 1811-1812, in Stephens, *Gen. Zool.* 8, p.198, Malimba, Portuguese Congo.

Alternative names: Little Purple-banded Sunbird, Little Bifasciated Sunbird, Bifasciated Sunbird, Short-billed Sunbird

IDENTIFICATION A small sunbird. In field appears dark or metallic green contrasting with black, but at close quarters blue breast-band in combination with dark underparts aids identification.

Similar species Smaller and with shorter, less decurved bill than Mariqua Sunbird *Cinnyris mariquensis* (116), male with bluer, less green uppertail-coverts, female and juvenile less heavily streaked on the chest and belly and with less yellow, *mariquensis* tending to have a yellowish patch mid-chest. Male of eastern race *microrhynchus* has non-breeding plumage confusable with eclipse male Copper Sunbird *C. cupreus* (138) but separable by green not purple on wing-coverts. Smaller than Orange-tufted Sunbird *C. bouvieri* (125), but male also with two breast-bands, lower narrower than in *bouvieri* but best distinguishing feature is black not chocolate-brown underparts. Tsavo Purple-banded Sunbird *C. tsavoensis* (122) has shorter bill and the male has a more purplish breast-band, female usually pale-throated whereas centre of throat dusky olivaceous in *bifasciatus*.

VOICE Call A *b-r-r-r-zi* by male, female replying with *b-r-r-r*. A distinctive *tsikit-y-dik*. **Song** A high-pitched descending trill and an oft-repeated *cherr-ip-chooo*. Race *microrhynchus*: a trilled *titititititi-trooo*, sometimes followed by a short warble. Also an emphatic half-second burst of *treeee-ti-ti-tooo*, the last syllable lower and slurred, repeated every 0.5-10 seconds.

Purple-banded
Sunbird

DISTRIBUTION East and Central Africa. Gabon, Republic of the Congo, Democratic Republic of the Congo, Rwanda, Uganda, Kenya, ?Somalia, Tanzania including Zanzibar and Mafia Island, Angola, Zambia, Malawi, Mozambique, Namibia (mainly in Caprivi Strip), extreme north of Botswana, Zimbabwe, Swaziland and South Africa.

HABITAT Partial to coastal bush, mangrove swamps and riverine environments including gallery forest, but also open savanna woodland with thickets and mixed broad-leaved woodland, miombo woodland, dry forest, moist evergreen forest, cultivated zones and bushland, banana plantations, tree nurseries, grassland and gardens.

STATUS Common resident in Angola, where the commonest sunbird of the dry woodlands in the escarpment zone. Not uncommon Democratic Republic of the Congo. Locally common in Kenya and Tanzania. Uncommon in Uganda. Common in Zanzibar. Threatened in Caprivi Strip by deforestation along rivers. Widespread and common throughout northern half of Zambia, less so in south.

MOVEMENTS Migrant in Zimbabwe, moving from lowveld to highveld in April–July, breeds, and returns November–January. Non-breeding visitor to southern Mozambique, November–May, with influx of birds possibly from Zimbabwe. In Tanzania moves up into mountains in cooler season and has bred at 900 m. Appears north-east Gabon, February–May. Only appears in Durban, South Africa, in southern winter.

FOOD Nectar, seeds and insects including Diptera and termites (Isoptera); spiders taken from webs and fed to fledglings by parents. Balls of rubber latex found in stomachs. Prefers small trees and frequents *Tecoma* bushes. **Known food-plants** *Acacia* spp., *Aloe* spp. including *A. arborescens*, unidentified Cactaceae close to *Opuntia quitensis*, *Cassia singuena*, unidentified mistletoes Loranthaceae parasitic on *Acacia albida*, *Leonotis* sp., *Manihot glaziovii*, *Mimusops caffra*, *Punica granatum*, *Syzygium codatum*, *Tecoma mollis*.

HABITS Occurs singly or in pairs and associates with White-breasted Sunbirds *Cinnyris talatala* (133) and Scarlet-chested Sunbirds *Chalcomitra senegalensis* (85). Aggressive and frenetic. Maximum longevity more than 8 years 6 months. Reduces metabolism at night by 48% at constant ambient temperature of 5°C and by 55% at 25°C. Host to *Leucocytozoon nectariniae* and *Trypanosoma* sp.

BREEDING Males chase females. When nest-building, sings from top of tree (e.g. *Acacia karoo*) and picks small pieces of lichen off trees. Both parents feed nestlings, sometimes with small seeds. One nest damaged and robbed of seed-down *Mondia whytii* lining by female *C. senegalensis*. **Nest** Small, oval, pear-shaped, made of dry grass, vegetable fibres and down and held together with cobwebs; profusely covered on the outside with dead leaves and lichens, wood chips and seeds, sometimes giving unkempt appearance, but some are tidy with bits of lichen giving a scaly look to the nest, and often with beard. Lining includes feathers and seed-down of the creeper *Mondia whytii*. Suspended 1-10 m above ground e.g. at the top of *Acacia* tree or bamboo, sometimes over ant-hills or termite mounds, road or dry riverbed. Less firmly fixed than nests of *C. mariquensis*. Entrance hole very small and young birds known to use secondary openings, below the entrance, through which to beg. 100-115 mm high x 45-70 mm wide. One nest of *microrhynchus* on Zanzibar within 15 cm of a wasp's nest, another (*microrhynchus*), Kenya, very inconspicuous, beautifully felted with material from a curious brownish small woolly cocoon, well decorated with lichens, pieces of bark, masses of minute caterpillar frass, bark strips, suspended from bush twig, 2 m above ground, in scrubby grassland, strongly bound with web, finely grass-lined, and with silky plant down, feathers from *Centropus* and doves. **Eggs** Race *bifasciatus*: c/1-2; 14.5-16.2 x 10.6-11.1; pale smoky-grey, or pale fawn, streaked with darker grey and speckled and lined with black and dark grey; *microrhynchus*: c/2; 14.5-17.8 (mean 15.1, n=15) x 10.3-11.8 (mean 10.6), slightly elongated, smooth with slight gloss or oily sheen; white, slate-grey, dark greenish or purplish-grey, with a few spots, streaks and smears of varying shades of grey, purple, dark purplish-black or black, mostly at larger pole. **Laying months** Angola: May, October; juvenile April, in breeding condition (Cabinda) August; Demo-

cratic Republic of the Congo: August; East Africa: January, March–December; Kenya: July; Malawi: May, August, October; Mozambique: September–November; South Africa: November; South Africa: September–November; Tanzania: January, August; Uganda: June, August, September; Zanzibar: March–December; Zambia: January, August–November, active gonads March and July; Zimbabwe: March, June and September–December.

DESCRIPTION *C. b. bifasciatus*
Adult male Head, upperparts and lesser wing-coverts metallic green with slight golden-gloss, merging into metallic deep blue on uppertail-coverts. Remiges, median and greater coverts black with dark blue gloss. Tips of lesser and median wing-coverts metallic green. Tail very dark blue with dull metallic bluish-violet fringes on outer-webs. Chin and throat metallic green with slight golden gloss. Upper breast-band metallic purplish-blue above purplish-red or reddish-maroon chest-band (6-9 mm deep, sometimes with a few blue feathers in it). Rest of underparts, axillaries and underwing-coverts brownish-black, undertail-coverts sometimes tipped blue. No pectoral tufts. Buccal cavity of male in nuptial plumage dark brown to black or dark grey, occasionally with yellow underlay. Iris dark hazel or brown. Bill, legs and feet black. **Non-breeding plumage** Wings and tail of breeding dress retained, and some metallic feathers remain on head, mantle, throat, breast, back, rump and uppertail-coverts, together with some black feathers on abdomen. See also under *microrhynchus*.
Adult female Lacks any metallic plumage. All brown above except for narrow white stripe over eye. Ear-coverts and lores darker brown than forehead. Wings dark brown, median and greater coverts darker. Primaries narrowly edged yellowish-white. Chin and throat whitish with slight olive tinge on throat. Breast, belly and undertail-coverts pale yellow, dark streaks on breast. Tail blue-black with T5-T6 edged white, T3 and T4 edged pale grey or off-white. Axillaries white, tipped pale yellow. Underwing-coverts white with yellow wash. Buccal cavity variable from off-white to pinkish-grey or yellow. Iris brown. Bill, legs and feet black.
Juvenile Immature male has distinctive plumage, being darker brown on upperparts than adult female with black chin and throat, rest of underparts yellowish with heavy black mottling. First metallic (adult) feathers appear on lesser wing-coverts and throat. Immature female similar to adult female but darker brown above, throat greyish concolorous with breast, and lower breast and belly washed yellow. Buccal cavity of both sexes orange-yellow or rich yellow (see also under *microrhynchus*, below).

GEOGRAPHICAL VARIATION
C. b. bifasciatus (Shaw, 1811) (Gabon to Cabinda, through Democratic Republic of the Congo to western Angola including northern Malanje, Cuanza Norte, Bengo and Luanda and south to Benguela, and along the coast and inland to north-eastern Namibe and central and northern Huíla; Namibia) Described above.
C. b. microrhynchus Shelley, 1876 (includes *strophium* Clancey & Williams, 1957) (Kenya, Uganda, eastern borders of Democratic Republic of the Congo to Katanga, Zambia. Also Zambesi area of Angola in north-eastern Moxico, Malawi, Mozambique, south to eastern Zimbabwe, South Africa in eastern Transvaal and northern KwaZulu-Natal; Zanzibar; Mafia island). Male with more glossy green head and upperparts

than *bifasciatus* and maroon breast broader (8-12 mm deep), less red and more suffused with violet. Female more heavily streaked below. Bill shorter (16-20 vs 21.5-23) in both sexes. Has an eclipse plumage, with male retaining glossy wing-coverts and uppertail feathers, dark wings, blackish throat and some dark on underparts; few in breeding dress by January in Zimbabwe, most by June. Birds in non-breeding dress in Malawi, October–April. Primary moult takes c.4 months. Juvenile has bright orange gape for first five months, becoming yellow until at least 15 months old and black at 20 months.

MEASUREMENTS Wing 55-59 (mean 57.3, 10 male *bifasciatus*), 52-62 (mean 57.0, SD 1.5, 36 male *microrhynchus*), 53.5-60 (imm male *microrhynchus*), 49.5-55 (mean 52.4, 10 female *bifasciatus*), 48.5-56 (mean 52.5, SD 1.4, 11 female *microrhynchus*), 51-54 (imm female *microrhynchus*); **tail** 35-40 (mean 38.1, 10 male *bifasciatus*), 33-45.5 (mean 37.2, 43 male *microrhynchus*), 35-43 (imm male *microrhynchus*), 31-35.5 (mean 33, 10 female *bifasciatus*), 29-37.5 (female *microrhynchus*), 33-37.5 (imm female *microrhynchus*); **bill** 20-23 (mean 20.7, 10 male *bifasciatus*), 16-20.0 (mean 18.5, 18 male *microrhynchus*), 16-19.5 (imm male *microrhynchus*), 18-20 (mean 19.6, 10 female *bifasciatus*), 15.5-18.0 (female *microrhynchus*), 15.5-18.0 (imm female *microrhynchus*); **tarsus** 16-17 (mean 16.7, 10 male *bifasciatus*), 14-16 (male *microrhynchus*), 14-16 (imm male *microrhynchus*), 15-17 (mean 16.1, 10 female *bifasciatus*), 13-15 (female *microrhynchus*), 13-15 (imm female *microrhynchus*); **mass** 6-8 (7 male *bifasciatus*), 6.3-9.0 (mean 7.3, 51 male *microrhynchus*), 6.3-8.8 (imm male *microrhynchus*), 6 (female *bifasciatus*), 6.0-9.0 (mean 6.5, 18 female *microrhynchus*), 6.0-7.3 (imm female *microrhynchus*).

REFERENCES Benson (1944), Brooke (1970), Chapin (1954), Clancey (1979), Clancey & Williams (1957), Edwards (1988), Hanmer (1981, 1989), Jones (1996), Prinzinger *et al.* (1989), Sclater & Moreau (1933), Skead (1967), Tree (1991, 1997b).

---

122   TSAVO PURPLE-BANDED SUNBIRD
Cinnyris tsavoensis   Plate 32

Cinnyris bifasciatus tsavoensis van Someren, 1922, *Novit. Zool.* 29, p.196, Tsavo, Kenya.

Taxonomic note Considered by some authors to be a subspecies of *C. bifasciatus*, whose range it splits in two.

IDENTIFICATION A small sunbird; male with metallic green upperparts, narrow maroon breast-band and black abdomen.
Similar species Very similar to Purple-banded Sunbird *Cinnyris bifasciatus* (121) but has shorter bill, male lacks eclipse plumage, and breast-band is narrower (3-5 mm deep), restricted to sides or lacking, and is more purplish. Female *tsavoensis* usually pale-throated, most female *bifasciatus* have centre of throat dusky olivaceous.

VOICE Call *Chi-chi-chi-chi.* **Song** A fast *tsusitiseesee, chuchititsi-tsi-tsi-tsi-sitisee-see-see-see-chitisee* or *sitisee-see-see tseu-tseu-tseu chiti-tisiti-see-swee.*

DISTRIBUTION Juba area of Somalia, southern Ethiopia and Sudan through dry eastern Kenya to Tsavo National

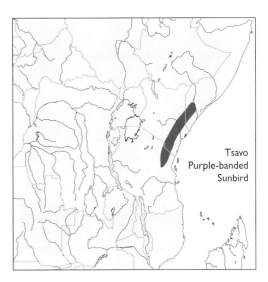

Park (East and West) and Kibwezi, and north-east Tanzania to Korogwe and Handeni.

HABITAT Dry *Acacia* and *Commiphora* savanna, and *Acacia* woodland along riverbanks and dry watercourses.

STATUS Fairly common, presumed resident, west of 46°E in southern Somalia. Also fairly common in dry woodland in Kenya e.g. Tsavo East National Park.

MOVEMENTS Apparently sedentary.

FOOD Nectar and insects.
Known food-plants *Delonix elata.*

HABITS Gleans twigs for insects and catches them in flight.

BREEDING Nest Only one described (Serle 1943). Elongated ellipse set vertically, suspended 2 m above ground, near end of slender lateral shoot of *Acacia* sp. Made of fine strips of wood fibre, grasses, dried *Acacia* sp. buds, bark, and tiny twigs bound together with gossamer, bark chiefly adhering to exterior; no feathers in nest. Opening directed away from the tree, supporting branch incorporated in fabric of upper pole of nest and small vertical offshoot traversed the posterior wall for half its length. 22 mm opening in anterior wall near upper pole of ellipse. No porch. Length of nest (excluding 30 mm of beard hanging from lower pole) 150 mm. Greatest breadth 50 mm. Greatest anterior-posterior depth 53 mm. Length of cavity 58 mm. Depth below lower lip of opening 30 mm. Nest compact. **Eggs** c/1; ovate, smooth and unglossed. Delicately and beautifully marked with pastel shades of grey. Ground palest grey, ashy shell-marks form suffusions, blotches and spots which are more condensed around the large end. Superimposed on them are a few scattered fine spots and speckles of grey-brown. 15.4 x 10.6. **Laying months** Kenya: October.

DESCRIPTION
Adult male Upperparts to rump, median and lesser wing-coverts, chin and throat iridescent green. Rump and uppertail-coverts also metallic but more bluish. Tail very dark brown, slightly glossed above and edged metallic green. Narrow (2 mm deep) breast-band violet above maroon chest-band, also narrow (3-5 mm deep). Rest of underside black. Wing black. Underwing-coverts and axillaries black. Iris black. Bill and legs black.

Adult female Greyish-green above, tail darker and slightly glossy. T4-T6 tipped white, outer feather also with white on outer margin. Narrow brownish-white supercilium. Sides of face greyish-brown. Underparts pale brownish-white, with yellow tinge below breast, which is streaked greyish-brown. Wing dark brown, edged olive except median and lesser wing-coverts which have greyer tips. Underwing-coverts and axillaries off-white. Iris black, Bill and legs black.

Juvenile Resembles adult female but chin and throat darker with pale malar stripes and abdomen more strongly barred dark brown.

GEOGRAPHICAL VARIATION None described.

MEASUREMENTS Wing 54-57 (mean 55.2, 9 males), 48-51 (mean 49, 4 females); **tail** 38-41 (mean 40.7, 9 males), 33-35 (mean 34.3, 4 females); **bill** 16-17 (mean 16.8, 9 males), 16-17 (mean 16.5, 4 females); **tarsus** 14-15 (mean 14.6, 9 males), 14-15 (mean 14.5, 4 females); **mass** 6.3-7.6 (mean 7.0, 10 males), 6.0-6.8 (mean 6.5, 5 females).

REFERENCES Clancey & Williams (1957), Fry *et al.* (2000), Lack (1985), Serle (1943).

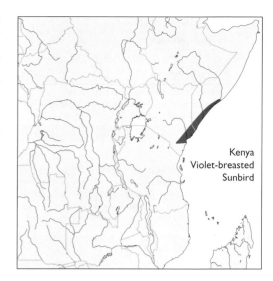

Kenya Violet-breasted Sunbird

---

123 KENYA VIOLET-BREASTED SUNBIRD
Cinnyris chalcomelas   Plate 32

Cinnyris chalcomelas Reichenow, 1905, *Vög. Afr.* 3., p.482, Kismaju, southern Somaliland.

Alternative name: Violet-breasted Sunbird (note: not to be confused with Kenya Violet-backed Sunbird *Anthreptes orientalis*, 57)

IDENTIFICATION Medium-sized sunbird. Male has metallic green upperparts and broad purple breast-band above a black abdomen.

Similar species Larger than Pemba Sunbird *Cinnyris pembae* (124) and Purple-banded Sunbird *C. bifasciatus* (121) (wing 61.5-63.5 vs 51.5-53 and 51-60 repectively) and longer-billed but shorter-tailed; male lacks maroon band present in Tsavo Purple-banded Sunbird *C. tsavoensis* (122) and *C. bifasciatus*, and throat is greenish-blue not golden-green. Head and upperparts greener, less glossy or bluish, than *pembae*, with no bluish-violet on lesser wing-coverts. Female paler and less streaked below than *tsavoensis* and *bifasciatus* and with more obvious supercilium than in female *tsavoensis*.

VOICE Call A *chut* and *chip*. **Song** A trilling *chrrrrrrrrssss wwwizzzzlllle* and a slower series of notes finishing with *chee-per-chichi-woo-per-chichi-chee-dzurr.*

DISTRIBUTION Southern Somalia, eastern Kenya.

HABITAT Thorn savannas in coastal lowlands from Juba valley to Mombasa and Tsavo.

STATUS Locally fairly common resident in Somalia south of 3°N. Uncommon Kenya.

MOVEMENTS May wander inland.

FOOD Probably nectar and insects.
Known food-plants *Acacia* sp., *Hibiscus* sp., *Millingtonia* sp.

HABITS More relaxed and less frenetic than most of its congeners, making more deliberate moves and sometimes remaining motionless for long periods. Up to 100 seen together at *Acacia* sp. flowers.

BREEDING Nest built by female only. **Nest** Undescribed. **Eggs** Unknown. **Laying months** Somalia: December, nest-building April, July, October.

DESCRIPTION
Adult male Upperparts iridescent emerald-green. Tail black, with slight blue sheen above. Lores blackish. Chin and throat iridescent blue-green. Broad (7-8 mm deep) band of violet on upper breast. Abdomen black. Median and lesser wing-coverts iridescent green. Wing blackish. Underwing-coverts and axillaries black. Iris dark brown. Bill and legs black. **Non-breeding plumage** Male like adult female but retains blue-black remiges and tail and iridescent wing-coverts: back, crown and cheeks grey-brown with patches of iridescent green. Grey line 3 mm broad stretching from base of bill to lower chest and grey patches amongst black of lower abdomen.

Adult female Greyish-brown above with light green tinge, uppertail-coverts darker. Tail very dark brown, slightly glossy above, some rectrices and especially outer one with whitish tips. Brownish-white supercilium. Sides of face brown. Underparts brownish-white with slight streaking on throat, breast and flanks. Yellow tinge to mid-rib. Wing dark greyish-brown edged greyish. Underwing-coverts dark brown, axillaries off-white. Bill and legs black.

Juvenile Male like adult female but black throat-streak with central part iridescent green. Iridescent green shoulder-patches. Some black on lower belly. Outer edges of inner primaries broadly edged white.

GEOGRAPHICAL VARIATION None described, but until recently was treated as subspecies of *C. pembae.*

MEASUREMENTS Wing 60-63 (mean 61.1, 8 males), 53-58 (mean 55.9, 6 females); **tail** 39-43 (mean 41.0, 7 males), 32-38 (mean 34.7, 6 females); **bill** 18-21 (mean 20.0, 8 males), 18-20 (mean 18.9, 6 females); **tarsus** 16-19 (mean 17.0, 8 males), 14.5-17 (mean 15.5, 6 females); **mass** 7.0-95 (mean 8.5, 4 males), 7 (female).

REFERENCES Ash & Miskell (1998), Clancey & Williams (1957), Fry *et al.* (2000).

124 PEMBA SUNBIRD
Cinnyris pembae   Plate 39

Cinnyris pembae Reichenow, 1905, *Orn. Monatsb.* 13, p.180, Pemba island, near Zanzibar.

Alternative names: Pemba Island Sunbird, Pemba Violet-breasted Sunbird

IDENTIFICATION The only purple-banded sunbird on Pemba Island.
Similar species Differs from Kenya Violet-breasted Sunbird *Cinnyris chalcomelas* (123) by smaller size (wing average 9 mm shorter and bill 2 mm shorter in male, wing 6 mm shorter in female) and in voice and plumage (patches of sheen on upperwing-coverts violet not green). Female plain below whereas female *chalcomelas* slightly streaked.

VOICE Call Distinctive, loud and repetitive *tslink-tslink-tslink* or *tslunk*, unlike any call of *C. chalcomelas*, uttered from bare exposed branches of tall trees. **Song** A crescendo of 6-15 *tslinks* with some *tsk*, culminating in a frantic warble of accelerating rising and falling notes lasting 1.5-2 seconds. The warble is sometimes elided into long bursts for more than a minute, without the introduction.

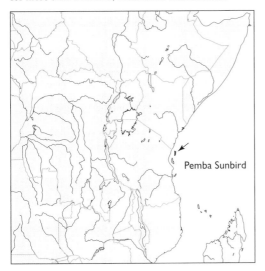

Pemba Sunbird

DISTRIBUTION Pemba island, off south-east Tanzania.

HABITAT Many habitats including towns and villages. Equally common in tropical moist forest dominated by *Quassia* (*Odyendea*) *zimmermannii*, coral rag forest dominated by *Manilkara sansibarensis*, *Mimusops obtusifolia* and *Diospyros consolatae*, coastal rag scrub dominated by *Acacia* spp., *Commiphora lindensis* and *Sorindeia madagascariensis*, plantations of clove *Syzygium aromaticum* and of rubber *Hevea brasiliensis* and farmland.

STATUS Common and widespread throughout Pemba island and on smaller off-shore islands, but listed as near-threatened by Collar *et al.* (1994) owing to restricted range.

MOVEMENTS Probably sedentary.

FOOD Nectar and fruits. Feeds on small creamy-white berries of *Flueggea virosa* by jabbing into them to extract and swallow small segments; smaller berries plucked and taken whole.

Known food-plants *Carica papaya, Cocos nucifera, Flueggea virosa, Hibiscus* sp., *Manihot esculenta, Musa* sp., *Phoenix reclinata, Syzygium aromaticum.*

HABITS Only sings during breeding season.

BREEDING Territorial. Males aggressive towards each other in breeding season. **Nest** Bag or purse-shaped nest suspended 1-2 m up from shrub or amongst foliage; thick-walled with side entrance, lined with fluffy down from seeds of *Imperata cylindrica*. **Eggs** c/2. Greenish-white background obscured by streaks and patterns of ashy-brown in a variety of shades. **Laying months** May–January.

DESCRIPTION
Adult male Upperparts, chin and throat and median wing-coverts iridescent green with blue reflections, especially on uppertail-coverts. Tail black with iridescent blue-green edges. Glossy violet band on upper breast above black abdomen. Wing black, greater wing-coverts edged iridescent green, but larger outer lesser wing-coverts iridescent green, smaller ones purple. Underwing-coverts and axillaries black. Iris dark brown. Bill and legs black. Moults from breeding dress to breeding dress, December–June, after breeding.
Adult female Greenish grey-brown above. Tail greyish-brown with dark blue gloss above, edged dark olive, T3-T5 with white tips, outer feather with white patch at tip of innerweb and outerweb edged white. White supercilium. Sides of face slightly darker brownish-olive than rest of upperparts. Below plain unstreaked pale creamy or pale yellow. Wing dark greyish-brown, edged pale yellowish. Underwing-coverts and axillaries white.
Juvenile Resembles adult female but chin and throat darker, with broad whitish malar stripe. Underparts mottled grey. Iridescent plumage of male first appears on throat and breast as it moults into immature plumage which sometimes includes some metallic bluish-violet on chest and metallic tips to head and body feathers.

GEOGRAPHICAL VARIATION None, but *C. chalcomelas* formerly considered to be a subspecies of *C. pembae*.

MEASUREMENTS Wing 51.5-54 (mean 53, 8 males), 48, 50 (2 females); **tail** 31-36 (mean 33.5, 8 males), 29, 30 (2 females); **bill** 16-18 (mean 17.3, 8 males), 16, 18 (2 females); **tarsus** 14-16 (mean 15.0, 8 males), 15, 16 (2 females); **mass** no data.

REFERENCES Archer & Parker (1993), Archer & Turner (1993), Catry *et al.* (2000), Clancey & Williams (1957), Fry *et al.* (2000), Pakenham (1979).

125 ORANGE-TUFTED SUNBIRD
Cinnyris bouvieri   Plate 30

Cinnyris bouvieri Shelley, 1877, *Monog. Nectariniidae*, p.227, pl.70, Landana Enclave of Cabinda.

Alternative names: Bouvier's Sunbird, Bouvier's Orange-tufted Sunbird

IDENTIFICATION Small sunbird with long, slightly curved bill. Male with all metallic plumage except on remiges, belly and upper throat. Female drab olive above, more yellowish and slightly streaked below, especially on throat.

293

Similar species About the same size as Purple-banded Sunbird *Cinnyris bifasciatus* (121), male of which also has two breast-bands. Lower one on *bouvieri* broader than in *bifasciatus* but best distinguishing feature is chocolate-brown not black underparts of *bouvieri*, although in poor light they still appear black. Purple forecrown, orange-yellow pectoral tufts and lack of blue sheen to metallic feathers also diagnostic, and similarly distinguish *bouvieri* from the larger Mariqua Sunbird *C. mariquensis* (116). Female difficult to separate from other species including Bates's Sunbird *C. batesi* (137) but straightish bill, dark on throat and slight malar stripe helpful. Tail is glossy black lacking olivaceous edges, outer feather paler with whitish outer margin and tip.

VOICE Call A *cheep* or *ziet* and *chip-ip*. **Song** A plaintive *tswee*, then a louder *tsi*, followed by a short warble ending in characteristic *tsi-pu, tsi-pu, tsi-pu, tsi-pu, tsi-pu, tsi-pu tsi* or *chieta-chieta-chieta-chit*. Bursts of *tsi-pu* sometimes preceded and/or followed by trill of *tr-tr-tr-tr-tr...* or by typical sunbird warbling twitters of rapid rising and falling notes. 4-second bursts of *tsi-pu, tsi-pu...* may be repeated every 5 or 6 seconds for 2 minutes or more.

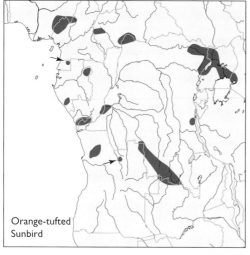

Orange-tufted Sunbird

DISTRIBUTION Central Africa. Obudu and Mambilla plateaus and Gahaka-Gumti Game Reserve, Nigeria, northern Cameroon, Central African Republic, Equatorial Guinea (Rio Muni), Gabon, Republic of the Congo, Democratic Republic of the Congo (edge of Congo forests and savannas of Congo west to Lualaba, Kasai, north-west Katanga at Sandoa, lower Congo), Angola from Cabinda south to Cuanza Norte, northern Malanje, adjacent Lunda Norte and northern Lunda Sul, Zambia (Zambezi rapids, northern Mwinilunga and River Mwombezhi in Solwezi District), Uganda, Kenya (Kakamega forest) and ?Rwanda.

HABITAT Mostly grassland, with bracken, thistles and other flowering species, and rocky country at high altitudes (1,300-2,000 m) in Cameroon, but also open parts of woods in savanna, shrubs and orchard-bush there. Lowland areas in Uganda including forest edge, scrub and forest patches, 700-1,800 m. Savanna around primary forest patches in Angola. Savanna and plantations in Democratic Republic of the Congo and up to 1,700 m in the Ruwenzoris. Edges of evergreen forest and perhaps also in rich miombo woodland in Zambia.

STATUS Generally uncommon but locally common in suitable habitat. Common at edge of montane forest, Nigeria. Common in Cameroon at 1,350-2,050 m in the northern highlands. Uncommon resident in Angola. Not uncommon in Gabon. Rare in Uganda where reported as not uncommon in the Entebbe region in 1930s and scarce near Kampala in 1960s; only one record since (Kifu forest, March 1972). Only known in Kenya since 1965, where not uncommon in Busia District and recorded Kakamega forest, 1,700 m.

MOVEMENTS Unclear; probably some sedentary and others migrate, perhaps as intra-African migrants. Recorded north-east Gabon, April and October. May make seasonal movements in Uganda, since few if any records in Lake Victoria region during height of rainy season.

FOOD Insects including small beetles. Coagulated rubber latex, from *Manihot glaziovii* found in stomachs; nectar. **Known food-plants** *Acanthus* sp., *Albizia zygia*, *Erythrina* sp., *Manihot glaziovii* and leguminous shrubs.

HABITS Usually seen singly but sometimes with other species of sunbird and forms assemblies at flowering trees, July–September, Uganda.

BREEDING Nest Domed, purse-shaped, made of fine grasses and gossamer, lined with plant-down, suspended <1 m above ground from thistle or higher from bush or tall grass stem. **Eggs** c/2, undescribed. **Laying months** Angola: breeding condition March; Cameroon: October; Democratic Republic of the Congo: breeding condition October; Kenya: c/2, Kakamega forest, November; Uganda: enlarged gonads November; Zambia: March.

DESCRIPTION
Adult male Forehead to eyes metallic purple, ear-coverts green with copper tinge, rest of upperparts metallic green, but uppertail-coverts bluer. Remiges, median and greater coverts dark brown. Tail black, middle feathers with dark blue gloss and metallic green fringes on both webs, and all others except outer pair with metallic green fringes on outerwebs. Chin and upper throat matt black, bordered with metallic purple. Rest of throat and upper breast metallic green. Narrow band of purple across chest above a broader band of dark maroon. Pectoral tufts orange above, tipped yellow, bright lemon-yellow below. Rest of underparts, axillaries and underwing-coverts dark brown. Feathers on inner edge of wing tipped metallic green. Lores black. Iris dark brown. Bill and feet black. Some evidence for the eclipse plumage described by Bannerman (1948) but convincing proof awaited.
Adult female Upperparts uniform mouse-brown, slight olive tinge on rump. Ear-coverts darker brown than head. Some have pale eye-stripe. Chest appears streaked with yellow interspersed with the grey-brown background. Belly pale yellow. Upper tips of tertials fringed off-white and outer edges of secondaries fringed buff. Tail black, outer feathers with white tips and margins. Undertail-coverts pale yellow. Underwing-coverts and axillaries pale yellow and white. Lores black. Iris brown. Bill black, feet black.
Juvenile Immature male like adult female but throat and breast dusky, belly less yellow.

GEOGRAPHICAL VARIATION *C. b. tanganyikae* Ogilvie-Grant, 1907 described from Ngombe in Kasai, but no longer considered valid.

MEASUREMENTS Wing 50-60 (mean 56.8, 11 males), 47-

56 (mean 52.9, 11 females); **tail** 35-42 (mean 39.3, 11 males), 29-37 (mean 34.2, 11 females); **bill** 18.5-23 (mean 21.1, 11 males), 16-24 (mean 19.6, 11 females); **tarsus** 16-18 (mean 16.9, 11 males), 15-17 (mean 15.7, 11 females); **mass** 7.0-10.0 (mean 8.4, 8 males).

REFERENCES Bannerman (1948, 1951), Benson (1966), Benson & Irwin (1966), Brosset & Erard (1986), Chapin (1954), Lippens & Wille (1976), Serle (1950).

---

126 PALESTINE SUNBIRD
Cinnyris oseus   Plate 30

Cinnyris osea Bonaparte, 1856, *Compt. Rend. Acad. Sci. Paris* 42, p.765, "Plaines de Jéricho," Palestine.

Alternative names: Orange-tufted Sunbird, Northern Orange-tufted Sunbird, Chad Orange-tufted Sunbird (*decorsei*)

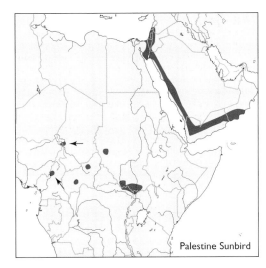

Palestine Sunbird

IDENTIFICATION A very small, fat-bodied sunbird, difficult to distinguish in field. Decurved bill, broad-ended wings, straight tail. Blue forehead and broad purplish-blue breast-band and black belly, but male looks all black at distance. Multi-coloured iridescent plumage visible at close range. When displaying or in hand, orange-red and yellow pectoral tufts of male distinctive. Female has dark wings and blackish tail contrasting with dull body. Non-breeding birds of both sexes and juvenile olive-grey above, dusky white below.

Similar species Male Orange-tufted Sunbird *Cinnyris bouvieri* (125) has slightly longer bill and maroon breast-band above non-metallic black abdomen. Female *oseus* is duller with less yellow below than female *bouvieri*, without streaking, and has bluish-green uppertail-coverts. Allopatric Shining Sunbird *C. habessinicus* (127) is 20% larger with gloss of male greener and broad red breast-band visible at close quarters.

VOICE Call Race *decorsei*: a weak *chip-ip-ip-ip-p*; *oseus*: *tsk* and a loud *tchoo-twit* or *tooo-weee* or *weet-to*, sometimes repeated again and again. *tiu, che-ew, ftift, seep seep, seep tchink tchink, pee-pee, dzee* and *teweeit te-weeit*. Male *seep*, answered by female *chew-it*. Alarm calls *tzik-tzik, che-VEEK* and *chaWEE*. **Song** Race *decorsei*: a metallic *chwing-chwing-chwing...* or *chwee-chwee-chwee...*; *oseus*: a high-pitched burst of *tsk, tsk, wee, wee, wee, tsk-choo, choo, choo*, lasting 1.5-2 seconds and repeated every 3-4 seconds. Also a typical sunbird warbling of high-pitched rising and falling notes in a rapid delivery. Much variation with reports of: (1) *tsi tsi tser-tser-tser-tser-tser* with first 2 notes slow, rest fast and lower-pitched recalling Blue Tit *Parus caeruleus*; (2) 2 loud whistles then rapid trill of *tweet-tweet chee-e-e-e-e-e*; (3) *soweett sooweet sooweet* and trill like start of song of Wren *Troglodytes troglodytes*; (4) fast high-pitched *dy-vy-vy-vy-vy-vy*; (5) rising *tveeit- tveeit- tveeit*; (6) accelerating *veet-tji veet-tji veet-tji*, culminating in trill. May mimic other species, recalling Lesser Whitethroat *Sylvia curruca*, Goldfinch *Carduelis carduelis* and *Hippolais* sp. warblers.

DISTRIBUTION North-central Africa. Savannas from Lake Chad, Cameroon, Central African Republic to Darfur, Ubangi-Shari, southern Sudan and upper Uelle of Democratic Republic of the Congo (migrant visitor) and north-west Uganda (Mt Kei) and Arabian peninsula

and south-west Palaearctic (Turkey, Jordan, Palestine, Egypt, Israel, Lebanon, Syria, Saudi Arabia, Yemen, Oman).

HABITAT Savannas, in both dry open grassland and rocky areas. Gardens, orchards, bushy riversides, rocky valleys and thick vegetation from sea-level to highlands, where found in *Juniperus* sp. woods. Up to 1,500 m in Jordan in groves of cypress *Cupressus* sp. In Yemen, not at sea-level but at 250-3,200 m.

STATUS Uncommon. In Jordan, common breeder in Rift margin highlands south to Petra, with small numbers wintering in Wadi Araba, rare in Wadi Rum and unknown at Azraq; some increases following settlements. Jordan populations 4-8 pairs per km^2 and 2-4 per km^2 when breeding. Restricted to south of Lebanon and extreme south-west of Syria. Recorded in extreme south of Turkey, but not since 1940s. Uncommon in Tihamah coastal plains of Saudi Arabia, but common breeding resident above 1,500 m in south-west Saudi Arabia. Common 250-2,800 m in north Yemen. Increasing in Israel since 1940s, possibly in response to intensive planting of gardens. Uncommon in Egypt where first noticed 1979 and first breeding record in 1984. Fairly common in southern Sudan. Uncommon Democratic Republic of the Congo.

MOVEMENTS *C. o. oseus*: resident, local wanderer and short-distance migrant; said to be present in Lebanon only from end July to early February, but once bred there, May (Kumerloeve 1960). Altitudinal movements occur in Jordan, where common at 800-1,400 m from early March. Nomadic during winter in Israel. Winter visitor to Syria. Apparently resident in Egypt and Saudi Arabia, but only reaches 1,600-2,000 m in Yanbu area of latter in winter. Disperses to higher altitudes after breeding in Oman and enters semi-desert there in late December to late February. *C. o. decorsei*: moves up to higher altitudes (2,000-3,000 m) in Jebel Marra, Sudan, to breed, September–January, departing March or April. No Sudanese specimens at NHM outside September–March period. Also, only present in Uelle grasslands, north Democratic Republic of the Congo, 8 October to March, where adults arrive with second-year birds, all in non-breeding condition, but then stay to breed January–February. Non-breeding quarters unknown.

FOOD Nectar, small fruits and ripe dates *Phoenix* sp., small seeds, spiders and insects including Diptera and larvae. *C. o. oseus* bores holes into flowers of *Malvaviscus arboreus* (an exotic from Brazil), when stimulated by protruding stylus. Pollinator of *Plicosepalus acaciae* and known in Arabic as *sultan el-zahar*, the king of the flowers. Nectar-robs e.g. *Hibiscus* sp.

Known food-plants *Acacia* sp., *Aloe* sp., *Anagyris foetida*, *Anchusa* sp., *Bauhinia* sp., *Begonia* sp., *Bougainvillea* sp., *Capparis* sp., *Citrus* sp., *Clerodendrum* sp., *Cordia* sp., *Convolvulus* sp., *Cytisus* sp., *Echinops* sp., *Euphorbia* sp., *Hibiscus* sp., *Jasminum* sp., *Lavandula* sp., *Lonicera etrusca*, unidentified mistletoes Loranthaceae, *Lupinus* sp., *Lycium* sp., *Malvaviscus arboreus*, *Moringa peregrina*, *Nicotiana* sp., *Otostegia* sp., *Phoenix* sp., *Plicosepalus acaciae* (parasite of *Acacia* sp. and *Ziziphus* sp.), *Punica* sp., *Pyrostegia ignea*, *Robinia* sp., *Tecoma capensis*, *Thevetia* sp., *Yucca* sp., *Zinnia* sp., *Zygophyllum* sp.

HABITS *C. o. oseus*: tame. In non-breeding season, usually solitary but forms small groups of up to 15 birds to feed. Restless, often flicking wings and tail. Reported as both shy and tame, nesting in habitations. Flight fast; flits from flower to flower with rapid wing-beats. Hovers in front of flowers to feed and makes sallies for flying insects. Hops. Roosts on branches. Group of 6 seen bathing in early morning.

BREEDING Pair-bonds formed and territories (0.3-14.3 ha) defended for nesting and feeding, but males promiscuous. Defence of territories may cease in non-breeding season. Extra-pair copulations regular with up to at least 6 males following receptive female for as long as 4 days before laying begins; thus males try to guard their females; but often unsuccessful. Amongst 25 pairs tested by DNA, 48% of the females had extra-pair young and 36% of the broods had at least one such chick. Indeed 23% of the 88 chicks tested were sired by extra-pair males. Intruders inspect rival's nest, perhaps to gauge if laying has started or not. Males sing from tree-tops or electric wires and in flight between perches. Also leave song-posts to attack intruding males. Rivals perform singing duels side by side until loser flies off being chased by winner. Interloping male interfered with female and attacked it when trying to feed nestling. Later presumed responsible for death of 2 young from this nest; 3 other cases of infanticide, including an experimental demonstration, in support of hypothesis that it serves to create a vacant territory for the invader (Goldstein *et al.* 1986). Courtship display involves male approaching female, exposing pectoral tufts, moving up and down whilst holding head erect and neck outstretched, tail spread and wings drooped. Only female builds nest, taking 8.4 (SD 2.7) days to complete, but heavy rain may prolong building to 21 days. Eggs laid daily in early morning. Only female incubates (for 13.1, SD 0.6, days) beginning with penultimate egg, leaving nest 4 times per hour during daylight. Only female broods young but both parents feed young and remove faecal sacs, with female making 2-3 times more feeds than male. Male effort greater with large broods. Nest-guarding rates higher the larger the brood, with male rates higher than females'. Experimental manipulation, adding weights of 0.3g to female tails, led to decreased feeding rates by females and partly compensatory increases by males but reduced nest-guarding by them. Removal of males caused females to increase provisioning rates for young but not enough to compensate for loss of mate, and without increase in nest-guarding effort but this and faecal sac removal rates

maintained at normal levels. Small nestlings fed insects and spiders, but never nectar (Markman *et al.* 1999) although other observations have suggested that after about day 11, regurgitated nectar is offered. On fledging, 14-21 days (mean 15.6, SD 1.6) after hatching, birds try to catch insects immediately and attempt to feed on nectar 5 days after leaving nest, but parents continue to feed them for up to 14 days. Fledglings return to roost in nest for 7-10 days after fledging, being led back by female. Double- or triple-brooded. Hatching rate 67%, fledging 47% of eggs laid; c/3 most successful, fledging 1.5 young. Egg losses attributable to infertility, desertion, egg disappearance, breakage and early death of embryo; chick losses caused by predation, disturbance by people, infanticide and starvation. Jay *Garrulus glandarius* is a predator of nests. Nests judged unsatisfactory may be dismantled and the materials used to construct elsewhere.

Nest Race *decorsei*: composed of dry thistle-leaves, lined with thistle-down, suspended from low bush, often <1 m from ground. Another, *Prinia*-like, was woven amid dead branches, a leaf formed the best part of one side, with woven of bits of dry withered cotton and much decorated with yellow bark flakes, apparently from *Gameza*. Race *oseus*: untidy pear-shaped nest composed of well-woven soft material, grasses, stems, roots, leaves, plant down, bark, paper and polythene shreds, bound with hair, wool and spiders' webs. Beard of leaves and twigs. Lined with feathers, wool, leaves and bits of paper. Height 180 mm, width 80 mm. Entrance hole on side near top, 25 mm in diameter, with short porch. Beard of leaves and twigs. Suspended 0.5-10 m above ground from bush or branch, e.g. of *Quercus* sp. or thorn-bush, or on verandahs or porches. One built inside trouser leg of pair of shorts left hanging to dry! Also builds inside houses. May have 2-3 broods per year, sometimes re-using nest. **Eggs** c/1-3 (mean 2.4, SD 0.74, for *oseus*); *decorsei*: c/2. 15 x 11, ovate, dull white, covered with fine grey or grey-brown spots, mostly at larger pole; *oseus*: subelliptical or long subelliptical, smooth and moderately glossy. White, very finely speckled reddish-brown on pale grey, yellowish-green or white background, with indistinct small violet-grey or brownish-grey spots and blotches in circle at larger pole. 15.2-16.2 (mean 15.4, n=8) x 10.5-11.4 (mean 11.2); weight 0.99 g (SD 0.06). **Laying months** Arabia: February, March, May and courtship September; Egypt: June; Israel: February–September on coastal plain, March–June at Eilat; Jordan: April, May; Lebanon, May. Sudan: Darfur, c/2 December, Jebel Marra, 2 nestlings December.

DESCRIPTION *C. o. decorsei*

Adult male Bill longish and fine, straight basally, then distinctly decurved. Purple forehead merging with metallic steel-blue and green on crown and nape. Uppertail-coverts dark metallic blue, rest of upperparts and lesser wing-coverts metallic green, appearing blue in some lights. Remiges, median and greater coverts dark brown. Lores black. Chin black, throat metallic purple with green gloss in lower part, cheeks metallic green. Breast violet with goldish reflections. Rest of underparts black without metallic sheen. Pectoral tufts orange-red, yellow underneath. Undertail-coverts black, tipped metallic blue when new. Underwing-coverts black. Bill, legs and feet black. Iris black or dark brown. **Non-breeding plumage** Undescribed for *decorsei*; *oseus* has upperparts like adult female but wings and tail as in breeding plumage, underparts dull black with iridescent patches, whitish near tail.

Adult female All upperparts dull brown, rump with slight olive wash. Wing-coverts darker brown than body. Tail black with blue gloss and metallic green fringes when new. All underparts light brown, belly washed yellow. Axillaries pale yellow. Underwing-coverts greyish-white with yellow and brown inter-mixed. No pectoral tufts. Iris dark brown. Bill and feet black.

Juvenile Young hatch blind and naked with some down; mouth orange-red, gape flanges pale yellow. Immature male as adult female but belly brighter yellow, gaining metallic feathers from age of 2-3 months. Males moulting into breeding plumage have much white interspersed with black on underparts, and are blotchy with metallic green patches above. Immature female as adult female but more olive above and more yellow below. Nestlings are dark olive-brown or greyish mouse-brown above with yellow breast and belly.

C. oseus oseus adult post-breeding moult partial involving head, body, lesser and median upperwing-coverts, tertials and tail, shortly before remiges moult in adult pre-breeding moult is complete, with primaries lost descendantly starting with inner primaries. Post-juvenile moult is partial as in adult non-breeding. First pre-breeding moult is partial or complete, starting immediately after completion of post-juvenile moult so birds can be in breeding plumage when only 2-3 months old.

GEOGRAPHICAL VARIATION

C. o. decorsei Oustalet, 1904 (includes *butleri* Sclater & Mackworth-Praed, 1918) (Lake Chad east to Lado district of Sudan, Bahr el Ghazal and Darfur; Cameroon, Central African Republic, migrant visitor to extreme north-east Democratic Republic of the Congo, north-west Uganda) Described above.

C. o. oseus Bonaparte, 1856 (Palestine, Egypt, Israel, Jordan, Lebanon, Oman, Saudi Arabia, South Yemen, Syria, Turkey) Differs from *decorsei* by being larger (male wing 54 mm, male bill 20 mm), and by a distinct metallic sheen on lower breast and belly, below violet-metallic patch, on adult male. Female paler and greyer below and greyer, less olive above.

MEASUREMENTS Wing 48-56 (mean 52.1, 14 male *decorsei*), 52-57 (mean 54.5, SD 1.23, 18 male *oseus*), 47-52 (mean 49, 5 female *decorsei*), 49-53 (mean 51.0, SD 1.27, 16 female *oseus*); **tail** 31-38 (mean 34.7, 14 male *decorsei*), 36-40 (mean 38.0, SD 1.41, 18 male *oseus*), 29-33 (mean 31.8, 5 female *decorsei*), 32-36 (mean 34.6, SD 1.09, 12 female *oseus*); **bill** 14.5-18.7 (mean 16.7, 13 male *decorsei*), 17-21.8 (mean 20.2, SD 1.01, 16 male *oseus*), 13.5-18 (mean 16.6, 5 female *decorsei*), 16-20.5 (mean 18.9, SD 0.96, 16 female *oseus*); **tarsus** 13-16 (mean 14.1, 14 male *decorsei*), 14.5-16.0 (mean 15.3, SD 0.40, 17 male *oseus*), 13-15 (mean 14.0, 5 female *decorsei*), 14.4-15.2 (mean 14.8, SD 0.29, 11 female *oseus*); **mass** mean 7.6 (SD 0.60, 8 male *oseus*), mean 6.8 (SD 0.73, 12 female *oseus*); mean mass of *oseus* hatchlings 0.79, SD 0.15, 80% of initial egg mass; mean mass of *oseus* fledglings 5.5-7.25 (mean 6.2, SD 0.46, 82% of adult male mass and 91% of adult female mass).

REFERENCES Andrews *et al.* (1999), Baha el Din (1985), Chapin (1954), Cramp & Perrins (1993), Eisikowitch & Nahari (1982), Gallagher & Woodcock (1980), Goldstein *et al.* (1986), Goldstein & Yom-Tov (1988), Harrison (1975), Kirwan *et al.* (1998), Kumerloeve (1960), Markman *et al.* (1995, 1996, 1999), Paz (1983), Rahmani *et al.* (1994), Sclater & Mackworth-Praed (1918), Zilberman *et al.* (1999).

127 SHINING SUNBIRD
Cinnyris habessinicus   Plate 31

Nectarinia (*Cinnyris*) *habessinica* Ehrenberg in Hemprich and Ehrenberg, 1828, *Symbolae Physicae.*, *Av.*, fol.a, pl.4, "ex Ora Habessiniae Ad Eilet," i.e., Eilet, Eritrea.

Alternative name: Abyssinian Sunbird

IDENTIFICATION A medium-sized sunbird. Male golden-green with a black belly and red breast-band, the conspicuousness of which varies with subspecies. Female told by uniformly pale or dark grey underparts.

Similar species Nominate male easily confused with male Mariqua Sunbird *Cinnyris mariquensis osiris* (116) unless red breast-band or yellow pectoral tufts seen; purple iridescence on crown also distinctive. Female *habessinicus* has uniform underparts but female *mariquensis* has heavy dark mottling on throat, breast and flanks. Juvenile resembles juvenile *mariquensis* but black throat-patch does not continue to reach breast and flanks as a series of large blackish spots, and lacks yellow wash on underparts. Male Palestine Sunbird *C. oseus* (126) may be confused with male race *hellmayri* but is smaller, lacks red breast-band and has orange-red and yellow pectoral tufts. Female separable from female Beautiful Sunbird *C. pulchellus* (115) and Black-bellied Sunbird *C. nectarinoides* (120) by larger size, longer, straighter bill and plain underparts without yellow.

VOICE Call A sharp *tsp, tsp, tsp* with notes uttered separately or a less harsh *tss tss tss* all run together, similar to call of Pygmy Sunbird *Hedydipna platura* (64). **Song** An attractive warble, usually delivered from top of thorn-tree, consisting of quick series of quite harsh *ch ch ch ch ch*, untypical of sunbirds, followed by two or three drawn-out sequences of *chee-chee-chee*, repeated again and again. Female produces a low subsong from amongst foliage.

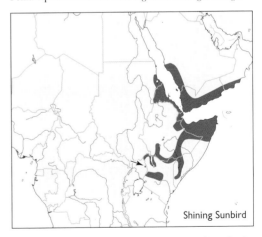

Shining Sunbird

DISTRIBUTION North-east Africa and Arabian Peninsula. Sudan, Ethiopia, Eritrea (migrant visitor), Djibouti, Somalia, Saudi Arabia, Oman, Yemen, Kenya, Uganda.

HABITAT Rocky or sandy broken country with thorn-bush, especially dry riverbeds with flowering trees and bushes, but also montane forest. In Ethiopia not found above 1,800 m. Also cultivated areas and gardens.

STATUS Very common in Red Sea hills of Sudan. Not uncommon in Ethiopia. Uncommon in northern Kenya. Common localised breeder 600-1,500 m in south-west Saudi Arabia, where fairly common in Tihamah coastal plains down to 120 m. Common 100-2,200 m in North Yemen.

MOVEMENTS Some seasonal drifting occurs in relation to flowering patterns of food-plants.

FOOD Nectar. Insects (including Coleoptera, Diptera, Hemiptera, Hymenoptera, Isoptera and Lepidoptera) and spiders often sought amongst *Usnea* sp. attached to juniper trees.
Known food-plants *Acacia* sp., *Aloe* spp., *Calotropis procera*, *Capparis* sp. including *C. decidua*, *Delonix elata*, *Ficus* sp., unidentified mistletoes Loranthaceae, *Salvadora persica* (especially its fruits), *Phoenix dactylifera*, *Salvia* sp., *Stereospermum* sp., *Ziziphus spina-christi*.

HABITS Singly, in pairs and in groups of up to 75. Active, feeding on flowers by probing from adjacent perch and by hovering in front of flowers. More tolerant of conspecifics than other sunbirds and four or five may feed together in the same tree. Host to *Haemoproteus* sp.

BREEDING Territorial. At start of display, male rears himself up with feathers held down and shuffles quickly along branch towards female, followed by swaying of body from side to side and sudden expansion of feathers and fanning of pectoral tufts. Female usually ignores advances, continuing to feed until forced to take off with male in pursuit. Male display sometimes interrupted by sudden vertical flight and return to original perch, followed by another burst of song. Nest built by female but male may accompany her when building. Both sexes feed the single nestling. May be double-brooded. **Nest** An oval or pear-shaped structure, about 100 mm long and 70 mm wide, with well-marked porch, suspended by bulky support at top of dome, from middle of a sloping branch in a thorny tree e.g. *Acacia* sp., shrub or *Euphorbia* sp., usually 3-4 m high but sometimes only 1-2 m high, and occasionally as much as 7 m up in a tree. May be exposed or hidden but round entrance faces into vegetation. Nest appears to have silver sheen as made of silvery-grey plant fibres with strands of withered grass, dead leaves and insect cocoons woven together with cobwebs and insect silk. Lined with orange-tinted plant wool from seeds of *Ipomoea* or paler *Calotropis* and feathers. **Eggs** c/1-2; *habessinicus*: white background with several large blotches of pale greyish-brown and a few scrawls of black at largest end. 19.5 x 15; *turkanae*: 19-19.5 x 13.5-14; slightly pointed ovals with little gloss; ground colour white, sometimes with zone of pale mauve-grey superimposed with blackish markings at larger end. **Laying months** Arabia: March–July; Egypt/Sudan: December–January, Gebel Elba; Eritrea: December–February along coast; April–June in highlands; Ethiopia: April; Kenya: April–July; Somalia: February–May.

DESCRIPTION *C. h. habessinicus*
Adult male Top of head shiny purple, rest of upperparts, chin to upper breast, lesser and median wing-coverts iridescent green, tinged gold; bluer on uppertail-coverts. Tail black with slight violet sheen, central rectrices edged metallic green. Narrow blue-green band above broad scarlet breast-band 7.5-11 mm deep. Apart from thin dark iridescent blue band below scarlet, rest of abdomen black. Pectoral tufts yellow. Wing blackish tinged violet. Underwing-coverts and axillaries black. Iris dark brown. Bill black. Legs black.

Adult female Pale greyish-brown above, with darker uppertail-coverts. Tail very dark brown with slight bluish sheen. Outer two pairs with tips whitish on innerwebs. Chin grey-white. Rest of underparts light brownish-grey, slightly mottled on throat and breast, belly tinged yellow, undertail-coverts greyish-white with dark streaks in centres. Wing dark greyish-brown, edged buff. Underwing-coverts whitish, darker at bases, axillaries light brown. Iris dark brown. Bill black. Legs black.
Juvenile Both sexes resemble adult female, but chin white, merging on throat into a black patch which extends onto breast, bordered on each side by line of whitish feathers. Male throat often blacker than female's. Immature tends to have darker centres to breast feathers, giving mottled effect. Immature plumage also similar to adult female's but chin to neck metallic green with traces of red chest-band.

GEOGRAPHICAL VARIATION
C. h. alter Neumann, 1906 (Somalia north of 7°N west to Ethiopia, up to 1,800 m) Breast-band slightly broader, female darker and bill larger than *habessinicus* (exposed culmen 22.5-25 in male *alter*, 18.5-20.5 in male *habessinicus*). Red breast-band of adult male 9-13 mm wide with well marked fringe of metallic bluish or violet-green. Female with greenish-orange breast-band often present.
C. h. habessinicus (Ehrenberg, 1828) (Red Sea province of Sudan, Eritrea up to 180 m, Ethiopia south to Harar and Yavello) Adult male has relatively narrow, deep red breast-band 7.5-11 mm wide, fringed below with a line of metallic bluish feathers. Adult female intermediate in colour between pale *turkanae* and darker *hellmayri* and *kinneari* and lacks ill-defined greenish-orange breast-band often present in adult female *alter*.
C. h. hellmayri Neumann, 1904 (Saudi Arabia, Yemen) Male has red breast-band obscured by subterminal greenish-blue bars; metallic crown blue not violet; female darker than *alter*.
C. h. kinneari Bates, 1933 (western Saudi Arabia from Asir to Hejaz) Male bill shorter (exposed culmen 18.5-20 vs 21.5-23) and red breast-band less obscured by bluish subterminal bars than in *hellmayri*, latter giving appearance of narrow red collar below metallic throat. Female very dark, more blackish-brown, making light fringes contrast more than in other forms, giving scaly appearance.
C. h. turkanae van Someren, 1920 (south-east Sudan, northern Uganda east over northern Kenya to upper River Juba in Somalia, west and south-west of southern Ethiopia; usually below 600 m and not above 1,200 m) Male with red breast-band broader (14-19 mm wide) and paler than in nominate, with little or no metallic fringe. Female paler below than any other race.

MEASUREMENTS Wing 69-72 (mean 70.4, SD 1.01, 28 male *alter*), 64-71 (mean 66.2, SD 1.03, 20 male *habessinicus*), 70-75 (mean 72, SD 1.82, 7 male *hellmayri*), 70-75 (mean 72, SD 0.59, 5 male *kinneari*), 66-69 (mean 67.1, SD 0.92, 23 male *turkanae*), 61-64 (mean 62.6, SD 0.9, 12 female *alter*), 56-62 (mean 59.3, 18 female *habessinicus*), 62-66 (mean 64.4, SD 1.26, 5 female *hellmayri*), 64, 65 (2 female *kinneari*), 58-60 (mean 58.8, SD 0.87, 11 female *turkanae*); **tail** 48-56 (mean 51.9, SD 2.01, 28 male *alter*), 44-51 (mean 46.4, SD 1.18, 20 male *habessinicus*), 51-56 (mean 54.4, SD 1.76, 7 male *hellmayri*),

51-57 (mean 54.6, SD 2.3, 5 male *kinneari*), 46-51 (mean 48.3, SD 1.55, 23 male *turkanae*), 43-49 (mean 45.3, SD 2.34, 12 female *alter*), 37-42 (mean 40.0, 18 female *habessinicus*), 44-49 (mean 46.4, SD 2.51, 5 female *hellmayri*), 49, 50 (2 female *kinneari*), 39-41 (mean 40.9, SD 0.53, 11 female *turkanae*); **bill** 21-24 (mean 22.7, 10 male *habessinicus*), 19-23 (mean 20.8, 10 female *habessinicus*); **exposed culmen** 22.5-25 (mean 23.5, SD 0.8, 28 male *alter*), 18.5-20.5 (mean 19.5, SD 0.67, 20 (male *habessinicus*), 21.5-23.0 (mean 22.3, SD 0.62, 7 male *hellmayri*), 18.5-20.0 (mean 16.4, SD 0.22, 5 male *kinneari*), 20-22 (mean 21.0, SD 0.67, 12 female *alter*), 21-23 (mean 21.9, SD 0.52, 23 male *turkanae*), 18-19 (mean 18.4, SD 0.44, 8 female *habessinicus*), 20-21.5 (mean 20.9, SD 0.54, 5 female *hellmayri*), 17.5, 19 (2 female *kinneari*), 29.5-21.5 (mean 20.4, SD 0.61, 11 female *turkanae*); **tarsus** 17-18 (mean 17.7, SD 0.24, 28 male *alter*), 15.5-17 (mean 15.8, SD 0.74, 20 male *habessinicus*), 16.5-17.0 (mean 16.8, SD 0.24, 7 male *hellmayri*), 17-17.5 (mean 17.2, SD 0.26, 12 female *alter*), 15-16 (mean 15.4, 8 female *habessinicus*), 16 (5 female *hellmayri*), 15.5, 16 (2 female *kinneari*), 16-16.5 (mean 16.3, SD 0.23, 11 female *turkanae*); **mass** 9.5-11.5 (mean 10.5, 16 male *habessinicus*), 9.0-11.5 (mean 10.0, 8 male *turkanae*), 7.5-9.5 (mean 8.6, 29 female *habessinicus*), 7.0-11.0 (mean 9.1, 13 female *turkanae*).

REFERENCES Archer & Godman (1961), Gallagher & Woodcock (1980), Rahmani *et al.* (1994), Williams (1954).

---

128 SPLENDID SUNBIRD
Cinnyris coccinigaster   Plate 40

Certhia coccinigastra Latham, 1801, *Lath. Ind. Orn.* Suppl. in *Gen. Synop. Birds*, Suppl. 2, p.35, Africa; restricted to Senegal by Grote, 1924, *Orn. Monatsb.* 32, p.71.

IDENTIFICATION Large sunbird. Adult male appears black at a distance but good views reveal the spectacular iridescent colours which give the species its name. Purple head, green back and wing-coverts, steel-blue reflections on mantle and rump, blue and scarlet breast, black belly and blue undertail all contribute to the distinctive multi-coloured appearance. Immature male has dark throat. Female dark brownish-grey above, yellow with grey and brown streaks below.
Similar species Male separated from male Superb Sunbird *Cinnyris superbus* (130) and Johanna's Sunbird *C. johannae* (129) by combination of violet-purple head, throat and upper breast and red and blue on lower breast above black belly and blue undertail-coverts. Female has dark bars on white throat, light streaking on underparts and belly plain yellow, whereas belly of *C. johannae* is heavily streaked with white chin and female *C. superbus* has orange undertail-coverts and distinct supercilium. Female and immature told from those of Red-chested Sunbird *C. erythroceria* (119) by larger size and longer bill, and from those of Scarlet-chested Sunbird *Chalcomitra senegalensis* (85) by paler, yellower underparts and less curved bill.

VOICE Call Clear flute-like calls, sparrow-like chirping and loud sequences of plaintive notes, repeated frequently especially in flight; *chee-iip, chip, tschup* and *choo*. Alarm call: *djew-djew-djew…* **Song** A series of 6-9 clear whistles gradually declining in strength, sounding as *chip-chee-cho-*

cho-choo-choo-choo-choo, or *pititew-tew-pitew-pitew-pitew*. Also a staccato song of 6-8 notes described as *"Oh–what–a–spLENdid–bird-I-AM"* (Serle 1956). Local variations maintained for up to 3 years, but apparently without habitat correlations or geographical differences although songs were more similar to those sung by the singers' neighbours than to those of more distant birds (Grimes 1974, Payne 1978, Schnell *et al.* 1985).

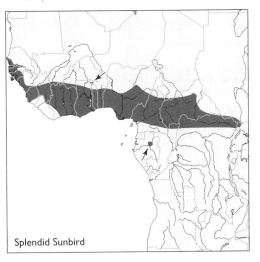

Splendid Sunbird

DISTRIBUTION West and Central Africa. Senegal, Gambia, Guinea-Bissau, Guinea, Sierra Leone, Liberia, Côte d'Ivoire, Ghana, Togo, Benin, Nigeria, Mali, Burkina Faso, Sudan, Cameroon, Central African Republic, Gabon, Democratic Republic of the Congo (Dramba in north-east), Angola (Cabinda, but no recent records) and ?Uganda (northern West Nile Province, but presence dubious).

HABITAT Savannas, secondary forest, forest edge, riversides, farmland, coastal thickets, inselbergs, scrubland, plantations, residential areas with adequate vegetation. In West Africa, occurs from the coast to about 10°N, except in mature forest. Reaches 1,500 m in Cameroon.

STATUS Common throughout most of its range. Density of 14 singing males per km^2 in Ghana. Seasonally common in Nigeria.

MOVEMENTS Some resident. Others migratory, in general travelling into northern savanna areas in the wet season, May–October, in West Africa, retreating south for the drier period (December–April); but in Liberia recorded only in north, October–January, and in Burkina Faso recorded November–May. Appears north-east Gabon, September–November.

FOOD Nectar, seeds and insects including bees and winged ants; catches termites on the wing and picks alates (e.g. those of *Pseudacanthotermes* cf. *militaris*) off leaves in thickets; spiders. Rubber latex found in stomachs, sometimes almost filling them.
Known food-plants *Berlinia grandiflora, Bombax* sp., *Caesalpinia pulcherrima, Carica papaya, Elaeis guineensis, Manihot glaziovii, Milletia thonningii, Parkia* sp.

HABITS Sing throughout the year except when moulting. Conspicuous, often perching on tops of bushes and shrubs or bare trees, 10 m or more high sometimes, and calling as it flies between them. Active bird when feeding, sometimes in groups of 12 or more in same tree, and joins other species of sunbirds at flowering trees. Hovers in front of tree-trunks in search of insects and at flowers and leaves. Probes bark of oil-palm *Elaeis guineensis* and feeds on their oozing sap. Type host of *Haemoproteus sequeirae*.

BREEDING Territorial. Song used by male to establish and maintain territory. Sings at dawn and repeatedly until late afternoon, from habitual perches. Males seen at top of tree crouching forward, bowing and advancing towards each other before taking off. Courtship involved male making erratic song-flight, alighting on branch 10 m up, being joined by female 1-2 m distant who held body stiff with neck stretched up and forward, with depressed tail and drooping wings. After a few seconds she shuffled towards the male but he took flight. Only females build, incubate and rear the young. Male may sing beside nest and accompany female on searches for nest material. One nest took 30 days to be built. May be double-brooded. **Nest** Exquisite domed pouch made of fibre, leaf skeletons, grass stems and bark, held together with cotton seed down, lined profusely with down, and bound by gossamer to a suspending twig or branch, 2-3 m above ground. Distinct porch but no beard. Usually well concealed amongst foliage. **Eggs** c/1-2. 18.0-19 (mean 18.3, n=6) x 12.3-15.3 (mean 13.1). Smooth, unglossed. Slightly pointed. Varied in colour. Some blotched and mottled very dark brown, mainly at larger pole, others with pale grey background, evenly marked with streaks and speckles of grey and brown. **Laying months** Gambia: July–October; Ghana: March, April, June, September, October, December, dependent young March–May, July, October, November; Nigeria: March–June, dependent young October; Senegal: September, October; Sierra Leone: September, October; Togo: nest-building March, April and August.

DESCRIPTION
Adult male Forehead to centre of crown and ear-coverts metallic purple. Hindcrown metallic steel-blue, merging into metallic golden-green on lower neck, mantle and back. Lores black. Lesser wing-coverts and scapulars metallic green, rest of wing black. Rump metallic golden-green merging into deep steel-blue on uppertail-coverts, some of which have purple fringes. Tail black with narrow metallic steel-blue or green fringes on outerwebs. Cheeks and throat metallic purple, merging with metallic steel-blue on breast. Latter appears barred as feathers have scarlet fringes. Long pale yellow pectoral tufts. Steel-blue band below breast. Lower breast, belly, flanks and thighs black. Undertail-coverts black with broad metallic steel-blue tips. Axillaries and underwing-coverts black. Margin of wing with metallic steel-blue border. Iris dark brown. Bill dark brown or black. Legs and feet blackish-purple or black. **Adult female** Forehead grey. Crown and neck brownish-grey with olive tinge. Lores black. Indistinct white stripe above eye. Upperparts brown with olive wash. Uppertail-coverts brown with olive fringes. Remiges and wing-coverts dark brown edged olive-green. Inner secondaries with pale tips. Tail blackish-brown, lightly glossed green, all feathers except central pair narrowly tipped white. Chin and throat white. Underparts pale yellow, mostly appearing mottled as feathers have grey centres, but middle of belly purer yellow. Axillaries pale yellow. Underwing-coverts white, some tipped yellow. Iris dark brown. Bill, legs and feet greenish-black. Plumage of female variable, becoming darker above and below with wear (Serle 1957).

Juvenile Immature male similar to adult female but lacks grey forehead and upperparts browner and ashier, less olive. Chin and throat greyish-black, becoming glossy-purple on subadult, other underparts pale yellow with some dark mottling on breast. Bill dark brown. During moult to adult, metallic on throat appears first, followed by seemingly random appearance of metallic feathers on body, giving bird scruffy look. Immature female darker brown on crown than adult female with less olive discernible and throat-patch less extensive than juvenile male. Underparts duller yellow, breast darker and more heavily mottled.

GEOGRAPHICAL VARIATION None described. Grote (1924) considered that females from Guinea-Bissau were greener above than those from Cameroon, and Chapin (1954) suspected that birds from the eastern end of the range might prove to be subspecifically distinct. Fry *et al.* (2000) reported that males in Côte d'Ivoire have glossy yellowish-green mantle and back, greenish-blue reflections to breast-band and greenish-blue undertail-coverts (a form which they also illustrated), but such characters are also observed in other parts of the species's range.

MEASUREMENTS Wing 66-73 (mean 71.1, 10 males), 61-67 (mean 64.4, 11 females); **tail** 39-46 (mean 43.2, 10 males), 35-38 (mean 37.0, 11 females); **bill** 23-28 (mean 25.7, 10 males), 22-26 (mean 24.4, 11 females); **tarsus** 16-19 (mean 17.1, 10 males), 16-17 (mean 16.6, 11 females); **mass** 12.3, 15.3 (2 males).

REFERENCES Blancou (1939), Chapin (1954), Fry *et al.* (2000), Grimes (1974), Grote (1924), Korb & Salewski (2000), Payne (1978), Schnell *et al.* (1985), Serle (1950, 1956, 1957), Walsh *et al.* (1990).

129 JOHANNA'S SUNBIRD
Cinnyris johannae   Plate 40

Nectarinia johannae J. & E. Verreaux, 1851, *Rev. Mag. Zool.* [Paris], ser. 2,3, p.514 [=314], Gabon.

Alternative names: Madame Verreaux's Sunbird, Johanna Sunbird

IDENTIFICATION A large forest species with very long bill and short tail. Male has distinctive colouring of purple and bright red below, with crown, head, throat and back metallic green. Female unmistakable, being the only sunbird in West Africa with heavily streaked underparts. **Similar species** Adult male told from Superb Sunbird *Cinnyris superbus* (130) by crown metallic green concolorous with rest of upperparts, underparts brighter red, throat green above and purple at base, and presence of (yellow) pectoral tufts. Female has white chin and throat, very heavily streaked underparts.

VOICE Call Race *fasciatus*: *wit* or *wit-wit-wit-wit-wit*; a plaintive descending whistle *tsioooo*, lasting nearly 0.5 seconds; *johannae*: *wit*, *wit-wit* and an emphatic 0.25-second *tswee*. **Song** Race *fasciatus*: a very complex high-pitched, somewhat whistling warble of rising and falling notes in a twittering delivery lasting more than a minute.

DISTRIBUTION West and Central Africa. Guinea, Sierra Leone, Liberia, Côte d'Ivoire, Ghana, Benin, Nigeria, Mali,

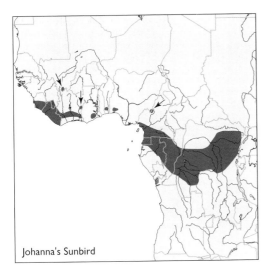

Johanna's Sunbird

Cameroon, Equatorial Guinea (Rio Muni), Gabon, Republic of the Congo, Democratic Republic of the Congo and Angola (Cabinda).

HABITAT Upper and middle strata of mature forest, in old secondary forest and along tracks and in clearings, but also, rarely, in gardens or cocoa plantations. Mostly in lowland humid southern forests in West Africa, but some records as far north as 8°19'N.

STATUS Common in Liberia but uncommon throughout rest of its range, rarer than both Splendid Sunbird *C. coccinigaster* (128) and *C. superbus*. Rare in Ghana. Rare in Nigeria, where only known from two records, one near Lagos, other at Sabon Gida, Gongola State. Widespread but uncommon, Gabon, where densities c.3-4 pairs per km². Uncommon resident in Cabinda. Scarce in Democratic Republic of the Congo.

MOVEMENTS Probably sedentary.

FOOD Insects including small caterpillars, spiders, pollen and nectar (confirmed by George Bates who tasted sweet stomach liquids from a specimen).
Known food-plants Unidentified mistletoes Loranthaceae, *Syzygium congolense*. Searches for invertebrates in *Usnea*. Fruits of *Macaranga assas* and *M. barteri*.

HABITS Usually seen singly at the top of a forest tree or in groups of 3-5 birds. Seldom ventures below the canopy layer. Usually 30-50 m in mature forest, but comes lower (>10 m) at edges and along riverbanks. Active, moving constantly from tree to tree, perching on branches <20 cm in diameter. Joins mixed-species flocks in upper strata of forests e.g. with Little Green Sunbird *Anthreptes seimundi* (60), Green Sunbird *A. rectirostris* (61), Blue-throated Brown Sunbird *Cyanomitra cyanolaema* (75) and Buff-throated Sunbird *Chalcomitra adelberti* (81). Probes flowers, forages for insects amongst leaves, shrubs and *Usnea*, and sallies for flying insects. Males seen performing group displays, May, Gabon, and December, Liberia. Host to feather mite *Anisodiscus dolichogaster*.

BREEDING Nest 220-300 mm long. Untidy structure made of fibrous inner bark of dead trees or green moss and lichen, held together by black fungus fibres (?*Marasmius*), lined with stiff palm fibres, attached to pinnate palm frond close to midrib or to liana, suspended 2-35 m high. Dead leaves and loose streamers forming ragged beard on exterior create illusion of rubbish. **Eggs** c/1-2; very pale blue, boldly spotted with red-brown, mostly at blunt end; *fasciatus*: 20.5 x 14-15 mm. **Laying months** Republic of the Congo: nest-building January; Democratic Republic of the Congo: indirect evidence of breeding February–July; Gabon: nest-building November; Ghana: July; Côte d'Ivoire at nest May, juvenile male May, nest-building January, February; Liberia: May, nest-building March, May, June; Sierra Leone: nest March.

DESCRIPTION *C. j. fasciatus*
Adult male Upperparts from forehead and crown to uppertail-coverts brilliant metallic golden-green. Lesser and median wing-coverts also brilliant metallic golden-green, other wing-coverts and remiges black. Lores black. Tail black with bluish-purple or plum-coloured gloss, narrowly edged metallic green if fresh. Cheeks, chin and upper throat brilliant metallic golden-green; lower throat and upper breast metallic purple. Middle and lower breast and upper flanks dark non-iridescent crimson-red. Upper of middle breast feathers with metallic purple subterminal band. Large lemon-yellow pectoral tufts. Belly, thighs, vent, undertail-coverts, axillaries and underwing-coverts black. Iris dark brown. Bill black. Feet black with yellowish soles.
Adult female Upperparts brownish-olive, rump feathers brown with olive margins. Narrow superciliary stripe, throat and cheeks to chin cream, chin and throat with fine dark brown streaks. Lores, ear-coverts and sides of neck dark olive. Remiges dark brown. Breast to flanks and belly pale olive-yellow. All underparts strongly streaked dark olive-grey, most heavily on breast and flanks. Upperwing dark greyish-brown, remiges narrowly edged olive, tertials and coverts narrowly edged pale olive. Tail blackish-brown tipped brownish-white, more broadly on T5-6. Undertail-coverts yellowish-white streaked with black. Axillaries pale yellow. Inner underwing-coverts white, those on margin of wing brown with white mottling. Iris dark brown. Bill black; feet black.
Juvenile Immature male resembles adult female and has striped underparts, but greyish streaking is denser and sides of throat, flanks and breast usually dusky.

GEOGRAPHICAL VARIATION
  C. j. fasciatus (Jardine & Fraser, 1852) (Sierra Leone to Benin and ?southern Nigeria, where subspecies unconfirmed) Described above.
  C. j. johannae (J. & E. Verreaux, 1851) (?southern Nigeria and southern Cameroon to Democratic Republic of the Congo at mouth of Congo, east to Kasai, upper Congo and Kivu) Underparts of male darker red than in *fasciatus* (deep crimson not almost scarlet). Female darker above and below.

MEASUREMENTS Wing 62-67 (mean 65.1, 10 male *fasciatus*), 70-72 (mean 71.6, 7 male *johannae*), 60-65 (mean 62, 10 female *fasciatus*); **tail** 32-37 (mean 35.7, 10 male *fasciatus*), 40-41 (4 male *johannae*), 30-35 (mean 32, 10 female *fasciatus*); **bill** 28-33 (mean 31.8, 10 male *fasciatus*), 31-37 (mean 35.7, 7 male *johannae*), 27-33 (mean 30.7, 10 female *fasciatus*); **tarsus** 16-18 (mean 16.7 10 male *fasciatus*), 17 (4 male *johannae*), 16-18 (mean 16.5, 10 female *fasciatus*); **mass** 12.6-14.7 (mean 13.7, 11 male *fasciatus*), 11-15 (mean 12.4, 3 female *fasciatus*).

REFERENCES Bannerman (1948), Gray (1986), Holman (1949), Zumpt (1961).

130 SUPERB SUNBIRD
Cinnyris superbus **Plate 40**

Certhia superba Shaw, 1811-1812, *Gen. Zool.* 8, p. 193, Malimba, Portuguese Congo.

IDENTIFICATION A large long-billed and short-tailed sunbird, the male beautiful and unmistakable if seen clearly, with metallic blue crown, iridescent green back, iridescent violet and blue throat, and maroon breast, but may appear all black in poor light or when silhouetted in the tree-tops. Female recognised by large size, olive and yellow colouring, unstreaked breast and orange-red wash on undertail-coverts. Young male similar to female.
Similar species More of a forest bird than the superficially similar Splendid Sunbird *Cinnyris coccinigaster* (128) from which it can be told by its larger size, longer bill and dark red underparts below the breast, metallic green or blue crown (violet in *coccinigaster*). Male Johanna's Sunbird *C. johannae* (129), also restricted to forests, appears similar but has brighter red below and crown, head, throat and back metallic green all over (*superbus* has steel-blue crown contrasting with golden-green back and blue or purple throat). Female *superbus* has long pale supercilium and yellower underparts than either *coccinigaster* or *johannae* (latter heavily streaked below). Orange undertail-coverts distinguish female *superbus* from both other species and longer bill also separates *superbus* from *coccinigaster*.

VOICE Call Race *ashantiensis*: a loud *chip* and *weeet*. **Song** Noisy jingling, recalling "*which to do?*" Race *ashantiensis*: a 3-6 note song varying on *weeto-choh-choo-weet*; *nigeriae*: similar with sequences involving *weet-choo weet-choo witchoo witch*; *weetch-doo, weetch-doo*; *superbus*: similar sequence of *tweetcho-weet-choo* or just a 3-note *tweet-choh-weet*.

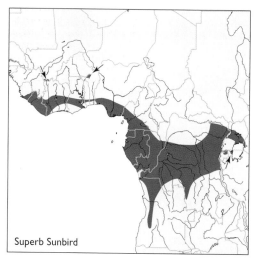

Superb Sunbird

DISTRIBUTION West and Central Africa. Mainly West African, but reaches Kenya, Uganda and Tanzania. Recorded from Guinea, Sierra Leone, Liberia, Côte d'Ivoire, Ghana, Togo, Benin, Nigeria, Mali, Burkina Faso, Cameroon, Central African Republic, Equatorial Guinea, Gabon, Republic of the Congo, Democratic Republic of the Congo, Uganda, Kenya (Kakamega forest, Mumias and Busia Districts), Tanzania (Bukoba) and Angola.

HABITAT In the canopy and in fairly dense undergrowth along streams in primary and secondary forest and coffee plantations, forest edges and clearings in wooded lowlands. More often in secondary habitats than *C. johannae*, frequenting gallery forests, savannas, mature mangroves, villages, tree nurseries, overgrown cultivations and bush near forest, seldom venturing more than 10 m away from forest edge. Reaches upper forest boundary at 1,400 m, Mt Nimba, Liberia, and to similar height at base of Ruwenzoris, but does not reach montane forest.

STATUS Not uncommon in forests. Usually rarer than Splendid Sunbird but commoner than Johanna's. Common, Liberia. Not uncommon in Ghana, Togo and Nigeria. Widespread and common, Gabon, at densities of 8-10 pairs per km². Locally common resident in Angola. Fairly common resident in Lake Victoria area, Uganda below 1,500 m.

MOVEMENTS Probably resident.

FOOD Nectar, confirmed by George Bates who tasted sweetness in stomach contents; insects including ants and midges; spiders; small green seeds. Catches chironomid midges in the air and hovers in front of food-plants.
Known food-plants *Berlinia grandiflora, Bombax* sp., *Carica papaya* (young fruit buds), *Citrus limon, C. sinensis, Erythrina abyssinica, E. indica, Markhamia* sp., *Musa* sp., *Ochthocosmus africanus* (fruits), *Spathodea* sp.

HABITS Usually seen singly or in pairs, sometimes in family parties. Timid, easily disturbed, but attacks own reflection in windows. Often feeds from flowers at tops of tall forest trees. Some territoriality in relation to flowering, maintained by males calling from tops of tall trees. Can feed while hovering in front of a flower, also leaf-gleans and sallies. Sometimes clings to branches like a creeper (*Certhia* sp. or *Salpornis* sp.), even facing downwards. Forages in the lower strata of trees at edges of clearings, and feeds at banana flowers in gardens. Flight strong, fast, undulating and with unpredictable zig-zags.

BREEDING Males may begin to breed before attaining full plumage. Display involves singing and rapid movements with wings stretched out. Nest construction, by female only, may take about a month but one built in 24 hours. Incubation by female only but male helps feed nestlings. **Nest** Loosely constructed untidy structure of dried grass or *Usnea*, concealed amongst foliage and suspended 2-10 m above ground from (e.g.) banana tree by pad (150-300 mm wide) of dried grass and fibres bound around horizontal branch of tree, or from climbing rose in open on a lawn near forest patch, or from bamboo, *Trema* sp. or *Harungana* sp., or from high-tension electric wires. Nest itself domed with side entrance near top, porch with lip; 300 mm from top to bottom, with loose trailing beard hanging for another 300-600 mm below, composed of fine dry grasses, fibres, strips of banana bark, dead leaves, finely shredded broad-leaved grasses, *Usnea*, moss and decorated with lichen, moss and dead leaves. Lining of fine grasses, fibres, banana bark or seed-down. At distance looks like untidy bunch of dead grass hanging from branch. **Eggs** Race *ashantiensis*: c/1. 18.0-20.8 (mean 19.4, n=6) x 12.5-15.0 (mean 13.6); *buvuma*: 18.7-21.5 (mean 20.6, n=4) x 13.9-15.0 (mean 14.5); *nigeriae*: 20.0 x 14.7; *superbus*: c/1-2. 20-21.5 x 14-15. Creamy-white or pale bluish-white, glossy, with grey, dark slate or purplish-black specks and blotches, sometimes concentrated at blunt end. **Laying months** Angola: December, in breeding condition August–

September; Cameroon: February, July, October, November; Democratic Republic of the Congo: probably breeds July–december; Gabon: October–March; Ghana: February, November, nest-building October, November, juveniles August; Liberia: dependent young November; Nigeria: July; Republic of the Congo: April; Togo: nest-building April; Uganda: March–May, July–September, nest-building February, April.

DESCRIPTION *C. s. superbus*

Adult male Forehead and crown dark metallic blue-green, appearing steel-green in some lights; nape to uppertail-coverts lighter, metallic golden-green or bronzy bluish-green. Metallic green stripe above eye, bordering crown. Ear-coverts and cheeks bronze. Wing, except for metallic green lesser and median coverts, black. Chin metallic purple, throat and upper breast deep metallic blue, also appearing purple in some lights. Rest of underparts, except for black middle and lower belly and thighs, dark red. No pectoral tufts. Axillaries, underwing-coverts and undertail-coverts black, latter with dark red tips. Lores black. Iris dark brown. Bill and feet black.

Adult female Crown and upperparts greyish-brown with olive wash. Broad yellowish-white stripe above eye from lores to behind blackish-brown ear-coverts. Lesser wing-coverts greyish-brown with yellow suffusion, rest of coverts and wing dark brown, remiges with light yellow or olive margins. Uppertail-coverts olive-green. Tail blackish-brown with white ends, except on central pair. Chin yellowish-white. Rest of underparts greenish-yellow, occasionally with brown mottling on breast, these feathers sometimes with reddish-orange tips. Undertail-coverts reddish-orange. Axillaries and underwing-coverts yellowish-white. Iris dark brown. Bill black, feet dark grey.

Juvenile Young male as female but slightly larger, some with green tinge on back. First adult colours appear on lesser wing-coverts, followed by others in seemingly random fashion giving birds untidy appearance. Flank feathers last to moult into adult dress.

GEOGRAPHICAL VARIATION

C. s. ashantiensis Bannerman, 1922 (Sierra Leone to Togo and ?Benin) Both sexes smaller than nominate (male wing 67-74, bill 26-29 vs 72-83, 28-33), male with the metallic cap extending less far back (not reaching nape).

C. s. buvuma van Someren, 1932 (north and northeast Democratic Republic of the Congo [Upper Congo], Uganda and Kenya) Slightly darker below than nominate and male upperparts darker, purer (less golden-) green. Larger; crown-patch sometimes stretches further back than in nominate.

C. s. nigeriae Rand & Traylor, 1959 (southern Nigeria) Male brighter and clearer red below than nominate.

C. s. superbus (Shaw, 1811) (Cameroon and Gabon to north Angola, south through Uíge to Cuanza Norte and along the escarpment through Cuanza Sul to Chongoroi in Benguela, and east through northern Malanje to northern Lunda Norte, east to Democratic Republic of the Congo at Kasai and south-west Katanga at Kasaji) Described above.

MEASUREMENTS Wing 67-75 (mean 70.6, 10 male *ashantiensis*), 77-83 (male *buvuma*), 72-79 (mean 74.8, 10 male *superbus*), 62-67 (11 female *ashantiensis*), 67-72 (mean 69.7, 10 female *superbus*); **tail** 40-45 (30 male *ashantiensis*), 45-51 (mean 46.7, 10 male *superbus*), 35-41 (11 female

ashantiensis), 39-47 (mean 42.7, 10 female *superbus*); **bill** 26-32 (mean 31.2, 10 male *ashantiensis*), 28-37 (mean 35.3, 10 male *superbus*), 26-30 (11 female *ashantiensis*), 26-37 (mean 35.3, 10 female *superbus*); **tarsus** 19-21 (30 male *ashantiensis*), 19-22 (mean 19.8, 10 male *superbus*), 18-19 (11 female *ashantiensis*), 19-21 (mean 19.8, 10 female *superbus*); **mass** 13.8-14.7 (mean 14.3, 3 male *ashantiensis*), 17-19 (mean 18.2, 5 male *buvuma*), 18 (male *superbus*), 13.2 (female *ashantiensis*), 17-20.6 (mean 18.2, 3 female *buvuma*), 15.4 (female *superbus*).

REFERENCES Bannerman (1948), Chapin (1954).

131 RUFOUS-WINGED SUNBIRD
Cinnyris rufipennis　　　　　　　　Plate 36

Nectarinia rufipennis Jensen, 1983, *Ibis*, 125, p.447. Udzungwa Mountains, Tanzania.

IDENTIFICATION At close quarters, males unmistakable with bronzy throat-patch and distinctive rufous red on wings, contrasting with violet upperparts, chestnut-red lower breast-band and greyish-green underparts; but rufous wings are not obvious if views poor. Female also distinctive with rufous on wings and spotted upper- and underparts. Some females do not have as much streaking on the lower belly as indicated in first accounts.

Similar species None; male superficially similar to Variable Sunbird *Cinnyris venustus* (134), but appears much bluer at close quarters, and as these species are allopatric confusion unlikely. Calls resemble those of Eastern Double-collared Sunbird *C. mediocris* (112), with which confusion possible if not seen well.

VOICE Call Squeaking and fizzing noises, including *see-it* when feeding. Loud *tyew* or *chow*, sometimes followed by *zew* or *zee* or *cha-zew*, perhaps from second bird; *tiddit*, sometimes trilled. Flight call: *drep-drep*. **Song** Soft high-pitched trilling very similar to that of Moreau's Sunbird *C. moreaui* (113) and, to a lesser extent, *C. mediocris*, but sounding less "electrical". Female accompaniment to male song a high-pitched chirping. Sings a lot at some times of year, presumably the breeding season.

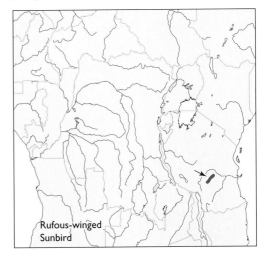

Rufous-winged Sunbird

DISTRIBUTION Only known from the eastern escarpment of the Udzungwa mountains in eastern Tanzania, where it occurs at 600-1,700 m, being commonest at 1,500-1,700 m where present in nearly all herbaceous glades.

HABITAT Moist montane forest with lichens, mosses and epiphytes, but also in glades within 20 m of forest edge.

STATUS Vulnerable. Endemic resident of Tanzania, where restricted to the eastern escarpment of the Udzungwa mountains and thus globally threatened. Locally fairly common in the 50 km² of the Mwanihana forest (7°45′S 36°35′E) within the Udzungwa Mountains National Park, where numerous 1,500-1,700 m, quite common 1,000-1,500 m and uncommon below 1,000 m. Also locally common from 1,350-1,600 m in the Ndundulu mountains (7°45′S 36°29′E) within the West Kilombero Scarp Forest Reserve and, especially, in the small Ukami forest in the Nyumbanitu mountains. The species's survival depends on the conservation of its mature forest habitat.

MOVEMENTS Appears to undertake altitudinal movements in response to availability of flowers and insects or to temperature changes. However, a few birds are always present at preferred locations.

FOOD Nectar and presumably insects.
Known food-plants *Achyrospermum carvalhi, A. radicans, Leucas densiflora,* unidentified mistletoes Loranthaceae, *Tecoma capensis.*

HABITS Noisy. Usually singly or in pairs, feeding actively within restricted area, about 1 ha, during two-day observation period. Often in light gaps with dense undergrowth and flowering plants. Feeds on flowers and shrubs at 0.5-8 m from the ground, occasionally up to 30 m in the canopy where it joins mixed-species groups. Also leaf-gleans. Highly territorial, defending patches of flowers in a small area for lengthy periods; also defends several patches of mistletoes at once, singing and feeding at them for an hour or more before moving on to another clump. Aggressive towards other sunbirds which approach the food sources, including Eastern Olive Sunbird *Cyanomitra olivacea* and *Cinnyris moreaui;* former sometimes dominant and may chase *rufipennis* away from flowers.

BREEDING Nest Only known from an empty nest (found by E. Mulungu), suspended 5 m above ground from a bamboo shoot *Sinarundinaria alpinum,* in a forest clearing. Typical sunbird type of nest, made of grass, rootlets and cobwebs (D. C. Moyer pers. comm.). **Eggs** Unknown. **Laying months** Juvenile being fed by female, January.

DESCRIPTION
Adult male Crown, face, nape, back and wing-coverts violet, with turquoise reflections in some lights. Triangular glossy bronze patch from base of lower mandible to upper chest. Upper breast-band violet, 4 mm deep, above second band of chestnut, 10 mm deep. Small pectoral tufts yellow. Upper belly greyish-white, merging with lime-green of lower belly and thighs. Undertail-coverts white. Uppertail black with violet gloss, particularly on outerwebs; undertail blackish-grey, tipped grey. Upper remiges black, but outer edges of secondaries bold cinnamon-rufous and outer edges of primaries the same but less extensively. Underwing has remiges dark grey, coverts pale grey. Iris dark brown. Bill long and curved, black. Legs black. **Non-breeding plumage** Shows some white patches in red chest-band and mottling on head.

Adult female Crown, face and nape greyish-olive, merging with olive-green back and upperwing-coverts, but crown, nape, upperwing-coverts and back, especially, with black centres creating mottled look. Nape, back and uppertail-coverts also glossed turquoise. Uppertail-coverts more greenish-olive than back. Uppertail black, outer margins brown with slight turquoise tinge and white tips. Undertail black, tipped white. Greater secondary coverts blackish-grey, with smoky-grey outer margins. Upper remiges blackish-grey with reddish-brown outer margins, narrow on primaries but broad on secondaries. Underwing-coverts grey. Legs, feet and bill black.
Juvenile Undescribed.

GEOGRAPHICAL VARIATION None described.

MEASUREMENTS Wing 57 (male), 55 (female); **tail** 43 (male), 38 (female); **culmen from base** 23.5 (male), 21.5 (female); **tarsus** 16 (male), 15 (female); **mass** 10.0 (male with large fat deposits), 8.7 (female).

REFERENCES Collar *et al.* (1994), Collar & Stuart (1985), Dinesen *et al.* (1993), J. Fjeldså (1999, pers. comm.), Fry *et al.* (2000), Jensen (1983), Jensen & Brøgger-Jensen (1992), D. C. Moyer (1999, pers. comm.), Stuart *et al.* (1987).

132 OUSTALET'S SUNBIRD
Cinnyris oustaleti   Plate 29

Nectarinia oustaleti Barbosa du Bocage, 1878, *Jorn. Sci. Math. phys. Nat. Lisboa* 6, p.254, Caconda, Huila, Angola.

Alternative names: Oustalet's White-bellied Sunbird, Caconda White-bellied Sunbird

IDENTIFICATION Male with violet reddish-coloured band across chest and lower neck. Chin and throat very dark blue appearing black in field. Above metallic green with bluish tinge. Tufts not visible in field. Female greyish-brown above, paler below. Call distinctive.
Similar species Smaller-billed than White-breasted Sunbird *Cinnyris talatala* (133), and curvature starts near tip. Head of male *oustaleti* greener, middle of throat bluer and maroon band broader than in *talatala;* pectoral tufts orange and yellow in *oustaleti,* yellow in *talatala.* In the field, female difficult to distinguish from female *talatala* but *oustaleti* is darker brown above and more heavily streaked below. In the hand told by less curved and shorter bill, duskier throat and yellower abdomen, with first primary usually longer (maximum 17 mm). Juvenile only separable by shorter, less decurved bill than juvenile *talatala.*

VOICE Call *Cheep* at a rate of 4 per second; *chip, tu, chip-chuu-chuu, tsip, weet-weet, tu-ter-twee, tu-ter-twee* with the *tu* higher-pitched than rest of call; a single or double *tchick* in flight; *tzzip* by both sexes when foraging. **Song** A jingling song of random rising and falling high-pitched notes delivered from a prominent perch; similar to but distinct from songs of *C. talatala* and Variable Sunbird *C. venustus* (134).

DISTRIBUTION Central Africa. Tanzania (two records Kiasasye and vagrant collected at Kigoma), western Angola, Zambia (Northern Province at Mwenzo, Mbala, Kasama and Mporokoso) and Malawi.

HABITAT *Brachystegia–Isoberlinia* woodland and secondary growth in slash-and-burn agricultural systems. Dense scrub.

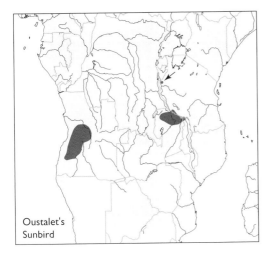

Oustalet's
Sunbird

STATUS Locally common resident in Angola. Rare in Malawi and Zambia.

MOVEMENTS Unknown, probably sedentary.

FOOD Insects (jassids or members of a similar family, larval Lepidoptera, small beetles, chalcids, Diptera) and small spiders.
Known food-plants *Diplolophium* sp., *Canna* sp., *Monotes* sp., *Parinari mobola.*

HABITS Restless and shy, often silent. Single or in small groups. Usually keeps low down but occasionally feeds in trees.

BREEDING Nest Undescribed. **Eggs** Unknown. **Laying months** Angola: October–February; Zambia: late March–end June.

DESCRIPTION *C. o. rhodesiae*
Adult male Top of head iridescent bluish-green, uppertail-coverts iridescent blue, rest of upperparts, sides of head, neck, median and lesser wing-coverts and scapulars iridescent green. Tail black with faint blue sheen. Webs of central rectrices and outerwebs of T2–T5 edged iridescent blue, outer feather brown with white tip on outerweb. Chin and throat iridescent greenish-blue. Band of shiny purple on upper breast with some maroon at base above a narrow brownish-black band. Rest of abdomen white. Orange and yellow pectoral tufts. Remiges very dark brown edged paler. Underwing-coverts and axillaries off-white. Iris dark brown. Bill and legs black. **Non-breeding plumage** Similar to adult female but greyer on throat and breast and separable by presence of orange and yellow pectoral tufts and metallic wing- and uppertail-coverts, with some sparse metallic feathering on body. Moult into eclipse plumage only involves body feathers apart from a few metallic wing- and uppertail-coverts.
Adult female Lores olivaceous-black; forehead, crown, sides of neck and upperparts greyish-yellow, ear-coverts darker; short indistinct pale streak above and behind eye; throat, breast and flanks dusky-white to pale greyish-olive or greyish-buff, feathers with whitish fringes giving an indistinct streaky appearance, becoming darker when worn and feather-bases exposed; rest of underparts creamy-white, merging to pale sulphur-yellow on lower breast and centre of abdomen; wings deep greyish-olive with pale

fringes; median and lesser wing-coverts usually fringed metallic oily-green; underwing-coverts yellowish-white; tail black, 2 or 3 pairs of central rectrices narrowly edged metallic oily-green, outer pair dusky white on outerweb and broadly tipped white on innerweb, rest of tail feathers narrowly tipped white; uppertail-coverts metallic oily-green; Iris dark brown; bill and feet black.
Juvenile Upperparts and wings dark greyish-brown, tail black, tips and outerwebs of outer pair of rectrices dusky white, rest except central pair narrowly tipped whitish; throat and breast dull grey with pale margins to feathers; rest of upperparts dusky white, tinged pale yellow in centre of abdomen.

GEOGRAPHICAL VARIATION
C. o. oustaleti (Bocage, 1878) (central Angola, from central and northern Huíla north through Huambo and northern Bié to Cuanza Sul). Bill longer (males 19–22) than *rhodesiae* (males 17–19).
C. o. rhodesiae Benson, 1955 (north-east Zambia from Kasuma and near Isalala basin close to Malawi border to 2 km across Tanzanian border at Kasesya in southwest Tanzania, where also recorded at Kigoma, December 1961) Described above.

MEASUREMENTS Wing 54–60 (mean 56.2, 13 male *oustaleti*), 52–55 (mean 53.3, 3 male *rhodesiae*), 51–55 (mean 52.4, 6 female *oustaleti*), 50–53 (female *rhodesiae*); **tail** 33–42 (mean 37.7, 13 male *oustaleti*), 34–37 (mean 36.3, 3 male *rhodesiae*), 31–36 (mean 33.8, 6 female *oustaleti*), 30–35 (female *rhodesiae*); **bill** 19–22 (mean 20.6, 13 male *oustaleti*), 17–19 (mean 18.8, 3 male *rhodesiae*), 18–21 (mean 19.7, 6 female *oustaleti*), 17 (2 female *rhodesiae*); **exposed culmen** 15–16.5 (female *rhodesiae*); **tarsus** 14–16 (mean 15.4, 13 male *oustaleti*), 14–16 (mean 15.0, 3 male *rhodesiae*), 14–15 (mean 14.8, 6 female *oustaleti*), 13.5–14 (female *rhodesiae*).

REFERENCES Aspinwall (1989), Dillingham (1984), Fry *et al.* (2000), Moyer (1983), Williams (1955).

---

133 WHITE-BREASTED SUNBIRD
Cinnyris talatala   Plate 29

Cinnyris talatala A. Smith, 1836, *Rep. Exped. C. Afr.*, p.53, between Orange River and Kurrichane, South Africa.

Alternative name: White-bellied Sunbird

IDENTIFICATION A small sunbird with long curved bill. Male has metallic green upperparts and throat and broad violet breast-band, contrasting with white belly. Female dull brown above but also with white belly and slight streaking on breast. Juvenile male resembles adult female but has black throat.
Similar species Oustalet's Sunbird *Cinnyris oustaleti* (132) very similar: see account for that species (above). Moulting male can be confused with that of Variable Sunbird *C. venustus* (134) and adult Plain-backed Sunbird *Anthreptes reichenowi* (50), but latter has metallic blue on forehead and lacks metallic shoulder-flash. Belly of female may vary from whitish to pale yellow and even pale greyish, when it may be mistaken for female of larger Miombo Double-collared Sunbird *C. manoensis* (102) or with young or female *C. venustus*, which have white-tipped tails. Very similar to allopatric white-bellied subspecies of *C. venustus*

albiventris. Juvenile confusable with that of Mariqua Sunbird *C. mariquensis* (116), but latter is larger with a more heavily streaked breast, markings sometimes reaching belly and flanks, and much more pronounced yellow wash below. Dusky Sunbird *C. fuscus* (135) also has white belly, but dark upperparts, throat and chest distinctive; female *fuscus* also darker above than female *talatala*.

VOICE Calls and songs may be mimetic with the following species sometimes being imitated: European Bee-eater *Merops apiaster*, Common Bulbul *Pycnonotus barbatus*, Cape Tit-babbler *Parisoma subcaeruleum*, Piping Cisticola *Cisticola fulvicapilla*, Rattling Cisticola *C. chiniana*, Black-chested Prinia *Prinia flavicans*, Scaly Weaver *Sporopipes squamifrons* and Streaky-headed Seed-eater *Serinus gularis*. **Call** *Tsk-tsk* or *tsiik-tsiik* or *chak-chak-chak*; utters a *chick-chick* or *chip-chip-chip* call when in food-plants and the *tsk-tsk* also in flight. A single *tsik* may be followed 5 seconds later by 3 in quick succession. **Song** An optional introduction of 2-6 *tsk*, then a 2-second burst of *tsweet-tsweet-tsi-tsi-tsi* followed by a trill or *weeah-weeah*, *tchwee-tchwee* then a rapid burst of 18 *tch* in a trill lasting 0.5-2 seconds. Full song involves expansion of the part after the introductory *tsk-tsk* into a melodic whistling warble of considerable complexity, which may last 2 minutes or more. Song may be uttered in characteristic song-flight (see under breeding), from prominent perch or from hidden position in thicket. Female also sings.

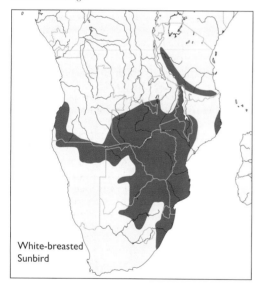

White-breasted Sunbird

DISTRIBUTION Democratic Republic of the Congo, south-east Tanzania, south-west Angola from Cunene west to Namibe, north along the coastal plain to southern Benguela, and from southern and western Huíla to western Huambo, Zambia (mostly in south), Malawi, Mozambique, northern Botswana, northern Namibia, Zimbabwe, Swaziland and South Africa (KwaZulu-Natal and Transvaal).

HABITAT Dry savanna woodland. *Acacia* savanna in Zimbabwe and South Africa, with *Acacia karoo*, *Aloe candelabrum*, *Ehretia rigida*. Also occurs in *Baikiaea*, miombo and mopane woodland, and gardens and parks in towns. Occasionally in riverine forest.

STATUS Abundant. Locally common resident in Angola.

Common in eastern South Africa. Widespread and abundant in southern Zambia. Common in Malawi and Zimbabwe. 1.5-3 birds per ha in Botswana.

MOVEMENTS Complex. Some migratory, others nomadic. Influx into Zimbabwe, May–September, probably from the west and from dry parts of Mozambique. Moves into Bulawayo area during the cooler months. At Mazabuka, in Zambia, common February–July, but rare August–January. Breeding visitor to Namibia, October–April. Active passage of migrants towards north-east observed in northern Botswana at Ngoma Bridge. Appears to move from more arid western and southern areas of southern Africa, where it breeds in summer, to wetter eastern and northern parts of its range in dry winter months. May winter further west if summer rains have been better than average.

FOOD Insects, including ants, aphids, Lepidoptera and Orthoptera, and nectar.

Known food-plants *Acacia sieberiana*, *Acrocarpus* sp., *Agapanthus* sp., *Aloe arborescens*, *A. cameronii*, *A. chabaudii*, *Baikiaea plurijuga*, *Bauhinia* sp., *Brunfelsia* sp., *Callistemon viminalis*, *Canna* sp., *Cassia singuena*, *Cestrum* sp., *Chaenomeles speciosa*, *Combretum mossambicense*, *C. paniculatum*, *Cordyla africana*, *Cotyledon* sp., *Dalbergia nitidula*, *Erythrina abyssinica*, *E. tomentosa*, *Eucalyptus* sp., *Euphorbia* sp., *Grewia* sp., *Halleria lucida*, *Hibiscus* sp., *Ipomoea lobata*, *Jacaranda mimosifolia*, *Kigelia* sp., *Kniphofia* sp., *Leonotis leonurus*, unidentified mistletoes Loranthaceae, *Petrea* sp., *Protea* sp., *Salvia* sp., *Schotia* sp., *Strelitzia* sp., *Tecoma capense*, *Tithonia tagetiflora*, *Watsonia* sp.

HABITS Occurs singly, in pairs and in loose groups. Active and noisy. Chases conspecifics and is quite gregarious, also joins mixed-species groups e.g. with Scarlet-chested Sunbird *Chalcomitra senegalensis* (85), Copper Sunbird *Cinnyris cupreus* (138), *C. venustus*, *C. mariquensis*, *C. fuscus* and Southern Double-collared Sunbird *C. chalybeus* (103). Yellow tufts seldom exposed but sometimes flashed when male singing in presence of female. Hovers in front of flowers to feed and can fly backwards when doing so. Drinks from bird-baths throughout the year in Botswana, even when plenty of food available, and also seen probing mud and drinking oozing water. Bathes in bird-baths, where aggressive e.g. juvenile seen to peck Violet-eared Waxbill *Uraeginthus granatinus*. Bill-wiping motion sometimes involves upper surface of upper mandible as head bent down and twisted below perch. Primary moult takes 4 months. Maximum longevity at least 16 years. Host to *Leucocytozoon nectariniae* and *Plasmodium* sp.

BREEDING Territorial. After copulation, male may fly off in song-flight with usual warbling song uttered whilst flying at half usual speed, using cupped wing-beats, in a semicircle of 5 m radius before returning to perch. Female builds nest in 4-8 days. Nests usually about 50 m apart but sometimes as close as 20 m. Incubation by female only starts after first egg in 64% of two-egg clutches and after the second egg in 36%. Incubation period 13-14 days, nestling period 14-15 days, with chicks brooded for first 5 days. Only female feeds young and removes faecal sacs in some nests, but male attends, whereas in other nests both sexes feed young and remove faecal sacs. Young fed aphids and grasshoppers, and when ants overran a nest these were fed by the female to the young. Nestlings utter a *tzick-tzick* call as female approaches nest; female replies with *tsweep*.

Eyes open on 5th day and fully open on day 8. After fledging, young return to nest to roost for up to 4 nights and continue to be fed by female for a week. Begging involves wing-quivering and *tseep-tseep* calls. Occasionally double-brooded. **Nest** Untidy, loosely knit, pear-shaped oval composed of dead plants, usually grasses, dead leaves and cobwebs. 128 mm high, 64-77 mm wide and entrance hole 25 mm in diameter. Some without porch, others with porch of dried grass, mainly *Eragrostis*. Sometimes decorated with dead leaves and miscellanea including newspaper. Some unlined, others thinly lined with vegetable down, sheep's wool, or feathers. Two-thirds of nests are free-hanging but rest are attached at top and back or top and side or top and front. Suspended 0.2-3.2 m above ground in thorny scrub especially *Opuntia* or small tree or thistle or creeper on tree. Occasionally nests in the recessed angles between ribs of cactus *Cereus peruvianus*. Sometimes nests within centre of spider's nest. One nest next to one of wasp *Belanogaster* sp. Nest success rate only 22% in South Africa, failures accountable to high winds, rain and predators including Slender Mongoose *Herpestes sanguineus*. **Eggs** c/1-2, with 83% of nests having c/2. 15.0-19.1 (mean 16.4, n=46) x 10.5 - 12.7 (mean 11.7). Two colour forms occur, with individual females only laying one type: type 1 white with purplish-grey and olive specks mainly at blunt end; type 2 indistinctly speckled and freckled with pale fawn and light ash. **Laying months** Angola: breeding condition November, December; Botswana: January, March, July, September–December; Malawi: January, April–October; Mozambique: February–August; Namibia: February–March; South Africa (KwaZulu-Natal): July–February, peak in September, October; (Durban): October–December; (Johannesburg): November; Zambia: September, October; Zimbabwe: June–December.

DESCRIPTION Occurs in three main categories according to belly colour, of either sex: (1) belly light-grey to dark grey, usually with a yellowish patch of variable size in centre of belly; (2) belly either pure white or, more often, white with yellowish patch of variable size in centre of belly; (3) yellow-bellied morphs ("butter-bellies") reported from Zimbabwe in which underparts completely or partly suffused pale yellowish (Tree 1991).
Adult male Crown, nape, ear-coverts, cheeks, neck and mantle iridescent green, basal two-thirds of feathers dull brown. Remiges, primary and greater coverts dull brown; outer edges of remiges white. Median and lesser wing-coverts iridescent green. Rectrices dull greenish-black, edged green except for outertail feathers. Outerweb of outertail feathers and tip of innerweb white, white sometimes also stretching along margin of innerweb. Uppertail-coverts iridescent bluish-green. Chin and upper throat iridescent deep blue, lower throat with green reflections. Upper breast-band blue above, purple below, bordered with black band edged brown distally. Yellow pectoral tufts. Belly, flanks and undertail-coverts yellowish-white (see above). Buccal cavity black. Iris dark brown. Bill and feet black. **Non-breeding plumage** Wing and tail as in breeding dress, but metallic feathers restricted to centre of chin, upper breast, head, back and uppertail-coverts, with rest of plumage resembling adult female. Hanmer (1981) reported that males in Malawi began entering eclipse plumage in September but were already moulting into breeding dress by late January, and that none was in full eclipse plumage but had some traces of old breeding plumage remaining. Indeed, a complete eclipse plumage

may not exist, at least not in some areas, as Tree (1990) suggested that records of non-breeding plumage (e.g. Mackworth-Praed & Grant 1945, Skead 1967) were erroneous and may refer to young males in female-like plumage prior to assuming breeding dress.
Adult female Head and upperparts greyish-olive or dull brown. Wings as male but coverts lack iridescent green. Tail olivaceous-black, two outer tail feathers darker. Outerweb of outertail feathers and tip and part of inner-web white. All except outer two pairs of rectrices with green gloss on outer margins. Underparts greyish-olive on throat and breast, yellow on belly or mostly off-white with greyish-olive on throat. Undertail-coverts very pale yellowish-white. Buccal cavity yellow-grey, occasionally brown. Bill and feet black. Some have gloss on lesser wing-coverts and uppertail feathers, leading to confusion with young males.
Juvenile Hatchling dark orange, browner on head and back. Eyes open on eighth day. Fledgling pale lime-yellow below, back olive-grey, wings and tail slate-brown. Gape bright orange for first three months. Buccal cavity of juvenile yellow, becoming yellowish-pink in male during post-juvenile moult. Juvenile male resembles adult female but has black throat (where first metallic feathers appear later) and touch of iridescence on forehead, shoulders and rump, although very young bird is washed yellow below. Has short whitish supercilium and conspicuous yellow edges to primaries. Outerwebs of outertail feathers edged white and underside of next pair have drop-shaped white markings. Tail as adult male. Older immature male has light brown upperparts, metallic green shoulder-flash, metallic blue chin, metallic green on throat and yellow belly. Gape becomes black after 20 months.

GEOGRAPHICAL VARIATION No subspecies accepted here. *C. t. aresta* described by Clancey (1962) is not considered to be valid, nor is *C. t. anderssoni* (Strickland, 1852), but birds from the north and west of the species's range, formerly ascribed to *anderssoni*, are smaller than the birds in the south. *C. t. lumbo* (van Someren, 1921) is also not recognised. *Cinnyris leucogaster* (Vieillot, 1819) is this species.

MEASUREMENTS Populations in middle Zambezi valley and eastwards smaller than those to south-west. **Wing** 55-70 (mean 59.6, SD 2.79, 22 males, Botswana), 51-55 (mean 53.0, SD 1.4, 26 males Malawi), 53-58.5 (males, Zimbabwe), 53-58.5 (juv/imm males, Zimbabwe), 50-65.5 (mean 55.6, SD 2.14, 20 females, Botswana), 48-51 (mean 49.4, SD 1.1, 25 females, Malawi), 49-55 (females, Zimbabwe), 49-55 (juv/imm females, Zimbabwe); **tail** 35.5-42 (males, Zimbabwe), 35.5-42 (juv/imm males, Zimbabwe), 31-41 (females, Zimbabwe), 31-41 (juv/imm females, Zimbabwe); **bill** 20.5-26 (males, Zimbabwe), 20.5-26 (juv/imm males, Zimbabwe), 19.0-23.0 (females, Zimbabwe), 19.0-23.0 (juv/imm females, Zimbabwe); **tarsus** 14-17.5 (males, Zimbabwe), 14-17.5 (juv/imm males, Zimbabwe), 14.0-17.5 (females, Zimbabwe), 14.0-17.5 (juv/imm females, Zimbabwe); **mass** 6.7-10.0 (mean 8.4, SD 0.61, 24 males, Botswana), 6.4-8.1 (mean 7.3, SD 0.5, 30 males, Malawi), 6.6-9.0 (males, Zimbabwe), 6.6-8.2 (mean 7.4, SD 0.5, 16 immature males, Malawi), 6.1-8.9 (juv/imm males, Zimbabwe), 6.8-10.0 (mean 7.7, SD 1.03, 21 females, Botswana), 5.3-7.8 (mean 6.6, SD 0.7, 31 females, Malawi), 6.0-8.8 (females, Zimbabwe), 5.6-7.6 (mean 6.4, SD 0.6, 18 immature females, Malawi), 5.8-8.3 (juv/imm females, Zimbabwe).

REFERENCES W. D. Borello (pers. comm.), Borello
(1992), Buchanan & Steyn (1965), Clancey (1962, 1967),
Cole (1992), Cyrus (1989), Earlé (1981a,b,c, 1982), Fry *et
al.* (2000), Hanmer (1981, 1989), Herremans (1992),
Hustler (1985), Mackworth-Praed & Grant (1945), Medland (1992), Saunders (1980), Skead (1967), Tree (1988,
1990, 1991, 1997f), Vincent (1949).

134 VARIABLE SUNBIRD
Cinnyris venustus   Plate 28

Certhia venusta Shaw & Nodder, 1799, *Nat. Misc.* 10, pl.369,
Sierra Leone.

Alternative names: Yellow-bellied Sunbird, Yellow-breasted
Sunbird, Buff-breasted Sunbird, Buff-chested Sunbird

IDENTIFICATION A small sunbird with a long curved
bill. Male metallic green above, with pale yellow, bright
orange-yellow, orange-yellow or white belly beneath broad
purple chest-band; throat and upper breast appear black
at a distance; orange and yellow or scarlet pectoral tufts
visible on perched bird. Female lacks metallic plumage
and chest-band and is yellowish below, greyish-olive above.
Similar species Nominate male and other races with yellow
bellies can be confused with Collared Sunbird *Hedydipna
collaris* (63) but are slimmer, with broad purple chest-band
and much longer bill. Female and immature resemble
those of Copper Sunbird *Cinnyris cupreus* (138) but supercilium less distinct. Subadult male or moulting male with
metallic blue chin, metallic green or blue throat and metallic green on wing-shoulder very closely resemble those
of White-breasted *C. talatala* (133) and adult male Plain-
backed Sunbirds *Anthreptes reichenowi* (50), but latter has
metallic blue forehead and lacks metallic on shoulder. The
white-bellied subspecies *Cinnyris venustus albiventris* is
restricted to the Horn of Africa and north-east Kenya.
Other subspecies differ from sympatric *C. talatala* by yellow
belly and violet not green forehead, violet-blue throat and
more orange pectoral tufts. May be confused with *C.
cupreus* with yellow belly. Early juvenile bird confusable
with that of Miombo Double-collared Sunbird *C. manoensis*
(102). Male told from all male double-collared sunbirds
by absence of scarlet breast-band.

VOICE Call *Chip, chop*; male and female twitter to each
other with a repeated *zi-zi-zi-zi* and when approaching a
food-plant call *chip-chip*. Male calls include *tsee-tsk-tsk* or
tser-tze-zip or *tsiu-tsé-tsé* or *tew-tew-tew*. Alarm call: *cheer-cheer*
or *tshwee, tshwee, tshwee*. **Song** A short, musical song;
falkensteini: a sequence lasting 1.5-2 seconds and repeated
every 2-4 seconds, consisting of 3-4 introductory notes, *te-
tch-weee*, then a rapid trill-like chatter of up to 15 *ch*; this
may then be followed by a long high-pitched warble of
rising and falling notes uttered rapidly. Subsong a *tsrrr*
trill followed by *tschi-pu*.

DISTRIBUTION West, Central and East Africa. Senegal,
Gambia, Guinea-Bissau, Guinea, Sierra Leone, Liberia,
Côte d'Ivoire, Ghana, Togo, Benin, Nigeria, Mali, Burkina
Faso, Sudan, Ethiopia, Eritrea, Somalia, Cameroon, Chad,
Central African Republic, Gabon, Republic of the Congo,
Democratic Republic of the Congo, Rwanda, Burundi,
Uganda, Kenya, Tanzania, Angola, Zambia, Malawi,
Mozambique, Zimbabwe and South Africa.

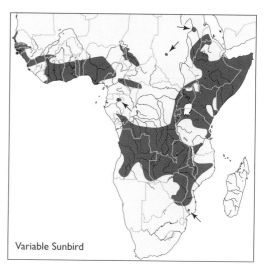

Variable Sunbird

HABITAT Thorn savannas north of the equator, but more
wooded areas including *Brachystegia* woodland further
south e.g. in miombo woodland in Angola. The nominate
race occurs in forest, forest edge, wooded ravines on hillsides, savanna, open farmland, and parks near the coast.
In Nigeria it occurs from semi-arid areas at Lake Chad up
to 1,100 m on the Ngaundere Plateau. Also found in open
coastal habitats, mangroves, coconut plantations, inselbergs, montane savanna, amongst *Pteridium* ferns and
Solanaceae in highlands and in gardens in urban areas.
Usually above 900 m in Ethiopia. In Uganda, occurs in
open forest, forest edge, clearings, bushland, woodland
(e.g. *Acacia*), gardens and cultivated areas and up to 2,700
m in Ruwenzoris. In South Africa and Zimbabwe avoids
dry areas and occurs from 300-2,500 m in riverine scrub,
herbaceous scrub, valleys, hillsides, *Brachystegia* woodland,
forest patches and slopes with *Protea* spp. In Zambia found
in moist areas especially rank vegetation along rivers or
streams, riverine forest, but also *Burkea* sp. savanna and
regenerating miombo.

STATUS Common over most of its range. Not uncommon
in Senegal and Gambia. Common along coast and in
northern highlands, Liberia. Common in Togo. Seasonally
common in Nigeria. *C. v. albiventris* is a common, almost
ubiquitous resident in Somalia. Locally common in
Ethiopia. Locally common resident in Angola. Common
and widespread in Uganda, except in north and north-
west. Common in Malawi, Zambia and Zimbabwe. Rare in
South Africa.

MOVEMENTS Partial intra-African migrant, but movements poorly understood. Present all year in coastal
savanna of Nigeria but absent in other southern habitats
there during the rains, April–October, when present in
northern Nigeria, at least for May–June. Passage through
Zaria, northern Nigeria, April–July, with return movements
September but destinations unknown. Present Gabon,
March–October. Some nomadic in Zimbabwe, where
recently colonised Harare to become commonest sunbird
in the city. Some individuals are probably resident, others
migratory.

FOOD Insects (sometimes taken from spiders' webs),
including ants, small Diptera and lepidopteran larvae;

spiders, nectar. Rubber latex found in stomachs.

Known food-plants *Acacia* sp. including *A. sieberiana*, *Acrocarpus fraxinifolius*, *Aloe* sp., *Albizia coriara*, *Berlinia grandiflora*, *Canna* sp., *Callistemon citrinus*, *C. viminalis*, *Calpurnia lasiogyne*, *Cestrum* sp., *Combretum mozambicensis*, *C. paniculatum*, *Erythrina humeana*, *Faurea speciosa*, *Fuchsia* sp., *Gardenia tigrina* (nectar-robbed), *Grevillea banksii*, *G. robusta*, *Grewia similis*, *Halleria lucida*, *Hibiscus* sp., *Jacaranda mimosifolia*, *Kalanchoe* sp., *Kniphofia* sp., *Lantana rhodesiensis*, *Lathyrus odoratus*, *Leonotis mollissima* (nectar-robbed), *L. nepetifolia*, unidentified mistletoes Loranthaceae, *Melia azedarach*, *Pedilanthus tithymaloides*, *Phragmanthera dschallensis* (parasite of *Acacia* spp., especially *A. drepanolobium*), *Protea* sp., *Prunus* sp., *Salvia* sp., *Schotia brachypetala*, *Symphonia globulifera*, *Tecoma* sp., *Thevetia peruviana*, *Tibouchina multiflora*, *Tithonia rotundifolia*, unidentified Zingiberaceae.

HABITS Very active, occurring singly, in pairs, in small parties with several males in the non-breeding season, and in mixed-species groups, especially at profusely flowering trees. Searches leaves for insects, as well as probing flowers. Sometimes hovers in front of flowers. Occasionally makes sallying flights to catch insects on the wing. Sits at tops of trees to preen. Wipes bill on branch after preening. Male displays to another by stretching upright and producing an uninterrupted sequence of *tsweuip-tsweuip-tsweuip-tsweuip...* Advertising display involves singing from exposed perch with tail spread. Responds to reflection in windows. Noted bathing in dew on creeper leaves together with Grey Waxbills *Lagonosticta perreini*. Reduces metabolism at night by 43% at constant ambient temperature of 5°C and by 47-63% at 25°C. Maximum longevity more than 8 years 6 months. Host to *Haemoproteus sequeirae*, *Leucocytozoon nectariniae* and *Plasmodium* sp. and to feather mites *Pterodectes hologaster* and *Xolalges glossopus*.

BREEDING Male sings from top of bush. Most building by female but male accompanies her on foraging flights and seen to help construct. Nest takes 10-20 days for completion. Only female incubates. Incubation period 14 days. Both sexes may feed young during 18-day nestling period. One nest raided for feathers by Scarlet-chested Sunbird *Chalcomitra senegalensis* (85), leading to breeding failure. Parasitised by Klaas's Cuckoo *Chrysococcyx klaas*. **Nest** May be built as low as 870 mm from the ground e.g. in *Clematis scabiosfolia*, 1 m high in dense *Lantana camara* or 1.5 m up on branch of small *Acacia*, also in *Bougainvillea*, at top of tall fern, in top of stunted maize plant, in hut and up to 2 m from ground. Nest oval or pear-shaped, untidy, resembling bundle of vegetation, flimsy-looking externally; made of grass or reeds, rootlets, fibres, flower-heads, white thread or dead leaves, held together with cobwebs. Material may stretch up around the attachment. Cup lined with vegetable down e.g. of *Clematis* sp., or feathers. Hood above entrance. Sometimes short beard. Nest proper of *venustus* 130 mm in length, 65 mm wide, 70 mm deep at level of 30 x 35 mm entrance hole, base of inside 35 mm below entrance. Nests of *falkensteini* 115-175 mm high, 58-76 mm wide, entrance hole 25-27 mm in diameter. Double-brooding noted in same nest for *venustus* in Nigeria. **Eggs** Race *albiventris*: c/1-2. 15.5 x 10.0-11.0; *falkensteini*: c/1-3; 13.9-17.3 (mean 15.7, n=36) x 10.4-12.1 (mean 11.2), ovate, unglossy, white, cream or greyish-white, mostly obscured by dense ashy-brown, brown, fawn or ash-grey speckling and freckling, particularly at larger

pole; *igneiventris*: 15.7 x 11.4-11.6; *venustus*: c/1-2. 13.5-17.2 (mean 16.2, n=8) x 10.2-12.1 (mean 11.1), greyish-green background overlain with purplish-grey blotches and with grey-brown spots and speckles concentrated at larger end. **Laying months** Angola: breeding condition November; Democratic Republic of the Congo: August, September; East Africa: January–December; Eritrea: June; Ethiopia: April–October; Gambia: March; Liberia: December, dependent young January–April; Malawi: March–June, August, December; Mozambique: April–September; Nigeria: October–January; Sierra Leone: October; Sudan: November–January; Togo: July; Uganda: February, March, September, October; Zambia: April, July–October; Zimbabwe: all year, peak February–October.

DESCRIPTION *C. v. venustus*
Adult male Front of crown metallic purple, merging into metallic green. All upperparts, ear-coverts, neck, rump and lesser wing-coverts metallic green. Lores black. Remiges, median and greater coverts brown. Greater coverts with olive edges. Uppertail-coverts metallic blue, appearing green in some reflections. Tail black or very dark blue with metallic blue or green fringes. Chin metallic purple, throat metallic green, upper breast metallic purple, merging with unglossy black area. Rest of underparts pale yellow. Pectoral tufts variable in colour, usually yellow and scarlet, sometimes only yellow. Undertail-coverts white with yellow tinge. Underwing-coverts white with black on wing border. Axillaries pale yellow or white. Iris dark brown. Bill, legs and feet black. A rare form of this nominate race has iridescent green upperparts washed pinkish-coppery.
Non-breeding plumage Males lose most of their metallic plumage for a short period in non-breeding season when they resemble adult females but are more olive-brown. Metallic feathers on chin, throat and upper breast, lesser wing-coverts and uppertail-coverts may be retained, sometimes with scattering of metallic feathers on back. Some populations may not have eclipse plumage (and see below under *falkensteini*). Primaries moulted in 1-10 sequence centrifugally, secondaries in 8,1,9,7,3,4,5,6 order counted centripetally.
Adult female Smaller than male. All upperparts ash-brown with olive wash on rump and lesser wing-coverts. Wing including median and greater coverts darker brown. Tail black with faint green gloss, all feathers tipped off-white, middle pair narrowly, outer ones more broadly; outer feathers with pale outerwebs. All underparts pale yellow except chin and throat white. Underwing-coverts and axillaries white with yellowish wash. Iris dark brown. Bill, legs and feet black.
Juvenile Immature male like adult female but lacks pale tips to outer tail feathers, throat and breast with dusky markings, those on throat sometimes very conspicuous, appearing as dark streak, as birds moult back into adult plumage with metallic blotches appearing. Immature female resembles adult female but appears smaller and scruffier with less black legs and feet. Buccal cavity (both sexes) dusky orange.

GEOGRAPHICAL VARIATION
C. v. albiventris (Strickland, 1852) (includes *blicki* Mearns, 1915) (Somalia, east and southern Ethiopia, north and eastern Kenya) Male with white abdomen. Female greyish-brown above, whitish below, faintly streaked on throat and breast.
C. v. falkensteini Fischer & Reichenow, 1884 (includes

niassae Fischer & Reichenow, 1899 and *kuanzae* Fischer & Reichenow, 1899) (Kenya [except east and north] north-west to west of Elgon and south-east Sudan, Tanzania, Malawi, Mozambique, Zambia, Zimbabwe, Gabon, lower Congo, Kasai, Angola from central Huíla, Huambo and Bié north to Luanda and Bengo, Cuanza Norte and Malanje, and east to Lunda Norte, Lunda Sul and northern Moxico to Democratic Republic of the Congo [Katanga]) Male has deeper yellow underparts than nominate. Young bird has orange gape, turning yellow after three months, black after two years. Not all males enter eclipse plumage. In immature plumage after post-fledging moult, male has only a small proportion (20%) of head, nape, mantle, breast and wing-coverts metallic. Older immature male has light brown upperparts, metallic green shoulder-flash, metallic blue chin, metallic green on throat and yellow belly. At end of first year, enters partial adult plumage with 50-80% of full metallic plumage. Only assumes full adult plumage after third moult at end of second year. Eclipse plumage closer to adult than in nominate, and this partial eclipse involves loss of 10-20% of metallic feathers and appearance of dusky feathers on crown and chest. Primary moult takes 3 months.

C. v. fazoqlensis (Heuglin, 1871) (includes *sukensis* van Someren, 1932) (Eritrea; Ethiopia [south-east to Harar and south-west to Yavello and Alghe] west to Sudan [east of the Nile from Khartoum southwards]) Belly colour similar to *falkensteini* but metallic green, not purplish-blue, on throat above purple breast.

C. v. igneiventris Reichenow, 1899 (mostly at 1,200-2,700 m, eastern Democratic Republic of the Congo from west of Lake Albert to Kivu, Rwanda, north-west of Lake Tanganyika, Uganda, Tanzania) Male differs from *falkensteini* in having mid-chest washed orange-scarlet and pectoral tufts scarlet, not orange or yellow.

C. v. venustus (Shaw & Nodder, 1799) (Senegal, Gambia and Sierra Leone to Nigeria, north Cameroon and Ubangi-Shari) Described above.

MEASUREMENTS Wing 54-58 (mean 55.4, 11 male *albiventris*), 48-57 (mean 51.7, SD 1.2, 28 male *falkensteini*), 53-56 (mean 53.3, 10 male *fazoqlensis*), 48-53 (mean 50.7, 10 male *venustus*), 49 (female *albiventris*), 46-53 (mean 48.6, SD 0.9, 25 female *falkensteini*), 45-53 (mean 47.5, 10 female *venustus*); **tail** 42 (male *albiventris*), 31.0-41.0 (male *falkensteini*), 30-37 (mean 34.4, 10 male *venustus*), 32 (female *albiventris*), 30.0-39.0 (female *falkensteini*), 27-35 (mean 30.4, 10 female *venustus*); **bill** 17 (male *albiventris*), 19.0-21.0 (mean 19.8, 3 male *falkensteini*), 17-20 (mean 18.0, 10 male *venustus*), 17 (female *albiventris*), 16-18 (mean 16.9, 10 female *venustus*); **tarsus** 16 (male *albiventris*), 14.1-18.4 (mean 16, 3 male *falkensteini*), 14-16 (mean 15.1, 10 male *venustus*), 17 (female *albiventris*), 13-16 (mean 14.1, 10 female *venustus*), 14.5-18.5 (unsexed *falkensteini*); **mass** 5.2-9.3 (mean 7.3, 27 male *falkensteini*, one bird 1 g heavier on recapture), 5.0-7.9 (mean 6.2, 25 male *venustus*), 5.3-10.0 (mean 7.5, 16 female *falkensteini*), 5.1-6.0 (mean 5.4, 6 female *venustus*).

REFERENCES Bannerman (1940), Blancou (1939), Cheke (1976), Elgood *et al.* (1973), Hanmer (1981, 1989, 1997), Hustler (1985), Irwin (1984, 1986), Lane (1995), Lees (1999), Prinzinger *et al.* (1989), Prinzinger & Jackel (1986), Sclater & Moreau (1933), Serle (1940), Siemens

(1983), Sievi (1974), Skead (1967), Tree (1997e), Traylor & Parelius (1967), Wilhelm *et al.* (1980, 1982), Zumpt (1961).

---

135 DUSKY SUNBIRD
Cinnyris fuscus   Plate 35

Cinnyris fuscus Vieillot, 1819, *Nouv. Dict. Hist. Nat.* nouv. éd. 31, p.506, Great Namaqualand.

Alternative name: White-vented Sunbird, Namaqua Sunbird

IDENTIFICATION A sombre sunbird, adult male appearing black above and white below unless orange pectoral tufts shown. At close quarters dark brown with metallic bronze-green and purple reflections above and on chest of male visible, contrasting sharply with white below. Male in non-breeding plumage and young male have black throats. Female greyish-brown above, white below.
Similar species White-breasted Sunbird *C. talatala* (133) is also white-bellied but male has metallic green upperparts and throat and female more streaked below.

VOICE Call A *tsk* and a whistling *weeeh, weeeh*. Also *skrrrrrr-eh* and a stammering *ts, ts, ts, tsk*; *ji-dit* in flight. **Song** A *tst* followed by a trill of *trr-trr-trr...* lasting 1.5-2 seconds, falling slightly after half-a-second when the pitch becomes a steady tone, abruptly ending with a sharp *tschut*. Trill is variable, sometimes more like *tt-tt-tt* or else the *trr-trr-trr...* may be deep and rasping. Other descriptions of song variants include *sweek, week, wee-aswirrik, e'e'e'e'; tsip-tsirra, riprip; ah, ree, ree, ree, reee*, followed by a tinny *weenkle, weenkle, ee, eenkle, eenkle, eenkle, ink*; a husky *shreep-chip, chip, chip, chip, chip, chip, chip, chip*. May sing from food-bush.

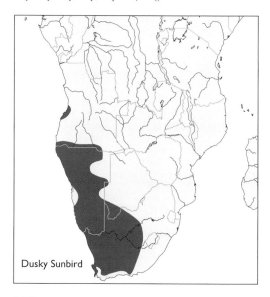

Dusky Sunbird

DISTRIBUTION South-west Africa. South-western Angola, western and southern Namibia, south-western Botswana, South Africa (east in the karoo to Colesburg in western Cape Province).

HABITAT Dry country, including semi-arid coastal plains with sand-dunes but not sandy desert. *Acacia* sp. scrub along watercourses. Inselbergs with scattered bushes, hillside scrub, orchards and gardens.

STATUS Locally common, nomadic resident in Angola. Locally common in Namibia, where may appear abundant when congregating in hundreds at large patches of *Nicotiana* sp.

MOVEMENTS Nomadic in search of food-plants in flower, but migration patterns unclear. Moves in response to droughts, when may irrupt into south-western Cape Province of South Africa.

FOOD Insects including moths and nectar.
Known food-plants *Acacia* sp., Acanthaceae, *Aloe* spp. including *A. asperfolia*, *A. dichotoma*, *A. gariepensis*, *A. grandidentata*, *A. hereroensis*, *A. littoralis*, *A. zebrina*, *Cadaba* sp., *Canna* sp., *Crassula* sp., *Crocosmia* sp., *Drosanthemum luderitzii*, *Hibiscus* sp., *Lantana* sp., *Leonotis oxymifolia*, *Lycium campanulatum*, unidentified mistletoes Loranthaceae, *Nicotiana glauca*, *Psilocaulon* sp., unidentified Scrophulariaceae.

HABITS Active, even in heat of day in semi-desert, and noisy. Flight fluttery and moth-like during male-male encounters, e.g. male flew in moth-like manner towards another, perched on bush, leant forward, fanned out tail and hopped aggressively towards feeding rival. Often in pairs, and associates with Scarlet-chested Sunbirds *Chalcomitra senegalensis* (85) and *Cinnyris talatala*, but dominant over Southern Double-collared Sunbird *C. chalybeus* (103). Congregates at major sources of nectar. Probes from perch and hovers in front of flowers. Hawks for insects. Drinks water from pools.

BREEDING Male defends territories aggressively with much singing and physically, and responds vigorously to play-back of taped calls. Courtship display aerial. Nests built in 6 days, with as long as 12 days between completion and first egg-laying. Only female incubates, for 12-13 days. Both parents feed chicks, but only female broods them. Nestlings remain in nest for 13-15 days. Female removes faecal pellets. Although 62% of broods were of two young and only 37.5% had three, which is the reverse of clutch sizes (see below), it is likely that hatch failures and both early and late chick mortalities occur. Young may return to roost in nest for up to 13 nights after fledging. Both parents feed fledglings for 2-3 weeks. Possibly double-brooded. Parasitised by Klaas's Cuckoo *Chrysococcyx klaas* (11% of clutches in Namibia), which matches egg colour to those of host well. Nest Close to ground, 0.1-1.65 m up, hanging from branches of shrub or tree e.g. in *Blepharis gigantea*, *Catophractes alexandri*, *Commiphora glaucescens*, *Euphorbia virosa*, *Iboza riparia*, *Kissenia capensis*, *Opuntia* sp., *Petalidium* sp., *Pluchea loeschuleubnitziae*, *Sporobolus consimilis*, *Suaeda plumosa* or *Ziziphus mucronota*, usually along streambanks or dry riverbeds. Oval, entrance at side, near top. Made of dry grass, fibres, bark and dry leaves, bound with cobwebs and decorated with wool or oddments such as tissue paper. Lined with plant down or hair from gemsbok *Oryx oryx*. Attached to substrate at back. 125 mm high x 75 mm wide; inside diameter of cup 40-50 mm. Eggs c/2-3; in Namibia 39% c/2, 61% c/3; 14.0-16.2 (mean 15.4, n=47) x 10.3-11.8 (mean 10.9), with differences of 0.9 mm in length and 0.6 mm in width in amongst same clutch; white, sparingly marked with large smudges,

mottles and spots of light and dark purplish-brown, lilac, slate-blue or brown. Laying months Namibia: all months with peak during late rains February–April; South Africa: August–March.

DESCRIPTION *C. f. fuscus*
Adult male Head very dark blackish-brown with slight purplish-blue iridescence. Neck, mantle and back very dark brown with slight blue, purple and bronze iridescence. Uppertail-coverts very dark brown with purplish sheen, occasionally with some white feathering. Rectrices black. Remiges, primary, greater and median wing-coverts brown. Lesser wing-coverts very dark brown. Throat and breast very dark blackish-brown with purplish and bronzy-green iridescence. Chest and upper belly white. Lower belly and undertail-coverts off-white or buffish. Axillaries and underwing-coverts dark brown. Pectoral tufts orange, sometimes yellowish-orange. Iris dark brown. Bill and feet black. Non-breeding plumage From April–July to September–December male loses black plumage except on throat and from head to rump, with a scattering of metallic feathers on upperparts and lesser wing-coverts; remains in eclipse until moults into nuptial dress, September–December. In years with early rains, may breed when still moulting out of eclipse plumage.
Adult female Head dull brown. Neck, mantle, back, rump and wings dull brown. Tail and uppertail-coverts very dark blackish-brown. Underparts very pale greyish-olive; lower belly and undertail-coverts off-white. Underwing-coverts white. Axillaries grey.
Juvenile Similar to adult female but greener above, with yellow tinge below. Nestling blackish-olive with yellow gape.

GEOGRAPHICAL VARIATION
C. f. fuscus Vieillot, 1819 (South Africa, Namibia, Botswana) Described above.
C. f. inclusa (Clancey, 1970) (coastal south-western Angola at River Cunene and Moçamedes in Namibe north to coastal plain at Benguela) Breeding-dress male differs from *fuscus* in having black area below metallic gorget glossy black with purple sheen, not matt sooty brownish-black, and flanks and undertail-coverts purer white without brownish feathers. Female said to be darker, more olive, above and with more pronounced pale greenish-yellow tinge below.

MEASUREMENTS Wing 56-61 (mean 58.6, 10 male *fuscus*), 56-61 (mean 57.8, 10 male *inclusa*), 50-54 (mean 52.5, 10 female *fuscus*), 51-53.5 (mean 52.1, 10 female *inclusa*); tail 38-43 (mean 40.2, 10 male *fuscus*), 30-35 (mean 32.7, 10 female *fuscus*); bill 21-24 (mean 22.4, 10 male *fuscus*), 18-21 (mean 19.8, 10 female *fuscus*); tarsus 17-19 (mean 18, 10 male *fuscus*), 15-17 (mean 16.2, 10 female *fuscus*); mass 9-10 (mean 9.7, 3 male *fuscus*), 7-10 (male *inclusa*), 6-7 (female *inclusa*).

REFERENCES Clancey (1970a), Fraser & Wheeler (1991), Harrison (1997b), Jensen & Clinning (1974), Molyneux (1976), Skead (1967), Williams *et al.* (1986).

136 URSULA'S SUNBIRD
Cinnyris ursulae   Plate 29

Cyanomitra ursulae Alexander, 1903, *Bull. Br. Orn. Club* 13, p.38. Mt St Ysabel, Fernando Po [= Bioko].

Alternative name: Ursula's Mouse-coloured Sunbird, Fernando Po Mouse-coloured Sunbird

IDENTIFICATION A small forest sunbird, mostly olive-green above and grey below (except yellow undertail-coverts); curved bill, short tail and orange pectoral tufts of male diagnostic. Also, the metallic grey-blue forehead appears shiny in good light.
Similar species None.

VOICE Call A *tsit-tsit*; second-long bursts of accelerating and slightly falling *tseep-tseep-tseep-tseep*, sometimes slurring into a single call: *tche-tchu*. **Song** A very high-pitched trill descending during its second-long duration; main song is a very complex sequence ("a low thin sweet song"), involving some *tzip-tzip-tzip*, a whistling high-pitched warble of rapid rising and falling twitters, interspersed with the trill, *tseep* and *weet*, lasting more than 1.5 minutes.

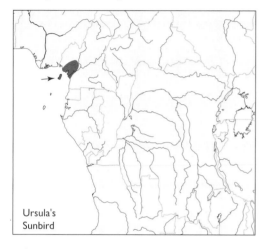

Ursula's Sunbird

DISTRIBUTION Cameroon: Bamenda-Banso highlands, Mt Bakossi, Mt Cameroon, Mt Kupé, Mt Manenguba, Mt Nlonako, and Rumpi hills. Equatorial Guinea, Bioko: north-east slopes of Pico Basile, the Caldera da Luba and south-east slopes of Pic Biao.

HABITAT Occurs in primary and secondary forest and in low shrubs at forest edges and in upland habitat. In Cameroon from 950-1,250 m on Mt Cameroon and from 950 m to the summit at 2,050 m on Mt Kupé. Highlands between 1,000 and 1,200 m on Bioko, especially in moss forest.

STATUS Generally regarded as uncommon but probably overlooked within its restricted habitat, as reported as common on Mt Cameroon, Mt Nlonako, Mt Kupé, in Rumpi Hills and Nta Ali Forest reserves. Dependent on small range of intact forest, so susceptible to deforestation and listed as near-threatened by Collar *et al.* (1994).

MOVEMENTS Unknown, presumably sedentary.

FOOD Insects including ants, spiders, nectar and seeds.
Known food-plants *Rauvolfia vomitaria*, unidentified Flacourtiaceae and Rubiaceae; blossoms of shrubs on forest floor as well as flowering trees.

HABITS Feeds at all heights in foliage of primary forest, usually solitary or in pairs but sometimes in mixed-species flocks or with Cameroon Sunbird *Cyanomitra oritis* (76). Active but secretive birds, frequenting small bushes and

isolated trees. Searches leaves and twigs and hovers in front of flowers.

BREEDING Young fed by both parents. **Nest** Unusual as not suspended. Composed mostly of moss, some small roots and cobwebs interspersed within compact structure which is loose like a cushion, hidden on low (3.5-4.2 m) moss-covered branches, creepers, lianas or shrubs. Circular side entrance with short moss porch and cottony lining. No beard. **Eggs** c/1-2. 14.9-15.2 x 11.2-11.3. White or white ovals with slight chestnut tinge. **Laying months** Cameroon: January, March, December. Equatorial Guinea, Bioko: moulting March.

DESCRIPTION
Adult male Forehead and fore-crown grey, with slight metallic blue wash, merging into olive-green posteriorly. Ear-coverts and eye-ring grey. Back of neck, rest of upperparts and uppertail-coverts yellowy-olive. Remiges, lesser wing-coverts and margins of greater and median coverts yellower but rest of wing blackish-brown. Tail blackish-brown with olive-yellow outer margins. Chin and throat pale brown with slight fawn wash, breast greyer. Belly, undertail-coverts and tips of elongated flank feathers pale olive with yellow tinge. Pectoral tufts orange-red. Axillaries and underwing-coverts white. Iris brown or hazel. Bill and legs black. Feet dark grey.
Adult female Resembles adult male but pectoral tufts less pronounced and duller orange. Iris red-brown. Bill black. Feet dark grey.
Juvenile Immature resembles adult but lacks pectoral tufts and metallic feathers, has mottled grey and off-white chin and upper throat, dark grey-green throat and upper chest (i.e. unlike smoky-grey of adults' from chin to chest), rest of underparts yellowish-olive, brightest on belly.

GEOGRAPHICAL VARIATION None described.

MEASUREMENTS Wing 46-49 (mean 48.1, 11 males), 44-48 (mean 46.2, 11 females); **tail** 25-28 (mean 26.6, 11 males), 23-26 (mean 24.7, 11 females); **bill** 16-20 (mean 19.4, 11 males), 17-19 (mean 18.1, 11 females); **tarsus** 14-17 (mean 14.7, 11 males), 14-15 (mean 14.2, 11 females); **mass** 5.3-7.3 (mean 6.5, 48 unsexed).

REFERENCES Bannerman (1948), Fry *et al.* (2000), Pérez del Val (1996), A. J. Stattersfield (*in litt.*), Stuart & Jensen (1986).

---

137 BATES'S SUNBIRD
Cinnyris batesi   Plate 18

Cinnyris batesi Ogilvie-Grant, 1908, *Bull. Br. Orn. Club* 23 p.19, River Ja, Cameroons and Camma river, Gaboon.

IDENTIFICATION A tiny dull green sunbird, distinguished by a short, curved bill, very short tail and yellowish belly.
Similar species Almost indistinguishable in the field from Little Green Sunbird *Anthreptes seimundi* (60), which has a straighter bill, longer tail and paler rectrices: *batesi* perches upright whereas *seimundi* holds itself more horizontal. Resembles small versions of Eastern *Cyanomitra olivacea* (78) or Western Olive Sunbird *C. obscura* (79) but bill shorter and straighter, tail shorter and darker, lacks buff patch in front of eye and eye-stripe does not extend so far back.

Can also be confused with female Olive-bellied Sunbird *Cinnyris chloropygius* (100) but belly brighter yellow. Difficult to tell from female Orange-tufted Sunbird *C. bouvieri* (125) but curved not straightish bill, paler throat and lack of malar stripe helpful.

VOICE Call A *ts* repeated over and over again, which may also be a song; sometimes *tsk* or *weet* or a very high-pitched *tseeep*. Also *tsp-tsp ch-ch-chur, chut chut-ut*. **Song** A barely audible trill followed by a harsh nasal *ts-tsp*.

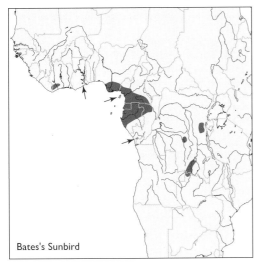

Bates's Sunbird

DISTRIBUTION West and Central Africa. Liberia, Côte d'Ivoire, Ghana, south-east Nigeria, Cameroon, Equatorial Guinea (Bioko and Rio Muni), Gabon, Republic of the Congo, Democratic Republic of the Congo (east over Congo basin to upper Congo, south to west Katanga), Angola (Cabinda), and north-west Zambia at Mwinilunga.

HABITAT The canopy of trees in primary forest, at the edges of primary forest, secondary growth and cultivated fields with tall trees.

STATUS Rare to uncommon, Liberia and Côte d'Ivoire. Rare, Ghana, where recorded Jukwa and Kakum forest. Uncommon Nigeria. Common Cameroon. Locally common in Equatorial Guinea and Gabon, where 30-60 birds per km². Uncommon resident in Cabinda.

MOVEMENTS Probably sedentary.

FOOD Insects, spiders and nectar from flowering trees, especially large flowers in the forest canopy. Berries, fruits. **Known food-plants** *Macaranga assas*.

HABITS A bird of the forest canopy. Usually seen in pairs at mid-height or tops of trees, but sometimes occurs in groups of up to 10 feeding on small fruits at the tops of trees in riparian forest. Also joins mixed-species flocks. Fond of branches with much moss and epiphytic growth. Reduces metabolism at night by 44% at constant ambient temperature of 5°C and by 55% at 25°C.

BREEDING Nest A hanging pocket without fibres in its composition and not even a hint of beard or porch. 100 mm high, 55 mm wide and 6 mm deep, made of pappus, dry leaves and cobwebs with green moss on outside, lined with cottony fluff, suspended 2-3 m above ground in

bushes or from electric flex in abandoned buildings. Entrance only 20 mm in diameter. **Eggs** c/1-2. 15.0-15.1 (mean 15.0 3) x 11.0-11.7 (mean 11.3). Short pointed oval, without gloss. Light pink with grey-green or pinkish spots and stains or brown or deep brown with a few irregular blotches of deep brown or yellowish-brown. 15.0-15.1 x 11.0-11.7. **Laying months** Cameroon: July, December; Democratic Republic of the Congo: February; Gabon: February, March; Nigeria: birds in breeding condition February, March, November.

DESCRIPTION

Adult male All upperparts dark olive, except indistinct pale stripe above eye. Underparts paler, dull grey-olive with pale whitish-yellow centre of belly. Wings dark brown with pale yellow fringes. Tail black with wide greenish-olive edges and dull olive tips to outer pair. Bannerman (1948) described long pale yellow pectoral tufts but Mackworth-Praed & Grant (1973) and Fry *et al.* (2000) stated there are none; in most specimens there are long wispy pale yellow feathers at the sides of the breast, paler, often white, at the base, resembling pectoral tufts, but these are difficult to distinguish from elongated axillaries or underwing-coverts and few seem to emanate from the pectoral region where the tufts of other species originate. Iris dark brown. Bill black except for pale base of lower mandible. Legs and feet black.

Adult female As male, but elongated underwing-coverts (pseudo-pectoral tufts) paler with less yellow and sometimes all white or reduced.

Juvenile Nestling similar to adult but belly feathers and undertail-coverts more lemon-yellow. Mouth and tongue orange. Iris grey. Bill horn. Legs and feet grey. Juvenile similar to adult.

GEOGRAPHICAL VARIATION None described.

MEASUREMENTS Wing 46-55 (mean 51.6, 18 males), 45-52 (mean 47.0, 15 females); **tail** 23-31 (mean 29.1, 18 males), 22-29 (mean 25.1, 15 females); **bill** 14-18 (mean 16.0, 16 males), 14-15 (mean 15.2, 13 females); **tarsus** 13-15 (mean 13.7, 10 males), 13-15 (mean 13.5, 10 females); **mass** 5.7-7 (mean 6.3, 5 unsexed).

REFERENCES Bannerman (1948), Bates (1911), Benson & Irwin (1966), Brosset & Erard (1986), Fry *et al.* (2000), Mackworth-Praed & Grant (1973), Pérez del Val (1996), Prigogine (1971), Prinzinger *et al.* (1989).

138 COPPER SUNBIRD
Cinnyris cupreus   Plate 35

Certhia cuprea Shaw, 1811-1812, *Gen. Zool.* 8., p.201, Malimba, Portuguese Congo.

Alternative name: Coppery Sunbird, Copper-coloured Sunbird

IDENTIFICATION Male appears completely black at a distance, but close views reveal the brilliant dark metallic plumage, appearing coppery or purple in the nominate and greenish in race *chalceus*, especially noticeable on the back. Female dull olive-green above, pale yellowish-buff below.

Similar species Western Violet-backed Sunbird *Anthreptes* *longuemarei* (56) is easily separable if white underparts seen. Female *C. cupreus* told from that of Beautiful Sunbird *C. pulchellus* (115) and Variable Sunbird *Cinnyris venustus* (134) by darker upperparts, brighter supercilium and pale yellow underparts. Male smaller and shorter-tailed than superficially similar Tacazze Sunbird *Nectarinia tacazze* (95) and Bronze Sunbird *N. kilimensis* (96). Female larger than Purple-banded Sunbird *Cinnyris bifasciatus* (121), more yellowish below, with dark lores and pale supercilium. Female *C. venustus* lacks supercilium.

VOICE Call Octosyllabic; also a scolding *pst* and *cht-cht* or *tsck-tsck* when flying between food-plants. Aggressive series of *keek* or *tzck* calls by territory-defending male. Alarm call: high-pitched *cher, cher, cher...* or *jid-jid-jid* or *jaaa-jaaa*. **Song** A loud chattering *ship-chip-chip*. Race *cupreus*: 18 *chip* notes, accelerating as they approach the final crescendo of a trill of 6-10 very rapid *chip* notes; repeated every 1.5-2 seconds. Race *chalceus*: a soft warble, interspersed with *tsck* notes, and a more excited version uttered with wings slightly open and tail fanned.

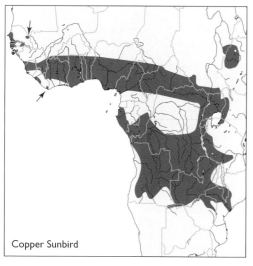

Copper Sunbird

DISTRIBUTION West, Central and East Africa. Senegal, Gambia, Guinea-Bissau, Guinea, Sierra Leone, Liberia, Côte d'Ivoire, Ghana, Togo, Benin, Nigeria, Mauritania (migrant visitor), Mali, Burkina Faso, Niger, Chad, Sudan, Ethiopia, Cameroon, Central African Republic, Gabon, Republic of the Congo, Democratic Republic of the Congo, Rwanda, Burundi, Uganda, Kenya, Tanzania, Angola, Zambia, Malawi, Mozambique, Namibia, Botswana (vagrant), Zimbabwe and South Africa.

HABITAT A predominantly savanna bird, preferring thorn-scrub but also found in degraded forest, woodlands, riverine woodland, swamps, mangroves, coastal thickets, cultivated areas, gardens and urban areas. Ascends up to 2,100 m in mountainous areas, but not above 1,800 m in Ethiopia.

STATUS Abundant throughout most of its range; rare in Mauritania. Not uncommon in Senegal and Gambia. Common in Togo and Nigeria. Common in southern Sudan, west of the Nile. Locally common resident in Angola. Common and widespread in Uganda, up to 1,800 m. Occurs at density of 30-35 pairs per km² in Odzala National

Park, Republic of the Congo. Widespread but sparse in Zambia, but locally common at some sites in Northern, Luapala and North-west Provinces. Similar status in Malawi, where seasonally common at Lilongwe.

MOVEMENTS Some resident populations but also partially migratory in West Africa, where moves north into the savanna during rains (April–October) to breed, moving south when the wet season ends. In Mauritania only recorded in wet season, August–October. Possibly altitudinal movements, Malawi, as only seen above 475 m in September–May; present Lilongwe, October–March, and at Nchalo in the south April–December only. Nomadic, Zimbabwe, concentrating on areas where nectar abundant, July–October. Recoveries in South Africa up to 43 km from ringing site.

FOOD Insects (ants, aphids, beetles, flies, caterpillars, leafhoppers, termites taken in flight), spiders and nectar. Sometimes hunts insects in trees such as *Brachystegia spiciformes* and *B. boehmii*; aphids taken from *Calodendrum capense*. A notorious nectar-robber but also probes. Found with balls of rubber latex in stomach, as much as 4 months after *Manihot* sp. had stopped flowering. Aphids, fruitflies, other insects including larvae, spiders and nectar fed to young.

Known food-plants *Acacia polyacantha*, *A. sieberana*, *Acrocarpus* sp., *Aloe cameronii*, *Antirrhinum* sp., *Azadirachta indica* (fruits), *Bauhinia petersiana*, *Berlinia grandiflora*, *Bougainvillea* sp., *Brachystegia boehmii*, *B. spiciformes*, *Calliandra* sp., *Callistemon viminalis*, *Caesalpinia* sp., *Canna* sp., *Ceiba* sp., *Combretum* spp. including *C. mossambicum*, unidentified Convolvulaceae, *Cuphea miniata*, *Erythrina latissima*, *Eucalyptus saligna*, *Gladiolus melleri*, *Gloriosa superba* (but probably for insects), *Hibiscus* sp., *Jacaranda acutifolia*, *J. mimosifolia*, *Juniperus procera*, *Kniphofia* sp., *Leonotis* sp. including *L. leonurus*, *Markhamia* sp., *Passiflora quadrangularis*, *Pentas* sp., *Prunus persica*, *Salvia* sp., *Sphenostylis marginata*, *Syzygium* sp., *Tapinanthus* sp., *Tecoma capense*, *Thalia geniculata*, *Thevetia* sp., *Thunbergia lancifolia*, *Tithonia rotundifolia*, *Trichodesma physaloides*, *Zinnia* sp.

HABITS Active with jerky, erratic flight. Usually found singly, but at times males congregate in loose groups of 12 or more birds. Joins some mixed-species flocks e.g. with Scarlet-chested Sunbird *Chalcomitra senegalensis* (85) at flowering trees. Hawks for insects and hovers in front of flowers. Aggressive, chasing away conspecifics and other sunbird species such as *Cinnyris venustus*. Territorial in breeding season. Bathes in dew. Reduces metabolic rate by 65% during night at 25°C. Maximum longevity more than 11 years. Host to *Haemoproteus* sp. and *Plasmodium vaughani*, the cestode *Staphylepis ambilateralis* and the feather mites *Anisodiscus dolichogaster*, *Boydaia nectarinia*, *Lasioseius cinnyris* and *Sternostoma nectarinia*.

BREEDING Assumes breeding plumage February–March, Nigeria. Male display involves flying to above tree height, followed by undulating flight with zig-zags, singing all the while and continuing to do so after landing. Male defends territory, adopting aggressive posture when any bird enters it. This involves leaning forward with tail bent down, rapidly raising and lowering feathers and uttering rapid series of *keek* or *tzck*. Intruders may be mobbed or struck. Species attacked include Masked Weaver *Ploceus velatus*, Black-headed Weaver *P. cucullatus*, House Sparrow *Passer domesticus*, Common Bulbul *Pycnonotus barbatus*, *Chalcomitra senegalensis*,

Fiscal Shrike *Lanius collaris*, Kurrichane Thrush *Turdus libonyanus* and Didric Cuckoo *Chrysococcyx caprius*. Territorial activity very intense during incubation, declining after hatching and ceasing half-way through nestling period.

Courtship behaviour involves postures similar to aggressive pose with birds leaning forwards, neck outstretched, bills horizontal and open, secondaries crossed over the rump, tail spread stiffly and twisted to one side, bodies puffed out and shivering, calling and facing each other for 12-14 seconds, followed by copulation lasting 3-7 seconds. During courtship dances, male advances towards female, who rocks from side to side with tail spread and twisted towards male while singing. Male then shivers with legs bent, wings lowered and half-spread before alighting on female.

Only female builds nest, but male attends. Male may perform distraction display near nest involving flight with exaggerated wing-flapping, accompanied by alarm calls. Both parents incubate and feed chicks (including after fledging), but sometimes only female incubates. Female removes faecal sacs and tidies nest. Incubation 13-14 days. Fledgling period 11-16 days. Parasitised by Didric Cuckoo *Chrysococcyx caprius* and by Klaas's Cuckoo *C. klaas*. **Nest** Elongated domed pear-shaped structure woven of fine dry grass with cobwebs joining bamboo leaves, other dead leaves, lichen, bark, other plant material and gossamer outside basic structure of roots, fibres and vegetable down with porch and beard of grass-heads and stems, thickly lined with fine roots and pappus, attached to tip of flame-tree branch or suspended 0.75-4.5 m above ground amongst creeper near a house, on nail under eaves of house or in bush or tree, e.g. *Bauhinia* sp., *Cassia* (now *Senna*) *singueana*, *Cedrella toona*, *Combretum erythrophyllum*, *Cussonia arborea*, *Erythrina abyssinica*, orange tree, mulberry tree. Entrance hole circular, 25 mm in diameter, at side of nest, sometimes with projecting canopy of dried grass flowers and sill projection at base forming lip. Length 130 mm including beard, width 60 mm, depth of nest cup 45 mm. Nests of *chalceus* 118-140 mm from top to bottom (147-159 including attachment), beard 121-234 mm, width 63-88 mm, depth 72-80 mm, height of entrance 36-41 mm, entrance width 30-33 mm, canopy length 70-108 mm, sill protrusion at base of entrance 4-6 mm. The tropical nest fly *Passeromyia heterochaeta*, whose larvae suck blood of nestlings, has been found in nests. **Eggs** c/1-3; *chalceus*: 15.6-17.0 (mean 16.5, n=9) x 11.0-12.2 (mean 11.8), pale greenish yellow-white (becoming more grey-green during development), irregularly marked with sepia and olive streaks and paler smears; *cupreus*: 15.1-17.5 (mean 16.1, n=30) x 10.2-12.2 (mean 11.4). Mass 5 g. Ovate, slightly glossed, colour variable but background usually pale brown, light grey, yellow or greenish-white washed light olive-brown, covered with blotches, spots and streaks of very dark brown, blackish- or purplish-brown or ashy-grey. **Laying months** Angola: April, November; Cameroon: September–October; Democratic Republic of the Congo: December–April, June; East Africa: January, March–September, November, December; Gambia: May, June, September, October; Ghana: June, July, dependent young May–June; Malawi: January–March; Nigeria: August–October, where double-brooded; Sierra Leone: August–October; Togo: July; Uganda; March–December; Zambia: December–March, June; Zimbabwe: September–February.

DESCRIPTION *C. c. cupreus*
Adult male Head, throat and neck metallic copper (appear-ing variously as golden- or reddish-copper, greenish-bronze or black, depending on angle of light), merging into more metallic purple on mantle, back, uppertail-coverts, lesser wing-coverts and breast. Rest of wing-coverts black with dark blue gloss. Tail black with dark purplish-blue gloss. Underparts below metallic breast black with slight gloss. Undertail-coverts, underwing-coverts and axillaries black. Iris dark brown, bill black, yellowish at base. Legs and feet black. Buccal cavity of male in nuptial plumage dark red or dusky mauve. **Non-breeding plumage** Male loses most metallic plumage in non-breeding season (in West Africa south of 8°N October–January; Tanzania June–September; Angola June–October), when upperparts olive, with a few metallic purple feathers. Lesser wing-coverts and uppertail-coverts tipped metallic purple. Underparts yellowish with some black feathers on belly and flanks. Black remiges and rectrices retained. In January–February West African and Sudanese birds begin moulting back into breeding dress when some have coppery stripe down throat to belly, indistinct supercilium and violet on uppertail. By March, most are in full breeding plumage. Birds are in breeding plumage, July–October, June, November–July, Democratic Republic of the Congo, Tanzania and Malawi.
Adult female Lacks any metallic colouring. Crown and rest of upperparts brownish-olive, ear-coverts brown. Narrow pale yellow supercilium from just before eye. Lores black. Remiges dark brown narrowly edged olive and tipped pale when fresh. Lores black. Tail black with dark blue gloss, outer feathers browner with pale terminal part and pale outerweb. Underparts from chin to undertail-coverts dull olive with yellow wash, especially on belly. Axillaries pale yellow, underwing-coverts white, yellowish at edges. Iris dark brown, bill, legs and feet black.
Juvenile Nestling very dark brown with off-white fluff on crown, orange palate, and yellow gape (but see under *chalceus* below). Legs and bill blackish-mauve, feet black. Immature male as eclipse male but lacks metallic feathers on lesser wing-coverts, so resembles female but has duskier throat. Immature female also like adult female but upperparts browner-olive rather than greyish-olive of adult. Buccal cavity orange in both sexes and remains so in male during post-juvenile moult.

GEOGRAPHICAL VARIATION
C. c. chalceus (Hartlaub, 1862) (includes *vaughan-jonesi* White, 1944) (Angola from central and northern Huíla north through Huambo and Bié to southern Cuanza Norte, Uíge, Malanje and adjacent Lunda Norte, northern Lunda Sul and Moxico; Zambia, south-east Democratic Republic of the Congo [Katanga], Malawi, northern Mozambique, northern Zimbabwe and ?south-west Tanzania) Males more greenish-bronze, less purplish-bronze and longer-winged than *cupreus*. In eclipse plumage, which lasts about a month, iridescence on head, mantle and throat replaced by dull olive-green but black wings, tail and metallic patch on wing-coverts and uppertail-coverts are retained. Immatures less than five months old with bright orange gape, older birds with bright yellow gape flanges, becoming duller yellow with age (15-18 months old) and black at 2 years. Primary moult takes 4 months, usually starting after breeding season but some delay for 2-3 months.
C. c. cupreus (Shaw, 1811) (includes *septentrionalis* Vincent, 1936) (Senegal to Cameroon and mouth of Congo, east to southern Sudan, Cabinda, Democratic

Republic of the Congo [except Katanga], western Ethiopia, Uganda, Kenya west of the Rift Valley, western Tanzania south to Kigoma). Described above. Clinal variation, as males from West Africa smaller (wing <60 mm).

MEASUREMENTS Wing 61-67 (mean 64.3, SD 1.5, 66 male *chalceus*), 54-66 (mean 59.6, 10 male *cupreus*), 59-63 (juv/imm male *chalceus*), 56-61 (mean 58.8, SD 1.6, 45 female *chalceus*), 52-56 (mean 52, 10 female *cupreus*), 55-60 (juv/imm female *chalceus*); tail 45-52 (mean 48.4, 10 male *chalceus*), 35-48 (mean 45.4, 10 male *cupreus*), 38.5-45 (juv/imm male *chalceus*), 41-44 (female *chalceus*), 30-43 (mean 35.8, 10 female *cupreus*), 36-43 (juv/imm female *chalceus*); bill 20.5-23.5 (mean 21.7, 10 male *chalceus*), 16-23 (mean 21, 10 male *cupreus*), 19-22.5 (juv/imm male *chalceus*), 20-22 (female *chalceus*), 16-22 (mean 17.8, 10 female *cupreus*), 19-22 (juv/imm female *chalceus*); tarsus 16-17 (male *chalceus*), 15-17 (juv/imm male *chalceus*), 15-17 (mean 15.5, 10 male *cupreus*), 16-17 (mean 14.5, 10 female *cupreus*), 14.5-16.5 (juv/imm female *chalceus*); mass 8.4-11.4 (mean 9.8, SD 0.7, 70 male *chalceus*), 6.8-8.4 (mean 7.7, 25 male *cupreus*, West Africa), 7.5-11.0 (mean 9.0, 63 male *cupreus*, Kenya), 8.2-10.5 (juv/imm male *chalceus*), 7.3-10.2 (mean 8.8, SD 0.8, 48 female *chalceus* significantly lighter than males P<0.001), 5.5-8.3 (mean 6.7, 18 female *cupreus*, West Africa, significantly lighter than males P<0.01), 7.2-8.9 (mean 8.1, 10 female *cupreus*, Kenya), 7.8-9.5 (juv/imm female *chalceus*).

REFERENCES Bannerman (1948, 1951), Chapin (1954), Davey & Davey (1990), Fain & Mariaux (1991), Fry *et al.* (2000), Hanmer (1981, 1989), Hicks (1959), Howells (1971), Irwin (1986), Mackworth-Praed & Grant (1945), Mariaux & Vaucher (1991), Oatley (1996b), Prinzinger & Jackel (1986), Tree (1990, 1991, 1997c), Zumpt (1961, 1966).

---

139 PURPLE SUNBIRD
Cinnyris asiaticus   Plate 30

Certhia asiatica Latham, 1790, *Lath. Index Orn.* 1, p.288, India; restricted to Gurgaon by Baker, 1926, *Fauna Brit. India, Birds*, 3, p.396.

Possibly forms a superspecies with *C. talatala*, *C. oustaleti*, *C. bouvieri* and *C. oseus*.

IDENTIFICATION Adult male appears black at distance; mostly metallic purple, blue and blue-green; narrow reddish band on lower breast; pectoral tufts yellow and scarlet. In non-breeding plumage, male is pale olive-brown above with blackish wings and tail; yellow below with dark mesial stripe on throat and breast. Adult female olive-brown above, dull yellow below.

Similar species Female like female Plain-throated Sunbird *Anthreptes malacensis* (53) but latter has eye-ring and brighter plumage; female Purple-rumped Sunbird *Leptocoma zeylonica* (88) has ashy throat and rufous wings; female Crimson-backed Sunbird *L. minima* (89) has red on rump; male Purple-throated Sunbird *L. sperata brasiliana* (90) has sooty-brown belly and vent, whereas the female *sperata* is olive above and brighter below; male Copper-throated Sunbird *L. calcostetha* (92) has belly and undertail-coverts black, and lacks reddish-brown band separating breast from belly, whereas female *calcostetha* has greyish-white

throat and white undertail-coverts; female Olive-backed Sunbird *Cinnyris jugularis* (140) from female of this species by much brighter plumage; Long-billed Sunbird *C. lotenius* (149) has larger bill, male has sooty-brown body, whereas female *loterius* is olive above and has white tips to tail. Resembles allopatric Palestine Sunbird *C. oseus* (126): bill of *asiaticus* less decurved and shorter, male with metallic plumage washed darker green and female washed yellow, not pale grey, below.

VOICE Call Single *chip*, and frequently uttered, loud *chweet*, a rising *sweep*, and *zik*. A shrill chirp uttered on wing. A loud harsh monotonous whistle. **Song** Usually by male, excited *cheewit-cheewit* repeated rapidly 2-6 times; bright warble *swi-swi-swi-a-col-a-oli* or *sisisi-sew-sew-sew*, sometimes from perch at top of tree.

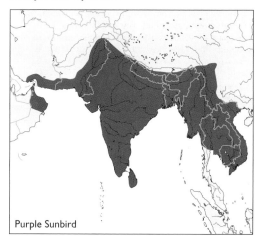

Purple Sunbird

DISTRIBUTION United Arab Emirates, northern Oman, south Iran, Baluchistan, Pakistan, India, Nepal, Sri Lanka, Bangladesh to Indochina and south Yunnan.

HABITAT Lowlands and hills generally to 1,500 m, but to 1,830 m in Nepal and 2,400 m in Nilgiri Hills, southern India. Gardens, cultivation, riverbeds, thorn-scrub, dry forest and light deciduous forest. Usually around flowering shrubs and trees.

STATUS Common throughout India south of Himalayan foothills, and partially migratory. Locally common in Sri Lanka, present throughout and at all altitudes but commonest in dry habitats. Common resident in northern Oman, but also partially migratory. Rare and local in Bhutan.

MOVEMENTS *C. a. brevirostris* migrates northwards to the northern foothills and Punjab plains in March–April and returns south, perhaps to western India south to Londa, at end August–early September; a few winter in Punjab, whereas in Sind resident population is augmented in winter by migrants from north. One ringed at Bharatpur, India, was recaptured 320 km north, 3 years later. The nominate undergoes vertical movements depending on season, and is a summer visitor to Punjab and the Himalayan foothills; in Sri Lanka it moves down from hills in early December and returns in July. In Nepal moves uphill after nesting; mainly resident to at least 365 m, and mainly a summer visitor above 900 m, but recorded at 2,065 m at Pati Bhanjyang 9 February and late March. In Oman, some move south to latitude of Masirah in winter.

FOOD Nectar when mistletoe fruits unavailable; small insects (tineid and geometrid larvae, *Myllocerus* weevils, *Trigona* bees, *Cydnus nigritus* bugs, jassids, small flies) and spiders; mistletoe fruits parasitic on gamer *Gmelina arborea* and teak *Tectona grandis*; grapes, which it damages by piercing and sucking out juice in orchards around Hyderabad, India, where considered a pest; fruits on periphery of vineyards are most affected; range of damage 3.2-45%. Also important as pollinator e.g. of *Loranthus longiflorus*, buds of which remain closed and unfertilised until bird opens them by gentle squeezing of tops of mature buds and probing for nectar, thereby attaching pollen from anthers for deposition on stigmata of another bud.

Known food-plants *Acacia pennata, Acanthus ilicifolius, Anisomeles indica, A. malabarica, Borassus* sp., *Callistemon* sp., *Canna* sp., *Caryota urens* (toddy palms, when being tapped), *Dendrophthoe falcata* (has slits in the corolla which, when penetrated by a sunbird bill, release the top of the corolla exposing pollen), *Elytranthe parasitica, Leonotis nepetifolia,* unidentified mistletoes Loranthaceae (including *?Loranthus longiflorus* and parasites of *Gmelina arborea* and *Tectona grandis*), *Macrosolen parasiticus, Madhuca indica, Musa* sp., *Scurrula obovata, S. parasitica, S. rhopalocarpa, Sesamum indicum, Thevetia peruviana, Tolypanthus lagenifera, Vitis* sp. The buds of *E. parasitica, S. obovata, S. parasitica, S. rhopalocarpa* and *T. lagenifera* have to be opened by birds, upon which they are dependent for pollination.

HABITS Pugnacious. Found singly, in pairs or small parties; noisy and restless. Always around flowering trees and *Loranthus* clumps where it probes blossoms, and is an important pollinator. Occurs in gardens. Hawks gnats like a flycatcher and, where these are abundant, may be found in groups of up to 40-50. Sometimes catches insects on ground. Swift and jerky flight. In display to female, male perches before her with slightly raised head and fluttering, partially opened wings to display pectoral tufts, and singing. Also hovers vertically for a few seconds, rapidly beating wings which become a blur, with pectoral tufts standing out in front. After some seconds the performance is repeated. Spends gradually less and less time feeding during the day, from 35 minutes per hour at 07h00-08h00 to 4 minutes per hour at 16h00, before an increase up to 14 in the hour just before dusk. Host to *Haemoproteus sequeirae*, microfilariae including those of *Splendidofilaria alii*, and *Plasmodium* sp.

BREEDING Parasitised by Plaintive Cuckoo *Cacomantis merulinus*. Only female involved in building nest and incubation, but male helps in feeding young. **Nest** An oblong purse of soft grass and fibres, leaves, cobweb, etc., decorated with detritus and rubbish including pieces of bark and caterpillar droppings, usually with a porch; lined with silky-white seed-down; suspended on twig usually up to 2, occasionally 6, but recorded up to 13 m from ground, often from inner branch of bush; may be hung from trelliswork, creepers, ropes, electric wires, chains, rafters, *Opuntia* bushes and amongst spiders' nest masses; once first stage built on wire and bulb holder, and brood chamber on 60W bulb with entrance on top, on veranda of inhabited house at Aurangebad, India, which was completed over 21-30 April, but bird always flew out when lamp switched on and eventually abandoned nest which contained two eggs. One nest collapsed to ground with mass of second brood. **Eggs** c/1-3. Race *asiaticus*: 14.1-18.0 (mean 16.0, n=100) x 10.9-12.4 (mean 11.6); *brevirostris*: 15.3-17.9 (mean 16.7, n=30)

x 10.9-12.1 (mean 11.6); *intermedius*: 14.2-18.1 (mean 15.9, n=35) x 10.8-12.5 (mean 11.5). Greyish-white, streaked chocolate forming band around broad end. **Laying months** Breeding season of nominate varies with climate and altitude, chiefly in the dry season, but recorded in all months. Nepal: Kathmandu Valley, May, Chitwan, Nepal Valley, chiefly June; season appears to be mid-April to mid-June. India: Bihar, February–May, 2 or more broods in rapid succession, sometimes in same nest; Haryana, March–June; Peninsular India: February–August, earlier in the south (January–June), beginning in Kerala in November, commonly double brooded; north India: May–August; Sri Lanka: January–June, occasionally to September, peak March–April. *C. a. brevirostris* end March–July; Oman: first half of year January–July, often double-brooded, enlarged ovary and young in nest July; Pakistan: April, May. *C. a. intermedius* January–June, peak April. Burma: February–May.

DESCRIPTION *C. a. asiaticus*
Adult male Above dark metallic blue and purple; throat and breast dark metallic purple, sides blue-green; belly dark purple separated from breast by narrow reddish-brown band; pectoral tufts bright yellow and scarlet. Iris orange-brown, brown or dark brown. Bill brownish-black, long, curved, and sharply pointed with serrations along cutting edges of both mandibles near tip. Feet brownish-black; mouth pinkish-yellow. **Non-breeding plumage** Above pale olive-brown, as adult female, but wings and tail blackish; below yellow with broad blue-black stripe down middle of throat, breast and belly; summer to late winter; October–January in Karachi.
Adult female Above olive-brown, below dull yellow.
Juvenile Like female but paler below.

GEOGRAPHICAL VARIATION
C. a. asiaticus (Latham, 1790) (whole of India from Himalayan foothills southwards where other forms do not occur; Sri Lanka) Described above.
C. a. brevirostris (Blanford, 1873) (south-east Oman, southern Iran, Baluchistan and Pakistan to western Gujarat and Rajasthan) From *asiaticus* by shorter bill, male greener above and reddish-brown pectoral band often absent; female paler. Juvenile whiter on flanks than female.
C. a. intermedius (Hume, 1870) (northern Andhra Pradesh, Orissa, Assam, Bangladesh to Indochina and south Yunnan) Male differs from *asiaticus* by more violet-purple upperparts, chin and throat. Juvenile buffier-grey below than female.

MEASUREMENTS Wing 54-60 (male *asiaticus*), 53-59 (male *intermedius*), 51-56 (female *asiaticus*), 50-55 (female *intermedius*), 55-57 (unsexed *brevirostris*); **tail** 31-38 (male *asiaticus*), 34-40 (male *intermedius*), 29-34 (female *asiaticus*), 30-35 (female *intermedius*), 34-35 (unsexed *brevirostris*); **bill** 19.5-22 (male *asiaticus*), 19-22 (male *intermedius*), 18-22 (female *asiaticus*), 19-20 (female *brevirostris*), 19-20 (female *intermedius*), 14-16 (unsexed *brevirostris*); **gape** 16.8-20.8 (male *intermedius*), 16.5-18.4 (male *brevirostris*), 14.6-16.9 (female *brevirostris*), 17.5-20.1 (female *intermedius*); **tarsus** 14-16 (male *asiaticus*), 14-15 (female *asiaticus*); **mass** 6.9-11 (male *asiaticus*), 5-10 (female *asiaticus*).

REFERENCES Ali (1931, 1932, 1969), Ali & Ripley (1974), Bharucha (1982), Das (1963), Davidar (1985), J. Elkin (pers. comm.), Fleming *et al.* (1976), Gallagher & Woodcock (1980), Grimmett *et al.* (1998), Henry (1955),

Kumar (1984), Kumar *et al.* (1984), Latham (1790), Majumdar (1980, 1981a), Mason & Lefroy (1912), McClure (1974), Meyer de Schauensee (1984), Rahman *et al.* (1993), Raju (1998), Raju & Reddy (1989), Smythies (1986), Suter (1945), Vyawahare (1989), Wait (1931), Whistler (1949).

---

140 OLIVE-BACKED SUNBIRD
Cinnyris jugularis   Plate 26

Certhia jugularis Linnaeus, 1766, *Syst. Nat.* ed. 12, p.185, Philippine islands.

Alternative names: Yellow-bellied Sunbird, Yellow-breasted Sunbird, Black-breasted Sunbird, Black-throated Sunbird

IDENTIFICATION Adult male is mostly olive-green above, brown in *C. j. teijsmanni*, with black wings and tail, latter tipped white; below chiefly yellow, black in *teijsmanni*, often with maroon or chestnut breast-band; varying amounts of black with iridescence on forehead, sides of neck, throat and breast; some have yellowish supercilium and/or moustachial stripe; yellow or orange pectoral tufts. Nonbreeding male, or juvenile male moulting into adult, has black confined to mesial throat-stripe. Adult female lacks all blackish, chestnut or maroon, and has a yellowish supercilium. Juvenile is usually paler and browner than female.
Similar species Female Plain *Anthreptes simplex* (52), Plain-throated *A. malacensis* (53), Red-throated *A. rhodolaema* (54) and Purple-throated Sunbirds *Leptocoma sperata* (90) lack white-tipped black tail, and first and last lack bright yellow below, whereas second has yellow eye-ring. Male black-bellied forms from Black Sunbird *L. sericea* (91) by olive or brown non-iridescent crown; female from *sericea* by supercilium and whitish or yellowish (not grey or orange) throat. Female Purple Sunbird *Cinnyris asiaticus* (139) is much duller; Apricot-breasted Sunbird *C. buettikoferi* (141) is olive-grey, not bright olive, above; female Flame-breasted Sunbird *C. solaris* (142) is greenish, not bright olive, above; female Apo Sunbird *Aethopyga boltoni* (151) has yellow rump; females of Flaming Sunbird *A. flagrans* (153) and Metallic-winged Sunbird *A. pulcherrima* (154) are duller yellow below; female Elegant Sunbird *A. duyvenbodei* (155) has dark olive band across lower throat, whereas male has scarlet ear-coverts, lores and nape; female Lovely Sunbird *A. shelleyi* (156) has much duller underparts; female Gould's Sunbird *A. gouldiae* (157) has grey throat and yellowish rump, and lacks white-tipped black tail; female Green-tailed Sunbird *A. nipalensis* (158) lacks bright yellow below; females of White-flanked Sunbird *A. eximia* (159) and Fork-tailed Sunbird *A. christinae* (160) are much duller below and lack white-tipped black tail; females of Black-throated Sunbird *A. saturata* (161) and Fire-tailed Sunbird *A. ignicauda* (166) have yellow rumps, and latter is much less yellow below.

VOICE Call Loud, rising *tweeet*. Wispy *sweet-sweet*. Short *chup-chup-chup* in flight; finch-like *twee-ez*. Thin nasal upslur, *sweei*, sometimes wavering; repeated *chip* or *tzip* notes. Mating call of male *pease*, repeated 8 times on a descending scale and repeated incessantly. Female utters persistent *tseep* or *sweet*. **Song** Discordant jumble of twittering notes. Musical chirps *cheep, cheep, chee weet*, and a short melody ending in a clear trill.

DISTRIBUTION Burma, Thailand, Indochina, Malay Peninsula; Andamans, Nicobars; south-east China, Hainan Island; Greater Sundas; North Natunas, Philippines; Wallacea; New Guinea, Solomon Islands, Bismarck Archipelago; north-eastern Australia. Once recorded in Bangladesh (Malumghat forest).

HABITAT Lowlands, but up to 1,700 m, in open country, scrub, mangroves, rain forest, riverine forest, at forest edge, *Eucalyptus* woodland, secondary growth, agricultural land, coconut and other plantations, and gardens. In northern Queensland, *Eucalyptus–Melaleuca* woodland on verge of seasonal swamps, with *Acacia* on higher ground, and understorey of *Ziziphus mauritiana*.

STATUS Common and sedentary in coastal northern Queensland (0.2-0.4 pairs/ha and 0.8 pairs/ha in suburban Townsville, Queensland) and coastal islands of Australia (from Cape York south to Staaten river on west coast and to Gladstone on central coast). Common in Andaman and Nicobar islands, Philippines, throughout Greater Sundas, Sumatra, New Guinea, but there absent from forest, throughout Sulawesi from sea-level to 800 m, and in Solomon Islands. Local populations may be destroyed by cyclones. Common in parts of southern Laos.

MOVEMENTS Attempted colonisation of Booby Island, Torres Straits, presumably from nearest occupied island 24 km away (see under Habits). More abundant around Townsville in wet summer months than in dry winter.

FOOD Nectar, small fruits, small insects including locustids and moths, spiders (dismembered whilst hovering in front of their webs). The long narrow tongue is frayed at the tip like a brush, which can be projected far beyond the bill, so that the bird can lap or suck pollen from deep in flowers and catch smaller insects.
Known food-plants *Bauhinia* sp., *Carica papaya*, *Cocos nucifera*, *Dendrophthoe pentandra*, *Dysoxylum gaudichaudianum* (fruits), *Erythrina* sp., *E. indica*, *Ficus* sp., *Firmiana colorata*, *Hemerocallis* sp., *Hibiscus* spp., unidentified mistletoes Loranthaceae, *Morinda* spp., *Moringa oleifera*, *Russelia juncea*.

HABITS Restless; singly, in pairs and sometimes in small parties. Direct flight, swift and darting. Tame near houses, where sometimes nests. Frequently feeds low; hovers to glean vegetation and take swarming insects; assertive and pugnacious. Joins mixed-species parties e.g. with white-eyes *Zosterops* or smaller honeyeaters. Competes ecologically with myzomelid honeyeaters. Male displays below and facing female, lifting head to expose black breast and everting axillary tufts, turning head from side to side, calling. Immature male ringed on Booby Island, Torres Straits, reconnoitred the island, which is 24 km west of Goods Island, staying 3 weeks; returned next year mated with a female and made an attempt to nest, the first landbird known to do so. Host to *Haemoproteus sequeirae*, *Leucocytozoon* sp. *Plasmodium vaughani*, *Trypanosoma* sp. and microfilariae. Type host of the cestode *Allohymenolepis palawanensis*.

BREEDING Nest built entirely by female. One bird made 27 building trips in 29 minutes. Parasitised in Australia by Gould's Bronze-Cuckoo *Chrysococcyx russatus*. Incubation 13-15 days; fledge after 13-15 days. Although clutch normally 2 in Borneo, usually only one chick fledges. Taken by monitor lizards and possibly rats and ground squirrels. **Nest** An oval purse with hooded side-entrance, of grass,

318

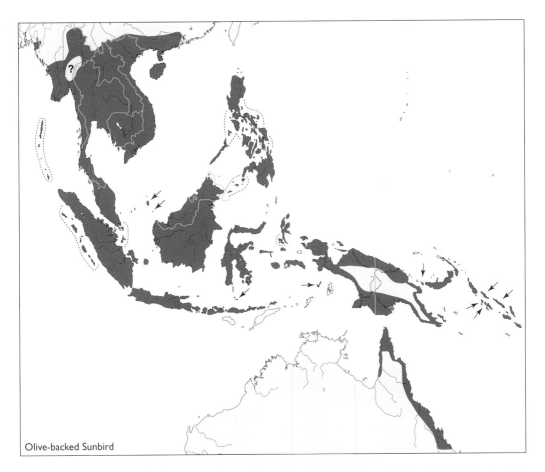

Olive-backed Sunbird

bark, cocoons, moss, lichens, leaf fragments and vegetable fibres, with "beard"; lined with bark or feathers; normally 0.5-1.5 m above ground, occasionally higher (up to 10 m in peninsular Malaysia); in Australia, nests generally low 0.3-7.6 m, mean 1.45 m, usually towards centre of vegetation, with entrances facing inwards. Nests 300-600 mm long, pendulous; may be found in spiny bushes, or suspended from palm fronds, creepers, cables and fence wires, or from roofs or other parts of houses. One, Marinduque, a neatly woven pocket with roofed entrance on side, made of fibre, dead grass and other debris, bound with spiders' web, lined with cotton and fine grass. **Eggs** c/2 (in Andamans, peninsular Malaysia and Australia 1-3, with mean 1.95 in Australia). Dull or faintly glossy. Greygreen or pale greyish-white to pale brown, mottled overall with brown, or mottling concentrated at broad end; may be speckled black; very variable. Marinduque: May 1888, c/3, 16 x 12; whitish with mottled grey undermarkings covering most of shell, and overmarkings pale brown with few spots of deep brown; *andamanica*: 15.0-18.0 (mean 16.6, n=48) x 10.7-12.0 (mean 11.5); *aurora*: 15.7-16.5 x 11.4-12.2; *clementiae*: 15.5-16.7 (mean 16.1, n=4) x 11.5-12.1 (mean 11.8); *flammaxillaris*: 14.4-16.2 (mean 15.3, n=40) x 10.5-12.2 (mean 11.2); *flavigaster*: 14.6-17.8 (mean 16.6, n=8) x 10.5-12.6 (mean 11.7); *frenata*: 15.0-17.8 (mean 16.8, n=39) x 10.5-12.6 (mean 11.8); *jugularis*: 15.2-17.9 (mean 16.4, n=9) x 12.0-13.2 (mean 12.4); *ornata*: 13.6-19.0 (mean 15.6, n=137) x 10.4-12.2 (mean 11.2);

plateni: 15.0-16.6 (mean 15.7, n=4) x 11.4; *proselia*: 14.8-17.0 (mean 15.9, n=10) x 10.7-12.1 (mean 11.2). **Laying months** Andaman islands: c/3, January–August, October; Sulawesi: January–February, and feeding young June, December–September, and on Butung and Hoga probably breeds throughout the year, peaking August–September; Buru: feeding fledged young November; Borneo: mostly January–August, but in all months of the year except October and December; nest building early January (twice); eggs February; feeding fledged young May; nestlings September (in Brunei). Australia: chiefly October–March, but nests found in all months; in northern Queensland generally September–February (70% of rain occurs December–March); 5 nests September, 3 in October, 6 in November; 4 clutches August–early September, 3 October, 4 November; very little breeding late February–June; Indonesia: Java, February–November, Moluccas, Seram, September; peninsular Malaysia: March, May; Burma: January–March, June–September, November; New Guinea: November in south; Nicobar Islands: January, March; Philippines: Sibuyan c/3 June, Basilan c/3 undated, Marinduque c/3 May, Palawan June. Attempted to nest Booby Island, Torres Straits; Thailand: January–May, July–September, November, December.

DESCRIPTION *C. j. ornatus*
Adult male Metallic purple-black forehead (amount variable), chin, throat, breast and sides of neck; rest of

underparts yellow to orange-yellow, with bright yellow pectoral tufts; upperparts olive-green, remiges blackish edged green, tail black tipped white. Iris dark brown, bill and feet black. **?Non-breeding plumage** (could be juvenile male moulting to adult plumage) Metallic purple-black confined to stripe down throat to upper breast; otherwise as female.

Adult female As male, but lacks purple-black, and has pale yellow supercilium.

Juvenile Similar to female; male develops dark glossy throat-streak; paler and browner on head and back in some forms.

GEOGRAPHICAL VARIATION Variation extensive, with some 21 subspecies recognised. In the following list, the last five form a distinctive group which might deserve specific separation, and indeed the last, *C. (j.) teijsmanni*, might itself merit separation, resulting in two or three species.

C. j. andamanicus (Hume, 1873) (Andamans) Male differs from *ornata* in being browner above, usually with no metallic colouring on forehead, metallic colouring of breast with blue-green tinge bordered with rusty band. Yellow of underparts paler than *proscelius*, and upperparts much less bright green. Female paler and duller than female *klossi*.

C. j. aurorus (Tweeddale, 1878) (Philippines – Agutaya, Balabac, Busuanga, Cagayancillo, Culion, Cuyo, Palawan, Dumaran and Calauit) Male differs from *jugularis* in having a bright orange spot or band of variable size on breast.

C. j. flammaxillaris (Blyth, 1845) (Burma, Thailand, Cambodia, north peninsular Malaysia) Male above, including sides of head and forehead, greeny-olive; wings brown, remiges edged green; tail blackish, slightly glossed blue. Chin and throat glossed blue at sides, purple in centre; upper breast glossed purple, with broad maroon band below. Lower breast and belly yellow, greyer on flanks; orange pectoral tufts. Female has blackish tail with slight bluish gloss.

C. j. flavigaster (Gould, 1843) (Solomon Islands and Bismarck Archipelago) Male is brighter and more yellow-green above than *ornatus*; throat to upper breast glossed purple. Tail blackish with slight purple gloss; short yellow line behind eye and moustachial stripe; underparts bright yellow; pectoral tufts orange-yellow. Female very bright yellow below, very similar to male above, with a yellow moustachial stripe.

C. j. frenatus (Müller, 1843) (Morotai, Bacan, ?Bisa, Mare, Moti, Ternate, Kayoa, Halmahera, Obi, Gomumu, New Guinea except where *idenburgi* occurs, northern Queensland, Australia) Male differs from *plateni* by much brighter yellow-olive upperparts, and a longer bill (20-24 mm). Male differs from *flavigaster* by more extensive metallic gloss on breast (but not in all), and more obvious yellow moustachial stripe.

C. j. infrenatus (Hartert, 1903) (Butung, Hoga and Tukangbesi) Male differs from *plateni* in being darker, and has no malar or superciliary stripe.

C. j. jugularis (Linnaeus, 1766) (Philippines, except where *aurorus* or *obscurior* occur) Male differs from *ornatus* in being darker yellow below, occasionally with a brown band bordering throat, and no gloss on forecrown.

C. j. klossi (Richmond, 1902) (includes *blanfordi* [Baker, 1921]) (Nicobars, except Car Nicobar) Male differs from *ornatus* in being brighter and more olive

above, centre of throat metallic purple (and usually forecrown also, latter sometimes purple-blue), and sides of breast metallic purple-blue, lacking maroon on breast; pectoral tufts orange-yellow. Female brighter than *flammaxillaris*.

C. j. obscurior Ogilvie-Grant, 1894 (north Luzon) Male has paler yellow underparts than nominate, and usually has brown border between throat and breast.

C. j. ornatus (Lesson, 1827) (includes *microleucus* Oberholser, 1919 and *pectoralis* [Horsfield, 1821]) (central and southern Malay Peninsula, Lombok, Sumbawa, Santonda, Sangeang, ?Komodo, Rinca, Flores, Paloe, Lomblen, ?Tanimbar, mainland Sumatra and most islands, Borneo) Described above.

C. j. plateni (Blasius, 1885) (Sulawesi, Talaud, Siau, Sangihe, Manadotua, Manterawu, Bangka, Togian and Salayar) Male has no metallic colour on front on face, a black glossed purplish-blue throat with a yellow stripe above it from base of bill under eye to auriculars, and a yellow supercilium. Both sexes similar to *frenatus* but male duller above.

C. j. polyclystus Oberholser, 1912 (Sumatra – Enggano Island) Similar to *ornatus* but much larger, particularly bill; yellow of posterior underparts and olive of upperparts much darker.

C. j. proscelius Oberholser, 1923 (Car Nicobar) Male similar to *andamanicus* and *klossi* but smaller, and differs from latter by having a purple-glossed throat.

C. j. rhizophorae (Swinhoe, 1869) (north Vietnam, Hainan Island) Male differs from *flammaxillaris* by broad maroon band across breast; pectoral tufts yellow; broad sooty band below maroon; rest of underparts greyish-white, more yellow on centre of belly; a minority have a bluish gloss on forecrown.

C. j. robustirostris Mees, 1964 (Banggai and Sula) Male has an even longer bill (26-27.5) than *frenatus*.

C. j. woodi (Mearns, 1909) (Philippines – Bongao, Jolo, Sibutu, Tawitawi, Dammi, Tres Islas, Sanga Sanga, Baluk Baluk, Sitanki, Papahag, Omapoy, Saluag, Simunul, Tumindao, Manuk Manka, Siasi and Simalae) Male differs from *aurorus* in having centre of throat metallic purplish-blue.

The following five subspecies form a group and arguably could be separated specifically from other forms. *C. j. teijsmanni* could even be separated from the other four, thus splitting *C. jugularis* into three species.

C. j. buruensis (Hartert, 1910) (Moluccas – Buru) Male is similar to *clementiae* but bill 16-17, rather than 18-20, and abdomen less black. Differs from *keiensis* in lacking maroon below, and in being brighter green above.

C. j. clementiae (Lesson, 1827) (Moluccas – Seram, Boano, Ambon, Saparua, Nusa Laut and Watubela) Female a little paler than *frenatus*. Male yellowish-olive above; no face-stripes; purplish throat and black abdomen; yellow pectoral tufts.

C. j. keiensis Stresemann, 1913 (Moluccas – Kai) Male similar to *clementiae* but has a slight maroon margin to purplish throat. Male golden-green above; flanks yellow-green; pectoral tufts yellow or orange-yellow; rest of underparts blackish tinged purple-maroon.

C. j. idenburgi Rand, 1940 (north-west New Guinea and Sepik Ramu) Male is dark olive-green above, and black glossed blue-green below, with ?orange pectoral tufts.

C. j. teijsmanni Büttikofer, 1893 (Tanahjampea, Kalao, Bonerate, Kalaota and Madu) Male brownish above, with a dark purplish, or purplish-green, throat, green at sides, and bordered below with dark chestnut (or maroon) band, with rest of underside black glossed purple; pectoral tufts yellow and orange. The female is greyish-olive above.

MEASUREMENTS Wing 51-54 (male *andamanicus*), mean 56.5 (SD 1.1, 10 male *frenatus*), 50-53 (male *klossi*), 53 (male *plateni*), 51 (male *ornatus*), 47-52 (male *proselius*), 50-51 (female *andamanicus*), mean 53.5 (SD 1.6, 10 female *frenatus*), 46-50 (mean 48.4, SD 1.70, 4 female *ornatus*), 47-49 (female *proselius*), 55 (unsexed *jugularis*); **tail** 32-33 (male *andamanicus*), 30-32 (male *klossi*), 36.5 (male *plateni*), 30-31 (male *proselius*), 30-32 (female *andamanicus*), 28 (female *proselius*), 32 (unsexed *jugularis*); **bill** 23-25 (male *andamanicus*), 17-23 (male *klossi*), 19.5 (male *plateni*), 18-19 (male *proselius*), 22-23 (female *andamanicus*), 19 (female *proselius*), 20 (unsexed *jugularis*); **culmen** mean 19.8 (SD 0.62, 10 male *frenatus*), mean 19.6 (SD 0.69, 10 female *frenatus*); gape 18.2 (male *ornatus*), 17.5-19.9 (mean 19, SD 1.15, 4 female *ornatus*); **tarsus** 14 (male *andamanicus*), 14 (male *klossi*), 14 (male *plateni*), 14 (male *proselius*), 14 (female *andamanicus*), 14 (female *proselius*), 14 (unsexed *jugularis*); **mass** 6.7 (male *ornatus*), 6.0-6.9 (mean 6.4, SD 0.38, 4 female *ornatus*), 8.8-10.5 (mean 9.7, S.D. 0.59, 7 male *flavigaster*), 7.1-9.1 (mean 8.4, S.D. 1.1, 3 female *flavigaster*).

REFERENCES Ali & Ripley (1974), Beehler *et al.* (1986), Bishop (1992), Blakers *et al.* (1984), Bruce (1986), M. Catterall (pers. comm.), Coates & Bishop (1997), Davison (in prep.), Deardorff *et al.* (1978), Eck (1974), Evans *et al.* (2000), Garnett *et al.* (1991), Grimmett *et al.* (1998), Holmes & Wood (1979), Jepson (1993), Kratter *et al.* (2001), Linnaeus (1766), Linsley (1995), Maher (1991, 1992), Mann (1996), McGregor (1905a), Medway & Wells (1976), Meyer de Schauensee (1984), Oberholser (1912), Ogilvie-Grant & Whitehead (1898), Pizzey (1980), Pizzey & Knight (1997), Rand & Gilliard (1966), Sheldon *et al.* (in press), Smythies (1981, 1986), Watling (1983), White & Bruce (1986), Zimmer (1918).

---

141 APRICOT-BREASTED SUNBIRD
Cinnyris buettikoferi   Plate 25

Cinnyris büttikoferi, Hartert, 1896, *Novit. Zool.* 3, p.581, Sumba island (Lesser Sunda islands).

Taxonomic note Possibly conspecific with *C. jugularis*.

IDENTIFICATION Adult male olive-brown above; dark metallic purplish bluish-green gorget; rest of underparts yellow, with orange patch on breast. Adult female is duller, and paler below, than male, with pale yellow or whitish throat, greenish sides to breast, rest of underparts yellow. **Similar species** Female Plain-throated Sunbird *Anthreptes malacensis* (53) has yellow eye-ring, lacking in female *buettikoferi*.

VOICE Call Sharp, high *chee* or *sip* in flight. **Song** 4-8 note repeats of *wee-chew, wee-chew, wee-chew, wee-chew-wee*. Long, sweet, high, tinkling warble.

DISTRIBUTION Endemic to Sumba (Lesser Sunda Islands).

HABITAT Forest edge, in low secondary forest, mixed

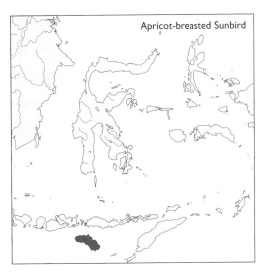

Apricot-breasted Sunbird

cultivation and scrub; in lowlands up to at least 950 m. Favoured habitat may be open/young secondary growth, particularly at low altitudes.

STATUS Common. Fieldwork in past 10 years suggests a population of over 750,000 birds.

MOVEMENTS Unknown.

FOOD Not known.
Known food-plants None.

HABITS Singly or in pairs; conspicuous; mainly in mid-storey to canopy, occasionally lower.

BREEDING Nothing recorded. **Nest** Unknown. **Eggs** Unknown.

DESCRIPTION
Adult male Crown grey-brown; neck and back brown with strong olive tinge; remiges brown edged green; tail blackish, slightly glossed, with brown tips. Chin to upper breast iridescent purplish blue-green; orange breast-patch; bright yellow pectoral tufts; white underwing coverts; rest of underparts yellow. Bill dark brown in female, black in male; feet blackish; iris dark brown.
Adult female As male, but whole underside yellow, paler on throat, with greenish-olive sides of breast.
Juvenile Unknown.

GEOGRAPHICAL VARIATION None.

MEASUREMENTS Wing 50.3-53 (males), 50, 51 (2 females); **bill** 20.9, 22.6, 22.9 (3 males), 20.6, 21.8 (2 females); **mass** no data.

REFERENCES Coates & Bishop (1997), Hartert (1896), Jones *et al.* (1994, 1955), White & Bruce (1986).

---

142 FLAME-BREASTED SUNBIRD
Cinnyris solaris   Plate 27

Nectarinia solaris Temminck, 1825, *Pl. Col., livr.* 58, pl.347, fig.3, Amboine; error = Timor, see Hartert, 1904, *Novit. Zool.* 11, p.214.

IDENTIFICATION Adult male chiefly green and golden above; wings and tail brown, latter with pale tips; forehead, crown, cheeks and throat metallic blue-green and purple; breast orange-red; pectoral tufts orange or yellow; rest of underparts orange, yellow and greeny-yellow. Adult female mostly greenish above; tail glossed black with large amount of white; below yellow. Juvenile greyer than female.
Similar species Female Plain-throated Sunbird *Anthreptes malacensis* (53) from both sexes by yellow eye-ring, and lack of white-spotted black tail; female Olive-backed Sunbird *Cinnyris jugularis* (140) from both sexes by bright olive not greenish upperparts, brighter underparts.

VOICE Call No information. **Song** 3-4 halting high-pitched sweet notes (duration 1 second) alternating up and down; repeated at half-second intervals. Sings from exposed perch in canopy.

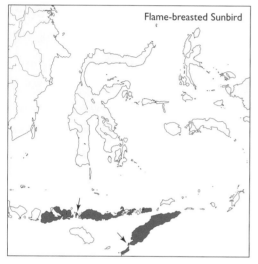

Flame-breasted Sunbird

DISTRIBUTION Endemic to Lesser Sundas, occurring on Sumbawa, Flores, Lomblen, Alor, Semau, Roti, Timor, Wetar and Komodo.

HABITAT Scrub, secondary monsoon forest, bushy and wooded places, at forest edge, in cultivation and suburban gardens; lowlands to 1,000 m (Flores).

STATUS Scarce to abundant, depending on island.

MOVEMENTS Unknown.

FOOD Not known.
Known food-plants None.

HABITS Singly, in pairs or up to 6 birds. Sings from exposed bare branches in canopy.

BREEDING Nothing recorded.

DESCRIPTION *C. s. solaris*
Adult male Dull green to golden above; wings and tail dark brown, former edged green, latter with slight bluish-black gloss; terminal third of outer tail feathers grey, tips of 2nd and 3rd greyish. Metallic blue-green forehead and crown, cheeks and throat, latter with purple centre forming contrasting stripe; breast orange-red, pectoral tufts orange or deep yellow; abdomen orange or yellow; underwing-coverts whitish; flanks more greeny-yellow. Bill blackish; feet blackish; iris blackish-brown.

Adult female Greenish above; yellow supercilium pronounced in some, lacking in others, wings brown edged green; tail blackish with slight green gloss, terminal half of outer feathers white and large whitish tips to second feathers. Underparts yellow, deeper on lower breast and belly.
Juvenile As female but greyer above and below; yellow confined to sides of neck, flanks and belly; underwing-coverts yellowish-white.

GEOGRAPHICAL VARIATION Clinal in males: dull green to golden above, pectoral tufts yellowish to orange. Dullest in Sumbawa and Flores, grading through Lomblen and Alor, brighter in Semau and Timor, and richest in Wetar. Female on Wetar bright (not sulphur-) yellow below.
>   *C. s. exquisitus* Hartert, 1904 (Wetar) Male has orange-yellow, not deep yellow pectoral tufts; female is bright yellow, not sulphur-yellow below. This form is doubtfully separable, perhaps being merely the end of a cline.
>   *C. s. solaris* (Temminck, 1825) (all range except Wetar) Described above.

MEASUREMENTS Wing 50-55 (mean 52.6, 20 males), 50, 50, 50 (3 females), 48 (unsexed juvenile); **tail** 27-35 (mean 31.9, SD 2.60, 10 males), 27-32 (mean 30.0, SD 2.16, 4 females); **bill** 18.8-21.9 (mean 20.2, SD 0.90, 10 males), 18.0-19.7 (mean 19.1, SD 0.78, 4 females); **gape** 17.1-20.7 (mean 19.3, 17 males), 18.5, 19.3, 19.6 (3 females), 17.4 (unsexed juvenile); **tarsus** 14-17 (mean 15.1, SD 0.99, 10 males), 14-16 (mean 14.5, SD 1.0, 4 females).

REFERENCES Bishop (1992), Bruce (1986), Coates & Bishop (1997), Temminck (1825), White & Bruce (1986).

143 SOUIMANGA SUNBIRD
Cinnyris sovimanga   Plate 27

Certhia sovimanga Gmelin, 1788, *Syst. Nat.* 1, p.471, Madagascar. (*souimanga* sometimes used instead of *sovimanga*, as latter meaningless form only used since no u available in Latin)

Alternative name: Sovimanga Sunbird

Probably forms a superspecies with *C. humbloti*, *C. comorensis* and *C. coquerellii* and possibly with *C. jugularis*, from which the others may be derived.

IDENTIFICATION Adult male dark green and olive-grey above; wings and tail dark brown; throat to breast glossy green and blue bordered dark brownish-red; rest of underparts variably sooty-brown, yellow or grey. Adult female is dark olive-brown above; throat to breast greyish with dark scaling; rest of underparts yellow and grey-green. Juvenile differs from female in lacking scaling.
Similar species Male differs from Madagascar Sunbird *Cinnyris notatus* (144) in smaller size and having olive-grey (not glossy dark green and blue) lower back, rump and uppertail-coverts, and dark reddish-brown (not glossy violet) band on lower breast; female differs from female *notatus* by lack of narrow white supercilium and heavy dark ventral mottling and streaking, and lack of whitish tips to tail feathers.

VOICE Call Loud chirps, including characteristic constant *pit* repeated up to 4 times. A plaintive diminishing *teeee*, followed by an oft-repeated *teeteeteetee*. *C. s. abbotti* utters *chissik* calls. **Song** Short warbling phrases. *C. s. abbotti* has a warbling song interspersed with harsher notes.

DISTRIBUTION Endemic to Madagascar, and the Glorieuses (Glorioso) and Aldabra Islands.

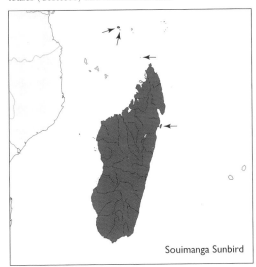

Souimanga Sunbird

HABITAT Forests, mangroves and secondary growth, and around habitation; lowlands to 2,300 m. In eastern Madagascar to 2,050 m. In south-east Madagascar much less common at 410 m than at 810-1,900 m. *C. s. apolis* occurs in spiny subdesert vegetation and adjoining plantations.

STATUS Abundant on Madagascar, occurring throughout the island, on Grande Glorieuse and Aldabra Archipelago.

MOVEMENTS Unknown. Becomes abundant in some areas where certain plants, e.g. *Aloe* spp., *Fernandoa* sp. and *Kalanchoe* sp., in flower.

FOOD Insects: Coleoptera (including Elateridae), Hymenoptera (including Apoidea and Formicidae), Hemiptera, Homoptera (including Jassidae), Orthoptera; spiders (including Salticidae), other small arthropods, nematodes, nectar. Pierces flower buds.
Known food-plants *Acacia farnessiana*, *A. sakalawa*, *A. rovumae*, *Albizia polyphylla*, sap from *Agave* sp. stalks gouged by ring-tailed lemurs *Lemur catta*, *Agave rigida*, *Aloe vaombe*, *A. divericata*, *Bakerella* spp., *Capparis chrysomeia*, *Citrus* sp., *Cynanchum* spp., *Cordia* spp., *Delonix regia*, *Dicoma* sp., *Eucalyptus citriodora*, *Euphorbia tirucalli*, *Fernandoa madagascariensis*, *Hibiscus mascarenhasia*, *Kalanchoe beharensis*, *Lantana camara*, *Liparis* sp., *Malva* sp., *Maerua filiformis*, *Medinilla torrentum*, *Opuntia* sp., *Plectranthus* spp., *Sarcostemma decorsei*, *Tamarindus indica*, Leguminosae.

HABITS Occurs in pairs in breeding season; gregarious at other times, gathering into groups of up to 6 or more. Joins mixed-species groups e.g. with *C. notatus*, Madagascar White-eye *Zosterops maderaspatana*, Common Jery *Neomixis tenella* and/or Common Newtonia *Newtonia brunneicauda*. Feeds by hovering as well as when perched. Swift direct flight. Guards *Aloe* flowers and aggressive towards *C. notatus*. Females dispute *Bakerella* sp. flowers. Host to microfilariae of *Cardiofilaria andersonii*.

BREEDING Female broods and feeds young; male occasionally feeds female; incubation 14 days. On Aldabra nesting stimulated when increase in nectar abundance precedes increase in insect abundance. **Nest** Suspended from buildings, coral overhangs and branches (*aldabrensis*) at c.2 m in outer branches. One on Aldabra 1 m up in mangroves, at least 16 m from dry ground. Nest on Madagascar like that of *C. notatus* but smaller, usually in darker places; occasionally in trees or from roots along roadside cuttings, usually in bushes 0.5-2.5 m above ground; camouflaged and hanging from drooping branch or root. Made of plant down, dry leaves, feathers, hair, bark and lichens, the latter also used as decoration; small porch over entrance one-third from top. **Eggs** c/1-3, commonest 2; *souimanga*: 54 nests with c/2, 2 with c/3, 2 with c/1; 108 eggs from 54 nests; 15.0-16.5 (mean 15.4, n=56) x 10.4-12.4 (mean 11.2). Pale greyish-white to brownish-grey, speckled brownish-grey, especially at larger pole; mass of 94 fresh eggs 0.65-1.11 g, mean 1.0. **Laying months** Madagascar: breeding begins at start of rains, October, ending in March in north-west and January in south-east. In the east it begins July–August, towards end of rains. Southeast Madagascar: October, fledglings September–November, enlarged gonads late September–late December; Aldabra: August–March, enlarged testes June, juvenile January, 2 young in nest and 2 eggs March (*aldabrensis*). Isles Glorieuses: January.

DESCRIPTION *C. s. sovimanga*
Adult male Crown, upper back, mantle and wing-coverts glossed dark green; lower back and rump dark olive-grey; tail dark brown with slight dark green gloss; wings dark brown, remiges edged green. Throat to upper breast glossed green with glossy blue lower border, and dark brownish-red band below this; rest of breast sooty-brown; pectoral tufts yellow; belly variable yellow to off-whitish, often yellower in centre; rest of underparts mixed yellow and grey; dark streaking on vent. Bill and feet black, iris brown.
Non-breeding plumage Male variable; may have many metallic feathers on head and breast, or almost completely lacks metallic feathering, and has odd red feather on chest. Subadult has yellow fleshy gape.
Adult female Dark olive-brown above; pale supercilium from just in front of eye; throat to breast greyish with dark fringes to feathers giving a variable scaled effect; centre of belly yellow, rest of underparts grey-green; indistinct dark streaking on breast and flanks, with more distinct streaking on vent.
Juvenile As female, but without scaling on throat.

GEOGRAPHICAL VARIATION
C. s. abbotti Ridgway, 1894 (Aldabra group – Assumption Island) Male differs from *buchenorum* in having paler brown underparts and greenish flanks.
C. s. aldabrensis Ridgway, 1894 (Aldabra Island) Male has red band of chest much broader than in nominate, rest of underparts sooty-brown. Female is darker than nominate.
C. s. apolis Hartert, 1920 (south-west Madagascar, east to Ankapoky) Male differs from nominate in having little yellow on centre of belly, which is creamy-white, underparts below sooty band off-white, breast-band darker and redder; female is greyer, less olive above, and paler below. Those at Petriky intermediate between *apolis* and *sovimanga*.
C. s. buchenorum Williams, 1953 (Aldabra group – Cosmoledo Island) Male differs from nominate in

323

having broader red band and rest of underparts, except pectoral tufts, dark sooty-brown, rump glossy green; female much darker on throat and breast.

C. s. sovimanga (Gmelin, 1788) (Madagascar where *apolis* does not occur; Isles Glorieuses) Described above. Population on Isles Glorieuses has slightly broader breast-band and narrower black abdomen, but not sufficiently significant to separate.

MEASUREMENTS Wing 54 (male *abbotti*), 51-55 (male *aldabrensis*), 54-55 (male *apolis*), 54 (male *buchenorum*), 51-56 (mean 54.1, 14 male *sovimanga*, Madagascar), 54-57 (mean 55.2, 6 male *sovimanga*, Isles Glorieuses), 48-52 (female *aldabrensis*), 47 (female *apolis*), 47-52 (mean 49.4, 14 female *sovimanga*, Madagascar), 49, 49, 50 (3 female *sovimanga*, Isles Glorieuses); **culmen from base** 20.5-24.0 (mean 22.0, 14 male *sovimanga*, Madagascar), 21.0-23.0 (mean 22.0, 6 male *sovimanga*, Isles Glorieuses), 19.0-21.5 (mean 20.5, 14 female *sovimanga*, Madagascar), 19.0, 19.5 (2 female *sovimanga*, Isles Glorieuses); **gape** 18.8 (male *abbotti*), 17.6-20.4 (male *aldabrensis*), 19.2-19.8 (male *apolis*), 18.8 (male *buchenorum*), 16.3-17.0 (female *aldabrensis*), 18.3 (female *apolis*); **mass** 6.2, 6.7, 7.0 (3 male *apolis*), 5.5-8.5 (mean 7.6, SD 0.8, 16 male *sovimanga*), 6.0, 6.0 (2 female *apolis*), 5.5-7.6 (mean 6.9, SD 0.6, 16 female *sovimanga*).

REFERENCES Benson (1984), Frith (1977), Goodman *et al.* (1997), Goodman & Parillo (1997), Goodman & Putnam (1997), Gmelin (1788), A. F. A. Hawkins (pers. comm.), Langrand (1990), Louette (1988), Milon (1949), Prys-Jones & Diamond (1984), Sinclair & Langrand (1998), Williams (1953).

---

144 MADAGASCAR SUNBIRD
Cinnyris notatus   Plate 39

Certhia notatus P.L.S. Müller, 1776, *Natursyst.*, Suppl. p.99, Madagascar.

Alternative names: Madagascar Green Sunbird, Long-billed Green Sunbird

IDENTIFICATION Adult male dark above, glossed green, blue and purple; chin to breast glossy green; glossy violet band on lower breast; rest of underparts blackish. Adult female olive-brown above; tail black with bluish sheen, edged and tipped white; thin white supercilium from just in front of eye; greyish throat and breast, with strong dark streaking and mottling. Juvenile more olive above, greyer below, with less mottling.

Similar species Male from male Souimanga Sunbird *Cinnyris sovimanga* (143) by black belly rather than yellow or whitish, by glossy dark green and blue rather than olive-grey lower back, rump and uppertail-coverts, and by glossy violet band on lower breast, rather than dark reddish-brown; female differs from all sympatric sunbird females by narrow whitish supercilium and heavy dark mottling and streaking below, and also from Humblot's Sunbird *C. humbloti* (146) and *C. sovimanga* by whitish tips to tail; male from male *C. humbloti* by glossy violet band on lower breast and blackish or blackish-brown posteriorly, rather than dull red band on breast grading into yellowish-green of belly and vent; male from Anjouan Sunbird *C. comorensis*

(147) by purple and green sheen on tail rather than blue, and violet gloss on carpal joint; male from male Mayotte Sunbird *C. coquerelLii* (148) by lack of orange-red below.

VOICE Call A loud penetrating nasal *chew-chew-chew* or *chip-chip-chip-chip*. Also, male utters an oft-repeated, piercing, *pti* or *ptii* from top of tree when breeding, with first two *pti* notes rising, middle group at same pitch and last two diminishing. Much less variable than *C. sovimanga*. **Song** Quiet, slow, warbling from cover.

DISTRIBUTION Madagascar and Comoro Islands.

Madagascar Sunbird

HABITAT In Madagascar wooded areas, *Eucalyptus* plantations, gardens, secondary forest, lowland forest, mid-altitude rain forest, dry forest, mangroves and parks. Up to 1,200 m in south-east Madagascar, and up to 2,050 m in eastern Madagascar. On Mohéli, Comoros, found in forest at all altitudes, most frequent at 400-500 m.

STATUS Common on Madagascar's high plateau in *Eucalyptus* plantations and gardens, fairly common in lowland forest and mid-altitude rain forest, less common in forest at high altitudes, and patchy in south-western dry forest. Widely but thinly distributed in the Comoro Islands, except in the heath zone on Mount Karthala; commonest in evergreen forest. Generally more numerous than *C. humbloti*.

MOVEMENTS Patchiness of records in south-western dry forest of Madagascar may be attributable to seasonal movements. Definitely absent from dry spiny forest in south-west for long periods; returns July–September, and an increase in some of areas of such forest July–February.

FOOD Ants, beetles (adults and larvae), caterpillars, grasshoppers, gastropods, spiders and nematodes; plant seeds and nectar.

Known food-plants *Agave rigida, Aloe divericata, A. vaombe, Bakerella tandrokensis*, ?*Dombeya* sp., *Eucalyptus* sp., *Fernandoa madagascariensis, Lonicera* sp., unidentified Leguminosae, *Medinilla* sp., *Musa sapientum, Ophiocoles comorensis*.

HABITS Occurs in pairs or groups of 3-5 in mixed-species flocks e.g. with *C. souimanga*, Madagascar White-eye *Zosterops maderaspatana* and/or Common Newtonia *Newtonia* *brunneicauda*. Noisy and territorial at flowering trees, males chasing others for long distances. Feeds high in canopy, particularly in *Eucalyptus* inflorescences. Feeds by hovering and from perches. Flies high with powerful flight. During interlude when chasing female, male perched with neck extended upwards, bill slightly agape and closed wings, lifted slightly away from body. Wings then raised and lowered several times. Chases *C. sovimanga* from *Fernandoa* sp. trees.

BREEDING Male occasionally feeds female, but female broods and feeds young; male once recorded feeding young. Young in nest 15-16 days. On Grand Comoro, nests in evergreen forest. Nest <2-5.5 m above ground, well camouflaged, hanging from drooping branch with broad attachment at top, looking like a *Eucalyptus* leaf in silhouette; small porch over entrance one-third from top. Made of plant down, dry leaves, feathers, hair, bark and lichen, which are also used for decoration. Race *moebii*: made of fine grass, covered with dark brown and black fibres, lined with soft moss and asclepiad and composite pappus; decorated with a few dried leaves and moss. Top to bottom 230 mm, entrance diameter 30 mm, top of entrance with overhanging lip 100 m from top of nest; *voeltzkowi*: similar to *moebii*, 8 m above ground in evergreen forest. **Eggs** Race *moebii*: 20.4 x 14.1, white, smooth, finely and fairly thickly streaked all over with light dull brown on pale grey, the underlying markings being mainly in confluent concentrations at top of large end; *notatus*: c/1 usually, but c/2 Tananarive at 1,200 m, July; 18.5-21 (mean 19.2, n=4) x 13-14 (mean 13.9); pale grey to sienna-brown with some grey-brown speckling forming band at broadest area. Fresh mass 1.69 and 1.78 g. **Laying months** Mohéli, Comoros: female and juvenile, February; female with brood-patch February, female which had recently laid September; enlarged testes September; Grand Comoro: enlarged testes Convalescence, September, nests August, September; Madagascar: breeding starts at beginning of rains, October–March in north-west, October–end January in southeast; starts towards end of rains, July–August, in east. Southeast Madagascar enlarged gonads October–November, fledgling September.

DESCRIPTION *C. n. notatus*
Adult male Head, back, scapulars, lesser wing-coverts and uppertail-coverts glossed green, rump glossed green and blue. Tail blackish with purple sheen with some glossy green edging. Wings blackish-brown with some violet gloss on carpal joint. Chin to breast glossy green; glossy violet band separates green from black and blackish-brown of rest of underparts. Undertail-coverts yellowish-white with dark brown centres, giving mottled look. Bill and feet black; iris dark brown. **Non-breeding plumage** Male similar to adult female but with sparse metallic feathers.
Adult female Above brown with olive tinge; very narrow off-white supercilium; darker feather centres on head and nape give slight scaling effect, appearing as conspicuous longitudinal streaking. Greyish throat and breast becoming yellower on lower breast and belly, with heavy dark mottling and streaking; undertail-coverts dark brown with pale edges. Tail blackish with bluish sheen; whitish tips to some feathers, and edges to outer feathers.
Juvenile As female, but chin to chest much greyer and with much less obvious mottling; more olive and less brown above.

GEOGRAPHICAL VARIATION
C. n. moebii Reichenow, 1887 (Grand Comoro Island)

Male differs from *notatus* in having much purple and violet gloss on chin to breast.
C. n. notatus (P. L. S. Müller, 1776) (Madagascar) Described above.
C. n. voeltzkowi Reichenow, 1905 (Mohéli Island, Comoros) Male differs from *notatus* in having duller gloss on chin to breast, with much blue mixed with green.

MEASUREMENTS Wing 74-78 (male *moebii*), 67-73 (male *notatus*), 71-77 (male *voeltzkowi*), 66-68 (female *moebii*), 57-65 (female *notatus*), 69-71 (female *voeltzkowi*); **tail** 40 (female *voeltzkowi*); **bill to feathers** 34 (female *voeltzkowi*); **gape** 31.7-38.3 (male *moebii*), 26.5-29.9 (male *notatus*), 33.3-37.7 (male *voeltzkowi*), 31.0-32.3 (female *moebii*), 25.3-30.2 (female *notatus*), 34.7-37.3 (female *voeltzkowi*); **mass** 16 (male *moebii*), 13.8-17.0 (mean 15.4, SD 1.2, 9 male *notatus*), 19.0-21.0 (mean 20.2, 6 male *voeltzkowi*), 12.0-16.0 (mean 13.8, SD 1.7, 5 female *notatus*), 13.0-21.0 (mean 18.7, 6 female *voeltzkowi*).

REFERENCES Benson (1960), Cheke & Diamond (1986), Forbes-Watson (1969), Goodman *et al.* (1977), Goodman & Parillo (1997), Goodman & Putnam (1996), A. F. A. Hawkins (pers. comm.), M. Herremans (pers. comm.), Langrand (1990), M. Louette (pers. comm.), Louette (1988), Milon (1949).

---

145 SEYCHELLES SUNBIRD
Cinnyris dussumieri   Plate 22

Nectarinia dussumieri Hartlaub, 1860, *J. Orn.*, 8, p.340, Seychelle islands.

Alternative name: Seychelles Blue-headed Sunbird

IDENTIFICATION Adult male is dark brownish-grey above; throat to breast glossy metallic darkish blue; rest of underparts grey-brown and off-white with yellow or orange pectoral tufts, but these are invisible on perched birds; short tail with white tips conspicuous in flight and broad white tips to undertail noticeable on perched bird. Adult female lacks gloss and pectoral tufts, and has pale grey scaling on brownish throat.
Similar species. None.

VOICE Call *Pseeeu*, at 2-second intervals from perch and *tsick-tsick* or *tseet* contact calls e.g. amongst flowers or in flight. Insect-like *tzit tzit*. *Chirr* when alarmed. Short *tsuu* or *tsee* by nest-building females; also used when entering or leaving nest. **Song** High-pitched squeaky and jumbled, from 6 to more than 20 notes, starting slow, *dze-dze-dze-dze*, then becoming faster, *der-tseet-tseet-tsit-tsit-tsit* or *pse-pser-eu-eu-tsit*, and sometimes lasting more than a minute. May be preceded by rattling trill; some notes more spaced out. A rapid purer trill, with notes less squeaky. A vehement complex trilling and a throbbing *chee-chee-chee* by males. A harsh *chesooty-choo* accompanies a head-back display posture and varying in intensity, rhythm and pitch. Female only sings occasionally, producing a slightly quieter, less harsh song than male. A quiet *tsuu* with varying rhythm and short repetitions of same syllable is uttered by male in a hunched posture.

DISTRIBUTION Endemic to the Seychelles; found on

Mahé, Praslin, Silhouette, La Digue, Frégate, Aride, Cousin and Cousine.

May be derived from Souimanga Sunbird *Cinnyris sovimanga* (143) or from Asian Olive-backed Sunbird *C. jugularis* (140) or Long-billed Sunbird *C. lotenius* (149) or is possibly related to Blue-throated Brown Sunbird *Cyanomitra cyanolaema* (75) of continental Africa and Socotra Sunbird *Chalcomitra balfouri* (87) of Socotra (see Benson 1984 for discussion). However, the generic arrangement followed here would make the last two unlikely.

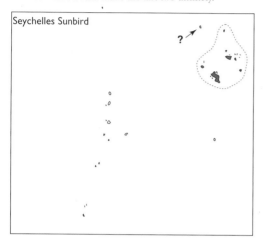

Seychelles Sunbird

HABITAT Occurs from sea-level to 900 m in forest, secondary growth, coconut plantations and farmlands, mostly confined to secondary forest on hills; occurs on "plateau" (low-lying flat area at sea-level) on La Digue and in other habitats on smaller islands. Found low on Mahé, Praslin, and Frégate amongst mangroves, plantations or gardens. Very tolerant of man-made habitats.

STATUS Common and conspicuous on all wooded islands of the Seychelles, where population estimated as well in excess of 10,000 birds in 1978, and has probably benefited from introductions of exotic flowering plants. Used to be absent from Aride but 10-12 birds (4 females) present there in 1993 (Anderson 1994) and pairs now breeding, some polygynously (Lucking 1996). About 5,700 estimated to inhabit Silhouette Island in 1996 (Cresswell *et al.* 1997) at densities of 5.0 per ha (lowland forest), 2.7 (highland forest and moss forest, >200 m), 1.9 (coconut plantations) and 0.3 (*glacis*, i.e. inselbergs or sheets of bare granite, with pockets of shrubs and small trees).

MOVEMENTS Some inter-island movements, as Aride recently re-colonised and bird recovered there which had previously been ringed 20 km south on Cousin Island.

FOOD Nectar, insects including larvae, ants, cockroaches; spiders and other arthropods. Drinks from standing water. **Known food-plants** *Albizia lebbek, Allamanda* sp., *Averrhoa bilimbi, Bougainvillea* sp., *Braunsia* sp., *Camellia thea, Caesalpinia* sp., *Canna* sp., *Carica papaya, Casuarina equisetifolia, Catharanthus roseus, Chrysobalanus icaco, Cocos nucifera, Cordia subcordata, Costus speciosus, Datura metel, Eucalyptus* sp., *Eugenia* spp., *Euphorbia pyrifolia, Ficus* spp., *Gastonia crassa, Gliricidia* sp., *Gossypium hirsutum, Hibiscus* sp., *Kalanchoe pinnata, Lantana camara, Mangifera indica, Morinda citrifolia, Musa* sp., *Nepenthes pervillei* (sweet secretory areas underneath flap above the pitcher only),

Petrea sp., *Phyllanthus casticum, Quiscalis indica, Randia* sp., *Spathodea nilotica, Stachytarpheta cuticifolia, S. jamaicensis, Tabebuia pallida, Tecoma stans, Thespesia populnea, Thevetia peruviana, Thunbergia alata, T. erecta, Turnera* sp. Forages for insects in *Pisonia grandis*.

HABITS Found singly or in pairs. Active, moving fast from flower to flower, remaining about 1 second on each. Usually forages at heights of 6-10 m. Pierces base of large flowers, over 20 mm deep, as well as feeding through corolla tube, but sometimes foiled if perianth is too tough as in *Hibiscus*. Hovers to take nectar e.g. from *Bougainvillea*, and gleans, probes, hovers and flycatches for insects; also takes food from ground, including by pecking down from perch on *Stachytarpheta cuticifolia*, but feeds on nectar in preference. Feeds in mixed flocks with *Foudia madagascariensis* and *Zosterops modestus*, and has been recorded following the latter, when sunbird probed leaves and bark of *Calophyllum inophyllum*. Collects insects from spiders' webs to feed chicks.

Two wing moult periods per year (January–May, but also August–September on Praslin).

Territorial, defending sites throughout the year. Some as small as 900 m². During courtship, male sings or calls from prominent perch of bare branch or flower, 2-10 m high, returning there regularly; while singing, has head back, chest expanded and pectoral tufts visible; may sway from side to side; after singing, may bend forward to c.30° above horizontal, rock c.10° from side to side, and make swallowing motions to emphasise blue gorget; female sings occasionally. Four birds, some of either sex, observed singing together in a *Terminalia latappa* tree. Male actively chases female and sometimes pecks their cloacas, possibly to elicit discarding of sperm if extra-pair copulations are taking place in this species, which is known to be polygynous (see below under breeding). Male also hangs upside-down beneath branches whilst moving towards a female, sometimes fluttering his wings. Female also hangs upside-down and rotates around a branch (in one case for up to 30 seconds while male poked under her tail). Male sometimes hops from one side of a female to the other, landing fleetingly on her back en route, and even two males at a time may do this. Prior to mating, the female crouches down with tail up and wings spread.

Displaying males usually face each other on a branch, about 30 cm apart, singing loudly in turn. Head is thrown back, chest is puffed out to extents commensurate with level of aggression, beak vertical and pectoral tufts well displayed. Sometimes one male alters position to a leaning-forward posture, swinging from side to side with neck outstretched, and occasionally both perform an exaggerated swinging display. Sessions are accompanied by a repetitive call and may last several minutes until one bird departs, chased by other. Such displays may occur during communal feeding in flowering trees.

In response to distant calls, presumably of territory-holding neighbours, single male sometimes adopts a hunched posture, with bill stretched up and forward, and wings held up towards head and about a third open, with body angled forward and drawn in, giving a lean appearance. This posture is accompanied by a quiet throttled-sounding call, with the birds motionless or turning slowly from side to side.

Unpaired adults and juveniles may congregate, especially May–July, on Cousin. Sometimes members of such groups sing at and chase each other. Courtship displays also occur amongst these birds, including homosexual interactions and mountings with swapping of roles with both "partners" playing male and female roles.

Preens for up to 2 minutes on secluded perch, movements including scratching cheek with foot. Often bill-wipes after landing on branch.

Adults taken by Seychelles Kestrel *Falco araea* and fallen eggs and chicks taken by skinks *Mabuya wrightii* and *M. seychellensis* and ghost crabs *Ocypode* sp. Fledglings known to become entangled in webs of palm spiders. Longevity up to at least 13 years.

BREEDING Male selects site, female does most or all building. Male contributes to earlier part of building, but not later. Female may occasionally seek nest material outside territory. One nest completed in 6 days. Pairs show nest-site fidelity. Male defends nest and territory, especially close to nest, and sings from prominent perch, but feeding territories of neighbours overlap. Both sexes are involved in territorial disputes, but usually with rivals of their own sex, on adjacent branches with much posturing and persistent singing. Breeding territories maintained all year. Some monogamous and bond in pairs for life, others polygynous, as male mated with at least two females and fed two sets of offspring, from nests 75 m apart. Another male, previously monogamous, found defending two territories about 300 m apart, each with separate nesting female. Female also defends area close to nest. Female incubates for 11-16 days; most (95% of 277 visits to nest on Aride Island at rate of 10 visits per hour) or all of feeding done by female, but polygynous males fed unfledged chicks with 16% of food items; up to 2 faecal pellets may be removed per hour; little feeding after fledging. On Cousin, some related "helpers", including a three-month-old chick, assist parents with feeding chicks. Young are fed insects only. Fledging success 44.4-75.8% during 3 years on Cousin, with better success usually in years with more rain. Fledglings leave to safety high up in tree near nest and remain in vicinity, dependent on their parents, for a month. Most pairs rear 1 chick per year, sometimes 2, occasionally 3 and one instance of 4, when male took over feeding of fledglings allowing female to nest again quickly. **Nest** Nest pear-shaped or coconut-shaped suspended 1-20 m above ground from end of branch or twig of tree (e.g. *Casuarina* sp., *Citrus* sp. or *Pisonia* sp.; on Cousin 36.5% in *Phyllanthus casticum*, 25% in *Pisonia grandis*, 14.5% in *Morinda citrifolia*, 12% in *Casuarina equisetifolia*, 3% in *Ficus reflexa*, 2% in *Euphorbia pyrifolia* and 7% in other species) or on end of leaf-stalks; 155 x 85 mm; entrance sheltered by porch half-way up; made of dead grass, some also with *Casuarina* needles, legume fruits, broad leaves, strips of bark or plant stems, strips of coconut fronds, spiders' webs, down, body feathers of birds especially seabirds, cotton, pieces of string, nylon string, plastic and other domestic debris, moss and palm fibres, lichens, tendrils, leaf skeletons, fine roots, skink skin; lined with kapok, cotton wool or feathers (these mostly downy feathers obtained from ground, occasionally from air, and even from living chicks of Fairy Tern *Gygis alba*). Many with tail up to 300 mm long. Nest hidden on Mahé and Silhouette where Seychelles Kestrels *Falco araea* occur. **Eggs** c/1, but up to 4 chicks reared per pair per year. Eggs dirty white spotted brown. 18.6-18.9 (mean 18.7) x 10.3-12.8 (mean 11.6, n=2). **Laying months** Some breeding activity in every month. Active nests declined September–December/January suggesting peak during first part of north-

west monsoon. Mahé 10 nests September–October, 8 concealed, 3 December–January; Silhouette 5 December–January, 3 concealed, La Digue 6 September, 5 exposed, height 3-8.4 m, 8 January, all exposed; Praslin 5 September, 3 exposed, 5 December–January, all exposed; Fregate 4 October, 3 exposed; Cousin 3 September, 1 exposed, 10 December, all exposed, breeding in all months except April–June.

DESCRIPTION
Adult male Sooty-brown above; throat to breast glossed metallic darkish blue; pectoral tufts lemon-yellow, yellow-orange or bright orange-red; rest of underparts grey-brown grading into whitish on vent and undertail-coverts; some show trace of maroon breast-band. Rectrices tipped white, broadly below, narrowly above. Bill black; iris grey, brown, maroon or black; feet dark slate or black.
Adult female Differs from male in lacking gloss and pectoral tufts, and has paler tips to throat and upper breast, giving a slight scaled effect in some. Remiges have olive edging, and tips of tail grey or white; underwing-coverts browny-white with or without a yellowish tinge.
Juvenile Slightly smaller-billed and underparts sparsely speckled. Males do not gain pectoral tufts until second moult.

GEOGRAPHICAL VARIATION None described; variation in colour of male's pectoral tufts is non-geographical.

MEASUREMENTS Wing 58-62 (mean 60.7, 18 males), 55-61 (mean 58.2, 5 females); **bill** 24-25 (7 males), 23-24 (4 females); **gape** 21.5-25.2 (mean 23.0, 14 males), 20.3-22.8 (mean 21.4, SD 1.27, 4 females).

REFERENCES Anderson (1994), Beckett (1996), Benson (1967, 1984), Cresswell *et al.* (1997), Delacour (1944), Diamond (1984), Gaymer *et al.* (1969), Greig-Smith (1978, 1980, 1986), Hall & Moreau (1970), Hartlaub (1860), Lucking (1996), Oliver (1991), Owen & Bresson (1987), Prys-Jones & Diamond (1984), Sinclair & Langrand (1998), Watson (1984), Williams (1953).

---

146 HUMBLOT'S SUNBIRD
Cinnyris humbloti   Plate 27

Cinnyris humbloti Milne-Edwards & Oustalet, 1885, *Compt. Rend. Acad. Sci. Paris* 101, p.220, Great Comoro.

IDENTIFICATION Adult male green above with dark gloss, or washed golden; throat to breast glossed green or purple bordered dull red; pectoral tufts yellow; rest of underparts yellowish-green. Adult female olive-green above, greyer on head, brighter on rump, unglossed; throat to belly greyish with dark mottling and streaking; rest of underparts yellowish-green; no pectoral tufts; white tips to tail; vent buffy-white.
Similar species Much smaller and shorter-billed than Madagascar Sunbird *C. notatus* (144). Male *C. notatus* has glossy violet band across breast and black or blackish band posteriorly to this, whereas *humbloti* has dull red band grading into yellowish-green of belly and vent. Female *notatus* differs from female *humbloti* by white supercilium, dark brown on undertail-coverts and lack of white tips to tail feathers.

VOICE Call scolding *tssk, tssk*. **Song** Jumbled, chippy, series of notes.

Humblot's Sunbird

DISTRIBUTION Endemic to West Comoro Islands.

HABITAT Found in forest at all altitudes (although less frequent than *C. notatus* on Mohéli), scrub and gardens; sea-level to 790 m.

STATUS Common endemic on Grand Comoro and Mohéli.

MOVEMENTS Unknown.

FOOD Insects including Diptera, Hemiptera, Coleoptera, larvae of Lepidoptera; spiders, vegetable matter and nectar.
Known food-plants *Cocos nucifera*, *Cussonia* sp., *Eucalyptus* sp., *Impatiens* sp.

HABITS Feeds by gleaning and hover-gleaning on coconut leaf-tips. Male displays pectoral tufts when excited or alarmed.

BREEDING Nest Race *humbloti*: Attached by moss to slender horizontal branches of *Philippia* bushes, 3-5 m above ground. Made of fine grass, thickly covered on outside with moss, lined with soft silken pappus (apparently from asclepiads) and a few feathers. Some with a few strands of *Usnea barbata* on outside. Average dimensions: top to bottom 130 mm, greatest width 80 mm, entrance diameter 20 mm, about equidistant from top to bottom. Race *mohelicus*: almost at sea-level, 2 m above ground, overhanging path. Made of fine grass, lined with asclepiad pappus. Another nest, generally similar but in evergreen forest at 700 m, had a little moss on the outside. Attached 3 m up to horizontal stem of a palm overhanging a well-frequented path. **Eggs** Race *humbloti*: c/1; 17.7 x 12.1; elongate and smooth, rather pointed for a sunbird; whitish-grey or very faintly tinged blue, finely but not thickly spotted and speckled all over with pale yellow-brown on underlying pale lilac-grey, with zone of concentration around the top; *mohelicus*: 16.3 x 11.3. elongate, smooth, whitish with very faint creamy tinge, otherwise as *humbloti*. All markings rather faint, grey underlying markings being scarcely distinguishable. **Laying months** Grand Comoro: 1,645-1,900 m, September, male with enlarged testes August; Mohéli: food-carrying February, males with enlarged testes and female with 1 mm oocytes September. Eggs and young in nest September.

DESCRIPTION *C. h. humbloti*
Adult male Crown, shoulder, throat to upper breast glossed green, bordered by narrow glossy purple band; hindcrown has some glossy purple. Wings dark brown edged green; tail blackish with slight green gloss. Rest of upperparts green with more golden wash on mantle; broad dull red band across breast grading into yellowish-green of belly and vent; underwing-coverts yellowish-white, pectoral tufts yellow; tail narrowly tipped grey. Iris dark brown, bill black, feet black with grey soles.
Adult female Olive-green above. Tail as male, but otherwise upperparts without gloss. Throat to upper belly greyish, feathers with dark centres giving scaled or speckled effect; rest of underparts yellowish with fine dark streaking becoming unmarked buffy-white on vent, some having golden wash on belly; no pectoral tufts.
Juvenile Male *mohelicus* resembles adult female but has maroon patches on sides of chest and dark olive-green on sides of belly, with a few metallic violet feathers on forehead and crown. Male *humbloti* blackish above, glossier on head and back, lower breast to belly brown, becoming greyer and paler on flanks and towards vent.

GEOGRAPHICAL VARIATION
C. h. humbloti Milne-Edwards & Oustalet, 1885 (Grand Comoro Island) Described above.
C. h. mohelicus Stresemann & Grote, 1926 (Mohéli Island) Slightly smaller than nominate. Male duller green above without golden wash and with more extensive glossy purple area on shoulder than nominate; larger grey tips to tail feathers. Glossy areas of head and throat to breast bronze-purple, with purple lower border to breast. Female duller above than nominate.

MEASUREMENTS Wing 50-54 (mean 51.7, 18 male *humbloti*), 49-52 (mean 50.6, SD 1.43, 10 male *mohelicus*), 47-49 (mean 47.9, SD 0.90, 7 female *humbloti*), 45-49 (mean 47.0, SD 1.30, 11 female *mohelicus*); **tail** 27-32 (mean 29.7, SD 2.16, 10 male *humbloti*), 26-33 (mean 28.8, SD 2.68, 5 male *mohelicus*), 29, 30 (2 female *humbloti*), 27-33 (mean 29.4, SD 2.22, 7 female *mohelicus*); **bill** 17-20 (mean 19.1, SD 1.10, 10 male *humbloti*), 17-18 (mean 17.3, SD 0.52, 6 male *mohelicus*), 18, 19 (2 female *humbloti*), 15-18 (mean 16.4, SD 0.92, 8 female *mohelicus*); **gape** 17.5-19 (mean 18.2, 8 male *humbloti*), 16.8-17.8 (mean 17.3, SD 0.41, 4 male *mohelicus*), 16.1-17.4 (mean 16.9, SD 0.60, 4 female *humbloti*), 15, 15.5, 15.5 (3 female *mohelicus*); **tarsus** 14-16 (mean 14.6, SD 0.70, 10 male *humbloti*), 15-16 (mean 15.5, SD 0.55, 6 male *mohelicus*), 15, 15 (2 female *humbloti*), 15-16 (mean 15.4, SD 0.53, 7 female *mohelicus*); **mass** 6.0-7.0 (mean 6.5, 14 male *humbloti*), 5.5-7.0 (mean 6.5, 6 male *mohelicus*), 6.0-8.0 (mean 6.5, 6 female *humbloti*), 5.5-7.0 (mean 6.3, 12 female *mohelicus*).

REFERENCES Benson (1960), Cheke & Diamond (1986), M. Herremans (pers. comm.), M. Louette (pers. comm.), Louette (1988), Milne-Edwards & Oustalet (1885), Sinclair & Langrand (1998).

147 ANJOUAN SUNBIRD
Cinnyris comorensis   Plate 30

Cinnyris comorensis Peters, 1864, *J. Orn.* 12, p. 161, Anjouan [= Johanna] Island, Comoro islands.

Probably forms a superspecies with *C. sovimanga*, or may be conspecific with it.

IDENTIFICATION Adult male blackish above, with blue-green or dark green gloss; throat to breast glossy blue-green, bordered dark maroon; pectoral tufts orange or vermilion; rest of underparts sooty-brown. Adult female mostly greenish-olive above; blackish tail showing whitish and grey; below greyish and yellowish with darker mottling and streaking. Juvenile differs from female by lack of mottling, and some, perhaps males, are more greenish below. **Similar species** Madagascar Sunbird *C. notatus* (144) male has purple and blue sheen on tail, not blue, and violet gloss on carpal joint; female has a narrow white supercilium, and heavier mottling and streaking below.

VOICE Call A sharp *pit pit* contact call. Female near nest utters *tweedle-di-diii*, answered by male with sharp chirp. Female also gives rising plaintive *cheep* at intervals of about 1 second until male appears, when she answers with *tweedle-di-diii*. Both birds utter *cheep* when searching for food near nest. Apparent alarm note *tswi*, uttered c.8 times increasing in rapidity and rising slightly in pitch, the male version being slightly deeper and less shrill. Male also gives a sweet *tswee, tswee, tswee, tswee*. **Song** A variable jumbled series of notes.

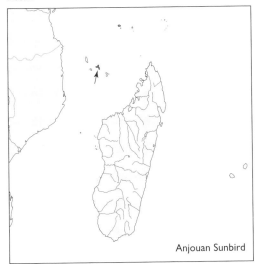

Anjouan Sunbird

DISTRIBUTION Anjouan in the Comoro Islands.

HABITAT Forest and thickets, 90-855 m.

STATUS Common endemic occurring throughout Anjouan Island.

MOVEMENTS Unknown.

FOOD Insects including Diptera; spiders, vegetable matter.
Known food-plants *Citrus* sp., *Impatiens sultani*, *Lantana* sp., *Musa* sp.

HABITS When excited, male flashes pectoral tufts.

BREEDING Nest In an *Acacia* sp. bush, 2 m above ground, made of very fine grass, covered on outside with coarser grass and tendrils. Decorated with very fine strips of curly bark and a little black fern fibre. Lined inside with very soft asclepiad pappus. suspended from horizontal branch

by many fine strips of bark about 1 mm wide, woven into top of nest. Similar nest found at 700 m. **Eggs** c/1; 16.0 x 12.0; white, faintly tinged bluish or greenish, boldly but not very thickly freckled all over with dull brown on underlying grey. **Laying months** October; males with enlarged testes September and October; juvenile September. Female with yolking oocyte September.

DESCRIPTION
Adult male Crown, upper back, mantle and throat to upper breast glossy blue-green; lower back, rump and tail blackish with slight dark blue gloss; wings blackish-brown. Narrow, very dark maroon band across breast; pectoral tufts orange or vermilion with yellow bases to feathers; rest of underparts sooty-brown. Iris dark brown, bill blackish, feet black with grey soles.
Adult female Greenish-olive above with darker mottling on crown; tail blackish with slight blue gloss and distal half of outer feathers greyish-white, next pair with large grey distal spots. Greyish on throat becoming yellowish on lower breast and belly; dark centres to feathers give mottled appearance to throat and breast and streaking to belly; undertail-coverts buffy-white.
Juvenile As female but lacks mottling; centre of throat and upper breast darker. One specimen much browner above. Presumed juvenile male as adult female above; below, sooty chin, dark grey-green throat and upper breast, flanks olive-grey, rest dark yellow with indistinct dark grey-green streaking; bill dark brown with pale fleshy base.

GEOGRAPHICAL VARIATION None.

MEASUREMENTS Wing 54-57 (55.7, 12 males), 48-53 (mean 50.7, SD 2.22, 4 females); **tail** 37-41 (mean 39.2, SD 1.79, 5 males), 35, 36 (2 females); **bill** 19-23.2 (mean 20.9, SD 1.56, 9 males), 17, 19 (2 females); **gape** 19.9-22 (mean 20.9, SD 0.95, 5 males), 18.6, 19.8 (2 females); **tarsus** 18-20 (mean 19.2, SD 0.84, 5 males), 17, 18 (2 females); **mass** 7.3-9.0 (mean 8.4, 5 males), 6.8, 7.5 (2 females).

REFERENCES Benson (1960), M. Herremans (pers. comm.), M. Louette (pers. comm.), Louette (1988), Sinclair & Langrand (1998).

148 MAYOTTE SUNBIRD
Cinnyris coquerellii Plate 30

Nectarinia coquerellii Hartlaub (ex J. Verreaux ms), 1860, *J. Orn.* 8, p.90, no locality; Mayotte Island, Comoro Islands, designated by Schlegel, 1866, *Proc. Zool. Soc. London* p.421.

Alternative name: Mayotte Buff-breasted Sunbird

IDENTIFICATION Adult male above, and throat to breast, chiefly iridescent dark green and purple; orange-red on breast; rest of underparts, including pectoral tufts, yellow, buffier on vent. Adult female grey-brown above with blackish tail; throat to breast grey with darker streaking; rest of underparts yellowish, whitish on vent. **Similar species** Male differs from male Madagascar Sunbird *C. notatus* (144) by orange-red underparts; female by much less obvious narrow whitish supercilium and much less heavy streaking and mottling below.

VOICE Call Various harsh chipping notes. **Song** Undescribed.

Mayotte Sunbird

DISTRIBUTION Endemic to the south-east Comoro Islands, including Mayotte.

HABITAT Avoids dense forest, preferring open areas and forest edge; sea-level to 460 m.

STATUS Common on Mayotte.

MOVEMENTS Unknown.

FOOD Insects including pupae of Cicadidae, small caterpillars; spiders and, presumably, nectar.
Known food-plants Baobab *Adansonia digitata*, papaya *Carica papaya*.

HABITS Found around *Acacia* sp. and *Mimosa* sp. Forages among leaves of coconut palms.

BREEDING Nest Similar in size to those of Anjouan Sunbird *C. comoroensis* (147) and Humblot's Sunbird *C. humbloti* (146), although top of entrance only 20 mm from top of nest. Made of fine grass, thickly lined with white silken asclepiad pappus, strands of fine grass straggling out for about 100 mm untidily from bottom of nest; suspended 3 m above ground. **Eggs** Unknown. **Laying months** Males with enlarged testes October–November, including one with unossified skull and not in full breeding plumage; female with oocyte yolking October. Female at nearly finished nest October. Nest-building November.

DESCRIPTION
Adult male Crown, sides of head, throat, shoulder and back to rump glossy dark green, with small amount of purple iridescence on uppertail-coverts and varying amounts on back; purple band across upper breast and some purple on throat. Centre of breast orange-red extending into a point through lower breast to belly; rest of underparts yellow, buffier on vent, pectoral tufts bright yellow. Remiges and rectrices black, tinged glossy blue. Iris dark brown, bill and feet black.
Adult female Grey-brown above, wings browner, tail blackish; throat to breast grey with indistinct darker streaking; rest of underparts yellowish, brighter in centre of belly, whitish on vent. Rump and uppertail-coverts greenish. Lower flanks and undertail-coverts greyish-white, underwing-coverts white, axillaries pale yellow. Remiges dark brownish-

grey, wing-coverts plain grey, rectrices glossy bluish-black. **Juvenile** Unknown.

MEASUREMENTS Wing 50-57 (mean 51.9, 23 males), 44-49 (mean 46.8, 16 females); **tail** 29-32 (mean 30.8, 19 males), 24-30 (mean 25.4, 11 females); **bill** 18.4-20.5 (mean 19.6, SD 0.64, 10 males), 17-21.3 (mean 18.5, SD 1.34, 8 females); **gape** 18.0-19.8 (mean 17.0, 10 males), 16.9-19.3 (mean 17.8, 7 females); **tarsus** 16 (male), 16, 17 (2 females); **mass** 9.0 (male), 7.0 (female).

REFERENCES Benson (1960), Hartlaub (1860), M. Herremans (pers. comm.), M. Louette (pers. comm.), Louette (1988), Sinclair & Langrand (1998).

149 LONG-BILLED SUNBIRD
Cinnyris lotenius   Plate 31

Certhia lotenia Linnaeus, 1766, *Syst. Nat.* ed. 12, 1, p.188, Ceylon.

Alternative names: Loten's Sunbird; Maroon-breasted Sunbird

IDENTIFICATION Bill long, slender and deeply arched. Adult male has whole of upperparts, and throat to breast, very dark, mostly glossed blue-green and purple; narrow dark crimson or maroon breast-band; yellow pectoral tufts; rest of underparts sooty-brown. In non-breeding plumage as female but broad dark patch from throat to upper breast. Adult female dull dark brownish-olive above, appearing brown in field; tail blue-black tipped white; dull yellow below, undertail-coverts white. Juvenile similar to female, but greyer below.
Similar species Male Purple Sunbird *C. asiaticus* (139) from male by dark purple belly, not sooty-brown, whereas female *asiaticus* is paler brown above, and lacks white tips to tail; female Purple-rumped Sunbird *Leptocoma zeylonica* (88) from female by grey throat and white-tipped blue-black tail; female Crimson-backed Sunbird *L. minima* (89) from female by crimson rump, and non-breeding male *minima* has mauve-violet back to uppertail-coverts and crimson band across wing-coverts and back.

VOICE Call Sharp metallic *chit, chit*. **Song** *Cheewit-cheewit-cheewit* quickly repeated 2-6 times; female has soft subsong; song in Sri Lanka described as a pleasing *titti-titu-weechi weechi weechi*.

DISTRIBUTION South Asia. Southern India (southern Deccan north to Bombay in west, Nallamalai Hills in east) and Sri Lanka; once Orissa.

HABITAT Low country and hills to 1,600 m in India, replaced by *L. minima* above 1,200 m in Karnataka, but up to 2,100 m in Sri Lanka. Moist deciduous biotope, in well-wooded but open country, gardens and farmland, amongst flowering trees and shrubs, occasionally in canopy of dense evergreen forest.

STATUS Generally common.

MOVEMENTS Possibly undergoes local movements in Nilgiris.

FOOD Nectar, spiders and tiny insects.
Known food-plants *Bombax* sp., *Dendrophthoe falcata* (has

slits in the corolla which, when penetrated by a sunbird bill, release a trigger such that the fused filaments straighten and separate at the top of the corolla which thus opens explosively allowing release of pollen), *Erythrina* sp., *Hibiscus* sp., *Lantana* sp., unidentified mistletoes Loranthaceae, *Macrosolen parasiticus*.

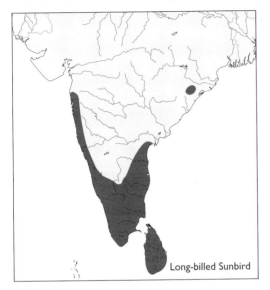

Long-billed Sunbird

HABITS Singly or in pairs; opens flower buds by pinching with bill; will pierce base of calyx to rob nectar of some flowers; hovers in front of flowers. In Kerala male pivots from side to side, raises and lowers wings and erects pectoral tufts whilst singing. In Sri Lanka, male tightens feathers, appearing very slim, erects pectoral tufts, and flies in deep loops whilst singing. Non-breeding plumaged male, Trivandrum, Kerala, India, observed probing cloacas of two fledgling Common Tailorbirds *Orthotomus sutorius*, perhaps mistaking them for flowers, and also occasionally pulling at wings and tails; parents were agitated and attempted to entice fledglings away, but did not attempt to prevent attacks. Host to *Haemoproteus* sp.

BREEDING Nest A pouch of fibres, lichens, rootlets, grass, moss, leaves etc., lined with vegetable down or wool with a porch; very untidy outside, covered with a variety of different particles, often forming a ragged tail; suspended from a twig, or wedged amongst creepers or in a bush 0.5-

3 m above ground in a shady place; in Sri Lanka, particularly, often a lined hollow in a dense mass of cobwebs. **Eggs** c/2-3; 15.9-18.1 (mean 17.0) x 11.2-12.4 (mean 12.0, n=50). Brownish-white with dull brown spots at small end, becoming larger blotches and forming a cap at large end, or greyish- or greenish-white marked with brown and grey. **Laying months** India: chiefly March–May, January–May in Kerala, but may occur in any month (*C. l. hindustanicus*); February–May in low country dry zone, and August–December in hills and wet zone (*C. l. lotenius*); Sri Lanka: January–July, 7 nests April–May, Negombo Lagoon in west.

DESCRIPTION *C. l. hindustanicus*
Adult male Whole head, back, shoulders and rump black glossed metallic green and purple; wings and tail dull blackish; throat metallic blue-green and purple, breast metallic purple; narrow dark crimson or maroon band across breast; bright yellow pectoral tufts; rest of underparts sooty-brown. Iris brown or reddish-brown, bill black, mouth pinkish-brown, feet horny-black. **Non-breeding plumage** Similar to female, but with broad black median patch from throat to upper breast, and no white on tail. **Adult female** Above dull dark brownish-olive; wings brown; tail blue-black tipped white, with white edging to outer feathers; dull yellow below, becoming white on vent and undertail-coverts.
Juvenile Similar to female but greyer below, with shorter bill and softer feathers.

GEOGRAPHICAL VARIATION
C. l. hindustanicus Whistler, 1944 (South India; Orissa) Described above.
C. l. lotenius (Linnaeus, 1766) (Sri Lanka) Larger and longer-billed than *hindustanicus*.

MEASUREMENTS Wing 56-60 (male *hindustanicus*), 58-60 (male *lotenius*), 53-56 (female *hindustanicus*), 50-57 (female *lotenius*); **tail** 36-40 (male *hindustanicus*), 37-41 (male *lotenius*), 32-35 (female *hindustanicus*), 33-36 (female *lotenius*); **bill** 27-29 (male *hindustanicus*), 30-32 (male *lotenius*), 26-28 (female *hindustanicus*), 30-31 (female *lotenius*); gape 25.8-28.5 (male *hindustanicus*), 27.0-29.6 (male *lotenius*), 23.6-27.9 (female *hindustanicus*), 26.0-27.1 (female *lotenius*); **tarsus** 15-16 (male *hindustanicus*), 14-15 (male *lotenius*), 14-16 (female *hindustanicus*), 14-15 (female *lotenius*); **mass** 8-11 (male *hindustanicus*), 7-8 (female *hindustanicus*).

REFERENCES Ali (1969), Ali & Ripley (1974), Davidar (1985), Khan (1977), Majumdar (1981b), Neelakantan (1975), de Silva (1992).

AETHOPYGA

Aethopyga Cabanis, 1851, *Mus. Hein* 1, p.103. Type by subsequent designation (G. R. Gray, 1855, *Cat. Gen. Subgen. Birds* p.19), *Certhia siparaja* Raffles.

Seventeen species in tropical Asia. Bill curved, slightly longer than head, with ridged culmen; nostrils bare, longitudinal and operculated. Tail graduated, and in many species central rectrices of male project far beyond others. Sexes different; male almost invariably, and female frequently, has contrasting yellow patch of variable size on lower back and rump. Long tongue rolled to form tube, which has two lateral splits towards tip, forming two groove-like structures, with a ventral plate, which may be used to convert the two lateral grooves into tubes (Figure 4d).

150 GREY-HOODED SUNBIRD
Aethopyga primigenius   **Plate 42**

Philippina primigenius Hachisuka, 1941, *Bull. Biogeogr. Soc. Japan* 11, p.6, Galog, 4,000ft., Mt Apo, Mindanao, Philippines.

Alternative names: Grey-headed Sunbird, Hachisuka's Sunbird

IDENTIFICATION Adult dark grey on top of head and neck with metallic green forehead in male; olive-green back with bright yellow rump; wings and tail dark olive-brown, latter tipped white; chin and throat dark grey; breast and centre of belly white, rest of underparts yellow. **Similar species** Apo Sunbird *Aethopyga boltoni* (151) has head and neck more olive-green, not grey, the male with yellow stripe on throat, and orange on breast, the female olive, yellow and orange below, and tail glossed black, not brown; Metallic-winged Sunbird *A. pulcherrima* (154) has tail glossed black and lacks white tips, and chin and throat bright yellow; from Lina's Sunbird *A. linaraborae* (152) by grey head and neck; tail brown, not glossed blue-black, and lack of orange below.

VOICE Call Up to about 6 *seek-seek*. **Song** Rapid metallic, high-pitched *tink-tink...*, becoming *see-see-see...*

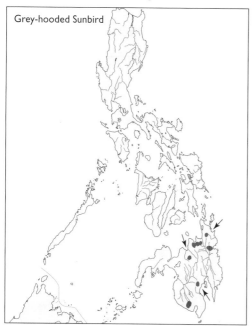
Grey-hooded Sunbird

DISTRIBUTION Endemic to Mindanao (Philippines) occurring on Mt Apo, Mt Busa, Mt McKinley, Mt Kitanglad, Mt Lamut, Civolig, Daggayan, Lake Sebu and Mt Hilong-Hilong (Diuata Mountains).

HABITAT Forest and forest edge above 1,000 m.

STATUS Uncertain, as little information available; although habitat relatively secure, treated as near-threatened owing to small total range.

MOVEMENTS Unknown.

FOOD Nothing recorded.
Known food-plants None.

HABITS Nothing recorded.

BREEDING Nest Unknown. **Eggs** Unknown. **Laying months** Probably in February. Males with enlarged testes, Katanglad, November–December.

DESCRIPTION *A. p. primigenius*
Adult male Top of head and neck dark grey, with iridescent bronze-green on forehead and a similar-coloured patch on ear-coverts; back olive-green; rump bright yellow; tail and wings dark olive-brown, tail tipped white; chin and throat dark grey; breast and centre of belly white; flanks and undertail-coverts yellow. Iris brick-red; bill blackish-brown, feet dark brown with pale soles.
Adult female As male, but lacks bronze-green patch on forehead and ear-coverts.
Juvenile Unknown.

GEOGRAPHICAL VARIATION
A. p. diuatae Salomonsen, 1953 (Mt Hilong-Hilong) Greyer below than nominate, and throat darker with indistinct central pale grey-white streak ending in yellow spot on breast in male (also present on one male nominate seen); white of belly greyer, with very indistinct darker grey streaking. Iridescence on male forehead more extensive than in nominate.
A. p. primigenius (Hachisuka, 1941) (whole range except Mt Hilong-Hilong) Described above.

MEASUREMENTS Wing 48-51 (mean 49.7, SD 1.03, 6 male *diuatae*), 50-53 (mean 52.5, SD 0.84, 14 male *primigenius*), 47-49 (mean 47.7, SD 0.96, 4 female *diuatae*), 46-51 (mean 48.8, SD 1.77, 7 female *primigenius*); **tail** 32-39 (mean 35.0, SD 1.86, 6 male *diuatae*), 34-39 (mean 36.3, SD 1.40, 13 male *primigenius*), 31-34 (mean 32.5, SD 1.29, 4 female *diuatae*), 30-37 (mean 33.0, SD 2.13, 7 female *primigenius*); **bill** 23-23.7 (mean 23.7, SD 1.10, 6 male *diuatae*), 21-25 (mean 22.3, SD 0.96, 13 male *primigenius*), 21-24.4 (mean 22.8, SD 1.42, 4 female *diuatae*), 20.3-23.3 (mean 21.5, SD 1.04, 7 female *primigenius*); **tarsus** 16-19 (mean 17.5, SD 1.0, 4 male *diuatae*), 17-19 (mean 17.7, SD 0.75, 12 male *primigenius*), 17, 18 (2 female *diuatae*), 17-18 (mean 17.4, SD 0.53, 7 female *primigenius*); **mass** no data.

REFERENCES Collar *et al.* (1999), Dickinson *et al.* (1991), duPont (1971b), Hachisuka (1941a).

151 APO SUNBIRD
Aethopyga boltoni   **Plate 42**

Aethopyga boltoni Mearns, 1905, *Proc. Biol. Soc. Washington*, 18, p.4, Mt Apo, 6,250 ft., Mindanao, Philippines.

IDENTIFICATION Adult male has metallic green forehead; head, back and wings dark olive-green, with pale yellow rump; graduated tail black glossed green and tipped white; below yellow, more orange on breast, more olive on belly; pectoral tufts orange. Adult female mostly olive-grey above, greener on back, little yellow on rump; whitish chin; throat to upper breast grey, tinged olive, indistinctly streaked pale; breast yellowy-green, merging with broad dull orange upper belly and streak down abdomen; rest of underparts yellow. Pectoral tufts pale yellow. Juvenile paler than adult, male lacking orange colour and pectoral tufts.

Similar species Male Lina's Sunbird *Aethopyga linaraborae* (152) has grey forehead, not green, metallic greater and lesser wing-coverts, and edges to tail; female has a yellowish throat, not greyish. Female Olive-backed Sunbird *Cinnyris jugularis* (140) lacks yellow rump. Grey-hooded Sunbird *A. primigenius* (150) has head and neck greyer, not olive-green, and tail brown, not glossed blue-black; male Metallic-winged Sunbird *A. pulcherrima* (154) lacks white tips to tail; Lovely Sunbird *A. shelleyi* (156) has much red above and red streaking below and lacks white tips to tail, and female is mostly olive, grey and whitish.

VOICE Call 1-6 bubbling *peep* notes whilst foraging; first note may be separated from remaining rapid notes. **Song** Rapid, squeaky, rising, high-pitched trill of up to c 15 notes. Rapid trill on same pitch, becoming slower and slower and a continuous series of *sip-sip-sip* or *clip-clip-clip...*

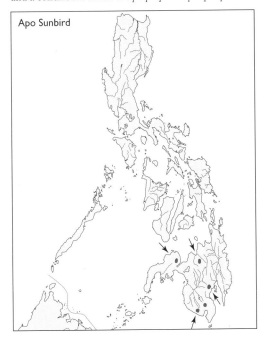

Apo Sunbird

DISTRIBUTION Endemic to Mindanao island, Philippines, where it occurs on Mt McKinley, Mt Apo, Mt Kitanglad, Mt Matutum, Mt Busa, Mt Malindang, Mt Pasian, Mt Parker and Lake Sebu.

HABITAT Flowering trees in forest, usually above 1,500 m, but recorded down to 823 m (race *malindangensis* 1,050-2,300 m, race *tibolii* in montane mossy forest at 820-2,300 m). Flowering trees and shrubs at all levels in stunted forest.

STATUS Although fairly common within relatively secure habitat, it is listed as near-threatened owing to its very small total range.

MOVEMENTS Unknown.

FOOD Nothing recorded.
Known food-plants None.

HABITS Occurs singly, in pairs or mixed flocks. Host to *Haemoproteus sequeirae*.

BREEDING Nest Pendulous, 80 mm wide x 160 mm, opening of 30 mm; composed of mosses, loosely woven and laced with several spider or insect egg-cases; suspended 2.4 m from ground at end of stem of tiger grass *Thysanolaena latifolia*. **Eggs** Unknown. **Laying months** 2,420 m on Mt Apo January, another nest on Mt Apo, July, enlarged ovary Mt Apo, March; *A. b. tibolii*: enlarged testis and ovary April.

DESCRIPTION *A. b. malindangensis*
Adult male Head, back and wings dark olive-green; metallic green forehead; rump light yellow; graduated tail black with metallic green gloss, feathers tipped white except central two; chin and throat light yellow with dark grey sides; breast orange-yellow with bright orange pectoral tufts; belly olive-yellow. Bill black; feet black with yellowish soles; iris red.
Adult female Crown olive-brown; sides of face brown; nape to upper back olive, becoming greener on wing-coverts and lower back; some yellow on rump. Remiges blackish edged bright olive; tail graduated, blackish with slight green sheen. Chin whitish; throat to upper breast olive-grey with indistinct paler stripes; rest of breast more yellowish, with dull orange suffusion on lower breast; rest of underparts yellow, brighter on flanks, with some orange on centre of belly. Underside of central 3 pairs of rectrices with large grey tips.
Juvenile See *A. b. tibolii*.

GEOGRAPHICAL VARIATION
A. b. boltoni Mearns, 1905 (Mt McKinley, Mt Apo and Mt Katanglad) Top of head, and underparts, particularly breast, duller than in *malindangensis*. Male has duller and less extensive orange centre to breast, with less light red on sides of breast; flanks and abdomen duller yellow and less iridescence on forehead and crown. Female has less extensive and duller orange on lower breast, and duller yellow flanks and abdomen.
A. b. malindangensis Rand & Rabor, 1957 (Mt Malindang) Described above.
A. b. tibolii Kennedy *et al.* 1997 (Mt Busa and Mt Matutum, southern Mindanao) Both sexes from *boltoni* by less rich coloration; lower breast and belly-patch orange-yellow, not orange; pectoral tufts paler. Female has edges of secondaries paler; chin and throat pale grey finely streaked white, not greyish-olive; belly paler yellow. Juvenile male *tibolii* paler than adult, less yellow on throat, lacking orange in breast and belly and pectoral tufts. Female paler than adult.

MEASUREMENTS Wing 51.7-55.9 (male *boltoni*), 50.8-58 (male *malindangensis*), 51.6-52.5 (male *tibolii*), 49.0-51.5 (female *boltoni*), 48.5-52.4 (female *malindangensis*), 47.3-49.8 (female *tibolii*); **tail** 44.0-49.6 (male *boltoni*), 44-53 (male *malindangensis*), 44.3-46.4 (male *tibolii*), 36.5-39.2 (female *boltoni*), 33.1-38.8 (female *malindangensis*), 36.9-38 (female *tibolii*); **bill** 22.2-24.5 (male *boltoni*), 22.1-23.8 (male *tibolii*), 19.0-21.2 (female *boltoni*), 19.1-21.2 (female *tibolii*); **gape** 20.2, 20.8 (2 male *malindangensis*), 21.3 (female *malindangensis*); **tarsus** 15.1-16.0 (male *boltoni*), 15.4-17 (male *malindangensis*), 14.9-15.3 (male *tibolii*), 14.6-15.5 (female *boltoni*), 14.1-15.2 (female *malindangensis*), 14.3-14.8 (female *tibolii*); **mass** 7.0-9.2 (male *boltoni*), 7.5-8.7 (male *malindangensis*), 4.9-7.8 (male *tibolii*), 6.6-7.2 (female *boltoni*), 6.1-8.5 (female *malindangensis*), 6.0-6.6 (female *tibolii*).

REFERENCES Collar *et al.* (1999), Dickinson *et al.* (1991), duPont (1971b), Hornskov (1996), Kennedy *et al.* (1997), Mearns (1905) Rand & Rabor (1960).

152 LINA'S SUNBIRD
Aethopyga linaraborae   Plate 42

Aethopyga linaraborae Kennedy, Gonzales and Miranda, 1997, *Auk* 114, p.3 and frontispiece, 1,200 m, near peak of Mt Pasian, Davao del Norte Province, Mindanao, Philippines.

IDENTIFICATION Adult male has forehead, cheek-patch, wing-coverts and uppertail-coverts mostly metallic green, with some blue; head and tail blackish-grey, latter edged violet and tipped white; back olive-green, rump yellow; below yellow, orange on breast, pectoral tufts scarlet. Secondaries and greater wing-coverts edged blue. Adult female differs from male by almost complete absence of metallic above, rump more olive; olive-green and yellow below streaked olive-yellow. Secondaries edged orange.
Similar species Male from Apo Sunbird *Aethopyga boltoni* (151) by grey head; metallic uppertail-coverts, ear-coverts, lesser and greater wing-coverts, and edges to scapulars and secondaries; tail dark grey with metallic edges rather than dark olive-brown with green edges. Female differs from *A. boltoni* in lacking well-defined yellow rump, blackish-grey tail edged metallic cobalt-blue rather green; secondaries edged orangish olive-yellow; clearly delineated throat with yellowish or greenish streaks, less orange but more extensively streaked below; graduated tail shorter; bill longer.

VOICE Nothing recorded.

DISTRIBUTION Endemic to eastern Mindanao island, Philippines, where it occurs on Mt Mayo, Mt Puting Batu and Mt Pasian.

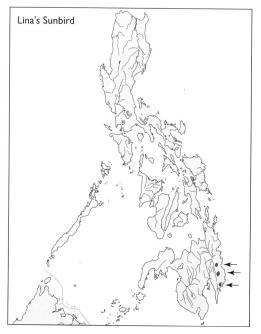

Lina's Sunbird

HABITAT Montane mossy forest from about 975-1,980 m and above.

STATUS Although fairly common within relatively secure habitat, it is listed as near-threatened owing to its very small total range.

MOVEMENTS Nothing recorded.

FOOD Nothing recorded.
Known food-plants None.

HABITS Found in middle and upper canopy, at 5-8 m. Accompanies mixed feeding flocks.

BREEDING Nest Unknown. **Eggs** Unknown. **Laying months** Two males with enlarged testes, one female with enlarged ovary, May.

DESCRIPTION
Adult male Forehead metallic emerald-green with hint of blue; head blackish-grey, crown feathers edged metallic blue; back olive-green; clearly defined rump sulphur-yellow; uppertail-coverts deep metallic emerald-green; tail feathers dark blackish-grey, edged violet with all except central feathers with whitish-silver tips. Ear-patch metallic cobalt-blue; lesser wing-coverts bright metallic emerald-green; greater wing-coverts metallic ultramarine; remiges dark brown; edges of scapulars and secondaries cobalt-blue; wing-lining white. Chin to upper breast, and undertail-coverts, sulphur-yellow; lower breast and belly yellow; small orange flecks on upper breast, and patch in centre of breast of same colour; scarlet pectoral tufts. Individual variation in brightness of yellow underparts and size of orange breast-patch. Iris dark brick- to blood-red; bill black; legs dark tannish-brown to black with pale ochre-yellow soles; skin around eye blackish-brown.
Adult female Colours more muted than in male and lacks metallic sheen on forehead, ear-coverts, uppertail-coverts and wing-coverts; no pectoral tufts or yellow between chin and upper breast. Head dark grey with trace of pale metallic emerald-green feather-edges; olive-green of back grades into olive sulphur-yellow at tail-base; throat yellowish olive-green, breast to belly yellowish-olive, with indistinct olive-yellow streaking and diffuse orange patch on centre of lower breast and belly; edges of tail feathers metallic cobalt-blue; wing-coverts olive-green; remiges edged orangish olive-yellow.
Juvenile Unknown.

GEOGRAPHICAL VARIATION None.

MEASUREMENTS Wing 51.7-55.8 (males), 46.6-50.2 (females); **tail** 36.4-40.4 (males), 32.1-34.4 (females); **bill** 22.3-26.3 (males), 19.3-22.8 (females); **tarsus** 14.5-16.3 (males), 14.1-15.4 (females); **mass** 5.7-8.7 (males), 6.0-7.0 (females).

REFERENCES Collar *et al.* (1999), Kennedy *et al.* (1997).

153 FLAMING SUNBIRD
Aethopyga flagrans   Plate 42

Aethopyga flagrans Oustalet, 1876, *Journ. Institut*, p.108, Lagune, Luzon, Philippines.

IDENTIFICATION Adult male has metallic blue-green

forehead, forecrown and uppertail-coverts; tail black edged metallic green; rest of upperparts olive-yellow with orange wash; metallic purple chin; throat and breast black with orange median stripe from throat to belly; white undertail-coverts, rest of underparts olive-yellow. Adult female olive-green above, grey below, yellowish on lower breast.

Similar species Male Purple-throated Sunbird *Leptocoma sperata* (90) has scapulars and mantle maroon, whereas female is yellower, less grey below; female Olive-backed Sunbird *Cinnyris jugularis* (140) from has much brighter yellow underparts than female *flagrans*; female Metallic-winged Sunbird *Aethopyga pulcherrima* (154) has yellow rump and is all grey below; female Lovely Sunbird *A. shelleyi* (156) much greyer below; female Crimson Sunbird *A. siparaja* (163) lacks yellowish patch on breast.

VOICE Not known.

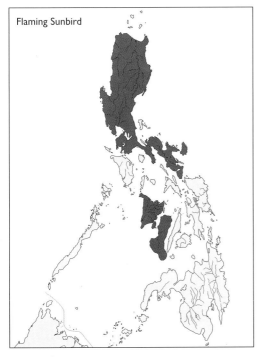

Flaming Sunbird

DISTRIBUTION Endemic to Philippines, occurring on Luzon, Catanduanes, Guimaras, Panay, Negros.

HABITAT Forest, forest edge and secondary growth up to 1,350 m.

STATUS Uncommon.

MOVEMENTS Unknown.

FOOD Not known.
Known food-plants None.

HABITS Singly, in pairs or in mixed flocks.

BREEDING Nest Unknown. **Eggs** Unknown. **Laying months** Southern Luzon: Male with enlarged testes April.

DESCRIPTION *A. f. flagrans*
Adult male Forehead and forecrown metallic blue-green; hindcrown, back and wing-coverts bright olive-yellow

washed orange; uppertail-coverts metallic blue-green; tail black edged metallic green; chin dark metallic purple; throat and breast dull black with bright reddish-orange median stripe to centre of belly; rest of belly and flanks olive-yellow; undertail-coverts whitish. Bill blackish; iris brown; feet dark brown.
Adult female Upperparts olive-green; underparts greyer with yellowish patch on lower breast.
Juvenile Unknown.

GEOGRAPHICAL VARIATION
   A. f. daphoenota Parkes, 1963 (Negros) Male has blood-red of mantle more extensive than *guimarasensis*, the orange underparts darker, and wing-coverts and edgings orange not greenish; female also has orange edgings, and is greener and less grey above.
   A. f. decolor Parkes, 1963 (north-east Luzon) Male differs from nominate in having dull olive-yellow upperparts, and breast-stripe and belly-patch less red. However, single specimen at Natural History Museum, Tring, does not differ from nominate in this respect.
   A. f. flagrans Oustalet, 1876 (Luzon, except north-east; Catanduanes) Described above.
   A. f. guimarasensis (Steere, 1890) (Guimaras, Panay) Male differs from nominate in having hindcrown to mantle blood-red, yellow below much brighter and less orange on belly.

MEASUREMENTS Wing 51 (male *decolor*), 47-50 (male *flagrans*), 47-49 (male *guimarasensis*), 45 (female *flagrans*); **bill** 18.8-20.7 (mean 19.5, SD 0.72, 7 male *flagrans*), 18.0, 18.6, 19.3 (3 male *guimarasensis*), 16.6 (female *flagrans*); **gape** 17.0-20.4 50 (male *flagrans*), 16.6-17.6 (male *guimarasensis*), 16.4 (female *flagrans*); **mass** no data.

REFERENCES Dickinson *et al.* (1991), duPont (1971b), Goodman & Gonzales (1990).

---

154 METALLIC-WINGED SUNBIRD
Aethopyga pulcherrima   Plate 42

Aethopyga pulcherrima Sharpe, 1876, *Nature* 14, p.297, Basilan, Philippines.

Alternative name: Mountain Sunbird

IDENTIFICATION Adult male has forehead, wing-coverts, uppertail-coverts and tail metallic purple-green and green; crown and back olive-yellow; rump and underparts yellow, more greyish on belly and small orange-red patch on breast. Adult female is olive-green above, with yellow rump; below olive-grey. Juvenile similar to adult female but yellower below.
Similar species Female Purple-throated Sunbird *Leptocoma sperata* (90) and Olive-backed Sunbird *Cinnyris jugularis* (140) lack yellow rumps, and former is yellowish-green below, the latter much yellower below; Grey-hooded Sunbird *Aethopyga primigenius* (150) from male by olive-brown not black tail glossed green and purple, and chin and throat grey; male Apo Sunbird *A. boltoni* (151) has white tips to tail; Flaming Sunbird *A. flagrans* (153) lacks yellow rump, and has yellow and whitish underparts; male Lovely Sunbird *A. shelleyi* (156) has upper back dark red; female Crimson Sunbird *A. siparaja* (163) lacks bright yellow rump.

VOICE Call Metallic *sink sink...*, becoming higher and faster, in some cases developing into a trill. Sharp *see* or *see-see*, *tsik tsik*, followed by short, rising trill. **Song** Longish trill, high-pitched, preceded by slower notes, with gaps, and becoming separate notes towards end.

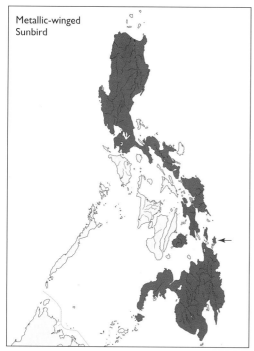

Metallic-winged Sunbird

DISTRIBUTION Endemic to Philippines; occurs on Luzon, Basilan, Dinagat, Leyte, Mindanao, Samar, Biliran and Bohol (?Siargao).

HABITAT Forests, forest edge, secondary growth and banana plantations; mostly submontane up to 1,500 m, but also in lowlands.

STATUS Fairly common.

MOVEMENTS None recorded.

FOOD Unknown.
Known food-plants None.

HABITS Occurs singly, or in mixed flocks.

BREEDING Nest On Samar one was attached to climbing fern 2.5 m above ground. **Eggs** c/3; *pulcherrima*: 13.7-14.0 (mean 13.9, n=3) x 10.7-11.2 (mean 11.0); dull pink, thickly mottled pinkish-grey especially towards broad end where distinct zone is formed, and deep brown rounded spots overmark egg. **Laying months** Philippines: Samar, June; Bohol, probably April–May; Luzon, male with enlarged gonads April.

DESCRIPTION *A. p. pulcherrima*
Adult male Forehead and spot behind eye metallic purplish-green or steel-blue; crown and back olive-green; rump bright yellow; uppertail-coverts and wing-coverts metallic green; tail black glossed metallic green; remiges olive-green; chin and throat bright yellow; breast yellowish with slight orange-red patch; belly greyish-yellow. Bill blackish, feet dark brown.

Adult female Differs from male by olive-green upperparts, except rump, and underparts dull olive-grey with some yellowish on upper breast.
Juvenile Differs from female in having rump and underparts paler yellow; bill brown, feet dark grey with ochraceous soles, iris yellowish-brown.

GEOGRAPHICAL VARIATION
A. p. decorosa (McGregor, 1907) (Bohol) Male differs from *jefferyi* in having remiges edged metallic purplish-blue, wing-coverts, tail and uppertail-coverts metallic blue not metallic green, and rump paler yellow; underparts much paler and red breast-spot almost or completely absent. Female from *jefferyi* by much lighter rump-patch.
A. p. jefferyi (Ogilvie-Grant, 1894) (Luzon) Male differs from *pulcherrima* in having dark metallic blue forehead, bright yellow lower back like rump, and metallic green of wing-coverts extending onto edges of remiges.
A. p. pulcherrima Sharpe, 1876 (Basilan, Dinagat, Leyte, Mindanao, Samar and Biliran) Described above.

MEASUREMENTS Wing 48 (male *decorosa*), 51 (male *jefferyi*), 49 (male *pulcherrima*), 43.7 (female *decorosa*), 43, 51 (2 female *jefferyi*), 45-49 (female *pulcherrima*); **tail** 24.6 (male *decorosa*), 22.4 (female *decorosa*), 22 (unsexed, unknown subspecies); **bill** 23.5 (male *jefferyi*), 19.0-22.4 (mean 20.0, SD 1.39, 5 male *pulcherrima*), 20.8, 22.3 (2 female *jefferyi*), 18.6-20.6 (mean 19.7, SD 0.75, 5 female *pulcherrima*); **gape** 18.0-21.3 (male *pulcherrima*), 18.2-19.8 49 (female *pulcherrima*); **culmen from base** 18.3 (male *decorosa*), 18.3 (female *decorosa*); tarsus 14 (unsexed, unknown subspecies).

REFERENCES Dickinson *et al.* (1991), duPont (1971b), Goodman & Gonzales (1990), Ogilvie-Grant & Whitehead (1898), Rand & Rabor (1960), Sharpe (1876).

155 ELEGANT SUNBIRD
Aethopyga duyvenbodei　　　Plate 42

Nectarinia duyvenbodei Schlegel, 1871, *Ned. Tijdsch. Dierk.*, 4, p.14, Sanghir island (north of Sulawesi).

Alternative name: Duyvenbode's Sunbird

May form superspecies with *A. shelleyi* and/or *A. pulcherrima*.

IDENTIFICATION Male has striking golden-yellow underparts, orange on sides of breast; yellowish-olive back; yellow band on rump; otherwise olive-green, with metallic green and blue areas on upperparts, maroon-red on sides of neck and nape; dark tail with white edges and tips. Female yellowish-olive above, rump paler, scaly crown and yellow underparts; dark tail edged pale.
Similar species Female from female Plain-throated Sunbird *Anthreptes malacensis* (53) by yellow on rump, and lack of yellow eye-ring; male from male Olive-backed Sunbird *Cinnyris jugularis* (140) by maroon-red ear-coverts, lores and nape, whereas female from female of that species by darker upperparts, and lack of large white tips to tail.

VOICE Call High-pitched rasping *treek* or *tseeeck*. Rapid *tit...* up to 4 times, sometimes as single note; *tsik-tsik* and squeaky noises from adult in presence of juvenile. **Song** Very short, high, insect-like trill from male; chipping notes run into high trill by male.

DISTRIBUTION Endemic to the Sulawesi area (Sangihe Island, and one specimen from Siau dated 1866). Recorded from Talawid Atas, Kedang, Gunung Awu, Petta, Manganitu, Gunung Sahendaruman (including adjacent Gunung Sahangbalira, Gunung Palenti and Kentuhang), Ulung Peliang, Tabukan and Tahuna.

Elegant Sunbird

HABITAT Little information; only known from specimens until 1985. Recorded from dense bamboo thicket in secondary woodland midway up Gunung Awu, Sangihe; also from mixed plantations (coconut, nutmeg, clove, banana and other fruit trees) where some some hardwood trees persist and preferably with scrubby undergrowth, remnant forest and secondary scrub and in tree-ferns. Altitudinal range 75-900 m on Sangihe, where occurs high on Gunung Awu and Gunung Sahangbalira, reaching Cycadaceae/Pandanaceae forest association.

STATUS Endangered. Common on Sangihe in cultivated areas containing forest remnants or other large trees but deforestation, followed by planting of coconut and nutmeg or gardens, now abandoned to secondary vegetation, has posed a major threat. Little or no forest remains on the volcanically active Siau island, and searches in 1995 and 1998 proved negative.

MOVEMENTS Unknown, but thought to be sedentary.

FOOD Gleans insects from vegetation and spiders' webs; nectar.
Known food-plants Bamboos, unidentified small tube-shaped scarlet flowers, clovers, *Pandanus*, *Areca* palm, *Cocos nucifera*, *Durio zibethinus*, *Syzygium aromaticum*, which in some cases may be visited for insects rather than plant products. Males and females sometimes feed in separate groups.

HABITS Singly or in pairs, occasionally in small groups and in mixed feeding flocks with other sunbirds and flowerpeckers – Purple-throated Sunbird *Leptocoma sperata* (90), Grey-sided Flowerpecker *Dicaeum celebicum* (42) and Yellow-sided Flowerpecker *D. aureolimbatum* (16). Four females and a male seen huddling together and calling.

BREEDING Nest Unknown. **Eggs** Unknown. **Laying months** Large gonads May; just emptied nest August; juveniles August and September; singing and lek-like behaviour November–December. These dates suggest two breeding seasons.

DESCRIPTION
Adult male Crown metallic green; sides of occiput, neck and auriculars maroon-red; back and mantle very dark green; wing-coverts glossed greeny-blue, shoulder glossed blue, remiges blackish with metallic blue edging to inner secondaries; rump deep yellow, uppertail-coverts metallic purple; rounded tail blackish-brown with whitish edging and tips. Lores and throat to upper breast yellow; sides of breast orange; rest of underparts orange-yellow; dark green of mantle extends as indistinct bar onto sides of breast. Iris black; bill black or blackish; feet blackish or reddish-pink.
Adult female Lores olive. Dark golden-olive above, indistinct scaling on forehead and crown; wings brownish, edged greenish, primaries noticeably darker, edged greenish-olive; tail blackish tipped grey. Throat to upper breast greenish-yellow; narrow darkish olive band across lower throat separating it from breast; rest of underparts bright yellow.
Juvenile Similar to female but with pale pinky-brown bill and legs.

GEOGRAPHICAL VARIATION None.

MEASUREMENTS Wing 55, 58, 58 (3 males), 51, 52 (2 females); **bill** 21.2, 21.5, 22.5 (3 males), 18.8, 19.1 (2 females); **gape** 19.1, 20.1, 20.3 (3 males), 18.3, 19.3 (2 females); **mass** no data.

REFERENCES BirdLife International (in prep.), Bishop (1992), Coates & Bishop (1997), Collar *et al.* (1994), Riley (1997), J. Riley (*in litt.*), Schlegel (1871), White & Bruce (1986).

---

156 LOVELY SUNBIRD
Aethopyga shelleyi   Plate 43

Aethopyga shelleyi Sharpe, 1876, *Nature* 14, p.297, Palawan, Philippines.

Alternative name: Palawan Sunbird

IDENTIFICATION Adult male has metallic crown, uppertail-coverts and tail; hindneck and sides of head to upper back dark red; lower back and rump yellow; chin and throat yellow bordered steel-blue and red; breast yellow streaked red; belly pale grey. Adult female olive-green above, greyish-yellow below.
Similar species Female Plain-throated Sunbird *Anthreptes malacensis* (53) from female by yellow eye-ring and brighter underparts; female Purple-throated Sunbird *Leptocoma sperata* (90) from female by more yellowish-green, less greyish and less olive underparts and whitish supercilium; female Copper-throated Sunbird *L. calcostetha* (92) from female by greyish-white throat; female Olive-backed Sunbird *Cinnyris jugularis* (140) from female by much brighter underparts; Apo Sunbird *Aethopyga boltoni* (151) has white tips to tail and lacks red streaking below; female Flaming Sunbird *A. flagrans* (153) is much greyer below, with yellow

confined to belly and lower breast; male Metallic-winged Sunbird *A. pulcherrima* (154) from male by olive-green upper back, female with yellow rump and dull olive-grey underparts.

VOICE A peculiar, very high, thin piping. Up to 9 high-pitched unhurried notes *tsip..tsip* and a much longer series of these, with short pauses, *ad infinitum*. Nine to 25 distinct, stressed notes on same pitch.

DISTRIBUTION Endemic to the Philippines, occurring on Balabac, Busuanga, Culion, Palawan, Luzon, Lubang, Mindanao, Samar, Leyte, Dinagat, Siargao, Cebu, Masbate, Negros, Panay, Ticao, Jolo, Tawitawi, Mindoro, Marinduque and Polillo.

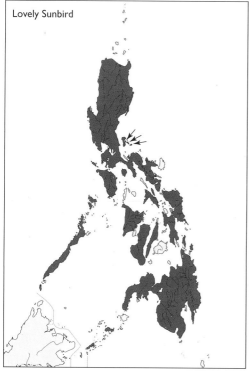

Lovely Sunbird

HABITAT Forest, at forest edge, in scrub and secondary growth below 2,000 m.

STATUS Fairly common.

MOVEMENTS Unknown.

FOOD Unknown. **Known food-plants** None.

HABITS Found singly or in mixed flocks. Host to *Plasmodium vaughani* and the hippoboscid *Ornithoica exilis*.

BREEDING Nest One on Samar was a long bag-shaped pocket with loose dangling beard of dead leaves; side entrance roofed over, dangling from bramble in old clearing some distance from forest. **Eggs** c/3. Pale pinkish-white, heavily marked with irregular zone of dull red towards large end; scattered spots and blotches of same colour over rest of shell, and underlying brown markings. Race *bella*: 12.7-13.5 (mean 12.9, n=3) x 9.7-9.9 (mean 9.8). **Laying months** Philippines: Cebu, June; Culion, February; Jolo, September; Negros, January; Samar, July.

DESCRIPTION *A. s. shelleyi*
Adult male Crown metallic purple and green; hindneck and upper back dark red; lower back and rump bright yellow; wings yellowy-green; uppertail-coverts and graduated tail metallic blue-green; sides of head dark red; chin and throat yellow with red margin; peacock blue-green malar stripes; breast yellow streaked red; belly pale grey. Bill and feet dark brown; iris black.
Adult female Upperparts olive-green; underparts greyish-yellow.
Juvenile As female, but much greyer below, with buffy centre of breast and belly.

GEOGRAPHICAL VARIATION The species appears to fall into two groups which may be specifically distinct.

Palawan group
A. s. shelleyi Sharpe, 1876 (Balabac, Busuanga, Culion and Palawan) Described above. This form is larger than others (except possibly for *arolasi*) with gloss to hindcrown (but without purple cheek-spot) and size differences between the sexes much more marked. These characters could, perhaps, be used to separate this form as a distinct species.

Philippine group
A. s. arolasi Bourns & Worcester, 1894 (Jolo and Tawitawi) Male is larger than *bella* and has heavier orange-red streaking on breast, and yellower abdomen and undertail-coverts, whereas female has less yellow on rump.
A. s. bella Tweeddale, 1877 (Mindanao, Samar, Leyte, Dinagat and Siargao) Male has glossy purple spot on cheek, no purple on crown. Green gloss on crown only extends to rear of eye; rest of crown and nape unglossed dark green; brighter yellow below and less red on breast than *shelleyi*, is slightly smaller, and female has a yellow rump.
A. s. bonita Bourns & Worcester, 1894 (Cebu, Masbate, Negros, Panay and Ticao) Male differs from *bella* in darker yellow lower back and rump, and breast heavily streaked red.
A. s. flavipectus Ogilvie-Grant, 1894 (north Luzon) Male has little or no red on breast. Only forecrown glossed green; rest of crown and nape unglossed dark green.
A. s. minuta Bourns & Worcester, 1894 (south and central Luzon, Mindoro, Polillo, Marinduque) Male similar to *arolasi* but smaller and throat pure yellow with no red or orange.
A. s. rubrinota McGregor, 1905 (Lubang) Male similar to *flavipectus* but breast much lighter yellow with no red or only traces of red in centre, and has glossy purple spot on cheek; female has yellow rump.

MEASUREMENTS Wing 40-45 (male *bella*), 42 (male *rubrinota*), 46-50 (male *shelleyi*), 41 (female *bella*), 43-45 (female *shelleyi*); **tail** 45 (unsexed *shelleyi*); **bill** 16 (unsexed *shelleyi*), 13.8-15.2 (mean 14.5, SD 0.65, 5 male *bella*), 14.2 (male *rubrinota*), 15.0-18.1 (mean 16.4, SD 0.80, 10 male *shelleyi*), 12.7, 14.3 (2 female *bella*), 14.1 (female *rubrinota*), 13.3-16.6 (mean 15.3, SD 0.99, 7 female *shelleyi*); **gape** 13.6-14.8 (male *bella*), 14.4 (male *rubrinota*), 14.4-15.9 (male *shelleyi*), 14.3 (female *bella*), 13.8-14.9 (female *shelleyi*); **tarsus** 14 (unsexed *shelleyi*); **mass** no data.

REFERENCES D. Allen (pers. comm.), Bourns & Worcester (1894), E. C. Dickinson (*in litt.*), Dickinson *et al.* (1991), duPont (1971b), R. S. Kennedy (*in litt.*), McGregor (1905, 1909-10), Maa (1966), Mann (in prep. a), Ogilvie-Grant & Whitehead (1898), Sharpe (1876), Zimmer (1918).

157 GOULD'S SUNBIRD
Aethopyga gouldiae   Plate 43

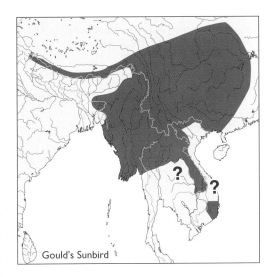

Gould's Sunbird

Cinnyris gouldiae Vigors, 1831, *Proc. Zool. Soc. London*, p.44, Himalayas; restricted to Simla-Almora district by Ticehurst & Whistler, 1924, *Ibis* p.471.

Alternative name: Mrs Gould's Sunbird

IDENTIFICATION Short-billed and male long-tailed. Adult male has metallic purple-blue crown, throat, sides of neck, uppertail-coverts and tail, latter with outer feathers tipped buff; rest of underparts yellow, usually streaked scarlet on breast, more olive on vent. Adult female has grey head and nape, yellow rump and rest of upperparts olive, olive-grey, or grey, olive and yellow; throat pale grey, rest of underparts yellow; graduated tail tipped whitish. Juvenile as female, but tail less graduated, and tips less white.
Similar species Female Plain-throated Sunbird *Anthreptes malacensis* (53) from female by yellow eye-ring, and lack of yellow on rump; both sexes from corresponding Purple-rumped Sunbird *Leptocoma zeylonica* (88) and Purple-throated Sunbird *L. sperata* (90) by yellow rump, and male also by long tail; female from female Copper-throated Sunbird *L. calcostetha* (92) by yellowish rump and lack of white below; female from female Olive-backed Sunbird *Cinnyris jugularis* (140) by grey throat and yellowish rump, and lacks white-tipped black tail; male Green-tailed Sunbird *Aethopyga nipalensis* (158) has olive-green middle of back, whereas female lacks yellow rump, has no yellow below, and has white tips to outer tail feathers; female Fork-tailed Sunbird *A. christinae* (160) lacks yellow rump; male Black-throated Sunbird *A. saturata* (161) lacks yellow on underparts, whereas female is greyish-olive below; female Crimson Sunbird *A. siparaja* (163) has less yellow below; male Fire-tailed Sunbird *A. ignicauda* (166) has scarlet uppertail-coverts and tail, whereas female lacks pale grey throat.

VOICE Scissors-like *tzit-tzit*; quick repeated *tzip*; alarm *tshi-stshi-ti-ti-ti*; lisping *squeeeee* rising in middle.

DISTRIBUTION Himalayas from Sutlej valley east to Nepal, Bhutan, Arunachal Pradesh, southern and southeast Tibet (Kobdo), Assam, Nagaland, Manipur, south to Chittagongs and north-west Burma; west, central and south China (vagrant Hong Kong); southern Laos and southern Vietnam.

HABITAT Various forest types, including oak, coniferous, and evergreen scrub jungle; altitude varies with geographical range, breeding 1,200-4,270 m, but 330-2,700 m in winter. In Nepal found in undergrowth and lower branches in damp ravines, usually near flowering *Rhododendron* and mistletoes in spring. In *Symplocos*-dominated ridgetop forest at 1,850 m, above *Fagus* forest in Guangxi, China.

STATUS Not uncommon in Burma. Vagrant to Hong Kong, Pakistan and Bangladesh. Widespread but uncommon in Nepal. Generally uncommon in India, locally common in east. Frequent in Bhutan.

MOVEMENTS Vertical movements in higher parts of range; some from east Nagaland and west China move to Manipur, north Cachar and Burma in winter. Female ringed on Doi Pui, Thailand, was recovered on another peak 5 km distant one month later.

FOOD Nectar, spiders and insects.
Known food-plants *Rhododendron* sp., parasitic plants.

HABITS Shy; restless and active like other sunbirds. Found at ground-level up to the canopy, particularly at parasitic plants. Drinks at pools at midday. Host to *Haemoproteus sequeirae*.

BREEDING Host to Asian Emerald Cuckoo *Chrysococcyx maculatus* in India. **Nest** Pear-shaped or oval, made of vegetable down, fibrous material, green moss, grass shreds and cobweb, entrance about two-thirds way up with reinforced rim; lined with soft cotton down, suspended from fern or twig low in bushes or brambles. 140 x 70 mm. **Eggs** Race *dabryii*: 17.0 x 12.0; *isolata*: c/2-3. 13.5-15.3 (mean 14.4, n=22) x 10.0-11.5 (mean 10.9). White freckled with small blotches of pale reddish-brown, slightly more numerous at larger end. **Laying months** Indian subcontinent: April–August; Nepal: mid-March to mid-June, breeding above Dhunche.

DESCRIPTION *A. g. gouldiae*
Adult male Crown, ear-coverts and patch on sides of neck metallic purple-blue; sides of head, neck, supercilium, nape and back crimson; rump bright yellow; uppertail-coverts and upper surface of tail metallic purple-blue, central feathers very long, outer feathers brown tipped buffish; throat metallic purple-blue; rest of underparts yellow variably streaked scarlet (absent in some) on breast, tinged olive on vent. Iris brown, reddish-brown or crimson; bill dark brown, lower mandible paler, or bill blackish; feet dark brown, soles paler.
Adult female Head and nape grey; rest of upperparts olive, yellowish on rump; throat pale grey, rest of underparts yellowish-grey.
Juvenile As adult female, but tail not so graduated or tips so whitish.

GEOGRAPHICAL VARIATION
A. g. annamensis Robinson & Kloss, 1919 (southern Laos, southern Vietnam, Thailand) Male has scarlet

on sides of breast, with crown and throat more lilac-purple, and lacks yellow on rump. Female from nominate female by yellow lower breast and belly, yellow of rump extending onto lower back and uppertail-coverts.

A. g. dabryii (Verreaux, 1867) (extreme east Nagaland, western, central and south China, and Pome, south-east Tibet; also in winter to Manipur, north Cachar, Burma) Male has scarlet breast, with crown and throat more lilac-purple than blue in some but more bluish in others.
A. g. gouldiae Vigors, 1831 (Himalayas from Sutlej valley east to Arunachal Pradesh, and Kobdo, southeast Tibet) Described above.
A. g. isolata Baker, 1925 (Assam south of Brahmaputra River, Nagaland, Manipur, south to Chittagong Hills and north-west Burma) Male has paler yellow on rump and breast than nominate, and purple rather than blue gloss.

MEASUREMENTS Wing 53-59 (male *dabryii*), 52-58 (mean 54.9, SD 1.45, 10 male *gouldiae*), 48-55 (mean 51.2, SD 2.99, 4 female *gouldiae*), 51-56 (unsexed *isolata*); **tail** 75-76 (male *dabryii*), 60-86 (male *gouldiae*), 35-47 (female *gouldiae*), 62-69 (unsexed *isolata*); **bill** 16.7-18.9 (mean 17.9, SD 0.86, 10 male *gouldiae*), 15.9-19.2 (mean 17.7, SD 1.36, 4 female *gouldiae*); **gape** 17.1-18.4 (male *annamensis*), 14.5-17.9 (male *dabryii*), 14.8-17.8 (male *gouldiae*), 16.0-17.4 (female *annamensis*), 15.3-17.8 (female *dabryii*), 16.4-19.5 (female *gouldiae*); **tarsus** 15-18 (male *gouldiae*), 14-15 (female *gouldiae*); **mass** 6.9 (male *annamensis*), 6.5-8 (male *gouldiae*), 6.1 (female *annamensis*), 4-6 (female *gouldiae*), 6-7 (unsexed *isolata*).

REFERENCES Ali & Ripley (1974), Deignan (1944), Fleming *et al.* (1976), Gatson (1989), Gretton (1990), Grimmett *et al.* (1998), Inskipp & Inskipp (1985), King *et al.* (1975), McClure (1974), Melville & Round (1984), Meyer de Schauensee (1984), Robson (1988), Vigors (1831), Vuilleumier (1993).

---

158   GREEN-TAILED SUNBIRD
Aethopyga nipalensis   Plate 43

Cinnyris nipalensis Hodgson, 1837, *India Review* p.273, Nepal; restricted to Chandrigari Pass, central Nepal by Ripley, 1961, *Synopsis Birds India Pakistan*, p.588.

Alternative name: Nepal Sunbird

IDENTIFICATION Male has long graduated white-tipped tail with elongated central rectrices. Adult has crown, nape and tail metallic blue-green; sides of neck and upper back crimson-brown or maroon; wings and middle of back olive-green; rump yellow; below yellow streaked scarlet on breast, except for black cheeks and metallic green throat. Adult female olive-green, with graduated tail with white tips to all feathers except central pair. Juvenile has a less graduated tail than female, with less obvious pale tips; male washed orange on breast.
Similar species Female Plain-throated Sunbird *Anthreptes malacensis* (53) has yellow eye-ring and yellow underparts, and lacks white tips to tail; female from female Purple-throated Sunbird *Leptocoma sperata* (90) by large white tips to all tail feathers except central, and darker olive-green underparts; Copper-throated Sunbird *L. calcostetha* (92)

has greyish-white throat and lacks white-tipped graduated tail; female Olive-backed Sunbird *Cinnyris jugularis* (140) from female of this species by brighter yellow underparts; male Gould's Sunbird *Aethopyga gouldiae* (157) has back entirely crimson, with no olive-green, whereas female has yellowish rump and yellow underparts, except for pale grey throat; male Fork-tailed Sunbird *A. christinae* (160) lacks crimson-brown/maroon band on upper back and sides of neck, whereas female is yellow below, and lacks white tips to outer tail feathers; male Black-throated Sunbird *A. saturata* (161) lacks bright yellow and scarlet below, and female has yellow rump and lacks white tips to outer tail feathers; female Crimson Sunbird *A. siparaja* (163) by greyish tinge on head and throat, greenish-yellow belly and undertail-coverts; male Fire-tailed Sunbird *A. ignicauda* (166) has scarlet uppertail-coverts and tail, whereas female has yellow rump and lacks white tips to tail.

VOICE Call A sharp *dzit*; *twit-zig-zig*; repeated *bee-tzree*; *tzweeeet*; contact call *reet*. **Song** A high *tchiss* followed by a low-rising-high *tchiss-iss-iss-iss*; in Nepal sings February to mid-June.

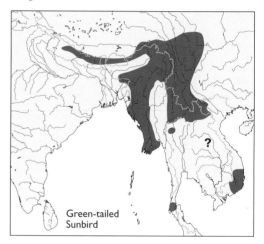

Green-tailed Sunbird

DISTRIBUTION Himalayas from Mussoorie to Nepal, Bhutan, Arunachal Pradesh, Meghalaya, Nagaland, Manipur, south to Chittagong Hills, Burma, Thailand, Laos, Vietnam (including Da Lat plateau) and north-west Yunnan; central and south-west China.

HABITAT Forest, including dense oaks, woodland, scrub jungle, rhododendrons, orchards and gardens; altitudinal range varies geographically, 300-3,665 m, lower in winter in higher parts of range. In Nepal chiefly 1,830-3,000 m, occasionally 3,505 m, in winter 915-2,745 m (but once 3,300 m), occasionally as low as 305 m.

STATUS Locally common in Burma above 1,800 m. Widespread and common in Nepal. India: uncommon in west, common in east. Common in Bhutan; only one recent record from Bangladesh.

MOVEMENTS Seasonal altitudinal movements in higher parts of range, but recorded at 3,300 m at Bolumche, Nepal, December.

FOOD Probably small arthropods and/or nectar.
Known food-plants *Caryopteris* sp., *Leucosceptrum* sp., *Pyrus communis*.

HABITS Found in winter in Nepal with *A. ignicauda, A. saturata* and *A. siparaja*, but not *A. gouldiae*. Solitary or in scattered groups. Frequently at flowering pear trees.

BREEDING Parasitised in India by Asian Emerald Cuckoo *Chrysococcyx maculatus*. One parasitised nest, Sikkim, contained two host eggs and one cuckoo's. **Nest** An untidy oval purse of vegetable down and green moss, suspended from the end of a twig 1.5-2 m from ground; entrance near top or half-way up, 25 mm diameter. No porch. Decorated with caterpillar excreta and bits of bark. 140 x 70 mm. **Eggs** c/2-3; *nipalensis*: 14.8-16.0 (mean 15.3, n=11) x 10.3-11.3 (mean 10.8); spotless or sparingly spotted and mottled dark brown. **Laying months** India: April–June; Nepal: April–June; Thailand: enlarged gonads April.

DESCRIPTION *A. n. nipalensis*
Adult male Crown and nape metallic blue-green tipped greyish-white except central feathers, bordered on upper back and sides of neck by crimson-brown or maroon band; wings and middle of back olive-green; rump bright yellow; tail metallic blue-green; cheeks black, throat metallic blue-green; rest of underparts bright yellow with scarlet streaking on breast. Iris brown or reddish-brown; bill and feet black or dark brown, underside of toes paler.
Adult female Olive-green with feathers of graduated tail tipped white.
Juvenile As adult female, but tail less graduated, and pale tips less obvious, the male having orange wash on breast.

GEOGRAPHICAL VARIATION
A. n. angkanensis Riley, 1929 (northern Thailand) Male has lower breast and upper belly scarlet.
A. n. australis Robinson & Kloss, 1923 (southern Thailand) Similar to *koelzi* but much smaller with little or no yellow on rump, and much less scarlet below.
A. n. blanci Delacour & Greenway, 1939 (Laos) From *ezrai* by breast and undertail-coverts flammulated with orange-red, as in *nipalensis*, instead of pure yellow; olive-green of back more golden; similar to *victoriae* but lacks yellow patch on back, and has much shorter bill.
A. n. ezrai Delacour, 1926 (southern Vietnam) Known from the type and one other specimen only. Has no yellow on lower back or rump; sides of neck brick-red slightly tinged yellow; yellow below with no scarlet.
A. n. horsfieldi (Blyth, 1842) (western Himalayas from Mussoorie and west Nepal, where it intergrades with nominate) Back and sides of neck olive-yellow with only a trace of maroon along margin of metallic-green of hindneck, and almost no scarlet on breast, and shorter bill than nominate. Similar to *victoriae* but red on sides of neck darker and duller.
A. n. karenensis Ticehurst, 1939 (south-east Burma) Similar to *victoriae* but no scarlet mixed with yellow below. Adult female has grey head to upper breast, rest of underparts yellowish.
A. n. koelzi Ripley, 1948 (Bhutan, Arunachal Pradesh, Meghalaya, Nagaland and Manipur south to Chittagong Hills, to north-west Yunnan and north Vietnam; central and south-west China, Tibet) Has a longer bill from skull (>24 mm compared to <23 mm) than nominate, and male has a smaller yellow patch on lower back and rump. Adult female has olive crown and nape, and hint of yellow on rump.
A. n. nipalensis (Hodgson, 1837) (west Nepal to Darjeeling and Sikkim) Described above.
A. n. victoriae Rippon, 1904 (western Burma) Similar to *koelzi* but with little or no maroon on back.

MEASUREMENTS Wing 51-52 (male *blanci*), 52 (male *ezrai*), 53-57 (mean 53.8, SD 1.47, 10 male *koelzi*), 51-58 (male *nipalensis*), 48-52 (mean 49.7, SD 1.28, 8 female *koelzi*), 47-52 (female *nipalensis*); **tail** 61-64 (male *blanci*), 71 (male *ezrai*), 58-64 (male *koelzi*), 58-70 (male *nipalensis*), 41-46 (female *koelzi*), 42-49 (female *nipalensis*); **bill** 17 (male *blanci*), 22.6-26 (mean 23.7, SD 0.98, 10 male *koelzi*), 20-23.6 (mean 22.2, SD 0.92, 10 male *nipalensis*), 20.1-23.2 (mean 22.3, SD 0.97, 8 female *koelzi*), 19.1-23.2 (mean 21.1, SD 1.03, 10 female *nipalensis*); **culmen** 17 (male *ezrai*); **gape**: 18.1-22.7 (male *horsfieldi*), 19.5-23.6 (male *koelzi*), 21.5-23.4 (male *nipalensis*), 18.5-20.4 (female *nipalensis*); **mass** 6.0-6.5 (4 male *angkanensis* or *australis*), 5.5-7.5 (male *koelzi*), 6.5, 8.0 (male *nipalensis*), 5.4 (female *angkanensis* or *australis*), 6.0-6.5 (female *koelzi*), 5-6 (female *nipalensis*), 5.6 (unsexed *angkanensis* or *australis*).

REFERENCES Ali & Ripley (1974), Delacour (1926), Delacour & Greenway (1939), Fleming (1968), Fleming *et al.* (1976), Grimmett *et al.* (1998), Inskipp & Inskipp (1985), King *et al.* (1975), Melville & Round (1984), Meyer de Schauensee (1984), Smythies (1986), Stepanyan (1985).

---

159 WHITE-FLANKED SUNBIRD
Aethopyga eximia   Plate 44

Nectarinia eximia Horsfield, 1821, *Trans. Linn. Soc. London* 13, p.168, Java.

Alternative name: Kuhl's Sunbird

IDENTIFICATION Adult male has crown and narrow band on throat metallic purple-blue; rump yellow; long tail blue-green; throat and upper breast red; long fluffy white flank feathers; back, wings and rest of underparts olive. Adult female has rounded tail; dark olive above; dark olive-green below, with greyer throat, and long white flank feathers.
Similar species All sympatric sunbirds lack white flanks. Females of Plain-throated Sunbird *Anthreptes malacensis* (53) and Olive-backed Sunbird *Cinnyris jugularis* (140) are much brighter yellow below and former has yellow eye-ring; female Copper-throated Sunbird *Leptocoma calcostetha* (92) differs from female of present species by greyish-white throat and white undertail-coverts.

VOICE Clear precise *tee-tee-tee-leet* and minor variations.

DISTRIBUTION Endemic to the mountains of Java (including Gede-Pangrango National Park).

HABITAT Uplands, 1,200-3,000 m. Flowering trees and vines, in low or middle storeys, in forest, forest edge, clearings and alpine scrub above tree-line.

STATUS Common, especially above 2,400 m.

MOVEMENTS Unknown.

FOOD Little recorded, but presumably includes nectar and/or small arthropods.
Known food-plants Unidentified mistletoes Loranthaceae.

HABITS Singly, in pairs or small parties close to ground, but visits flowers on creepers and in the canopy.

BREEDING Nest Unknown. **Eggs** Greyish-white, vaguely marked with small dark brown spots and clouds, with a

White-flanked Sunbird

heavy cap or zone, 15.8-18.4 (mean 16.9, n=23) x 11.2-12.5 (mean 11.9). **Laying months** Java: west Java, January, March, May, December.

DESCRIPTION

Adult male Long graduated tail; iridescent green crown, with some blue; bright olive nape, back and wing-coverts; lower back and rump yellow; remiges dark brown edged olive; uppertail-coverts iridescent blue-green; tail dark brown, proximal two-thirds of central rectrices iridescent blue-green, with some iridescence on sides of other feathers. Throat and breast red, with narrow iridescent purple throat-band; belly smoky-brown, becoming more olive towards vent; sides of breast olive-green; underwing-coverts and long flank feathers white; pectoral tufts white. Iris brown, bill black and feet black or brownish-black.

Adult female Tail much shorter. Dull olive above, greyer on head, dark olive-green below, greyish on throat, with white underwing-coverts, pectoral tufts and flanks; tail rounded, not elongated.

Juvenile As female but darker grey on throat and more brownish, particularly below.

GEOGRAPHICAL VARIATION None described.

MEASUREMENTS Wing 54-58 (mean 56.4, SD 1.26, 10 males), 48-54 (mean 51.2, SD 1.58, 8 females); **bill** 20.4-22.8 (mean 21.6, SD 0.75, 10 males), 16.7-19.3 (mean 18.1, SD 1.17, 8 females); **gape** 18.0-21.2 (males), 15.0-20.4 (females); **mass** no data.

REFERENCES Hellebrekers & Hoogerwerf (1967), Mac-Kinnon & Phillipps (1993).

160 FORK-TAILED SUNBIRD
Aethopyga christinae   Plate 44

Aethopyga christinae Swinhoe, 1869, *Ann. Mag. Nat. Hist.* ser. 4, 4, p.436, Hainan (China).

IDENTIFICATION Adult male has crown, nape, uppertail-coverts and elongated central tail feathers metallic green.

Central tail feathers end in long blackish points up to 13 mm long; outer rectrices with large white tips, back and wings yellowish-olive, rump yellow; rest of tail and sides of head black; throat and breast maroon-crimson; metallic moustachial stripe, rest of underparts olive-yellow. Adult female has brownish or blackish crown, rest of upperparts olive-green, below yellowish-grey chin to breast, rest of underparts buffish-yellow.

Similar species Female Plain-throated Sunbird *Anthreptes malacensis* (53) from female by much yellower underparts and yellow eye-ring; female Purple-throated Sunbird *Leptocoma sperata* (90) is yellow below, brighter on belly; female from female Copper-throated Sunbird *L. calcostetha* (92) by lack of greyish-white throat; female Olive-backed Sunbird *Cinnyris jugularis* (140) is brighter yellow below, and has a white-tipped black tail; female from that of Purple Sunbird *C. asiaticus* (139) by olive-green plumage; female Gould's Sunbird *Aethopyga gouldiae* (157) from female by yellowish rump; male Green-tailed Sunbird *A. nipalensis* (158) has crimson-brown/maroon band on upper back and sides of neck, whereas female is darker below and has white tips to outer tail feathers; female Black-throated Sunbird *A. saturata* (161) is less yellow below, and has yellow rump; female Crimson Sunbird *A. siparaja* (163) is much less yellow below; female Fire-tailed Sunbird *A. ignicauda* (166) has yellow rump.

VOICE Call Single or double *twisk*, or up to 5 rapid *twisk* notes. *Chip-chip* becoming trill of 5-8 notes slightly descending. **Song** "Weird and monotonous" (Caldwell & Caldwell 1931); *pe-et, pe-et, pit, pit*, first note or so on a slightly ascending pitch, and becoming more rapid.

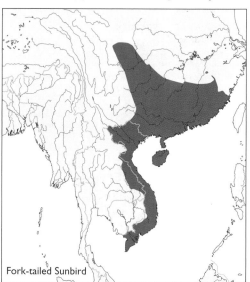

Fork-tailed Sunbird

DISTRIBUTION Central and south-east Laos, Vietnam and south-east China (Fukien, Kwangtung, Kwangsi, southern Hunan, eastern Szechuan, Hong Kong, Hainan Island).

HABITAT Forest and forest edge, generally on lower hills up to 1,400 m, occasionally in gardens.

STATUS Common in southern China; fairly common within range in South-East Asia.

MOVEMENTS Winter influxes occur in southern Kwang-tung (but apparently resident in north-west) and central Fukien.

FOOD Seeds; presumably also nectar and small arthropods.
Known food-plants None.

HABITS Reduces metabolism at night by 50% at constant ambient temperature of 5°C and by 72% at 25°C.

BREEDING **Nest** Pear-shaped, suspended from leaves on branch, and made of grasses, mosses and fibrous material, sometimes decorated with lichens. **Eggs** c/2-4; greenish-greyish ground colour, marked purplish, with reddish-brown tinge with dusky dots. **Laying months** China: April "onwards".

DESCRIPTION *A. c. latouchii*
Adult male Crown and nape metallic green, back and closed wings yellowish-olive; rump yellow; uppertail-coverts and central tail feathers metallic green, latter ending in narrow black points protruding 13 mm from rest of tail, outer feathers tipped white, rest black; sides of head blackish, throat and breast maroon-crimson; brilliant metallic blue-green moustachial streak; rest of underparts light olive, yellowish in centre of belly. Bill black or reddish-brown; feet brown; iris brown or dark brown.
Adult female Crown dull brownish or blackish with greyish-olive edging giving scaly appearance; upperparts olive-green; chin, throat and breast light yellowish-green, rest of underparts greenish-yellow.
Juvenile As female, but greyer above and on throat and upper breast; male develops longer tail and yellow rump before iridescence.

GEOGRAPHICAL VARIATION
  A. c. christinae Swinhoe, 1869 (Hainan Island) Back black rather than yellowish-olive as in *latouchii*; chin, throat and breast dark red.
  A. c. latouchii Sclater, 1891 (south-east China, north Vietnam and central Laos) Described above.
  A. c. sokolovi Stepanyan, 1985 (south Vietnam) Male from male *latouchii* by darker olive back; blackish sides to head have a reddish tinge; yellow area on upperparts larger and darker in tone; breast, belly and undertail-coverts olive-green to green, rather than golden olive-green.

MEASUREMENTS **Wing** 46.5 (male *christinae*), 46-52 (mean 49.9, SD 1.63, 10 male *latouchii*), 48.9, 48.5 (2 male *sokolovi*), 44-49 (female *latouchii*); **tail** 38.5 (male *christinae*), 29.8-45.4 (mean 40.0, SD 7.8, 6 male *latouchii*), 34.1, 34.2 (2 male *sokolovi*); **bill** 14.0 (male *christinae*), 13.6-15 (mean 13.9, SD 0.53, 6 male *latouchii*), 13.9, 14.8 (2 male *sokolovi*); **gape** 11.9 (male *christinae*), 15.5-16.9 (mean 12.0, SD 0.29, 6 male *latouchii*), 12.1, 13.5 (2 male *sokolovi*), 14.8-18.0 (female *latouchii*); **mass** 4.7-5.9 (mean 5.2, 12 unsexed of unknown subspecies).

REFERENCES Caldwell & Caldwell (1931), Corlett (1996), King *et al.* (1975), Meyer de Schauensee (1984), Prinzinger *et al.* (1989, 1992), Robson (1994, 2000), Stepanyan (1985).

161 BLACK-THROATED SUNBIRD
Aethopyga saturata   Plate 44

Cinnyris saturata Hodgson, 1837, *India Rev. Journ. Foreign Sci. Arts* 1, p.273, Nepal.

Alternative name: Hodgson's Sunbird

IDENTIFICATION Adult male appears almost black but has crown, nape, uppertail-coverts and elongated tail metallic purple or blue; back and sides of neck crimson-brown; wings blackish-brown; rump yellow; throat and breast blackish or blackish and scarlet; malar stripe purple or blue; rest of underparts greyish-olive or yellowish. Adult female has grey crown, yellow rump, rest of upperparts olive-green; tail graduated and tipped white; underparts olive and yellow. Juvenile differs from adult female by less graduated tail with less obvious white tips.
Similar species Female differs from Plain Sunbird *Anthreptes simplex* (52), Purple-throated Sunbird *Leptocoma sperata* (90), Copper-throated Sunbird *L. calcostetha* (92) and Olive-backed Sunbird *Cinnyris jugularis* (140) by yellow on rump; male Gould's Sunbird *Aethopyga gouldiae* (157) has yellow on underparts, whereas female has pale grey throat and rest of underparts yellow; male Green-tailed Sunbird *A. nipalensis* (158) is bright yellow and scarlet below, whereas female lacks yellow on rump, and white tips to outer tail feathers; female Fork-tailed Sunbird *A. christinae* (160) is more yellow below, and lacks yellow on rump; male Crimson Sunbird *A. siparaja* (163) from male by lack of blackish on throat and breast, and both sexes differ in having much less yellow on rump; male Fire-tailed Sunbird *A. ignicauda* (166) from male by scarlet uppertail-coverts and tail, and female *ignicauda* from female by lack of white tips to tail.

VOICE **Call** Repeated, quick, high-pitched, thin *tit*, *tit-tit* and *tiss-it*, etc. **Song** A lively twitter consisting of an uneven series of sharp high-pitched *swi*, *tis* and *tsi* notes, interspersed with rapid metallic trills *swi'it'it'it'it'it* and *swi'i'i'i'i'i*; heard in Nepal February to mid-July.

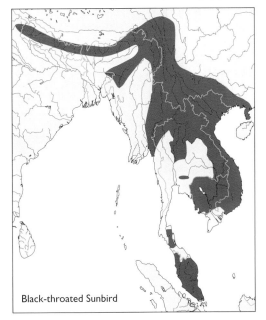

Black-throated Sunbird

343

DISTRIBUTION Himalayas, from Garhwal, Mussoorie and Rajaji National Park, east to Nepal, Bhutan, southeast Tibet, Arunachal Pradesh, Assam, Meghalaya, Bangladesh, Nagaland, Manipur; western and south-east Yunnan, western Kwangsi; Burma, Thailand, Indochina and peninsular Malaysia.

HABITAT Bushes in forest, at edge of dense jungle, in thin forest, scrub, secondary growth and banks of shady streams; usually 1,000-2,200 m, but down to 305 m in winter.

STATUS Common in Burma. Widespread and frequent in Nepal. Fairly common in India and Bhutan. May no longer occur in Bangladesh. Uncommon in Thailand.

MOVEMENTS Seasonal altitudinal movements in higher parts of range.

FOOD Probably includes nectar and/or pollen and insects. **Known food-plants** *Caryopteris* sp., *Elettaria cardamomum*, *Holmskjoldia* sp., *Leucosceptrum* sp., *Prunus* sp.

HABITS Occurs singly or in pairs. Down to ground-level at cardamom flowers. Maximum longevity record 4 years. Host to *Haemoproteus sequeirae*, *Hepatozoon* sp., *Plasmodium* sp. and *Trypanosoma* sp.

BREEDING Nest of *saturata* pear-shaped, made of vegetable down or dry grass, moss (especially on upper half), lichens, rootlets, fibre from fern rhizomes and cobweb, decorated outside with woodchips and bamboo leaves, lined with soft seed down; entrance hole one-third from top with (or without) 20-30 mm porch; attached to thin branches of bushes or creepers, or tips of tree-fern fronds up to 4 m above ground. **Eggs** c/1-3. White, speckled, spotted and blotched inky-black, inky-grey or muddy-brown; *sanguinipectus*: 17.5 x 12.2; *saturata*: 14.0-15.3 (mean 14.6, n=26) x 10.5-12.1 (mean 11.3). **Laying months** India: *assamensis*: January, March–July; *saturata*: May, July; Burma: April; Nepal: February–May, but as late as September, Chitlang Valley (*wrayi*); Thailand: enlarged gonads April.

DESCRIPTION *A. s. saturata*
Adult male Crown and nape metallic purple; back and sides of neck crimson-brown; wings blackish-brown; variably narrow yellow band on rump, absent in some; uppertail-coverts and upper surface of tail metallic purple, central feathers elongated; throat and breast blackish; broad metallic purple malar stripe; rest of underparts greyish-olive. Iris brown; bill brownish-black to black; feet dark horny-brown to dark brown.
Adult female Olive-green above, crown grey, yellow band on rump; underparts greyish-olive; tail graduated with white tips.
Juvenile Like adult female, but tail not so graduated, and white tips not so distinct.

GEOGRAPHICAL VARIATION
A. s. anomala Richmond, 1900 (southern Thailand to Trang) Male has lower breast to vent greyish with yellowish band across breast; throat to upper breast dull smoky-black bordered with glossy purple; no yellow on rump.
A. s. assamensis (McClelland, 1839) (north-east India, north Burma to west Yunnan) Male more richly coloured than *saturata*, with slightly more yellow on rump; belly dull olive-green and grey. Female has entire underparts greenish, with little or no yellow tinge.

A. s. cambodiana Delacour, 1948 (south-west Cambodia) Male as *sanguinipectus* but red on back darker.
A. s. galenae Deignan, 1948 (north-west Thailand) Male differs from *saturata* by having breast mixed yellow and scarlet; lower breast, belly and flanks greenish-grey. Male differs from *petersi* by sulphur-yellow breast-patch more extensive posteriorly and less clearly separated from olivaceous-yellow (not greyish olive-green) of rest of underparts. Female from that of *petersi* by yellowish posterior underparts, not greyish olive-green.
A. s. johnsi Robinson & Kloss, 1919 (southern Vietnam) Male has entire breast scarlet, narrowly streaked yellow, belly, vent and flanks olive-green or greyish-green; female has entire underparts greenish, with little or no yellow tinge.
A. s. ochra Deignan, 1948 (southern Laos and central Vietnam) Male has more extensive yellow below than *petersi* or *wrayi*. Female has entire underparts greenish, with little or no yellow tinge.
A. s. petersi Deignan, 1948 (eastern Burma, northern Thailand, Laos, northern Vietnam, south-east Yunnan, western Kwangsi) Male has glossy blue crown and moustachial stripe, chin to breast unglossed black, lower breast sulphur-yellow streaked scarlet, belly, flanks and vent olive-yellow. Female similar to *sanguinipectus*.
A. s. sanguinipectus Walden, 1875 (south-east Burma) Male similar to *galenae* but entire throat except centre of chin metallic blue-violet, and less red streaking on chest.
A. s. saturata (Hodgson, 1837) (Himalayas from Garhwal and Mussoorie east to Nepal, Bhutan and south-east Tibet) Described above.
A. s. wrayi Sharpe, 1887 (Malay Peninsula south of Trang) Male has very little yellow on rump; breast sooty-black with yellowish tips to feathers. Belly, flanks and vent greyish olive-green; less red streaking on breast than *petersi*.

MEASUREMENTS Wing 52-56 (male *assamensis*), 51-58 (mean 54.3, SD 1.22, 9 male *saturata*), 44-48 (female *assamensis*), 47-50 (mean 48.4, SD 0.97, 11 female *saturata*); **tail** 69-77 (male *assamensis*), 63-81 (male *saturata*), 32-37 (female *saturata*); **bill** 20-21 (male *assamensis*), 20-25.6 (mean 23.0, SD 1.27, 9 male *saturata*), 18-19 (female *assamensis*), 18.7-24.8 (mean 21.1, SD 1.75, 11 male *saturata*); **gape** 20.2-21.9 (male *saturata*), 18.9-20.8 (female *saturata*); **tarsus** 14-17 (male *saturata*), 14 (female *saturata*); **mass** 6.0-6.5 (male *saturata*), 5.5-5.7 (3 males, Thailand), 5.0 (female, Thailand).

REFERENCES Ali & Ripley (1974), Deignan (1948), Fleming *et al.* (1976), Grimmett *et al.* (1998), King *et al.* (1975), McClure (1974), Medway & Wells (1976), Melville & Round (1984), Meyer de Schauensee (1984), Smythies (1986).

162 WESTERN CRIMSON SUNBIRD
Aethopyga vigorsii   Plate 45

Cinnyris vigorsii Sykes, 1832, *Proc. Zool. Soc. London*, p.98, Ghauts, Dukhun, (western India).

Alternative names: Vigors's Yellow-backed Sunbird, Yellow-backed Sunbird

Taxonomic note Previously considered conspecific with *A. siparaja*.

IDENTIFICATION Adult male has forehead to centre of crown, uppertail-coverts, central tail feathers and edges of others, metallic green; rest of tail blackish-brown with some blue iridescence; rump pale yellow; back dark, dull crimson-red; throat to breast crimson-scarlet with obvious yellow streaks, and bordered with thin blackish collar; metallic violet or blue moustachial streaks and cheek spots; rest of underparts grey, darker, more brownish on breast; wings blackish-brown. Adult female chiefly olive-green above; tail black; olive-grey from throat to breast, whitish-grey on chin, rest of underparts grey. Central rectrices elongated but not as long in proportion to body as in Crimson Sunbird *A. siparaja* (163).

Similar species Female can be distinguished as follows from the following females: Purple-rumped Sunbird *Leptocoma zeylonica* (88) is browner above, with rufous wings, has shorter bill and whitish-grey chin to upper breast, rest of underparts yellow; Crimson-backed Sunbird *L. minima* (89) is smaller, with a much shorter bill, crimson rump and uppertail-coverts and is much brighter yellow below; Long-billed Sunbird *Cinnyris lotenius* (149) has a much longer, more curved bill, is browner above, and whitish-grey below with buffy-yellow centre of belly; Purple Sunbird *C. asiaticus* (139) is greyer above, much yellower, not grey, below.

VOICE Call A sharp, harsh but lively *chi-chwee*, reminiscent of Black-naped Monarch *Hypothymis azurea*. **Song** No information.

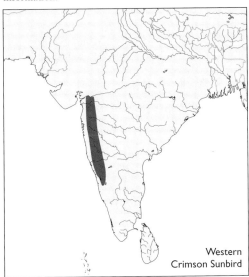

Western Crimson Sunbird

DISTRIBUTION India, in the Western Ghats from Narbada river south to North Kanara, the Nilgiris, and possibly further south in Kerala.

HABITAT Evergreen and moist deciduous biotopes around flowering trees and shrubs. Up to 900 m in Nilgiris, preferably foothills in evergreen and moist-deciduous biotope.

STATUS Common.

MOVEMENTS Unknown.

FOOD Nectar, and probably insects and spiders.
Known food-plants *Elytranthe parasitica, Scurrula obovata, S. parasitica, S. rhopalocarpa, Tolypanthus lagenifera* (all these species are dependent on birds opening their buds for pollination).

HABITS Unknown.

BREEDING Nest Coarse compared to other sunbirds and without cobweb coverings, suspended from bushes or exposed roots along earth cuttings in hilly country. One nest was purse-like, delicately woven with porch, attached to twig over stream, ornamented with scraps of bark, paper and caterpillar frass. **Eggs** c/1-3; 14-18.3 (mean 17.1, n=4) x 10-12.8 (mean 12.4); white or cream, speckled brown or reddish-brown or almost completely covered with a brown suffusion, darker in places. **Laying months** India: June–October. Nest with eggs in cutting on roots 9 September, Borivli National Park. In Bombay area most nests in winter; 17 & 21 September at Bhor Ghat; in hills many nests June–September.

DESCRIPTION
Adult male Forehead to centre of crown dark metallic green, back deep dull crimson-red, lower back and rump pale yellow; uppertail-coverts and lengthened, narrow, central tail feathers blackish-brown edged metallic blue with outer feathers tipped dark grey, and edges of other feathers metallic blue-green; chin to breast scarlet streaked yellow; moustachial streaks and cheek spots glossed metallic blue; rest of underparts grey, darkish, more blackish-grey below scarlet. Remiges brown, without olive edges. Underwing-coverts and axillaries white. Iris red-brown to crimson; bill blackish, dark brown below; feet dark brown to blackish.
Adult female Crown, nape and upper mantle greyish-olive, back olive brightening to olive-yellow on rump and uppertail-coverts; tail black, outerwebs tipped olive, inner white, central feathers olive; wings dark brown edged olive; chin whitish-grey, throat to breast olive-grey, rest of underparts grey. Some have chin to breast dull orange-scarlet.
Juvenile Male occasionally like adult female, but with dull scarlet throat and breast, possibly a transition from immature plumage. Female as adult female but greyer below.

GEOGRAPHICAL VARIATION None.

MEASUREMENTS Wing 61-65 (males), 54-57 (females); **tail** 50-58 (males), 35-38 (females); **bill** 23-27 (males), 21-24 (females); **tarsus** 15-16 (males), 15-16 (females); **mass** 7,9 (2 males), 7,8 (2 females).

REFERENCES Ali (1969), Ali & Ripley (1974), Fleming *et al.* (1976), Inskipp & Inskipp (1985), Mann (in prep. a), Mukherjee (1981), Robson (2000).

---

163 CRIMSON SUNBIRD
Aethopyga siparaja Plate 45

Certhia siparaja Raffles, 1822, *Trans. Linn. Soc. London* 13, p.299, Sumatra.

Alternative names: Yellow-backed Sunbird, Goulpourah Sunbird

Taxonomic note Previously included *A. vigorsii*.

IDENTIFICATION Adult male has forehead to centre of crown, and elongated central tail feathers, metallic bronze-green or blue; rest of tail black; hindcrown crimson or olive, rump olive and grey or blackish, latter with yellow patch; back crimson; throat to breast scarlet; metallic moustachial streaks; rest of underparts olive and grey. Adult female is chiefly olive, grey and yellow with yellow on rump and undertail-coverts; tail black; yellowish streaking on belly; long yellowish-white flank feathers. Juvenile male is like adult female, but has scarlet chin and centre of throat. Juvenile female greyer and less yellow than adult female.
Similar species Plain Sunbird *Anthreptes simplex* (52) lacks yellow below; females of Plain-throated Sunbird *A. malacensis* (53), Red-throated Sunbird *A. rhodolaema* (54) and Purple-throated Sunbird *Leptocoma sperata* (90) are much yellower below, and the first has a yellow eye-ring; female Black Sunbird *L. sericea* (91) has yellow on belly; Copper-throated Sunbird *L. calcostetha* (92) has white undertail-coverts; female Flaming Sunbird *Aethopyga flagrans* (153) has yellowish patch on breast; female Metallic-winged Sunbird *A. pulcherrima* (154) has bright yellow rump; female Gould's Sunbird *A. gouldiae* (157) has much more yellow below; female Green-tailed Sunbird *A. nipalensis* (158) has white tips to tail feathers; both sexes of White-flanked Sunbird *A. eximia* (159) have white flank feathers, and male also has long tail; female Fork-tailed Sunbird *A. christinae* (160) has much more yellow below; male Temminck's Sunbird *A. temmincki* (165) has scarlet tail, whereas female is more yellowish-olive, less grey below, and lacks white on flanks; male Javan Sunbird *A. mystacalis* (164) has iridescent purple tail and more yellow on rump, whereas female is duller and has red wash on wings and tail; male Fire-tailed Sunbird *A. ignicauda* (166) has long scarlet tail, whereas female has more yellow on rump and underparts. Male Scarlet Honeyeater *Myzomela sanguinolenta* has red forecrown and rump.

VOICE Call Likened to opening and closing of scissors. **Song** A chirping trill, or a loud sharp trill, often uttered on the wing. Soft *siesiep-siepsiep* (Java).

DISTRIBUTION The Himalayan foothills from Kangra east through Nepal to Bhutan and Arunachal Pradesh, south through Assam, Meghalaya, Manipur and Bengal to east Bihar and Chittagong Hills; Yunnan, Indochina, Thailand, Burma, south through Malay Peninsula; Nicobars; Sumatra and islands, Borneo, Natunas, Java; Sulawesi; west-central Philippines.

HABITAT Various forest types, generally at the edge, including riverine forest, *Melaleuca* forest and peatswamp forest, and fairly open country, including grassland and scrub, mangroves, woodland, coconut groves, secondary growth and gardens. Usually below 915 m, but from 50 m up to 1,500 m in Sulawesi, 1,800 m in Nepal in summer, to 1,190 m in Borneo, and at 1,690 m in Bhutan.

STATUS Usually common. Rare to uncommon on Butung.

MOVEMENTS Seasonal vertical movements in Himalayas.

FOOD Nectar, insects and spiders.
Known food-plants *Butea monosperma*, *Canna* sp., *Caryopteris* sp., *Erythrina indica*, *Gliricida* sp., *Hibiscus* sp., *Leucosceptrum* sp., unidentified mistletoes Loranthaceae, *Prunus* sp., *Salmaria malabarica*, *Woodfordia* sp., unidentified Zingiberaceae.

HABITS Usually forages low, but occasionally in canopy, singly, in pairs and occasionally in family parties; rather acrobatic. Males sing from exposed branches in canopy, and are extremely aggressive towards each other. Pierces corolla bases. Reduces metabolism at night by 54% at constant ambient temperature of 5°C and by 62% at 25°C. Host to *Leucocytozoon* sp.

BREEDING Parasitised in India by Asian Emerald Cuckoo *Chrysococcyx maculatus*. Observed feeding a juvenile Yellow-billed Malkoha *Phaenicophaeus calyorhynchus* at Dumoga-Bone National Park, North Sulawesi, January 1986. **Nest** Attached to palm fronds, sometimes very low, attenuated pear-shaped, usually with porch; constructed of vegetable down, rootlets, moss, grass, cobweb, decorated with oddments or clothed with rootlets on outside; under overhanging bank (Gunung Kinabalu, Sabah). **Eggs** c/1-3; dull or faintly glossy; variable colouring. Pinkish, rather sparingly marked with small dark reddish-brown spots (penumbrae) and hairlines, and by larger light reddish-brown clouds, mainly at blunt end; or densely covered with small spots giving uniform impression. Race *beccarii*: 16.7 x 12.4; *cara*: 12.2-14.9 x 10.6-11.1; *flavostriata*: 15.0 x 11.0; *heliogona*: 13.5-16.0 (mean 14.6, n=27) x 10.2-11.5 (mean 10.7); *labecula*: white or cream, speckled brown or reddish-brown, very variable; *magnifica*: 16.5-17.3 (mean 16.9, n=5) x 12.2-12.7 (mean 12.5); *seheriae*: 14.2-16.3 (mean 15.2, n=53) x 10.3-12.0 (mean 11.4); *siparaja*: pale salmon-pink blotched and speckled dark red (Gunung Kinabalu), 13.2-15.3 (mean 14.1, n=14) x 10.2-11.4 (mean 10.6). **Laying months** April–July (*labecula*); Borneo, Gunung Kinabalu, April (*siparaja*); India: Assam, May–July (*seheriae*); Sikkim, May, July, August (*seheriae*); Java: West Java, March–July, September, December; Butung, Sulawesi: young September (*beccarii*); peninsular Malaysia: March (*siparaja*); probably February (nominate or *trangensis* peninsular Malaysia); Burma: January–February, June (*cara*), April, May (*seheriae*); Nepal: Amlekghang and Chitwan, mid-February–mid-July (*seheriae*); Philippines: Negros, February–April, Cebu, June (*magnifica*); Sumatra: Deli, April (*siparaja*).

DESCRIPTION *A. s. seheriae*
Adult male Forehead to centre of crown metallic bronzy-green, hindcrown dark olive, back crimson, rump olive

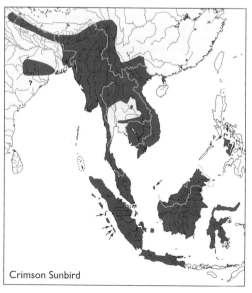

Crimson Sunbird

346

with concealed golden-yellow patch; uppertail-coverts and lengthened, narrow central feathers metallic bronzy-green, rest of tail black with outer feathers tipped dark grey; throat and breast scarlet; moustachial streaks glossed metallic purple and blue; rest of underparts light olive to olive-grey. Lesser wing-coverts crimson, rest of wing feathers dark brown edged olive. Iris dark brown; upper mandible dark brown, black at base, lower mandible horny-brown; feet dark brown. **Non-breeding plumage** Male loses most of crimson on head and breast.

Adult female Crown, nape and upper mantle greyish-olive, back olive brightening to olive-yellow on rump and uppertail-coverts; tail black edged red, outerwebs tipped olive, inner white, central feathers olive; wings dark brown edged ochraceous-olive; throat light grey, breast olive-grey, rest of underparts light olive with some yellowish streaking on upper belly; undertail-coverts yellow, long yellowish-white flank feathers.

Juvenile Male like adult female, but chin and centre of throat scarlet; female as adult female but greyer, not so yellow, below.

GEOGRAPHICAL VARIATION

A. s. beccarii Salvadori, 1875 (central, south and south-east Sulawesi, Butung, Muna and Kabaena) Female differs from nominate in having a red back.

A. s. cara Hume, 1874 (southern Burma, Thailand) Green gloss on crown of male.

A. s. flavostriata (Wallace, 1865) (northern Sulawesi) Male differs from nominate in having much more pronounced yellow streaking on red throat, and female has an olive back with slight carmine tipping to feathers. Male has metallic blue forecrown, moustachial stripes and tail; rest of foreparts red; broad yellow rump; dusky belly.

A. s. heliogona Oberholser, 1923 (Java) Very similar to nominate but some orange in yellow of rump, and grey of belly paler (see van Balen 1993).

A. s. insularis Delacour & Jabouille, 1928 (Phuquoc Island in Cambodia) Very similar to *siparaja*, but belly, lower breast and flanks paler grey.

A. s. labecula (Horsfield, 1839) (eastern Himalayas in Bhutan and Arunachal Pradesh, south through Assam, Meghalaya, Nagaland, Manipur and Bangladesh south to the Chittagong Hills) Both sexes are darker and richer above and below than *seheriae*.

A. s. magnifica Sharpe, 1876 (Philippines, on Cebu, Marinduque, Negros, Panay, Sibuyan, Tablas, ?Leyte) Male from *seheriae* by metallic purplish gloss on black forehead and tail, crown dark red, rump bright orange-yellow, and belly to undertail-coverts black, whereas female has head, back and rump dark olive-green, with varying amounts of red on scapulars, remiges, wing-coverts and back, red edging to black tail, and grey-green underparts. Larger than *flavostriata*, with stronger bill.

A. s. mangini Delacour & Jabouille, 1924 (south-east Thailand, central and southern Indochina) Similar to *siparaja* but crown of male glossed purple.

A. s. natunae Chasen, 1934 (Natuna Islands) From *siparaja* by paler grey underparts.

A. s. nicobarica (Hume, 1873) (Great and Little Nicobars, Kondal Island, Meroe Island) Male as *labecula*, but crown and tail violet-purple.

A. s. owstoni Rothschild, 1910 (Nachan, south China) Male differs from *seheriae* in colour of abdomen which is consistently olive-green rather than light olive to olive-grey. Differs from *cara* in having a darker crimson throat, with blackish rather than yellowish bases to feathers, with nape brown, not red, and more elongated middle rectrices.

A. s. seheriae (Tickell, 1833) (Himalayan foothills from Kangra east to Sikkim, south to eastern Bihar, north Bengal, western Bangladesh and ?hills of north-eastern Deccan; through central Burma to south Yunnan, south to west Tonkin, extreme north-west Thailand) Described above.

A. s. siparaja (Raffles, 1822) (Malay Peninsula south of Kedah in west and Narathiwat in east, Sumatra, except Aceh, and islands, Borneo and islands, except Natunas; possibly includes *heliogona* of Java) Male has a dark grey belly, and female has no red in tail. Gloss on crown of male purple-green; rump yellow and, in a few, uppertail-coverts glossed green; tail glossed purple and central rectrices much less elongated than in *seheriae*; throat to upper breast scarlet, rest of underparts less olive than *seheriae*. Much smaller, with shorter, less curved bill than this form, and female has much shorter central rectrices.

A. s. tonkinensis Hartert, 1917 (north-east Vietnam and south-east Yunnan) Male has central tail feathers shorter than *seheriae*, not conspicuously narrowed; more extensive yellow on rump and upper back than *siparaja*; no green on uppertail-coverts.

A. s. trangensis Meyer de Schauensee, 1946 (southern Thailand and Malay Peninsula north of nominate) Male differs from nominate in having lower breast and belly more olive, less grey, becoming yellowish in centre; wing-edges more olive.

MEASUREMENTS Wing 49-52 (male *natunae*), 50-52 (male *nicobarica*), 55.5-59.5 (male *owstoni*), 46-60 (male *seheriae*), 47-53 (female *seheriae*), 61 (male *siparaja*); **tail** 81 (male *labecula*), 40-45 (male *nicobarica*), 51-55 (male *owstoni*), 62-76 (male *seheriae*), 43 (male *siparaja*), 46 (female *natunae*), 32-33 (female *nicobarica*), 34-39 (female *seheriae*); **bill** 20-23 (male *seheriae*), 19-21 (female *seheriae*); **culmen from skull** 17 (male *siparaja*); **gape** 16.9-20.0 (male *flavostriata*), 22.7-25.3 (male *magnifica*), 17 (male *natunae*), 16.5-21.1 (male *seheriae*), 16.8 (female *flavostriata*), 21.0-23.7 (female *magnifica*), 18.0-20.3 (female *seheriae*); **tarsus** 14-16 (male *seheriae*), 14-16 (female *seheriae*); **mass** 6-9 (male *labecula*), 4.8-7.9 (male *seheriae*), 6 (female *labecula*), 5.0 (female *seheriae*).

REFERENCES Ali & Ripley (1974), van Balen (1993), Bourns & Worcester in McGregor (1909-1910), M. Catterall (pers. comm.), Chasen (1934), Coates & Bishop (1997), duPont (1971b), Dickinson *et al.* (1991), Fleming *et al.* (1976), Hellebrekers & Hoogerwerf (1967), Inskipp & Inskipp (1985), Inskipp *et al.* (2000), King (1975), King *et al.* (1975), MacKinnon & Phillipps (1993), Mann (1996, in prep. a), van Marle & Voous (1988), Medway & Wells (1976), Nash & Nash (1985a), Ogilvie-Grant & Whitehead (1898), Prinzinger *et al.* (1989), Prinzinger & Jackel (1986), Rothschild (1910), Rozendaal & Dekker (1989), Sengupta (1974), Smythies (1960, 1981, 1986), White & Bruce (1986).

164 JAVAN SUNBIRD
Aethopyga mystacalis   Plate 46

Nectarinia mystacalis Temminck, 1822, *Pl. Col., livr.* 21, pl.126, Java.

Alternative name: Scarlet Sunbird

IDENTIFICATION Adult male has bright crimson head, breast and back; crown except forehead, malar stripe, uppertail-coverts and long graduated tail iridescent purple; rump yellow; flight feathers blackish; belly grey and flanks whitish. Adult female mostly olive and grey, paler on throat, yellower on belly. Juvenile is greyer than adult female.
Similar species Female Plain-throated Sunbird *Anthreptes malacensis* (53) is yellow below and has yellow eye-ring; female Copper-throated Sunbird *Leptocoma calcostetha* (92) has greyish-white throat and white undertail; both sexes of White-flanked Sunbird *Aethopyga eximia* (159) have white flanks; male Crimson Sunbird *A. siparaja* (163) has a bronzy-green tail, less yellow on rump, and lacks red forehead, whereas female is paler and brighter, and lacks red wash on wings and tail; the very similar Temminck's Sunbird *A. temminckii* (165) is allopatric.

VOICE Soft, ringing *tzeep-tzeep, cheet-cheet.*

Javan Sunbird

DISTRIBUTION Endemic to Java (including Gunung Gede-Pangrango National Park).

HABITAT Hill dipterocarp and lower montane forest, secondary forest and edge; generally 800-1,985 m, once 2,300 m, but occasionally much lower (a specimen in the Natural History Museum, Tring, is from Wynkoops Bay, presumably at or near sea-level).

STATUS Not uncommon on Java.

MOVEMENTS Unknown.

FOOD Presumably nectar and/or small arthropods.
Known food-plants Unidentified mistletoes Loranthaceae.

HABITS In pairs in upper canopy; noisy. Host to microfilariae.

BREEDING Nest Undescribed. **Eggs** Dull or faintly glossy; white or greyish-white sparingly marked with greyish-brown spots with a slight zone. 13.6-16.6 (mean 15.0, n=13) x 10.0-11.4 (mean 11.1). **Laying months** West Java, January, April–June, October.

DESCRIPTION
Adult male Crown, except forehead which is crimson, malar stripe, lower rump, uppertail-coverts and long graduated tail dark iridescent purple; head, breast, lesser wing-coverts and back crimson; yellow streaking on breast; rump pale yellow, wings blackish, belly pale grey. Iris dark brown, bill and feet brown.
Adult female Grey head, paler on throat; rest of plumage olive, paler below, flanks whitish.
Juvenile As female, but greyer above and below.

GEOGRAPHICAL VARIATION None.

MEASUREMENTS Wing 46-49 (males), 43-48 (females); **bill** 15.4, 17.2, 18.5 (3 males), 15.0, 17.2, 17.9 (3 females); **gape** 15.4-15.7 (males), 13.6-16.8 (females); **mass** no data.

REFERENCES van Balen (1992, 1993), Holmes (1996), MacKinnon & Phillipps (1993).

---

165 TEMMINCK'S SUNBIRD
Aethopyga temmincki   Plate 46

Nectarinia temmincki S. Müller, 1843, *Land. Volk.*, in Temminck, *Verh. Nat. Gesch. Nederland. Overz. Bezit*, 1, (1839-1844), p.173, Mount Singalang, 1,600 ft., 0°24'S 100°20'E, Sumatra.

Taxonomic note Previously included in *A. mystacalis* and known as Scarlet Sunbird.

IDENTIFICATION Adult male chiefly scarlet above, including tail with elongated central feathers; lower rump brown glossed purple, rest of rump yellow; sides of crown, nape, moustachial stripe and uppertail-coverts metallic purple-violet; chin to breast scarlet, rest of underparts grey, yellower on centre of belly and whiter on flanks. Adult female has wing-coverts, and back to rump, golden-olive and tail edged orange; rest of plumage various shades of grey, with some olive and yellow wash below. Juvenile greyer below than adult female.
Similar species Javan Sunbird *A. mystacalis* (164) is allopatric; female from Plain-throated Sunbird *Anthreptes malacensis* (53) and Red-throated Sunbird *A. rhodolaema* (54) females by much duller underparts, and also from former by lack of eye-ring; female from female Plain Sunbird *A. simplex* (52) by red wash on wings and tail; female Purple-throated Sunbird *Leptocoma sperata* (90) is olive-green above and lacks grey head, whereas female Copper-throated Sunbird *L. calcostetha* (92) has greyish-white throat and white undertail-coverts, and both lack red; male Crimson Sunbird *Aethopyga siparaja* (163) lacks scarlet tail, whereas female is greyer above and lacks white on flanks.

VOICE Call Soft *cheet-cheet.* **Song** No information.

DISTRIBUTION South-west Thailand, peninsular Malaysia, Sumatra and Borneo.

HABITAT Lowland and hill dipterocarp forests, lower

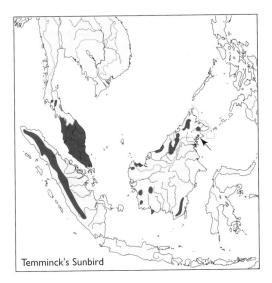

Temminck's Sunbird

montane forest and peatswamp forest. Generally sub-montane, but recorded from close to sea-level to 1,985 m.

STATUS Uncommon.

MOVEMENTS Unknown.

FOOD Probably nectar and/or small arthropods.
Known food-plants Unidentified mistletoes Loranthaceae.

HABITS Often forages low, as well as in canopy; very active.

BREEDING Nest Suspended from small twig. Egg-shaped with pointed apex forming an attachment. Made of dry grass and vegetable down, also lined with down, with a few decorations of paper, bark and other plant material. Entrance hole one-third way down from top, with small porch. 125 x 60 mm. **Eggs** c/3; undescribed. **Laying months** Peninsular Malaysia: February. Mt Mulu, Sarawak, October, 1,200 m (nest in Natural History Museum, collected by Charles Hose, 24 October, year unknown).

DESCRIPTION
Adult male Centre of crown, broad supercilium, nape and sides of head, mantle, back and wing-coverts scarlet; lower rump brownish glossed purple, rest of rump yellow. Sides of crown, nape and moustachial stripe, also uppertail-coverts, glossed purple and violet. Tail blackish-brown with scarlet edging, elongated central feathers mostly scarlet with dark centres. Wings dark brown with golden-olive edging. Below scarlet from chin to chest; rest of underparts grey with yellowish centre of belly. Iris brown. Bill and feet black.
Adult female Shorter-tailed. Top and sides of head grey with dark mottling; wing-coverts, back, mantle and rump golden-olive; tail dark brown with orange edging; flight feathers with golden to pale orange edging. Chin to chest greenish-grey, becoming greyer on belly and flanks, with yellowish centre to belly.
Juvenile As female but greyer on throat to breast.

GEOGRAPHICAL VARIATION None.

MEASUREMENTS Wing 46-54 (males), 44-49 (females); **bill** 15.3-18.8 (mean 17.8, SD 1.10, 10 males), 14.1-17.6 (mean 15.5, SD 1.14, 10 females); **gape** 14.2-17.9 (males), 13.6-16.0 (females); **mass** 4.8, 6.1 (2 males), 5.0 (female), 6 (unsexed).

REFERENCES Gaither (1994), MacKinnon & Phillipps (1993), Medway & Wells (1976), Smythies (1957, 1960, 1981).

166 FIRE-TAILED SUNBIRD
Aethopyga ignicauda   Plate 46

Cinnyris ignicauda Hodgson, 1837, *India Review* 1, p.273, Nepal.

IDENTIFICATION Adult male has metallic purple crown, olive wings and yellow rump; rest of upperparts, including elongated tail, scarlet; throat metallic purple, and rest of underparts yellow washed orange on breast and greyer towards vent. Non-breeding male as adult female, but tail longer, and more yellow below, with red on uppertail-coverts, tail and sometimes on underparts. Adult female olive, head grey, with yellow on rump and belly. Juvenile male as adult female, but brighter yellow below, and often with some red on throat and breast.
Similar species Female Plain-throated Sunbird *Anthreptes malacensis* (53), Purple-throated Sunbird *Leptocoma sperata* (90) and Olive-backed Sunbird *Cinnyris jugularis* (140) are much more yellow below, lack yellow on rump, and first also has yellow eye-ring; male Gould's Sunbird *Aethopyga gouldiae* (157) has uppertail-coverts and tail metallic purple-blue, whereas female has pale grey throat; male Green-tailed Sunbird *A. nipalensis* (158) has uppertail-coverts and tail metallic blue-green, whereas female lacks yellow rump and has white tips to tail; female Fork-tailed Sunbird *A. christinae* (160) lacks yellow rump; male Black-throated Sunbird *A. saturata* (161) has metallic purple uppertail-coverts and tail, whereas female has white tips to tail; male Crimson Sunbird *A. siparaja* (163) lacks long scarlet tail and female has less yellow above and below.

VOICE A high-pitched, monotonous *dzidzi-dzidzidzidzi* continually repeated (*ignicauda*) or a very high, sharp piping, *tsitsitsitsi...tsi...tsi...tsi*, with last two notes slower (*flavescens*).

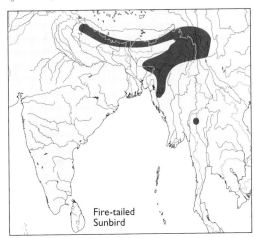

Fire-tailed
Sunbird

DISTRIBUTION The Himalayas from Rajaji National Park and Garhwal east through Nepal, Bhutan and Arunachal Pradesh, then south through Nagaland, Manipur, Assam

349

and Meghalaya to Bangladesh (Chittagongs and Sylhet); east to west Szechuan, central Yunnan and Tibet, and to south China; Chin Hills (Burma).

HABITAT Coniferous forest with dense undergrowth, particularly amongst *Rhododendron*, and above tree-line; 3,000-4,880 m in summer, 610-2,900 m in winter. Oak forests in Kumaon Himalaya.

STATUS Widespread and fairly common in Nepal, Bhutan and India; may no longer occur in Bangladesh. Very common above tree-line (3,900 m) in Adung valley (Burma), and not uncommon further south. Uncommon in lower Garhwal Himalayas; frequent at Thrumshimgla National Park, Bhutan.

MOVEMENTS Seasonal vertical movements in Himalayas. One record of migrant to Thailand.

FOOD Insects, spiders and nectar.
Known food-plants *Berberis* sp., *Callistemon* spp., *Caryopteris* sp., *Elaeagnus* sp., *Leucosceptrum* sp., *Loranthus longiflorus*, *Rhododendron arboreum*, *R. campanulatum*.

HABITS Pursue each other in flight whilst singing, and also dance; active and aggressive. Catch insects in the air. In winter in parties and mixed flocks.

BREEDING Male gives little if any assistance in nest-building. **Nest** Oval, one with small entrance near top, of moss, rootlets, cobweb, papery bark, lined with vegetable down, fine grass and feathers, suspended from branch of dwarf bamboo or bush within 2 m of ground; 140 x 70 mm. Another composed of fine seed down from fallen pods of a simul tree *Bombax malabarica*, held together with spiders' webs, scraps of moss, long shreds of grass, attached by grass and moss to a bracken frond. A third decorated with scraps of moss and caterpillar frass and a fourth made of lichen. **Eggs** c/2-3, pale violet-white covered with purplish speckles or brick-red with darker brick-red freckles (Himalayas), or white with tiny brown blotches forming a broad ring at the large end (Assam); *ignicauda* 14.3-17.0 (mean 15.6,

n=14) x 11.0-12.5 (mean 11.8). **Laying months** North-east India: April–June; Nepal (Gapte Cave): building May.

DESCRIPTION *A. i. ignicauda*
Adult male Crown metallic purple; sides of face blackish; sides of crown, nape, back, uppertail-coverts and elongated tail scarlet; rump yellow; wings olive; throat metallic purple; rest of underparts yellow, brighter with some scarlet on breast, greyer towards vent. Iris dark brown; bill and feet blackish-brown. **Non-breeding plumage** (October to February, but breeding plumage males occur in all months) As female, but underparts brighter yellow, sometimes with orange or red; uppertail-coverts and tail red, tail longer.
Adult female Mainly olive, more yellow on rump and belly becoming whitish on vent, with head and chin to upper breast grey.
Juvenile Male as adult female, but brighter yellow below with variable amount of red between throat and breast.

GEOGRAPHICAL VARIATION
A. i. flavescens Baker, 1921 (Chin Hills, Burma) Male differs from *ignicauda* in having much less scarlet in yellow of breast.
A. i. ignicauda (Hodgson, 1837) (includes *exultans* Baker, 1925) (range of species except where *flavescens* occurs) Described above.

MEASUREMENTS Wing 52-57 (male *flavescens*), 55-60 (male *ignicauda*), 48-52 (female *flavescens*), 52-58 (female *ignicauda*); **tail** 109-157 (non-breeding c.48; male *ignicauda*), 18.7-21.4 (mean 20.3, SD 1.12, 5 female *ignicauda*); **gape** 18.5-20.8 (male *flavescens*), 19.6-22.0 (male *ignicauda*), 17.8-20.3 (female *flavescens*), 19.1-21.7 (female *ignicauda*); **tarsus:** 16 (male *ignicauda*); **mass** 7.5, 9 (2 male *ignicauda*).

REFERENCES Ali & Ripley (1974), Fleming *et al.* (1976), Grimmett *et al.* (1998), Inskipp & Inskipp (1985), Inskipp *et al.* (2000), Meyer de Schauensee (1984), Singh (2000), Smythies (1986), Sultana & Khan (2000).

SPIDERHUNTERS
ARACHNOTHERA

Arachnothera Temminck, 1826, *Pl. Col., livr.* 65 pl. 388, in text to fig. 1. Type by monotypy *Nectarinia chrysogenys* Temminck.

Ten species in tropical Asia. Robust, and larger than almost all sunbirds. Sexes similar and, unlike other sunbirds, both sexes incubate; no metallic plumage; mostly greenish. Bill long, at least twice length of head; stout, strongly curved, with ridge between nostrils. Long tongue rolled to form a complete tube for most of its length, but has two lateral splits on distal 10%, which are rolled to form two tubes completed by the ventral section as in *Aethopyga*.

167 LITTLE SPIDERHUNTER
Arachnothera longirostra   Plate 47

Certhia longirostra Latham, 1790, *Lath. Index Orn.* 1, p.299, Bengal; restricted to Tippera District, Bengal State, Pakistan [= Bangladesh], by Deignan, 1963, *Bull. U.S. Natn. Mus.* 226, p.208.

IDENTIFICATION Bill very long, stout and curved. Adult olive above, with dark brown tail tipped white; black moustachial stripe; throat and breast greyish-white; rest

of underparts yellow. Male has orange pectoral tufts. Juvenile is browner.
Similar species From female sunbirds by much longer, curved bill; from all other spiderhunters by greyish-white chin and throat, and lack of streaking below.

VOICE Call Harsh metallic *cheet* or *chee-chee* similar to Asian Paradise-Flycatcher *Terpsiphone paradisi*. Short plaintive call note; persistent *chee chee chee*; series of up to 25 harsh loud notes *sheep sheep...*; repeated *chip cheep cheep*; loud *chip chip*, endlessly repeated. Repeated *ship ship...* when feeding.
Song Monotonous *which-which...*, twice per second for

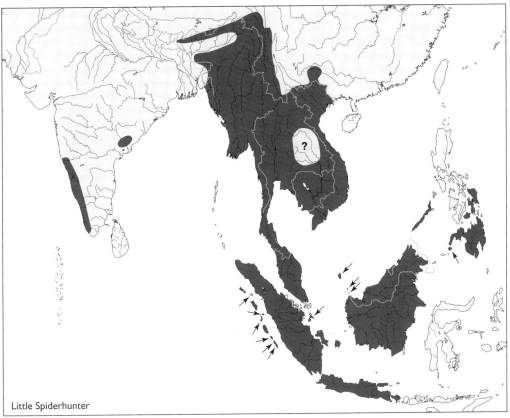

Little Spiderhunter

about two minutes, recalling Common Tailorbird *Orthotomus sutorius*. Continuous *tee-chu*, first note rising, second falling, repeated dozens of times. Territorial song an incessant whistle-like squeak, *chew-chew-chew-chew...*

DISTRIBUTION From Chitwan (central Nepal) and south-east Nepal to Arunachal Pradesh, Meghalaya, Assam, Manipur and Bangladesh south to Chittagongs; Western Ghats, from north Kanara to western Tamil Nadu and Kerala; Eastern Ghats; Burma, Thailand, Indochina, western Yunnan; North Natunas, Greater Sundas including Riau and Lingga Archipelagos, and Philippines.

HABITAT Understorey of various forest types including montane, alluvial, deciduous, evergreen, heath and peat-swamp, at forest edge, in coastal vegetation, mangrove swamp, scrub jungle, coconuts, bamboos, secondary growth, clearings with bananas or gingers, *Albizia*, rubber, cardamon, sholas *Aeschynomene* sp., plantations and gardens, and also in watered ravines and along streams. Generally below 1,000 m, but up to at least 2,000 m in Sumatra (possibly to 2,200 m), Java and Bali, and 2,100 m in China; 1,400 m on Borneo; up to 1,500 m in southern India; between 75 and 305 m in Nepal.

STATUS Common throughout Thailand except eastern parts. Widespread in Burma where common in Tenasserim, but rare elsewhere. Frequent in western Ghats, India, and locally common in north-east India. Rare in Bhutan; locally common in Bangladesh. Very scarce and local in south-east Nepal. Not uncommon Sumatra. Uncommon in the Philippines. Common in Borneo. Common in parts of southern Laos.

MOVEMENTS Two ringed on Gunung Mulu, Sarawak, were recaptured 490 m higher on the mountain 8 and 9 days later. Probably undergoes local movements in Nilgiris. Nomadic in parts.

FOOD Spiders, insects and nectar. Pierces corollas of *Canna* sp. Takes insects from spiders' webs and pools of water in epiphytes and ferns.
Known food-plants *Canna* sp., *Erythrina*, unidentified mistletoes Loranthaceae, *Melastoma* spp., *Musa* sp., *Spathodea* sp., unidentified Zingiberaceae.

HABITS Occurs singly or in pairs; inquisitive and restless; feeds acrobatically and pecks at flowers; probes corolla tubes of banana flowers whilst clinging to bracts; flight rapid. Highly mobile. Greatest longevity recorded 5 years. Host to *Haemoproteus sequeirae*, *Leucocytozoon* sp. and microfilariae.

BREEDING In India brood-parasitised by Violet Cuckoo *Chrysococcyx xanthorhynchus*, Asian Emerald Cuckoo *C. maculatus*, Common Cuckoo *Cuculus canorus bakeri*, Large Hawk-Cuckoo *Hierococcyx sparverioides* and Hodgson's Hawk-Cuckoo *H. fugax*; in Thailand by *C. xanthorhynchus*.
Nest A compact cup 10 cm deep, of leaf skeletons, soft grass and vegetable down neatly felted together and attached by rim to underside of banana leaf by cobwebs or vegetable cotton passed through leaf and knotted on upper surface; semi-circular entrance hole on one side. Another made of rootlets, dead leaves, plant fibres, and cobwebs in a tunnel made by sewing up ginger and plantain leaves. India: may have two entrances; placed under *Khydia* leaf,

351

or in elephant grass, or under giant creeper, or large dock leaf or on castor-oil plant; may be as little as 0.5 m above ground; lined with fine grass. **Eggs** c/2-3. Dull; (a) white or creamy, with heavy zone of reddish-brown or purplish-brown spots; (b) almost completely unmarked except for a few brown spots. *buettikoferi*: 18.1 x 13.0; *longirostra*: unglossed, pinkish-white to salmon-pink, sparsely stippled all over reddish with sharply defined ring of reddish-brown spots around larger end; 16.3-19.1 (mean 18.3, n=100) x 12.3-13.9 (mean 13.1) (India); 17.1-17.5 x 12.8-13.4 (peninsular Malaysia); *prillwitzi*: 16.2-20.2 (mean 18.3, n=100) x 12.4-14.7 (mean 13.3). **Laying months** Borneo: eggs in oviduct November, juveniles July and August, probably breeds opportunistically, Sabah, July, food-carrying May and November, eggs in oviducts or active gonads January, March, April, July, September–December; India, Assam: January–November, chiefly May–August; south-western India: December–August, chiefly January–May; Java: January, February, April–June, September, October, December; peninsular Malaysia: February–May (nestlings April), October (nestlings), December, and juveniles all months, most May and June, least September–December. Nepal: Krui, believed to breed in March–September. Sumatra: May–June, probably Mamas River, August; Thailand, January.

DESCRIPTION *A. l. longirostra*
Adult male Very long, stout, curved bill; above olive, crown feathers dark centred; wing-coverts olive, remiges dusky-brown edged olive; tail dark brown tipped white; lores white, short black moustachial streak; throat and breast greyish-white, latter tinged yellow; rest of underparts bright yellow; orange pectoral tufts. Iris brown to dark brown; bill horny-brown, greyer on gonys and at base of lower mandible, or black upper mandible, pale grey lower; feet black, blackish-grey or bluish-grey.
Adult female As male but smaller, and lacks pectoral tufts.
Juvenile As adult female but browner.

GEOGRAPHICAL VARIATION
A. l. atita Oberholser, 1932 (South Natunas) From *rothschildi* by longer bill; yellow of underparts less greenish, deeper, brighter and more golden.
A. l. buettikoferi van Oort, 1910 (Borneo) Browner and less olive above than *longirostra*, and with paler pectoral tufts.
A. l. cinereicollis (Vieillot, 1819) (peninsular Thailand and peninsular Malaysia south of Isthmus of Kra, Sumatra and satellite islands) Grey of sides of head, neck and throat bluish; black at corner of mouth; upperwing and -tail greenish-brown; breast to vent yellow, except for white undertail-coverts; white tips to tail feathers, greyish below; bill very long.
A. l. dilutior Sharpe, 1876 (Palawan) From nominate by more olive-brown crown, brown lores, upperparts more olive-green; flanks washed sulphur-yellow, rest of underparts ashy-whitish; pectoral tufts dull orange.
A. l. flamifera Tweeddale, 1878 (Bohol, Leyte, Mindanao, Samar, Dinagat, Biliran) From *dilutior* by faint orange-green wash on upperparts, and flanks, belly and undertail-coverts yellow; pectoral tufts bright orange.
A. l. longirostra (Latham, 1790) (India, in Western Ghats from Kanara south to west Tamil Nadu and Kerala; Eastern Ghats; south-east Nepal, Darjeeling, Bhutan, Arunachal Pradesh, Meghalaya, Manipur, Bangladesh south to Chittagong Hills, through Burma to west Thailand south to Kra; west Yunnan) Described above.

A. l. niasensis van Oort, 1910 (Nias Island) From *cinereicollis* by longer bill and wing, and very pale yellow underparts.
A. l. pallida Delacour, 1932 (includes *zharina* Oberholser, 1912) (south-east Thailand, central Indochina) Much shorter bill than nominate; above paler and greyer olive-green, throat very white, rest of underparts very pale yellow.
A. l. prillwitzi Hartert, 1901 (Java) From *longirostra* by having brighter yellow on underparts, and more orange pectoral tufts.
A. l. randi Salomonsen, 1953 (Basilan) Similar to *flamifera* but has a much longer bill.
A. l. rothschildi van Oort, 1910 (North Natunas) Yellow below as in *cinereicollis* but bill, and usually wing, shorter.
A. l. sordida La Touche, 1921 (south and south-east Yunnan, north-east Thailand, northern Indochina) Similar to *longirostra* in dull grey throat and breast, but dull whitish-grey lores and much shorter bill.

MEASUREMENTS Wing 66.5 (male *atita*), 65-74 (mean 69.7, 136 male *buettikoferi*, Brunei), 67-73 (mean 69.7, 19 male *buettikoferi*, Sabah), 65-71 (mean 68.1, 7 male *cinereicollis*), 60-67.5 (male *longirostra*), 66-69 (male *pallida*), 70 (male *niasensis*), 64 (male *rothschildi*), 61 (female *atita*), 59-59-66 (mean 62.5, 75 female *buettikoferi*, Brunei), 67-73 (mean 69.7, 19 female *buettikoferi*, Sabah), 59-63 (mean 61.2, 5 female *cinereicollis*), 60 (female *longirostra*), 62 (female *niasensis*), 58-62 (female *pallida*), 58 (female *rothschildi*), 63 (unsexed *sordida*); **tail** 40-42 (male *longirostra*); **bill** 34-37 (male *longirostra*), 42 (male *niasensis*), 35 (male *rothschildi*), 32-33 (female *longirostra*), 38 (female *niasensis*), 31 (female *rothschildi*); **exposed culmen** 38.5 (male *atita*), 34 (male *pallida*), 35.5 (female *atita*), 32 (unsexed *sordida*); **gape** 37.0-45.9 (male *buettikoferi*, Brunei), 40-45 (mean 43.1, 18 female *buettikoferi*, Sabah), 38-43 (male *longirostra*), 36-41 (female *longirostra*), 31-39.7 (female *buettikoferi*, Brunei), 40-45 (mean 43.1, 18 female *buettikoferi*, Sabah); **tarsus** 15 (male *longirostra*); **mass** 10.3-16.1 (mean 14.0, 134 male *buettikoferi*, Brunei), 12.9-15.6 (mean 14.0, 7 male *cinereicollis*), 8.8-13.7 (mean 11.1, 77 female *buettikoferi*, Brunei), 10.8-14.0 (mean 12.2, 5 female *cinereicollis*), 9-16 (mean 12.6, 47 unsexed *buettikoferi*, Tanjung Puting).

REFERENCES Ali (1969), Ali & Ripley (1974), Andrew (1985), G. W. H. Davison (in prep.), Delacour (1932), Evans *et al.* (2000), Fleming *et al.* (1976), Gaither (1994), Grimmett *et al.* (1998), Hellebrekers & Hoogerwerf (1967), Holmes (1996), Inskipp & Inskipp (1985), Khan (1977), La Touche (1921), Mann (1996), McClure (1974), Medway & Wells (1976), Nash & Nash (1988), Oberholser (1932), van Oort (1910), Rajathurai (1996), Sheldon *et al.* (in press), Smythies (1960, 1981, 1986), Thompson (1966), Wells *et al.* (1978), Zimmer (1918).

168 THICK-BILLED SPIDERHUNTER
Arachnothera crassirostris   Plate 47

Arachnocestra crassirostris Reichenbach, 1854, *Handb. spec. Orn., Icon. Synops. Avium, Scansoriae, Tenuirostres, continuatio* XI, p.314, pl. 592, fig. 4016, no locality; Sumatra designated by Robinson and Kloss, 1923, *Journ. Fed. Malay*

States *Mus.* 8, p.353; later restricted, without comment, to "Settlement of Malacca" by Robinson 1928, *Birds Malay Pen.*, 2, p.297.

IDENTIFICATION Long, thick, curved bill. Adult is chiefly dark olive above; chin to breast greyish-yellow, rest of underparts greenish-yellow or yellow; greyish-yellow tips and edging to tail; male has orange-yellow pectoral tufts. Juvenile is browner, with paler bill.

Similar species From female sunbirds by much longer and more curved bill; from Little Spiderhunter *Arachnothera longirostra* (167) by greenish, not greyish throat; from Streaky-breasted Spiderhunter *A. affinis* (174), Grey-breasted Spiderhunter *A. modesta* (173) and Streaked Spiderhunter *A. magna* (175) by lack of ventral streaking; from Spectacled Spiderhunter *A. flavigaster* (170) and Yellow-eared Spiderhunter *A. chrysogenys* (171) by dark patch through eye and through yellow orbital ring.

VOICE Call A "wheezing rattle" in the hand, and a hard, nasal *chit chit; chissie-chissie*; contact call *tch-tch*. **Song** No information.

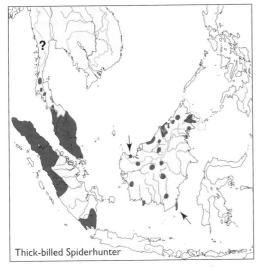

Thick-billed Spiderhunter

DISTRIBUTION The Malay Peninsula (including southern Thailand and Singapore where recently re-discovered), Sumatra (including Berbak Game Reserve; West, Lampung, Jambi) and Borneo.

HABITAT Forest and secondary growth, mangroves (one record), *Albizia*, *Eucalyptus*, bananas and wild gingers in lowlands and lower hills to 1,350 m (to 1,220 m in peninsular Malaysia and 1,300 m in Sumatra).

STATUS Uncommon and local resident of lowland forest in Borneo. Uncommon in Thailand, rare in Sumatra.

MOVEMENTS Unknown.

FOOD Soft insects; butterflies and nectar.
Known food-plants Unidentified Musaceae, unidentified Zingiberaceae.

HABITS Little recorded. Usually forages low. Flies fast through foliage as other spiderhunters; aggressive and bold. Direct flight.

BREEDING Nest Similar to Long-billed Spiderhunter *A.*

robusta (169), but smaller. **Eggs** Unknown. **Laying months** Borneo, Sabah: enlarged testes, January.

DESCRIPTION
Adult male Dark olive-brown above; flight feathers with greeny-yellow edging; chin to breast greyish-yellow; pectoral tufts yellowish-orange; rest of underparts greeny-yellow becoming yellow on undertail-coverts and flanks; tail has greyish-yellow tips, and edging to outer feathers. Iris brown or dark brown; bill black, horn at base; feet blackish with orange soles.
Adult female Like male but lacks pectoral tufts.
Juvenile Thought to be similar to female, but browner and with paler bill.

GEOGRAPHICAL VARIATION None.

MEASUREMENTS Wing 72-79 (males), 64-69 (females); **bill** 30.3-33.9 (mean 32.1, SD 1.48, 4 males), 30.2-36.1 (mean 32.8, SD 2.22, 6 females); **gape** 29.7-33.5 (males), 27.6-31.8 (females); **mass** 15.5, 16.4 (2 males).

REFERENCES Gretton (1990), Holmes (1996), Hornskov (1987), MacKinnon & Phillipps (1993), Mann (1996, in prep. b), van Marle & Voous (1988), Medway & Wells (1976), Sheldon *et al.* (in press), Smythies (1957, 1960, 1981).

---

169 LONG-BILLED SPIDERHUNTER
Arachnothera robusta   Plate 47

Arachnothera robusta S. Müller and Schlegel, 1845, *Verh. Nat. Gesch. Zool.* (Aves), p.68, pl. xi, fig. 1, Indrapoera, western Sumatra.

IDENTIFICATION Very long, curved bill. Adult is olive above, with dark tail tipped white; chin white, rest of underparts yellow streaked green on throat and breast. Male has orange-yellow pectoral tufts.
Similar species From female sunbirds by extremely long curved bill; from Little Spiderhunter *Arachnothera longirostra* (167), Thick-billed Spiderhunter *A. crassirostris* (168), Spectacled Spiderhunter *A. flavigaster* (170) and Yellow-eared Spiderhunter *A. chrysogenys* (171) by streaked underparts; from Streaky-breasted Spiderhunter *A. affinis* (174), Grey-breasted Spiderhunter *A. modesta* (173), Streaked Spiderhunter *A. magna* (175) and Whitehead's Spiderhunter *A. juliae* (176) by yellow on underparts.

VOICE Call High-pitched *chit-chit, chit-chit* in flight, or a monotonous harsh *chuu-luut chuu-luut* from high tree perch. **Song** Rising *choi, choi, choi, choi...*

DISTRIBUTION The Malay Peninsula from Trang in southern Thailand southwards, Sumatra (Aceh, Barat, Lampung, Jambi, Riau, North), Borneo and Java.

HABITAT The canopy in lowland and hill dipterocarp forests, heath forest and peatswamp forest, coniferous forest, rubber estates, *Albizia*, *Eucalyptus*, tobacco and other plantations, edges of rubber plantations and gardens; occasionally in secondary growth. Occurs from sea-level to at least 1,000 m on Borneo, from sea-level to at least 1,380 m in peninsular Malaysia, and between sea-level and 1,700 m on Sumatra.

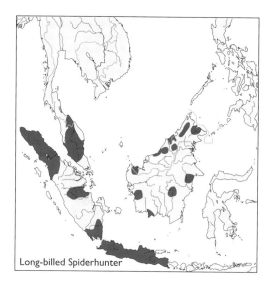

Long-billed Spiderhunter

STATUS Scarce in Borneo. Rare in Thailand, Sumatra and Java, where locally common at sea-level.

MOVEMENTS Unknown.

FOOD Spiders, caterpillars, other soft insects, small flowers and fruits of invasive creepers, and nectar. **Known food-plants** *Macrosolen* sp.

HABITS Solitary and aggressive; usually high in trees; has been observed flying backwards. Greatest longevity 5 years.

BREEDING Nest Bottle- or trough-shaped, of grass stems woven together and held against underside of banana leaf by cobweb slings, knotted on surface of leaf; entrance tunnel opening towards tip of leaf; 43 cm long, including entrance tunnel, entrance 11.5 cm wide, and chamber 10 x 6.5 cm. At Mawao, Sabah, built by sewing together the edges of banana leaf to form tube holding a large mass of plant materials. **Eggs** c/2. Matt white or faintly glossy with handsome zone of black spots and pencillings around broadest part; *armata*: 21.9 x 14.9; *robusta*: 17.9-22 (mean 21.8) x 15-16 (mean 15.7). **Laying months** Java: West Java, January, April–July, December; peninsular Malaysia: building February–June, eggs March, April, young June; Sumatra: nest-building, using coconut fibre under large leaf on small tree, Berbak, Jambi, September. Sarawak: eggs May. Borneo, Kalimantan Tengah, Barito Ulu: juveniles September; Sabah: nest with 2 chicks March, active gonads June; Sarawak: Samunsam, adult carrying nest material June, and carrying leaf skeletons into hole on underside of bough, 20 m up trunk of forest tree, locality unknown, December.

DESCRIPTION *A. r. robusta*
Adult male Very long bill; upperparts olive; remiges edged yellowish; slight dark scaling on crown; tail blackish-brown, outer two pairs of feathers tipped white; underparts dull yellow, brighter on belly and undertail-coverts, streaked green on throat and breast; orange-yellow pectoral tufts. Underwing-coverts pale yellow. Iris brown, bill black, feet blackish-olive.
Adult female As male, but smaller and lacks pectoral tufts.
Juvenile Unknown.

GEOGRAPHICAL VARIATION
    A. r. armata S. Müller & Schlegel, 1845 (Java) Less heavily streaked than nominate and much smaller.
    A. r. robusta S. Müller & Schlegel, 1845 (whole range except Java) Described above.

MEASUREMENTS Wing 81-90 (male *robusta*), 76.5 (female *armata*), 76-84 (female *robusta*); **tail** 52, 62 (2 male *robusta*), 60 (female *robusta*); **bill** 55.6-64.7 (mean 60.7, SD 3.36, 6 male *robusta*), 44.3 (female *armata*), 55.8-60.9 (mean 58.2, SD 1.77, 6 female *robusta*); **gape** 54.3-61.0 (male *robusta*), 50.4-58.8 (female *robusta*); **tarsus** 18, 19 (2 male *robusta*), 18 (female *robusta*); **mass** no data.

REFERENCES Hellebrekers & Hoogerwerf (1967), Holmes (1996), MacKinnon & Phillipps (1993), Mann (in prep. b), van Marle & Voous (1988), McClure (1974), Medway & Wells (1976), Sheldon *et al.* (in press), Smythies (1999), Wilkinson *et al.* (1991).

---

170 SPECTACLED SPIDERHUNTER
Arachnothera flavigaster   Plate 47

Anthreptes flavigaster Eyton, 1839, *Proc. Zool. Soc. London*, p.105, "Malaya".

Alternative names: Large Spiderhunter, Greater Yellow-eared Spiderhunter

IDENTIFICATION Long thick curved bill. Mostly olive, greener above, and yellower on edges of flight feathers, flanks and belly; broad eye-ring and large yellow ear-patch. **Similar species** From female sunbirds by large size and very long bill; combination of unstreaked yellow underparts and broad yellow orbital ring not bisected by dark line distinguish it from all other spiderhunters except Yellow-eared Spiderhunter *Arachnothera chrysogenys* (171), which is smaller with a longer, finer bill, has a larger ear-patch, a narrower eye-ring, and is streaked on throat and breast.

VOICE Call High-pitched *chit-chit*. **Song** No information.

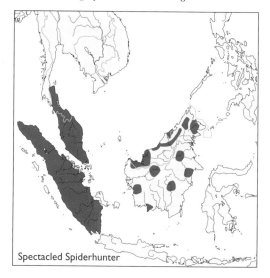

Spectacled Spiderhunter

DISTRIBUTION Peninsular Thailand and Malaysia, Sumatra and Borneo.

HABITAT Upper and middle storey of lowland diptero-carp forest, peatswamp forest and secondary forest, and at forest edge; also in cleared areas, cultivation, coconut groves, abaca, plantains, *Albizia*, rubber and oil-palm plantations and gardens; sea-level to 610 m in Malaysia, to 1,680 m (possibly 1,800 m) on Borneo, and to 1,500 m on Sumatra.

STATUS Not uncommon in open forest in Sumatra; uncommon to rare in Borneo.

MOVEMENTS Unknown.

FOOD Pollen, nectar, fruit, insects and spiders.
Known food-plants *Elaeis guineensis*, unidentified Musaceae, *Polygala* sp., *Spathodea campanulata*, unidentified Zingiberaceae.

HABITS Aggressive; active. Usually forages high in trees where it is not easy to observe.

BREEDING Nest On underside of coconut frond 8-13 m above ground or between large rubber tree leaves sewn together. Eggs Unknown. Laying months Borneo: April; Borneo, Sabah: nest, probably with young, April, enlarged testes July and August. Peninsular Malaysia: (?eggs) end February–March.

DESCRIPTION Sexes similar.
Adult Mostly olive; more greenish above, and yellower on flanks, belly and edges of remiges; large yellow ear-patch; broad yellow eye-ring; long thick curved bill. Iris brown. Bill blackish, feet yellowish-brown.
Juvenile Unknown.

GEOGRAPHICAL VARIATION None.

MEASUREMENTS Wing 99-107 (males), 93-106 (females); bill 39.2-44.4 (mean 42.2, SD 1.88, 5 males), 39.5, 44.2, 41.1 (3 females); gape 40.8-45.0 (males), 39-44.6 (females); mass no data.

REFERENCES King *et al.* (1975), MacKinnon & Phillipps (1993), Medway & Wells (1976), Sheldon *et al.* (in prep.).

171 YELLOW-EARED SPIDERHUNTER
Arachnothera chrysogenys   Plate 47

Nectarinia chrysogenys Temminck, 1826, *Pl. Col., livr.* 65, pl. 388, fig. 1, Bantam district, Java.

Alternative name: Lesser Yellow-eared Spiderhunter

IDENTIFICATION Long fine curved bill. Adult olive-green above, yellow below with indistinct dark streaking on breast; large cheek-patch and narrow eye-ring yellow; male has grey pectoral tufts.
Similar species From female sunbirds by massive size and large bill; combination of indistinctly streaked yellow underparts and yellow orbital ring, not bisected by dark line, distinguishes it from all other spiderhunters except Spectacled *Arachnothera flavigaster* (170), which is larger, shorter and thicker-billed and has a smaller ear-patch, broader eye-ring, and no indistinct streaking on throat and breast.

VOICE Call High *twit-twit-twit-twee-ee* in flight with last note prolonged. Song No information.

DISTRIBUTION The Malay Peninsula, Sumatra (including islands), Borneo and West Java.

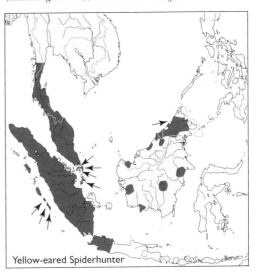
Yellow-eared Spiderhunter

HABITAT The canopy of primary forests, including peatswamp forest, and secondary forest, at forest edge, alluvial areas and mangroves, banana plantations, abaca, *Eucalyptus*, *Albizia* and other tree plantations, wooded gardens and villages; lowlands up to 1,400 m, and as high as 1,835 m in peninsular Malaysia.

STATUS Local and uncommon in Sumatra. Rare in West Java. Very scarce in Borneo. In Burma occurs north to Mergui.

FOOD Nectar, pollen, small fruits, seeds, spiders and insects.
Known food-plants *Hibiscus* sp., ?Musaceae, ?Zingiberaceae.

HABITS Usually forages high, singly, occasionally in pairs; fluttering, indirect flight; searches bark and broken branches. Hovers and hangs upside-down. Host to *Leucocytozoon* sp.

BREEDING Nest Similar to those of Long-billed Spiderhunter *A. robusta*, and attached by sewing. Size 39 x 13 cm, slung from undersurfaces of palm fronds and banana leaves, 1.5-13 m above ground, with or without long entrance tunnel. Made of reddish-brown fibres from rotting leaf-bases. Inner cup of finer material. Eggs c/2; 21.9 x 15.1; white with larger end ringed with fine black lines or dirty greyish-white, heavily flecked with sepia and grey-brown, particularly at broad end. Laying months Sumatra: Krui, Lampung, May–June. Sarawak: Baram, September; Borneo: Brunei, February and March; Kalimantan Barat, Tanjung Puting National Park, juveniles June; Sabah, enlarged gonads May, July and August.

DESCRIPTION A. c. chrysogenys
Adult male Upperparts olive-green becoming brighter on rump, large yellow cheek-patch and narrow eye-ring of filoplumes; underparts yellowish-green from throat to breast (with indistinct greenish streaks), becoming brighter yellow on belly, lower flanks and undertail-coverts. Edges

355

of remiges bright yellow. Grey pectoral tufts. Iris brown. Bill blackish, feet pale brown.
Adult female As male but lacks pectoral tufts.
Juvenile Unknown.

GEOGRAPHICAL VARIATION
A. c. chrysogenys (Temminck, 1826) (southern Burma, southern Thailand, peninsular Malaysia, Sumatra, western Borneo, Java) Described above.
A. c. harrissoni Deignan, 1957 (eastern Borneo) Differs from *chrysogenys* by mantle being almost devoid of golden suffusion, nearly concolorous with crown; exposed parts of closed wing much less strongly diffused with golden-bronze, i.e. lighter and duller.

MEASUREMENTS Wing 82-90 (male *chrysogenys*), 75-85 (female *chrysogenys*); **bill** 37.8-41.7 (mean, 39.8, SD 1.59, 6 male *chrysogenys*), 41.7, 36.8 (2 female *chrysogenys*); **gape** 41.1-45.0 (male *chrysogenys*), 39 (female *chrysogenys*); **mass** no data.

REFERENCES Deignan (1957), Gibson-Hill (1950b), Harrison (1968), Holmes (1996), MacKinnon & Phillipps (1993), Mann (1996, in prep. b), Medway & Wells (1976), Mitra & Sheldon (1993), Nash & Nash (1988), Sheldon *et al.* (in press), Smythies (1957, 1960, 1981, 1999).

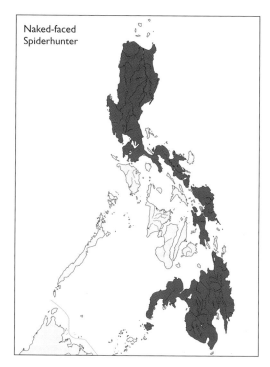

Naked-faced Spiderhunter

172 NAKED-FACED SPIDERHUNTER
Arachnothera clarae   Plate 48

Arachnothera clarae Blasius, 1890 (Apr. 15), *Braunschweigische Anzeigen*, no. 87, p.877 (desc.); 1890 (Apr. [= Aug.]), *J. Orn.* 38, pp.144, 146, 148 (desc. and type locality), Davao, Mindanao, Philippines.

Alternative name: Philippine Spiderhunter

IDENTIFICATION Long, stout, slightly curved bill. Olive-green above; edges of remiges brownish; pinkish naked lower face and forecrown; underparts green, paler on vent and undertail-coverts.
Similar species From female sunbirds and Little Spiderhunter *Arachnothera longirostra* (167) by much larger size and naked pink face-patch; also from former by much larger bill, and from latter by green underparts.

VOICE Call Very high, long, insect-like *seee*. Low harsh croaking *crrr* with quality recalling Corncrake *Crex crex*. Rapid insect-like *trrrik*. Rapid rattling trills, rising and falling, or on level pitch. **Song** No information.

DISTRIBUTION Endemic to Philippines, occurring on Luzon, Leyte, Samar, Biliran and Mindanao.

HABITAT Below 1,350 m in forests, forest edge, scrub and around bananas in clearings. Race *malindangensis* occurs at 1,050-1,400 m.

STATUS Not uncommon.

FOOD Presumably includes nectar and small arthropods.
Known food-plants None.

HABITS Occurs singly or in pairs.

BREEDING Nest Unknown. **Eggs** Unknown. **Laying months** Bird in breeding condition on Mt Kitanglad in March.

DESCRIPTION *A. c. luzonensis* Sexes similar.
Adult Bare skin in front of eye black. Upperparts olive-green; edges of remiges burnt-orange. Underparts green, greyer on throat to breast with dark centres to feathers giving indistinct streaking; paler, more yellowish on belly and lower flanks; no pectoral tufts. Naked face-patch pinkish; bill blackish; feet dark brown; iris black.
Juvenile Unknown.

GEOGRAPHICAL VARIATION
A. c. clarae Blasius, 1890 (Davao, on Mindanao) Differs from *malindangensis* in having paler olive-grey, less greenish underparts. Forehead feathered.
A. c. luzonensis Alcasid & Gonzales, 1968 (Luzon – Sierra Madre mountains, and Mt Isarog) Described above.
A. c. malindangensis Rand & Rabor, 1957 (Mindanao – Mt Malindang, Civolig, and possibly Basilan, although this may belong to an undescribed form) Differs from *luzonensis* by lighter olive-green upperparts, golden edges to remiges and underparts olive-grey. From *philippensis* by darker and duller green upperparts, and in being greyer below with less of a greenish wash.
A. c. philippinensis (Steere, 1890) (Leyte, Samar, Biliran) Differs from nominate in having the forehead also naked and underparts greener.

MEASUREMENTS Wing 86-92 (mean 90, 5 male *malindangensis*), 85 (unsexed *luzonensis*), 84-87 (female *malindangensis*); **tail** 42 (unsexed *luzonensis*); **bill** 35 (unsexed *luzonensis*), 39.3, 38.3, 36.5 (3 male *philippensis*), 43.7 (female *philippensis*); **gape** 40.0-43.5 (male *philippensis*), 45.8 (female *philippensis*); **culmen from base** 38-41 (mean 39.7, 5 male *malindangensis*), 41-42 (female *malindangensis*); **tarsus** 19 (unsexed *luzonensis*); **mass** no data.

REFERENCES Dickinson *et al.* (1991), duPont (1971), Ripley & Rabor (1961).

173 GREY-BREASTED SPIDERHUNTER
Arachnothera modesta   Plate 48

Anthreptes modesta Eyton, 1839, *Proc. Zool. Soc. London*, p.105, Malaya.

Previously included in *A. affinis*; *A. a. everetti* was at times considered a separate species and at times included in *affinis*. Some field observers did not distinguish between the two species on Borneo, and therefore some documentation could refer to either.

IDENTIFICATION Long, stout, slightly curved bill. Golden olive-green above; olive-grey below with narrow dark streaking from chin to breast, and slightly streaked on flanks and belly; sexes similar. Juvenile lacks streaking.
Similar species From female sunbirds by much longer bill; from all other spiderhunters except Streaky-breasted *Arachnothera affinis* (174) by grey underparts streaked dark; from *A. affinis* in having throat and breast less heavily marked with streaking which does not extend to abdomen and undertail-coverts; abdomen greyer, less white; less green and more golden above; smaller, with a shorter and much less robust bill.

VOICE Call Apparently undocumented. **Song** A continuous *tee-chu*, first note rising, second falling, very similar to that of Little Spiderhunter *A. longirostra.*

Grey-breasted Spiderhunter

DISTRIBUTION Southern Burma, Thailand, ?Cochinchina, peninsular Malaysia, Sumatra (including Mentawai Islands) and Borneo.

HABITAT In all storeys of lowland and hill dipterocarp forests, at peatswamp forest edge, in dry coastal forest, open secondary forest, banana plantations, orchards, coastal scrub and coconut groves; up to 1,200 m.

STATUS Common in Sumatra and Thailand. Rare in Burma. Uncommon on Borneo.

FOOD Spiders, black ants and nectar.
Known food-plants *Erythrina* sp., unidentified Musaceae, unidentified Zingiberaceae.

HABITS Forages at various heights, but frequently in low and middle storeys. Very active, flying rapidly through foliage, and not easy to observe.

BREEDING Nest Against trunk of palm. **Eggs** c/2; smooth, glossy, unevenly coloured with olive-brown, with darker brown ring at broad end; 21 x 15-15.5. **Laying months** Borneo: February; peninsular Malaysia: eggs April, juveniles May–August. Sumatra, Pematangsiantar, Simulungun, nest, date unknown.

DESCRIPTION *A. m. modesta* Sexes similar.
Adult Upperparts golden olive-green; underparts olive-grey, narrowly streaked brown on chin, throat and upper breast. Remiges blackish-brown edged yellowish-green; tail green with blackish-brown tips, all except central feathers with white subterminal spots. Bill medium to blackish-brown with paler lower mandible; feet fleshy to brown; iris brown.
Juvenile Lacks streaking.

GEOGRAPHICAL VARIATION
A. m. caena Deignan, 1956 (southern Burma, Thailand) Paler, less streaked and more yellowish, less buffish below, above more golden or yellow-green than *modesta*. This form is not well marked, and intergrades with nominate in southern Burma, peninsular Thailand and northern peninsular Malaysia.
A. m. concolor Snellemann, 1887 (Sumatra, including Mentawai Islands) Not well differentiated from *modesta* but darker green above, and some individuals less streaked below.
A. m. modesta (Eyton, 1839) (Thailand south of Kra, peninsular Malaysia, Borneo except where *pars* occurs) Described above.
A. m. pars Riley, 1939 (eastern Borneo) From *modesta* by less greenish-yellow underparts, throat and breast more heavily streaked dusky, slightly more greenish and less yellowish above. May be synonymous with *A. affinis everetti.*

MEASUREMENTS Wing 78-88 (mean 82.4, SD 2.99, 7 male *modesta*, Malay Peninsula), 74, 78, 81 (3 male *modesta*, west Borneo), 72-78 (mean 77.5, SD 7.19, 4 female *modesta*, Malay Peninsula), 69-85 (mean 74.8, 13 female *modesta*, Borneo), 74-84 (5 unsexed *modesta*, west Borneo), 80-95 (mean 85.8, SD 6.46, 5 unsexed *modesta*, Brunei), 76-89.5 (mean 82.4, 5 unsexed *pars*, Kalimantan Timur); **tail** 39.5-52.0 (mean 45.5, 14 unsexed *modesta*, Malay Peninsula), 44.5-57 (mean 49.6, 5 unsexed *pars*, Kalimantan Timur); **bill** 36.8-38.6 (mean 37.7, SD 0.78, 7 male *modesta*, Malay Peninsula), 36.0 (male *modesta*, west Borneo), 34.4 (female *modesta*, Malay Peninsula), 34.5, 36.8 (2 unsexed *modesta*, Malay Peninsula), 32.7-39.9 (mean 36.5, SD 2.70, 5 unsexed *modesta*, west Borneo); **gape** 32.9, 33.6, 35.8 (3 male *modesta*, west Borneo), 39.1, 40.6 (2 female *modesta*, west Borneo), 40.3-43.4 (mean 41.2, SD 1.46, 4 unsexed *modesta*, Brunei); **culmen** 33-40 (mean 35.7, 14 unsexed *modesta*, Malay Peninsula), 35-40 (mean 37.3, 5 unsexed *pars*, Kalimantan Timur); **mass** 20.5-24.9 (mean 22.6, 4 male *modesta*, Malaysia), 20.6 (female *modesta*, peninsular Malaysia), 20.1-25.5 (mean 23.4, SD 2.35, 4 unsexed *modesta*, Brunei).

REFERENCES Gibson-Hill (1949), MacKinnon & Phillipps (1993), Mann (1996, in prep. b), van Marle & Voous (1988), Medway & Wells (1976), Nash & Nash (1985), Riley (1939), Smythies (1960, 1981, 1999).

174 STREAKY-BREASTED SPIDERHUNTER
Arachnothera affinis   Plate 48

Cinnyris affinis Horsfield, 1822, *Trans. Linn. Soc. London*, 13, (1821) p. 166, Java.

Alternative name: Bornean Spiderhunter

Previously included *A. modesta*, but not always *A. a. everetti* in the past, and many observers did not distinguish between these forms. Therefore some documentation is suspect.

IDENTIFICATION Long stout curved bill. Adult green above, more golden on wings; below grey with pronounced dark streaking from chin to vent. Juvenile is less streaked below, rufous on hindcrown, and buffy on throat and upper breast.
Similar species From female sunbirds by larger size and longer bill; from all other spiderhunters except Grey-breasted *Arachnothera modesta* (173) by grey underparts streaked dark; from *A. modesta* by larger size, and ventral streaking extending onto flanks and abdomen.

VOICE Call Various raucous, piercing ringing calls. **Song** *Chee-wee-dee-weet... tee-ree, chee chee-chur.*

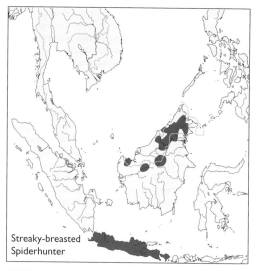

Streaky-breasted Spiderhunter

DISTRIBUTION Borneo, where known from a few localities in Sarawak, including Gunung Dulit, Kelabit highlands, Gunung Penrissen, Belaga, in Sabah including Gunung Kinabalu area and Gunung Magdalena, Bettotan Rayoh, Gunung Trus Madi, in Kalimantan Barat, including Gunung Liang Kubung, Kalimantan Timur – upper Mahakam River and possibly Sungai Berau, and one untraced locality, Rumah Lassa; Java and Bali.

HABITAT Hill dipterocarp and lower montane forests, at forest edge and amongst plantains; 900-1,600 m, sometimes as low as 305 m.

STATUS An uncommon and little-known species in Borneo, commoner in Bali and Java.

FOOD Presumably as in other spiderhunters: nectar, spiders and insects.

Known food-plants *Erythrina* sp., unidentified Musaceae.

HABITS Apparently similar to other spiderhunters; associated with plantains. Often feeds high; flies fast and low through forest. Host to *Haemoproteus sequeirae*, *Leucocytozoon* sp. and microfilariae.

BREEDING (presumed *A. a. everetti*) **Nest** A cup suspended from underside of large leaf by spiders' web; of bright brown silky substance from fern fronds, plant down, and covered with small flower and plant stems stuck together with spiders' web (Sharpe 1889, who identified the birds involved as *A. modesta*). **Eggs** c/1-2; smooth and glossy; (a) liver-coloured, with somewhat darker cap; (b) olive greenish-white or deep olive-brown, almost completely covered with a dark brownish shade. Very pale, hardly visible, grey mottling scattered all over shell, largely concentrated at blunt end, forming a faded cap of olive-greyish clouds. Occasionally a very few well-defined dark scribbles or thread-like markings of sepia tinged black; *affinis*: 19.5-23.0 (mean 21.4, n=18) x 14.3-15.5 (mean 14.8); *everetti*: 21.0-21.9 (mean 21.3, n=8) x 15.0-15.5 (mean 15.3). **Laying months** Borneo: Sabah, Gunung Kinabalu, February–March; Java, West Java, April, October, December.

DESCRIPTION *A. a. everetti* Sexes similar.
Adult Dark green above with dark scaling on crown; remiges and rectrices blackish-brown edged green; central rectrices with much green except for tips, and all except central feathers have large white subterminal spots, and tips brown. Below grey, heavily streaked grey-brown from chin to belly, with some streaking on flanks, and whitish barring on undertail-coverts. Iris hazel, chocolate-brown, dark brown or green. Bill black or blackish-brown with paler lower mandible; feet flesh, pale brown or brownish-pink.
Juvenile Differs from adult in lacking streaking below, and in race *affinis* by buffier subterminal tail spots.

GEOGRAPHICAL VARIATION
A. a. affinis (Horsfield, 1822) (Java and Bali) More golden above, and less green, than *everetti*, tinged yellow below; streaking below is brown rather than grey-brown; tips to tail paler brown; averages smaller.
A. a. everetti (Sharpe, 1893) (Borneo) Described above.

MEASUREMENTS Wing 79-91 (mean 86.0, SD 4.90, 7 male *affinis*), 86-98 (mean, 90.3, SD 3.35, 7 male *everetti*), 78, 83, 83 (3 female *affinis*), 80-93 (mean, 86.3, SD 5.12, 9 female *everetti*), 73-90 (6 unsexed *affinis*); **bill** 33.5-38.4 (mean 36.2, SD 1.70, 7 male *affinis*), 39.4-43.5 (mean 41.5, SD 1.70, 6 male *everetti*), 36.7-42.3 (mean, 40.2, SD 1.92, 6 female *everetti*), 34.1-39 (6 unsexed *affinis*); **gape** 40.2-43.3 (mean 42.0, 6 male *everetti*), 35.7-43.8 (mean 40.5, 8 female *everetti*); **mass** no data.

REFERENCES Hellebrekers & Hoogerwerf (1967), MacKinnon & Phillipps (1993), Mann (in prep. b), Sharpe (1889, 1893), Smythies (1957, 1960, 1981, 1999).

175 STREAKED SPIDERHUNTER
Arachnothera magna   Plate 48

Cinnyris magna Hodgson, 1837, *India Review* 1, p.272, Nepal.

IDENTIFICATION Long stout curved bill; bright yellow feet. Adult is golden-olive above, heavily streaked black; black subterminal band to tail, and buff tips; below yellowish-white with heavy black streaking. Juvenile is less green and yellow, more buffy and greyish.
Similar species From all spiderhunters and sunbirds by heavy black streaking above and below.

VOICE Noisy. **Call** Sharp, metallic chirruping *chiriririk* or *chirik, chirik* also *chisikik* or *chee-chee-chee...* Soft *ug-ug-ug* when angry. Flight-call a repeated *ka-tik*; also a loud musical trill in flight; persistent *chip* whilst feeding; repeated *chittit, chittittitit*. **Song** Begins with a soft *vijvitte vij* then gains speed to become rapid and monotonous song.

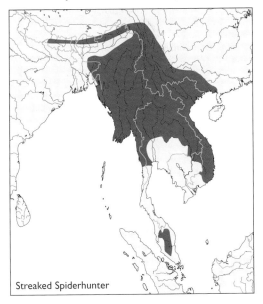

Streaked Spiderhunter

DISTRIBUTION Sutlej valley (last record 1868) east through Nepal (westernmost locality in 20th century was Chitwan), Sikkim, Bhutan, Arunachal Pradesh, south through Nagaland, Meghalaya and Bangladesh to Chittagongs, Burma, north-west and south-west Thailand, Laos, north and central Vietnam, west and south Yunnan, and Malay Peninsula.

HABITAT In Nepal, in *terai* and lower hills up to 450 m, but recorded up to 2,135 m in Arun Valley, in sal forests and amongst tangled thickets. In India in evergreen forest, abandoned cultivation and gardens; 600-2,200 m, lower in winter. In Malay Peninsula montane forest and forest edge from 915 to at least 1,835 m. In Burma teak, oak and evergreen forests, villages and gardens. As low as 500 m in northern Vietnam.

STATUS Not uncommon in teak forests of the Pegu Yomas in Burma, but local in Shan States and very rare in Tenasserim. Frequent at Thrumshimgla National Park, Bhutan.

MOVEMENTS Seasonal vertical movements in northern parts of range. Once recorded flying at night at Fraser's Hill, Malay Peninsula.

FOOD Insects, spiders and nectar. Snatches spiders from their webs.
Known food-plants Papaya *Carica papaya*, unidentified Musaceae, unidentified Zingiberaceae.

HABITS Found singly or in pairs, sometimes in mixed parties; usually quite high, but also found low amongst bananas and gingers; movements rapid and jerky; flight swift with fast wing-beats and slight undulations. Noisiness and sunbird-like behaviour make it conspicuous. Host to *Haemoproteus sequeirae, Leucocytozoon* sp. and microfilariae.

BREEDING Parasitised by Large Hawk-Cuckoo *Hierococcyx sparverioides*, Indian Cuckoo *Cuculus micropterus*, Common Cuckoo *C. canorus bakeri* and Lesser Cuckoo *C. p. poliocephalus*. **Nest** Neat inverted dome of leaf skeletons joined together with cobwebs, lined with grass and leaf skeletons; sewn by vegetable down and cobwebs to underside of broad leaf, usually a banana. Others on underside of giant creeper leaf, large ginger, teak leaf, thorny creeper or huge dock leaf; may have two entrances; may be oblong; may be as little as 0.5 m from ground. **Eggs** c/2-3. Brown or olive-brown, darker at broad end; *aurata*: 20.0-23.2 (mean 21.3, n=8) x 14.5-15.5 (mean 15.4); *magna*: 19.5-24.2 (mean 22.7, n=100) x 15.0-16.5 (mean 15.9). **Laying months** India: March–July; peninsular Malaysia: April and September, South Annam, enlarged testes March; Burma: April, July, August.

DESCRIPTION *A. m. magna*
Adult Sexes similar. Above golden yellowish-olive streaked black; tail tipped buff, with blackish subterminal band; below very pale yellowish-white with bold black shaft-streaks. Iris brown, bill blackish-brown; feet chrome-yellow to orange-yellow.
Juvenile Less golden-green above, more buffy and greyish, less yellow below than adult.

GEOGRAPHICAL VARIATION
A. m. aurata Blyth, 1855 (east and central Burma, west and south Yunnan; intergrades with *magna* in Karen Hills) Slightly smaller than *magna* and has rump and uppertail-coverts golden; undertail-coverts dusky-olive broadly tipped yellowish-white.
A. m. magna (Hodgson, 1837) (north and north-east India, Nepal, Sikkim, Bhutan and Bangladesh, to north Burma and peninsular Malaysia) Described above.
A. m. musarum Deignan, 1956 (south-east Burma, north Thailand, north Laos) Less suffused golden above than *magna*, and ground colour of underparts, especially abdomen and undertail-coverts, only washed pale yellow. Possibly slightly larger than *magna*.
A. m. pagodarum Deignan, 1956 (southern Burma, south-west Thailand) Upperparts duller and greener, less suffused golden than in *musarum* and striations less clearly defined. From *aurata* by stronger striations above, and streaks of underparts broad and bold as *musarum*.
A. m. remota Riley, 1940 (Vietnam) More greenish, less golden above than *magna*; black centres of head and back feathers smaller and less conspicuous; bend of wing and undertail-coverts deeper yellow, underparts more yellowish. From *aurata* by brighter yellow underparts, heavier black streaking; bend of wing and undertail-coverts deeper yellow and underparts more greenish-yellow.

MEASUREMENTS Wing 78-93 (male *aurata*), 84-96 (mean 92.8, 4 male *magna*), 93 (male *remota*), 77-79 (female *aurata*), 78-90 (female *magna*); **tail** 44-52 (male *magna*), 39-48 (female *magna*); **bill** 36.4-45.1 (male *aurata*), 44.7-47 (male *magna*), 37.6-39.3 (female *aurata*), 41.9-44 (female *magna*); **culmen** 43.5 (male *remota*); **gape** 36.2-44.8 (male *aurata*), 41.1-45.3 (male *magna*), 42.3-44.3 (male *musarum*), 41.5-44.9 (male *remota*), 36.6-40.5 (female *aurata*), 38.5-44.8 (female *magna*), 38.2-43.8 (female *musarum*), 36.9-40.1 (female *remota*); **tarsus** 20-21 (male *magna*), 20-22 (female *magna*), **mass** 28-34.5 (mean 31.5, 4 male *magna*), 23.9 (female *magna*).

REFERENCES Ali & Ripley (1974), Deignan (1956), Fleming *et al.* (1976), Hill (2000), Inskipp *et al.* (2000), Medway & Nisbet (1968), Medway & Wells (1976), Riley (1940), Smythies (1986).

---

176 WHITEHEAD'S SPIDERHUNTER
Arachnothera juliae   Plate 48

Arachnothera juliae Sharpe, 1887, *Ibis* p.451, pl.14, Mt Kinabalu, North Borneo.

IDENTIFICATION Long stout curved bill. Adult mostly blackish and blackish-brown, heavily streaked white on head and body; rump and undertail-coverts yellow. **Similar species** None.

VOICE Call Repeated loud shrieking calls in flight or from tree perch; long twittering call; wheezy 2-note call, first falling, second rising *whit-whiiII* and *whiII*; a short sharp bleat. *Swee-ee*, first note rising, second falling. Nasal, slurred, *swee-urr*, first note rising, second falling; *teeh-teeh-wee*, last note rising; *tee-tee-swee-eee*, third note rising, last falling. *See-wee see-wee; swee-eee-eee*. **Song** High-pitched squeaking.

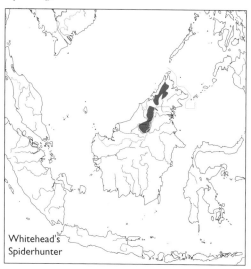

Whitehead's
Spiderhunter

DISTRIBUTION Endemic to Borneo, occurring in Sarawak (Gunung Dulit, Gunung Kalulong, Gunung Murud, Gunung Selidang, Usun Apau Plateau, Kelabit Highlands and Gunung Mulu), Sabah (Gunung Kinabalu, Gunung Trus Madi and Crocker Range) and Kalimantan Timur (upper Bahau river and Gunung Lanjut). Possibly occurs on other mountains in Borneo.

HABITAT Hill dipterocarp forest, lower and upper montane forests and at forest edge, 930-2,100 m.

STATUS Listed as near-threatened by Collar *et al.* (1994). Locally common in montane forests, 1,000-1,500 m.

MOVEMENTS Unknown.

FOOD Presumably includes berries, nectar and small arthropods.
Known food-plants *Rhododendron* sp.

HABITS Most often seen singly, but occasionally in pairs or small groups. Usually in tree-tops, often amongst orchid clusters, but sometimes forages lower. May perch for long periods on exposed branches.

BREEDING Nest Unknown. **Eggs** Unknown. **Laying months** Sabah: active nest March, enlarged testes June and November.

DESCRIPTION Sexes similar.
Adult Mainly brown. Crown streaked buffy-white. Neck and back narrowly streaked white; rump bright yellow. Throat with small brownish-white streaks. Undertail-coverts bright orange yellow; rest of underparts broadly streaked white. No pectoral tufts. Iris brown, bill and feet black.
Juvenile Unknown.

GEOGRAPHICAL VARIATION None.

MEASUREMENTS Wing 81-86 (males), 76-81 (females); **bill** 47.8-51.2 (mean 48.1, SD 1.72, 6 males), 43.5-46.8 (mean 45.1, SD 1.35, 4 females); **gape** 45.4-52.7 (males), 42.9-47.5 (females); **mass** no data.

REFERENCES Babbington (1992), van Balen (1997), Collar *et al.* (1994), MacKinnon & Phillipps (1993), Mann (in prep. b), Sharpe (1887), Sheldon *et al.* (in press), Smythies (1957, 1960, 1981).

REFERENCES

Ade, B. (1984) Birds attendant at *Cassia singuena. Honeyguide* 30: 33-34.

Akinpelu, A. (1989) Competition for the nectar of *Tecoma stans* flowers between Olive Sunbird (*Nectarinia olivacea*) and insects. *Malimbus* 11: 3-6.

Alam, M. K. & Rahman, M. M. (1988) Some observations on the feeding of *Scurrula parasitica* Linn. (Loranthaceae) seeds by birds. *Bano-Biggya-Patrika* 17: 89-90.

Alexander, F. (1995a) Ulugulu (*sic*) Violet-backed Sunbird *Anthreptes neglectus* at Sable Valley wildlife sanctuary, Shimba Hills. *Kenya Birds* 4: 30-31.

Alexander, F. (1995b) Active anting by Collared Sunbirds. *Kenya Birds* 4: 31-32.

Ali, S. (1931) The role of sunbirds and flowerpeckers in the propagation and distribution of the tree-parasite *Loranthus longiflorus* Desr. in the Konkan (W. India). *J. Bombay Nat. Hist. Soc.* 35: 144-9.

Ali, S. (1932) Flower-birds and bird-flowers in India. *J. Bombay Nat. Hist. Soc.* 35: 573-605.

Ali, S. (1969) *Birds of Kerala.* Oxford University Press, Madras, India.

Ali, S. & Ripley, S. D. (1974) *Handbook of the birds of India & Pakistan,* Vol. 10. Oxford University Press, Bombay, India.

Ali, S. & Ripley, S. D. (1983) *Handbook of the birds of India & Pakistan.* Compact edition. Oxford University Press, Bombay, India.

Allan, D. G. & Tree, A. J. (1997) Bluethroated Sunbird *Anthreptes reichenowi.* p.522 in *The atlas of southern African birds.* Vol. 2. *Passerines.* Harrison, J. A., Allan, D. G., Underhill, L. G., Herremans, M., Tree, A. J., Parker, V. & Brown, C. J. (eds.). BirdLife South Africa, Johannesburg.

Allport, G. (1989) West of the Dahomey Gap. *World Birdwatch* 11: 9.

Amadon, D. (1951) Le pseudo-souimanga de Madagascar. *Oiseau et R.F.O.* 21: 59-63.

Anderson, C. (1994) Seychelles sunbirds (*Nectarinia dussumieri*) on Aride Island. *Phelsuma* 2: 67-70.

Andrew, P. (1985) An annotated checklist of the birds of Cibodas-Gunung Gede Nature Reserve. *Kukila* 2: 92-95.

Andrews, I. J., Khoury, F. & Shirihai, H. (1999) Jordan bird report 1995-97. *Sandgrouse* 21: 10-35.

Anon. (1980) Rare birds of southern Africa. Neergaard's Sunbird *Nectarinia neergardi* (Grant) *African Wildl.* 34: inside back cover.

Antikainen, E. (1990) Bronze Sunbird catching food in a classroom. *Bull. E. Afr. Nat. Hist Soc.* 20: 12-13.

Archer, A. L. & Parker, I. S. C. (1993) Fruit-eating sunbirds. *Scopus* 17: 60-61.

Archer, A. L. & Turner, D. A. (1993) Notes on the endemic species and some additional new birds occurring on Pemba island, Tanzania. *Scopus* 16: 94-98.

Archer, G. & Godman, E. M. (1961) *The birds of British Somaliland and the Gulf of Aden: their life histories, breeding habits, and eggs.* Vol. IV. Oliver & Boyd, Edinburgh and London.

Ash, J. S. (1994) Comments. *Scopus* 18: 55-56.

Ash, J. S. & Miskell, J. E. (1983) *Birds of Somalia, their habitat, status and distribution. Scopus* Special Supplement, pp. 1-97.

Ash, J. S. & Miskell, J. E. (1998) *Birds of Somalia.* Pica Press, Sussex.

Aspinwall, D. R. (1971) Olive Sunbirds near Lusaka. *Bull. Zambian Orn. Soc.* 3: 58.

Aspinwall, D. R. (1989) Oustalet's White-bellied Sunbird on Malawi/Zambia border. *Nyala* 14: 39-40.

Atkins, J. D. (1994) An isolated population of the Olive-bellied Sunbird *Nectarinia chloropygia* in Ethiopia. *Scopus* 18: 54-56.

Atkinson, P. W., Dutton, J. S., Peet, N. B. & Sequeira, V. A. S. (1994) A study of the birds, small mammals, turtles and medicinal plants of São Tomé with notes on Príncipe. BirdLife International Study Report No. 56. BirdLife International, Cambridge.

Attenborough, D. (1995) *The private life of plants.* BBC Books, London.

Atyeo, W. T. (1971) Analgoid mites (Proctophyllodidae) from the Dicaeidae (Aves: Passeriformes). *J. Austral. Ent. Soc.* 10: 37-42.

Backhurst, G. C. (1973) East African bird ringing report 1971-1972. *J. East Afr. Nat. Hist. Soc.,* November 1973, no. 144, 15pp.

Backhurst, G. C. (1977) East African bird ringing report 1974-1977. *J. East Afr. Nat. Hist. Soc.* 31: 1-10.

Baha el Din, S. M. (1985) The occurrence of the Palestine Sunbird (*Nectarinia osea*) in Egypt. *Bull. Orn. Soc. Middle East* no. 14: 1-2.

Baha el Din, S. M. (1992) Ornithological report for Egypt. *Courser* 3: 59-67.

Baker, E. C. S. (1934) *The nidification of birds of the Indian Empire.* 4 vols. Taylor & Francis, London.

van Balen, B. (1992) Gunung Gede-Pangrango National Park, Java. *Oriental Bird Club Bull.* 15: 23-29.

van Balen, B. (1993) The identification of tit-babblers and red sunbirds on Java. *Oriental Bird Club Bull.* 18: 26-28.

van Balen, S. (B.) (1997) Faunistic notes from Kayan Mentarang with new records for Kalimantan. *Kukila* 9: 108-113.

Ballingall, B. (1990) Parental care and feeding of nestlings in the Mistletoebird *Dicaeum hirundinaceum. Australian Birdwatcher* 13: 174-177.

Banks, J. & Banks, J. (1986) Sri Lanka – a note on some birdwatching areas. *Oriental Bird Club Bull.* 3: 18-22.

Bannerman, D. A. (1921a) Exhibition and description of a new species of sunbird (*Anthreptes ogilvie-granti*) from Cameroon. *Bull. Brit. Orn. Club* 42: 8-9.

Bannerman, D. A. (1921b) The birds of southern Nigeria including a detailed review of the races of species known to occur there. *Rev. Zool. Bot. Afr.* 9: 254-426.

Bannerman, D. A. (1948) *The birds of tropical West Africa.* vol. 6. The Crown Agents, London.

Barlow, C., Wacher, T. & Disley, T. (1997) *A field guide to birds of the Gambia and Senegal.* Pica Press, Robertsbridge, U.K.

Barnicoat, F. C. (1984) Breeding the Black Sunbird *Nectarinia* (*Chalcomitra*) *amethystina amethystina. Avicult. Mag.* 90: 86-87.

Bartels, M. (1914) Ueber eine anscheinend neue Art *Dicaeum* von Java. *Orn. Monatsb.* 22: 125-126.

Bartlett, C. M. & Anderson, R. C. (1987) Additional comments on species of *Pelecitus* (Nematoda: Filarioidea) from birds. *Canad. J. Zool.* 65: 2813-2814.

Bates, G. L. (1911) Further notes on the birds of southern Cameroon. Part II. With descriptions of the eggs by W. R. Ogilvie-Grant. *Ibis* (9)5: 581-631.

Bates, G. L. (1927) Notes on some birds of Cameroon and the Lake Chad region: their status and breeding-times. *Ibis* (12)3: 1-64.

Bates, G. L. (1934) Birds of the Southern Sahara and adjoining countries in French West Africa. Part V. *Ibis* (13)4: 685-717.

Beckett, B. (1996) Relationship between sunbirds and pitcher plants *Nepenthes pervillei. Birdwatch* 17: 20.

Beehler, B. M. (1978) *Upland birds of northeastern New Guinea.* Wau Ecology Institute Handbook no.4, Wau, Papua New Guinea.

Beehler, B. M., Pratt, T. K. & Zimmerman, D. A. (1986) *Birds of New Guinea.* Princeton University Press, Princeton, U.S.A.

Beesley, J. S. (1972) Birds of the Arusha National Park, Tanzania. *J. East Afr. Nat. Hist. Soc.* no. 132, June 1972, 30 pp.

Bennett, G. F. & Bishop, M. A. (1991) The haemoproteids (Apicomplexa: Haemoproteidae) of the flowerpeckers of the avian family Dicaeidae (Passeriformes). *Syst. Parasitol.* 18: 159-164.

Bennett, G. F. & de Swardt, D. H. (1989) First African record of *Leucocytozoon anellobiae* (Apicomplex: Leucocytozoidae) in Gurney's Sugarbird *Promerops gurneyi. Ostrich* 60: 71.

Bennett, G. F., Whiteway, M. & Woodworth-Lynas (1982) Host parasite catalogue of the avian haematozoa. *Memorial Univ. Nfld. Occas. Pap. Biol.* no. 5.

Bennett, G. F., Peirce, M. A. & Caines, J. R. (1985) Avian Haemoproteidae 19. The haemoproteids of the sunbirds (family Nectariniidae) and morphometric variation in *Haemoproteus sequeirae. Canad. J. Zool.* 63: 1371-1376.

Bennett, G. F., Earlé, R. A. & Peirce, M. A. (1992) The Leucocytozoidae of South African birds (Passeriformes). *Onderstepoort J. Vet. Res.* 59: 235-247.

Bennun, L. (1986) Montane birds of the Bwindi (Impenetrable) forest. *Scopus* 10: 87-91.

Benson, C. W. (1944) Notes from Nyasaland. *Ibis* 86: 445-480.

Benson, C. W. (1949) A new race of sunbird from Nyasaland. *Bull. Brit. Orn. Club* 69: 19-20.

Benson, C. W. (1960a) Sunbirds of the Indian Ocean, illustrated by Chloe Talbot Kelly. *Animals* 12: 497.

Benson, C. W. (1960b) The birds of the Comoro Islands: results of the British Ornithologists' Union Centenary Expedition 1958. *Ibis* 103b: 5-106.

Benson, C. W. (1966) Some misidentified female sunbirds. *Bull. Brit. Orn. Club* 86: 65-66.

Benson, C. W. (1984) Origins of Seychelles land birds. Pp.469-486 in D. R. Stoddart (ed.) *Bioegeography and ecology of the Seychelles Islands.* W. Junk, The Hague.

Benson, C. W., Beamish, H. H., Jouanin, C., Salvan, J. & Watson, G. E. (1975) The birds of the Isles Glorieuses. *Atoll Research Bulletin* 176.

Benson, C. W. & Benson, F. M. (1977) *The birds of Malawi.* Mountfort Press, Limbe, Malawi.

Benson, C. W., Brooke, R. K., Dowsett, R. J. & Irwin, M. P. S. (1971) *The birds of Zambia.* Collins, London.

Benson, C. W. & Irwin, M. P. S. (1966) The sunbirds *Nectarinia bouvieri* and *batesi. Bull. Brit. Orn. Club* 86: 62-65.

Benson, C. W. & Prigogine, A. (1981) The status of *Nectarinia afra prigoginei. Gerfaut* 71: 47-57.

Berrington, W. (1997) Seed-eating sunbird. *Bee Eater* 48: 47.

Bharucha, E. K. (1982) Sunbirds fostering fledglings of Plaintive Cuckoos. *J. Bombay Nat. Hist. Soc.* 79: 670-671.

Bhunya, S. P. & Das, K. M. (1991) Karyological study of four Indian birds. *Caryologia* 44: 187-194.

BirdLife International (in prep.) *Threatened birds of Asia.*

BirdLife International (2000) *Threatened Birds of the World.* Barcelona and Cambridge, U.K.

Birkhead, T. R. & Møller, A. P. (1992) *Sperm competition in birds: evolutionary causes and consequences.* Academic Press, New York & London.

Bishop, K. D. (1985) Scarlet-headed Flowerpecker *Dicaeum trochileum:* a new bird for Sumatra. *Kukila* 2: 7-8.

Bishop, K. D. (1992) New and interesting records of birds in Wallacea. Part II. Miscellaneous observations. Part III. Preliminary lists of small and ornithologically previously unexplored islands. *Kukila* 6: 13-34.

Blackwell, K. F. & Wells, D. R. (1965) Collared Sunbird feeding on berries. *Bull. Niger. Orn. Soc.* 2: 81.

Blakers, M., Davies, S. J. J. F. & Reilly, P. N. (eds.) (1984) *The atlas of Australian birds.* Melbourne University Press, Melbourne.

Blancou, L. (1939) Contribution à l'étude des oiseaux de l'Oubangui-Chari occidental (Bassin supérieur de l'Ouham). Fin. II. Liste des espèces. *Oiseau et R.F.O.* n.s. 9: 410-485.

Blanford, W. T. (1873) Description of new species of *Nectarinia, Sitta* and *Parus* from Persia and Baluchistan. *Ibis* (3)3: 86-90.

Blasius, W. (1886) Beiträge zur Kenntniss de Vogelfauna von Celebes II & III. *Zeitschr. Ges. Orn.* 3: 81-179, 196-210.

Blasius, W. (1888) Die Vögel von Gross Sanghir. *Ornis* 4: 527-646.

Borello, W. D. (1992) An incidence of mass sunbird migration in northern Botswana. *Babbler* no. 23: 18-21.

Booth, A. (1969) The Orange-bellied Flowerpecker *Dicaeum trigonostigma. Avicult. Mag.* 75: 273-274.

Bostock, N. & Sujanika (1993) Birding itineries in Indonesia. *Oriental Bird Club Bull.* 18: 30-46.

Bourns, F. S. & Worcester, D. C. (1894) Preliminary notes on the birds and mammals collected by the Menage Scientific Expedition to the Philippine Islands. *Occas. Pap. Minn. Acad. Nat. Sci.* 1: 64pp.

Bourns, F. S. & Worcester, D. C. (1909-1910) in McGregor, R. C. *A manual of Philippine birds.* Bureau of Science, Manila.

Bowler, J. & Taylor, J. (1989) An annotated checklist of the birds of Manusela National Park Seram. Birds recorded on the Operation Raleigh Expedition. *Kukila* 4: 3-29.

Britton, P. L. & Britton, H. A. (1977) Sunbirds nesting inside buildings at the Kenya coast. *Scopus* 1: 68-70.

Britton, P. L. & Britton, H. A. (1978) Notes on the Amani Sunbird *Anthreptes pallidigaster* including a description of the nest and eggs. *Scopus* 2: 102-103.

Broekhuysen, G. J. (1959) The biology of the Cape Sugarbird. *Ostrich* Supp. 3: 180-221.

Broekhuysen, G. J. (1963) The biology of the Orange-breasted Sunbird *Anthobaphes violacea* (Linnaeus). *Ostrich* 34: 187-234.

Broekhuysen, G. J. (1971) Partial albino sugarbird. *Ostrich* 42: 70.

Brooke, R. K. (1964) Avian observations on a journey across central Africa and additional information on some of the species seen. *Ostrich* 35: 277-292.

Brooke, R. K. (1970) Buccal colours, weights and races of *Nectarinia bifasciata. Bull. Brit. Orn. Club* 90: 11-14.

Brooke, R. K. (1976) Buccal colours of sunbirds as an age character. *Bull. Brit. Orn. Club* 96: 58-59.

Brooks, T. M., Evans, T. D., Dutson, G. C. L., Anderson, G. Q. A., Asane, D. C., Timmins, R. J. & Toledo, A. G. (1992) The conservation status of the birds of Negros, Philippines. *Bird Conserv. Internatn.* 2: 273-302.

Brosset, A. (1974) La nidification des oiseaux en forêt gabonaise: architecture, situation des nids et prédation. *Terre et Vie* 28: 479-510.

Brosset, A. & Erard, C. (1986) *Les oiseaux des régions forestières du nord-est du Gabon.* Vol. 1. Société Nationale de Protection de la Nature, Paris.

Bruce, M. D. (1986) The birds of Wallacea: some opportunities for field study. *Oriental Bird Club Bull.* 3: 23-26.

Bruce, M. D. (1987) Additions to the birds of Wallacea. 1. Bird records from smaller islands in the Lesser Sundas. *Kukila* 3: 38-44.

Buchanan, D. & Steyn, P. (1964) The incubation and nestling periods of the White-breasted Sunbird, *C. talatala,* Smith. *Ostrich* 35: 65.

Bullen, J. (1969) Zululand South Africa birds. More comments on some unfamiliar species. *Bokmakierie* 21: 40-41.

Burd, M. (1995) Pollinator behavioural responses to reward size in *Lobelia deckenii:* no escape from pollen limitation of seed set. *J. Ecology* 83: 865-872.

Burger, A. E., Siegfried, W. R. & Frost, P. G. H. (1976) Nest-site selection in the Cape Sugarbird. *Zoologica Africana* 11: 127-158.

Burger, L. (1987) A sunbird. *Witwatersrand Bird Club News* no. 138: 22-23.

Butchart, S. H. M., Brooks, T. M., Davies, C. W. N., Dharmaputra, G., Dutson, G. C. L., Lowen, J. C. & Sahu, A. (1993) Preliminary report of the Cambridge Flores/Sumbawa conservation project 1993. Unpublished.

Büttikofer, J. (1893) On two new species of birds from South Celebes. *Notes Leyden Mus.* 15: 179-181.

Büttikofer, J. (1894) Ornithologische Sammlungen aus Celebes, Saleyer und Flores. *Weber's Zool. Ergeb. Reise Nederl. Ost-Ind.* 3: 269-306.

Button, J. A. (1967) The birds of Ilaro. II. Forest and savannah residents (Passerines). Part B: Campephagidae to Ploceidae. *Bull. Niger. Orn. Soc.* 4: 10-19.

Butynski, T. (1994) Uluguru Violet-backed Sunbird *Anthreptes neglectus* at Tana, Kenya. *Scopus* 18: 62-64.

Caldwell, H. R. & Caldwell, J. C. (1931) *South China birds.* Hester May Vanderburgh, Shanghai, China.

Cane, W. P. & Carter, M. F. (1988) Significant range extension for *Nectarinia reichenbachii* in West Africa. *Bull. Brit. Orn. Club* 108: 52-54.

Capanna, E. & Geralico, C. (1982) Karyotype analysis in ornithological studies. 2. The chromosomes of four species of African birds (Nectariniidae, Ploceidae and Sturnidae). *Avocetta* 6: 1-9.

Catry, P., Mellanby, R., Suleiman, K. A., Haji Salim, K., Hughes, M., McKean, M., Anderson, N., Constant, G., Heany, V., Martin, G., Armitage, M. & Wilson, M. (2000) Habitat selection by terrestrial birds on Pemba Island (Tanzania), with particular reference to six endemic taxa. *Biol. Conserv.* 95: 259-267.

Cave, F. O. & Macdonald, J. D. (1955) *Birds of the Sudan: their identification and distribution.* Oliver & Boyd. London.

Chabaud, A. G. (1979) *Chandlerella inversa* n. sp., filaire parasite de nectariniidés au Gabon. *Bull. Mus. Natn. Hist. Nat. Paris* (Zool. Biol. Ecol. Anim.) no. 2, 1979: 295-297.

Chapin, J. P. (1954) *The birds of the Belgian Congo.* Part 4. *Bull. Amer. Mus. Nat. Hist.* 75B.

Chapin, J. P. (1959) Breeding cycles of *Nectarinia purpureiventris* and some other Kivu birds. *Ostrich* Suppl. 3: 223-229.

Chapin, R. T. (1978a) Brief accounts of some central African birds based on the journal of James Chapin. *Rev. Zool. Afr.* 92: 805-836.

Chapin, R. T. (1978b) Breeding behaviour of the Bronzy Sunbird *Nectarinia kilimensis. East Afr. Nat. Hist. Soc. Bull.* 1978: 52-55.

Chasen, F. N. (1931) Birds from Bintang Island in the Rhio Archipelago. *Bull. Raffles Mus.* 5: 114-120.

Chasen, F. N. (1934) Nine new races of Natuna birds. *Bull. Raffles Mus.* 9: 92-7.

Chasen, F. N. (1939a) Preliminary diagnoses of new birds from North Sumatra II. *Treubia* 17: 183-184.

Chasen, F. N. (1939b) *The birds of the Malay Peninsula.* vol. 4. Witherby, London.

Chasen, F. N. & Kloss, C. B. (1930) On a collection of birds from the lowlands and islands of North Borneo. *Bull. Raffles Mus.* 4: 1-112.

Chattopadhyay, S. (1980) Egg-bound death of a Purple-rumped Sunbird at Baj Baj, West Bengal. *J. Bombay Nat. Hist. Soc.* 77: 333.

Cheke, A. S. & Diamond, A. W. (1986) Birds on Moheli and Grande Comore (Comoro Islands) in February 1975. *Bull. Brit. Orn. Club* 106: 138-148.

Cheke, R. A. (1971a) Feeding ecology and significance of interspecific territoriality of African montane sunbirds (Nectariniidae). *Rev. Zool. Bot. Afr.* 84: 50-64.

Cheke, R. A. (1971b) Temperature rhythms in African montane sunbirds. *Ibis* 113: 500-506.

Cheke, R. A. (1972) Birds of the Cherangani montane forests and their parasites. *E. Afr. Wildl. J.* 10: 245-249.

Cheke, R. A. (1976) Notes on a nesting Variable Sunbird. *Bull. Brit. Orn. Club* 96: 5-8.

Cheke, R. A. (1978) Records of birds and their parasites from the Cherangani Mountains, Kenya. *E. Afr. Wildl. J.* 16: 61-64.

Cheke, R. A. (1999) Vocalisations of the Mouse-brown Sunbird *Anthreptes gabonicus. Malimbus* 21: 51.

Cheke, R. A. (2001) Confirmation of the position of the likely type-locality of *Nectarinia rubescens stangerii. Bull. Brit. Orn. Club* 121: 62-63.

Cheke, R. A. & Walsh, J. F. (1996) *The birds of Togo.* B.O.U. Checklist no. 14, British Ornithologists' Union, Tring, Herts.

Chenaux-Repond, R. (1975) Ersatz sunbird's nest. *Honeyguide* 81: 37.

Chittenden, H. (1995) On the nest of Neergaard's Sunbird. *Birding in Southern Africa* 47: 85.

Christy, P. & Clarke, W. V. (1994) *Guide des oiseaux de la Réserve de la Lopé.* ECOFAC, Gabon, Libreville.

Christy, P. & Clarke, W. V. (1998) *Guide des oiseaux de São Tomé et Príncipe.* ECOFAC, São Tomé.

Clancey, P. A. (1952) A systematic account of the birds collected on the Natal Museum expedition to the Lebombo Mountains and Tongaland, July, 1951. *Ann. Natal Mus.* 12: 227-274.

Clancey, P. A. (1962) Miscellaneous taxonomic notes on African birds. XIX. *Durban Mus. Novit.* 6: 181-194.

Clancey, P. A. (1967) On variation in *Nectarinia talatala. Bull. Brit. Orn. Club* 87: 153-157.

Clancey, P. A. (1968) The name of the Grey Sunbird. *Bull. Brit. Orn. Club* 88: 150-151.

Clancey, P. A. (1969) A catalogue of birds of the South African subregion. Supplement No. 1. *Durban Mus. Novit.* 8: 275-324.

Clancey, P. A. (1970a) Miscellaneous taxonomic notes on African birds. Part 30. *Durban Mus. Novit.* 9: 1-11.

Clancey, P. A. (1970b) Miscellaneous taxonomic notes on African birds. Part 31. *Durban Mus. Novit.* 9: 25-28.

Clancey, P. A. (1973) Miscellaneous taxonomic notes on African birds. Part 37. *Durban Mus. Novit.* 10: 1-22.

Clancey, P. A. (1975) Miscellaneous taxonomic notes on African birds. Part 43. *Durban Mus. Novit.* 11: 1-24.

Clancey, P. A. (1978a) Miscellaneous taxonomic notes on African birds. 52. On the southern and eastern races of *Nectarinia olivacea* (Smith), 1840. *Durban Mus. Novit.* 11: 317-327.

Clancey, P. A. (1978b) Miscellaneous taxonomic notes on African birds. 52. On the validity of *Nectarinia olivacea lowei* (Vincent), 1934. *Durban Mus. Novit.* 11: 327-330.

Clancey, P. A. (1979) Miscellaneous taxonomic notes on African birds. 53. The valid subspecific criteria and ranges of the two eastern races of *Nectarinia bifasciata* (Shaw). *Durban Mus. Novit.* 12: 15-17.

Clancey, P. A. (1986) Miscellaneous taxonomic notes on African birds 67. *Durban Mus. Novit.* 14: 7-27.

Clancey, P. A. (1992-1993) The status of *Nectarinia olivacea* (Smith, 1840); a unitary species or two polytypic allospecies? *Gerfaut* 82-83: 25-29.

Clancey, P. A. & Irwin, M. P. S. (1978) Species limits in the *Nectarinia afra/Nectarinia chalybea* complex of African double-collared sunbirds. *Durban Mus. Novit.* 11: 331-351.

Clancey, P. A. & Williams, J. G. (1957) The systematics of the Little

Purple-banded Sunbird, *Cinnyris bifasciatus* (Shaw) with notes on its allies. *Durban Mus. Novit.* 5: 27-41.

Clarke, G. (1985) Bird observations from northern Somalia. *Scopus* 9: 24-42.

Classen, R. (1987) Morphological adaptations for bird pollination in *Nicolaia elatior* (Jack) Horan (Zingiberaceae). *Gardens' Bull.* (Singapore) 40: 37-43.

Close, D. H. (1991) Mimicry by Mistletoebird. *South Australian Orn.* 31: 74.

Coates, B. J. (1990) *The birds of Papua New Guinea including the Bismarck Archipelago and Bougainville.* vol. II. Dove Publications, Alderley, Australia.

Coates, B. J. & Bishop, K. D. (1997) *A guide to the birds of Wallacea. Sulawesi, the Moluccas and Lesser Sunda Islands, Indonesia.* Dove Publications, Alderley, Australia.

Coe, M. J. (1961) Notes on *Nectarinia johnstoni* on Mt. Kenya. *Ostrich* 32: 101-103.

Coe, M. J. (1967) *The ecology of the alpine zone of Mount Kenya.* W. Junk, the Hague.

Cole, D. T. (1992) Whitebellied Sunbirds take to nesting Cereusly. *Babbler* no. 23: 33-35.

Colebrook-Robjent, J. F. R. (1990) The nest and eggs of Bannerman's Blue-headed Sunbird *Nectarinia bannermani. Bull. Brit. Orn. Club* 110: 13-14.

Collar, N., Crosby, M. J. & Stattersfield, A. J. (1994) *Birds to watch 2: the world list of threatened birds.* BirdLife International, Cambridge.

Collar, N. J., Mallari, N. A. D. & Tabaranza, B. R. (1999) *Threatened birds of the Philippines.* Haribon Foundation and BirdLife International, Makati City, Philippines.

Collar, N. J. & Stuart, S. N. (1985) *Threatened birds of Africa and related islands: the ICBP/IUCN Red Data Book,* Part 1. Third Edition. International Council for Bird Preservation, Cambridge, U.K.

Collins, B. G. (1983a) Seasonal variations in the energetics of territorial Cape Sugarbirds. *Ostrich* 54: 121-125.

Collins, B. G. (1983b) Pollination of *Mimetes hirtus* (Proteaceae) by Cape Sugarbirds and Orange-breasted Sunbirds. *J. South Afr. Bot.* 49: 125-142.

Collins, B. G. (1983c) A first approximation of the energetics of Cape Sugarbirds *Promerops cafer* and Orange-breasted Sunbirds *Nectarinia violacea. South Afr. J. Zool.* 18: 363-369.

Collins, B. G., Grey, J. & McNee, S. (1990) Foraging and nectar use in nectarivorous bird communities. Pp.110-122 in Morrison, M. L. *et al.* (eds.) *Studies in avian biology, no. 13. Avian foraging: theory, methodology, and applications.* Cooper Ornithological Society, Los Angeles, California.

Colston, P. R. & Curry-Lindahl, K. (1986) *The birds of Mount Nimba, Liberia.* British Museum (Natural History), London.

Compton, S. G., Craig, A. J. F. K. & Waters, I. W. R. (1996) Seed dispersal in an African fig tree: birds as high quantity, low quality dispersers? *J. Biogeography* 23: 553-563.

Coomans de Ruiter, L. (1951) Vogels van het dal van de Bodjoriviere (Zuid-Celebes). *Ardea* 39: 261-318.

Cooper, G. (1991) Plain Flowerpecker at Ho Sheung Heung. The first record for Hong Kong. *Hong Kong Bird Report* 1990-1991: 117-118.

Corlett, R. (1998) Frugivory and seed dispersal by birds in Hong Kong shrubland. *Forktail* 13: 23-27.

Cowles, R. B. (1936) Observations on the Amethyst Sunbird, *Chalcomitra amethystina amethystina* (Shaw). *Auk* 53: 28-30.

Craib, C. L. (1981) Gurney's Sugarbird (R750). *WBC Newssheet* 113: 4-7.

Craig, A. J. F. K. & Hulley, P. E. (1994) Sunbird movements: a review, with possible models. *Ostrich* 65: 106-110.

Craig, A. & Simon, C. (1991) Sunbird and sugarbird seasons. *Safring News* 20: 9-12.

Cramp, S. & Perrins, C. M. (eds.) (1993) *The birds of the western Palearctic,* vol. 7. Oxford University Press, Oxford.

Cresswell, W., Irwin, M., Jensen, M., Mee, A., Mellanby, R., McKean, M. & Milne, L. (1997) Population estimates and distribution changes of landbirds on Silhouette Island, Seychelles. *Ostrich* 68: 50-57.

Cunningham-van Someren, G. R. (1996) Active anting by weavers and sunbirds at Karen, Kenya. *Ostrich* 67: 165.

Curio, E. (1994a) Zum Bedrohungs-Status endemischer Vögel auf den Philippinen: eine Expedition der Ruhr-Universität Bochum (1993). *Zool. Ges. Arten- u. Populationsschutz Mitt.* 10: 5-7.

Curio, E. (1994b) Ornithological observations during a (preliminary) Philippines conservation expedition in 1993. *Ökol. Vögel* 16: 613-631.

Curio, E., Diesmos, A. C., Mallari, N. A. D. & Altamirano, R. A. N. (1996) The Mindoro Scarlet-collared Flowerpecker *Dicaeum retrocinctum* – an alleged single island endemic. *J. Orn.* 137: 361-366.

Cyrus, D. (1989) Unusual plumage of Whitebellied Sunbird confusing birders? *Bokmakierie* 41: 10.

D'Albertis, L. M. & Salvadori, T. (1879) Catalogo degli uccelli raccolti da L. M. D'Albertis durante la 2a. e 3a. esplorazione del Fiume Fly negli anni 1876 & 1877. *Ann. Mus. Civ. Genoa* 14: 21-147.

Danielsen, F. & Heegaard, M. (1995) The birds of Bukit Tigapuluh, southern Riau, Sumatra. *Kukila* 7: 99-120.

Das, A. R. K. (1963) On the honey-sucking habits of the Purple Sunbird *Nectarinia asiatica* (Latham). *Pavo* 1: 60-65.

Davey, J. K. A. & Davey, L. (1990) Wintering Coppery Sunbirds in Harare. *Honeyguide* 36: 42.

Davidar, P. (1985a) Ecological interactions between mistletoes and their avian pollinators in South India. *J. Bombay Nat. Hist. Soc.* 82: 45-60.

Davidar, P. (1985b) Feeding territories of the Small Sunbird (*Nectarinia minima* Sykes). *J. Bombay Nat. Hist. Soc.* 82: 204-206.

Davidson, D. A. G. (1945) *Loranthus* attack in *Sal* plantations. *Indian For.* 71: 181-182.

Davies, N. B. (1983) Polyandry, cloaca-pecking and sperm competition in Dunnocks *Prunella modularis*. *Nature* 302: 334-336.

Davies, N. B. (1987) Studies of West Palearctic birds: 188. Dunnock. *British Birds* 80: 604-624.

Dean, R. & Milton, S. (1998) Ground-foraging Malachite Sunbirds. *Promerops* 236: 11.

Dean, W. R. J. (2000) *The birds of Angola. An annotated checklist.* B.O.U. Check-list No. 18, Tring, Herts.

Deardorff, T. L., Schmidt, G. D. & Kunze, R. E. (1978) *Allohymenolepis palawanensis* new species (Cyclophyllidea, Hymenolepidae) from the Philippine bird *Nectarinia jugularis*. *J. Helminthology* 52: 211-214.

Deignan, H. G. (1943) New forms of *Anthreptes* and *Seicercus* (Aves) from the Indo-Chinese Sub-region. *Proc. Biol. Soc. Washington* 56: 29-30.

Deignan, H. G. (1944) The type locality of *Nectarinia dabryii* Verreaux. *Auk* 61: 133-135.

Deignan, H. G. (1945) The birds of northern Thailand. *U.S. Natn. Mus. Bull.* 186: 1-616.

Deignan, H. G. (1948) The races of the Black-throated Sunbird. *J. Washington Acad. Sci.* 38: 21-23.

Deignan, H. G. (1956) New races of birds from Laem Thong, the Golden Chersonese. *Proc. Biol. Soc. Washington* 69: 207-211.

Deignan, H. G. (1957) A trio of new birds from tropical Asia. *Proc. Biol. Soc. Washington* 70: 43-44.

Deignan, H. G. (1960) Remarks on the flowerpecker, *Dicaeum agile* (Tickell). *Bull. Brit. Orn. Club* 80: 142-144.

Delacour, J. (1926a) *Aethopyga ezrai* sp.nov.; *Anthreptes hypogrammica lisettae* subsp.nov. *Bull. Brit. Orn. Club* 47: 21-22.

Delacour, J. (1926b) Les oiseaux de la mission zoologique Franco-Anglo-Américaine à Madagascar. *Oiseau et R.F.O.* N.S. 2: 1-96.

Delacour, J. (1932b) Etude systematique de quelques oiseaux nouveaux ou interessant obtenus par la VIe expedition en Indochine. *Oiseau et R.F.O.* 2: 431-432.

Delacour, J. (1944) A revision of the family Nectariniidae (Sunbirds) *Zoologica* 29(4): 17-38.

Delacour, J. (1946) Notes on the taxonomy of the birds of Malaysia. *Zoologica* 31: 1-8.

Delacour, J. & Jabouille, P. (1928) *Dicaeum beccarii cambodianum* subsp. nov. *Bull. Brit. Orn. Club* 48: 135.

Delacour, J. & Mayr, E. (1946) *Birds of the Philippines*. Macmillan, New York.

Demey, R. (1986) Two new species for Ivory Coast. *Malimbus* 8: 44.

Demey, R. & Njabo, K. Y. (2001) A new sight record in Cameroon of the distinctive race *crossensis* of Green-throated Sunbird *Nectarina rubescens*. *Malimbus* 23: 66-67.

Diamond, A. W. (1984) Biogeography of Seychelles land birds. Pp.487-504 in D. R. Stoddart (ed.) *Bioegeography and ecology of the Seychelles Islands*. W. Junk, The Hague.

Dickinson, E. C., Kennedy, R. S. & Parkes, K. C. (1991). *The birds of the Philippines*. British Ornithologists' Union Checklist No.12, London.

Dillingham, I. H. (1984) The record of the Angola White-bellied Sunbird *Nectarinia oustaleti* from Kigoma in western Tanzania. *Scopus* 8: 80.

Dinesen, L., Lehmberg, T., Svendson, J. O., & Hansen, L. A. (1993) Range extensions and other notes on some restricted-range forest birds from West Kilombero in the Udzungwa Mountains. *Scopus* 17: 48-59.

Doughty, C., Day, N. & Plant, A. (2000) *Birds of the Solomons, Vanuata and New Caledonia*. Christopher Helm (A. & C. Black), London.

Downs, C. T. (1997) Sugar digestion efficiencies of Gurney's Sugarbirds, Malachite Sunbirds, and Black Sunbirds. *Physiological Zool.* 70: 93-99.

Downs, C. T. (2000) Ingestion patterns and daily energy intake on a sugary diet: the Red Lory *Eos bornea* and the Malachite Sunbird *Nectarinia famosa*. *Ibis* 142: 359-364.

Downs, C. T. & Perrin, M. R. (1996) Sugar preferences of some southern African nectarivorous birds. *Ibis* 138: 455-459.

Dowsett, R. J. (1983) Diurnal weight variation in some montane birds in south central Africa. *Ostrich* 54: 126-128.

Dowsett, R. J. (1993) Afrotropical avifaunas: annotated country checklists. Pp.1-322 in Dowsett, R. J. & Dowsett-Lemaire, F. (eds.) *A contribution to the distribution and taxonomy of Afrotropical and Malagasy birds*. Tauraco Research Report No. 5.

Dowsett, R. J. & Dowsett-Lemaire, F. (1984) Breeding and molt cycles of some montane forest birds in south-central Africa. *Rev. Ecol. Terre Vie* 39: 89-112.

Dowsett, R. J. & Dowsett-Lemaire, F. (1993) A contribution to the distribution and taxonomy of Afrotropical and Malagasy birds. *Tauraco Res. Rep.* 5: 1-389.

Dowsett, R. J., Dowsett-Lemaire, F. & Bulens, P. (1993) Additions and corrections to the avifauna of Congo. *Malimbus* 15: 68-80.

Dowsett, R. J. & Prigogine. A. (1974) The avifauna of the Marungu Highlands. *Hydrobiological survey of the Lake Bangweulu Luapula River basin*. 19. Cercle Hydrobiologigue de Bruxelles, Brussels.

Dowsett-Lemaire, F. (1988) On the breeding behaviour of three montane sunbirds *Nectarinia* spp. in northern Malawi. *Scopus* 11: 79-86.

Dowsett-Lemaire, F. (1989a) Food plants and the annual cycle in a montane community of sunbirds (*Nectarinia* spp.) in northern Malawi. *Tauraco* 1: 167-185.

Dowsett-Lemaire, F. (1989b) Ecological and biogeographical aspects of forest bird communities in Malawi. *Scopus* 13: 1-80.

Dowsett-Lemaire, F. (1990) Enquête faunistique et floristique dans la forêt de Nyungwe, Rwanda. *Tauraco Res. Rep.* 3: 31-85.

Dowsett-Lemaire, F. (1996) Avian frugivore assemblages at three small-fruited tree species in the forests of northern Congo. *Ostrich* 67: 88-89.

Dowsett-Lemaire, F. & Dowsett, R. J. (1999) Birds of the Parque Nacional de Monte Alen, mainland Equatorial Guinea, with an updating of the country's list. *Alauda*: 67: 179-188.

Dranzoa, C. (1997) The survival of understorey birds in the tropical rainforest of Ziika, Uganda. *Ostrich* 68: 68-71.

Duckworth, J. W. & Hedges, S. (1998) Bird records from Cambodia in 1997, including records of sixteen species new for the country. *Forktail* 14: 29-36.

Duckworth, J. W., Wilkinson, R. J., Tizard, R. J., Kelsh, R. N. & Evans, M. I. (1997) Bird records from Similajau National Park, Sarawak, Malaysia. *Forktail* 12: 117-154.

duPont, J. E. (1971a) Notes on Philippine birds (no. 1). *Nemouria* no. 3: 1-6.

duPont, J. E. (1971b) *Philippine birds*. Monograph Ser. 2. Delaware Museum of Natural History, Greenville, Delaware.

duPont, J. E. & Rabor, D. S. (1973) Birds of Dinagat and Siargao, Philippines: an expedition report. *Nemouria* 10: 111.

Durrer, H. & Villiger, W. (1962) Schillerfarben der Nektarvögel (Nectariniidae). *Revue Suisse Zool.* 69: 801-814.

Dutson, G. C. L., Evans, T. D., Brooks, T. M., Asane, D. C., Timmins, R. J. & Toledo, A. (1992) Conservation status of birds on Mindoro, Philippines. *Bird Conserv. Internatn.* 2: 303-325.

Dutson, G. C. L., Magsalay, P. M. & Timmins, R. J. (1993) The rediscovery of the Cebu Flowerpecker *Dicaeum quadricolor*, with notes on other forest birds on Cebu, Philippines. *Bird Conserv. Internatn.* 3: 235-243.

Dymond, N. (1994) A survey of the birds of Nias Island, Sumatra. *Kukila* 7: 10-27.

Earlé, R. A. (1981a) Weights of southern African sunbirds (Aves: Nectariniidae). *Durban Mus. Novit.* 13: 21-40.

Earlé, R. A. (1981b) Factors governing avian breeding in *Acacia* savanna Pietermaritzburg South Africa. 2. Intrinsic factors. *Ostrich* 52: 74-83.

Earlé, R. A. (1981c) Factors governing avian breeding in *Acacia* savanna Pietermaritzburg South Africa. 3. Breeding success, recruitment and clutch size. *Ostrich* 52: 235-243.

Earlé, R. A. (1982) Aspects of the breeding biology and ecology of the White-bellied Sunbird *Nectarinia talatala*. *Ostrich* 53: 65-73.

Earlé, R. A. (1983) Notes on bird parties in some Transvaal South Africa indigenous forests. *Ostrich* 54: 176-178.

Eccles, S. D. (1985) Reichenbach's Sunbird *Nectarinia reichenbachii* new to Ivory Coast. *Malimbus* 7: 140.

Eccles, S. D. (1988) The birds of Sao Tome – record of a visit, April 1987 with notes on the rediscovery of Bocage's Longbill. *Malimbus* 10: 207-217.

Eck, S. (1974) Katalog der ornithologischen Sammlung des Staatlichen Museums für Tierkunde Dresden. *Zool. Abh. Mus. Tierk. Dresden* 33.

Edington, J. M. & Edington, M. A. (1983) Habitat partitioning and antagonistic behaviour among the birds of a West African scrub and plantation plot. *Ibis* 125: 74-89.

van Eeden, T. C. (1981) "Anting" in the Kruger National Park. *Laniarius* 13: 7.

Eisentraut, M. (1965) Über einige Vogelrassen von der Insel Fernando Po. *J. Orn.* 106: 218-219.

Eisikowitch, D. & Nahari, N. (1982) Discrimination of *Malvaviscus arboreus* flowers by the sunbird *Nectarinia osea*. *Acta Bot. Neerl.* 31: 55-58.

Elgood, J. H., Fry, C. H. & Dowsett, R. J. (1973) African migrants in Nigeria. *Ibis* 115: 375-411.

Elgood, J. H., Heigham, J. B., Moore, A. M., Nason, A. M., Sharland, R. E. & Skinner, N. J. (1994) *The birds of Nigeria: an annotated check-list*. B.O.U. Check-list no. 4 (second edition). British Ornithologists' Union, London.

Erard, C. (1979) What in reality is *Anthreptes pujoli* Berlioz? *Bull. Brit. Orn. Club* 99: 142-143.

Evans, D. J. (1992) A Nile Valley Sunbird nest in Egypt. *OSME Bull.* 28: 24.

Evans, D. J. & Dijkstra, K. D. (1993) The birds of Gezira, Egypt. *OSME Bull.* 30: 20-25.

Evans, M. R. (1991) The size of adornments of male Scarlet-tufted Malachite Sunbirds varies with environment conditions as predicted by handicap theories. *Anim. Behav.* 42: 797-804.

Evans, M. R. (1996) Nectar and flower production of *Lobelia telekii* inflorescences, and their influence on territorial behaviour of the Scarlet-tufted Malachite Sunbird (*Nectarinia johnstoni*). *Biol. J. Linn. Soc.* 57: 89-105.

Evans, M. R. & Barnard, P. (1995) Variable sexual ornaments in Scarlet-tufted Malachite Sunbirds (*Nectarinia johnstoni*) on Mount Kenya. *Biol. J. Linn. Soc.* 54: 371-381.

Evans, M. R. & Hatchwell, B. J. (1992a) An experimental study of male adornment in the Scarlet-tufted Malachite Sunbird. I. The role of pectoral tufts in territorial defence. *Behav. Ecol. Sociobiol.* 29: 413-419.

Evans, M. R. & Hatchwell, B. J. (1992b) An experimental study of male adornment in the Scarlet-tufted Malachite Sunbird. II. The role of the elongated tail in mate choice and experimental evidence for a handicap. *Behav. Ecol. Sociobiol.* 29: 421-427.

Evans, M. R. & Thomas, A. L. R. (1992) The aerodynamic and mechanical effects of elongated tails in the Scarlet-tufted Malachite Sunbird: measuring the cost of a handicap. *Anim. Behav.* 43: 337-347.

Evans, T. D. (1996) Note on the field identification of Uluguru Violet-backed Sunbird *Anthreptes neglectus*. *Bull. Afr. Bird Club* 3: 38-39.

Evans, T. D. (1997) Records of birds from the forests of the East Usambara lowlands, August 1994–February 1995. *Scopus* 19: 92-108.

Evans, T. D. & Anderson, G. (1993a) Results of an ornithological survey in the Ukaguru and East Usambara mountains, Tanzania. *Scopus* 17: 40-47.

Evans, T. & Anderson, G. Q. A. (1993b) Notes on Moreau's sunbird *Nectarinia moreaui*. *Scopus* 17: 63-64.

Evans, T. D., Towll, M. C., Timmins, R. J., Thewlis, R. M., Stones, A. J., Robichaud, W. G. and Barzen, J. (2000) Ornithological records from the lowlands of southern Laos during December 1995–September 1996, including areas on the Thai and Cambodian borders. *Forktail* 16: 29-52.

Fain, A. & Mariaux, J. (1991) Notes on two mesostigmatid mites (Acari, Mesostigmata) recorded from sunbirds (Nectariniidae) in the Ivory Coast. *Rev. Suisse Zool.* 98: 319-324.

Farquhar, M. R., Lorenz, M., Rayner, J. L. & Craig, A. J. F. K. (1996) Feather ultrastructure and skeletal morphology as taxonomic characters in African sunbirds (Nectariniidae) and sugarbirds (Promeropidae). *J. Afr. Zool.* 110: 321-331.

Feehan, J. (1985) Explosive flower opening in ornithophily: a study of pollination mechanisms in some Central African Loranthaceae. *Bot. J. Linn. Soc.* 90: 129-144.

Field, G. D. (1971) Juvenile plumage of the Upper Guinea race of the Collared Sunbird *Anthreptes collaris subcollaris*. *Ibis* 113: 366-367.

Fjeldså, J. (1999) The impact of human forest disturbance on the endemic avifauna of the Udzungwa Mountains, Tanzania. *Bird Conserv. Internatn.* 9: 47-62.

Fjeldså, J., Howell, K. & Andersen, M. (1997) An ornithological visit to the Rubeho Mountains, Tanzania. *Scopus* 19: 73-82.

Fleming, R. L. (1968) Winter observations on the ecology and distribution of birds on the Kosi-Gandak Watershed Ridge, central Nepal. *Pavo* 6(1-2): 1-11.

Fleming, R. L. Snr., Fleming, R. L. Jnr. & Bangdel, L. S. (1976) *Birds of Nepal*. Fleming, Kathmandu, Nepal.

Forbes, H. O. (1903) *The natural history of Socotra and Abd el Kuri*. Henry Young & Sons, Liverpool.

Fletcher, T. B. & Inglis, C. M. (1924) *Birds of an Indian garden*. Thatcher, Spink & Co., Calcutta & Simla.

Follet, B. (1990) Lesser Doublecollared Sunbird rearing Klaas Cuckoo. *Promerops* no. 196: 13-14.

Forbes-Watson, A. D. (1969) Notes on birds observed in the Comoros on behalf of the Smithsonian Institution. *Atoll Res. Bull.* 128: 1-23.

Ford, H. A. (1995) Plain Sunbird *Anthreptes simplex* feeding on arils of *Acacia* seeds. *Forktail* 10: 181-182.

Fraser, M. W. (1989) Short-term responses of birds to fire in old mountain fynbos. *Ostrich* 60: 172-182.

Fraser, M. W. (1997a) Malachite Sunbird *Nectarinia famosa*. Pp.488-490 in *The atlas of southern African birds*. Vol. 2. *Passerines*. Harrison, J. A., Allan, D. G., Underhill, L. G., Herremans, M., Tree, A. J., Parker, V. & Brown, C. J. (eds.). BirdLife South Africa, Johannesburg.

Fraser, M. W. (1997b) Orangebreasted Sunbird *Nectarinia violacea*. Pp.492-493 in *The atlas of southern African birds*. Vol. 2. *Passerines*. Harrison, J. A., Allan, D. G., Underhill, I. G., Herremans, M., Tree, A. J., Parker, V. & Brown, C. J. (eds.). BirdLife South Africa, Johannesburg.

Fraser, M. W. (1997c) Lesser Doublecollared Sunbird *Nectarinia chalybea*. Pp.500-501 in *The atlas of southern African birds*. Vol. 2. *Passerines*. Harrison, J. A., Allan, D. G., Underhill, L. G., Herremans, M., Tree, A. J., Parker, V. & Brown, C. J. (eds.). BirdLife South Africa, Johannesburg.

Fraser, M. W. (1997d) Cape Sugarbird *Promerops cafer*. Pp.484-485 in *The atlas of Southern African Birds*. Vol. 2. *Passerines*. Harrison, J. A., Allan, D. G., Underhill, L. G., Herremans, M., Tree, A. J., Parker, V., & Brown, C. J. (eds.) BirdLife South Africa, Johannesburg.

Fraser, M. & McMahon, L. (1991) Orangebreasted Sunbird feeding from *Agapanthus* flowers. *Promerops* no. 198: 13.

Fraser, M. & McMahon, L. (1992) Habitat change by Cape Sugarbirds and Orangebreasted Sunbirds in an apparent response to fire in old mountain Fynbos. *Safring News* 21: 51-54.

Fraser, M., McMahon, L., Underhill, L. G., Underhill, G. D., & Rebelo, A. G. (1989) Nectarivore ringing in the southwestern Cape. *Safring News* 18: 3-18.

Fraser, M. & Wheeler, L. (1991) Dusky Sunbirds at Rondevlei. *Promerops* no. 199: 6.

Friedmann, H. (1931) The Tanganyikan form of *Anthreptes orientalis*. *Occas. Pap. Boston Soc. Nat. Hist.* 5: 383-384.

Friedmann, H. & Stager, K. E. (1969) Results of the 1968 Avil expedition to Mt. Nyiru, Samburu District, Kenya. Ornithology. *Los Angeles County Museum Contrib. Sci.* no. 174: 1-30.

Frith, H. J. (ed.) (1984) *Birds in the Australian high country*. Revised ed. Angus & Robertson, London, Sydney, Melbourne.

Frost, S. K. & Frost, P. G. H. (1980) Territoriality and changes in resource use by sunbirds at *Leonotis leonurus* (Labiatae). *Oecologia* 45: 109-116.

Frost, S. K. & Frost, P. G. H. (1981) Sunbird pollination of *Strelitzia nicolai*. *Oecologia* 49: 379-384.

Fry, C. H. (1965) A nest of the Buff-throated Sunbird. *Bull. Niger. Orn. Soc.* 2: 81-82.

Fry, C. H. (1970) Migration, moult and weights of birds in Northern Guinea Savanna in Nigeria and Ghana. *Ostrich* suppl. 8: 239-263.

Fry, C. H., Keith, S. & Urban, E. K. (eds.) (2000) *The birds of Africa*. Vol. 6. Academic Press, London.

Fuggles-Couchman, N. R. (1984) The distribution of, and other notes on, some birds of Tanzania – Part II. *Scopus* 8: 81-92.

Fuggles-Couchman, N. R. (1986) Breeding records of some Tanzanian birds. *Scopus* 10: 20-26.

Gaither, J. C. (1994) Weights of Bornean understorey birds. *Bull. Brit. Orn. Club* 114: 89-90.

Gallagher, M. & Woodcock, M. W. (1980) *The birds of Oman*. Quartet Books, London.

Ganguly, J. K. (1986) Co-operative feeding of chicks of the Purple-rumped Sunbird *Nectarinia zeylonica*. *J. Bombay Nat. Hist. Soc.* 83: 447.

Gardiner, J. & Meikle, J. (1985) Note on the breeding habits of the Bronze Sunbird. *Honeyguide* 31: 58-59.

Gardner, L. L. (1925) The adaptive modifications and the taxonomic value of the tongue in birds. *Proc. U.S. Natn. Mus.* 67(19): 1-49.

de Garine-Witchatitsky, M., Cheke, R. A. & Lazaro, D. (in press) Effects of tsetse targets on mammals and birds in the Kasungu National Park, Malawi. *Biodiversity & Conservation*.

Garnett, S. T., Williams, A. C., Hindmarsh, R. W. H. & Hindmarsh, N. L. (1991) Island colonisation after possible reconnaisance by the Yellow-bellied Sunbird *Nectarinia jugularis*. *Emu* 91: 185-186.

Gaston, A. J. (1989) Andrew Leith Adams: a pioneer of Himalayan ornithology. *Forktail* 4: 3-8.

Gatter, W. (1997) *The birds of Liberia*. Pica Press, Robertsbridge, Sussex, U.K.

Gaugris, Y. (1976) Additions à l'inventaire des oiseaux du Burundi (Decembre 1971–Decembre 1975). *Oiseaux et R.F.O.* 46: 273-289.

Gaugris, Y., Prigogine, A. & Vande weghe, J.-P. (1981) Additions et corrections à l'avifaune du Burundi. *Gerfaut* 71: 3-39.

Gaymer, R., Blackman, R. A. A., Dawson, P. G., Penny, M. & Penny, C. M. (1969) The endemic birds of Seychelles. *Ibis* 111: 157-176.

Genelly, R. E. (1969) Birds of the Mole Game Reserve, Ghana. *Nigerian Field* 34: 171-182.

Gibson-Hill, C. A. (1952) A revised list of the birds known from the Rhio-Lingga Archipelago. *Bull. Raffles Mus.* 24: 361.

Gill, F. B. (1969) Additions to the birds known from the West Sumatran islands. *Ardea* 57: 89-91.

Gill, F. B. (1971) Tongue structure of the sunbird *Hypogramma hypogrammica*. *Condor* 73(4): 485-6.

Gill, F. B. & Conway, C. A. (1979) Floral biology of *Leonotis nepetifolia* (Labiatae). *Proc. Acad. Nat. Sci. Philadelphia* 131: 244-256.

Gill, F. B. & Wolf, L. L. (1975a) Foraging strategies and energetics of East African sunbirds at mistletoe flowers. *Amer. Naturalist* 109: 491-510.

Gill, F. B. & Wolf, L. L. (1975b) Economics of feeding territoriality in the Golden-winged Sunbird. *Ecology* 56: 333-345.

Gill, F. B. & Wolf, L. L. (1977) Nonrandom foraging by sunbirds in a patchy environment. *Ecology* 58: 1284-1296.

Gill, F. B. & Wolf, L. L. (1978) Comparative foraging efficiencies of some montane sunbirds in Kenya. *Condor* 80: 391-400.

Gill, F. B. & Wolf, L. L. (1979) Nectar loss by Golden-winged Sunbirds to competitors. *Auk* 96: 448-461.

Giraudoux, P., Degauquier, R., Jones, P. J., Weigel, J. & Isenmann, P. (1988) Avifaune du Niger: état des connaissances en 1986. *Malimbus* 10: 1-140.

Goldstein, H., Eisikovitz, D. & Yom-Tov, Y. (1986) Infanticide in the Palestine Sunbird *Nectarinia osea*. *Condor* 88: 528-529.

Goldstein, H., Verbeek, N. A. M., Eisikowitch, D. & Yom-tov, Y. (1987) Sunbirds prefer to feed in the sun. *Ardea* 75: 293-295.

Goldstein, H. & Yom-Tov, Y. (1988) Breeding biology of the Orange-tufted Sunbird in Israel. *Ardea* 76: 169-174.

Goodman, S. M. & Gonzales, P. C. (1990) The birds of Mt. Isarog National Park, southern Luzon, Philippines, with particular reference to altitudinal distribution. *Fieldiana* N.S. 60.

Goodman, S. M. & Parillo, P. (1997) A study of the diets of Malagasy birds based on stomach contents. *Ostrich* 68: 104-113.

Goodman, S. M., Pidgeon, M., Hawkins, A. F. A. & Schulenberg, T. S. (1997) The birds of south-eastern Madagascar. *Fieldiana Zool.* 87: 1-132.

Goodman S. M. & Putnam, M. S. (1997) The birds of the eastern slopes of the Réserve Naturelle Intégrale d'Andringitra, Madagascar. In Goodman, S. M. (ed.) *A floral and faunal inventory of the eastern slopes of the Réserve Naturelle Intégrale d'Andringitra, Madagascar, with reference to elevational variation. Fieldiana Zool.* N.S. 85.

Gore, M. E. J. (1990) *Birds of the Gambia*. Second edition. B.O.U. Check-list no. 3, British Ornithologists' Union, Tring, Herts.

Grant, C. H. B. & Mackworth-Praed, C. W. (1943) A new race of sunbird from the southern Belgian Congo. *Bull. Brit. Orn. Club* 63: 63.

Gray, G. R. (1860) List of birds collected by Mr. Wallace at the Molucca Islands, with descriptions of new species, etc. *Proc. Zool. Soc. Lond.*: 348.

Gray, H. H. (1986) Johanna's Sunbird in Nigeria. *Malimbus* 8: 44.

Green, A. A. (1990) The avifauna of the southern sector of the Gashaka-Gumti Game Reserve, Nigeria. *Malimbus* 12: 31-51.

Green, C. A. (1991) First sight record of Yellow-vented Flowerpecker for Bali. *Kukila* 5: 143-144.

Greig-Smith, P. W. (1978) Imitative foraging in mixed-species flocks of Seychelles birds. *Ibis* 120: 233-235.

Greig-Smith, P. W. (1980) Foraging, seasonality and nesting of Seychelles Sunbirds *Nectarinia dussumieri*. *Ibis* 122: 307-321.

Gretton, A. (1990). Recent reports. *Oriental Bird Club Bull.* 11: 40-48.

Grimes, L. G. (1971) Notes on some birds seen at Buea and on Mount Cameroon. 30 Dec. 1970–Jan. 1971. *Bull. Niger. Orn. Soc.* 8: 35-45.

Grimes, L. G. (1974) Dialects and geographical variation in the song of the Splendid Sunbird *Nectarinia coccinigaster*. *Ibis* 116: 314-329.

Grimes, L. G. (1987) *The birds of Ghana*. B.O.U. Check-list no. 9, British Ornithologists' Union, London.

von Grote, H. (1924) Neue Formen aus Westafrika. *Orn. Monatsb.* 32: 68-72.

Gyldenstolpe, N. (1924) Zoological results of the Swedish Expedition to Central Africa 1921, Birds. *Kungl. Sv. Vet. Akad. Handl.* 3: 91.

Hachisuka, M. (1941) Description of a new genus and species of sunbird from the Philippine Islands. *Bull. Biogeogr. Soc. Japan* 11(2): 5-8.

Hadden, D. (1981) *Birds of the North Solomons*. Wau Ecology Institute Handbook no. 8., Wau, Papua New Guinea.

Hale, M. (1996) Thick-billed Flowerpecker – a first record for Bali. *Kukila* 8: 155-157.

Hall, B. P. (ed.) (1974) *Birds of the Harold Hall Australian Expeditions 1962-70*. British Museum (Natural History), London.

Hall, B. P. & Moreau, R. E. (1970) *An atlas of speciation in African passerine birds*. British Museum (Natural History), London.

Hamilton, W. D. & Zuk, M. (1982) Heritable true fitness and bright birds: a role for parasites? *Science* 218: 384-387.

Hanmer, D. B. (1979) The Grey Sunbird *Nectarinia veroxii* in southern Malawi. *Bull. Brit. Orn. Club* 99: 71-72.

Hanmer, D. B. (1981) Mensural and moult data of nine species of sunbird from Moçambique and Malawi. *Ostrich* 52: 156-178.

Hanmer, D. B. (1987) Much ado about Bluethroated Sunbirds. *Witwatersrand Bird Club News* no. 138: 11-12.

Hanmer, D. B. (1989) The end of an era – final longevity figures for Nchalo. *Safring News* 18: 19-32.

Hanmer, D. B. (1997) Bird longevity in the eastern highlands of Zimbabwe – drought survivors. *Safring News* 26: 47-54.

Harebottle, D. M. (1999) Nestling period of the Greater Doublecollared Sunbird *Nectarinia afra*. *Bird Numbers* 8: 22-23.

Harrison, C. (1975) *A field guide to the nests, eggs and nestlings of British and European birds with North Africa and the Middle East*. Collins, London.

Harrison, J. A. (1997a) Greater Doublecollared Sunbird *Nectarinia afra*. Pp.504-505 in *The atlas of southern African birds*. Vol. 2. *Passerines*. Harrison, J. A., Allan, D. G., Underhill, L. G., Herremans, M., Tree, A. J., Parker, V. & Brown, C. J. (eds.). BirdLife South Africa, Johannesburg.

Harrison, J. A. (1997b) Dusky Sunbird *Nectarinia fusca*. Pp.510-511 in *The atlas of southern African birds*. Vol. 2. *Passerines*. Harrison, J. A., Allan, D. G., Underhill, L. G., Herremans, M., Tree, A. J., Parker, V. & Brown, C. J. (eds.). BirdLife South Africa, Johannesburg.

Harrison, J. A., Allan, D. G., Underhill, L. G., Herremans, M., Tree, A. J., Parker, V. & Brown, C. J. (eds.) *The atlas of southern African birds*. Vol. 2. *Passerines*. BirdLife South Africa, Johannesburg.

Hartert, E. (1896) An account of the collection of birds made by Mr. William Doherty in the Eastern Archipelago. VII. List of birds collected in Sumba. *Novit. Zool.* 3: 576-590.

Hartert, E. (1897) On the birds collected by Mr. Everett on the island of Savu. *Novit. Zool.* 4: 263-273.

Hartert, E. (1901) Some notes on Java birds. *Novit. Zool.* 8: 52.

Hartert, E. (1903) On the birds collected on the Tukang-Besi Islands and Buton, south-east of Celebes, by Mr. Heinrich Kuhn. *Novit. Zool.* 10: 18-38.

Hartert, E. (1904) The birds of the South-West Islands of Wetter, Roma, Kisser, Letti and Moa. *Novit. Zool.* 11: 174-221.

Hartert, E. (1906) On the birds of the island of Babber. *Novit. Zool.* 13: 288-302.

Hartert, E. (1918) *Dicaeum trigonostoma megastoma* subsp. nov., *Dicaeum trigonostigma flaviclunis* subsp. nov. *Bull. Brit. Orn. Club* 38: 73-75.

Hartert, E. (1920) Types of birds in the Tring Museum. *Novit. Zool.* 27: 425-505.

Hartert, E. (1926a) On the birds of Feni and Nissan Islands, east of South New Ireland. *Novit. Zool.* 33: 41.

Hartert, E. (1926b) On the birds of the district of Talasea in New Britain. *Novit. Zool.* 33: 122-145.

Hartlaub G. (1860a) Systematsche Uebersicht der Vögel Madagascar. *J. Orn.* 8: 81-112.

Hartlaub G. (1860b) Drei neue africanische Vögel der Pariser Sammlung. *J. Orn.* 8: 340-341.

Hartley, I. R. & McGowan, P. J. K. (1991) Moult and biometrics in five birds endemic to Palawan, Philippines. *Forktail* 6: 74-77.

Haugaard, J. (1995) Unusual aggression by sunbird. *Vocifer* 2: 6.

Hellebrekers, W. P. J. & Hoogerwerf, A. (1967) A further contribution to our oological knowledge of the island of Java (Indonesia). *Zool. Verhandl.* 88: 164.

Hellmayr, C. E. (1912) Descriptions of two new birds from the Timor group of islands. *Novit. Zool.* 19: 210-211.

Henderson, C. L. & Cherry, M. I. (1998) Testing alternative hypotheses of provisioning in the Cape Sugarbird *Promerops cafer*. In Adams, N. J. & Slotow, R. H. (eds.) Proc. 22 Internatn. Orn. Congr., Durban. *Ostrich* 69: 253.

Hendrickx, F. L. & Massart-Lis, Y. (1952) *Cinnyris rockefelleri* Chapin. *Ibis* 94: 531-532.

Henry, G. M. (1955) *A guide to the birds of Ceylon*. Oxford University Press, Bombay.

Henry, G. M. (1971) *A guide to the birds of Ceylon*. 2nd. edition. Oxford University Press, Bombay.

Hernandez, H. M. (1981) The reproductive ecology of *Nicotiana glauca*, a cosmopolitan weed. *Bol. Soc. Bot. Mex.* 41: 47-74.

Herremans, M. (1992) Indirect evidence for the existence of movements of sunbirds in Botswana. *Babbler* no. 24: 149.

Herremans, M. (1997) Marico Sunbird *Nectarinia mariquensis*. Pp.494-495 in *The atlas of southern African birds*. Vol. 2. *Passerines*. Harrison, J. A., Allan, D. G., Underhill, L. G., Herremans, M., Tree, A. J., Parker, V. & Brown, C. J. (eds.). BirdLife South Africa, Johannesburg.

Hicks, E. A. (1959) *Check-list and bibliography on the occurrence of insects in birds' nests*. The Iowa State College Press, Ames, Iowa.

Hicks, E. A. (1962) Check-list and bibliography on the occurrence of insects in birds' nests. Supplement I. *Iowa State J. Sci.* 36: 233-348.

Hicks, E. A. (1971) Check-list and bibliography on the occurrence of insects in birds' nests. Supplement II. *Iowa State J. Sci.* 46: 123-338.

Hill, M. (2000) Bird fauna of two protected forests in northern Vietnam. *Forktail* 16: 5-14.

Hindwood, K. (1966) *Australian birds in colour*. A. H. & A. W. Reed, Sydney.

Hipkiss, A. J., Watson, L. G. & Evans, T. D. (1994) The Cambridge-Tanzania rainforest project 1992: brief account of ornithological results and conservation proposals. *Ibis* 136: 107-108.

Holman, F. C. (1949) The nest and eggs of *Cinnyris johannae*. *Ibis* 91: 351-352.

Holmes, D. A. (1994) A review of the land birds of the West Sumatran Islands. *Kukila* 7: 28-46.

Holmes, D. A. (1996) Sumatra Bird Report. *Kukila* 8: 9-56.

Holmes, P. & Wood, H. (1979) Report of the Ornithological Expedition to Sulawesi. Unpublished report.

Hoogerwerf, A. (1966) Nouvelles notes sur les sous-espèces Indonesiennes du soui-manga à gorge rousse (*Anthreptes malacensis* Scop.). *Oiseau et R.F.O.* 36: 51-62.

Hoogerwerf, A. (1967) A new subspecies of the Ruby-cheek (*Anthreptes singalensis*) (Gmelin) from Java. *Bull. Brit. Orn. Club* 87: 5-10.

Hopkins, G. H. E. & Clay, T. (1952) *A check list of the genera and species of Mallophaga*. British Museum (Natural History), London and H. M. Stationery Office, London.

Hopkins, M. T. E., Demey, R. & Barker, J. C. (1999) First documented records of Green-throated Sunbird *Nectarinia rubescens* for Nigeria, with a discussion of the distinctive race *crossensis*. *Malimbus* 21: 57-60.

Hornskov, J. (1987) More birds from Berbak Game Reserve, Sumatra. *Kukila* 3: 58-59.

Hornskov, J. (1996) Recent observations of birds in the Philippine Archipelago. *Forktail* 11: 1-10.

Howells, W. W. (1971) Breeding of the Coppery Sunbird at Salisbury, Rhodesia. *Ostrich* 42: 99-109.

Hume, A. O. (1870) Letter. *Ibis* (2)6: 435-438.

Hume, A. O. (1875) Novelties? *Stray Feathers* 3: 296-303.

Hustler, K. (1985) Which sunbird was it? *Honeyguide* 31: 173-174.

Hutton, J. (1985) Another Greater Doublecollared Sunbird (785). *Witwatersrand Bird Club News* no. 128: 9.

Inskipp, C. & Inskipp, T. (1985) *A guide to the birds of Nepal*. Croom Helm, London.

Inskipp, C., Inskipp, T. & Sherub (2000). The ornithological importance of the Thrumshingla National Park, Bhutan. *Forktail* 16: 147-162.

Irwin, M. P. S. (1961) Notes on the South African forms of the Collared Sunbird *A. collaris* (Vieillot) with the description of a new race. *Durban Mus. Novit.* 6: 105-111.

Irwin, M. P. S. (1984) Final comment on yellowbellied sunbirds. *Witwatersrand Bird Club News* no. 127: 8.

Irwin, M. P. S. (1993) What sunbirds belong to the genus *Anthreptes*? *Honeyguide* 39: 211-216.

Irwin, M. P. S. (1995a) The Plain-backed Sunbird in the Transvaal and Zimbabwe. *Honeyguide* 41: 26-27

Irwin, M. P. S. (1995b) On the affinities of the Plain-backed Sunbird *Anthreptes reichenowi*. *Honeyguide* 41: 47-48.

Irwin, M. P. S. (1999) The genus *Nectarinia* and the evolution and diversification of sunbirds: an Afrotropical perspective. *Honeyguide* 45: 45-58.

Itino, T., Kato, M. & Hotta, M. (1991) Pollination ecology of the two wild bananas, *Musa acuminata* ssp. *halabanensis* and *Musa salaccensis*: chiropterophily and ornithophily. *Biotropica* 23: 151-158.

Iwarson, M. (1979) Pollen from bills of African sunbirds (Nectariniidae). *Botaniska Notiser* 132: 349-355.

Jackson, H. D. (1970) Unusual nest of a Bronze Sunbird. *Ostrich* 41: 262-263.

Jackson, S., Nicolson, S. W. & van Wyk, B.-E. (1998) Apparent absorption efficiencies of nectar sugars in the Cape Sugarbird, with a comparison of methods. *Physiological Zool.* 71: 106-115.

Jardine, W. (1843) *The natural history of the Nectariniadae* [sic] *or sunbirds*. Pp.147-277 in W. Jardine, (ed.) *The Naturalist's Library*, vol. 5: *Ornithology: sun-birds*. W. H. Lizars, Edinburgh.

Jennings, M. C. (1995) *An interim atlas of the breeding birds of Arabia*. National Commission for Wildlife Conservation and Development. Riyadh, Kingdom of Saudi Arabia.

Jensen, F. P. (1983) A new species of sunbird from Tanzania. *Ibis* 125: 447-449.

Jensen, F. P. & Brøgger-Jensen, S. (1992) The forest avifauna of the Uzungwa Mountains, Tanzania. *Scopus* 15: 65-83.

Jensen, R. A. C. & Clinning, C. F. (1974) Breeding biology of two cuckoos and their hosts in south-west Africa. *Living Bird* 13: 5-50.

Jepson, P. (1993) Recent ornithological observations from Buru. *Kukila* 6: 85-109.

Johnson, D. N. (1997) Neergaard's Sunbird *Nectarinia neergaardi*. P.499 in *The atlas of southern African birds*. Vol. 2. *Passerines*. Harrison, J. A., Allan, D. G., Underhill, L. G., Herremans, M., Tree, A. J., Parker, V. & Brown, C. J. (eds.). BirdLife South Africa, Johannesburg.

Jones, J. M. B. (1996) Purple-banded Sunbird breeding in Marondera north. *Honeyguide* 42: 35-36.

Jones, M., Juhaeni, D., Banjaransari, H., Banham, W., Lace, L., Linsley, M. D. & Marsden, S. (1994) The status, ecology and conservation of the forest birds and butterflies of Sumba, Indonesia. A report to the Indonesian Directorate General of Forest Protection & Nature Conservation, the Indonesian Institute of Sciences and BirdLife International, Department of Biological Sciences, Manchester Metropolitan University.

Jones, M. J., Linsley, M. D. and Marsden, S. J. (1995) Population sizes, status and habitat associations of the restricted-range bird species of Sumba, Indonesia. *Bird Conserv. Internatn.* 5: 21-52.

Jones, P. J. & Tye, A. (1988) A survey of the avifauna of São Tomé and Príncipe. ICBP Study Report no. 24. International Council for Bird Preservation, Cambridge.

Jones, P. J. & Tye, A. (in press) *The birds of São Tomé, Príncipe and Annobón (Gulf of Guinea)*. British Ornithologists' Union Checklist, Tring, Herts.

Jullard, J. P. (1980) Notes sur quelques oiseaux des Seychelles. *Alauda* 48: 56-67.

Junge, G. C. A. (1952) New subspecies of birds from New Guinea. *Zool. Meded.* 31(22): 247-250.

Kahindi, O. & Kageci, J. (1995) Violet-backed repels Black-bellied Sunbird. *Kenya Birds* 4: 36.

Keith, G. S. (1968) Notes on birds of East Africa, including additions to the avifauna. *Amer. Mus. Novit.* 2321.

Keith, G. S. & Gunn, W. W. H. (1971) *Sounds of nature: birds of the African rain forests*. Federation of Ontario Naturalists and the American Museum of Natural History.

Kennedy, R. S., Gonzales, P. C. & Miranda, H. C. (1997) New *Aethopyga* sunbirds (Aves: Nectariniidae) from the island of Mindanao, Philippines. *Auk* 114: 1-10.

Khan, M. A. R. (1977) Local movements of the Small Sunbird *Nectarinia minima*. *Bangladesh J. Zool.* 5: 77-78.

King, B. F., Woodcock, M. & Dickinson, E. C. (1975) *A field guide to the birds of South-East Asia*. Collins, London.

Kirkpatrick, C. E. & Smith, T. B. (1988) Blood parasites of birds in Cameroon. *J. Parasitology* 74: 1009-1013.

Kirkup, D. (1998) Pollination mechanisms in African Loranthaceae. Pp.37-60 in Polhill, R. & Wiens, D. (1998) *Mistletoes of Africa*. Royal Botanic Gardens, Kew, U.K.

Kirwan, G. M., Martins, R. P., Eken, G. & Davidson, P. (1998) A checklist of the birds of Turkey. *Sandgrouse* Supplement 1: 1-32.

Koenig, L. (1956) Zum Vorkommen einiger Sprinte zwischen Tessalit und Niamey (Franzosich West Africa). *J. Orn.* 97: 384-402.

Korb, J. & Salewski, V. (2000) Predation on swarming termites by birds. *Afr. J. Ecol.* 38: 173-174.

von Korff, J. (1997) Lesser Double-coloured Sunbird's unusual nest. *Bee Eater* 48: 47.

Kramer, G. (1975) Nischentrennung beim Grünkopfnektarvogel (*Cyanomitra verticalis*) und Bronzenektarvogel (*Nectarinia kilimensis*) (Fam. Nectariniidae, Aves) im Kivuhochland (Republik Zaire, Afrika). *Oecologia* 20: 143-156.

Kratter, A. W., Steadman, D. W., Smith, C. E. & Filardi, C. E. (2001) Reproductive condition, moult, and body mass of birds from Isabel, Solomon Islands. *Bull. Br. Orn. Cl.* 121: 128-144.

Krienke, W. (1941) Nesting of the Nyasa Violet-backed Sunbird on Elvington farm, Beatrice District, Southern Rhodesia. *Ostrich* 12: 24-25.

Kumar, S. T., Reddy, A. R. & Lakshminarayana, K. (1984) A new record of sunbirds as avian pests on grape around Hyderabad. *J. Bombay Nat. Hist. Soc.* 81: 475-476.

Kumerloeve, H. (1960) On the occurrence and breeding habits of the Palestine Sun-bird, *Cinnyris osea osea* (Bonaparte) in Beirut. *Alauda* 28: 30-33.

Kunkel, P. (1964) Ausdrucksbewegungen des Grünkopfnektarvogels *Cyanomitra verticalis* (Latham). *Vogelwelt* 85: 150-158.

Kuroda N. (1920) Notes on and descriptions of the flower-peckers of Formosa. *Tori* 2: 230-232.

Lack, P. (1976) Nesting of Hunter's Sunbird. *Bull. East Afr. Nat. Hist. Soc.* 1976: 49.

Lack, P. (1985) The ecology of the land-birds of Tsavo East National Park, Kenya. *Scopus* 9: 2-23, 57-96.

Lamarche, B. (1981) Liste commentée des oiseaux du Mali. 2ème partie: passereaux. *Malimbus* 3: 73-102.

Lamarche, B. (1988) Liste commentée des oiseaux de Mauritanie. *Etudes Sahariennes et Ouest-Africaines* 1: 1-164.

Lamba, B. S. (1978) Nidification of some common Indian birds 13: the Purple-rumped Sunbird, *Nectarinia zeylonica* Linnaeus. *Indian J. For.* 1: 329-344.

Lambert, F. R. (1991) Fruit-eating by Purple-naped Sunbirds *Hypogramma hypogrammicum* in Borneo. *Ibis* 133: 425-426.

Lambert, F. R. (1992) The consequences of selective logging for Bornean lowland forest birds. *Phil. Trans. R. Soc. Lond.* B 335: 443-457.

Lambert, F. R. (1994) Some key sites and significant records in the Philippines and Sabah. *Bird Conserv. Internatn.* 3: 282-297.

Lane, S. (1992) Miombo Doublecollared Sunbird in Limbe. *Safring News* 21: 39-40.

Lane, S. (1995) Eclipse plumage in Yellow-bellied Sunbird *Nectarinia venusta*. *Nyala* 19: 54-55.

Langrand, O. (1990) *Guide to the birds of Madagascar*. Yale University Press, New Haven.

La Touche, J. D. D. (1921) Descriptions of new birds from S.E. Yunan. *Bull. Brit. Orn. Club* 42: 29-32.

Leandri, J. (1950) Points de vue sur le problème de l'ornithophilie. *Terre et Vie* 97(2): 86-100.

LeCroy, M. & Peckover, W. S. (1998) Misima's missing birds. *Bull. Brit. Orn. Club* 118: 217-238.

Ledger, J. A. (1980) *The arthropod parasites of vertebrates in Africa south of the Sahara*. Vol. IV. *Phthiraptera (Insecta)*. Publications of the South African Institute for Medical Research no. 56., Johannesburg.

Lees, S. G. (1999) Scarlet-chested Sunbird pirating nesting material from Yellow-bellied Sunbird. *Honeyguide* 45: 27.

Lekagul, B. & Cronin, E. W. (1974) *Bird guide of Thailand*. 2nd ed. Kurusapa Ladprao Press, Bangkok.

Lekagul, B. & Round, P. D. (1991) *A guide to the birds of Thailand*. Saha Karn Bhaet Co. Ltd., Bangkok.

Leon, B. & Nicolson, S. W. (1997) Metabolic rate and body temperature of an African sunbird, *Nectarinia chalybea*: daily rhythm and the effect of ambient temperature. *South Afr. J. Zool.* 32: 31-36.

Lewis, A. & Pomeroy, D. (1989) *A bird atlas of Kenya*. A. A. Balkema, Rotterdam.

Linsley, M. D. 1995. Some bird records from Obi, Maluku. *Kukila* 7: 142-151.

Lippens, L. & Wille, H. (1976) *Les oiseaux du Zaïre*. Lannoo, Tielt, Belgium.

Lloyd, P. (1989) Sucrose concentration preferences of two southern African sunbirds. *Ostrich* 60: 134-135.

Lloyd, P. (1991) Feeding responses of captive Greater Double-collared Sunbirds (*Nectarinia afra*) to changes in sucrose food concentrations, and their relation to optimal foraging models. *South African J. Sci.* 87: 67-68.

Lloyd, P. & Craig, A. J. F. K. (1989) Morphometrics, molt and taxonomy of the *Nectarinia afra*–*Nectarinia chalybea* complex of South African double-collared sunbirds. *Ann. Cape Prov. Mus. Nat. Hist.* 18: 135-150.

Löhrl, H. (1979) Tagesaktivität, Nestbaumethode und Brutverhalten des Honigsaugers *Nectarinia* (*aidemonia*) *kilimensis* in Zentralafrika. *J. Orn.* 120: 441-450.

Longmore, W. (1991) *Honeyeaters and their allies of Australia*. Angus & Robertson, Harper Collins, Sydney, Australia.

Lott, D. F. (1991) Bronzy Sunbirds tolerate intrusion on foraging territories by female Golden-winged Sunbirds that perform "begging" display. *J. Field Orn.* 62: 492.

Lott, D. F. & Lott, D. Y. (1991) Bronzy Sunbirds *Nectarinia kilimensis* relax territoriality in response to internal changes. *Ornis Scand.* 22: 303-307.

Lotz, C. N. & Nicolson, S. W. (1996) Sugar preferences of a nectarivorous passerine bird, the Lesser Double-collared Sunbird (*Nectarinia chalybea*). *Functional Ecology* 10: 360-365.

Lotz, C. N. & Nicolson, S. W. (1998) A terrestrial fish: adaptations of an African sunbird for nectar feeding. *Ostrich* 69: 230.

Louette, M. (1976) The populations of *Nectarinia preussi* in the Cameroon mountain area. *Abstr. 4th. Pan-African Orn. Congr.* Mahé, Seychelles.

Louette, M. (1988) Les oiseaux des Comores. *Ann. Mus. Roy. Afr. Centr.*, serie in-8°, Sci. Zool., no. 255.

Louette, M. (1989) Additions and corrections to the avifauna of Zaire (4). *Bull. Brit. Orn. Club* 109: 217-225.

Lucking, R. S. (1996) Polygyny in the Seychelles Sunbird *Nectarinia dussumieri*. *Bull. Brit. Orn. Club* 116: 178-179.

Maa, T. C. (1966) Studies in Hippoboscidae (Diptera). *Pacific Insects Monograph* 10: 1-148.

Maa, T. C. (1969a) Revision of *Icosta* Speiser (= *Lynchia* auctt.) with erection of a new related genus *Phthona* (Diptera: Hippoboscidae). *Pacific Insects Monograph* 20: 25-236.

Maa, T. C. (1969b) A revised checklist and concise host index of Hippoboscidae (Diptera). *Pacific Insects Monograph* 20: 261-299.

Mabberley, D. J. (1997) *The plant book: a portable dictionary of the vascular plants*. Second edition. Cambridge University Press, Cambridge.

Macdonald, D. (1985) Greater Doublecollared Sunbird. *Witwatersrand Bird Club News* no. 128: 9.

Macdonald, J. D. (1958) Notes on *Cinnyris manoensis* Reichenow. *Bull. Brit. Orn. Club* 78: 7-9.

MacKinnon, J. & Phillipps, K. (1993) *The birds of Borneo, Sumatra, Java and Bali*. Oxford University Press, Oxford.

Mackworth-Praed, C. W. & Grant, C. H. B. (1945) On the plumages and moults of males of sunbirds occurring in East Africa. *Ibis* 87: 145-158.

Mackworth-Praed, C. W. & Grant, C. H. B. (1955) *African handbook of birds. Series 3: Birds of eastern and north eastern Africa.* Vol. 2. Longmans.

Mackworth-Praed, C. W. & Grant, C. H. B. (1973) *African handbook of birds. Series 3: Birds of west central and western Africa.* Vol. 2. Longmans.

Madge, S. G. (1986) Display of Thickbilled Flowerpecker *Dicaeum agile*. *J. Bombay Nat. Hist. Soc.* Centenary supplement: 213.

Magsalay, P., Brooks, T., Dutson, G. & Timmins, R. (1995) Extinction and conservation on Cebu. *Nature* 373: 294.

Maher, W. J. (1991) Growth and development of the Yellow-bellied Sunbird *Nectarinia jugularis* in north Queensland. *Emu* 91: 58-61.

Maher, W. J. (1992) Breeding biology of the Yellow-bellied Sunbird *Nectarinia jugularis* in northern Queensland. *Emu* 92: 57-60.

Maina, L. W. (1999) Analyses and taxonomic significance of the vocalisations of Afro-tropical sunbirds. M.Sc. thesis, Natural Resources Institute, University of Greenwich, Chatham, Kent.

Majumdar, N. (1980) Occurrence of the Bengal Black Robin, *Saxicoloides fulicata erythrura* (Lesson) [Muscicapidae: Turdinae] and the Assam Purple Sunbird, *Nectarinia asiatica intermedia* (Hume) [Nectariniidae] in Orissa state. *J. Bombay Nat. Hist. Soc.* 77: 334.

Majumdar, N. (1981a) New records from Andra Pradesh. *J. Bombay Nat. Hist. Soc.* 78: 382-383.

Majumdar, N. (1981b) *Nectarinia lotenia hindustanica* range extension. *J. Bombay Nat. Hist. Soc.* 78: 383-384.

Mann, C. F. (1985) An avifaunal study in Kakamega Forest, Kenya, with particular reference to species diversity, weight and moult. *Ostrich* 56: 236-262.

Mann, C. F. (1996) The avifauna of Belalong forest, Brunei Darussalam. Pp.101-116 in Edwards, D. S., Booth, W. E. & Choy, S. C. (eds.) *Tropical rainforest – current issues*. Kluwer, Dordrecht.

Mann, C. F. (in prep. a) Taxonomic comments on some Asian sunbirds and flowerpeckers (Aves, Nectariniidae). *Zool. Verhand.*

Mann, C. F. (in prep. b) *A check-list of the birds of Borneo*. B.O.U. Check-list, Tring, U.K.

Mariaux, J. & Vaucher, C. (1991) A new species of *Staphylepis* Spassky & Oshmarin, 1954 (Cestoda: Hymenolepididae) found in West African nectariniid birds. *Rev. Suisse Zool.* 98: 261-286.

Markman, S., Yom-Tov, Y., & Wright, J. (1995) Male parental care in the Orange-tufted Sunbird: behavioural adjustments in provisioning and nest guarding effort. *Anim. Behav.* 50: 655-669.

Markman, S., Yom-Tov, Y., & Wright, J. (1996) The effect of male removal on female parental care in the Orange-tufted Sunbird. *Anim. Behav.* 52: 437-444.

Markman, S., Pinshow, B. & Wright, J. (1999) Orange-tufted

Sunbirds do not feed nectar to their chicks. *Auk* 116: 257-259.

van Marle, J. G. & Voous, K. H. (1988) *The birds of Sumatra*. British Ornithologists' Union Checklist No.10, London.

Martin, J. (1953) Rapid building of Cape Sugarbird. *Ostrich* 24: 129.

Martin, R. (1983) Possible eclipse plumage in the Lesser Doublecollared Sunbird. *Bokmakierie* 35: 67.

Martin, R., Martin, J. & Martin, E. (1991) Lesser Double-collared Sunbirds: new breeding areas. *Promerops* no. 198: 14.

Martin, R. & Mortimer, J. (1991) Fynbos: too frequent burning poses threat to Cape Sugarbirds. *Promerops* no. 199: 6-8.

Martins, R. P., Porter, R. F. & Stone, F. (1993) Preliminary report of the OSME survey of southern Yemen and Socotra spring 1993. Ornithological Society of the Middle East, unpublished report, Sandy, Bedfordshire, U.K.

Mason, C. W. & Maxwell-Lefroy, H. (1912) The food of birds in India. *Mem. Agr. Dept. India, Entomological Series* Vol. 3.

Mayr, E. (1936) New subspecies of birds from the New Guinea Region. *Amer. Mus. Novit.* 869.

Mayr, E. (1944) The birds of Timor and Sumba. *Bull. Amer. Mus. Nat. Hist.* 83: 127-194.

Mayr, E. (1945) Birds collected during the Whitney South Sea Expedition, LV. Notes on the birds of northern Melanesia. *Amer. Mus. Novit.* 1294.

Mayr, E. & Amadon D. (1947) A review of the Dicaeidae. *Amer. Mus. Novit.* 1360.

Mayr, E. & Amadon, D. (1951) A classification of recent birds. *Amer. Mus. Novit.* 1496.

McCardle, J. E. (1989) Lesser Doublecollared Sunbird 783 *Nectarinia chalybea*. *Mirafra* 6: 119.

McClure, H. E. (1974) *Migration and survival of the birds of Asia*. Applied Scientific Research Corporation of Thailand, Bangkok.

McGregor, R. C. (1905a) Birds of the islands of Romblon, Sibyan, and Cresta da Gallo. *Bur. Govt. Laboratories, Manila Publ.* 25: 5-23.

McGregor, R. C. (1905b) Further notes on birds from Ticao, Cuyo, Culion, Calayan, Lubang, and Luzon. *Bur. Govt. Laboratories, Manila Publ.* 25: 25-34.

McGregor, R. C. (1907) The birds of Bohol. *Phil. J. Sci.* 2(Sci.A): 315-333.

McGregor, R. C. (1909-1910) A manual of Philippine birds. *Bur. Sci. Manila* 2 (2 parts).

McGregor, R. C. (1914) Description of a new species of *Prionochilus* from the highlands of Luzon. *Phil. J. Sci.* 9: 531-533.

McGregor, R. C. (1927) New or noteworthy Philippine birds, V. *Phil. J. Sci.* 32: 513-527.

Mearns, E. A. (1905) Descriptions of eight new Philippine birds, with notes on other species new to the islands. *Proc. Biol. Soc. Washington* 18: 83-90.

Medland, R. D. (1991) Souza's Shrike attacking Violet-backed Sunbird. *Nyala* 15: 49.

Medland, R. D. (1992) Song-flight of White-bellied Sunbird. *Nyala* 16: 29-30.

Medway, Lord (1972) The Gunong Benom Expedition 1967. 6. The distribution and altitudinal zonation of birds and mammals on Gunong Benom. *Bull. Brit. Mus. (Nat. Hist), Zoology* 23: 103-154.

Medway, Lord & Nisbet, I. C. T. (1968) Bird report: 1966. *Malayan Nature J.* 21: 34-50.

Medway, Lord & Wells, D. R. (1976) *The birds of the Malay Peninsula*. Vol. 5. Witherby, London.

Mees, G. F. (1964) Four new subspecies of birds from the Moluccas and New Guinea. *Zool. Meded.* 40(15): 125-130.

Mees, G. F. (1965) Revision of *Nectarinia sericea* (Lesson). *Ardea* 53: 38-56.

Mees, G. F. (1966) A new subspecies of *Anthreptes malacensis* (Scopoli) from the Soela Islands (Aves, Nectariniidae). *Zool. Meded.* 41(18): 255-257.

Melville, D. S. & Round, P. D. (1984) Weights and gonad conditions of some Thai birds. *Bull. Brit. Orn. Club* 104: 127-138.

Meyer, A. B. (1874) Uber neue und ungenugend bekannte Vögel von New-Guinea und den Inseln der Geelvinksbai. *Sitzingsb. K. Akad. Wiss. Wien, Math. Naturwiss. Cl.* 69: 1-39; 70: 120-124.

Meyer, O. (1933) Vogeleier und Nester aus Neubrittanien, Sudsee. *Beitr. Fortpfl. Biol. Vögel* 9: 122-136.

Meyer de Schauensee, R. M. (1940) The birds of the Batu islands. *Proc. Acad. Nat. Sci. Philadelphia* 92: 23-42.

Meyer de Schauensee, R. M. (1984) *The birds of China*. Oxford University Press, Oxford, U.K.

Meyer de Schauensee, R. M. & Ripley, S. D. (1939) Zoological results of the George Vanderbilt Sumatran Expedition, 1936-1939. Part III. Birds from Nias Island. *Proc. Acad. Nat. Sci. Philadelphia* 91: 399-413.

Milne-Edwards, A. & Oustalet, E. (1885) Observations sur la faune de la Grande Comore. *Compt. Rend. Acad. Sci. Paris* 101: 218-220.

Milon, P. (1949) Notes d'observation sur les soui-mangas Malgaches. *Terre et Vie.* 1949 no.4: 1-10.

Milstein, P. le S. (1963) Nesting behaviour of Marico Sunbird and Greater Double-collared Sunbird. *Ostrich* 34: 46.

Moffet, J. (1990) The Malachite Sunbird. *Mirafra* 7: 7-8.

Moore, A. (1995) More anecdotal evidence for the type-locality of *Chalcomitra rubescens stangerii. Bull. Brit. Orn. Club* 115: 134-135.

Molyneux, T. G. (1976) Notes on birds of the northeastern Namib Desert Park, South-West Africa, and adjoining farms. *Madoqua* 9: 45-52.

Moreau, R. E. (1944) Some weights of African and of wintering Palaearctic birds. *Ibis* 86: 16-29.

Moreau, R. E. & Moreau, W. (1937) Biological and other notes on some East African birds. *Ibis* (14)1: 321-345.

Moreau, R. E. & Moreau, W. (1940) Incubation and fledging periods of African birds. *Auk* 57: 313-325.

Morel, G. J. & Morel, M.-Y. (1990) *Les oiseaux de Sénégambie. Notices et cartes de distribution.* Editions de l'ORSTOM, Paris.

Morioka, H. (1992) Tongue of two species of *Prionochilus* from the Philippines, with notes on feeding habits of flowerpeckers (Dicaeidae). *Japanese J. Orn.* 40(3): 85-92.

Mortimer, J. & Martin, E. (1991) Lesser Double-collared Sunbirds: new breeding areas. *Promerops* no. 198: 14.

Mostert, D. P., Siegfried, W. R. & Louw, G. N. (1980) *Protea* nectar and satellite fauna in relation to the food requirements and pollinating role of the Cape Sugarbird. *South Afr. J. Sci.* 76: 409-413.

Moyer, D. C. (1983) A record of the Angola White-bellied Sunbird *Nectarinia oustaleti* from Kesesya in southwestern Tanzania. *Scopus* 7: 52.

Moulton, J. C. (1914) Handlist of the birds of Borneo. *J. Straits Branch Royal Asiatic Soc.* 67: 125-191.

Mukherjee, P. (1981) A curious accident to the nest of a sunbird. *J. Bombay Nat. Hist. Soc.* 78: 170-171.

Müller, S. (1843) Bijdragen tot de kennis van Timor en eenige andere naburige eilanden. *Verh. Nat. Gesch. Ned. Overz. Bezitt. Land-en Volkenk.* 129-320.

Mundy, P. J. & Cook, A. W. (1972) Birds of Sokoto. Part 2. *Bull. Niger. Orn. Soc.* 9: 61-76.

Murphy, S. R., Reid, N., Yan, Z. & Venables, W. N. (1993) Differential passage time of mistletoe fruits through the gut of honeyeaters and flowerpeckers: effects on seedling establishment. *Oecologia* 93: 171-176.

Murray, R. M. (1968) St Lucia Park, South Africa, October: Scarlet-chested Sunbird *Nectarinia senegalensis. Lammergeyer* 9: 51.

Nash, A. D. & Nash, S. V. (1985) Breeding notes on some Padang-Sugihan birds. *Kukila* 2: 59-63.

Nash, S. V. & Nash, A. D. (1986) The ecology and natural history of the birds of Tanjung Puting National Park, Central Kalimantan, Indonesia. WWF/IUCN Project 1687.

Nash, S. V & Nash, A. D. (1988) An annotated checklist of the birds of Tanjung Puting National Park, Central Kalimantan. *Kukila* 3: 93-116.

de Naurois, R. (1979) The Emerald Cuckoo of São Tomé and Príncipe islands (Gulf of Guinea). *Ostrich* 50: 88-93.

de Naurois, R. (1983) Les oiseaux réproducteurs des iles de São Tomé et Príncipe: liste systematique commentée et indications zoogéographiques. *Bonn. Zool. Beitr.* 34: 129-148.

de Naurois, R. (1994) *Les oiseaux des iles du Golfe de Guinée (São Tomé, Prince et Annobon).* Instituto de Investigação Científica Tropical, Lisbon, Portugal.

Neelakantan, K. K. (1975) Curious behaviour of a Loten's Sunbird (*Nectarinia lotenia*). *J. Bombay Nat. Hist. Soc.* 72: 858-9.

Neumann, O. (1905) Vögel von Schoa und Süd Athiopien. *J. Orn.* 53: 229-300.

Newby, J. E. (1980) The birds of the Ouadi Rime–Ouadi Achim faunal reserve. A contribution to the study of the Chadian avifauna. *Malimbus* 2: 29-55.

Newby-Varty, B. V. (1945) Observations made on Umvukwe Ranch, 27 miles north of Banket, S. Rhodesia. *Ostrich* 16: 218-220.

Neuby [*sic*] Varty, B. V. (1948) Some nests and eggs. *Ostrich* 19: 158-160.

Newman, K., Johnston-Smith, N. & Medland, B. (1992) *Birds of Malawi. A supplement to Newman's Birds of southern Africa.* Southern Book Publishers, Halfway House, South Africa.

Ng'weno, F. (1990) Sunbird flying backwards. *Bull. East Afr. Nat. Hist. Soc.* 20: 27-28.

Oatley, T. B. (1995a) Selected recoveries reported to SAFRING: July 1994–December 1994. *Safring News* 24: 27-38.

Oatley, T. B. (1995b) Selected recoveries reported to SAFRING: January 1995–June 1995. *Safring News* 24: 68-75.

Oatley, T. B. (1996) Selected recoveries reported to SAFRING: July 1995–December 1995. *Safring News* 25: 31-38.

Oatley, T. B. (1996b) SASOL report on selected recoveries received at SAFRING: January 1996–June 1996. *Safring News* 25: 60-67.

Oatley, T. B. (1997) Selected recoveries reported to SAFRING: July 1996–December 1996. *Safring News* 26: 25-33.

Oatley, T. B. & Best, C. C. (1997) Selected recoveries reported to Safring: January 1997–June 1997. *Safring News* 26: 72-80.

Oberholser, H. C. (1912) Descriptions of one hundred and four new species and subspecies of birds from the Barussan Islands and Sumatra. *Smiths. Misc. Coll.* 60(7): 1-22.

Oberholser, H. C. (1923) A review of the genus *Prionochilus* Strickland and its closest allies. *Ohio J. Sci.* 23: 287-294.

Oberholser, H. C. (1932) The birds of the Natuna islands. *U.S. Natn. Mus. Bull.* 159: 1-137.

Ogilvie-Grant, W. R. (1894) *Aethopyga flavipectus* sp.n., *Eudrepanis jefferyi* sp.n., *Cinnyris obscurior* sp.n., *Cinnyris whiteheadi* sp.n., *Dicaeum luzoniense* sp.n., *Dicaeum obscurum* sp.n. *Bull. Brit. Orn. Club* 3: 49-50.

Ogilvie-Grant, W. R. & Whitehead, J. (1898) On the nests and eggs of some rare Philippine birds. *Ibis* (7)4: 231-247.

Oliver, P. J. (1991) Seychelles Sunbird *Nectarinia dussumieri* piercing flowers. *Bull. Brit. Orn. Club* 111: 174-175.

Ollerton, J. (1998) Sunbird surprise for syndromes. *Nature* 394: 726-727.

van Oort, E. D. (1911) On some new or rare birds from Sumatra, Java, Ceram and the Poeloe-Toedjegroup, north of Ceram. *Notes Leyden Mus.* 34: 59-65.

Owen, H. & Bresson, R. (1987) A 3-year study of the Seychelles Sunbird *Nectarinia dussumieri* on Cousin Island, Seychelles. Unpubl. report to ICBP, Cambridge.

Oxlee, D. (1988) "Crimson-throated" Black sunbird. *Witwatersrand Bird Club News* no. 142: 14.

Packenham, R. H. W. (1979) *The birds of Zanzibar and Pemba.* British Ornithologists' Union Check-list no. 2., London.

Parkes, K. C. (1962) New subspecies of birds from Luzon, Philippines. *Postilla* 67.

Parkes, K. C. (1963) The races of the Flaming Sunbird (*Aethopyga flagrans*). *Bull. Brit. Orn. Club* 83: 7-8.

Parkes, K. C. (1988) Three new subspecies of Philippine birds. *Nemouria* 30: 8.

Parkes, K. C. (1989) Notes on the Menage collection of Philippine birds 1: revision of *Pachycephala cinerea* (Pachycephalidae) and an overlooked subspecies of *Dicaeum trigonostigma* (Dicaeidae). *Nemouria* 33: 9.

Parrott, S. & Andrew, A. (1996) An annotated checklist of the birds of Way Kambas National Park, Sumatra. *Kukila* 8: 57-85.

Paton, D. C. & Collins, B. G. (1989) Bills and tongues of nectar-feeding birds: a review of morphology, function and performance with intercontinental comparisons. *Austral. J. Ecol.* 14: 473-506.

Pauw, A. (1998) Pollen transfer on birds' tongues. *Nature* 394: 731-732.

Payne, R. B. (1978) Microgeographic variation in songs of Splendid Sunbirds *Nectarinia coccinigaster* – population phenetics, habitats and song dialects. *Behaviour* 65: 282-308.

Paynter, R. A. (ed.) (1967) *Check-list of birds of the world: a continuation of the work of James L. Peters*, vol. 12. Museum of Comparative Zoology, Cambridge, Massachusetts, U.S.A.

Paz, U. (1983) Portrait of the Palestine Sunbird. *Israel – Land and Nature* 9: 7-10.

Pearson, D. S. (1975) A preliminary survey of the birds of Kutai Reserve, Kalimantan Timur, Indonesia. *Treubia* 28: 157-162.

Penny, M. (1974) *The birds of the Seychelles and the outlying islands.* Collins, London.

Pérez del Val, J. (1996) *Las aves de Bioko, Guinea Ecuatorial: guía de campo.* Edilesa, León, Spain.

Pettet, A. (1977) Seasonal changes in nectar feeding by birds at Zaria, Nigeria. *Ibis* 119: 291-308.

Pfeffer, P. (1961) Etude d'une collection d'oiseaux de Borneo. *Oiseau* 31: 9-29.

Pizzey, G. (1980) *A field guide to the birds of Australia.* Collins, Sydney.

Pizzey, G. & Knight, F. (1997) *The field guide to the birds of Australia.* Angus Robertson/Harper Collins, Australia.

Polhill, R. & Wiens, D. (1998) *Mistletoes of Africa.* Royal Botanic Gardens, Kew, U.K.

Porter, R. & Martins, R. (1993) OSME in Southern Yemen and Socotra. *OSME Bull.* 31: 1-4.

Porter, S. (1956) Nesting of Malachite Sunbird. *Avicult. Mag.* 62: 46-53.

Prendergast, H. D. V. (1983) Competition for nectar between sunbirds and butterflies. *Malimbus* 5: 51-53.

Priest, C. D. (1938) The breeding habits of the Violet-backed Sunbird *A. longuemarei nyassa,* Neumann. *Ostrich* 9: 99.

Priest, C. D. (1948) *Eggs of birds breeding in southern Africa.* Glasgow University Press, Glasgow.

Prigogine, A. (1952) Quatre nouveaux oiseaux du Congo Belge. *Rev. Zool. Bot. Afr.* 46: 407-415.

Prigogine, A. (1971) Les oiseaux de l'Itombwe et de son hinterland, vol. 1. *Ann. Mus. Roy. Afr. Centr.* 8ᵉ, Sci. Zool., 185: 1-298.

Prigogine, A. (1972) Nids et oeufs récolté au Kivu. 2. (République du Zaire). *Rev. Zool. Afr.* 85: 203-226.

Prigogine, A. (1975) Etude taxonomique de *Nectarinia alinae* et description de trois nouvelles formes de la République du Zaire. *Rev. Zool. Afr.* 89: 455-480.

Prigogine, A. (1977) Populations of the Scarlet-tufted Malachite Sunbird, *Nectarinia johnstoni* Shelley in central Africa and description of a new subspecies from the Republic of Zaire. *Mitt. Zool. Mus. Berlin* 53: 117-125.

Prigogine, A. (1978) Les oiseaux de l'Itombwe et de son hinterland, vol. 2. *Ann. Mus. Roy. Afr. Centr.* 8ᵉ, Sci. Zool., 185: 1-134.

Prigogine, A. (1979) Subspecific variation of Stuhlmann's Double-collared Sunbird, *Nectarinia stuhlmanni,* around the Albertine rift. *Gerfaut* 69: 225-238.

Prigogine, A. (1984) Les oiseaux de l'Itombwe et de son hinterland, vol. 3. *Ann. Mus. Roy. Afr. Centr.* 8ᵉ, Sci. Zool., 243: 1-146.

Prinzinger, R. & Jackel, S. (1986) Energy metabolism respiration frequency and oxygen-consumption per breathing act in 11 different sunbird species during day and night. *Experientia* 42: 1002-1003.

Prinzinger, R., Lubben, I. & Schuchmann, K.-L. (1989) Energy metabolism and body temperature in 13 sunbird species (Nectariniidae). *Comp. Biochem. Physiol. A. Comp. Physiol.* 92: 393-402.

Prinzinger, R., Schafer, T., Schuchmann, K.-L. (1992) Energy metabolism respiratory quotient and breathing parameters in two convergent small bird species the Fork-tailed Sunbird *Aethopyga christinae* (Nectariniidae) and the Chilean Humming-bird *Sephanoides sephaniodes* (Trochilidae). *J. Therm. Biol.* 17: 71-79.

Prys-Jones, R. P. & Diamond, A. W. (1984) Ecology of the land birds of the granitic and coralline islands of the Seychelles, with particular reference to Cousin Island and Aldabra Atoll. Pp.529-5558 in D. R. Stoddart (ed.) *Bioeography and ecology of the Seychelles Islands.* W. Junk, The Hague.

Pucheran, J. (1853) Voyage au Pole Sud et dans l'oceanie sur les corvettes L'Astrolabe et La Zelee 1837-1840. *Zoologie* 3 (Mamm. et Ois.): 47-158.

Pyke, G. H. (1979) The economics of territory size and time budget in the Golden-winged Sunbird. *Amer. Nat.* 114: 131-145.

Quantrill, B. & Quantrill, R. (1998) The birds of the Parcours Vita, Yaoundé, Cameroon. *Malimbus* 20: 1-14.

Rabor, D. S. (1977) *Philippine birds and mammals.* U.P. Science Education Center, Quezon City.

Rahman, M. M., Baksha, M. W. & Sterringa, J. T. (1993) Ethological observations on the Purple Sunbird (*Nectarinia asiatica* Latham): a mistletoe-frequenting bird. *Indian For.* 119: 388-403.

Rahmani, A. R., Shobrak, M. Y. & Newton, S. F. (1994) Birds of the Tihamah coastal plains of Saudi Arabia. *OSME Bull.* 32: 1-19.

Rajathurai, S. (1996) The birds of Batam and Bintan Islands, Riau Archipelago. *Kukila* 8: 86-113.

Raju, A. J. S. (1998) Foraging of sunbirds on some plant species of sub-tropical India. In Adams, N. J. & Slotow, R. H. (eds.) Proc. 22 Internatn. Orn. Congr., Durban. *Ostrich* 69: 375.

Raju, A. J. S. & Reddi, C. S. (1989) Pollination biology of *Anisomeles indica* and *A. malabarica* (Lamiaceae). *Plant Species Biol.* 4: 157-167.

Rand, A. L. (1941) Results of the Archbold Expeditions. No. 32. New and interesting birds from New Guinea. *Amer. Mus. Novit.* 1102.

Rand, A. L. (1942a) Results of the Archbold Expedition. No. 42. Birds of the 1936-37 New Guinea Expedition. *Bull. Amer. Mus. Nat. Hist.* 79: 289-366.

Rand, A. L. (1951) Review of the subspecies of the sunbird *Nectarinia jugularis. Fieldiana Zool.* 31: 597-607.

Rand, A. L. (1961) The tongue and nest of certain flowerpeckers (Aves: Dicaeidae). *Fieldiana Zool.* 39: 581-587.

Rand, A. L. (1967) The flower-adapted tongue of a Timaliinae bird and its implications. *Fieldiana Zool.* 51: 53-63.

Rand, A. L. & Gilliard, E. T. (1967) *Handbook of New Guinea birds.* Weidenfeld and Nicholson, London.

Rand, A. L. & Rabor, D. S. (1957) New birds from the Philippines. *Fieldiana Zool.* 42: 13-18.

Rand, A. L. & Rabor, D. S. (1960) Birds of the Philippine Islands: Siquijor, Mount Malindang, Bohol and Samar. *Fieldiana Zool.* 35: 221-441.

Rand, A. L. & Rabor, D. S. (1967) New birds from Luzon, Philippine Islands. *Fieldiana Zool.* 51: 89.

Rand, A. L. & Rabor, D. S. (1969) New birds from Camiguin South, Philippines. *Fieldiana Zool.* 51: 157-168.

Rebelo, A. G. (1987a) Sunbird feeding at *Satyrium odorum* Sond. flowers. *Ostrich* 58: 185-186.

Rebelo, A. G. (1987b) Visits to *Oldenburgia grandis* (Thunb.) Baillon (Asteraceae) by the Cape Sugarbird *Promerops cafer. Ostrich* 58: 186-187.

Rebelo, A. G. (1991) Community organisation of sunbirds in the Afro-tropical region. Pp.1180-1187 in Bell, B. D., Cossee, R. O., Flux, J. E. C., Heather, B. D., Hitchmough, R. A., Robertson, C. J. R. & Williams, M. J. (eds.) *Acta 20 Congressus Internationalis Ornothologici.* Vol. 2. New Zealand Ornithological Congress Trust Board, Wellington.

Redman, N. J., Lambert, F. & Grimmett, R. (1984) Some observations of scarce birds in Nepal. *J. Bombay Nat. Hist. Soc.* 81: 49-53.

Reed, B. E. (1971) Near misses with van Hasselt's Sunbird. *Avic. Mag.* 77: 22-23.

Reid, N. (1983) Seasonal occurrence of the Mistletoebird in the inner northeastern suburbs of Adelaide. *South Austral. Orn.* 29: 60-63.

Reid, N. (1987) The Mistletoebird and Australian mistletoes: co-evolution or coincidence? *Emu* 87: 130-131.

Reid, N. (1989) Dispersal of mistletoes by honeyeaters and flowerpeckers: components of seed dispersal quality. *Ecology* 70: 137-145.

Reid, N. (1990) Mutualistic interdependence between mistletoes *Amyema quandang* and Spiny-cheeked Honeyeaters and Mistletoebirds in an arid woodland. *Austral. J. Ecol.* 15: 175-190.

Reid, N. (1997) Behaviour, voice and breeding of the Mistletoebird *Dicaeum hirundinaceum* in arid woodland. *Victorian Naturalist* 114: 135-148.

Rensch, B. (1928) Neue Vogelrassen von den Kleinen Sunda-Inseln III. *Orn. Monatsb.* 36: 80-81.

Rensch, B. (1931) Uber einige Vogelsammlungen des Buitenzorger Museums von den Kleinen Sunda-Inseln. *Treubia* 13: 371-395.

Richardson, D. M. & Baker, A. J. (1981) Last record of the Cebu Island subspecies of the Orange-bellied Flowerpecker *Dicaeum trigonostigma pallidius. Bull. Brit. Orn. Club* 101: 275-276.

Richardson, K. C. & Wooller, R. D. (1988) The alimentary tract of a specialist frugivore the mistletoebird *Dicaeum hirundinaceum* in relation to its diet. *Austral. J. Zool.* 36: 373-382.

Richmond, C. W. (1912) Descriptions of five new birds from the west coast of Sumatra. *Proc. Biol. Soc. Washington* 25: 103-105.

Ridgway, R. (1894) Descriptions of some new birds from Aldabra, Assumption, and Gloriosa Islands, collected by Dr. W. L. Abbott. *Proc. U.S. Natn. Mus.* 17: 371-373.

Riley, J. (1997) The birds of Sangihe and Talaud, North Sulawesi. *Kukila* 9: 3-36.

Riley, J. H. (1935) Three new forms of birds from the Philippine Islands and Siam. *Proc. Biol. Soc. Washington* 48: 147-148.

Riley, J. H. (1939) A genus and three new forms of birds from Borneo. *J. Washington Acad. Sci.* 29: 39-41.

Riley, J. H. (1940) Three new forms of birds from South Annam. *Proc. Biol. Soc. Washington* 53: 79-80.

Ripley, S. D. (1959a) Comments on birds from the Western Papuan Islands. *Postilla* 38.

Ripley, S. D. (1959b) Competition between sunbird and honeyeater species in the Moluccan islands. *Amer. Nat.* 93: 127-132.

Ripley, S. D. (1960) Two new birds from Angola. *Postilla* 43.

Ripley, S. D. & Rabor, D. S. (1961) The avifauna of Mount Katanglad. *Postilla* 50.

Ripley, S. D. & Rabor, D. S. (1966) *Dicaeum proprium*, new species (Aves: family Dicaeidae). *Proc. Biol. Soc. Washington* 79: 305-306.

Robinson, H. C. & Kloss, C. B. (1918) On two new species of flowerpeckers (Dicaeidae) from the Malay Region. *J. Fed. Mal. States Mus.* 7: 239.

Robson, C. (1988) Recent reports. *Bull. Oriental Bird Club* 7: 38.

Robson, C. (1992) Recent reports. *Bull. Oriental Bird Club* 15: 45.

Robson, C. (2000) *A field guide to the birds of South-East Asia.* New Holland, London.

Robson, C., Buck, H., Farrow, D. S., Fisher, T. & King, B. F. (1998) A birdwatching visit to the Chin Hills, West Burma (Myanmar), with notes from nearby areas. *Forktail* 13: 109-119.

Robson, C. & Davidson, P. (1996) Some recent records of Philippine birds. *Forktail* 11: 162-167.

de Roo-de Ridder, A. & de Roo-de Ridder, F. (1969) The first records of *Cinnyris "ogilvie-granti"* (Bannerman) from the Congo Republic. *Rev. Zool. Bot. Afr.* 80: 391-396.

Rothschild, W. & Hartert, E. (1896) Contributions to the ornithology of the Papuan Islands IV. List of a collection made by Albert S. Meek on Fergusson, Trobriand, Egum and Woodlark Islands. *Novit. Zool.* 3: 233-251.

Rothschild, Lord & Hartert, E. (1914) *Dicaeum geelvinkianum rosseli* subsp.n. *Bull. Brit. Orn. Club* 35: 32.

Rothschild, Lord & Hartert, E. (1926) On the avifauna of Yunnan, with critical notes. *Novitat. Zool.* 33: 189-343.

Rozendaal, F. G. & Dekker, R. W. R. J. (1989) An annotated checklist of the birds of the Dumoga-Bone National Park, North Sulawesi. *Kukila* 4: 85-108.

Salomonsen, F. (1933) Zur Systematik und Biologie von *Promerops.* *Orn. Monatsber.* 41: 37-40.

Salomonsen, F. (1953) Miscellaneous notes on Philippine birds. *Vidensk. Medd. Dansk naturhist. Foren.* 115: 205-281.

Salomonsen, F. (1960a) Notes on flowerpeckers (Aves, Dicaeidae) 1. The genera *Melanocharis, Ramphocharis* and *Prionochilus. Amer. Mus. Novit.* 1990.

Salomonsen, F. (1960b) Notes on flowerpeckers (Aves, Dicaeidae) 2. The primitive species of the genus *Dicaeum. Amer. Mus. Novit.* 1991.

Salomonsen, F. (1960c) Notes on flowerpeckers (Aves, Dicaeidae) 3. The species group *Dicaeum concolor* and the superspecies *Dicaeum erythrothorax. Amer. Mus. Novit.* 2016.

Salomonsen, F. (1961) Notes on flowerpeckers (Aves, Dicaeidae) 4. *Dicaeum igniferum* and its derivatives. *Amer. Mus. Novit.* 2057.

Salomonsen, F. (1964) Some remarkable new birds from Dyaul Island, Bismarck Archipelago, with zoogeographical notes. *Biol. Skrift. Kong. Dansk Vidensk. Selsk.* 14: 1-37.

Salomonsen, F. (1967) Dicaeidae. Pp.166-208 in R. A. Paynter (ed.) *Check-list of birds of the world,* vol. 12. Museum of Comparative Zoology, Cambridge, Massachusetts.

Salvadori, T. (1878) Intorno agl'individui del genere *Hermotimia* dell'isola del Duca di York. *Atti R. Acad. Sci. Torino* 13: 529-534.

Salvadori, T. (1880) Prodromus ornothologiae Papuasiae et Moluccarum. *Ann. Mus. Civ. Stor. Nat. Genova* 16: 62-82.

Sargeant, D. E. (1994) Recent ornithological observations from São Tomé and Príncipe Islands. *Bull. Afr. Bird Club* 1: 96-102.

Scammell, K. M. (1963) Breeding in Malachite Sunbird. *Avicult. Mag.* 70: 158-162.

Schlamowitz, R., Hainsworth, F. R. & Wolf, L. L. (1976) On the tongues of sunbirds. *Condor* 78: 104-107.

Schlegel, H. (1871) Observations zoologiques IV. *Ned. Tijdsch. Dierk.* 4: 1-32.

Schmidt, R. K. (1964) The Lesser Double-collared Sunbird, *Cinnyris chalybeus* (Linnaeus) in the south-western Cape. *Ostrich* 35: 86-94.

Schmidt, R. (1991) Lesser Double-collared Sunbirds nesting in gardens. *Promerops* no. 197: 12.

Schnell, G. D., Watt, D. J. & Douglas, M. E. (1985) Statistical comparison of proximity matrices: applications in animal behavior. *Anim. Behav.* 33: 239-253.

Schodde, R. (1977) Contributions to Papuasian ornithology VI. Survey of the birds of southern Bougainville island, Papua New Guinea. *Div. Wildlife Res. Tech. Pap.* 34, CSIRO, Australia.

Schoeman, M. E. (1990) Behaviour observations of Greater Double-collared Sunbird. *Hornbill* 23: 22-23.

Schönwetter, M. (1980-1984) *Handbuch der Oologie.* Vol 3. Akademie-Verlag, Berlin.

Schouteden, H. (1949) Contribution à l'étude de la faune ornithologique du Katanga (Congo Belge). *Rev. Zool. Bot. Afr.* 42: 158-174.

Schouteden, H. (1959) Un nectariniidé nouveau pour la faune congolaise: *Nectarinia bocagei* Shell. *Rev. Zool. Bot. Afr.* 59: 326-328.

Sclater, P. L. (1877) On the birds collected by Mr. George Brown, C.M.Z.S., on the Duke of York Island, and on adjoining parts of New Ireland and New Britain. *Proc. Zool. Soc. Lond.* 96-114.

Sclater, P. L. (1883) On birds collected in the Timor-Laut or Tenimber group of islands by Mr. Henry O. Forbes. *Proc. Zool. Soc. Lond.:* 48-58.

Sclater, P. L. & Hartlaub, G. (1881) On the birds collected in Socotra by Prof. I. B. Balfour. *Proc. Zool. Soc. Lond.:* 165-175.

Sclater, W. L. (1930) *Systema Avium Aethiopicarum: a systematic list of the birds of the Ethiopian Region.* Part II. British Ornithologists' Union, London.

Sclater, W. L. & Mackworth-Praed, C. (1918) A list of the birds of the Anglo-Egyptian Sudan, based on the collections of Mr. A. L. Butler, Mr. A. Chapman and Capt. H. Lynes, R.N., and Major Cuthbert Christy, R.A.M.C. (T.F.). Part II. Alaudidae – Hirundinidae. *Ibis* (10)6: 602-720.

Sclater, W. L. & Moreau, R. E. (1933) Taxonomic and field notes on some birds of north-eastern Tanganyika Territory. *Ibis* (13)3: 187-219.

Seddon, N., Ekstrom, J. M. M., Capper, D. R., Isherwood, I. S., Muna, R., Pople, R. G., Tarimo, E. & Timothy, J. (1999) Notes on the ecology and conservation status of key bird species in Nilo and Nguu North Forest Reserves, Tanzania. *Bird Conserv. Internatn.* 9: 9-28.

Seiler, H. W. & Fraser, M. W. (1985) Ageing & sexing guide: Cape Sugarbirds *Promerops cafer. Safring News* 14: 91-92.

Seiler, H. W. & Prys-Jones, R. P. (1989) Mate competition, mate guarding, and unusual timing of copulation in the Cape Sugarbird (*Promerops cafer*). *Ostrich* 60: 159-164.

Seiler, H. W. & Rebelo, A. G. (1987) A sexual difference in the Cape Sugarbird's role as pollinator of *Protea lepidocarpodendron? Ostrich* 58: 43-45.

Serle, W. (1940) Field observations on some northern Nigerian birds. Part II. *Ibis* (14)4: 1-47.

Serle, W. (1943) Notes on East African birds. *Ibis* 85: 55-92.

Serle, W. (1949) The birds of Sierra Leone, Part IV. *Ostrich* 20: 114-126.

Serle, W. (1950) A contribution to the ornithology of the British Cameroons. *Ibis* 92: 602-638.

Serle, W. (1951) The Double-collared Sunbird *Cinnyris reichenowi* Sharpe. *Nigerian Field* 16: 20-21.

Serle, W. (1956) The Splendid Sunbird (*Cinnyris coccinigaster* (Latham). *Nigerian Field* 21: 78.

Serle, W. (1957) A contribution to the ornithology of the Eastern Region of Nigeria. *Ibis* 99: 371-418, 628-685.

Serle, W. (1963) A new race of sunbird from West Africa. *Bull. Brit. Orn. Club* 83: 118-119.

Serle, W. (1965) A third contribution to the ornithology of the British Cameroons. *Ibis* 107: 60-94, 230-246.

Serventy, D. L. (1970) Torpidity in Australian birds. *Emu* 70: 201-202.

Sevastopulo, D. G. (1980a) Sunbird building in close proximity to a wasp's nest. *Entomologist's Mon. Mag.* 115: 26.

Sevastopulo, D. G. (1980b) Collared Sunbird (*Anthreptes collaris* Vieillot) building near wasps' nests. *Entomologist's Mon. Mag.* 116: 3.

Sharpe, R. B. (1876a) Contributions to the ornithology of Borneo. Part I. *Ibis* (3)6: 29-52.

Sharpe, R. B. (1876b) Prof. Steere's expedition to the Philippines. *Nature* 14: 297-298.

Sharpe, R. B. (1876c) Mr. O. C. Stone's expedition to New Guinea. *Nature* 14: 338-339.

Sharpe, R. B. (1877) Contributions to the ornithology of Borneo. Part II. *Ibis* (4)1: 1-25.

Sharpe, R. B. (1879) A list of the birds of Labuan Island and its dependencies. *Proc. Zool. Soc. Lond.*: 317-353.

Sharpe, R. B. (1881) On the birds of Sandakan, northeast Borneo. *Proc. Zool. Soc. Lond.*: 790-800.

Sharpe, R. B. (1889) On the ornithology of northern Borneo with notes by John Whitehead. Part IV. *Ibis* (6)1: 409-443.

Sharpe, R. B. (1893) Bornean notes, no. I. *Ibis* (6)5: 547-563.

Sharpe, R. B. (1897) *Dicaeum hosii* n.sp. *Bull. Brit. Orn. Club* 6: 48.

Sheldon, F. H. (1985) The taxonomy and biogeography of the Thick-billed Flowerpecker complex in Borneo. *Auk* 102: 606-612.

Sheldon, F. H., Moyle, R. G. & Kennard, J. (in press) *Ornithological history, gazetteer, and annotated checklist of Sabah, north Borneo.* Ornithological Monographs.

Shelley, G. E. (1876-1880) *Monograph of the Nectariniidae.* Published by the author, London.

Sheppard, D. M. (1958) Bird notes from Molo 2. The garden. *J. East Afr. Nat. Hist. Soc.* 23: 6-8.

Showler, D. A. & Davidson, P. (1996) The Socotra Sunbird *Nectarinia balfouri. Sandgrouse* 17: 148-150.

Sibley, C. G. & Ahlquist, J. E. (1974) The relationships of the African sugarbirds (*Promerops*). *Ostrich* 45: 22-30.

Sibley, C. G. & Ahlquist, J. E. (1983) The phylogeny and classification of birds based on the data of DNA-DNA hybridization. *Current Orn.* 1: 245-292.

Sibley, C. G. & Ahlquist, J. E. (1990) *Phylogeny and classification of the birds of the world.* Yale University Press, New Haven.

Sibley, C. G. & Monroe, B. L. (1990) *Distribution and taxonomy of birds of the world.* Yale University Press, New Haven.

Sibley, C. G. & Monroe, B. L. (1993) *A supplement to distribution and taxonomy of birds of the world.* Yale University Press, New Haven.

Siegfried, W. R. (1985) Nest site fidelity of Malachite Sunbird and parasitism by Klaas's Cuckoo. *Ostrich* 56: 277.

Siegfried, W. R., Rebelo, A. G. & Prys-Jones, R. P. (1985) Stem thickness of *Erica* plants in relation to avian pollination. *Oikos* 45: 153-155.

Siemens, L. (1983) Field notes from AUEA biology department. *East Afr. Nat. Hist. Soc. Bull.*: 71.

Sievi, J. R. (1974) Breeding habits of the Yellow-bellied Sunbird. *Honeyguide* 79: 42-43.

da Silva, R. (1992) High tide at Negombo Lagoon. *Oriental Bird Club Bull.* 15: 15-17.

Simpson, K. N. G. (1997) A brief review of the Mistletoebird *Dicaeum hirundinaceum* (Shaw) 1793 (Aves: Dicaeidae) and an introductory bibliography. *Victorian Naturalist* 114: 143-148.

Simpson, K. & Day, N. (1984) *The birds of Australia.* Lloyd O'Neil, South Yatta, Australia.

Sinclair, I. & Langrand, 0. (1998) *Birds of the Indian Ocean islands.* Struik, Cape Town.

Singh, A. P. (2000) Birds of lower Garhwall Himalayas: Dehra Dun valley and neighbouring hills. *Forktail* 16: 101-124.

Singh, P. (1995) Recent bird records from Arunachal Pradesh, India. *Forktail* 10: 65-104.

Skead, C. J. (1953) A study of the Black Sunbird, *Chalcomitra a. amethystina* (Shaw). *Ostrich* 24: 159-166.

Skead, C. J. (1954) A study of the Larger Double-collared Sunbird, *Cinnyris a. afra* (Linnaeus). *Ostrich* 25: 76-88.

Skead, C. J. (1962) A study of the Collared Sunbird, *Anthreptes collaris. Ostrich* 33: 38-40.

Skead, C. J. (1967) *The sunbirds of southern Africa; also the sugarbirds, the white-eyes and the spotted creeper.* A. A. Balkema, Cape Town.

Skead, C. J. (1972) A juvenile Klaas Cuckoo *Chrysococcyx klaas* with its hosts in late June 1971. *Ostrich* 43: 134.

Skinner, N. J. (1969) Notes on the breeding of the Pygmy Long-tailed Sunbird *Hedydipna platura* at Zaria. *Bull. Niger. Orn. Soc.* 6: 124-126.

Smythies, B. E. (1957) An annotated checklist of the birds of Borneo. *Sarawak Mus. J.* 7(9): 523-818.

Smythies, B. E. (1960) *The birds of Borneo.* Oliver & Boyd, Edinburgh.

Smythies, B. E. (1981) *The birds of Borneo.* 3rd edition. Sabah Foundation, Kota Kinabalu, and Malayan Nature Society, Kuala Lumpur (Ed. Earl of Cranbrook).

Smythies, B. E. (1986) *The birds of Burma.* 3rd edition. Nimrod Press, Liss, Hampshire, U.K.

Smythies, B. E. (1999) *The birds of Borneo.* 4th edition. Natural History Publications (Borneo), Sdn. Bhd., Kota Kinabalu, Sabah (Ed. G. W. H. Davison).

Snow, D. W. (1950) The birds of São Tomé and Príncipe in the Gulf of Guinea. *Ibis* 92: 579-595.

Spottiswood, C. (1993) Orangebreasted Sunbirds feeding on the ground. *Promerops* no. 208: 16-17.

Stattersfield, A. J., Crosby, M. J., Long, M. J. & Wege, D. C. (1998) *Endemic Bird Areas of the world: priorities for biodiversity conservation.* BirdLife International (Conservation Series 7), Cambridge, U.K.

Stepanyan, P. S. (1985) *Aethopyga christinae sokolovi* Stepanyan, ssp. nov. (Nectariniidae, Aves) from South Vietnam. *Ornitologiya* 20: 133-138. [In Russian]

Stewart, D. R. M. & Stewart, J. (1964) Anting behaviour in the Bronze Sunbird. *J. East Afr. Nat. Hist. Soc. Coryndon Mus.* 5: 92.

Steyn, P. (1973) A nest of Gurney's Sugarbird. *Honeyguide* 73: 29-30.

Steyn, P. (1997) Cape Sugarbird: pollinator of proteas. *Africa: Birds & Birding* 2: 27-32.

Stones, A. J., Lucking, R. S., Davidson, P. J. & Wahyu Raharjaningtrah (1997) Checklist of the birds of the Sula Islands (1991), with particular reference to Taliabu Island. *Kukila* 9: 37-55.

Stresemann, E. (1929) Eine Vogelsammlung aus Kwangsi. *J. Orn.* 77: 323-337.

Stresemann, E. (1940) Die Vögel von Celebes. *J. Orn.* 88: 1-135.

Stresemann, E. & Grote, H. (1926) *Cinnyris humbloti mohelica* subsp. nov. *Orn. Monatsb.* 34: 147.

Stresemann, E. & Paludan, K. (1932) Vorlaufiges uber die ornithologischen Ergebnisse der Expedition Stein 1931-2. I. Zur Ornithologie der Insel Waigeu. *Orn. Monatsb.* 40(6): 13-18.

Stuart, S. N. & Hutton, J. M. (eds.) (1977) The avifauna of the East Usambara Mountains, Tanzania. Unpublished.

Stuart, S. N. & Jensen, F. P. (1985) The avifauna of the Uluguru Mountains, Tanzania. *Gerfaut* 75: 155-197.

Stuart, S. N. & Jensen, F. P. (1986) The status and ecology of montane forest bird species in western Cameroon. Pp.38-105 in Stuart, S. N. (ed.) *Conservation of Cameroon montane forests. Report of the ICBP Cameroon montane forest survey, November 1983– April 1984.* International Council for Bird Preservation, Cambridge, U.K.

Stuart, S. N., Jensen, F. P. & Brøgger-Jensen, S. (1987) Altitudinal zonation of the avifauna in Mwanihana and Magombera forests, eastern Tanzania. *Gerfaut* 77: 165-186.

Stuart, S. N. & van der Willigen, J. A. (1980) Is Moreau's Sunbird *Nectarinia moreaui*, a hybird species? *Scopus* 4: 56-58.

Subramanya, S. & Radhamani, T. R. (1993) Pollination by birds and bats. *Current Sci.* 65: 201-209.

Sultana, A. & Khan, J. A. (2001) Birds of the oak forests in the Kumaon Himalaya, Uttar Pradesh, India. *Forktail* 16: 131-146.

Svendsen, J. O., Hansen, L. A., Fjeldså, J., Rahner, M. C., Pedersen, L. B., Kisbye, H., Edvardsen, E. & Kiure, J. (1995) Section 5. Ornithology. Pp.33-54 in J. O. Svendsen & L. A. Hansen (eds.) *Report on the Uluguru Biodiversity Survey 1993.* Royal Society for the Protection of Birds, Danish Centre for Tropical Biodiversity and Tanzania Forestry Research Institute, Sandy, Bedfordshire, U.K.

de Swardt, D. H. (1989) Some observations on the local movements of Gurney's Sugarbird in the Lydenburg area, Transvaal. *Safring News* 18: 31-32.

de Swardt, D. H. (1990) Ageing and sexing. Gurney's Sugarbird *Promerops gurneyi. Safring News* 19: 57-60.

de Swardt, D. H. (1991a) The seasonal movements of Gurney's Sugarbird *Promerops gurneyi* in the Lydenburg area, Transvaal. *Ostrich* 62: 40-44.

de Swardt, D. H. (1991b) Measurements and moult in the Greater Doublecollared Sunbird. *Safring News* 20: 21-25.

de Swardt, D. H. (1992a) Distribution, biometrics and moult of Gurney's Sugarbird *Promerops gurneyi. Ostrich* 63: 13-20.

de Swardt, D. H. (1992b) Olive Sunbird breeding at the Natal botanical gardens. *Albatross* no. 312: 17-18.

de Swardt, D. H. (1995) Malachite Sunbird ringing in the Free State. *Safring News* 24: 15-18.

de Swardt, D. H. (1997) Gurney's Sugarbird *Promerops gurneyi.* Pp.486-487 in *The atlas of Southern African birds.* Vol. 2. Passerines. Harrison, J. A., Allan, D. G., Underhill, L. G., Herremans, M., Tree, A. J., Parker, V., & Brown, C. J. (eds.) BirdLife South Africa, Johannesburg.

de Swardt, D. H. & Bothma, N. (1992) Notes on the breeding biology of Gurney's Sugarbird. *Ostrich* 63: 136-137.

de Swardt, D. H. & Buys, P. J. (1992) Cape Sugarbird at Jagersfontein, southern Orange Free State. *Ostrich* 63: 136.

de Swardt, D. H. & Schoeman, S. (1997) Sunbird recaptures and seasonal movements at Lydenburg, Mpumalanga Province. *Safring News* 26: 13-15.

Swinhoe, R. (1870) On the ornithology of Hainan. *Ibis* (2)6: 240.

Swynnerton, C. F. M. (1908) Further notes on the birds of Gazaland. *Ibis* (9)2: 1-107.

Swynnerton, C. F. M. (1916) Short cuts by birds to nectaries. *J. Linn. Soc. Bot.* 43: 381-415.

Sykes, D. T. (1984) Unusual nest site of Collared Sunbird. *Witwatersrand Bird Club News* no. 124: 2.

Tarboton, W. R., Kemp, M. I. & Kemp, A. C. (1987) *Birds of the Transvaal*. Transvaal Museum, Pretoria.

Taylor, J. S. (1946) Notes on the Malachite Sunbird, *Nectarinia famosa*. *Ostrich* 17: 254-257.

Thiollay, J.-M. (1985) The birds of Ivory Coast: status and distribution. *Malimbus* 7: 1-59.

Thompson, M. C. (1966) Birds from North Borneo. *Univ. Kansas Publs. Mus. Nat. Hist.* 17: 377-433.

Thonnerieux, Y., Walsh, J. F. & Bortoli, L. (1989) L'avifaune de la ville de Ouagadougou et ses environs (Burkina Faso). *Malimbus* 11: 7-40.

Ticehurst, C. B. (1918) The plumage of the Purple Honeysucker (*Aracnecthra asiatica*). *J. Bombay Nat. Hist. Soc.* 26: 286-287.

Travis, J. (1982) A method for the statistical analysis of time energy budgets. *Ecology* 63: 19-25.

Traylor, M. A. & Archer, A. L. (1982) Some results of the Field Museum 1977 expedition to south Sudan. *Scopus* 6: 5-12.

Traylor, M. A. & Parelius, D. (1967) A collection of birds from the Ivory Coast. *Fieldiana Zool.* 51: 91-117.

Tree, A. J. (1988) Ringing report for the Association 1986/87. *Honeyguide* 34: 86-88.

Tree, A. J. (1991) A ringing guide to selected species of Zimbabwean sunbirds. *Safring News* 20: 13-20.

Tree, A. J. (1997a) Bronze Sunbird *Nectarinia kilimensis*. P.491 in *The atlas of southern African birds*. Vol. 2. *Passerines*. Harrison, J. A., Allan, D. G., Underhill, L. G., Herremans, M., Tree, A. J., Parker, V. & Brown, C. J. (eds.). BirdLife South Africa, Johannesburg.

Tree, A. J. (1997b) Purplebanded Sunbird *Nectarinia bifasciata*. Pp.496-497 in *The atlas of southern African birds*. Vol. 2. *Passerines*. Harrison, J. A., Allan, D. G., Underhill, L. G., Herremans, M., Tree, A. J., Parker, V. & Brown, C. J. (eds.). BirdLife South Africa, Johannesburg.

Tree, A. J. (1997c) Coppery Sunbird *Nectarinia cuprea*. P.498 in *The atlas of southern African birds*. Vol. 2. *Passerines*. Harrison, J. A., Allan, D. G., Underhill, L. G., Herremans, M., Tree, A. J., Parker, V. & Brown, C. J. (eds.). BirdLife South Africa, Johannesburg.

Tree, A. J. (1997d) Miombo Doublecollared Sunbird *Nectarinia manoensis*. Pp.502-503 in *The atlas of southern African birds*. Vol. 2. *Passerines*. Harrison, J. A., Allan, D. G., Underhill, L. G., Herremans, M., Tree, A. J., Parker, V. & Brown, C. J. (eds.). BirdLife South Africa, Johannesburg.

Tree, A. J. (1997e) Yellowbellied Sunbird *Nectarinia venusta*. Pp.506-507 in *The atlas of southern African birds*. Vol. 2. *Passerines*. Harrison, J. A., Allan, D. G., Underhill, L. G., Herremans, M., Tree, A. J., Parker, V. & Brown, C. J. (eds.). BirdLife South Africa, Johannesburg.

Tree, A. J. (1997f) Whitebelled Sunbird *Nectarinia talatala*. Pp.508-509 in *The atlas of southern African birds*. Vol. 2. *Passerines*. Harrison, J. A., Allan, D. G., Underhill, L. G., Herremans, M., Tree, A. J., Parker, V. & Brown, C. J. (eds.). BirdLife South Africa, Johannesburg.

Tree, A. J. (1997g) Grey Sunbird *Nectarinia veroxii*. Pp.512-513 in *The atlas of southern African birds*. Vol. 2. *Passerines*. Harrison, J. A., Allan, D. G., Underhill, L. G., Herremans, M., Tree, A. J., Parker, V. & Brown, C. J. (eds.). BirdLife South Africa, Johannesburg.

Tree, A. J. (1997h) Olive Sunbird *Nectarinia olivacea*. Pp.514-515 in *The atlas of southern African birds*. Vol. 2. *Passerines*. Harrison, J. A., Allan, D. G., Underhill, L. G., Herremans, M., Tree, A. J., Parker, V. & Brown, C. J. (eds.). BirdLife South Africa, Johannesburg.

Tree, A. J. (1997i) Scarletchested Sunbird *Nectarinia senegalensis*. Pp.516-517 in *The atlas of southern African birds*. Vol. 2. *Passerines*. Harrison, J. A., Allan, D. G., Underhill, L. G., Herremans, M.,

Tree, A. J., Parker, V. & Brown, C. J. (eds.). BirdLife South Africa, Johannesburg.

Tree, A. J. (1997j) Black Sunbird *Nectarinia amethystina*. Pp.518-520 in *The atlas of southern African birds*. Vol. 2. *Passerines*. Harrison, J. A., Allan, D. G., Underhill, L. G., Herremans, M., Tree, A. J., Parker, V. & Brown, C. J. (eds.). BirdLife South Africa, Johannesburg.

Tree, A. J. (1997k) Violetbacked Sunbird *Anthreptes longuemarei*. P.521 in *The atlas of southern African birds*. Vol. 2. *Passerines*. Harrison, J. A., Allan, D. G., Underhill, L. G., Herremans, M., Tree, A. J., Parker, V. & Brown, C. J. (eds.). BirdLife South Africa, Johannesburg.

Tree, A. J. (1997l) Collared Sunbird *Anthreptes collaris*. Pp.524-525 in *The atlas of southern African birds*. Vol. 2. *Passerines*. Harrison, J. A., Allan, D. G., Underhill, L. G., Herremans, M., Tree, A. J., Parker, V. & Brown, C. J. (eds.). BirdLife South Africa, Johannesburg.

Tree, A. J., Hustler, K., Aspinwall, D. R. & Fernsby, N. (1991) Shelley's Sunbird in Zimbabwe: the first certain record south of the Zambesi. *Honeyguide* 37: 120-122.

Tristram, H. B (1889a) *A catalogue of a collection of birds belonging to H. B. Tristram*. Durham.

Tristram, H. B. (1889b) On a small collection of birds from the Louisiade and d'Entrecasteux Islands. *Ibis* (6)1: 553-558.

Turner, D. A. & Forbes-Watson, A. (1979) *Nectarinia adelberti* au Cameroon. *Oiseau et R.F.O.* 49: 158.

Tweeddale, A. Marquis of (1877a) Reports on the collections of birds made during the voyage of HMS Challenger. No. II. On the birds of the Philippine Islands. *Proc. Zool. Soc. Lond.*: 534-551.

Tweeddale, A. Marquis of (1877b) Contributions to the ornithology of the Philippines. No. II. On the collection made by Mr. A. H. Everett in the island of Zebu. *Proc. Zool. Soc. Lond.*: 755-769.

Tweeddale, A. Marquis of (1877c) Descriptions of four new species of birds from the Indian Region. *Ann. Mag. Nat. Hist.* (4)20: 94-96.

Tweeddale, A. Marquis of (1877d) Description of some new species of birds. *Ann. Mag. Nat. Hist.* (4)20: 533-538.

Tye, A. & MacAulay, L. R. (1993) The races of Olive Sunbird *Nectarinia olivacea* on the Gulf of Guinea Islands. *Malimbus* 14: 65-66.

Tyler, D. (1992) Black Sunbird at Dassies Hoek. *Promerops* no. 206: 15.

Underhill, L. G. & Fraser, M. W. (1989) Bayesian estimate of the number of Malachite Sunbirds feeding at an isolated and transient nectar source. *J. Field Orn.* 60: 382-387.

Uys, C. J. (1981a) Lesser Double-collared Sunbird (760) nesting in suburban garden, Newlands. *Promerops* no. 146: 6-7

Uys, C. J. (1981b) Malachite Sunbird nesting in unusual site. *Promerops* no. 147: 6.

Verheught, W. J. M., Skov, H., Danielsen, H. & Danielsen, F. (1993) Notes on the birds of the tidal lowlands and floodplains of South Sumatra Province, Indonesia. *Kukila* 6: 53-84.

Vernon, C. J. (1971) Owl foods and other notes from a trip to southwest Africa. *Ostrich* 42: 153-154.

Vigors, N. A. (1831) [A collection of birds from Manila.] *Proc. Zool. Soc. Lond.* 1831: 96-98.

Vincent, A. W. (1949) On the breeding habits of some African birds. *Ibis* 91: 313-345.

Viney, C. & Phillipps, K. (1978) *A colour guide to Hong Kong birds*. Government Printer, Hong Kong.

Viney, C. & Phillipps, K. (1988) *Birds of Hong Kong*. 4th edition. Government Printer, Hong Kong.

Vuilleumier, F. (1993) Notes on birds observed in beech (*Fagus*) forests in the Maoersham Natural Reserve, Guanxi Autonomous Region, China. *Bull. Brit. Orn. Club* 113: 152-166.

Wait, W. E. (1931) *Manual of the birds of Ceylon*. 2nd. edition. Dulau & Co. Ltd., London.

Walden, A. Viscount (1870) On the sunbirds of the Indian and Australian Regions. *Ibis* (2)6: 18-51.

Wallace, A. R. (1863) List of birds collected in the island of Bouru (one of the Moluccas), with descriptions of the new species. *Proc. Zool. Soc. London*: 18-32.

Wallace, A. R. (1865) Descriptions of new birds from the Malay Archipelago. *Proc. Zool. Soc. London*: 474-481.

Walsh, [J.] F. (1966) A nest of the Violet-backed Sunbird. *Bull. Niger. Orn. Soc.* 3: 70-71.

Walsh, [J.] F. (1967) Inland records of the Mouse-brown Sunbird. *Bull. Niger. Orn. Soc.* 3: 74-75.

Walsh, J. F., Cheke, R. A. & Sowah, S. A. (1990) Additional species and breeding records of birds in the Republic of Togo. *Malimbus* 12: 2-18.

Waltert, M. & Faber, K. (2000) Olive-bellied Sunbird *Nectarinia chloropygia* host to Cassin's Honeybird *Prodotiscus insignis*. *Malimbus* 22: 86.

Watling, D. (1983) Ornithological notes from Sulawesi. *Emu* 83: 247-261.

Watson, J. (1984) Land birds: endangered species of the granitic Seychelles. Pp.513-528 in D. R. Stoddart (ed.) *Bioegeography and ecology of the Seychelles Islands*. W. Junk, The Hague.

Welch, G. & Welch, H. (1998) Mystery birds from Djibouti. *Bull. African Bird Club* 5: 46-50.

Wells, D. R. (1966) The Violet-backed Sunbird nesting in Nigeria. *Bull. Niger. Orn. Soc.* 3: 72-74.

Wells, D. R., Hails, C. J. & Hails, A. J. (1978) A study of the birds of the Gunung Mulu National Park, Sarawak, with emphasis on those of the lowland forest. Unpublished report to the Royal Geographical Society, London.

Wetmore, A. (1930) A systematic classification for the birds of the world. *Proc. U.S. Natn. Mus.* 76: 1-8.

Wetmore, A. (1940) A systematic classification of the birds of the world. *Smithsonian Misc. Coll.* 99: 1-11.

Wetmore, A. (1951) A revised classification for the birds of the world. *Smithsonian Misc. Coll.* 117: 1-22.

Wetmore, A. (1960) A classification for the birds of the world. *Smithsonian Misc. Coll.* 139: 1-37.

Whistler, H. (1949) *A popular handbook of Indian birds*. 4th. edition. Gurney & Jackson, London.

White, C. M. N. (1963) *A revised check-list of African flycatchers, tits, tree-creepers, sunbirds, white-eyes, honeyeaters, buntings, finches, weavers and waxbills*. Government Printer, Lusaka.

White, C. M. N. & Bruce, M. D. (1986) *The birds of Wallacea (Sulawesi, the Moluccas and Lesser Sunda Islands, Indonesia): annotated checklist*. British Ornithologists' Union Checklist no. 7, London.

Whitehead, J. (1899) Field-notes on birds collected in the Philippine Islands in 1893-6. *Ibis* (6) 1: 81-111, 210-246, 381-399, 485-501.

Wilhelm, K., Comtesse, H. & Pflumm, W. (1980) Influence of the food supply on the song of the male Yellow-bellied Sunbird (*Nectarinia venusta*). *Zeitschr. Tierpsychol.* 54: 185-202.

Wilhelm, K., Comtesse, H. & Pflumm, W. (1982) Influence of sucrose solution concentration on the song and courtship behaviour of the male Yellow-bellied Sunbird (*Nectarinia venusta*). *Zeitschr. Tierpsychol.* 60: 27-40.

Wilkinson, R., Dutson, G., Sheldon, B., Darjono & Yus Rusila Noor (1991) The avifauna of the Barito Ulu region, central Kalimantan. *Kukila* 5: 99-116.

Wille, H. (1964) *Nectarinia bocagei* Shelley, een nieuwe soort voor Kongo. *Gerfaut* 54: 77-83.

Williams, A. A. E. (1978) Accidental parasitization of an Eastern Double-collared Sunbird by a Variable Sunbird. *Scopus* 2: 25-26.

Williams, A. J., Braine, S. G. & Bridgeford, P. (1986) The biology of the Dusky Sunbird in S.W.A./Namibia: a review. *Lanioturdus* 22: 4-9.

Williams, J. B. (1993a) Energetics of incubation in free-living Orange-breasted Sunbirds in South Africa. *Condor* 95: 115-126.

Williams, J. B. (1993b) Nest orientation of Orange-breasted Sunbirds in southern Africa. *Ostrich* 64: 40-42.

Williams, J. G. (1950a) A new race of *Cinnyris regius* from Tanganyika. *Ibis* 92: 644-645.

Williams, J. G. (1950b) On the status of *Cinnyris mediocris moreaui*. *Ibis* 92: 645-647.

Williams, J. G. (1950c) Further notes on *Cinnyris moreaui*. *Ibis* 92: 647.

Williams, J. G. (1951a) Notes on *Scepomycter winifredae* and *Cinnyris loveridgei*. *Ibis* 93: 469-470.

Williams, J. G. (1951b) *Nectarinia johnstoni*: a revision of the species, together with data on plumages, moults and habits. *Ibis* 93: 579-595.

Williams, J. G. (1951c) Notes on *Anthreptes reichenowi yokanae*. *Bull. Brit. Orn. Club* 71: 48-50.

Williams, J. G. (1952) Notes on the African Sunbird *Cinnyris afra graueri* Neumann. *J. East Afr. Nat. Hist. Soc.* 20: 440-442.

Williams, J. G. (1953a) On the status of the Seychelles Sunbirds, *Cyanomitra dussumieri* and *Cyanomitra mahei*. *Ibis* 95: 545.

Williams, J. G. (1953b) Revision of *Cinnyris sovimanga*: with description of a new race. *Ibis* 95: 501-504.

Williams, J. G. (1953c) *Cinnyris mediocris*: a revision of the species and description of a new race. *Bull. Brit. Orn. Club* 73: 8-11.

Williams, J. G. (1953d) On the nest and eggs of *Anthreptes reichenowi yokanae*. *Bull. Brit. Orn. Club* 73: 33.

Williams, J. G. (1954) A systematic revision and natural history of the Shining Sunbird of Africa. *Condor* 57: 249-262.

Williams, J. G. (1955) *Cinnyris oustaleti*: notes on plumages and habits. *Ibis* 97: 150-153.

Williams, J. G. (1956) A new Golden-winged Sunbird from Kenya. *Bull. Brit. Orn. Club* 76: 136-139.

Winterbottom, J. M. (1962) Breeding season of Long-tailed Sugarbird *Promerops cafer* (L.). *Ostrich* 33: 77.

Winterbottom, J. M. (1964) Notes on the comparative ecology of the Long-tailed Sugarbird and the Orange-breasted Sunbird. *Ostrich* 35: 239-240.

Witherby, H. F. (1905) On a collection of birds from Somaliland. *Ibis* (8) 5: 507-524.

Wolf, L. L. (1975) Energy intake and expenditure in a nectar-feeding sunbird. *Ecology* 56: 92-104.

Wolf, L. L. & Gill, F. B. (1986) Physiological and ecological adaptations of high montane sunbirds and hummingbirds. Pp.103-119 in F. Vuilleumier & M. Monasterio (eds.) *High altitude tropical biogeography*. Oxford University Press/American Museum of Natural History, New York.

Wolf L. L. & Wolf, J. S. (1976) Mating system and reproductive biology of Malachite Sunbirds. *Condor* 78: 27-39.

Wolters, H. E. (1965) *Nectarinia chalybea pintoi* und *Nectarinia seimundi traylori* nomina nove. *J. Orn.* 106: 357.

Wolters, H. E. (1977) Die Gattungen der Nectariniidae (Aves, Passeriformes). *Bonn Zool. Beitr.* 28: 82-101.

Wolters, H. E. (1979) *Die Vogelarten der Erde*. Lief. 4. 241-320. Paul Parey, Hamburg and Berlin.

Woodcock, M. W. (1980) *Collins handguide to the birds of the Indian sub-continent including India, Pakistan, Bangladesh, Sri Lanka and Nepal*. Collins, London.

Wooler, R. D. (1982) Feeding interactions between sunbirds and sugarbirds. *Ostrich* 53: 114-115.

van Wyk (1984) Malachite Sunbirds take a shower. *Witwatersrand Bird Club News* 126: 17.

Young, T. P. (1982) Bird visitation, seed-set, and germination rates in two species of *Lobelia* on Mount Kenya. *Ecology* 63: 1983-1986.

Young, T. P. & Evans, T. P. (1993) Alpine vertebrates of Mount Kenya, with particular notes on the rock hyrax. *J. East Afr. Nat. Hist. Soc. & Natn. Mus.* 82: 55-79.

Zedlitz, O.(1910) Einige neue Formen aus Nordost-Africa. *Orn. Monatsb.* 18: 57-59.

Zilberman, R., Moav, B. & Yom-Tov, Y. (1999) Extra-pair paternity in the socially monogamous Orange-tufted Sunbird (*Nectarinia osea osea*). *Israel Journal of Zoology* 45: 407-421.

Zimmer, J. T. (1918) Some notes on the birds of southern Palawan and adjacent islands. *Phil. J. Sci.* 13: 327-357.

Zimmerman, D. A., Turner, D. A. & Pearson, D. J. (1996) *Birds of Kenya and northern Tanzania*. Christopher Helm, London.

Zumpt, F. (ed.) (1961) *The arthropod parasites of vertebrates in Africa south of the Sahara (Ethiopian Region)*. Vol. I. *(Chelicerata)*. Publications of the South African Institute for Medical Research vol. 9 no. 50, Johannesburg.

Zumpt, F. (ed.) (1966) *The arthropod parasites of vertebrates in Africa south of the Sahara (Ethiopian Region)*. Vol. III. *(Insecta excl. Phthiraptera)*. Publications of the South African Institute for Medical Research vol. 13 no. 52, Johannesburg.

INDEX

Species are listed by their vernacular name (e.g. Olive-backed Sunbird) and by their scientific name. Specific scientific names are followed by their generic name as used in the book (e.g. *jugularis, Cinnyris*) and subspecific names are followed by both the specific and generic names (e.g. *aurorus, Cinnyris jugularis*). Numbers in *italic* refer to the first page of the relevant systematic entry. Numbers in **bold** type refer to the colour plate numbers.

abbotti, Cinnyris sovimanga 84, *323*
Abyssinian Sunbird. *See* Shining Sunbird
acik, Chalcomitra senegalensis 76, *236*
adelberti, Chalcomitra 76, *227*
adelberti, Chalcomitra adelberti 227
aeneum, Dicaeum 48, *165*
aeneum, Dicaeum aeneum 165
aeruginosum, Dicaeum agile 38, *142*
Aethopyga 331
Aethopyga, pulcherrima 335
afer, Cinnyris 96, *273*
afer, Cinnyris afer 274
affine, Dicaeum agile 142
affinis, Arachnothera 126, *358*
affinis, Arachnothera affinis 358
agile, Dicaeum 38, *140*
agile, Dicaeum agile 142
albiventris, Cinnyris venustus 86, *309*
albopunctatum, Dicaeum geelvinkianum 48, *163*
aldabrensis, Cinnyris sovimanga 323
alfredi, Cyanomitra olivacea 222
alinae, Cyanomitra 70, *219*
alinae, Cyanomitra alinae 220
alter, Cinnyris habessinicus 298
Amani Sunbird **16** 62, 181, 196, *205*
Amethyst Sunbird **22** 74, 211, 228, 229, *231*, 234, 283
Amethyst-throated Sunbird. *See* Amethyst Sunbird
amethystina, Chalcomitra 74, *231*
amethystina, Chalcomitra amethystina 233
amicorum, Cinnyris manoensis 264
Anabathmis 207
anambae, Anthreptes malacensis 185
anchietae, Anthreptes 56, *182*
Anchieta's Sunbird **13** 56, *182*
andamanicus, Cinnyris jugularis 320
anderseni, Cinnyris regius 275
angkanensis, Aethopyga nipalensis 341
angolensis, Anthreptes longuemarei 60, *190*
Anjouan Sunbird **30** 90, 324, *328*
annae, Dicaeum 38, *140*
annae, Dicaeum annae 140
annamensis, Aethopyga gouldiae 116, *339*
anomala, Aethopyga saturata 118, *344*
Anthobaphes 211
anthonyi, Dicaeum 40, *148*
anthonyi, Dicaeum anthonyi 149
Anthreptes 181
antioproctis, Dicaeum trigonostigma 154
apo, Dicaeum ignipectum 169
Apo Sunbird **42** 114, 318, *332*, 335, 337
apolis, Cinnyris sovimanga 84, *323*
Apricot-breasted Sunbird **25** 80, *321*
Arachnothera 350
ardens, Promerops gurneyi 32, *131*
armata, Arachnothera robusta 354
arolasi, Aethopyga shelleyi 338
arturi, Nectarinia kilimensis 104, *252*

ashantiensis, Cinnyris superbus 303
Ashy Flowerpecker **8** 46, *161*
asiaticus, Cinnyris 90, *316*
asiaticus, Cinnyris asiaticus 317
aspasioides, Leptocoma sericea 80, *244*
assamensis, Aethopyga saturata 118, *344*
assamensis, Chalcoparia singalensis 58, *178*
assimile, Dicaeum trigonostigma 154
atita, Arachnothera longirostra 352
aurantium, Anthreptes 62, *192*
aurata, Arachnothera magna 359
aurea, Chalcomitra fuliginosa 228
aureolimbatum, Dicaeum 40, *147*
aureolimbatum, Dicaeum aureolimbatum 147
auricapilla, Leptocoma sericea 245
auriceps, Leptocoma sericea 80, *245*
aurora, Cinnyris jugularis 82
aurorus, Cinnyris jugularis 320
australe, Dicaeum 42, *150*
Australian Flower Swallow. *See* Mistletoebird
Australian Flowerpecker. *See* Mistletoebird
australis, Aethopyga nipalensis 341
axantha, Leptocoma sperata 243
axillaris, Deleornis 56, *180*

balfouri, Chalcomitra 72, *238*
Banded Green Sunbird. *See* Banded Sunbird
Banded Sunbird **16** 62, *196*. *See also* Purple-naped Sunbird
bannermani, Cyanomitra 72, *215*
Bannerman's Blue-headed Sunbird. *See* Bannerman's Sunbird
Bannerman's Sunbird **21** 72, 213, *215*
bansoensis, Cyanomitra oritis 68, *219*
bantenensis, Chalcoparia singalensis 178
batesi, Cinnyris 66, *312*
Bates's Sunbird **18** 66, 179, 194, 198, 221, 222, 294, *312*
batuense, Dicaeum cruentatum 175
Beautiful Long-tailed Sunbird. *See* Beautiful Sunbird
Beautiful Sunbird **41** 112, 201, 259, *281*, 286, 287, 288, 297, 314
beccarii, Aethopyga siparaja 347
beccarii, Dicaeum ignipectum 169
becki, Dicaeum aeneum 165
bella, Aethopyga shelleyi 338
bensoni, Cinnyris mediocris 278
besti, Dicaeum trigonostigma 154
bicolor, Dicaeum 40, *149*
bicolor, Dicaeum bicolor 149
Bicoloured Flowerpecker **15** 40, 137, 143, 147, *149*, 155, 159
Bifasciated Sunbird. *See* Purple-banded Sunbird
bifasciatus, Cinnyris 108, *289*
bifasciatus, Cinnyris bifasciatus 290
bineschensis, Cinnyris chloropygius 261
birgitae, Anthreptes malacensis 186

Black Sunbird **25** 80, 162, 164, *243*, 318. *See also* Amethyst Sunbird
Black-bellied Sunbird **41** 112, 281, 287, *288*, 297
Black-belted Flowerpecker **6** 42, *151*
Black-breasted Sunbird. *See* Olive-backed Sunbird
Black-fronted Flowerpecker **10** 50, *166*, 171
Black-sided Flowerpecker **11** 52, 136, 138, 157, *169*
Black-throated Sunbird **44** 118, 183, 242, 246, 318, 339, 340, 342, *343*, 349. *See also* Olive-backed Sunbird
blanci, Aethopyga nipalensis 341
Blood-breasted Flowerpecker **11** 52, 136, 153, 166, 167, 169, *171*
Blue Sunbird. *See* Western Violet-backed Sunbird
Blue-headed Sunbird **20** 70, 213, 216, *219*. *See* Bannerman's Sunbird; Cameroon Sunbird
Blue-naped Sunbird. *See* Purple-naped Sunbird
Blue-throated Brown Sunbird **21** 72, 187, 207, 213, *216*, 218, 219, 229
Blue-throated Little Sunbird. *See* Plain-backed Sunbird
Blue-throated Sunbird. *See* Blue-throated Brown Sunbird; Plain-backed Sunbird
bocagei, Nectarinia 102, 247
Bocage's Montane Double-collared Sunbird. *See* Montane Double-collared Sunbird
Bocage's Sunbird **36** 102, *247*
boehndorffi, Cyanomitra verticalis 215
boltoni, Aethopyga 114, 332
boltoni, Aethopyga boltoni 333
bonga, Dicaeum ignipectum 169
bonita, Aethopyga shelleyi 338
Bornean Spiderhunter. *See* Streaky-breasted Spiderhunter
borneana, Chalcoparia singalensis 178
borneanum, Dicaeum concolor 158
borneensis, Anthreptes malacensis 185
bouvieri, Cinnyris 90, 293
Bouvier's Orange-tufted Sunbird. *See* Orange-tufted Sunbird
Bouvier's Sunbird. *See* Orange-tufted Sunbird
brasiliana, Leptocoma sperata 78, 243
brevirostris, Cinnyris asiaticus 317
Bronze Sunbird **37** 104, 248, 249, *251*, 253, 255, 314
Bronzy Sunbird. *See* Bronze Sunbird
Brown Sunbird. *See* Mouse-brown Sunbird
Brown-backed Flowerpecker **4** 38, 135, 140, *143*, 155
Brown-throated Sunbird. *See* Plain-throated Sunbird
buchenorum, Cinnyris sovimanga 323
buettikoferi, Arachnothera longirostra 352
buettikoferi, Cinnyris 80, 321
Buff-bellied Flowerpecker. *See* Fire-breasted Flowerpecker
Buff-breasted Sunbird. *See* Variable Sunbird
Buff-chested Sunbird. *See* Variable Sunbird
Buff-throated Sunbird **23** 76, *227*
bungurense, Dicaeum everetti 143
buruensis, Cinnyris jugularis 320
buvuma, Cinnyris superbus 303
Buzzing Flowerpecker **7** 44, 140, 147, 148, 149, 150, *155*

Caconda White-bellied Sunbird. *See* Oustalet's Sunbird
caena, Arachnothera modesta 357
caeruleogula, Leptocoma sericea 245
cafer, Promerops 32, 131
cagayanensis, Anthreptes malacensis 185
cagayanensis, Dicaeum hypoleucum 156

calcostetha, Leptocoma 80, 246
cambodiana, Aethopyga saturata 344
cambodianum, Dicaeum ignipectum 50, 169
Cameroon Blue-headed Sunbird. *See* Cameroon Sunbird
Cameroon Sunbird **19** 68, 207, *218*
cameroonensis, Deleornis fraseri 180
Cape Long-tailed Sugarbird. *See* Cape Sugarbird
Cape Sugarbird **1** 32, 129, *131*
cara, Aethopyga siparaja 347
Carmelite Sunbird **22** 74, *228*, 229, 231
Cebu Flowerpecker **6** 42, *150*, 159
celebensis, Anthreptes malacensis 185
celebicum, Dicaeum 52, 170
celebicum, Dicaeum celebicum 171
centrale, Dicaeum geelvinkianum 163
cephaelis, Cyanomitra obscura 224
ceylonense, Dicaeum erythrorhynchos 157
Chad Orange-tufted Sunbird. *See* Palestine Sunbird
chalceus, Cinnyris cupreus 100, 316
chalcomelas, Cinnyris 94, 292
Chalcomitra 226
Chalcoparia 177
chalybeus, Cinnyris 92, 264
chalybeus, Cinnyris chalybeus 266
changamwensis, Cyanomitra olivacea 222
chapini, Cinnyris stuhlmanni 268
Chestnut-headed Sugarbird. *See* Gurney's Sugarbird
chlorigaster, Anthreptes malacensis 186
chlorolaema, Leptocoma sericea 80, 245
chloropygius, Cinnyris 98, 259
chloropygius, Cinnyris chloropygius 260
christianae, Leptocoma sericea 80, 245
christinae, Aethopyga 118, 342
christinae, Aethopyga christinae 343
chrysochlore, Dicaeum chrysorrheum 145
chrysogenys, Arachnothera 124, 355
chrysogenys, Arachnothera chrysogenys 355
chrysorrheum, Dicaeum 38, 144
chrysorrheum, Dicaeum chrysorrheum 145
cinereicollis, Arachnothera longirostra 352
cinereigulare, Dicaeum trigonostigma 42, 154
Cinnyris 259
clarae, Arachnothera 126, 356
clarae, Arachnothera clarae 356
clementiae, Cinnyris jugularis 82, 320
cnecolaemum, Dicaeum trigonostigma 154
coccinigaster, Cinnyris 110, 299
cochrani, Leptocoma sericea 245
Coguno Double-collared Sunbird. *See* Neergaard's Sunbird
Collared Sunbird **17** 64, 181, 187, 195, *197*, 201, 203, 308
collaris, Hedydipna 64, 197
comorensis, Cinnyris 90, 328
concolor, Arachnothera modesta 357
concolor, Dicaeum 44, 157
concolor, Dicaeum concolor 158
congensis, Cinnyris 106, 286
Congo Black-bellied Sunbird. *See* Congo Sunbird
Congo Sunbird **38** 106, *286*
convergens, Anthreptes malacensis 186
Copper Sunbird **35** 100, 247, 281, 289, 308, *313*
Copper-coloured Sunbird. *See* Copper Sunbird
Copper-throated Sunbird **25** 80, 183, 184, 187, 242, *246*, 316, 337, 339, 340, 341, 342, 343, 348

377

Coppery Sunbird. *See* Copper Sunbird
coquerelli, Cinnyris 90, *329*
corinna, Leptocoma sericea 245
cornelia, Leptocoma sericea 245
crassirostris, Arachnothera 124, *352*
cretum, Dicaeum igniferum 167
Crimson Sunbird **45** 120, 183, 184, 187, 242, 244,
    246, 335, 339, 340, 342, 343, *345*, 348, 349
Crimson-backed Sunbird **24** 78, *240*, 316, 330, 345
Crimson-breasted Flowerpecker **3** 36, *136*, 137, 138,
    168, 169, 171
Crimson-crowned Flowerpecker **8** 46, *160*, 167, 170
crossensis, Chalcomitra rubescens 230
cruentata, Chalcomitra senegalensis 236
cruentatum, Dicaeum 54, *174*
cruentatum, Dicaeum cruentatum 175
culionensis, Prionochilus plateni 137
cupreonitens, Nectarinia famosa 104, *255*
cupreus, Cinnyris 100, *313*
cupreus, Cinnyris cupreus 315
cyanocephala, Cyanomitra verticalis 72, *215*
cyanolaema, Cyanomitra 72, *216*
cyanolaema, Cyanomitra cyanolaema 217
Cyanomitra 213

dabryii, Aethopyga gouldiae 116, *340*
daphoenota, Aethopyga flagrans 335
dartmouthi, Nectarinia johnstoni 257
davao, Dicaeum pygmaeum 159
dayakanum, Dicaeum trigonostigma 154
decolor, Aethopyga flagrans 335
decorosa, Aethopyga pulcherrima 336
decorsei, Cinnyris oseus 296
Deleornis 178
deminuta, Chalcomitra amethystina 74, *233*
derooi, Cyanomitra alinae 220
Dicaeini 134
Dicaeum 139
dilutior, Arachnothera longirostra 352
diuatae, Aethopyga primigenius 114, *332*
diuatae, Dicaeum nigrilore 148
diversum, Dicaeum geelvinkianum 163
djamdjamensis, Hedydipna collaris 200
dolichorhynchum, Dicaeum ignipectum 169
dorsale, Dicaeum trigonostigma 154
Drepanorhynchus 258
Dreptes 210
Dusky São Tomé Sunbird. *See* São Tomé Sunbird
Dusky Sunbird **35** 100, 306, *310*
dussumieri, Cinnyris 74, *325*
duyvenbodei, Aethopyga 114, *336*
Duyvenbode's Sunbird. *See* Elegant Sunbird

Eastern Double-collared Sunbird **33** 96, 259, 263,
    270, 271, *277*, 279, 280, 303
Eastern Olive Sunbird **18** 66, 194, 195, 213, *221*,
    222, 225, 312
Eastern Violet-backed Sunbird. *See* Kenya Violet-backed
    Sunbird
eboensis, Chalcomitra adelberti 76, *228*
eichhorni, Leptocoma sericea 245
elachior, Hedydipna collaris 200
Elegant Sunbird **42** 114, 318, *336*
emmae, Leptocoma sperata 243
erlangeri, Cinnyris nectarinoides 112, *289*
erythroceria, Cinnyris 106, *287*

erythrorhynchos, Dicaeum 44, *156*
erythrorhynchos, Dicaeum erythrorhynchos 157
erythrothorax, Dicaeum 46, *160*
erythrothorax, Dicaeum erythrothorax 161
eumecis, Leptocoma sperata 243
everetti, Arachnothera affinis 358
everetti, Dicaeum 38, *143*
everetti, Dicaeum everetti 143
eximia, Aethopyga 118, *341*
eximium, Dicaeum 48, *164*
eximium, Dicaeum eximium 165
exquisitus, Cinnyris solaris 322
extremus, Anthreptes malacensis 186
ezrai, Aethopyga nipalensis 341

falkensteini, Cinnyris venustus 86, *309*
famosa, Nectarinia 104, *253*
famosa, Nectarinia famosa 255
fasciatus, Cinnyris johannae 301
fazoqlensis, Cinnyris venustus 86, *310*
finschi, Dicaeum agile 38, *142*
Fire-breasted Flowerpecker **10** 50, 136, 138, 140,
    153, 157, *168*, 169
Fire-tailed Sunbird **46** 122, 242, 318, 339, 340,
    342, 343, *349*
fischeri, Cyanomitra veroxii 68, *226*
flagrans, Aethopyga 114, *334*
flagrans, Aethopyga flagrans 335
Flame-breasted Flowerpecker **8** 46, *160*
Flame-breasted Sunbird **27** 84, 184, 318, *321*
Flame-crowned Flowerpecker **5** 40, 143, *148*, 155
flamifera, Arachnothera longirostra 352
Flaming Sunbird **42** 114, 242, 318, *334*, 335, 337
flammaxillaris, Cinnyris jugularis 82, *320*
flavescens, , Aethopyga ignicauda 350
flaviclunis, Dicaeum trigonostigma 154
flavigaster, Arachnothera 124, *354*
flavigaster, Cinnyris jugularis 320
flavipectus, Aethopyga shelleyi 338
flaviventris, Leptocoma zeylonica 240
flavostriata, Aethopyga siparaja 120, *347*
Fork-tailed Sunbird **44** 118, 177, 242, 246, 318,
    339, 340, *342*, 343, 349
formosum, Dicaeum ignipectum 169
fraseri, Deleornis 56, *179*
fraseri, Deleornis fraseri 179
Fraser's Sunbird. *See* Scarlet-tufted Sunbird
frenatus, Cinnyris jugularis 82, *320*
fuelleborni, Cinnyris mediocris 96, *278*
fugaensis, Dicaeum pygmaeum 159
fulgidum, Dicaeum hirundinaceum 54, *173*
fuliginosa, Chalcomitra 74, *228*
fuliginosa, Chalcomitra fuliginosa 229
fuscus, Cinnyris 100, *310*
fuscus, Cinnyris fuscus 311

gabonicus, Anthreptes 60, *187*
gadowi, Nectarinia kilimensis 104, *252*
galenae, Aethopyga saturata 344
garguensis, Hedydipna collaris 200
geelvinkianum, Dicaeum 48, *162*
geelvinkianum, Dicaeum geelvinkianum 163
Giant Sunbird. *See* São Tomé Sunbird
Golden-rumped Flowerpecker **4** 38, *140*
Golden-winged Sunbird **38** 106, *258*
gouldiae, Aethopyga 116, *339*

gouldiae, Aethopyga gouldiae 339
Gould's Sunbird **43** 116, 184, 239, 242, 246, 318,
   339, 340, 342, 343, 349
Goulpourah Sunbird. *See* Crimson Sunbird
granti, Cyanomitra obscura 224
graueri, Cinnyris stuhlmanni 268
grayi, Leptocoma sericea 80, 245
Greater Double-collared Sunbird **33** 96, 264, 266,
   267, 269, 270, *272*
Greater Yellow-eared Spiderhunter. *See* Spectacled
   Spiderhunter
Green Sugarbird. *See* Malachite Sunbird
Green Sunbird **16** 62, 179, *195*, 196, 198, 221, 223
Green-headed Olive Sunbird. *See* Green-headed
   Sunbird
Green-headed Sunbird **21** 72, 207, *213*, 215, 216,
   218, 219, 222, 227
Green-tailed Sunbird **43** 116, 184, 242, 246, 318,
   339, *340*, 342, 343, 349
Green-throated Sunbird **22** 74, 228, *229*, 231, 234
Grey Sunbird. *See* Mouse-coloured Sunbird
Grey-bellied Double-collared Sunbird. *See* Southern
   Double-collared Sunbird
Grey-breasted Spiderhunter **48** 126, 353, *357*, 358
Grey-chinned Sunbird. *See* Green Sunbird
Grey-headed Sunbird **13** 56, 179, *180*, 194. *See also*
   Grey-hooded Sunbird
Grey-hooded Sunbird **42** 114, *332*, 333, 335
Grey-sided Flowerpecker **11** 52, 147, 160, 167, 169, *170*
Grey-throated Sunbird. *See* Plain-throated Sunbird
griseigularis, Anthreptes malacensis 58, 186
Guimaras Flowerpecker. *See* Black-belted Flowerpecker
guimarasensis, Aethopyga flagrans 114, 335
Guinean Olive Sunbird. *See* Western Olive Sunbird
guineensis, Cyanomitra obscura 224
Gunning's Sunbird. *See* Plain-backed Sunbird
gurneyi, Promerops 32, 129
gurneyi, Promerops gurneyi 130
Gurney's Long-tailed Sugarbird. *See* Gurney's Sugarbird
Gurney's Sugarbird **1** 32, *129*, 131
gutturalis, Chalcomitra senegalensis 76, 236

habessinicus, Cinnyris 92, 297
habessinicus, Cinnyris habessinicus 298
Hachisuka's Sunbird. *See* Grey-hooded Sunbird
haematostictum, Dicaeum 42, 151
hanieli, Dicaeum sanguinolentum 172
harrissoni, Arachnothera chrysogenys 356
hartlaubii, Anabathmis 70, 208
Hartlaub's Sunbird. *See* Príncipe Subird
haussarum, Anthreptes longuemarei 190
Hedydipna 197
heliocalus, Anthreptes malacensis 186
heliogona, Aethopyga siparaja 347
heliolusius, Anthreptes malacensis 186
hellmayri, Cinnyris habessinicus 298
henkei, Leptocoma sperata 78, 243
hindustanicus, Cinnyris lotenius 331
hirundinaceum, Dicaeum 54, 172
hirundinaceum, Dicaeum hirundinaceum 173
Hodgson's Sunbird. *See* Black-throated Sunbird
hofmanni, Cinnyris shelleyi 286
horsfieldi, Aethopyga nipalensis 341
hosei, Dicaeum cruentatum 175
humbloti, Cinnyris 84, 328
humbloti, Cinnyris humbloti 328

Humblot's Sunbird **27** 84, 324, *327*
hunteri, Chalcomitra 76, 237
hunteri, Chalcomitra hunteri 237
Hunter's Sunbird **23** 76, 233, *237*
hypodila, Hedydipna collaris 200
Hypogramma 206
hypogrammicum, Hypogramma 64, 206
hypogrammicum, Hypogramma hypogrammicum 206
hypoleucum, Dicaeum 44, 155
hypoleucum, Dicaeum hypoleucum 156

idenburgi, Cinnyris jugularis 320
idius, Deleornis fraseri 180
igneiventris, Cinnyris venustus 86, 310
ignicapillus, Prionochilus percussus 36, 136
ignicauda, Aethopyga 122, 349
ignicauda, Aethopyga ignicauda 350
ignicolle, Dicaeum hirundinaceum 173
igniferum, Dicaeum 50, 166
igniferum, Dicaeum igniferum 167
ignipectum, Dicaeum 50, 168
ignipectum, Dicaeum ignipectum 169
ignitum, Dicaeum cruentatum 175
ignotum, Dicaeum pectorale 162
inclusa, Cinnyris fuscus 311
Indian Purple-rumped Sunbird. *See* Purple-rumped
   Sunbird
inexpectatum, Dicaeum bicolor 40, 149
infrenatus, Cinnyris jugularis 320
insularis, Aethopyga siparaja 347
intermedium, Dicaeum trigonostigma 154
intermedius, Cinnyris asiaticus 90, 317
internota, Chalcoparia singalensis 178
interposita, Chalcoparia singalensis 178
iris, Anthreptes malacensis 186
isidroi, Dicaeum trigonostigma 155
isolata, Aethopyga gouldiae 340
itombwensis, Nectarinia johnstoni 257

jacksoni, Nectarinia tacazze 102, 250
Javan Sunbird **46** 122, *348*
jefferyi, Aethopyga pulcherrima 114, 336
johannae, Cinnyris 110, 300
johannae, Cinnyris johannae 301
Johanna's Sunbird **40** 110, 299, *300*, 302
johnsi, Aethopyga saturata 118, 344
johnstoni, Nectarinia 104, 255
johnstoni, Nectarinia johnstoni 257
jugularis, Cinnyris 82, 318
jugularis, Cinnyris jugularis 320
juliae, Arachnothera 126, 360
juliae, Leptocoma sperata 78, 243

kaboboensis, Cyanomitra alinae 220
kampalili, Dicaeum anthonyi 40, 149
karenensis, Aethopyga nipalensis 116, 341
keiense, Dicaeum hirundinaceum 173
keiensis, Cinnyris jugularis 320
kempi, Cinnyris chloropygius 261
Kenya Violet-backed Sunbird **15** 60, *190*, 191, 288
Kenya Violet-breasted Sunbird **32** 94, *292*, 293
kilimensis, Nectarinia 104, 251
kilimensis, Nectarinia kilimensis 252
kinneari, Cinnyris habessinicus 92, 298
kirkii, Chalcomitra amethystina 233
klossi, Cinnyris jugularis 320

koelzi, Aethopyga nipalensis 116, *341*
koratensis, Chalcoparia singalensis 178
kruensis, Anthreptes seimundi 66, *194*
kuehni, Dicaeum celebicum 171
Kuhl's Sunbird. *See* White-flanked Sunbird

labecula, Aethopyga siparaja 347
lamperti, Chalcomitra senegalensis 236
Large Spiderhunter. *See* Spectacled Spiderhunter
Larger Double-collared Sunbird. *See* Greater Double-
collared Sunbird
laterale, Dicaeum aureolimbatum 147
lathburyi, Drepanorhynchus reichenowi 259
latouchii, Aethopyga christinae 118, *343*
layardorum, Dicaeum eximium 48, *165*
Legge's Flowerpecker. *See* White-throated Flowerpecker
Leptocoma 239
Lesser Double-collared Sunbird. *See* Southern Double-
collared Sunbird
Lesser Yellow-eared Spiderhunter. *See* Yellow-eared
Spiderhunter
linaraborae, Aethopyga 114, *334*
Lina's Sunbird **42** 114, 332, 333, *334*
lisettae, Hypogramma hypogrammicum 64, *207*
Little Bifasciated Sunbird. *See* Purple-banded Sunbird
Little Green Sunbird **18** 66, 179, *193*, 198, 221,
223, 312
Little Purple-banded Sunbird. *See* Purple-banded
Sunbird
Little Spiderhunter **47** 124, *350*, 353, 356
Long-billed Green Sunbird. *See* Madagascar Sunbird
Long-billed Spiderhunter **47** 124, *353*
Long-billed Sunbird **31** 92, 239, 241, 316, *330*, 345
Long-tailed Congo Sunbird. *See* Congo Sunbird
Long-tailed Emerald Sunbird. *See* Malachite Sunbird
Long-tailed Sugarbird. *See* Cape Sugarbird
longirostra, Arachnothera 124, *350*
longirostra, Arachnothera longirostra 352
longuemarei, Anthreptes 60, *188*
longuemarei, Anthreptes longuemarei 190
Longuemare's Sunbird. *See* Western Violet-backed
Sunbird
lotenius, Cinnyris 92, *330*
lotenius, Cinnyris lotenius 331
Loten's Sunbird. *See* Long-billed Sunbird
Louisiade Flowerpecker **9** 48, 162, *163*
Lovely Sunbird **43** 116, 242, 246, 318, 333, 335, *337*
loveridgei, Cinnyris 100, *280*
Loveridge's Sunbird **35** 100, 277, 279, *280*
ludovicensis, Cinnyris 94, *270*
ludovicensis, Cinnyris ludovicensis 270
Ludwig's Double-collared Sunbird. *See* Montane
Double-collared Sunbird
luzonensis, Arachnothera clarae 126, *356*
luzoniense, Dicaeum ignipectum 50, *169*

Macklot's Sunbird. *See* Copper-throated Sunbird
maculatus, Prionochilus 34, *135*
maculatus, Prionochilus maculatus 135
Madagascar Green Sunbird. *See* Madagascar Sunbird
Madagascar Sunbird **39** 108, 322, *324*, 328, 329
Madame Verreaux's Sunbird. *See* Johanna's Sunbird
maforense, Dicaeum geelvinkianum 48, *163*
maforensis, Leptocoma sericea 245
magna, Arachnothera 126, *358*
magna, Arachnothera magna 359

magnifica, Aethopyga siparaja 120, *347*
magnirostrata, Cyanomitra cyanolaema 218
malacensis, Anthreptes 58, *184*
malacensis, Anthreptes malacensis 185
Malachite Sunbird **37** 104, 131, 211, 249, 251, *253*,
255
malaitae, Dicaeum aeneum 165
malindangensis, Aethopyga boltoni 333
malindangensis, Arachnothera clarae 356
mangini, Aethopyga siparaja 347
manoensis, Cinnyris 92, *263*
manoensis, Cinnyris manoensis 263
mariae, Hypogramma hypogrammicum 207
mariae, Leptocoma sericea 245
Marico Sunbird. *See* Mariqua Sunbird
Mariqua Sunbird **39** 108, *283*, 286, 289, 294, 297, 306
mariquensis, Cinnyris 108, *283*
mariquensis, Cinnyris mariquensis 284
Maroon-breasted Sunbird. *See* Long-billed Sunbird
marungensis, Cyanomitra alinae 220
Marungu Sunbird. *See* Prigogine's Double-collared
Sunbird
masawan, Dicaeum anthonyi 149
maugei, Dicaeum 50, *167*
Mayotte Buff-breasted Sunbird. *See* Mayotte Sunbird
Mayotte Sunbird **30** 90, 324, *329*
mecynorhyncha, Leptocoma sperata 243
mediocris, Cinnyris 96, *277*
mediocris, Cinnyris mediocris 278
megastoma, Dicaeum trigonostigma 154
melanogastra, Cinnyris pulchellus 112, *282*
melanoxanthum, Dicaeum 38, *145*
Metallic-winged Sunbird **42** 114, 242, 318, 332, 333,
335, 338
metallica, Hedydipna 64, *203*
microrhynchus, Cinnyris bifasciatus 108, *290*
Midget Flowerpecker **9** 48, *165*
mindanense, Dicaeum hypoleucum 156
minima, Leptocoma 78, *240*
minor, Anthreptes seimundi 194
minullum, Dicaeum concolor 158
minullus, Cinnyris 98, *261*
minuta, Aethopyga shelleyi 338
Miombo Double-collared Sunbird **31** 92, 231, 259,
263, 270, 277, 285, 305, 308
Miombo Sunbird. *See* Miombo Double-coloured
Sunbird
misoriense, Dicaeum geelvinkianum 163
Mistletoe Flowerpecker. *See* Mistletoebird
Mistletoebird **12** 54, 164, 169, *172*
mjobergi, Anthreptes malacensis 185
modesta, Arachnothera 126, *357*
modesta, Arachnothera modesta 357
modestum, Dicaeum agile 142
moebii, Cinnyris notatus 108, *325*
mohelicus, Cinnyris humbloti 84, *328*
Montane Double-collared Sunbird **32** 94, 263, 267,
269, 270, 273, 277
monticolum, Dicaeum 52, *169*
Moo-ne-je-tang. *See* Mistletoebird
moreaui, Cinnyris 100, *278*
Moreau's Sunbird **35** 100, 277, *278*, 280, 303
Mottled Flowerpecker **9** 48, *166*
Mountain Sunbird. *See* Metallic-winged Sunbird
Mouse-brown Sunbird **15** 60, *187*, 188, 216
Mouse-coloured Sunbird **19** 68, 221, *225*. *See also*

Mouse-brown Sunbird
Mrs Gould's Sunbird. *See* Gould's Sunbird
musarum, Arachnothera magna 359
mysorensis, Leptocoma sericea 245
mystacalis, Aethopyga 122, 348

Naked-faced Spiderhunter **48** 126, *356*
Namaqua Sunbird. *See* Dusky Sunbird
Nandi Double-collared Sunbird. *See* Northern Double-collared Sunbird
Natal Long-tailed Sugarbird. *See* Gurney's Sugarbird
Natal Sugarbird. *See* Gurney's Sugarbird
natunae, Aethopyga siparaja 347
natunense, Hypogramma hypogrammicum 207
natunensis, Prionochilus maculatus 135
Nectarinia 247
Nectariniidae 129
Nectariniinae 134
Nectariniini 177
nectarinoides, Cinnyris 112, 288
nectarinoides, Cinnyris nectarinoides 288
neergaardi, Cinnyris 98, 266
Neergaard's Sunbird **34** 98, 264, *266*, 273, 286
neglecta, Cyanomitra olivacea 222
neglectum, Dicaeum maugei 168
neglectus, Anthreptes 60, 191
nehrkorni, Dicaeum 46, 160
Nepal Sunbird. *See* Green-tailed Sunbird
newtoni, Anabathmis 70
newtonii, Anabathmis 209
Newton's Sunbird **20** 70, *209*
niasense, Dicaeum cruentatum 175
niasensis, Arachnothera longirostra 352
nicobarica, Aethopyga siparaja 347
nigeriae, Cinnyris superbus 303
nigrilore, Dicaeum nigrilore 148
nigrilore, Dicaeum 40, 147
nigrimentum, Dicaeum cruentatum 54, 175
nigriscapularis,Leptocoma sericea 245
Nile Valley Sunbird **17** 64, 201, *203*, 281
nipalensis, Aethopyga 116, 340
nipalensis, Aethopyga nipalensis 341
nitidum, Dicaeum 48, 163
nitidum, Dicaeum nitidum 164
Northern Double-collared Sunbird **33** 96, 198, 259, 267, *271*, 274, 277
Northern Orange-tufted Sunbird. *See* Palestine Sunbird
notatus, Cinnyris 108, 324
notatus, Cinnyris notatus 325
nuchale, Hypogramma hypogrammicum 207
nyassae, Anthreptes longuemarei 190

oblitus, Prionochilus maculatus 135
obscura, Cyanomitra 66, 222
obscura, Cyanomitra obscura 224
obscurifrons, Dicaeum geelvinkianum 163
obscurior, Cinnyris jugularis 320
obscurum, Dicaeum hypoleucum 44, 156
obsoletum, Dicaeum agile 142
ochra, Aethopyga saturata 344
octaviae, Cyanomitra cyanolaema 218
oenopa, Leptocoma sperata 243
olivacea, Cyanomitra 66, 221
olivacea, Cyanomitra olivacea 222
olivaceum, Dicaeum concolor 44, 158
olivaceus, Prionochilus 34, 134

olivaceus, Prionochilus olivaceus 134
olivacina, Cyanomitra olivacea 222
Olive Sunbird. *See* Eastern Olive Sunbird; Western Olive Sunbird
Olive-backed Flowerpecker **2** 34, *134*
Olive-backed Sunbird **26** 82, 183, 184, 187, 242, 244, 316, *318*, 333, 335, 337, 339, 340, 341, 342, 343, 349. *See also* Elegant Sunbird; Green-headed Sunbird
Olive-bellied Sunbird **34** 98, 194, *259*, 261, 271, 277, 286, 313
Olive-capped Flowerpecker **5** 40, *147*, 149, 155
Olive-coloured Sunbird. *See* Eastern Olive Sunbird
Olive-crowned Flowerpecker **8** 46, *162*, 164
Orange-bellied Flowerpecker **6** 42, 138, 145, *153*, 168, 171, 174
Orange-breasted Sunbird **19** 68, *211*, 264
Orange-tufted Sunbird **30** 90, 289, *293*, 295, 313. *See also* Palestine Sunbird
orientalis, Anthreptes 60, 190
oritis, Cyanomitra 68, 218
oritis, Cyanomitra oritis 219
ornatus, Cinnyris jugularis 319
orphogaster, Cinnyris chloropygius 261
oseus, Cinnyris 90, 295
oseus, Cinnyris oseus 298
osiris, Cinnyris mariquensis 108, 285
oustaleti, Cinnyris 88, 304
oustaleti, Cinnyris oustaleti 305
Oustalet's Sunbird **29** 88, *304*
Oustalet's White-bellied Sunbird. *See* Oustalet's Sunbird
owstoni, Aethopyga siparaja 347

pagodarum, Arachnothera magna 359
Palawan Flowerpecker **3** 36, 136, *137*, 138, 148, 149, 159
Palawan Sunbird. *See* Lovely Sunbird
palawanorum, Dicaeum pygmaeum 159
Pale-billed Flowerpecker **7** 44, 140, 145, *156*, 157
Palestine Sunbird **30** 90, *295*, 297, 316
pallescens, Dicaeum agile 142
pallida, Arachnothera longirostra 352
pallida, Chalcoparia singalensis 178
pallidigaster, Hedydipna 62, 205
pallidius, Dicaeum trigonostigma 155
panopsia, Chalcoparia singalensis 178
paraguae, Anthreptes malacensis 185
pars, Arachnothera modesta 357
parsoni, Prionochilus olivaceus 34, 134
pectorale, Dicaeum 46, 162
pectorale, Dicaeum pectorale 162
Pemba Island Sunbird. *See* Pemba Sunbird
Pemba Sunbird **39** 108, 292, *293*
Pemba Violet-breasted Sunbird. *See* Pemba Sunbird
pembae, Cinnyris 108, 293
percussus, Prionochilus 36, 136
percussus, Prionochilus percussus 136
petersi, Aethopyga saturata 118, 344
phaeopygium, Dicaeum eximium 165
Philippine Spiderhunter. *See* Naked-faced Spiderhunter
philippinensis, Arachnothera clarae 126, 356
phoenicotis, Chalcoparia singalensis 178
pintoi, Cinnyris manoensis 264
Plain Flowerpecker **7** 44, 140, 143, 145, 155, 156, *157*, 168, 169

Plain Sunbird **14** 58, *183*, 184, 186, 242, 246, 318, 343, 348

Plain-backed Little Sunbird. *See* Plain-backed Sunbird

Plain-backed Sunbird **13** 56, *181*, 205, 305, 308

Plain-throated Sunbird **14** 58, 177, 183, *184*, 186, 242, 244, 246, 316,318, 321, 337, 339, 340, 341, 342, 348, 349. *See also* Elegant Sunbird

plateni, Cinnyris jugularis 82, 320

plateni, Prionochilus 36, *137*

plateni, Prionochilus plateni 137

platura, Hedydipna 64, *201*

Plum-coloured Sunbird. *See* Western Violet-backed Sunbird

poensis, Cyanomitra oritis 219

polyclystus, Cinnyris jugularis 320

pontifex, Dicaeum hypoleucum 44, *156*

porphyrolaema, Leptocoma sericea 245

preussi, Cinnyris reichenowi 96, *272*

Preuss's Double-collared Sunbird. *See* Northern Double-collared Sunbird

prigoginei, Cinnyris 94, *269*

Prigogine's Double-collared Sunbird **32** 94, 267, *269*

prillwitzi, Arachnothera longirostra 352

primigenius, Aethopyga 114, *332*

primigenius, Aethopyga primigenius 332

Prince's Island Sunbird. *See* Príncipe Subird

Príncipe Sunbird **20** 70, *208*

Prionochilus 134

Promeropinae 129

Promerops 129

proprium, Dicaeum 38, *143*

proscelius, Cinnyris jugularis 320

proserpina, Leptocoma sericea 245

pryeri, Dicaeum cruentatum 175

Pryer's Flowerpecker. *See* Scarlet-backed Flowerpecker

pulchellus, Cinnyris 112, *281*

pulchellus, Cinnyris pulchellus 282

pulcherrima, Aethopyga 114, *335*

pulcherrima, Aethopyga pulcherrima 336

Purple Sunbird **30** 90, 184, 239, 241, 242, 246, *316*, 318, 330, 342, 345

Purple-banded Sunbird **39** 108, 266, 283, *289*, 291, 292, 294, 314

Purple-breasted Sunbird **36** 102, *248*

Purple-naped Sunbird **17** 64, *206*

Purple-rumped Sunbird **24** 78, *239*, 241, 316, 330, 339, 345

Purple-throated Sunbird **24** 78, 183, 184, 187, *241*, 246, 316, 318, 335, 337, 339, 340, 342, 343, 348, 349

purplish, Dicaeum maugei 167

purpureiventris, Nectarinia 102, *248*

pygmaeum, Dicaeum 44, *159*

pygmaeum, Dicaeum pygmaeum 159

Pygmy Flowerpecker **7** 44, 137, 143, 149, 150, 151, 152, *159*

Pygmy Long-tailed Sunbird. *See* Pygmy Sunbird

Pygmy Sunbird **17** 64, 197, *201*, 203, 281. *See also* Nile Valley Sunbird

quadricolor, Dicaeum 42, *150*

ragazzii, Cyanomitra obscura 224

Rainbow Bird. *See* Purple-breasted Sunbird

randi, Arachnothera longirostra 352

rectirostris, Anthreptes 62, *195*

rectirostris, Anthreptes rectirostris 196

Red-and-blue Sunbird. *See* Anchieta's Sunbird

Red-banded Flowerpecker **9** 48, *164*

Red-breasted Sunbird. *See* Greater Double-collared Sunbird

Red-capped Flowerpecker **9** 48, *162*, 164

Red-chested Flowerpecker **10** 50, 160, *167*, 170, 171

Red-chested Sunbird **38** 106, *287*, 299

Red-collared Sunbird. *See* Southern Double-collared Sunbird

Red-crowned Flowerpecker. *See* Red-capped Flowerpecker

Red-keeled Flowerpecker. *See* Black-belted Flowerpecker

Red-striped Flowerpecker **6** 42, 137, *150*, 151, 152, 159

Red-throated Sunbird **14** 58, 177, 183, 184, *186*, 242, 246, 318, 348

Red-tufted Malachite Sunbird. *See* Red-tufted Sunbird

Red-tufted Sunbird **37** 104, 251, 253, *255*

Regal Sunbird **34** 98, *274*, 276

regius, Cinnyris 98, *274*

regius, Cinnyris regius 275

regulus, Prionochilus percussus 136

reichenbachii, Anabathmis 68, *207*

Reichenbach's Sunbird **19** 68, *207*, 213, 218

reichenowi, Anthreptes 56, *181*

reichenowi, Anthreptes reichenowi 182

reichenowi, Cinnyris 96, *271*

reichenowi, Cinnyris reichenowi 272

reichenowi, Drepanorhynchus 106, *258*

reichenowi, Drepanorhynchus reichenowi 258

remota, Arachnothera magna 359

retrocinctum, Dicaeum 42, *152*

rhizophorae, Cinnyris jugularis 82, 320

rhodesiae, Cinnyris oustaleti 88, *305*

rhodolaema, Anthreptes 58, *186*

rhodopygiale, Dicaeum sanguinolentum 172

robusta, Arachnothera 124, *353*

robusta, Arachnothera robusta 354

robustirostris, Cinnyris jugularis 320

rockefelleri, Cinnyris 100, *275*

Rockefeller's Sunbird **35** 100, 274, *275*

rosseli, Dicaeum nitidum 164

rothschildi, Arachnothera longirostra 352

rubescens, Chalcomitra 74, *229*

rubescens, Chalcomitra rubescens 230

rubrigena, Anthreptes malacensis 186

rubrigulare, Dicaeum geelvinkianum 163

rubrinota, Aethopyga shelleyi 116, *338*

rubritorques, Anthreptes 62, *196*

rubrocoronatum, Dicaeum geelvinkianum 163

rubropygium, Dicaeum trigonostigma 154

Ruby-cheeked Sunbird **18** 58, 177, 184, 186

Rubycheek. *See* Ruby-cheeked Sunbird

rufipennis, Cinnyris 102, *303*

Rufous-throated Sunbird. *See* Red-throated Sunbird

Rufous-winged Sunbird **36** 102, *303*

Ruwenzori Blue-headed Sunbird. *See* Blue-headed Sunbird

Ruwenzori Double-collared Sunbird. *See* Stuhlmann's Double-collared Sunbird

Rwanda Double-collared Sunbird. *See* Stuhlmann's Double-collared Sunbird

saliens, Cinnyris afer 274

salomonseni, Dicaeum pygmaeum 160

salvadorii, Dicaeum maugei 168
salvadorii, Leptocoma sericea 245
salvadorii, Nectarinia johnstoni 257
samarensis, Prionochilus olivaceus 134
San Cristobel Midget Flowerpecker. See Mottled
    Flowerpecker
sanghirense, Dicaeum celebicum 171
sangirensis, Leptocoma sericea 80, 245
sanguinipectus, Aethopyga saturata 344
sanguinolentum, Dicaeum 52, 171
sanguinolentum, Dicaeum sanguinolentum 172
São Tomé Giant Sunbird. See São Tomé Sunbird
São Tomé Sunbird 20 70, 210
saturata, Aethopyga 118, 343
saturata, Aethopyga saturata 344
Scarlet Sunbird. See Javan Sunbird
Scarlet-backed Flowerpecker 12 54, 153, 174, 175
Scarlet-breasted Flowerpecker 2 34, 136, 138, 153, 168
Scarlet-chested Sunbird 23 76, 233, 237, 299
Scarlet-collared Flowerpecker 6 42, 150, 151, 152, 159
Scarlet-headed Flowerpecker 12 54, 153, 167, 171,
    174, 175
Scarlet-tufted Malachite Sunbird. See Red-tufted
    Sunbird
Scarlet-tufted Sunbird 13 56, 179, 194
schistaceiceps, Dicaeum erythrothorax 46, 161
schubotzi, Cinnyris stuhlmanni 268
sclateri, Cyanomitra obscura 66, 224
seheriae, Aethopyga siparaja 120, 346
seimundi, Anthreptes 66, 193
seimundi, Anthreptes seimundi 194
Seimund's Little Green Sunbird. See Little Green
    Sunbird
senegalensis, Chalcomitra 76, 233
senegalensis, Chalcomitra senegalensis 236
septentrionalis, Prionochilus maculatus 34, 135
sericea, Leptocoma 80, 243
sericea, Leptocoma sericea 244
setekwa, Dicaeum geelvinkianum 163
Seychelles Blue-headed Sunbird. See Seychelles Sunbird
Seychelles Sunbird 22 74, 325
shelleyi, Aethopyga 116, 337
shelleyi, Aethopyga shelleyi 338
shelleyi, Cinnyris 106, 285
shelleyi, Cinnyris shelleyi 285
Shelley's Double-collared Sunbird. See Shelley's Sunbird
Shelley's Sunbird 38 106, 263, 264, 266, 273, 283,
    285
shellyae, Drepanorhynchus reichenowi 259
Shining Sunbird 31 92, 283, 295, 297
Short-billed Sunbird. See Purple-banded Sunbird
sibutuense, Dicaeum trigonostigma 42, 155
sibuyanicum, Dicaeum trigonostigma 155
siccata, Chalcomitra hunteri 238
simalurense, Dicaeum cruentatum 175
simplex, Anthreptes 58, 183
singalensis, Chalcoparia 58, 177
singalensis, Chalcoparia singalensis 178
siparaja, Aethopyga 120, 346
siparaja, Aethopyga siparaja 347
Small Sunbird. See Crimson-backed Sunbird
Smaller Black-bellied Sunbird. See Black-bellied Sunbird
Smaller Double-collared Sunbird. See Southern Double-
    collared Sunbird
Socotra Island Sunbird. See Socotra Sunbird
Socotra Sunbird 21 72, 238

sokolovi, Aethopyga christinae 343
solaris, Cinnyris 84, 321
solaris, Cinnyris solaris 322
sollicitans, Dicaeum concolor 158
Solomons Flowerpecker. See Midget Flowerpecker
somereni, Hedydipna collaris 200
sordida, Arachnothera longirostra 352
Souimanga Sunbird 27 84, 322, 324
Southern Bifasciated Sunbird. See Mariqua Sunbird
Southern Double-collared Sunbird 31 92, 211, 263,
    264, 266, 273, 286
sovimanga, Cinnyris 84, 322
sovimanga, Cinnyris sovimanga 323
Sovimanga Sunbird. See Souimanga Sunbird
Spectacled Spiderhunter 47 124, 353, 354, 355
sperata, Leptocoma 78, 241
sperata, Leptocoma sperata 242
Splendid Sunbird 40 110, 234, 299, 302
splendidum, Dicaeum maugei 50, 168
stangerii, Chalcomitra rubescens 74, 230
Streaked Spiderhunter 48 126, 353, 358
Streaky-breasted Spiderhunter 48 126, 353, 357, 358
stresemanni, Dicaeum trochileum 176
striatissimum, Dicaeum agile 142
Striped Flowerpecker. See Thick-billed Flowerpecker
stuhlmanni, Cinnyris 94, 267
stuhlmanni, Cinnyris stuhlmanni 268
Stuhlmann's Double-collared Sunbird 32 94, 267,
    269, 271, 273, 274
suahelicus, Cinnyris mariquensis 108, 285
subalaris, Cinnyris chalybeus 266
subcollaris, Hedydipna collaris 64, 200
Sugarbird. See Cape Sugarbird
sulaense, Dicaeum celebicum 171
sumatrana, Chalcoparia singalensis 178
sumatranum, Dicaeum agile 142
sumatranum, Dicaeum cruentatum 54, 175
sumbavense, Dicaeum annae 140
Superb Sunbird 40 110, 299, 300, 302
superbus, Cinnyris 110, 302
superbus, Cinnyris superbus 303

tacazze, Nectarinia 102, 249
tacazze, Nectarinia tacazze 250
Tacazze Sunbird 36 102, 249, 251, 253, 255, 314
talatala, Cinnyris 88, 305
talautense, Dicaeum celebicum 52, 171
talautensis, Leptocoma sericea 80, 245
tanganjicae, Cyanomitra alinae 220
teijsmanni, Cinnyris jugularis 82, 321
temmincki, Aethopyga 122, 348
Temminck's Sunbird 46 122, 183, 184, 187, 242,
    246, 348
tephrolaema, Anthreptes rectirostris 62, 196
Thick-billed Flowerpecker 4 38, 135, 140, 143,
    145, 146, 149, 155, 156, 157, 168
Thick-billed Spiderhunter 47 124, 352, 353
thomensis, Dreptes 70, 210
thoracicus, Prionochilus 34, 138
tibolii, Aethopyga boltoni 333
Tickell's Flowerpecker. See Pale-billed Flowerpecker
tinctum, Dicaeum agile 142
Tiny Sunbird 34 98, 259, 261
tonkinensis, Aethopyga siparaja 347
trangensis, Aethopyga siparaja 347
trigonostigma, Dicaeum 42, 153

trigonostigma, Dicaeum trigonostigma 154
tristrami, Dicaeum 48, *166*
trochileum, Dicaeum 54, *175*
trochileum, Dicaeum trochileum 176
Tsavo Purple-banded Sunbird **32** 94, 288, 289, *291*, 292
tsavoensis, Cinnyris 94, *291*
turkanae, Cinnyris habessinicus 298

uchidai, Dicaeum concolor 158
Uganda Violet-backed Sunbird. *See* Western Violet-backed Sunbird
Uluguru Violet-backed Sunbird **15** 60, 190, *191*
ursulae, Cinnyris 88, *311*
Ursula's Sunbird **29** 88, *311*
Usambara Grey-chin Sunbird. *See* Banded Sunbird
usambaricus, Cinnyris mediocris 96, *278*

Variable Sunbird **28** 86, *181*, 198, 263, 274, 281, 303, 305, *308*, 314
venustus, Cinnyris 86, *308*
venustus, Cinnyris venustus 309
veronica, Leptocoma sericea 245
veroxii, Cyanomitra 68, *225*
veroxii, Cyanomitra veroxii 226
Verreaux's Sunbird. *See* Mouse-coloured Sunbird
verticalis, Cyanomitra 72, *213*
verticalis, Cyanomitra verticalis 214
vicina, Leptocoma sericea 245
victoriae, Aethopyga nipalensis 341
vigorsii, Aethopyga 120, *344*
Vigors's Yellow-backed Sunbird. *See* Western Crimson Sunbird
vincens, Dicaeum 40, *146*
violacea, Anthobaphes 68, *211*
violaceum, Dicaeum geelvinkianum 163
Violet-backed Sunbird. *See* Western Violet-backed Sunbird
Violet-breasted Sunbird. *See* Kenya Violet-breasted Sunbird
Violet-headed Sunbird. *See* Orange-breasted Sunbird
Violet-tailed Sunbird **16** 62, *192*
virescens, Dicaeum concolor 158
viridisplendens, Cyanomitra verticalis 215
viridissimum, Dicaeum bicolor 149
Visayan Flowerpecker,. *See* Black-belted Flowerpecker
voeltzkowi, Cinnyris notatus 325
vulneratum, Dicaeum 46, *161*

Wedge-tailed Sunbird. *See* Orange-breasted Sunbird
Western Bifasciated Sunbird. *See* Mariqua Sunbird
Western Crimson Sunbird **45** 120, 241, *344*
Western Olive Sunbird **18** 66, 179, 194, 195, 213, 221, *222*, 225, 312
Western Violet-backed Sunbird **15** 60, 187, *188*, 190, 191, 193, 313
Whiskered Flowerpecker **4** 38, *143*, 148, 149, 159
White-bellied Sunbird. *See* White-breasted Sunbird
White-breasted Sunbird **29** 88, *181*, 263, 283, 304, *305*, 308, 310
White-flanked Sunbird **44** 118, 184, 246, 318, *341*, 348
White-throated Flowerpecker **5** 40, 140, *146*
White-vented Sunbird. *See* Dusky Sunbird
Whitehead's Spiderhunter **48** 126, 353, *360*
whytei, Cinnyris ludovicensis 271

wiglesworthi, Anthreptes malacensis 186
wilhelminae, Dicaeum sanguinolentum 52, *172*
woodi, Cinnyris jugularis 320
wrayi, Aethopyga saturata 344

xanthopygium, Dicaeum trigonostigma 155
xanthopygius, Prionochilus 36, *137*

Yellow-backed Sunbird. *See* Crimson Sunbird; Western Crimson Sunbird
Yellow-bellied Flowerpecker **4** 38, 140, *145*, 153, 156, 157
Yellow-bellied Sunbird. *See* Olive-backed Sunbird; Variable Sunbird
Yellow-breasted Flowerpecker **2** 34, *135*, 140, 143, 144
Yellow-breasted Sunbird. *See* Olive-backed Sunbird; Variable Sunbird
Yellow-chin Sunbird. *See* Green Sunbird
Yellow-chinned Sunbird. *See* Green Sunbird
Yellow-eared Spiderhunter **47** 124, 353, 354, *355*
Yellow-rumped Flowerpecker **3** 36, 136, *137*, 138, 169
Yellow-sided Flowerpecker **5** 40, *147*
Yellow-tufted Malachite Sunbird. *See* Malachite Sunbird
Yellow-vented Flowerpecker **4** 38, 135, *144*
yokanae, Anthreptes reichenowi 56, *182*

Zambesi Blue-headed Sunbird. *See* Plain-backed Sunbird
Zambesi Valley Double-collared Sunbird. *See* Shelley's Sunbird
Zambesi Valley Sunbird. *See* Shelley's Sunbird
zambesiana, Hedydipna collaris 200
zanzibarica, Cyanomitra veroxii 226
zeylonica, Leptocoma 78, *239*
zeylonica, Leptocoma zeylonica 240
zeylonicum, Dicaeum agile 142
zuluensis, Hedydipna collaris 200